W0018511

RESEARCH AND PRACTICAL ISSUES OF ENTERPRISE INFORMATION SYSTEMS II

VOLUME 1

IFIP – The International Federation for Information Processing

IFIP was founded in 1960 under the auspices of UNESCO, following the First World Computer Congress held in Paris the previous year. An umbrella organization for societies working in information processing, IFIP's aim is two-fold: to support information processing within its member countries and to encourage technology transfer to developing nations. As its mission statement clearly states,

> *IFIP's mission is to be the leading, truly international, apolitical organization which encourages and assists in the development, exploitation and application of information technology for the benefit of all people.*

IFIP is a non-profitmaking organization, run almost solely by 2500 volunteers. It operates through a number of technical committees, which organize events and publications. IFIP's events range from an international congress to local seminars, but the most important are:

- The IFIP World Computer Congress, held every second year;
- Open conferences;
- Working conferences.

The flagship event is the IFIP World Computer Congress, at which both invited and contributed papers are presented. Contributed papers are rigorously refereed and the rejection rate is high.

As with the Congress, participation in the open conferences is open to all and papers may be invited or submitted. Again, submitted papers are stringently refereed.

The working conferences are structured differently. They are usually run by a working group and attendance is small and by invitation only. Their purpose is to create an atmosphere conducive to innovation and development. Refereeing is less rigorous and papers are subjected to extensive group discussion.

Publications arising from IFIP events vary. The papers presented at the IFIP World Computer Congress and at open conferences are published as conference proceedings, while the results of the working conferences are often published as collections of selected and edited papers.

Any national society whose primary activity is in information may apply to become a full member of IFIP, although full membership is restricted to one society per country. Full members are entitled to vote at the annual General Assembly, National societies preferring a less committed involvement may apply for associate or corresponding membership. Associate members enjoy the same benefits as full members, but without voting rights. Corresponding members are not represented in IFIP bodies. Affiliated membership is open to non-national societies, and individual and honorary membership schemes are also offered.

RESEARCH AND PRACTICAL ISSUES OF ENTERPRISE INFORMATION SYSTEMS II

VOLUME 1

IFIP TC 8 WG 8.9 International Conference on Research and Practical Issues of Enterprise Information Systems (CONFENIS 2007) October 14-16, 2007, Beijing, China

Edited by

Li D. Xu
Old Dominion University, USA

A. Min Tjoa
Vienna University of Technology, Austria

Sohail S. Chaudhry
Villanova University, USA

Library of Congress Control Number: 2007937257

Research and Practical Issues of Enterprise Information Systems II
Volume 1
Edited by L. Xu, A. Tjoa, and S. Chaudhry

p. cm. (IFIP International Federation for Information Processing, a Springer Series in Computer Science)

ISSN: 1571-5736 / 1861-2288 (Internet)
ISBN: 978-0-387-75901-2
eISBN: 978-0-387-75902-9
Printed on acid-free paper

Printed in the United States of America.

9 8 7 6 5 4 3 2 1
springer.com

Table of Contents

Volume 2

Preface

Enterprise information systems (EIS) have become increasingly popular over the last 15 years [1-2]. EIS integrate and support business processes across functional boundaries in a supply chain environment [3-5]. In recent years, more and more enterprises world-wide have adopted EIS such as Enterprise Resource Planning (ERP) for running their businesses. Previously, information systems such as CAD, CAM, MRPII and CRM were widely used for partial functional integration within a business organization. With global operation, global supply chain, and fierce competition in place, there is a need for suitable EIS such as ERP, E-Business or E-Commerce systems to integrate extended enterprises in a supply chain environment with the objective of achieving efficiency, competency, and competitiveness. As an example, the global economy has forced business enterprises such as Dell and Microsoft to adopt ERP in order to take the advantage of strategic alliances within a global supply chain environment. Today, not only the large companies, but also the medium companies are quickly learning that a highly integrated EIS is more and more a required element of doing business. Businesses all over the world are investing billions of dollars in acquiring and implementing EIS in particular ERP systems by SAP and Oracle. As a result, there is a growing demand for researching EIS to provide insights into challenges, issues, and solutions related to the design, implementation and management of EIS.

There is no doubt that the topic of EIS is new, popular and having important long-term strategic impact on global business and world economy. Due to the importance of the subject, there is a significant amount of ongoing research in the area. To respond the market needs from both academic researchers and practitioners for communicating their research outcomes, and contribute to, and often lead, progresses in the state-of-knowledge and state-of-the-art in EIS, the First IFIP TC8 International Conference on Research and Practical Issues of Enterprise Information Systems (CONFENIS 2006) was held at Vienna, Austria, April 2006 (http://www.confenis.org/?q=node). Two months after, the International Forum of Information Systems Frontiers (IFISF) —Xian International Symposium, was held in June 29-30, Xian, China. This is the first international symposium on information systems frontiers that is sponsored by a major Chinese research institution and held in China. One of the main themes of this conference is Enterprise Information Systems. Due to the success of these two premier international conferences, the Second IFIP TC8.9 International Conference on Research and Practical Issues of Enterprise Information Systems (CONFENIS 2007) is to be held in Beijing, China, October 2007 (http://www.keylab-imie.org/confenis2007/general/index.aspx).

CONFENIS 2007 is a primary international event which provides an opportunity for EIS academicians and practitioners in the world to gather, exchange ideas, and present original research in their fields. The purpose of the conference is to report on the state-of-the-art of, and emerging trends in, research and practice in EIS. The conference called for original contributions on significant research findings, reflecting advanced technological research and applications in the field, and state-of-the-art survey papers and reviews on future directions of enterprise information systems.

CONFENIS 2007 received about five hundred submissions with selected ones included in these two volumes of proceedings. CONFENIS 2007 is to establish an international forum on the increasingly important area of Enterprise Information Systems. Distinguished scholars invited as keynote speakers include: John Warfield (George Mason University, USA), Shoubo Xu (Chinese Academy of Engineering and Beijing Jiaotong University), Xiaohong Guan (Tsinghua University, China), William McCarthy (Michigan State University, USA), G. Swanson (International Federation for Systems Research) and Yushun Fan (Tsinghua University, China).

We hope that this proceedings will serve our authors as an avenue to contribute to the progresses in the state-of-knowledge and state-of-the-art in EIS and its applications; meanwhile, we hope it will serve information systems professionals worldwide as an avenue to gain a new perspective on how the global business and world economy are impacted by EIS. We are very grateful to have the sponsorship of Beijing University of Posts and Telecommunications and Beijing University of Aeronautics and Astronautics for this conference. We would specially like to thank Dean Tingjie Lu, Professor Huaying Shu, Associate Dean Zhanhong Xin and Dr. Jiayin Qi of the School of Economics and Management of Beijing University of Posts and Telecommunications, Professor Lu Liu and Professor Guoping Xia of Beijing University of Aeronautics and Astronautics, former Chair of IFIP TC8, Professor J. Dewald Roode (South Africa), former Vice-Chair of IFIP TC8, Professor David Avison (France), Secretary of IFIP TC8, Professor Isabel Ramos (Portugal), and Vice-Chair of IFIP TC8, Professor Jan Pries-Heje (Denmark), for their encouragement and guidance throughout this endeavor. We are also deeply grateful to many individual reviewers who worked with us so diligently.

Special thanks also go to managing editors, Dr. Shan Wang of Renmin University of China and Dr. Jiayin Qi of Beijing University of Posts and Telecommunications, and the editorial staff Xiaoyan Huang, Rong Liu, Shan Jiang, and Nan Jiang of Beijing University of Posts and Telecommunications for providing professional support in managing and editing manuscripts.

Li Da Xu
IFIP TC8 WG8.9, Chair

A Min Tjoa
IFIP TC8 WG8.9, First Vice-Chair

Sohail Chaudhry
CONFENIS 2007 Program Committee Co-Chair

REFERENCES

1. M. Elmes, D. Strong and O. Volkpff, Panoptic empowerment and reflective conformity in enterprise systems-enabled organizations, *Information and Organization*. Volume 15, pp.1-37, (2005).
2. L. Xu, Editorial: inaugural issue, *Enterprise Information Systems*. Volume 1, pp.1-2, (2007).
3. G. Shanks and P. Seddon, Editorial, *Journal of Information Technology*, Volume 15, pp. 243-244, (2000).
4. S. Wang and N.P. Archer, Electronic marketplace definition and classification: literature review and clarification, *Enterprise Information Systems*. Volume 1, pp.89-112, (2007).
5. J. Warfield, Systems science serves enterprise integration: a tutorial, *Enterprise Information Systems*. Volume 1, pp.235-254, (2007).

The Theory of Material Flow

Shoubo Xu

School of Economics and Management, Beijing Jiaotong University, Beijing 100044, P.R. China
Academy of Material Flow, Beijing Jiaotong University, Beijing 100044, P.R. China
xusb@263.net

Abstract. On basis of research for years, the paper for the first time presents 7 main theories under "The MF", namely "Material flow theory", "Comprehensive MF theory", "MF element theory", " MF nature theory", "MF science & technology theory", " MF engineering theory" and " MF industry theory". The paper points out that the MF, as the collective term for fluidity of macroscopic goods and that of microcosmic substances, is purposeless behaviors and all purposeful behaviors including administrative behaviors; the Material Flow is not only economic phenomena, but also social and natural ones. There is not only economic MF, but also social and natural ones. Economic MF is the core for the MF, and Social and Natural MF is the basis for the MF; no matter whether in nature, society or economic circles, MF comprises of five basic elements: Material, Flow, Owner, Region and Time, among which Material is the core one; MF is divided into intrinsic and extrinsic ones by nature. Its intrinsic natures include Material (M), Flow (F), Owner (O), Region (R) and Time (T); its extrinsic natures include Party (P), Service (S), Management (M), Technology (T) and Economy (E). MF science and technology is a scientific and technological field with very strong comprehensibility, dealing with subjects including natural science, engineering technology and science and human and social studies; MF engineering is a syntheses comprising of 6 MF elements or 6 MF forces. MF's hard science and technology and its soft science and technology will be applied for the national economy in the most efficient way, with the fundamental purpose to benefit the human kind; MF is not only one industry, but also one backbone industry, and even a backbone industry group.

Keywords: *The MF, Material flow theory, Comprehensive MF theory, MF element theory, MF nature theory, MF science & technology theory, MF engineering theory, MF industry theory*

1. INTRODUCTION

Since I put forward a new concept for "MF" for the first time in 1985[1-2], I have carried out specialized studies on the issue of MF science theory over the years. Having been presented on meetings and publications home and abroad, some of my research achievements got recognition from fellow experts and leaders of China's concerned authorities. Those experts sum my series of research achievements on MF scientific theory as "the Material Flow Theory" [3] for which I feel very grateful.

As all know, Karl Marx began his research with the merchandise and merchandise circulation, putting an emphasis on capital production, circulation and general process of capitalist production from the value form point of view, and in the end finished his great work *On Capital*, which contributes a great deal to the social and scientific development. Thus, the author views that the significant task in the research of "the MF theory" is to carry out the research on the process of manufacturing, circulation and consumption, focusing on the practical form, beginning from the research of merchandise. Fig. 1 shows 7 basic theories for the MF Theory and their interrelationship.

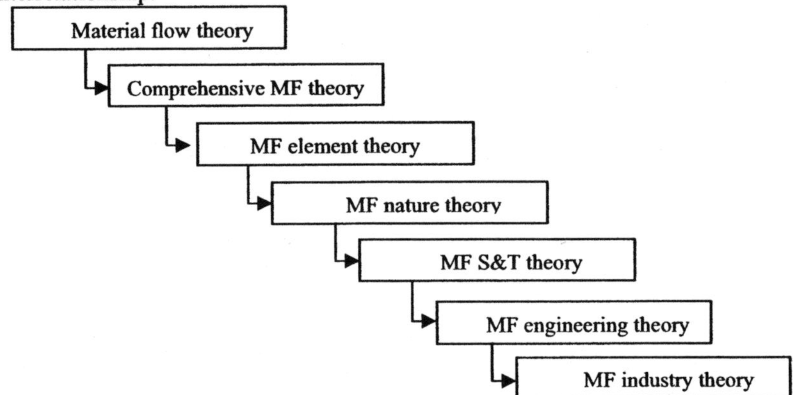

Figure 1. Relationship between 7 Basic Theories for the MF Theory

The following individually illuminates 7 major theories under "the MF Theory": firstly, "the Material flow theory" put forward according to the research on the MF science and technology concept; secondly, "Comprehensive MF theory" put forward according to the research on the MF objective matter and phenomena, thirdly, "The MF element theory" put forward according to the research on the MF composition elements, fourthly, "The MF nature theory" put forward according to the research on the MF nature; fifthly, "The MF science & technology theory" put forward according to the research on the MF science and technology system; sixthly, "The MF engineering theory" put forward according to the research on the MF engineering; seventhly, "The MF industry theory" put forward according to the research on the MF industrial development.

2. MATERIAL FLOW THEORY

As the most important portion put forward according to the research on MF's scientific concept, Material flow theory [4-8] is the foundation and source for "The MF". Table 1 compares the concept of MF in China with that of P.D or Logistics in Japan and western countries. From the table, we can find that the new concept "material flow (MF)" in China is different from the concept of PD or Logistics in Japan and western countries, no matter in its English term, earliest mentioned time and its attribute, connotations, nature and applying domain. The concept of "Material Flow" based on "The MF" in China has laid a very good theoretic foundation and given a correct direction for the development of China's MF undertaking and MF science and technology. In actuality, so-called "The Material Flow" is the collective term for fluidity of macroscopic goods and that of microcosmic substances, and should be translated into English as MF instead of Logistics. The concept of MF embraces that of PD and Logistics. To put the other way round, compared to the MF, PD and Logistics are only part of the MF. The term "Material Flow", firstly used by the US to represent the flow of materials in its manufacturing enterprises, although the same in English expression is not used to a large extent but to a small one.

Table 1. Comparison between the Concept of MF in China and That of P.D or Logistics in Japan and Western Countries

Country	China	Japan	The U.S.	The U.S.
Concept	Material Flow (MF)	Circulation of merchandise (PD)	Physical distribution of merchandise (PD)	Manoeuvre of military materials, staff and equipment (Logistics)
The earliest mentioned time	1985	1965	1915	1905
The earliest attributes of the concept	Belonging to natural, social and economic facts	Belonging to the economic facts	Belonging to the economic facts	Belonging to the military facts
Connotations of the concept	Collective term for fluidity of macroscopic goods and that of microcosmic substances	Physical moving of materials from supply to demand	Physical distribution of merchandise (PD)	Manoeuvre of military materials, staff and equipment (Logistics)
The behavioral character of the concept	Purposeless behaviors and all purposeful behaviors including administrative behaviors	Purposeful economic behaviors	Purposeful economic administration behaviors	Purposeful military rear-services management at the earliest stage, now being part of the whole supply management
The plying domain of the concept	The economic, social and natural domains	The circulation domain	The circulation domain	The military domain as well as the whole supply chain

3. COMPREHENSIVE MF THEORY

Comprehensive MF theory [4, 5, 8, 9] reveals the essence of MF objects and phenomena. The MF in the natural world exists before the appearance of human society. Its characters include: materials exist in the natural world and are not economic commodities; the impetus for flow originates from the natural world rather than economic activities of the mankind; there are not any purposes for they are not acts by the mankind. The MF in the natural world can benefit human beings (e.g., electric power generation by water, wind and tide); on the other hand, it can also bring natural disasters to the human world (e.g., flood, windstorm, sand storm, debris flow, sandstorm and polluted atmospheric currents and water currents and so on).

The MF in the social world is the material flow phenomena peculiar to the human society. Since there are human living consumption and agricultural production at the primitive society, kinds of relevant primitive materials flows also appeared. MF has been the substantial foundation for human's existence since its beginning, and one cannot survive without MF. The MF concerning residents' living and waste is inevitable behavior. The social aspect has not any economic objective and is fundamental and indispensable in any society. MF in the social sphere also includes the military logistics and the disaster relief MF. This type of MF is a non-profiting social behavior, rather than economic one, serving the mankind's own survival and development as well as the society. Its characters include: materials exist in the natural world and can also be economic commodities; the impetus for flow originates from the mankind's social activities; this kind of MF is a non-profiting social behavior.

The MF in the economic sphere is an important MF phenomenon emerging at the latest stage. Since commodity exchange and social labor division emerges from the production and development of agricultural society, the MF in the economic sphere develops more and more quickly due to the demands on economic development. However, restricted by the MF impetus, it's small-scaled. By the beginning of the industrial society, the development of traffic and transportation greatly expedite the MF in the economic domain. The MF in the economic world, the so-called source of third profits in the modern society, has got more and more emphasis from people. The MF in the economic world includes the material flows of each area, industry, trade and enterprise; the flow of various materials; the material flow of various activity natures, etc.. As one important component of mankind's economic behaviors, it's a business behavior aiming to crease values and surplus values. Its characteristics include: materials are economic commodities; the impetus for flow originates from the mankind's economic activities; this kind of MF is a profiting economic behavior.

To sum up, the MF is a very important objective matter and phenomenon. It exists not only in the economic world but also in the social world and natural world; it's not only an economic phenomenon, but also a social and natural phenomenon. There is not only economic MF, but also social and natural ones. What's more, there are relationships between them. It can be said that objectively there exists a complex MF phenomenon rather than a simple MF phenomenon. Therefore, they are called as comprehensive MF phenomena. The theoretical viewpoints based on comprehensive MF phenomena are "Comprehensive MF theory".

Fig 2 gives a chart of Comprehensive Material Flow, reflecting the MF in the economic world, the MF in the social world and the MF in the natural world as well as their interrelationship, also presenting various material flows in the MF in the economic world. Compared to the Material Flow, the MF in the economic world, the MF in the social world and the MF in the natural world are only one important component rather than all of the Material Flow. Among them, the MF in the economic world is the core for the Material Flow, while the MF in the social world and the MF in the natural world are the foundation for the Material Flow.

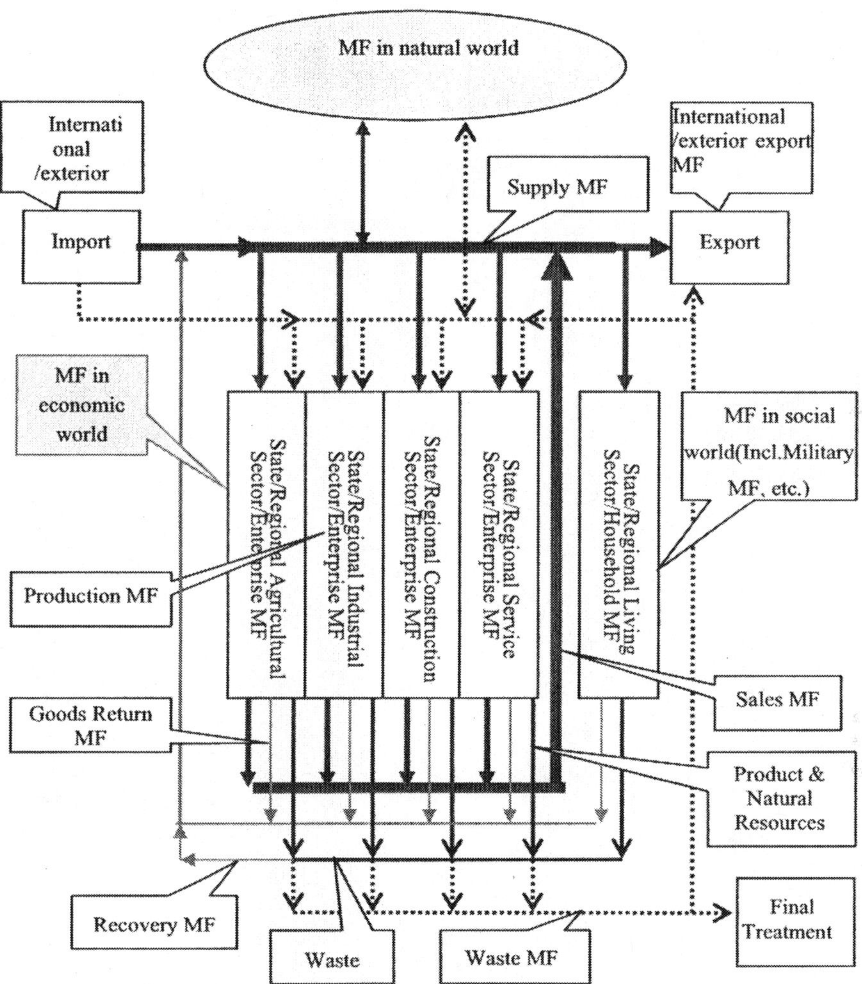

Figure 2. Comprehensive Material Flow

4. MF ELEMENT THEORY

MF element theory reveals the composition of MF objects. The author conducted a research and concluded that the MF in whatever form comprises of five basic elements: Material, Flow, Owner, Region and Time, namely MFROT theory. The MF in the natural world, the MF in the social world and the MF in the economic world all possess these five most basic elements. Of course, among these five elements, the Material element is the most important and core one. All materials requiring movement and flow possess owner, region and time. Therefore, the elements of Flow, Owner, Region and Time shall be closely related to the core element Material. From this, we can see that any MF must simultaneously possess five basic elements. The MF will not exist if lacking any one of these elements. This is the theory of five MF elements (MFORT). Table 2 shows list of elements (MFORT) for Natural MF, Social MF and Economic MF.

Table 2. Elements (MFORT) for Natural MF, Social MF and Economic MF

Class	Material Flow	MF in the natural world (Natural MF)	MF in the social world (Social MF)	MF in the economic world (Economic MF)
English term	Material Flow (MF)	Natural Material Flow (NMF)	Social Material Flow (SMF)	Economic Material Flow (EMF)
M (Material)	Macroscopic/microcosmic substances (incl. living and lifeless substances)	Materials exist in the natural world and are not economic commodities	Materials exist in the natural/social world and can also be economic commodities	Materials are economic commodities
F (Flow)	Impetus for flow originates from the natural world and social/economic activities of the mankind; regular movement with carrier and regular/irregular movement without carrier	Impetus for flow originates from the natural world rather than social/economic activities of the mankind; regular/irregular movement without carrier	Impetus for flow originates from social activities of the mankind; regular movement with carrier	Impetus for flow originates from economic activities of the mankind; regular movement with carrier
O (Owner)	Owner of natural, social and economic worlds	Owner of natural world	Owner of social world	Owner of economic world
R (Region)	Within the region spaces of natural, social and economic worlds	Within the region spaces of natural world	Within the region spaces of social world	Within the region spaces of economic world
T (Time)	In ancient/modern/contemporary times	In ancient/modern/contemporary times	In ancient/modern/contemporary times	In ancient/modern/contemporary times

5. MF NATURE THEORY

MF nature theory reveals the nature of MF. Based on the research, we put forward that the MF has both intrinsic nature and extrinsic nature. MF's intrinsic nature reflects the intrinsic characteristics of the MF's basic elements, which are the objective nature possessed by the MF and not transformed with the human subject willpower. Fig 3 is a chart of the MF nature theory. From the chart, we can see that corresponding to five MF elements (MFORT), there are five characters for the MF's intrinsic nature: Material (M), Flow (F), Owner (O), Region (R) and Time (T).

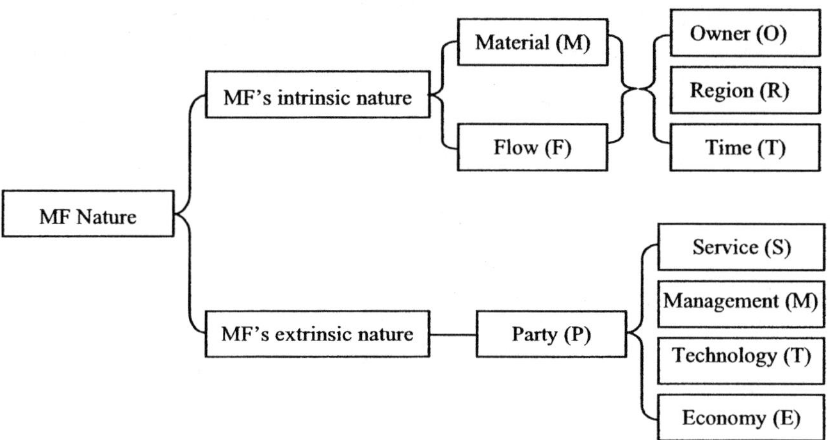

Figure 3. Material Flow Nature

MF's extrinsic nature reflects the extrinsic characteristics of MF's non-basic elements, which can be selected according to the subject will of the MF Party. From the chart, we can also find that there are also five extrinsic natures for the MF, including Party (P), Service (S), Management (M), Technology (T) and Economy (E). From the research, the author views that the MF has only one basic intrinsic attribute, which is the nature of the MF itself. The nature of the MF itself is determined by Nature of Material. The nature of material decides that of flow. For example, as materials have different natures, the requirements are different concerning the following: transportation means, packaging, MF processing and storing. To sum up, the fundamental characteristics for MF are the nature of material.

The natures of material include Material (M) and Flow (F). Any material is substantial and one form of objective existence. Therefore, Material (M) is the fundamental attribute for the material. According to Marxism philosophy, movement is the basic attribute for material and the manner of material existence. Object and movement cannot be separated. "Movement, from its most common meaning ...... includes all changes and processes occurring in the universe, from simply position displacement to thought."[1] The location displacement here refers to the material flow.

[1] See P491, Volume 3, *Selected Works from Marx & Engels.*

Therefore, Flow (F) is also the fundamental attribute for material. These two natures of material are integrated and cannot be separated from each other.

Owner Nature of Material Flow (O). The MFs in the natural, social and economic worlds all have their owners. The owner for the MF in the natural world is the natural world, the owner for the MF in the social world is the social world, and the owner for the MF in the economic world is the economic world. The Party of Material Flow (PMF) is determined by the Owner Nature of material. The natural world comprises of various living and lifeless natural substances, including stars, soils, sands, mountains, deposits, rivers, water, sunshine, air, forest, organisms and micro-organisms. Different natural substances are different owners for the MF in the natural world. The owners for the MF in the economic world include enterprises, industries, trades, units and departments. The owners for the MF in the social world include families, units and armies. Different owners produce different natures for owners and different material flows.

Region Nature (R) of the Material Flow. The region nature is the attribute shared by the MFs in the natural/social/economic worlds. All materials, either microscopic substances or macroscopic items, possess their own regional spaces and locations; also all flows possess their own flowing regional ranges. Therefore, the material flow possesses the attribute of region. The regional space possesses the nature of hierarchy. There are difference levels for regional space attributes of the natural, social and economic worlds. Take the MFs in the social/economic world as examples, viewing from the global scope, the highest regional level is at the international one(including five continents and all large regions), what comes next are countries, and then every region/area in each country (including provinces, cities, prefectures, states, counties, townships and communities).

Time nature (T) of the Material Flow. The time nature is the attribute shared by all the materials, and of course the MFs in the natural/social/economic worlds. According to the research on China's history, it's usually to call the period before the 1850s as the ancient times, the period from the 1850s to the May 4th Movement of 1919 as the modern times, and the period after that as the contemporary times. Various material flows at different times have their own characteristics.

Scientific classification can be conducted on complex material flow phenomena according to the theory of MF element (MFORT) nature. Fig 4 explains the nature of five MF elements (MFORT) and their classification method. Of course, classification can also be conducted according to the MF's extrinsic nature (PSMTE).

6. MF SCIENCE & TECHNOLOGY THEORY

For a long time, it's viewed that the material flow is equal to circulation of commodities or doing business, without not many sciences and technologies. Therefore, the Material Flow science and technology has not been recognized properly by the people. Since the reform and opening up, what is extensively promulgated on textbooks, journals and news media are the western definition of "PD". So people mistakenly viewed that "MF management is equal to the MF". The MF science and technology only has the subject of MF management. Just as the people only cared for the material management in the past, they now only care for the MF management. This kind of thought seriously influenced the comprehensive development of the MF science and technology in China.

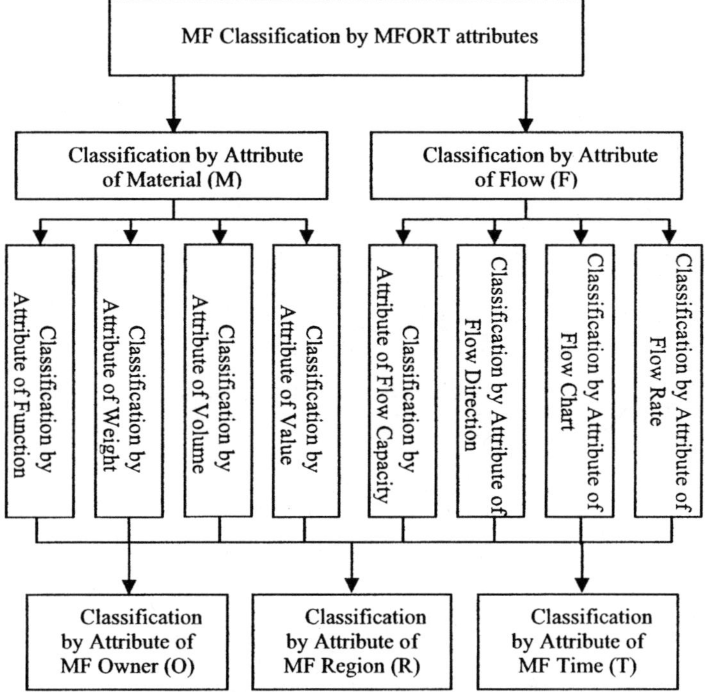

Figure 4. The Nature of Five MF Elements (MFORT) & Their Classification Method

Based on the researches, we bring forward that MF science and technology is one of the integrated fields and the same as energy science and technology, environment science and technology, etc. To develop MF science and technology requires the involvement of various subjects, including natural science, engineering technology and human society science. Since China's opening-up and reform, appearance of some new integrated science and technology, such as energy or environment branches, is both the demand of objective world and development of science and technology, whose smooth development has formed their independent system. But the research and development of MF science and technology has far lagged behind without its independent system up to now.

In our view, the principles that science and technology are the primary productive forces and strategies of rejuvenating country by science and education urgently demand more research and development on "MF science and technology" with great efforts. Therefore, it is necessary to create the independent subject system for MF science and technology for purpose of promoting its R&D. We propose that the MF science and technology subjects system consist of the following four parts:

fundamental subjects of MF science and technology; MF engineering and technological subjects; theoretical subjects of MF science and technology; the rest subjects of MF science and technology (See Table 3).

Table 3. MF Science and Technology Subjects System

I. The fundamental subjects of MF science and technology	Distribution engineering
MF physics	Loading/unloading engineering
MF mathematics	Storage engineering
MF chemistry	Packaging engineering
MF astronomy	MF processing engineering
MF geography	MF information engineering
MF biology	MF simulation technology
The rest of fundamental subjects of MF science and technology	MF examining and monitoring technology
II. MF engineering and technological subjects	MF safety engineering
Comprehensive material flow engineering	**III. Theoretical subjects of MF science and technology**
Economic MF engineering	MF system and MF network
Regional MF engineering	MF technological economics
Section MF engineering	MF economics
Recycling MF engineering	MF management
Social MF engineering	MF pedagogy
Military MF engineering	MF sociology
Natural MF engineering	MF law
MF infrastructure engineering	MF history
MF facilities engineering	Other subjects of MF science
Transportation engineering	**Iv. The rest of subjects of MF science and technology**

It should be pointed out that the MF science/technology subject system in table 3 is just a frame and suggestion. Continuous revision, complementation and perfection need to be made in line with the development of MF subjects. Table 2 shows that the majority of MF subjects are untouched, which leaves room to explore and a time mission to complete.

Different from the western MF science theory based on the thought that "The MF is actually the management over it", China's "MF science & technology theory" [4-5] is based on "the Material flow theory" and "Comprehensive MF theory". It can be said that "the MF science & technology theory" in China is one important component of the MF Theory, and the MF management subject in the west is only one branch under the MF science & technology theory.

7. MF ENGINEERING THEORY

Through studies, we view that MF engineering is a syntheses from 6 MF elements or 6 MF forces, applying the MF science and technology into the national economy in the most effective way and benefiting the mankind [7]. The concept of MF engineering contains four points: firstly, it points out that the MF engineering is a syntheses from 6 MF elements or 6 MF forces; secondly, it points out that MF engineering applies science and technologies, including the MF hard science and technologies and the MF soft science and technologies; thirdly, it points out that MF engineering should be applied to the national economy in the most effectively way; fourthly, it points out that the fundamental purpose of MF engineering is to benefit the mankind. This concept of MF engineering is used in its extensive meaning. The concept of MF engineering usually mainly referring to the MF civil engineering is used in its narrow meaning.

The 6 MF elements include: (1) MF laborers, meaning various persons engaging in the MF, including the MF management staff; (2) Objects to be worked on in the MF, meaning various “materials”; (3) Means of labor for the MF, meaning various equipment required for MF labor; (4) MF work environments, meaning various natural, social and political environments relating to the MF; (5) MF labor space, meaning various MF work sites and occupied lands; (6) MF labor time, meaning construction time and operation time for various kinds of MF facilities.

The 6 MF forces include: (1) Labor power, meaning persons engaging in the MF work; (2) Material resources, meaning energy and raw materials required for the engagement of MF labor; (3) Financial resources, meaning fixed assets, current assets and so on required for the engagement of MF labor; (4) Transport capability, meaning transportation and traffic required for the engagement of MF labor; (5) Natural forces, meaning such natural resources as water, land and air required for the engagement of MF labor; (6) Time forces, meaning the time required for the engagement of MF labor.

No MF engineering can be void of any of the 6 elements or 6 forces above. Equipment manufacturing, facilities construction, services, scientific and technological development, planning, designing and so on of the MF all require the 6 elements or 6 forces above. This is the hexa-structure theory for the MF engineering. Those 6 elements are the same as those 6 forces in essence, but different in the expressions. Some “elements” and “forces are in perfect agreement, such as the “element” of persons and human “forces”, time “element” and time “force”; some “elements” and “forces are not in perfect agreement, e.g., financial “force” means not only the labor asset “element” of fixed assets including factory, plant and equipment, but also the occupation of current assets, namely the “element” of objects of labor. Therefore, “force” and “element” is not consistent completely. However, both these 6 elements and these 6 forces are independent basic primitives, and there is no repeatability between each element and each force, both of which have their independence.

MF engineering is hexa-structured. Different nature, quality, quantity and percentage in this hexa-structure will decide different nature of the MF engineering. MF engineering has multiple types: transportation, storage, loading/unloading, packaging, circulating/processing, distribution, information and management; capital technology intensive, physical labor intensive and intellectual labor intensive; technologically advanced, technologically common, and technologically lagging behind; intensive and extensive; etc. For example, automated storage engineering falls under the capital technology intensive and technologically advanced type; general storage engineering falls under the labor intensive and not very technologically advanced type, but “applicable” one. The 6 MF elements can be alternative to a certain degree. For example, capital and technology element can replace labor element and natural force element. Along with the development of MF science and technology, there are more and more scientific and technological contents in the structure of six MF elements. This is determined by the hexa-structure theory of the MF theory.

MF engineering contains not only single MF engineering, but also comprehensive MF engineering. Single MF engineering generally refers to the MF engineering for a certain object, e.g., coal MF engineering, petroleum MF engineering, electric power MF engineering, raw material MF engineering, machinery and equipment MF engineering, commodity MF engineering, etc.; Single MF engineering also refers to transportation, distribution, storage, loading, packaging, circulation and processing, information processing and other types of engineering. Unlike the single MF engineering, the comprehensive MF engineering is not the simple addition of single MF engineering, but has its own special comprehensive MF engineering technology. The relationship between single MF engineering technology and comprehensive MF engineering technology is just like that between the manufacturing technology of automobile engine parts and the total design and manufacturing technology of automobiles. The single MF engineering technology cannot replace comprehensive MF engineering technology, and vice versa.

All the theoretical opinions above based on the MF engineering in its extensive meaning are "MF engineering theory". It's the important component of "The MF ".

8. MF INDUSTRY THEORY

As all know, national economy is made up of three domains: manufacturing, circulation and consumption. We put forward that national economy has three forms: first, the practical form; second, the value form; the third is integrated forms including practical form and value form. Therefore, manufacturing, circulation and consumption have three forms accordingly, actually with the national economy existing in the integrated forms. For the sake of research convenience, however, the research will be conducted from the aspect of practical form and value form. Karl Marx has carried out a detailed study over the rule of merchandise movement from the value form, contributing a great deal to both social and scientific developments. "The MF " studies the rule of merchandise movement with an emphasis on the material form point of view.

Viewing from practical form, the whole national economy is made up of the three big domains: material manufacturing, material flowing and material consuming, thus it can be also said that the whole national economy consists of the three big backbone industry groups: manufacturing, MF and consumption. We regard MF not only as a backbone industry, but also as a backbone industry group, since it deals with a number of industries, such as transportation, distribution, storing, packing, circulation manufacturing, MF information, MF infrastructure construction, MF facilities production, MF technology development, MF education, MF service, MF management, and so on. Historically development of national economy in the various countries relies on the first backbone industry group of "manufacturing" and the second group of "consumption". Naturally MF comes to be the third group, which guarantees the national economy in every society.

For a long time, people think that the material flow is only material management and MF management, and not an industry. Through studies, we view that the MF is not only an industry, but also a backbone industry, and even a backbone industry group, just like production and consumption. This is called as "The MF industry group theory", and also as "The MF industry theory". "The MF industry theory:" is the important component of "the MF Theory". To really develop well the whole material flow undertaking, it's not sufficient to only hold the thought of MF industry. We must set the thought of "The MF industry theory" [4-5].

Above are the main contents in seven basic theories under The MF. They will play an effective role on not only the great development of China's MF science and technology in the new century but also that of China's MF undertaking. The key to realize the fast development of China's economy and society as well ass the peaceful uprising is to effectively carry out the work of Material Flow.

1. We should actively promote and popularize the new MF concept and expedite the comprehensive development of MF science and technology.
2. We should not only develop modern Material Flow, but also reasonably develop traditional Material Flow.
3. We should develop the third party MF, and further develop X Party Material Flow (XPMF).
4. We should energetically develop urban material flow, and even further develop rural material flow.
5. We should energetically and effectively carry out domestic material flow, and even further develop international material flow.
6. We should effectively develop Economic MF, and even further Social MF and Natural MF.

REFERENCES

1. S. Xu, Research on several issues of Wu Liu technological economics, *Wu Liu of China*. Volume 1, pp.16–18, (1985).
2. S. Xu, *Technological Economics* (People's Press: Jiangsu, 1988).
3. J. Ding, On work of China MF Association and academic research on China MF —— Speech on the 3rd annual meeting of China MF academic study and the 2nd session of 1st board of directors of China MF Association (October 15, 2004); http://www.chinawuliu.com.cn
4. S. Xu, A new discipline in the era of knowledge economy: Material Flow science and technology, *Systems Research and Behavioral Science*. Volume 23, Number 2, pp. 251-257, (2006).
5. S. Xu, Prospect of Research and Development on MF Science and Technology in *Proceedings of 2004 International Conference on MF/Logistic* (Beijing Jiaotong University Press: Beijing, 2004).
6. S. Xu, Research on Scientific Classification of MF, *Journal of Beijing Jiaotong University (Social Sciences Edition)*. Volume 1, Number 2, pp 21-24, (2002).
7. S. Xu, Research on Several Problems of MF Engineering, *Journal of Beijing Jiaotong University (Social Sciences Edition)*.Volume 2, Number 1, pp 21-22, (2003).
8. S. Xu, Scientific Classification on Material Flow (Cont.), *Journal of Beijing Jiaotong University (Social Sciences Edition)*. Volume 4, Number 4, pp 11-15, (2005).

9. S. Xu, Some Issues on Wu Liu Theory (Continuation), *Journal of Beijing Jiaotong University (Social Sciences Edition).* Volume 2, Number 3, pp 25-28, (2003).
10. S. Xu, Some Issues on MF Theory, *Journal of Beijing Jiaotong University (Social Sciences Edition).* Volume 1, Number 1, pp 1-4, (2002).

Optimization-Based Production Scheduling for Large Enterprises

Xiaohong Guan

Department of Automation, Tsinghua University, Beijing 100084, P.R. China
Systems Engineering Institute, SKLMS Lab, Xian Jiaotong University, Xi'an 710049, P.R. China xhguan@tsinghua.edu.cn xhguan@sei.xjtu.edu.cn

Abstract. Production scheduling of many industrial systems with complicated operating dynamics and constraints in large enterprises such as electric power generation, batch chemical process, etc is very important with significant economic impact. In this speech, a new method is presented to solve the scheduling problem of a class of production systems with hybrid dynamics and constraints. Within Lagrangian relaxation framework, the exact optimal solutions to the subproblems are efficiently obtained without discretizing the continuous production levels or introducing intermediate levels of relaxation. A novel definition of the discrete state associated with a consecutive time period is introduced so that solving each subproblem is decomposed into solving a continuous and a discrete optimization problem separately. The optimality principle is applicable for both continuous and discrete problems. A double dynamic programming method is developed to solve the entire subproblem. To deal with the issues caused by homogenous subproblems, the successive subproblem solving (SSS) method is presented in this speech. With the introduction of the convex penalty terms associated with the system constraints, individual subproblems are solved successively to obtain a proper surrogate subgradient direction for the high level dual problem. In this way, the solutions to the homogenous subproblems can be differentiated in the dual solution. More dual solution patterns can be generated by the SSS method than by the standard LR method, and it is possible to modify the dual solution into better feasible schedules. The testing results for the practical problems of power generation scheduling and generation resource bidding demonstrate that the methods presented in the speech are efficient and effective.

Keywords: *Production scheduling, Resource allocation, Dynamic programming, Lagrangian relaxation*

1. INTRODUCTION

Production scheduling of many industrial systems in large enterprises such as electric power generation, batch chemical process, etc is very complicated since both discrete decision variables such as up/down of a production unit, and continuous decision variables such as production levels along a time horizon need to be determined. There may be many complicated operating dynamics and constraints such as minimum up/down time requirements of individual production units, ramping limits of production levels, total energy availability, etc. Due to huge social and economic impact on production costs, energy consumption and environmental pollution, scheduling such systems has been active research topics for many decades [1-6]. One of such scheduling problems is power generation scheduling, also called unit commitment or hydrothermal scheduling [1, 4-6]. A one percent savings of production (generation) cost could means more than 10 millions US dollars for a large generation company. Although the electrical power industries worldwide are being deregulated and their operating patterns are changing, the optimization based production scheduling is the core for market clearing computation and for analyzing and developing good bidding strategies [7].

Obtaining the optimal production schedule is usually extremely difficult since production scheduling is usually an NP-hard hybrid optimization problem [1-8]. It is more desirable to have efficient approaches for near-optimal solutions [8]. Among various near-optimal approaches, Lagrangian Relaxation (LR) is one of the most successful ones for problems with decomposable structure [1, 3, 4, 6]. In the LR solution framework, the system wide constraints are relaxed by Lagrange multipliers and the problem is solved in a two-level optimization structure. The decomposed subproblems are solved at the low level with much smaller dimensions and less complexity and the multipliers are updated at the high level dual problem. However, the solution obtained in this framework, called dual solution, is generally infeasible. That is, the once relaxed system wide constraints are not satisfied. A method, usually heuristic, is needed to modify the dual solution into a near optimal feasible solution. The most obvious advantage of the LR approach is its computational efficiency since its computational complexity increases almost linearly with the problem size. Furthermore since the dual cost is a lower bound of the original primal cost, solution quality can be quantitatively evaluated. Besides, Lagrange multipliers have some important economic interpretations as system shadow prices. They can be utilized to perform quick what-if studies. The LR based approaches have been successfully applied for manufacturing job shop scheduling, power generation, supply chain planning, and even routing and wavelength assignment of optimal networks, etc.[1-9].

Although the subproblems within the LR framework are much easier to solve than the original problem, the hybrid dynamics and constraints coupling each other may still be very difficult to handle. The commonly applied approaches are heuristics, dynamic programming by discretizing production levels or adding additional level of relaxation for continuous constraints with heuristics to obtain feasible schedules [10-13]. The optimal solutions to the subproblems may not be obtained. In such a case, the convergence basis for the LR based approaches may be violated [14]. Moreover, the computational efficiency of the LR approach would be offset due to a large number of states caused by discretization or many additional iterations at the intermediate level. Therefore it is desirable to have a systematic method to deal with the subproblems with hybrid dynamics and constraints in the LR framework.

Another serious but inherent issue in applying Lagrangian relaxation based methods is caused by the homogeneous subproblem solutions associated with the identical production units [15, 16]. That is, if some subproblems are homogenous or identical, no matter how the multipliers are updated, the solutions to these subproblems will always be the same. For example, suppose in the optimal schedule,

5 of the 10 identical production units should be in production and rest 5 units should be idle at a particular time. However, in the LR framework, the solutions to the subproblems associated with these identical units are the same. These 10 units will be either scheduled in production or idle simultaneously, possibly causing serious solution oscillations with a slight change of the multipliers. Moreover, the identical schedule for these units obtained in the dual solution may be far away from the optimal schedule and gives little information to construct feasible solution with the dual solution structure. This issue has long been recognized as a major obstacle in applying Lagrangian based approach for production scheduling especially for systems with a significant number of identical or very similar production units.

In this speech, the scheduling problem of a class of production systems with hybrid dynamics and constraints is discussed with practical backgrounds. A new method is presented to obtain the exact optimal solutions to the subproblems with hybrid dynamics and constraints efficiently without discretizing the continuous production levels or introducing intermediate levels of relaxation [17, 18]. A novel definition of the discrete state associated with a consecutive time period is introduced so that solving each subproblem is decomposed into solving a continuous and a discrete optimization problem separately. With this new definition, the optimal discrete state transition is not affected by the historical continuous states and discrete states and the optimality principle is still applicable for both continuous and discrete problems. The double dynamic programming method is developed to solve the entire subproblem.

To deal with the issues caused by homogenous subproblems, the successive subproblem solving (SSS) method is presented in this speech [15, 16]. Although the subproblems are no longer decomposable with the introduction of the convex penalty terms associated with the system constraints, individual subproblems are solved successively to obtain a proper surrogate subgradient direction for the high level dual problem [19]. As a result the solutions to the homogenous subproblems can be differentiated in the dual solution. This method can generate more dual solution patterns than the standard LR approach and make it easier to modify the dual solution into good feasible schedules.

Numerical testing is shown for the practical problems of power generation scheduling and generation resource bidding. The testing results demonstrate that the methods presented in the speech are efficient and effective for scheduling the production systems with hybrid dynamics and constraints. In comparison with the standard subgradient and surrogate subgradient method [19], the new SSS method can generate much better feasible solutions with much less oscillations.

REFERENCES

1. Cohen and V. Sherkat, Optimization-Based Methods for Operations Scheduling, in *Proceedings of IEEE*. Volume 75, Number 12, pp.1574-1591, (1987).
2. R.F.H. Muiser and L.B. Evans, An Approximated Method for the Production Scheduling of Industrial Batch Process with Parallel Units, *Computers Chem. Eng*. Volume 13, Number 2, pp.229-238, (1989).

3. H. Chen and C. Chu, A Lagrangian Relaxation Approach for Supply Chain Planning with Order/Setup Costs and Capacity Constraints, *Journal of Systems Science and Systems Engineering*. Volume 12, Number 1, pp.98-110, (2003).
4. X. Guan, E. Ni, R. Li, and P.B. Luh, An Optimization-Based Scheduling Algorithm for Scheduling Hydrothermal Power Systems with Cascaded Reservoirs and Discrete Hydro Constraints, *IEEE Transactions on Power Systems*. Volume 12, Number 4, pp.1775-1780, (1997).
5. C.H. Bannister and R.J. Kaye, A Rapid Method for Optimization of Linear Systems with Storage, *Operations Research*. Volume 39, Number 2, pp.220-232, (1991).
6. A. Renaud, Daily Generation Management at Electricite de France: From Planning towards Real Time, *IEEE Transactions on Automatic Control*. Volume 39, Number 7, pp.1080-1093, (1999).
7. B.F. Hobbs, M.H. Rothhopf, R.P. Oneill, and H. Chao (eds.), *The Next Generation of Electric Power Unit Commitment Models* (Kluwer Academic Publishers: 1999).
8. X. Guan, S. Guo, Q. Zhai, W. Gong, and C. Qiao, A New Method for Solving Routing and Wavelength Assignment Problems in Optical Networks, *IEEE/OSA Journal of Lightwave Technology* (forthcoming).
9. D.S. Hochbaum (eds), *Approximation Algorithms for NP-Hard Problems* (PWS Publishing Company: Boston, 1995).
10. X. Guan, P.B. Luh, and H. Yan, An Optimization-Based Method for Unit Commitment, *International Journal of Electric Power & Energy Systems*. Volume 14, Number 1, pp.9-17, (1992).
11. J.F. Bard, Short-term Scheduling of Thermal-Electric Generators Using Lagrangian Relaxation, *Operations Research*. Volume 36, Number 5, pp.756-766 (1988).
12. M.S. Salam, K.M. Nor, and A.R. Hamdan, Hydrothermal Scheduling Based Lagrangian Relaxation Approach to Hydrothermal Coordination, *IEEE Transactions on Power Systems*. Volume 13, Number 1, pp.226-235, (1998).
13. W.L. Peterson and S.R. Brammer, A Capacity Based Lagrangian Relaxation Unit Commitment with Ramp Rate Constraints, *IEEE Transactions on Power Systems*. Volume 10, Number 1, pp.1077-1084, (1998).
14. A.M. Geoffrion, Lagrangian Relaxation for Integer Programming, *Mathematical Programming Study*. Volume 2, pp.82-114, (1974).
15. X. Guan, Q. Zhai, and F. Lai, A New Lagrangian Relaxation Based Algorithm for Resource Scheduling with Homogenous Subproblems, *Journal of Optimization: Theory and Applications*. Volume 113, Number 1, pp.65-82, (2002).
16. Q. Zhai, X. Guan, and J. Cui, Unit Commitment with Identical Units: Successive Subproblem Solving Method Based on Lagrangian Relaxation, *IEEE Transactions on Power Systems*. Volume 17, Number 4, pp.1250-1257, (2002).
17. W. Fan, X. Guan, and Q. Zhai, A New Method for Unit Commitment with Ramping Constraints, *Electric Power Systems Research*. Volume 63, Number 3, pp.215-224, (2002).
18. Q. Zhai and X. Guan, Production Scheduling with Hybrid Dynamics and Constraints, *Proceedings of 42nd IEEE Conference on Control and Decision* (IEEE, Bahamas Island: December 15-18, 2004), pp.2780-2785.
19. X. Zhao, P. B. Luh, and J. Wang, The Surrogate Gradient Algorithm for Lagrangian Relaxation, *Journal of Optimization: Theory and Applications*. Volume 100, Number 3, pp.699-712, (1999).

The REA Enterprise Ontology: A New Accounting Infrastructure for Enterprise Systems

William McCarthy

Accounting & Information Systems Department, Michigan State University, East Lansing 48824, MI, U.S.A

Abstract. The data infrastructure for many present-day enterprise (ERP) systems can be traced back to the accounting-oriented legacy systems of the 1970s and 1980s. Most of this infrastructure was derived from these sources:

- customer and vendor master files (receivables and payables);
- open-purchase and open-sales order files (special journals);
- raw material, and finished goods files (inventory);
- work-in-process and manufacturing files (job and process costing);
- employee master and training files (payroll); and
- the general ledger files.

The REA (resource-event-agent) enterprise ontology re-factors and extends this data infrastructure by discarding double-entry accounting artifacts and using in their stead a single business process design pattern consisting of the following temporal layers or components:

- a representation of ***what has occurred*** in business transactions (resources, events, agents);
- a representation of ***what could be or should be*** in business transactions (its business rules expressed as connected abstractions of resources, events, and agents); and
- a representation of ***what is planned or scheduled*** in business transactions (its contracted or scheduled commitments).

REA also connects the evolving states of the business entities in the REA pattern to both (1) their planned and accomplished workflows, and (2) their roles within the overall value chain of a single company and within the supply chains of collaborating companies.

This keynote speech will explain the components of the REA ontology and explore their use in developing enterprise systems. A UML class diagram detailing the REA pattern is shown in Figure 1.

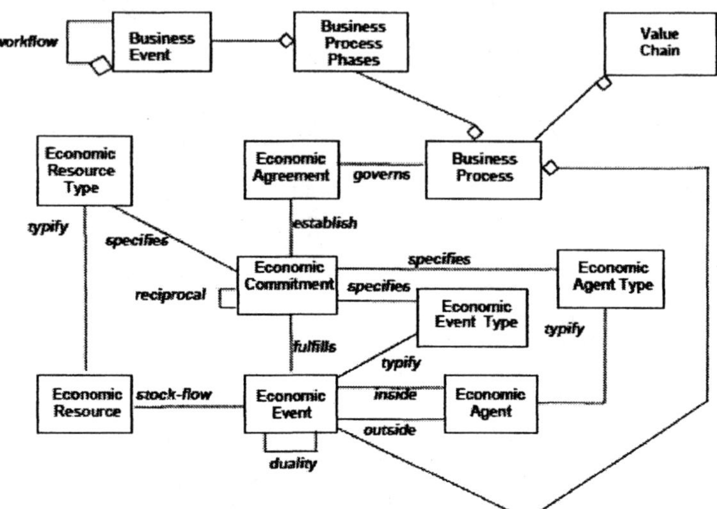

Figure 1 REA Enterprise Ontology-Base Classes

SOURCE: Adapted from Guido L. Geerts and William E. McCarthy "The Ontological Foundations of REA Enterprise Information Systems,"Working Paper, Michigan State University, 2007

A Hybrid Approach for Business Process Verification

Bing Li and Junichi Iijima

Graduate School of Decision Science and Technology, Tokyo Institute of Technology
W9-66, 2-12-1 Ookayama, Meguro, Tokyo, Japan {li.b.ab, iijima.j.aa }@m.titech.ac.jp

Abstract. Business Process Verification (BPV) works as one of the important functions in the emerging Business Process Management Systems. Current proposed approaches are not yet well applied because of the gap between formal models defined in the academia and informal models used in the industry. This paper attempts to propose a hybrid approach to solve this problem. XPDL will be used to describe business processes and Situation Calculus will be employed as the formalism to perform the function of BPV. A typical order fulfillment process is exemplified to illustrate the approach and the demonstration system implements the automatic transformation from the XPDL-defined process and performs the logical verification.

Keywords: *Business process verification, XPDL, Situation calculus*

1. INTRODUCTION

As part of modern enterprise information systems, Business Process Management Systems (BPMS) are increasingly important and receive greater consideration from the enterprise's executives and IT engineers. BPMS can be defined as a generic software system that is driven by explicit process designs to enact and manage operational business processes from the perspective of IT system engineers [1]. Business process design is important in the emerging BPMS.

Many previous and current research efforts are related to business process design, also called workflow modeling or business process modeling. These approaches can be classified into two categories. Applications of formal methods in business process modeling fall in the category of formal approaches, which usually employ mathematical logic [2-4]. The obvious strength of these approaches resides in the precise and inferable process model that can be verified mathematically and automatically. But since these formal approaches emphasize mathematical notation and calculi, they are not yet well applied to the BPM industry. On the other hand, informal approaches are more supported by BPMS vendors. They usually define a process in graphical or text-based languages. Then the defined process is simulated and tested to uncover potential errors that have been existent in the design phase. The merit of these informal approaches is their friendliness to general users. But the function of business process verification is obviously insufficient and detection of design errors is possibly postponed to the simulation phase or even to the execution phase.

Please use the following format when citing this chapter:

Li, B., Iijima, J., 2007, in IFIP International Federation for Information Processing, Volume 254, Research and Practical Issues of Enterprise Information Systems II Volume 1, eds. L. Xu, Tjoa A., Chaudhry S. (Boston: Springer), pp. 1-9.

A hybrid approach integrating both informal and formal approaches in business process design, promises to combine the aforementioned separate strengths in BPMS. This paper attempts to elucidate such a hybrid approach for business process verification (BPV), which is especially important in dynamically designing business processes. A typical order fulfillment process will be used to explain the approach and implementation of model transformation from the XPDL-defined process. A general explanation and the detailed underlying formalization can be found in Li et al. [5] and [6].

2. EXAMPLE

2.1 Order Fulfillment Process

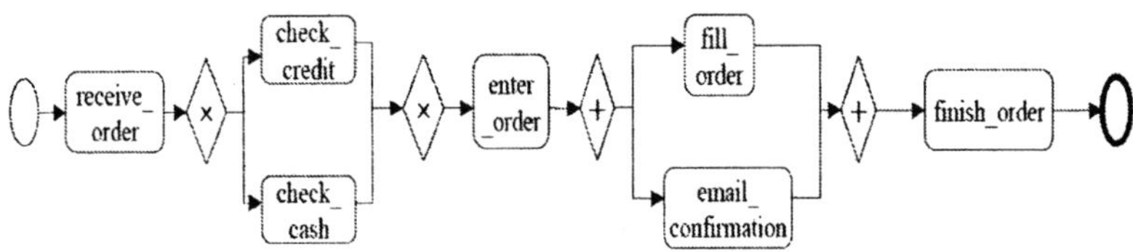

Figure 1. Order Fulfillment Process (BPMN)

As shown in Figure 1, a simple but typical example – order fulfillment process – is used to explain the approach in this paper. This process can include the five basic workflow patterns found in Havey [7]. For convenience, in this paper these workflow patterns will be referred to as XOR-Split, XOR-Join, AND-Split, And-Join and Sequence. To avoid displaying the whole lengthy process definition in XML syntax, Business Process Modeling Notation (BPMN) [8] is used to illustrate the process graphically and intuitively. From this BPMN-defined process model, the constituent activities and the transition routing can be clearly shown. BPMN can undoubtedly provide the communication convenience to some extent. However, it can not precisely represent a process model or allow for easy analysis. Therefore we prefer to use an XML-syntaxed language in this research.

2.2 XML Process Definition Language (XPDL)

XPDL[9] is an industrial standard which is supported by many BPMS developers and vendors. This approach selects XPDL as the source process model for its analyzability in XML syntax. XPDL focuses on the business logic and can specify transition relations in business processes. Constituents in a process are represented by using the concepts such as *Workflow Process*, *Activity*, *Transition* and so on. By employing this process specification standard, the approach will make it easy to integrate the industrial efforts and put them into practice. For example, the XPDL specification related to the activity "check_credit" is shown as follows. Referring to Figure 1 helps to understand the XML-based specification intuitively. The activity can be referred by using the id of "check_credit"; the activity will be implemented by an application, which can be a software application or another process; the input parameters are "CardNo" and "Rate" that refer to the NO. Of the credit card and the rating of the credit; the performer information can be provided. The control flows are represented by transitions. There are one incoming transition – from "xor_split" to "check_credit" and one outgoing transition – from "check_credit" to "xor_join"; the transition conditions can be represented by using equations or other mathematical expressions.

```
...
<Activity Id="check_credit">
   <Implementation>
            <Tool Id="check_credit_app" Type="APPLICATION">
                     <ActualParameters>
                              <ActualParameter>CardNo</ActualParameter>
                              <ActualParameter>Rate</ActualParameter>
                     </ActualParameters>
            </Tool>
   </Implementation>
   <Performer>orderProcessor</Performer>
   <ExtendedAttributes/>
</Activity>
...
<Transition From="xor_split" Id="order_fulfillment_tra2" To="check_credit">
   <Condition Type="CONDITION">
            PayWay= ="credit" CreditStatus= ="none"
   </Condition>
</Transition>
...
<Transition From="check_credit" Id="tra3" To="xor_join">
   <Condition Type="CONDITION">
            CreditStatus = = "valid"
   </Condition>
</Transition>
...
```

The above XML script specifies the activity from the perspectives of input parameters, performers and transitions. In particularly, transition relations construct the control flow of a business process and related errors can lead to deadlock or unreachable activities. This paper concentrates on the control flow perspective, but the approach is possibly applied to verify other aspects of business processes such as global constraints [2].

In XPDL, the complex transitions can be represented by routing activities that correspond to the gateways in BPMN. In the above example, the "xor_split" and "xor_join" are routing activities. A transition has some conditions and only when these conditions are satisfied, the transition can happen.

In respect to transition conditions, the repressiveness of the current XPDL specification is not so robust. This problem can be overcome by clearly defining the format of conditions or directly using some XML-syntaxed rule languages.

3. FORMAL VERIFICATION

3.1 Motivation of Formal Verification

Formal verification is necessary in the emerging BPMS[10]. Expanding and fast changing business needs require that business processes should be designed and deployed quickly. Human-designed processes are prone to containing potential errors or bugs, which may increase development time and cost. But formal verification of a business process before execution can greatly reduce errors in the design phase.

In detail, formal verification can bring the following benefits. First, it can remove any ambiguity from a business process and make it more precise. Formal verification will employ a formal language, which is usually a mathematical logic. Based on such a formal language, business processes can be specified in a precise and concise way. Second, this formal process specification will enable inference functions, including automatic verification, process analysis, etc.

But a gap exists between the industrial standard process description language, such as XPDL, and formal languages that are used in the academic research. This is why the function of verification is still not sufficient in BPMS products. This hybrid approach attempts to bridge this gap between XPDL and a formal language – Situation Calculus. This strategy is also meaningful to other BPM languages such as Business Process Execution Language (BPEL).

3.2 Formalism of Situation Calculus

Situation Calculus was first introduced by John McCarthy and later extended by Ray Reiter. Much research work has been done in this formalism and it has become a formal language to model dynamical domains.

Situation Calculus has strength of reasoning about actions. This formalism can be applied to business process modeling including verification [4].The semantic transformation from XPDL to Situation Calculus seems intuitive and uncomplicated. Furthermore Situation Calculus is extensible to include some dynamic features such as concurrency and reactiveness. Some basic concepts including action, situation and fluent will briefly introduced. Detailed explanations can be found in Reiter [11] and Brachman et al. [12].

Actions are represented by action functions that consist of functional symbols and corresponding arguments. Situations are world histories represented by the sequence of actions. Fluents are functions and predicates that are dependent on the situation, which can represent the status and changes of the modeling world.

A domain model in Situation Calculus mostly consists of actions. An action is specified by precondition and successor state axioms. These axioms will be constructed by action functions, situations and fluents. Truth values of the fluents in these axioms will separately ensure executability of the action and satisfiability of the successor states.

The underlying concept is that the execution of an action will change the world states by making the related fluents become true; thus the new world state may satisfy the precondition of another action; then, this will result in the execution of an action sequence, that is, a situation starting from the initial world state.

3.3 Transformation from XPDL

XPDL is in XML syntax and has no obvious relationship with formal languages, which make it hard to be verified directly. Formal languages usually enable reasoning, including automatic verification, thanks to the underlying formal semantics. Thus transformation from XPDL is meaningful and Situation Calculus is selected for the strength explained in the section above. The specification in Situation Calculus will provide a precise and inferable process model for future analysis.

This research focuses on the control flow perspective of a business process and the transformation of transition relations in XPDL to Situation Calculus is most part of our work. As explained in Section 2.2 (XPDL) and Section 3.2 (Situation Calculus), the activities in XPDL correspond to the actions in Situation Calculus; the parameters correspond to the arguments in the action functions. Thus the obvious gap lies between the transition conditions in XPDL and the precondition and successor state axioms in Situation Calculus.

To bridge the gap between XPDL and Situation Calculus, we devise XML Situation-calculus Specification Language (XSSL), which attempts to represent some concepts in Situation Calculus by using XML syntax. In this format, the transformation will be convenient to introduce. Moreover, XSSL will enable the separation of activity specification from process specification, which can improve reusability of some common activities or processes.

Furthermore, it potentially improves the usage of Situation Calculus with more extension work to improve the expressiveness of XSSL. The key is to define XSSL more independently from XPDL, and represent more concepts of Situation Calculus in XML syntax.

The following XML script specifies the action of "check_credit", which actually expresses the elements of XSSL. The XPDL-defined process specification can be automatically transformed into the XSSL-defined one. From the XSSL script, the important element is "Action", which corresponds to the "Activity" in XPDL. An action is represented with its arguments, preconditions and postconditions. These concepts can be directly mapped into the formalism of Situation Calculus.

```
...
    <Action Id="check_credit">
            <args>
```

```
                <arg>CardNo</arg>
                <arg>Rate</arg>
        </args>
        <preconditions>
                <precondition>OrderStatus= ="received"</precondition>
                <precondition>PayWay= ="credit"</precondition>
                <precondition>CreditStatus= ="none"</precondition>
        </preconditions>
        <postconditions>
                <postcondition>CreditStatus= ="valid"</postcondition>
                <postcondition>OrderStatus= ="checked"</postcondition>
        </postconditions>
    </Action>
...
```

When comparing this XSSL-defined activity with the XPDL-defined one, the main difference can be found to be in the transformation from the transition conditions in XPDL to the preconditions and postconditions in XSSL. This transformation is implemented based on the formal definition in Li et al. [6]. The defined mappings process different types of routing activities and calculate the preconditions and postconditions.

3.4 Logic Based Verification

The formalism of Situation Calculus can be implemented by a Prolog Interpreter [11]. Similarly, the logical process model – a formal specification in Situation Calculus – can be implemented by Prolog programs. Thus XSSL-defined process specification can be transformed into a Prolog format, which is an inferable model that can to be verified automatically. The following Prolog script specifies the action of "check_credit" based on the formalism of Situation Calculus.

```
...
poss(check_credit(PID,CardNo,Rate),S):-
    order_status(PID,received,S),
    pay_way(PID,credit),
    credit_status(PID,none,S),
    card_no(PID,CardNo),
    rate(PID,Rate).

credit_status(PID,valid,do(A,S)):-
    A=check_credit(PID,CardNo,Rate);
    credit_status(PID,valid,S).

order_status(PID,checked,do(A,S)):-
    A=check_credit(PID,CardNo,Rate);
    order_status(PID,checked,S),
    not A=enter_order(PID,OrderInfo).
...
```

The above Prolog-defined process specification can be automatically generated from the XSSL-defined one. Moreover, some extra processing work should be done such as the introduction of the process id (PID), which enables the process concurrency and instances, and recovery of data relations. This kind of information is expressed in XPDL and can also be extracted into XSSL. It will be our extension work to study on how to represent extra information such as data relation in XSSL while keeping the independence of XSSL from XPDL.

In order to improve the performance of verification in Prolog, some extra processing work is introduced. For example, backtracking on situations will lead to memory overflow from our development experience. To solve this problem, situations are constructed from the transition routing information in XPDL. That is, the possible routes can be extracted from XPDL, enabling the construction of action sequences – situations.

4. DEMONSTRATION OF THE BPV SYSTEM

The interface of the implemented demonstration system is shown in Figure 2.

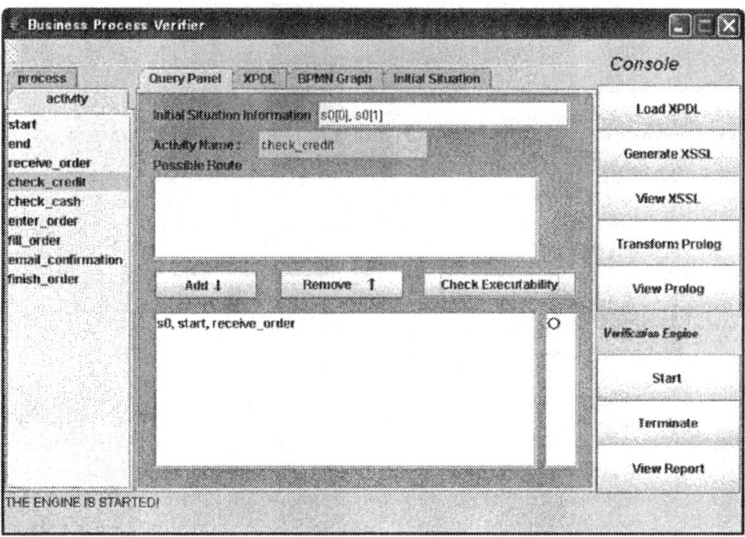

Figure 2. User Interface of the Demonstration System

A business process is defined in XPDL. This XPDL-defined business process can be defined with the aid of some XML editors or directly transformed from some graphical process model such as a BPMN-defined process one, which is currently not the focus of this research.

Load XPDL will parse the XPDL file and show the constituent activities in the left panel and other related information such as initial situations for testing. **Generate XSSL** will automatically generate the XSSL file from the XPDL file, and **Transform Prolog** will automatically transform the XSSL file into the Prolog file. These Prolog files will finally be used to build up the knowledge base for the background Prolog engine to make verification – to check the queries from the users.

The system is currently implemented at the activity level, that is, the whole process is verified after checking each activity involved. E.g., to check the activity of "check_credit", there is only one possible route according to the XPDL definition (referring to Figure 1). First, select it to construct the situation to be verified and also set the initial situation or use the default settings (**Add ↓**); second, **Start** will start the prolog engine and build up the related knowledge base; **Check Executability** will query this engine and show the result as "o" for success and "×" for failure. The current result show that the route will succeed under the default initial situation settings – that is, there is an order paid by credit card in the initial situation; and after executing the activity of "receive_order", the activity of "check_credit" can be executed.

The successful result shows that the checked activity is executable in a certain situation. After each activity involved in a process is verified, the whole process is actually ensured to be executable. It is direct to make the whole process verification if we encapsulate the checking for each involved activity and just check the last activity in the transition route. When there is an error, it is necessary to backtrack and find where the problem occurs – that is, the transition condition can not be satisfied.

The verification employs action reasoning in Situation Calculus, which enables automatic verification at the semantic level. The precondition of each activity is verified to ensure that there is no deadlock in the process. The successor state condition interconnects the activities and represents the state changes in the process, thus making the whole process verification possible.

5. CONCLUSIONS AND FUTURE WORK

In this paper we proposed a hybrid approach for business process verification and explained it focusing on the model transformation from an XPDL-defined process. The underlying formalization was explained in Li et al. [6] that provided the theoretical foundation for this paper. The implementation of the prototype system and the internal automatic transformation demonstrated the feasibility of the approach.

This hybrid approach integrates the informal language – XPDL, and the formal language – Situation Calculus. By linking them to cooperate in business process verification, we can obtain some meaningful results. Practicability and robustness are two direct benefits. Besides, the formalized process specification is more precise and becomes inferable, enabling more potential analysis of business processes.

Much work still needs to be done in the future research. Only some concepts in XPDL are currently mapped to Situation Calculus. In order to put this approach into large-scale industrial application, some further extension of the transformation should be done. Furthermore, this approach is currently only applied to business process verification and it could be also used to dynamically aid process design such as providing some recommendation for process composition.

REFERENCES

1. M. Weske, W.M.P. Van Der Aalst, and H.M.W. Verbeek, Advances in business process management, *Data & Knowledge Engineering.* Volume 50, pp.1-8, (2004).
2. S. Mukherjee, H. Davulcu, M. Kifer, P. Senkul, and G. Yang, Logic Based Approaches to Workflow Modeling and Verification, *Logics for Emerging Applications of Databases* (Springer, 2003).
3. G.K. Janssens, J. Verelst, and B. Weyn, Techniques for Modeling Workflows and Their Support of Reuse, in *Business Process Management*, LNCS1806 (Springer, 2000), pp.1-15.
4. M. Koubarakisa, and D. Plexousakis, A formal framework for business process modeling and design, *Information Systems.* Volume 27, (2002), pp.299-319.
5. B. Li, and J. Iijima, Bridging The Gap Between XPDL And Situation Calculus: A Hybrid Approach For Business Process Verification, in *Proc. of the 5th International Workshop on Modeling, Simulation, Verification and Validation of Enterprise Information Systems – MSVVEIS 2007* (INSTICC, 2007), pp. 151-156.
6. B. Li, and J. Iijima, Formal Verification of XPDL-based Business Process Definition, *The International Journal of Business Process Integration and Management* (submitted, 2007).
7. M. Havey, *Essential Business Process Modeling*, 1st edition (O'Reilly: 2005).
8. OMG, *Business Process Modeling Notation Specification* (2006).
9. WfMC, *Process Definition Interface – XML Process Definition Language*, Version 2.0 (2005).
10. W.M.P. Van Der Aalst, and A.H.M. Ter Hofsede, Verification of Workflow Task Structures: A Petri-Net-Based Approach, *Information Systems.* Volume 25, Number 1, pp.43-69, (2000).
11. R. Reiter, *Knowledge in Action: Logical Foundations for Specifying and Implementing Dynamical Systems* (MIT Press: Massachusetts, 2001).
12. R. Brachman and H. Levesque, *Knowledge Representation and Reasoning* (Morgan Kaufmann, 2004).

Grid-Based Information Aggregation Architecture for Supply Chain Coordination

Ding Fang and Jie Liu

Department of Information System and Information Management, Fudan University, Shanghai 200433, P.R. China fangding_fd@126.com liujie@fudan.edu.cn

Abstract. To support supply chain coordination management model's development and popularization, information platform must be able to integrate information resources in the supply chain and make them collaborate dynamically. Grid technologies and infrastructures support the sharing and coordinated use of diverse resources in dynamic, distributed virtual organizations. It's regarded as the promising foundation for constructing supply chain system. This paper proposed grid-based information aggregation architecture for supply chain coordination based on the analysis of the supply chain coordination problem.

Keywords: *Supply chain coordination, Grid technology, Information aggregation, Enterprise application integration, Inter-enterprise collaboration*

1. INTRODUCTION

To survive today's business environment, an enterprise needs to consider leveraging resources in an area beyond the boundary of itself. Now the competition of enterprises is indeed the competition of supply chains. After about 20 years' development, both the academic research and enterprise practice indicate that coordination management is the trend of the supply chain management. Currently, the coordination management model for the supply chain information flow and production flow mainly includes VMI (Vendor Managed Inventory), JMI (Jointly Managed Inventory) and CPFR (Collaborative Planning, Forecasting and Replenishment) [1].

It's well known that information technology and the information system (IT/IS) is the enabler of modern business model. Many literatures take IT/IS as one of the key successful factor of the implementation of VMI, JMI and CPFR model. However, because traditional supply chain coordination system has flaws of inflexibility and closeness, they are not sufficient for today's dynamic and adaptive business environment. In order to support the development and popularization of the supply chain coordination management model, information platform must have capability of supporting heterogeneous resources integration and collaboration dynamically. On the other hand, grid technologies are emerging as an infrastructure for next generation business computing, enabling distributed resource management, and large-scale computational problems in science, engineering and commerce [2]. With the

Please use the following format when citing this chapter:

Fang, D., Liu, J., 2007, in IFIP International Federation for Information Processing, Volume 254, Research and Practical Issues of Enterprise Information Systems II Volume 1, eds. L. Xu, Tjoa A., Chaudhry S. (Boston: Springer), pp. 11-18.

characteristics of openness, heterogeneity, distribution and autonomy, grid technology will be the promising foundation for constructing supply chain coordination system.

The rest of this paper is structured as follows. In the next section, we first introduce the research background from the practice and theory aspect respectively. In section 3 we analyze the supply chain coordination problem. In section 4 we present grid-based information aggregation architecture for supply chain coordination with each major function and key issues explained in detail. We summarize the paper and discuss the future work in the last section.

2. RESEARCH BACKGROUND

1) Practice Background

Without the support of IT/IS, modern business model could not be implemented. The supply chain coordination system's objective is to connect business partners, suppliers, dealers, retailers and even the end customers together, leveraging resource sharing and collaboration of the supply chain, supporting the enterprises to compose dynamic alliance, dealing with the volatile market environment together. Now, many manufacture enterprises and MIS software suppliers both home and abroad have paid much attention to supply chain coordination system. Taking steel and automobile industry as example, Shanghai Baosteel Company, a leading company in china steel industry, has developed collaborative commerce platform with Faw-Volkswagen automotive company and Shanghai General Motors respectively. Chang-an Automobile also developed its collaborative commerce platform with its supplier. Main MIS software suppliers such as SAP, Oracle, i2 have also added the supply chain coordination model to their products.

However, traditional supply chain coordination systems have some critical flaws. The main flaws among them are inflexibility and closeness. These flaws make it difficult for information to share effectively and hard for enterprises to join the collaboration system dynamically. These flaws strictly handicap the development and popularization of coordination management model. For example, the coordination system between Baosteel and Shanghai GM can not automatically integrate the sale plan information, production plan information and stock data of the third logistic company, which can't meet the requirement for the smooth transformation from VMI to JMI and CPER model. Besides, because of the closeness of the system, it will be very hard for other automobile company to join Baosteel's coordination system dynamically. Thus, Baosteel have to develop a new system for every automobile enterprise. The long developing period and high cost (almost 1 million RMB for one system) make the coordination management model only can be implemented with few important partners. To support development and popularization of coordination management model, the supply chain coordination system must have the capability of supporting integration of distribution, dynamic and heterogeneous resources and seamless collaboration of them.

2) Theory Background

Grid computing has gained tremendous popularity in the last five years and remains a major topic. The early development of Grid technologies was motivated by the problems of creating scientific resource sharing applications, e.g., collaborative visualization of large scientific data sets, and increasing functionality and availability by coupling scientific instruments and remote computer and archives.

More recently, attempts have been made to open grids to other application fields. Indeed grids appears a promising candidate infrastructure paradigm for managing applications distributed over MAN/WAN and designed to share information and service among users. Thus, aside from computing grids, information grids, knowledge grids and manufacturing grids are now considered with a very high interest.

Ian Foster, who is the head of the distributed systems lab at Argonne National and also an authority in grid field, define grid as a distributed computing infrastructure, coordinated resource sharing and problem solving in dynamic, multi-institutional virtual organizations [3]. In industry community, IBM define grid as any of a variety of levels of virtualization along a continuum, thus, from local area, inside organization, outside organization to global area [4].

Grid has proven itself a viable infrastructure for distributed resource sharing platforms for scientific computing domain. Grid promises to offer solutions to the construction of reliable, scalable, and distributed systems, all of which are very important characteristics of supply chain coordination system [5]. Thus grid technology will be the promising foundation for constructing supply chain coordination system.

3. SUPPLY CHAIN COORDINATION PROBLEMS

In VMI model, vendors make the decision of replenishment time, replenishment amount and transportation way by monitoring the stock situation and sales information of the retailer. However, VMI model only transfer risks to the suppliers, the whole supply chain performance is not been improved essentially. Based on the VMI model, two advanced coordination model-JMI and CPFR-has been developed. JMI is a much more detailed extension of VMI but the goals and premise are quite similar. JMI put more emphasis upon managing stock together within partners. JMI included some factors of CPFR, and is considered the transition model form the VMI to CPFR. CPFR's goal is to improve the partnership between trading partners through collaborative processes and shared information. CPFR automates and improves sales forecasting and replenishment between trading partners, enabling participants to share improvements in inventory costs, revenue, and customer service. VICS (American Volunteer Inter-industry Commerce Standards Association) presented CPFR reference operation process [6].

From the CPFR's mission and operation process, we can see that successful CPFR depends on the effective sharing of the information among partners. Advanced Planning and Scheduling（APS）is the plan tool of the supply chain coordination. APS is also a plan method based on the theory of constraints (TOC). In order to make feasible coordination plan, enterprises in the supply chain must share customer requirement information, order information, stock information, product data information and production constraint information with their partners. But this information is separated in different system such as PDM, PLM, ERP, CRM, WMS and OA system. Coordination forecasting needs to use information in the CRM and ERP system. Coordination logistics need to use information in the TMS, GPS and GIS system. However, these systems have heterogeneity both in the technology platform and information semantics. For example, these systems were often developed in the different programming environment, such as .Net, J2EE and CORBA, some legacy system even use mainframe environment and COBOL. Meanwhile, for lack of the uniform semantic repertory, information semantics in the supply chain often conflict or wrap with others. All of these are the obstacles of the information aggregation.

4. GRID-BASED INFORMATION AGGREGATION ARCHITECTURE FOR SUPPLY CHAIN COORDINATION

Grid architecture identifies fundamental system components, specifies the purpose and function of these components, and indicates how these components interact with one another. Currently there are many researches about the grid architecture [2-3, 7-8]. In this paper we divided these architectures into two categories: general grid architectures and application grid architecture. We will introduce them respectively in the following.

General grid architectures are not limit in certain application field. They only present instructive, abstract architecture framework and could be applied to other application grid, such as computation grid, information grid, manufacturing grid and knowledge grid. Currently there are two important general grid architecture, one is the five-level hourglass framework [2] provided by Foster in 2001, the other is OGSA (open grid service architecture) [3] also provided by Foster etc.

The five-level hourglass framework is a profound structure, which is protocol-centered, and it emphasizes the importance of service, API and SDK. However, its emphasis is not on concrete definition of protocol, but on qualitative description. The five-level framework separates the operation, management and use of sharing resource to five layers by the components and distance of sharing resource. The five layers are fabric layer, connectivity layer, resource layer, collective layer and application layer from the bottom up.

Grid technologies are evolving toward an Open Grid Services Architecture (OGSA) in which a Grid provides an extensible set of services that virtual organizations can aggregate in various ways. Building on concepts and technologies from both the Grid and Web services communities, OGSA defines uniform exposed service semantics (the Grid service); defines standard mechanisms for creating, naming, and discovering transient Grid service instances; provides location transparency and multiple protocol bindings for service instances; and supports integration with underlying native platform facilities. The open source Globus Toolkit described in the “OGSA and the Globus Toolkit” sidebar has emerged as a de facto standard for construction of Grid systems. Based on OGSA, Chunming Hu, Jinpeng Huai and Hailong Sun proposed a web service-based grid architecture, which points out how to apply web service into the grid system construction [7]. J. Luo, L. Xu and J. P. Jamont proposed architecture of agent grid, which is an intelligent platform that enables the agents to interact with one another to form dynamic services on the Grid [8].

Application grid architecture could be designed on the base of the domain problems' properties in combination with general grid architecture. For example, Yanli He, Haicheng Yang and Weiping He proposed a manufacturing grid architecture [9]; Mario Cannataro and Domenico Talia proposed knowledge grid architecture [10]. Jin Zhang and Dongyuan Yang proposed logistic information grid architecture [11]. All of these grid architectures are based on the layer structure provided by the general grid architecture.

Since supply chain coordination grid's objective is to solve the integration and collaborative problem of the heterogeneous information resources and application resources in the supply chain, it's an information grid in essence. This paper proposed grid-based supply chain coordination system architecture based on the analysis of the supply chain coordination problems, which is illustrated in figure 1. The follows will explain each layer's function and key problems in detail.

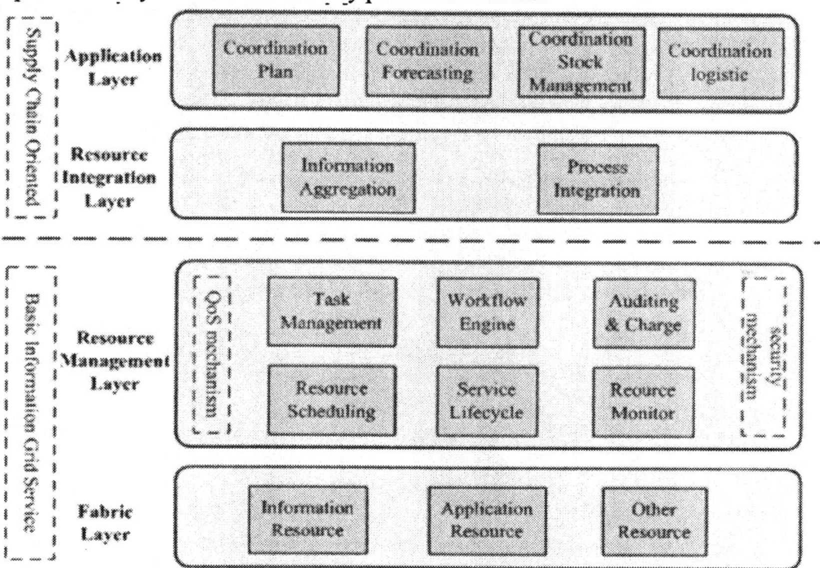

Figure 1. Grid-based Supply Chain Coordination System Architecture

4.1 Fabric Layer

This layer provides a set of tools and APIs controlling local resources. In the computation grid, resource means CPU, band width and storage. In the Information grid and knowledge grid resource mainly means information and application resource. In the manufacturing grid resource includes equipment and instrument. Like information grid, resource in the grid-based supply chain coordination system includes data resource, meta-data resource, ontology resource and application resource. Data resource covers one enterprise's product technology, customer requirement, stock, order, finance, production and product constraint information. Application resource is the software and agent that contains management science model (production and plan model, forecasting model, logistic model, etc.) and other computation function (such as data mining).

4.2 Resource Management Layer

Resource management layer provides the running environment of the resource. Grid services standard provide a standard programming model, which makes it possible for resource to be published, discovered and invoked. The web service protocols cluster provides open, scalable and standard foundation for the implementation and interoperation of resources. For example, WSDL could be used to describe services; UDDI and WS-Inspection could be used to implement service discover and dynamic binding; SOAP could be used to implement service invoking; WS-Security could be used in the security mechanism; BPEL4WS could be used in the service orchestration and workflow management. Based on these protocols, service management and interoperation model could be built.

4.3 Resources Integration Layer

In this layer, abstract resource is seamlessly integrated together to provide service to upper layers. According to the dependency degree to the information, resource aggregation could be divided into information aggregation and process integration.

4.3.1 Information Aggregation Sub-layer

Information aggregation means sharing understandable data among enterprise in the supply chain. For example, enterprise in the upstream of the supply chain need to know order fulfillment, production capability and production constraint information of downstream enterprises; enterprise in the downstream of the supply chain need to know customer requirement, stock, sales plan information of upstream enterprises.

Information semantic heterogeneity is the main obstacle for the information aggregation in the information grid. Because ontology has good concept structure, support formal definition of the term and support logistic reasoning, it's a promising candidate technology for the information aggregation in information grid. This paper proposed information aggregation architecture based on compound ontology, which is illustrated in figure 2. Data in the grid unit could be abstracted into 3 categories: Meta-data Resource (MR), Data Resource (DR) and Ontology Resource (OR). These resources are represented by grid services and could be invoked by the upper layer through the service protocol. The second layer (Resource management layer) is in charge of the management of the lifecycle and availability of these resources. There is an ontology merge & reasoning module in the information aggregation sub-layer, which could merge local ontology resources into global ontology resource. In combination with the local Meta Data resource and data resource, global aggregation data view could be built.

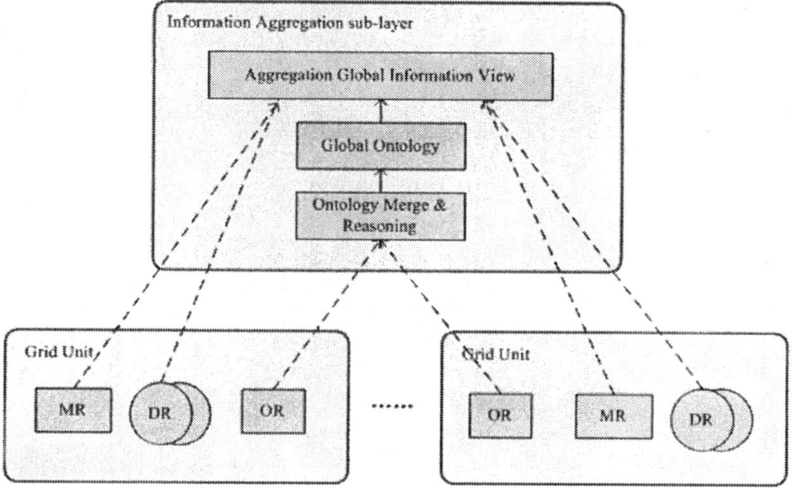

Figure 2. Ontology-Based Information Aggregation Model for Information Grid

4.3.2 Process Integration Sub-layer

Information aggregation is the entry-level of the supply chain integration. Process integration's goal is to implement the business process automation. The key issues of the process integration include: business process's description, modeling and decomposition; the orchestration of the business process; the coordination and transaction control of execution of business process.

4.4 Application Layer

This is the top layer of the architecture. This layer provides supply chain coordination application service to the user based on the information aggregation and process integration module. Supply chain application services include coordination plan, coordination forecasting, coordination stock management and coordination logistics. The key issues in this layer are the construction and solving method of the management science model.

5. SUMMARY AND FUTURE WORK

In this paper, we have presented a Grid-based information aggregation architectural framework for supply chain coordination. Meta-data, data, ontology and application in the supply chain enterprise are modeled as grid resource and represented by grid services. The components function and every layer's key issues have been described in this paper. The primary focus of our future work in this area will be on the development of more sophisticated ontology based information aggregation module. We are also interested in the business process integration under grid environment and CPFR models in steel and automotive supply chain.

REFERENCES

1. B. Fugate, F. Sahin, and J.T. Menzter, Supply Chain Management Coordination Mechanisms, *Journal of Business Logistics.* Volume 27, Number 2, pp.129-161, (2006).
2. I. Foster, C. Kesselman, and J.M. Nick, *Physiology of the Grid: An Open Grid Services Architecture for Distributed Systems Integration. Global Grid Forum.* http://www.globus.org/research/papers/ogsa.pdf(Accessed July 24, 2006).
3. I. Foster, C. Kesselman, and S. Tuecke, The Anatomy of the Grid: Enabling Scalable Virtual Organizations, *The International Journal of High Performance Computing Applications.* Volume 15, Number 3, pp.200-222, (2001).
4. B. Jacob, M. Brown, and K. Fukui, *Introduction to Grid Computing,* IBM Corporation. http://www.redbooks.ibm.com/redbooks/pdfs/sg246778.pdf (Accessed May 5, 2007).
5. J. Jeng, H. Chang, and J. Chung, BPMM: A Grid-Based Architectural Framework For Business Process Meta Management, in *Proc. of The 2003 Symposium On Applications And The Internet,* eds. S. Helal, Y. Oie, C. Chang, and J. Murai, pp.84-94 (IEEE Computer Society: Washington, DC, USA, 2003).
6. J. Andraski, C. Bremant, and G. Cantwell, *Collaborative Planning, Forecasting and Replenishment Version 2.0.,* Voluntary Interindustry Commerce Standards Association. http://www.vics.org/committees/cpfr/voluntary_v2/CPFR_Tabs_061802.pdf (Accessed May 22, 2007).
7. C. Hu, J. Huai, and H. Sun, Web Service-Based Grid Architecture and Its Supporting Environment, *Journal of Software (in Chinese).* Volume 15, Number 7, pp.1064-1073, (2004).
8. J. Luo, L. Xu, and J.P. Jamont, Flood Decision Support System on Agent Grid: Method and Implementation, *Enterprise Information Systems.* Volume 1, Number 1, pp.49-68, (2007).
9. Y. He, H. Yang, and W. He, Framework of Cross-Enterprise Collaborative Manufacturing Based On Grid Theory, *Computer Integrated Manufacturing Systems.* Volume 11, Number 5, pp.636-641, (2005).
10. M. Cannataro and D. Talia, The Knowledge Grid: Designing, Building, and Implementing an Architecture for Distributed Knowledge Discovery, *Communications of the ACM.* Volume 46, Number 1, pp.89-93, (2003).
11. J. Zhang and D. Yang, Architecture of Logistics Information Grid, *Science and Technology Review.* Volume 23, Number 10, pp.48-51, (2005).

What is Business Process Management: A Two Stage Literature Review of an Emerging Field

Charles Møller[1], Carsten J. Maack[2] and Rune D. Tan[3]

[1]Aalborg University, DK-9220 Aalborg charles@production.aau.dk
[2]Aarhus School of Business, DK-8210 Aarhus V carsten@ma2ck.dk
[3]Vestas Wind Systems A/S, DK-8900 Randers rdtan@vestas.com

Abstract. Business Process Management (BPM) is an emerging new field in business. However there is no academically agreed upon conceptual framework. The aim of this paper is to establish a conceptual framework grounded in the recent literature. The purpose of this work is to ensure a better foundation for future research and to discussion of the implications of BPM on Enterprise Information Systems (EIS). The starting point of this study is a focused literature review of the BPM concept. This literature review leads to the formulation of a conceptual framework for BPM which is evaluated using a quantitative lexical analysis of a broader literature sample. Finally the implication of the BPM on EIS is discussed and potential future research opportunities are outlined.

Keywords: *Business process management (BPM), Work flow management, Business transformation*

1. INTRODUCTION

Business Process Management (BPM) is a new concept that is gaining an increased recognition in the management literature [1, 2]. Recently we have seen that traditional computer science research in workflow management is extending its perspective towards BPM [3]. However there is no academically agreed upon conceptual framework for BPM, and the concept of BPM is often used for commercial purposes, which makes it hard to grasp the fundamental idea of BPM [4]. Analyst Terry Schurter defines (BPM) as a natural and holistic management approach to operating business that produces a highly efficient, agile, innovative, and adaptive organization that far exceeds that achievable through traditional management approaches [5]. This definition makes no explicit reference to IT, but rather agility is pivotal. Agility is vital to contemporary business and the role of IT in shaping agility is obvious [6]. Consequently a common fframework across business, technology and Information Systems (IS) is needed.

BPM is often proclaimed as a new management principle that gives companies the competitive advantages that is needed to support more agile and flexible business processes. Enterprise Information Systems (EIS), on the other hand, are described as tightly coupled system because they are built upon specific reference data models and process models, but still they are claimed inadequate to support agile business

Please use the following format when citing this chapter:

Møller, C., Maack, C. J., Tan, R. D., 2007, in IFIP International Federation for Information Processing, Volume 254, Research and Practical Issues of Enterprise Information Systems II Volume 1, eds. L. Xu, Tjoa A., Chaudhry S. (Boston: Springer), pp. 19-31.

processes. However, contemporary EIS is rapidly evolving towards BPM oriented principles [7]. The lack of agility and flexibility is thus the Achilles heel of many EIS. BPM appears to be the solution to this problem, but what is BPM really about and what are the implications to EIS? Therefore the aim of the paper is to present a comprehensive study and common framework for the concept of BPM in an EIS perspective. The purpose of this work is to ensure a better foundation for future research and discussion of the implications of BPM on EIS. The starting point of this study is a focused literature review of the BPM concept. The research methodology is discussed in the next section. This literature review presented in the next chapter leads to the formulation of a conceptual framework for BPM which is evaluated using a quantitative lexical analysis of a broader literature sample. Finally the implication of the BPM on EIS is discussed and potential future research opportunities are outlined.

1.1 Methodology

The analysis of BPM and the preparation of this paper is done on basis of the tree books: [1], [3] and central chapters of [2]. These books have contributed to the understanding of the conceptual terms in the BPM literature, which again has formed the foundation and pre-understanding in which the authors possess. Articles used for this paper was located through the databases/sources shown in table 1.

Table 1. Located Papers Used in This Article

Database/source	< 2003	2004	2005	2006	2007	Total
The ACM Portal	2	2	0	4	0	8
Emerald	3	0	10	9	2	24
ScienceDirect / Elsevier	8	4	5	7	4	28
Gartner	3	0	17	14	0	34
Google Scholar	6					6
Waria.com				8		8
The 2006 BPMS Report				4		4
Total	*22*	*6*	*32*	*46*	*6*	*112*

Due to the authors pre-understanding based on the mentioned books, the search for articles in table 1 is based on a subjective approach where different combinations of words with "Business Process Management" and "agility", "advantage", "ERP", "SOA" etc. to make a more a comprehensive covering of the subject BPM. With in the number of located articles 43 articles were read. Based on the 43 articles 29 keywords were defined which seemed to cover the main characteristics of BPM.

After the preparation of the 29 keywords it was clear that several words were substituted or just synonyms. Therefore the keywords were reduced to 13 concepts in two groups: 1) Agent/rules: Benefits/Motivation/Expectations; BPMS; History; Implementation; Management/Organizational culture; and Maturity, and 2) Processes: Simulation/Modeling; Standardization/Automation; Strategy; Webservices & SOA; Workflow systems.

In our search for a framework for BPM we need to find out whether the 43 articles are representative to the total number of articles gathered, which we believe to cover the literature of BPM. In order to document whether this is the case a lexical analysis is used for this purpose. A lexical analysis of all 112 articles was performed using the program Leximancer (http://www.leximancer.com/). Leximancer is a tool to analyse text files, it generates concepts based on context and the frequency of words. Further more the size of each concepts generated indicates how prominent the concepts are in the literature. Using Leximancer now makes it possible to find out what the total number articles is primarily about. But our research is about BPM and therefore we need to look at the generated concepts in relation to BPM, which is also possible through Leximancer. By pre-programming "Business Process Management" as a concept Leximancer makes it possible to see which concepts explains the most of BPM. The result of the lexical analysis is a total number of 84 concepts describing BPM where the four largest concepts in the perspective of BPM explains 63.5% of the lexical content of BPM. The four major concepts were *Management*, *Technology*, *Support* and *Approach*. Each of these concepts resulted in a number of quotes where e.g. BPM and Management were described. These quotes were then sorted in relation to keywords and discussed in relation to the overlaying concept.

2. BUSINESS PROCESS MANAGEMENT

2.1 Management in a BPM Perspective

The most frequent word appearing in the lexical analysis was "management". Management is an often-used word in combination with other management disciplines e.g. Customer Relationship Management, Process management, Supply Chain Management, Content Management, Workflow Management, Knowledge Management etc.

The literature reviewed mostly agree on BPM as a management discipline [8], or a management philosophy [9] and how much companies will benefit from this discipline in gaining more effective leverage of information across their business [10]. The philosophy of BPM compared to earlier management disciplines is that BPM is a journey of continuous process improvement [11] opposite e.g. Business Process Reengineering (BPR) that is only a one time process improvement, and due to that agility and more effective business processes will disappear. BPM is though emerged from earlier management disciplines/theories such as total quality management (TQM), LEAN, Six Sigma, and Business Process Reengineering (BPR) [12]. BPM is about developing management disciplines and deploying technology to be able to handle exceptions in standard procedures so that exceptions becomes standard procedure [13]. To do so the literature also advocates that BPM is used as a formal and structured approach employing governance, methods, policies, metrics, practice and tools to ensure that it defines, manages and continually optimizes its business processes [14, 15]. The deployment of BPM requires like any other discipline full attention from management, which is often overlooked, the people involved in the processes needs day-to-day management [16]. Further more deployment of BPM is different from traditional technology deployments because BPM initiatives is not the IT departments responsibility but the "process management" [17].

Management culture is mentioned as an important factor in having success on BPM, often the emphasis lies on the business processes and the underlying complexity of the technology in how to obtain bottom-line profitability [18, 19]. A wide holistic approach towards BPM as a management discipline and the management commitment to organizational transformation will ensure success [20]. When managing BPM projects the management should also remember the importance of managing the people who work within the processes and how their mutual collaboration can contribute to the quantity of work being done. To be able to manage people in organizations and to set key performance indicators and hereby getting the maximum benefit from BPM, companies need to manage the people interface [21]. Effective management information is necessary for planning and decision making [22].

2.2 Technology in a BPM Perspective

Technology in a BPM perspective concerns the crucial importance that technology plays in generating value and underpinning the philosophy of BPM by delivering an infrastructure that drives work though the firm, enabling a regime of monitoring, optimization and traceability [23]. It allows businesses to prepare different scenarios and make the right changes immediately, more effectively and hereby contribute with competitive advantages. Furthermore the technology provides the needed infrastructure to translate strategic choices into concrete plans of action and letting the businesses become more proactive [24].

The objective of BPM is to increase employee and customer value through innovative, flexible and efficient processes but in such a process-managed organizations is more about business transformation then about technology [25]. Simply to view BPM as a label for new technology is a misunderstanding [26] nor an updated version of BPR [27]. Reluctant behavior by thinking of BPM is not surprising while BPM like BPR emphasizes process thinking as a method to lower cost, increase quality of service and improve personal productivity. BPM and BPR are quite similar but the major difference is that BPM is defined as a continuous performance improvement methodology [28] while BPR is not iterative. Both have technology as an enabler but BPM technology at that time in the 1980's did often obstruct process change. In addition the code behind the systems required specialized skills and significant time to change and last, it was proprietary independent of each other applications before the ability to automate the entire process appeared. Today's thinking regarding continual process improvement has significantly changes since the BPR era [29].

The standards as SOA, XML and Web service has all contributed the advance of BPM technology [8] and undertaking a BPM initiative without SOA it is nearly unthinkable [16]. These standards deliver great flexibility and make it a lot easier to invoke complex application processing in BPMS products [8] and often this lack of interoperability can be solved by various web services [18]. BPM and SOA can be thought as a new way of linking the business and IT department together however, BPM is fundamentally a top-down approach whereas SOA is a bottom-up [16]. A big technological challenge is therefore to identify the commonalities and resolve the differences [16], and this need can very well be increasing in the future until the BPM technology mature and find its full potential. BPM technology is a new era of software *"that uses process models to drive the work through the organization by routing tasks to the relevant employee"*. This includes a wide range of software spanning from process modeling interfaces, process engines, business rules engines and activity monitoring and analytics components all integrated in a BPM Suite [21].

By the ability to model business processes a process engine is acquired to keep track of the work being done, integrating with third party applications, and hereby ensure later traceability in the processes [22]. Also modeling provides critical capabilities in bringing business intelligence into focused action [9]. The unique about BPM modeling is that changing a process step is as easy as drawing a line between two boxes. This becomes possible because of the models created in a BPMS are linked or integrated directly to the applications and databases by orchestrating the underlying infrastructure completely [11]. Thereby the process engine can be seen as a software server that keeps track of each individual work item and routing it along to the next task when finished [9]. In this context the rule engine becomes a central element in the technology perspective of BPM while it is the place where the business can respond to the continual optimization needs of its processes [23, 24]. In addition it is recommended that these BPM-based applications is frequently updated and fine-tuned, which means at least once a quarter or even twice as much [15].

BPM has in many cases evolved from a feature of workflow to a flexible way of providing strategic value to the business [18]. Various ways leads to BPM but the "right" choice depend on the leaders understanding of BPM and the commitment to organizational transformation [8]. And the businesses needs to appreciate that BPM technology is a lifelong cycle and not a one-off deployment [25].

2.3 Support in a BPM Perspective

The third most frequent word was "Support". The literature emphasizes how Technology/BPM suites support the lifecycle of processes. *Supporting lifecycles from vision through modelling, deployment, execution, performance monitoring, and modification is the very core of BPM initiatives [30].* The future BPM systems will support a business transactions/events from the beginning to end and at the same time adding rules and policies needed to support the organizations [27]. Knowledge management, knowledge bases and knowledge sharing is an important factor in obtaining better BPM. The imposing of information flows which support knowledge creation and sharing through out the entire process is a prerequisite for BPM [28]. BPM systems are challenged in how to facilitate and support human-application-level interactions [31] as well as on system-to-system level. Even though many systems support these interactions many BPM system do not accomplish to support human-to-human requirements as effectively [32] this could be e.g. task handling and sharing information across the organization. Besides the human-human interaction problems, ad hoc processes is yet another kind of processes that sets high demands for BPM systems and to the human-human interaction due to the requirements of knowledge and collaboration between workers in such processes. To support Ad hoc processes BPM systems needs to incorporate and support collaboration through shared whiteboards, forums content management capabilities etc. within longer running processes where participants can discuss aspects of the current process [21]. Close collaboration is also needed to support business and IT professionals through the entire process to enhance the amount of control and management of business processes.

Generally the literature mentions BPM suites/systems as a tool to support automation of business decision through a set of business rules that are able to structure loose informal business practices and policies to support processes [30]. The use of business rules can also simplify how processes are developed as well as sharing common processes in different problems [9]. BPM systems also offers automation of repetitive steps in integration application for supporting complex decisions-making [30].

2.4 Approach in a BPM Perspective

When talking about approach in a BPM perspective it refers to a broad range of sub-concepts with reference to a strategic understanding of the main subject Business Process Management in an EIS perspective. Beyond that the concept "approach" is used in relationship to a broad definition of BPM and issues at the implementation stage. For that reason is seems like there are three main sub-concepts: definition, strategy and implementation, which are linked together by motivating factors in the search for business benefits, agility, flexibility, high performance, optimization, competitive advantages and so on. All words which are typically wrapped around benefits in the context to insure the semantic perception.

Quite often the use and definition of BPM in the literature is visionary and in addition hard to transform into something "easy-to-implement". A more holistic approach is therefore applied as a result of the difficulties in generalization [28]. At the other hand it is claimed that a holistic approach to BPM is needed to embrace all relevant parties and not just to solve pain point in the business or used by the IT department on its own [25]. This difference in the approach gives naturally different perceptions and views of BPM. For instance as a way to standardize business operations in the belief that reducing variation is a viable strategy, or as a method to squeeze cost out inspired by the Business Process Re-engineering theories popular in the 90s [9]. BPM require an approach that fundamental shift from function-centric to process-centric thinking and by that BPM provide visibility into and control over business processes [10]. Despite that the BPM literature is not exhaustive described the scope and definitions it possible to gather [33]. So due to the different perceptions of BPM and the conflicts occurring, understanding BPM might relate in how to use BPM instead of misunderstanding of the potential and the need for process thinking. This lack of process skills in the workforce result in different process management approaches within the entire organization [4] and is for that reason vital to eliminate for receiving the added value to the corporate business thought BPM. Clearness about what the senior management mean of BPM and how they intend to use it is of huge importance [28] likewise is the top management commitment and the executive sponsorship [22, 34]. This commitment is essential for receiving success and is crucial to achieve. A further requirement is an alliance between IT and the business leaders to drive a successful process transformation [35].

The approach perspective in the literature selected for this study also embraces a differentiation between different styles in implementing process-enables products like BPM. One strategy is the "pure-play" invented by Gartner Group in 2003 which consists of a holistic application-independent approach there through generic and adaptable technology deals with any business problem [29, 31]. A alternative solution is separately tailor each problem though specific applications supported by many niche applications [31]. The third alternative is a combination between the to worlds by taking the best and by that layering on top of the existent functionality [31]. This combination refers to frameworks, templates, accelerators and are more dependent of vendors terms [31].

Important to keep in mind is that the need for change intervals are getting shorter and shorter to get effective methodologies and get around the business optimization cycle quickly enough [15]. As regards creating a specification of requirements is waste of time [15, 36] because nothing stays the same and such a document is not sufficient dynamic. By not acting so can kill a BPM project as it distracts from the critical requirements of proving the efficacy of the BPM approach to the business [36]. Beside that forget all about the waterfall implementation methodology that it is seeking to answer functional requirements [24]. Business leaders often think in re-engineering and transforming the organization, but these process-focused technologies is "built-to-change" rather than "built-to-last" [24]. Creating a Center of Excellence (COE) provide a repository for knowledge and best practices development [15] is recommended while the need for coordination and integration increases accordingly BPM projects [22]. Moreover the COE becomes a direct descendant of the steering group and is usually responsible for supporting the BPM projects across the business and keeping momentum going across the organization [22]. Educate users to understand the iterative nature of BPM gives the best chance of success in the initial project [22]. In addition to this the big challenge is to help the business managers to understand that the approach is fundamentally different from the traditionally waterfall or "big bang" implementation approach [31]. The vendors do often describe their support as "round-tripping" with reference to a spiral implementation, which means that their approach is concentrating about analysis, through development, into deployment and then monitoring and optimization [36]. The proposal is to hold short cycles of iterations, which improve the behavior of the application over time and focus on a particular topic, each with "playback" [36]. This methodology ensures flexibility to change quickly as needed and with no surprises emerging [36].

Most organization that has embraced process management has implemented a hybrid or matrix-style approach [9, 28]. This means that the Line of Business manager (LOB) still run their operations as normal, but for the important process that cross the organizational boundaries is taking care of by a process owner [9]. An effective BPM approach therefore needs a description of the relationships between executives, LOBs, process owners, process architects and process developers [9].

Key considerations in the development of a successful BPM projects include unambiguous intensions, a business case to gain executive sponsorship, a clear link between BPM – the method and the strategy, acquisition of process competencies, process discipline, improvement and cross-process integration, strategic alignment, culture and leadership, governance, skills and knowledge [24, 28, 33]. Furthermore is the ability to build coalitions and facilitate collaboration among the organization that may have conflicting objectives imperative [4] and the top management commitment [34]. BPM is also about a change in culture and does not success simply through having good systems and the right structure in place [37]. Viewing BPM as "just another development tool" ought to expect conflicts and frustrations [38] and the way to gaining success require a deep understanding of business processes before thinking in implementation a BPM suite [22].

3. DISCUSSION OF FINDINGS

A comparison of the keywords from the non-lexical analysis and the keywords (sub-concepts) emerged from the lexical analysis are interesting to make to find out whether the read literature are representative to the located literature about BPM. The identified keywords/sub-concepts in the two analyses was compared and in general the two sections of keywords identified are mostly similar to each other. After the execution of the lexical analysis is has now become clearer what the literature actually tells about "benefits" due to that we are able to differentiate what we actually meant by benefits in the non-lexical analysis. The keyword "process" from the non-lexical analysis is typically used in the context and reference to cross-functional possibilities, getting rid of organizational boundaries, understand the information flow or the ability to model the entire infrastructure of the organization. In some cases it is necessary to have insight and knowledge about the foundation of BPM because articles can have the same approach for explaining a topic in BPM. For example talking about knowledge-management, knowledge bases, and knowledge sharing can often be conceived with creating a Centre of Excellence.

On the basis of our research the following sections we will discuss our perception of BPM, where the literature need more research and were have we done the most emerging observations.

Through out this research of the BPM literature we found four major concepts where each of these explaining their perception in relation to BPM. The concept Management cover BPM as a management discipline and methodology where the concept Technology treats more specific relations to architecture and process modelling. These two concepts represent two different parts of what BPM is about where the two other concepts are in between. This makes it difficult to understand what BPM is about. Is it a management discipline or a technology or maybe both? The authors of this article find that BPM can be separated in to two areas: BMP as a management discipline and BPM technology. On this basis we have developed the framework for understanding BPM.

3.1 BPM Discipline

BPM as a management discipline or philosophy is concerning integration of organisational process thinking, as well as keeping management sponsorship etc. BPM is based on management disciplines like Lean, Six Sigma, TQM and BPR, which makes the differences in BPM difficult to clearly define. The literature in our research focuses in the ability to operate agile, make changes immediately and use it as a method to become more proactive to changes. We find that BPM have focus on developing highly flexible business processes as a mean to get competitive advantages. Working with a BPM project in its early stages is in our conviction not different from adopting another management discipline. It is all about changing the organizational culture and to collaborate though the organizational boundaries, getting the management commitment and to settle the project in the entire organization and not just in the IT department. The whole business needs to feel ownership and start working in new ways, which is not special for BPM projects. It is still relevant to educate users and nothing is really new about this. The literature mentions a shift in function-centric thinking to view the entire business though process-centric thinking as an essential starting point for the BPM project. Having the right systems and structure in place does not assure success. Adapting and using BPM to embrace the entire business needs a holistic perception from start. So what is different by using BPM?

The BPM literature often use the word agility to explain one of the benefits by adopting BPM in to the business, but why is the ability to react agile so important and how can it be a competitive advantage is not explicit clarified in the articles but Fingar and Smith are though spending much energy on this topic in the book the Third Wave [1]. We understand agility in relation to BPM as a capability to immediately adapt and react on marked changes. Through interactions with customers, orchestration of internal operations and utilization of the business ecosystems of external business partners [6]. Further we find it of huge importance to be agile and we perceive agility as a prerequisite to BPM. But to use agility in a proactive manner must be done with respect to the business strategy, which can be a challenging balance to manage. The ability of reacting and adapt fast to market changes can be of more importance than be the first to develop a new product. To help the business manage this balance BPM and BPMS are in our opinion inseparable while the technology makes it possible to model the flexible processes and this in co-ordinance with the business rules.

3.2 BPM Technology

BPMS is considered as the practical part and mean to deploy and establish BPM. SOA and web-services are important technologies for creating and establish a BPM environment. Based on these technologies and reference models business process management systems /suites makes it possible to model processes that can directly be executed in to the company. The technology such as BPMS is the foundation for making fully use of the BPM potential. The ability handle hundreds or maybe thousands of processes at the same time or simulate changes in processes and measure their impact as well as establishing rules so that processes automatically adapt to changes in the market makes BPMS a truly advantage compared to the systems that we use to day. We perceive that BPMS and the underlying technology in relation to BPM is the mean to make better BPM it can be compared to the 5 principles used in LEAN to make better LEAN.

The vision of having all business people in the organisation modelling their business processes due to their knowledge in their field of expertise seams unlikely but never the less the focus on automating and modelling business processes are of high importance to secure quality, performance and agility. Gartner predicts that the fully potential of BPM won't be accomplished before 2017 [8] due to this we recommend the companies are standing by in investing in new BPMS. EIS systems are already now implementing better process handling which take time not only the development of technology but also the organizations and companies needs to mature to adopt BPM. This doesn't mean that companies shouldn't work with BPM. You don't need technology to make use of BPM but prepare and make the organization mature to think in processes and cross functional.

3.3 Validity

The research method used in this paper can be split in to 4 steps or 2 stages: obtaining a pre-understanding, manual reviewing 43 articles, defining keywords on basis of the read articles and preparing the lexical analysis.

To secure consistency in the research each author used the same method in defining keywords. First the keywords were located on basis of what the authors have read (see table 1) hereafter each keyword in every article were ranked according to number of topics and the size of the topics in the articles. This was done independently by each author to secure some sort of objectivity, by not influencing each other. On this basis a comparison of the topics size were made to find out whether the authors had the same perception and strength of keywords in read articles. This comparison was tremendously painless which might be an incident or indicator for the same understanding of the literature, only small adjustments were made.

The lexical analysis serves several purposes, first of all it would be nearly impossible for a human to preserve a complete objective overview of so much literature as covered in this paper and therefore the lexical analysis is a great tool. Further more the lexical analysis is able in a fast way to give an indication of whether the read articles are representative to the rest of the literature and to ensure that the authors haven't chased non-existing topics. The only problem experienced in using a lexical analysis is the usability of the generated output. Programs such as Leximancer are programmed to generate output (quotes) in a context based on mathematical algorithms, but the quality of the contexts are often not as good as hoped, which also have an impact on our conclusion of this research. The profound work in manually analysing the output is very comprehensive but necessary to get quality data about the contents of the literature.

The validity of this research paper must be considered strong due to the wide use of both subjective and objective research methods where a qualitative approach in using common human sense together with a quantitative research method through the lexical analysis must be a strong way of ensuring a correct interpretation of the literature. The result of the research is also well documented through the two step analysis first an analysis of the read articles and then an analysis of the entire number of articles.

4. CONCLUSIONS

Our main conclusion is that BPM is a practically oriented concept with a weak academic foundation. BPM is a holistic management discipline that uses technology to control and operate the entire business through rules that clearly defines business processes. BPM is about continuous improvement and optimizing processes to ensure high performance and by that achieving agility and flexibility as a tool to gain competitive advantages. We have proposed a framework for BPM which identify a set of conceptual clusters. However we have found no evidence of linkages to the academic field of Management of EIS. The lexical analysis was attempted as a supplementary literature analysis. The combination of a weak conceptual foundation and concept analysis revealed that this approach is less suited to analyze an emerging field. Nevertheless the analysis brought up consistent conceptual clusters.

BPM is obviously a relevant challenge to practice and more research is needed. However future research should make an effort to bridge existing research on EIS and BPM. For space saving reasons tables, references and comparisons have been omitted from this paper. This is available on request in an unabridged paper.

REFERENCES

1. H. Smith and P. Fingar, *Business Process Management: The Third Wave* (Meghan-Kiffer Press: Tampa, Fl, 2003).
2. P. Fingar and J. Bellini, *The Real-Time Enterprise: Competing on Time with the Revolutionary Business SEx Machine* (Meghan-Kiffer Press: USA, 2004).
3. M.A. Dumas, W.M.P. Van der Aalst and A.H.M. Hofstede, *Process-aware Information Systems: Bridging People and Software through Process Technology* (John Wiley & Sons, Inc., Hoboken, NJ, 2005).
4. M.J. Melenovsky, *Business Process Management as a Discipline*. Gartner Research, G00139856 (Gartner Inc., 2006), p.6.
5. T. Schurter, Let's talk about BPM - what it really means (2007). http://www.bpmg.org/Zpost1759.php (Accessed May 16, 2007).
6. V. Sambamurthy, A. Bharadwaj, and V. Grover, Shaping agility through digital options: reconceptualizing the role of information technology in contemporary firms, *MIS Quarterly*. Volume 27, Number 2, p.237, (2003).
7. C. Møller, ERP II: a conceptual framework for next-generation enterprise systems? *Journal of Enterprise Information Management*. Volume 18, Number 4, pp.483-497, (2005).

8. J.B. Hill, J. Sinur, D. Flint, and M.J. Melenovsky, *Gartner's Position on Business Process Management*, G00136533 (Gartner Inc., 2006), p.26.
9. D. Miers, BPM – Driving Business Performance (BPM Focus Inc., 2006), p.13.
10. M.J. Melenovsky, J. Sinur, J.B. Hill, and D.W. McCoy, *Business Process Management: Preparing for the Process-Managed Organization*, Gartner Research, G00129461. (Gartner Inc., 2005), p.8.
11. M.J. Melenovsky, *Business Process Management Offers a World Where Exceptions No Longer Exist*, Gartner Research, G00134777 (Gartner Inc., 2005), p.4.
12. M.J. Melenovsky and K. Harris, *Business Process Management Leverages Organizational Knowledge to Create Better Business Value*, Gartner Research, G00136713 (Gartner., 2006), p.4.
13. D. Miers, *BPM – Too Much BP but not Enough of the M. BPM Focus* (Lighthouse Point, FL, 2006), p.6.
14. M.J. Melenovsky, *Business Process Management's Success Hinges on Business-Led Initiatives,* Gartner Research, G00129411 (Gartner Inc., 2005), p.8.
15. D. Miers, Best Practice BPM, *ACM Queue.* Volume 4, Number 2, pp.40-48, (2006).
16. D. Miers, *Issues and Best Practices for the BPM and SOA Journey* (BPM Focus Inc., Lighthouse Point, FL, 2006).
17. B. Rosser and R. Buchanan, *Business Process Management and Enterprise Architecture: The New Synergy*, Gartner Research, G00143201 (Gartner Inc., 2006), p.7.
18. M. Chen, D. Zhang, and L. Zhou, Empowering collaborative commerce with Web services enabled business process management systems, *Decision Support Systems.* Volume 43, Number 2, pp.530-546, (2007).
19. L. Verner, The Promise and the Challenge, *ACM Queue.* Volume 4, Number 2, p.9, (2004).
20. M.-A.A. Pantazi and N.B. Georgopoulos, Investigating the impact of business-process-competent information systems (ISs) on business performance, *Managing Service Quality.* Volume 16, Number 4, pp.421-434, (2006).
21. D. Miers, *Process Innovation and Corporate Agility: Balancing Efficiency and Adaptability in a Knowledge-centric World* (BPM Focus Inc., 2006), p.17.
22. D. Miers, *The Keys to BPM Project Success* (BPM Focus Inc., 2006), p.19.
23. J. Sinur, J.B. Hill and M.J. Melenovsky, *Selection Criteria Details for Business Process Management Suites*, Gartner Research, G00134657 (Gartner Inc., 2005), p.16.
24. M.J. Melenovsky, J. Sinur, *BPM Maturity Model Identifies Six Phases for Successful BPM Adoption*, Gartner Research, G00142643 (Gartner Inc., 2006), p.14.
25. P. Redshaw, *How Banks Can Benefit from Business Process Management*, Gartner Research, G00126515 (2005), p.15.
26. D. Miers, P. Harmon, and C. Hall, The 2006 BPM Suites Report, *BPTrends* (2006).
27. J. Sinur, *Business Process Management Suites Will Be the 'Next Big Thing'*, Gartner Research, G00125461 (Gartner Inc., 2005), p.6.
28. J.-P. Pritchard and C. Armistead, Business process management - lessons from European business, *Business Process Management Journal.* Volume 5, Number 1, (1999).
29. J.B. Hill, J. Sinur, D. Flint, and M.J. Melenovsky, *Distinguishing Business Process Management From Business Process Re-engineering*, Gartner Research, G00136775 (Gartner Inc., 2005), p.5.

30. D. Miers, P. Harmon, and C. Hall, *A Detailed Analysis of BPM Suites, in The 2006 BPM Suites Report Release 2.0,* eds. D. Miers, P. Harmon, and C. Hall (2006), p.21.
31. D. Miers, BPM Solution Frameworks: Achieving Revolutionary Objectives through Evolutionary Change. *BPM Focus* (2006), pp.14-.
32. J. Sinur, D.W. McCoy, and T. Bell, Creating a BPM and Workflow Automation Vendor Checklist, *Gartner Research*, COM-19-1332 (Gartner Inc., 2003), pp.8.
33. R.G. Lee and B.G. Dale, Business process management: a review and evaluation, *Business Process Management Journal.* Volume 4, Number3, pp.214-225, (1998).
34. M.A. Mashari, A.A. Mudimigh, and M. Zairi, Enterprise resource planning: A taxonomy of critical factors. *European Journal of Operational Research.* Volume 146, Number 2, pp.352-364, (2003).
35. J.P. Roberts, How IT Departments Support Business Process Management. *Gartner 7* (2006).
36. D. Miers, Getting Past the First BPM Project: Developing a Repeatable BPM Delivery Capability, *BPM Focus* (2006), pp.17.
37. M. Zairi, Business process management: a boundaryless approach to modern competitiveness, *Business Process Management Journal.* Volume 3, Number 1, (1997).
38. D.W. McCoy, Re-examine Your Process Mentality to Avoid Business Process Management Pitfalls, *Gartner Research*, G00127431 (Gartner Inc., 2005), pp.5.

Grid-VirtuE: A Layered Architecture for Grid Virtual Enterprises

Alfredo Cuzzocrea[1,2], Alessandro D'Atri[3], Andrea Gualtieri[4], Amihai Motro[5] and Domenico Saccà[1,2]

[1] ICAR Institute, Italian National Research Council, Cosenza, Italy
[2] DEIS Department, University of Calabria, Cosenza, Italy
cuzzocrea@{icar.cnr.it, si.deis.unical.it} sacca@{icar.cnr.it, si.deis.unical.it}
[3] CeRSI, Luiss "Guido Carli" University, Rome, Italy datri@luiss.it, gualtieri@exeura.it
[4] Exeura, Cosenza, Italy
[5] CS Department, George Mason University, Fairfax, VA, USA ami@gmu.edu

Abstract. A *grid virtual enterprise* is a community of independent enterprises concerned with a particular sector of the economy. Its members (nodes) are small or medium size enterprises (SME) engaged in bilateral transactions. An important principle of a grid virtual enterprise is the lack of any global "guiding force", with each member of the community making its own independent decisions. In this paper we describe Grid-VirtuE, a three-layer architecture for grid virtual enterprises. The top layer of the architecture, representing its ultimate purpose, is an environment in which grid virtual enterprises can be modeled and implemented. This layer is supported by middleware infrastructure for grids, providing a host of grid services, such as node-to-node communication, bilateral transactions, and data collection. The bottom layer is essentially a *distributed data warehouse* for storing, sharing and analyzing the large amounts of data generated by the grid. Among other functionalities, the warehouse handles the dissemination of data among the members of the grid; it confronts issues of data magnitude with an aging mechanism that aggregates old data at a lower level of detail; and it incorporates privacy-preserving features that retain the confidentiality of individual members. Warehouse information is also used for data and process mining, aimed at analyzing the behavior of the enterprise, and subsequently inducing evolutionary changes that will improve its performance.

Keywords: *Enterprise engineering, Enterprise information architecture, Enterprise Information Integration (EII), Enterprise Information Systems (EIS), Enterprise integration, Enterprise modeling and integration*

1. INTRODUCTION

A *grid virtual enterprise* is a community of independent enterprises concerned with a particular sector of the economy, such as automotive, fashion, or entertainment. Its members (nodes) are small or medium size enterprises (SME) engaged in bilateral transactions. An important principle of a grid virtual enterprise is the lack of any global "guiding force": Each member of the community makes its own

Please use the following format when citing this chapter:

Cuzzocrea, A., D'Atri, A., Gualtieri, A., Motro, A., Saccá, D., 2007, in IFIP International Federation for Information Processing, Volume 254, Research and Practical Issues of Enterprise Information Systems II Volume 1, eds. L. Xu, Tjoa A., Chaudhry S. (Boston: Springer), pp. 33-42.

independent decisions, such as the products it offers, the prices it charges, and the members it wishes to do business with.

In this paper we describe Grid-VirtuE, a three-layer architecture for grid virtual enterprises.

1. The top layer of the architecture, representing its ultimate purpose, is an *environment for modeling grid virtual enterprises*. This environment incorporates and expands on features and properties that have been defined in earlier work (particularly, the VirtuE model).
2. The top layer is supported by *middleware infrastructure for grids*, providing a host of grid services, such as node-to-node communication, bilateral transactions, and data collection.
3. The bottom layer is essentially a *distributed data warehouse* for storing, sharing and analyzing the large amounts of data generated by the grid. Among other functionalities, the warehouse handles the dissemination of data among the members of the grid; it confronts issues of data magnitude with an aging mechanism that aggregates old data at a lower level of detail; and it incorporates privacy-preserving features that retain the confidentiality of individual members. Warehouse information is also used for data and process mining, aimed at analyzing the behavior of the enterprise, and subsequently inducing evolutionary changes that will improve its performance.

The focus of this paper is mostly on the top and bottom layers, as these layers incorporate most of the novel aspects of Grid-VirtuE. Section 2 describes the modeling layer, and Section 3 is dedicated to the data warehouse layer. Section 4 places this work in the context of other research, and Section 5 concludes with a brief summary and discussion of future work.

2. THE MODELING LAYER

The modeling environment of Grid-VirtuE is largely based on previous work on the VirtuE model [1-3]. In this section we review the features of the VirtuE model that have been adapted for Grid-VirtuE.

2.1 Members and the Catalyst

A *virtual enterprise-breeding environment* (VBE) [4] is a community of business entities that are potential participants in business coalitions. The launching of a new virtual enterprise begins when a VBE player assumes the role of catalyst [5]. The catalyst has a business plan, knowledge of the additional expertise and resources needed to accomplish the business plan, and information on VBE players that can satisfy these needs. The catalyst then chooses the enterprise members from the VBE, and becomes a privileged member of the virtual enterprise, with several exclusive roles, such as changing the membership of the enterprise or modifying its goals (i.e., end products). In Grid-VirtuE, the catalyst role consolidates several distinct organizational roles, such as broker, planner and coordinator [4].

The members of the new enterprise are independent but have shared interests. They are independent in the sense that they remain autonomous and maintain their own assets. These assets include human, equipment or financial resources, as well as business expertise, such as knowledge about their production and delivery processes. Their shared interests are reflected in that they agree to cooperate with each other to produce joint products that are provided to common clients. After the community had been established, it could evolve because a new member joins or an exiting member departs. This form of evolution provides the virtual enterprise with flexibility and allows it to adapt to new market situations.

2.2 Products and the Product Dictionary

In practice, virtual enterprises may produce many different kinds of products. In Grid-VirtuE, we consider only *information* products, of the type that can be delivered over computer networks. Information products are provided by members of the enterprise to their clients. This provision is the ultimate purpose of an enterprise. Information products are also exchanged among the members of the enterprise in the production phase that precedes the provision of a product to a client. We distinguish between two kinds of information products: *content* and *process*. Content is an information item; for example, a specific data table, a specific document, or a specific image. Process is an operation that modifies given content to provide new content; for example, summarization of a data table, encryption of a document, or compression of an image.

All products, contents as well as processes, are classified into product *types*. A product type describes the common attributes of all products of that type. For example, all images could be instances of the content type *Image*, and all compression processes could be instances of the process type *Compression*. We assume that all intensional information (i.e., types and their attributes) is maintained in an enterprise-wide resource called the *dictionary*. This global knowledge resource is available to every member of the enterprise. Every product in the virtual enterprise is an instance of a type described in the dictionary. The purpose of the dictionary is to assure semantic consistency across the enterprise.

2.3 Local Inventories and the Global Catalog

The products either used or created by each enterprise member are described in a local resource called *inventory*. Items in the inventory are *instances* of product types described in the dictionary. Among other information, the inventory specifies the *source* and *target* of each product. The source is either *native* or *import*: A native product is produced locally, whereas an import product is procured from another member of the enterprise. The target is either *internal* or *export*: An internal product is an intermediate product used by this member in the manufacturing of other products, whereas an export product may be delivered to other enterprise members.

The product *catalog* is an enterprise-wide resource that lists the products that are available for procurement from enterprise members; i.e., it is the union of the products marked "export" in all inventories. Each member *publishes* his list of export products in this catalog and is responsible for keeping it updated. Note that products in the catalog are *instances* of the types in the dictionary. Hence, the dictionary *regulates* the catalog.

2.4 Production Plans

Another designation of inventory products is whether they are *basic* or *complex*. A product is complex if it is derived from other products; otherwise, it is basic. For native complex product, production plans must be provided. A production plan specifies how other contents and processes are combined to derive the new product. In particular, it specifies the dependence of a product on products that must be procured from other members. Production plans are provided for both complex contents and complex processes, and a product may have multiple (alternative) production plans.

2.5 Transactions

Since component products are often obtained from other enterprise members, a procurement mechanism is necessary. Procurement is executed in bilateral *transactions*. A transaction begins when a request for a catalog product (content or process) is sent from one participant to another, and terminates when the request is satisfied. There are two types of transactions in a virtual enterprise. An *external* transaction is a request for a product that is submitted from a client to one of the members of the virtual enterprise. The member processes the request and provides a solution. A member of the virtual enterprise who processes an external transaction acts in the role of a *provider*. To satisfy an external transaction, a provider may decide to purchase products from other members. Such transactions are *internal*. A member of the virtual enterprise who processes an internal transaction acts in a role of a *subcontractor*. The execution of external transactions is the ultimate purpose of the virtual enterprise. Each member of a virtual enterprise may act as a provider on some transactions and as a subcontractor on other transactions.

2.6 Times and Logging

Grid-VirtuE incorporates a concept of time. Time is simply a system-wide clock that is stamped on transactions and other enterprise events. Enterprise events, such as execution of transactions, updates of the catalog, or changes in membership, are recorded in a log. Log records provide essential information on each such event and the time of its occurrence. There are two types of log: local and global. Every enterprise member maintains his own local log, and, in addition, there is an enterprise-wide log. Local logs may be used by members to improve their operations.

The global log can be used for studying enterprise-wide performance, as well as for communication among members.

2.7 Performance Indicators and Constitutional Rules

Grid-VirtuE allows the definition of *performance indicators*, which are formulas that capture various quantitative characteristics of the virtual enterprise; for example, the enterprise assets, interdependence levels, the number of transactions performed over a period of time, or the average turnaround time.

Another feature of Grid-VirtuE is *constitutional rules*, which are constraints that express behavior standards that are expected. Such rules enable virtual enterprises with different style or flavor; for example, an organization without any competition (similar products are not available from different members), or an organization that resembles a free market. Rules may be established that require members to maintain activity at some minimal frequency, or limit the number of transactions in a given period. Compliance with constitutional rules is monitored and disseminated, but not enforced.

2.8 Information Dissemination and Behavior Mining

Altogether, Grid-VirtuE incorporates four global information resources: the product dictionary, which describes products and types; the product catalog, which lists the products available from members; the log, which chronicles the activities of the enterprise; and the constitution, which establishes the conventions of the enterprise. These resources are managed by the catalyst. It is important to note that the information in these global resources is maintained and processed in a manner identical to any other content. Thus, the catalyst can supply other members with products that calculate performance indicators, or assess compliance with constitutional rules. This information is exchanged using the ordinary transaction mechanism of Grid-VirtuE.

The information derived from the enterprise information resources need not be limited to the calculation of performance measures or the validation of constitutional rules. The global log, and to some degree the other information resources, can be subjected to a wide array of data mining techniques. The overall purpose is to study the performance and behavior of the enterprise, and to associate the outcome with various evolutionary decisions. Log mining is further discussed in Section 3.5.

3. THE DATA WAREHOUSE LAYER

The choice of a data warehouse [6] for the latent layer of Grid-VirtuE is well-justified, as data warehouses can sustain computational grids [7] efficiently. A data warehouse will thus provide all the necessary support for the functionalities of Grid-VirtuE. In this section we describe the main aspects of the data warehouse layer of Grid-VirtuE.

3.1 Data Fragmentation and Dissemination

A *virtual data warehouse* maps its overall data domain onto a set of geographically distributed grid nodes. It then provides a wide variety of functionalities (e.g., data integration, data querying, and metadata services) over the entire distributed environment, while maintaining complete transparency to its users (i.e., users need not be aware of the placement of data). Each Grid-VirtuE enterprise encapsulates such a virtual data warehouse.

In this paradigm, the fragmentation and dissemination of data among the member nodes is an important process, as its efficiency has critical impact on the performance of all ensuing data management and query processing activities.

Fragmentation techniques have been studied extensively in the context of distributed databases [8], and can be classified in two main variants. In data-oriented techniques, the fragmentation process is driven by dimensional parameters of data; for example, the size and number of attributes in relational data, or the depth and fan-out degree in XML data. In *semantics-based techniques*, the fragmentation process is driven by the semantics of data; for example, relational data could be fragmented so that each fragment satisfies a given constraint set expressed as functional dependencies; and XML data could be fragmented so that each fragment stores semantically-related elements (e.g., a "book_author" element will be stored with its "book_title", "year", and "price" subelements). Most likely, the second variant is more appropriate for the Grid-VirtuE architecture.

3.2 Data Alimentation, Acquisition and Registration

In Grid-VirtuE, the data stored in individual nodes, termed *local data repositories*, could be alimented by stream data sources located outside the grid environment. To this end, the grid provides data acquisition and registration services. These services can be managed in a distributed manner based on the *Universal Description Discovery and Integration* (UDDI) paradigm [9]. This distributed data acquisition and registration mechanism, which can be reasonably intended as a "natural" application of the well-known Web services paradigm to grids, was proposed in our earlier work on the *SensorGrid* system [10], a high-performance system based on a data compression and approximation paradigm, for efficiently representing and querying sensor network data on grids.

3.3 Data Aging and Aggregate Information Processing

To deal with the massive amounts of data expected in virtual grid enterprises, Grid-VirtuE adopts a *data aging mechanism*: As time passes, data are progressively aggregated in information blocks of lower level of detail; these blocks, described by patterns, provide succinct description of the original information content. This data aging mechanism provides tangible benefits in the data management and query processing layer of different applications for virtual grid enterprises, including business intelligence, supply chain management, and market analysis.

In an earlier work [11] we used a similar grid-based approach for handling massive amounts of multidimensional data repositories generated by sensor networks, where streams of data are delivered by sensors that monitor environmental parameters of a given geographical area, and we demonstrated the advantage of data aging and aggregate information processing. Here, we argue the applicability of these methods in "business" contexts as well, for example for supply chain management.[1]

3.4 Preserving Privacy

Preserving data privacy has become an important issue in all environments where data is collected, maintained and accessed (e.g., repositories of census, medical, or financial data). Grid architectures, such as Grid-VirtuE, are naturally prone to privacy breaches, as malicious members could join the virtual enterprise only to extract sensitive information. Hence, an important issue in Grid-VirtuE is to preserve the privacy of the local data repositories (the components of the virtual data warehouse).

To support privacy preservation, members retrieve information from local data repositories under an *accuracy-privacy contract*. Such contracts are based on the generally accepted trade-off between data accuracy and data privacy: Data privacy increases as its accuracy decreases, and vice versa. Thus, when data mining tools generate accurate data (i.e., data that is specific and of high quality), they are also likely to breach the privacy of the data (i.e., disclose information that should be protected). An accuracy-privacy contract balances these concerns, by specifying the maximal level of accuracy of delivered data that meets the privacy concerns of the owner of the data.

To meet these privacy concerns, schemes must be devised that represent data in various degrees of accuracy (i.e., at different levels of specificity), to meet different levels of required privacy. Obviously, different approximation ("compression") techniques must be devised for different types of data (e.g., relational, multidimensional, XML).

The collaborative nature of grid virtual enterprises poses further challenges to privacy preservation, as members can extend their individual capabilities for inferring protected information, by forming coalitions with other grid members. Thus, members with knowledge on different, non-overlapping portions of data could combine their efforts, thereby acquiring knowledge to which they are not entitled. The reason for this deficiency is that privacy-preserving schemes that work well against transgressions of a single member might fail under an attack coordinated by multiple members.

3.5 Process Mining on Event Logs

As already explained in Section 2.8, Grid-VirtuE enterprises continuously log their business activities. These event logs can be used for computing various performance

[1] Like sensor networks, a supply chain management based on Radio Frequency Identification (RFID) produces continuous data streams.

indicators and for extracting useful knowledge by means of process mining techniques.

Knowledge thus extracted can then be used in ex post analysis for re-engineering the activities of the virtual enterprise, or for constructing advanced deployment scenarios. Grid-VirtuE members can perform process-mining activities in a *collaborative* manner, and can thus benefit from the possibility of correlating different process mining results. As grid executions are easily modeled with workflows (e.g. [12]), the workflow mining techniques we proposed in [13] can be adapted for Grid-VirtuE.

4. BACKGROUND

Virtual enterprises and grid architectures have been researched quite extensively, so we only review here briefly efforts that combine both technologies.

The convergence between grid technologies and virtual enterprises has been introduced by Foster *et al.* [7], which asserted that logical components of a virtual enterprise can be mapped onto technological components that are grid nodes or software components (e.g., resources, protocols, or middleware). This work has influenced heavily all subsequent initiatives in grid computing research, with particular emphasis on computational issues; in contradistinction, our aim is to realize this philosophy in the rather different domain of virtual enterprises.

Lican *et al.* [14] extend these concepts towards the definition of a *Virtual and Dynamic Hierarchical Architecture* (VDHA) for *e*-science grids. VDHA incorporates certain P2P characteristics, and efficiently supports scalable and highly dynamic virtual architectures for *e*-science computing. Compared with our approach, VDHA is specifically tailored to high performance computing environments, whereas we are mostly concerned with business intelligence environments. However, VDHA and Grid-VirtuE share many points in common, as the idea of supporting *dynamism* within virtual enterprises.

In [15], Foster *et al.* propose models and architectures for efficiently implementing *virtual data grids*, a novel computational paradigm aimed at sharing available computational and data resources on grids, to improve the performance of time consuming activities on very large repositories of data. These architectures are useful in *e*-science settings found in areas such as high-energy physics and astronomy. Although designed for different environments, virtual data grids bear similarities to the data warehouse layer of Grid-VirtuE.

5. CONCLUSION

We proposed a layered architecture for grid virtual enterprises, an architecture that combines the features of a virtual enterprise model such as VirtuE, with the operational advantages of a grid organization. Many of the innovations of Grid-VirtuE arise from adopting a distributed data warehouse organization for its underlying level.

Much work remains to be done, and we mention here three interesting research directions. First and foremost is the need for significant case studies, to test the applicability of Grid-VirtuE in real-life settings (as already mentioned, supply chain management may provide a particularly attractive example). Second, in Section 3.3 we suggested using patterns to reduce the *volume* of data, and in Section 3.4 we suggested using approximation schemes to reduce the *specificity* of data to meet privacy requirements. These are two related forms of data abstraction, and we plan to investigate and exploit their relationship (for example, concise patterns are often achieved at the cost of precision). One of the most promising directions for virtual enterprises is the possibility of evolving them rationally on the basis of their recent history and performance. The third research direction is to develop suitable process mining techniques, and to embed them in a system that will intelligently associate their conclusions with suitable corresponding evolutionary changes.

ACKNOWLEDGEMENT

This work has been performed within *Interop: Interoperability Research for Networked Enterprises Applications and Software*, European Network of Excellence IST-508011 (http://interop-noe.org), and has been partially supported by the SFIDA-PMI project.

REFERENCES

1. A. D'Atri and A. Motro, VirtuE: Virtual Enterprises for Information Markets, in *Proc. of 10th European Conference on Information Systems* (2002), pp.768-777.
2. A. D'Atri and A. Motro, VirtuE: A Formal Model of Virtual Enterprises for Information Markets, *Journal of Intelligent Information Systems* (forthcoming, 2007).
3. A. D'Atri and A. Motro, Evolving VirtuE, in *Proc. of 8th IFIP Working Conference on Virtual Enterprises* (forthcoming, 2007).
4. H. Afsarmanesh and L.M. Camarinha-Matos, A Framework for Management of Virtual Organization Breeding Environments, in *Proc. PRO-VE 05: Collaborative Networks and their breeding environments, IFIP 6th Working Conference on Virtual Enterprises* (2005), pp.35-48.
5. A. D'Atri, Organizing and Managing Virtual Enterprises: the ECB Framework, in *Proc. of 4th IFIP Working Conference on Virtual Enterprises* (2004), pp.171-178.
6. W.H. Inmon, *Building the Data Warehouse*, 2nd Edition (John Wiley & Sons: New York, NY, USA 1996).
7. I. Foster, C. Kesselman, and S. Tuecke, The Anatomy of the Grid: Enabling Scalable Virtual Organizations, *Journal of High Performance Computing Applications*. Volume 15, Number 3, pp.200-222, (2001).
8. M.T. Özsu and P. Valduriez, *Principles of Distributed Database Systems* (Prentice-Hall: Englewood Cliffs, NJ, USA, 1999).
9. F. Curbera, M. Duftler, R. Khalaf, W. Nagy, N. Mukhi, and S. Weerawarana, Unraveling the Web Services Web: An Introduction to SOAP, WSDL, and UDDI, *IEEE Internet Computing*. Volume 6, Number 2, pp.86-93, (2002).
10. A. Cuzzocrea, F. Furfaro, G.M. Mazzeo, and D. Saccà, A Grid Framework for Approximate Aggregate Query Answering on Summarized Sensor Network Readings, in

Proc. of the 1st International Workshop on Grid Computing and its Application to Data Analysis, LNCS, Volume 3292 (2004), pp.144-153.

11. A. Cuzzocrea, F. Furfaro, E. Masciari, D. Saccà, and C. Sirangelo, *Approximate Query Answering on Sensor Network Data Streams*, in *Sensor-Based Distribution Geocomputing*, eds. A. Stefanidis and S. Nittel (CRC Press: 2004), pp.53-72.
12. E. Deelman, J. Blythe, Y. Gil, C. Kesselman, G. Mehta, K. Vahi, K. Blackburn, A. Lazzarini, A. Arbree, R. Cavanaugh, and S. Koranda, Mapping Abstract Complex Workflows onto Grid Environments, *Journal of Grid Computing*. Volume 1, Number 1, pp.25-39, (2003).
13. G. Greco, A. Guzzo, G. Manco, and D. Saccà, Mining and Reasoning on Workflows, *Transactions on Knowledge and Data Engineering, IEEE*. Volume 17, Number 4, pp.519-534, (2005).
14. H. Lican, W. Zhaohui, and P. Yunhe, Virtual and Dynamic Hierarchical Architecture for E-Science Grid, *International Journal of High Performance Computing Applications*. Volume 17, Number 3, pp.329-347, (2003).
15. I. Foster, J.-S. Vöckler, M. Wilde, and Y. Zhao, The Virtual Data Grid: A New Model and Architecture for Data-Intensive Collaboration, in *Proc. of the First Biennial Conference on Innovative Data Systems Research* (2003).

Value Network Positioning of Expected Winners: Analysis of the Top Software Business Start-ups

Juhani Warsta and Veikko Seppänen

Department of Information Processing Science, University of Oulu, P.O. Box 3000, Oulu, Finland juhani.warsta@oulu.fi veikko.seppanen@oulu.fi

Abstract. The focus of this paper is on trying to answer the question how the most promising ICT start-ups are positioned with regard to value creation in growing markets. The results of the study show that there are clearly a few most promising positions in the value network of emerging markets: either an infrastructure or application software supplier, or an application service provider.

Keywords: *ICT, Start-up, Value network analysis, Business ecosystem*

1. INTRODUCTION

Plenty of efforts have been paid to understand how start-up companies develop to future winners. Research data has often been gathered from individual case companies or from small groups of companies. For this reason many of the studies have been qualitative in their nature, and have thus tried to generalize findings from a rather restricted volume of primary company-specific data [1-3]. In this study we have chosen a different approach as far as the research approach is concerned. We decided to use secondary data that has been put forward by market analysis practitioners with regard to the industry as a whole, and by individual companies themselves for external observers. In order to make explicit and understand the positioning of companies in value networks, we selected a group of fast growing companies suggested as potential winners by business analysts. We analyzed their market position using the basic software value network framework proposed by Messerschmitt and Szyperski (later M-S) [4], to see also if this framework can help in explaining why certain positions are favored for rapid growth. The companies were selected for the study from the Red Herring lists of the *Top 100 Private Companies in North America*. The chosen companies are high-tech firms that can be categorized to software or software-intensive product and service companies, as well as to hardware companies.

In the following we will first discuss the M-S framework that is applied in this study. We will then present the data collection principles and analyze the value network positions of selected companies, in order to understand why they have sought for certain positions. Finally, we will augment the contemporary frameworks based on

Please use the following format when citing this chapter:

Warsta, J., Seppänen, V., 2007, in IFIP International Federation for Information Processing, Volume 254, Research and Practical Issues of Enterprise Information Systems II Volume 1, eds. L. Xu, Tjoa A., Chaudhry S. (Boston: Springer), pp. 43-52.

the results of the analysis, i.e. propose a justified view to winning positions in the value network of emerging markets.

2. SOFTWARE BUSINESS ANALYSIS FRAMEWORKS

Perhaps the most extensive present view to software industry is provided by the study of the software ecosystem in a treatise by M-S [4]. They present a framework that describes the value network of the software industry, Figure 1. In this framework software development includes eight business functions and their linkages to each other to form the overall value network.

As illustrated in Figure 1, the *industry consultant* analyzes and conveys the needs of a vertical industry segment or horizontal business functions. The *business consultant* spreads these results into practice, when the same or similar applications have been addressed in other companies. Basically the industry consultant focuses on the needs of all firms and the business consultant on adapting applications in specific firms.

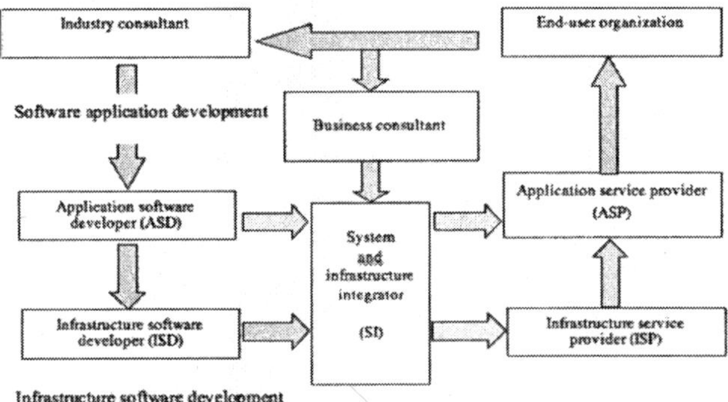

Figure 1. The Software Value Network Framework [4]

The *applications software developer (ASD)* produces the software application. The ASD thus tries to maximize its market share by attempting to meet the needs of the multiple end-user markets, and emphasizing the company's core competences, such as technical and project management skills in software development. The *infrastructure software developer (ISD)* has knowledge of a wide range of applications, requirements and the needs of application developers. The ISD thus benefits from the economics of scale from infrastructure related standardization processes and outcomes.

The *system and infrastructure integrator (SI)* specializes in the provisioning of software. It acquires application and infrastructure software from ASD and ISD supplier companies, making all the software to work together as well as installing and testing the whole system. The *application service provider (ASP)* licenses and operates applications, whereas the *infrastructure service provider (ISP)* purchases and operates the required software and hardware infrastructures, like computers, operating systems, networks and data storages.

3. PRINCIPLES OF DATA GATHERING AND ANALYSIS

The U.S. based Red Herring magazine publishes annually a list called *Red Herring 100* that features each year's most promising high-tech companies in the article *Top 100 Private Companies in North America*. We examined all the one hundred companies posted to these lists in May 2005 and May 2006, using not only the data found in the article, but also the information given in the listed companies' web sites.

We started the analysis by classifying the two hundred companies according to the value chain framework presented by M-S [4]. First we categorized the empirical data coarsely to fall either into the framework or outside of it. From the two analyzed lists of 100 companies we found 61, respectively 60 companies to fall inside the framework. In a few cases a company could be classified in two categories, e.g. companies that were both infrastructure developers and infrastructure providers. Therefore the total count of businesses summed up over the respective number of individual companies.

The analyzed companies fell in software business categories as shown in Table 1. One of the immediate findings was that there were no companies belonging in any of the two consultant business categories of the framework, although [4] see these as an integral part of the software value network. This may indicate that to be a notable consulting start-up company is not an easy task, especially qualifying the requirements set up by this sample group.

Table 1. Distribution of the Data

2005	Developers	System Integrators	Providers
Application Software	11	0	12
Infrastructure Software	31	0	7
Total	42	0	19
2006	Developers	System Integrators	Providers
Application Software	10	0	8
Infrastructure Software	31	0	11
Total	41	0	19

Table 1 shows clearly that businesses focus on the developer side, in particular on infrastructure software supply. This indicates that especially infrastructure software provisioning businesses are still under development. However, among the data set application software provisioning already matches with the level of application software development, which may reflect the overall change from shrink-wrapped software products to software-as-service type of offerings.

The most striking finding from the data was that there were absolutely no firms represented in the system integrators' category. Intuitively, this may be due to the small size and short existence of the analyzed companies, as system integrator operations demand an established position in the middle of the value network based on a wide set of business relationships and a strong resource base, cf. the analysis of system house type software businesses in Sallinen as an example [5]. Yet, the current business trends are favoring system integration, as big customer companies are concentrating on their core businesses and are more and more reducing the number of their direct subcontractors, thus giving space and opportunities for companies that are capable to integrate and supply various entities for brand owners [6]. It thus seems that system integration business opportunities are not in the focus of or are missed by the fast growing start-up companies.

Among the analyzed data Infrastructure Software Developers (ISD) are represented best. One may thus ask, if growth-seeking software business is more lucrative in the infrastructure field. In other words, it seems that there is a large potential for various infrastructure related software offerings. On the other hand, the supply side may also be more interesting for an infrastructure company, because markets are possibly more standardized than on the Application Software Developer (ASD) side. The ISD business may be either more lucrative for growth-seeking software start-up companies or just 'easier' to enter, compared to ASD business. In any case, the distribution of the supplier side business categories shown in Table 1 is interesting, as it indicates that the "secrets of software success" may after all not stem from the classic application software product supply position [7].

4. PARTNERING AND BUSINESS ROLES IN THE DEVELOPER SIDE

We analyzed the software supplier category more thoroughly in order to find out patterns of partnership development for value creation among these companies. Our aim was to find out the "direction of arrows" in the M-S framework, i.e. what is the partnering behavior in the supplier and developer side, using the classification shown in Table 2. This classification was based on actual findings of the data available on each companies own websites, rather than on any pre-conceptualization of the types of business relationships of software companies. Classifying the data we used the membership categorization device -method as described by Silverman [8].

4.1 Application Software Developers

The analyzed data shows a tendency of application software developers to form networks with several different partner categories. Though, the data varies between the analyzed years, but to this may influence the fact that two websites of these 10 companies (year 2006) lacked totally any information about partnering and one of the companies did not have any website at all. In other words, their business relationships are created, in terms of the M-S framework, horizontally towards service provider businesses. On the other hand, the figures indicate also clear partnering intention with *Consultants*. Analyzing the information available on the web sites of these companies, we found out that consulting partners were sought mainly for *software selling and distribution* purposes.

Table 2. Partnering Tendency of Application Software Developers (ASD)

Year	SI	Strategic partner	Technology partner	Service and implementation partner	Channel	Consulting partner	ASP	Number of companies
2005	6	2	5	5	5	6	5	11
2006	-	-	3	2	3	1	-	10

This is contrary to the M-S value creation thinking, where consultants are more or less seen as knowledge distributors from a specific industry to software supplier and system integrator businesses. Therefore, the data indicates that this part of the value network is functioning in a reversed direction compared to the M-S framework.

4.2 Infrastructure Software Developers

Table 3 shows the respective distribution of partnering tendency among the ISD businesses represented in the data. These figures show a clear difference compared to the partnering tendency of the ASD businesses described in Table 2. The interest of ISD businesses is to seek partnering with technology providers, so that such relationships can be strategic or operational in their nature. M-S discuss the role of technology in software business to some extent, but the data indicates that on the supplier side the importance of technology-driven business relationships is very high indeed. Therefore, the lower left-hand corner (Figure 1.) of the basic software value network should be expanded to describe the role of strategic and operational technology suppliers, too, especially for the needs of ISD businesses.

Table 3. Partnering Tendency of Infrastructure Software Developers (ISD)

Year	SI	Strategic partner	Technology partner	Service and implementation partner	Channel	Consulting partner	Number of companies
2005	12	10	14	5	32	7	31
2006	3	2	10	4	14	6	31

ISD businesses have also strong interests in finding channel partners. This may indicate a better possibility, compared to ASD businesses, to sell more standardized software products via SI and service provider channels. The products that ISD businesses included in the data offer are mostly network related.

The above analysis describes networking of ISD businesses with intermediary organizations of the value network, as described in the M-S framework. In other words, it supports the idea of coordinated value creation activities spanning from suppliers via integration and service provisioning to end-customers. However, most of the studied ISD businesses have relationships directly with end-customers, too. Altogether 28 businesses had direct sales (year 2005) operations (90%) and 5 of these businesses practiced also Web-based sales. This behavior may be due to the small size and emergent stage of the businesses. On the other hand, it can also indicate the importance of being able to short-circuit the value network by having direct access to end-customers, keeping in mind that one of the most fundamental aspects of software business is a tendency of winning companies to gather most of the customers in a specific market [7]. The rapidly growing ISD start-ups that are conceptually located farthest away from the end-customers in the value network, may this way seek for ensuring their future market position.

5. TOWARDS AN EXTENDED SOFTWARE VALUE NETWORK

In the analyzed context three main types of businesses exist: *development, integration*, and *provisioning*. The M-S framework illustrates well the relationships between these types of businesses. However, based on the analyzed data we were able to identify several interesting features that are not found in the aforesaid framework, as the real life operates differently from a conceptual framework, Figure 2.

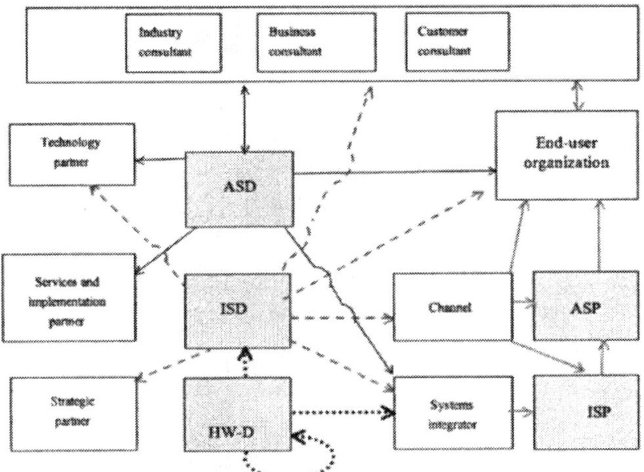

Figure 2. Landscape of the Most Promising High-tech Companies

The four main findings are as follows:

1) Value network short-circuits. In 90% of the analyzed cases the value network is short-circuited between the software developers (ASD or ISD) and the end-users (customers).

2) The different role of consultants. The consultants did not only act as information relaying actors from customers towards developers, instead the ISD and especially ASD businesses used consultants as their promotion channel towards end-customers.

3) Lack of system integrator businesses among these start-ups.

4) The HW developing firms belong organically to the ecosystem and have an important role especially for ISD businesses.

Figure 2 shows the value creation landscape derived from the data. In the figure we have depicted only those actors that emerge as the most interesting elements or partners, ref. Table 2 and Table 3. Next, we will discuss the four main findings.

5.1 Short-circuiting

With the term short-circuiting we mean the information and process flow for end-user access, contrary to the M-S framework. The empirical data shows clearly ISD and ASD types of companies had established or were interested to develop their cooperation directly with end-user organizations, without relying solely on different kinds of channel partners. This way of action may originate from several reasons that occur during the evolution and growth of the developer type firms in question:

- The developers have not yet established any extensive supply channel network or are under their way of building this.
- The firms have learned in the past to operate using direct end-user contacts, as in the early stages of development there have been only a few customers and interaction with them is economical and controllable.
- Some of the analyzed firms run this business also using the Internet that may indicate a new way of getting end-users involved.

Internet can also be used as a complementing sales channel or the companies can use it as their main channel especially when they are searching international customers [9]. This development can be justified also by the fact that firms interacting directly with their end-users secure continuous and current feedback concerning their product development and innovations in the market. This gives a better visibility to start-ups that operate with their own brand name instead being hidden behind partners. However, in the future problems can emerge for these companies, because when their business evolves, they must growingly trust on channel partners in order to attain larger markets.

5.2 The Role of Consultants

Short-circuiting can be also found between consultants and ASD and ISD businesses, as these firms use relationships to an opposite direction compared to the M-S framework. Information is not flowing from the industrial and business consultants to developer firms. Instead, according to our findings, the flow of information and relationships (or aspirations towards relationships) between ASD or ISD firms and consultants are established in order to use the latter as new business lead finders and promotional partners.

This phenomenon gains strength, when "moving up" in the value network from HW-D to ISD and ASD, i.e. consultants are most useful for firms that operate in or with the application environment. Hardware firms do not need consultants, they know what they need and are buying, but this is not the case with software. It may also be the case that product needs and possibilities are unclear between software provider companies and end-users, and thus they need intermediate actors that can facilitate and communicate the needs of both sides. Consultants operate thus in several capacities: lead finders, implementators and information distributors.

5.3 The Role of System Integrators

Davies [10] emphasizes that "Recent literature on business strategy argues that firms should concentrate less on making stand-alone physical products and more on delivering high-value services and customer-focused solutions". He further argues that new successful businesses are "built on new forms of vertical integration".

From this standpoint the observed lack of the SIs in the analyzed group of firms was a surprise. There may be several reasons for this, though. As being an SI firm, the company must have a wide-ranging knowledge base, enough own resources, as well as an extensive complementing partner network. This is seldom the case for a new start-up. On the contrary, it may have difficulties to convince a bigger company of its resources and integration capabilities that are a strategic issue for the customer. The occurrence of SIs can also depend on the maturity and competition level of the industry in question [11]. This is again a question of when and how SIs start to develop, i.e. when the industry is mature enough to support SIs in the value network.

According to our former studies on the Finnish software industry, the most promising stage in technology lifecycle to establish integration business is when the secondary or customer industry is in a turning point, just before a steady state of the industry development [12]. At this turning point key business processes, core technologies and system interfaces have typically been standardized, industry segments' have become rather homogenous and markets grown, and thereby enough room for integration business has been created. Later on, during a steady state, the customer industry has typically reached a technologically mature phase, the markets have been divided among big actors, and system supply and integration networks have been optimized.

5.4 The Role of Hardware Developers

The hardware development business in the left hand lower corner of Figure 2 is an interesting element not only in relation to software businesses, but also because it has contacts inside the business branch. In other words, HW-D firms carry out businesses between themselves. Thus, some of these companies play a developer's role and other a system integrator's role. Especially ISD and HW-D partners (technology or strategic) are typically hardware, software, Internet, and networking companies, and act at the same time as developers and customers.

HW-D firms were not in our main focus in this study, but it is clear that they would deserve a separate in-depth analysis, referring to the kind of research work that has been done for introducing M-S type of value-creating framework. The reason is that, as opposed to being far away from rapidly growing software businesses, HW-D companies seem to play an important role in the overall ICT value creating system.

6. CONCLUSIONS

Our focus in this paper was to answer the question how the most promising ICT start-ups are positioned with regard to value creation in growing markets. In particular, we were interested in why these companies are obviously able to position themselves better in the value network in terms of the evolving market than their competitors. In order to understand this we selected a group of top-ranked companies and analyzed them using the software value network framework proposed by Messerschmitt and Szyperski. We found it to fit well with the reality, but at the same time to be somewhat too robust to describe the entire ICT industry ecosystem as a whole. We found the following major proposals to improve the framework:

a) Hardware producing companies should be integrated in the framework, in order to reflect more holistically the software and hardware business interplay and dependency from each other.

b) The framework should also describe how companies establish and maintain relationships with other companies in direct ways, without making use of any middlemen.

c) The analyzed companies use consultants in a different way than what is proposed in the framework, as many companies have established or sought for relationships with consultants as business lead hunters and sales force.

In real life the HW-D businesses form an essential element in ISD business development, because ISD businesses typically build their infrastructure software innovations, development, and usage opportunities on advance knowledge of hardware innovations. Thus, the closer the cooperation with technology innovators and hardware developers, the better business opportunities and possibilities to grow and succeed in competition.

In our analysis of ISD businesses we found that they characteristically establish direct relationships with end-user organizations. This may be due to the fact that the companies are young firms that have started their business with direct customer contacts, and only later extend their business relationships to include intermediaries in customer interfaces. The need for fast and direct feedback and ideas from customers is obviously a stronger value creating force for start-ups than a well-organized and orchestrated distribution channel. Moreover, companies that are positioned in this way in the value network make heavily use of business consultants, but not in the way that M-S have proposed. In Figure 2, it is shown how ASD businesses approach end-user organizations directly, whereas consultants can be seen operating in both directions. From end-users they give feedback, market information, and technology development information to ASD businesses. On the other hand they represent ASD businesses as a marketing and sales channel, thus forming another distribution channel for ASD businesses than SIs and service provisioning companies. Yet, ASD businesses cooperate with technology partners and service and implementation partners, too. ISD businesses also benefit from technology and strategic partners, and approach directly end-user organizations. They seek for networking with consultants, not for acquiring market needs information, but for using them as selling partners and new business opportunities trackers.

Finally, the results of the study show that there are clearly a few most promising positions in the value network of emerging markets: either an infrastructure software developer or application software developer, or an application service provider. According to our findings based on the *Red Herring 100* companies start-up companies have understood the demands of business, as they are very relationship-minded in order to grow their businesses as fast as possible in highly volatile and rapidly emerging markets. The partnering tendency strengthens their internal knowledge base and reduces business risks.

From all the analyzed business categories we found infrastructure software developers (ISD) to be the most promising business category that has the best potential to grow rapidly. Furthermore, an interesting aspect among the analyzed start-ups was the total lack of system integrator (SI) companies, even though this line of business has a strong potential for future growth – as well illustrated by the world's biggest ICT companies.

REFERENCES

1. M. Cusumano, *The Business of Software: What Every Manager, Programmer, and Entrepreneur Must Know to Thrive and Survive in Good Times and Bad* (Free Press: 2004), p.35.
2. M. Giarratana, The birth of a new industry: entry by start-ups and the drivers of firm growth - The case of encryption software, *Research Policy*. Volume 33, pp.787-806, (2004).
3. S. Nambisan, Software firm evolution and innovation–orientation, *Journal of Engineering and Technology Management*. Volume 19, pp.141-165, (2002).
4. D. Messerschmitt and C. Szyperski, *Software Ecosystem: Understanding an Indispensable Technology and Industry* (The MIT Press: 2003), p.432.
5. S. Sallinen, *Development of industrial software supplier firms in the ICT cluster - An analysis of firm types, technological change and capability development*, Academic Dissertation presented to the Faculty of Economics and Industrial Management, University of Oulu, Oulu (2002).
6. J. Warsta, V. Seppänen, and P. Tyrväinen, Evolution of Secondary Software Product Businesses: Momentum of Concurrent Enterprising, in *Proc. of 11th International Conference on Concurrent Enterprising* (University BW Munich: Germany, 2005).
7. C.R. Roeding, G. Purkert, S.K. Kindner, R. Muller, and D.J. Hoch, *Secrets of Software Success* (Harvard Business School Press: Boston, 1999), p.312.
8. D. Silverman, *Interpreting Qualitative Data, Methods for Analyzing Talk, Text and Interactio,* Second Edition (SAGE Publications Ltd.: London, 2001), p.325.
9. P. Arenius, V. Sasi, and M. Gabrielsson, Rapid internationalisation enabled by the Internet: The case of a knowledge intensive company, *Journal of International Entrepreneurship*. Volume 3, pp.279-290, (2006).
10. A. Davies, Moving base into high-value integrated solutions: a value stream approach, *Industrial and Corporate Change*. Volume 13, Number 5, pp.727-756, (2004).
11. J. Warsta, S. Juntunen, and V. Seppänen, Who is our Customer? Analysis of Software Company's Value Creation Strategies, in *IMP-2004 Industrial marketing and purchasing group* (Copenhagen, 2004).
12. P. Tyrväinen, J. Warsta, and V. Seppänen, Toimialakehitys ohjelmistoteollisuuden vauhdittajana - Uutta liiketoimintaa lähialoilta (In Finnish), in *Teknologiakatsaus 151/ 04. Tekes: Helsinki* (2004), p.71.

A Review on the Relationship Between New Variables and Classical TAM Structure

Yuanquan Li, Jiayin Qi and Huaying Shu

School of Economics & Management, Beijing University of Posts & Telecommunications, Beijing 100876, P.R. China Leo8410@gmail.com ssfqjy@263.net shuhy@bupt.edu.cn

Abstract. Integration of different theories and expansion of research areas are the main trends in the research domain of IS adoption. Classical TAM structure has been largely expended by newly added variables. Prior studies [1] have analyzed relationships among variables in TAM and found the stability of classical structure, but what about relationships between new variables and classical structure? We selected 30 articles from the main international journals for analyses. It is found that, SE, SN and PBC are used mostly in extended TAM. The relations between SE, PBC and TAM are consistently significant, but the integration of SN into TAM is not so ideal. In our review scale, this relation is inconsistent. Other variables and relations are also discussed in this article. The conclusions of this article will provide guidance for future researches about extended TAM model building.

Keywords: *TAM, TAM classical structure, New variables, Variable relations*

1. INTRODUCTION

Although Information System (IS) has played an important role in modern enterprises, the implementation of IS is costly and has a relatively low success rate. Since the middle of 1980s, researchers have begun to concentrate on predicting the effect of IS implementations by exploring user's adoption mechanism for IS. Among these researches, TAM (Technology Acceptance Model) is one of the most important models, which was proposed in the doctoral thesis of Davis (1986). With the development of nearly 20 years, TAM has become to be the mainstream model to explain the mechanism of IS adoption.

Based on different theories, many researchers have added some new variables into the classical TAM structure. For example, based on TPB (Theory of Behavior), Patrick Y.K. et al. added SN (Subject Norm) and PBC (Perceived Behavior Control) into TAM [2], S.-S. Liaw added PE (Perceived Enjoyment) by introducing SCT (Social Cognitive Theory) into TAM [3], and Chorng-Shyong Ong & Jung-Yu Lai added CSE (Computer Self-Efficacy) depending on studies of Attribution Theory and Social Cognitive Theory [4].

Introduction of new variables into classical TAM has enhanced the explanatory power. However, the relations between new variables and classical TAM variables are inconsistent [5] and lack of relevant studies. In this article, we attempt to analyze

Please use the following format when citing this chapter:

Li, Y., Qi, J., Shu, H., 2007, in IFIP International Federation for Information Processing, Volume 254, Research and Practical Issues of Enterprise Information Systems II Volume 1, eds. L. Xu, Tjoa A., Chaudhry S. (Boston: Springer), pp. 53-63.

these relations by reviewing previous studies and try to provide a reference for future research in IS adoption domain.

2. CLASSICAL TAM STRUCTURE AND VARIABLES

TAM was proposed by Davis in 1989 [6], two main variables are mentioned in the classical TAM (Figure 1): Perceived Ease of Use (PEOU) and Perceived Usefulness (PU). External variables have effects on Attitude toward Using (AT) and Behavior Intention (BI) through PEOU and PU, and finally affect the Use (U) of IS.

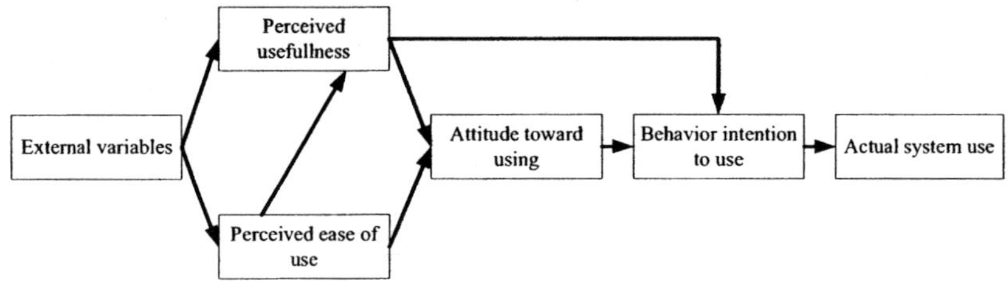

Figure 1. Classical Structure of TAM [6]

Different researchers in different researches used different TAM structures. They get extended models by adding some new variables or relations into classical TAM. However, we find most extended TAM models are still built on the classical TAM structure that is made by PU, PEOU, AT, BI and USE [1].

3. NEW VARIABLES IN EXTENDED TAM

In this research, the term 'new variables' is defined as the variables that do not exist in classical TAM structure but have initial theory supports, such as SN (based on SCT&TRA), PBC (based on TPB). In our research, we only choose the new variables that be used widely and have theoretical supports. Depending on this criterion, we select Self-efficacy, SN (Subject Norm), Enjoyment, PBC (Perceived Behavior Control), Anxiety, Credibility, Compatibility, Innovation, Cost, Trust and Image which are described in the table below.

Table 1. Explanation of New Variables

	Explanation	Theory
Self-efficacy	People are more likely to make internal attributions when the event outcome is positive [7].	Attribution Theory
	Self-Efficacy is composed by level of ability, intensity of beliefs and generalizability of ability.[8]	SCT [8]
	individual perceived ability to use computer.[10]	CSE [10]
SN	Observed behaviors of others influence the observer to emulate those behaviors.[8]	SCT [8]
	Beliefs that specific individuals or groups approve or disapprove of performing the behavior.[11]	TRA [9] TPB [11]
Enjoyment	The extent to which the activity of using the technology is perceived to be enjoyable in its own right, apart from any performance consequences that may be anticipated[12]	MM. [12]
PBC	Presence or absence of requisite resources and opportunities [11]	TPB [11]
Anxiety	Computer anxiety was studied by Henderson et al. as an element of the computer attitude scale (CAS) developed by Loyd and Gressard [13].	CAS[13]
Credibility	Credibility can be simply defined as believability.[4]	
Compatibility	Compatibility refers to the degree to which an innovation is perceived as consistent with the existing values, past experiences and needs of potential adopters.[14]	DOI [14]
Innovation	Describes the extent to which the individual has an innate propensity toward adopting a new IT [15].	PIIT [15]
Trust	Trust is basically seen as a common mechanism for reducing social complexity and perceived risk of transaction[16]	Social Exchange [16, 17]
Image	TAM2 theorized that subjective norm achieved its effect on perceived usefulness partially by altering image.[18]	TAM2 [18]

In our research, we care about there types of relations between new variables and classical TAM structure, which are positive significant effect (marked as POS.), negative significant effect (marked as NEG.) and none significant effect (marked as NS.).

4. RESEARCH METHODOLOGIES

The literatures we select come from the journals as follows:

- MIS Quarterly;
- Decision Sciences;
- Management Science;
- Journal of Management Information Systems;
- Information Systems Research;
- Information & Management;
- Journal of Information Technology;
- International Negotiation;
- Academy of Management Journal;
- Computer Standards & Interfaces;
- Government Information Quarterly;

- Human-Computer Studies;
- Decision Support Systems

The selected literatures were published from 1980s to 2006, and most articles are about model applications. These applications are not rigidly adhered to the fruits of predecessors, but creating many new improved models by combining other related theories. In summary, we get 108 articles. And further more, we choose 30 articles for analyzing based on the following three criteria: firstly, TAM is used in an empirical study; secondly, some new variables were added in the research model; finally, the research methodology is well described and the research results are available and complete.

5. FINDINGS OF RESEARCH

Through analyzing of literatures been selected, we get the results bellow:

Table 2. Relations between New Variables and Classical TAM

New variables		PU	PEOU	AT	BI	USE
SE	N.S.					1
	NEG.					
	POS.	4	10		4	1
SN	N.S.			2	4	
	NEG.	2				
	POS.	1			9	1
PE	N.S.		1	1	2	
	NEG.					
	POS.	1	3	4	3	1
PBC	N.S.				1	1
	POS.		4		5	1
Anxiety	N.S.					1
	NEG.	2	5			
Credibility	POS.	2		1	2	
Compatibility	N.S.	1				
	NEG.	1				
	POS.	2	4		1	
Innovation	N.S.					
	POS.	1	2	2		
Cost	NEG.			1	2	
Trust	POS.			1	1	
Image	POS.	1		1	1	

Notes: figures in the table above are the frequency this relation appears in our selected articles.

In order to describe the relations in the table above more clearly and easily understood, we design a structure below. In the center of this structure, that is classical TAM structure and around it that is 8 new variables. Cost, Trust and Image are not included in this structure, because these variables in our literature review are used seldom (less than 4 times).

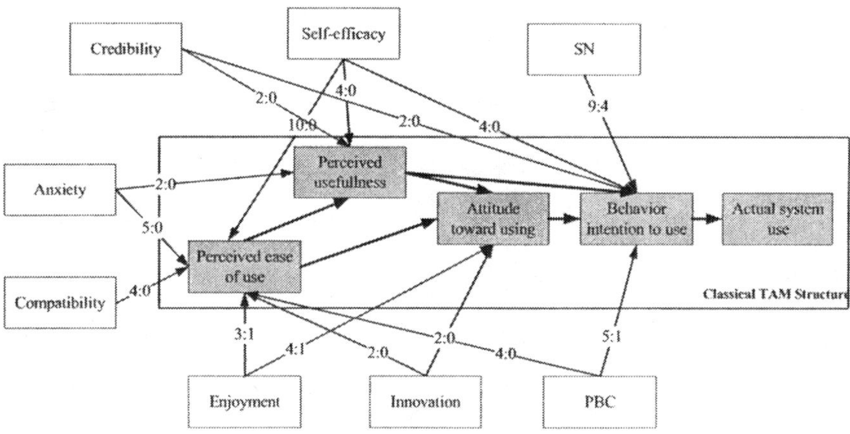

Figure 2. Relations between New Variables and Classical TAM

Notes: the left figure in the relation arrow means the number of significant relations; the right figure means the number of insignificant relations.

There exist consistent positive significant relations between Self-Efficacy and PU, PEOU and BI, no NEG. or N.S. effects were found. SN has 9 POS. relations with BI, but we also find 4 NEG. relations, so this relation is inconsistent, the SN-PU relation is all significant but lack of evidence to decide its effect type (POS. or NEG.). Relations between Enjoyment and PEOU and AT are consistent positive significant (POS.: N.S. is 3:1 and 4:1), but Enjoyment-BI relation is inconsistent (POS.:N.S. is 3:2). PBC has positive significant relation with PEOU and BI (POS.:N.S. is 4:0 and 5:1). Anxiety has significant negative relations with PU and PEOU (NEG.: N.S. is 2:0 and 5:0). Credibility has significant positive relations with PU and BI (POS.:N.S. is 2:0 and 2:0). Relation between Compatibility and PEOU is significant positive (POS.:N.S. is 4:0), but Compatibility-PU is inconsistent (POS.:NEG.: N.S. is 2:1:1). Relations between Credibility, Innovation, Cost, Trust, Image and classical TAM are so fewer in our literature review scale that can not describe their relation types. So in this study these relations are not mentioned.

6. DISCUSSIONS AND CONCLUSIONS

The relations between SE and PU, PEOU and BI are all positive significant in our results. Self-Efficacy refers to an individual's judgment of his or her ability to use a computer [10]. This may influence an individual's PEOU and acceptance. Such effects can also get theoretical support from the Self-Efficacy Theory. However, SE and PU relationship has been studied less in contrast to SE-PEOU and SE-BI, but in some special areas such as e-shopping [4], on-line tax [19] and broadband Internet

[20], this relation has been mentioned in relevant hypothesis and empirical evidence shows a positive significant relation-ship between them.

SN-BI relation is inconsistent; the same results can also be got from previous studies. Jiayin Qi & Yuanquan Li found SN-BI relation is 3 significant but 4 insignificant [1]. Although SN is an important variable in TRA and TPB, empirical evidence supporting its roles has been mixed [21, 22]. So we think SN-BI is an important relation in TAM research but more deeply and widely studies should be done.

Prior IS research suggested that PBC might be a determinant of PEOU [23]. In our re-search, PBC - PEOU is consistent positive significant which validates the hypothesis above. PBC – BI is an important relation in TPB [11], an indirect effect through BI is based on the notion that PBC will have a motivating influence based on an individual's assessment of likelihood of success. Though our research, this effect is supported.

Perceived Enjoyment is an important intrinsic motivation variable which is seen as a determinant of system-specific perceived ease of use [24]. Our result shows that, Enjoyment actually has significant effect on PEOU (3:1). But prior researches believed Enjoyment -PEOU relation changes over time. With increasing experience, PEOU is expected to reflect the unique attributes of enjoyment as it relates to the user-system interaction [24]. We also find Enjoyment has positive significant effect on AT (4: 0), lots of previous researches support this relation, Heijden added PU and verified that it positively affected AT and BI towards personal website adoption [25]. Moon & Kim's study showed that intrinsic motivation was positively related to attitude towards using the Web [26].

Some researchers believe there are no relationships between computer anxiety and computer-based performance [27, 28, 29, 30]. But others found consistent relations between them. In our research, Anxiety has consistent significant negative effect on PU and PEOU. This consistent relationship is partly due to its independence of prior experience and gender [31], Self Efficacy Theory also conceives Experience and Anxiety as independent factors. So we think that Anxiety has significant negative effect on USE through PU and PEOU.

Agarwal & Prasad asserted a positive relationship between an individual's prior compatible experiences and the new information technology acceptance [32]. They found that PU and PEOU non-trivially contributed in mediating the effects of compatibility to attitude. However, we only found positive relation between Compatibility and PEOU, Compatibility-PU relationship is inconsistent.

In some special areas like Internet tax-filing [33] and mobile banking [34], PC (Perceived Credibility) is one of the most important factors affecting the use intention, so in this kind of area, relations of PC – BI and PC – PU is concerned a lot [33, 19, 35], and we find both of the relations are positive significant.

7. FUTURE RESEARCHES

In the previous study, relationships among TAM structure were analyzed [1], this article follows that study and further researches the relationships between new variables and classical TAM structure. In future, more intentions will be paid on the effects of control variables in extended TAM. These three researches will exhibit a panoramic view of the TAM research domain and provide theoretical and practical support for further studies.

REFERENCES

1. J. Qi, Y. Li, and S. Shi, Adoption of IS: Theoretical development and practices in China, in *CNAIS 2006 Symposium on IT/IS Adoption* (Chengdu, China, 2006).
2. Y.K. Patrick, P. Chaua, and Hu. Jen-Hwa, Investigating Healthcare Professionals' Decisions to Accept Telemedicine Technology: An Empirical Test Of Competing Theories, *Information & Management.* Volume 39, pp.297-311, (2002).
3. S.S. Liaw, Understanding User Perceptions of World-Wide Web Environments, *Journal of Computer Assisted Learning.* Volume 18, pp.137-148, (2002).
4. C. Shyong and O.J.Y. Lai, Gender Differences in Perceptions and Relationships Among Dominants of E-Learning Acceptance, *Computers In Human Behavior.* Volume 22, pp.816–829, (2006).
5. H. Sun and P. Zhang, The role of moderating factors in user technology acceptance, *Int. J. Human-Computer Studies.* Volume 64, pp.53-78, (2006).
6. F.D. Davis, Perceived usefulness, perceived ease of use, and user acceptance of information technologies, *MIS Quarterly.* Volume 13, Number 3, pp.319-340, (1989).
7. V. Venkatesh and F.D. Davis, A model of the antecedents of perceived ease of use: development and test, *Decision Sciences.* Volume 27, Number 3, pp.451-481, (1996).
8. A. Bandura, Self-efficacy: Toward a unifying theory of behavioral change, *Psychological Review.* pp. 191-215, (1977).
9. M. Fishbein and I. Ajzen, *Belief, Attitude, Intention and Behavior: An Introduction to Theory and Research* (Addison-Wesley, Reading, MA, 1975).
10. D.R. Compeau and C.A. Higgins, Computer Self-Efficacy: Development of a Measure and Initial Test, *MIS Quarterly.* Volume 19 Number 2, pp.189-221, (1995).
11. I. Ajzen, From intentions to actions: a theory of planned behavior, in *J.A.J.K., Action Control: From Cognition to Behavior*, eds. Beckmann (Springer: Verlag, New York, 1985), pp.11-39.
12. F.D. Davis, R.P. Bagozzi, and P.R. Warshaw, Extrinsic and intrinsic motivation to use computers in the workplace, *Journal of Applied Social Psychology.* Volume 22, pp. 1111–1132, (1992).
13. B.H. Loyd and C.P. Gressard, Reliability and factorial validity of computer attitude scales, *Educational and Psychological Measurement.* Volume 44, pp.501-505, (1984).
14. E.M. Rogers and F.F. Shoemaker, *Communication of Innovations,* 2nd (New York, 1971).
15. Y.M. Yi, D.J. Jackson, S.J. Park, and C.J. Probst, Understanding information technology acceptance by individual professionals: Toward an integrative view, *Information & Management.* Volume 43, pp.350-363, (2006).
16. H.H. Kelley and J.W. Thibaut, *Interpersonal Relations: A Theory of Interdependence* (Wiley: New York, 1978).
17. H.H. Kelley, *Personal Relationships: Their Structure and Processes* (Lawrence Erlbaum Associates: Mahwah, NJ, 1979).
18. V. Venkatesh and F.D. Davis, A theoretical extension of the technology acceptance model: Four longitudinal field studies, *Management Science.* Volume 46, pp.186-204, (2000).

19. I.L. Wu and J. Chen, An extension of Trust and TAM model with TPB in the initial adoption of on-line tax: An empirical study, *Int. J. Human-Computer Studies*. Volume 62, pp.784-808, (2005).
20. O. Sangjo, A. Joongho, and K. Beomsoo, Adoption of broadband Internet in Korea: the role of experience in building attitudes, *Journal of Information Technology*. Volume 18, pp.267-280, (2003).
21. E. Karahanna, D.W. Straub, and N.L. Chervany, Information technology adoption across time: a cross-sectional comparison of pre-adoption and post-adoption beliefs, *MIS Quarterly*. Volume 23, Number 2, pp.183-213, (1999).
22. K. Mathieson, Predicting user intentions: comparing the technology acceptance model with the theory of planned behavior, *Information Systems Research*. Volume 2, Number3, pp.173-191, (1991).
23. V. Venkatesh, Determinants of perceived ease of use: integrating control, intrinsic motivation, and emotion into the technology acceptance model, *Information Systems Research*. Volume 11, Number 4, pp.342-365, (2000).
24. M. Igbaria, J. Iivari, and H. Maragahh, Why do individuals use computer technology? A Finnish case study, *Information and Management*. Volume 29, pp.227-238, (1995).
25. H. Heijden, Factors influencing the usage of websites: the case of a generic portal in The Netherlands, *Information and Management*. Volume 40, Number 6, pp.541–549, (2003).
26. J.W. Moon, Y.G. Kim, Extending the TAM for a World-Wide-Web context, *Information and Management*. Volume 38, Number 4, pp.217-230, (2001).
27. M.C. Kernan and G.S. Howard, Computer anxiety and computer attitudes: An investigation of construct and predictive validity issues, *Educational and Psychological Measurement*. Volume 50, pp.681-690, (1990).
28. C.F. Munger and B.H. Loyd, Gender and attitudes towards computers and calculators: The relationship to math performance, *Journal of Educational Computing Research*. Volume 5, pp.167-177, (1989).
29. B. Szajna, An investigation into the predictive validity of computer anxiety and computer attitude, *Educational and Psychological Measurement*. Volume 54, pp.926-934, (1994).
30. B. Szajna and J.M. Mackay, Predictors of learning performance in a computer-user training environment: A path-analytic study, *International Journal of Human Computer Interaction*. Volume 7, pp.361-369, (1995).
31. B. Whitely, Gender differences in computer related attitudes. It depends on what you ask, *Computers in Human Behavior*. Volume 12, pp.275-289, (1996).
32. R. Agarwal and J. Prasad, Are individual differences germane to the acceptance of new information technologies, *Decision Sciences*. Volume 30, Issue 2, pp. 361-391, (1999).
33. I.C. Chang, Y. Li, W. Hung, and H.G. Hwang, An empirical study on the impact of quality antecedents on tax payers' acceptance of Internet tax-filing systems, *Government Information Quarterly*. Volume 22, pp.389-410, (2005).
34. P. Luarn and H.H. Lin, Towards an understanding of the behavioral intention to use mobile banking, *Computers in Human Behavior*. Volume 21, pp.873-891, (2005).
35. Y. Wang, The adoption of electronic tax filing systems: an empirical study, *Government Information Quarterly*. Volume 20, pp.333-352, (2002).
36. A.l. Gahtani, S. Said, and M. King, Attitudes, satisfaction and usage: factors contributing to each in the acceptance of information technology, *Behaviour and Information Technology*. Volume 18, No. 4, pp. 277-297, (1999).
37. D. Compeau, C.A. Higgins and S. Huff, Social cognitive theory and individual reactions to computing technology: a longitudinal study, *MIS Quarterly*. Volume 23, No. 2, p.145-158, (1999).
38. M.J. Brosnan, Modeling technophobia: a case for word processing, *Computers in Human Behavior*. Volume 15, pp. 105-121, (1999).

39. P. Roberts and R. Henderson, Information technology acceptance in a sample of government employees: a test of the technology acceptance model, *Interacting with Computers*. Volume 12, pp. 427-443, (2000).
40. V. Venkatesh and M. G. Morris, Why Don't Men Ever Stop to Ask for Directions? Gender, Social Influence, and Their Role in Technology Acceptance and Usage Behavior, *MIS Quarterly*. Volume 24, Number. 1, pp.115-139, (2000).
41. J.Y.L. Thong, W. Hong, and K.Y. Tam, Understanding user acceptance of digital libraries: what are the roles of interface characteristics, organizational context, and individual differences, *International Journal of Human-Computer Studies*. Volume 57, Number 3, pp. 215-242, (2002).
42. P. Jen-Hwa Hu, T.H.K. Clark, and W.W. Ma, Examining technology acceptance by school teachers: a longitudinal study, *Information & Management*. Volume 41, pp. 227–241, (2003).
43. C.L. Hsu and H.P. Lu, Why do people play on-line games? An extended TAM with social influences and flow experience, *Information & Management*. Volume 41, pp. 853–868, (2004).
44. E. Yoh, M. L. Damhorst, Stephen Sapp, and Russ Laczniak, Consumer adoption of the Internet: The case of apparel shopping, *Psychology and Marketing*. Volume 20, Issue 12, pp. 1095-1118, (2003).
45. C.K. Riemenschneider, D.A. Harrison and P.P. Mykytyn, Understanding IT adoption decisions in small business: integrating current theories, *Information & Management*. Volume 40, Issue 4, pp. 269-285, (2003).
46. H.P. Shih, An empirical study on predicting user acceptance of e-shopping on the Web, *Information & Management*. Volume 41, Issue 3, pp. 351-368, (2004).
47. M. Pagani, Determinants of adoption of third generation mobile multimedia services, *Journal of Interactive Marketing*. Volume 18, Issue 3, pp. 46-59, (2004).
48. H. Van der Heijden, User Acceptance Of Hedonic Information Systems, *MIS Quarterly*. Volume 28, Number 4, pp. 695-704, (2004).
49. S.Y Hung and C.M. Chang, User acceptance of WAP services: test of competing theories, *Computer Standards & Interfaces*. Volume 27, Issue 4, pp. 359-370, (2005).
50. K.C.C. Yang, Exploring factors affecting the adoption of mobile commerce in Singapore, *Telematics and Informatics*. Volume 22, Issue 3, pp. 257-277, (2005).
51. I.L. Wu and J.L. Chen, An extension of Trust and TAM model with TPB in the initial adoption of on-line tax: An empirical study, *International Journal of Human-Computer Studies*. Volume 62, Issue 6, pp. 784-808, (2005).
52. J.H. Wu and S.C. Wang, What drives mobile commerce? An empirical evaluation of the revised technology acceptance model, *Information & Management*. Volume 42, Issue 5, pp. 719-729, (2005).
53. D.J. Mcfarland and D. Hamilton, Adding contextual specificity to the technology acceptance model, *Computers in human behavior*. Volume 22, No. 3, pp. 427-447, (2006).
54. Y. Liu, Y. Chen, and C. Zhou, Exploring Success Factors for Web-based E-Government Services: Behavioral Perspective from End Users, *Information and Communication Technologies*. Volume 1, pp. 937- 942, (2006).
55. J. Yu, I. Ha, M. Choi, and J. Rho, Extending the TAM for a t-commerce, *Information & Management*. Volume 42, Issue 7, pp. 965-976, (2005).
56. M.S. Featherman, *Evaluative Criteria and User Acceptance of Internet-Based Financial Transaction Processing Systems*. Ph.D Thesis, Hawaii University (2002).

APPENDIX

Table 3. Articles We Used for This Research

Studies / New variables	SN	Image	PBC	Innovation	Self-efficacy	Cost	Anxiety	Enjoyment	Compatibility	Credibility
A.l. Gahtani, S. Said, and M. King [36]		+						+	+	
D. Compeau, C.A. Higgins, and S. Huff [37]					+		+			
M.J. Brosnan [38]					+		+	+		
P. Roberts and R. Henderson [39]	+						+	+		
V. Venkatesh [23]			+		+		+	+		
V. Venkatesh and M. G. Morris [40]	+									
Y.K. Patrick, P. Chaua, and Hu. Jen-Hwa [2]	+		+							
J.Y.L. Thong, W. Hong, and K.Y. Tam[41]					+					
Y. Wang [35]					+					+
S.-S. Liaw [3]					+			+		
P. Jen-Hwa Hu, T.H.K. Clark, and W.W. Ma [42]	+				+				+	
C.L. Hsu and H.P. Lu [43]	+									
O. Sangjo, A. Joongho, and K. Beomsoo [20]					+				+	
E. Yoh and M. L. Damhorst [44]	+									

C.K. Riemenschneider, D.A. Harrison and P.P. Mykytyn [45]	+		+							
H.P. Shih [46]					+					
M. Pagani [47]				+		+		+		
H. Van der Heijden [48]								+		
S.Y Hung and C.M. Chang [49]	+		+	+	+	+				
I.C. Chang, Y. Li, W. Hung, and H.G. Hwang [33]										+
K.C.C. Yang [50]				+						
I.L. Wu and J.L. Chen [51]	+		+							+
P. Luarn and H.H. Lin [34]					+	+				+
J.H. Wu and S.C. Wang [52]						+			+	
Y.M. Yi, D.J. Jackson, S.J. Park, and C.J. Probst [15]	+	+	+	+	+					
D.J. Mcfarland and D. Hamilton [53]					+		+			
Y. Liu, Y. Chen, and C. Zhou [54]			+		+					+
J. Yu, I. Ha, M. Choi, and J. Rho [55]	+							+		
M.S. Featherman [56]	+	+								

Notes: The mark "+" means relevant new variable used in this article

A Study on Self-adaptive Heterogeneous Data Integration Systems

Yan Cao, Yan Chen and Buyuan Jiang

College of Economics and Management, Dalian Maritime University, Dalian 116026, P.R. China caoy123@163.com chenyan_dlmu@163.com sophyblaze@hotmail.com

Abstract. Along with the rapid development of Internet and the extensive use of information technology in various fields, large amount of heterogeneous data has been produced. The way of integrating these heterogeneous data has been a hot issue. In this paper, from the problems which enterprise information integration faced, a framework of self-adaptive heterogeneous data integration system (AHDIS) has been given, and by using ontology, semantic similarity, web service and XML techniques, a self-adapted heterogeneous data integration platform which can be dynamically regulated has been built up successfully. With this integrated platform, the global data model can automatically or semi-automatically be adjusted while a change has been made to the local data model, so that it can realize the data sharing among heterogeneous data sources.

Keywords: *Data integration, AHDIS, Schema mapping, Semantic similarity, Web Services*

I. INTRODUCTION

In the process of information construction, the enterprise has constructed many information systems to manage the enterprise data. For differences in business, functions and phases of information system construction of every department etc, enterprise's internal data has obvious distributives, autonomy and the heterogeneity (platform, application, data format and semantic heterogeneity). However in many situations, enterprise needs sharing information among several applications more and more which is distributed in different positions in the network to improve their operating efficiency and provide the support for high-level consolidated decision. Therefore, it's imperative to establish the integration system. A good integration system should not only meet the needs for existing application, but also have good extensibility; enterprise's future application system should be able to add to the integration system conveniently, the adaptive heterogeneous data integration system is designed for the need.

Self-adaptive Heterogeneous Data Integration System--AHDIS, means to complete the adjustment of global data pattern automatically or semi-automatically when heterogeneous local data pattern changes and it can enable the system to continue steady operation. In this paper, we bring forward a self-adaptive heterogeneous data

Please use the following format when citing this chapter:

Cao, Y., Chen, Y., Jiang, B., 2007, in IFIP International Federation for Information Processing, Volume 254, Research and Practical Issues of Enterprise Information Systems II Volume 1, eds. L. Xu, Tjoa A., Chaudhry S. (Boston: Springer), pp. 65-74.

integration model based on correlative technology, using XML Schema to express the data pattern of heterogeneous data source; Using correlative technology such as ontology to solve semantic heterogeneity; Using Web Service to solve mutual operation between heterogeneous systems, and realize actual operation to the data source; completing construction and modification to the heterogeneous data integration system automatically or semi-automatically.

2. HETEROGENEOUS DATA INTEGRATION METHOD

Schema mapping is a key technology in realizing the heterogeneous data source integration, it usually takes more than half the efforts to produce schema mapping during the process of integration, and may cause mapping redefinition when the data source pattern changes. Because of the increasing complexity of the data source's local schema or the integration system's global schema, manual and detailed definition of schema mapping becomes the biggest bottleneck in realizing integration systems. Therefore, reducing manual participation as far as possible and intensifying automation of Schema mapping become the universally- pursued goal.

Schema mapping mainly uses form definitions, such as GAV (Global As View), LAV (Local As View), GLAV etc. Global schema in GAV is established basing on the data view of data source, it's made up of a series of elements; each element corresponds to an query of data source which shows data structure and operation of corresponding data source. In LAV, the global schema is firstly constructed and the data view of data source is defined on the basis of it, and obtained by the global schema according to inferring with certain rules. GLAV is the united product of GAV and LAV, made by uniting goal pattern view and the source pattern view, so it combines the above two's advantages or has the higher expression ability. Integration system with the GAV mapping description deals with inquiry through the unfolding technology, so though its efficiency is higher, its expansibility is bad and it's unsuitable for application of the data source's dynamic changing; Integration system with the LAV mapping description deals with query through the rewriting technology, its complexity is higher but expansibility is better. In this paper, we absorb the advantages of GAV, to the disadvantages of GAV, we solve semantic heterogeneity with correlative technology such as ontology etc; Use Web Service to solve mutual operation between heterogeneous systems, and then realize actual operation to the data source; complete construction and modification to the heterogeneous data integration system automatically or semi-automatically, improve expansibility of the entire heterogeneous data integration system.

3. THE SYSTEM STRUCTURE OF AHDIS

In the heterogeneous data integration system, data schemas of each local data source are all established at the different time by different users according to different needs, so there may be kinds of differences and conflicts between them. In order to realize users' transparent visit to multi-data sources system, it needs to establish a global layer in the integration system to shield these differences and conflicts. In the heterogeneous data integration system, the global schema constitutes a virtual database. The global schema is visited by users, but their actual data needs to be obtained from each local data source.

In order to establish mapping from the global schema to the local schema in the integration system, the following problems must be solved:

(1) To seek one kind of unified method to express each local data schema,

(2) To establishing a common data model of integration system,

(3) To transform users' inquiry of the global schema to one or multi-sub inquires.

If heterogeneous data integration system of GAV pattern changes in the local schema, its global schema can realize auto-adapted adjustment in certain degree, following functions are needed:

(1) The system has the function of monitoring local schema's changes,

(2) The system has the function of adjusting the global schema according to the local schema's changes.

Therefore, the auto-adapted heterogeneous data integration system, ought to be able to provide the matching algorithm for users, enables user to complete the mapping of synonymous elements between each data source and establish the global schema conveniently (provide the keys to the unified visit connection to outsiders). The operation to data is through invoking Web service, and completed by each data source's subsystem. The self-adaptive heterogeneous data integration system can modify data source and invoke its corresponding Web service conveniently. General structure for Heterogeneous data integration is shown in figure 1:

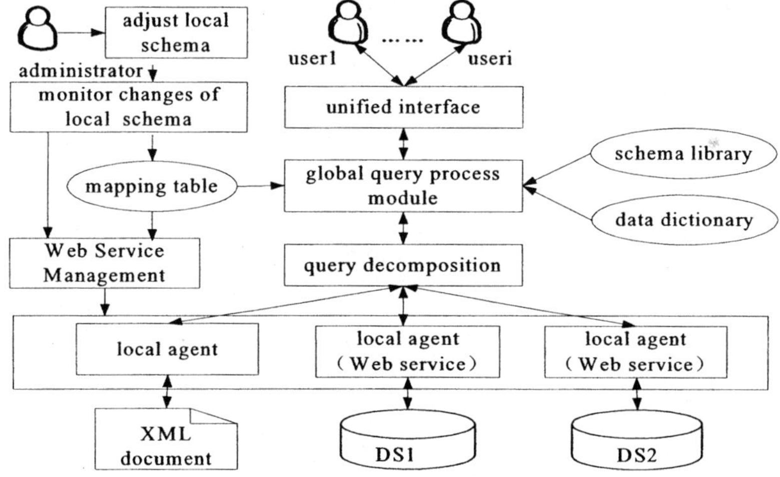

Figure 1. The Framework of Self-Adaptive Heterogeneous Data Integration System

It mainly includes the following several parts: data dictionary, common data model, decomposition of query, local pattern change monitor and Web Service management etc.

4. THE DESIGN OF AHDIS FRAMEWORK

4.1 Data Dictionary

This paper manages data source by establishing data dictionary for it, which is convenient to establish the mapping. And it divides metadata which describes the data source into three kinds, which is schema information, position (navigation) information and other corresponding information [1-2].

Using XML Schema sets modeling for metadata of the data source, establishes metadata dictionary (MDD) of the data source. Because the heterogeneous data integration system usually has many heterogeneous data sources, we let each data source firstly register in MDD before integrating, describing the position and type of the data source, and providing detailed schema structure and semantic information. Metadata descriptions of many data sources compose MDD of data source. Mapping rules between relational data model and XML Schema are as follows:

- Tables of relational data model correspond to ComplexType complex types of XML Schema;
- Each field in a table is mapped to an attribute or sub-element of ComplexType type;
- Attributes or elements which are mapped by table's primary keys are defined as key attributes, mapped by foreign keys are defined as keyref attributes;
- Create sub-elements based on relations of primary keys and foreign keys in a table. If foreign keys of a table are as primary keys or a part of primary keys in another table, then the table with the identical field as foreign key is mapped to the father element, while the other table is mapped to the sub-element [3].

4.2 Common Data Model

In order to solve heterogeneity of each member's system data model in the integration system, the system which integrates many data models has to provide a mapping for concepts in a model to another model, the most common method is to provide a Common Data Model(CDM), each member model is mapped on CDM. Choosing common data model and common data language generally follows the two principles [4]:

- The common data model and common data language should be easily converted with the member database system data model and data language. This requests that common data model should be as simple as possible.
- The common data model and common data language should be able to conveniently express the data and treating process in integration system, and support dealings with the structural and semi- structural data.

In the realization process, global schema in the integration system is expressed with the global ontology, here global ontology can be understood as a sharing glossary storehouse, and uses XML Schema as the description language of common data model (CDM), is used to describe the inner structure of data source, determine mapping from the integrated pattern to each data source's local schema, and transform queries which are based on the integrated pattern to sub-queries of each data source.

The naming of heterogeneity is the main reason for the semantic conflicts between patterns, we can solve synonym problem through assigning a unified name for field information of each data source in CDM, and renaming in CDM. Take the vehicle license plate number for example, use vehicle_no to express in one data source but vehicle_num in another one, use vehicle_no to express uniformly in CDM, <Field name= "vehicle_num" type= "String" > vehicle_no </Field>.

4.3 Query Decomposition

In the heterogeneous data integration system, users can operate global schema directly, therefore system's query processing function need automatically realize transformation from global query to sub-query of each local data source transformation. System's query processing generally includes several following stages: standardization of query, query decomposition, query transformation and result synthesis. This paper uses XQuery language to query the global schema, query processing module transforms query of global schema to one or multi-sub-query. If local data source is XML documents, it can directly return to the child result, if the local data source is the relational database, it firstly transforms XQuery into SQL sentence.

4.3.1 Algorithm of Query Decomposition

The purpose of query decomposition is decomposing global query which involves many data sources to a group of local sub-query operated on single data source. Global query decomposition should follow the following principles [5-7]):

(1) Decomposition of global query take data source as a unit, and decompose query of one local data source in one sentence, each local sub-query can only involve the object of one local data source.

(2) Nesting query in global query should be decomposed and then be distributed to each sub-query before executing.

(3) Query conditions should be decomposed to sub-query according to the mapping.

According to query decomposition principles, here we give steps of query decomposition algorithm as follows:

- Take out the correlative mapping MapList from the mapping table according to the 'for' sentence.
- Traverse MapList according to conditional expression in the where sentence, establish a where sub-sentence for each mapping, and add to sub-query subsets Qs.
- Confirm the 'for' sentence of sub-query according to the where sub-sentence of each sub-query.
- Search the mapping in MapList for each return element in the return sentence. To each mapping glossary, if its data source section and data table section match with the 'for' sentence of sub-query in Qs, then establish the return sub-sentence and add it to the sub-query sentence.
- Transform XQuery to sub-query to SQL which is for local data source.

For example, one company uses two kinds of GPS vehicles monitoring system during different periods, the vehicle marked with "SB3327" have used different system successively, the vehicle's location information is stored in different systems, XQuery sentences for querying the vehicle's whole localization information through the integration system are as follows:

```
for $i in document("GobalDB.xml")//vehicle
where $i//vehicleno="SB3327"
return $i//mobileno, $i//timegps, $i//vehiclelatitude, $i//vehiclelongitude
```

Fragments of XML pattern structure for two data sources and its ontology structure are shown in figure 2.

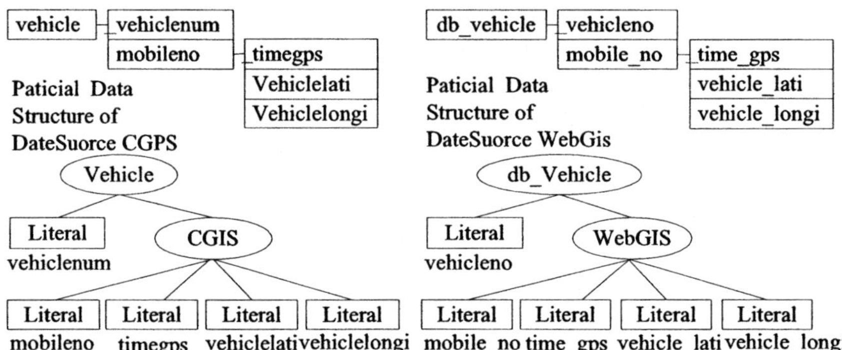

Figure 2. XML Schema Structure for Part of Data Source and their Ontology Structure

The steps of query decomposition are as follows: according to the mapping, we establish sub-query: the "where sentence", then according to sub-query: the where sentence, we establish sub-query: the "for sentence", according to the return sentence and the maplist, we get the sub-query after reorganizing:

```
for $i in document("WebGIS.xml")//db_vehicle where $i//vehicleno="SB3327"
    return $i//mobile_no,$i//time_gps,$i//vehicle_lati,$i//vehicle_longi;
for $i in document("CGPS.xml")//vehicle where $i//vehiclenum="SB3327"
    return $i//mobileno,$i//timegps,$i//vehiclelati,$i//vehiclelongi;
```

According to data dictionary, we transform it to the SQL sentence:

```
Select mobile_no,time_gps,vehicle_lati,vehicle_longi
    from db_gps_normal where mobile_no in select mobile_no
    from db_vehicle where vehicleno="SB3327";
Select mobileno,timegps,vehiclelati,vehiclelongi
    from gpsinform where mobileno in select mobileno
    from vehicle where vehiclenum="SB3327"
```

4.4 Inspection of Local Schema's Change

The adaptability of heterogeneous data integration system means: in the process of integration system construction, when we use GAV to pattern integration, once the local schema changes, global schema can realize auto-adapted adjustment in certain degree. When the data schema of Data Source changes, the manager submits the changes of local schema to the AHDIS, it makes some adjustments according to the changes. The flow is shown in figure 3. It mainly completes the pattern mapping.

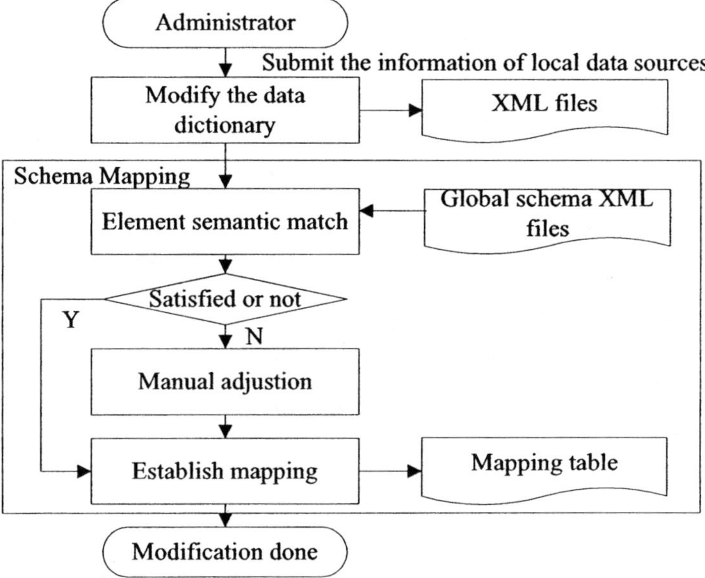

Figure 3. Schema Modify Flowchart

4.4.1 Schema Mapping

The schema mapping can be divided into two steps: schema matching and mapping generation. The target of schema matching is to discover the relations among the schema elements; the goal of the latter is to create logic expressions of equality and containing which are in accordance with schema semantic restriction among element gatherings.

To realize the automatic regulation of the global schema, firstly we need to identify the relations between the changing schema elements of local schema and the elements of global, and determine whether there is any difference on the semantics (for there is one mapping between every pair of the same semantic elements in the local and global schema) and structure, and then process accordingly. This paper can complete the schema mapping better by calculating the similarity of the semantics and description.

4.4.1.1 Schema Matching

(1) The semantic similarity: in the research of the Linguistics, the distance between words is an important relationship between them. It's a real number in [0, $+\infty$] [8]. The distance from one word to itself is 0. Generally speaking, there is a tight

relationship between the distance and the semantic similarity. The distance between two phrases is longer, their similarity is lower, and vice versa. The similarity functions to definite objects x and y are below:

- sim(x, y)$\in$[0..1];
- sim(x, y) =1, then x=y, the two objects are equivalent;
- sim(x, y)=0, it represents that there is no common characteristic between the two objects;
- sim(x, y) = sim(y, x), it represents that the two objects' similarity is symmetrical.
- sim(x, y) $\geq\lambda$, $\lambda\in$[0..1], if the similarity of the objects is equal to or above λ, they are similitude.

(2) Semantic similarity computation: in the foundation of paper [8], similarity computational method of the newly-added data source concepts and global pattern concepts in this article is: obtain by attribute semantic similarity and attribute description similarity weighted array. Princeton University's WordNet is a tree shape English semantics dictionary. In the tree diagram the distance between two leaves are two concepts' semantic distance, and semantic similarity can be further obtained by the semantic distance. In this foundation, two words and expressions C_1 and C_2 similarity can be recorded as Sim(C_1, C_2), and their distance can be recorded as Dis(C_1, C_2). Then their semantic similarity can be obtained through formula (1):

$$\text{Sim}(C_1, C_2) = \frac{\alpha(l_1 + l_2)}{(\text{Dis}(C_1, C_2) + \alpha) \times 2 \times \text{maxl} \times \max(|l_1 - l_2|)} \quad \textbf{(1)}$$

In the formula, l_1 and l_2 are the layers which C_1 and C_2 locate, α is the parameter which can be adjusted and ordinary $\alpha>0$. Dis(C_1, C_2) is the ontology tree's most short-path between concept C_1 and C_2, maxl refers to the text trees' greatest depth. Elimination here by this parameter makes it convenient to normalize computation results.

The practice indicated that it's available to obtain good similarity by comparing the regular words using WordNet. However, in the data integration system, the concept (namely field name) is often the irregular abbreviations for example: vehicle_no, carNo and so on. In view of this kind of situation, the results of the match are not very ideal. To solve this problem, we may define the sharing glossary storehouse in advance. For example: in the actual situation, the database design of the logistics information system, here is the sharing glossary listed in table 1.

Table 1. Sharing Words Table

Target Words	Sharing Words
vehicle_no	chepai , chepaiNo, carNo, vehicleno
driver_no	sijiNo, driNum , driverno
company_no	group_no
mobile_no	Sim, telno
...	...

(3) The description similarity computation: in data integration, description similarity is calculated through the description information of its attributes, for

example: data type, data length, key or not and whether it is allowed null or not. In this way, the attributes can be regarded as a vector, and each description of the attributes is a characteristic vector of the vector such as s1 (data type, data length, key or not and whether it is allowed null or not). After separate calculation of each characteristic vector's similarity of the two vectors, we can obtain the weighted average as these two vectors' similarity. It is showed as formula (2):

$$\mathrm{Sim}(s_1,s_2)=\sum_{i=1}^{sum}\mathrm{W_i Sim}_i(s_1,s_2),\qquad \sum_{i=1}^{sum}\mathrm{W}_i=1,\quad \mathrm{W}_i\in[0,1] \tag{2}$$

In the formula, $\mathrm{Simi}(s_1, s_2)$ represents the similarity of s_1 and s_2's characteristic vector numbered i and W_i is their weight, sum represents the number of the characteristic vectors.

The similarity which is obtained through the two computation methods can be respectively recorded as LSim, DSim. Finally the semantic similarity of concept is calculated by the formula $\mathrm{Wsim}(s_1, s_2)$=Wdesc Dsim+(1-Wdesc)Lsim. Wdesc shows the relative importance of semantic similarity and description similarity.

4.4.1.2 The Mapping Output

The system can set the weight value Wdesc and the threshold value λ which are used in the semantic match calculation. If the similarity is bigger than λ, the two vocabularies are regarded to have the same semantics. The system establishes the direct mapping between the local schema and global schema to the concepts with same semantics. If there is no semantic match, it's necessary to add into the global schema. Then the system will establish the schema mapping. Tables are used in the system to display matching results. It also can realize automatic matching in certain degree. Because the semantic matching is an extremely complex process, the matching precision is influenced by kinds of factors; therefore, the users can realize the result revision manually.

4.5 Management of Web Service

In the AHDIS model of this article, the actual operations to the data sources are completed by different local systems distributed in various regions. When the system decomposes the inquiries, it can transform the XQueries of the sub-inquiries to SQL sentences which operate to the local data sources. Then we encapsulate these data operations to local data sources in Web Service. In this way, data processing can be realized in the system which provides Web Service through the long-distance transfer. And the maintenance of the transferred Web Service such as addition, deletion and modification will be carried on by the management of Web Service. The main work of Web Service management is to manage the Web service naming, the transfer ways and some simple semantic description information.

Usually when we need to transfer Web Service in our programs, we "insert the Web quotation", and then the VS.NET environment will generate service proxy for us, and transfer corresponding Web service. This measure can have certain limitations: when the Web service's physical location has changed, the client code must be modified, otherwise the transfer will fail. Considering this, we need the ability to transfer Web Service dynamically. We may preserve the Web Service URL in the configuration document (a kind of Web Service information documents). We only need to modify the configuration document correspondingly when the service URL changes.

5. SUMMARY AND FUTURE WORK

The AHDIS model in this paper can simplify the foundation process of the heterogeneous data integration system to some extent. The realization of automatic or semiautomatic foundation of the system will provide much convenience to modify, add and delete the data sources dynamically in it. As the operations to data in this scheme are completed by each local data source, the consistency and real-time of data will be well ensured. Based on the semantic information acquired, the conception similarity can be further divided into two parts-semantic similarity and description similarity. By calculating the semantic similarity from various angles, the precision of the semantic matching will be improved. Although this paper has resolved some problems in the semiautomatic foundation of the heterogeneous data integration system, there are still much to be further researched in future: improve and perfect the concept similarity model to calculate the concepts' similarity better, thus enhance the accuracy rate of the output mapping relations.

REFERENCES

1. S. Zhang, H. Li, and Z. Lu, MetaData Management Model Design in WEB Data Integration System, *Computer Engineering and Applications*. Number 21, pp.189-191, (2005).
2. J. Song, W. Zhang, W. Xiao, and G. Li, Research on Metadata Based Heterogeneous Data Management in the Same Domain, *Computer Engineering and Applications*. Number 14, pp.168-171, (2005).
3. H. Thompson, D. Beech, M. Maloney, and N. Mendelsohn, *XML schema part 1: structures*, W3C Recommendation (2001). http://www.w3.org/TR/2001/REC-xmlschema-1-20010502/
4. R. Li, *Query Processing and Optimization in Heterogeneous Information Integration*. Ph.D Thesis, Huazhong University of sience and Technology (2004).
5. N. Wang and N. Wang, Query Decomposition and Optimization in Heterogeneous Data Integration System, *Journal of Software*. Volume 11, Number 2, pp.222-228, (2000).
6. R. Li, Z. Lu, W. Wu, and W. Xiao, A Study of Algorithm on Query Decomposition in Mutidatabase Systems, *Mini-micro Systems*. Volume 22, Number 4, pp.488-491, (2001).
7. X. Chen, Z. Pan, and Q. Zhao, A Schema-Reusable Method on Heterogenous Databases Access and Integration in Grid Environment, *Journal of Software*. Volume 17, Number 11, pp.8-17, (2006).
8. Q. Liu and S. Li, Word Similarity Computing Based on Hownet, *Computational Linguistics and Chinese Language Processing*. Volume 7, Number 2, pp.59-76, (2002).

Design and Implementation of Enterprise Spatial Data Warehouse

Yin Liang[1, 2] and Hong Zhang[1]

[1]School of Environment Science and Spatial Informatics, China University of Mining and Technology, XuZhou 221008, P.R. China hongzh@cumt.edu.cn
[2]Department of Computer Science and Technology, Xuzhou Normal University, XuZhou 221116, P.R. China liangyinq86@xznu.edu.cn

Abstract. Traditional enterprise data warehouse, an integral part of decision support systems (DSS), provides a variety of granularity data to satisfy requirements of different users. It is estimated that about 80% of the information stored in data warehouse is geo-spatial related. However, traditional data warehouse cannot efficiently process spatial data. With the increasing amount of spatial data stored in spatial databases, how to utilize these spatial data is becoming a critical issue of data warehouse. In this paper, we focus on designing and implementing the enterprise spatial data warehouse for spatial decision-making. We propose three methods of building enterprise spatial data warehouse, and extend traditional enterprise data warehouse model into spatial multidimensional data model, which consists of both spatial and non-spatial dimensions and/or measures. Spatial index with the pre-aggregated results is built on spatial dimension and use the groupings of the index to define a hierarchy. Methods for computation of spatial measure are studied. Extended enterprise spatial data warehouse can accelerate spatial OLAP operations and support the spatial data analysis for decision-making support purposed.

Keywords: *Spatial data warehouse, Spatial measure, Spatial dimension hierarchy*

1. INTRODUCTION

At present, many enterprises have built data warehouse (DW) on which users can carry out their analysis, and obtained much benefit. It is estimated that about 80% of multi-granularity data stored in DW integrates spatial or location information [1], such as supplier address and client address. However, during design and implementation of enterprise data warehouse (EDW), these spatial data is usually represented in an alphanumeric, non-map manner, and lost many spatial characteristic. For example, a certain store address is represented as character string "HuaiHai Street 123". With the popular use of satellite telemetry system, RS, GPS, and other computerized data collection tools, a huge amount of spatial data has been stored in spatial database (SDB), geographic information systems (GIS), and other spatial information repositories. How to utilize these spatial data to provide analysis environment of more perfect for enterprise decision-making and improve capabilities of spatial data analysis and visualization is becoming a critical issue of DW.

Please use the following format when citing this chapter:

Liang, Y., Zhang, H., 2007, in IFIP International Federation for Information Processing, Volume 254, Research and Practical Issues of Enterprise Information Systems II Volume 1, eds. L. Xu, Tjoa A., Chaudhry S. (Boston: Springer), pp. 75-83.

Existing EDWs are neither able to store nor to manipulate spatial data. The management of spatial data is usually carried out by GIS. Therefore, it is an efficient method to combine EDW and GIS to construct enterprise spatial data warehouse (ESDW) for spatial decision-making. On the one hand, DWs Technology can offer efficient access methods and management of a huge amount of data. Furthermore, most on-line analytical processing (OLAP) operations, such as slice, dice, pivot, roll-up, drill-down, and experiences of managing aggregate data, can be used to manage spatial data in SDW. On the other hand, GIS Technology has a long experience in managing spatial data. Especially, spatial index structures, spatial storage management, spatial query and analysis, and spatial information visualization are lucubrated, and applied extensively. However, building ESDW cannot be reduced to simple coupling of EDW and GIS. New techniques for spatial conceptual multidimensional modeling, physical storage, and query optimization are studied to manage high volumes of spatial data. ESDW has been recognized as a key technology for decision-making support [2].

The rest of paper is organized as follows. Section 2 refers to related works. Section 3 details three methods of building ESDW. Section 4 introduces a prototype system. Finally, section 5 gives conclusion and future works of the study.

2. RELATED WORKS

In the ESDW, spatial data and non-spatial data are considered as dimension or measure. In this paper, we present three methods of building ESDW. Before proposing our new methods, we first review related technologies of EDW and GIS.

2.1 EDW

In an EDW, data are organized by multidimensional data model. A multidimensional data model is usually represented as a star schema or snowflake schema consisting of a large fact table and a set of smaller dimensional tables joined to the fact table [3]. The fact table stores the primary keys of all the related dimensional tables and numerical measure, such as sales. The dimensional tables can store not only attributes that form a hierarchy, such as day-month-year, but also descriptive attributes, such as store's name. The dimensions usually represent different analysis perspectives, like customers, product and time, and allow the users to analyze the data from multiple perspectives. Multidimensional data model has been widely applied for non-spatial data, but it is seldom used for spatial data modeling. This is because current multidimensional database technologies do not support the spatial data structures [4]. Therefore, building a multidimensional data model for spatial data is still a challenge. In addition EDW and OLAP tools cannot fully exploit spatial data because spatial data does not have implicit or explicit concept hierarchy.

2.2 GIS

GIS can handle both spatial and non-spatial data to satisfy requirements of some specific domain. GIS not only are powerful tools used to manipulate, manage and visualize spatial databases, but also provide various functions to analyze spatial data. Therefore, the GIS technology is appropriate for a variety of usages including resource management, land surveying, and business planning. However, current GIS cannot effectively and expediently analyze geographical data based on multidimensional data structure. Especially, GIS cannot provide overall information for decision-maker. Since data structure and manipulation of various GIS application are not uniform criterion, resulting in spatial data of the same type in different GIS systems are inconsistent. In this case, it is difficult to obtain overall and consistent data for decision-making support.

2.3 Combining EDW and GIS

The ESDW, which combines EDW and GIS, is built to share spatial information and support decision-making analysis. Recently, SDW is widely studied. In [5], Stefanovic et al. propose a framework of SDW. They extend concept of dimension and measure in DW into spatial dimension and spatial measure. Dimensions in a spatial data cube can be nonspatial dimension, spatial-to-nonspatial dimension and spatial-to-spatial dimension, and measures are both numerical measure and spatial measure. In [6], Rivest et al. extend the definition of spatial measures. In [7], Ferri et al refer to the integration of GIS and DW/OLAP environments. In [8], Fidalgo et al. propose model based on star schema. However, the model does not include the notion of spatial measure, while dimension are classified in a rather complex way. In [1] Bimonte et al. present a multidimensional data model which is able to support complex objects as measures, inter-dependent attributes for measures and aggregation functions. Based on existing model of EDW, spatial information can be integrated into multidimensional data models as dimension or measure to build ESDW.

3. METHODS OF BUILDING ESDW

In this section we present three methods of building ESDW. The first method is the introduction of spatial dimension, the second is introduction of spatial measure, and the third is both spatial dimension and spatial measure.

3.1 Multidimensional Data Model with Spatial Dimension

3.1.1 Conceptual Model

A multidimensional model includes spatial dimensions without spatial measures. Spatial dimension can be one or more. If spatial dimension is more than one, a topological relationship is considered. Each spatial dimension includes both description attributes and geometry attributes related to geometry object. Spatial information is represented as spatial dimension, when it is only perspective for analyzing data object property.

When users present a query such as "total sales of products of category A in 2006 in given stores location", *stores location* is represented as spatial dimension, as shown on Figure 1. In *stores location* table *name*, *city* and *address* are description attributes of store dimension, and location is geometry attribute. This is the case for one spatial dimension.

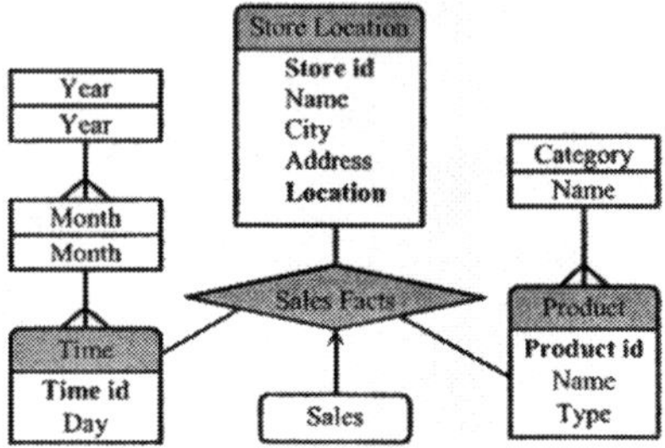

Figure 1. A Star Schema with a Spatial Dimension

If a model includes more than one spatial dimension, a spatial join is required between two or more spatial dimension. Further, the spatial join predicate is specified in the fact table. Figure 2 shows a star schema for the analysis of customer's buying behavior in every city, which relates two spatial dimensions, *customer* represented as type point and *city location* represented as type area, as well as two non-spatial dimensions, *time* and *product*. Spatial join predicate is *contains* for two spatial dimensions.

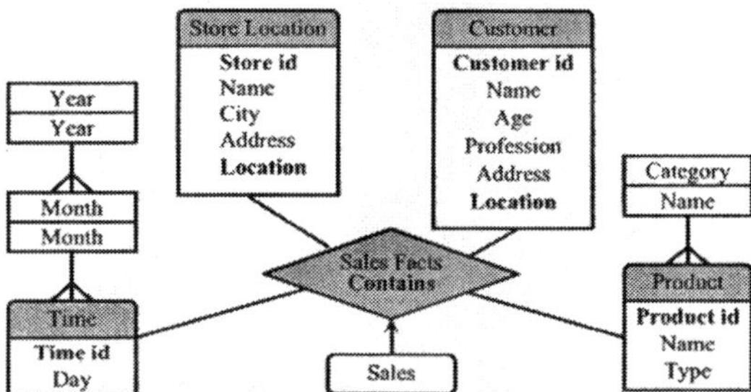

Figure 2. A Star Schema with Two Spatial Dimensions

In this multidimensional model, the aim of multidimensional analysis is sales, location of store, customer and city is different perspectives to analyze sales.

3.1.2 Hierarchy of Spatial Dimension

Each dimension in EDW can be consisted of one or more attribute, and the dimensions are organized as hierarchies of these attributes to represent different degree of generalization, such as day-month-year and city-state-country, etc. In order to improve response performance of OLAP, combinations of different dimensional hierarchies can be pre-computed and stored. Moreover, aggregation results of high dimensional hierarchies can be directly obtained from ones of lower dimensional hierarchies. However, in SDW the spatial dimensions different from non-spatial dimensions since spatial dimensions do not have implicit or explicit concept hierarchies. Set-grouping hierarchies at the spatial dimensions are more complex. During design SDW, dimensional hierarchies may be unknown, or more. Especially, some predefined regions or random ad-hoc query windows created by the users require grouping based on maps, which are computed on the fly. Therefore, we cannot directly apply materialized views techniques widely used in DW to SDW. To solve the problem, two technologies are considered as follows:

1. There may exist some default groupings in some applications. For example, stores in Nanjing are a grouping, and another grouping for stores are covered by Shanghai. Spatial dimensions are organized into multiple hierarchies based on default groupings. If the aggregation results of each default groupings are materialized, the queries that involve these grouping can directly obtain query result.

2. A spatial index is constructed on the objects of the finest granularity on spatial dimension and hierarchy is defined based on the groupings of the index [9]. Each spatial dimension needs to build a spatial index tree.

Figure 3 depicts spatial locations of stores and corresponding R-tree which indexes a set of five store, c1,···, c5, whose MBRs are R2 and R3. Based on all the aggregation paths from the bottom to the top of the index tree, data cubes are constructed and conceptual hierarchies on spatial dimension are generated automatically, as shown in Figure 4. By constructing the spatial index tree, we can take advantage of materialized views techniques that exist for EDW to implement spatial views selection, pre-computation, and materialization. This method not only keeps star schema of EDW, but also provides capability to process spatial data.

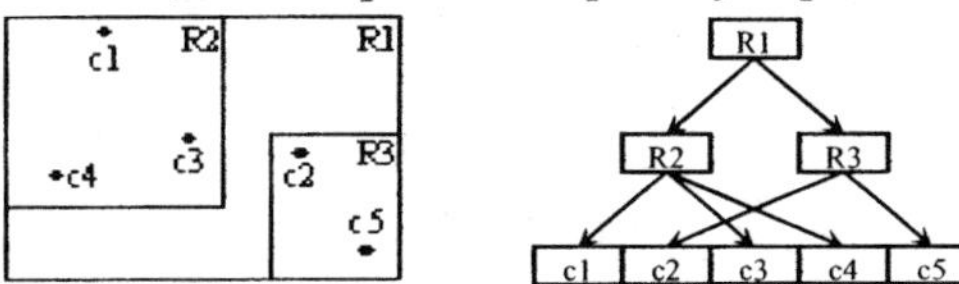

Figure 3. Spatial Data and the Corresponding R-tree

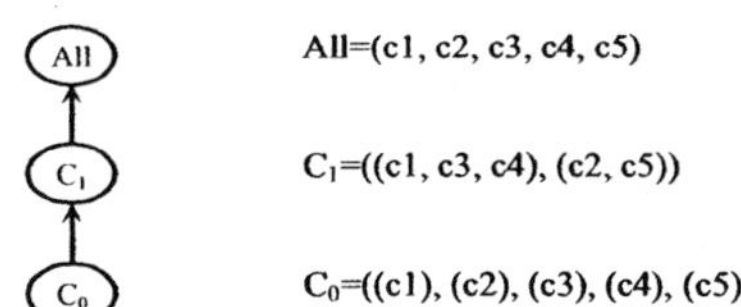

Figure 4. A Spatial Dimensional Hierarchy for the R-tree of Figure 3

In addition, taken spatial index tree as the conceptual hierarchies on spatial dimension, ad-hoc of spatial OLAP can be efficiently processed. In order to obtain aggregation results from non-leaf nodes of spatial index tree and reduce access numbers of nodes to improve query performance, AR-tree, aRB-tree and aCR-tree are used as the hierarchy on spatial dimension.

3.2 Multidimensional Data Model with Spatial Measure

3.2.1 Conceptual Model

A multidimensional model includes spatial measures but no spatial dimensions. Spatial measure is usually represented as a collection of spatial pointers to the corresponding spatial objects. Spatial measure is the aim of multidimensional analysis. It is analyzed by non-spatial dimensions. To apply the roll-up and drill-down operations to some dimensional hierarchies, spatial aggregation function should also be defined.

When the user presents the query such as " which cities are customers that buy products of category A in 2006 in?" Geography location of cities is represented as spatial measure. Furthermore, amalgamation aggregation function should be defined to merge border upon cities as a big spatial object. Figure 5 depicts that *City location* is spatial measure and *union* is spatial aggregation function. In this model, *City location* is subject of multidimensional analysis and the users can get information about product sale influenced by geography location of cities.

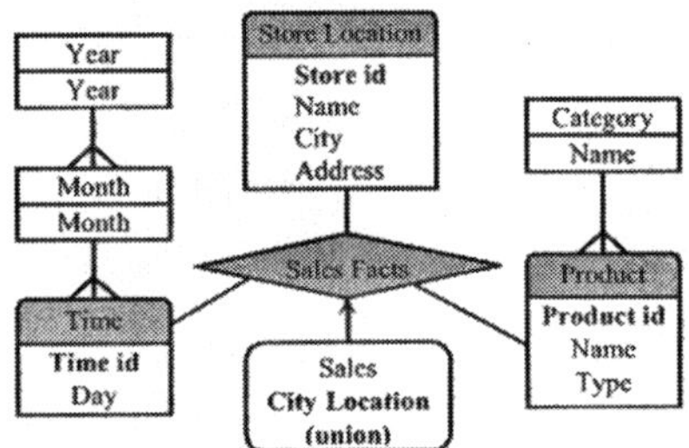

Figure 5. A Star Schema with a Spatial Measure

3.2.2 Computation of Spatial Measure

Spatial measure is similar to numerical measure. According to computing property, aggregation functions for spatial data are also divided into three types of functions [10]: (1) spatial distributive functions, such as convex hull, union, intersection, and length; (2) spatial algebraic functions, such as center of n geometric points or center of gravity; and (3) spatial holistic functions, such as equi-partition and min-distance.

However, spatial measure differs from numerical measure. There are four differences as follows: (1) Numerical measure is simple type and its semantics is limited to quantify description, and spatial measure is complex type; (2) Aggregation result of numerical measure is new numerical value, and aggregation result of spatial measure is a collection of pointers to the corresponding spatial objects and connected spatial objects are merged into a new spatial object; (3) Computing cost of numerical measure is small, and Computing cost of spatial measure is more expensive and it is more required to materialize some spatial queries to improve response time; and (4) Storage space of spatial measure is larger than numerical measure's, and storage space of a spatial object may take kilo- to mega-bytes in storage space. Therefore, it is unpractical to materialize all spatial queries. According to different application, we can use three methods to compute spatial measure as follows:

1. Collection of spatial pointer

Spatial objects are represented by a set of pointers. Advantage of this method is that the storage space is relatively small, and similar to that for non-spatial measures. However, aggregation operations of a group of spatial objects, when necessary, have to be performed on-the-fly. It is a good method if only few spatial objects are aggregated in any pointer collection.

2. Approximate computation of spatial measure

This method is to precompute rough approximation of spatial measure and store. Accuracy of results is not high, but storage space and computing time may be smaller. Due to the users focus on trend change for decision-making analysis, in this case, rough approximation can satisfy requirement of the users. Therefore, this method has been widely studied. The method based on minimum bounding rectangle (MBR) is presented in [5]. The methods based on rotation minimum bounding rectangle (RMBR), multilevel extractive points, and data precision transformation are introduces in [11].

3. Selective materialization of spatial measure

Partial spatial objects selected from objects of aggregation operations are precomputed and stored. Thus, the users can not only obtain accurate results, but also reduce computing time of on-the-fly. Spatial greedy algorithm, pointer intersection algorithm, and object connection algorithm are usually used to determine which sets of spatial objects should be precomputed.

3.3 Multidimensional Data Model with Spatial Dimension and Spatial Measure

The multidimensional data model includes both spatial dimensions and spatial measure. Spatial index tree can be used as set-grouping hierarchy on spatial dimensions. Spatial measure can be not only represented by a collection of pointers to the corresponding spatial objects, but also obtained by applying spatial or topological operators, and is analyzed by both spatial and non-spatial dimensions. When some spatial information is analysis aim, the others are analysis perspectives; this model is a good choice.

Figure 6 illustrates the star schema for the analysis of store location, which closes highway and residential area. The *Highway*, *Store Location*, and *Resident Location* are the spatial dimensions in DW. The fact table is *Sales*, which specify *Distance* operation between spatial dimensions. Aggregation function of spatial measure is *Min-distance*.

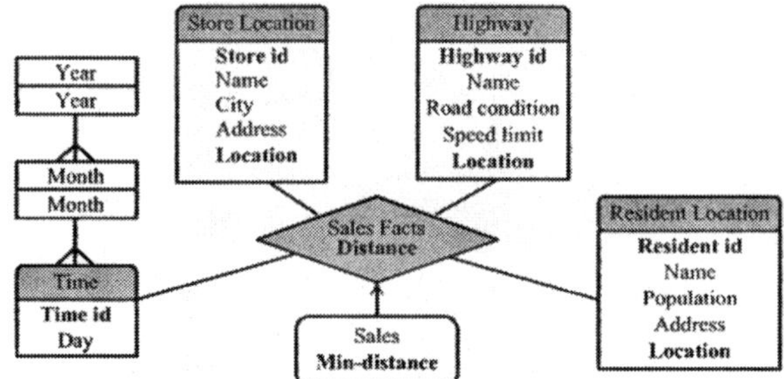

Figure 6. A Star Schema with Spatial Dimension and Spatial Measure

4. A PROTOTYPE

We develop a prototype based on three methods above. The prototype is a three tier architecture. Figure 7 depicts architecture of the prototype. In the prototype, different analytical subject can adopt one of three methods. The designers consider the following three cases to determine which of these models can represent requirements of the users:

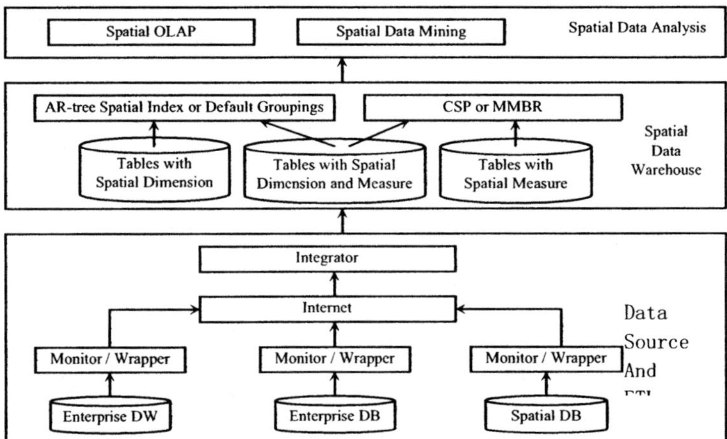

Figure 7. Prototype Architecture

1. If spatial information only needs to be visualized, any one of three models is used to implement. For example, when we find store location with sales more than 500 thousand yuan in 2006, *store location* may be spatial dimension or spatial measure.

2. When the users require comparison of data in different area, or analysis data in some specific area, spatial information is only represented as dimension. The

prototype provides both default groupings and AR-tree as hierarchy on spatial dimensions.

3. If spatial objects need to aggregate location, spatial information is represented as spatial measure, but no spatial dimension. Collection of spatial pointer (CSP) and the method based on minimum bounding rectangle (MMBR) are provided in our prototype.

5. CONCLUSIONS

To integrate spatial information into existing EDW, we propose three methods of building ESDW to improve analysis ability of spatial decision-making. We introduce the corresponding multidimensional data model and key technologies respectively, and apply them to our prototype. The prototype shows feasibility of the methods above. Future study is to further improve query performance for ESDW.

REFERENCES

1. S. Bimonte, A. Tchounikine, and M. Miquel, Towards a spatial multidimensional model, in *Proc. of the 8th ACM international workshop on Data warehouse and OLAP* (2005), pp.39-46.
2. J. Han, R. Altman, V. Kumar, H. Mannila, and D. Pregibon, Emerging scientific applications in data mining, *Communication of the ACM*. Volume 45, Number 8, pp.54-58, (2002).
3. R. Kimball, M. Ross, and R. Merz, *The Data Warehouse Toolkit: The Complete Guide to Dimensional Modeling* (John Wiley & Sons: New York, NY, 2002).
4. G. Pestana, M.D. Silva, and Y. Bedard, Spatial OLAP modeling: An overview base on spatial objects changing over time, in *Proc. of ICCC 2005 - IEEE 3rd International Conference on Computational Cybernetics Proceedings* (2005), pp.149-154.
5. N. Stefanovic, J. Han, and K. Koperski, Object-based selective materialization for efficient implementation of spatial data cubes, *IEEE Transactions on Knowledge and Data Engineering*. Volume 12, Number 6, pp.938-958, (2000).
6. S. Rivest, Y. Bedard, and P. Marchand, Toward better support for spatial decision making: Defining the characteristics of spatial on-line analytical processing (SOLAP), *Geomatica*. Volume 55, Number 4, pp.539-555, (2001).
7. F. Ferri, E. Pourabbas, M. Rafanelli, and F. Ricci, Extending geographic databases for a query language to support queries involving statistical data, in *Proc. of the 8th ACM Symposium on Advances in Geographic Information Systems* (2000), pp.220-230.
8. R.N. Fidalgo, V.C. Times, J. Silva, and F. Souza, GeoDWFrame: A framework for guiding the design of geographical dimensional schemas, in *Proc. of the 6th International Conference on Data Warehousing and Knowledge Discovery* (2004), pp.26-37.
9. F.Y. Rao, L. Zhang, X.L. Yu, Y. Li, and Y. Chen, Spatial hierarchy and OLAP-favored search in spatial data warehouse, in *Proc. of the 6th ACM International Workshop on Data Warehousing and OLAP* (2003), pp.48-55.
10. S. Shekhar and S. Chawla, *Spatial Databases: A Tour* (Prentice Hall: New Jersey, 2003).
11. Y.H. Tong, K.Q. Xie, and S.W. Tang, Spatial data warehouse model and spatial data cube computation methods, *Computer Science*. Volume 29, Number 10, pp.1-5, (2002).

The Uncertainty Decision-Making of ERP Investment

Feng Wu[1,3], Huaizu Li[1], LK Chu[2] and Kun Gao[1]

[1] School of Management, Xi'an Jiaotong University, Xi'an 710049, P.R. China
fengwu@mail.xjtu.edu.cn hzli@mail.xjtu.edu.cn kgao@mail.xjtu.edu.cn
[2] Department of Industrial and Manufacturing System Engineering,
The University of Hong Kong, Pokfulam Road, Hong Kong SAR, P.R. China
lkchu@hkucc.hku.hk
[3]Key Lab of Information Management & Information Economics of Education Ministry,
Beijing 100080, P.R. China

Abstract. Investment in ERP projects has become a dominant part of IT investment of many enterprises. Traditional approaches used for such project evaluation are mainly based on Internal Rate of Return (IRR) and Net Present Value (NPV). However these approaches completely lack the ability to deal with the uncertainties in decision making process of the ERP investment. On the base of risk and uncertain analysis, this study employs a mathematical model to design an ERP decision analytical model based on real option. The model has accounted for the uncertainties and management flexibilities, it is more appropriate to evaluate ERP project investment in uncertainty.

Keywords: *ERP, Real option, Uncertainty decision-making, Investment, Risk*

1. INTRODUCTION

ERP investment projects involve a variety of risks and uncertainties, and the investment return is difficult to assess. Therefore, it is by no means easy to decide on the appropriate investment strategies for technology investment projects of such nature [1, 2]. Traditionally, project evaluation approaches such as internal rate of return (IRR) and net present value (NPV) are widely used to determine the appropriateness of an investment project. However, these traditional project evaluation approaches generally use expectations of future cash flows in calculating IRR or NPV and assume passive decision makers who do not dynamically respond to the changing investment environment [3]. Without recognizing the possibility that a proactive decision maker could exercise the managerial flexibilities and takes correct actions in response to the developing investment environment, such approaches are apparently inappropriate for valuating technology projects under uncertainty. On the other hand, the real-option approach overcomes the drawbacks of the traditional investment decision approaches, and provides a new approach for enterprises to carry through ERP project investment with managerial flexibility [4-6].

There are various reasons that explain the failures of investment decision making for ERP projects [7, 8]. One of the most critical ones can be attributed to the uncertainty of input cost and benefit of an ERP project [9]. Therefore, the evaluation

Please use the following format when citing this chapter:

Wu, F., Li, H., Chu, L. K., Gao, K., 2007, in IFIP International Federation for Information Processing, Volume 254, Research and Practical Issues of Enterprise Information Systems II Volume 1, eds. L. Xu, Tjoa A., Chaudhry S. (Boston: Springer), pp. 85-95.

of the cost and benefit of IT project is a prerequisite to effectively solve decision making issues of ERP.

The valuation of real options is central to the decision making of an ERP investment project. Compared with the commonly used lattice simulation and finite difference method, stochastic programming is much more suitable for compound real option evaluation and thus a better approach to solving multistage decision making problems under uncertainty [10-12].

2. ANALYSIS OF ERP PROJECT RISK AND REAL OPTION OF INVESTMENT

2.1 Risk Analysis of ERP Project

According to the published reports on ERP implementations, it is found that firms are in general exposed to investment risks manifested by a high failure rate of ERP projects. These risks could be categorized into external and internal risks. The former types of risk include marketing risks, potential regulation risks, unpredictable risks and agent risks which could mainly derive from the uncertainties of demand of products in the future, government deregulation, and the emergence of inexpensive or more advanced technologies in the market. The internal risks consist of technology risks, management risks, resource risks and implementation risks. These risks are due to uncertainties arising from long-term investment capability of the firm (e.g. running out funds to complete the project), the internal competence in managing the new technology and the suitability of an ERP system to the business processes of a firm.

Traditional approaches to risk management aim at controlling either external or internal risk factors. Unfortunately, most risk factors are uncontrollable. Therefore, the effectiveness of these approaches is limited. Fortunately, the real-option approach could effectively solve the issues discussed above. There are numerous risks and uncertainties existing in the process of ERP investment. By maximizing the value of real options embedded in an ERP investment project, it is possible for decision makers to actively respond to unfavorable investment environment and take right actions to mitigate investment risks.

2.2 Real Options of ERP Investment

During the course of an ERP investment project, or even before the project is approved and commissioned, a technology manager will have a number of options open to him/her. Before committing any resource to the ERP project, he/she may decide on whether it is appropriate to kick start the project or adopt a wait-and-see approach. When the project has been rolled out, he/she still has to monitor the project continuously and decide on whether the project should still be confined to the pilot level, or to change the scale of investment (to expand or to withhold) or to abort it all together (if the project turns out to be a failure). Within the framework of real options, the decision to take a particular option depends on a number of factors which are collectively represented as uncertainty. Therefore, the framework provides a kind of roadmap for the technology manager to make the appropriate investment decisions amidst uncertainties. The following options are some of the best known options and are considered to be pertained to ERP investment projects, which include the option to wait, the option to abandon, the option to change the project investment scale and the option to learn.

3. INVESTMENT APPROACHES TO ERP PROJECTS

3.1 Investment Strategy of ERP Project

An enterprise might choose to achieve a complete as opposed to a partial implementation at the beginning of an ERP implementation project. Two possible investment strategies have been identified and given as follows:

Strategy S-1

Purchase the complete, integrated ERP system from a leading ERP solution provider. A comprehensive suite of major modules are available to support business functions (finance, production, human resource, market and sales). This is followed by the project rollout whose tasks include process analysis and design, implementation tasks including system configuration, installation of software components, customization, development of interfaces, training, etc.

Strategy S-2A

Select the minimum system configuration to provide a software solution for major function departments in an enterprise;

Strategy S-2B

Enhance the system capabilities by including other application components for use by other departments; design and develop interface software (which is used to connect application programs) and perform overall system integration (Figure 1).

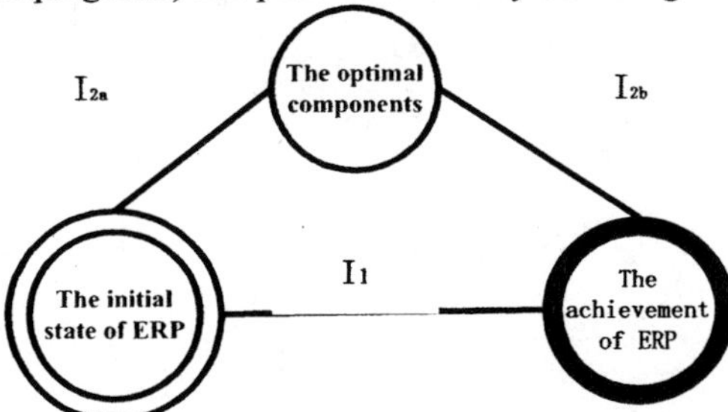

Figure 1. Investment Strategies of an ERP Project

Suppose that the investment decisions for an ERP project will be made over a multiple-period time horizon from period 1 to T, the decision maker is assumed to possess managerial flexibilities or options with respect to investment timing and scale at each decision making period or investment evaluation stage $t \in \{1,\ldots,T\}$. In the selection of an appropriate investment strategy, two assumptions are made:

- Assumption 1: at each decision evaluation period $t \in \{1,\ldots,T\}$, the decision maker can randomly select either strategy S-1 or S-2, or can choose to wait and invest until more information is gathered or uncertainties are resolved.
- Assumption 2: once the decision maker selects investment strategy S-2A, investment strategy S-2B must be selected before the investment valuation terminated at period T.

3.2 Investment Process Analysis of an ERP Project

An enterprise has the opportunity to input certain expense (I) for the implementation of an ERP system in ERP project investment. The cost of investment is determinate but the future change of I is uncertain on every time point $t \in \{1,\ldots,T\}$ in decision period T.

τ is the period starting from the project inception when the investment is made to the point in which the project has formally resulted in income for the enterprise. Let the capital investment for the ERP project be $I(t)$ at time point t. The initial investment $I(0)$ but $I(t)$ is uncertain for $t > 1$. τ periods after the initial investment the enterprise begins to receive income C in various forms until the end of system lifecycle $T*$. However, the enterprise can also delay its investment by choosing to bide time because of the uncertainties that arise from the ERP investment cost and on the possible incomes that could be attained. So, there exists an option to wait in the investment project. The time-dimensional analyses of two major investment strategies are shown as Figure 2 and Figure 3 respectively:

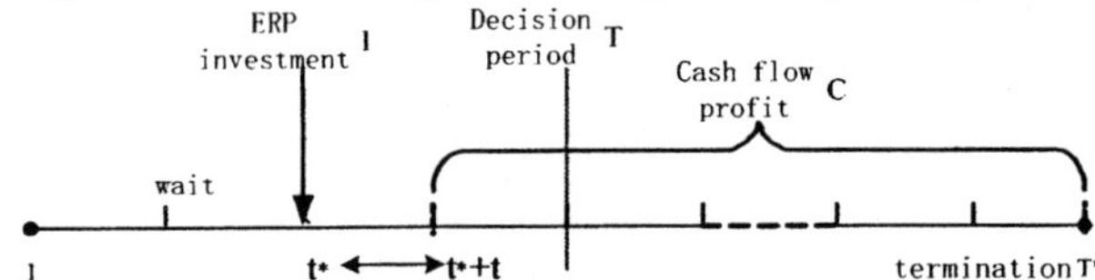

Figure 2. Time-Dimensional Analysis of Investment Strategy S-1

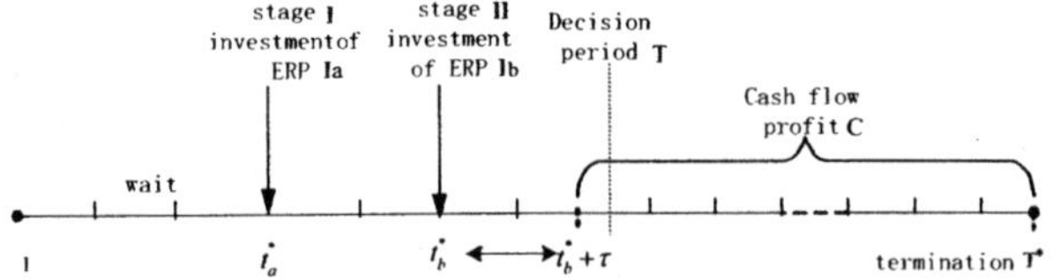

Figure 3. Time-Dimensional Analysis of Investment Strategy S-2

Assume that income are uncertain, the decision to wait for a certain period before making the investment would seem to be a better approach. If the value of any ERP assets decreases by the time, that will justify this decision to wait until the right timing. However, the lifecycles of ERP systems are becoming shorter and shorter with the advent and development of new technologies, waiting means the enterprise is gradually losing out on new technology initiatives, thus reducing its capability to enhance its revenue and some other less tangible benefits. Therefore, these two factors must be jointly considered in order to make the optimal decision.

4. THE ANALYSIS OF UNCERTAINTY – INVESTMENT BENEFITS

The benefits derived from an ERP project are the fundamental considerations in the investment decision process. Compared with other types of capital investment projects, it is difficult to assess the costs and benefits of an ERP investment project due to the tremendous uncertainty that might occur during the project lifecycle. Since the valuation of such a project within the real-option framework involves a trade-off between these uncertain quantities, some appropriate approaches for their evaluation are required. This section will be devoted to the discussion on those pertained to benefits.

The benefits that are derived from an ERP project can be categorized either as tangible or intangible. The former includes the reduction of production cost and inventory expenses, and increased productivity. On the other hand, the intangible types of benefit consist of improving product quality, reducing lead time, increasing the flexibility of firms, and promoting corporation image, among others. Unfortunately, such intangible benefits of ERP are difficult to assess and as a result, most valuation approaches are incapable of addressing these benefits. Also, the large uncertainty associated with such intangible benefits in technology projects makes their assessment even more difficult. However, for valuating an ERP project, this aspect is clearly a very important factor to consider. If the intangible benefits are ignored, any similar initiative for productivity improvement will probably receive a similar, negative valuation. On the other hand, tangible benefits that can be derived from an ERP project also contain significant uncertainties. It is apparently that, in today's competitive environment, no certain future demand and hence income can be guaranteed.

4.1 Assessment of Tangible Benefits under Uncertainty

Given G^t to be the total demand of an enterprise's product in the market in year t, it is commonly observed that G^t is a process of production pervasion [13]. Geometric Brownian motion (GBM) is therefore appropriate for describing such a process because the tangible profit for an enterprise will become uncertain after the implementation of ERP. With this assumption, the differential coefficient of G^t is given as

$$dG^t = \alpha G^t dt + \sigma G^t dW \qquad (1)$$

$\ln(G^t)$ follows a simple Brownian motion with drift because the demand is non-negative. Thus,

$$dg^t = (\alpha - \frac{1}{2}\sigma^2)dt + \sigma dW, \quad t \in \{1,...,T\}, \quad g^t = \ln G^t \qquad (2)$$

where α is the growth rate of income accrued during the project lifecycle. α can be positive or negative. σCdW represents the stochastic deviation of C.

With the assumption of risk neutrality, the change of cash flow C can be described by Eq. (1) and (2) and the uncertainty of demand

$$dC = (\alpha - \eta_c)Cdt + \sigma CdW^* = \alpha^* Cdt + \sigma CdW^* \qquad (3)$$

where η_c is the risk premium of uncertainty of cash flow, and dW^* is the increment of Gauss-Wiener process that is linked with the entire economic activity with the assumption of risk neutrality.

So, the income with uncertainty can be deduced from Eq. (3),

$$V(C^t,t) = E_Q[\int_{t+\tau}^{T^*} C(\tau)e^{-r_f\tau}d\tau] = -\frac{C^t}{r_f - \alpha^*}[e^{-(r_f-\alpha^*)\tau} - e^{-(r_f-\alpha^*)(T^*-t)}] \qquad (4)$$

Eq. (4) represents the tangible benefits that the ERP project would bring to the enterprise when the investment decision for the ERP software system is made at the decision point t, see table 1.

Table 1. Definitions of Variables in Eq. (4)

C^t :	$G^t \bullet p$
E_Q :	Measure of risk neutrality
α^* :	$\alpha - 1/2\sigma^2$
r_f :	Risk-free interest rates
p :	Net profit of unit product

4.2 Assessment of Intangible Benefits under Uncertainty

The intangible benefits derived from ERP are, by their nature, difficult to assess. Especially, such benefits vary widely and are very hard to assess quantitatively. This study will adopt the model of Kalafut and Low [14] as the basis for assessing the enterprise intangible benefits. Based on this model, a fuzzy assessment method will be developed in this study to evaluate the intangible benefits derived from an ERP system implementation.

The net profits D^t in time t brought to an enterprise due to the ERP project are related to market demand of product G^t. Therefore, it is also uncertain.

$$D^t = G^t \bullet p \tag{5}$$

p is net profit of unit product. Similar to the calculating process of tangible benefit $V(C^t,t)$, the enterprise's total net profit value $V(D^t,t)$ within years of applying ERP system can be calculated by using

$$V(D^t,t) = -\frac{D}{r_f - \alpha^*}[e^{-(r_f-\alpha^*)\tau} - e^{-(r_f-\alpha^*)(T^*-t)}] \tag{6}$$

Total intangible profit cash flow of ERP

$= \delta\ \times$the total net profit of enterprise in the lifecycle of ERP system.

$$= \delta \times V(D^t,t) \tag{7}$$

5. CASE STUDY

Datang Telecom (CDMA) was founded in April 1993 to deal in the high-tech businesses. The company mainly engages in product R&D, production, sales and service in the field of telecom and information. In order to solve the management problem, enhance the management level, and achieve the long-run development strategy programming, the company decided to adopt SAP's advanced ERP management information system. The project period was from 1999 to 2002. This case study represents a retrospective analysis of the project valuation process using the proposed framework based on real options.

5.1 The Decision Model

Cost information provided by Datang Telecom is given as follows. The sunk costs due to the project are given in Table 2.

Table 2. Value of ERP Sunk Cost

Decision point	1	2	3	4
I_1	586	556	540	530
I_{2a}	397	385	375	368
I_{2b}	159	142	136	129

Also, according to the market forecast, the volatility rate σ is taken to be 0.3 and b=30 Yuan/Line (unit product saved cost) and p=100 Yuan/Line (unit product net profit) from data provided by the company.

In terms of prediction for VCI by ERP implementation experts, δ in this case is 10%.The value of consultancy, training and other expenses are:

$$K_0^{\,1} = 2.33 \text{ Million(yuan) } \quad G_0^{\,1} = 663.5 \text{ K Lines}$$

$$\mu_k = \ln 2.62,\ \rho_k = 0.0012,\ \sigma_k = \ln 0.5$$

$$\gamma = 5\%,\ E = 200K(Yuan)/year;\ v_1 = 1.2,\ v_2 = 1.6$$

$$L = 902K(Yuan),\ \alpha^* = 0.52,\ r_f = 0.82,$$

$$P_1 = 823K(Yuan),\ P_{2a} = 432K(Yuan),\ P_{2b} = 341K(Yuan)$$

The constraint of expense budget:

$$I = 12000K(Yuan),\ I' = 8000K(Yuan)$$

Set the initial feasible portfolio 1 of decision variables to be {1,0,0,0,0,0,0,0,0,0,0,0}, the sub-problems and the corresponding deterministic programs can be solved (**NB.** the model is developed in Visual C++ using the solver ILOG). Since the results obtained from solving these deterministic programs are unbounded, constraints will be added to the main problem. Then, by using the ILOGHybrid20 package, the main problem of the 0-1 integer program can be solved. After 5 iterations, portfolio 8, {0,0,0,0,1,0,0,0,1,0,0,0}, is substituted into the sub-problem. The result obtained for this portfolio is $S_{\max} = 2425.6$ K (Yuan). According to this portfolio, the decision maker did not invest in the first year but adopted S-2A in the second year due to the uncertainty of income and consultancy expense. S-2B was then implemented in the third year. The maximum of the NPV of the ERP investment project with real options was 2425.6K Yuan.

5.2 Solving NPV_{static}

The static NPV is obtained based on the following information, see table 3.

Table 3. The Definitions of Variables of Static NPV

NPV_{static}	The NPV that is to adopt investment strategy S-1 and invest immediately without considering the flexibility of ERP investment at period $t = 1$.
V	The net cash flow of total profit that the implementation of ERP that would bring to the enterprise. It is estimated by the expert team of the ERP project. V =9,895K (Yuan)
M	NPV of the operation and maintenance total expense from ERP system go-live to the end of the ERP project = 9x200K(Yuan)

I_a	Total cost required by employing S-2A = Consultant cost + software cost + project cost
I_l	=7,860K (Yuan)
γ	Risk-free rate = 0.05
τ	The time required for the implementation of the ERP system if S-1 is adopted = 1 (year)

$$NPV_{static} = \frac{V}{(1+r)} - \frac{I_1}{(1+r)} - \frac{M}{(1+r)^2}$$

$$= 942.4 - 748.5 - 163.2 = 307 \text{ K (Yuan)}$$

The total ROV of ERP project investment was:

$$ROV = \max\left(NPV_{option} - NPV_{static}, 0\right) = 2118\text{K (Yuan)}$$

It is obvious that the NPV of investing portfolio 8 is larger than that of adopting S-1 at period $t = 1$. The reason is that the value of managerial flexibilities are explicitly considered in portfolio 8, including the value of real options such as the option of waiting, option to learn, option to abandon and option to change the project investment scale are used in project investment.

6. CONCLUSION AND FINDINGS

6.1 A Comparative Study of the Real-Option Approach and the Traditional NPV Method

Under the real option framework, the compound real options are considered. These include the option to learn and the option derived from the flexibility of decision-making management and the uncertainty of benefit and cost in ERP project investment. Also, the model employs investment portfolio 8, which will enable the firm to achieve the maximum NPV including the real options of the project. Therefore, the optimal investment strategy, portfolio 8, should be selected. In contrast, the traditional financial evaluation method will take no account of the uncertainty and value of real options in the project investment, and the value of NPV is negative. Consequently, the firm will miss the optimal opportunity of investment.

6.2 Findings and Significance of the Research

For the analysis of ERP investment strategy, the approach used in this paper, the decision-making model of stochastic programming, counts in the intangible benefit after ERP project go-live in quantity, and takes uncertainty of consultant expense of investment cost into consideration, which will make the decision-making model more in accordance to real investment environment. In previous studies on the valuation of ERP investment projects, few authors have considered the intangible benefits that could be derived from the ERP system. However, the motivation for such investments is due more to the potential value that could be created as a result of the introduction of the advanced management approaches and information systems. Unfortunately, such intangible benefits are known to be difficult to assess. In traditional financial valuation methods, due to a lack of an effective quantitative approach for the assessment of intangible benefits - the benefits of ERP usually have not been given a more rigorous evaluation and will lead to overrating or undervaluing of the benefits of ERP for the firm. With the option values added to the static NPV, the real-option framework will provide a basis for better approaches for valuating technology investment projects.

ACKNOWLEDGEMENTS

The authors gratefully acknowledge fundings received from the Nation Natural Science Foundation of China (NSFC) No. 70572038), and the Key Lab of Information Management & Information Economics of Education Ministry, China, F0607-39.

REFERENCES

1. G. Alesii, VAR in real options analysis, *Review of Financial Economics*. Volume 14, Number 3-4, pp.189-208, (2005).
2. M. Benaroch, Option-based management of technology investment risk, *IEEE Transactions on Engineering Management*. Volume 48, Number 4, pp.428-444, (2001).
3. S. Sarkar, The effect of mean reversion on investment under uncertainty, *Journal of Economic Dynamics and Control*. Volume 28, Number 2, pp.377-396, (2003).
4. F. Black and M. Scholes, The pricing of options and corporate liabilities, *The Journal of Political Economy*. Volume 81, Number 2, pp.637-654, (1973).
5. A. Duku-Kaakyire and D.M. Nanang, Application of real options theory to forestry investment analysis, *Forest Policy and Economics*. Volume 6, Number 6, pp.539-552, (2004).
6. S.R. Grenadier and N. Wang, Investment timing, agency and information, *Journal of Financial Economics*. Volume 75, Number 3, pp.493-533, (2005).
7. P. Ifinedo and N. Nahar, ERP systems success: an empirical analysis of how two organizational stakeholder groups prioritize and evaluate relevant measures, *Enterprise System Systems*. Volume 1, Number 1, pp.25-48, (2007).
8. D.L. Olson, and F. Zhao, CIO's perspectives of critical success factors in ERP upgrade projects, *Enterprise System Systems*. Volume 1, Number 1, pp.129-138, (2007).

9. K. Gao, F. Wu, and H.Z. Li, The uncertainty investment analysis of ERP based on real option, *System Engineering _Theory & Practice.* Volume 27, Number 2, pp.17-26, (2007).
10. M. Benaroch, Managing information technology investment risk: A real options perspective, *Journal of Management Information Systems.* Volume 19, Number 2, pp.43-84, (2002).
11. J.R. Birge, Decomposition and partitioning methods for multistage stochastic linear programs, *Operations Research.* Volume 33, Number 5, pp.989-1007, (1985).
12. J.R. Birge, Stochastic programming computation and applications, *Journal on Computing*. Volume 9, Number 2, pp.111-133, (1997).
13. G. Premkumar, K. Ramamurthy, and S. Nilakanta, Implementation of electronic data interchange: An innovation diffusion perspective, *Journal of Management Information Systems*. Volume 11, Number 2, pp.157-186, (1994).
14. P.C. Kalafut and J. Low, The value creation index: quantifying intangible value, *Strategy and Leadership.* Volume 29, Number 5, pp.9-15, (2001).

Service-Oriented Process-Driven Enterprise Cooperative Work with the Combined Rule Strategies

Wen-an Tan, Yun Yang, Zhenhong Lv and Zhonglong Zheng

Institute of Computer Software, Zhejiang Normal University, Jinhua 321004, Zhejiang, P.R. China {jk76, zhonglong, jhlzhxch}@zjnu.cn

Abstract. The key to enterprise process simulation and process enactment is to implement enterprise process cooperative schedule, i.e., how to control the execution order of the scheduled activities according to cooperative behavior rules under resource constraints. This paper proposes a dynamic PERT/CPM approach using a compound number, and discusses its applications to dynamic enterprise process scheduling for Computer Supported Cooperative Work (CSCW). By using the compound number, activity's duration, the earliest start time, and the latest start time of activities in a process model can be defined and calculated effectively to facilitate the enterprise process flexible scheduling and process forecast during process enactment. A framework to role-oriented process-driven enterprise cooperative work is proposed, some schedule strategies and the algorithm implementation are discussed, as well as the process-driven enterprise application integration.

Keywords: *Enterprise process engine, CSCW, Dynamic PERT/CPM, Process simulation and enactment*

1. INTRODUCTION

It is very difficult to address the issues of enterprise cooperative work using conventional mathematical programming. Service oriented enterprise architecture via enterprise dynamic modeling, focusing on business process modeling, simulation, optimization, and enactment, is the new paradigm [1]. Using business process simulation, computer-aided solutions can be economically obtained to support enterprise cooperative work in enterprise process enactment environment.

Because of the non-deterministic nature of the enterprise business problem, the business process model has two non-deterministic means, i.e., the non-determinism of the process model structure and the non-determinism of model parameters, such as the duration of activity and the probability of product arrived. Therefore, the simulation of the process model is non-deterministic [2].

In order to describe the non-deterministic of the duration of activities in the project network, Fuzzy number is imported, and bring out the PERT (Program Evaluation and Review Technique) which suggests using three different estimates: optimistic, most likely, and pessimistic value [3]. The durations of all activities satisfy β-distribution. It could be calculated as following formula:

Please use the following format when citing this chapter:

Tan, W., Yang, Y., Lv, Z., Zheng, Z., 2007, in IFIP International Federation for Information Processing, Volume 254, Research and Practical Issues of Enterprise Information Systems II Volume 1, eds. L. Xu, Tjoa A., Chaudhry S. (Boston: Springer), pp. 97-109.

$$\text{Duration} = \left[\frac{\text{Optimistic } + 4\times(\text{most likely}) + \text{Pessimistic}}{6} \right] \quad (1)$$

As same as using CPM (Critical Path Method) to describe the duration time in project network, conventional PERT is still a static method which could not present the uncertainty during the process enactment. Most of process simulation tools usually use rule FCFS (First Come First Serve), HPFS (Highest Priority First Serve) and RS (Radon Selection) and the combined rules to schedule process activities. It is appropriated for the service industries. But for manufacturing industries and engineering project, these are not suitable and enough, especially in the forecast of project process schedule.

In order to present different behavior characters in the business process to support process flexible scheduling for enterprise cooperative work, compound number is proposed to define the non-deterministic of process model, such as duration, the earliest start time and the latest start time of the activities in process models, by according to the definition of fuzzy centre-number and the expression of complex number [4]. A compound number can be defined as the sum of a deterministic number and a non-deterministic number which expression is as $x=a+b\ i$[5]. We have proposed a framework of enterprise process cooperative work and developed 8 kinds of process schedule rules algorithms for enterprise modeling. Using these algorithms to define enterprise collaborative model, a kind of combined rules, the customized model can be flexible simulated according to the characteristic of the industrial sector and the enterprise individual requirement. We can use the proposed techniques to support enterprise process dynamic scheduling with computer supported cooperative work environment.

The rest of paper is organized as follows: Section 2 proposes a compound number to define the non-deterministic of process parameter, such as activity's duration, the earliest start time and the latest start time; Section 3 proposes a framework of enterprise process cooperative work and discusses the implementation of enterprise process collaborative scheduling; Section 4 summarizes the paper.

2 COMPOUND NUMBER APPLICATION

2.1 Compound Number Definition

Definition1. Let x=a+b i, then x is called a compound number, if a and b is a deterministic number, and i is a non-deterministic real number and i∈[-1,1]. i is called compound factor determined by the practice. The following theorems and properties can be proved easily according definition1.

Theorem1. Addition operation rule: Let $x_1=a_1+b_1i$, $x_2=a_2+b_2i$, sum x of x_1 and x_2 is:

$$x = (a_1+ a_2) + (b_1+b_2)\ i. \quad (2)$$

Theorem2. Subtraction operation rule: Let $x_1=a_1+b_1i$, $x_2=a_2+b_2i$, then difference x of x_1 and x_2 is:

$$x = (a_1 - a_2) + (b_1+b_2)\, i. \tag{3}$$

Property1. Upper limit and lower limit: Let $x_1=a_1+b_1i$, $x_2=a_2+b_2i$,..., $x_n=a_n+b_n i$,

(1) The upper limit of set $\{x_1, x_2, ..., x_n\}$ is also a compound number $x = a + bi$, which can be defined as:

$$x = sup(x_1, x_2, ..., x_n)\,. \tag{4}$$

and satisfying:

$$a=\frac{\max(a_1+b_1,a_2+b_2,...,a_n+b_n)+\max(a_1-b_1,a_2-b_2,...,a_n-b_n)}{2},$$

$$b=\frac{\max(a_1+b_1,a_2+b_2,...,a_n+b_n)-\max(a_1-b_1,a_2-b_2,...,a_n-b_n)}{2}$$

(2) The lower limit of set $\{x_1, x_2, ..., x_n\}$ is also a compound number $x = a + bi$, which can be defined as:

$$x = inf(x_1, x_2, ..., x_n). \tag{5}$$

and satisfying:

$$a=\frac{\min(a_1+b_1,a_2+b_2,...,a_n+b_n)+\min(a_1-b_1,a_2-b_2,...,a_n-b_n)}{2},$$

$$b=\frac{\min(a_1+b_1,a_2+b_2,...,a_n+b_n)-\min(a_1-b_1,a_2-b_2,...,a_n-b_n)}{2}$$

2.2 Compound Number Applied in PERT/CPM

The duration Dk, the earliest start time Ek and the latest start time Lk of activity Ak can be described with compound number as following formula (6):

$$\begin{aligned} D_k &= a_k + b_k i \\ E_k &= a_{e\_k} + b_{e\_k} i \\ L_k &= a_{l\_k} + b_{l\_k} i\,. \end{aligned} \tag{6}$$

Each compound factor "i" is a random number valued in [-1,1], which of Dk is created by the random number generator algorithm according to the distribution property (e.g., Constant, Uniform, Normal, Poisson distribution) defined in the activity, and i of Ek is calculated by comparing the real time Treal to the plan time of Ek.

$$i = \frac{T_{real} - a_{e\_k}}{b_{e\_k}}\,. \tag{7}$$

We can use it for the approximate calculation of Lk in order to dynamically control the schedule of activities by the schedule rule defined in the cooperative model.

2.2.1 The Calculation of the Earliest Start Time

(1)Activity Ak in sequential structure

Ek can be obtained by the rule of addition operation and the property of upper limit. If the activity Ak has only one predecessor activity Ak-1, the relationship can be illustrated simply as following structure

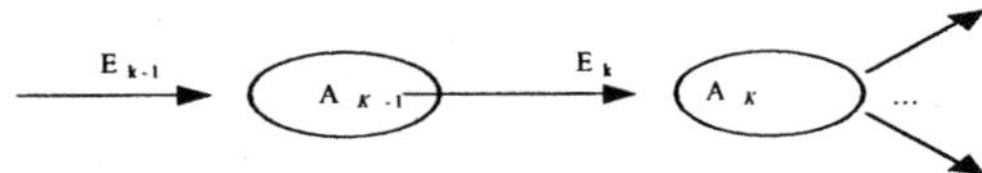

Figure 1. Sequential Structure of Activities A_k and A_{k-1}

E k of the activity Ak is the sum of the earliest start time Ek-1 of the activity Ak-1 and its duration. It can be calculated by following formula:

$$E_k = (a_{e\text{-}(k\text{-}1)} + a_{(k\text{-}1)}) + (b_{e\text{-}(k\text{-}1)} + b_{(k\text{-}1)})\, i. \tag{8}$$

(2)Activity A_k in Parallel Structure

Figure 2 illustrated one parallel structure in Process model. If activity A_k has more than one predecessor (A_{k-1}, A_{k-2}, …,A_{k-j}), the earliest start time E_k of A_k can be calculated as following two steps:

①E^1_k, E^2_k,…,E^j_k can be calculated one by one according to the rule of addition operation from the E_{k-1},E_{k-2}, …, E_{k-j} with formula (8);

②E_k of A_k can be calculated according to the property of the upper limit:

$$E_k = sup(E^1_k, E^2_k, \ldots, E^j_k)\,. \tag{9}$$

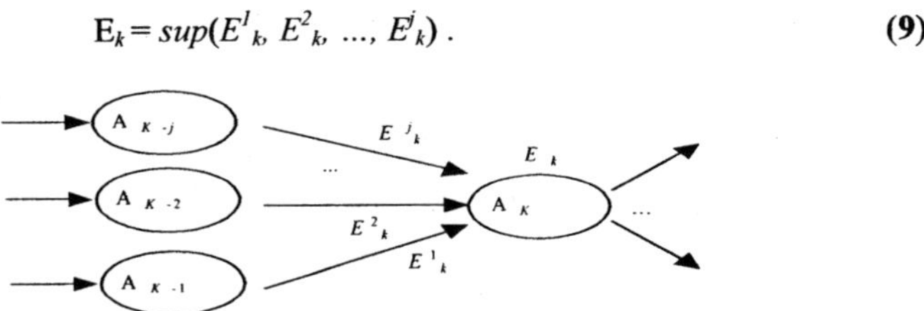

Figure 2. Activity A_K with Multiple Predecessors

2.2.2 The Calculation of the Latest Start Time

We can search out all paths (*path*$_1$, …, *path*$_k$) from the sources to the finished products in the process model by process tracking. Let E^r be the finish time of the *r-th* path.

$$E^r = a_r + b_r i,\ \ r=[1..k]\ . \qquad \textbf{(10)}$$

Definition2. Let set A={$E^1, E^2, ..., E^j$}, $a=max(a_r|\ a_r+b_r i \in A)$, $b=max(b_r|a_r+b_r i \in A$ *and* $a_r=a)$, $A_1=\{a_r+b_r i|\ a_r+b_r i \in A,\ a_r=a,\ r=1,...,k\}$, $A_2=\{\ a_r+b_r i|\ a_r+b_r i \in A,\ a_r-b_r \geq max(E^j),\ r$ *and* $j=1,...,k,$ *but* $r \neq j\}$, $A_3=\{\ a_r+b_r i|\ a_r+b_r i \in A\ ,\ a_r+b_r < a+b$ *and* $a_r-b_r > a-b\}$, then all paths corresponding to A_1 are called *dynamic-time-critical-path,* and the static cycle of the project is a. If there are A_2, then A_2 corresponds with the absolutely *time-critical-path.* $E = a+bi$ is the project dynamic cycle, and the associated path is called *main-time-critical-path,* and all paths corresponding to A_3 are called *hypo-critical-paths.*

Within the enterprise process simulation or process enactment, the *main-critical-path* and the *hypo-critical-path* usually could be transferred each other.

Based on the proposed definition, each A_k's L_k can be calculated in reverse from the finished products using the rule of subtraction operation and the property of lower limit of compound number.

(1) Activity A_k in sequential structure

In the Figure 3, the sequential structure of process model is illustrated as that activity A_k has only one successor A_{k+1}.

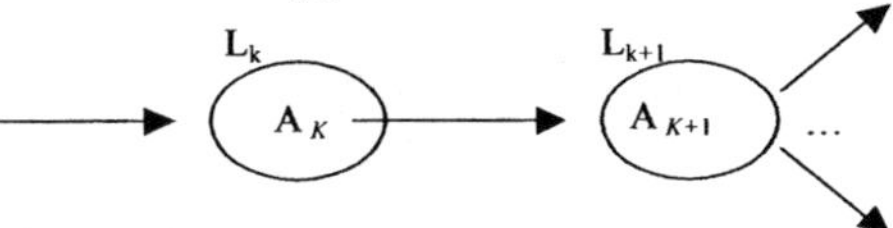

Figure 3. Sequential Structure of Activities A_k and A_{k+1}

The latest start time L_k of activity A_k is the difference of the latest start time L_{k+1} of its successor and the duration D_k of A_k. L_k can be calculated by the following formula:

$$L_k = (a_{l\text{-}(k+1)} - a_k) + (b_{l\text{-}(k+1)} + b_k)\ i\ . \qquad \textbf{(11)}$$

(2) Activity A_k in parallel structure

Figure 4 illustrates that the activity A_k has some successors A_{k+1}, A_{k+2}, ..., A_{k+j}. Now, Let $L_{k+1}, L_{k+2}, ..., L_{k+j}$ *are the* latest start times of these succeeding activities. L^1_k, L^2_k, ..., L^j_k are the latest start time of A_k reversed calculated from A_{k+1}, A_{k+2}, ..., A_{k+j} in the method of sequential structure.

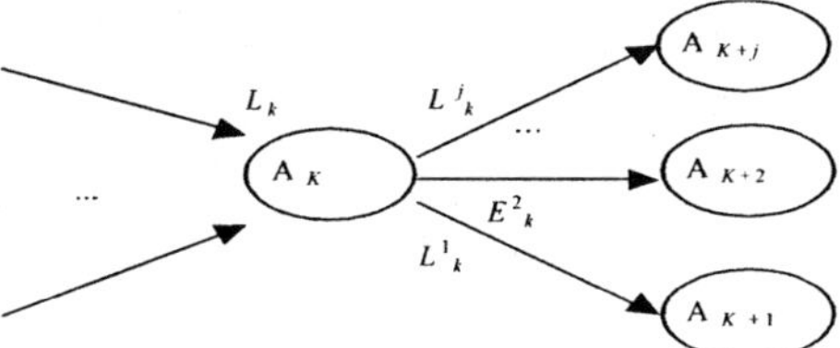

Figure 4. Activity A_k with Multiple Successors

The latest start time L_k of A_k can be obtained according to the following two steps:

① $L^1_k, \ldots, L^j_k$ can be obtained by reverse calculations from the successors using the rule of subtraction operation with $L_{k+1}, \ldots, L_{k+j}$ to the duration of $\mathbf{A}_k$ as formula (11);

② L_k can be calculated accord the property of lower limit:

$$L_k = inf(L^1_k, L^2_k, \ldots, L^j_k) \quad \textbf{(12)}$$

3. PROCESS-DRIVEN ENTERPRISE COOPERATIVE WORK

The enterprise applications with computer supported cooperative work have three level means. Firstly, it is the definition of the cooperative model. One is that dynamic PERT/CPM technique can be used to support flexible scheduling in process simulation interpreted by VPML [6] according to the cooperative behavior rules defined in the cooperative model. Another is that it can provide the assistant function with cooperative scheduling in enterprise process enactment, i.e., task schedule, which supports enterprise applications integration and process integration.

In the process definition environment, the customized enterprise model can be defined flexibly from process, infrastructure, behavior, cooperative and information. It is a static tool to describe and analyze the enterprise process.

In the process simulation environment, readyEventQueue is a queue used to store the events of activity readiness ordered by the cooperative schedule rules. Process simulation can flexibly simulate enterprise business processes, and activate the ready activities as the requirement of the enterprise in practical work.

In the process enactment environment, the information system will build a role-oriented Task-table for each personnel role defined in the enterprise process model. The Role-Oriented Task-table will store the work task ordered according to the cooperative rules. It can be used to assist each manager to execute the tasks as the requirements of cooperative work.

This section is organized as follows. Section 3.1 proposes a framework of process engine for role-oriented process-driven enterprise cooperative work; Section 3.2 introduces the flexible schedule strategies; Section 3.3 presents the implementation of the proposed strategies; Section 3.4 discusses process driven enterprise applications integration

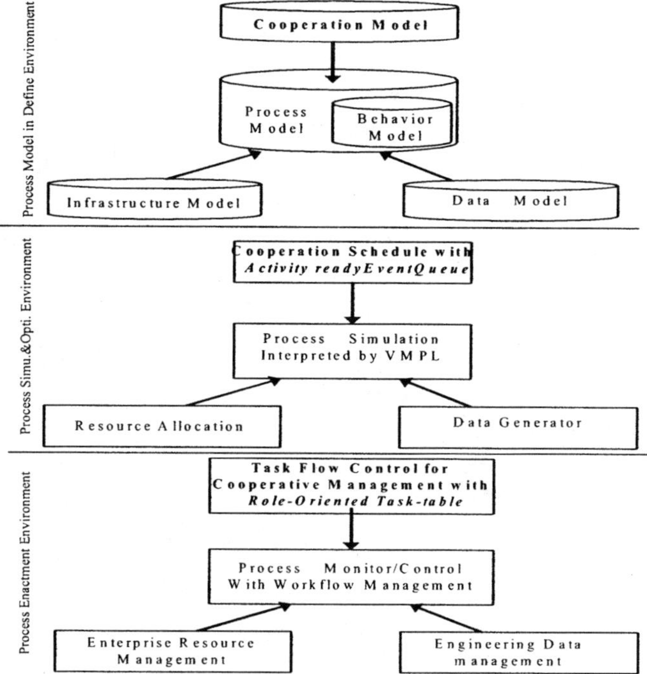

Figure 5. Dynamic Enterprise Modeling for Cooperative Work Framework

3.1 Role-Oriented Process-Driven Enterprise Cooperative Work Engine

Enterprise processes execution is based on event stream mechanism. We can define different process cooperative model, i.e., different combined schedule rules, for the individual processes. And there is an organization need to support a sub-process, i.e., a combined activity, as well as some roles or a resource group are require to support a leaf artificial activity. So, during process simulation, all activities in each sub-process can be activated driven by process schedule engine according to the activityReadyQueue, as well as during process enactment, each role may cooperatively work based on business process model according to the task schedule. Process schedule engine is illustrated as figure 6.

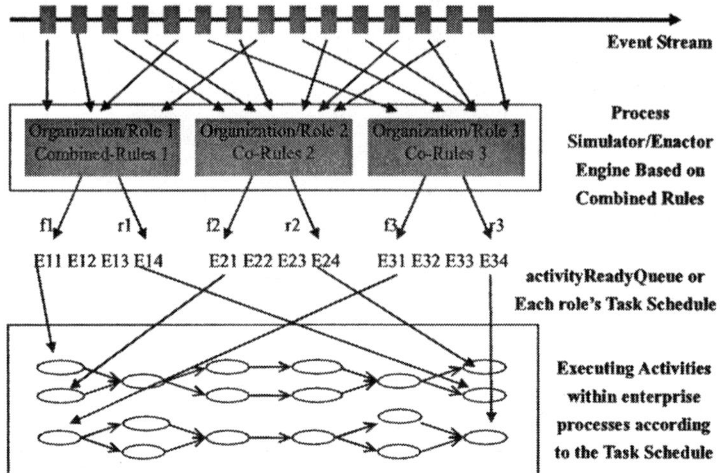

Figure 6. Role-oriented Process-driven Enterprise Cooperative Work Engine

3.2 Flexible Schedule Strategies

While simulating or enacting the enterprise process model, the key is how to control the execution order of the scheduled activities according to cooperative behaviour rules under resource constraints.

Activating activities is based on the queuing model and the discrete event spring mechanism. The events made by activity completing are put in the output-stream. For Output-OR sub-structure, events will put in different stream paths according to the probability of path defined by the modeling engineers.

In the proposed modeling environment, cooperative behavior editor provides a set of 8 kinds of schedule strategies. Process modeling engineers can define their own rules within cooperative behavior editor. The following schedule strategies exist [5]:

- Rule 1: HPFS (Highest Priority First Serve);
- Rule 2: MS (Minimum slack time first Serve);
- Rule 3: FCFS (First Come First Serve);
- Rule 4: SOT (Shortest Operation Time);
- Rule 5: LOT (Longest Operation Time);
- Rule 6: LRPT (Longest Remaining Processing Time);
- Rule 7: SRPT (Shortest Remaining Processing Time);
- Rule 8: SIRO (service in random order) etc.

In the above rules, MS, SOT, LOT, LRPT and SRPT need supporting of dynamic PERT/CPM technique. The combination of these rules can be used to schedule the manufacturing process or the project process.

By this method, all ready activities can be flexibly scheduled. All resources can be allocated to the business activities for which they are needed.

3.3 The Implementation of Schedule Strategies in Process Simulation

3.3.1 Random number generator.

Random number generator is the basic tool used to construct random variables according to the probability distribution. Here, we use compound number to present the non-deterministic process model parameters. The compound factor i of the duration D_k of activity A_k is created by the random number generator according the distribution property (e.g., Constant, Uniform, Normal, Poisson) defined in the activity attribute. In order to guarantee the independence and reappearance in the multi-simulation of the process model, the proposed system provides two ways for random number generating: random mode and fixed mode. For the random mode, the random variables are created randomly every time, and they are different. For the fixed mode, it is necessary to generate a random number to input a seed variable. If the seed variable is the same, the random number generator will construct one stream using the same random number. Thus, the process simulations can be reappearance.

3.3.2 The algorithms of the schedule strategies

In order to implement all above schedule strategies, we have to modify the schedule's algorithm based on rule FCFS in the original PMSE (process model simulation environment) developed by the Software Engineering Institute at BeiHang University, China.

We have improved and extended some of functions of process simulation environment. A structure variable *ReadyEventQueue* was proposed to store the activity ready events sorted according to the proposed schedule strategies, and these activity ready events will not still stored in the *EventQueue*. But *EventQueue* still store the rest events according to FCFS and HPFS, such as activity active events, activity complete events. The schedule algorithm can process these activity ready events according to the schedule strategies defined by user.

Figure 6 illustrates the cooperative work of the ready activities controlled by 4 levels of combined rules in the proposed strategies. After location-analyzing according to the combined rules, the activity-ready-events will be located in the reasonable position in the pool of activity-ready-events. Then scheduler will allocate resources for the activities required and active these activities orderly.

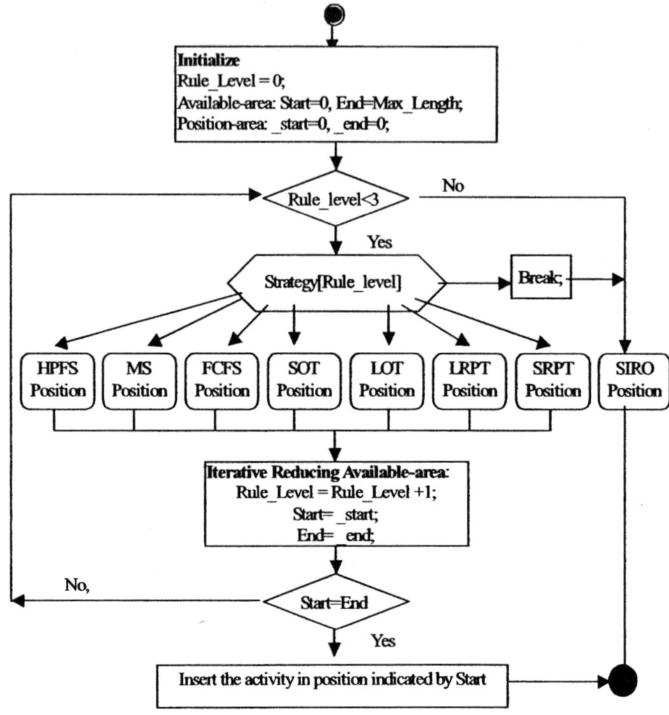

Figure 7. The Location Process of Ready Activity in Ready-Pool

Above these location-analyzing algorithm will reduce the size of position area of activity-ready-events from Available-Area [Start..End] to Position-Area [_start .. _end] besides SIRO-location-analyzing. If pointer _start and pointer _end point to the same position, the activity-ready-event will be inserted there. While the first iterative location-analyzing, the Available-Area is the whole-space of readyEventQueue. SIRO-Position is usually used as the last level rule, so that if the former 3 levels Location-analyzing cannot locate the activity-ready-event, i.e., there are still exist conflicts in the process of resource-allocation, the activity-ready-event will be located in random position in available area in readyEventQueue.

Here give the pseudo-code of MS rule's locate-analyzing algorithm as one example of locate-analyzing algorithm.

Table 1. The Pseudo-code of Algorithm for MS Rule

```
Boolean simReadyPool::reduceByMS(int Start, int End,
int* _start, int* _end, simActClone* act)
{
Boolean Result = FALSE;
//There are not activity which thelastStartTime is
//equal to *act
```

```
double lastTime←LastStartTime (*act);
for(int pos=Start;  pos<End;  pos++){
double lastTime_pos←LastStartTime(simActClone(pos));
if(lastTime_pos > lastTime) { break;}
if ((lastTime_pos == lastTime) && (!Result))
{ Result= TRUE;  *_start = pos; }
//Record _start position
if ((lastTime_pos >= lastTime) && (Result))
{*_end= pos;  break; }
//Record the end position _end
}
if (!Result) {*_start=pos; *_end=pos; }
return Result;
}
```

All activity-ready-events are stored orderly in the readyEventQueue. This order is a kind of dynamic priority, so that, readyEventQueue need dynamic updating. Re-calculating the compound factor i of the current event start time Ek and the Lj of all readied activities are required after advancing simulator clock.

3.4 Process Driven Enterprise Applications Integration

Enterprise Applications Integration (EAI) is the set of tools and technologies developed to integrate various dissimilar applications within the organization. Mostly, they consist of flowcharts or maps for invoking applications or sending and receiving messages in specific orders.

Many EAI products have some tools that enable a business to automate business processes by superimposing them across existing applications. BPMS [7] is a mechanism which rapidly develops and evolves custom business automation solutions by directly integrating with legacy and packaged systems as an implementation detail.

One of the goals of adaptive process engineering is to leverage these legacy systems while providing an easy migration path to model-based systems, by accessing legacy systems transparently.

Process models may be deeply nested within many levels. Each model manages its own affairs yet they all work together to solve higher-level business problems. The software architecture which supports the model-based approach consists of horizontal layers rather than vertical applications. The models occupy the middle layer and form the integrating structure of the systems. It is called the process integration server. An example is Biztalk developed by Microsoft Corporation. The model can be used to automatically estimate the time and cost to carry out a manual task [8]. By connecting the models through the Work-Flow-Management mechanism, many activities can be scheduled rapidly and intelligently. The conventional integration methods are usually based on the uniform strategies such as event-oriented FCFS, HPFS. But they do not provide the flexible definition function or selection of cooperation strategies to control the active order of ready activities.

A cooperation model was built within the enterprise model to attack the impact issues. The cooperation model selector provides the selection/definition function of the proposed multilevel cooperative strategies for control task scheduling, allocating resources to assistant managers doing their work. These are following 8 strategies can be selected: HPFS, MSFS, FCFS, SIRO, SOT, LOT, LRPT, SRPT etc,. By combining these rules, all ready activities can be flexible scheduled, and all resources can be allocated availably to the ready activities.

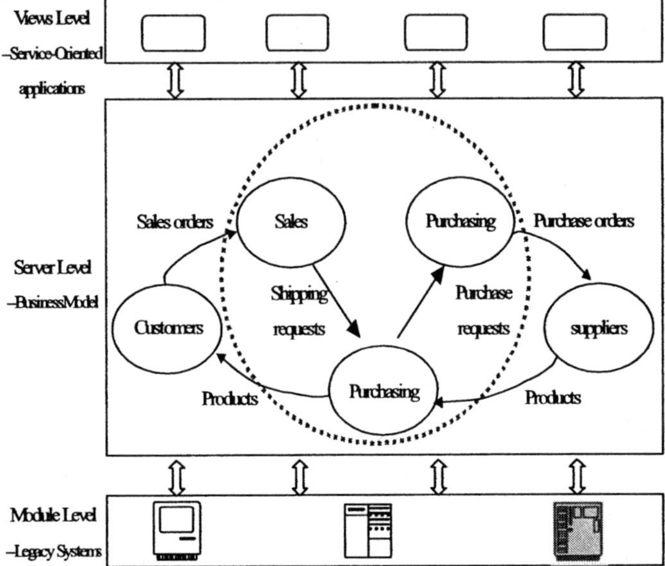

Figure 8. Architecture of Applications Integration for a Distributor Business Model

Within enterprise process enactment, relative services-oriented applications could be provided for the correlation role users [9]. It is very important to protect the investment of IT legacy systems. We usually use Web services to wrap legacy software systems for integration with modern IT systems. Each role user has a *Role-Oriented Task-table* which orderly stores all work tasks associated with the role according to the above cooperative rules. It is similar with aforementioned structure, *readyEventQueue*. The difference is that the *Role-Oriented Task-table* is only one real assistant schedule tool to assist the role users to work effectively, and the final determination and works are still determined by the managers [10].

4. CONCLUSIONS

The flexible scheduling of resources for activities is very important in process simulation or process enactment. In this paper, the dynamic PERT/CPM technique with compound number and its applications to enterprise management with computer supported cooperative work were discussed detail. A framework to process-driven enterprise cooperative work is proposed, and 8 kinds of scheduling rules and the combined strategies algorithm implementation are discussed to implement an intangible cooperative work relationship in the manufacturing stream-like process or the project-oriented process model, as well as the process-driven enterprise application integration. It is very useful for the enterprise management in the domains of analyzing and optimizing the enterprise business processes.

ACKNOWLEDGEMENTS

The majority of the work presented in this paper was done by the first author during his Ph.D studies in BeiHang University, China. Appreciations should be given to Prof. Bosheng Zhou, the Ph.D supervisor and the team members in BeiHang University. This work was partially supported by the National Natural Science Foundation of Zhejiang province of China (Grant No. Y106039) and the Key Research Foundation for Zhejiang Education of China (Grant No. 20060491).

REFERENCES

1. B.S. Zhou, H. Xu, and L. Zhang, The Principle of Process Engineering and Introduction to Process Engineering Environments, *Journal of Software*. Number 8 (Supplement), pp.519-534, (1997).
2. L. Zhang and L. Wang, Process Simulation Technique and its Support Environment, *Journal of Software*. Number 8 (Supplement), pp.565-575, (1997).
3. C.S. McChahon, Using PERT as an Approximation of Fuzzy Projection-Network Analysis, *IEEE Transaction on Engineering Management*. Volume 40, Number 2, pp.146-153, (1993).
4. X. He, *The Theory and Technology of Fuzzy Number Knowledge* (National Defence Industry Press: Beijing, 1994).
5. W. Tan, B. Zhou, and L. Zhang, Research on the Flexible Simulation Technology for Enterprise Process Model, *Journal of software*. Volume 12, Number 7, pp.1080-1087, (2001).
6. B. Zhou, Visual Process Modeling Language VPML, *Journal of Software*. Number 8(Supplement), pp.535-545, (1997).
7. E.D. Jenz, *BPMS and Web Services: An Unbeatable Team.*www.webservies.org
8. W. Tan, *A Study and Development for Dynamic Optimizing Enterprise Process Technique and its Supporting Environment.* Ph.D Thesis, BeiHang University (2001).
9. D.A. Taylor, *Business Engineering with Object Technology* (John Wiley & Sons: New York, 1995).
10. Y. Rezgui, Role-based service-oriented implementation of a virtual enterprise: A case study in the construction sector, *Computers in Industry*. Volume 58, Number 2, pp.74-86, (2007).

Global Logistics Intelligent Decision System of Medical Equipment Manufacturing

Sk Ahad Ali[1], Hamid Seifoddini[2] and Jay Lee[3]

[1]University of Puerto Rico-Mayaguez, Puerto Rico, USA
[2]University of Wisconsin-Milwaukee, Wisconsin, USA
[3]University of Cincinnati, Cincinnati, USA

Abstract. Global logistics aim to optimize and control the material/product flow and the information flow so that materials/products can be moved at a desired pace, in a proper fashion and at the right volume. The production processes in the medical equipment manufacturing industries are highly automated and dynamic and the orders are customized. This study presents an intelligent global logistics system for scheduling and planning of medical equipment production systems to minimize logistics cost. The optimization technique for production scheduling in the supply chains of medical equipments shows how an intelligent logistics system can effectively solve real-world problem. This research develops an intelligent decision system for global logistics of medial equipment manufacturing system. The proposed system is verified with real-world application. Medical equipment manufacturers can get benefit of the proposed optimization system.

Keywords: *Global logistics, Supply chain, Medical equipments*

1. INTRODUCTION

Nowadays companies want to establish relationships with external partners to identify their demands and effective responses. Supply chain management is the process of strategically managing the market oriented, manufacturing based and logistics supported movement and storage of materials, parts and finished inventory from suppliers through the company and onto customers. Figure 1 shows a typical supply chain how suppliers, manufacturers and customers are integrated for their inter-related businesses. It also show different types of dynamics (logistics/supplier related uncertainty, operations related uncertainty, workforce related uncertainty, machine related uncertainty and demand related uncertainty) in the different stages of supply chain.

Please use the following format when citing this chapter:

Ali, S. A., Seifoddini, H., Lee, J., 2007, in IFIP International Federation for Information Processing, Volume 254, Research and Practical Issues of Enterprise Information Systems II Volume 1, eds. L. Xu, Tjoa A., Chaudhry S. (Boston: Springer), pp. 111-124.

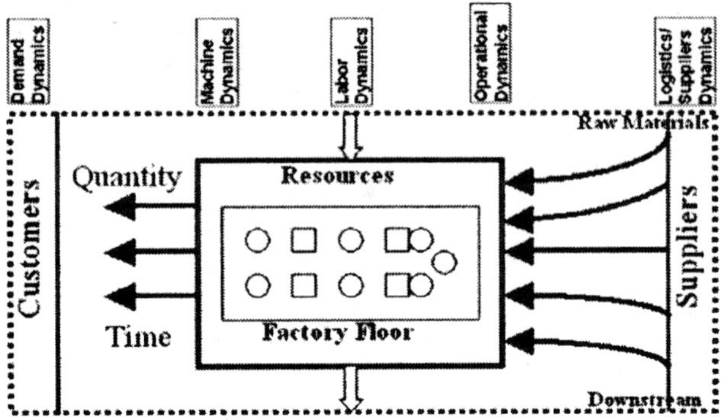

Figure 1. A Typical Supply Chain

Healthcare is gaining more attention from practitioners as well as manufacturing sectors. Due to cheap labor, less union problem and some other factors, companies are shifting their facilities overseas from United States. Global logistics systems are becoming more challenging due to outsourcing. A global logistics network for medical equipment manufacturing system is shown in Figure 2. The managing such logistics systems are needed to be considered for best customer services due to lot of dynamics are involved in the systems. Forrester illustrates the effect in a series of case studies and points out that it is a consequence of industrial dynamics or time varying behaviors of industrial organizations [1]. Within the area, industrial dynamics research has concentrated on logistics information and delay in the supply chain system [2-4]. Industrial dynamics research has concentrated on logistics information and delay in the supply chain system [5]. The decisions for supply chain management are mainly of two categories such as strategic (external) and operational (internal). Strategic decisions are made typically over a long time horizon which is closely linked to the corporate strategy and guides supply chain policies from a design perspective. Arntzen et al. [6] provide the most compressive deterministic model for supply chain management to minimize a combination of cost and time elements. Nicholson et al. addressed the issue of managing inventory costs in a healthcare setting [7]. It found, that the recent trend of outsourcing to distribute non-critical medical supplies directly to the hospital departments using them (i.e., the two-echelon network) results not only in inventory cost savings but also does not compromise the quality of care as reflected in service levels.

Spekman et al. [8] develop the concept of supply chain management and argues that only through close collaborative linkages through the entire supply chain, can one fully achieve the benefits of cost reduction and revenue enhancing behaviors. Wilding [9] provides a framework for understanding the generation of uncertainty within supply chains. On the other hand, operational decisions are short term and focused on activities over a day-to-day basis. The effort in these types of decisions is to effectively and efficiently manage the product flow in the internal supply chain. Burnham addresses the systematic logistics improvement principles where Global Logistics Systems (GLS) has been addressed strategic and tactical issues for timely and accurate delivery, availability, and lowest total cost [10]. Stock explores and develops the concept of enterprise logistics as a tool for integrating the logistics activities both within and between the strategically aligned organizations of the extended enterprise [11]. It is indicated that enterprise logistics is a necessary tool for the coordination of supply chain operations that are geographically dispersed around the world. However, for a pure network structure, a high level of enterprise logistics integration alone does not guarantee improved organizational performance. The paper ends with a discussion of managerial implications and directions for future research.

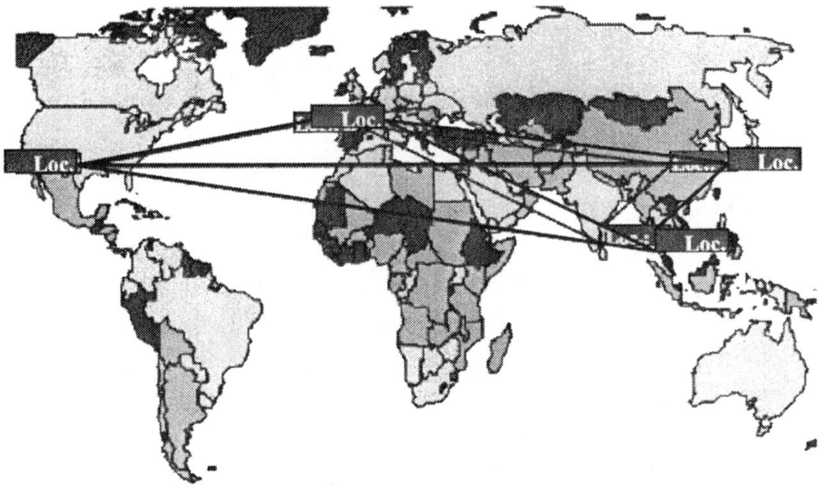

Figure 2. Global Logistics Network of Medical Equipment Manufacturing

With global competition intensifying and companies battling to keep market share, it is imperative that they carefully manage costs while maintaining service levels. Many companies are considering outsourcing transportation and distribution functions as a way to reduce costs. Companies need ways to measure service. Well-defined metrics can help a company measure costs and service and analyze tradeoffs between the two. Byers develops a list of potential metrics for distribution and transportation operations, and constructs a conceptual framework [12]. Pontrandolfo et al. focuses on the issues of coordination in the area of logistics (i.e. supply, manufacturing and distribution phases) of global manufacturing networks and propose a framework that systematically addresses the global manufacturing planning (GMP) problem by identifying and classifying the variables involved therein [13]. In recent years, researchers and practitioners alike have devoted a great deal of attention to supply chain management (SCM). The main focus of SCM is the need to integrate operations along the supply chain as part of an overall logistic support function. At the same time, the need for globalization requires that the solution of SCM problems be performed in an international context as part of what we refer to as Global Supply Chain Management (GSCM). An approach to study GSCM problems using an artificial intelligence framework is proposed and called reinforcement learning (RL) [14]. The

RL framework allows the management of global supply chains under an integration perspective.

1.1 Supply Chain Decision System

The main goal of supply chain management is to integrate and optimize the business and operational functions of an enterprise. Stewart [15] gives the first cross-industry framework for evaluating and improving enterprise-wide supply-chain performance and management, which is known as the supply-chain operations reference (SCOR) model. The SCOR methodology developed by the supply chain council addresses and benchmarks supply chains. These entities receive and process information from both the supply and demand management systems so as to derive the optimized enterprise supply chain infrastructure. As planning for the inbound, manufacturing and outbound functions are clustered together in this model, it is deemed necessary to have a logical separation between inbound, manufacturing and outbound. This is to allow further examinations of the activities that have occurred within each of these functions. In upstream inbound planning, manufacturers have to co-ordinate the inbound materials. Down stream manufacturers have to plan the outbound distribution strategy. Both the streams have unique physical distribution network topologies. These planning strategies and distribution topologies are documented and observed by small to medium size enterprises. It involves balancing the company's needs on both the supply side and the demand side and in harmonizing this with all the actors in the supply chain to achieve demand pipeline leadership, which is shown in Figure 3.

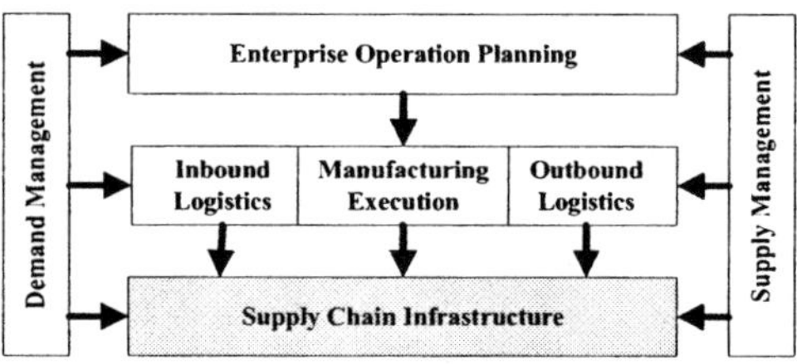

Figure 3. SCM Decision System

1.2 Enterprise Operation Planning (EOP)

EOP function resides within the manufacturing decision system function. The primary utilization of EOP is to provide global visibility of forecasts, inventory and production by consolidating data from multi-sites and databases. It has a centralized planning function to support global supply chain management and the relationships between demand and supply. This information is then translated to allocation of production demands to various sites. The EOP function links the high-level manufacturing enterprise business planning with medium to short-term planning and execution activities. Tactically, EOP optimizes target inventory and production levels by identifying variances between planned and actual performance. It also develops site and production line schedules in a typical high-mixed, high-volume manufacturing company.

In one-way or another, EOP enables supply chain integration to meet the customers' demands across the entire virtual enterprise which includes the immediate company, all its suppliers and customers. This is different from the traditional integration focus, which creates imbalance between the demand side (i.e. the customers, corporate entities, sales and marketing) and supply side (i.e. design, logistics, manufacturing and supplier). Although many companies that used the traditional integration methodology are able to integrate one side (supply or demand side) or the other, however, there has been little interaction between the two.

The mapping of a real life problem involves a wide range of knowledge such as production knowledge and mathematical knowledge, which actually make it very difficult to be used in supply chain management. That is to say, the planner should decide the quantity of each combination to meet the demand, concerning the full utilization of material at the same time. The product combination scenario is shown in Figure 4. Of course, it is very difficult for the planner to solve this large problem as a mathematical model efficiently and correctly without the help of computer and an effective algorithm of optimization. So how to model such large-scale problem more easily and more accurately is the attention of the research. As genetic algorithms have proved their contribution to complex problems, the system may be solved easily and more accurately.

2. MATHEMATICAL FORMULATION

The mathematical formulation has been described in respect to a real problem scenario. The global logistics problems are considered in terms of logistics cost minimization. It can provide proper information about production control to improve customer service. This scenario is basically for the medical equipment supply chains. The detailed configuration and design structure of the logistics network is shown figure. In order to identify the various factors that influence the overall logistics cost, a cause and effect diagram will be developed. There are many possible causes that have a direct influence on the overall logistics cost such as capacity, lead time, inventory cost, manufacturing cost, forecasting and shipping cost. Based on the determination of important factors, the following mathematical formulation has been developed to minimize the cost.

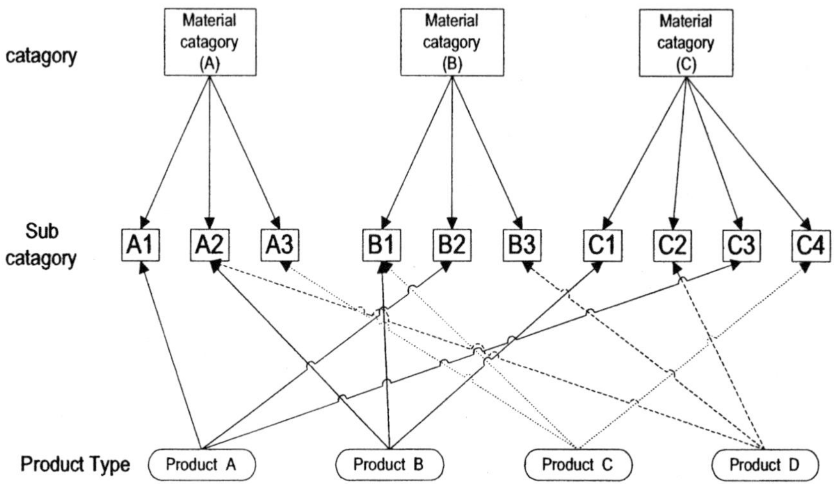

Figure 4. Product Combination Scenario

Product types: P1, P2,........, Pn , where n is the type of products
Demand quantity, D1, D2,........, Dn, in respect of product type P1, P2,........, Pn
Locations: L1, L2,......,Lm, where m is the number of locations
Manufacturing cost: MC1, MC2, ..., MCm
Shipping cost (finished products): FC11, FC12, ..., FCmm
Shipping cost (sub assembles): SC11, SC12,......, SCmm
Inventory cost: IC1, IC2, ..., ICm
Shipping plan: SP11, SP12, ..., SPmm
Total shipping cost = [D1, D2,..........., Dn] * [SC11, SC12,......., SCmm] + [D1, D2,..........., Dn] * [MC1, MC2, ..., MCm] + [D1, D2,..........., Dn] * [IC1, IC2, ..., ICm] + [SP11, SP12,..., SPmm] * [FC11, FC12,........., FCmm]

2.1 Constraints

The constraints of the global logistics systems are following:

Capacity Constraints

Each product needs to be checked with the customer order against available capacity of the real shop floor. This capacity check will give the customer committed demand that will assist to provide optimal logistics scenario for each product.

$$D_1 \leq C_1$$
$$D_2 \leq C_2$$
$$\cdots\cdots\cdots$$
$$D_n \leq C_n$$

Where $C_n(k = 1, 2, \cdots\cdots\cdots, N)$ is the capacity of the nth product that depends upon real time shop floor level. This real time capacity gives more realistic logistic strategy.

Sub Assembles Constraints

Sub Assembles constraints state that the total number of type components consumed in every moving window cannot exceed the maximum number of components needed, i.e.,

$$\sum_{i=1}^{n} SA_i \leq \sum_{i=1}^{n} CA_i$$

SA – Sub assembles, CA – Capacity assembles

Demand Constraints

The commit demand must be equal to or less than the product demands of the customer i.e. commit demand cannot exceed the customer demand that can be expressed as:

$$\sum_{\substack{i=1\\j=1}}^{m,m} SP_{ij} \leq \sum_{\substack{i=1\\j=1}}^{m,m} DP_{ij}$$

Where, SY_{ij} and DP_{ij} are the shipping plan and demand plan respectively.

Logistics Fuzzy Rules as Constraints

The suppliers' behaviors are needed to be identified to consider the supplier dynamics. The supplier's behavior is characterized based on timely delivery, quality and flexibility. The IF-THEN rule based fuzzy rules are used for the supplier's behavior.

Rule 1: IF x_1 is A_1^1 and (or) … and (or) x_n is A_n^1
THEN y_1 is B_1^1 and (or) … and (or) y_m is B_m^P

. . .

. . .

Rule k: IF x_1 is A_1^k and (or) … and (or) x_n is A_n^k
THEN y_1 is B_1^P and (or) … and (or) y_m is B_m^q

Where,

$x_{1 \ldots n}$ independent fuzzy variables (antecedent)
$y_{1 \ldots m}$ independent fuzzy variables (consequent)
$A_i^{1 \ldots P}$ fuzzy sets corresponding to x_i
$A_j^{1 \ldots q}$ fuzzy sets corresponding to y_j

2.2 Objective Function

The total logistics cost is considered as objective function and the cost should be minimized.

$$TC = \sum_{i=1, j=1}^{n,m} ([D_i] \times [\{MC_j\}, \{SC_{jj}\}, \{FC_{jj}\}, \{IC_j\}])$$

Where, TC = Total cost
i = the type of product as 1,2,....,n
j = the number of location as 1,2,.....,m
D = Demand
MC = Manufacturing cost
SC = Shipping cost for sub-assembles
FC = Shipping cost for finish products
IC = Inventory cost

3. CASE STUDY: MEDICAL EQUIPMENT MANUFACTURING SYSTEM

In order to achieve high economies of scale and shorten the logistics and supply chain lead-times, medical equipment manufacturing system has its manufacturing operations set up in various parts of the globe. Whatever be the location of these facilities, the company has identified "continuous improvement" as the driving factor for its consistent growth year after year. The company has embraced Internet as a key tool in reducing cost. Whether it is improving its responsiveness to the customers in order to offer better equipment diagnostics or sharing of information, it has exploited the benefits of internet to the maximum and has improved its bottom line.

This research provides an effort to optimize the logistics performance of one of medical equipment manufacturing system's key products, X-Ray Scanner. The product has three models that are made in three different locations. Company does not manufacture all the parts needed for assembly at one location. This means that some of the parts are procured from other locations and these are then assembled at a particular facility, tested for quality and sent to the customer i.e. the hospital. When an order is received for a specific model, the company has to identify the best location for its assembly and manufacture of an X-Ray model to maintain high customer service level and at the same time minimize the overall logistics cost. The following objectives are identified to solve logistics problems:

- To build an LP optimization model using Arena OptQuest for minimizing the overall logistics cost
- Identify the uncertainty of factors that affect the overall logistics cost using Design of Experiments
- Propose best practices in the industry for global logistics

3.1 Problem Formulation

Due to the constraints on the level of data that was available, the project focused on formulation as an important step. It will generate an optimal solution, however the company can use the factors considered in the formulation steps to improve this optimal solution and further minimize its logistics cost in the future.

The product X-Ray Scanner has the following components/parts:

- Gantry 1 (premium)
- Gantry 2 (mid tier)
- Gantry 3 (3rd tier)
- Console 1
- Console 2
- Console 3
- Table
- Accessories

An X-Ray Scanner consists of a gantry, console, table and accessories. There are three different models that can be assembled from this product mix. Tables and accessories are the same for any kind of model with variations in gantries and consoles. The locations in which these parts are made are given in Table 1.

Table 1. Manufacturing Locations for Various Parts

Location A	Location B	Location C	Location D
Gantry 2	Gantry 1	Gantry 1	Accessories
Gantry 3	Gantry 2	Console 1	
Console 2	Console 1		
Console 3	Console 2		
Table			

It can be seen from the table that a gantry and console of similar types are made in the same manufacturing location. Hence, for purpose of simplicity we grouped each gantry and console type and call them under a generic name of product type. Thus, Location A makes product type 2 and 3. Location B manufactures product type 1 and 2 and Location 3 manufactures only product type 1. Tables are manufactured only in Location A. Thus assembly of X-Ray Scanners is two locations. Tables are supplied from Location A. Location D makes only accessories and supply it to all three plants that manufacture and assemble the X-Ray scanners. Location and customers maps are shown in Figure 5.

In order to identify the various factors that influence the overall logistics cost, a cause and effect diagram is built. As seen from Figure 6, the six possible causes are identified that have a direct influence on the overall logistics cost. They are capacity, lead time, inventory cost, manufacturing cost, forecast and shipping cost. Based on the determination of important factors and the availability of data, the model has been developed.

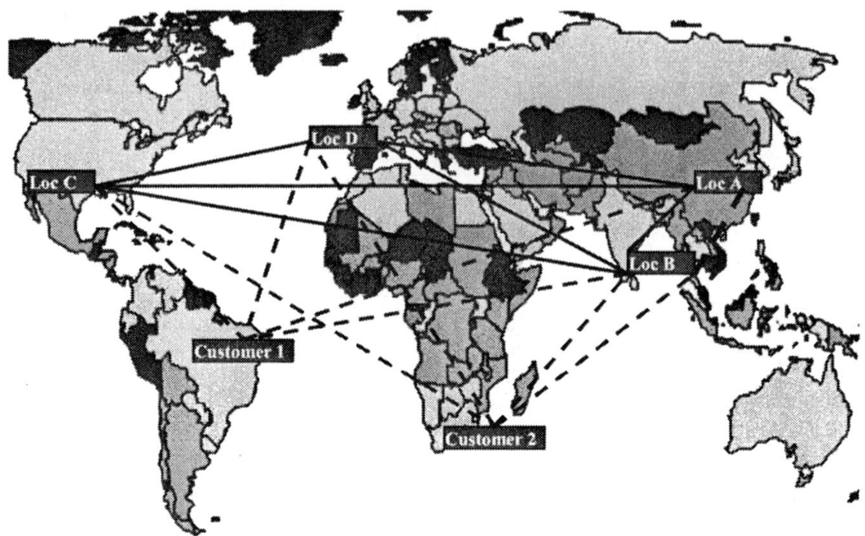

Figure 5. Global Logistics Network with Customers

3.2 Optimal Algorithm

The algorithm is developed for the logistics and supply chain networks of their distribution center and plants to optimize their logistics networks using LINDO. The objective is to minimize total logistics cost for a specific product type, given the capacity constraints in the specific plants. The demand, all cost related on shipping, manufacturing, inventory and shipping plan are in Table 2 –7.

Table 2. Demand for X Ray Scanners

	Location A	Location B	Location C	Location D
P1	250	100	250	329
P2	0	0	0	0
P3	0	0	0	0

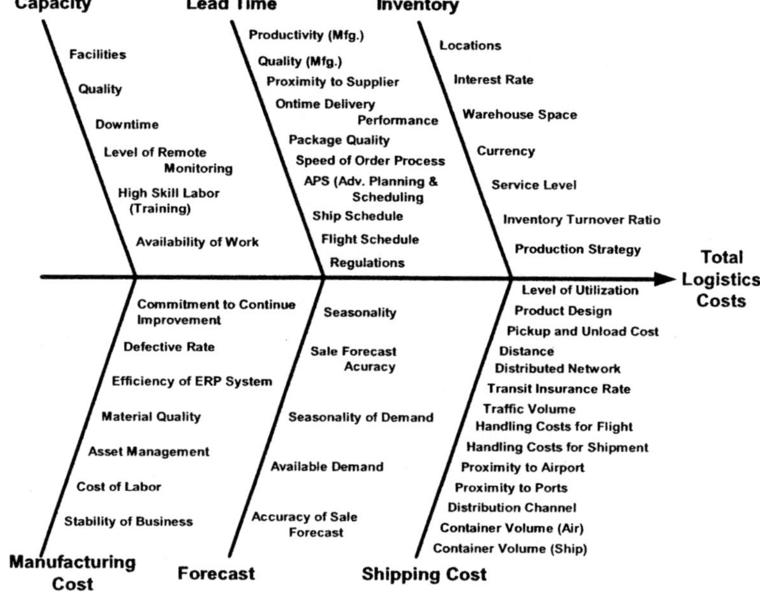

Figure 6. Logistics Cost Factor Analysis

Table 3. Transportation Cost (Finished Products)

	Location A	Location B	Location C	Location D
Location A	50	500	575	625
Location B	500	50	600	700
Location C	575	585	45	250
Location D	625	700	350	50

Table 4. Shipping Plan

	Market					
	Loc. A	Loc. B	Loc. C	Loc. D	Total Production	Capacity
Location A	0	0	0			
Location B	250	100	54	0	404	4750
Location D	0	0	196	329	525	525
Total	250	100	250	329	929	

Table 5. Transportation Cost (Sub-assembles)

	Loc. A	Loc. B	Loc. C	Loc. D
Loc. A		300	250	275
Loc. C	225	275		125

Table 6. Manufacturing Cost

	Loc. A	Loc. B	Loc. C	Loc. D
Accessories			110	
Tables	200			
P1		100		225
P2				
P3				

Table 7. Inventory Cost

	Loc. A	Loc. B	Loc. C	Loc. D
Accessories			25	
Tables	30			
P1		50		45
P2				
P3				

3.3 Effect of Factor Uncertainty

We used a DOE (design of experiment) model to identify the effect of each factor on the response variable, i.e. the total logistics cost. Five-key factors (interest rate, traffic volume, handling cost, distribution cost and labor cost) influencing the overall logistics cost are identified. We assigned weights to each factors and carried out 1/2 factorial design.

Table 8. Design Matrix for DOE and Results

Interest Rate	Traffic Volume	Handling Cost	Distr. Cost	Labor Cost	Inventory Cost	Mfg. Cost	Tran. Cost	Optimal Rate
1	1	-1	-1	1	1	1.00000	0.96	632943
1	1	1	1	1	1	1.00000	1.00	648465
-1	-1	1	-1	-1	0.94	0.98000	0.96	625997
1	-1	-1	-1	-1	1	0.97330	0.96	627149
-1	-1	1	1	1	0.94	0.99333	1.00	644414
-1	-1	-1	1	-1	0.94	0.98666	0.96	627444
-1	1	1	1	-1	0.94	1.00000	0.96	630339
-1	1	-1	1	1	0.94	0.99333	1.00	644414
1	-1	1	1	-1	1.00	0.99333	0.94	623735
-1	1	1	-1	1	0.94	0.98666	1.00	642966
-1	**1**	**-1**	**-1**	**-1**	**0.94**	**0.98000**	**0.94**	**618238**
1	1	1	-1	-1	1	0.98666	0.94	622287
1	-1	1	-1	1	1	0.98000	1.00	644125
1	1	-1	1	-1	1	0.99333	0.94	623735
1	-1	-1	1	1	1	0.98666	1.00	645570
-1	-1	-1	-1	1	0.94	0.97330	1.00	640073

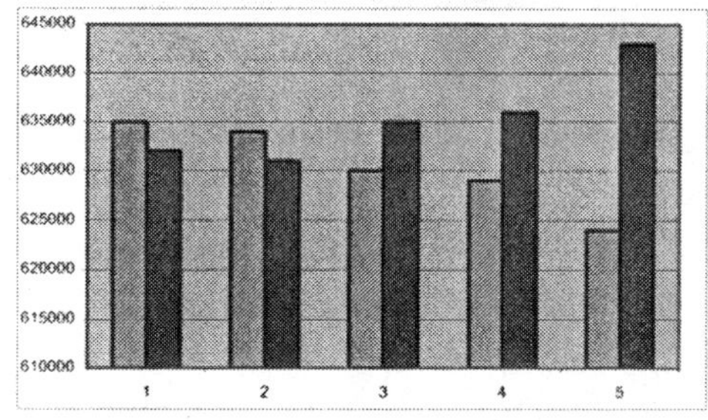

1- Interest rate
2-Traffic volume
3-Handling cost
4-Distribution cost
5-Labor cost

Figure 7. Effect of the Factors Considered

The results of the DOE are given in Figure 7, which indicates that the effect of labor cost, distribution cost and the handling cost have a significant impact on the overall logistics cost. From the results, we observe that labor cost has the greatest impact on the optimal cost. In the future, this factor needs to be taken care of.

4. CONCLUSIONS

The global logistic network has been pointed out to show the impact of the different cost factors considered for medical equipment manufacturing systems. The formulation of the logistics network has been shown in details and a case sudsy has been done on medical system and shows the optimal production and cost scenario. The proposed methodology can be used to improve the any logistics systems specifically in medical equipment manufacturing systems.

REFERENCES

1. J.W. Forrester, Industrial Dynamics (MIT Press: Boston, MA 1961).
2. J.L. Burbidge, The New Approach of Production, Production Engineer. Volume 40, pp.769-784, (1961).
3. D.R. Towill, Supply Chain Dynamics, Computer Integrated Manufacturing. Volume 4, pp.197-208, (1991).
4. D.R. Towill, Supply Chain Dynamics-The Change Engineering Challenge of the Mid 1990s, in Proceedings of the Institution of Mechanical Engineers Volume 206 (1992), pp.233-245.
5. D.R. Towill, Industrial Dynamics Modelling of Supply Chains, International Journal of Physical Distribution and Logistics Management. Volume 26, Number 2, pp.23-42, (1996).
6. B.C. Arntzen, G.G. Brown, T.P. Harrison, and L.L. Trafton, Global Supply Chain Management at Digital Equipment Corporation, Interfaces. Volume 25, Number 1, pp.69-93, (1995).
7. L. Nicholson, A.J. Vakharia, and S.S. Erenguc, Outsourcing Inventory Management Decisions in Healthcare: Models and Application, European Journal of Operations Research. Volume 154, Number 1, pp.271-290, (2004).

8. R.E. Spekman, J.W. Kamauff, and N. Myhr, An Empirical Investigation into Supply Chain Management: A Perspective on Partnerships, Supply Chain Management. Volume 3, Number 2, pp.53-67, (1998).
9. R. Wilding, The Supply Chain Complexity Triangle: Uncertainty Generation in the Supply Chain, International Journal of Physical Distribution and Logistics Management. Volume 28, Number 8, pp.599-616, (1998).
10. J.M. Burnham, Systematic Logistics Improvement: Integrating Principles and Practices, in Proceedings of the APICS 35th International Conference and Exhibition (1992), pp.500-510.
11. G.N. Stock, N.P. Greis, and J.D. Kasarda, Enterprise Logistics and Supply Chain Structure: The Role of Fit, Journal of Operations Management. Volume 18, Number 5, pp.531-547, (2000).
12. J.E. Byers, T.L. Landers, and S. Anderson, Framework for Logistics System Metrics, in Proc. of the 1996 ASME International Mechanical Engineering Congress and Exposition, Volume 4 (Atlanta, 1996), pp.773-781.
13. P. Pontrandolfo and O.G. Okogbaa, Global Manufacturing: A Review and a Framework for Planning in a Global Corporation, International Journal of Production Research. Volume 37, Number 1, pp.1-19, (1999).
14. P. Pontrandolfo, A. Gosavi, O.G. Okogbaa, and T.K. Das, Global Supply Chain Management: A Reinforcement Learning Approach, International Journal of Production Research. Volume 40, Number 6, pp.1299-1317, (2002).
15. G. Stewart, Supply Chain Operations Reference Model (SCOR): The First Cross-Industry Framework for Integrated Supply Chain Management, Logistics Information Management. Volume 10, Number 2, pp.62-67, (1997).

Gentelligent® Parts: A Decentralized Information System for Enterprises

Matthias Schmidt, Felix S. Wriggers, Frank Fisser and Peter Nyhuis

Institute of Production Systems and Logistics, Gottfried Wilhelm Leibniz Universitaet Hannover, 30823 Garbsen, Germany
schmidt@ifa.uni-hannover.de wriggers@ifa.uni-hannover.de
fisser@ifa.uni-hannover.de nyhuis@ifa.uni-hannover.de

Abstract. Gentelligent® Parts are components that function as storage mediums. They can record information, save it, process it and communicate it. Due to these characteristics, Gentelligent® Parts can serve as decentralized Enterprise Information System (EIS). It follows that along the product's evolutionary process and during the utilization phase extensive potential for improving the logistic and technical processes results. This article provides insight into both the principle of Gentelligent® Parts as well as the corresponding data structure and targeted process improvements.

Keywords: *EIS for manufacturing sector, Inter-and Intra-organizational information systems, Supply chain management (SCM), Supply chain planning and execution, Production planning and controlling, Logistics operations*

I. INTRODUCTION

In addition to the price and product quality, a high logistic efficiency, implicated through short delivery times and high delivery reliability, is an increasingly significant factor for a company's success [1-3]. Logistics is thus a key factor in global competition. This is not the least due to businesses concentrating on their core competences and trying to design factories accordingly. Through the intensive outsourcing of secondary processes and the complete outsourcing of modules that are to be manufactured to system suppliers, the vertical integration is radically reduced. Subsequently within an enterprise there is a shifting of complexity. Externally seen, this means that the performance demanded by the customer has to be produced from clearly longer and complexer value adding chains [4]. Adequately providing information is increasingly significant for managing these extended value adding chains.

In order to stand up to the globalized markets steadily increasing stress of competition, enterprises have to constantly increase their efficiency along their internal value adding chain as well as along those links reaching beyond them. This concerns both logistic and technical processes. Efficient management requires that economical decisions are made on every hierarchical level and at every link of the supply chain throughout the entire product evolutionary process. Adequately

Please use the following format when citing this chapter:

Schmidt, M., Wriggers, F. S., Fisser, F., Nyhuis, P., 2007, in IFIP International Federation for Information Processing, Volume 254, Research and Practical Issues of Enterprise Information Systems II Volume 1, eds. L. Xu, Tjoa A., Chaudhry S. (Boston: Springer), pp. 125-134.

supplying the right information to the right person and the right process at the right time is therefore essential [5]. In the future, information, its availability and its usefulness will be core competences for a successful company [6].

2. CURRENT AND FUTURE INFORMATION PROCESSING

Up until recently the talk was about "Economy of Speed". The focus was on optimizing the production factor "time" in the sense of production and delivery time. Now, at the start of the "Economy of Information", more and more factors such as uniqueness, innovatability and the ability to learn stand in the foreground. The paradigm of "individual production" will dominate production technology for a long time and is already reflected in decisive tendencies [7]. In order to realize an "individual production" customer specific information for each product has to be backed up by corresponding information technology.

Production companies are already developing enormous logistic potential through currently available information technology such as RFID or barcodes. Nevertheless, with this technology information about parts or processes along the value adding chain can not be completely provided. Moreover, due to the physical separation of the parts and information (cf. Figure 1) it can not occur in real time.

Currently, parts and their related information are a single unit only in the form of a virtual component during the development phase, that is during the first phase of the products evolution. Further in the lifecycle (production, utilization, disposal) the information is generally separated from the physical part. The production date, production history, quality information, materials, state of change, product model and additional information are no longer directly available. In order to be able to access the information of an individual component, the serial number – as long as a unique one exists – has to be read out and subsequently accessed from a databank located elsewhere. Usually though, individual part information is not maintained or is maintained only for a short time span in a databank. At best, the information for a series of parts can be accessed. Direct access of information about a component has thus been impossible up until now.

The RFID technology can help to reduce the lack of information about the real world in the virtual "planning world" [8]. Due to the new possibilities for applying RFID technology in order to combine products and product information for example shown by ten Hompel [9], this technology exhibits a trend for exponential growth. However, as a result of the materials limited durability and their physical constraints there are boundaries to the application of RFID technology, particularly in production processes.

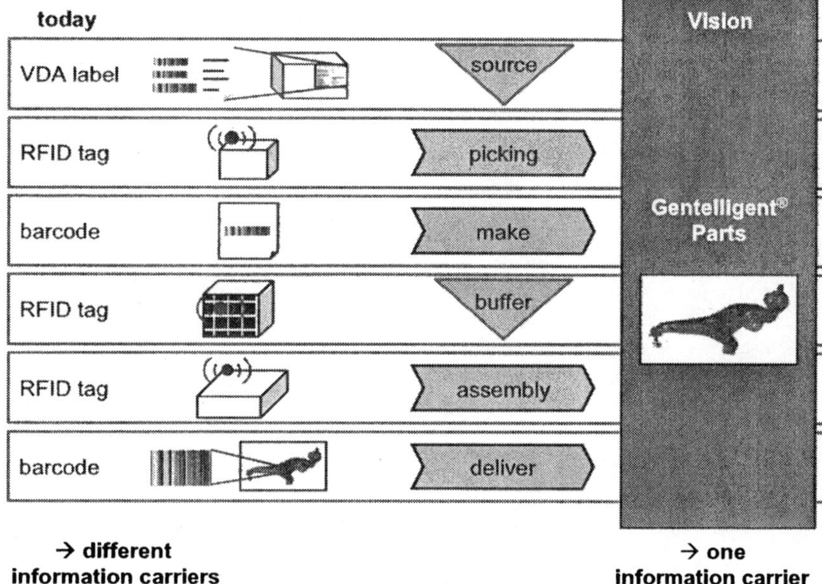

Figure 1. Part Relevant Information Storage: Today and in the Future

As a study from Seliger and Reichl [10] demonstrated, there is however a high demand for cost efficient information systems in production enterprises. These information systems should for example, as embedded systems, be able to be used flexibly for different technical systems and applications. With information systems that accompany the production, the continuous monitoring of standard units during the utilization phase should for example be possible in order to punctually arrange adaption processes such as maintenance and repairs. Such fundamental changes to the provision of information, not only impact the information in the production, but also open up both new potential and requirements for machines. Production systems will have to communicate and organize themselves in the future [11].

3. GENTELLIGENT® PARTS

In order to fulfil the abovementioned conditions, the foundation for a changing the paradigm in production technology will be created within the collaborative research centre (SFB) 653 "Gentelligent® Parts in the Lifecycle" (which is being conducted at the Leibniz Universitaet Hannover. The longterm goal of SFB 653 is the abolition of the physical separation of components and the information relevant to them. This will be accomplished through the development and utilization of a new type of components, the so called Gentelligent® Parts. These are characterized by their ability to record information, store it on the part and process it. The information is maintained throughout the lifecycle and can thus also be inherited by a future generation of parts. The components are thus genetic and intelligent (GI), or simply "Gentelligent®"

In order to realize this vision of Gentelligent® Parts a variety of technologies will be developed. For example foreign objects will be inserted in sinter parts. Through the existence and the size of foreign particles in a matrix array, information such as an identification number can be directly and irreversibly stored in the part [12].

However, there will also be methods developed which allow saved information to be changed. As Bach et al. [13] and Wu et al. [14] pointed out information can be saved, deleted and re-written similarly to on a harddrive through the introduction of magnetized magnesium under a keeper layer on the component.

Furthermore, the Gentelligent® Parts will be equipped with sensor functions, so that information from their surroundings can be recorded and saved. An example of this is the production of mechanical stress sensors through the placement of local strains. According to Behrens et al. [15] through this it is possible to record the load on a part over its lifecycle.

4. GENTELLIGENT® PARTS AS A DECENTRALIZED INFORMATION SYSTEM

Through the new component properties outlined above, the conditions for an Enterprise Information System (EIS) based on decentralized information stored on parts are met. Above all, the available decentralized information generates potential for the implementation in logistic processes, since these processes are characterized by a great amount of data. The goal is to reduce external storage mediums and to store a large portion of all the part relevant information – created through the production and utilization of the part – on the part directly. The use of additional data carriers such as externally placed RFID tags or barcodes will be refrained from. Through this alone, mistakes on error prone interfaces between the frequently different data carriers should be avoided, because no duplication or loss of data can occur here.

4.1 The Concept of Data for Gentelligent® Parts

Planning and Controlling logistic and technological production processes during the manufacturing of parts is based on information management. Which information should be decentrally stored on a component when – that is for conducting which processes – is thus critical for the development of information systems based on Gentelligent® Technology (GI Technology). In order to determine this, information, which on the one hand flowed into processes as input information and on the other hand flowed out of processes as output information, was collected from generic processing models such as the Supply Chain Operations Reference Model published by the Supply Chain Council [16].

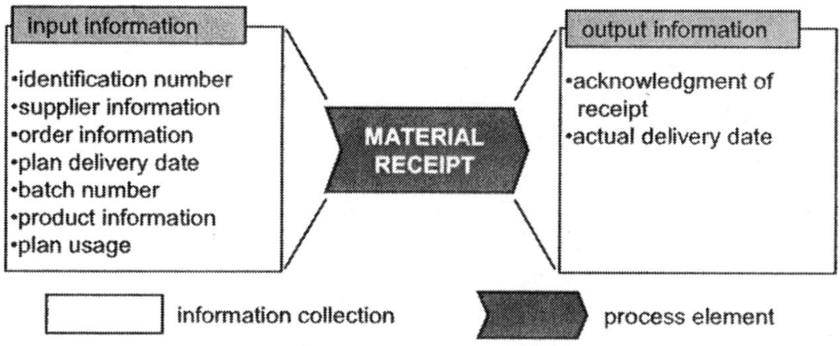

Figure 2. Input and Output Information for the "Material Receipt" Process

This is illustrated in Figure 2, using the example of the process element "material receipt". The "material receipt" process result in the confirmation of the goods input and the booking of them in a materials management system. The actual delivery date is also recorded, so that a supplier control can be conducted.

First to be noted as input information for this process, are the identification of the part and the supplier. Together with information regarding the ordering and the planned delivery dates (in some circumstance also the batch number), the correctness of the delivery can be determined. Information about the product and the planned usage is also helpful for the more expedient forwarding of goods, quality control and direct disposal of them onto the line.

As exemplarily presented here, the processes for procurement, production, assembly, distribution and return were analyzed with their process elements. Based on this matrix it could be identified which information could be advantageously stored decentrally on the part. Once the data model is developed, it will structure the information that is required and/or created during the production processes of Gentelligent® Parts (and is to be stored on the components) in a process oriented way. This model is a requirement for the consistent and redundancy-free processing of information.

The storage capacity of Gentelligent® Parts is – at least according to current technology – limited, however it will continue to be expanded in the future. The concept of the data model has to reflect this. The plan therefore is to gradually extend the data to be stored on the part, depending on the storage capacity of the Gentelligent® Parts. An excerpt from the data model is presented in Figure 3. The central information of a Gentelligent® Parts is without a doubt its identification. It thus forms the first step of the data model. This distinct, part specific, information already facilitates a number of process simplifications and reduces the process' susceptibly to errors. In a second step, information documenting the production process is to be stored on the Gentelligent® Parts. Included in this are data for clearly identifying all the links in the supply chain, as well as all the batch numbers along the evolutionary process. The part is thus unmistakably traceable. At the same time, through the uniqueness of the combination of different information a protection against plagiarism is implemented on the component.

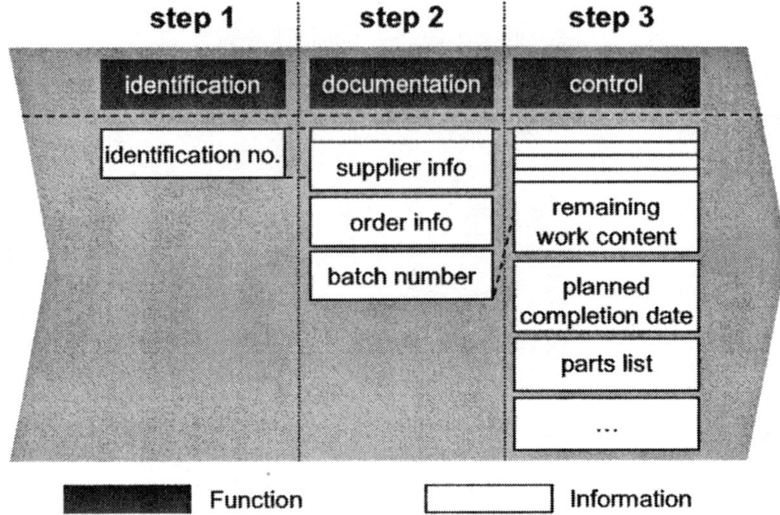

Figure 3. Excerpt from the Data Model for Gentelligent® Parts

In a third stage of development, the available data model is supplemented by further data. Here, information which enables a desired function of the Gentelligent® Parts is to be saved. If for example, a real time capable, part driven control of the assembly area is to be realized, then static information such as a part list of the components which are to be mounted can on the one hand be stored. On the other hand, dynamic information such as remaining work content (in planned hours) or the desired and realizable completion dates for an order can also be saved. Furthermore, the information part list stored on a key part enables a part driven picking to prepare an assembly process. The worker can identify the parts to be picked for assembly with the help of the Gentelligent® Key Part. Accordingly information relevant to other utilizations of Gentelligent® Parts can also be stored.

4.2 Utilizing a Decentralized Information System in Production Processes

GI Technology makes it possible to design simpler, leaner and more error resistant processes. In order to elucidate this, the application of GI Technology on a number of processes will be exemplarily presented here. The procurement process will be considered first. It is outlined in Figure 4, on the third level of the SCOR model using the five process elements: “scheduling material delivery”, “material receipt”, “material testing”, “material transport” and “release of supplier payment”.

As indicated in Figure 4, GI Technology almost affects all five process elements. The scheduling of the material delivery can be activated through Gentelligent® Parts. They log out of the store when they are used and activate a new order operation when a minimal stock level is breached. A quasi GI Kanban is thus implemented.

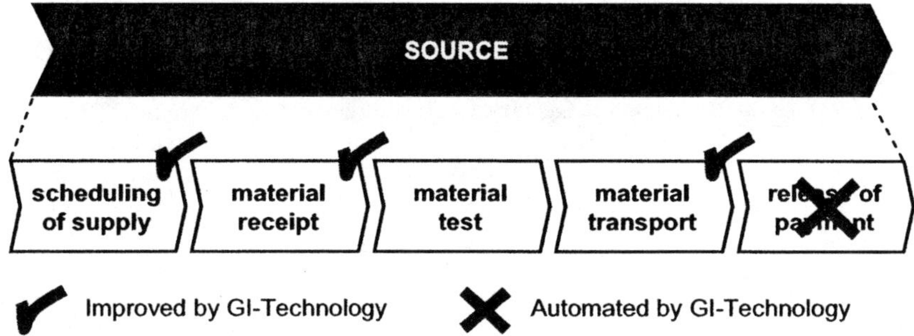

Figure 4. Process Improving the Procurement Process through GI Technology

Through the GI Technology the subprocess "material receipt" including verifying the identity can be simplified when the delivered materials are simple and clearly identifiable.

This is the case, when an identification number is directly written on the part and can be identified error-free through an active or – depending on the type of GI Technology implemented – passive scanner. Personal expenditures and costs due to errors caused by mistakes on both the receiver's and deliverer's side can be avoided, because whether or not the delivered part is correct can be determined by directly comparing the part and system data.

The material transport from the receipt of the goods to a downstream stocking echelon can also be simplified: By clearly identifying the part, a storage location will be assigned to it through the EDP system and if applicable directly written on the Gentelligent® Parts. The risk of mistakes during storage is thus minimized.

The material transport from the receipt of the goods to a downstream stocking echelon can also be simplified: By clearly identifying the part, a storage location will be assigned to it through the EDP system and if applicable directly written on the Gentelligent® Parts. The risk of mistakes during storage is thus minimized.

Furthermore, it is plausible that the release of the suppliers' payment could be automated by activating it with GI Technology. By exactly identifying the number of received parts, the payment process would be initiated based on the components. It can be activated either directly after the receipt of materials or when applicable, after they have been tested. All of the parts, which meet the standards for the technical quality, are registered after they have passed through the process elements "material receipt" or "material testing". The value deposited in the EDP system, will be credited to the supplier, whose identification is also stored on the part. These accounts will then be settled in a specific cycle e.g., weekly or monthly. It is also conceivable that this application could be extended by storing the price of the part directly on it, so that the billing can be conducted through decentrally accumulated, part specific information. This billing data then only has to be collected in the form of credit accounts in the EDP system.

Within the frame of the production process, a part driven control of assembly parts will also be implemented. Of the four production control tasks, identified by Lödding [17] – order creation, order release, sequencing and controlling capacities – this method will regulate the order release and sequencing. However, it will also have an impact on controlling the capacities.

For each of the groups which are to be assembled, a key part will be determined, which can communicate with the remaining components in its group. The key part knows from the start of the manufacturing what the target completion date for the group is. Based on the inter-operation time which remains to the target completion date, the components will decide amongst themselves the sequencing of the processing on the workstations. Thus if a part falls behind, and others have enough time to wait, a decentralized order sequencing change will be carried out. The goal of the algorithm that this is based on is to maintain the given targeted completion date and ensure that all parts in a group arrive at an assembly workstation simultaneously. As soon as all of the parts to be manufactured and assembled have passed through the production, the key part will trigger the picking of the remaining parts from the stores based on the deposited part list for the assembly order. This method should increase the scheduling reliability and reduce both the WIP as well as the handling effort required during the assembly.

Since the remaining work content and the completion date for the individual operation are deposited on each of the parts, existing back logs on any of the workstations can be decentrally reacted to by increasing capacities as long as a corresponding flexibility of capacities is permitted.

As demonstrated here based on the example of procurement, process simplifications can be identified throughout the complete production process. A number of these simplifications are so extensive that the process elements can almost be automated.

4.3 Utilizing a Decentralized Information System during the Product Evolutionary Process

Further important utilization aspects of GI Technology can be identified outside of the production process. An example of this is the documentation of the evolutionary process of Gentelligent® Parts. Every link of a supply chain irreversibly encodes and writes its identification and where applicable the batch number on the corresponding part. Through this, the evolutionary process of the Gentelligent® Parts is continuously written. This can protect enterprises from claims for recourse in relation to parts which are not produced by them, but are rather copied. Moreover, the traceability of products, which is already demanded in many industrial sectors, is easily ensured.

The intelligence of Gentelligent® Parts arises through its technical ability to compile, process and store information during the utilization phase such as influencing forces, accelerations, and temperatures. This occurs through suitable materials and sensors, which are integrated in or linked to the part. The entirety of information that is stored on the Gentelligent® Parts can as required be communicated to the user of the part or read out during its removal/replacement.

The information recorded during its implementation should be applied to determine causes of failures and based on that the probability of failure and the length of remaining life, as well as for determining dynamic maintenance intervals. The information gained is passed back to the company through the maintenance process or through a return process, so that the information can be passed down to the next generation of parts. New parts can therefore be designed with the help of real load profiles, which are determined during the utilization phase of the previous parts.

5. SUMMARY

A decentralized Enterprise Information System based on Gentelligent® Parts offers an enormous potential for making improvements and for avoiding errors in the logistic and technical production processes, particularly with regards to the supply chain which extends beyond the enterprise. This potential was tentatively outlined in both production processes and utilization phases. In order to realize this potential, a corresponding data model, which is oriented on the Gentelligent® Parts' still small but steadily growing storage capacity, was discussed in detail. Through this, errors at interfaces between companies and at interfaces between firms and information systems can be avoided.

ACKNOWLEDGEMENTS

The research results presented here were acquired within the context of the collaborative research centre 653, sponsored by the German Research Foundation.

REFERENCES

1. H. Wildemann, *Logistik-Chek*, 5th edition (TCW Transfer-Zentrum: München, 2007).
2. B. Enslow, *Best Practices in International Logistics, Benchmark Report* (Aberdeen Group: Boston, 2006).
3. K.K.B. Hon, Performance and Evaluation of Manufacturing Systems, *Annals of the CIRP*. Volume 54, Number 2, pp.675-690, (2005).
4. H. Baumgarten and J. Thoms, *Trends und Strategien in der Logistik: Supply Chains im Wandel* (Bereich Logistik TU Berlin: Berlin, 2002).
5. E. Turban, J.E. Aronson, and T.P. Liang, *Decision Support Systems and Intelligent Systems*, 7th edition (Prentice Hall: Upper Saddle River, 2004).
6. L. Monostori1, J. Váncza1, and S.R.T. Kumara, Agent-Based Systems for Manufacturing, *Annals of the CIRP*, Volume 55, Number 2, pp.697-720, (2006).
7. T. Teich, Extended Value Chain Management für hierarchielose regionale Produktionsnetze, *3. Paderborner Frühjahrstagung* (Paderborn, 2001).
8. C. Zhang and Y. Fan, Complex event processing in enterprise information systems based on RFID, *Enterprise Information Systems*. Volume 1, Number 1, pp.3-23, (2007).
9. M. Ten Hompel, Selbst ist das Paket – RFID und Selbstorganisation ermöglichen das Internet der Dinge, in *8. Karlsruher Arbeitsgespräche* (Forschungszentrum Karlsruhe GmbH: Karlsruhe, 2006), pp.101-108.
10. G. Seliger, H. Reichl, *Einsatz produktbegleitender Informationssysteme und ihre Auswirkungen auf die Produktionstechnik*, Ergebnisbericht der Voruntersuchung im Auftrag des PFT. http://www.epi.tu-berlin.de (Accessed December 4, 2002).

11. E. Westkämper, *Intelligente Maschinen müssen kommunizieren*, Siemens-Pictures of the Future (2002).
12. B.A. Behrens, F. Lange, A. Bouguecha, and E. Gastan, Plagiatschutz: Fremdpartikel als Informationsträger in Sinterbauteilen, *KEM.* Volume 11, pp.128-129, (2006).
13. F.W. Bach, M. Schaper, M. Bosse, G. Gershteyn, and M. Nowak, *Casting of Magnesium alloys with magnetic properties, in "Magnesium-broadhorizons", Number 2,* (Moskau, 2006), pp.16-19.
14. K.H. Wu, O. Traisigkhachol, and H.H. Gatzen, Development of a recording head for magnetic storage of information on machine components, in *Proc. of ECS 2006 - 210th meeting of the electrochemical society* (Cancun, Mexico, 2006).
15. B.A. Behrens, M. Kamp, O. Pösse, and K. Weilandt, Smart materials - intelligent components by means of metal forming, *Steel Grips.* Volume 3, Number 4, (2005).
16. Anonymous, *Supply Chain Operations Reference Model*, Supply Chain Council (2007) http://www.supply-chain.org(Accessed March 12, 2007).
17. H. Lödding, *Verfahren der Fertigungssteuerung, Grundlagen, Beschreibung, Konfiguration* (Springer: Berlin, 2005)

Virtual Enterprise in Closed-Loop Supply Chain and Performance Evaluation Based on Exergoeconomics

Guojun Ji

School of Management, Xiamen University, Xiamen 361006, Fujian, P.R. China
jiking@xmu.edu.cn

Abstract. Based on analyzing the difficulties of closed-loop supply chain operation management, considering the new environment as the economic society developing continuously and discussing the feasibility of virtual enterprise, an operation management mode for the closed-loop supply chain based on virtual enterprise is presented in this paper. The organization framework, the operational process, the dynamic durative of virtual enterprise with traditional management mode is expounded in detail. Using the exergoeconomics theory, the closed-loop supply chain is regarded as a huge energy system with the new view, and the sustainability of the closed-loop supply chain system is discussed under the circumstance of exergoeconomics in this paper, and then the metric about "system negative environment effect" is introduced to measure closed-loop supply chain system performance from the point of energy. Finally a case study illustrates our conclusion.

Keywords: *Closed-loop supply chain, Virtual enterprise, Exergoeconomics*

1. INTRODUCTION

Rapidly globalizing markets, production and distribution systems operating within complex and fluid capital markets have triggered exceptional economic and competitive pressures in national economies. Consequent microeconomic reform, deregulation and the corporatization and privatization of national market places have been no less significant and have further impacted on nation-wide, as well as international, global logistics systems so that change is now pervasive, urgent and transforming. For buyers of freight services, whether manufacturers, rural and primary producers or retail giants, the pressing need to control costs in supply chains has spawned numerous strategies within a broader supply chain management framework that seeks sophisticated levels of operational as well as corporate integration–and ideally, fully integrated corporate and intercorporate business processes. For sellers of freight services–traditional "transport" providers now best described as third party logistics providers or fourth party service providers. They provide the outsourcing service of reverse logistics to the companies, intervene between buyer or shipper and customer–the focus on value delivery in competitive markets and are underlying urgent attempts to expand control over freight activities and to capture an increased share of value over the entire movement chain. It is resulting in rapidly restructuring corporate and value delivery systems. Therewith,

Please use the following format when citing this chapter:

Ji, G., 2007, in IFIP International Federation for Information Processing, Volume 254, Research and Practical Issues of Enterprise Information Systems II Volume 1, eds. L. Xu, Tjoa A., Chaudhry S. (Boston: Springer), pp. 135-143.

over the last several years, changes in environmental laws and the new returns demands of market returns have raised the requirement for effective reverse logistics to a new level, reverse logistics issues are gaining justifiable popularity among society, governments and industry worldwide. They are mainly regulatory-driven in Europe, consumer-driven, market-driven and profit-driven in North America and in incipient stage in other parts of the world, including China, where both consumer awareness and globalization are likely to lead to greater economic, consumer and regulatory pressures in the coming future. Only very recently, some companies in consumer durables' and automobile sectors in China have introduced exchange offers to tap customers who already own such products. Presently, these returned products are either resold directly or after repair and refurbishment by firm franchisee/ local remanufacturers in the seconds' market. They are not remanufactured or upgraded by original equipment manufacturers (OEMs). In Chinese society is particularly price sensitive and to a little extent quality sensitive (quality for a given price) but not environment sensitive in its buying and promotion behavior in past years. Therefore, reverse logistics has not received the desired attention and is generally carried out by the unorganized sector for some recyclable materials such as paper and metal. As well, manufacturers must deal with returns from retailers, the channels of distribution, or end customers with warranty issues. To the cement supply chains, they are faced with environmentalist, so they must consider return activities, such as exhaust emission and waster disposal, dismoded cement recall etc. For example, in 2005 there was more the emitted cement tunnage's amount than two cement factories outputs, reported by Chinese News. In 2001 there were about 40 million desktops and mobile Personal Computers sold. About 9 million (23%) of these were sold through retail stores. The retailer experienced a return rate of about 10% or 900,000 Units. Each of these units is estimated to cost the retailer $40-$50 to process and ship back to the manufacturer or to dispose of the units. The manufacturers estimate that each return costs them about $500 each. This adds up to a whopping $486 million. Each return is taking the manufacturers from 4 to 12 weeks to fully process. Returns are a small percentage of sales for the retailer or manufacturer, however, in high volume environments like consumer goods, this small percentage adds up to a large reverse logistics problem [1].

The term closed-loop supply chain (CLSC) has not appeared as such in the literature on supply chain and operations management until the beginning of this century. Several authors have spoken of 'reverse supply chains', a topic which was mainly discussed in practitioner circles [2]. However, a clear definition of CLSC only seems to have emerged thereafter. In their earlier work, CLSCs for refillable containers, photocopier remanufacturing and the re-use of consumer electronics are discussed in [3]. Probably the first contributors in designing a CLSC were Thierry et al. with their model of an 'integrated supply chain' [4]. This chain of companies has been defined as a supply chain, which comprises service, product recovery, and waste management activities. In this model, products return from the end-user to undergo a product recovery operation, such as re-use, repair, remanufacture or recycling. Thereafter, products are integrated back into the 'forward' supply chain. CLSC Management includes processes and operations that can not be found in conventional supply chain management. Krikke et al. explain that a CLSC consists of a forward and a reverse chain [5]. Guide and Van Wassenhove [6] further add that the additional activities the reverse supply chain includes comprise product acquisition, reverse logistics, test, sort, disposition, refurbish as well as distribution and marketing. While there are a variety of theoretical considerations for conventional supply chain management, there is still a lack of a theory for CLSC management, particularly with regard to the additional elements that the reverse supply chain incorporates. The rapid change of science and technology results in the diversity reduction which based on the production cost and the core technology. CLSC management has become an important strategy for enterprises and even countries to seizure the global plateau. With the industrial ecology issues are extensive popularity among the fields of society, government and industry etc. such as 3R (reducing, reusing and recycling) strategies, cost-saving ecological ideas and programmes, green teams and so on. On the other hand, the leading actors in today's markets have transformed from sellers to buyers, whether or not meet customers' individuation demands become an important factor to show enterprises' talents in the competitive environment. The concept of virtual enterprise was proposed by Kenneth Preiss, Steven L. Goldman, and Roger N. Nagal in 1991 in their report called "21st Century Manufacturing Enterprises Strategy: An Industry-Led View" [7]. The way of only depending on a single enterprise to respond rapidly to changing market opportunities and intensely global competition have been inapplicable. The key technique determined by utilizing agile manufacturing practices is based on virtual enterprise. CLSC operation management is restricted by the cost, the practice, and the human resource etc. Considering the environmental consciousness and the policy impact, the outsourcing for the segmental activities (such as reverse logistics) of CLSC is the better selection for the enterprises driven by economic profit. In order to make full use of the third provider services' advantage, virtual enterprise will be most appropriate.

The concept of exergy, a parameter in thermodynamics, was presented at first by Z. Rant in 1956. With several decades of development, the exergy analysis has become the basic theory and a useful tool in analyzing the energetic system and has obtained attention and application widely. Thermodynamics considered economics appears the exergoeconomics. Based on the theory of exergetic cost, it is applied in design analysis and optimization, operation optimization and diagnostics etc. Exergy has been proved to be suitable as a common quantifier of the sustainability of a system by Marc A. Rosen et al. and Ibrahim Dincer, etc [8]. Supply chain management by using exergoeconomics is nearly a new field. Based on the traditional exergoeconomics theory, Bai et al. [9] introduced environment effect factor as the measurement of supply chain system evaluation considered the sustenance of environment and resource. However, there are limitations in identification of the coefficient and no case study supported.

In this paper, an operation management mode for CLSC based on virtual enterprise is presented in this paper. The organization framework, the operational process, the dynamic durative of virtual enterprise, and the comparison with traditional management mode are expounded in detail. Based on the exergoeconomics theory, the sustainability of CLSC system is discussed, and then the metric about "system negative environment effect" is introduced to measure CLSC system performance in the point of energy, a case study illustrates our conclusion.

2. VIRTUAL ENTERPRISE AND CLSC OPERATION

2.1 The Framework of Organization

The difficulties of CLSC management are enlarged by lots of partners and their flexibility. Hence a "leader enterprise or organization" is necessary to administer the virtual enterprise, namely the core enterprise. The sponsor manufacturer always plays the role of core enterprise; the reverse activities depend on the fourth service provider is also an appropriate option.

Comparing with the traditional organization structure, the virtual enterprise organized by two layers (core enterprises and non-core enterprises) is flat, availing interaction of partners. The flat structure is easy to respond the rapid changing market, as well as to eliminate the information distortion effectively. There are three main reverse logistic functions: collection, inspection/sort, and reprocessing. Collection refers to bringing the products from the customer to a point of recovery, including return, transportation, and storage. At this point the products are inspected, i.e. their quality is assessed and a decision is made on the options of disposal, according to that the products are sorted. The disposal of reprocessing includes the following options: direct reuse, repair, recycling, remanufacturing and harmless disposal. The type of recovery can be separated between product recovery, component recovery, material recovery and energy recovery. The abovementioned functions are necessary for CLSC. Based on virtual enterprise operation, subdividing the functions to several independent enterprises by integrating their core competencies is just the advantage we seek for, e.g., lowering cost, evading risk, etc. Therefore, the organization frame of CLSC operation management based on virtual enterprise can presented, as shown in figure 1.

2.2 The Process of Operation Management

Table 1 depicts the process of CLSC operation management based on virtual enterprise, which follows four phases:

Identifying opportunity: In order to utilizing the rapid response attribution of virtual enterprise with respect to the uncertainties of CLSC, enterprises in CLSC have to track the trends of market development timely. A mass of collected data using for forecasting should be from enterprises, customers, industries, markets, legislation and so on. The useful information will be evaluated relative to reliability, worthiness, feasibility.

Constructing organization: Based on abovementioned, virtual enterprise means the integration of the core competencies for participating in supply chain. Therefore identifying the core competency, evaluating the alternative enterprises and estimating the entire performance are crucial, that directly influence the operation efficiency of CLSC. The core competencies concerning CLSC reflect return channels, logistics capabilities, research & development technology, manufacture arts and crafts, assets proprietary etc., determined by the relevant decision support system (DSS). Information system and the logistics network are necessary absolutely to support the virtual enterprise.

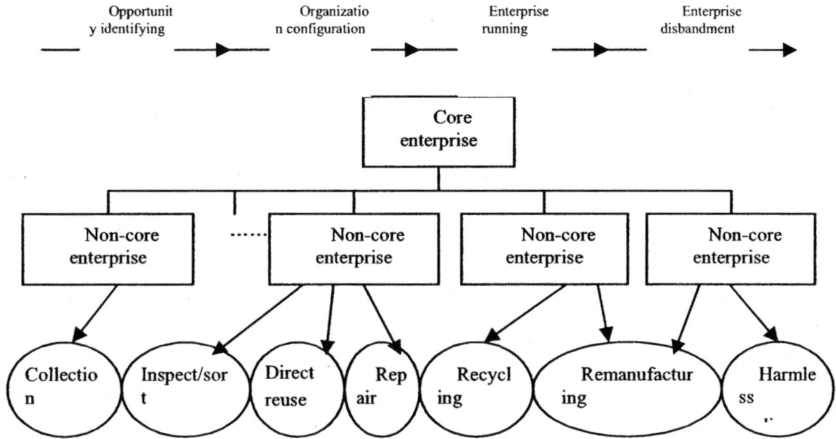

Figure 1. The Organization Framework of Virtual Enterprise for CLSC

Table 1. The Operation Management Mode of CLSC Based on Virtual Enterprise

Opportunity identifying
✓ information collection ✓ data mining ✓ analysis and estimate
Organization configuration
✓ the core competency identifying ✓ evaluating and selecting partners ✓ the information system and CLSC network ✓ estimating the holistic performance
Enterprise running
✓ coordination mechanism ✓ dynamic contract ✓ risk identification and control ✓ monitor system and improvement
Enterprise disbandment
✓ the assets liquidation ✓ knowledge management

Organization operation: The organization form of virtual enterprise is at the expense of coordination among partners. It implies that the excellent organization management is the precondition of virtual enterprise operation. The operation management is extended to the application of coordination mechanism, dynamic contract by stages, risk identification and control etc. As the dynamic developing, examine the operation status continuously, and improve the process according to the feedback.

Organization disbandment: The disbandment of virtual enterprise takes place after the disappearance of market opportunity. There is the assets liquidation among partner enterprises. The knowledge management runs through the whole operation management of virtual enterprise.

3. MODEL INTRODUCED AND CASE STUDY

Firstly, the exergy analysis is extended to take the environmental impacts of CLSC system into consideration. CLSC system influences the environment because of the waste discharged by it which includes two parts: one is from the emitted heat; the other is the physical exergy and chemical exergy of the waste itself. However, the various components in the wastes, with different chemical nature, bring different harm to the environment. A harm coefficient can be defined to denote this. Environment negative effect is defined as ENE , $ENE = \sum_i B_i E_{x,i}$, where $E_{x,i}$ denotes the physical and chemical exergy of the component i in the system's wastes; and B_i is the harm coefficient of component i to the environment.

Secondly, the exergy analysis can be extended to assess the comprehensive effect of CLSC system considered resource and environmental impact. So, while dealing with the total effect of CLSC system, the exergy discharge loss should be considered twice, resource waste in the total exergy loss of the system, and impact on the environment in the ENE . However, the resource waste and the environment pollution can not be considered as equal, so the effect coefficient is introduced to use here. The system negative effect (SNE) is defined as $SNE = C_1 E_{xl,tot} + C_2 ENE$, where, $E_{xl,tot}$ is the total exergy loss of the system; C_1 and C_2 are the effect coefficients. It is difficult to determine the effect coefficient of the system's negative effect, since resource waste cannot be compared with environmental pollution in a direct way. To solve this problem, the economic losses often are used to determine the effect coefficients. Let the exergy loss of the system represents as $E_{xL} = \Delta M + \Delta P + R$, where ΔM is the material loss of the system, ΔP is the product loss of the system, and R denotes the residual of the system. Then the economic loss caused can be calculated by the equation that $E_{eL} = \sum E_{xL} P_{in}$, where P_{in} denotes the average input exergy cost of the system.

SNE is an absolute variable, which can be used to evaluate different models of the systems with the same type or the different designed systems, but cannot be used to evaluate the different types systems. So a relative variable $SNEF$ is defined as $SNEF = \frac{SNE}{E_{x,in}}$, where, $SNEF$ is factor of SNE , and $E_{x,in}$ denotes the system's input exergy.

We consider that two cement CLSC systems, A and B, are as follows. The flow charts of system A and B are shown in figure 2.

In succession, using by exergoeconomics and in view of the resource utilization and environmental impact, the calculation and analysis of the sustainability of the abovementioned cement CLSC systems performance is considered as follows.

(1) Calculate the input exergy, the output exergy, the whole system exergy and the physical and chemical exergy of all wastes in these two CLSC systems. Since the harm coefficients are hard to determined, we use the emissions limit for secondary standard in Cement Factory Atmosphere Emissions Standard constituted by China Environment Protection Department (GB 4915-1996) as the harm coefficients. So the environmental negative effect in supply chain system A is

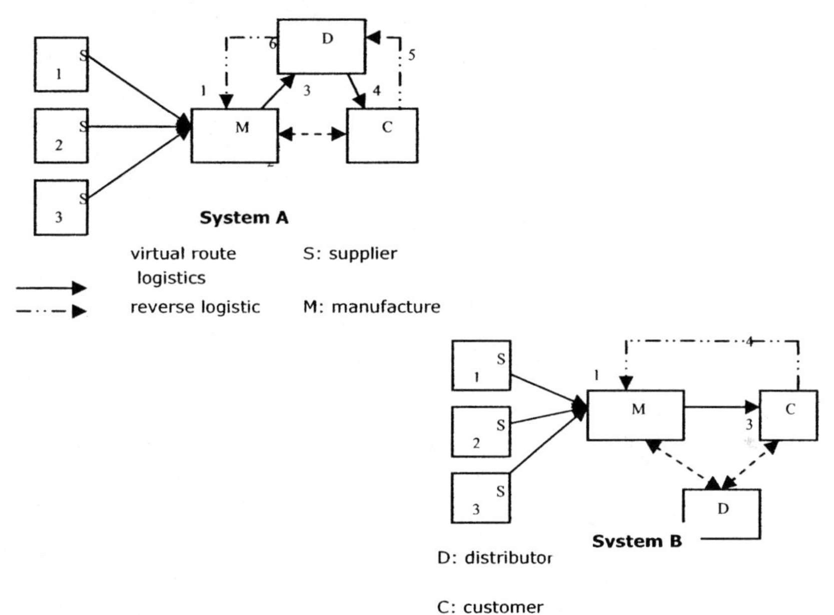

Figure 2. Flow Charts of Cement CLSC Systems A and B

$$ENE = 0.00006 \times 10^{6} \times 0.9 + 21.1318 \times 10^{6} \times 1.0$$
$$+ 0.0006 \times 10^{6} \times 2.4 + 0.2376 \times 10^{6} \times 0.03 = 2.12 \times 10^{7}\, kj / T$$

and that in system B is $ENE = 4.57 \times 10^{6}\, kj / T$.

(2) Calculate the economic loss caused by resource waste. It can be deduced by the average input exergy cost of a system multiplying the total exergy loss of the system. So the economic losses of resource waste in system A is 1,590,800￥/a, and that in system B is 1,538,000￥/a.

(3) Calculate the economic loss of environmental impact which caused mainly by the powdery dust, CO_2, SO_2 and other oxides emitted from the cement CLSC system. It can be divided into two parts, one is the influence on the natural environment and the other is that on human health. It is hard to quantify the economic loss of the natural environment caused by the system. To some extent, the pollutant penalties are established by the Environment Protection Departments, the processing cost to handle the contamination in the factories, cost of dust catcher and cloth for enveloping the powdery dust on trucks can reflect the approximate costs, so we can use the sum of these to denote the economic loss of environment effect in cement system A is 222,000￥/a, and that in system B is 191,000￥/a.

The economic loss caused by the influence on human health can be calculated by the sum of direct and indirect economic loss. Cement powdery dust is a kind of harmful substances. Once one inbreathe it at the definite amount can result in diseases, such as lung disease, and it deteriorates the working ambience. Direct economic loss concludes medical cost, income loss and cost on dust protection measures for workers. Indirect economic loss is comprised of economic loss based on work delay and food pollution. Therefore, the economic loss of human health caused by both cement CLSC systems is 24,710￥/a. And then we can calculate the total economic loss of the cement supply chain system A is 249,410￥/a, and that of system B is about 215,710￥/a.

(4) So, we can calculate that, for system A, SNE is 2.888 and $SNEF$ is 0.0174; for system B, SNE is 0.272 and $SNEF$ is 0.0016.

The calculation process and results show that the system negative effect factor can finally evaluate the resource utilization and environmental influence in CLSC system which are the two key aspects of the sustainability and can be used as an objective to further optimize CLSC. The results show a less effect coefficient of environment negative effect. This is because that in the method effect coefficient is calculated by economic loss. In the present system of price and pollution penalty, the resource waste plays a primary role in system negative effect. But with the increasing recognition of the environmental protection, much more restrict criteria of contamination discharge will be issued. Besides, the need for CLSC forces companies to think more of the reverse logistics. If not be responsible for the whole product life cycle, company will be punished or even excluded from the market place. Therefore, the proportion of the influence to the environment will rise as well.

It can be seen from the results that the main contamination released by the cement supply chain system is cement powdery dust. So the system should be improved by reducing the outgoing of powdery dust, for example, utilizing the advanced dust catcher and regulations for envelopment of the trucks and route or time period for the loading trucks. The negative effect coefficient of cement CLSC system B is much less than that of system A, this means that system B is much better than system A in sustainability. It can be easy to see that cement flow in system A is more complicated than system B, thus resource waste increases, environment aggravates. In fact, according to reported in Chinese News, there are released amounts more than two cement factories annually. Therefore, sustainability of CLSC system decreases and system performance gets worse.

ACKNOWLEDGEMENTS

This work is supported by new century outstanding talent plan in Fujian.

REFERENCES

1. G.J. Ji, Market-motivated value systems, reverse logistics and the evaluation model for the third party reverse logistics providers, *International Logistics and Trade*. Volume 4, Number 1, pp.53-92, (2006).
2. Morrell and A. L., The forgotten child to the supply chain, *Modern Materials Handling*. Volume 56, Number 6, pp.33-36, (2001).
3. V.M. Smith and G.A. Keoleian, The value of remanufactured engines, *Journal of Industrial Ecology*. Volume 8, Number 1-2, pp.193-221, (2004).
4. M. Thierry, M. Solomon, N.J. Van, and W.L. Van, Strategic issues in product recovery management, *California Management Review*. Volume 37, Number 2, pp.114-137, (1995).
5. H.R. Krikke, J.B. Ruwaard, and L.N.V. Wanssenhove, Concurrent product and closed-loop supply chain design with an application to refrigerators, *International Journal of Production Research*. Volume 41, Number 16, pp.3689-3719, (2003).
6. V.D.R. Guide and L.N.V. Wassenhove, *Business Aspects of Closed-Loop Supply Chains: Exploring The Issues* (Carnegie Mellon University Press: Pittsburgh, PA, 2003)
7. P. Kenneth, L.G. Steven, and N.N. Roger, *21st Century Manufacturing Enterprises Strategy: An Industry-Led View* (Leihigh University Press: New York, NY, 1991)
8. Y.F. Wang and X. Feng, Exergy analysis involving resource utilization and environmental influence, *Science in China (Series B)*. Number 1, pp.86-95, (2001).
9. S.Z. Bai, X.J. Zheng, and S.B, Wang, Application of exergoeconomics in supply chain management, *Logistics Technology*. Volume 10, Number 1, pp.1-2, (2005).

A Study on the Relationship Between ERP Logic and Direct Consume Coefficient of I/O Table

Lingling Zhang[1], Jun Li [2], Qin Wang[3], Rencheng Tong[4], Yuejin Zhang[4] and Xingsen Li[4]

[1]School of Management, Graduate University of Chinese Academy of Sciences, Chinese Academy of Sciences, Research Center on Data Technology and Knowledge Economy, Beijing, 100080, P.R. China zhangll@gucas.ac.cn
[2]School of Management, Graduate University of Chinese Academy of Sciences, Chinese Academy of Sciences; Research Center on Data Technology and Knowledge Economy, Beijing 100080, P.R.. China lijun@huatai-serv.com
[3]Institute of Computing Technology of the Chinese Academy of Sciences, Beijing 100080, P.R. China wangqin@ict.ac.cn
[4]School of Management, Graduate University of Chinese Academy of Sciences, Beijing 100080, P.R. China tongrch@gucas.ac.cn zhangyuejin05@mails.gucas.ac.cn lixingsen@126.com

Abstract. The paper analyzes necessity and possibility of integrating ERP with Input-Output technology (I/O). It studies relationship between ERP logic and the direct consume coefficient of manufacture enterprise I/O table, and proves that it is feasible to convert basic data of ERP to direct consume coefficient and entire consume coefficient of enterprise I/O table. It also proves that it is convenient to use ERP basic data to make manufacture enterprise I/O table, and to analyze and improve decision making.

Keywords: *Workflow net (WF-net), Workflow model, Colored petri net, Agent, Workflow resource management, Business process analysis*

1. INTRODUCTION

Enterprise Resource Planning, ERP, has been widely used by international manufacture enterprise as an information system recently. But, with the development of the innovation and technology progress, and the counterchange of the market demand, some function of traditional ERP can't satisfy the needs of a few enterprises. It mainly behaves like this, the operation model's dynamic ability to meet emergency and decision sustain is too bad, the building circle is too long, as well as the cost is too high. Those result in the difficult of the population and success of EPR.

In order to solve those problems, this paper brings forward some thinks about the applying of enterprise I/O technology into ERP. Contrast ERP and enterprise I/O model, they have some communications in the referring objects, inside logic, main functions, and the ranger they deal with. For these reason they have the possibility to associative. But they emphasize particularly on different things. Thus, to apply the enterprise I/O model into ERP have several advantages. On one hand, we can utilize

Please use the following format when citing this chapter:

Zhang, L., Li, J., Wang, Q., Tong, R., Zhang, Y., Li, X., 2007, in IFIP International Federation for Information Processing, Volume 254, Research and Practical Issues of Enterprise Information Systems II Volume 1, eds. L. Xu, Tjoa A., Chaudhry S. (Boston: Springer), pp. 145-152.

this modern model technology to systems analysis, afford many kinds of administer information, strengthen the ability of decision-making and sustain, flexible, optimize and dynamic ability to meet emergency of ERP. On the other side, as to I/O model, it also combines with strongly ERP , making use of the company technology to real time manage mass of information in enterprise, strengthen its maneuverability in enterprise, achieving the predominance mutualism.

To implement the aims just referred, many problems should be settled first. The chief problem is the feasibility of the associative of ERP and I/O technology. As to I/O model, through accounting and analysis of the manufacture course, make plans of the enterprise, as well as offering some bases on enterprise decision-making, the first thing is to make I/O table, which is the key and foundation to utilize I/O model. But how to get data conveniently and truly is the key to make I/O table. From the research discover, the ERP logic ,which is the foundation of ERP, has huge comparability with consume relationship of I/O Table in principle, can implement the conversion between ERP foundation data and I/O table, which assure the feasibility of directly make I/O table from the ERP intrinsic data and make ground for the further research.. This paper will discuss this topic.

ERP has been widely used by manufacture enterprise as an information system recently. Meanwhile, the research on machine enterprise I/O model is mature. This paper studies the relationship between ERP logic and the direct consume coefficient of machine enterprise I/O table, and proves that converting basic data of ERP to direct consume coefficient and entire consume coefficient of enterprise I/O table is feasible. And it is also feasible using the basic data of ERP to make the I/O table, to analyze and improves decision.

2. ERP LOGIC, RELEVANT DEMAND, CONSUME OF ENTERPRISE I/O TABLE

Doctor Joseph A. Orlicky, IBM, divide materiel into Independent demand and Dependent demand. He thought the materiel requirement in product framework is relevant. In his theory , it contract accessory、discreteness、parts、whole、raw and processed materials, considering different materiel has different match relation. And, bring time subsection into materials stock station. On the bases of main manufacture plan, bill of materiel and stock station, make sure of the demand time-sharking. MRP in 60s, closed loop MRP in 70s, MRPII in 80s and ERP in 90s are all based on this. Thus, no matter how strong the ERP is, the base of it is relevant demand theory.

Material requirement planning is not only a technique for planning "material" requirements. It is also a logic that relates all the activities in a company to customer demands. People can manage all the resources in a company by using MRP logic together with data processing in other areas. This entire system is called a Manufacturing Resources Planning System, or MRP II. With the introduction of technological enhancements such as open systems platforms and client/server architecture, MRP II systems are now evolving into Enterprise Resource Planning Systems (ERP). An ERP system plans not only the allocation of manufacturing resources but also other resources, and has applications in service as well as manufacturing industries.

Nature of Demands All systems are implemented to satisfy customers' demand. There are different sources of demand for a product and its component items. Some item requirements are determined by the needs of other items while others are specified by customers. The former requirements also come from customers, but indirectly. Item requirements can be classified as dependent and independent demands.

Independent demand Demand for an item that is unrelated to the demand for other items. Demand for finished goods, parts required for destructive testing, and service part requirements are examples of independent demand.

Dependent demand Demand that is directly related to or derived from the bill of material structure for in other items or end products. Such demands are calculated and need not be forecasted. Concretely to say, the relevant demand means that, a kind of materiel demand is directly relevant to another kind, or can be directly calculated by other materiel. In ERP, relevant demand embodied by product framework, while product framework is described by BOM（Bill of Material）. So, BOM（Bill of Material）is important data in ERP, it embodies the relationship among finally items and the parts, the module, the accessory and raw and processed materials.

As for this case, from the BOM, we can conclude that when produce a ball-pen, it will cost a ball-hat. However, when produce a ball-hat, it will cost 0.005g PE, others can analogy like this. Thus, we can get all the costs if we produce a ball-pen (the parts, the module, the accessory and raw and processed materials, frock mould). But all the functional modules in ERP contain produce and manage module, stock module, repertory manage module, finance manage module, which were built on basic data. So we can say ERP is the same with the produce condition that making accessories into output when considering enterprise's type. MRP is a Manufacturing Resources Planning System of parts. As long as to make out the main manufacture plan, any manufacture enterprise can use MRP.

So from the analysis, the Consume relation detonated among materiel by BOM has the following characteristics.

1) Consume relation among materiel is unilateralism. Any machine manufacture produce can be described like the parts, the module, the accessory and framework of raw and processed materials. Consume relation detonated among materiel is from the top down. For example, the accessory as the most important portion, only cost raw and processed materials, but not modules、parts、and finished product. Modules cost only accessory and raw and processed materials but not parts. Others like this.

2) Consume dosage among materiel is indicated in substantiality, show every connection of quantity dependence, all use substantiality as unit.

3) Manufacture framework and Consume relation is each independent but between then are associate. From chart 1, Manufacture framework reflects machine manufacture enterprise layered product framework and organizing character, which framework is dendriform, having father item, children item. Similarly, BOM can be expressed like multilayer BOM, but also father item, children item BOM, which distinctly describe the constitution and consume of every accessory, parts, and module. When detached, they each have its absolute system. Ball-pen's components ball-hat's BOM, and ball-core, writing skill also have their monolayer BOM.

4) BOM not only describes the Consume relation among materiel, but also describes the Consume relation with frock mould during the materiel process.

5) BOM has greatly agility. When designing software, it can add attribute when necessary. Whether the attributes are abundant and complete is an important scale to measure whether ERP is strong.

3. MACHINE MANUFACTURE ENTERPRISE SUBSTANTIAL I/O TABLE AND CHARACTERISTIC

The I/O table of enterprise is based on the manufacture characteristic and using require. Setting corresponding module in the table to describe the consume and occupy in every resource by Self manufacture. Commonly, it is need to set ① Consume relation matrix about self manufacture to self manufacture to describe the technical and economic contact among them; ②Consume relation matrix about self manufacture to external manufacture to describe the consume relation of external manufacture.; ③Consume relation matrix about self manufacture to charge to describe the consume relation to charge; ④Consume relation matrix about self manufacture to manufacture equipment and hour to describe the consume relation to equipment and hour.

Compared with other enterprise, machine manufacture enterprise have some vivid characteristic: ① The output of machine manufacture enterprise is mostly assembling framework, to be divided into four layers , accessory, parts, module, and complete product according to process. Their execution process is in layer and sequence. Their consume relation is unilateralism, no converse contact. ② The complexity of machine manufacture is mainly behaved into accessory ,module, parts and the variety of the technology. Accessory is different with the framework and the capability, its process arts and flow are different. ③ The character of the machine process is the consume of energy sources , frock module and labor hour mostly happen with carrying equipment, the equipment can be divided into currency and expert. ④ Besides process hours ,tool, apparel, mole, jamming of cartridge and mould (can be called by a joint name frock mould) are absolutely necessarily in machine manufacture enterprise , a great deal of them is made by enterprise itself. ⑤ the reckon of machine manufacture enterprise is too great, from the request of management, it is necessary to account exactly the consume by every process and frock mould to element and the cost .

Table 1 is machine manufacture enterprise substantial I/O table. It contains 6 matrixes. ①self manufacture × self manufacture consume relation matrix. Self manufacture is divided into four layers according to the characters of machine manufacture enterprise, accessory, parts, module, and complete product according to process. ②self manufacture × frock mould consume relation matrix., to describe the consume relation of frock mould. ③self manufacture × raw and processed materials consume relation matrix, to describe the consume relation to raw and processed materials, which only behaved by accessory. ④self manufacture × energy sources consume relation matrix, to describe the consume relation to energy sources. It mostly happen with carrying equipment. ⑤self manufacture × labor hour consume relation matrix, to describe the consume relation to labor hour. ⑥ self manufacture × equipment process hour consume relation matrix, to describe the consume relation to equipment.

If a_{ij} express dosage when yielding unit materiel j .(substantiation)

In I/O model, direct consume coefficient express the consume to product and labor when manufacturing unit substantial product. For example the self manufacture × self manufacture direct consume coefficient matrix:

$\tilde{a}_{ij} = \tilde{q}_{ij} / \tilde{Q}_j$ express the dosage of substantial product i when yielding unit materiel j

$\tilde{a}_{ij}$ is direct consume coefficient about j to i, express the dosage of substantial product i when yielding unit substantial product j . $\tilde{Q}_j$ is the output of j during the reporting period. Other direct consume coefficient in direct consume matrix are analogized like this.

Table 1. Machine Manufacture Enterprise Substantial I/O Table

Input / output		Interspace				Finally product	Totally output
		accessory	module	parts	complete product		
self manufacture	accessory	q_{ij}				$\tilde{\gamma}^i$	$\tilde{Q}_i$
	module						
	parts						
	complete product						
frock mould		$\tilde{Z}_{ij}$					
raw and processed materials		$\tilde{G}_{ij}$					
energy sources		$\tilde{W}_{ij}$					
labor hour		$\tilde{T}_{1ij}$					
equipment process hour		T_{2ij}					

If $\tilde{b}_{ij}$ express the total dosage of product i when yielding unit self manufacture j

$$\tilde{b}_{ij} = \tilde{a}_{ij} + \sum_{k=1}^{n} \tilde{a}_{ik}\tilde{a}_{kj} + \sum_{s=1}^{n}\sum_{k=1}^{n} \tilde{a}_{is}\tilde{a}_{sk}\tilde{a}_{kj} + \cdots\cdots \qquad i.j = 1,2\cdots n$$

$\widetilde{a}_{ij}$ is direct consume coefficient , the latter are first second……indirect consume coefficient, using $k,s\cdots$ as agency. As to table 1, the equation above first quadrant can be written like matrix as follows:

$$\widetilde{B}=\widetilde{A}+\widetilde{A}^2+\widetilde{A}^3+\widetilde{A}^4+\cdots=(I-A)^{-1}-I$$

$\widetilde{A}$、$\widetilde{B}$ are direct consume coefficient matrix and totally consume coefficient matrix

4. THE RELATION AND TRANSFORM BETWEEN ERP LOGIC AND CONSUME COEFFICIENT

From the analysis above, Machine manufacture enterprise substantial I/O model is emphasize produce and process, recognize product as analyze object. Every element in matrix in table 1 separately described the consumption and occupy of the self manufacture to kinds of resources during the process. ERP is built on the bases of independent demand and dependent demand. ERP system plans not only the allocation of manufacturing resources but also other resources, and has applications in service as well as manufacturing industries. In nature, both are coherent. We can reduce them into table 2.

Table 2. ERP Logic and Enterprise Substantial I/O Model

Element	ERP logic	Enterprise substantial I/O model
Industry	Machine manufacture enterprise	Machine manufacture enterprise
Expressing element	a_{ij} : express dosage when yielding unit materiel j	$\widetilde{a}_{ij}=\widetilde{q}_{ij}/\widetilde{Q}_j$ express the dosage of substantial product i when yielding unit materiel j
Express	Consum relationship among meteriel and to all kinds of resources	The consume and occupy of self manufacture to all kinds of resources
Source	Dosage attribute in BOM	$\widetilde{a}_{ij}=\widetilde{q}_{ij}/\widetilde{Q}_j$
Express mode	Substantiation	Substantiation
Consume relationship	Unilateralism	Unilateralism
To totally consume	No describetion	Described by total consume coefficient

There is the relationship above, so we can clearly to elicit:

$$\widetilde{a}_{ij}=a_{ij}$$

Thus, in practicality handle, we can use BOM in ERP to directly transform into direct consume coefficient A in I/O table. And we can get B from $B=(I-A)^{-1}$ .Using ball-pen as an example, we get direct consume coefficient matrix when transform the BOM. Then we can get the totally consume coefficient matrix. It is easy in computer.

The characters when transforming into direct consume coefficient from BOM:

1) Through ERP data sharing and transforming directly, we get the direct consume coefficient in the quadrants in enterprise substantial I/O table .They are in reason, and the results are right and feasible.

2) Through transforming, we can use another mode to describe the direct consume relation, which is avail to plan the manufacture. Using pen-core for example, from the rows, besides ball-pen is 1, other direct consume coefficient to pen-core is o. From the lines, ball-core has consumed to pinpoint, pen-oil, pen-pipe and pen-core assemble center, there are 1piece, 0.002kg, 1piece, and 0.0025kg. The whole direct consume coefficient express all materiel's consume to other resources and other materiel.

3) From direct consume coefficient matrix A we can get totally consume coefficient matrix B . Direct consume coefficient matrix describe all materiel's consume to other resources and other materiel during the process, which is avail to plan the manufacture. Totally consume coefficient matrix describe the all materiel's consume to all the other materiel during the process. Using ball-pen for example, the most right line describe he all materiel's consume to all the other materiel during the ball-pen process. It describe the substance consume relation during the process in another angle, which is avail to manage analyze and make decision.

4) The course of ERP foundation data transforming into direct consume coefficient is exact and rapid.

5) We can go on manage sustain and decision-making sustain, for example, whole cost reckon and analyze, fix a price, consume analyze, balance the ability of equipment

5. CONCLUSIONS

Using enterprise I/O model to calculate and analyze the process, and to offer thereunder for enterprise when making decision, the first thing is make I/O table, which is the key and foundation to utilize I/O model. This paper studies the relationship between ERP logic, discuss the feasibility when transforming the ERP foundation data into the direct consume coefficient and totally consume coefficient in I/O table. We can see ,if the products are complex and various, this transform can converse mass data into the corresponding element in I/O table and making table automatically according some rules. And, the transformed I/O table can contain more things than ERP foundation data. Meanwhile, utilizing the analyis and account of I/O model, we can get the data to sustain manage decision. This study makes ground for further research.

ACKNOWLEDGEMENTS

This research has been partially supported by grants from National Natural Science Foundation of China (No. 70501030 and Innovation Group 70621001), and Beijing Natural Science Foundation of (No.9073020).

REFERENCES

1. J.E. Hunton, B. Lippincott, and J.L. Reck, Enterprise resource planning systems: comparing firm performance of adapters and nonadapters, *International Journal of Accounting Information Systems*. Number 4, pp.165-184, (2003).
2. A. Lee, Researchable directions for ERP and other new information technology, *MIS Quartely*. Volume 24, Number 1, pp.3-7, (2000).
3. V.A. Mabert, A. Soni, and M.A. Venkataraman, Enterprise resource planning survey of US manufacturing firms, *Production and Inventory Management*. Volume 41, Number 2, pp.52-58, (2000).
4. P. Bibgi, M.K. Sharma, and J.K. Godla, Critical Issues Affecting an ERP Implementation, *Information System Management*. Volume 16, Number 3, pp.7-14, (1999).
5. R.J. Murray and D.E. Trefts, The IT Imperative In Business Transformation, *Information System Management*. Volume 17, Number 1, pp.1-6, (2000).
6. T. Rencheng, The Input-Output Table with Two Factors, *Chinese Economic Planning and Input-Output Analysis* (Oxford Univ. Press), p.19.

On Bill of Knowledge Resources during ERP Implementation

Jiagui Zhong, Hui Li, Yanhui Chen and Yang Wu

School of Information, Renmin University of China, Beijing 100872, P.R. China
zhongjg@ruc.edu.cn lihui504819@sina.com chenyh_0418@yahoo.com.cn
wuyang1017@yahoo.com.cn

Abstract. It is the key of whether the ERP system can be applied successfully to definitude, organize and manage the knowledge resources during ERP implementation scientifically. In this paper, we use the analyzing method of project management to formulate the basic plan of ERP implementation. Based on that, we analyze the required knowledge according to the phases of ERP implementation, elaborate the knowledge from many angles, and form the bill of knowledge resources. This will help enterprises to make the knowledge resources plan during ERP implementation, guide their practice, and increase the success rate and efficiency of ERP implementation.

Keywords: *Enterprise resource planning, Knowledge management, Project management*

1. INTRODUCTION

ERP (Enterprise Resource Planning) is an administrative thinking and method of modern enterprises. It is market and customer demand-oriented, to optimize resource allocation and eliminate all the null and void labor and resources in the process of production and operation, so as to achieve the organic integration of information flow, material flow, capital flow, value flow and the business flow [1]. Nevertheless, the success rate of ERP Implementation is not very high. How to implement ERP successfully has always been a difficult problem confusing enterprises, software vendors and consulting firms.

In this paper, we firstly establish a plan for the implementation of the project mainly according to the basal processes of ERP Implementation for enterprises, using the theory of project management. Basing on that, we extract the different knowledge resources required in each stage of implementation from the perspective of knowledge management, then illustrate them from various angles, and bring forward the concept of bill of knowledge resources during ERP Implementation with a detailed plan for acquiring and applying the knowledge.

Please use the following format when citing this chapter:

Zhong, J., Li, H., Chen, Y., Wu, Y., 2007, in IFIP International Federation for Information Processing, Volume 254, Research and Practical Issues of Enterprise Information Systems II Volume 1, eds. L. Xu, Tjoa A., Chaudhry S. (Boston: Springer), pp. 153-161.

2. THE FLOW AND THE INITIAL SCHEDULE OF ERP IMPLEMENTATION

We usually manage ERP implementation as a project, which can be divided into two phases, the preparation phase and the implementation phase [2]. Given the implementation phase is the main part of the lifecycle of ERP implementation, we focused our study on this stage. Following the theory of project management, we set down the initial schedule of ERP implementation, as shown in figure 1. The width of the blue rectangle in the figure denotes the relative length of time, the beginning and the end of each process.

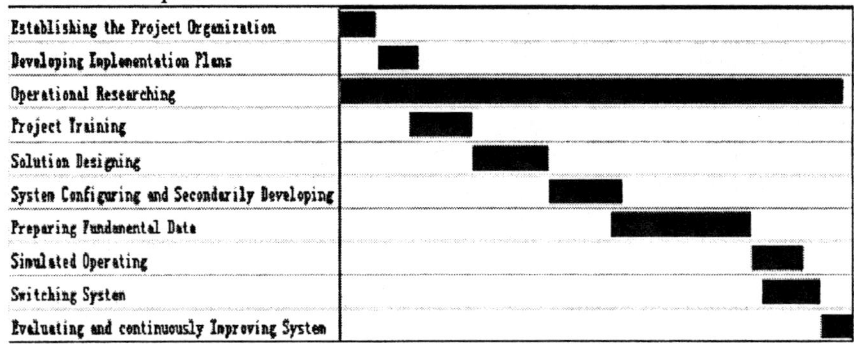

Figure 5. Initial Schedule of ERP Implementation

3. BILL OF KNOWLEDGE RESOURCES

Figure 1 clearly shows the key processes of ERP implementation and correlations of these processes. In the following paragraphs, we will point out the main knowledge that is required by the enterprises during ERP implementation, elaborate the knowledge from various angles of view, and finally form the bill of knowledge resources.

3.1 Establishing the Project Organization

According to the actions during ERP implementation, we divide the organization of the project into three levels, the leading group, the implementing group and the applying group. The required knowledge is as follows:

3.1.1 Project Management Knowledge

The project management in this phase mainly involves human resource management. We fractionalize the work using the method of Work Breakdown Structure (WBS), and manage human resource according to the requirements of the fractionized work as well as the employees' competence, which requires a project manager with rich experience.

3.2 Developing Implementation Plans

In this phase we should make out the concrete plans for the following implementation. The required knowledge is as follows:

3.2.1 Project Management Knowledge

Firstly, we should definitude the object of the project and the exact implementation range. Then we can map out the schedule of the project with sufficient estimations of the changes and risks that may occur, and the consulting firm should bring forward a prevention solution. Therefore, this knowledge is partly from the enterprise and partly from the consulting firms.

3.2.2 Financing Management Knowledge

According to the initial cost and budget plan and the schedule of the whole project, we make out the concrete plan for controlling the cost and the budget. Although we can get this knowledge from books, it is impossible to master it during the short time of setting down the implementation plans. Therefore, enterprises require the accountants who have mastered the knowledge.

3.2.3 Computer Software Application Knowledge

With the help of computer software assistant tools, we can break down the work, make out schedules, manage human resource, work out the concrete implementation plans and follow up the execution. For instance, the Microsoft Project is one of the most useful tools. Similarly with the knowledge of financing management, this requires the excellent technicians.

3.3 Operational Researching

Operational Researching is a process that enterprises and cooperators (consulting firms, software vendors) join together to understand the business flow of enterprises. The required knowledge is as follows:

3.3.1 Human Resource Management Knowledge

In this part, our emphasis is the investigation and analysis. We should be clear about the organizational structure, jobs offered and responsibilities of each department to make sure the following work can go smoothly.

3.3.2 Business Flow Knowledge

We should accurately identify the business of the enterprises, make the business flow clear, and collect relevant bills of document, report forms, etc. A little part of the knowledge is apparent, which we can get from books. But the main part depends on the accumulated experience of relevant staffs.

3.3.3 Investigation Knowledge

We should choose the appropriate one according to the circumstances. And the execution processes require kills. Therefore, the investigators with rich experience are required.

3.3.4 Document Management Knowledge

After investigations and repeated discussions with the departments, we will gain the business flow documents of each department, such as ledger, receivables, payables, assets, stocks, distributions, etc, then compile them and make reports of current business situations, in order to make good data preparations for the following work.

3.4 Project Training

ERP is a normative system. However, only with our management, it can work effectively. The training has two meanings, education and exercises. The former emphasizes particularly on principles and conceptions, mainly explaining "why we should work in this way, what are necessaries, what are benefits". The later emphasizes particularly on application methods, mainly explaining "how to do". The required knowledge is as follows:

3.4.1 Training Management Knowledge

The training is supported by consulting firms and software vendors. The implementing group should be trained about the functions of the software; the applying group should be trained about manipulating techniques. At the same time, the training should be carried out step by step.

3.4.2 Expert's Thinking and Experience

The experts who are invited as training instructors can pour the required knowledge and skills into relevant staffs in different degrees. This embodies the progress of knowledge transfer.

3.5 Solution Designing

Basing on the third phase, an appropriate solution scheme should be designed according to the current circumstances and future demands. The required knowledge is as follows:

3.5.1 Organizational structure of the Enterprise Knowledge

Enterprises should optimize and rebuild their organizational structures rationally according to the characteristics of their business, including administrative levels, business functions, etc, to make their business implementation more effective.

3.5.2 Business Requirements Knowledge

In this phase, we should definitude enterprises' different business requirements, match them with the functions of the software, decide whether to make a secondary development, and form the complete solution scheme. Therefore, the knowledge we need emphasize investigation. And we should pay attention to the accuracy of the materials.

3.5.3 BPI or BPR knowledge

ERP implementation should be combined with BPI or BPR. We should build a rational and orderly administrative system, organizational structure, and working methods to operate the implementation smooth. The knowledge required is usually from consulting firms, with cooperation with the enterprises.

3.5.4 Professional Consulting Skills

Implementing consultants should guide the project teams to make practical simulations under a testing environment, train all members about the application of the software, discuss the feasibilities of different schemes, and report results to the leading group to be examined and approved.

3.6 System Configuring and Secondarily Developing

To install the system, the users should firstly set users' privileges and other basic information, and then secondarily develop or improve and reorganize the business process according to the designed solutions. The required knowledge is as follows:

3.6.1 Software System Application Knowledge

Technical staffs from software vendors are required to assist business staffs to install the system and set parameters according to the concrete conditions of the enterprise.

3.6.2 Secondary Development Knowledge

When the software and the actual situations do not match, and the former may be polished less easily to match the latter, we should secondarily develop the system. In this situation, the knowledge required is mainly from software vendors who will make specific solutions for the secondary development.

3.6.3 Business Process Reorganization (BPI) Knowledge

Once small-scale secondary development of the software can not solve this problem, the business process of the enterprise should be reorganized. The relevant knowledge is mainly from consulting firms, who will guide the implementation by virtue of their experience wealth.

3.7 Preparing Fundamental Data

The preliminary data preparation is a key to guarantee correct operations of the system. Relevant knowledge includes the extraction of the basic data, transaction data entry, data coding, the use of information technology tools and the progress of project management.

3.7.1 Fundamental Data Extracting Knowledge

The fundamental data includes basic material information, product structure information or BOM, product process, accounting subjects, basic staff information, customer data, vendor data, etc. To avoid data leakage, the work should be completed by the enterprise itself. In addition, attention should also be paid to the accuracy and integrality of the data.

3.7.2 Transaction Data Entry Knowledge

Transaction data includes sales orders, purchase orders, inventory information, financial information, etc. And these dynamic data should be formally input in the system switching stage.

3.7.3 Data Coding Knowledge

Every item of data to be input into the computer should be classified and coded. Usually, this is done by consulting firms.

3.7.4 Information Technology Tools Using Knowledge

Information technology tools will significantly increase the efficiency to manage the massive data. It's up to the enterprise itself to choose an information technology tool and recruit or train related operators.

3.7.5 The Progress of Project Management Knowledge

In the data preparation phase, the benefit of the new system is not notable. Therefore, it should be shorten by a restraint system in the enterprise.

3.8 Simulated Operating

After the customization or secondary development, a practical operation simulation is necessary, including the software functions simulation, the practical operation simulation and the parallel operation. The relevant knowledge includes system testing and document management.

3.8.1 System Testing Knowledge

During the testing stage, users should hear software vendors detailing the functional parameters of the system and input representative data to maximize the testing scope of the system. At the same time, software vendors should correct the system faults arising from bugs. Therefore, this work should be completed by the enterprise with supports from software vendors.

3.8.2 Document Management Knowledge

Archive the records of the simulated operation process, which can offer the basis for further improvements. Accuracy and integrity is still the basic principles in this phase.

3.9 Switching System

The running of the ERP system is a switching process, during which the new one gradually replaces the old one. The required knowledge is as follows:

3.9.1 Switching Modes Choosing Knowledge

According to the actual situations of the simulated operation, there are three switching ways, direct, parallel, and grading. As a highly integrated system, the direct one may be the best choice considering the integration of information. Even for the grading one, business processes should not be split to avoid destroying information integration. To ensure a smooth switching work, it should be completed under the guidance of consulting firms.

3.10 Evaluating and Continuously Improving the System

After the system runs successfully and sustains a period of stable operation, we should evaluate and continuously amend the system to make it more effective. The relevant knowledge includes project evaluation and BPI.

3.10.1 Project Evaluation Knowledge

We can evaluate the operation from many aspects, such as the integration of the systems, the rationalization of business processes, dynamic performance monitoring, and the continued improvement in management, etc. What's more, as an asset of the enterprise, return of investment should be taken into account. In order to ensure the validity of the evaluation results, enterprises should hire professionals to complete the work.

3.10.2 BPR Knowledge

To improve the efficiency of the system, enterprises should firstly achieve automations with human resource liberated, and then improve its business processes, optimize them or even make some major and fundamental changes, which can be called BPR.

4. HOW TO GET THE KNOWLEDGE RESOURCES ABOVE

According to Armstrong and Novins, enterprises should not only concern with the content of the knowledge but also distinguish them according to their sources and characteristics.

To enable enterprises to obtain relevant knowledge more easily, we sum up three major sources for the knowledge above, consulting firms, software vendors and enterprises themselves, and divide the knowledge from two dimensions, sources of the knowledge and steps of ERP Implementation. The results are shown in table 1.

Table 1. Knowledge Resources List

Knowledge Resources		Knowledge Sources		
		ERP Consulting Firms	ERP Vendors	User Enterprises
Steps of the ERP Implementation	Establishing the Project Organization	Project Management		
	Developing Implementation Plans	1. Project Management 2. Computer Software Applications		Financial Management
	Operational Researching	Investigation		1. Human Resources Management 2. Business Process 3. Document Management
	Project Training	1. Training Management 2. Expert's Thinking and Experience	1. Training Management 2. Expert's Thinking and Experience	
	Solution Designing	1. BPI or BPR Knowledge 2. Professional Consulting Skills		1. Organizational Structure of the Enterprise 2. Enterprise Business Needs
	System Configuring and Secondarily Developing	BPR Knowledge	1. Application of the Software System 2. Secondary Development	
	Preparing Fundamental Data	Data Coding		1. Fundamental Data Preparing 2. Transaction Data Entry 3. Information Technology Tools Using 4. Progress of the Project Management
	Simulated Operating		System Testing	1. System Testing 2. Document Management
	Switching System	Switching Modes Choosing		
	Evaluating and continuously Improving System		Project Evaluation	BPR Knowledge

5. CONCLUSIONS

Successful project management and knowledge management is prerequisite to a successful ERP implementation. In the paper, we apply the theory of project management and knowledge management synthetically. Based on the key processes of ERP implementation, we list the detailed knowledge required during the implementation, and form a bill of knowledge resources. The significance of this paper lies: Through providing such a bill of knowledge resources to enterprises which need to implement ERP system, it will make them definitely understand the knowledge required during implementation. And through illustrating the relevant knowledge from different angles, it will help enterprises fully comprehend the knowledge and apply it better, and help build the knowledge system of ERP implementation and finally integrate it into the enterprise culture, which will improve the success rate of ERP implementation and bring greater competitive advantages and economic benefits for enterprises.

ACKNOWLEDGEMENTS

This paper has been financed by Information Economy and Information Management Key Laboratory of Ministry of Education of China. The project name is The Simulation of Knowledge Flow: Research of Knowledge Innovation based on CAS, and the project number is F0607-18.

REFERENCES

1. L. Xie and A. Wu, The execution and exploration on enterprise's ERP project, *Journal of Changchun University*. Volume 16, Number 6, pp.22-, (2006).
2. J. Zhu, N. Lu, and H. Wei, *Enterprise Resource Planning,* pp.195-228 (Guangdong Economy Press: Guangzhou, Guangdong, 2006).
3. Q. Chen, *ERP—Step Forward from Internal Integration,* pp.289-290 (Electronic Industry Press: Beijing, 2005).
4. Anonymous, *Ten main points of ERP implementation planning*, Setways (2005). http://www.ithook.com/html/2005-03-08/20050308_02704.html (Accessed July 15, 2007).

Dynamic Ontology for Supply Chain Information Integration

Wei Yang[1] and Fan Yang[2]

[1]Computer School, Wuhan University, Wuhan 430072, P.R. China
william_yang2005@163.com
[2]School of Information Management, Wuhan University, Wuhan 430072, P.R. China
yzf_613@163.com

Abstract. In this paper, ontology technology is applied to Supply Chain information integration, in order to provide unified interface for semantic data and to share, reuse knowledge among information resources. Ontology can solve well the semantic heterogeneity problem of distributed, heterogeneous and autonomous data sources; and the problem of semantic interoperability. Since the objects on Supply Chain are highly dynamic and unpredictable, the information to be integrated is often changing along with the objects, which means that the corresponding ontology also needs to be changed. The process and methods how supply chain dynamic ontology changes is mainly discussed.

Keywords: *Supply Chain (SC), Information integration, Dynamic ontology, Global ontology, Local ontology*

1. INTRODUCTION

As the development of E-Commerce and information technology, SC becomes more and more agile: the architecture of SC changes rapidly according to the diverse and individual requirements of customers; competition shifts from among enterprises to among SCs; SC management in internal enterprise has extended to the whole industry chain; the resource management has extended too, from internal enterprise (eg. ERP) to external (B2B); the cooperation of enterprises on chain becomes more and more closer--from VMI (Vendor Managed Inventory), JMI (Jointly Managed Inventory) to CPFR (Collaborative Planning, Forecasting). The agility of SC boosts enterprises to constitute Dynamic Alliance, which can integrate information among different enterprises and can easily merge the one that wants to join the alliance into SC information system [1].

Information integration among enterprises on SC is the foundation of the whole SC integration, which means information share among internal and external members on SC. The information includes anything that may affect the behavior of other SC members. Since every enterprise on SC has its own information center, database, operation system, application software and user interface that are always separate from others, many *isolated information islands* emerge. The principal task of SC is to break the isolation and to increase the interoperability of application. It is urgent to integrate these SC data resources that are distributed in physical condition, autonomic

Please use the following format when citing this chapter:

Yang, W., Yang, F., 2007, in IFIP International Federation for Information Processing, Volume 254, Research and Practical Issues of Enterprise Information Systems II Volume 1, eds. L. Xu, Tjoa A., Chaudhry S. (Boston: Springer), pp. 163-172.

in management and heterogeneous in model and to make these SC data can be understand by the computer. To deal with these problems, we introduce the ontology into SC information integration in this paper. Ontology can precisely define knowledge concept and the relationship between them [2], therefore, it can effectively reduce ambiguous understanding, promote information integration and realize information sharing of SC. Ontology provides the guarantee to each node enterprise to communicate conveniently so that improves the operational efficiency of SC enterprises.

There are many researches on ontology building and integration. So far, the main methods of building ontology include TOVE [3], METHONTOLOGY [4] ENTERPRISE [5], KACTUS [6], SENSUS [4], IDEF5 [7], SEVEN STEPS [8] etc. At present, the study on ontology integration has been launched. Reference [9] studied ontology integration from the linguistic point of ontology language, reference [10] studied from the architecture of integration and reference [11] studied from the association of ontology library.

SC is dynamic, so the information integration objects are continuously changing, so is virtual organization ontology. That is, SC ontology is dynamic. In this paper, how to build ontology is not the main concern, but the process and method of how SC dynamic ontology changes are discussed.

2. SC DYNAMIC ONTOLOGY

2.1 The Origin of SC Dynamic Ontology

The SC is a complex, separate and dynamic network system, of which information increasingly presents its characteristics, such as, high heterogeneity, large quantity, dynamic content and distributed data sources. In view of this point we use ontology to integrate information. SC ontology is dynamic, continuously changing, so we called it dynamic ontology in this paper.

SC is dynamic, which is its main characteristic, because the node enterprises on SC need constantly changing according to business strategy and fluctuation of market requirement.

2.2 The Cases of Dynamic Ontology Changing

This paper studies on the process of ontology changing, on condition that original ontology already exists. It emphasizes on the changes of ontology when the internal and external environment have changed. There are cases of environment changes as following:

1. The user has changed the requirement of SC. E.g. some product has been eliminate in the competition, the SC want to produce new product.

2. Technology transforms. E.g. using new technology resulted in SC structure changing.
3. SC node enterprises have changed. E.g. some collaborators quit, and new collaborators enter.
4. The internal structure of SC node enterprise has changed. E.g. a node enterprise wants to add a new department.

In summary, there are two kinds of environment changing: SC structure changing and SC node enterprise changing.

2.3 The Content of Dynamic Ontology Changing

According to section 2.2, SC environment changing contains two aspects, so the SC ontology changing from two aspects. The changes of SC structure correspond with the changes of global ontology, e.g. adding a distribution enterprise. The changes of SC members correspond with the change of local ontology, e.g. carrying out personnel restructuring in manufacturing enterprise. Figure 1 shows the SC changing (E. stands for Enterprise), and figure 2 shows the corresponding ontology changing (O. stands for Ontology).

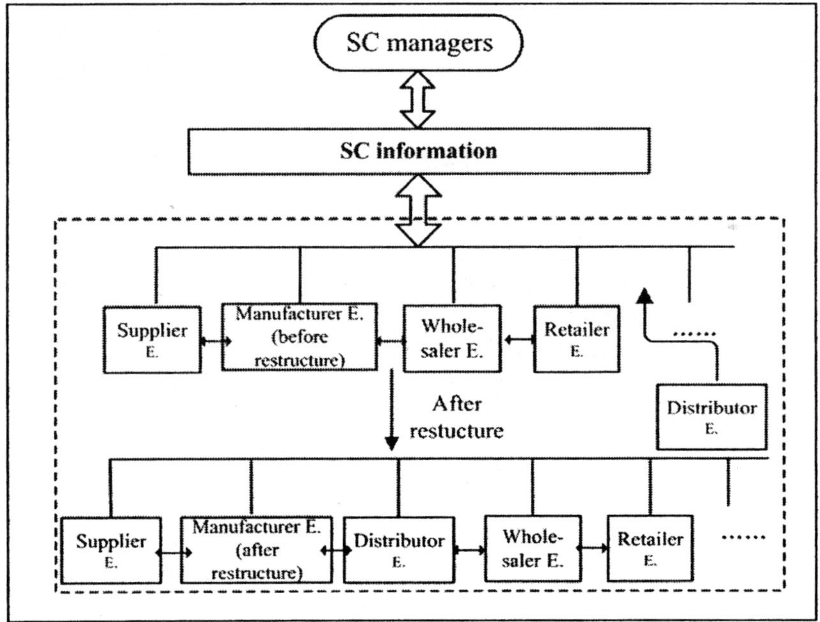

Figure 1. The SC Changing (E. Stands for Enterprise)

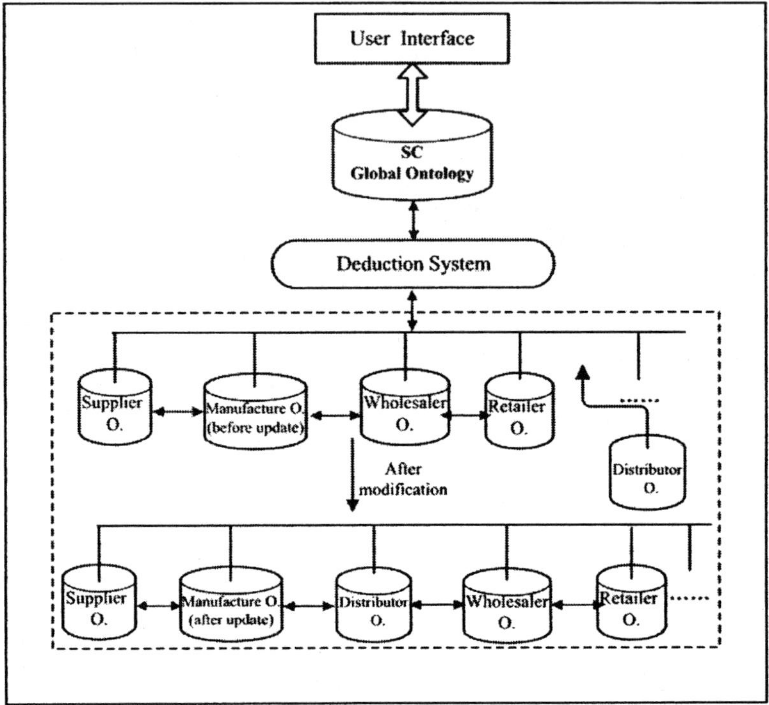

Figure 2. Ontology Changing (O. Stands for Ontology)

3. THE METHODS OF DYNAMIC ONTOLOGY CHANGING

According to the analysis in above sections, there are two kinds of SC ontology changing: global ontology and local ontology, each one needs its suited method.

3.1 The Method of SC Global Ontology Changing

The changing of SC global ontology includes adding, deleting and updating each node enterprise (member) on SC. The character of adding is the same as deleting; deleting is the contrary process of adding; so this section mainly discusses the method of adding objects. The method of updating objects will be discussed in the next section about local ontology changing, for a SC ontology object is a local ontology.

Adding an ontology object means integrating a new ontology object into the global ontology. This process uses the theory in PowerLoom deduction system [12] and OTPM [13]. New ontology can be added based on the degree of similarity or dissimilarity among terms. In this paper, we use similarity to form new global ontology. We take integrating distributor ontology into SC ontology for an example. We only discuss a certain part abstracted from the actual ontology, for the actual one is very complex. The method how to add distributor ontology is illustrated in detail with the following figures.

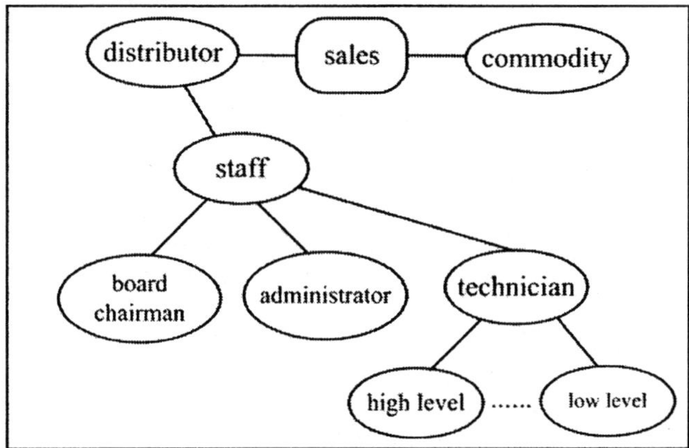

Figure 3. Distributor Ontology P (Abstract from Real Distributor Ontology)

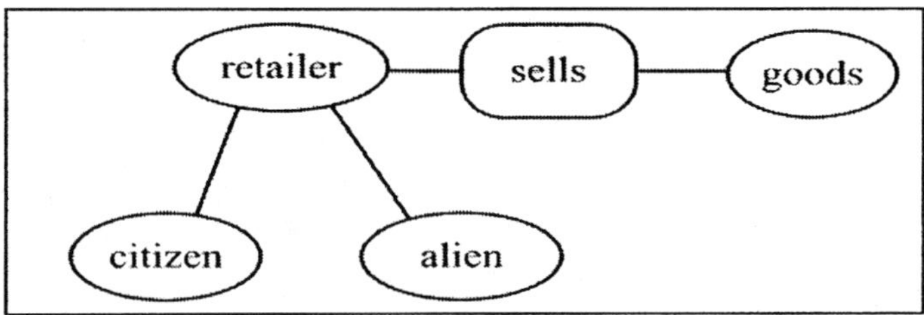

Figure 4. Retailer Ontology Q (Abstract from Real Retailer Ontology)

There are four levels of similarity degree among term connotations: equivalence, specialty, overlap and disjointness. Two terms, pt and qt, respectively belongs to distributor ontology p and retailer ontology q. $\oint$ stands for the mapping from the term to its connotation. The relationship between term pt and qt are defined as follows:

1. Equivalence.

pt and qt are equivalent, that is pt = qt. If and only if their connotation's definitions are the same:

$$(pt=qt)\Leftrightarrow(\oint[pt] \equiv \oint[qt]) \quad \textbf{(1)}$$

For example, *commodity* in Fig.3 distributor ontology and *goods* in Fig.4 retailer ontology, their connotations are the same, so the two terms are equivalent, that is *commodity=goods.*

2. Specialty.

pt is a specialty of qt, that is pt≤qt . If and only if their connotations' intersection is the same as the term pt's connotation:

$$(pt \leqslant qt)) \Leftrightarrow ((\oint[pt] \cap \oint[qt]) \equiv \oint[pt]) \tag{2}$$

For example, *staff* in Fig.3 is a specialty of *distributor* in Fig.4, that is *staff≤ distributor.*

3. Overlap.

pt and qt overlap, that is pt∽qt, if and only if their connotations' intersection is not null (connotations' intersection concept T is always true).

$$(pt \backsim qt) \Leftrightarrow (((\oint[pt] \cap \oint[qt]) \equiv \oint[T]) \wedge \neg \oint[T] \equiv False) \tag{3}$$

For example, *staff* in Fig.3 and *alien* in Fig.4 overlap, that is *staff∽alien.*

4. Disjointness.

pt and qt disjoint. If and only if their connotations' intersection is null:

$$\neg(pt \backsim qt) \Leftrightarrow ((\oint[pt] \cap \oint[qt]) = \Phi)\ (\Phi \text{ stands for null}) \tag{4}$$

For example, *staff* in Fig.3 and *goods* in Fig.4 are two disjoint terms.

There are several integration regulations, too. Disjointness doesn't matter much with integration, so we don't discuss this case in this paper.

5. **Regulation 1.** Equivalence integration. If two terms' definition D1 and D2 are equivalent, we can combine these two definitions into one (D1 or D2). E.g. *commodity=goods*, so we can use *commodity* only instead of *commodity* and *goods*.

6. **Regulation 2.** Specialty integration. If definition D1 is a specialty of definition D2, we can build the special relationship between them. E.g. *staff≤distributor.*

7. **Regulation 3.** Overlap integration. If definition D1 and D2 overlap, we can create 3rd definition D3 to stand for their intersection. D3 can have its instance or not, it depends on the experts. E.g. *staff∽alien*, we use new definition *foreign staff* instead of their intersection. Foreign staff has no instances.

According to the above regulations, we join distributor ontology (shown in Fig.3) and retailer ontology in SC global ontology (shown in Fig.4) into a new SC global ontology (shown in Fig.5).

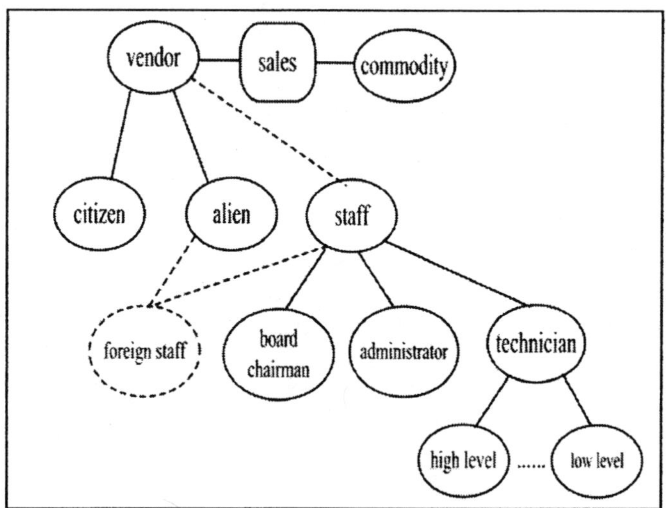

Figure 5. The Result of Adding Distributor Ontology into SC Global Ontology (Abstract from the Real One)

3.2 The Method of SC Local Ontology Changing

Local ontology means certain domain ontology, such as manufacture ontology and distributor ontology etc. We can also call it member ontology. At present, this topic attracts many attentions. There are several ways to call ontology changing, for example, ontology evolving and ontology updating etc. But they are the same in nature; all of them modify ontology concepts and the relationship among them, in order to suit the changing environment. M. Klein and D. Fensel bring forward that ontology changing contains three aspects: changing in domain, changing in concept, changing in regulation [14]. Compared to SC global ontology changing, local ontology changing is more detailed in recent researches.

There are many methods of local ontology changing [15, 16]. We use *OWL-Oriented Evolution of the Ontology*, referring to [17]. This method describes the relationship among concept, slot and side. It achieves the Related-Concept set of changing objects through *Get-Related-concept* algorithm, and updates through *Change-Related-Concept* algorithm. In view of SC, changing should place mainly on concept, instance and application of the ontology that needed modification. E.g. to carry out personnel restructuring in manufacture enterprise, we should change concepts and corresponding relationships involving in personnel.

4. THE CHANGING PROCESS MODEL OF SC DYNAMIC ONTOLOGY

In the above sections, we introduce the reason, content and methods of SC dynamic ontology changing. To sum up, we put forward the changing process model of SC dynamic ontology. This model also consists of two kinds of updating: SC global ontology and node enterprise (member) ontology, as shown in Fig.6.

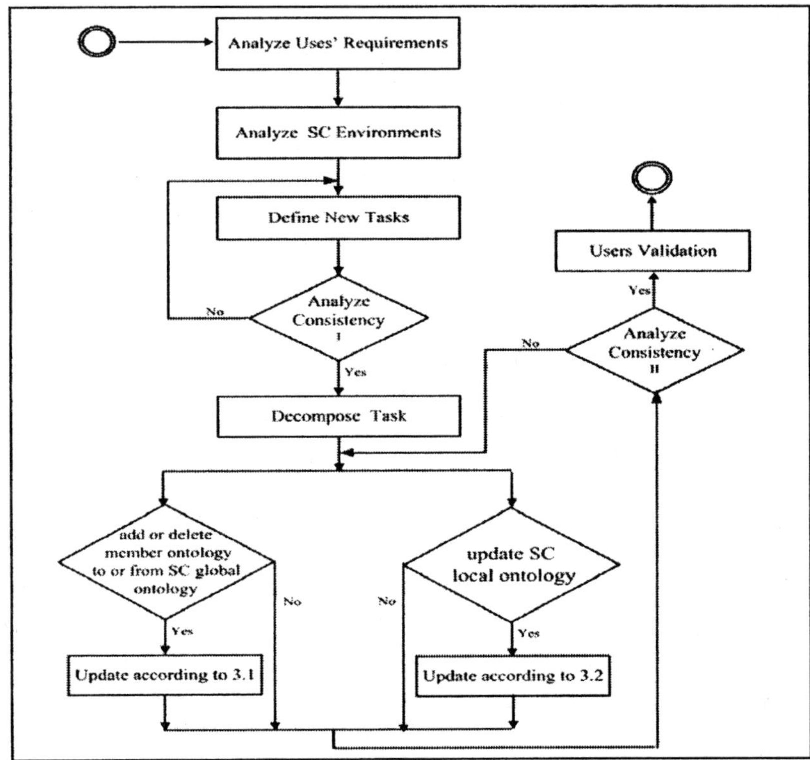

Figure 6. The Changing Process Model of SC Dynamic Ontology

In figure 6, at first, the users ask for changing ontology. Then, the ontology managers analyze the requirements of users and the internal and external environment of SC. Subsequently managers define ontology changing task. If the task is complex enough, it should be disassembled. If global ontology of SC needs changing, it could be changed following the method discussed in section 3.1; else if local ontology of node enterprise needs changing, it could be changed following the method mentioned in section3.2. Finally, the users check the updating results. If users validate, SC dynamic ontology changing will finish. If there are other requirements, the next updating cycle will begin.

Consistency analysis, which aims to reduce conflicts, appears twice in the process model. It deals with semantic conflicts among ontology concepts, data error of instances and function error of applications caused by ontology changing. But the tasks of the two kinds of consistency analysis are not the same with each other. The former one occurs before the implementation of changing. It analyzes all kinds of conflicts, which may be occurred while in updating process of SC system, to make sure the feasibility of ontology changing. The latter one occurs after the updating tasks. Its task is to ensure the consistency of the whole SC system.

In this paper, the changing of dynamic ontology is emphasized, so the way in which ontology changes is mainly described in the process model. Other topics of dynamic ontology, such as bulletin management and version management, are not mentioned.

5. CONCLUSIONS AND FUTURE WORK

In this paper, the research background is SC, and we mainly study its dynamic ontology. Through the example of adding distributor ontology to SC global ontology and implementing personnel restructuring in manufacture department, we analyzed the origin, reason and content of dynamic ontology changing, bought forward the corresponding method and suggested the dynamic ontology changing process model. All changing issues focus on two aspects: global ontology of SC and local ontology of node enterprise.

In this paper, the examples abstracted from the actual ontology are very simple, but the actual ones are much more complex and can change at different granularity [16]. Therefore, we should pay more attention to the popularization of content, process and method discussed in this paper, and we will study the applicability of SC dynamic ontology changing regulations in future.

REFERENCES

1. D. Fensel and C. Bussler, The Web Service Modeling Framework WSMF, *Electronic Commerce Research and Applications*. Volume 1, Number2, pp.113-137, (2002).
2. T.R. Gruber, *A translation approach to portable ontology specifications*, Tech Rep: Logic-92-1, Stanford University (1993).
3. M. Gruninger, Designing and Evaluating Generic Ontologies, in *Proc. of ECAI96's Workshop on Ontological Engineering* (1996), pp.53-64.
4. M. Fernándz, Overview of Methodologies for Building Ontologies, in *Proc. of IJCAI99's Workshop in Ontologies and Problem Solving Methods: Lessons Learned and Future Trends* (1999).
5. J. Stader, Results of the Enterprise Project, in *Proc. of the 16th Int. conference of the British Computer Society Specialist Group on Expert Systems* (Cambridge, UK, 1996).

6. N. F. Noy, S. Kunnatur, M. Klein, and M.A. Musen, Tracking Changes During Ontology Evolution, in *Proc. of the 3rd International Semantic Web Conference (ISWC-04)*, (2004).
7. KBSI.IDEF5 *Ontology Description Capture Overview.* http://www.idef.com/idef5.html (Accessed October 1, 2003).
8. Natalya F. Noy and Deborah L. McGuinness, *Ontology Development 101: A Guide to Creating Your First Ontology* (Augest, 2001). http://protege.Stanford.edu/publications/otology_development/ontolog101.pdf (Accessed October 12, 2002).
9. M. Klein, Combining and Relating Ontologies: An Analysis of Problems and Solutions, in *Proc. Of IJCAI'01 Workshop on Ontologies and Information Sharing* (Seattle, WA, 2001), pp.53-62.
10. H. Wache and T. Vgele, Ontology-based Integration of Information--a survey of Existing Approaches, in *Proc. of the Workshop Ontologies and Information Sharing*, (2001).
11. M. Prasenjit, A Graph-oriented Model for Articulation of Ontology Interdependencies, in *Proc. Of EDBT'00* (Springer: Verlag, 2000), pp.86-100.
12. M.R. MacGregor, H. Chalupsky, and E.R. Melz, *PowerLoom Manual*, University of Southern California (November, 1997). http://www.isi.edu/isd/LOOM/PowerLoom/documentation/manul.pdf .
13. Y. Zhang, H. Zhang, and W. Zhang, Ontology-Based Information Integration Mapping Construction Between Global View and Local Views in Virtual Organization, *MINI-MICRO SYSTEMS.* Volume 3, Number 27, pp.253-257, (2006).
14. M. Klein and D. Fensel, Ontology Versioning on the Semantic Web, in *Proceedings of the International Semantic Web Working Symposium* (2001), pp.75-91.
15. G. Elouris, D. Plexousakis, and G. Antoniou, Evolving Ontology Evolution, in *SOFSEM 2006, LNCS 3831,* eds. J.Wiedermannetal (Springer: Verlag Berlin Heidelberg, 2006), pp.14-29.
16. L. Stojanovic, A. Maedche, B. Motik, and N. Stojanovic, User-Driven Ontology Evolution Mangement, in *EKAW 2002, LNAI 2473*, eds. A. Gómez-Pérez and V.R. Benjamins, (Springer: Verlag Berlin Heidelberg, 2002), pp.285-300..
17. M. Zhou, J. Gao, and F. Li, OWL-Oriented Evolution of the Ontology, *Journal of Computer-aided design &computer graphics.* Volume 3, Number 17, pp.584-591, (2005).

An Enterprise Content Management Solution Based on Open Source

Rogerio Atem de Carvalho

Federal Center for Technological Education of Campos (CEFET Campos), R. Dr. Siqueira, 273, Campos/RJ, CEP 28030-130, Brazil ratem@cefetcampos.br

Abstract. Spread out on the Internet, mail servers, and hard-drives everywhere, unstructured information in the form of Web pages, email, RSS feeds, office documents, images, video, and sound, accounts for approximately ten times the structured information stored in databases. Seeking to organize their large volume of non-structured content, companies implement Enterprise Content Management (ECM) systems to make this information more accessible for users and make these systems communicate with relational database backed solutions through a single interface. Small and medium enterprises (SMEs) and local governments also have the same need for unstructured information organization. However, most of times, they cannot afford the high acquisition and customization costs, or don't want to become dependent of proprietary ECM solutions. This paper aims to present NSI^2, an ECM solution totally built on top of open source software that offers the functionalities demanded by this kind of system.

Keywords: *Enterprise content management, EIS for public sector, Enterprise information integration, Open source, Small and medium enterprises*

1. INTRODUCTION

Scattered on the Internet, mail servers, and hard-drives everywhere, unstructured information in the form of Web pages, email, RSS feeds, office documents, images, video, and sound, account for approximately ten times the structured information stored in databases. The ever growing convergence of Information and Communication Technologies confirms this tendency for the years to come. Seeking to organize their large volumes of unstructured content and integrate them to the traditional, database backed enterprise systems, companies implement Enterprise Content Management (ECM) systems to make this information more accessible for users through a single point of access. Small and medium enterprises (SME), education and research institutions, and government organisms also have the same need for unstructured information organization and integration to foster their business processes and become compliant to regulations and modern accountability practices. However, most of times, they cannot afford the high acquisition and customization costs - or don't want to become dependent - of proprietary ECM solutions. This paper aims to present NSI^2, an ECM solution totally built on top of open source software, that offers all the basic - and some not so basic - functionalities demanded by this

Please use the following format when citing this chapter:

de Carvalho, R. A., 2007, in IFIP International Federation for Information Processing, Volume 254, Research and Practical Issues of Enterprise Information Systems II Volume 1, eds. L. Xu, Tjoa A., Chaudhry S. (Boston: Springer), pp. 173-183.

kind of system. NSI^2 is a play with the acronym of Information Systems Research Group (NSI in Portuguese, where it is developed), and Non-Structured Information (NSI).

This paper is structured as follows: after this introduction, the main issues on ECM and how NSI^2 address them are presented. Its content management structure comes next, followed by sections describing its infrastructure and current applications. Finally, concluding remarks are given on the last section.

2. NSI2 AND ENTERPRISE CONTENT MANAGEMENT

Enterprise Content Management (ECM) integrates the management of structured, semi-structured, and unstructured information, and related software and metadata in solutions for content production, publication, utilization, and storage in organizations [1], emphasizing the coexistence of technical and social aspects within the content management [2]. It is an emerging topic that have been attracting new commercial and academic players, including the professional forums such as AIIM International, which defines itself as "the ECM association" (http://www.aiim.org).

ECM is related to, and some times confused with, a series of other topics, which include Knowledge Management, Content Management Software, and Web Portals. However, it represents a new area since it focuses on the management of textual and multimedia content across and between enterprises, seeking to establish an integrated perspective on information management, through the integration of content with organizational databases and applications [1]. Moreover, like every enterprise-wide initiative, an ECM system deployment raises many issues. How NSI2 addresses issues identified by [1], [3], and [4], are now briefly discussed.

2.1 Return on Investment (ROI)

ROI is calculated as the present value of the benefits divided by the present value of costs [3], in other words, a combination of cost savings, improved profit margins, and sales enhancements. However, ECM ROI normally is associated to cost savings only. According to [1], these savings can be obtained through a composition of different cost drivers, like reduced time on information searching, lower printing costs, and multi-lingual technical publishing. On the other hand, other indirect benefits must be considered, like the need to answer to external and internal regulations and the development of future capabilities on enterprise systems technologies. Obviously, investment costs also must be taken into account [3]: software licensing fees, hardware and physical infrastructure, bandwidth, support, and management.

If the benefits can vary for each case, costs savings can be obtained for almost all cases – at least for small and medium deployments - by the use of Free/Open Source Software (FOSS) and commodity hardware. In fact, the sole use of FOSS, in general, reduce the Total Cost of Ownership (TCO) [5] [6] and, simultaneously, broaden the user base for a given solution [7]. Following this approach, NSI^2 is totally based on

FOSS components that can run on clusters of commodity hardware, since it is aimed at SME, educational institutions, and local governments. For these cases, cost has been a major hindrance to the widespread ECM adoption, in special in developing countries. Since NSI^2 is a young solution, detailed ROI calculations are yet to be obtained, but observed cost reductions on its first user organization is about 65% in hardware, and 100% in software licensing.

2.2 Content Model

The core of any ECM solution is to understand the role of content in the organization context [1]. According to [8], content is normally organized under two different approaches: database-based and document-based. The first evolved from the database community and consists basically of storing documents and their components as database objects, while the other emerged from the publishing communities, and consists basically of defining document templates. Relying on Zope, NSI^2 uses a hybrid approach, based on the concept of *typed content*, where document templates are defined as classes. Therefore, according to the specific necessities, a content element can be treated as a document or as an object. While keeping all the advantages of an object stored in Zope Object Database (ZODB), like versioning, use of semantic relations, semantic checking, and undo; for content producers it is a document that can be edited (using a built-in text editor) and exported as a XML object if needed. Objects are stored in a hierarchical folder structure, and are accessed through their URL, which is constructed from the server name followed by the object path in ZODB. Zope also offers default templates that provide different types of metadata that can be customized for specific uses. Following the types identified by [9], template sheets provide content (keywords, title, language and other Dublin Core fields), data lineage (date created, date modified, change log etc), and technical (content type, encoding etc) metadata. Using object-orientation, new types can be created by both composition and inheritance from basic template sheets.

2.3 Infrastructure

According to [1], for wide-scale ECM initiatives, information technology involves a number of challenges, all addressed by NSI^2:

1) Integration of standardized applications and tools: NSI^2 uses Zope's features on relational databases access and XML processing for integration with other applications. When needed, Python scripts can be implemented to build-up more sophisticated integration routines.
2) Developing user-friendly content management: the Zope based Plone Content Management system is used to manage content in NSI^2. This tool allows users to edit documents through the web, and specific workflows can be created to administer content publishing.
3) Updates in software and hardware (scalability): NSI^2 relays on a series of FOSS with strong developer communities that have been keeping the software up-to-date for years. In terms of hardware, clusters of commodity

hardware are used, which reduces costs and the need for more specialized support personnel.

4) XML and other open format compliance: although Zope has its own object-oriented storage formats and algorithms, it is possible to convert every object into a XML document. In the contrary way, XML objects can be easily converted into Zope objects.
5) Information security issues: content is secured through Zope's fine-grained and flexible access routines, built around the concept of "safe delegation of control", that allows to turn control over parts of collections of documents to certain user roles. More restricted security measures can rely on proxy roles, where a user only has the right to run a certain script that indirectly execute operations on ZODB.

2.4 Customization

Customization is a key issue for ECM, due to its considerable costs, being functional customization the main issue on this matter. ECM customization and can be divided in three main areas:

1) Content Model Management: functionality for structuring of content, metadata model, taxonomy, and templates.
2) Content storage and delivery management: user roles, versioning, classification, transformation, retention and tracking.
3) Process support and automation: workflows.

For the first two areas, besides taking advantage of Zope and Plone features, NSI^2 extends both to manage automatically fragments of documents and store huge collections of indexable objects, as will be seen afterwards in this article. Workflows are used as Zope offers them.

3. NSI2 CONTENT MANAGEMENT STRUCTURE

NSI^2 content management structure is built on top of Plone (http://www.plone.org), a Content Management Systems (CMS) based on the Zope (http://www.zope.org) object publishing and application server. Extensions are also provided to enhance the CMS capabilities of Plone. The next topics will discuss briefly each of these components of NSI^2.

3.1 Zope and Plone

Zope stands for the Z Object Publishing Environment, it is and open source web application server implemented in Python language, and can run on a variety of operational systems that include Unixes, Linux, Windows, and Macintosh. Zope offers an integrated solution for web applications that relies on an object oriented and transaction enabled database (ZODB), an administrative interface (ZMI), a web server, a search engine (Zcatalog), and a workflow engine. Also, it can connect to all major relational database management systems, work together with Apache, and is XML-RPC, DOM, WebDAV and other open standards enabled. It also offers more than three hundred plug-ins (called products) developed by the community, which address e-Commerce, content, integration with other tools and environments, helpers, internationalization, navigational, visualization, and user management. It also has around it a strong and active community of developers that interact through mail lists and wikis that account for thousands of entries a month. In other words, Zope supplies the entire infrastructure to develop web-based applications, in special, content-driven solutions, its original focus.

Plone is a CMS that works on top of Zope. It is highly extensible, with more than six hundred plug-ins for a variety of uses such as layout and presentation, versioning, communication, object storage, media management, project management, calendars, statistics, and many others. It offers all basic content types like folders, links, files, documents, events, images, news items, and dozens of more sophisticated types in the form of plug-ins. All content types have a rich metadata set associated to it, based on the Dublin Core Metadata Initiative (http://www.dublincore.org), providing content, lineage and technical metadata. Content objects can have keywords, historical data, type, and even discussion threads associated to them. Using specific plug-ins it is possible to have enhanced search options through the implementation of ontologies.

Plone is highly extensible and even users with very basic programming skills can create new content types, define views and security roles, and implement workflows to manage the new type. Using a code generation tool denominated ArchGenXML, it is possible to model in UML new sets of related content types, managed by specific workflows, and generate all the code necessary to implement a new application. Also, new layouts and default content views can be configured through a series of specific forms, liberating content managers of deep HTML knowledge. It also supplies basic accessibility features.

Analyzing other ECM and CMS solutions, like the one presented in [11], it is clear that the Zope/Plone infrastructure addresses all the basic features demanded by this kind of applications. More than that, it can be used to implement highly sophisticated Knowledge Management solutions [12].

3.2 NSI^2 Extensions

A Web Services based architecture [13] is envisioned for future developments of NSI^2, however, current efforts focuses on improving user experience and solution scalability, as described by the following topics.

Granular Document

An ECM system must be a content application tailored to a specific audience, instead of a limited search engine. According to [14], modern content applications should deal with the representation of semi-structured content – stored and indexed securely in a content repository. Following this reasoning, NSI^2 extends Plone with a new type, named Granular Document. Granular documents can be divided into grains or fragments according to their representation inside the document. For instance, a research article stored as granular document can have its paragraphs, tables, formulas, and figures indexed and accessed separately from the composite (the own document). This concept is related with the learning objects concept from distance learning [15] and fragment concept from caching of web pages [16]. The first concept refers to those pieces of information inside a learning content that can be identified themselves as smaller learning objects. Fragments are pieces of information that can be reused in different contents and, therefore, can be served and cached as such, reducing network traffic and I/O tasks, and also improving user experience.

Granular Document is implemented in a very straightforward way: the XML representation of a document is parsed for identifiable grains of information, like paragraphs, images and tables. These grains inherit the metadata from the owner document and also have their own metadata and text automatically associated in proper indexes. For instance, an image with a specific caption can be found through its owner document's full text and metadata, and also by its own metadata (for instance, related to its format) and the caption text. When a user opts for a granular search, he or she will get a results page with a hierarchy of documents and their respective grains. Granular search can be restricted by all kinds of metadata, like format, type, date of upload, author, and such, to reduce the result set size. Moreover, if ontology is in use, and the user also opts for an enhanced granular search, the grains inherit the semantic network associated to the owner document. In that way, it is possible to give users the option of a more focused search, like "return all images about fuzzy aggregation operators" – where image is the grain type and "fuzzy aggregation operators" the full text term to search for. If the search is based on ontologies, documents containing related terms and their grains would be returned too.

When created, a Granular Document object first converts HTML or MS-Office to XML and then parses it in the search for grains. Documents in ODT format, like the ones from Open Office, are unzipped and then parsed. The user can view and save documents and grains in plain HTML, PDF or in its original format. These options can be configured by the system administrator, according to the enterprise content reuse policies. It is important to note that, since grains are also objects, they are cached separately from their owner documents.

Self Service

Self-Service is a product that works on top of Granular Document and is similar to solutions like SafariU (http://www.safariu.com), which let users build new textbooks from parts of existent ones, providing automatic table of contents and index. Self-Service allows a user to search a NSI^2 catalog and tick the grains (or whole documents) of interest. Then Self Service will build a new document, in HTML or Open Office format, with the selected grains, including the source for each object and a complete reference list at the end. With this document the user will have a basis for creating new content, like reports, articles, news, and learning material.

Enhanced User

Enhanced User is a way of stimulating the continuous use of the solution, giving registered users (not simple guests) features like search storage, push and RSS services according to selected document categories, file and grain cabinet, polls and a series of customization options. Also included is a Personal Information Management (PIM) structure that can hold email with full text search (including in attachments, even when zipped), personal contacts, *personal* calendar, text notes, and instant messaging.

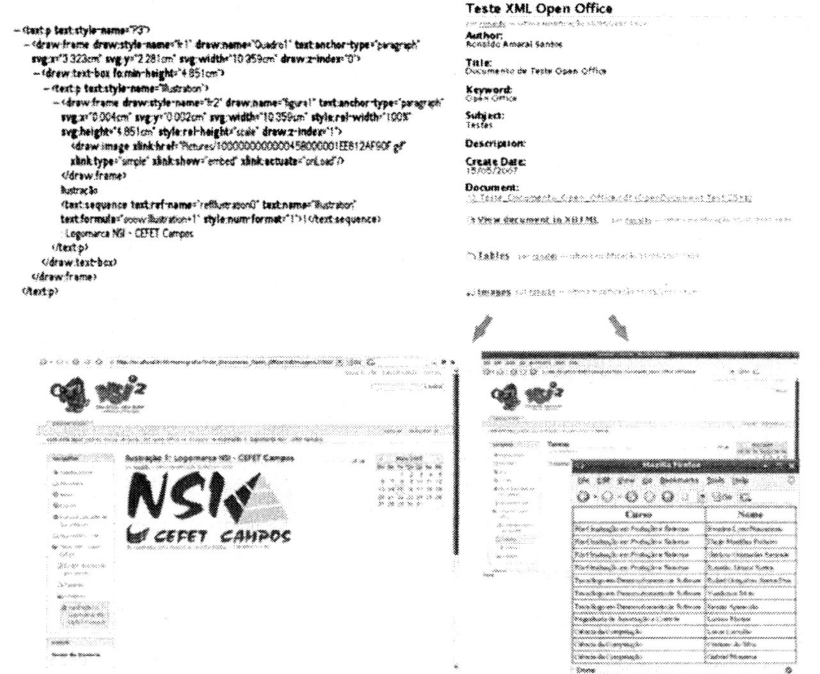

Figure 6. Granular Document Grain Extraction From XML That Represents the Original Document. Grains Can be Opened and Saved in Original, HTML or PDF Format.

Enhanced File System Storage

Zope stores objects and indexes inside its object database, ZODB, which, however, looses efficiency when it comes to store more than tens of gigabytes of objects. Moreover, no software is better than the operational system to store and serve large collections of files, making it a better choice, providing that a good retrieval method is offered. Although Plone already offers a content type (FSFile) that keeps metadata on ZODB and stores the file itself on a specific directory in the file system, this solution also have some limitations when dealing with a large number of files in the same place. To overcome these deficiencies, NSI^2 extends Plone by offering a content type called Enhanced File System File (EFSFile).

This new type uses the same philosophy of FSFile, however, it is optimized to transparently work with the PVFS2 file system and the Lucene search engine, which are used to enhance NSI^2 scalability, as will be presented in the Deployment Architecture section. When referenced on a search result page, EFSFile objects are viewed as ordinary Zope objects, but their content and index entries are stored outside ZODB. In that way, file serving and search processing can be delegated to specialized software running on dedicated clusters, while developers still take advantage of all object-oriented resources of Zope, and users still access these objects as "first-class content", since for both groups, it is like the objects were inside ZODB.

4. NSI2 DEPLOYMENT ARCHITECTURE

An ECM solution to be effective must be scalable and be available in a 24x7 fashion. In NSI^2, scalability and availability are understood as a composition of three elements: access, storage, and indexing. The structure used to comply to these requirements (Figure 2) is based on a set of open source software that guarantees both load balancing and failover:

Access: provided by LVS (Linux Virtual Server) servers that distribute HTTP and FTP requests over a farm of Zope servers. Additionally, ZEO (Zope Enterprise Objects) cluster makes Zope servers share a common content objects collection.

Storage: the PVFS2 distributed file system stores files in a cluster of storage servers, as they were a single server.

Indexing: the Lucene search engine is a more scalable and manageable replacement to the built-in Zope search and indexing functionalities, allowing the setup of a grid of machines exclusively dedicated to run parallel searches and store the indexes.

Using this structure, if one server fails, another one is automatically elected to replace it, in a transparent way. Moreover, it is possible to add new servers "on the fly" to any of the clusters, thus keeping the quality of services when the number of users and information stored and indexed grow.

5. APPLICATIONS

Besides various smaller applications for local governments, NSI^2 is the basis of a series of initiatives sponsored by the Secretary for Professional and Technological Education of the Brazilian Ministry of Education (Setec/MEC) in collaboration with Unesco. Those initiatives offer a series of services for the Professional and Technological Education (PTE) network, which accounts for approximately three thousand public and private institutions in Brazil. Starting on 2009, NSI^2 will form the basis for extending these services to Mercosul (common market for South American countries) and Portuguese-speaking countries in Africa, like Angola and

Mozambique. This deployment of NSI² based solutions in development countries shows the two-pronged importance of the use of FOSS to implement it: reduce TCO and foster information technology development – through the availability of all source code and documentation. Currently, four different NSI² applications are in development, all in the realm of the PTE:

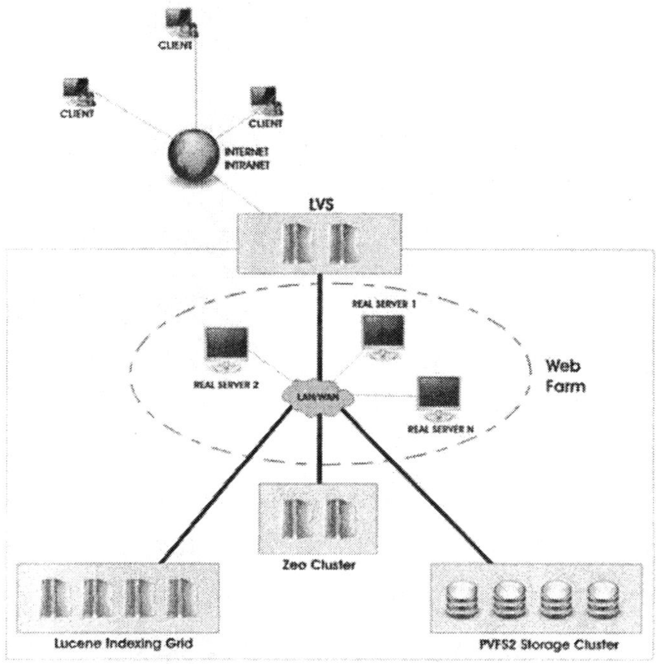

Figure 2. NSI² Deployment Architecture: Users View a Single Point of Access for the ECM Solution

1) Digital Library: a library of articles and thesis will concentrate the academic work on PTE in Brazil. Workflows for revision, translation, metadata association, and publishing will support the correct upload of these documents.
2) Digital Document Center: using a series of Open Office templates and proper workflows, the administrative documents from Setec/MEC will be generated, managed, and stored using NSI². In the medium term, taking advantage of the structure offered by the Granular Document objects, a XML Datawarehouse [17] will be created, allowing analytic operations on the document collection stored in the solution. This document warehouse will be used for statistics, governmental accountability, and historical data analysis purposes.
3) Observatory of the PTE: similar to the Digital Library, it stores analytical documents on various statistics about labor positions and alike related to the PTE. Using the Self-Service option for Granular Documents, new reports and case studies will be better supported.

4) Learning Objects Catalog: a catalog that will maintain references to learning material stored on various PTE institutions. Also using the Self-Service functionality, new learning material can be built from the material obtained through the catalog.

These applications are all in prototype state, and are scheduled to be fully functional by the end of this year.

6. CONCLUSIONS

The solution here presented currently has limitations related to advanced search capabilities, like natural language usage. Also, image and sound files searching are limited to their metadata. However, it is envisioned that these capabilities can be incorporated in the future, thanks to its flexible, object-oriented architecture.

Although NSI^2 is aimed at smaller budgets, it is believed that this solution is compliant to most ECM needs. In fact, even bigger private and public organizations can be satisfied by the use of a proven content management system, a platform that easily integrates to other platforms using open standards, and the scalable infrastructure and extensions provided.

REFERENCES

1. T. Paivarinta and Munkvold, B.E. Enterprise Content Management: An Integrated Perspective on Information Management, in *Proc. of the 38th Annual Hawaii International Conference on System Sciences* (2005).
2. P. Tyrvainen, A. Salminen, and T. Paivarinta, Introduction to the enterprise content management minitrack, in *Proc. of the 36th Annual Hawaii International Conference on System Sciences* (2003).
3. H.E. McNay, Enterprise content management: an overview, in *Proc. of the IEEE International Professional Communication Conference* (2002), pp.396-402.
4. S. Nordheim and T. Paivarinta, Customization of enterprise content management systems: an exploratory case study, in *Proc. of the 37th Annual Hawaii International Conference on System Sciences* (2004).
5. B. Fitzgerald and T. Kenny, Developing an information systems infrastructure with open source software, *IEEE Software*. Volume 21, Number 1, pp.50-55, (2004).
6. S. Krishnamurthy. An Analysis of Open Source Business Models, *Perspectives on Free and Open Source Software*, eds. M. Cusumano,C. Shirky, J.Feller, B. Fitzgerald, S.A. Hissam, K.R. Lakhani (MIT Press, 2005), pp.279-296.
7. D. Riehle, The Economic Motivation of Open Source Software: Stakeholder Perspectives, *IEEE Computer*. Volume 40, Number 4, pp.25-32, (2007).
8. M. Grossniklaus and M.C. Norrie, Information concepts for content management, in *Proc. of the Third IEEE International Conference on Web Information Systems Engineering* (2002), pp.150- 159.
9. W. Kim, On metadata management technology: status and issues, *Journal of Object Technology*. Volume 4, Number 2, pp.41-47, (2005).

10. S. Nordheim and T. Paivarinta, Customization of enterprise content management systems: an exploratory case study, in *Proc. of the 37th Annual Hawaii International Conference on System Sciences* (2004).
11. D. Krechel, M. Hartbauer, and K. Maximini, LENUS - The Hospital Content Management System, in *Proc. of the 19th IEEE International Symposium on Computer-Based Medical Systems* (2006).
12. J. Hartmann and Y. Sure, An infrastructure for scalable, reliable semantic portals, *IEEE Intelligent Systems*. Volume 19, Number 3, pp.58-65, 2004.
13. K.H.S. Kwok and D.K.W. Chiu, A Web services implementation framework for financial enterprise content management, in *Proc. of the 37th Annual Hawaii International Conference on System Sciences* (2004).
14. S. Buxton, Beyond search: content applications, *IEEE IT Professional*. Volume 9, Number 1, pp.29-35, (2007).
15. A.A. Khaing and N.L. Thein, Efficiently Creating Dynamic Web Content: A Fragment Based Approach, in *Proc. of the 6th Asia-Pacific Symposium on Information and Telecommunication Technologies* (2005).
16. P.A. Moumoutzis, N. Christodoulakis, and S. ASIDE, An Architecture for Supporting Interoperability between Digital Libraries and eLearning Applications, in *Proc. of the Sixth IEEE International Conference on Advanced Learning Technologies* (2006), pp.257-261.
17. V. Nassis, T.S. Dillon, R. Rajugan, and W. Rahayu, An XML Document Warehouse Model, in *Proc. of the 11th Int. Conf. on Database Systems for Advanced Applications* (2006).

A Quality Control Model for Extended Enterprises and Its Implementation

Yongtao Qin, Liping Zhao, Yiyong Yao and Damin Xu

State Key Laboratory for Manufacturing Systems Engineering, School of Mechanical Engineering, Xi'an Jiao Tong University, Xi'an 710049, P.R. China
qinyt23419@126.com lipingzh@mail.xjtu.edu.cn
yyyao@mail.xjtu.edu.cn daminxu@gmail.com

Abstract. Along with the intensification of global competition and the complexity of manufacturing products, cooperation among enterprises becomes more intimately, and the range of quality control extends from internal to the external enterprises. Consequently, previous quality control methods for internal enterprise have been difficult to meet the demands of extended enterprises. To effectively realize the quality control of extended enterprises, it is necessary to research the quality control model which adapt to extended enterprise. To meet the demand of extended enterprises' quality control, in this paper, on the basis of the fractal characteristic of quality control in extended enterprises, based on fractal method, combine with complex networks, quality control fractal network is established by constraint relationship among nodes and node. Base on quality control fractal network, quality control model is constructed by some methods to manipulate and operate node and constraint relationship. Finally, Based agent technology, the implementation method of quality control model is studied to meet the demand of quality control, and it can provide an approach to solve quality control problems for extended enterprises.

Keywords: *Quality control, Extended enterprise, Manufacturing*

I. INTRODUCTION

Along with the intensification of global competition and the complexity of manufacturing products, cooperation among enterprises becomes more intimately, the range of quality control extends from internal to external enterprises, these issues engender it more difficult to quality control for extended enterprises in modern networking manufacture, so that the previous methods of intra-enterprise quality control has been difficult to apply to inter-enterprise quality control. In order to control effectively extended enterprise quality, a new model must be established to adapt to the requirement of quality control for extended enterprise [1-7].

Therefore, some researchers in domestic and overseas studied a lot about it, and fractal theory present a new approach to resolve problems in complex systems, but current fractal theory mostly focuses on the study about the quality control of internal enterprises, and with a view to realizing the quality control of extended enterprises,

Please use the following format when citing this chapter:

Qin, Y., Zhao, L., Yao, Y., Xu, D., 2007, in IFIP International Federation for Information Processing, Volume 254, Research and Practical Issues of Enterprise Information Systems II Volume 1, eds. L. Xu, Tjoa A., Chaudhry S. (Boston: Springer), pp. 185-194.

meeting the demand of quality control's open and extensibility feature for extended enterprises [8]. In this paper, based on fractal method, firstly quality control model for extended enterprises is established, and the implementation of quality control for extended enterprises is presented in this paper.

2. QUALITY CONTROL MODEL FOR EXTENDED ENTERPRISE

2.1 Fractal Characteristic of Quality Control in Extended Enterprises

The quality control for extended enterprises integrates the quality control information of internal enterprises which has their own quality control system according to some strategies under the commend of core enterprise, and meet the demand of products quality, exerts overall benefit, so that it has some fractal characteristic in quality control function [9-10].

When the quality control for extended enterprises has been seen as a total unit, the general target of quality control has been decomposed after the extended enterprises chose cooperative partners, and created some executable child quality control units with restricted a certain conditions and associated each other. The child quality control units also could be thought as parent units, and these units' function will be achieved by sub-quality control units' effect. Quality control units can be divided as core enterprises, partner enterprises, manufacturing cell, equipment unit and until the quality control of a specific unit or a part according to the hierarchical structure of extended enterprises. Each unit which can be seen as a relatively independent part to some extent reappears and reduces entirety, and has independent action, adjusting goal, self-similarity feature. Figure 1 show the quality control unit that has common function in extended enterprises.

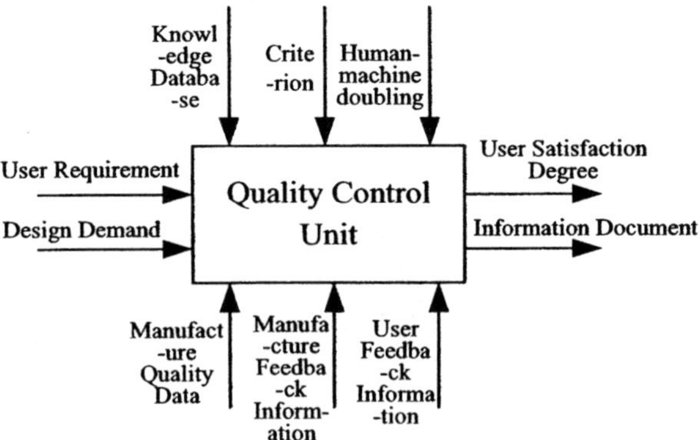

Figure 1. The Quality Control Unit

Under a certain strategy, quality control system with complex and fantastic characteristic for extended enterprises has been constructed by constraint relationship among nodes on the basis of management or coordination rule among quality control units. An open and extensibility organization structure can be established based this system. The organization structure has self-similarity feature. As a result, quality control in extended enterprises has fractal characteristic.

2.2 Quality Control Model for Extended Enterprise

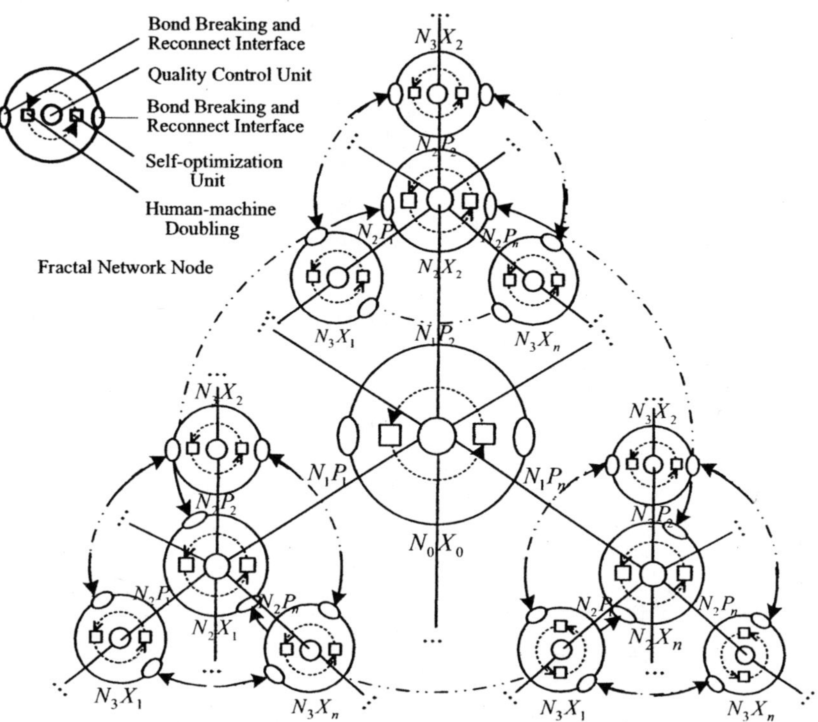

Figure 2. The Quality Control Model for Extended Enterprise

Base on the principle of interest optimization, extended enterprise ally with some cooperative enterprises on the premise of profit maximization, and meet the quality control demand. With view to accurate express quality control state for extended enterprise and research some optimization method, coordinate quality control for better improve quality control effect, further study the rules of quality control for extended enterprise. Therefore, based on fractal method, combined with complex networks, quality control fractal network has been established by constraint relationship among nodes and node. Base on quality control fractal network, quality control model is constructed by some method to manipulate and operate node and constraint relationship. Quality control model for extended enterprise is shown in figure 2.

Real line in figure 2 shows management constraint relationship of upper layer's to lower layer's nodes; dotted line shows constraint relationship of coordinated among same layer's nodes; the constraint relationship can express relationship and connection among nodes, and information's reconstruction. Management constraint of upper layer's to lower layer's nodes and coordinated cooperation constraint among same layer' nodes is unilateral. That is to say the connection among nodes is undirected.

There are definitions for further describe the model:

(1) Node

The N_iX_j node is described as below:

$$N_iX_j = \{N_i, X_j\} \,\big|\, 0 \le i < n, 0 < j < m \tag{1}$$

N_i represents the i layer node. X_j represents the j node.

The value is decided by actual quality control system, for example, i =4 for extended enterprise generally, that is to say extended enterprise is divided into 4 layers, which are core enterprise layer, partner enterprise layer, manufacture cell layer and equipment layer.

Based on quality control function unit, fractal network node is constructed by modularization and object - oriented methodology. The node constitution (NC) is constructed as below:

$$NC = \{N_iX_j, IQ, OQ, QC, DS, CT\} \tag{2}$$

N_iX_j represents the j node in the i layer;

IQ represents input quality information which includes input information by manual work or quality information of other nodes;

OQ represents output quality information which denotes communication information among nodes by unified encapsulation and standardized expression.

QC represents quality control unit:

$$QC=\{G,D,A,S,F\} \tag{3}$$

G: quality goal analyzing cell; D: quality assignment allocation cell;
S: quality information integration cell; F: quality decision and prediction cell;
A: quality assignment action and monitor cell.

DS represents requirement of quality control, such as standard, user demand, technical condition, production capacity, and so on;

CT represents communication unit which express transmission and acceptance of quality control information among nodes.

(2) Constraint Relationship

Based on centralized and distributive management strategy, constraint relationship among nodes is constructed:

$$CB = \{ R_i, C\} \tag{4}$$

CB represents constraint relationship;

R_i represents constraint relationship type;

i ranges from 1 to 2, R_1 is the constraint relationship between upper and lower layer's nodes; R_2 present the constraint relationship among same layers:

$$R_1 = \{RM, N_i P_k\} \tag{5}$$

RM represents management constraint between upper and lower layer's nodes;

$N_i P_k$ represents weights of management constraint among layers;

$$N_i P_k = \{N_i, P_k\} \mid 0 \le i < n, 0 < k < p \tag{6}$$

N_i represents the i layer node. P_k represents weight value is k.

According to differences in production output, human resource and cooperation condition, management constraint between upper and lower layer's nodes have different weights.

$$R_2 = \{RL_l, DL\} \tag{7}$$

RL_j represents coordinated constraint relationship among same layers, value j is 1, 2, or 3 , which represents exclusion relationship, necessity relationship and optional relationship respectively;

DL represents dynamic reconfiguration, value j is 0 or 1 which represents quality control can reconstruct, value j is 2 which represents quality control can not reconstruct.

Based on the construction of node and complex connection created by constraint relationship, fractal network can be established. The network structure has diversity and randomly selectivity, can adjust action by constantly collection feedback information, evaluation spontaneous information received [11-12]. It reflected the self-organization, self-optimization, and self-organization characteristic of network.

Based on fractal network, the quality control model for extended enterprise is constructed by the quality information capsulation based template schemes, or BOM with object-oriented programming, some quality control methods such as SPC, control chart, QFD to manage the quality information among nodes, some optimization algorithms to coordinate the interaction among node such as cooperation, conflict, centralized, and distribution strategy such as constraint logic programming to constraint the quality control relationship among nodes such reconstruction.

3. IMPLEMENTATION OF QUALITY CONTROL MODEL

3.1 Implementation Framework of Quality Control Model

According to characteristic and requirements of quality control for extended enterprise, based on fractal method, quality control model is established. The model can be implemented through studying implementation method. The implementation framework of quality control for extended enterprise was shown in figure 3.

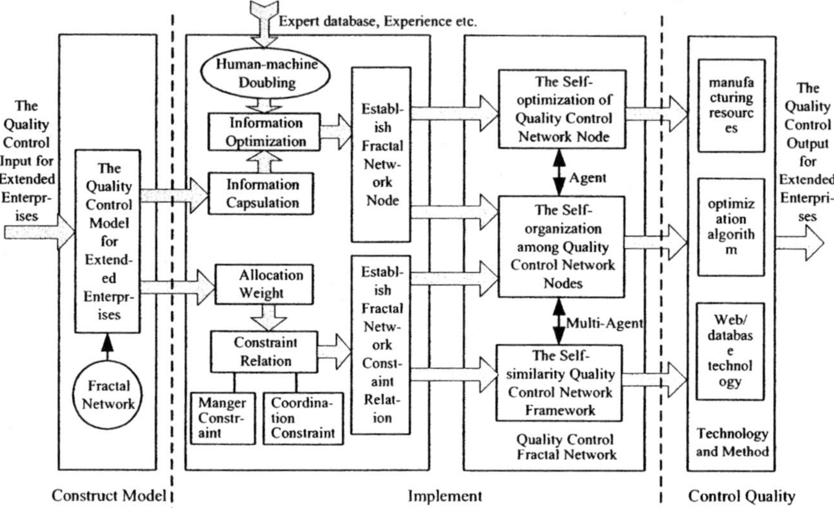

Figure 3. Implementation Framework of Quality Control Model

The framework of quality control model has several steps to realize implementation, as follows:

Firstly, based on fractal network, the quality control model is constructed. Secondly, node is established by information optimization, capsulation, human-machine doubling, experience, and so on. The template or BOM can be used in information capsulation, and CORBA, XML and ontology can be used in the standard expression of information. Constraint relation among nodes is established by external enterprises structure, product configuration, and so on. Weight allocation, constraint logic programming can be used in constraint's construction. Thirdly, base on agent technology, fractal agent is established to realize the node function, and has self-optimization characteristic. Multi-agent strategy is established to realize constraint relation by centralized and distribution strategy, discrete particle swarm optimization algorithm, and quality control methods, so that fractal network structure has self-similarity, self-organization characteristic. In conclusion, quality control can be achieved by some technologies and methods such as Web and database technology, optimization algorithm, and outer condition, and some manufacturing resources.

3.2 The Implementation Method of Quality Control Model

3.2.1 Quality Control Fractal Agent

Because network node is the key and basis of quality control model for extended enterprise, the fractal network node must be established to control quality for extended enterprise firstly. Accordingly, based on quality control unit, quality control fractal agent is constructed by agent technology, modularization and object - oriented methodology so as to realize node function, and has self-optimization characteristic. The structure of quality control fractal agent as illustrated in Figure 4.

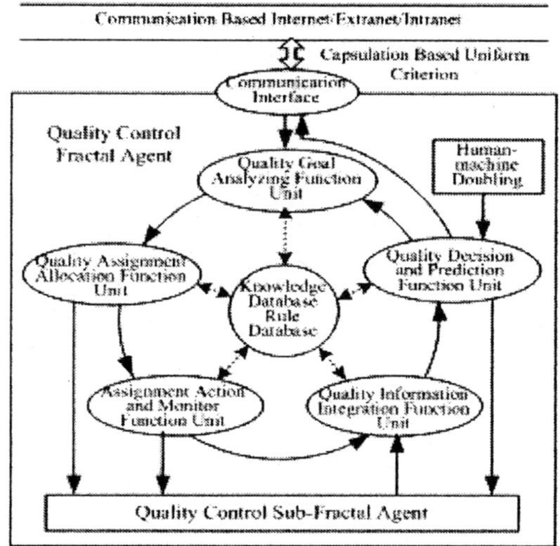

Figure 4. The Structure of Quality Control Fractal Agent

The structure of quality control fractal agent has several processes to realize its functions, as follows:

In the quality control fractal agent, Firstly, quality goal analyzing function unit analyzed the quality information form communication interface, constructed quality control goals and transfer to other units. The input's information is communicated by Internet/Extranet/Intranet, and capsulation based uniform criterion. Secondly the quality assignment allocation function unit allocated and assigned the goals to sub-agent. Thirdly, assignment action and monitor function unit execute and monitor quality control. Fourthly, quality information integration function unit integrate quality information. Finally, quality decision and prediction function unit can predict and evaluate quality information, and feed back information to quality goal analyzing function unit on the basis of knowledge, rule database and Human-machine doubling, so as to it can modify and accommodate quality control goal and achieve self cycle optimization. Fractal agent is describing:

$$Fractal\ agent=\{\sum Unit_i, QC\} \Big| \ i = 1, 2...., n \quad \textbf{(8)}$$

① *Fractal agent* represents quality control fractal agent;

② QC represents quality control unit;

③ $\Sigma Unit_i$ represents organization structure, the set consisted of sub-organization is a recursion nesting, and may be an organization that possess function such as technology, manufacture. The sub-organizations that constituted fractal agent are labeled sub-fractal agent.

3.2.2 Logical Structure of Implementation Method

To the characteristic and demand of quality control for extended enterprise, the quality control method can realize by quality control model constructed for extended enterprise. Firstly, fractal network node is established by agent technology, CORBA, XML, ontology. Secondly, constraint relationship is produced on the basis of Soft Bus among quality control fractal agents. Eventually quality control fractal network is built to control quality. The logical structure of implementation method is presented in figure 5.

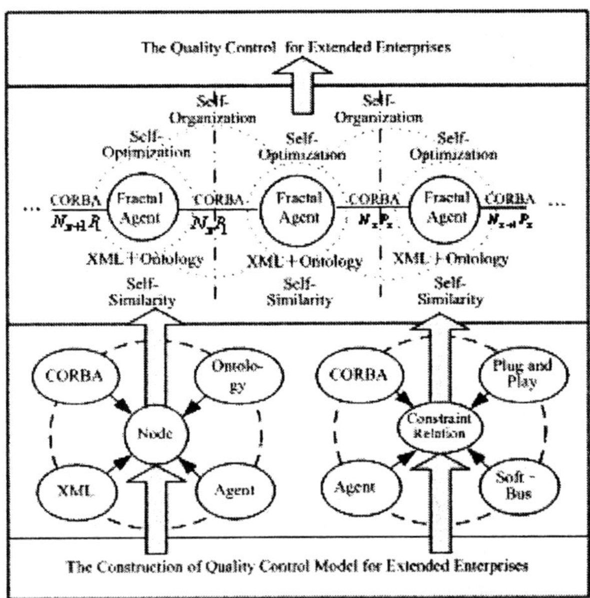

Figure 5. The Logical Structure of Implementation Method

Constraint relationship between management and coordinated are established by making use of "soft-bus" structure that is produced by CORBA and a certain control strategy on the basis of the characteristic of enterprises. Fractal agents are connected by Plug and Play with the registration function of network. Then, based on database and information environment by Intranet/ Extranet/Internet, ontological expression by XML, communication among agents, CORBA's support to transmission protocol, so that quality control information that transmit among agents can smoothly communicate through the environment of heterogeneous systems and protocol[13-15].

Constraint relationship among fractal agents is established by "soft bus" structure and "Plug and Play" mode in self-organization network. Fractal network structure of quality control which has self-similarity, self-optimization, and self-organization is constructed by network complicated evolution. On the basis of open and extensibility feature of the fractal network, using Web technology by Internet/Extranet/Intranet to assure Real-time control, cooperation based the fractal network, the quality of extended enterprises can be control which can implement quality establishment, allocation, and action from core enterprise layer to equipment layer, and achieve quality evaluation, judgment, and prediction from equipment layer to core enterprise layer.

4. CONCLUSIONS

In this paper, on the base of the self-similarity Characteristicistics in the quality control of extended enterprises, based on fractal method and complex networks, depended on constraint relationship among nodes and node, the self-similarity, self-optimization, self-organization fractal network structure is established. Based on fractal network, the quality control model for extended enterprise is constructed by quality information capsulation based template schemes or BOM with object-oriented programming, some quality control methods to manage the quality information among nodes and manipulate constraint relationship among nodes, some optimization algorithms to coordinate the interaction among node, centralized and distribution strategy to constraint the quality control relationship among nodes. Finally based on agent technology, the implementation method of quality control model is studied by CORBA, XML, ontology, and so an, so that this model has open and extensibility feature for extended enterprises, can meet the demand of quality control, and it brings an approach to solve quality control problems for extended enterprises.

ACKNOWLEGEMENTS

This work was supported by grant No. 2006AA04Z149 form the National High - Tech. R&D Program for Contemporary Manufacturing Integrated Technology, China.

REFERENCES

1. J.L. Paris and H. Pierreval, Modelling and Simulation of Manufacturing Systems and Extended Enterprises, *Simulation Modeling Practice and Theory.* Volume 15, pp.111-112, (2007).

2. F. Chan, R. Swarnkar, and M. Tiwari, Infrastructure for co-ordination of multi-agents in a network–based manufacturing system, *The International Journal of Advanced Manufacturing Technology*. Volume 31, pp.1028-1033, (2007).
3. F. Linington, A Unified Behavioural Model and a Contract Language for Extended Enterprise, *Data & Knowledge Engineering*. Volume 51, Number 1, pp.5-29, (2004).
4. Y. Hu, T. Yu, L. Liu, and H. Sun, Knowledge Enterprise: Intelligent Strategies in Product Design, Manufacturing, and Management, in *Proc. of International Federation for Information Processing (IFIP)* eds. K. Wang, G. Kovacs, M. Wozny, and M. Fang (Springer: Boston, MA, 2006), pp.902-907.
5. M. Palaciosa, E. Alvarez, M. Alvarez, and J. Santamaria, Lessons learned for building agile and flexible scheduling tool for turbulent environments in the extended enterprise, *Robotics and Computer-Integrated Manufacturing*. Volume 22, pp.485-492, (2006).
6. O. Bayazita and B. Karpak, An analytical network process-based framework for successful total quality management (TQM): An assessment of Turkish manufacturing industry readiness, *International Journal Production Economics*. Volume 105, pp.79-96, (2007).
7. W. Wei, L. Zhao, and Y. Yao, Collaborative quality tracking model based on workflow, *Computer Integrated Manufacturing Systems*. Volume 12, Number 10, pp.1586-1590, (2006).
8. S. Zhang and B. Wang, Managing Access in Extended Enterprise Networks Web Service-Based, *Lecture Notes in Computer Science*. Volume 3251, pp.963-966, (2004).
9. H. Dong, ·D. Liu, Y. Zhao, and Y. Chen, A novel Approach of Networked Manufacturing Collaboration: Fractal Web-based Extended Enterprise, *The International Journal of Advanced Manufacturing Technology*. Volume 26, Number 11, pp.1436-1442, (2005).
10. M. Shin, Y. Cha, K. Ryu, and M. Jung, Conflict Detection and Resolution for Goal Formation in the Fractal Manufacturing System, *International Journal of Production Researc*. Volume 44, Number 3, pp.447-465, (2006).
11. P. Melin and O. Castillo, An intelligent hybrid approach for industrial quality control combining neural networks, fuzzy logic and fractal theory, *Information Sciences*. Volume 177, pp.1543-1557, (2007).
12. Y. Yao, G. Lin, and A. Trappey, Using Knowledge-Based Intelligent Reasoning to Support Dynamic Equipment Diagnosis and Maintenance, *International Journal of Enterprise Information Systems*. Volume 2, Number 1, pp.17-31, (2006).
13. M. Lim and D. Zhang, An integrated agent-based approach for responsive control of manufacturing resources, *Computers & Industrial Engineering*. Volume 46, pp.221-232, (2004).
14. O. Lopez-ortega and M. Ramirezr, A STEP-based manufacturing information system to share flexible manufacturing resources data, *Journal of Intelligent Manufacturing*. Volume 16, pp.287-301, (2005).
15. M. Sakthivel, S. Devadasan, S.R. Raman, and S. Sriram, Design and Development of a Quality Management Information System, *International Journal of Enterprise Information Systems*. Volume 2, Number 4, pp.18-37, (2006).

Secure Enterprise Information Systems: A Mutual Authentication Scheme for Roaming Users Using Memorable Information

Lin Yang, Xinghua Ruan, Jingdong Xu and Gongyi Wu

College of Information Technical Science, Nankai University, Tianjin 300071, P.R. China
cameling_yang@yahoo.com.cn {ruanxinghua, xujd, wgy}@nankai.edu.cn

Abstract. In enterprise information systems, personal mobility provides the ability for roaming users to access enterprise network services from anywhere at anytime. However, methods for mutual authentication between roaming user and servers are still far from satisfied. In this paper, we focus on such a mutual authentication scheme, by which users can only use memorable information to log in servers with confidence. The scheme is designed in a threshold fashion to improve system's availability and robustness. It can resist known attacks, such as replay attack, password guessing attack and verifier stolen attack. We believe this scheme is suitable for enterprise computing scenarios, in which network environments are confidential and closed.

Keywords: *Enterprise information systems, Security, Privacy, Trust, Password, Mutual authentication, Identity-based cryptography*

1. INTRODUCTION

Personal mobility provides the ability for roaming users to access proper network service at anytime, from anywhere. This problem is of growing importance as Internet-enabled computing devices become ever more prevalent and versatile. A common scenario in enterprise information systems is described as follows: a big enterprise with many departments possesses sufficient numbers and abundant variety of computing devices for its employees; each employee belongs to one particular department and has rights of accessing to dedicated services provided by that department; an employee can log in his or her department's network from any of these devices using one enterprise-wide unique interface.

One crucial issue of above scenario is mutual authentication between the employee and his or her department's network. This would be straightforward if users can only use memorable information, such as names and passwords, to complete mutual authentication. However, memorable passwords are very susceptible to exhaustive search or dictionary attacks [1-3].

In this paper, we propose a new threshold password-and-names-based mutual authentication scheme for roaming users. The proposed scheme is based on elliptic curve cryptography [4]. Password is used for authenticating user to servers in a threshold fashion [5], and identity-based cryptography techniques [6] is used to solve

Please use the following format when citing this chapter:

Yang, L., Ruan, X., Xu, J., Wu, G., 2007, in IFIP International Federation for Information Processing, Volume 254, Research and Practical Issues of Enterprise Information Systems II Volume 1, eds. L. Xu, Tjoa A., Chaudhry S. (Boston: Springer), pp. 195-200.

the problem of authenticating servers to user. The roaming user can achieve mutual authentication with his or her department's networks by only keeping three pieces of information in mind. They are his or her user name, relative password and his or her department's name. We assume all these pieces of information are memorable, since two names are familiar to users, and password can be weak and short.

2. PROPOSED SCHEME

There are four kinds of entities in proposed scheme, namely the dealer, the server, the client and the user. The scheme consists of mainly three phases: the setup phase, the registration phase and the authentication phase. For reader's convenience, we first list the notations used in our scheme in Table 1.

Table 1. Notations

Symbol	Meaning
E	an Enterprise's dealer
D	a particular department
N_D	the department's name
(t,n)	the parameters of the department's threshold system
A	a collection of n servers in the department
B	a subset of A and $\|B\|$ equals to t
S_i	a server in the department, $i \in \{1,2,...,n\}$
(Sk_i, Pk_i)	the server S_i 's private/public key pair
C	a client terminal
nonce	a nonce selected by client in authentication phase
U	a roaming user
N_U	the user's username
P_U	the user's password
G_1	an additive cyclic group of order prime q
G_2	a multiplicative cyclic group of order prime q
P	a generator of G_1
$\hat{e}$	a bilinear map that maps $G_1 \times G_1$ to G_2
H_1	a hash function that maps $\{0,1\}^*$ to G_1
H_2	a hash function that maps $\{0,1\}^* \times G_1$ to $\mathbb{Z}_q^*$
H_3	a hash function that maps $\{0,1\}^* \times G_1 \times G_1$ to $\mathbb{Z}_q^*$
s	a secret held by dealer for the enterprise
r	a secret held by dealer for the department
r_i	the secret share of r stored in server S_i

Dealer has the responsibility for initializing enterprise-wide parameters and then distributing them. Servers respond to user's request and verify its validity distributedly. At meanwhile, every server involved in authentication phase should authenticate itself to the user too. Each server has a name in format of {*department name* || *ID*}, where "||" means concatenation. The registered user can accomplish mutual authentication with department's servers in authentication phase. Note that s is the one and only one enterprise-wide secret. On the contrary, there should be several different r s, each for one particular department. We will demonstrate later that s is used in authenticating servers while r is used in authenticating users.

2.1 Detailed Scheme

2.1.1 Setup Phase

In setup phase, the enterprise's dealer E is in charge of initializing enterprise-wide parameters and generating the secrets stored in every server.

Step 1: E randomly chooses a number $s \in \mathbb{Z}_q^*$ and computes $P_{pub} = sP$. The system parameters are $\{G_1, G_2, q, P, P_{pub}, \hat{e}, H_1, H_2, H_3\}$, which should be distributed safely to all of this enterprise's servers and clients. s is kept secretly in E.

Step 2: Suppose department D with name N_D is organized by E. D has a set of servers, denoted by $S_i \in A, i = 1,...,n$. For each server $S_i \in A$, E assigns an arbitrary unique string ID_i to it and computes $Pk_i = H_1(N_D \,||\, ID_i)$, $Sk_i = sPk_i$ then sends ID_i and Sk_i to S_i secretly. Now, every server $S_i \in A$ has a unique ID_i and a private/public key pair (Sk_i, Pk_i), in which Sk_i should be kept secretly, while Pk can be easily rebuilt with the knowledge of N_D and ID_i.

Step 3: After generating private and public key pair for ever server, E can now initialize secrets for user registration and authentication. E randomly chooses a number $r \in \mathbb{Z}_q^*$ and $a_1, a_2, ..., a_{t-1} \in \mathbb{Z}_q$, then it constructs a polynomial of degree of $t-1$: $f(x) = (r + a_1 x + a_2 x^2 + \cdots + a_{t-1} x^{t-1}) \bmod q$. After that E computes the secret share $r_i = f(i) \bmod q$ for each $S_i \in A, i = 1,...,n$ and distributes them safely to each server. The secret r is held by E while secret share r_i is kept secretly by

$S_i \in A, i = 1,...,n$. If there is another department, E repeat the process in step 2 and step 3 to initialize secrets for its servers.

2.1.2 Registration Phase

In order to get registration to department D, user U first chooses a password P_U, which is easy to memorize, and then sends it with his or her username N_U secretly to E. E computes user U 's mater key $K_U = rH_1(N_U \,||\, P_U)$ and his or her shared secrets $K_i = H_2(ID_i, K_U)$ with every $S_i \in A, i = 1,...,n$, where ID_i is the arbitrary unique string assigned to S_i in the setup phase. Then the couple $\{N_U, K_i\}$ is sent to S_i secretly. After that, E can erase any information about P_U, K_U and K_i, and then the registration phase is done. K_i is obviously a strong secret and should be kept secretly in S_i. We can see later that after the authentication phase, it can be used to derive a secure session key between U and S_i.

2.1.3 Authentication Phase

We assume the network between client terminal C and servers of D is insecure. The user U roams up to C and wants to get mutual authentication with D. The method U used to accomplish such an authentication is to provide three pieces of memorable information: the department's name N_D, his or her username N_U and his or her password P_U. The dealer E can be offline in this phase.

Step 1: After user U inputs N_D, N_U and P_U to the client C, C first chooses t out of n servers in department D. We denote the selected servers as $S_i \in B$ where B is a subset of A. We also denote the index of these t servers by set $I = \{i_1, \ldots, i_t\}$ where I is a subset of $\{1, \ldots, n\}$. Then, C selects a random element $x \in \mathbb{Z}_q^*$ and computes $R = xH_1(N_U \| P_U)$. After that, C chooses a *nonce* to indicate this authentication process with $S_i \in B$, and sends $\{\text{Requese}, nonce, N_U, R\}$ to them.

Step 2: On receiving C's request, the server S_i first retrieves the corresponding $\{N_U, K_i\}$ indicated by N_U from its local storage, and then computes $R_i = r_i R$. After that, S_i randomly picks a number $y_i \in \mathbb{Z}_q^*$ and computes $Y_i = y_i P$, $h_i = H_3(nonce, R_i, Y_i)$ and $Z_i = y_i P_{pub} + h_i Sk_i$, where Sk_i is S_i's private key generated in the setup phase. Finally, $\{\text{Reply}, nonce, ID_i, R_i, Y_i, Z_i\}$ is send to C as a reply, in which ID_i is the arbitrary unique string assigned to S_i in the setup phase.

Step 3: On receiving replies with the proper *nonce* from these t servers, C first rebuilds the public key Pk_i for each $S_i \in B, i \in I$ by computing $Pk_i = H_1(N_D \| ID_i)$, where N_D is inputted to C by user U in step 1, and then verifies these servers one by one. To accomplish this, C computes $h_i = H_3(nonce, R_i, Y_i)$, $V_i = Y_i + h_i Pk_i$ for every S_i's reply, and checks that $\hat{e}(P, Z_i) = \hat{e}(P_{pub}, V_i)$. If it does not hold, C can send a complaint to S_i, or send a request to another server. This step is over when all verifications are passed.

Step 4: We assume that all the servers $S_i \in B$ sent the correct reply. After confirming these replies, the client C computes $K_U = \sum_{i \in I} \lambda_i x^{-1} R_i$ for the user U, where $\lambda_i = \prod_{j \in I, j \neq i} \frac{-j}{i-j} \bmod q$ is the coefficient of Lagrange interpolation formula. After that, C can compute $K_i = H_2(ID_i, K_U)$ to obtain the shared strong secret with every S_i. At this point, the roaming user U can safely log into $S_i \in B, i \in I$ from C with the help of K_i. One feasible, but not only method is using this shared long secret to protect a Diffie-Hellman key exchange between C and S_i, to derive a secure session key for further communication.

3. CONCLUSIONS

Due to the space limitation, the formal analysis of our scheme's correctness, security and performance is given in the full version of this paper [7]. To the best of our knowledge, we are the first to introduce identity-based cryptography techniques into distributed password-based authentication protocols to achieve efficient and explicit mutual authentication in enterprise information systems. The characteristics of our scheme are summarized as follows: 1) legal roaming users can log in networks safely with their hands empty; 2) the scheme can achieve mutual authentication between user and distributed servers; 3) user's password cannot be revealed by the administrator of the server; 4) the system secret won't leak out even if some of the servers are compromised; 5) the system is still available even if some of the servers are unavailable; 6) the scheme reaches high efficiency in network communication; and 7) the scheme resists replay attack, password guessing attack, stolen-verifier attack and insider attack. Benefit from these characteristics, our mutual authentication scheme can be deployed for enterprise information security frameworks, and at meanwhile provide roaming users with ideal mobility and convenience.

REFERENCES

1. S. Bellovin and M. Merritt, Encrypted key exchange: Password-based Protocols Secure Against Dictionary Attacks, in *Proc. of IEEE Symposium on Research in Security and Privacy 1992* (Oakland, CA, USA, 1992), pp.72-84.
2. W. Fork and B. Kaliski, Server-assisted generation of a strong secret from a password, in *Proc. of 9th International Workshops on Enabling Technologies: Infrastructure for Collaborative Enterprises 2000* (Gaithersburg, MD, USA, 2000), pp.176-180.
3. D. Jablon, Password authentication using multiple servers, in *Topics in Cryptology*, CT-RSA April 8-12, 2001, LNCS, Volume 2020, (Springer-Verlag: Heidelberg, 2001), pp.344-360.

4. D. Boneh and M. Franklin, Identity-based encryption from the Weil pairing, in *Proc. Of Advances in cryptology 2001, LNCS, Volume 2139* (Springer-Verlag: Heidelberg, 2001), pp.213-229.
5. A. Shamir, How to share a secret, *Communications of the ACM.* Volume 22, Number 11, pp.612-613, (1979).
6. X. Cheng, J. Liu and X. Wang, An Identity-based Signature and Its Threshold Version, in *Proc. of 19th International Conference on Advanced Information Networking and Applications AINA 2005*(28-30 March 2005), pp.973-977.
7. L. Yang, X, Ruan, J. Xu, and G. Wu, *A Mutual Authentication Scheme for Roaming Users Using Memorable Information*, Unpublished work, available by email request (cameling_yang@yahoo.com.cn).

The Research and Application of Web Services in Enterprise Application Integration

Yan Cao, Yan Chen and Yiting Shen

College of Economics and Management, Dalian Maritime University, Dalian 116026, P.R. China caoy123@163.com chenyan_dlmu@163.com atingle_cn@hotmail.com

Abstract. At present, most enterprises have a heterogeneous environment of legacy application, which lead to many "information isolated islands". Enterprises become more and more eager to share data in business processes over different systems. Traditional Enterprise Application Integration (EAI) methods usually integrate applications from peer to peer which has many defects. In This paper, a kind of EAI framework based on Web Services (WSEAI) has been put forward, which has nothing with any platform and programming language, so it can make the enterprise applications integrated together without gap. We have been successfully putting the EAI framework in one logistical company's WebGPS system and realized the integration based on Web Services.

Keywords: *EAI, WSEAI, Web services, WebGPS system*

I. INTRODUCTION

Text Enterprise Application Integration (EAI) refers to the seamless application systems integration of two or more enterprises by tying in the operation flow, application software, hardware and a variety of standards, so that the enterprises could work like one in business processing and information sharing. Traditional EAI uses distributed object technology-based point-to-point integration like RMI, CORBA, DCOM, etc., which usually could not meet the requirement of the enterprises and result in high cost and low efficiency. Therefore, a new solution is needed.

With the maturity of the Web Services technology, it has broken through the restriction of the traditional point-to-point application integration solution, and exerted great impact on the EAI. Considering current heterogeneous platforms, the main aim of the Web Services technology is to build a general-purpose technology level regardless of the platforms and languages, by which to realize the connection and integration [1].

In this Paper, based on the Web Services technology, we put forward the Web Services-based EAI Framework which is called as WSEAI, and its biggest difference between the traditional EAI solutions lays in its inter-enterprise integration, and at the same time its consideration of the interaction of the Web Services in different platforms, which could successfully integrate the legacy systems on Web Services base. The WSEAI make the integration of different application systems easier, cost-

Please use the following format when citing this chapter:

Cao, Y., Chen, Y., Shen, Y., 2007, in IFIP International Federation for Information Processing, Volume 254, Research and Practical Issues of Enterprise Information Systems II Volume 1, eds. L. Xu, Tjoa A., Chaudhry S. (Boston: Springer), pp. 201-205.

efficient and dynamically expandable, and even partial realization of the EAI will be very useful.

2. DESIGN OF WSEAI

Traditional EAI solution, for example, point-to-point integration or distributed object-based middleware integration, features with its standard processing of the interfaces of different information systems for integration, which lacks of flexibility and adaptability. But through standard Web protocols (HTTP, SMTP, etc.) and series standard protocols (XML, SOAP, WSDL, UDDI, etc), the standard Web Services technology has provided a new solution for the EAI.

Both the Intra-EAI and Inter-EAI have been taken into consideration in designing the Web Services-based EAI Framework.

As the basis of EAI, currently the Intra-EAI mainly needs to solve the communication problem of different modules. Different from the traditional EAI modules that use special protocol, by using the Web Services Technology, the modules' interfaces could be altered to standard Web Services interfaces before connecting with the external equipments. So by wrapping the interfaces modules of different intra-enterprise application systems through the Web Services technology, and publishing it to the private UDDI Registry, then the other application systems of the enterprise could realize its own function by invoking the Web Services. This could realize the communication of the scattered legacy systems, and consequently realize the Intra-EAI.

The virtual enterprise and Inter-EAI is one of the highlights in the future informatization. While by making use of the reuse mechanism of Web Services, there will be no need of external service programming, and the only requirement is to republish the Web Services to the public UDDI registry, and then the other enterprises could invoke the Web Services on the Internet, which could break through the regional restriction and realize the Inter-EAI.

Accordingly, the Web Services technology is very feasible to realize the EAI. In view of the need of the enterprise, in this Paper we designed the Web Services-based EAI Framework (WSEAI), and it is shown as Figure 1[1-2].

According to the Figure 1, the Web Services-based EAI Framework could be built on the platform of J2EE and NET, and the functions of its main modules are as follows:

(1) Web Services Adapter: Web Services adapter mainly alters the current application systems to the Web Services interface format and processes the binding invocation of the Web Services.

(2) SOAP Router: As key part of the integration framework, the SOAP router is used to transfer messages, its two main functions are: SOAP message router and message format conversion.

(3) Web Server: As the core of the integration framework, the main function of the Web Server is to provide interactive Web pages and transmit the request of the upper level to SOAP router, and then communicate with the client-side and SOAP processor by the HTTP and HTTPS.

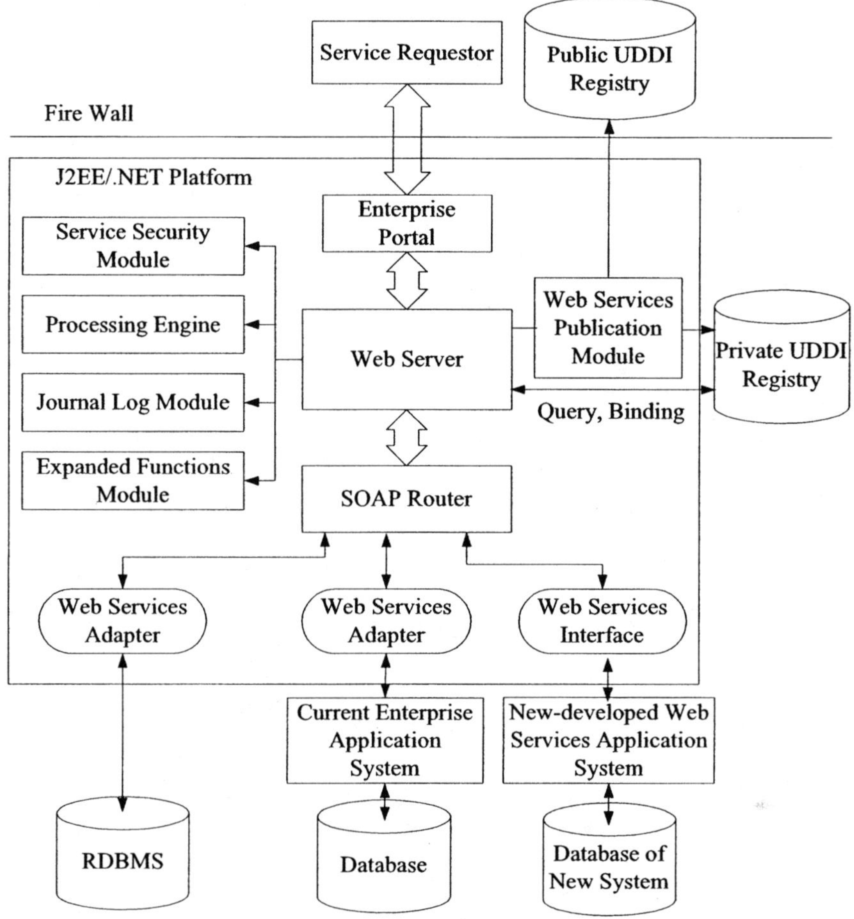

Figure 1. Web Services-based EAI Framework (WSEAI)

(4) Web Services Publication Module: Under the .NET platform, we could use the UDDI SDK programming to publish the Web Services to the private and public UDDI Registry in batch.
(5) UDDI registry: Public UDDI registry is open and could be used to realize the Inter-EAI; while the private UDDI registry shall be wrapped first and all the relevant Web Services Description Language (WSDL) shall be registered in the registry.

As the bridge of various application systems, the integration framework interface is coupled loosely, i.e., any application system could invoke its corresponding interface to connect to the system in a flexible and fast manner, and realizes the so-called "Plug & Play" [3].

To integrate new application system, we need to describe its service with WSDL by Web Services adapter, and then publish the message to the UDDI registry through the SOAP. For intra-enterprise integration, the message shall be registered in the private UDDI registry. The message shall be published to the public UDDI registry for inter-enterprise integration, which is useful for the partner enterprises or the prospective partners to find and invoke the services and realize the inter-enterprise application system integration.

3. APPLICATION OF WSEAI

There is a Logistic Company in Dalian, Liaoning, China. The frame of its information system is shown as Figure 2.

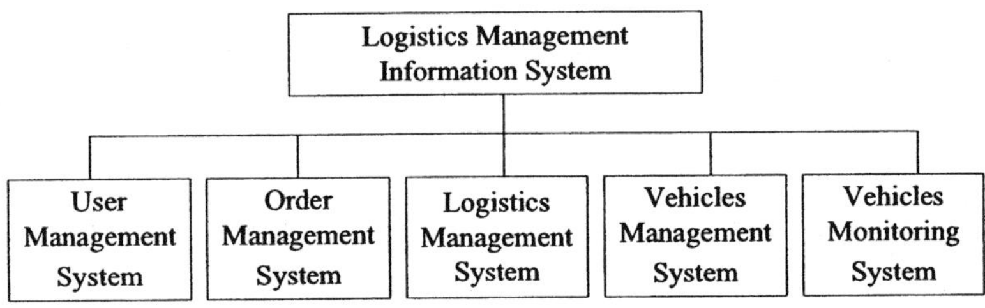

Figure 2. The Frame of Information System

According to Figure 2, the original information system of the logistics company has five sub-systems, in which the Vehicle Monitoring System is mainly used to monitor the transport vehicles by GPS. Almost without data communication with other systems, the Vehicle Monitoring System is relatively independent. The vehicle management department uses the GSM number to manage the vehicles. To facilitate the clients to follow the position of their goods, the company needs to establish a B/S vehicles monitoring system network, which we called WebGPS system. One of the main functions of the WebGPS is that after passing the authentication, the client could check the position of the transport vehicle by submitting the order number, and the position could be demonstrated in the electronic map on the Internet. It would be a waste of manpower and material resources if we develop a new WebGPS, which involves the sub-systems like User Management System, Order Management System and Logistics Management System, etc., and the redesign of the data flow. What's more, redevelopment of the monitoring module needs to use the GPS technology, serial port operation technology, GSM data communication protocol and GPS data decode, etc. But we could make full use of the original system by the thought of EAI. The following is an example of realizing the WSEAI in the WebGPS system

Based on the thought of EAI framework, we use Web Services to renew the original system, and expose the required functions of the original systems through the Web Services interface, which could be invoked by the WebGPS system, and the entire system framework of the .NET platform is as Figure 3:

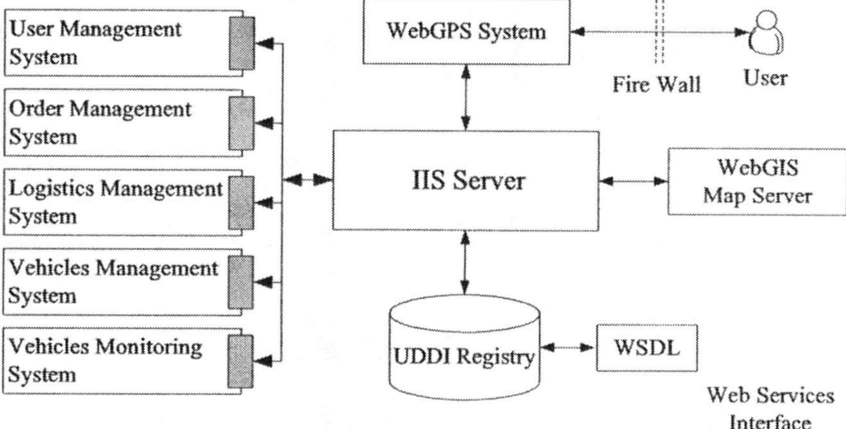

Figure 3. Web Services-based WebGPS Integration System

4. SUMMARY

In conclusion, compared with the traditional EAI solution, the application of the Web Services technology is more flexible and efficient. By wrapping the legacy systems, the original system is still independent. The wrapped interfaces are all in XML data format, and the service request and response is based on the SOAP protocol, which can easily realize the integration of the legacy systems and the newly developed Web Services application systems, etc. What's more, formed by a series of standards, the Web Services owns independent platform and language, which is more suitable for the heterogeneous platforms integration. In addition, the UDDI registry could help to realize the dynamic Web Services invocation, which has great advantage over the traditional static integration solutions.

REFERENCES

1. X. Chai and Y. Liang, *Technology, Framework and Application of Web Services* (Electronic and Industrial Press: Beijing, 2003).
2. V.N. Gudivada and J. Nandigam, Enterprise Application Integration Using Extensible Web Services, in *Proc. of the IEEE International Conference on Web Services (ICWS'05)* (2005), pp.41-48.
3. X. Chai. *SOAP Technology and B2B Application Integration* (2001). http://www.ibm.com/developerworks/cn/xml/soap/index.html

Integration of Product Design Process and Task Management for Product Data Management Systems

Rui Lu, Wu-liang Peng and Cheng-en Wang

Key Laboratory for Process Industry Automation, Ministry of Education, Northeastern University, Shenyang 110004, Liaoning, P.R. China
luruihappy@163.com peng-wuliang@163.com wangc@mail.neu.edu.cn

Abstract. Product design is an evolving process which is characterized with creativity and uncertainty. The task management in this process is different from traditional ones because it involves more specific factors such as user specifications, product design specifications, reengineering, design process, and design data. In this article, we aim to analyze product design process with the viewpoint of project management and task management, and propose an integrated approach to interconnect those constraints, functional and non-functional factors coming from both product design and task management processes. In the presented approach, utilizing workflow technique, the design process and task management are directly and closely interconnected at process and data level by using the shared model and the shared database. Therefore, we can easily obtain the work breakdown structure (WBS) for project management. Implemented as part of PDM (Product data management) systems, the proposed method has been tested that it can facilitate the product design.

Keywords: *Project Management, Workflow, Product data management systems, Iteration, Product design process, Task management*

1. INTRODUCTION

As the early stage of the product development, product design is becoming vital to the prosperity of enterprise and is critical in product development lifecycle. In order to develop high quality and high performance products with short time-to-market, management of product design information is paramount. As an evolving process of problem solving, design process is characterized with creativity and uncertainty. This tends to iteration in design (see figure 1), i.e. having to go back to earlier stages to correct mistakes when the design choices were flawed or impossible to match the specifications. As the product developments become more and more complicated, the hundreds of thousands of design information generated from product design, and more constraints (management, prototyping and organization) involved in design process are more than any single individual can handle. In a typical product development lifecycle, CAD/CAM tools, PDM systems and Workflow Management Systems are used to follow a design-prototype-implement cycle. On the other hand, Product design implies the definition of a project, the identification of the

Please use the following format when citing this chapter:

Lu, Rui, Peng, W., Wang, C. 2007, in IFIP International Federation for Information Processing, Volume 254, Research and Practical Issues of Enterprise Information Systems II Volume 1, eds. L. Xu, Tjoa A., Chaudhry S. (Boston: Springer), pp. 207-218.

technologies to be used, the establishment of a schedule, an evaluation of the load, communicating with the clients [1]. A Product design process composes several successive stages and is a complex task involving more and more disciplines coming from functional and non-functional aspects. Task management is an important feature of design frameworks [2]. A proper task management approach can facilitate the design process and eventually improve the efficiency of product development.

Product design process and task management are both around enterprise business and producing activity, and they have overlapping and resemblance. Furthermore, product developing project/task always followed by a great business reengineering or great renovations of technology and management, more factors (redesign and reengineering, design data, task resources and their capacities, task execution and monitor, etc.) must be taken into account.

Nightingale [3] provided a framework linking products to innovation processes and described how knowledge, technology and organization are all interrelated. Li et al. [4] discussed an integrating framework of process and project management and presented the mapping method between them. The CRISTAL system was described in [5] and how to integrate product data and workflow management systems was discussed. There are some other research works reported [6-8]. We have also reviewed some commercial tools. Microsoft Project is often used as general task management. However, it offers limited team support and cannot support information flow. Furthermore it doesn't ties to any single example or domain. Other solutions such as SMARTEAM, TEAMCENTER etc are reviewed too. All of researches and commercial products only focus on partial aspect of design and task process. The design data and task data are only conceptually connected or very loose with little data level commutation and communication. Thus we try to analyze product design with the viewpoint of project management and task management, associate design process with task management, and integrate factors coming from design and task management process to help to design the large-scale complex product.

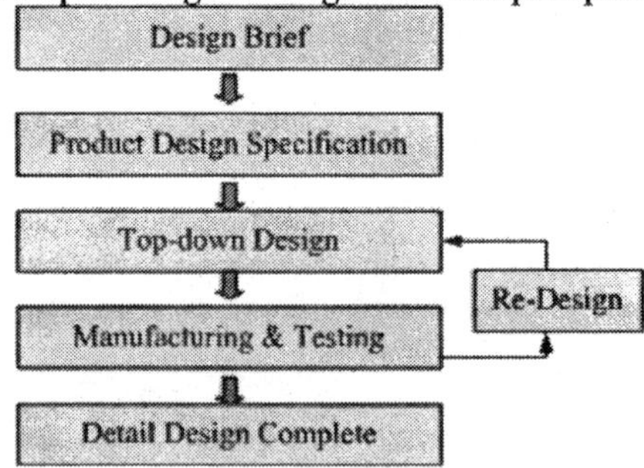

Figure 1. Iterative Product Design Process

In this paper, an approach of integrating the product design process and task management is proposed. The benefits of this solution are that it (a) enables the design process to synchronize with the design task, (b) integrates task information and design data from definition through releasing and execution, (c) facilitates the collection and exchange of design data, (d) facilitates the tracing and monitoring of task management and design process, as well as re-engineering of tasks and processes by utilizing workflow technique, and (e) associates task with the product specification to ensure the quality of both tasks and processes.

The next section describes the characteristics of task management in product design process and the difference between task management in design process and the typical task management. In the third section, an integrated approach is proposed to interconnect the design and task management processes. This section contains a short introduction to the integrated framework. The proposed approach is described via the general design task management process. The shared database is also described. In the forth section, an integrated task management system is given to illustrate the application of the proposed approach in design projects and design processes. The last section contains the conclusions.

2. TASK MANAGEMENT IN ITERATIVE PRODUCT DESIGN PROCESS

The key concept of design process is activities and their sequent relationships. The core of task management is the work breakdown structure and the dependency among tasks. Design Task management system are closely related to product design processes, user specifications, product specifications, design data, design resources, design tasks and task execution and monitoring process[9]. Furthermore, redesign feedback loops can have impact on cost and project schedules. Therefore, reengineering is another important factor should be considered in design task management. Since it is closely related to those factors, the differences between design task management and the traditional one are depicted as following:

a) The outcome of task in product design process is design data, such as product structure profile, graph documents, etc.
b) More constraints or factors coming from design and task management processes should be taken into account. Task management should link functional and non-functional knowledge from two processes.
c) Product data and task data are closely related. Task management should be integrated with design process and eventually integrated with product development lifecycle process.
d) Due to the iteration, which is fundamental characteristic of complex design project, the task duration and task result are stochastic during the task execution.

In manufacturing systems, engineers use PDM to coordinate and control access to documented versions of product designs, and project managers use PM and Task Management tools to control task plan and execution. In the market, few task management factors are currently taken into account by PDM systems although PM and Task Management are considered indispensable function in PDM systems. Our main objective in this paper is to integrate the design process with task management by means of shared model and shared database, and utilize workflow technique to control and monitor both design and task management process. For that, we propose an integrated task management approach which will be described here below.

3. INTEGRATED TASK MANAGEMENT APPROACH

Figure 2 addresses the proposed task management approach and the integration between the product design and task management process by utilizing workflow model. The product design and general design task management processes are illustrated in this figure.

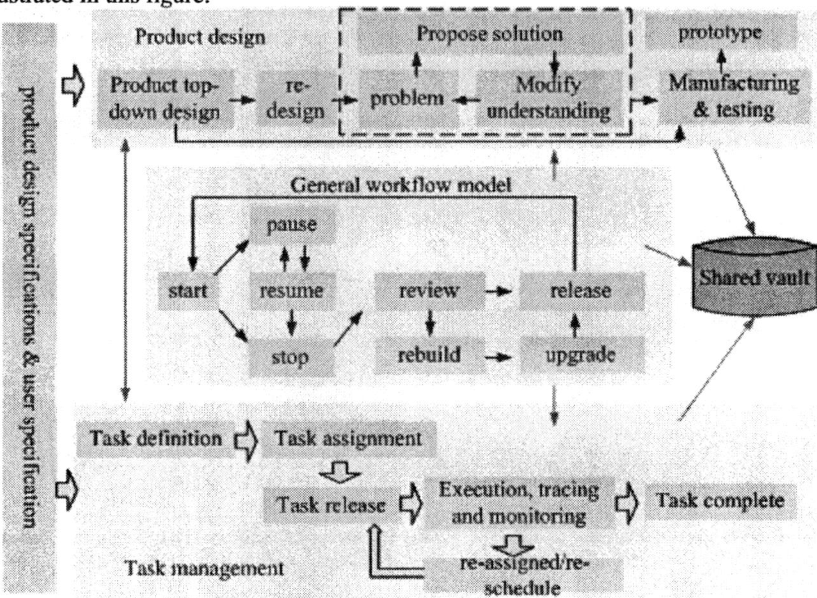

Figure 2. Proposed Approach and its Integration with Design Process

3.1 The Integrated Framework

In this framework, product design data and task management information share the same database and the same model. In enterprise, design process is constructed based on experience and experts' knowledge, therefore, is more 'harder'. That means that product design process is not expected to change during the execution of the process. At first, we define a process model with sequence steps in light of the feature of the product design project, product and user specifications, etc. At the same time, several quality activities are appointed to perform at each step. An appointed quality activity consists of design data documents (such as CAD documents), quality documents which is used to control design quality, and reference documents. Those documents are required to download/ submit at the start/ end of the certain step. The information model is shown in Figure 3. At every step, workflow models are defined to perform those quality activities automatically during the execution. Then, this rationalized process model is used as the template of task plan. Furthermore, process model is used as the basement of process management and is traced and recorded. Once the designer finds that there are some faults during the process execution, he then raises the problems and finds solutions to solve them. Then the process knowledge is fed back and the process reusability can be improved.

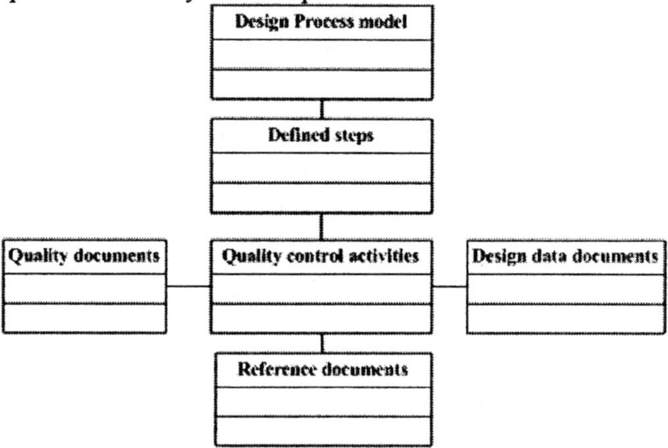

Figure 3. Information Model of Design Process Model

On the other hand, due to the inherent iteration of product development, there are loops that exist in design process. Furthermore, under the execution of tasks, it is common to have a number of unexpected events. As task management does not support conditional branching, recursion or loops, these events are solved by workflow model. For a proper defined workflow instance, it is easy to coordinate the flow of tasks and monitor the collaborative product development process in product development lifecycle. Those defined workflow model can be rebuilt, updated and upgraded and more reasonable and effective service can be supplied.

3.2 Proposed Task Management Approach

Hagerman [2] summarized that task management consists of task creation (building a task tree), task resolution/assignment (select tools and data) and task execution (running the tools). In this integrated approach, we propose the general process of task management as steps (task definition, task assignment, task release, task execution, tracing and monitoring, task re-schedule and task re-assignment), as illustrated in Figure 2.

3.2.1 Task Definition

Once the user specifications and product design specifications are finalized and released to design department, design tasks can begin. In the discussed integrated framework, design project managers and task supervisors are authorized to create tasks according to specifications. On the product design side, product structures are hierarchical in nature and product breakdown is often strictly hierarchical in form.

Attributes can be assigned to each part or sub-part. In industry, product breakdown is often referred to as "Bill of Materials" (BOM). On the more detailed management level in task side, the objective of task creation is to decomposing overall task into hierarchical, smaller, more traceable sub-tasks. The outcome of task definition is Work Breakdown Structure (WBS). The objective of this section is to create the relationship between PBS and WBS in order to help task managers to obtain task tree structure.

Top-down design leads to clear and complete tree-based overall product components or parts view. In reality, PBS represents architecture of components or parts on the side of product design. And the tree structure often implies the design task definition on task management side. This tree-based architecture of tasks is associated with product and its specification and quality control documents. The next step is to map the PBS representation onto design tasks according to functional and nonfunctional parameters. In our framework, this step is called "aggregation/ decomposition and mapping", as shown in figure 4. At this stage of development, at first, design supervisors or managers aggregate and/ or decompose product parts and/ or components according to some parameters (such as function representation, performance, experience and knowledge feedback, reusability of components, qualities, costs and delays, etc). At this stage, the procedure is completely manual and relies on experience obtained in past success and failures. The data coming form the knowledge database provide engineers with the necessary decision supports. The second step consists of defining tasks with three estimated durations-optimistic, most likely, and pessimistic-for their expected duration, creating relations between them, determining delays, costs and tools of them. Following that, those functional representations are mapped onto certain project tasks. At last, we get the work breakdown structure corresponding with product information and quality control documents.

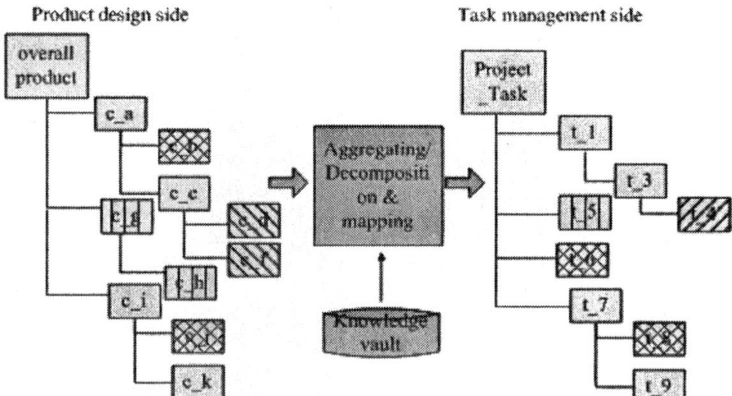

Figure 4. Product Breakdown Structure to Work Breakdown Structure

3.2.2 Task Assignment

The team responsible for carrying out the design process is usually being part of the established organization of enterprise, while the designer team responsible for the realization of tasks usually disbanded when the design project is completed. In order to integrate the organization with design department, we create project-based organizations which called "design project organizations" in our framework. This organization allows resources to be efficiently allocated in the design project. The defined design tasks are assigned to the designers by design supervisors. One of the benefits of integration of process and task management is to compute the designers' planned workloads from project and resource calendar, and capture their actual daily workloads in real-time from the execution of process. This workload profile will benefit evaluation of task resources' performances. At the same time, designers' workload capacities and availabilities are important parameters that impact on the task schedule. Consequently, they are considered during the task plan and execution and shared during design and task management lifecycle.

3.2.3 Task Execution and Monitor

After a task has been assigned to designers, it can be released for execution which means to maintain a schedule, to monitor the plan, to trace the states of task completion and to do re-planning if necessary.

WFMSs as well as PM provide essential functionality for work management (planning and execution support for processes) [10]. In this approach, our aim is to utilize workflow to "mediate" and "glue" the processes, design data and task information as well as different organizations and designers, and eventually to seamlessly integrate the design process and task management. The information model of this approach is illustrated in Figure 5. In this approach, three workflow models (schedule change, quality activities control, and workload calculation workflow model) are defined to monitor and control the task execution.

Quality activities control workflow model: As mentioned previously, the key outcome of design task is design data. In product design process, almost each part or component definition has one or more workflow definition assigned to it to collecting design data, to checking design quality, and to getting approval from supervisor or related organization. We define a workflow model to obtain and control design data created by designers and to monitor information generated from tasks. A FTP service and a relation database are used to contain design data and task information. Designers often submit design documents and data at the end of one stage. The workflow instance is started to perform those functions and return the results. If only the workflow instance return approval, the task can enter the next step through the task flow.

Workload calculation workflow model: As the design process synchronizes with task, a workload calculation workflow model is created to perform the function of tracing and updating the designers' actual workloads and available capacities. The task resource's work load capacity and working performance help to avoid the conflict of task resource assignment.

Schedule change workflow model: Although task plan is made, some of tasks are usually executed in a different order, by unplanned resources with significant and unexpected delays. Due to the quick variations of the environments, as well as the dynamic task schedule change, task execution process is driven by workflow engine. Workflow technology has been reported to be effective in specifying, executing, monitoring, and coordinating the flow of tasks within a distributed environment, while reinforcing flexibility [11]. The trigger point of the workflow is the occurrence of an unexpected situation (event) such as overloaded resources, unexpected delays, and etc. As soon as the task is ready to be executed, task schedule workflow instance takes place in the light of the task plan laid out for it. Any changes in the planned schedule can be reflected in the execution of workflow instance without delay. Once the task plan has to be rescheduled, task supervisor should start the workflow instance to run algorithm to do re-schedule, and any changes can be sent to the WFMS. At the same time, task status, such as completion, can be reflected throughout its execution.

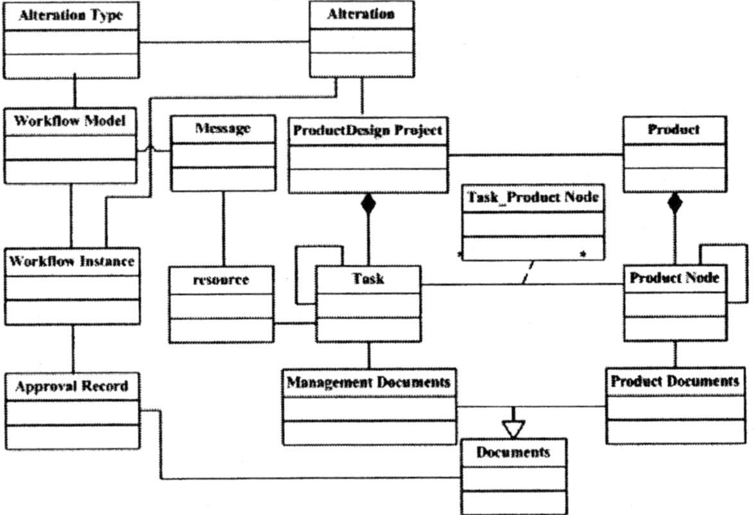

Figure 5. Information Model of Design Task Management

3.2.4 Task Re-assignment and Re-schedule

During the execution of the task, when events occur, the schedule sometimes needs to change and may be re-assigned to another designer. For example, if design task T_a is not finished after the planned days working, design supervisors decide that the task will continue for several days. Under this circumstance, all related designers (designers of T_a, as well as the task supervisors of the tasks that have T_a as a predecessor) are notified by message sending strategy. The delay of one task will postpone the completion and cause the whole design project delay eventually. Facing this problem, other designers may be assigned to help in T_a in order to shorten duration. These events handling procedure is defined as a schedule change workflow model and automatically handled in the proposed approach.

During the execution of design task, two situations of delay (task delay and iteration) could postpone the project. Both of them are considered in our approach. Assuming that task T_a is delayed. The effects of the entire project should be re-calculated. The procedure is described as two steps: a) tracing for the successors via the chain of dependency relationship until all the affected tasks are identified, and b) revising the time pair (start time and finish time) of all identified tasks. All independent tasks are not considered because there is no dependency relationship between them.

As aforementioned, iteration and overlap are important features in product design project. An iterative project network is distinguished from project network without iteration is that the task properties in project is dynamic, meaning that the task sequence is variable, a task duration in each state is stochastic, as well as the task results. When iteration arises, the over-run caused by iteration is usually a fraction of the original duration of task because of each task resource's learning curve [12-14] improvement over the performing stage of the project is considered in our approach. Learning curve measures a characteristic of task when it repeats. The iteration model assumes that the learning curve improves in each repetition until it reaches the minimum fraction of the original duration when a task does the same work repeatedly. Therefore, the time required for later iteration tends to shorter than previous iteration. The duration of tasks that required iteration is re-estimated and computed by the algorithm running in schedule change workflow instance.

Three different re-scheduling methods are used in our approach, namely, revise schedule by averaging, revise schedule manually, and revise schedule based on the weight of tasks [15]. The last method uses numeral ($1 \le w \le 10$) to represent the importance of each task. The amount of time to be shortened for task T_a is computed by using equation (1):

$$t_{is} = \frac{t_d}{\sum_{j=1}^{k}(t_j^2/(w_j \times \sum_{j=1}^{k} t_j))} \times (t_i^2/w_i \times \sum_{j=1}^{k} t_j) \tag{2}$$

Where t_{is} : the shortened time of the *i*th task; t_d : the overdue time of the entire schedule; t_j : the duration of the *j*th task ($1 \le j \le k$); w_j : the weight of the *j*th task ($1 \le w_j \le 10$).

3.3 The Shared Database

So far the design and task management are traced by workflow model and become active. And the information flow is also automatic, as all relevant information is stored in the unique database, allowing concurrent multiple authorized users to extract useful information. The shared database stores the static and dynamic data structures of processes and tasks. It contains structural information such as tasks and their relations, planned task duration and resources assigned to tasks. It also stores the dynamic information about the real-time status of tasks and design processes, as well as the historical task records. Considering the design data generated from design task and process combines multiple formats, a FTP server is created to contain the unstructured data such as graph documents.

With the proposed approach, as a product go through its design lifecycle, design process synchronizes with task management process. The design task is linked with product and designers' workloads. And the actual workload is updating under the task execution. Product specification, quality and reference documents are directly routed to designers by workflow. Design data and task detail information are collected under the workflow model execution. The integrated approach has been implemented as part of a PDM system; the next section gives scenario of its integrated task management subsystem.

4. AN INTEGRATED TASK MANAGEMENT SYSTEM

The integrated system has been deployed as the part of PDM systems. It can facilitate the collection and exchange of design data, reduce the "time-to-market", and improve the efficiency of design process.

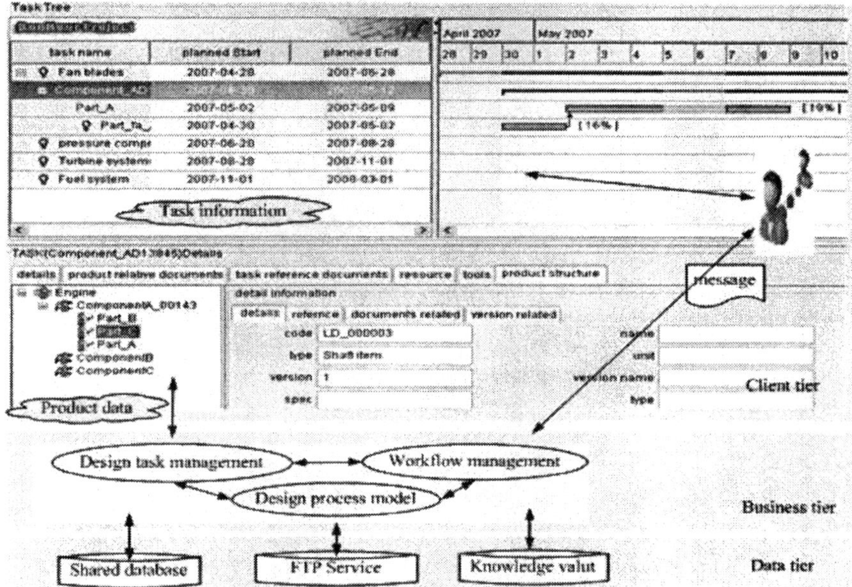

Figure 6. Three-tiered Architecture

The integrated system is built on the J2EE platform. Conceptually, the architecture takes a three-tiered approach (see Figure 6). On the client tier, the workbench provides GUI which comprises design data and task management interface for product definition, task planning and performing. The business logic tier consists of application logic and provides typical services for design process and task management. On the data tier, the data is stored in a SQL Server 2000 database and all design documents generated from design process are managed through FTP service using Microsoft IIS.

5. DISCUSSION

When mapping the PBS representation onto design tasks, human intervention is needed. However, the proposed approach does not support the functionality that can validate the mapping made by engineers. Furthermore, in case of multiple mapping alternatives, there is no method to allow the planner to simulate the entire processes of each alternative. Therefore, the proposed approach can be extended by support the functionality of mapping and simulation.

On the other hand, we assume that task resources and their capacities are sufficient for design project. However, in reality, the resource conflicts are one of the bottlenecks which actually affect the project schedule. So this approach can be further extended by taking variable resource capacity and requirements into account.

6. CONCLUSIONS

As the early step of product development, design is critical for enterprise. One strategy for reducing time-to-market development is to take constraints that usually appear during the product design project into account. The main ambition of the research is to consider all functional and non-functional factors coming from both design and task management processes. We proposed an integrated approach to facilitate seamlessly interconnection between product design process and design task management, and thereby providing consistency between design data and task status and information and eventually improving product design efficiency. As related previously, task management during design process is different from the traditional one. The outcome of design task is usually the product structure profile and design documents. Therefore, task is directly related with product node and design data generate from designers. In our approach, workflow technology acts as a "media" and a "glue" to automate the processes design tasks, tracking and monitoring task status, collecting design data emerging from design process and task execution, and triggering defined workflow instance to maintain product quality and feeds experience database with feed-back records which will be benefit for future similar product or product design projects.

REFERENCES

1. C. Gutierrez, C. Baron, L. Geneste, P. Clermont, D. Esteve, and S. Rochet, How to interconnect Product Design and Project Management including Experience Feedback and Reusability, in *Proc. of Information Reuse and Integration, Conf. 2005. IRI–2005 IEEE International Conference* (IEEE: 2005), pp.294-299.
2. J.W. Hagerman and S.W. Director, Improved Tool and Data Selection in Task Management, in *Proc. of the 33rd ACM/IEEE Design Automation* (IEEE: Las Vegas, USA, 1996), pp.181-184.
3. P. Nightingale, The Product-Process-Organization relationship in complex development projects, *Research Policy*. Volume 29, pp.913-930, (2000).

4. Q. Li, Y. Chen, and Q. Wang, Integration of Process and Project Management System, in *Proc. 2002 IEEE Region 10 Conference on Computers, Communications, Control and Power Engineering, Volume 3* (IEEE: 2002), pp.1582-1586.
5. R. McClatchey, Z. Kovacs, F. Estrella, J-M. Le Goff, G. Chevenier, N. Baker, S. Lieunard, S. Murray, T. Le Flour, and A. Bazan, The Integration of Product Data and Workflow Management System in a Large Scale Engineering Database Application, in *Proc. of Database Engineering and Applications Symposium* (IEEE: Cardiff, UK, 1998), pp.296-302.
6. V. Bellotti, N. Ducheneaut, M. Howard, and I. Smith, Taking Email to Task: The Design and Evaluation of a Task Management Centered Email Tool, in *Proc. of the SIGCHI conference on Human factors in computing systems, Volume 5, Number 1* (IEEE: Florida, USA, 2003), pp.345-352.
7. J. Moore, J. Stader, A. Macintosh, A.C. Mont, and P. Chung, Intelligent Task Management Support for New Product Development in the Chemical Process Industries, in *Sixth International Product Development Management Conference (PDM 99)* (Cambridge, UK, 1999), pp. 787-796.
8. F. Maurer, B. Dellen, S. Goldmann, H. Holz, B. Kotting, and M. Schaff, Merging Project Planning and Web-Enabled Dynamic Workflow Technologies, *IEEE internet computing, IEEE*. Volume 4, Issue 3, pp.65-74, (2000).
9. W. He, I.B.H. Lee, E.W. Lee, and W. He, An integrated design Task management approach for product development lifecycle, in *Proc. of Industrial Informatics, 2006 IEEE International Conference* (IEEE: 2006), pp.554-559.
10. C. Bussler, Workflow Instance Scheduling with Project Management Tools, in *Proc. of Database and Expert Systems Applications (1998)* (IEEE: Vienna, Austria, 1998), pp.753-758.
11. H.M. Shih and M.M. Tseng, Workflow technology–based monitoring and control for business process and project management, *International Journal of Project Management*. Volume 14, Number 6, pp.373-378, (1996).
12. T.R. Browning and S.D. Eppinger, Modeling Impacts of Process Architecture on Cost and Schedule Risk in Product Development, *IEEE transactions on engineering management*. Volume 49, Number 4, pp.428- 442, (2002).
13. E.Z. Huang and S.J. Chen, Estimation of Project Completion Time and Factors Analysis for Concurrent Engineering Project Management: A Simulation Approach, *Concurrent engineering: Research and Applications*. Volume 14, Number 4, pp.328-341, (2006).
14. S.H. Cho and S.D. Eppringer, A Simulation-Based Process Model for Managing Complex Design Projects, *IEEE Transactions on Engineering Management*. Volume 52, Number 3, pp.316-328, (2005).
15. C.H. Chen, S. Ling, and W. Chen, Project Scheduling for collaborative product development using DSM, *International Journal of Project Management*. Volume 21, Number 4, pp.291-299, (2003)

An Industrial Knowledge Reuse Oriented Enterprise Modeling Framework for Enterprise Management Information Systems

Shiliang Wu

School of Management Science and Engineering, Nanjing University of Finance and Economics, Nanjing 210046, P.R. China shiliang.wu@163.com

Abstract. Existing enterprise modeling architectures can not provide effective support on expressing and reusing industrial knowledge. Industrial knowledge reuse oriented enterprise modeling for integrated management information systems (MIS) should be located between general purpose enterprise modeling and concrete enterprise application scheme, and an enterprise modeling framework for integrated MIS which is industrial knowledge reuse oriented is put forward in this paper. In this framework, a new lifecycle dimension was constructed by extending traditional lifecycle dimension and combing the multiple views mechanism of ARIS, knowledge reuse dimension was introduced to support the modeling and reusing industrial knowledge, and the language, methodology and tools dimension was introduced to express the sets of languages, methods and tools used in constructing, validating, maintaining and evolving enterprise models. Finally, the cement production industry was adopted as an example to illustrate how the framework can be employed to guide the reuse of industrial knowledge.

Keywords: *Knowledge management, Enterpriser model, Enterprise Resource Planning (ERP)*

1. INTRODUCTION

Enterprise model is a tool used to describe enterprise knowledge from multiple views, which provides a general problem-solving schema for enterprise repetitive problems under certain settings [1]. There are many famous enterprise model or enterprise reference architecture in the world, for example CIMOSA [2], PERA [3], GERAM[4], etc. Enterprise informatization practice shows that successful implementations of enterprise information systems can be expected and knowledge accumulation for specific industries can be realized [1]. Nowadays, successful enterprise informatization projects are still rare. We think one of main reasons is that the industry knowledge reuse enterprise modeling theory and implementation methodology has not given enough attention. Research on enterprise reference architectures which are industry knowledge reuse oriented is still deficient. In China, several national high-tech (863/CIMS) and national science projects aiming at building industry-specific enterprise reference models were launched. However, the research outcomes in this domain are still rare.

Please use the following format when citing this chapter:

Wu, S., 2007, in IFIP International Federation for Information Processing, Volume 254, Research and Practical Issues of Enterprise Information Systems II Volume 1, eds. L. Xu, Tjoa A., Chaudhry S. (Boston: Springer), pp. 219-228.

This paper studied on industry knowledge reuse oriented enterprise modeling framework. The main contribution is that an enterprise modeling framework for integrated MIS which is industrial knowledge reuse oriented was advanced and each components of this framework were analyzed.

2. LIMITATIONS OF EXISTING ENTERPRISE MODELING FRAMEWORKS

During the last decade, the information and telecommunication technology advanced dramatically. The external and internal environments enterprises faced have changed. The management theories and methodologies on which traditional enterprise reference architecture depended have evolved [1]. We should rethink about existing enterprise modeling frameworks. Several limitations of them are given below:

1. Generally, existing enterprise modeling architectures provide general frameworks and methodologies for enterprise engineering and enterprise integration, which can not provide sufficient support for industry-specific enterprise informatization engineering. For instance, in instantiation dimension, the division of generic and partial components was too generalized, which degraded the ability of modeling and reusing industry-specific knowledge.
2. Existing enterprise modeling architectures provide a group of static views aiming at single enterprise, which can not meet the needs of enterprise integration at different levels such as information integration, resource integration, business process integration and integration among enterprises.
3. The lifecycle dimension in existing enterprise modeling architectures generally was divided into three phase, namely, requirement definition, design and implementation, respectively. The lack of evolvement phase in most existing enterprise modeling architecture make it unable to be used to guide the continuous improvement and maintenance of enterprise information systems. Meanwhile, most existing enterprise modeling architectures have not provided modeling mechanisms for automatic modeling conversion and execution, thus can not meet the needs of managing models and systems during the maintenance phase.

3. POSITION OF INDUSTRY KNOWLEDGE REUSE ORIENTED ENTERPRISE MODELING FOR INTEGRATED MANAGEMENT INFORMATION SYSTEMS

The position of industry knowledge reuse oriented enterprise modeling should be located between generalized enterprise modeling and customized enterprise modeling (see Figure 1). It is not to put forward a brand-new enterprise reference architecture, but to revise existing general enterprise reference architecture to highlight the reuse of industrial knowledge at each stage in lifecycle dimension. Typical characteristics of industry knowledge reuse oriented enterprise modeling architecture are such as strong industry pertinence which means that the reference architecture for target industry (or family of industries sharing large quantities of similarities) can be reused in concrete enterprises belong to same industry readily, version based evolvement mechanism which means that sound industrial knowledge can be inherited, accumulated and reused for future versions. Obviously, this kind of industrial knowledge reused oriented enterprise modeling architecture is intend to offer a mechanism and methodology to realize knowledge reuse by means of abstracting managerial characteristics of target industry and reusing application solutions of all kind components (e.g. various generators, functions, subsystems, and related documents) which can be used in most different industries. Therefore, this architecture is very helpful to accelerate the popularity of mass customization of enterprise MIS systems. Here customization is industry oriented and version based.

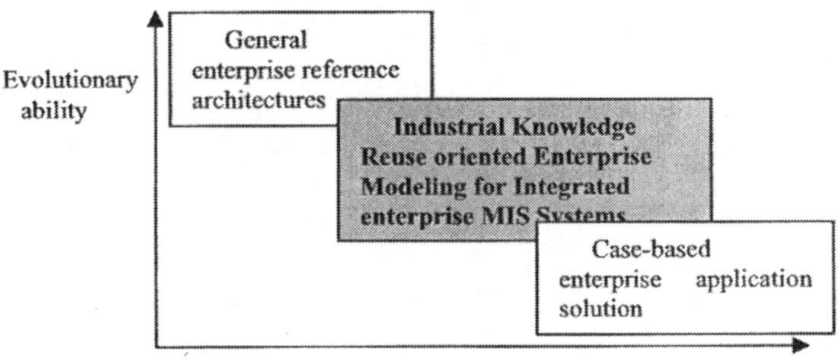

Figure 1. Position of Industrial Knowledge Reuse Oriented Enterprise Modeling for Integrated Enterprise Management Information Systems

4. AN INDUSTRIAL KNOWLEDGE REUSE ORIENTED ENTERPRISE MODELING FRAMEWORK FOR ENTERPRISE MANAGEMENT INFORMATION SYSTEMS

Based on above discussion, we present an industry knowledge reuse oriented enterprise modeling framework for integrated enterprise management information systems (MIS) (see Figure 2).

This framework emphasizes the roles in guidance of constructing and implementing industry specific enterprise information systems played by enterprise reference models, which is achieved by absorbing the advantages of multi-views and multi-dimensional enterprise modeling methodology, meanwhile considering the needs of knowledge reuse, especially software assets based systematic knowledge reuse. Compared with other traditional enterprise reference architectures, there are mainly three enhancements. First, this framework revised the dimension of stepwise particularization into knowledge reuse to accentuate the important roles of this dimension in realizing industrial knowledge reuse. Second, the lifecycle dimension in traditional enterprise reference architectures was extended by integrating multi-views modeling mechanism in which process view as the central view and worked in harmony with other views. Thirdly, the language, method and tool dimension was introduced to express the toolsets used to build, verify, maintain and evolve enterprise models.

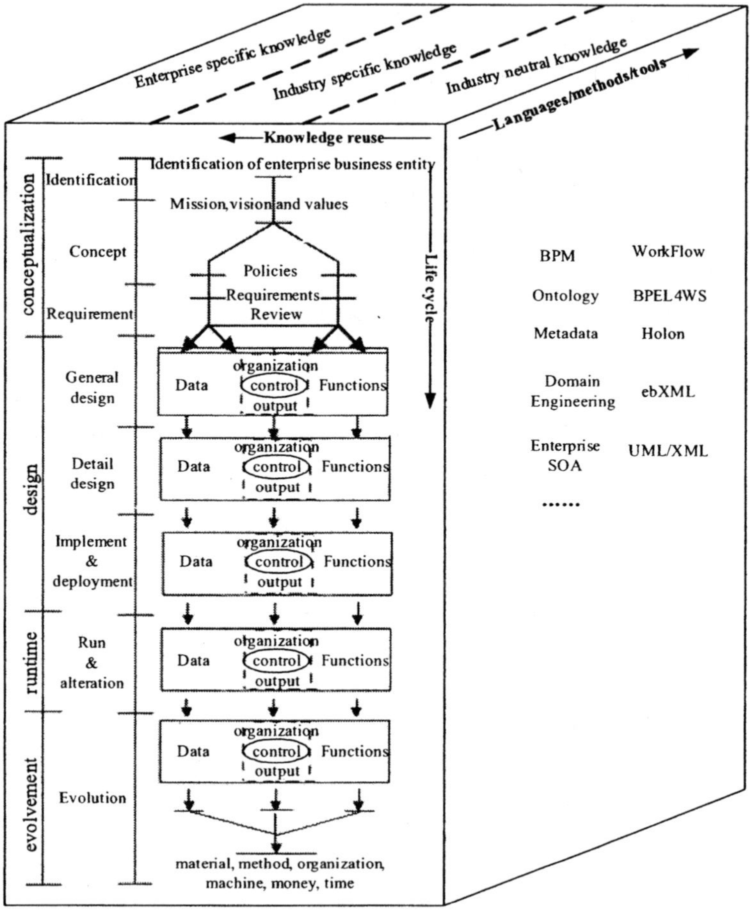

Figure 2. An Industrial Knowledge Reuse Oriented Enterprise Modeling Framework

4.1 Lifecycle Dimension

Life cycle is time dimension of the integrate enterprise modeling framework, which can be further divided into four sections: conceptualization, design, runtime and evolvement. There are several stages at each section. Generally, the outputs of one stage can be the input of the next stage, and continuous optimizing activities occur at each stage. When necessary, new tasks should be added at each stage in order to satisfy the reuse of industrial knowledge. Activities of each stage are discussed briefly blow.

1. Identification. Objects involved in knowledge engineering activities, such as entities, their boundary, external environments, etc, are identified, described and documented. Typical entities are enterprises, departments, teams, products and materials.
2. Concept. The entities obtained at identification stage are generalized to form concepts, which may involve the setup of domain of characteristic values. Typical characteristic value type is missions, visions, values, strategy, tacit, etc.
3. Requirement definition: At this stage, operating requirements for various entities are extracted and their feature sets are built. This task can be achieved along two threads. One is on the main outputs of target enterprises, usually involving products, services or both. The other is on management and control activities. Industrial feature sets involve many elements such as enterprise entities functions, behaviors, information, capabilities, strategy policies, etc. As to industries without industry reference models, the requirement definition documents may be built on the analysis of group of case enterprises belong to same industry or industries sharing large quantities of similarities.
4. General design. At this stage, a general schema for target industry is formed at a top level. The business components logically enabling enterprise systems belonging to target industry or industries are specified. Similar to general design stage of software engineering, the components' hierarchy, their interfaces and constraints are emphasized, while the internal logic of components are ignored at this stage.
5. Detail design. At this stage, the customizable, industry specific reference models are acquired by refining the general schema produced at previous stage. The industry specific models are the most important knowledge carriers which can be reused on many occasions. For instance, during the construction of industry specific enterprise management information systems, the analysis and design time can be reduced dramatically and the design quality can be guaranteed by reusing industry specific models of high quality. On the other hand, when applied in enterprise management information system implementation projects, industry specific reference models will be very helpful because enterprise specific models can be acquired easily by customizing relative industry reference models.
6. Implement & deployment. This is in fact a process of configuring and reengineering enterprise knowledge systems, which involves all kinds of knowledge engineering activities, such as combination of existing knowledge features and structures, knowledge finding, reference model configuration and customization, etc. According to the trend of software reuse and the ideas of model driven architecture, we think implementation and deployment is in fact a process of modeling because formal models are general be ready to execute.
7. Run & alteration. At this stage, IT system as an important enabler system is linked to enterprise entities tightly. IT system is used to accelerate information process and transmission in products and service processes provided by enterprises. When enterprise requirements change, if necessary, the enterprise model instance

embedded in IT system is altered and matched automatically to keep effective, which means the self-study and self-alteration mechanism should be provided in enterprise reference model library. The assimilation of new knowledge and evolvement of existing knowledge mechanism is indispensable at this stage.

8. Evolution. There is no evolution stage in most of existing enterprise architecture such as CIMOSA, Purdue, GERA, etc. The reason of introducing this stage is that generally enterprise information systems have long lifecycle and alterations and evolutions of information systems are indispensable. Enterprise models, enterprise management information systems, enterprise knowledge on enterprise modeling and enterprise models, have in essence is dynamic and evolutionary. Evolution stage concentrates on the management of industrial knowledge revision and maintenance. Evolution is made up of continuous and repetitive processes. Each process enriches existing enterprise modeling knowledge. Knowledge management at this stage is also version-based.

Another important enhancement in lifecycle dimension is that the multi-views are integrated, which greatly strengthen the modeling ability and operability of lifecycle dimension. Firstly, the traditional lifecycle dimension of ARIS was extended and the conceptualization section was refined. The refinement of conceptualization section makes it operable to acquire and share industrial knowledge. Secondly, modeling objects are extended to encompass manufacturing resources and production controls thus can meet the needs of information integration in enterprise job shop level. Thirdly, by integrating ARIS views into lifecycle dimension, the outputs at one stage can refining and evolve continuously at next stage, which means that the evolvement management on enterprise model has more operability.

To meet the needs of enterprise modeling for integrated information systems, modeling emphasis should be put on both the static enterprise entities (e.g. data, functions, organization, and outputs) and dynamic business process description. Enterprise information system logically incarnates material, information and finance flows of real enterprise. We think resources managed by MIS can be classified into five categories: organization related (e.g. employee, customer, supplier, team), material related (e.g. product, raw material, work in process product), machine related (e.g. workshop, device), method related (e.g. product process), money related (finance management), time related (e.g. factory calendar). During industrial knowledge reuse oriented enterprise modeling activities, the modeling on material information should be given enough attention. The organization and operation pattern of an enterprise usually relates with features of products and raw materials at great degree. Besides, the primary and secondary processes can be easily identified when attention was paid to products and materials related features and processes.

4.2 Knowledge Reuse Dimension

Knowledge reuse dimension serves the process of knowledge aggregation and reuse activities, which is the spatial dimension of enterprise modeling framework. There are three levels in this dimension.

1. Industry neutral knowledge level

There are many similarities exists in organize pattern, business domain, product organization among different industries. Naturally, industry neutral knowledge can be built by mining and generalizing knowledge commonly used in different industries. This level is made up of basic elements of enterprise modeling architecture, mainly the basic modeling components produced at different stages and model constraints, rules, glossary, services and protocols.

From semantic angle, the knowledge forms maybe industry neutral components, such as MRP (material requirement planning) computing component, BOM (bill of material) components, document component (e.g. invoice, contract, and order), calendar component, etc.

2. Industry specific knowledge level

On the basis of reusing and refining industry neutral knowledge, this level produces industry specific reference models. What this level concerns most is the expression and encapsulation of industry specific knowledge, and the outcome of encapsulation is usually the industrial components for different business domains. This level is aiming at different sub-industries belong to manufacturing industry, such as textile, mechanical manufacturing, medicine, food production, petrol and steel industry etc. Sometimes certain industry need to be further divided into smaller industries, thus industry tree occurs.

3. Enterprise specific knowledge level

What concerns most at this level is enterprise models for concrete enterprises, which are usually constructed by reusing and customizing relevant industry reference models. Knowledge about enterprise individualities at this level can be refined, generalized and transformed during knowledge evolvement cycle.

Industry neutral knowledge level and industry specific knowledge level sometimes are called industry reference model level, which is key points to implementing enterprise model knowledge reuse due to the fact that reference model level is built on aggregating and abstracting common enterprise requirement features from many enterprise informatized engineering projects. Industry reference model can be reused widely in business optimization, production plan, manufacturing control, etc., in enterprise engineering project. Shorter enterprise modeling time, higher modeling quality can be obtained by reusing industry reference models effectively.

4.3 Languages, Methods and Tools

In order to maximize the industrial knowledge reuse, we think three research fields should be paid close attention. The first is model driven architecture (MDA)[5], which offers a novel approach to solving the contradiction between the increasing complexity of enterprise applications and higher customer expectance. According to MDA theory, all kinds of models, especially those described formally, are in fact the most important reusable knowledge assets. The modeling process is also the application development process. Therefore, when combined with systematic software reuse methods, process and management practice knowledge, will be very helpful to guide the process of customization, reconfiguration and evolution of industry oriented management information systems. The second is domain engineering (DE)[6], which is the activity of collecting, organizing, and storing past experience in building systems or parts of systems in a particular domain in the form of reusable assets (i.e. reusable work products), as well as providing an adequate means for reusing these assets (i.e. retrieval, qualification, dissemination, adaptation, assembly, etc.) when building new systems. We think the industry reference models which incarnate industrial knowledge can be built by means of applying domain engineering in target industry (or similar industries). Actually, domain specific software architecture (DSSA) and other reusable components are important knowledge assets which usually have definite industry orientation. Furthermore, when considering the combination of domain engineering and enterprise service oriented architecture (ESOA), the more flexible, reusable industrial knowledge and the more agile IT solution for target industries can be achieved in theory. The third is about ontology. Ontology can be defined as an explicit formal specification of the terms in the domain and relations among them [7]. In the context of enterprise application, enterprise ontology refers to a set of glossary and definition related to enterprise businesses. From the angle of knowledge sharing, enterprise ontology can act as an ideal communication medium between different people and enterprise applications. We think well defined enterprise ontology can be a good start to build information view which is a part of enterprise modeling framework, which will promote the industrial knowledge reuse greatly.

5. CASE STUDY

The industrial knowledge reuse oriented enterprise modeling framework was used in the CIMS project of Pan-gu cement production enterprise group. By maximizing process industry knowledge reuse in cement enterprise informatization project, we finished project analysis and design, application system selection and system implementation with high quality.

The significance of the framework presented in this paper in prompting cement enterprise informatization was in three aspects. The knowledge reuse dimension was used to aggregate and reuse knowledge of cement industry, the lifecycle dimension was used to process management and control in the whole life of cement industry informatization engineering, and the languages, methods, and tools dimension provided expression methods and supporting tools for knowledge representation, reuse and management. Here, we put the emphasis on applying knowledge reuse dimension in overall solution for cement industry informatization.

According to industrial knowledge, we did not develop an overall solution from scratch, but from reusing and customizing existing industrial knowledge assets, such as general solutions for manufacturing industry, process industry reference framework, etc. The cement production industry can be regarded as a process industry, which has typical features of process industry. There are some typical features of process industry, for example, many kinds of sensors such as sensors for detecting temperature, pressure, location, velocity are widely used in production process; requirements of collecting, processing and visualizing data on line are very common; multiple systems coexists including automatic systems at device level, process control systems at job shop level, management information systems at business operating level; information integration requirements among different systems are urgent. Based on our industrial knowledge reuse framework, by means of maximizing reusing existing process industry knowledge, we advanced a reference framework for cement industry informatization, which are divided into five levels (See Figure 3).

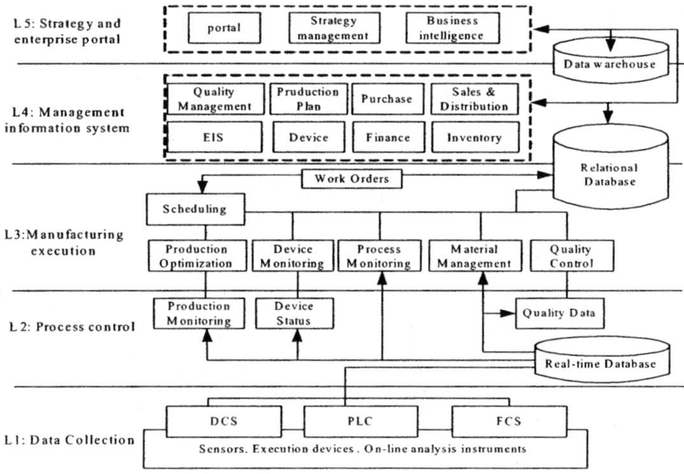

Figure 3. A Reference Framework for Cement Industry Informatization

1. L1: Data collection level. This level is composed of infrastructure systems such as distributed control system (DCS), programmatic logic control systems (PLC), etc, which collects control information from production fields. By installing relating sensors and on-line analyzing devices at target sites, real-time data about production process can be collected and then stored in real-time databases.
2. L2: Process control level. What this level concerns is the optimization of working operation and device control. This level accepts instructions from manufacturing execution level, dissolves them into concrete control instructions and passes them to control devices at data collection level. Device operating status and production data collected at data collection level is passed to manufacturing execution level via process control level.
3. L3: Manufacturing execution level. This level is the key to integrating enterprise management information systems and production control systems. Compared with management information system level, what this level concerns are production field resources, such as device utilization, production process, work in progress, etc. Some typical functions of this level are accepting work orders from management information systems level, scheduling and monitoring order execution activities, allocating device resources, and feeding information about resource utilization and inventory level back to management information system level.

4. L4: Management information system level. Most of modules (e.g. purchasing management, sales management, human resource management) in typical management information systems (e.g. enterprise resource planning, ERP) can be reused in cement industry. Some modules, e.g. quality management, device management, production plan, material management, need to be enhanced or reengineered when used in cement industry.
5. L5: Strategy and enterprise portal level. The aim of this level is to deepen the informatization of cement industry. Typical modules are business intelligence, e-commerce, etc.

6. CONCLUSIONS

This paper think that researches on industrial knowledge reuse oriented enterprise modeling provides a promising approach to solving problems such as low industry pertinence, high complexity of information system, too long implementation cycle, etc, which commonly exist in commercial general purpose enterprise management information systems. Based on the analysis on existing enterprise reference architecture, this paper advanced an industrial knowledge reuse oriented enterprise modeling framework for integrated information system, and gave a case study in cement industry. Our research indicates the industry specific information modeling and informatization can be improved greatly by maximizing the reuse of industrial knowledge.

REFERENCES

1. F. Arbab, M. Bonsangue, and J.G. Scholten, *State of the Art in Architecture Frameworks and Tools*, ARDIN Institute (2002). https://doc.telin.nl/dscgi/ds.py/Get/File-22327 (Accessed May 10, 2006).
2. K. Kosanke, F. Vernadat, and M. Zelm. CIMOSA: enterprise engineering and integration. *Computers in Industry*. Volume 40, Number 1, pp.83-97, (1999).
3. T.J. Williams, *The Purdue Enterprise Reference Architecture and Methodology (PERA)* Institute for Interdisciplinary Engineering Studies, Purdue University (2000). http://www.ecn.purdue.edu/IIES/PLAIC/Enterprise-Handbook_PERA.pdf (Accessed June 4, 2005).
4. Anonymous, *GERAM: Generalised Enterprise Reference Architecture and Methodology (version 1.6.3)* IFIP–IFAC Task Force on Architectures for Enterprise Integration (1999). http://www.cit.gu.edu.au/~bernus/taskforce/geram/versions/geram1-6-3/GERAMv1.6.3.pdf (Accessed October 9, 2004).
5. Anonymous, *MDA Guide (Version 1.0.1)* (Object Management Group: 2003). http://www.omg.org/cgi-bin/apps/doc?omg/03-06-01.pdf (Accessed May 20, 2007).
6. K. Czarnecki and U. Eisenecker, *Generative Programming: Methods, Techniques, and Applications* (Addison-Wesley: Boston, MA, 1999).
7. T.R. Gruber, A translation approach to portable ontologies, *Knowledge Acquisition*. Volume 2, Number 2, pp.199-220, (1993).

Service Level Driven Stock Allocation: A Model Based Enterprise Information System

Felix S. Wriggers[1], Matthias Schmidt[1], Rouven Nickel[2] and Peter Nyhuis[1]

[1]Institute of Production Systems and Logistics, Gottfried Wilhelm Leibniz Universität Hannover, Hannover, Germany wriggers@ifa.uni-hannover.de schmidt@ifa.uni-hannover.de
[2]Institute of Integrated Production Hannover, Hannover, Germany nickel@iph-hannover.de

Abstract. The conflict between the objectives for logistic efficiency and storage costs largely influences inventory management. The positioning in this tension field poses a challenge to decision makers. The Logistic Storage Analysis (LSA) is an industry proven control model used to dimension stock within this field of tension. To this end, the LSA offers a variety of tools, derived from Logistic Operating Curves, for aggregating and visualizing data and is thus an ideal foundation and starting point for the Enterprise Information System (EIS) currently being developed.

Keywords: *EIS for manufacturing sector, Logistic operations, Logistic operation curves, Stock allocation, Supply chain management, Supply chain planning and execution*

1. INTRODUCTION

Like the price and quality of the products, the logistic efficiency of industrial firms has become an important criterion for purchasing during the last two decades. The trend to consider parameters for logistic efficiency as well as the qualities of a company or a product has established itself in both national and international markets [1-2]. The logistic objectives, shorter delivery times and high due date reliability have thus taken on added significance with this development [3-5].

In order to meet these demands, the central logistic challenge in the controlling of procurement, storage and distribution processes turns out to be ensuring the availability of required parts for the customer at the planned time.

The availability of parts is ensured in operating plants through inventory management in that from a logistic viewpoint, the stock in the procurement or distribution stores has to be adequately dimensioned. In addition to availability, costs related to maintaining stock have to be considered in order to economically dimension it [6]. Here, we see the classical Dilemma of Inventory Management: A balance has to be found between a high availability of parts on the one hand and low stock costs on the other hand [2, 7-8].

As the primary goal, the firm's profitability is defined in accordance with the economical goals [7]. Consequently, efficiently managing costs and minimizing running costs are basic prerequisites for remaining competitive.

Please use the following format when citing this chapter:

Wriggers, F. S., Schmidt, M., Nickel, R., Nyhuis, P., 2007, in IFIP International Federation for Information Processing, Volume 254, Research and Practical Issues of Enterprise Information Systems II Volume 1, eds. L. Xu, Tjoa A., Chaudhry S. (Boston: Springer), pp. 229-237.

Stock dimensioning plays a major role here, as the costs related to extensive capital tie-up significantly influences the production costs. If some of the capital tie-up can be resolved, the freed capital might be directly utilized for investments and thus for generating future cash flows.

Nevertheless, from both the procurement and distributions sides, industrial firms' storage strategies are frequently not oriented on demand. Parts which are often required regularly and in large numbers are often out of stock, whereas those sporadically required are often stored in large amounts and for long periods. Thus for example stock accounts for ca. 22% of the balance sheet total in the German automobile ancillary industry [9].

In order to support companies in improving their inventory management it is necessary to develop a simple, field oriented Enterprise Information System. Such a system should offer decision making support for the Logistic Positioning of stock levels within the field of tension between the need for greater storage efficiency (higher service level, lower delivery delay) and low stock costs (low stock level). At the same time this system has to provide decision makers with up to the minute information including operating figures and when necessary, visualize them [10]. Building on Throughput Diagrams, Storage Operating Curves and Ranking Lists the Logistic Storage Analysis presents an ideal basis for such a system.

2. THE LOGISTIC STORAGE ANALYSIS

The Logistic Storage Analysis is a method with which a firm can analyze its stock and uncover potential for a greater service level. It is theoretically well established in numerous publications [7-8, 11] and has proven to be a useful instrument for analysis in a large number of applications including those in the field [e.g. 12-13]. Currently the Logistic Storage Analysis is being expanded to implement interdependencies of service levels and a different service level definition.

The Logistic Storage Analysis consists of a variety of methods (cf. Figure 1) such as the Storage Throughput Diagram, Storage Operating Curves and Ranking Lists. These can be used to transparently represent storages processes as well cause and effect relations, in addition to indicating problem areas and identifying potentials [8].

During a Logistic Storage Analysis the required modeling methods are linked together with one another, whereby scenarios with different boundary conditions are created through systematically varying the parameters which determine the stock level.

Taking into consideration different boundary conditions makes it possible to derive laws as well as to estimate the consequences of prospective measures identify problem articles and define objectives. Dimensioning the required safety stock level for example, leads to an increased reliability in storage processes and thus to an improved service level.

Experiences in practical applications have shown that the results can only be sustained and the potential can only be used over the long term, when a regular storage analysis is supported through the development of a logistic objective control.

This is due to the continual changes in a company and thus also to the shifting logistic environment, which requires the stock to be continuously monitored and adjusted.

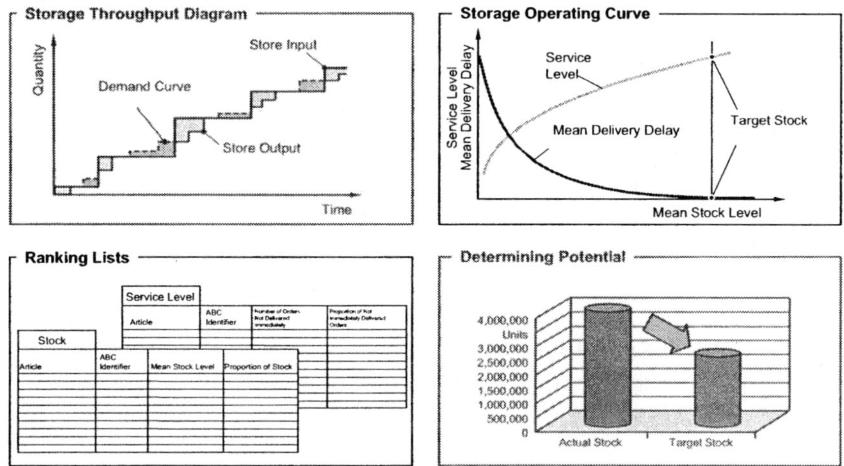

Figure 1. Logistic Storage Analysis Methods

Applying the Logistic Storage Analysis in the industrial field demonstrated a number of possibilities for improving it, particularly with regards to implementing inventory analyses and controls. On the one hand it became clear that the required data was not easily drawn from the system and that an intensive validation process had to be undertaken. On the other hand, there were problems in a few cases when converting it to a continuous control: The effort necessary to generate important figures from the data could not be justified and the problem could not be clearly visualized near to real time.

The idea to develop an Enterprise Information System, which offers users support in the decision making process thus emerged. After an initial storage analysis and dimensioning, this system should contribute to the continual analysis and control of the stores. At the same time this system should take into consideration two important further developments of the Logistic Storage Analysis: the Allocation Diagram and the unweighted Service Level Operating Curves.

3. EXPANDING THE LOGISTIC STORAGE ANALYSIS

3.1 The Unweighted Service Level

The service level is a common operating figure in the industrial field and offers an approach for evaluating the trade-off between stock costs and stock-out costs [14].

Generally, the service level, which can be either weighted or unweighted, describes the degree to which the demands on the stores are fulfilled. Up until now, the Logistic Storage Analysis only took into consideration the weighted service level.

Since the unweighted service level is however more frequently applied than the weighted service level in the industry, expanding the Logistic Storage Analysis to include the unweighted Service Level Operating Curve offers a better possibility to meet practical demands [7].

The weighted service level ($SERL_w$) is determined from the ratio of punctually withdrawn demanded parts to the total demanded quantity. The demanded orders are thus weighted with their respective amounts.

Through this weighting with the demand lot size, the significance and influence of the different order sizes is reflected on the logistic efficiency of a stocking echelon. Based on the C_{norm} function, LUTZ developed a weighted Service Level Operating Curve, which expresses the cause and effect relations between the Work in Process and weighted service level [7].

The unweighted service level ($SERL_{uw}$) corresponds to the ratio of demands that are met both time wise and quantity wise to the total demand.

Just as the weighted Service Level Operating Curve represents the service level over the mean stock level per article, so does the newly developed unweighted Service Level Operating Curve. Similarly, the C_{norm} function is also employed as a basis.

The correlation between the two service levels, allow inferences to be drawn about a store's distribution behavior. Thus when $SERL_w > SERL_{uw}$ it indicates that few large demands were punctually served, and that many smaller demands also faced delays. In contrast, the reverse situation, where $SERL_{uw} > SERL_w$, indicates that many small demands are punctually served and only a few large orders are delayed.

With regards to the criteria relevant to making decisions, a method for choosing the Logistic Operating Curve best suited for the respective problem was developed. This method also permits for the first time, inferences to be made from a stores' target service level about the article service level. In doing so, the degree of correlation (if applicable) between individual articles in the store is considered.

Further, factors influencing the C_{norm} function's shape were identified and structured according to their effects. Future work to determine an equation for the shape depending on the identified influencing factors is conducted at present.

3.2 The Allocation Diagram

When the customer is not separated from the production through a store, then the customer's desired service level is primarily dependent on the logistic synchronization between the firm's manufacturing and assembly areas. In order for a company to have a high logistic efficiency it is a prerequisite that all of the manufacturing orders required for an assembly order be completely available and allocated from the store for the planned assembly start date.

When single part orders are late being filled it frequently leads to delays in the corresponding assembly orders and thus has a direct, negative impact on the completion date. If a completion date in contrast is met earlier than planned or a part of it is retrieved too early and the assembly starts only at the planned date, the corresponding part has to be buffered. Costs then accumulate for the resulting Work in Process buffer through the tied up capital costs, handling and required floor space.

The Allocation Diagram developed in order to analyze the scheduling situation for the order network and to improve the analysis of adjusting the manufacturing and assembly processes [15-16]. The goal of this diagram is to visualize and precisely synchronize the provisions from the store and/or the preceding manufacturing.

An Allocation Diagram consists of two curves. The first curve represents the connection of the points in time at which the first position of an assembly order is allocated. The Completion Curve in contrast delivers the completion time of all an assembly order's positions, accumulated and sorted according to the point in time of the last allocated manufacturing order (Figure 2).

The area which is created between the two curves corresponds to the Work in Process of the partially allocated manufacturing orders. In order to be able to transparently represent the scheduling situation of different assembly orders, the respective planned requirement dates are normalized, that is set to zero. According to NICKEL the Allocation Diagram can be utilized for depicting the loss of value due to badly adjusted processes also [16].

So that the Work in Process buffers and scheduling deviations can be reduced in the output, a simultaneous and punctual allocation should be strived for. With reference to the diagram, that means that the two curves should approximate one another as closely as possible in the area before the normalized requirement date i.e. the point of origin.

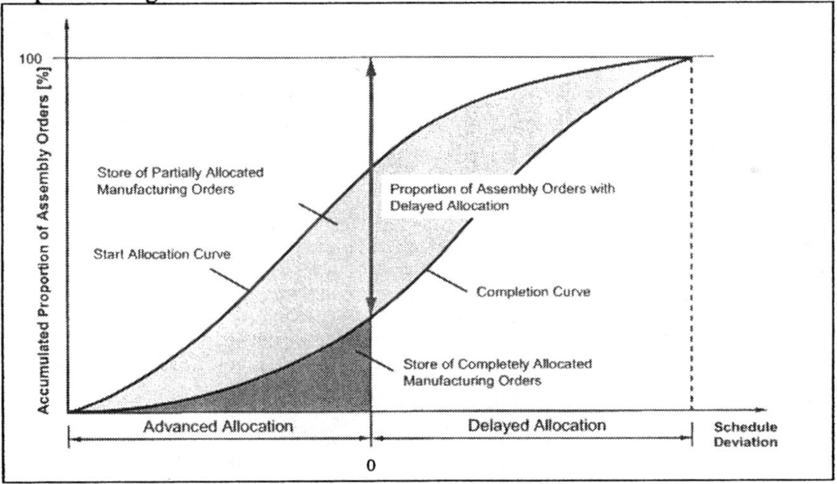

Figure 2. The Allocation Diagram

The Allocation Diagram might be deployed for diverse purposes. Both analysis of the current state of allocation processes and derivation of measures to improve upon the current state are furthered [16]. With the Allocation Diagram it is possible to indicate potential for improving the delivery reliability and reducing unnecessary stock, as well as to derive the measures required for developing these identified potentials [17].

Measures such as sequencing according to the slack rule, can further the punctual allocation. In order to support the simultaneous completion of the orders though, a reactive schedule oriented release is required which is based on realistic, order specific, planned throughput times. Dates determined through backwards scheduling have to be consistently used. Should however, an individual order's completion be delayed in an order network; it is advisable to shift the planned completion date for all other manufacturing orders in order to avoid an unplanned Work in Process buffer.

So that orders are punctually allocated, the flexibility of the capacities can be increased in the manufacturing area and/or the allocation of the manufacturing capacities can be distributed according to demands. Further measures, which promote the punctual and simultaneous availability of manufacturing orders include scheduling controls in both the manufacturing and assembly areas, as well as developing products that enable the complexity of an order's work content structure to be reduced.

4. DEVELOPMENT OF THE ENTERPRISE INFORMATION SYSTEM

By expanding the Logistic Storage Analysis to include the unweighted Service Level Operating Curves and the Allocation Diagram, the field of application for the Logistic Storage Analysis can also be extended. With the assistance of a further method, which can be applied in order to choose the most suitable Service Level Operating Curve, the direct back-coupling of a target service level (for the entire inventory) can occur for the first time based on the target stock levels of individual articles. In this way, it is possible to optimally structure the stores in the entire inventory with regards to costs (Figure 3).

Experiences during the development of the LogiAs Enterprise Information System for the make process, demonstrated that modeling with methods from the Logistic Operating Curves presented an almost ideal basis for such a system with regards to the ratio of required effort and illustrative quality. NICKEL AND VOGEL describe this EIS (LogiAs) and the applicability of the Logistic Operating Curve Theory in great detail [18]. LogiAs applies the Logistic Operating Curve Theory in order to control near to real time production processes. In doing so a variety of variables and Logistic Operating Curves are available for the user, which are supplemented through additional instruments (e.g., portfolios, scenarios, and ranking lists). These variables and Logistic Operating Curves are determined near to real time, based on the validated data from the data warehouse and are visualized according to the users wish.

It can thus be presumed that the above mentioned aspects of the expanded Logistic Storage Analysis form a very good basis for an Enterprise Information System. Therefore the Enterprise Information System currently under development at the Institute for Production Systems and Logistics will utilize the Logistic Storage Analysis and the Methods included therein.

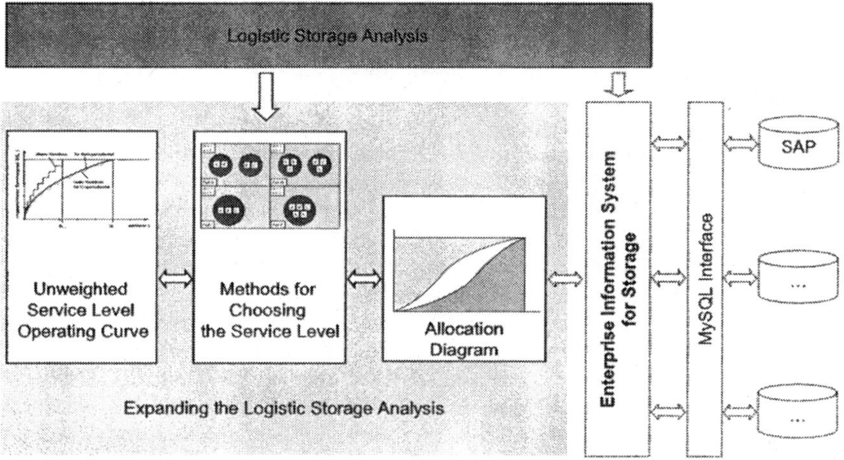

Figure 3. Locating the Enterprise Information System for Storage within the Field of Research on Storage Analysis

Building on real data gathered in an ample investigation period of the near past and validated for accuracy and correctness the System may then be used for several purposes in the field of stock dimensioning. An overview of the Logistic Stock Analysis capabilities is given in Figure 4.

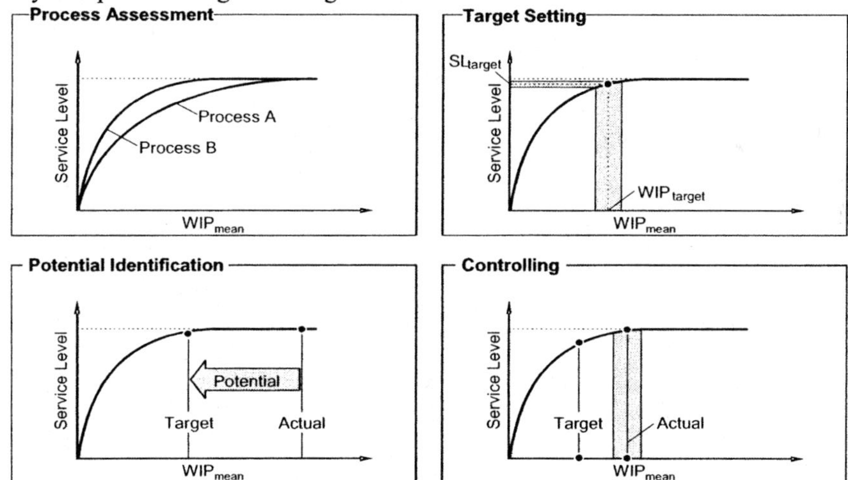

Figure 4. Capabilities of the Logistic Storage Analysis

On field of application for the Enterprise Information System is the assessment of alternative processes. Since the input parameters of Logistic Operating Curves are the parameters of upstream processes, alternative shapes of the curve result subject to their efficiency. For instance if the upstream process is a sourcing process involving suppliers, the suppliers can be assessed by means of Logistic Operating Curves. For each supplier individual Operating Curves can be generated establishing the option to evaluate the supplier quality. The supplier to be favored is the one sporting the best Operating Curve.

Service Level Operating Curves may also be generated if the upstream process is in-house. For this purpose the process's target variances can be used since the shape of the Operating Curve depends on them. Varying of these parameters poses the chance to study effects of process improvements (e.g. an improvement of on time delivery). Resulting Work in Process levels and Service Levels can be compared and thus the potential for optimization can be analyzed.

Besides for process assessment Service Level Operating Curves and respectively the Enterprise Information Systems can be utilized in setting targets. Service Level Operating Curves have to fulfil two functions for this purpose: Both the process of target setting and of target assessment. By using the Operating Curves it can be determined if aimed at targets are consistent with Service Levels and Work in Process. If the targeted Work in Process is not part of the Service Level Operating Curve the targeted Service Level is not obtainable for the targeted Work in Process for existing boundary conditions. Therefore measures have to be derived, to change the Operating Curves shape.

An essential field of application for Service Level Operating Curves is the determination of Work in Process necessary to achieve targeted Service Levels. The Enterprise Information System will be able to achieve this goal by calculating the Work in Process corresponding with the targeted Service Level. This Work in Process can then be used as target Work in Process. If the targeted Service Level is given with a range of tolerance, a likewise range of tolerance can be calculated for Work in Process. This range of tolerance can then be utilized for definition of action limits.

Service Level Operating Curves can be used to depict actual and target operating points. They are thus suited for a logistical Work in Process and Warehouse controlling. The Enterprise Information System thus aids a quick visualization of actual and target Work in Process and Service Levels. Considering influences fields of action can be derived. Effects of derived measures on the processes may also be evaluated. Thus an assessment as well as a concerted application of measures is aided by the Enterprise Information System.

Last but not least the potential inherent in the process can be discerned by comparing actual and target Work in Process. Expanding this comparison to all articles in stock results in the cumulative Work in Process adjustment necessary for one warehouse. This adjustment might be a reduction as well as an increase in overall Work in Process. It is imperative to check for further measures if the necessity for increase in Work in Process is determined.

ACKNOWLEDGEMENTS

The authors would like to thank the German Research Foundation (DFG), which financially supports the expansion of the Logistic Storage Analysis within the context of the project "Developing a Method for Increasing Part Availability in Assembly Areas through Service Level Oriented Inventory Dimensioning".

REFERENCES

1. T. Tracht and S. Reinsch, *Erfolgsfaktor Logistikqualität: Vorgehen, Methoden und Werkzeuge zur Verbesserung der Logistikleistung*, 2nd Edition, eds. H.P. Wiendahl (Springer: Berlin, 2002), pp.1-7.
2. H. Wildemann, *Logistik-Check - Identifikation und Erschließung von Logistikpotenzialen*, 5th Edition (TCW: München, 2007).
3. K.K.B. Hon, Performance and Evaluation of Manufacturing Systems, *Annals of the CIRP*. Volume 55, Number 2, (2005).
4. P. Nyhuis, F. Wriggers, and A. Fischer, Knowledge Enterprise: Intelligent Strategies in Product Design, Manufacturing, and Management, in *Proc. of The International Federation of Information Processing (IFIP), Volume 207*, eds. K. Wang, G. Kovacs, M. Wozny, and M. Fang (Springer: Boston, 2006).
5. B. Enslow, *Best Practices in International Logistic* (Aberdeen Group: Boston, 2006).
6. J. Gläßner, *Modellgestütztes Controlling der beschaffungslogistischen Prozesskette*, Fortschritt-Berichte VDI, Series 2, Number 337 (VDI: Düsseldorf, 1995).
7. S. Lutz, *Kennliniengestütztes Lagermanagement*, Fortschritt-Berichte VDI, Series 13, Number 53 (VDI: Düsseldorf, 2002).
8. P. Nyhuis and H.P. Wiendahl, *Logistische Kennlinien – Grundlagen, Werkzeuge und Anwendungen*, 2nd Edition (Springer: Berlin, 2003).
9. K. Gerhardt and C. Sarantidis, *Automobilzulieferer – Bericht zur Branche*, IKB Information Dezember 2003 (IKB: Düsseldorf, 2003).
10. M. Shah and M. Littlefield, *There is No Execution without Integration – MES Adoption Drives Performance* (Aberdeen Group: Boston, 2007).
11. S. Lutz and H. Lödding, and H.P. Wiendahl, Logistics-oriented inventory analysis, *International Journal of Production Economics*. Volume 85, Number 6, pp.217-231, (2003).
12. M. Vogel, M. Schmidt, D. Emminger, and A. Mix, Entwicklung eines Beschaffungskonzepts im Maschinenbau, *Supply Chain Management*. Volume 6, Number 2, pp.39-44, (2006).
13. F.S. Wriggers, T. Busse, and M. Schmidt, Logistische Lageranalyse und Methodenvalidierung im Elektronikwerk Amberg, *Industrie Management*. Volume 23, Number 5, publication pending, (2007).
14. J. Alscher, H. Schneider, Zur Interdependenz von Fehlmengenkosten und servicegrad, *Kostenrechnungspraxis*. Volume 6, pp.257-271, (1982).
15. P. Nyhuis, R. Nickel, and T. Busse, Logistisches Controlling der Materialverfügbarkeit mit Bereitstellungsdiagrammen, *Zeitschrift für wirtschaftlichen Fabrikbetrieb*. Volume 101, Number 5, pp.265-268, (2006).
16. R. Nickel, *Logistische Modelle für die Montage* (PZH: Hannover, 2007), publication pending.
17. P. Nyhuis, R. Nickel, and D.Grabe, Synchronisationspotenziale in der Logistik identifizieren und bewerten, *PPS-Management*. Volume 12, Number 2, pp.66-69, (2007).
18. R. Nickel and M. Vogel, Entwicklung eines Assistenzsystems für das Produktionscontrolling, *Industrie Management*. Volume 22, Number 4, pp.61-64, (2006).

The Human Side of ERP Implementations: Can Change Management Really Make a Difference?

Susan Foster[1], Paul Hawking[2] and Cindy Zhu[3]

[1]Faculty of Information Technology, Caulfield School of IT, Monash University, Melbourne Australia sue.foster@infotech.monash.edu.au
[2]School of Information Systems, Victoria University, Melbourne, Australia
[3]Beijing Jiaotong University, Beijing, P.R. China

Abstract. In the lead up to large-scale change bought about by enterprise system implementations, there are multiple complex influences at play that impact perceptions that the organisation might not be ready for the change effort. These influences manifest in uncertainty, ambiguity in roles and responsibilities and in many cases, information overload. Organisational change management (OCM) is often considered to be one of the most important success factors for enterprise system implementations and has even be referred to as a critical success factor. In this paper a definition of OCM will be proposed and outcomes of an investigation into the effectiveness of integrating OCM when implementing enterprise resource planning projects will be discussed. For the purposes of this investigation large scale enterprise resource planning systems were chosen as the software of choice to study. These systems by virtue of their complexity and implementation costs often cause long reaching impacts on the organization. Often to the point where organizations can wait for long periods of time to obtain any real benefit realisation. In this study 208 European organisations responded to a survey. Findings in brief indicated that experts who applied CM in their projects evaluated their projects as more successful than projects without CM.

Keywords: *ERP, Organizational change management (OCM), CSFs, Organizational readiness for change*

1. INTRODUCTION

The benefits that enterprise systems provide organisations have been well documented by many researchers identifying a range of factors contributing to the growth in the uptake of ERP systems; the need to streamline and improve business processes and better manage information systems expenditure. Clearly such systems are essential for modern businesses [1-6]. However, these systems are complex and for many companies, implementations are associated with project overruns and lack of benefit realisation.

Please use the following format when citing this chapter:

Foster, S., Hawking, P., Zhu, C., 2007, in IFIP International Federation for Information Processing, Volume 254, Research and Practical Issues of Enterprise Information Systems II Volume 1, eds. L. Xu, Tjoa A., Chaudhry S. (Boston: Springer), pp. 239-249.

1.1 Enterprise System and Change

The very nature of enterprise systems causes enterprise wide business process changes, job redesign and often an associated reduction in head count [7]. It is clearly evident that these are direct employee impacts. As many as 75% of organisational change efforts involving technology fail as a result of people's negative reactions to changes in their work practices, organisational business processes and in the use of the technology leading people to resist the change [8,9]. Consequently, it is the way in which staff are enabled to positively adapt to this change in their work practices, that has been identified as one of the leading critical success factors in successful implementations; the associated interventions are referred to as "change management" [10-13].

One such study indicated that respondents were very aware of the importance of effective change management in ERP implementations [13]. A qualitative question in this survey required IT professionals to provide a short description or definition of change management in order to assess their understanding of this concept [13]. From an analysis of the descriptions, an aggregated definition was developed:

Change management is defined as the process of assisting the organisation in the smooth transition from one defined state to another, by managing and coordinating changes to business processes and systems. Change management involves the effective communication with stakeholders regarding the scope and impact of the expected change; formal processes for assessing and monitoring the impact of the change on the stakeholders and their work processes, and identifying and developing effective and appropriate techniques to assist stakeholders to cope and adapt to the new technology.

It is argued that this definition is inclusive in that it clearly identifies some of the main critical factors involved in change management and takes a holistic approach. The definition applies to change management in a specific condition; that of technology change.

In this paper the impact of enterprise systems, specifically the implementation of SAP (ERP system) will be assessed on organizational change in European countries. The outcome of this assessment on organizational change will be discussed.

1.2 Survey

The main objective of this study was to analyze the role of change management (CM) within SAP projects and to learn the adopters' experiences with Change Management.

The ability to successfully implement an SAP system calls for involving the affected business departments and individuals in the change process and convincing them of the project's overall benefits. Overcoming resistance and obtaining user buy-in for new systems and methods of working are just some of the key elements of an effective organizational CM program. This study was designed to answer the following questions:

1. What role does change management (CM) play within large scale enterprise system implementations such as SAP?

2. What are the key drivers for applying CM?
3. Which CM measures have been applied?
4. What is the impact of CM on the project's success?

1.2.1 Survey Design

An online anonymous study was used. The questionnaire was primarily constructed of closed questions with preformulated answer categories. Some open, explorative questions were included in the questionnaire to provide additional support to closed answers. The questionnaire was structured into six parts: Demographic information about the participating organization, General information about the project, Training, Organizational CM, project success and future prospects.

1.2.2 Description of the Sample

In total 208 organizations responded to the survey, mainly from Germany, Switzerland, Austria, the Netherlands, France, Spain Sweden and the United Kingdom. Of these 155 organizations indicated that they had applied CM within their projects; 53 had not. The participating organizations represented a broad range of industries and sizes in terms of the number of employees and annual revenue.

2. RESULTS

In total approximately 50% of the participating organizations belonged to the manufacturing industry sector. One third of the participants were service industries and 18% were from financials and public sector. Nearly one third of the polled organizations employ up to 1000 people. Another third employ between 1000 and 5000 people. And 11% have more than 50,000. It is probably not surprising to note that the higher the application of CM in SAP projects linked to the higher the number of employees. Almost 90% of organizations with more than 5000 employees applied CM in their SAP projects, only about half of the organizations with fewer than 1000 employees did. Further, companies with higher revenues tended to integrate CM more than those with lower annual incomes.

2.1 Description of Projects

Project Phase and Duration

Over half of the projects (46%) had already been completed by the time of the Survey enabling organizations to contribute experiences from the whole implementation cycle. More than one-third of the SAP projects lasted one year, and one-third lasted two to three years. Long-term projects with a duration of four years or longer made up 23% of the sample. The decision to apply CM in a SAP project did not depend on the project's duration.

Project budget

Participants were asked to estimate the total budget for the SAP projects (including licenses and consulting and support services). The majority of the projects (54%) budgeted less than €2.5m. A third of the projects had a budget between €2.5m and €20m and 20% had a budget of more than €20m. By comparing projects with and without CM, a general trend was observed: The higher the total project budget, the higher the percentage of projects with CM.

Project complexity

The sample mainly consisted of small projects. Nevertheless, comparing projects with and without CM reveals a connection between the use of CM and project size: With increasing project size, CM was applied more frequently, and nearly all large SAP projects were supported by CM. In more than 50% of the projects, the implementation of SAP software caused large organizational changes. This clearly underscores the fact that SAP projects are organizational projects. The data analysis revealed a light trend: The more international the project scope, the more prevalent was CM.

2.2 Levels of Employee Resistance

Participating experts were asked to evaluate the resistance of different stakeholder groups within their organization toward the SAP project. As Figure 1 demonstrates, the level of resistance correlates with the hierarchical level of the stakeholder groups: the lower the level the higher the resistance.

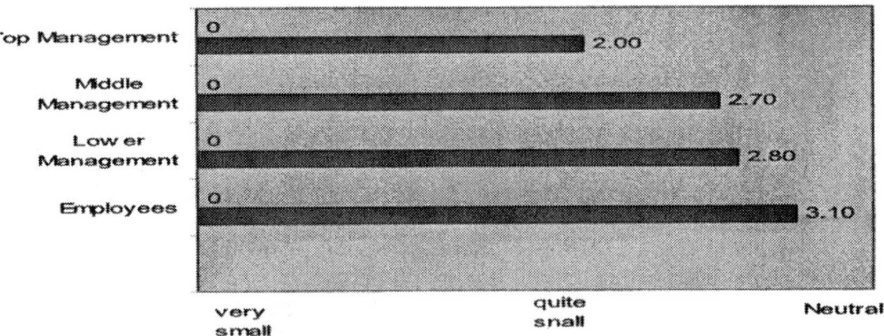

Figure 1. Expected Resistance by Stakeholder Groups

Further analysis indicated there was less resistance for smaller projects compared with midsize or large projects. Findings did indicate that the greater internationality of a SAP project, the higher the probability of resistance.

2.3 Obstacles in SAP Projects

The experts were asked to describe the main obstacles encountered in their SAP projects. The answers were grouped into five categories: organizational changes*, technical changes, cultural changes*, lack of involvement* and project management. Only three groups (*) are discussed below and include selected statements from participants:

Table 1. Obstacles in SAP Projects

Groups	Main obstacle	Qualitative answer
Organizational changes	Lack of definition of process scope and new processes	The main obstacle was an agreement on standardized definitions and processes
	Process standardization and harmonization	From regional processes to global processes and the corresponding responsibilities
	Consideration of local requirements	Country specific legal requirements
	Lack of transparency on organizational changes	The impact was not made clear for the organization and this has been a major obstacle
	Losing Power	International support for the project was sliding away because of shifting power balance between countries and BU organization
	New Roles	Change in roles and responsibilities Change in work content
Cultural Changes	Change of mindset new way of working	Old habits Get used to SAP way of working Stick to the old; new processes are always worse Cultural differences between countries
	Language barriers	Lack of English capabilities
	Transparency	Affected people in some areas (who) didn't want to put their cards on the table to emphasize their importance or to save their workplace.
Lack of involvement	Missing top management support	Increased centralization worries top management in business units
	Missing involvement of business departments (such as experts	Due to overlapping activities and missing understanding
	Missing commitment of middle and lower management	Top management was involved but middle management was expecting that 'the team' would solve all issues." Middle management fear the SAP implementation (will) not let them have their own results anymore

2.4 Change Management

The study shows a clear connection between experience with CM and later use of it: Nearly all organizations with high and very high CM experience used CM to support their SAP projects. In contrast, only about 40% of the organizations with very low CM experience decided to incorporate CM in their SAP project.

The following summarises the participants' answers to questions focusing on the use of CM in SAP implementation projects. Organizations that decided against applying CM were asked for their reasons. Summarising these answers, three reasons are identified:

1. First they just did not see the necessity of CM.

   Comments included: "Change management was not implemented explicitly and rather (was) applied on demand". It was "not formally done. Change was managed as project issues occurred". They believed also that "the technical and organizational implementation is absolutely sufficient for realising a SAP project." Furthermore, CM was considered "a management task."
2. Secondly they lacked experience with CM: "*The term 'change management' was not known in the project.*"
3. And finally, many organizations did not provide the project with the necessary financial and/or personnel resources. Linking to the lack of change management in smaller projects.

Experts were asked who made the decision to establish CM in the SAP project. In most projects it was either the project manager (59%) or the steering committee (44%). Less frequently the decision was made by the organizational top management. A further 22% viewed external partners as the responsible decision makers!

Change Management objectives

Study participants were asked to choose their three most important objectives from a predetermined list. As shown

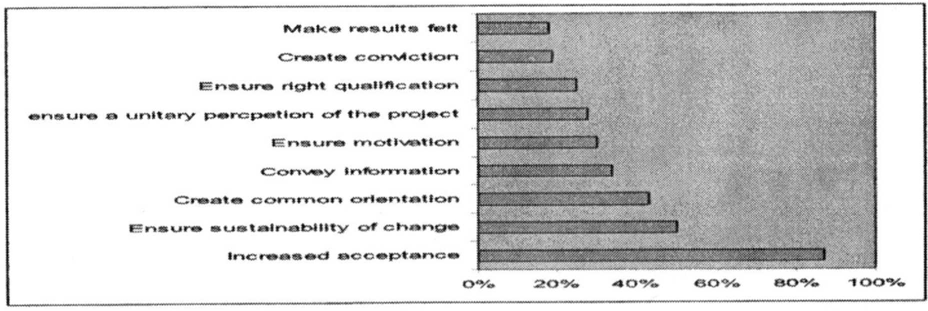

Figure 2. Change Management Objectives

Change Management Budget

A key issue for any CM project is the financial resources provided for the planned CM activities. Participants were asked to estimate the percentage of their project's total budget spent for CM activities not including end user and project team training.

Almost half of the projects allocated less than 5% of the overall project budget to CM activities.

Change Management Measures

Change management encompasses a large number of different measures. For the survey, the measures were clustered into five groups: Change management analysis, information and communication, training, participation, and further supporting measures. In general a CM analysis (for instance communication and training) is usually applied at the beginning of a project.

As shown in Fig.3 almost all organizations systematically identified the employees affected by the project (92%) and were convinced that this is a value-adding activity. To a lesser extent, the participating organizations were convinced of the analysis of information and communication requirements (75%) and the analysis of consequences of the process changes (70%) for the affected employees.

Only 50% of the participating organizations analysed the attitudes and expectations of the affected employees. These organizations risk miscommunication as a result of not focusing on the real needs of the affected employees.

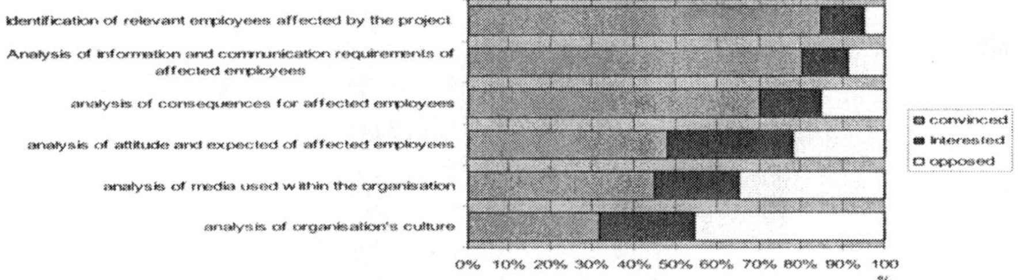

Figure 3. Change Management Analysis

2.5 Information and Communication

SAP projects typically affect numerous target groups of an organization, including SAP end users, middle and top level management, IT experts and internal consultants. This section examined how communication occurs and what it consists of in SAP projects.

Communication was identified under three categories: personal, electronic and paper-based. Personal information was identified as being; informational meetings, workshops and personal exchanges. These types of communication measures are considered the most effective ones for supporting change processes.

Electronic communications measures that are inexpensive and easy to handle, such as e-mails, electronic newsletters and intranet pages are favoured over more complex measures such as videos and DVDs. Paper-based communication was used less frequently than electronic.

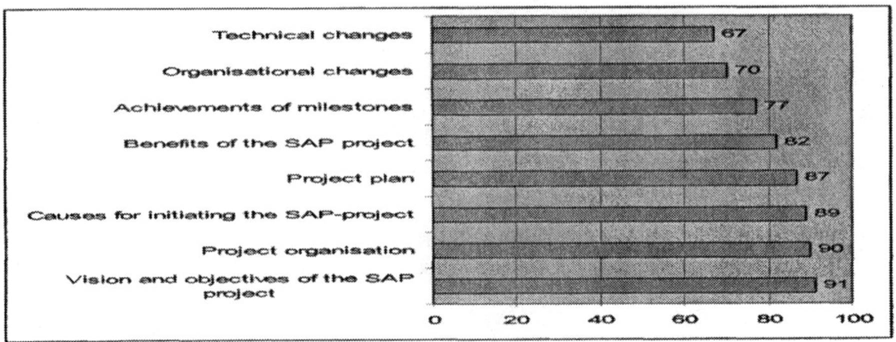

Figure 4. CM Communication Content

In addition to the types of communication, participants were asked about the content of their communication activities. More than 90% stated that generic topics such as vision, objectives and reasons for implementing SAP software, as well as the project plan and the project organization were especially communicated. A positive finding is that more than 70% of the participants said they informed their employees about organization and technical changes.

2.6 Training

The majority of the participating experts considered training activities as part of CM. The key results can be summarized as follows: Eighty percent of the experts had applied traditional training measures such as classroom training for end users and "train the trainer" concepts. In contrast e-learning tools were used in only every fifth project, but there is a clear trend to apply this newer training tool method more often in future projects. Many organizations were convinced of the "train the trainer" concept. Therefore, external resources were mostly used to train project team members and prospective trainers. Consequently, end users were mainly enabled internally.

2.7 Evaluating Benefits of CM

Participant's experiences with CM controlling activities were identified as being around 40% of the participants developed a specific business case (cost benefit analysis for CM). In addition an equal percentage of experts saw a high possibility of evaluating the benefits of CM. Obviously a prerequisite of such measurement is properly defining KPIs. Defining the right KPIs to measure the benefits of CM is an important precondition but it is also necessary to define the right tools or methods to obtain this information. One of the favoured KPIs is employees' acceptance of new processes and systems after go-live. The participating experts mentioned several tools or methods to evaluate this:

- Surveys and interviews covering different topics, such as satisfaction and acceptance Indicated most often) - More than 60% of the experts were convinced of the value of interviewing end users; surveys were conducted in only half of the projects.
- Workshops with the business and/or key users
- Pre- and post-go-live evaluations – "Find out the expectations of people before the project and ask them again after the project is six months live"
- Comparison of projects with and without CM
- Benchmarking against own projects and/or other companies' projects

2.8 Impact of Change Management on Project Success

Participants were asked to evaluate the influence of CM on the overall success of SAP projects; 90% who applied CM considered the influence on project success to be very high. Interestingly two thirds of the experts who did not apply CM in their projects also rated the influence of CM on a project's success. To evaluate the exact impact of CM on the overall success of SAP projects, projects with and without CM were compared with 11 listed success factors; such as: The end users are satisfied with the new SAP solution. In all instances projects with CM performed better on all counts than projects without CM.

Many participants offered comments pointing out the importance of CM in their SAP projects. Insights into their perceptions of CM are highlighted by the following comments:

- "CM is one of the critical success factors of a big implementation project, especially when organizational changes are involved."
- "CM is really an added value in an SAP implementation."
- "It is conditional for the success of an SAP project."
- "To make a major change in work processes combined with new tools without CM is simply not an option. Without CM an SAP implementation is a recipe for disaster, as the work would grind to halt."
- "There can be no lasting change (sustainability) without CM."

Summary

The impact of CM activities on SAP project successes identified that nearly all experts who applied CM in their projects rated the impact of CM on the overall project as very high or quite high. Even the majority of participants who did not apply CM in their actual projects considered CM to have a noticeable impact on a project's success. Further across all project success criteria, projects with CM were evaluated as more successful than projects without CM.

Limitations

Interpretations of the described results must take into account that the results are based on personal ratings and subjective expert judgments related to the implementation of a large enterprise system. CM should be further evaluated from a different – and broader – perspective, and surveys of affected business departments and end users are recommended. Furthermore, longitudinal case studies could be used to identify deeper insights in to the effects of different measures and would allow concrete practical recommendations to be deduced.

3. DISCUSSION

Enterprise Systems offer a wide variety of benefits to organizations who implement them. However, these systems are fraught with complexity to the point where they often overwhelm a successful implementation leading to project overruns and continued lack of benefit realization. It is hypothesized in this paper that change management plays an important role in the success of large scale enterprise system implementations. In fact organisational change management is often referred to as one of the most important success factors for any enterprise system implementation. To analyse this fact a survey was prepared and sent out to 208 European organizations implementing SAP. The Survey aimed to analyse the role of change management within SAP projects and to learn from the adopters experiences who had implemented CM.

The sample consisted mainly of small projects. However, the comparison of projects with and without CM reveals a connection between the use of CM and project size: With increasing project size, CM was applied more frequently with nearly all large SAP projects being supported by CM. Further in more than 50% of the projects, the implementation of SAP software caused large organizational changes. The data analysis revealed a slight trend: the more international the scope of the projects, the more prevalent was CM. This could be a reflection on the larger scale of global implementations and the importance of getting 'it' right the first time.

4. CONCLUSIONS

The survey findings conclude that CM is an 'effective' strategy to ensure a successful implementation of a large scale enterprise system. Results indicate that CM supports the transition process that is inherent in any SAP project and therefore contributes to the project's overall success. This was demonstrated on the basis of various success criteria – for instance, short-term project success factors (time, scope and budget) – as well as end-user acceptance and behaviour and long-lasting criteria such as the organisations' ability to accept and learn the new system: Organisational efficacy.

However, CM should be further evaluated from a different – and broader – perspective, and surveys of affected business departments and end users are recommended. Firstly that CM must be considered to be integral to any SAP implementation project and, secondly, that it is identified as a critical success factor covering the human side of SAP software implementations.

REFERENCES

1. T. Davenport, *Enterprise Systems Revisited: The Director's Cut.* Accenture (2003).
2. M. Hammer, How Process Enterprises Really Work, *Harvard Business Review.* Number11-12, pp.108-118, (1999).
3. *Looking for Payback, MIS*, eds T. Iggulden (1999), pp.75-80.
4. T. Somer and K. Nelson, The impact of Critical Success Factors across the Stages of Enterprise Resource Planning Systems Implementations, in *Proc. of the 34th Hawaii International Conference on System Sciences* (2001).
5. M.L. Markus, S. Axline, D. Petrie, and C. Tanis, Learning from Adopters' Experiences with ERP—Successes and Problems, *Journal of Information Technology.* Volume 15, Number 4, pp.245-265, (2000).
6. P. Hawking, A. Stein, and S. Foster, ERP Post Implementation: A New Journey, in *Proc. of the 14th Australasian Conference on Information Systems (ACIS)* (Perth, 2003).
7. T. Davenport, J. Harris, and S. Cantrell, *The Return of Enterprise Solutions*, Accenture (2002).
8. M.L. Markus, Technochange management: Using IT to drive organizational change, *Journal of Information Technology.* Volume 19, pp.4-20, (2004).
9. M.L. Markus and R.I. Benjamin, The magic bullet theory in IT enabled transformation, *Sloan Management Review.* Volume 38, Number 2, pp.55-68, (1997).
10. T.M. Somers and K. Nelson, The impact of Critical Success Factors across the Stages of Enterprise Resource Planning Systems Implementations, in *Proc. of the 34th Hawaii International Conference on System Sciences* (2001).
11. F.F.H. Nah and L.J. Kuang, Critical factors for successful implementation of enterprise systems, *Business Processes Management Journal.* Volume 7, Number 3, pp.285-296, (2001).
12. S. Shang and P.B. Seddon, A comprehensive framework for classifying the benefits of ERP systems, in *Proc. of the sixth Americas Conference on Information Systems* (2000).
13. S. Yang and P.B. Seddon, *Benefits and Key Project Success Factors from Enterprise Systems Implementations: Lessons from Sapphire 2003. ACIS 2004* (2004), pp.1-10.
14. S. Foster, P. Hawking, and A. Stein, Change Management: The Forgotten Critical Success Factor in Enterprise Wide System Implementations, in *Proc. of the 15th Australasian Conference on Information Systems (ACIS)* (Hobart, 2004).

Research on Implementing ERP in a Northeastern Enterprise Based on Information Orientation Theory

Lei Ye and Yuqiang Feng

School of Management, Harbin Institute of Technology, Harbin 150001, Heilongjian, P.R. China mis_yelei@126.com fengyq@hit.edu.cn

Abstract. Based on information orientation theory, the entire process of ERP implementation in enterprise is analyzed in detail from information behaviors and values, information management practice, and information technology practice. Advantages and disadvantages are both listed to show the benefits or barriers to the implementing of ERP in northeastern enterprises. After the analysis of an empirical ERP implementation of a northeastern pharmacy group, suggestions and problems that need to be awared in ERP implementation of northeastern enterprises are given.

Keywords: *Information orientation theory, ERP, Implementation, Northeastern enterprise, Regional specificities*

1. INTRODUCTION

ERP was suggested as a managerial tool for enterprise to govern all related resources inside and outside of enterprise to ensure sustainable competitive advantages. Most of ERP researches concern mainly on implementation methods or factors that lead to successful implementation. By constructing new evaluation frameworks for ERP implementation effectives, some researchers justified their work through sample enterprises. Others' work consider about methodologies that start from requirement analysis to technical support after implementation. Though all resources inside of enterprise are coded as digital information in kinds of management software, it's rarely to see researches about how information are located, and managed in ERP, needless to say researches about using and creating of information.

Information system research has long been developed mainly from two approaches--user satisfaction [1] and technology acceptance [2]. Both of the two approaches take the influence of information as a mediator. Researches from user satisfaction field point out that users' evaluation about information has a great influence to user satisfaction which contains completeness, accuracy, and format of information [3]. On the other hand, Davis, one of the pioneers in technology acceptance research, suggested information quality in his TAM2 model. However, there are little researches or theories take information as a determinant, not to say as a target. That's the reason we consider Information Oriented Theory as our research tool.

Please use the following format when citing this chapter:

Ye, L., Feng, Y., 2007, in IFIP International Federation for Information Processing, Volume 254, Research and Practical Issues of Enterprise Information Systems II Volume 1, eds. L. Xu, Tjoa A., Chaudhry S. (Boston: Springer), pp. 251-256.

Information orientation theory was first brought up by Marchand [4]. Marchand figured that a successful and effective use of information technologies was composed by three parts: information technology practice, information manage practice, and information behaviors &values, and company must achieve competence and synergy across all these capabilities of effective information use as a precondition to achieve superior business performance" [5-6].In his articles, Marchand pointed out that information's value are greatly underestimated in enterprise. The consideration of information as a container instead of a target lead to greatly information redundancy or information waste which aggravate the burden of information system.

How to consider information during ERP project implementation is a question that needs to focus on. Project managers, either from enterprise or implementation party, take project completion in time as their final goal. All they care about are functions in ERP system, and sometimes about the precise of data, but seldom if any about the usage or reuse of information, which leads to great loss for enterprise after implementation party leaves. Based on information orientation theory, we suggest that both of implementation party and client party should integrate the three capabilities about information during their implementation process. Our research is done during an ERP implementation process of a certain northeastern enterprise. Notification and suggestions about how to integrate are given and discussed.

2. INFORMATION TECHNOLOGY PRACTICE (ITP) AND RELATED IMPLEMENTATION MEASURES

ITP includes four parts: IT managerial support, IT business process support, IT operational support and IT innovation support. All these four parts are related more to software foundations rather than human resource or organization structure.

IT managerial support refers to IT technologies that assist managers to make decisions. After being processed completely, information flows to this module. Managers then can use them to make decisions. Nowadays, many ERP software suppliers afford data analyzing modules in their products to complete this task.

IT business process support aims at optimizing the business process. Information can flow much more rapidly and effectively through organized and efficient process. Valuable information comes from both inside and outside, like from supply chain or demand chain. While doing ERP implementation, consultants usually make adjustments to business process in order to make system works efficiently.

IT operation support deals with specific business matters including accounting, manufacturing, sale and etc. With these steps of operation, Lot of information is generated or collected. Matters that influence the operation support include system function, training, hardware configuration and etc.

IT innovation support is mainly discussed in R&D departments which are responsible for new products/services, and creativity-exploration improving. Information system relates to IT innovation support refers to Groupware, CAX, Enterprise Knowledge Portals and so on. As ERP system is concerned, it should consider appropriate integration with those specific systems.

Table 1 concludes related ERP behaviors to ITP mentioned above. Compared to capabilities, ITP is the least underestimated part during implementation.

Table 4. Related ERP Behaviors to ITP

	ITP Support	Types of knowledge workers	ERP assistance/related
Making better things	ITP of management	Executives/senior managers	Data analyzing modules
	ITP of innovation	R&D workers	Integration with other systems
Making things better	ITP of BP	Process managers	BPR
	ITP of operation	Operational workers supervisors	Modules, training.

3. INFORMATION MANAGEMENT PRACTICE (IMP) AND RELATED IMPLEMENTATION MEASURES

IMP is a process that neglected by project managers. It manages information effectively over the life cycle of information use including sensing, collecting, organizing, processing, and maintaining information [6].

Information sensing is essential to high level of IMP maturity as companies must continuously identify events, trends and changes in business conditions and make sense out of them to collect appropriate information, develop new strategies, or make decisions [6]. Information movement is the usage process of information, while sensing is the start of information movement. ERP system do not usually automatically contain module that realizing such function, but do afford interface to input them. Take purchase price as an example. After sensing material price, clerks in purchase department are required to collect and key in them into ERP system. In other words, information's sensing and collecting are done simultaneously.

After information sensing and collecting, much information in system should be organized next. Due to different macro factors like economy environment, characters of industry, content of fierce competition, and micro factors like enterprise's purpose, availability of human resource etc., different enterprises have different classification. That's the reason why classification of information organization is different in different enterprise. According to Marchand, information organizing depends on collecting phase and on good IT supports [6].

Besides information sensing, information processing is one of the most critical aspects of IMP. Marchand deems information processing including evaluation of information's relevance and importance to decide whether maintain for the future use or not. However, that's not the only reason for enterprise to evaluate and process information in our case of ERP implementation. Information processing is also responsible for valuable operational information, such as Return of Investment (ROI) calculation. Many ERP systems afford module to generate such kind of indirect information by processing raw information.

Maintaining is the last step for IMP. After processing, information is maintained for reusing and refreshing to avoid expensive and time-consuming double collection

[7]. Maintaining implies a thing that manager level should decide which information is valuable enough to be maintained. The process of decision is a clarification of enterprise's core competencies. Users can take advantages of various rules in ERP system to filter and maintain required information.

4. INFORMATION BEHAVIORS AND VALUES (IBV) AND RELATED IMPLEMENTATION MEASURES

IMP depicts the flow movement of information while IBV describes movement of human being involved with information. Marchand deems there are six IBV capabilities: proactiveness, sharing, transparency, control, formality, and integrity.

Specifically speaking, integrity aims at defining the type of information by their privacy in order to protect confidential information. We view integration as an efficient way to eliminate noises and useless information or redundant one. There is much information in enterprise especially for manufacturing industry. Much of them overlap. For example, storage department is usually responsible for the delivery statistics, while logistics does the same thing too. ERP system can decrease such phenomena by integrating information.

Formality is the necessary process for following steps. Information from different origins differs in coding, meaning and many other ways. Hasty using without pre-process leads to misunderstanding and mistakes. Unification through information transforming is the premise for maximal and reasonable use of information.

Information control indicates the information using circumstance by employees from all levels of enterprise. It mainly controls the flow direction of information. Business process reengineering is one of the important ways that influences information controls by change its direction.

Transparency, sharing and proactiveness are considerations about information openness. While in our research, as ERP system is concerned, information openness is inhibited by rules in enterprise and controlled by system modules. Table 2 concludes related ERP behaviors to IMP and IBV mentioned above.

5. CASE STUDY

The enterprise we focus on is in the pharmacy industry locates in Northeast and has some certain regional specificities. As a group, it has three sub-companies locate in different provinces. Two of them are in Harbin, Heilongjiang province, the third one is in Hezhou, Guangxi Province. The ERP supplier they choose is INSPUR, one of the biggest domestic ERP suppliers. The system they choose is a group level product.

Start from ITP, things goes well through IT managerial support and IT innovation support. However, problems happened in rest processes. Being accustomed to their financial software, it's necessary to input existed data into new systems. The most difficult thing is to solve the problem that users always compare the new system's shortcomings to the old one's which influence their satisfaction and work efficiency. Due to the culture difference, people lived in northeastern tend to be more conservative and stubborn. Existed experiences block the progress of ERP project.

Training and direct commands from superior are intensified simultaneously to prompt ERP implementation.

Table 2. Related ERP Behaviors to IMP&IBV

		Influence Factors
IMP	Sensing/Collection	ERP
	Organizing	Inside\Outside Environment
	Processing	ERP
	Maintaining	Rules
	Integrity	ERP
IBV	Formality	ERP
	Control	BPR
	Transparency	Rules
	Sharing/ Proactiveness	

BPR is another field that encounters problems. Being a former state-owned enterprise, one of its sub-companies has many cockamamie and out of date business processes. Taking the approval of purchase capital as an example, after the approval of manager from purchase department, it should then be checked by manager account for production for right material and then be checked by financial manager for right amount, while material requirement plan is brought up by production department. We rearranged the process after the implementation by cutting off the double check of production manager.

There are problems in information collecting for IMP. For example, due to incomplete market economy, some suppliers don't afford value added tax invoice or change the title of invoice which hamper the account processing. The direct result is that the name in value added tax invoice doesn't coincide with the name in the purchase order, which confuses information collecting. Since it is impossible to control supplier, we recommend the purchase department request right invoice before signing the purchase contract. The availability of IT human resource of enterprise interferes with the information organizing during the ERP implementation process. Information department in this pharmacy enterprise is built up in a hurry and qualified employees are in a short. Problems can't be solved in time, sometime even cannot be treated kindly which hurt the interests of users from other departments. We intensify the training for the final users to increase their understanding to the ERP system and hand out more operational handbook on one hand; On the other hand, we picked out key nodes that must be paid full attention by information department.

As listed above, IBV concerns each movement of human being involved with information. While sharing is talked, we find that managers of each department prefer to keep information their own instead of sharing. One of the purchase managers even requests us to keep the name of supplier as a department secret, and not to share with other departments. Distributed channel managers also keep all of their information as secrets. Aimed at maximizing information's value, communicated with superior manager, they released a series rules to share these kind of information.

From the analysis above, it can be safely drawn that information itself should be taken seriously while doing ERP implementation. By dividing the process of implementation into ITP, IMP and IBV, ERP consultants and project managers can take more specific and pertinent measures.

6. CONCLUSIONS

Based on Information Orientation Theory, we suggest measures related to information during ERP implementation process. For example, when stubborn user kept on hanging around previous system, we suggest an intensification of vertical command. Employees' behavior of refusing share key information is exposed when IBV is considered.

Information orientation theory views information as its target. Starting from information technology, it mainly research about the management, behavior and values of information. As ERP implementation is concerned, integrating the information management with operation of ERP system affords an opportunity to manage information well.

Another side about information management is related to Competitive Intelligence (CI) and Counterintelligence system. In fact, the two aspects do have some common thing in their process which beyond this paper's discussion which will be our next research topic.

REFERENCES

1. N. Melone, A theoretical assessment of the user-satisfaction construct in information systems research, *Management Science*. Volume 36, Number 1, pp.76-91, (1990).
2. V. Venkatesh, M. Morris, G. Davis, and F. Davis, User acceptance of information technology: Toward a unified view, *MIS Quarterly*. Volume 27, Number 3, pp.425-478, (2003).
3. H.W. Barbara and A.T. Peter, A Theoretical Integration of User Satisfaction and Technology Acceptance, *Information Systems Research*. Volume 16, Number 1, pp.85-102, (2005).
4. D.A. Marchand, *Competing with information: A manager's guide to creating business value with information content* (John Wiley and Sons: Chichester, England, 2000).
5. D.A. Marchand, W.J. Kettinger, and J.D. Rollins, Information orientation: People, technology and the bottom line, *MIT Sloan Management Review*. Volume 4, Number 41, pp.69-80, (2000).
6. D.A. Marchand, W.J. Kettinger, and J.D. Rollins, *Information orientation: The new business performance metric* (Oxford University Press: Oxford, Great Britain, 2001).
7. D.A. Marchand, W.J. Kettinger, and J.D. Rollins, *Making the invisible visible: How companies win with the right information, people and IT* (John Wiley and Sons: Chichester, England, 2001).

Business Interoperability on E-Marketplace

Jingzhi Guo

Department of Computer and Information Science, University of Macau Av. Padre Tomás Pereira, S. J. Taipa, Macau, P.R. China jzguo@umac.mo

Abstract. The increasing demand for doing business online calls for higher business interoperability on e-marketplaces (EMp). This drives the development of integration technologies for improving EMp functions. This paper argues that by comparing the cost of business interoperability on EMp brought by the integration technology, firms will more favour joining in public EMp than self-building private EMp. In this shift, three integration factors of standard flexibility, service provision and semantic integration are constantly improving EMp functions, which lead to an overall reduction of interaction cost for business interoperation. This will change business behaviours and corporate strategies of most firms and have important implications for firms to make strategies of how to treat EMp to increase business interoperability.

Keywords: *Electronic market place, Inter- enterprise interoperation, Business integration, Electronic business (E-business), E-commerce*

1. INTRODUCTION

In the past two decades, the business integration technologies have undergone a drastic transition from internal functions integration within a firm to external marketplace functions integration between firms [14]. These innovations have radically reduced the cost and time of business interoperation within and between firms that require for information sharing, exchanged data understanding and underlying systems integration [5]. This, in turn, brought many changes in the ways e-marketplaces are built and used. Underlying these changes are more fundamental changes in how firms adopt their e-marketplace patterns to connect with each other for rebuilding value-added chains online. In this paper, we address more basic issue of how advances in integration technologies developed in the context of e-commerce are affecting the business interoperability on e-marketplaces and discuss the options these changes present for corporate strategies.

Electronic marketplace (EMp) is a product of Internet computing technology and is one of the quickest development areas of e-commerce. It is a common information space [7], where e-business information exchange is enabled to allow EMp functions to be presented with certain information exchange efficiency and/or financial cost in use. With a historical perspective [7], the development of EMp was highly related to

Please use the following format when citing this chapter:

Guo, J., 2007, in IFIP International Federation for Information Processing, Volume 254, Research and Practical Issues of Enterprise Information Systems II Volume 1, eds. L. Xu, Tjoa A., Chaudhry S. (Boston: Springer), pp. 257-267.

the development of integration technology, from an intra-enterprise EMp (e.g. a tradition ERP system integrating discrete departments to enable better information exchange), to an inter-enterprise EMp (e.g. a community-oriented SCM system integrating heterogeneous firms for inter-enterprise information exchange), and to a regional or a global EMp (e.g. a global trading system like Alibaba.com integrating unknown firms to enable irregular international trade). *Integration technology* here can be defined as any type of IT technologies that enable better business information exchange on Internet between any business entities. Speaking from the levels of integration, these technologies can be the enablers of the exchanges of business concepts, documents and processes between either homogeneous or heterogeneous business applications or systems belonging to discrete business entities. It is obvious that the purpose of developing integration technologies is to provide a better business information exchange system, that is, a common business information space in terms of an EMp. Furthermore, the achievement of a better EMp is to improve the ability of business interoperation between any business entities, or in another word the *business interoperability* that can be defined as the capability of business collaboration between business partners for the fulfilment of certain business functions at certain cost and efficiency. Thus, a logical sequence can be found such that to improve integration technology is to formulate a more cost-effective EMp and finally is to increase business interoperability.

In this paper, we argue that new integration technologies lead to an imbalance development of EMp between public electronic marketplaces (*public EMp* run by an industry consortium or a third-party) and private electronic marketplaces (*private EMp* run by a single firm), where the cost and time of joining in public EMp is tremendously improved. Thus, there is a shift towards the more joining in of public EMp than self-building private EMp, transferring more *participants* (i.e. facilitators [7] and/or users) from traditional markets or private EMp. Some innovative firms will become public EMp facilitators but not users. Many financially and technically strong firms will become the both facilitators and users of the private EMp tightly integrating their business partners. Most firms will benefit from the emergence of the new integration technologies for better business interoperability.

The analytical framework, on which our argument is based, follows the transaction cost theory [12, 23], which is useful in explaining the EMp pattern changes brought by the development of integration technologies, as well as predicting the consequences of the changing business interoperability. The past two decades provides some clue of integration technologies for us to understand how they impact on the changes of cost and efficiency of EMp construction and hence possibly change people's attitude on adopting different types of EMp.

2. ANALYTICAL FRAMEWORK

A precondition of online business is to establish and use e-channel between business partners [19]. The cost and efficiency of building and using the e-channels determine the business interoperability. The e-channels can be researched in the context of EMp such as e-portal [21] (e.g. Amazon.com, CTrip.com and Dell.com), e-hub [18] (e.g. Tradecard.com and Alibaba.com), or simply an Internet-based software package sold to firms to form supply chain (i.e. e-package as we called, e.g. SAP SCM systems or global trading systems). For all these EMp forms, the business interoperability on them is measured by the cost and efficiency of these EMp's available business functions such as the services of matching buyers and sellers, facilitation of transaction, and institutional infrastructure [10].

In this section, we propose our framework to state that EMp participants tends to more favour one type of EMp if its use cost for achieving business interoperability is less than that for using another type of EMp.

2.1 Definitions of Private EMp and Public EMp

EMp has two basic forms for achieving business interoperability [15]: public EMp or many-to-many public exchanges, and private EMp or one-to-one/one-to-many private exchanges. A general decision that a firm has to make is whether it should join in a public EMp or self-build a private EMp to increase the same business interoperability. *Public EMp* is a business information exchange mechanism that provides the business interoperability between firms and is run by an e-marketplace facilitator, such as an industry consortium or a third-party dot-com firm (e.g. plasticsnet.com), to orient towards a perfect market for a group of buyers and sellers. It strives to reach industry- and market-based efficiency through managing interactions among EMp users. The EMp Facilitators as third-party determine the provided exchange functions based on the market demand, legal environment, profitability and maturity of EMp technologies. Firms using the public EMp could compare the cost and benefit of the available business interoperation functions between all public EMp and choose the one that is best appropriate to them. The major thought of adopting a public EMp by firms for business interoperability is that, by means of building a closer external partner relationships through service outsourcing, firms can be reconstructed as a light-weighted organization and thus decrease the management overhead. *Private EMp*, on the other hand, is a business information exchange mechanism for business interoperability *within a firm* (i.e. a firm acting as both EMp facilitator and a sole EMp user) by means of merging more external exchange partners. It is driven by a single seller or buyer and typically involves a firm automating its own supply chain and customer base where participation is generally open to suppliers or customers of the firm. Firms that have perfected this model include Dell, Cisco, and Wal-Mart. The philosophy behind it is that the excellence of management technique can make business interoperation more efficient by building a self-owned EMp than the external use of one or more third-party EMp, because the cost and time of coordinating external technical, social and legal relationships could be minimized. In addition, customer loyalty and trusted partner relationships can be maintained.

Variants or different naming of the two pure forms for business interoperability exist (e.g. auctions, vertical and horizontal exchanges, e-portals, e-hubs and community exchanges), but can usually be categorized into the above two forms. In general, when a technically and/or financially strong firm is a dominant seller or buyer in markets, it tends to increase business interoperability through a self-owned private EMp, for example, Boeing Company [20]. On the other hand, when a firm is both financially and technically weak such as small and medium sized enterprises (SMEs), it often favours to be the users of public EMp (e.g. users of Alibaba.com) to increase business interoperability, because this form offers more opportunities for finding potential buyers and creditable sellers.

2.2 Factors Favouring Public and Private Electronic Marketplaces

Following the transaction cost theory [23, 12], the EMp can be discussed in terms of management costs and interaction costs. The *management costs* refer to the costs of the setup, maintenance and use of an EMp, while the *interaction costs* denote the costs of purchase, integration and use of an EMp. Adopting the comparative advantage theory [17] often used in economics, a general statement can be derived such that trade-offs exist between firms with regard to the management costs and interaction costs, assuming that the *equal* business interoperability is desired (i.e. same efficiency and quantity of EMp functions at cost) by the EMp participants. The comparison between the two types on costs is opportunistic, which determines the intent of a firm on selecting either private EMp via building by itself or public EMp by joining in as a user. Table 1 summarizes the statement relevant to our argument.

Table 1. Relative Cost for Private and Public EMp

	Management Cost	Interaction Cost
Private EMp (self-building as a single buyer or seller)	*High*	*Low*
Public EMp (joining in as a competitive buyer or seller)	*Low*	*High*

In Table 1, the "Low" and "High" give a relative comparison of management cost and interaction cost between private EMp and public EMp. They reflect the comparative advantages and disadvantages of each specific EMp. For private EMp, the advantages are that a firm is not necessary to purchase the membership from public EMp and spend any money to integrate its own business systems to the external heterogeneous public EMp systems. The disadvantages are its own bearing of the costs by the firm for the EMp setup and maintenance. For public EMp, the advantages are that a firm has no need to cost its own to setup and maintain a specialized EMp for business interoperation. Its disadvantages are the firm's costs of purchasing the EMp services and the integration of its business systems into the accessed EMp. What's more, the public EMp themselves may not be well functionally integrated to provide business interoperability, e.g. the failure lesson from CommerceOne [6], which provided immature public EMp technology.

Table 1 is consistent with the traditional analysis of electronic hierarchy and electronic markets [12], where the concept is opportunistic. In this analysis, the choice between private EMp and public EMp depends on the cost by comparing the management costs and interaction costs between the two EMp. If an EMp offers lower cost than another, it would be favoured by the related firms.

There are many factors that affect cost hence the choice between private EMp and public EMp for business interoperation, such as information privacy, customer loyalty, trust relationship, market power, financial strength and technical ability. Other things remaining unchanged, two factors play an important role in comparing costs. They are business standard flexibility and business concept complexity. The issue of business standard flexibility has been discussed in the researches of standard integration [1, 12] while the reduction of business concept complexity has been investigated in ontology-based approach [11, 10], community-based/usage-centric technique (WebCatalogPers) [16], and collaboration-based/concept-centric approach (CONEX) [8].

Business standard flexibility. Business standard can be classified as international standards (e.g. UNSPSC.org), de facto industrial standards (e.g. ebXML.org), enterprise standards (i.e. used within a firm), and non-standards that most SMEs adopt. Business standard flexibility refers to the application ability of a standard from a given scope to another scope. It is an ability of integrating the internal legacy business systems into the external heterogeneous systems. Its opposite term business standard rigidity that can be compared with the concept of *asset specificity* [12] such that the latter emphasizes on the movability of physical goods off Internet while the former focuses on the exchangeability of electronic data on Internet. Business standards are the most important building blocks of EMp for business interoperability such that one business system can interoperate with another by following the same standards. However, business standard rigidity becomes an issue, because the desired increasing business interoperability asks for the more and more flexibility of business standards to adapt to a wider scope of integrating more distributed and more heterogeneous e-business systems.

Due to the above reason, a firm often favours to achieve business interoperability on a private EMp if it has a set of rigid enterprise-wide business standards and more depends on these legacy standards. This is because the change of existing rigid business standards in use will pay a higher cost for interaction than for management in e-business systems integration. In contract, firms in general favour to achieve business interoperability on public EMp if they have flexible business standards or they are less dependent of these legacy standards. This is because the cost paid to integrating their e-business systems into the public EMp is less than the cost of building their own private EMp for the same level of business interoperability.

Business concept complexity refers to the amount of effort for representing and using the syntactically and semantically interoperable business concepts. A business concept denotes a broad business connotation including the presentation and use of a business vocabulary, a business document, a business processes and even a whole business service [9]. For example, a business process is a sequence of operation concepts operated on a set of business documents that are in exchange. A business document is a set of business terms and values. All these business processes, documents, terms and values are business concepts. The business concept complexity can be regarded as a critic extension to the traditional understanding of business complexity in terms of the *complexity of product descriptions* [12].

Other things being equal, a firm tends to achieve business interoperability on private EMp if it is able to reduce the business concept complexity by turning the systems of complex concept representation and use into the systems of simple concept representation and use. This is because a simpler system, which can maintain the same business interoperability, is less in financial cost. For example, if a firm like Boeing Company [20] can force its business partners to adopt a uniform business concept representation system that is consistent with its legacy business systems (i.e. simplify the overall system in the eye of Boeing), it will be no doubt that a private EMp will be favoured by Boeing. In contrast, a firm favours to achieve business interoperability on public EMp if it is unable to handle the business concept complexity or there are no legacy business concept representation systems. This is because the handling financial cost of complex business concepts is much higher in maintaining or creating a private EMp by itself than simply joining in a ready-made public EMp. For instance, SMEs have non-standard business concept representation systems, which are most complex in business concept integration. They are also technically and financially weak in building private EMp for handling complex business concepts. What's more, they are less influential in forcing its business partners to join in their private EMp if any. Thus, SMEs, in general, seek public EMp to achieve their business interoperability.

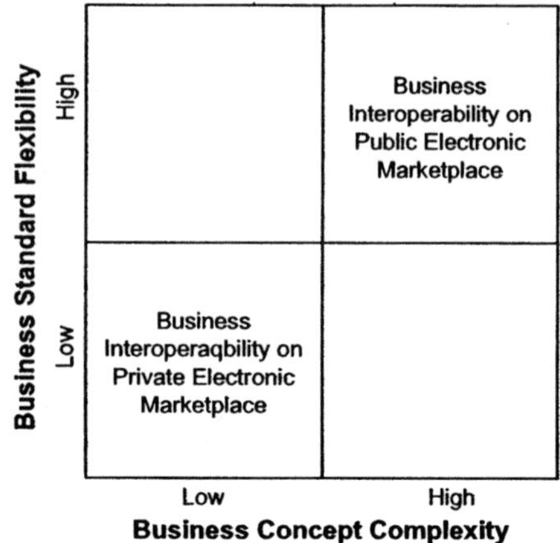

Figure 1. Factors Affecting E-Marketplace

Figure 1 shows that when a firm has more flexible business standards and is unable to reduce business concept complexity, it tends to use public EMp for business interoperability. In contrary, when a firm has more rigid business standards and is able to reduce business concept complexity, it tends to adopt private EMp for business interoperability.

3. INTEGRATION TECHNOLOGY AND ITS IMPACTS

The development of integration technology is changing the factors of business standard flexibility and business concept complexity that affect the cost for choosing between public EMp and private EMp for achieving business interoperability. This reflects in three aspects of the development of flexible standards, the evolution of service provision, and the emergence of semantic integration, which are shown in Table 2, 3 and 4.

3.1 The Development of Flexible Standards for Electronic Marketplaces

Table 2 shows that EMp standards for integration are moving from proprietary standards to open standards. This trend signifies that the standards are becoming more and more flexible. It implies that various e-business systems are easier to be integrated on EMp with less cost and time for interaction. This is because the open standard has proved its advantages in reusability and easy deployment [5].

Table 2. Development of Flexible Standards for EMp

Evolving stage	**proprietary standard**	**open standard**
Characteristics	pre-design, rigid	open, statically pre-designed
Examples and cases	EDIFACT (www.unece.org/trade/untdid)	UNSPSC, ecl@ss, etc. for business, and ebXML, SOAP, WSDL, BPML etc. in interoperability services
Cost and time	high cost in design & long time to deploy	less time in design and less cost to deploy and reuse

3.2 The Evolution of Service Provision in Electronic Marketplaces

Table 3 shows that the evolution of service provision from the cases of early rigid and non-reusable EDI systems to the open and highly reusable web services [3]. The evolving stages have proved that acquiring services from EMp (e.g. EDI systems, ASP networks, Web service oriented integration systems) is becoming easier and easier with less cost and time. It implies that EMp participants can find more desirable services through the outsourcing in public EMp, and there is no necessity to design and build any private EMp by their own.

Table 3. Evolution of Service Provision in EMp

Evolving stage	**electronic connection and EDI**	**application service provision (ASP)**	**web service (WS)**
Characteristics	- one-to-one connection - trusted partners on VPN - data transaction on ANSI X12 and Edifact for inter- and intra-industry - connectivity with trade documents - governed by standards of specific industry consortium	- one-to-many connection - trusted partners on proprietary network - data transaction on proprietary standards - connectivity with trade documents - governed by standards of vendors	- many-to-many connection - dynamically joined partners on Internet - Data transaction on XML SOAP in WSDL - connectivity with application-to-application - governed by standards of W3C, OASIS and WS-I
Examples and cases	- electronic connection e.g. American Hospital Supply Corporation (AHS) to many hospitals (1970s) - built-in house EDI e.g.	- Web EDI (outsourcing) eg.covalentworks.com, dicentral.com, datatrans-inc.com, spscommerce.com. - outsourcing enabled	- WebserviceX.net - Oracle: www.oracle. com/technology/tech/webserv ices; IBM: www-128.ibm. com/developerworks/webserv

	TRADANET/TRADACOM (Ghobadian et al, 1994)	application, e.g. ariba.com, Autodesk.com, Salesforce.com	ices; Microsoft: msdn. microsoft.com/webservices
Cost and time	- high cost in installation and maintenance - time-consuming for deployment	- configurable cost by outsourcing - less time in deployment	- low cost in deployment - less time in maintenance through increased reusability

3.3 The Emergence of Semantic Integration on Electronic Marketplaces

Table 4 shows that the emergence of semantic integration technology on EMp has characterized a path that the difficulties of business information exchange between heterogeneous e-business systems, or their conflicting business understanding, are gradually reducing. The overall cost and time of processing the business concepts with the same complexity is decreasing. This implies that the interaction cost between EMp participants is lowering.

Table 4. Emergence of Semantic Integration on EMp

Evolving stage	**keywords**	**metadata**	**ontologies**	**collaborative concepts**
Characteristics	- no semantic conflict resolution - semantic consistency depends on the hidden meanings	- pre-designed semantic consistency on meta-data level - semantic conflicts on data level	- pre-designed semantic consistency for all terms in one or several integrated ontologies - concept and concept value are not separated	- collaboratively designed semantic consistency for all concepts - partially resolved semantic conflicts for concept values - separate concepts from concept value
Examples and cases	- search engines, e.g. Yahoo.com, Google.com, Microsoft.com, Altavista.com	- organize resource and specify search, e.g. CERES/NBII (ceres.ca.gov/thesaurus/), MMUG (marinemetadata.org)	-ontology management: AlphaWorks (www.alphaworks.ibm.com/tech/snobase) -ontology editing, e.g. protege.stanford.edu	- collaborative concept creation systems, e.g. CONEX (www.sftw.umac.mo/~jzguo/pages/ConexDemo/index.html
Cost and time	- additional cost and time for resolving semantic conflicts from hidden meanings	- additional cost and time to maintain semantic consistency between metadata and resolving data-level semantic conflicts	- additional cost and time for integrating heterogeneous ontologies and resolving semantic conflicts from monolithic terms	- distributed cost in collaborative concept design - lower cost and less time for maintaining semantic consistency between heterogeneous concept systems

The above changes in standards, service provision and semantic integration technologies have signified the following trends:

- Business standards are becoming more flexible, which becomes a strong drag of EMp participants to more favour just joining in public EMp than building private EMp by themselves.

- Complex business concepts are becoming easier and cheaper to be processed in public EMp because of the new way of service provision and semantic integration.

These two trends support the argument that firms will more favour public EMp than private EMp for business interoperability with the development of integration technology.

3.4 Impact of More Favouring Public EMp than Private EMp

The more favouring public EMp than private EMp may have several important impacts on corporate behaviours and strategies.

- Firms will gradually abandon the practice of the full purchase of high cost hardware and software to set up a private EMp. Instead, they may buy reusable and interoperable business services from public EMp, because firms will find that this practice will save more costs.
- Strategic alliances will be formed between firms more than ever, because the purchase of non-core component services will be comparatively cheaper than the self-development in house, and it also increases the speed of time-to-market to win the market competition.
- Collaborative design of various types of things such as business knowledge, products, processes and services will become popular, because the semantically integrated and enlarged EMp provides an unprecedented, global, collaborative, and virtual space for firms to work together.
- More firms will participate in public EMp, especially those SMEs that previously have no way of joining in EMp for sharing the benefit of business interoperability, because the entry fee for public EMp is drastically reduced to only membership fee but the working together functionality is increased.

Exceptions will continue to existing during the above shift. Large firms with strong market position and financial status such as Boeing Company [20] and DaimlerChrysler will continue to build and improve their own private EMp because it more complies with their corporate interests.

4. CONCLUSION

The integration technologies are proved more and more important to construct interoperable EMp for increasing business interoperability. The framework we have developed helps explain this change. We have seen that integration technologies have evolved along three major directions in standardization, service provision and semantic integration in a result of more flexible business standards and cheaper and easier of handling complex business concepts in public EMp. Such changes make the interaction cost on public EMp less and less and thus attract more and more firms from self-building of private EMp to joining in public EMp.

This shift has several implications for practitioners and technology developers:

- Public EMp will not any more be a failure place in the case of CommerceOne [6]. All firms should realize the emerging business opportunities on public EMp brought by integration technology development.
- Most firms should consider certain forms of strategic alliances to benefit from the new advances of service provision supported by public EMp.
- Nearly all firms should be aware of the power of collaboration on EMp to increase corporate productivity.
- SMEs should seize the new opportunities by subscribing the integration services to join in public EMp for increasing their business interoperability.

In short, the development of integration technology, especially standardization, service provision and semantic integration, will lead to an overall increase of business interoperability on EMp, making firms more efficient and less cost in doing e-business on EMp.

The research conducted in this paper only describes the argument that firms will more favour joining in public EMp than self-building private EMp for business interoperability with the development of integration technology. The future work will verify this argument by an empirical research on the case analysis of the historical data from the selected EMp cases.

REFERENCES

1. T. Malone, J. Yates, and R. Benjamin, Electronic Markets and Electronic Hierarchies, *Communications of the ACM.* Volume 30, Number 6, pp.483-497, (1987).
2. R.H. Coase, The Nature of the Firm, *Economica.* Volume 4, pp.386-405, (1937).
3. Gilbert, *Commerce One sells e-marketplace unit* (9 December 2002). CNET News.com
4. M. Chen, A. Chen, and B. Shao, The Implications and Impacts of Web Services to E-Commerce Research and Practices, *Journal of Electronic Commerce Research.* Volume 4, Number 4, pp.128-139, (2003).
5. R. Torrens, *An Essay on the External Corn Trade* (1815). http://cepa.newschool.edu/het/profiles/torrens.htm.
6. J. Leukel and G. Maniatopoulos, A Comparative Analysis of Product Classification in Public vs. Private e-Procurement, *The Electronic Journal of e-Government.* Volume 13, Number 4, pp.201-212, (2005).
7. P. Rossen, *Electronic Trading Hubs: Review and Research Questions*, Centre for International Business Studies, Dalhousie University, Canada (2001). http://cibs.management.dal.ca/n700-research.htm.
8. R. Sommer, T. Gulledge, and D. Bailey, The n-Tier Hub Technology, *SIGMOD Record.* Volume 31, Number 1, pp.18-23, (2002).
9. D. Ricardo, *The Principles of Political Economy and Taxation*, introduction by P.M. Fogarty (London: Dent & Dutton, 1912).
10. Y. Bakos, The Emerging Role of Electronic Marketplaces on the Internet, *Communications of the ACM.* Volume 41, Number 8, pp.35-42, (1998).
11. T. Matz, Universal Business Integration: an Idea Whose Time has Come, *Business Integration Journal.* pp.10-13, (March, 2004).
12. C.S. Langdon and M. Shaw, Emergent Patterns of Integration in Electronic Channel Systems, *Communications of the ACM.* Volume 45, Number 12, pp.50-55, (2002).

13. S.G. Thompson, M. Cioffi, H. Gharib, N. Giles, Y. Li, and T.D. Nguyen, From trips to telcos - next generation service portals, *BT Technology Journal*. Volume24, Number 1, pp.27-39, (2006).
14. H.Y. Paik, B. Benatallah, and R. Hamadi, Dynamic Restructuring of E-Catalog Communities Based on User Interaction Patterns, *World Wide Web: Internet and Web Information Systems 5*. pp.325-366, (2002).
15. E-Business Watch, e-Business Interoperability and Standards: a Cross-Sector Perspective and Outlook, Enterprise & Industry Directorate General (European Commission, 2005).
16. S. Bergamaschi, F. Guerra, and M.Vincini, A Data Integration Framework for e-Commerce, *Lecture Notes in Computer Science*. Volume 2342, p.379, 2002.
17. S. Lee, T. Lee, S. Lee, D. Lee, J. Kim, C. Lee, and J. Shim, Practical Issues for Building a Product Ontology System, in *Proceedings of the 2005 Int'l Workshop on Data Engineering Issues in E-Commerce (DEEC'05)* (IEEE Computer Society, 2005).
18. M. Hepp, The True Complexity of Product Representation, in *Proceedings of 14th European Conference on Information System (ECIS 2006)* (Sweden 12-14/06/2006).
19. J. Guo, Achieving Transparent Integration of Information, Documents and Processes, in *Proceedings of IEEE Int'l Conf. on e-Business Engineering (ICEBE 2006)* (IEEE Computer Society, 2006), pp.559-562.
20. C. Nøkkentved, *Collaborative Processes in e-Supply Networks*, ECoE Research Report, PriceWaterhouseCoopers (2000).
21. J. Guo and C. Sun, Global Electronic Markets and Global Traditional Markets, *Electronic Markets*. Volume 14, Number 1, pp.4-12, (2004).
22. J. Guo, *Integration Ad Hoc Electronic Product Catalogues through Collaborative Maintenance of Semantic Consistency*. PhD Thesis, Griffith University (2004). http://www4.gu.edu.au:8080/adt-root/public/adt-QGU20050824.125257/index.html.
23. Product Classification, in *Proceedings of ISWC 2002* (LNCS 2342, 2002), pp.379-393.
24. E. Williamson, Markets and Hierarchies: Analysis and Antitrust Implications (Free Press: New York, NY, 1975).

The Relationship Between Supply Chain Management and ERP in E-Business

Dawei Liu

Institute of Management Science and Information Engineering, Hangzhou Dianzi University, Hangzhou 310018, P.R. China hduldw@163.com

Abstract. Supply Chain Management (SCM) in today's global environment, especially the E-business is important to create significant competition advantages to firms and business partners worldwide. Since the objectives and goals are essential factors in the study of supply chain management in the E-business. The purpose of this research paper is to present the research question, review the conceptual framework, ERP and environment for SCMS, study their objectives, impact of SCM and utilize any useful theories that may help to identify the critical factors of SCM. The differences of Pre-Internet and E-business are also presented to clarify further research opportunities in this field.

Keywords: *Supply chain management, SCM, E-business, ERP*

1. SUPPLY CHAIN MANAGEMENT AND E-BUSINESS

Supply Chain Management (SCM) is the systematic theory and practical tools to provide integrated supply chain to the "Supply Value Chain" in order to meet customers' satisfaction needs and expectation requirement [1]. The process of SCM is from suppliers of raw materials through manufacturing and on to end-customers. With the quick development of Internet, E-commerce is not simply about business transactions that run over the internet, but is fundamentally about the flow of information [2]. The boundaries of organizations are more fluid and flexible than they used to be 20 years before.

Supply chain management drives companies to streamline the ways they manufacture, distribute, and sell products and finally will change the strategies of firm. The supply chain cycle starts with a customer's requirement and the manufacturer delivers the order through the process of the firm, for example, sales, marketing, producing, distribution, purchasing, and selling. In regular style the manufacturer may search the outside support from suppliers, utilities, transportation, and other providers of goods and services that are essential to make the products and services customer required [4]. The information exchange pertains to such matters as requests for quote, bids, purchase orders, order confirmations, shipping documents, invoices and payment information et.. In this procedure multiple enterprises within a limited market collaboratively plan, practice, and manage the flow of goods, services, and information along the value system in the same way to increase customer-perceived value and optimizes the efficiency of the chain.

Please use the following format when citing this chapter:

Liu, D., 2007, in IFIP International Federation for Information Processing, Volume 254, Research and Practical Issues of Enterprise Information Systems II Volume 1, eds. L. Xu, Tjoa A., Chaudhry S. (Boston: Springer), pp. 269-273.

There is no arguing that cutting the cost is a critical challenge for firms. Creating more value and cutting costs raise a question for the practitioners to solve with the intensive competition globalization. New methods and theories, such as OTM, Zero Deposit, CRM, ERP, are take to satisfy stock owners' desire [5]. Among these new inventions, expanded inventories stand out as the most critical that have a huge impact on the company's bottom line. Inventories include raw materials, work in progress, and finished products. Businesses incur costs associated with storing, distributing, warehousing and transporting these products. It is discussed that the product manufacturing usually occurs between the business entities that include the manufacturer, the distributor, and the retailer [6]. This chain, mainly consisted by the three parts is referred to as the supply chain. According to Kehoe, Dennis, and Nick the supply chain is a set of three or more companies directly linked by one or more of the upstream and downstream flows of products, services, finances, and information from a source to a customer [7, 8].

The question focused on the companies that are trying to thrive in a difficult business environment is: What kind of strategies can practitioner take to operate the firm in lower operational costs, boost performance, and enhance upstream and downstream collaboration in order to survive and grow in today's competitive global environment? While recognizing the importance of the answer, it is as important to understand what lies ahead for Supply Chain Management (SCM) [9].

The aim of this paper is to study the prospects of the research question: How is the objectives of SCMS in future business, especially in E-business? The justification for the research question is that it provides a direction for organization on up-to-date technologies that can prove useful and would lead to building a successful SCMS. Factors, such as ERP, CRM, ECT, EDI, that have an influence on organization's decision to use a certain kind of "new" technology. Practitioners may focus on opportunities to influence the critical factors, while scholars may point out common factors among different technologies and may generalize to a wider scope, including traditional fields and high-tech fields.

2. SUPPLY CHAIN MANAGEMENT STRUCTURES

Supply Chain Management, claimed to be the next cost cut strategy and tool by many scholars is defined as a set of approaches utilized to integrate suppliers, manufacturers, warehouses, and stores [10]. In this condition merchandise is produced and distributed at the right quantities, to the right locations, and at the right time, in order to minimize system wide costs and raise profit while satisfying the requirements from the customers. SCM functionality for manufacturers includes full management of the scheduling and acquisitions of the materials needed for production [11].

SCM is integrated greatly with internal functions of the enterprises that may include HR, sales and marketing, manufacturing, and finance through Enterprise Resource Planning Systems (ERP). Enterprises are leaning more towards improving their supply chains due to the growth in the number of suppliers that require them to have more efficient and effective SCM systems. At the same time firms dependence on outsourcing logistics of the supply chain is also asking their improvement to meet customers' needs. Enterprises are aiming to create transparency and visibility into the supply chain in order to fulfill their business objectives [12]. Supply chain partners are able to cooperate when there is transparency in the supply chain. Vendors and suppliers can support the chain more efficiently and effectively when information moves across the chain in a timely manner.

Stephen and Gaughran argue the inevitable change of organizational structure in their discussion on the integration of supply chain. They insist that firms need to adopt new systems that cannot be observed in the traditional organization structure where independent functional areas such as production and marketing prevail, in order to shift to integrated supply chain management. Therefore a total new department should be founded to take charge of the changes caused by SCM. In other words, organization type which considers the role and status of independent department responsible for supply chain management (SCM) activities, should be clearly established. There is no arguing that many firms recognizing the importance of supply chain management have begun adopting new organizational structure [13]. However, it is a hard task to describe a single type of organization that is suitable for all the styles of supply chain management.

A hard choice have to be made by enterprises because even if a firm makes the establishment of a new department for supply chain management. Whether the new department is located in an independent place or incorporated into an appropriate existing department must be made. The decision will relocate the power and resources in the firm. Also, in case of creating a new independent department, the determination on operational role and hierarchical relationship within organization between new SCM department and existing departments should be followed [14]. And various industrial and environmental characteristics of each firm should be recognized. This difficulty makes the position of SCM department within an organization extremely sensitive, which is a rarely seen phenomenon in production or sales departments because the independent and solid status of these departments does not change regardless of how a firm may be restructured.

3. SUPPLY CHAIN MANAGEMENT AND ERP

Enterprise Resources Planning (ERP) system offers a viable management capability to helping enterprise in particular manufacturing enterprises manage the resources. The rapid growth in technologies and innovation in manufacturing and information processing is pushing companies into a new paradigm shift. Numerous companies that have successfully implemented ERP systems testified to its life-saving importance [15]. However, enterprises must not be haste to embrace ERP projects. The urgent project planning and poor adoption of ERP may mean realigning the enterprises' comparative advantage position which enterprises can dearly afford.

ERP projects adoption has been the most important tool of the larger organizations. Features and business process flow have been designed based on practices by practitioners in the large organizations. Consulting and project management methodologies are normally specified based on such experiences. The needs, operating requirements, logistics fulfillment and financial capabilities of the SME manufacturers are vastly different from that of the large and medium sized manufacturers. For small and medium firms, development of information technologies is key factors for the objective of their own. Adoption of information technology by small and medium firms in managing their ERP projects is also limited [16]. While ERP is sufficiently flexible to cope with the general manufacturing enterprises, we need to take a closer look at the strategic and operational needs of small and medium firms before we can properly develop a project management strategy for them.

As discussed above, enterprise resources in the firms are subjected to the effect of interactions. The interdependencies move in different ways to achieve its own set of objectives. Various enterprise resources should be coordinated and integrated for the pursuit of the firm's interdependencies. Given the complexities in understanding the dynamics involved in managing these resources in a firm, the less important part of the ERP is a three-level ERM architecture combining system dynamics modeling with multi-agent-based approach. This model reduces the cluster dynamics existing amongst the various enterprise resources within the firms, the understanding will greatly aid in project management of ERP systems in enterprises. The various enterprise resources in a firm can be segregated into different agents. An agent must have at least an objective or goal. When realizing the objective, the agent acts autonomously. The act matches the organization dynamics relationship well. Like the operational managers in a firm, agents can have several roles in the procedure of the organization operation.

In this three-level ERM architecture, each agent plays only one of the roles, e.g. execution, planning, and coordination. The plan of the ERM considers the possible decentralization of information, resources, and the decision-making processes commonly found in firms. Also this three-level model rejects the ''low levels of management structure'' typical of enterprise. The first level, the operational level, consists of execution agents which receive plans from the planning agent. The second level, the decision level, comprises of the various planning agents (typically associated with the planning and operational management in the SME). At the top level lies the coordination agent, who provides "global'' information and strategic directions for the planning agents to produce quality multi-agent plans.

4. CONCLUSIONS

With the understanding of SCM objectives and its future in E-business, more attention should be paid to search a high effective way to promote the ability of SCM. Customer intimacy and customer loyalty are the base of our SCM to gain extra profit in E-business, which means enterprises must adapt the new tendency to gain the advantage in the competition. And these can be approach by:

Firstly, ability to respond quickly to customers' requests for proposals and requests for changes by involving the appropriate technical and management skills at all project sites;

Secondly, better exploitation of the network resources, thanks to a decision-support environment which is aware of co-operation possibilities (e.g. roles to be fulfilled in a project under planning) and available partners' skills and capacities;

Thirdly, prompt negotiation of planning and re-planning options, by means of a communication infrastructure that circulates decisions and events between the appropriate actors, crossing companies and organizational unit boundaries.

REFERENCES

1. S. Chen, B. Mulgrew, and P.M. Grant, A clustering technique for digital communications channel equalization using radial basis function networks, *IEEE Trans. Neural Networks.* Volume 4, pp.570-578, (1993).
2. M. Heller, Will XML Ever Make Good On Its Promise?, *CIO.* pp.114-119, (May 2001).
3. M. Stein and F. Voehl, *Macrologistics Management* (St. Lucie Press: 1998), pp.55-69.
4. R.R. Levary, Better Supply Chains Through Information Technology, *Industrial Management.* Volume 42, Number 3, pp.24-30, (2000).
5. J. Herman, XML e-business Standards Converge, *Business Communication Review.* Volume 31, Number 10, pp.24-26, (2001).
6. J.H. Dobbs, *Competition's New Battleground: The Integrated Value Chain* (Cambridge Technology Partners: 1998).
7. D. Kehoe and N. Boughton. Internet Based Supply Chain Management A Classification Of Approaches To Manufacturing Planning And Control, *International Journal of Operations & Production Management.* Volume 21, Number 4, pp.44-57, (2001).
8. H. Lucas and V. Spitler, Technology Use and Performance: A Field Study of Broker Workstations, *Decision Sciences.* Volume 30, Number 2, pp.291-311, (1999).
9. A. Patrizio, XML Passes From Development To Implementation, *InformationWeek.* Volume 830, pp.116-120, (2001).
10. Patterson, A. Kirk, C.M. Grimm, and M.C. Thomas, Diffusion of Supply Chain Technologies, *Transportation Journal.* Volume 43, Number 3, pp.5-24, (2004).
11. C. Robson, *Real World Research: A Resource for Social Scientist and Practitioners,* 2nd Edition (Blackwell Publishers: 2002), pp.472-481.
12. S. Levi, E. David, and P. Kaminsky, *Designing and Managing the Supply Chain* (McGraw-Hill Higher Education: 2000), pp.16-19.
13. S.Z. Sleeper, Dynamic Supply Chains Combine EDI, XML In An Effort To Transition To The Web, *High-Tech Supply On-the-Fly.* pp. 87-92, (November 2000).
14. W.H. Delone and E.R. McLean, Information Systems Success: The Quest for the Dependent Variable, *Information Systems Research.* Volume 3, Number 1, pp.60-95, (1992).
15. R.W. Schmenner, *Production/Operations Management* (Science Research Associates: Chicago, 1987).
16. Z.G. Zacharia, The Evolution and Growth of Information Systems in Supply Chain Management, in *Supply Chain Management*, eds. J.T. Mentzer (Sage Publications: 2001), pp.289-319.

Model Analysis of Data Integration of Enterprises and E-Commerce Based on ODS

Zhigang Li, Yan Huang and Shifeng Wan

College of Information Management, Chengdu University of Technology, Chengdu 610059, Sichuan, P.R. China
cdlglzg@163.com cherrishhy@163.com wanshifeng2004@21cn.com

Abstract. Based on the discussion of ODS (Operational Data Store), enterprise data environment features and data integration requirement, three granularity level data models of Web logs in e-commerce are analyzed. Further, data updating and collecting train of thought has been expressed which is realized by granularity manager. Finally, a model is put up, which integrates e-commerce data and other enterprises' data by ODS.

Keywords: *ODS, Electronic commerce (E-commerce), Enterprise data, Integration*

1. INTRODUCTION

Electronic commerce systems are the ones that are built on the Internet and other networks to realize enterprise's business objectives. They can meet the needs of production, sales and services and also can support enterprise's collaborations with its business partners. The electronic commerce systems improve level of enterprises' information automation, management and decision-making. In addition, they offer enterprises a commercial intelligent computing system. As we know, E-commerce brings about enormous competition and business opportunities for the global economy, so e-commerce systems become global information systems. With increasing needs of e-commerce and pressure from enterprise internal development and external competition and collaboration, in enterprises, the demands for information system support are ever increasing as well. Information became the critical resource to enterprise's survival and development. So E-commerce systems are facing big challenges, which are evidenced in that they are required to be open, capable of connecting with other various application systems to integrate enterprises' information resources and improving enterprise's ability of developing markets. However, the more the layers of enterprise's system are, the more difficult data integration is. Thus, Operational Data Store is a better option to solve the data integration problems of e-commerce data and enterprises' other systems data [1, 2].

Please use the following format when citing this chapter:

Li, Z., Huang, Y., Wan, S., 2007, in IFIP International Federation for Information Processing, Volume 254, Research and Practical Issues of Enterprise Information Systems II Volume 1, eds. L. Xu, Tjoa A., Chaudhry S. (Boston: Springer), pp. 275-282.

2. THE REQUIREMENTS OF ENTERPRISES' DATA ENVIORNMENT AND DATA INTEGRATION

Because of the differences among enterprises' sizes, types and industries, data environment varies from different enterprises, so does the requirement of data environment. Data environment characteristics of big enterprise are as follows: firstly, on the whole, there is an operational data environment, and analysis data environment is at the rudimental level, then long-term data has been accumulated, finally, data are relatively canonical. While small and Medium-sized enterprises' characteristics are: firstly, some have operational data environment, but lack the qualifications of building large-scale analysis data environment, then they don't own accumulating long-term data, finally they lack unified data canonical [2].

Enterprise information system is complicated and its information processing contains several courses which are information collection, information management and information controlling. What's more, in connection with different levels and applied aims, it processes information at different abstract level. Then we may find that some terms which are used to describe the processing course, such as data processing, information processing and knowledge processing. At the same time, these terms also reflect the complexity of information processing. With development of E-commerce systems, information system integration is not only the integration of different data information, but also will become integration of knowledge.

The demands of information determine the demands of data integration function. And the purpose of enterprise data integration is to effectively integrate information which distributes in autonomic and isomerous partial data source, so as to realize sharing information among subsystems. Meanwhile, information integration also needs to solve the problems of information, knowledge (experience included) and transformation among data. Because different enterprise data distribute in different business systems, a unified platform is needed to show the analysis results. But this platform is lacking, so a unified enterprise data view can't be offered to the decision-makers. In this case, we need a platform to show the analysis results. We may find that it breaks the barriers among systems, then integrates management information and business information, and offers a unified enterprise production data view and operation data view for the decision-makers and executive officers. Next, some requirements are also needed which are data consistence, data security and efficient use of data [3]. Finally, the ultimate goal of data integration application is to realize enterprise decision-making supporting, which is the real significance.

3. DATA CHARATERISTICS IN ODS

ODS is a kind of store technology, lying between Data Base (DB) and Data Warehouse (DW). Comparing to Data Base, the way of organizing data for ODS also faces to subjects and integration, just like Data Warehouse. The structure of ODS is mixed, supporting operational transaction process and analysis process. ODS data is integrated, variable, specific and the current data or approaching current data and faces to subjects [4]. In addition, when running a system, ODS is the place for enterprise to release information, and the information is real time and about to real time. Meanwhile, other systems of the enterprise can use the information also, including Data Warehouse. But there still are some differences between ODS and Data Warehouse. Firstly, their data magnitude varies greatly. In terms of storing time, DW contains lots of historical data, whose amount greatly exceeds the current data and the latest data of ODS. And then their applying demands are different. DW is used for long-term strategy analysis, which mainly faces to professional data analyst and top management [5, 6]. But ODS is mainly used to global OLTP and the latest LOAP, which faces to middle management for daily management and short-term decision.

When processing lots of historical data, Data Warehouse exerts great efficient, but it can't do well to some old systems. Due to various reasons, these old systems lack synthesis, which makes it difficult to analyze data, dispose data and supply data to Data Warehouses. However, ODS can deal with the data offered by old systems better, in a short time and at lower costs, through redesigning data and data processing model [3].

Moreover, an important online technology is also needed, which can actively offer our customers with their interested subject information to gain more potential customers. According to customer's individual needs, this technology also can automatically search data, collect data, filter data and adjust data at the background, and finally supply customers with their needed information, which reduces customers' works in online searching, comparison and negotiation. These high-powered operations are too hard to proceed in Data Warehouses. But in ODS structure, these can be easily done. Once the incorporative and refined results which coming from enterprise's Data Warehouses are stored in ODS, they can benefit e-commerce web environment. Thus, in the web environment, ODS is one of the key structures for enterprise data processing, data in the web environment can be mostly withdrawn from ODS [7].

4. INTEGRATION MODEL FOR WEB DATA AND OTHER ENTERPRISES' DATA

Data model can help users to review how diversified data are integrated and help users to comprehend the final results. When the products are delivered, Data model also ensures the same expectation between the model builder and the end users. The use of data model helps to reduce the originating rate of redundancy. For data model can make redundancy obvious and delete it. So we may see data model is helpful to reduce the overall risk of the program. If data model were not used, e-commerce workmen will find it is very difficult to withdraw data from web daily and integrate them with other enterprises' date, for more interfaces are required to startup the circular developing process. Without the support of data model, it will be a big challenge for enterprises if they want to manage enterprise data as the critical resource [7].

In order to analyze the enormous data from daily web and then integrate them with other excessive enterprises' data, data granularities at different levels must be disposed. In e-commerce environment, daily web data are at the lowest level of granularity. In a day, the daily data can be taken from the web at a certain length of time [8] [9]. The daily web data can be directly introduced into the DBMS of the ODS in the website, which is the level 0. The introduction process of web log to the DBMS can be designed, or can be completed by the practical tools. From level 0, the daily data and enterprises' data are integrated in the ODS, which is level 1. For example, the customer information from the web log is integrated with the data in the enterprises' ODS. Finally, these data from one day or several days are integrated in ODS is the level 2, which can be used for quick report access [7] [8]. All these three levels of granularity need data models.

Web site data need to integrate with other enterprises' data. To support the integration, many data models will be used, every one of which plays a very important role. These models include [7]: Subject Model, Enterprise Logic Data Model, data models of Data Warehouse and data mart, ODS Model of web sites and Enterprise ODS model.

Subject Model—used to better understand all areas, such as product classification area.

Enterprise Logic Data Model (Enterprise Data Model)—used to connect different subjects, such as the connection between customers and products.

Data Warehouse Model and Data Mart Model-- used to meet the purposeful operational demands, such as doing sales report forms.

Website ODS Model—used to take use of website log's path information.

Enterprise ODS Model-- used to integrate web data and other enterprises' data.

Next this paper will mainly introduce the Enterprise ODS Model:

The structure of Enterprise ODS Mode is integrated and subject-orientated. What makes it different from Data Warehouse is that enterprise ODS is timeliness, including limited historical data. In the e-commerce environment, enterprise ODS is regarded as the Level 1 granularity. Enterprise ODS is renewed from the source systems (Web site ODS and other business systems), and other business operational systems or data mart [6, 8]. In other words, the enterprise ODS is the combination of all kinds of ODS.

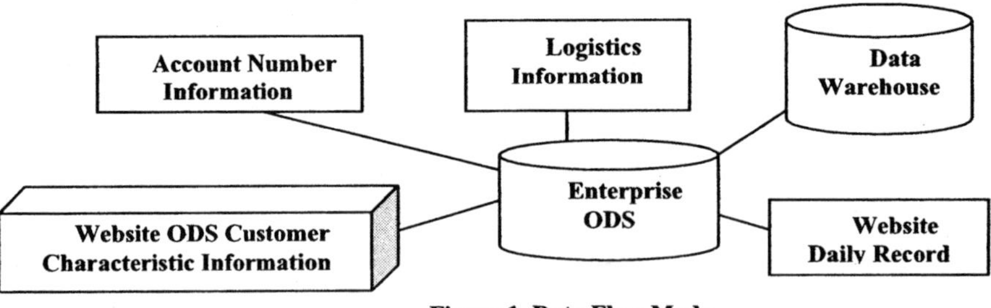

Figure 1. Data Flow Mode

Enterprise ODS environment may be very complicated. According to WH Inmon's analysis and giving consideration to the factual situation of enterprise's website [7, 9], we can design a data flow model. From this model we can see all the data flows form the source systems, Data Warehouses and data marts

Enterprise ODS supplies data to website ODS, so it can make some processes run together, which can take advantages of the parallel structure of this platforms and ETL tools. Internal customer entity of the enterprise ODS plays a very important role in the e-commerce environment. Figure 2 shows some of the data models established for customer entity in enterprise ODS.

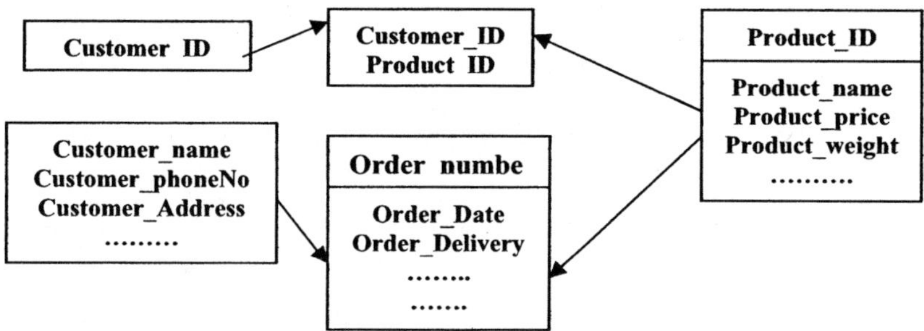

Figure 2. Data Model of Customer Entity in the Enterprise ODS

Using the Granularity Manager, ODS can fit different levels of data granularity (Level 0, Level 1, Level 2). Through using the three levels in web environment, we can successfully implement data updating and summary. And the levels of granularity need different data models, which based on different levels of summarization and corresponding actions taken by the website visitors in the interactive process.[5][7].

5. STRUCTURE PLAN FOR ENTERPRISES' DATA INTEGRATED BY ODS

There are two structures in analysis of enterprises' data environment [2]. One is two-layer structure like DB-DW, which is directed at the overall situation's analysis application. The other one is three-layer structure like DB-ODS-DW, which not only can solve problems of overall situation's analysis application just like the two-layer structure, but also can solve the problems of daily business demands. We can choose these two constructive strategies of Data Warehouse according to enterprise's characteristics and specific demands. However, when DB, ODS and DW exist at the same time, ODS has many advantages. For example, we can implement OLTP in enterprise-class and instant OLAP analysis by ODS. What's more, ODS can simplify data transition interface of DW and its management of data. Although not all constructions of DW needs ODS, the strategies made by it in the three-layer of DB-ODS-DW have the characteristics of integration and enterprise-class. In enterprise management, if information of long-term and daily strategies are both needed, the choice of building the three-layer of DB-ODS-DW maybe better.

Based on data warehouse technology, ODS is a kind of data environment concept which is overall situation consistent and faces to subject. In the process of enterprise information construction, it offers multi-layer data processing environment and builds up the three-layer structure of DB/ODS/DW. In this structure, ODS is the middle layer. On one hand, it includes the overall consisting data and detailed real time data, which can do overall online operational disposal. On the other hand, it is a kind of subject-oriented and integrated data environment, and with small quantity of data. It is helpful to complete data analysis processing of daily decision-making. At present, most enterprises have established perfect database application system, and it is impossible for them to give up all these systems because of the large amount of money in re-investing. So it is more feasible to withdraw data from these application systems to build the ODS, and finally form a technology route of a perfect application system structure. Thus, according to the research of Wei Fang [3], ODS is the best choice for the integration of enterprise information systems and E-commerce data, as shown in Figure 3.

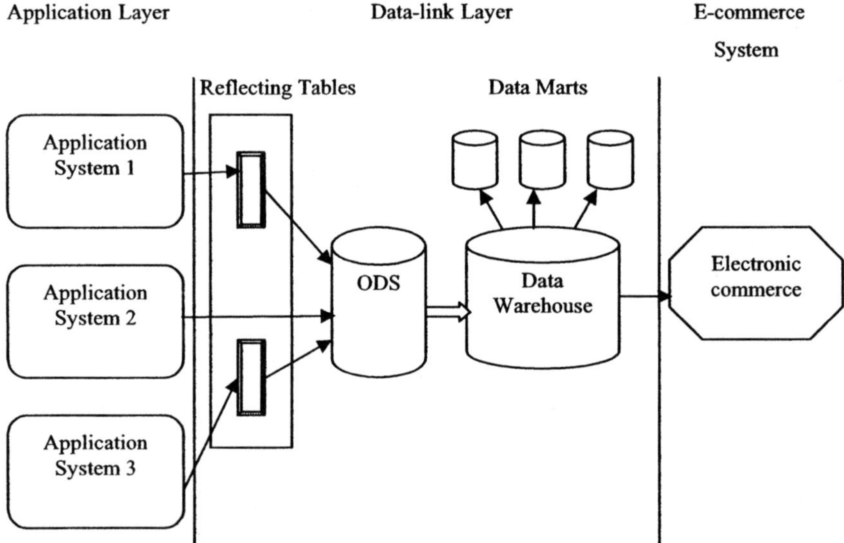

Figure 3. Structure Diagram of ODS and the Application System, Data Warehouse & E-Commerce System

The customer summarization of data and integration can be completed in the enterprise ODS. The summarization and integration of customer data from all enterprise systems and Internet can supply necessary information for successful Customer Relationship Management. In this environment, the data of website information like visiting traffic flow, customer order history (purchasing behavior), customer personal information and customer business activity information etc. can be melted into a data structure, which can offer business group the quick response and excellent reporting form. Then, individual customer-oriented marketing activities can be initiated, using all these customer information.

In fact, there are two kinds of ODS in the e-commerce environment: Web ODS and Enterprise ODS. They are designed for different purposes [7]. Enterprise ODS is a genuine data processor, which can hold much more data than Web ODS. Web ODS only offers services for internal affairs coming form the web server. Thus, it is a kind of "local" ODS, while Enterprise ODS has real enterprise data which can largely be used for processing. Therefore, Enterprise ODS is a kind of "global" server. And web ODS integrates with Enterprise ODS all day long at different intervals. Giving consideration to the capability and throughput, Web ODS and enterprise ODS are not usually stored in the same server [4].

In the Figure 3, data of the Application System 2 are directly stored in ODS, while data of the other application systems are firstly transformed by mapping table, then renovated, and finally stored into the ODS. The processed data stored in the ODS can be supplied to the data warehouse. These reorganized data which stored in the ODS can be provided to data warehouse. Besides, data in ODS and data warehouse can also be provided to e-commerce systems [3].

6. CONCLUSIONS

Development of modern enterprises needs statistics and analysis, which basis is data integration. With the development of E-commerce and business on the Internet, enterprises urgently need a set of data integration system which is reliable, safe, flexible and easy to extend. Data integration can implement integration and automation of design and production, while lacking of the means to optimize global production process. Strategy-supporting puts emphasis on building up enterprises' optimizing models and strategy supporting systems. And these models can offer supporting for top management to solve problems like sales, price, investment and production plan. With the expanding of enterprise's production scales and fields, also associated with the deep researching on production, the models we build are more and more complicated, and models' dependency relationship to data is stronger and stronger. If these models doesn't base on data integration, accuracy of data and timeliness can't be guaranteed [8]. Data integration plan of enterprise system is based on the rules of practicality and robustness. The suitable plan should be chosen according to the requirements of enterprises system construction. In addition, before choosing the suitable one, we should thoroughly analyze the merits and demerits of the plans. Some people think ODS can partly take the place of data warehouse. In fact, ODS and data warehouse have their respective characteristics, and they have no conflicts with each other, so they can not replace each other. Since ODS is more close to the area of operating systems, it can greatly improve the synthesis of the operating systems. In the process of data integration, if Chinese large enterprises can better utilize the advantages offered by ODS, it will benefit for them and offer them a better environment in their future data warehouse projects.

REFERENCES

1. E.F. Codd, S.B. Codd, and C.T. Salley, Beyond Decision Support, *Computer world.* Number 6, pp.46-50, (1993).
2. X. Su, J. Yang, N. Jiang, and X. Shu, *Data Warehouse and Data Mining* (Tsinghua University Press: Beijing, 2006).
3. W. Fang, C. Zuo and Y. Sun, Realize Data Integration of Big Business, *Computer Engineering and application.* Number 6, pp.218-220, (2002).
4. W.H. Inmon, R.H. Terdeman, J.N. Montanari, and D. Meers, *Data Warehousing for E-Business* (John Wiley & Sons Corp: New York, 2004).
5. Z. Li, *Principle and Application of Strategy Support System*, eds. Y. Liu (Higher Education Press: Beijing, 2005).
6. H. Xia, *Data Warehouse and Data Mining Technology*, eds. X. Chen (Science Press: Beijing, 2005).
7. Z. Li, Effects and Methods of Strategy management analysis technology in MIS Plan Construction, *Science Management and Technology Management Research.* Number 1, pp.211-214, (2005).
8. W.H. Inmon, *The Operational Data Store* (China Machine Press: Beijing, 2001).
9. R. Kimball and R. Merz, *Building the Web-Enabled Data Warehouse* (John Wiley & sons, 2000), pp.47-151.
10. Q. Guo, J. Yu, S. Liu, J. Zhao, and Y. Qi, *Theory and Practice of Enterprise Data Mining* (Huanghe Water Economy Press: Zhenzhou, Henan, 2005)

An Empirical Research of Successful ERP Implementation Based on TAM

Dong Cheng, Dehong Yang, Jidong Han and Yuanfang Song

School of Business, Renmin University of China, Beijing 100872, P. R. China
chengdong@ruc.edu.cn dehong.yang@wincor-nixdorf.com hjdruc@gmail.com, rucsongyuanfang@yahoo.com.cn

Abstract. The issues of enterprise resource planning (ERP) implementation have been given much attention due to its high failure rate. Some researches were focused on the influence of perceived use (PU) and perceived ease of use (PEU) on attitude and symbolic adoption based on the theory of technology acceptance model (TAM). Others studied the critical success factors from organizational or personal aspects. However, few scholars put them together to examine the influence of critical success factors on PU and PEU, which are key factors to user acceptance to ERP system. This study develops an integrative framework that links leadership's support, training abilities, change management abilities, business processing abilities and learning abilities with PU and PEU. The present structural equation model encompasses these relationships on the basis of a survey of 340 managers and end-users. This paper highlights two main results. First, leadership's support and training abilities have significant impacts on organizational business processing abilities. Second, change management abilities, business processing abilities and learning abilities, have significant impacts on user perceived ease of use. These findings will help managers to understand that user's perceived ease of use should be considered on organizational level in the construction and implementation of an ERP system.

Keywords: *Enterprise resource planning (ERP), Enterprise management, Enterprise information systems, Enterprise systems organizational issues, Human resource management, Business process reengineering, Technology acceptance model, Critical success factors*

1. INTRODUCTION

The enterprise resource planning (ERP) systems were introduced to enterprise mainly for improving information share and communication at first. Some researchers tried to find out what influences the acceptance of information system like ERP. They treat ERP as a new information technology. The technology acceptance model (TAM) was introduced as the fundamental model. A lot of variables were studied to test their impacts on user perceived use (PU) and perceived ease of use (PEU). Other researches were concentrated on the critical success factors. They try to find out some critical success factors to predict the adoption and implementation effectiveness of ERP systems. There are more than twenty factors identified. But how these factors

Please use the following format when citing this chapter:

Cheng, D., Yang, D., Han, J., Song, Y., 2007, in IFIP International Federation for Information Processing, Volume 254, Research and Practical Issues of Enterprise Information Systems II Volume 1, eds. L. Xu, Tjoa A., Chaudhry S. (Boston: Springer), pp. 283-292.

influence the adoption and implementation effectiveness is still unknown. They may have direct impact on adoption or they may influence adoption through other variables like PU or PEU. Some critical success factors may be mediate. This study tried to find out the impacts of some critical success factors on PU and PEU of TAM. An integrative framework was developed which links leadership's support (LD), training abilities (TR), change management abilities (CM), business processing abilities (CM) and learning abilities (LG) with PU and PEU. The present structural equation model encompasses these relationships on the basis of a survey of 340 managers and end-users. The paper highlights two main results. First, LD and TR have significant impacts on organizational BP. Second, CM, BP and LG have significant impacts on PEU. These findings will help the manager to understand that user's perceived ease of use should be considered on organizational level in the construction and implementation of an ERP system.

2. LITERATURE REVIEW

The proposed framework in this research is based on researches in several fields, which concern technology acceptance, diffusion of innovation and critical success factors. These literatures which provided the necessary theoretical foundations in this study were briefly discussed in the following sections.

2.1 Researches on the Technology Acceptance

User attitude and behavioral intention have received much attention in literatures. Several models were developed from the aspect of social psychology: the theory of reasoned action (TRA) was proposed by Fishbein et al. [1] and Ajzen et al. [2]; the theory of planned behavior (TPB) was proposed by Ajzen [3, 4]; the technology acceptance model (TAM) was proposed by Davis [5]. TPB was an extension of TRA by taking into account of the effects of a use's volitional control on behavioral intention. TAM focuses on user acceptance of new technology. The PU, PEU and AT are three main aspects of TAM. They are the key determinants of user intentions. In parsimonious TAM [6], the attitude which was treated as a mediating variable was excluded.

In the implementation of ERP system, the adoption of ERP package is mandatory in most cases. Thus, a new variable was needed to substitute for behavioral intention to examine users' acceptance. Some researches [7, 8] proposed a new construct called symbolic adoption, which refers to one's mental acceptance to a new technology.

2.2 Researches on Diffusion of Innovation

Diffusion of innovation (DOI) is a similar model to TAM. Tornatzky et al. [9] reported the relationship between innovation characteristics, relative advantage, complexity and compatibility with adoption behavior. Relative advantage was found similar to the notion of usefulness and complexity similar to ease of use [5]. In this research, we use TAM as our primary model.

2.3 Researches on Critical Success Factors

The concept of critical success factors has been well established in the information system literatures. While the implementations of ERP differ from traditional information systems in many aspects such as scale, complexity, business changes, etc., a more suitable theoretical frame or variables need to be developed for a successful ERP implementation.

Holland et al. [10] proposed a framework for understanding success and failure in ERP implementation. In that research, the critical success factors were divided into the strategic and tactical headings. Based on literature review, Nah et al. [11] identified 11 key critical factors for successful ERP implementation. Somers et al. [12] proposed a comprehensive list of 22 critical success factors through an extensive review of the literature. Based on these three researches, a lot of studies were conducted from different aspects [13-20]. Most of these researches were trying to find out the relationship between critical success factors and implementation effectiveness.

3. MODEL AND HYPOTHESES

In this study, TAM is proposed as the fundamental model using symbolic adoption which substitutes for the traditional behavior intention. Therefore, it is hypothesized that:

H1: PEU will have a positive effect on PU.
H2: PEU will have a positive effect on AT.
H3: PU will have a positive effect on AT.
H4: AT will have a positive effect on SA.
H5: PEU will have a positive effect on SA.
H6: PU will have a positive effect on SA.

Altogether 11 to 22 critical success factors were proposed in literatures to explore their impacts on user acceptance or implementation effectiveness. Some critical success factors work on organizational level or personal level both. Others only work on personal level.

The learning ability (LG) refers to activities a company taken to identify cutting-edge ERP technique and pilot-test new methods of using capabilities of ERP system [21]. These organizational activities will improve the use of ERP on personal level. User perceived ease of use of ERP system may by improved through constant learning and pilot-testing of new way of using. Therefore, it is hypothesized that:

H7: LG will have a positive effect on PEU.

The business process ability (BP) refers to a clear process definition and strict compliance with the process. In most case, ERP packages were built around best practices in specific industries, they may not fit the practices of a special corporation. A company needs to customize the package or change its business process [22]. BP will help employees to understand how the business operates and predict the impact of a particular action on the rest of the enterprise [23]. The business process of an enterprise will influence the fluency of user's work and then his perceived ease of use of an ERP system. Therefore, it is hypothesized that:

H8: BP will have a positive effect on PEU.

No matter how detailed the package or reengineering business process is customized, the work style of employees may change more or less. The change management ability (CM) refers to the managerial efforts which could help employees to adapt to or lower their worry of new process after implementation of ERP. These efforts will ease user attitude to change. Employees who have positive attitude to organizational change trend to believe that using new information system will help them attain gains in job performance. They believe that the system will give benefits to individuals and organization. User involvement in the design of a new information system may improve his attitude toward change [24]. The impacts of attitude to change on PU and PEU were reported [25]. Therefore, it is hypothesized that:

H9: CM will have a positive effect on PU.

H10: CM will have a positive effect on PEU.

The impacts of the degree of resistance to change from users across the organization on degree of BPR execution were reported [26]. An adequate change management can help employees understand how to adapt to their new duties. Members in organization will benefit from this to understand how the business operates and predict the impact of their own work on organizational goal. Therefore, it is hypothesized that:

H11: CM will have a positive effect on BP

Training ability (TR) refers to activities a company taken to teach general ERP concepts or hands-on operational skills. It included the need specification, preparation of material and training execution. All these require an overall consideration from organizational and business level. Therefore, it is hypothesized that:

H12: CM will have a positive effect on TR.

Training could help employees to understand how ERP affects the work of individuals, how to deal with conflicts created in implementation and how to adjust individual working process etc. Members in organization will benefit from this to understand and strictly comply with the process after the implementation. Therefore, it is hypothesized that:

H13: TR will have a positive effect on BP.

Since ERP implementation includes technological, operational, managerial components from strategic and organizational aspects, ERP may differ from other information technology or information system [27]. ERP is an enterprise-wide, cross-functional implementation. Both business process re-engineering and change management are beyond the scope of middle level manager and need to be promoted in the whole organization [13, 14]. The champion of ERP from leadership (LD) may minimize user resistance to change and hence improve the adoption through the whole organization [22]. Therefore, it is hypothesized that:

H14: LD will have a positive effect on CM.

H15: LD will have a positive effect on BP.

H16: LD will have a positive effect on SA.

The model we proposed is demonstrated in Figure 1.

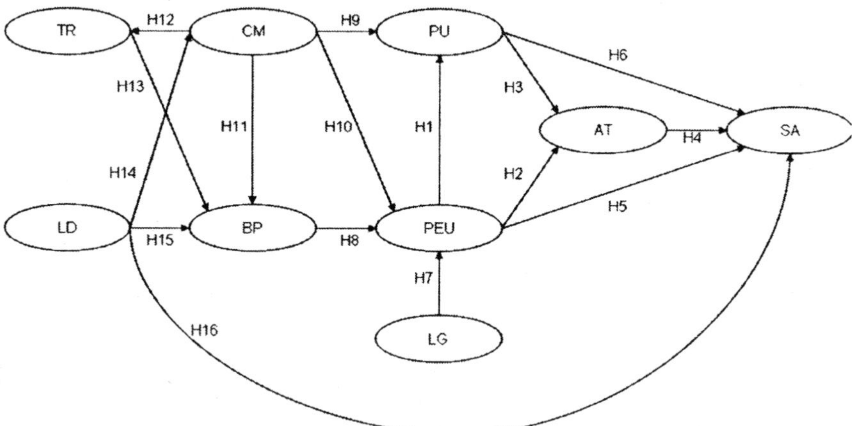

Figure 1. Proposed Structure Model

4. RESEARCH METHOD

Data were collected though questionnaires to test the hypotheses. The sample for this study consisted of ERP manager and users in more than thirty organizations. After five months, we obtained valid 340 answers out of 420 feedback questionnaires. The questionnaire items used a 5-point Likert-type scale. Each of these measures contained subscales ranging from 2 to 7 items.

A scale is thought to have content validity if the scale's items form a representative sample in the theoretical domain of the construct [28, 29]. In this study, we use the usual method of ensuring content validity which is extensive review of literatures. To ensure the content validity of the scale, items used in this study were mostly adopted and modified from previous studies which had been tested.

The most common method to measure the reliability of Likert scales is Cronbach's alpha. Normally, Cronbach's alpha more than 0.6 could be accepted. Cronbach's alpha within the range from 0.7 to 0.9 means high level of reliability. Cronbach's alpha and regression coefficient (R^2) were used to test the reliability and validity of the measures. Cronbach's alpha of all the variables in this research all stay above the level of acceptance. The measurement model was evaluated by completely standardized factor loadings and t-values. The values are showed in Table 1.

5. RESULTS

The data were analyzed using the LISREL structural equation modeling program (LISREL 8.72). To determine model quality, multiple gauges of goodness of fit were used. Absolute, incremental and parsimony fit indices [30] of the proposed model were reported in Table 2, 3, 4.

Table 5. Related Statistical Values of Factors and Scales

Factor	Indicator	Completely Standard factor loading	T-value	R^2	Cronbach's α
BP	BP1	0.721		0.519	0.862
	BP2	0.717	12.675	0.514	0.863
	BP3	0.696	12.297	0.484	0.867
	BP4	0.768	13.580	0.590	0.858
	BP5	0.678	11.991	0.460	0.867
	BP6	0.723	12.787	0.523	0.862
	BP7	0.703	12.436	0.495	0.867
TR	TR1	0.667		0.444	0.870
	TR2	0.751	12.204	0.565	0.860
	TR3	0.819	13.100	0.672	0.852
	TR4	0.792	12.752	0.628	0.854
	TR5	0.706	11.573	0.498	0.862
	TR6	0.636	10.559	0.404	0.872
	TR7	0.665	10.987	0.442	0.869
CM	CM1	0.856		0.732	0.848
	CM2	0.808	18.165	0.653	0.855
	CM3	0.674	13.948	0.454	0.869
	CM4	0.685	14.249	0.469	0.866
	CM5	0.649	13.248	0.421	0.867
	CM6	0.775	17.020	0.600	0.848
PU	PU1	0.876		0.768	0.892
	PU2	0.906	23.430	0.821	0.864
	PU3	0.882	22.364	0.778	0.892
PEU	PEU1	0.818		0.670	0.822
	PEU2	0.791	16.114	0.625	0.845
	PEU3	0.872	18.052	0.760	0.776
AT	AT1	0.937		0.878	
	AT2	0.919	29.073	0.844	
SA	SA1	0.866		0.749	
	SA2	0.564	11.476	0.318	
LD	LD1	0.705	14.269	0.496	0.824
	LD2	0.778	16.383	0.606	0.814
	LD3	0.684	13.723	0.468	0.832
	LD4	0.731	15.010	0.535	0.820
	LD5	0.721	14.723	0.520	0.814
LG	LG1	0.709	14.138	0.502	0.825

Factor	Indicator	Completely Standard factor loading	T-value	R^2	Cronbach's α
	LG2	0.777	16.016	0.604	0.789
	LG3	0.790	16.400	0.625	0.787
	LG4	0.760	15.526	0.577	0.802
overall					0.958

Table 6. Absolute Fit Indices of the Proposed Model

Fit Indices	Absolute					
Name	X^2 / df	GFI	RMSEA	RMR	SRMR	AGFI
Value	3.601	0.831	0.087	0.094	0.061	0.893

Table 7. Incremental Fit Indices of the Proposed Model

Fit Indices	Incremental		
Name	CFI	NNFI	IFI
Value	0.962	0.959	0.962

Table 8. Parsimony Fit Indices of the Proposed Model

Fit Indices	Parsimony	
Name	PGFI	PNFI
Value	0.641	0.873

The model exhibited an overall good fit, with several exceptions. GFI at 0.831 and AGFI at 0.893 were slightly below but close to the recommended level 0.90. Although the GFI level could be improved by dropping some items, the dropping procedure was stopped by the consideration on the content of the measurement. RMSEA at 0.087 and SRMR at 0.061 were slightly above but close to the recommended level.

The structural model was evaluated by standardized path estimates and t-values. Path coefficients of latent variable refer to direct influence of reason variables to result variables. Absolute T value greater than 1.96 (α=0.05) means significant level. Parameter Estimates are showed in Table 5. Fifteen among sixteen proposed direct relationship are statistically significant. H1, H2, H3, H4 and H6 were supported, the results confirmed the TAM. The result indicates that AT should be a mediate variable to the impact of PEU on SA. H7 was supported, the result indicated that learning activities a company taken will improve user perceived ease of use of ERP system. H8 was supported, the result indicated that a clear process definition and strict compliance with the process will help employees to understand how the business operates, thus improve their perceived ease of use of the ERP systems. H9 and H10 were supported, the results indicated that managerial efforts on change management will improve user perceived use and ease of use of an ERP system. H11 was supported, the result indicated that an adequate change management can help employees understand and comply with the new business process after the implementation of ERP. H12 was supported; the result indicated that change management from organizational and business level will help employees to get benefit from training activities. H13 was supported; the result indicated that training could help employees to deal with conflicts created in implementation and adjust individual working process to comply with the ERP business process. H14, H15 and H16 were supported; the results indicated that leadership support is a fundamental factor which will influence change management, business process and symbolic adoption.

Table 9. Parameter Estimates and Hypotheses Test

Hypotheses		Std. loading	T-value	Conclusion
H1	PEU→PU	0.518	8.353	Supported
H2	PEU→AT	0.486	6.746	Supported
H3	PU→AT	0.293	4.269	Supported
H4	AT→SA	0.920	16.104	Supported
H5	PEU→SA	-0.095	-1.502	
H6	PU→SA	0.149	2.704	Supported
H7	LG→PEU	0.207	3.439	Supported
H8	BP→PEU	0.268	3.059	Supported
H9	CM→PU	0.354	6.176	Supported
H10	CM→PEU	0.272	3.167	Supported
H11	CM→BP	0.276	3.233	Supported
H12	CM→TR	0.685	10.268	Supported
H13	TR→BP	0.213	3.353	Supported
H14	LD→CM	0.730	12.864	Supported
H15	LD→BP	0.438	5.928	Supported
H16	LD→SA	0.110	2.589	Supported

6. CONCLUSIONS

The critical success factors have been identified and tested in literatures for years, but in which way these critical success factors influence implementation of ERP system is still unclear. This research tested the impacts of some critical success factors on the user perceived use and ease of use based on TAM. The results confirmed the impacts of change management, business process and learning ability on perceived use and ease of use. Change management ability will contribute to the definition and clarification of business process. Good change management could provide suitable and enough training to employees, helping them to understand and comply with the new business process. Leadership champion of ERP plays a fundamental part in the support of change management, business process and the overall symbolic adoption of ERP system.

In general, the results imply that the implementation environment such as leadership support, change management, business process are critical to user perceived use and ease of use of an ERP system, they influence the adoption then the implementation effectiveness of an ERP system. To pursue a successful implementation, it is vital to create a suitable atmosphere around the enterprise. The more useful and easier to use an ERP system, the more value the system will produce.

REFERENCES

1. M. Fishbein and I. Ajzen, *Belief, Attitude, Intention, and Behavior: an Introduction to Theory and Research* (Addison-Wesley: Reading, MA, 1975).
2. I. Ajzen and M. Fishbein, *Understanding Attitudes and Predicting Social Behavior* (Prentice-Hall: Englewood Cliffs, NJ 1980).
3. I. Ajzen, From intentions to actions: A Theory of Planned Behavior, in *Action-control: From cognition to behavior*, eds. J. Kuhl and J. Beckman (Springer: Heidelberg, 1985), pp.11-39.
4. I. Ajzen, The Theory of Planned Behavior, *Organizational Behavior and Human Decision Processes*. Volume 50, Number 2, pp.179-211, (1991).
5. F.D. Davis, Perceived Usefulness, Perceived Ease of Use and User Acceptance of Information Technology, *MIS Quarterly*. Volume 13, Number 3, pp.319-340, (1989).
6. F.D. Davis, R.P. Bagozzi, and P.R. Warshaw, User Acceptance of Computer Technology: A Comparison of Two Theoretical Models, *Management Science*. Volume 35, Number 8, pp.982-1003, (1989).
7. E. Karahanna, D.W. Straub, and N.L. Chervany, Information Technology Adoption across Time: A Cross-sectional Comparison of Pre-adoption and Post-adoption Beliefs, *MIS Quarterly*. Volume 23, Number 2, pp.183-213, (1999).
8. P. Rawstorne, R. Jayasuriya, and P. Caputi, An Integrative Model of Information Systems Use in Mandatory Environments, in *Proc. of the Nineteenth International Conference on Information Systems*, eds. J. I. DeGross, R. Hirschheim, and M. Newman (Association for Information Systems: Atlanta, GA, 1998), pp.325-330.
9. L. Tornatzky and K. Klein, Innovation Characteristics and Innovation Adoption Implementation: a Meta Analysis of Findings, *IEEE Transactions on Engineering Management*. Volume 29, Number 1, pp.28-45, (1982).
10. C. Holland and B. Light, *A Framework for Understanding Success and Failure in Enterprise Resource Planning System Implementation*, in *Second-wave Enterprise Resource Planning Systems*, eds. G. Shanks, P.B. Seddon, and L.P. Willcocks (Cambridge University Press: Edinburgh, 1999), pp.180-195.
11. F.F. Nah, J.L. Lau, and J. Kuang, Critical Factors for Successful Implementation of Enterprise Systems, *Business Process Management Journal*. Volume 7, Number 3, pp.285-296, (2001).
12. T.M. Somers and K.G. Nelson, The Impact of Critical Success Factors across the Stages of Enterprise Resource Planning Implementations, in *Proc. of the 34th Annual Hawaii International Conference on System Sciences* (IEEE Computer Society: Washington, DC, 2001), pp.8016.
13. H. Akkermans and K. Helden, Vicious and Virtuous Cycles in ERP Implementation: a Case Study of Interrelations between Critical Success Factors, *European Journal of Information Systems*. Volume 11, Number 1, pp.35-46, (2002).
14. C.F. Ho, W.H. Wu, and Y.M. Tai, Strategies for the Adaptation of ERP Systems, *Industrial Management + Data Systems*. Volume 104, Number 3, pp.234-251, (2004).
15. P. Kraemmergaard and J. Rose, Managerial Competences for ERP Journeys, *Information Systems Frontiers*. Volume 4, Number 2, pp.199-211, (2002).
16. J. Magnusson and A. Nilsson, A Conceptual Framework for Forecasting ERP Implementation Success: A first step towards the creation of an implementation support tool, in *Proceedings of the 6th International Conference on Enterprise Information*

Systems, eds. I. Seruca, J. Filipe, S. Hammoudi, and J. Cordeiro (Universidade Portucalense: Porto, Portugal, 2004), pp.447-453.

17. F.F. Nah, K.M. Zuckweiler, and J.L. Lau, ERP Implementation: Chief Information Officers' Perceptions of Critical Success Factors, *International Journal of Human-Computer Interaction*. Volume 16, Number 1, pp.5-22, (2003).
18. F.F. Nah and S. Delgado, Critical Success Factors for Enterprise Resource Planning Implementation and Upgrade, *The Journal of Computer Information Systems*. Volume 46, Number 5, pp.99-113, (2006).
19. P. Ifinedo and N. Nahar, ERP Systems Success: an Empirical Analysis of How Two Organizational Stakeholder Groups Prioritize and Evaluate Relevant Measures, *Enterprise Information Systems*. Volume 1, Number 1, pp.25-48, (2007).
20. D.L. Olson and F. Zhao, CIOs' Perspectives of Critical Success Factors in ERP Upgrade Projects, *Enterprise Information Systems*. Volume 1, Number 1, pp.129-138, (2007).
21. J.K. Stratman and A.V. Roth, Enterprise Resource Planning (ERP) Competence Constructs: Two-Stage Multi-Item Scale Development and Validation, *Decision Sciences*. Volume 33, Number 4, pp.601-628, (2002).
22. S. August-Wilhelm, and F. Habermann, Making ERP a Success, *Communications of the ACM*. Volume 43, Number 4, pp.57-61, (2000).
23. A.V. Roth, J. Julian, and M.K. Malholtra, Assessing Customer Value for Reengineering: Narcissistic Practices and Parameters from the Next Generation, in *Business process change: Reengineering Concepts, Methods, and Technologies*, eds. W. Kettinger and V. Grover (Idea Group Publishing: Harrisburg, PA, 1995), pp.453-474.
24. D. Elizur and L. Guttman, The Structure of Attitudes toward Work and Technological Change within an Organization, *Administrative Science Quarterly*. Volume 21, Number 4, pp.611-623, (1976).
25. K. Kwahk, ERP Acceptance: Organizational Change Perspective, in: Proceedings of the 39th Annual Hawaii International Conference on System Sciences (IEEE Computer Society: Washington, DC, 2006), pp.1726.
26. C.S. Yu, Causes Influencing the Effectiveness of the Post-implementation ERP System, *Industrial Management + Data Systems*. Volume 105, Number 1, pp.115-132, (2005).
27. M.A. Mashari, A.A. Mudimigh, and M. Zairi, Enterprise Resource Planning: A Taxonomy of Critical Factors, *European Journal of Operational Research*. Volume 146, Number 2, pp.352-364, (2003).
28. G.A. Churchill, A Paradigm for Developing Better Measures of Marketing Constructs, *Journal of Marketing Research*. Volume 16, Number 3, pp.64-73, (1979).
29. E.J. Pedhazur and L.P. *Schmelkin, Measurement, Design, and Analysis: An Integrated Approach* (Lawrence Erlbaum Associates: Hillsdale, NJ, 1991).
30. K.A. Bollen, Overall Fit in Covariance Structural Models: Two Types of Sample Size Effects, *Psychological Bulletin*. Volume 107, Number 2, pp.256-259, (1990).

Design and Implementation of Ontology-Based Query Expansion for Information Retrieval

Fang Wu[1, 2], Guoshi Wu[1] and Xiangling Fu[1]

[1] School of Software Engineering, Beijing University of Posts and Telecommunications, Beijing 100879, P.R. China w-fang@hotmail.com xiangling.fu@263.net
[2] Department of Computer Science, Cangzhou Medical College, Cangzhou 061001, Hebei, P.R. China wuguoshi@email.buptsse.cn

Abstract. In Information Retrieval (IR), the user's input query conditions usually are not detailed enough, so the satisfactory query results can not be brought back. Query expansion of IR can help to solve this problem. However, the common query expansion in IR cannot get steady retrieval results. In this paper, we propose and implement query expansion method which combines domain ontology with the frequent of terms. Ontology is used to describe domain knowledge; logic reasoner and the frequency of terms are used to choose fitting expansion words. By this way, higher recall and precise can be gotten as user' query results. Experimental results show that compared with the results of common query expansion, the method described in this paper can get statistically significant improvement in recall and precise combination.

Keywords: *Search engine, Ontology, Web ontology language (OWL), Knowledge management, Enterprise search*

I. INTRODCTION

In information retrieval (IR), even the best system has a limited recall. Users may miss many important documents which they really need usually. There are two fundamental reasons for this problem. The first one is word mismatch, which means that concepts (or key words) of user queries are often different from the words of the resource documents although these words have similar meanings. Another is that users submit short queries which are not detailed enough for IR, so the bad search performance ensues. Query expansion (QE) can effectively alleviate the problem by adding additional terms which have similar meaning to the original query.

In this study, we proposed a new expansion method which is based on domain ontology and frequency of keyword occurrence in resource documents to filter expansion words. It achieves better performance in both precision and recall.

Please use the following format when citing this chapter:

Wu, F., Wu, G., Fu, X., 2007, in IFIP International Federation for Information Processing, Volume 254, Research and Practical Issues of Enterprise Information Systems II Volume 1, eds. L. Xu, Tjoa A., Chaudhry S. (Boston: Springer), pp. 293-298.

2. RELATED RESEARCH

QE approaches can be roughly classified into three groups: interactive QE, semantic dictionary QE and the QE method based on documents set. In this section, each approach is briefly explained.

Interactive QE [1]: In interactive QE, a user is shown a list of terms suggested by the system after entering his query. Through human-machine interaction, undesired terms will not be added to the query string. The system can get good result, but the method need people familiar with the professional domain knowledge, that is often beyond normal users' capacity.

Semantic Dictionary [2-5] QE: Many researchers have tried to use semantic dictionary, such as WordNet for QE. But the results have not been as good as expected. In WordNet, a concept may include many related words. In those words, some are useless for query and can bring noises to the result, and they also are added to queries. In addition, WordNet is too broad and can not be used into special domain.

The QE based on Documents Set [6-9]:

Automatic Global Analysis: Global analysis is based on corpus wide statistics such as co-occurrence statistics about all possible pairs of terms, which normally results in a similarity matrix among terms. The terms, which are the most similar to the query, will be used to expand a query. Since the co-occurrence information for every pair of terms in the whole corpus is normally needed, the processing is computational resource consuming.

Automatic Local Analysis: The method assumes that the top-n retrieved documents are relevant, the system uses the terms contained in those documents as expansion terms and retrieves again. But when the top-n documents happen to be irrelevant, the QE will fail.

User Relevance Feedback: It requires users to read every retrieved document and tell the system that which documents are relevant. Terms are extracted from these documents for QE. This method is seldom deployed in practice because it puts burden on users and often irritates users.

Most of the existing methods get the improved recall, but at the same time, some terms added to the query bring noises to the result, and the IR returns many irrelevant documents, which lead to low precision. Avoiding noises when expanding queries is a researchable problem. In this paper, our research range is short query and professional domain IR, and the important research is how to choose expansion words. Because of wide and dim meaning of semantic dictionary, we use ontology instead of it to describe domain knowledge, and logic reasoner and the frequency of terms are used to choose fitting expansion words. The experiments show that the method we propose can get higher recall with the least decrease of precision.

3. RELATED CONCEPT: ONTOLOGY

Ontology [10] can be defined as a formal, explicit specification of a shared conceptualization. That means ontology defines accepted concepts and their relations in some special domain. It is machine-readable and can be reused.

4. SYSTEM ARCHITECTURE

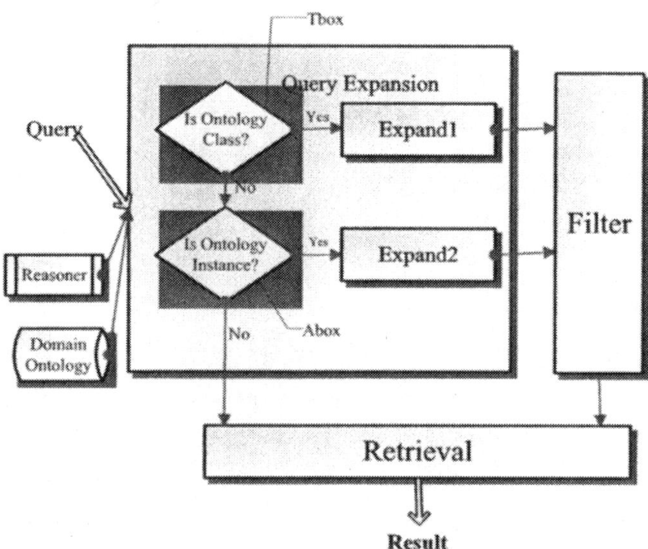

Figure 1. The Framework of Our System

Figure 1 sketches the architecture of our retrieval system. It is made up of Query Expansion, Filter and Retrieval modules. When user inputs a query which includes the terms in the Ontology, QE module provides a preliminary list of expansion words by using Pellet reasoner and domain ontology. Then, Filter module filters out some useless words, and delivers the new list to retrieval module. If the initial query does not include the words which belong to the ontology, it will be delivered to retrieval directly.

QE Module: The module expands the concept with the support of Pellet reasoner and domain ontology. The reasoner judges that the concept is a class or an instance in the ontology, then the module expands the concept by the judgment.

Reason: For a ontology user, the function of a reasoner is to obtain the cryptic knowledge from a ontology. There are two reason modes: TBOX and ABOX. TBOX: Terminology in a special domain, its task is to check the satisfiability of a concept in ontology. ABOX: Assertions about instance, its function is to check an instance belongs to which concept.

In QE module, firstly, a query will be checked if it is a concept in the ontology by TBOX. If it is, its subclasses, equivalent classes, and subinstances will be listed as expansion words ("expand1"in Figure 1). If the query is not a concept in the ontology, it will be check if it is an instance under a concept in the ontology. If it is, its brother instances will be list as expansion words ("expand2"in Figure 1).

Filter Module: The function of filter module is filtering out useless words in expansion words list. Filtering relays on the frequency of the word in document. If the occurrence frequency of a word is higher than a value, the word will be kept. If the frequency is lower than the value, the word will be filtered out. The principle is explained as follow.

1. Two documents: document I and document II

Document I: “徐华在北京工作，我也在北京工作。”

Document II: “他曾经在上海工作。”

2. Word Segment: Filter out useless words, and keep keywords.

Keywords of document I: “ 徐华 北京 工作 我 北京 工作 ”.

Keywords of document II: “ 他 上海 工作 ” .

3. Build Reverse Index:

Table 1. Reverse Index

Keyword	The name of document[Occurrence frequency]	Position
徐华	I[1]	1
北京	I[2]	2,5
工作	I[2],II[1]	3,6,3
我	I [1]	4
他	II[1]	1
上海	II[1]	2

From table1, we can know that “工作” occurs in document I twice and document II once. In the third column, “3,6” means occurrence position in document I, and “3” means the position in document II.The system stores above data as term dictionary, frequencies and positions files. Term dictionary stores the pointer to frequencies and positions. By the pointer, we can obtain keywords' occurrence frequencies in a document rapidly. Then, we can filter expansion words by the frequencies files.

Retrieval Module: The module is a full text IR which is made by Lucene.

5. ALGORITHM

```
1. Short query from user: Q
{ if (Q belongs to Domain Ontology)
    { Query Expansion;
      Filtering Expansion;}
else {delivers Q to Retrieval.}
}
Query Expansion//
If (Q is a concept in ontology){
    Listing its subclasses, equivalent classes and subinstances.}
else{
    If (Q is a instance in ontology){
Check which class the instance belongs to;Listing the subinstances of the class;}
```

}
Filtering Expansion//

For each expansion word, if its occurrence frequency from 'frequencies file is higher than some value, keep it. Otherwise, filter out the word from expansion word list.

2. Documents set:
{
Word segment;
Building frequencies file;}

6. EXPERIMENTS

Our system has two characters: One is domain ontology for QE is closer to the professional documents set than common semantic dictionary, and that can improve the performance of professional IR. Another is that the choice of expansion words is based on text collection. This overcomes noises in IR affectively.

In order to evaluate the performance of our system, we made some experiments. The text collection comes from Sina or Yahoo , and consists of 82 articles. The searching domain is travel knowledge .

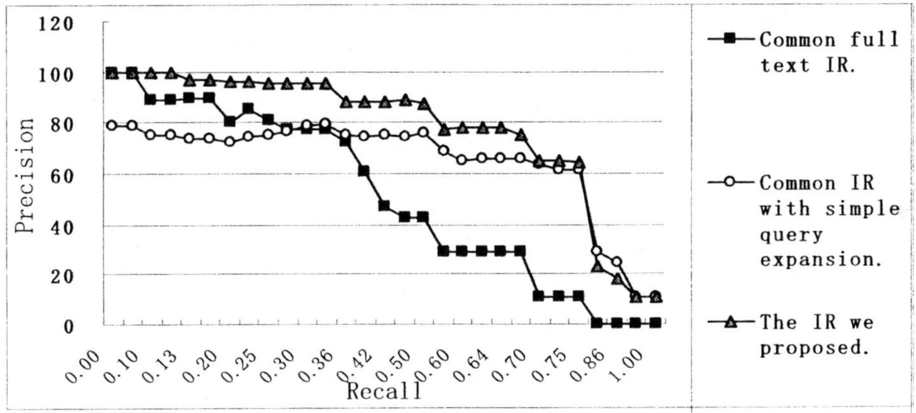

Figure 2. Average Precision/Recall Curves

Three search engines were built: common full text IR, IR with simple QE based on ontology and the IR we proposed in this paper. The average precision/recall curve [11] is effective to evaluate IR performance. Figure 2 shows that compared with full text IR, IR with simple query can not improve the performance of the IR consistently. With the increasing recall, the precision of the system is decreasing. However, the method we proposed in this paper increases the recall and does not decrease the precision.

7. CONCLUSIONS

We proposed a QE method based on ontology and occurrence frequency. This model overcomes two drawbacks in traditional QE: weak description in domain knowledge and noises caused by QE. With the new expansion method, recall and precision are improved at the same time. But in our system, the perfection of ontology affects the performance of IR, perfecting the ontology is an important work.

REFERENCES

1. H. Lee, S. Lin, and C. Huang, Interactive Query Expansion Based on Fuzzy Association Thesaurus for Web Information Retrieval, in *Proc. of the 10th IEEE International Conference on Fuzzy System* (IEEE Press: Melbourne, Australia, 2001), pp.724-727.
2. J. Gonzalo, F. Verdejo, and I. Chugur, Using Eurowordnet in a Concept-Based Approach to Cross-Language Text Retrieval, *Applied Artificial Intelligence*. Volume 13, Number 7, pp.647-678, (1999).
3. E.M. Voorhees, Using WordNet to Disambiguate Word Senses for Text Retrieval, in *Proc. of the Sixteenth Annual Intl. ACM SIGIR Conf. on Research and Development in Information Retrieval* (ACM Press: New York, NY, USA, 1993), pp.171-180.
4. R. Mandala, T. Tokunaga, and H. Tanaka, Combining multiple evidence from different types of thesaurus for query expansion, in *Proc. of the 22nd Annual International ACM SIGIR Conference on Research and Development in Information Retrieval* (ACM Press: Berkeley, CA, USA, 1999), pp.191-197.
5. G.A. Miller, R. Beckwith, C. Fellbaum, D. Gross, and K. Miller, Introduction to WordNet: an on-line lexical database, *International Journal of Lexicography*. Volume 3, Number 4, pp.235-244.
6. M.E. Maron and J.L. Kuhns, On Relevance, Probabilistic Indexing and Information Retrieval, *Journal of the Association for Computer Machinery*. Volume 7, Number 3, pp.216-244, (1960).
7. J.J. Rocchio, *Relevance feedback in information retrieval*, in *The SMART Retrieval System*, eds. G. Salton (Prentice-Hall, Inc.: Englewood Cliffs, NJ, 1971), pp.313-323.
8. G. Salton and C. Buckley, Improving retrieval performance by relevance feedback, *Journal of the American Society for Information Science*. Volume 41, Number 4, pp.288-297, (1990).
9. L. Song, Y. Cheng, and Q. Shan, Relevance Feedback for Information Retrieval System, *Journal of the China Society for Scientific and Technical Information*. Volume 24, Number 1, pp.34-41, (2005).
10. P. Paggio, B.S. Pedersen, and D. Haltrup, Applying Language Technology to Ontology-Based Querying: the Ontoquery Project, *Applied Artificial Intelligence*. Volume 17, Number 8 & 9, pp.817-833, (2003).
11. B.Y. Ricardo and R.N. Berthier, Retrieval Performance Evaluation, in *Modern Information Retrieval*, eds. X. Sui (China Machine Press: Beijing, 2005), pp.51-57.

Enterprise Java Applications and SAP R/3 System Integration Using JCO

Jitao Yang[1], Hongqi Su[1], Yuanfeng Wu[1] and Junwei Liu[2]

[1] Department of Computer Science, China University of Mining & Technology, Beijing 100083, P.R. China iipapaya@gmail.com shq@cumtb.edu.cn yuanfengwu@126.com
[2] Industry Application Division, Tsinghua Tongfang Co. Ltd, Computer System Business Group, Beijing 100085, P.R.China liujunwei@thtfpc.com

Abstract. Enterprise computing often takes the form of automation islands, and lots of business operations must be built on these islands. Then reusing existing components and creating integrated, flexible, reliable applications which can be combined for maximum productivity have become the imperative for an enterprise to survive and thrive in the new competitive and dynamic business environment. In the company with SAP as its ERP software, it is an obvious choice for the enterprise to target SAP R/3 Enterprise as its data source. But the question is how to achieve the integration when the company used Java EE as its platform for developing enterprise applications? JCO (Java Connector) is a new and economical solution that is introduced in this paper for the integration.

Keywords: *Data synchronization, Design pattern, Electronic data interchange, Business process integration, SAP, JCO*

1. INTRODUCTION

Business collaboration through enterprise application integration is an absolute competitive differentiator in an increasingly global economy, and the goal of enterprise integration is to provide timely and accurate exchange of consistent information between business functions to support strategic and tactical business goals in a manner that appears to be seamless [1]. However, problems often emerge from overly ambitious or imprecise requirements resulting from inadequate plans for integrating different systems.

Integration of information systems is expensive and time consuming. A lot of labor costs can be traced to the storage and reconciliation of data. In addition, most of codes in corporate software systems are dedicated to moving data from system to system. In this paper, we describe the challenges associated with the integration of SAP R/3 Enterprise and provide a road map toward a solution.

Please use the following format when citing this chapter:

Yang, J., Su, H., Wu, Y., Liu, J., 2007, in IFIP International Federation for Information Processing, Volume 254, Research and Practical Issues of Enterprise Information Systems II Volume 1, eds. L. Xu, Tjoa A., Chaudhry S. (Boston: Springer), pp. 299-309.

2. PRELIMINARIES

2.1 Problem Description

In the company using SAP R/3 as its ERP software, it is clear for the company to use SAP as its data source, and integrate the other non-SAP systems, such as a e-business system based on Java EE platform, a .NET platform and so on. The integration requires regular or real-time customers, materials, and other main data from the SAP ERP system, ensuring the consistency of the data used in the business operations and the internal SAP ERP main data.

Currently, SAP XI (Exchange Infrastructure) will complete this job well, but the cost is expensive and its configuration is relatively cumbersome. Then, how to design a flexible using and simple configuration data synchronization framework based on the enterprises' business operation reality, which not only let the ERP software play the central role in the allocation of enterprise resources, but also maintain the existing heterogeneous platform systems run smoothly and stably without a lot of changes, is more concerned by the ERP enterprise.

Based on an actual project, the paper provides a solution using JCO to make the other heterogeneous systems' developers and the end users use the SAP data in a comparatively transparent manner.

2.2 Data Classification

The data required by the enterprise's business operation can be broadly classified into the following two types:

The first category of data: basic data for business operation, such as the types of customers, the customers' respective sale regions, province information, products transportation methods and etc. Such data is characterized by relatively small changes, and belongs to system enumeration values.

The second category of data: main data for business operation, such as material main data, customer information main data, shipment information and BOM (Bill of Material) data. Features of such data will be incremental or periodically changed which means have to be dynamic updated, and its real-time requirements are relatively high.

These two types of data need to design two different data synchronization programs.

2.3 Data Synchronization Design

Based on the reality, we designed a middle layer between the SAP ERP system and the non-SAP systems for data exchange, as shown in Figure 1. The SAP data can be read through designed BAPI (Business Application Programming Interface), the middle layer is responsible for calling the data through JCO, and make the queried data transfer to the entity JavaBeans in the form of type security using Java Proxy, then the entity JavaBeans take charge to produce a series of SQL statements and store the data to the non-SAP systems' background databases or store the data in the form of xml.

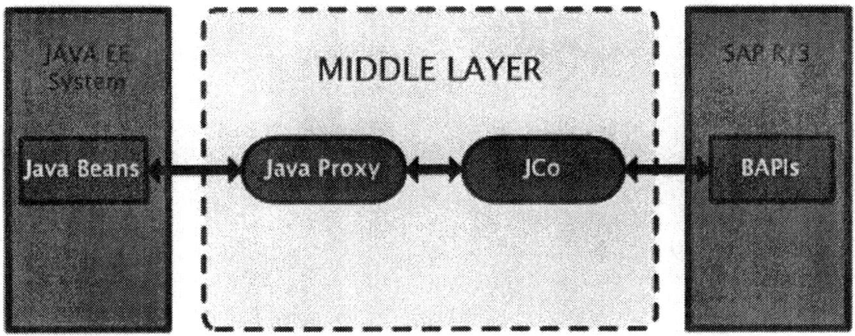

Figure 1. The Middle Layer Model

The data classification results to design different BAPI interfaces:

The first type of data: BAPI has no input parameters. Procedures for this category of data synchronization are clearing up the counterpart tables in the Java EE platform databases first, and insert the queried data from SAP one by one into the Java EE platform databases.

The second type of data: BAPI has input parameters: start-up time, termination time. The synchronization programs automatically synchronize daily based on the queried records' establish time, and the synchronization procedures do not clear Java EE databases' historical data, only incrementally synchronize.

2.4 Connect to SAP Using JCo

JCo is a high-performance, JNI-based middleware for SAP's RFC (Remote Function Call) protocol. JCo allows to build both client and server applications. JCo supports two programming models for connecting to SAP: direct connections, and connection pools. These two models also can be combined in one application. JCo's ability to use connection pools makes it an ideal choice for web server applications that are clients of an SAP system, and it also supports developing desktop applications [2]. Parts of the connection codes are shown below.

```
    import com.sap.mw.jco.*;
// direct connection
try{
    JCO.Client jcoClient = JCO.createClient(
                        "600",                      // SAP client
                        "<userID>",             // userid
                        "******",               // password
                        "EN",                   // language
```

```
                "<hostnsme>",  // application server host name
                "21");                    // system number
         jcoClient.connect();
        }
        catch (Exception ex) {
        ex.printStackTrace();
        }
        finally{
        jcoClient.disconnect();
        }

        // connection pool
        static final String POOL_NAME = "SapPool";
        JCO.Client mConnection;
        try {
                JCO.Pool                    pool                    =
JCO.getClientPoolManager().getPool(POOL_NAME);
                if (pool == null) {
                        OrderedProperties logonProperties =
                        OrderedProperties.load("/logon.properties");
                        JCO.addClientPool(POOL_NAME,          // pool
name
                        5,
                        // maximum number of connections
                        logonProperties);
        // properties
                }
                mConnection = JCO.getClient(POOL_NAME);
                System.out.println(mConnection.getAttributes());
        }
        catch (Exception ex) {
                ex.printStackTrace();
        }
        finally {
                JCO.releaseClient(mConnection);
        }
```

3. DATA SYNCHRONIZATION MIDDLE LAYER DESIGN AND IMPLEMENTATION

3.1 The Middle Layer Framework

According to business needs, customers issue requests, the Servlet deployed on the SAP NetWeaver server distribute the requests to entity JavaBeans, JavaBeans pass the input parameters to BAPI through JavaProxy, BAPI execute the queries using the parameters, and return the results to the entity JavaBeans through JavaProxy, then the Servlet select to deal by JSP pages, or store the data into the background database of the business systems or into the xml files. Here, Servlet play the role of controller, JSP is used to display data, entity JavaBeans responsible for handling business model. The system framework is shown in Figure 2:

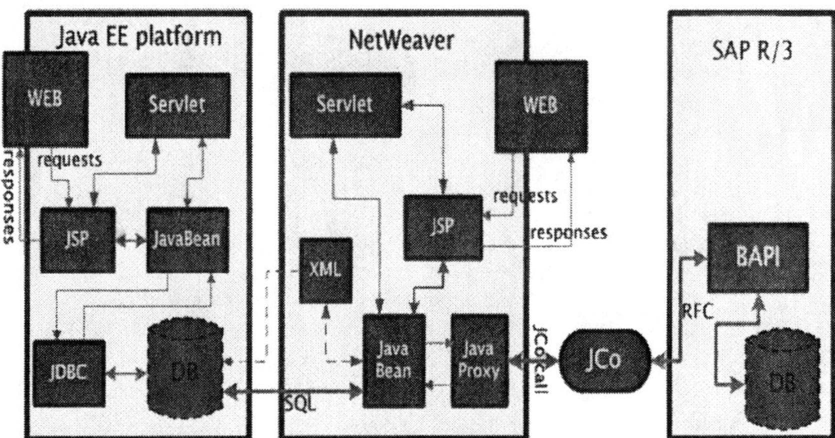

Figure 2. The System Framework

3.2 The First Category of Data Synchronization Process

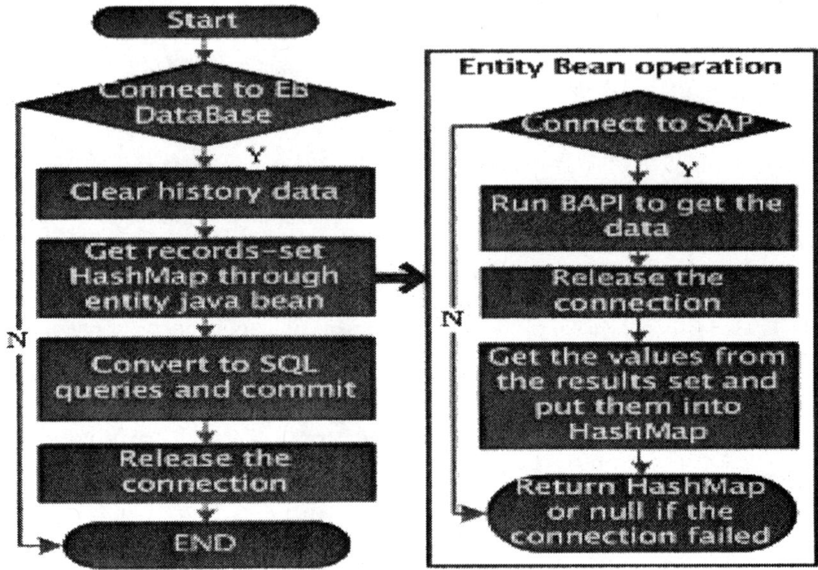

Figure 3. The First Category of Data Synchronization Process

For the first category of data, the queried results set by the implement of BAPI is stored in HashMap as a buffer, then the provisional data in the HashMap can be written as XML documents for the other heterogeneous data sources' read, or organized as SQL sequences and inserted into the heterogeneous business database directly. Process is shown in Figure 3.

3.3 The Second Category of Data Synchronization Process

This kind of data synchronization procedure is incremental synchronization which requires discriminate the queried records' creation time and the business needs, the records will be inserted into business database tables, or updated to the database tables by the primary keys. The insert operation will be changed to update when there are duplicate primary keys. If the query records' creation time is null, these records will be inserted into the business tables, and similarly, changed to update operation when the primary keys duplicate. Procedure is shown in Figure 4:

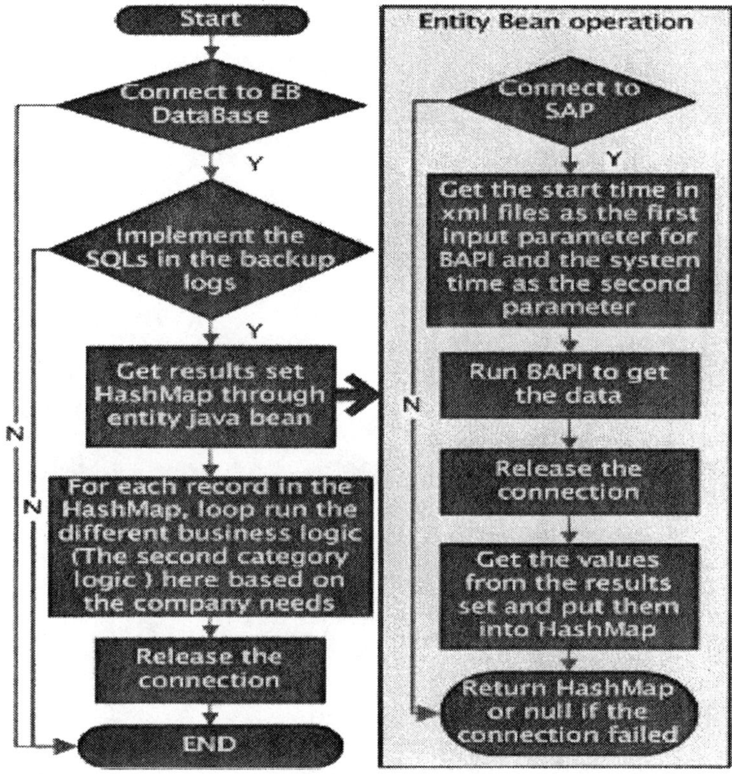

Figure 4. The Second Category of Data Synchronization Process

Based on the creation time of the data in the ERP system, BAPIs query the data from SAP conforming to the business needs, and in accordance with each record in the results set, loop run the second category logic. The second category logic is shown in Figure 5:

Definition:

ST: records query start-time // BAPI input parameter

ET: records query end-time // BAPI input parameter,

//the server's system date

CT: creation time //creation time of the main data in ERP

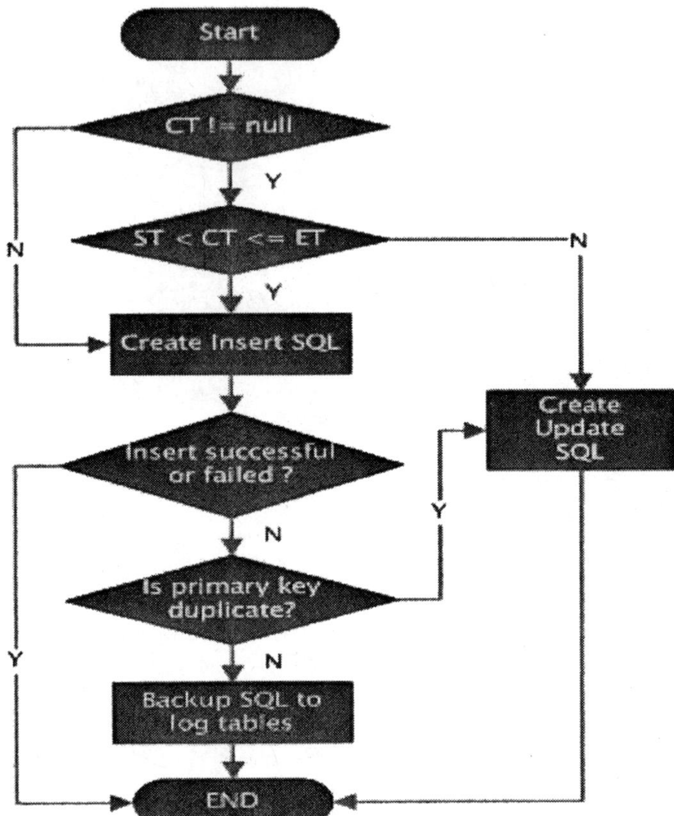

Figure 5. The Second Category Logic Process

3.4 Data Synchronization Time Nodes Storage

During the second category of data synchronization, the system time must be recorded after each operation and the recorded time will be as the start–time parameters to be inputed into BAPI in the next synchronous operation. Recording each BAPI implementation's system time in the following format:

```
… …
    <!--salers-->
            <bapi name="XSHOU_SL" date="2005-12-01" />
            <!--consignment sign-->
            <bapi name="FHUO_CS" date="2005-01-01" />
            <!--standard bom-->
    <bapi name="BPEI_STB" date="2005-12-01" />
     <!--variant bom-->
```

```
<bapi name="BSHI_VC" date="2006-12-11" />
 <!--material data-->
<bapi name="WLIAO_MD" date="2006-12-11" />
<!--customer main data-->
<bapi name="KHU_CMD" date="2006-12-11" />
… …
```

3.5 Field Mapping and Type Security

Heterogeneous systems using the relational data tables may be inconsistent with the SAP-data field's name, type or length. For the field name, use the XML document to establish the mapping relationship between the two systems:

```
… …
    <sapbapi name="DATA_BAPI_VC"> //BAPI interface name
                <H name="FN_EB"/>
//destination database field name
                <S name="FN_SAP"/>
//SAP-data field name
                <H name="VW_EB"/>
                <S name="VW_SAP"/>
    </sapbapi>
… …
```

For the field data-types, if the two system's field data-types are compatible, use JavaProxy for data-type conversion. If the data-types are not compatible, it will need to amend the e-business system's corresponding table's field data-types, and expand the length of the field to let it be able to receive the data from SAP.

3.6 Data Synchronization Logs Audit

In order to ensure the reliability of data synchronization, the middle layer records detail information of data synchronization procedures for the data calibration in the future. We use the open source component Log4J to detailed record the every operation step information. Log4J's related configuration information is shown below:

```
… …
 #root records log's level is INFO, the log information below the level is going to
 #be neglected, define an Appender named logConsole for the root recorder
log4j.rootLogger=INFO,logConsole
 #define a sapEB recorder, if there is no log level, it will inherit the root
 #recorder's level, define an Appender named logConsole for sapEB recorder,
 #sapEB is going to inherit the root recorder's Appender
log4j.logger.sapEB=,logFile
#define an Appender named logConsole and its type is ConsoleAppender
```

```
log4j.appender.console=org.apache.log4j.ConsoleAppender
#logConsole Appender's Layout is simplelayout
log4j.appender.console.layout=org.apache.log4j.SimpleLayout
#define an Appender named logFile and its type is RollingFileAppender
log4j.appender.logFile=org.apache.log4j.RollingFileAppender
log4j.appender.logFile.MaxFileSize=10MB
log4j.appender.logFile.MaxBackupIndex=2
#define logFile Appender's output path and its filename
log4j.appender.logFile.File=E:\\dataSyn\\sapEB\\ dataSyn.log
#using patternlayout as logFile Appender's layout
log4j.appender.logFile.layout=org.apache.log4j.PatternLayout
#define the output format of the logFile
    log4j.appender.logFile.layout.ConversionPattern=%d            {yyyy-MM-dd
  HH:mm:ss} [%c]-[%-5p] %l "#" %m%n%n

……
```

Add the configuration file information to the initializing servlets, then when NetWeaver server starting deploying, it will load the initialization servlets first, thus completing the Log4j environment configuration.

4. SYSTEM ANALYSIS

SAP Java Connector is SAP's Java middleware, the SAP Java Connector allows SAP customers and partners to easily build SAP-enabled components and applications in Java. JCO supports both inbound (Java calls ABAP) and outbound (ABAP calls Java) calls in desktop and (web) server applications [2]. Java Proxy encapsulates JCO call to ensure data type security, and improve the client-end's system stability.

Data classification makes each distributed data node decide what data to synchronize according to needs and achieve local data autonomy.

The whole middle layer is developed in SAP NetWeaver Developer Studio development platform, and is deployed on the NetWeaver server, so that the whole framework's development, deployment and management are very simple and efficient, and the framework is very reliable and robust.

5. CONCLUSIONS

Based on enterprise SAP ERP's implementation and integration cases, the paper discussed in detail how to achieve the SAP system and other heterogeneous business systems' integration, proposed to use data exchange middle layer to allow developers and end-users in a transparent manner using the SAP data.

The middle layer supports heterogeneous data sources' data synchronization - transferring data between SAP and other heterogeneous data sources such as sybase, oracle, mysql and so on. The middle layer is data synchronization reliable - distributed heterogeneous system nodes using the main data consistent with the SAP main data. The middle layer is local data nodes autonomy - each node will be able to decide on their own what is acceptable data, and how to access and update the data nodes. The middle layer is centralization data management facile - the maintenance of distributed data nodes is conveniently.

In conclusion, the program is stable, flexible, user-friendly and efficient in the enterprise SAP ERP's implementation and integration.

REFERENCES

1. D. Smith, L. O'brien, K. Kontogiannis, and M. Barbacci, *Enterprise Integration.* http://www.sei.cmu.edu/news-at-sei/columns/the_architect/2002/4q02/architect-4q02.htm(Accessed July 8, 2007).
2. G.S. Thomas, Developing Applications with the "SAP Java Conne-ctor" (JCo), *ARAsoft GmbH* (2001-2002). www.ARAsoft.de
3. Anonymous, *SAP Java Connector.* http://help.sap.com/saphelp_47x200/helpdata/en/6f/1bd5c6a85b11d6b28500508b5d5211/frameset.htm (Accessed December 26, 2006).
4. K. Kessler, P. Tillert, and P. Dobrikov, *JAVA Programming with the SAP Web Application Server* (Oriental Press: Beijing, 2005).
5. M.N. Huhns, and P.S Munindar, Service-Oriented Computing: Key concepts and Principles, *IEEE Internet Computing.* Volume 9, pp.75-81, (2005).
6. Anonymous, *Eye on integration.* http://www.sei.cmu.edu/news-at-sei/Columns/eye-on-integration/eye-on-integration.htm (Accessed December 20, 2006).
7. M. Gangwani, *Java SAP R/3 Integration*, Persistent White Paper (November 2004).

Organizational Coordination Theory and Its Application in Virtual Enterprise

Xiuquan Deng, Tong Chen and Dongdi Pan

School of Economics and Management, Beihang University, Beijing 100083, P.R. China
dengxiuquan@126.com chting714@gmail.com

Abstract. As one of the most important theories, coordination appears in a lot of fields and becomes a remarkable subject. This paper sums up the frame of the organizational coordination theory by refining the meaning of coordination, and with the support of this frame, studies the virtual enterprise's coordination mechanism in two layers which are the strategy layer and the task layer according to the characteristic of the dependences among the member companies. In the strategy layer, the trust relation in the virtual enterprise is built to coordinate the member companies' cooperating relations. And in the task layer, the task is decomposed and coordinated smoothly to make sure the achievement of the virtual enterprise's aim.

Keywords: *Organizational coordination theory, Virtual enterprise, Coordination mechanism, Trust mechanism, Resource estimation*

In the process of organization activities, coordination is a very widespread problem. Because of the large volume of communication, coordination is considered a very great need to virtual organization.

1. ORGANIZATIONAL COORDINATION THEORY

Coordination is the behavior that manages the interdependent relationships of activities with common object; the coordination mechanism is the mechanism that manages the dependent relationship effectively [1]. According to this definition, coordination contains two fields of knowledge: knowledge of the activity interdependences and knowledge of managing the independent relationship (the management performs as coordination mechanism) [2].

The study of organizational coordination theory should include the organizational dependence, coordination mechanisms and the factors affect its establishment (technical, structural and organizational task types) [3].

Please use the following format when citing this chapter:

Deng, X., Chen, T., Pan, D., 2007, in IFIP International Federation for Information Processing, Volume 254, Research and Practical Issues of Enterprise Information Systems II Volume 1, eds. L. Xu, Tjoa A., Chaudhry S. (Boston: Springer), pp. 311-316.

2. VIRTUAL ENTERPRISE COORDINATION MECHANISM

2.1 The Essence of Virtual Enterprise

Virtual Enterprise is opposed to the traditional enterprises. Its substance is that member enterprises operate with outside helps, integrating the external resources, achieving the function that they do not have and creating a powerful competitive advantage. In cooperation way, member enterprises can achieve functions such as research, development, production, sales and marketing, and other specific functions.

2.2 The Constitution of Virtual enterprises Coordination Mechanism

In this paper, the so-called virtual enterprises coordination mechanism refers to ways and means that the virtual enterprise members use to make normal communication and coordination, thus to achieve the coordination between all members of enterprises. In order to study the virtual Enterprise coordination mechanism, we must study the interdependent relationship between the virtual enterprise members. So far, there is not a recognized classification to it. According to the formation and operation process of virtual enterprise, we should class the dependence into levels: confidence dependent relationship on strategic level, and activity dependent relation on task level. (See Figure.1)

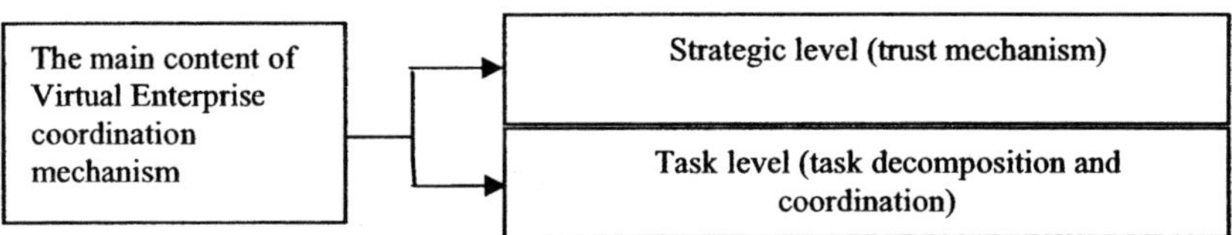

Figure 1. Virtual Enterprise Coordination Mechanism System Map

2.3 Virtual Enterprise Strategic Level Coordination

We class the confidence dependent relationship, taking the establishment and development of the confidence relationship as the basis for demarcation, considering about the time dimension, as follows: the initial trust and the continual trust.

The so-called initial trust is the trust relationship forms in the gestation period and the formation period of virtual enterprise. Initial trust may be just established relations or a continuation of former cooperation or transferred from the third party. Its biggest feature is the complication of the relationship. The so-called continual trust is the trust relationship forms in the operation period or the disintegration period. Continual trust is dynamic developed relations. Generally speaking, the level is higher, but it does not rule out the trust of low level and even the breakdown of a trust relationship caused by the opportunistic behaviors of cooperation partner.

With the virtual enterprise creation, growth, maturity, disintegration and reorganization, Virtual Enterprise's relationship of trust constitutes a "chain of trust": the initial trust-> continual confidence-> initial trust.

There are two kinds of trust relationship modes fit the characteristics of Virtual Enterprise: relation-based market model and credibility model [4].

The so-called relation-based market model is the model that member enterprises invest in specific field via their respective relation-network to build up mutual trust. However, the specificity of the trust investment is always strong; the cost of conversion is high or even cannot change. When cooperation between the members is made a temporary suspension, these investments will have difficulty in using for other purposes, which may cause excessive dependence of one member on the other or substantial control. Thereby it limits the establishment of a trust relationship in virtual enterprise and the flexibility of development. Meanwhile, the trust relationship based on the "personal relationship circles" is relatively fragile; the bad behaviors of some individual enterprises can easily destabilize the entire virtual enterprise.

The credibility model is the model that the virtual enterprise via the establishment of a mechanism to build and maintain a trust relationship. Corporate credibility is the comprehensive evaluation, gained in the business activities, on the capacity, efficiency, business philosophy and corporate culture, and other aspects. Corporate credibility can be conveyed by the market, supported by legal and moral, its formation needs a long-term accumulation, having greater stability.

The confidence in virtual Enterprise is uncertainty-and-risk-related; consequently, to increase the credibility, it is necessary to make security measures.

In a virtual enterprise which members have different interest objectives, it is necessary to consider the balance of interests and the establishment of an effective incentive system or mechanism. Meanwhile, a fair distribution of benefits can also bound the deception of partners.

2.4 Virtual Enterprise Task Level Coordination

Members in virtual enterprise generally use or consume some of the logistics resources in the activities of implementation process, particularly exclusive resources; the dependent relationship of member enterprises can be divided into three categories: 1-1-dependence, N-1-dependence and 1-N-dependence.

Because virtual enterprise is composed of members with same geographical distribution, but different self-interests, so the characteristic of incomplete information, as well as the powerless control to members is prominent, thus the task decomposition of virtual enterprise compared to the individual enterprises is more difficult, it needs a task decomposition method as a guide which can adapt to the characteristics of virtual enterprise.

Members of virtual Enterprise need task coordination, the basic idea is as follows(See Figure.2): The first step is the core enterprise to find market opportunities, as well as analysis for market opportunities to determine each sub-task required resources (including core competencies); The second step is based on the capacity-demand information to identify potential partners, choose the partners who are competent for the sub-tasks; The third step is to allocate the tasks to member enterprises, member enterprises provide a detailed production plan in accordance with the requirements of sub-tasks and submit its conclusions back to the core enterprise; The fourth step, the core enterprise make optimization, integration, modification to the sub-enterprises' programs, and then revise the results to member enterprises; The fifth step, member enterprises consider the feedback and analyze whether they have the ability and quality to timely complete the volume of production. If the capacity allows, task decomposition and the process of planning coordinating ended, and the members sign the contract of sub-tasks; or consulate with the core enterprise, if succeeded, the task decomposition process and plan coordination accomplish; if the negotiation failed, the core enterprise look for new cooperating partners.

3. CONCLUSIONS

Being a key management method for the formation and operation of virtual enterprise, Coordination theory has an important impact on the results that the virtual enterprise achieved in the production and operation process. In this paper, the results of the study are expected to design an appropriate coordination mechanism for virtual enterprises, thus the members of virtual enterprise can establish strategic cooperative partnership, then rationally distribute the profits, share risks, improve information sharing, reduce inventory, lower total system cost and eventually realize the profit maximization.

4. EMPIRICAL ANALYSIS

About the empirical analysis, we have already made preliminary work, but because of limited space, it is not showed here.

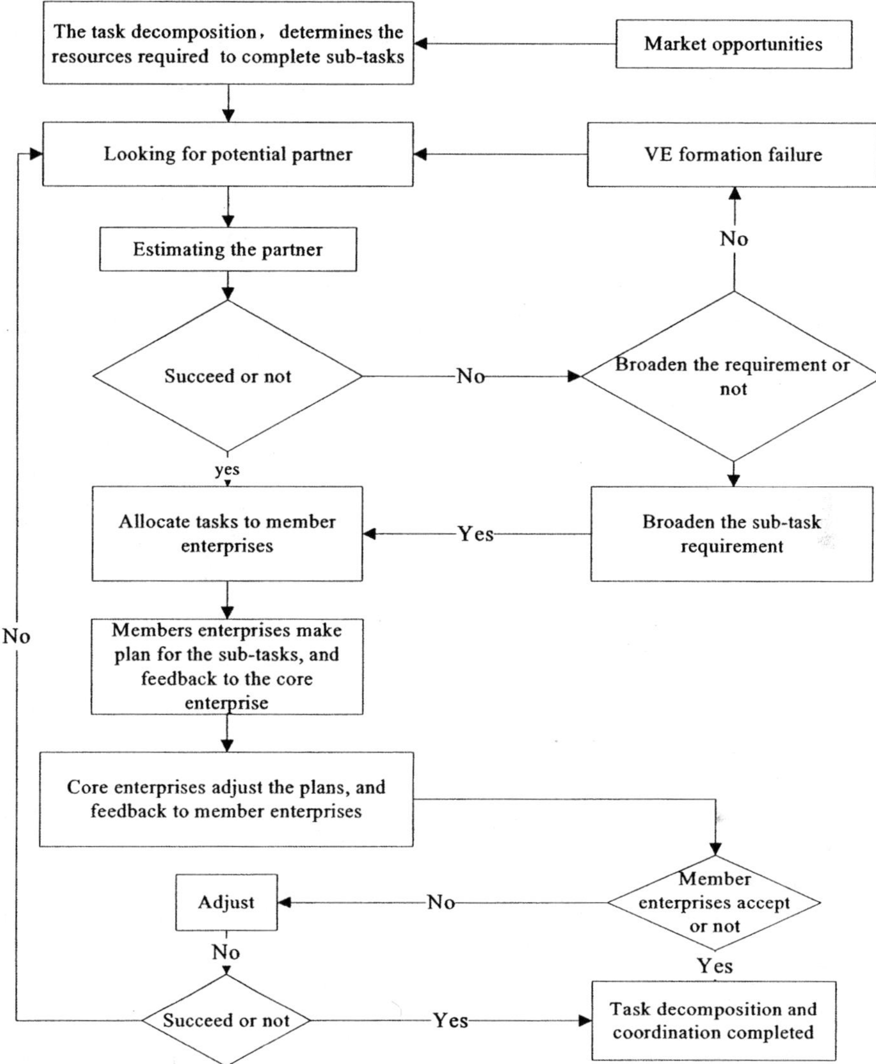

Figure 2. The Basic Ideas of Virtual Enterprise Task Decomposition and Coordination

ACKNOWLEDGMENT

This paper was supported by the grants from Aviation Science Foundation of China (No.2006ZG51080) and BUAA "New Star in Blue Sky" Plan.

REFERENCES

1. T.W. Malone and K. Crowston, The interdisciplinary study of coordination, *ACM Computing Surveys*. Volume 26, Number 1, pp.87-119, (1994).
2. T.W. Malone, and K. Crowston. Tools for inventing organizations: toward a handbook of organizational processes, *Management Science*. Volume 45, Number 3, pp.425-443, (1999).
3. H. Jing and Y. Xi. Retrospect and Prospect to Organizational Coordination theoretical research, *Management Review*. Volume 18, Number 2, pp.50-55, (2006).
4. M. Granovetter, Economic action and social structure: the problem of embeddedness, *American Journal of Sociology*. Volume 91, pp.481-510, (1985).
5. K. Crowston, *A Taxonomy of Organizational Dependencies and Coordination Mechanisms* (1994). http://ccs.mit.edu/tom.html

A Mechanism of Timely Knowledge Push on Demand Based on ECA and Multi-Agent Techniques

Jianlin Wu, Shuangshuang Lou, Yan Xiong and Bai Wang

Beijing Key Laboratory of Intelligent Communications Software and Multimedia, Beijing University of Posts and Telecommunications, Beijing 100876, P.R. China
jlwu@bupt.edu.cn loushuangshuang@gmail.com xiongyan@tseg.org
wangbai@bupt.edu.cn

Abstract. The knowledge organizations have already deployed or are deploying their Knowledge Management systems. And the knowledge service is the key mechanism for knowledge sharing in an organization. There are two mechanisms to implement knowledge service: "Pull" and "Push". The "Push" mechanism is widely used to push the right knowledge to the right person at the right time actively. At present, the publish/subscribe strategy is adopted mostly to implement the active push of knowledge. However, it can not guarantee the timely knowledge push. Based on the ECA and Multi-Agent techniques, a framework to implement Timely Information & Knowledge Push Service (TIKPS) is put forward in this paper. In the framework, ECA rules are utilized to represent the knowledge consumers' requirements. And a rule engine is designed to implement the timely knowledge push mechanism integrated with Multi-Agent techniques. Finally, an application example of the mechanism is given under telecom enterprise information and knowledge service environment.

Keywords: *Knowledge management, Knowledge push, ECA, Multi-Agent*

1. INTRODUCTION

One of the recent trends in information service is the active personalized service mechanism, also called "information push". Active services are popular because they provide R4 Service: the Right information at the Right time in the Right way to the Right person [1]. Another trend in enterprise information management is Knowledge Management (KM) [2-4]. Many organizations have already deployed or are deploying their Knowledge Management systems. And the knowledge service becomes the key factor for knowledge sharing in an organization.

Researchers have addressed the problems of efficient information & knowledge service and have proposed many approaches aiming at active personal information delivery [5-10], including Ontology-Based and XML-based Personalized information push, RSS, agent-based active information service etc.. The ontology-based user requirements modeling [6] can represent the semantic relative of user profile well, but the event-driven and timely push requirements can hardly be satisfied. The publish/subscribe strategy in RSS [8] and the agent-based push method [9] are applied

Please use the following format when citing this chapter:

Wu, J., Lou, S., Xiong, Y., Wang, B., 2007, in IFIP International Federation for Information Processing, Volume 254, Research and Practical Issues of Enterprise Information Systems II Volume 1, eds. L. Xu, Tjoa A., Chaudhry S. (Boston: Springer), pp. 317-326.

to implement the active push of certain knowledge. However, it can not guarantee the timely knowledge push (e.g. when some incidents occur, the user needs some specific knowledge).

There are also some projects that have tackled the issue of active personalized information & knowledge push service: compound knowledge push system [11], Knowledge active push for product design [12] and AACP [1]. The first two systems both adopt the workflow-driven knowledge push method, the former system also uses Agent technology to implement real time knowledge push; the latter implement the specific knowledge active push for product design. The AACP paradigm adopts a push-based, event-driven, interest-related, adaptive and active information service mode. However, none of the three projects considers the situation of conditional event-driven information & knowledge push service need (which occurs frequently), and consequently could not guarantee the timely push of needed information & knowledge most of the time.

In this paper, the combination of ECA and Multi-Agent techniques is firstly used to represent user's requirements in order to implement the timely information & knowledge push service (TIKPS) under various situations.

In the distributed and multi-task context, the usage of Multi-Agent framework appears very promising [13-14]. Active information & knowledge push on demand service mainly includes obtaining user's requirements, monitoring and searching the required information from distributed information sources, and pushing the needed information to the user at the right time. Multiple agents can collaboratively fulfill the information source monitoring task, the information query requirements, and the information delivery task.

Since the information & knowledge push requirements are mostly driven by data change events, each of these agents generally performs data oriented and event-driven actions. So Event-Condition-Action (ECA) rules can be efficiently employed to implement timely information & knowledge push.

The remainder of this paper is organized as follows. In section 2 we give a motivating example of TIKPS scenarios. In section 3 we present the proposed TIKPS framework and elaborate on the implement mechanism of agents with ECA rules. Then, section 4 discusses how the proposed solution can be used for the motivating example of section 2. Finally, section 5 concludes the paper.

2. MOTIVATING EXAMPLE

Typically, there are four situations of information & knowledge needs for business manager in the telecom enterprise. 1) The manager usually needs to read any reports about business performance per month. 2) The manager wants to know any new information and knowledge of one specific subject any time, e.g. the subject of "Customer Segmentation". 3) When some business incidents occur, the manager should know them immediately. For example, when the rate of "customer churn" reaches its threshold value (e.g. 2%), the manager needs to know these customers profile, the history "customer churn" value of the last 3 months, and the relevant knowledge of "customer churn" and solutions of "customer churn" incidents in history. 4) when the manager check in, he/she want to receive all subscribed interesting information & knowledge.

Supposing the manager is a user of TIKPS, after his (supposing the manager is male) register and first log on to the system, he submit his information & knowledge requirement to system, including 4 situations as described in the former part of this section. The system will create a **user agent** for the manager, responsible for all the issues of information & knowledge push service for this user. Then according to the requirement of the user, this user agent will responsible for generating a **Requirement Modeling agent** (RM agent) and several specific **push agents** for each type of push mode. The RM agent will abstract the manager's requirement to be ECA rules. The specific push agents, corresponding with the 4 situations as described in the former part of this section, will be Time-Sensitive push agent (TS push agent), Real-Time push agent (RT push agent), Conditional Event-Driven push agent (CED push agent), and User Event-Driven push agent (UED push agent).

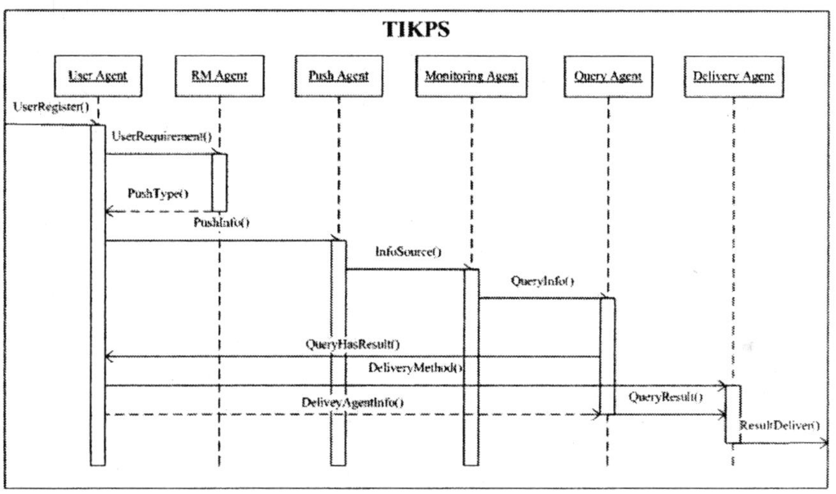

Figure 1. The Collaboration of Agents

Each push agent encapsulates the specific type of information & knowledge push task. The push agent will find the information & knowledge sources with the user given subjects or keywords. For each source, it will form and deploy a **monitoring agent**. The target of this agent is to monitor the information source, capture the matched event, and take the relevant action. According to the ECA rules, the action may be forming another agent e.g. query agent if the condition satisfied, or processing a computation (when complex event or condition). The **query agent** will search the needed information & knowledge, and then inform the User Agent to deploy a **delivery agent,** which will deliver the discovered information & knowledge to user by a certain method (may be different according to the user's state, e.g. email, SMS etc.). The figure1 illustrates the collaboration between agents.

3. TIKPS FRAMEWORK & AGENTS ARCHITECTURE

3.1 TIKPS Framework

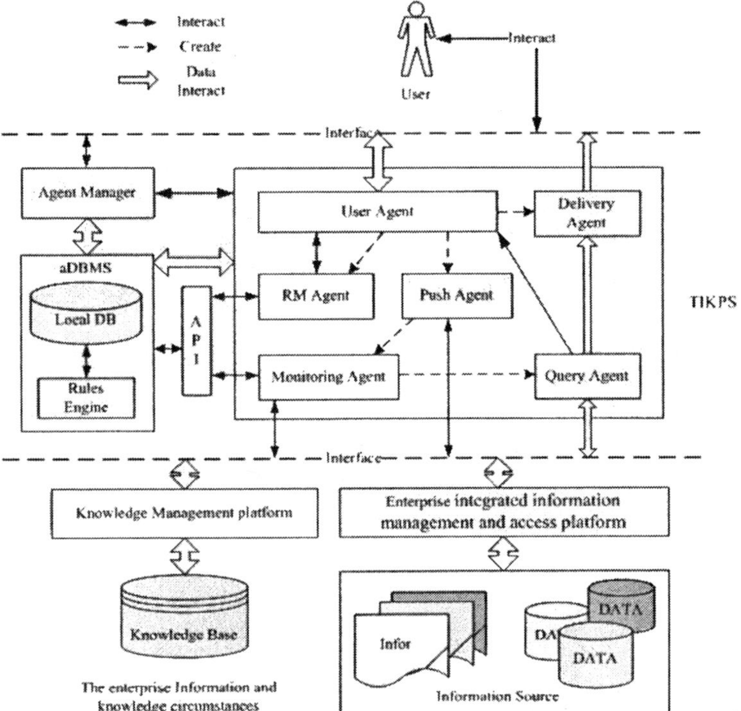

Figure 2. TIKPS Architecture

The proposed framework of TIKPS system is summarized in Figure 2. There are three layers: User layer, TIKPS layer and the enterprise information & knowledge circumstances layer. Two interfaces: information access interface and user interface. The scope of TIKPS system is between the two interfaces. The system consists of three main modules: Agent Manager (AM), Multi Agents and aDBMS.

Agent Manager. AM works as a lifecycle manager of the multi agents. More specifically, AM is responsible for the storage, creation and activation of the agents. The creation of an agent mainly concerns the definition of type, properties and roles of the agent. The activation of an agent mainly concerns the deployment of the incorporated ECA rules in the aDBMS. Furthermore, AM manages meta-information about the agents, which is also stored in the aDBMS. For example, AM could check the credential of an agent and set the appropriate privileges to the agent's ECA rules.

Multi Agents. The multi agents are the behavior entities to implement the system's function with collaboration between each other and the support of other modules of the system. Each agent has a specific task since it was created. And a set of ECA rules are deployed to handle the agents' behavior. The following describes the main task of each agent.

- User Agent: Interact with system user; obtain user information and user requirement information.
- RM Agent: Analyze and modeling user requirement to be ECA rules.
- Push Agent: manager the information of a certain push mode, e.g. the information & knowledge source add and cut. The behavior of Push Agent may influence Monitoring Agent, e.g. a new information source added will result a new monitoring agent to be created and deployed.
- Monitoring Agent: monitor the information source, capture the matched event, and take the relevant action. According to the ECA rules, the action may be forming another agent e.g. query agent if the condition satisfied, or processing a computation (when complex event or condition).
- Query Agent: search the enterprise information & knowledge platform according to the user given subject and keywords.
- Delivery Agent: deliver the discovered information & knowledge to user, the delivery method is designated by user agent according to user information when it is created.

The collaboration of agents has been illustrated in Figure1 in section 2.

aDBMS stores all·the local data of TIKPS system, including the data come from Agent Manager (AM), the data from user interface and the ECA rules. aDBMS provides API for external access.

3.2 The Definition Language: ECA Rules

The ECA rules are represented by the following general form:

When <event expression>
(If <condition expression>)
Then <action expression>
(Else <action expression>)

The rules can be parametrical; thus, they may contain parameters that acquire values when the rule is triggered.

Event Expression. A wide range of events may be supported. Typical basic events include time relevant events, database events, external events, user events, message transfer events, etc. Several basic events can compose a complex event through events operations [15]. The event can be identified by its parameters, e.g. event type, event occur time, event source, event description etc. Event can be described by formal expression as follow.

Event ::= <Basic Event> | <Basic Event> <logic operator> <Basic Event> **(1)**

Basic Event ::= [time relevant event | database event | external event | user event | message transfer event]

Logic Operator ::= "and" | "or"

Condition Expression. The condition part of the ECA rule is a Boolean expression or function defined on the set of values returned by a database query (in SQL for example). Generally, Condition can be described by formal expression as follow.

Condition ::= <Simple Condition> | <Simple Condition> <logic operator> <Simple Condition> **(2)**

Simple Condition ::= <Property condition> | <true | false>

Property condition ::= <expression> < relational operator> <expression>

Expression ::= variable | variable <operator> variable

Operator ::= + | - | * | /

Relational Operator ::= "equal to" | "unequal to" | "more than" | "less than" | "not more than" | "not less than"

Action Expression. The action part is a list of actions that have to be executed with a specific order in the same transaction. This is because all the actions have to be executed successfully. In case that at least one of them fails, the ones that have been executed have to roll back and the ones that are pending have to be canceled. The actions can be database operations, ECA rule handling operations (activation/deactivation) or calls to functions of AM (functions for management of local agents, e.g. form a new agent), or even other arbitrary functions. Typically, Action can be described by formal expression as follow.

Action ::= <function> | <data modify> **(3)**

<Function> ::= function name "(" <parameter list> ")"

Parameter list ::= <parameter> [{, <parameter>}]

Parameter ::= variable | constant

Data modify ::= variable "set to" <expression>

3.3 Monitoring Agent with ECA Rules

Monitoring Agent is the core agent to implement the timely and active push of information & knowledge. The purpose of a monitoring agent in TIKPS system is to achieve the following three tasks: 1) monitor the possible information source to capture the matched event, 2) Check whether the condition is satisfied, and 3) if satisfied, generate relevant query agent to get the needed information & knowledge. As already claimed, we propose the agents to be implemented through ECA rules. Therefore, each monitoring agent is defined using a number of ECA rules and a number of datasets. The ECA rules represent the logic of the agent while the datasets can contain initial parameters, agent state information as well as results that have been collected and computed by the agent.

Monitoring & push rules: the main purpose of the rules is to achieve the task of monitoring agent. The rules are responsible for executing of information & knowledge query and delivery or not. The rules are expressed by ECA rules as described in 5.2. The types of events here are most database events, time relevant events and user events.

Datasets: we propose the existence of two datasets that accompany each agent. The first one is the control dataset that is necessary for agent to find the right monitoring object, the control dataset also have the state and the lifecycle information of agent. The second one is the information & knowledge requirement dataset, including the information query requirement. These two datasets along with the agent's code, the ECA rules, represent the memory of the agent.

Other agents of the system, i.e. User agent, RM agent, push agent, query agent and delivering agent can be also implemented with ECA rules. However, the tasks and rules of each agent are differently assigned. The events activating the agent may be external events, message transfer events among agents, etc. For example, as illustrated in Figure1 in section 2, When the Query Agent has any query result, a message will generated and send to User Agent, this message event activate User Agent to take action, which is forming a Delivery Agent. Overall, the structure and the work mechanism of agents are the same. In this paper, we emphasize the implementation of Monitoring Agent with ECA rules.

4. APPLICATION EXAMPLE OF TIKPS

Following the motivating example of section 2, let's assume that the User Agent has obtained the user's requirement, the four situations of information & knowledge needs. These four cases refer to 3 different types of events and 4 coupling mode of event and condition.

1. Time-trigger event;
2. Data change event, no condition;
3. Data change event, with condition;
4. User interaction event.

Time-trigger event: One type of the time-related basic events. Time-related events can be divided into two types: instantaneous event and inter-zone time event. Each event has an event ID (eID), and is composed of attributes such as begin time B(e), end time E(e), during D(e) and event level. In our motivating example, the Time-trigger event is an instantaneous event, which can be expressed as

- CURRENT_TIME (time0): Occurs when the current time is equal to time0.

Data change event: One type of the database-related events – when the content, state, or attributes of database change, Change (X). In our motivating example, the two data change event can be expressed as follow.

- NEW (X, Subject,"Customer Segmentation"): A new entry X is inserted, and the remark "subject" of X is"Customer Segmentation".
- CHANGE (customer churn) and CURRENT_VALUE (customer churn) >= 2%: The value of customer churn changes and the value are not less than 2%.

User interaction event: when user takes some actions within the system, or user profile changes, or the state of user changes. In our motivating example, the user interaction event can be expressed as follow:

- LOG_ON (manager_id): Occurs when manager log on to the system.

The RM agent will analyze and model the user requirements to be ECA rules. According to the analyze result, User Agent will form relevant Push Agents. Push Agent then form and deploy Monitoring Agents to information source. And the monitoring agent monitors the data source and takes action according to these ECA rules. In our motivating example, the ECA rules are described as follow.

R1:

```
When  CURRENT_TIME (time0)
Then  NEW(QueryAgent, qa);
      DEPLOY_ QueryAgent (qa, data_source, key_words)
```

R2:

```
When  NEW (X, Subject,"Customer Segmentation")
Then  NEW(DeliveryAgent, da);
      DEPLOY_ DeliveryAgent (da, X)
```

R3:

```
When  CHANGE (customer churn)
If    CURRENT_VALUE (customer churn) >= 2%
Then  NEW(QueryAgent, qa);
      DEPLOY_ QueryAgent (qa, data_source_set, key_words)
```

R4:

```
When  LOG_ON (manager_id)
Then  NEW(QueryAgent, qa);
      DEPLOY_ QueryAgent (qa, data_source, key_words)
```

In the above rules we use the following variables:

- QueryAgent: an agent type.
- DeliveryAgent: an agent type.

- qa: an agent entity.
- Da: an agent entity.
- data_source: the target database where information & knowledge query executed.
- key_words: the key words used to search information & knowledge.
- data_source_set: numbers of target databases where information & knowledge query executed.

And the following functions:

- NEW(Agent_Type, agent_entity): form a new agent entity "agent_entity" of the type "Agent_Type".
- DEPLOY_ QueryAgent (agent_entity, data_source, key_words): deploy an agent entity "agent_entity" of the type of QueryAgent, and the query source is within "data_source", with the key words—"key_words".
- DEPLOY_ DeliveryAgent (agent_entity, result_set): deploy an agent entity "agent_entity" of the type of DeliveryAgent, and the information & knowledge delivered is in the "result_set".

When the events occur and the condition satisfied, the actions are taken to deploy Query Agents. Then the Query Agents search the needed information & knowledge, and the Delivery Agent will push the information & knowledge to user.

5. CONCLUSIONS

In this paper, a mechanism of timely information & knowledge push is proposed with ECA and Multi-agent techniques, and TIKPS framework is introduced. We argue that the proposed approach leads to a feasible solution for timely, actively information & knowledge push service in a knowledge organization: a problem still to be solved.

Multi-Agent system, in which each autonomous Agent is responsible for a specific task, interacting and collaborating with others, can deal with the heterogeneity and distribution of the information sources, and provide a robust and flexible solution. For example, Multi-Agent system can be well adapting the change of user's requirements by generating or destroying information monitoring and query agents, without influencing other requirements' satisfaction. The fact that we are using ECA rules to define user's requirements and agent logic does not restrict the functionality of the agent: i.e. the action part of the ECA rules can be allowed to contain arbitrary functions. The events that can trigger the activation of some agent's function are clearly stated in the event part of the corresponding rule while the condition part defines additional requirements for the function to be activated. Beside, the usage of ECA rules effectively implements the timely push of information & knowledge. Overall, this declarative way influences positively a number of aspects of the system like optimization opportunities, efficiency and flexibility.

REFERENCES

1. Z. Xin, J. Zhao, C. Chi, and J. Sun, Information Push-Delivery for User-Centered and Personalized Service, *Lecture Notes in Computer Science, Volume 3613/2005* (Springer: Berlin, Heidelberg, 2005), pp.594-602.
2. O'Leary and E. Daniel, Enterprise knowledge management, *Computer*. Volume 31, Number 3, pp.54-61, (1998).
3. L. Sui and R. Yang, Study of knowledge sharing and strategy in enterprise knowledge management, in *Proc. of the Annual Southeastern Symposium on System Theory, v 37, Proceedings of the Thirty-Seventh Southeastern Symposium on System Theory* (SST05 2005), pp.336-340.
4. M. Wooldridge and NR. Jennings, Intelligent Agents: Theory and Practice, *Knowledge Engineering Review*. Volume 10, Number 2, pp.115-152, (1995).
5. S. Albayrak, S. Wollny, N. Varone, A. Lommatzsch, and D. Milosevic, Agent Technology for Personalized Information Filtering: The PIA-System, in *Proc. of the 2005 ACM symposium on Applied computing* (2005), pp.54-59.
6. H. Pan, H. Lin, and J. Zhao, Ontology-Based Personalized Recommendation System, *Computer engineering and application*. Volume 41, Number 20, pp.176-180, (2005).
7. L. Yuan, H. Yan, and S. Wang, Information Push Service and Its Realization Based on XML, *Information Science*. Volume 21, Number 6, pp.619-620, (2003).
8. H. Yang, Web-based RSS Information Push Service, *Science and technology progress and Countermeasures*. pp.170-172, (2005).
9. Y. Zhang, L. Li, and C. Wang, Research of implementing active personalized information service, *Journal of Information*. pp.71-72, (2005).
10. C. Suo, Theory and Practice on Developing the IIPP-based Active Information Service System, *New Technology of Library and Information Service*. Volume 53, pp.49-51, (2004).
11. Z. Fan, Y. Feng, Y. Sun, B. Feng, and T. You, A framework on compound knowledge push system oriented to organizational employees, in *Proc. of Lecture Notes in Computer Science, v 3828 LNCS, Internet and Network Economics - First International Workshop, WINE 2005, Proceedings* (2005), pp.622-630.
12. S. Wang, X. Gu, J. Guo, J. Ma, and H. Zhan, Knowledge active push for product design, *Computer Integrated Manufacturing Systems, CIMS*. Volume 13, Number 2, pp.234-239, (2007).
13. N.R. Jennings, On agent-based software engineering, *Artificial Intelligence*. Volume 117, Number 2, pp.277-296, (2000).
14. B. Brewington, R. Gray, K. Moizumi, D. Kotz, G. Cybenko, and D. Rus, *Mobile agents in distributed information retrieval,* in *Intelligent Information Agents*, eds. Mathias Klusch (Springer: Verlag, New York, 1999), pp.355-395.
15. Z. Wang and Y. Hua, Research on Technology of Active Spatial Information Service, *Acta Geodaetica et Cartographica Sinica*. Volume 35, Number 11, pp.379-384, (2006).

E-Government for Construction: The Case of Singapore's CORENET Project

Bee-Hua Goh

Department of Building, School of Design and Environment, National University of Singapore, Singapore bdggohbh@nus.edu.sg

Abstract. In 1999, the Singapore Government envisioned a need to transform the construction industry through the Construction 21 Blueprint by a strategic vision. In line with the broader plan to develop Singapore into a knowledge-driven economy, this industry aspires to become 'a World Class Builder in the Knowledge Age'. And earlier, as part of the IT 2000 master plan for Singapore, the Construction Real Estate Network (CORENET) project has been set up in July 1993 to serve as a major information technology (IT) initiative. The goal of CORENET is to "re-engineer the business processes of the construction industry to achieve a quantum leap in turnaround time, productivity and quality." Specifically, its efforts are targeted at developing a set of infrastructure and industry projects, involving various government agencies and other industry players, to meet this goal. On the infrastructure projects, one thrust looks at providing Government to Business infrastructure to facilitate electronic building plans submission, checking and approval processes. Applying the concept of process re-engineering through the adoption of IT to the traditional building plans submission, checking and approval processes, the CORENET has now an infrastructure for: (i) One-stop Submission (OSSC) of building plans for approval; (ii) Buildable Design Appraisal (eBDAS); and (iii) Integrated Building Plan (IBP) and Integrated Building Services Plan (IBS) checking. The prevailing success and benefits of the three implemented projects are examined and discussed in relation to their re-engineered IT-enabled processes as well as feedback from a survey of the industry.

Keywords: *Business process reengineering, Inter-Enterprise interoperation, Strategic business transformation, Work flow model*

1. SINGAPORE'S CORENET

In January 1991, the National Computer Board (now IDA) initiated the IT 2000 study to examine how IT can create new competitive advantages and enhance the quality of life in Singapore. As such, the study group known as CORENET (Construction and Real Estate NETwork) was set up in July 1993. Since then, CORENET has come a long way to become a major IT initiative led by the Ministry of National Development and driven by the Building and Construction Authority (BCA) in collaboration with other public and private organizations. The goal of CORENET is to "re-engineer the business processes of the construction industry to achieve a quantum leap in turnaround time, productivity and quality." In order to

Please use the following format when citing this chapter:

Goh, B.-H., 2007, in IFIP International Federation for Information Processing, Volume 254, Research and Practical Issues of Enterprise Information Systems II Volume 1, eds. L. Xu, Tjoa A., Chaudhry S. (Boston: Springer), pp. 327-336.

achieve this, CORENET revolves around developing IT systems and key infrastructure to integrate the four major processes of a building project life cycle. Broadly, the effort is focused on developing a set of infrastructure and industry projects in order to:

i) provide Information Services to allow businesses to speed up business planning and decision making processes;

ii) provide Government to Business infrastructure to facilitate electronic building plans submission, checking and approval processes;

iii) provide Business to Business enablers to facilitate building project collaborations and business transactions;

iv) provide a set of standards to improve business communications; and

v) provide a series of promotional, training and incentive programmes to create awareness and encourage adoption.

The key Government to Business infrastructure projects completed to date is the One-Stop Submission Centre (OSSC), the Electronic Buildable Design Appraisal System (eBDAS) and the Integrated Building Plan and Building Service Plan Checking System (IBP/IBS). Other infrastructure projects to be developed include the Enterprise Content Management System (ECMS), the Integrated Structural Plan Checking System (ISP) and the Design Objects Library (DOL).

2. AIM OF THE PAPER

The paper aims to describe the Government to Business infrastructure projects developed and implemented in Singapore through a discussion of their benefits derived from the re-engineered IT-enabled processes as well as the feedback obtained from a survey of the users of the new IT infrastructure.

3. THE TRADITIONAL BUILDING DESIGN PROCESS

Traditionally, the whole construction process comprises four distinct sequential stages. They are design, tender documentation and selection, construction, and handover and maintenance. In the first stage, the key activities of design consist of developing concept and schematic designs, and obtaining planning approvals. As planning approvals are granted by the various regulatory bodies, the building owner through the appointed design consultant (or the Qualified Person) needs to submit the building plans to these bodies separately to apply for the approvals. The complex process of submitting the application, checking against planning requirements, evaluating the proposal, re-submission for non-compliance and issuing approval involves many parties and uses different channels of communication. The workflow for building plan submission in Singapore is depicted in Figure 1.

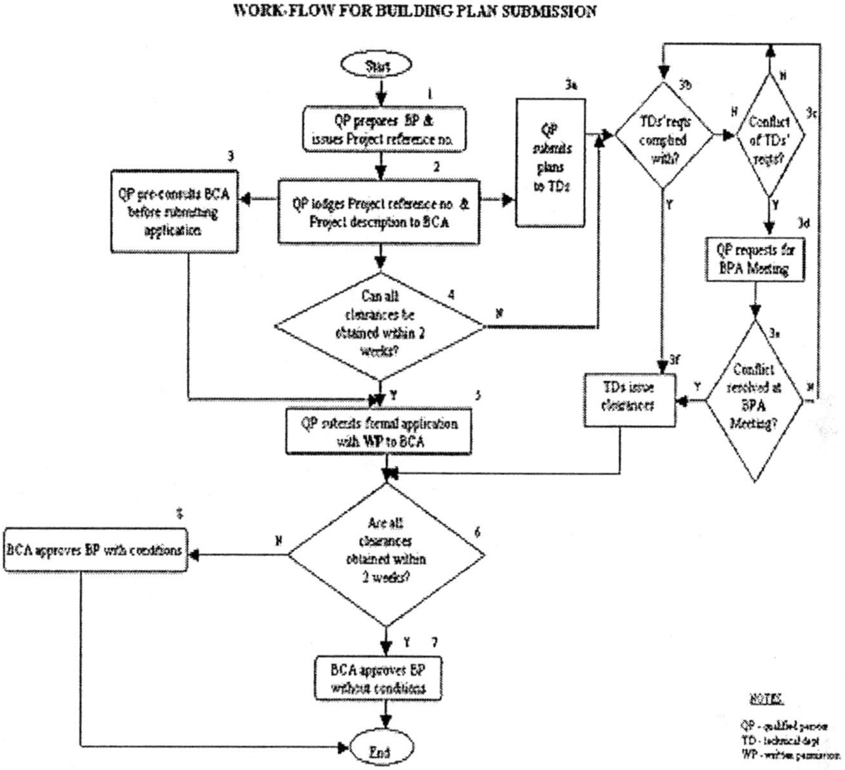

WORK-FLOW FOR BUILDING PLAN SUBMISSION

Figure 1. Workflow for Building Plan Submission in Singapore (Source: [5])

During the design stage, consultants in Singapore have to take into consideration, among other regulations, compliance with a regulation pertaining to buildable design. Under the Building Control Act, the regulation on buildable design was introduced in 2001 to improve the efficiency and standardisation of designs, processes, construction techniques, products and materials. In order to reduce the number of workers on site and achieve better site productivity, the industry has to adopt more labour efficient designs and use pre-assembled products. Hence, the regulation requires building designs to have a minimum buildability score as compliance. The Buildable Design Appraisal System (BDAS) was developed by the BCA as a scoring system to measure the potential impact of a building design on the usage of labour. The buildability score formula is based on the design of three components which are the structural system, wall system and other buildable design features.

4. APPLYING PROCESS RE-ENGINEERING TO THE TRADITIONAL BUILDING PLAN APPROVAL ACTIVITIES

In order to examine the benefits derivable from the completed Government to Business infrastructure projects, namely OSSC, eBDAS and IBP/IBS, there is a need to look at the traditional process and compare it with the re-engineered process that is enabled by IT. According to Hammer and Champy [1], technology enables the processes that are the essence of re-engineering to be re-designed. As they have explained in simple terms, without re-engineering, IT delivers little payoff; without IT, little re-engineering can be done.

In Table 1, a brief description of each of the systems is given, followed by the main elements of the re-engineered process that are enabled by IT. In addition, the traditional process for each of the building plan approval activities is explained for the purpose of highlighting the benefits to be derived from using each of the developed systems.

Table 1. Process Re-engineering Applied to Building Plan Approval (See details: [6])

Type of Project	Re-engineered Process	Traditional Process
OSSC Provides a network infrastructure that supports electronic submission of building project documents to regulatory agencies for processing and approval through a secure environment.	OSSC provides a virtual one-stop round the clock 'counter' to facilitate: • electronic submission to multiple regulatory agencies; • on-line enquiry of submission status; • integration of application forms and fee collection; • faster processing and turnaround time; and • elimination of printing of plans and forms.	A 'Qualified Person' makes multiple submissions resulting in time and money wasted for multiple trips. There is: • voluminous paper documents; • manual processing of submission and building plans; • insufficient physical storage space; and inefficient exchange of project information and coordination of project team members.
eBDAS It is an electronic module to compute the buildability score and check compliance of building plans with the "Code of Practice on Buildable Design".	The developed system is an electronic geometric-based Buildable Design Appraisal System as part of the BDAS legislation exercise to provide both the 'Qualified Person' and BCA officer an electronic tool to assist them in the preparation, measurement, consolidation, reporting, verification and analysis of buildability scores.	On most occasions, the 'Qualified Person' and BCA officers need to perform manual quantity taking-off from hardcopies of computer-aided design (CAD) files in order to compute the buildability score according to the BDAS requirements. • This computational process can be time consuming.

IBP/IBS It is an artificial intelligence checking system that automatically checks electronic plans for compliance with regulatory requirements.	The IBP/IBS system provides an expert tool to enhance overall effectiveness and efficiency of building plan and building services approval process. • There is a consistent way of interpretation of regulatory codes and regulations. • It serves the purpose of a 'Qualified Person' with self-checking capabilities to aid in the design process prior to submission for approval.	The plan checking is manually performed by experienced staff. • Staff will require in-depth knowledge of codes and regulations. • Interpretation of clauses may differ from individual to individual.

5. INDUSTRY FEEDBACK ON THE DEVELOPED INFRASTRUCTURE PROJECTS

A mailed questionnaire survey was conducted in 2003 to solicit views of industry players on the benefits that had been derived by using the new IT infrastructures. A total of 754 companies operating in the construction industry in the areas of architecture, engineering, quantity surveying, property development, construction, and product manufacturing and supplies had been sent a copy of the questionnaire. A breakdown of the sampling population and the rate of response by category are shown in Tables 2 and 3. Responses from the survey were analyzed using the SPSS software version 11.0. Missing data or incomplete entry for each question has been excluded from the analysis of total response.

Table 2. A Breakdown of the Sampling Population, in Number and Percent

Category	No. of Companies	Per cent
Architecture	361	47.9
Engineering	131	17.4
Quantity Surveying	19	2.5
Property Development	23	3.0
Construction	129	17.1
Product Manufacturing and Supplies	91	12.1
Total:	**754**	**100.0**

Table 3. The Rate of Response for the Survey, in Number and Percent

Category	No. of Targeted Companies	No. of Respondent Companies	Per cent of Respondent Companies
Architecture	361	38	10.5
Engineering	131	15	11.5
Quantity Surveying	19	5	26.3
Property Development	23	2	8.7
Construction	129	10	7.8
Product Manufacturing/Supplying	91	1	1.1
Multi-disciplinary	-	13	N.A.
Total:	**754**	**84**	**11.1**

Among the list of 39 questions, two questions (Questions 38 and 39) have been dedicated to soliciting feedback on the speed of implementation of the CORENET projects and whether benefits had been derived by the users, and whether the amount of promotion and training provided by the BCA was sufficient so as to equip industry players with skills to use these IT infrastructures. The actual questions are shown in Figure 2.

38. How would you assess the following aspects of the CORENET projects?

Speed of Implementation (Please circle: 1 for 'too slow' and 5 for 'too fast'.):

a. Information standardisation

- CAD standards (CP83)……………………1 2 3 4 5

- Cost Classification (CP80).....................1 2 3 4 5
- Resources Classification (CP93)..............1 2 3 4 5
- Electronic Measurement standard 1 2 3 4 5

b. One-Stop Submission 1 2 3 4 5

c. Electronic Buildable Design Appraisal System (eBDAS) 1 2 3 4 5

d. e-Collaboration 1 2 3 4 5

e. e-Marketplace 1 2 3 4 5

<u>Benefits Derived at Work</u> (Please tick √ the appropriate box.):

a. Information standardisation Yes ☐ No ☐

b. One-Stop Submission Yes ☐ No ☐

c. Electronic Buildable Design Appraisal System (eBDAS)

Yes ☐ No ☐

d. e-Collaboration Yes ☐ No ☐

e. e-Marketplace Yes ☐ No ☐

39. Do you think the amount of promotion and training on the use of CORENET is sufficient? (Please tick √ the appropriate box.)

Yes ☐ No ☐

(Note: The IBP/IBS project was only completed after the survey.)

Figure 2. Questions Relating to the CORENET Projects

On the infrastructure projects, namely OSSC and eBDAS, a majority of the respondents had selected the neutral option '3', that is, neither too slow nor too fast for the speed of implementation. And, the percentages obtained are 50.7% for OSSC and 55.0% for eBDAS. For respondents who had indicated that it was too slow, the percentages are 9.0% for OSSC and 8.3% for eBDAS. While for too fast, they are 19.4% for OSSC and 16.7% for eBDAS.

The majority of respondents had indicated 'Yes' for benefits derived at work from the OSSC (77.1%) and eBDAS (53.2%). The respective percentages had given a general indication of the level of adoption as well as extent of successful implementation of the two projects.

On promotion and training, there were a higher percentage of respondents who had indicated 'No' (64.9%) on whether the amount provided by the BCA was sufficient. There were 35.1% who responded 'Yes'. The results had given a strong signal for the need to increase promotional and training activities so as to achieve higher adoption of the projects by the industry.

6. DISCUSSION OF FINDINGS

While the response percentages for benefits derived at work from using the OSSC and eBDAS had been found to be the majority, 77.1% and 53.2%, respectively, it was appropriate to note that only 11.1% of the 754 targeted companies (or 84 companies) had responded to the survey. Hence, it could be implied that there would have been many more companies that had either not used these systems or not derived benefits from them.

A vital prerequisite for companies to use the Government to Business infrastructure is the adoption of a set of national IT standards upon which the platforms are based. In Singapore, the Singapore Standard Code of Practice for Construction Computer-Aided Design (SS CP83: 2000; 2004) [2] come in parts - Part 1: Organisation and naming of CAD layers; Part 2: CAD symbols; Part 3: Organising and naming of CAD files; Part 4: CAD drafting conventions; and Part 5: Colour and line-type. Together, they provide a set of standards to enable architectural companies to prepare CAD drawings for electronic transmission (or submission) of their applications to the OSSC. Based on the same survey, the results had indicated that adoption of the SS CP83 by the industry had been moderately low. Only 38.8% of the respondents had indicated they use the standard.

Hence, to begin with, a way forward to helping to increase the use of the Government to Business infrastructure is for the BCA to promote the SS CP83 together with the completed projects such as the OSSC, eBDAS and IBP/IBS. With reference to the survey results, a majority of the respondents (64.9%) had indeed indicated that promotional and training activities had been insufficient and, therefore, this aspect could be improved upon.

7. GENERAL CONCLUSIONS

Government policies are crucial in mapping the vision and setting the directions for large-scale change as evident in the area of IT. As a case in point, a very active government policy to reduce the administrative burden on companies had worked well for Denmark, winning her the title of the world's web-savviest nation in 2004 [3]. She has put in place a government portal that integrates five ministries and 24 other organisations where companies can access a broad range of services.

From the company's viewpoint, innovation through continuous improvement ensures that business and operational processes are constantly aligned with prevailing practice. And, the goal is to satisfy changing customer demand and expectations within the country and even beyond. Hence, process re-engineering is vital in ensuring that practices stay current and enterprises remain relevant in a globalising business environment. In the course of standardisation, the basic value is derived from the need to re-engineer some aspects of the existing process and consider new approaches to arriving at an improved process. In other words, challenging generally accepted practices and established strategies would bring about process innovation and improvement. By standardising practices, it will also mean businesses could offer a quicker and higher quality service through, possibly, using IT to become more efficient and customer centric [4].

ACKNOWLEDGEMENTS

The Singapore IT Barometer 2003 Survey was wholly funded by the National University of Singapore.

REFERENCES

1. M. Hammer and J. Champy, *Reengineering the Corporation: A Manifesto for Business Revolution* (HarperBusiness: USA, 2001).

2. Singapore Standard, *Code of Practice for Construction Computer-Aided Design (CAD)*, CP 83: Part 1, 2, 3, 4, 5 (Spring: Singapore, 2000, 2004).
3. The Straits Times, *Danes the Web-savviest* (Singapore Press Holdings: Singapore, 20 April 2004).
4. B.H. Goh, Towards iN2015 – Implications for the Construction Industry on its Future Standardisation and ICT Programmes, *Synthesis Journal 2006, Information Technology Standards Committee, Standards, Productivity and Innovation Board* (SPRING Singapore, 2006), pp.125-138.
5. Building and Construction Authority (BCA). http://www.bca.gov.sg.
6. Construction and Real Estate Network (CORENET). http://www.corenet.gov.sg.

Generalized Association Rule Mining Algorithms Based on Multidimensional Data

Hong Zhang and Bo Zhang

School of Computer Science and Technology, China University of Mining and Technology, Xuzhou 221008, Jiangsu, P.R. China hongzh@cumt.edu.cn

Abstract. This paper proposes a new formalized definition of generalized association rule based on Multidimensional data. The algorithms named BorderLHSs and GenerateLHSs-Rule are designed for generating generalized association rule from multi-level frequent item sets based on Multidimensional Data. Experiment shows that the algorithms proposed in this paper are more efficiency, generate less redundant rules and have good performance in flexibility, scalability and complexity.

Keywords: *Multi-dimension, Multidimensional data, Date mining, Generalized association rule, Formalization*

1. INTRODUCTION

Association rule mining is one of the most active research focuses in data mining. It was firstly proposed in the article written by Agrawal, Imielinski and Swami in 1993 [1]. And then many researchers did much hard work in association rule mining theory, algorithm design, parallel association rule mining and quantitative association rule mining. They also tried their best to improve the efficiency, adaptability and applicability of the mining algorithms and promote the application of them [1-5].

According to the limitations of the existing association rule formalization and the generalized association rule mining algorithms based on multidimensional data, this paper presents the formalized definition of generalized association rule, and designs algorithms for generating generalized association rule from multi-level frequent item sets based on multidimensional data.

2. MINING GENERALIZED ASSOCIATION RULE

2.1 The Formalization of Generalized Association Rule

The formalized description of multi-level association rule in n-dimension data set $R = (D, M, D_{str})$ is as follows:

Please use the following format when citing this chapter:

Zhang, H., Zhang, B., 2007, in IFIP International Federation for Information Processing, Volume 254, Research and Practical Issues of Enterprise Information Systems II Volume 1, eds. L. Xu, Tjoa A., Chaudhry S. (Boston: Springer), pp. 337-342.

Definition 1: an item is a 2-dimension of (d,v), item sets $I=\{(d,v)|d\in D, v\in DOM(d)\}$, where D is dimension set, $DOM(d)$ is the range of d.

Definition 2: set item $x=(d_x,v_x)\in I, y=(d_y,v_y)\in I$, if $d_x=d_y$, and $v_x\in Child(v_y)$. Then y is the father item, x is the filial item, record it as $y=\hat{x}=(d_x,\hat{v}_x)$.

Definition 3: set item sets $Z\subset I, \hat{Z}\subset I$, if Z and $\hat{Z}$ contains same items, and we can get $\hat{Z}$ by using its' father item to replace one or several items in Z, then we call $\hat{Z}$ the father item sets of Z, and Z is the filial item sets of $\hat{Z}$.

Definition 4: k-itemsets $X=\{(d_{i1},v_{i1}),(d_{i2},v_{i2}),\ldots,(d_{ik},v_{ik})\}\subset I$, where $\forall 1\le p,q\le k$, $d_{ip}\ne d_{iq}$. $\Pr(X)$ is defined as the number of transactions in original transaction database that contains the all items in item sets X. $\Pr(X)=F(d_{i1}=v_{i1},d_{i2}=v_{i2},\ldots,d_{ik}=v_{ik})$, where F refers to the function dependence relationship from the dimension set D in multi-dimension set R to measure attribute M_{count} ,set X is the support degree of $\sup(X)=\Pr(X)$.

Definition 5: Generalized association rule is an implication expression like $X\Rightarrow Y$, where $X\subset I$,$Y\subset I$, $X\cap Y=\phi$, and $\forall x\in X$, all $\hat{x}\notin Y$. The support degree of the rule $X\Rightarrow Y$ is $\sup(X\Rightarrow Y)=\sup(X\cup Y)$, confidence degree is $confidence\ (X\Rightarrow Y)=\sup(X\cup Y)/\sup(X)$.

2.2 Algorithms of Generalized Association Rule Mining

Descriptions of these two algorithms as follows.

2.2.1 BorderLHSs Algorithms

We can use the downward closure property based on LHS of the association rule to find the dividing line of LHSst through reverse searching means of BorderLHSs(A) under the conditiong of the given minimum support value, Description of BorderLHSs Algorithms is follows:

[Input]: Frenquent Itemset *A*

[Output]: Rule Condition (LHS) Dividing Lines (*LHSs)*

① *FIFO*={*A*}; *LHSs*= ϕ;

② while(*FIFO*≠ ϕ) do{

③ Dequeue *B* from the head of *FIFO*;

④ onBorder=*TRUE*;

⑤ For each ($|B|$ -1)-subset C of B do {

if($P(C) \le P(A)/\min\_conf$) then {

onBorder=*FALSE*;

⑥ if (C is not in *FIFO*) then Enqueue C to the end of *FIFO*;

}

}

if (onBorder==*TRUE*) then add B to *LHSs*;

}

⑦ Answer= *LHSs*;

BorderLHSs(A) will decrease the complexity enormously, because once the item set of *LHSs* was found, the searching algorithms will stop searching other subset. Even in the worst condition, the complexity of this Algorithms is $O\left(2^{|A|}\right)$.

2.2.2 GenerateRule Algorithms

GenerateRule Algorithms was obtained by deleting one frequent itemset LHSs and making it not cross with any superset or subset.

There are m frequent itemsets $A_1, A_2, \dots, A_m$, where any itemset is the superset of (|A|+1) layer of A or subset of A. Set $B \in (\text{BorderLHSs(A)} - \bigcup_{i=1}^{m} BorderLHSs(A_i))$, relative to any other rules, $B \to (A - B)$ is irredundant.

Descriptiong of GenerateRule Algorithms is as follows:

[Input]: All Frequent Itemset L

[Output]: Irredudant Association Rule AR

① For each $A \in L$ do {

② $LHS(A) = BorderLHSs(A)$;

③ For each $C \in L$ such that C is a $(|A|+1)$ -superset or a child itemset of A do {

$LHS(A) = LHS(A)$ -$BorderLHSs(C)$;

}

④ For each $B \in LHS(A)$ do {

add rule "$B \to (A-B)$" to AR;

}

}

Answer= AR;

This Algorithm gets the least and irredundant association rule. The efficiency of the association rule is improved greatly. If the processing time of every frequent itemset in set L is the same, then the computing complexity of the Algorithm and the value of set L are linearly dependent.

3. EXAMPLE VERIFICATION AND ANALYSIS

3.1 Sales Database

Given a sales database. It has four attributes: transaction identifier tid, customer's age, income and buys, where age and income are all numerical attributes,buys are category attributes, shown in table 1.

Table 1. Transaction Database of Sales

tid	age	income	buys
100	25	45k	{ IBM Laptop, HP Color Printer }
200	28	40k	{HP Desktop , Canon Color Printer }
300	44	45k	{IBM Desktop, HP Desktop }
400	21	20k	{HP Desktop, Epson b/w Printer }
500	36	40k	{ IBM Laptop }
600	32	30k	{HPLaptop, Epson b/w Printer }

3.2 Creating Association Rule

Suppose the threshold value of minimum confidence is *min_conf*=60%, according to the algorithm of GenerateLHSs-Rule, association rules are generated as shown in Table 2.

Table 2. Association Rule generated by GenerateRule (L) Algorithms

Multi-layer Association Rule	Support degree	Confidence degree
(buys, Printer) $\Rightarrow$ (age, [20,29])	3	75%
(income, [40 k,49 k]) $\Rightarrow$ (buys, Computer)	4	100%
(buys, Computer) $\Rightarrow$ (income, [40 k,49 k])	4	66.7%
(buys, Desktop) $\Rightarrow$ (age, [20,29])	2	66.7%
(age, [30,39]) $\Rightarrow$ (buys, Laptop)	2	100%
(buys, Laptop) $\Rightarrow$ (age, [30,39])	2	66.7%
(buys, Desktop) $\Rightarrow$ (income, [40 k,49 k])	2	66.7%
(buys, Laptop) $\Rightarrow$ (income, [40 k,49 k])	2	66.7%
(age, [20,29]) $\Rightarrow$ (buys, HP Desktop)	2	66.7%
(buys, HP Desktop) $\Rightarrow$ (age, [20,29])	2	66.7%
(buys, HP Desktop) $\Rightarrow$ (income, [40 k,49 k])	2	66.7%
(buys, IBM Desktop) $\Rightarrow$ (income, [40 k,49 k])	2	100%
(age, [20,29]) $\Rightarrow$ (income, [40 k,49 k]) $\wedge$ (buys, Computer)	2	66.7%

(income,[40 k,49 k]) ∧ (buys, Printer) ⟹ (age,[20,29])	2	100%
(age,[20,29]) ⟹ (income,[40 k,49 k]) ∧ (buys, Color Printer)	2	66.7%
(buys,Color Printer) ⟹ (income, [40 k,49 k]) ∧ (age [20,29])	2	100%

3.3 Interpretation of Result

- 31 association rules are generated by using general algorithms , in contrast, only 16 association rules are generated by using the algorithms in this paper. Thus, our algorithms can decrease the reduntant rules efficiently.
- Algorithms of Cumulate, Stratify and ML_T2L1 need larger store space and also have distinct limitation. However, when counting the support of itemset using the algorithms proposed in this paper, it only needs to access the relevant cell, does not need to scan the whole data cube. So it decreases the number of the candidate itemsets and improves the efficiency of generating frequent itemsets.
- Algorithm of *BorderLHSs*(*A*) guarantees that every subset of *A* can be visited one time. Once the itemset of the condition border *LHSs* was found, the searching algorithm will stop searching all the subset, which makes the complexity less than $O\left(2^{|A|}\right)$, so it can decrease the complexity of the algorithm greatly.

4. CONCLUSIONS

This paper proposes the formalized definition of generalized association rule and designs the BorderLHSs and GenerateLHSs-Rule Algorithms of generalized association rule mining based on multidimensional data, which decrease the number of redundant rules efficiently. Experiment shows that the algorithms in this paper is superior on algorithms efficiency and generating irredundant rules. At the same time, the algorithms have good performance in flexibility, scalablicity and complexity. This paper also has great theorical meaning and practical value on generalized association rule mining based on multidimensional data.

This paper is supported by the Natural Science Foundation of Jiangsu Province (serial number: BK2005021).

REFERENCES

1. R. Agrawal, T. Imielinski, and A. Swami, Mining association rules between sets of items in large databases, in *Proc. of ACM SIGMOD Conference on Management of Data*, eds. P. Buneman and S. Jajodia (ACM Press: Washington D.C, 1993), pp.207-216.
2. G. Piatetsky-Shapiro and W.J. Frawley, *Knowledge Discovery in Databases* (AAAI/MIT Press: Menlo Park, California, 1991).
3. J. Han and M. Kamber, *Data Mining——Concept and Technology* (China Machine Press: Beijing, 2001).
4. J. Li and H. Gao, Multidimensional Data Modeling for Data Warehouses, *Journal of Software*. Volume 11, Number 7, pp.908-917, (2000).

5. M. Chen, J. Han, and P.S. Yu, Data mining: An Overview from a Database Perspective, *IEEE Trans. on Knowledge and Data Engineering*. Volume 8, Number 7, pp.866-883, (1996).

Enterprise Integration Modeling for Extended Enterprise in ERP Systems

Luciana Rocha dos Santos[1], Simone Vasconcelos Silva[2] and Renato de Campos[3]

[1]Estácio de Sá University, Avenida 28 de Março, 423 - Centro – Campos dos Goytacazes - Brazil www.estacio.br lurochas@yahoo.com.br
[2]Federal Center for Technological Education of Campos, Rua Dr. Siqueira, 273 - Parque Dom Bosco – Campos dos Goytacazes - Brazil simonevs@cefetcampos.br
[3]São Paulo State University, Av. Eng. Edmundo Carrijo Coube, nº 14-01 – Bauru – Brazil rcampos@feb.unesp.br

Abstract. Currently, the companies overcome its organization barriers stimulated by the necessity of market expansion, minimize the enterprise costs, search for competitive advantages and need to absorb the fast market changes. New forms of organizations arise and are called extended and agile enterprises with new factors to be observed in the implementation of the integrated systems such as enterprise resources planning (ERP). Defining business processes of these organizations turn the task of modeling of the system integrated information sufficiently complex. In order to control all these variables of the businesses world and minimize the effect of the high risk of investment, it is necessary to use adequate methodologies. This article presents the main difficulties in the implantation of ERP systems and proposes a modeling methodology for networking enterprise with CIMOSA and UML.

Keywords: *Business process modeling, Enterprise agility, Extended enterprise, Enterprise resource panning (ERP), UML, CIMOSA.*

I. INTRODUCTION

Large organizations have invested greatly on complex systems, such as: ERP (Enterprise Resource Planning). With globalization, the systems need to adapt themselves to the constant changes and environments that extend the is organizational barriers with new business partners. New organizational paradigms are established such as: the Agile Enterprise and the Extended Enterprise.

Trends of the industries would be characterized by: globalization, parallelization, agility, virtual company, customer's satisfaction and quality. In this perspective, the challenge is to integrate and coordinate the business processes efficiently, in an inter-organizational environment and in continuous changing, and for that is necessary to model and plan the enterprise [1].

This article makes one brief description of organizational paradigms, ERP systems, business process, enterprise modeling and proposes to integrate the best business modeling practical as: CIMOSA and UML. The next section detaches the organizational paradigms as: Agile enterprise and Extended enterprise. In section 3 it

Please use the following format when citing this chapter:

Rocha dos Santos, L., Silva, S. V., de Campos, R., 2007, in IFIP International Federation for Information Processing, Volume 254, Research and Practical Issues of Enterprise Information Systems II Volume 1, eds. L. Xu, Tjoa A., Chaudhry S. (Boston: Springer), pp. 343-347.

is done an explanation regarding ERP systems showing, difficulties and perspectives. Section 4 shows the necessity of the business process modeling. Section 5 presents the enterprise modeling using CIMOSA and UML. In section 6 it is presented a proposal to the modeling of ERP systems, based on the development processes CIMOSA and UML; and in the section there are the 7 final considerations.

2. ORGANIZATIONAL PARADIGMS

The enterprises are live things. They constantly need to be redesigned to adjust themselves with the necessary agility to the alignment of new technologies, and to guarantee intra and inter-organizational improvements. The challenges faced by the enterprises in more dynamic and competitive markets take the definition of organizational paradigms as Agile enterprise and Extended enterprise [2-3].

The agile enterprise is the ability of an organization to detect the environment change and to answer efficiently and effectively to these changes, and thus to compete successfully in an of uncertain and unexpected business environment. The agility requires the integration of some factors: flexible production technologies, a competent work force, knowledge, and management of organizational structures that promote and stimulate cooperative initiatives between the enterprises [4-5].

The context of an Extended Enterprise represents the organizations in which "the main" enterprise, that is, dominant, "extends" its limits to suppliers or business partners, based mainly on contracts that establish rules for the collaboration net, however, an existing difficulty is the information exchange and knowledge among the collaboration of net partners, that is, to follow the production process or entire service, inside the organization until the associated organization or extended [6].

3. ERP SYSTEMS

The ERP is standardized software designed to integrate the internal value chain of an enterprise, based on an integrated database and consists on diverse modules aiming specific business functions [7].

Currently, to wait on the enterprise demands, it is verified a strong trend in the use of free software, which possesses advantages as reduction of costs and differentiated technical characteristics [3]. The ERP5 proposal is innovative because it uses object oriented database technology, it combines ERP and content management, and it is projected to be distributed with specific characteristics. Multilingual it deals with several currencies. Multi-user, it allows several enterprises. Meta-ERP in Meta-Planning manages a group of companies that belong to the same holding or manages an abstract organization. Synchronization, it is projected to be implemented in several places through the Internet and has characteristics of EDI (Electronic Data Interchange) standard [8].

To implant an ERP system can be a difficult and risky process. Typically, it has an impact on the entire organization, and generally, it is associated to the reengineering of business process, being necessary a strong management and control of the organizational changes. Some elements of risk threaten the success of ERP projects, and when the risks are not immediately detected and corrected, each subsequent phase inherits the problems not resolved. The implantation of the ERP requires abilities such as: change management, risk management, business process reengineering, beyond technical knowledge of execution [9-10].

4. BUSINESS PROCESS MODELING

In complex systems, business processes, components and then interactions they are in constant changing, so, it is not possible to establish them definitive by. The business processes integration and the information technology has been one of the key factors for a successful execution of an integrated enterprise system [11].

With the reference models, the modifications of alignment lessen their costs, time and complexity. The business processes modeling is essential to adjust the gaps between ERP system and the business model of the enterprise. The future of the ERP is to integrate the diverse aspects that compose ERP system with the external environment [1].

5. ENTERPRISE MODELING USING CIMOSA AND UML

Modeling the enterprise is an essential pre-requirement to capture the variables of the businesses world and to get an approach of the enterprise reality. The models of business process directly influence the construction of information systems [12].

CIMOSA constitutes one of the main efforts in the direction to provide an architecture, to modeling, analysis and design of enterprise systems. It is composed of three main components: Integration Infrastructure; Life Cycle of the enterprise System; and enterprise Modeling Structure. Makes possible the attainment of an integrated enterprise model, which captures and structures the essential characteristics of the enterprise beyond supplying conditions to define an infrastructure which supports the integration of the enterprise operations and, defines constructors for the principle of the particularization, where it builds a generic model or reference model which can be customized in accordance with a specific enterprise [1, 13].

The unified modeling Language (UML) contains notations and rules to express oriented objects models [14-15]. But it does not define how the work must be done, that is, it does not possess a development process. Larman [16], based on the best practical of development process of oriented objects systems and UML models, created the Process and Models Recommended (PMR), which will be used together with CIMOSA as follow.

6. MODELING PROPOSAL

Modeling an extended enterprise requires the creation of business process models correspondent to the sub-nets of different enterprise units. To implement such cooperation and to absorb the fast changes are the challenges of the dynamic models that must allow different enterprise parts to be integrated. The availability of these models can significantly increase the operation understanding of an enterprise and improve its coordination and management [6].

CIMOSA establishes that the modeling process "**Figure 1.**" initiates with the Requirements Definition Model (RDM), where it is necessary to find the keys areas or Domains (DMi) of the enterprise, and after established the Domain Processes (DPi) of each DMi of the enterprise. For each DPi it is defined the Enterprise Activities (EAi), that are defined by Objects View (OVi).

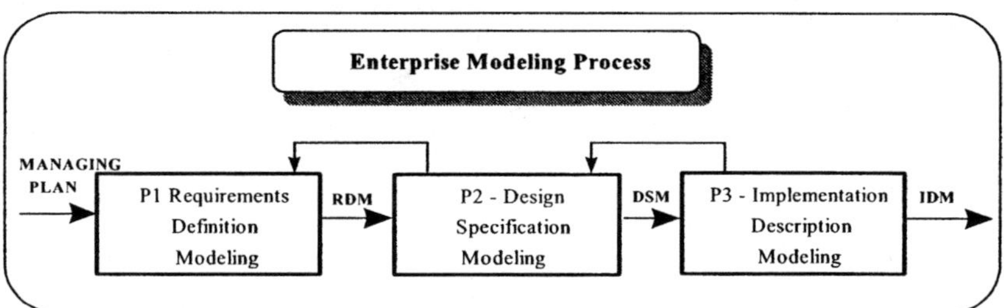

Figure 1. Main Step of the CIMOSA Process Modeling by Vernadat [1]

The modeling process considered by Larman Process and Models Recommended (PMR), also establishes 3 stages, represented in the "**Figure 2.**" to follow:

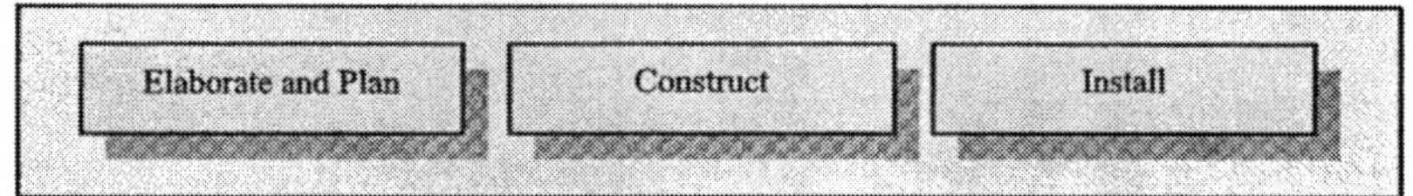

Figure 2. Steps Development in Mcro Lvel by Larman [16]

During the modeling process, in first CIMOSA stage (RDM), domain process is equivalent to the use cases of UML of PMR. Each item of CIMOSA model is represented in written form in explanatory template and it is detailed throughout the modeling process.

In the second phase of the modeling CIMOSA (PMS) the templates are reviewed and detailed. In this phase the PMR, Each cycle treats a relatively small set of requirements, and the system incrementally grows, whenever each cycle is completed. The main used diagrams are: Use Case Diagrams that represent the main EAi; Class Diagram; and Sequence Diagrams.

The third phase, is implementation description Modeling of (IDM) CIMOSA and the Install UML stage are equivalents, therefore they define tests, installation, training and other stages of system release. The model of the information system uses all pieces of information raised in the enterprise model. It has a generic character, and doing so, it is considered to be adaptable to the enterprise of different acting areas.

7. FINAL CONSIDERATIONS

The new organizational paradigms impose an accelerated rhythm of adaptation in order to make the enterprises to get competitive advantages, characterized by the continuous search of the new: markets, products, business partners and technologies. The agile enterprise and the extended enterprise represent this dynamics of the markets.

The modeling based on business processes, supported by techniques of great capacity of expression as CIMOSA and UML, aims to reduce the distance among the implantation of ERP systems in dynamic and complex organizations and also to make possible its continued maintenance.

REFERENCES

1. F.B. Vernadat, *Enterprise Modeling and Integration, Principles and Applications* (Chapman & Hall: Londres, 1996).
2. F.G. Goethals, M. Snoeck, W. Lemahieu, and J. Vandenbulcke, Management and enterprise architecture click: The FAD (E) E framework, *Information Systems Frontiers*. Volume 8, pp.67-79, (2006).
3. R.R. Campos and E.W. Cazarini, *Aspects of installation technician in developed integrated systems management of under the model of free software: perspective of use in the small company* (XIII Simpep, Brazil, 2006).
4. A.L. Azevedo, The emergency of virtual enterprise and the requirements for information systems, *Gestão e Produção*. Volume 7, Number 3, (2000).
5. J.L. Zhao, M. Tanniru, and L.J. Zhang, Services computing as the foundation of enterprise agility: Overview of recent advances and introduction to the special issue, *Information Systems Frontiers*. Volume 9, pp.1-8, (2007).
6. A. Kuczynski, D. Stokic, and U. Kirchhoff, Set-up and maintenance of ontologies for innovation support in extended enterprises, *International Journal of Advanced Manufacturing Technology*. Volume 29, pp.398-407, (2006).
7. C. Møller, ERP II: a conceptual framework for next-generation enterprise systems? *Journal of Enterprise Information Management*. Volume 18, pp.483-497, (2005).
8. J-P. Smets-Solanes and R.A. Carvalho, *An abstract model for an open source ERP system: the ERP5 proposal* (Enegep, Brazil, 2005).
9. S.V. Grabskia and S.A. Leechb, Complementary controls and ERP implementation success, *Inter. J. Accounting Inf. Systems*. Volume 8, pp.1-72, (2007).
10. M. Daneva and R.J. Wieringa, A requirements engineering framework for cross-organizational ERP systems, *Requirements Engineering*. Volume 11, pp.194-204, (2006).
11. F.P.C. Silva and N.A. Pereira, Modeling of processes business in the ERPs implementation in PMEs national, *Produção*. Volume 16, Number 2, pp.341-352, (2006).
12. L.R. Santos, S.V. Silva, and R. Campos, *Usage of enterprise modeling processes and information systems design to forecast demand* (Confenis, Áustria, 2006).
13. F.B. Vernadat, *Enterprise Modeling: Objectives, constructs & ontologies, Tutorial held at the EMOI-CAISE Workshop* (Riga, Latvia, 2004).
14. G. Booch, J. Rumbaugh, and I. Jacobson, *Unified Modeling Language User Guide* (Addisson Wesley: Massachusetts, 1999).
15. H. Eriksson and M. Penker, *Business Modeling with UML: business patterns at work* (Wiley: Canada, 2000).
16. C. Larman, *Applying UML and Patterns* (Prentice Hall PTR: New York, 2004).

Research on Process-Oriented Enterprise Knowledge Modeling and Integration Management Based on Ontology

Ziyu Liu[1, 2] and Lei Huang[1]

[1]College of Economics and Management, Beijing Jiaotong University, Beijing 100044, P.R. China purpleyuliu@sohu.com

[2]College of Information Science & Engineering, Hebei University of Science & Technology, Shijiazhuaug 050018, P.R. China

Abstract. The society is entering into knowledge-based economy, managing experience knowledge effectively is more important. Process-oriented knowledge management aims is the integration of business process and knowledge management, in order to solve the problem of process knowledge exchange and sharing in enterprise or between enterprises, an ontology-based approach to modeling and integrating enterprise process knowledge was proposed and an Enterprise Process Ontology (EPOnt) was developed. Its fundamental information is represented by the IDEF5 language graphically based on the reasons that most of ontologies have formal semantics but lack of graphical representation currently. Moreover, its precise syntax and formal semantics are defined in the Ontolingua language characterized by traits such as stronger expressiveness and compatibility with multiple representation languages and systems. Based on those, an actual Guangzhou Port Group business case was illustrated to show the application of the EPOnt and the architecture of an EPOnt-based enterprise knowledge integration management platform was presented. The proposed approach provides a common understanding of a relevant vocabulary of terms and enhances the semantic interoperability, reuse and share of process knowledge for improving server efficiency and quality of enterprise.

Keywords: *Process-oriented, Ontology, knowledge management, IDEF5 language, Ontolingua language*

I. INTRODUCTION

BPR (Business Process Reengineering) that swept the world in 90s of the 20th century has gradually faded out of people's vision. Instead, the newly emerging knowledge management (KM) is drawing people's attention. Process-oriented knowledge management (PKM) is to combine process-oriented method with knowledge management [1-2]. By providing the necessary knowledge for the value-added activities of business process, PKM can enhance organizational performance. The results of the first global Delphi study on prospects of Knowledge Management

Please use the following format when citing this chapter:

Liu, Z., Huang, L., 2007, in IFIP International Federation for Information Processing, Volume 254, Research and Practical Issues of Enterprise Information Systems II Volume 1, eds. L. Xu, Tjoa A., Chaudhry S. (Boston: Springer), pp. 349-357.

showed that integrating knowledge management into the business process is not only the most urgent issues that need to be solved about theoretical research, but also the most practical way to solve the problems in the practice of knowledge management [3]. Combining knowledge with business process can improve organizational knowledge management and process management. At present most studies on knowledge management in not only the theory, but also the construction of knowledge management system deal with the acquisition, collate and reuse process [4-7]. China's Cui Shuyin and Ren Hao from Tongji University made preliminary study on process-oriented knowledge management strategy in terms of the management [8]. However, it is rare to see the practices about combining business processes with knowledge management.

With the rapid development of the Internet and information technology, departments inside the enterprise or enterprises need to cooperate to provide users with better services. Therefore, we need to realize electronic service to improve enterprise efficiency and quality of decision-making, and reduce operating costs. In the efficient services of enterprises, all enterprises and departments need good cooperation with each other to exchange and share business process knowledge, such as the services that activities need and the correct logic dependence relationship. However, the business service systems inside enterprise or in different enterprises are independently constructed, and do not share the same program of business process knowledge modeling. These systems may use different names, such as the operation or mission, and lack definitions and descriptions of the full semantic of concepts and terms when they express the same concept. Not clearly definition of the concept and duplication of interpretation lead to inconsistencies of explanation and the use of business process knowledge, make it difficult for different systems within the enterprise or between different enterprises to automatic exchange and share process knowledge, eventually lead to the low efficiency, and even make service impossible.

Therefore, in view of the above questions, this paper proposes the modeling of business process knowledge based on Ontology without ambiguity for different enterprises or enterprise business systems to understand and effectively exchange and integrate process knowledge. Ontology can precisely define and depict the knowledge concept and public terms of relations and semantics, thus can effectively promote the common understanding and interaction of knowledge and semantic interoperability of heterogeneous systems. Currently, the majority of ontology modeling takes on the formal semantics, but lack icons, so it is difficult to express the information of ontology. Therefore, we developed the EPOnt (Business Process Ontology). First we adopted the visual charts ICAM to express Ontology basic information, and use Ontolingua with strong expression and compatibility of many languages and systems to accurately depict grammar and formal semantics. Based on those, an actual Guangzhou Port Group business case was illustrated to show the application of the EPOnt. Finally, we propose the integration architecture of enterprise knowledge management based on EPOnt.

2. PROCESS-ORIENTED AND ONTOLOGY

2.1 Process-oriented

During the 1990s, Hammer and Champy proposed the theory of business process reengineering [9]. It emphasizes that organization should put business process as the center but not functions. The process can describe the most of activities in organization in some case more than 90% [10]. The process is made up of activities, and a shallow definition of the process is a group of related activities [11]. For enterprise organizations, business is a series of activities that is engaged in by them to achieve operational objectives, and that is also the main daily work of enterprises. The business process is the activity of changing one or more input into output that is valuable for the customers. Process-oriented stresses the process, the output of the process and the customer satisfaction.

2.2 Ontology

Ontology that originates from philosophy is widespread paid attention to among the field of information science in recent years [12-13], and its importance has been demonstrated in many ways and has been widely recognized [12][14-15]. There are a number of definitions about the ambiguous term “ontology”, and different definitions have different level of detail and logic. Gruber’s theory and Guarino’s theory are two representations [12][16]. Gruber’s definition of Knowledge System Laboratory (KSL) of Stanford University is at large accepted: An ontology is an explicit specification of a conceptualization [16]. Ontologies embody human knowledge via symbols that are machine processible. Therefore, ontologies benefit machine reading the data when we use ontologies to index data and to express the metadata [17]. Ontology facilitates capture and construction of domain knowledge and enables representation of skeletal knowledge to facilitate integration of knowledge bases irrespective of the heterogeneity of knowledge sources [18].

2.3 Ontology Description Language: IDEF5, Ontolingua

IDEF5 is developed by KBSI of America [19]. Figure 1 shows parts of IDEF5 schematic language symbols, and kind and individual of IDEF5 are corresponding to class and instance of ontolingua. Ontolingua is developed by Knowledge System Laboratory (KSL) of Stanford University, and it can express class, class hierarchy, n variables relationship, function, axiom and instance etc [20]. The definition of ontolingua includes three parts: the head part of the definition, the non-formal definition part that is described by natural language and the formal definition part.

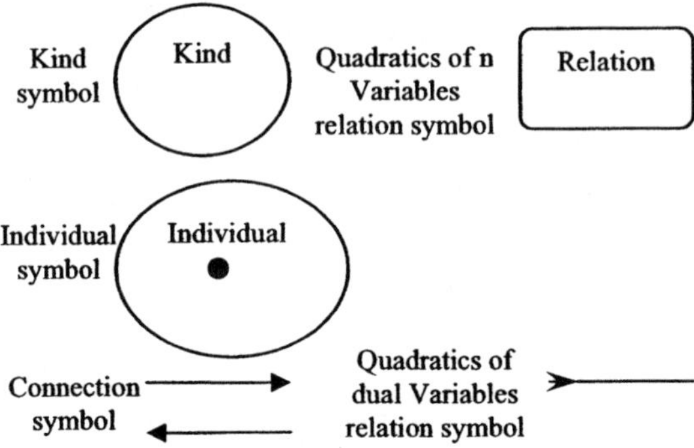

Figure 1. Parts of IDEF5 Schematic Language Symbols

3. PROCESS-ORIENTED ENTERPRISE KNOWLEDGE MODELING BASED ON ONTOLOGY

The purpose of developing EPOnt is to provide shared vocabulary for describing the transfer process of business. The whole business process can be said by a "flow" activity. Each activity is associated with input, output, resource and constraint, and it also has a proper logical links with other related activities. This expression method that is unified and activity-oriented is helpful to construct modular process activities base, and it can add or delete process activity independently [21]. EPOnt includes framework ontology and parameter constraint ontology, and that can help we reuse its vocabulary, such as individual-thing and constraint etc. Figure 2 shows parts of the fundamental information of the EPOnt represented by IDEF5 schematic language. Here we omit the analysis of main entities and formal description of EPOnt.

4. CASE STUDY

The business of Guangzhou port, such as scheduling business, the container business and so on, can be described by the terminology and precise semantics of EPOnt. EPOnt can describe the activities, parameters and connectivity relationship of specific activities and establish the process knowledge of specific business areas that is exchangeable and sharable. All these are the content of knowledge base. Now we give the knowledge describes for cargo handling cost service of Guangzhou port that is based on EPOnt.

Figure 3 shows the flow of cargo handling cost service, and it includes three activities: submitting cargo kind and quantity, computing cargo handling cost and paying cargo handling cost. These three activities form sequential connection relationship.

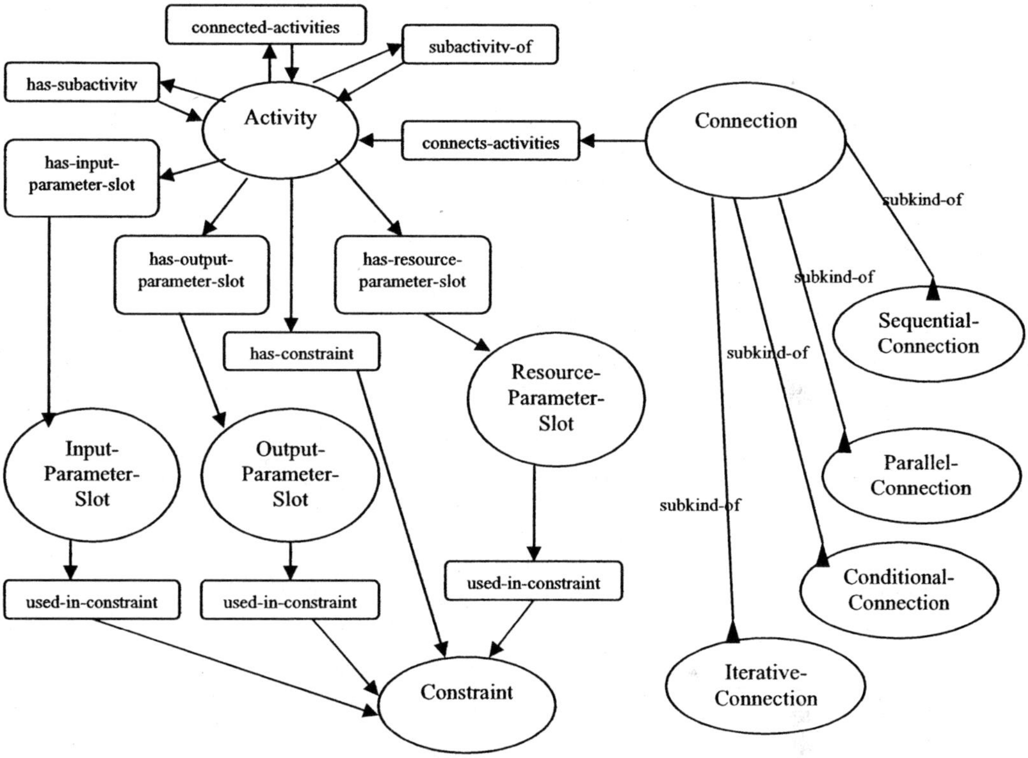

Figure 2. Fundamental Information of the EPOnt Represented by IDEF5 Schematic Language

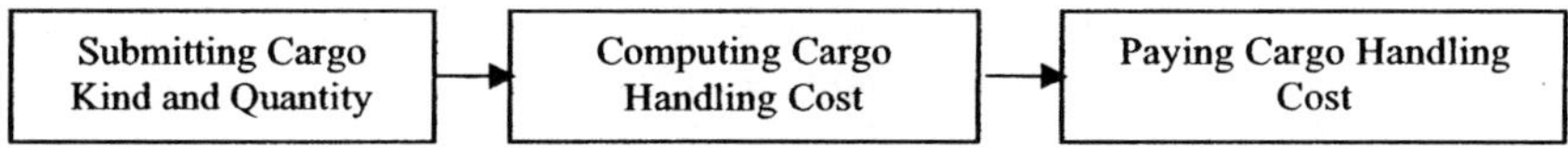

Figure 3. Cargo Handling Cost Service Flow Chart

Figure 4 shows the process knowledge for cargo handling cost service

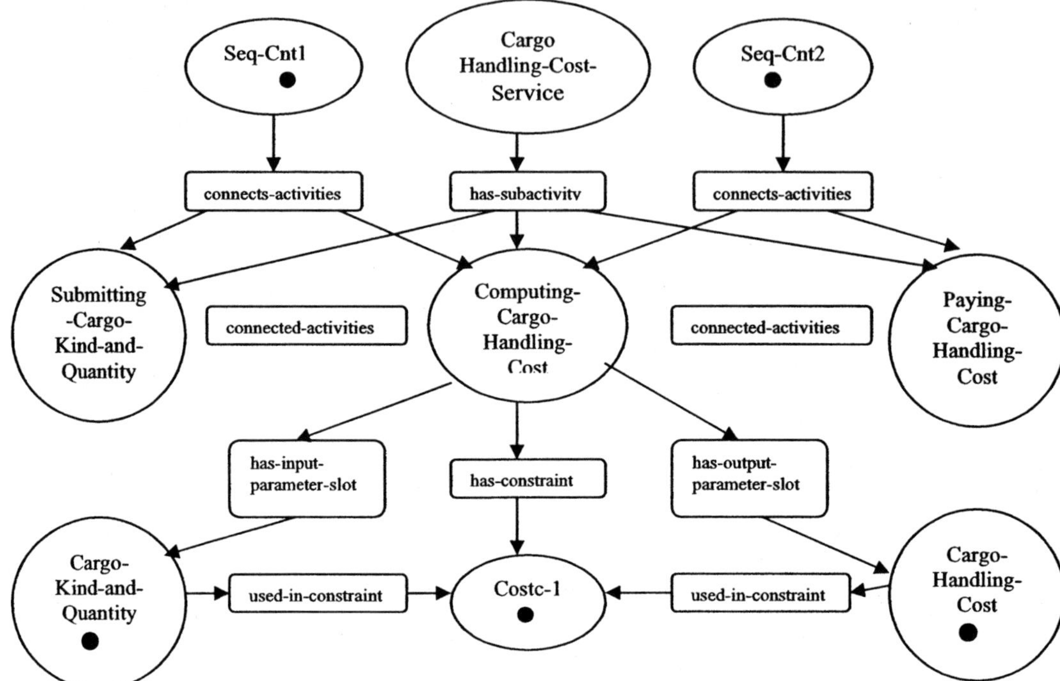

Figure 4. Process Knowledge Chart for Cargo Handling Cost Service

Cargo-Handling-Cost-Service is the sub-activity of *activity*. The following is the definition of *Computing-Cargo-Handling-Cost* that is included in *Cargo-Handling-Cost-Service*.

```
(define-class Computing-Cargo-Handling-Cost (?x)
  : def(and (Activity ?x)
  (has-input-parameter-slot ?x Cargo-Kind-and-Quantity)
  (=(value-cardinality?x Cargo-Kind-and-Quantity)1)
  (has-output-parameter-slot ?x Cargo-Handling-Cost)
  (=(value-cardinality?x Cargo-Handling-Cost)1)
  (has-constraint?x Costc-1)
  (exist?y(=>Submitting-Cargo-Kind-and-Quantity?y)
      (connected-activities?x?y))
  (exist?z(=>Paying-Cargo-Handling-Cost?z)
      (connected-activities?x?z))
```

Among them, the two *value-cardinality* clauses provide only one input *Cargo-Kind-and-Quantity* and one output *Cargo-Handling-Cost*. The process of transforming input into output is limited by constraint instance *Costc-1*, and the content of *Costc-1* is defined by relevant provisions about cargo handling charges from the ministry of communications, contractual agreement signed with users. Here we omit its formal definition.

In addition, there are two sequential connection instances, one is between *Submitting-Cargo-Kind-and-Quantity* and *Computing-Cargo-Handling-Cost* that is named *Seq-Cnt1*, the other is between *Submitting-Cargo-Kind-and-Quantity* and *Paying-Cargo-Handling-Cost* that is named *Seq-Cnt2*. The following is the definition of *Seq-Cnt2*.

```
(define-instance Seq-Cnt2(Sequential-Connection)
    : assertions(exist(?y?z)
    (=> (and(Computing-Cargo-Handling-Cost?y)
    (Paying-Cargo-Handling-Cost?z)
    (connects-activities Seq-Cnt2?y)
(connects-activities Seq-Cnt2?z))))
```

5. THE ARCHITECTURE OF PROCESS-ORIENTED ENTERPRISE KNOWLEDGE INTEGRATION MANAGEMENT PLATFORM

Figure 5 shows the EPOnt-based enterprise knowledge integration platforms. The main function of this platform is to support the exchange of process knowledge and semantic interoperability for business systems in enterprise or between enterprises.

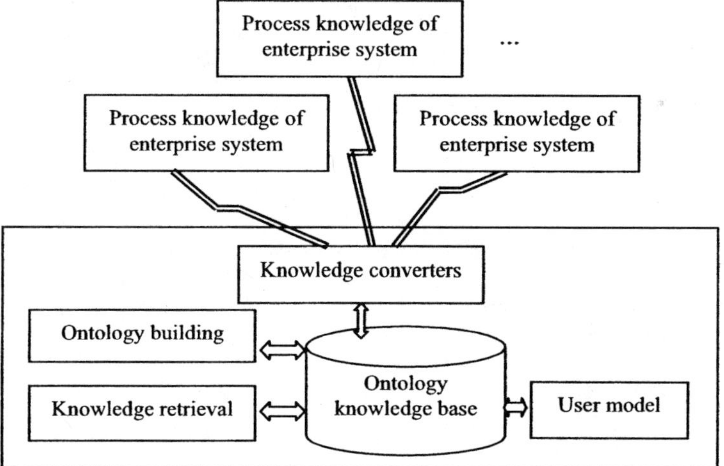

Figure 5. EPOnt-based Enterprise Knowledge Integration Platforms

Ontology knowledge base is an important foundation for system running, and the process ontology and process knowledge instance are stored in it. The ontology of the business systems involved in one operational service has defined syntax, terminology and the semantic in process knowledge. Different enterprises look EPOnt as the intermediate exchange format, and knowledge converters achieve semantic interoperability of process knowledge between multiple heterogeneous systems. EPOnt-based process knowledge integration includes three steps: (1) Terminology mapping. (2) Grammar conversion. (3) Semantic change. Through these three steps, it can change the terminology, semantics and grammar of different enterprise systems into EPOnt's.

Ontology building provides graphical defining way and formal definition modes to update ontology or create ontology-based process knowledge. The process knowledge that are converted from or created by users is stored in knowledge base. Through the function of knowledge retrieval, users can search process knowledge that can be used directly or modified according to the need. In the process of retrieval, users can give query conditions and weight on the basis of vocabulary and terminology. User model provides the function of editing the type of process knowledge and other forms of personal preference etc.

6. CONCLUSIONS

In order to integrate business process in enterprise or between enterprises, it requires integrating the services and exchanging flow knowledge of the services. But the business service systems of different enterprises and sectors have not provided clear and consistent semantic for the terms and terminology of the process knowledge. So this paper proposes an ontology-based approach to modeling and integrating enterprise process knowledge and describes the architecture of an EPOnt-based enterprise knowledge integration management platform. Ontology provides semantic foundation for the exchange of knowledge, and it can effectively promote common awareness for knowledge and semantic interoperability for heterogeneous system. EPOnt that is developed in this paper, its fundamental information is represented by the IDEF5 language, and its precise syntax and formal semantics are defined in the Ontolingua language. Using the EPOnt, we can construct the process knowledge of specific business areas. EPOnt can provide public terminology and vocabulary for the different operational systems, which can promote the semantic interoperability, reuse and sharing of business process knowledge in enterprise or between enterprises. That can enhance business efficiency and service quality of enterprise, and promote the achievement of the integration of business.

The application of the EPOnt in Guangzhou Port Group business case shows that EPOnt is a flexible and efficient tool. In this paper, the study of process-oriented enterprise modeling and integration of knowledge management based on ontology is only a preliminary result. In future we also have a lot of work to do.

REFERENCES

1. T.H. Davenport, S.L. Jarvenpaa, and M.C. Beers, Improving Knowledge Work Processes, *Sloan Management Review*. Volume 37, Number 4, pp.53-65, (1996).
2. R. Maier and U. Remus, Implementing Process oriented Knowledge Management Strategies, *Urnal of Knowledge Management*. Volume 7, Number 4, pp.62-74, (2003).
3. K. Mertins, P. Heisig, and J. Vorbeck, *Knowledge management* (Tsinghua University press: Beijing, 2004)
4. A. Maedche, B. Motik, L. Stojanovic, R. Studer, and R. Volz, Ontologies for enterprise knowledge management, *IEEE Intelligent Systems*. Volume 4, Number 3, pp.26-33, (2003).
5. D. Fensel, Ontology-Based knowledge management, *Computer*. Number 12, pp.56-59, (2002).
6. B. Liu, Study on key technologies of ontology based knowledge management, *JCSSTI*. Volume 24, Number 1, pp.75-81, (2005).
7. X. Huang, X. Xu, and G. Xu, Research of knowledge management system based ontology, *Science technology and engineering*. Volume 5, Number 6, pp.351-356, (2005).
8. S. Cui and R. Hao, Research on Process-oriented Knowledge Management Strategies, *Scientific Management Research*. Volume 24, Number 5, pp.76-79, (2006).
9. M. Hammer and J. Champy, *Reengineering the Corporation: A Manifesto for Business Revolution* (Harper Co llins: New York, 1993)
10. C.S. Amaravadi and I. Lee, The Dimensions of Process Knowledge, *Knowledge and Process Management*. Volume 12, Number 1, pp.65-76, (2005).
11. D. Garvin, The processes of organization and Management, *Sloan Management Review*. Volume 39, Number 4, pp.35-50, (1997).
12. N. Guarino, Formal ontology and information systems. in *Proc of the 1st Int'l Conf on Formal Ontology in Information Systems Trento* (IOS Press: Italy, 1998), pp.3-15.
13. M. Uschold and M. Gruninger, Ontologies: Principles, methods, and applications, *Knowledge Engineering Review*. Volume 11, Number 2, pp.93-155, (1996).
14. T. Berners-Lee, J. Hendler, and O. Lassila, The semantic Web, *Scientific American*. Volume 284, Number 5, pp.34-43, (2001).
15. T. B. Lee, Semantic Web road map (1998). http://www.w3.org/DesignIssues/Semantic.html
16. T. Gruber, A Translation Approach to Portable Ontology Specifications, *Knowledge Acquisition*. Volume 5, Number 2, pp.199-220, (1993).
17. J. Rogers, *Developing and applying ontologies: experiences from the medical domain*, Medical Informatics Group, University of Manchester (2002).
18. R. Studer, V.R. Benjamins, and D. Fensel, Knowledge engineering: Principles and methods, *Data and Knowledge Engineering*. Number 25, pp.161-197, (1998).
19. Y. Chen, IDEF Modeling analysis and design method (Tsinghua University press: Beijing, 1999), pp.256-292.
20. T.R. Gruber, Ontolingua: A mechanism to support portable ontologies. ftp://ksl.stanford.edu/pub/KSL-Reports/KSL-91-66.ps.gz. 2005-06-01.
21. Y. Yan, D. Yang, Z. Jiang, J. Lu, and X. Lan, Ontology-based e-Government process knowledge modeling and integration management, *Journal of shanghai jiaotong university*. Volume 40, Number 9, pp.1549-1555, (2006).

GeoOlap: An Integrated Approach for Decision Support

Rodrigo Soares Manhães[1], Sahudy Montenegro González[2], Giovanni Colonese[3], Rogério Atem de Carvalho[4] and Asterio Kiyoshi Tanaka[5]

[1,2]Universidade Candido Mendes, Rua Anita Peçanha, 100, 28040-320, RJ, Brazil
rmanhaes@gmail.com sahudy@ucam-campos.br
[3]Faculdade Salesiana Maria Auxiliadora, Rua Monte Elísio, 27943-180, RJ, Brazil
colonese@gmail.com
[4]Centro Federal de Educação Tecnológica de Campos, 28030-130, RJ, Brazil
ratem@cefetcampos.br
[5]Universidade Federal do Estado do Rio de Janeiro, 22290-240, RJ, Brazil
tanaka@uniriotec.br

Abstract. The integration of information from different sources within the enterprise is one of the basis for implementing successful Decision Support Systems (DSS). Typically a DSS supplies analytical information obtained and transformed from large data warehouses. Recently, the geographical component of information has become more important due to the growing use of this type of information in logistics, marketing, and other applications. This work describes GeoOlap, a decision support approach that proposes a method to develop decision support applications that integrates analytical and georeferenced elements from the ground up - at the design stage - and OLAP (On-Line Analytical Processing) and GIS (Geographical Information System) technologies to visualize the results. Additionally, this paper describes PostGeoOlap, an open source general-purpose tool, which supports GeoOlap and that allows developers to easily build decision support applications. A case study is presented to validate the proposed ideas.

Keywords: *Data warehousing, Open source, decision support system, Data integration, Enterprise modeling and integration*

1. INTRODUCTION

Many applications used for business intelligence are often built by using data warehousing tools. Data integration appears with increasing frequency as the volume and the need to share existing data. The capability to analyze aggregated data integrated from several sources makes a Data Warehouse (DW) allied to an OLAP (On-Line Analytical Processing) application, valuable tools for the decision makers. Another technology historically used for decision-making support is the Geographical Information System (GIS), which deals with spatial data and produces maps to help users to analyze data with geographical references.

Many researchers are working on the integration of analytical and geographical technologies. This idea provides better support to the decision-making process

Please use the following format when citing this chapter:

Manhães, R. S., Gonzáles, S. M., Colonese, G., de Carvalho, R. A., Tanaka, A. K., 2007, in IFIP International Federation for Information Processing, Volume 254, Research and Practical Issues of Enterprise Information Systems II Volume 1, eds. L. Xu, Tjoa A., Chaudhry S. (Boston: Springer), pp. 359-369.

allowing analysis under business perspectives, time and space. Most of the recent works regarding analytical and geographical data integration focuses the merge of already existent GIS and OLAP applications to produce an intersection among their results. This fusion generates a third application involving the desired integration. A few proposals present a spatial OLAP without modeling techniques to design an application from the conceptual level.

This paper presents GeoOlap. It proposes an approach to develop decision support applications integrating analytical and georeferenced data. Also describes PostGeoOlap, an open source decision support tool based on GeoOlap proposal. To model an application from its initial conception it's very important to reflect the real world where the coexistence of the spatial and temporal dimensions is essential. The main goal of PostGeoOlap is to be an open source and a general-purpose tool used to easily yield a decision support application. Recently, PostGeoOlap was approved by the Bisgrez initiative to add OLAP functionalities to the BizGres project.

The remainder of this paper is organized as follows. In Section 2 we present a breve review of the previous DW and GIS integration proposals. Section 3 describes the GeoOlap project. Section 4 presents PostGeoOlap tool in junction with case study screens. The case study was useful to validate the proposed ideas. Section 5 presents the conclusions and future directions.

2. RELATED WORK

There are several works related to GeoOlap project. These works have different approaches to develop geographical and analytical data integration.

GOAL in Kouba [1], SIGOLAP in Ferreira [2] and GOLAPA in Fidalgo [3] do not use a unified model with geographic and analytical concepts. Instead they treat these two technologies separately and propose an integration module that maps requests and data. Works in Stefanovic [4] and Papadias [5] are similar to GeoOlap but do not propose any technique for modeling the system as a whole from its conceptual abstraction level. GeoOlap intends to be an open source platform to develop decision support applications integrating OLAP and GIS technologies. Applications are modeled using GeoOlap's modeling technique and developed using the PostGeoOlap tool as it will be described in the next sections.

3. THE GEOOLAP PROJECT

Medium and small businesses have needs when it comes to data management and analytical processing to take important decisions about reducing billing costs and increase customer satisfaction. In the world of small and medium sized business, finding the right software solutions can be challenging. GeoOlap project in Colonese [6] is considered a solution for this kind of companies. It offers a low cost environment (using free software solutions) to develop decision support applications from its conceptual level until its visualization.

GeoOlap proposes a unified method to model multidimensional systems with geographical components. We define *spatial data warehouses* as DW where one or more dimensions (using a star schema) have spatial attributes. Spatial DW is conceptually modeled using a UML diagram with geographical stereotypes to represent the geographical classes. According to Trujillo [7], the use of UML can be explained because it considers the information system's structural and dynamic properties at the conceptual level more naturally than the classic approaches such as Entity-Relationship Model. Further, UML provides OCL (Object Constraint Language) for embedding user requirements and constraints in the conceptual model. In addition, UML also provides support to represent stereotypes, which simplify the representation of extensive hierarchies of objects. A representative icon or symbol associates a class to the whole extensive hierarchy.

The GeoOlap project is meant to easily model applications where the analytical and geographical functionalities are present from its conceptual phase.

At the end, the use of the PostGeoOlap implies the correct understanding and development of the application model. The process comprises the following activities: (1) modeling the data warehouse using UML with spatial stereotypes (for the geographical dimensions); (2) mapping the spatial DW schema (dimensional-relational) from the UML model (conceptual level); (3) using PostGeoOlap to manipulate the data warehouse in order to provide on-line capabilities to analytically and geographically query the data and to visualize the results both on a grid and on a map.

3.1 Spatial Stereotypes

The OpenGIS Consortium (OGC) defines specifications to allow interoperability in the processing of geographical data. It provides the OpenGIS Geometric Object Model for the geographical universe. Any real geographical object can be modeled and represented. The same data type defined in the conceptual model will be used in the logical model and also in the database implementation with no transformation nor conversion of concepts.

We propose to model a DW integrating the dimensional and spatial concepts in a unique diagram. We use geographical stereotypes to represent the geographical classes and no stereotypes to represent conventional or non-geographical classes (such as the fact class).

The stereotype representation (1) simplifies diagrams, (2) keeps semantic wealth and (3) facilitates the coexistence of different domains concepts (in this case, analytical and geographical concepts). Figure 2 uses a stereotype to represent the association between the `River` dimension and the `LineString` hierarchy as an abbreviation of `LineString` extended hierarchy shown in Figure 1.

4. THE POSTGEOOLAP TOOL

As part of the GeoOlap project was proposed PostGeoOlap. It is a tool for creating spatial OLAP solutions on top of PostGreSQL DBMS and PostGIS, its spatial extension. The name PostGeoOlap was assigned because of the integration of geographical properties, OLAP technology and PostGreSQL.

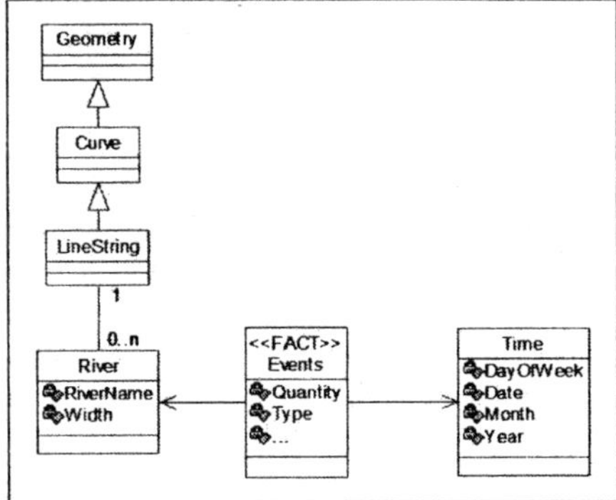

Figure 1. Association with an Extensive Hierarchy for the Dimension River

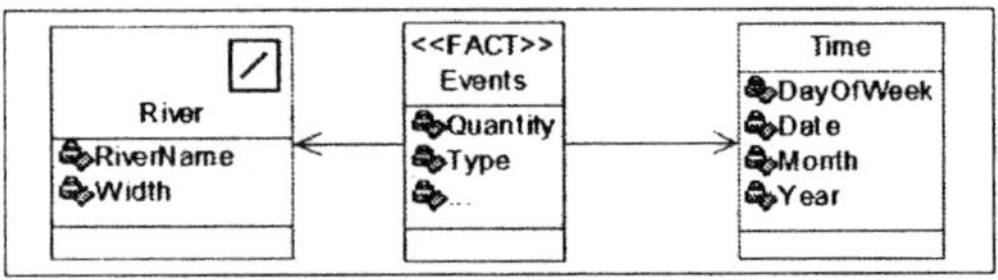

Figure 2. Stereotype to Represent the Association of River to LineString

PostGreSQL has PostGIS geographical extension, indispensable for this work. A feasibility study of PostGreSQL DBMS for data warehousing in Cunha [8] concludes that PostGreSQL version 7.4.x is not suitable for this kind of application. It mainly fails in the query optimizer and aggregation features. The current versions, 8.x, solves many of these negative aspects and has substantial improvements in the query optimizer. Recently, the BizGres initiative (yield by the PostGreSQL developers) works to make PostGreSQL a robust DBMS for Business Intelligence and data warehousing. The PostGeoOlap tool was approved by this initiative to provide OLAP functionalities to the BizGres project.

4.1 Design Principles

PostGeoOlap means to be a general-purpose tool for OLAP analysis of conventional and geographic data. We adopt the open-source and free software paradigm as project definition. The visualization classes and all APIs, frameworks and database software used in this project are open source. This plays an important role because it provides access to small and medium organizations to develop applications and to make use of data warehouse and GIS technologies, which have forbidding costs in their proprietary incarnations.

PostGeoOlap has adopted ROLAP as its data warehouse storing model to take advantage of the object-relational DBMS capabilities to store conventional and geographic information to use spatial and aggregate functions and to define new ones. Thus, both analytical and geographical queries are processed and answered by the PostgreSQL, and all data (from the base level to the aggregations) are kept in the relational model.

4.2 Main Goals

The main goals of PostGeoOlap are: (1) to provide to applications a mechanism to perform queries with analytical and geographic features on their data warehouses, and (2) to provide to application developers an easy-to-use GUI tool to build their decision support applications.

4.3 PostGeoOlap Metadata and Architecture

The metamodel in Figure 3 represents the metadata used by PostGeoOlap for the manipulation of the data maintained in the data warehouse. The Schema class represents the PostGreSQL database containing the DW. The `Cube` class represents each business perspective of data to be analyzed. The `Table` class represents all relations existing on data warehouse. The `Dimension` class is a subclass of `Table` and refers to all components of a cube (both the fact and dimension tables). The `Attribute` and `Field` class represents the data existing, respectively, in each dimension and table. The self-association indicates a conventional attribute as a label for a geographical one. The `Aggregation` class refers to the data aggregations implemented to improve the system performance. The `Hierarchy` class represents the several hierarchies for the attributes of a dimension. The `HierarchyItem` class allocates each attribute to a hierarchy.

The Figure 4 shows the architecture of the current implementation. PostGeoOlap is implemented in Java and it uses classes from the JUMP Unified Mapping Platform (JUMP) Java framework to perform visualization of maps and results of geographical queries. JUMP is a GUI application for presenting and processing spatial data. It has a number of functions for analysis and handling geospatial data. PostGeoOlap implementation utilizes the fact that JUMP exposes all its functionality for full programmatic access, including its map visualization classes. Other advantage of the use of JUMP is to provide a spatial object model compliant to OpenGIS Consortium specifications. This eliminates the need to map between them. The PostgreSQL representation of geographic data can be directly used as JUMP objects.

PostGeoOlap uses PostgreSQL to store the metadata, to make use of the standard spatial data types and to perform any standard SQL aggregation functions on the data (i.e. sum, max, min, avg, count) and all geographical functions defined by the OpenGIS Consortium (i.e. `touches`, `overlaps`, `crosses`, `distance`, `within`).

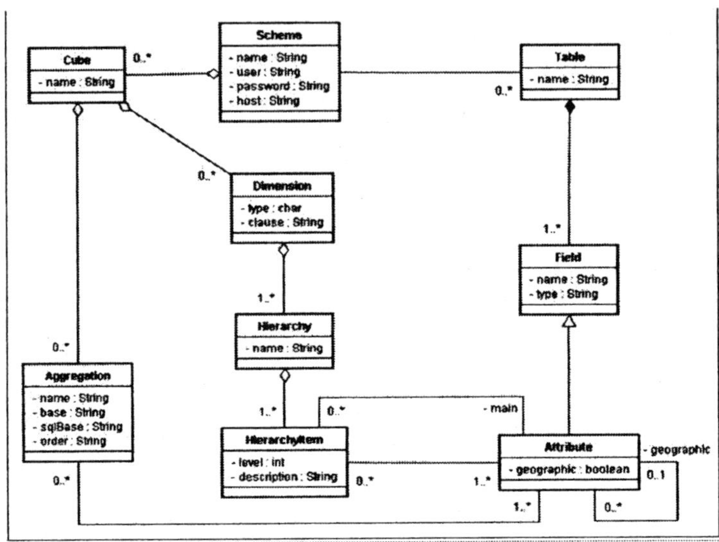

Figure 3. PostGeoOlap Metamodel

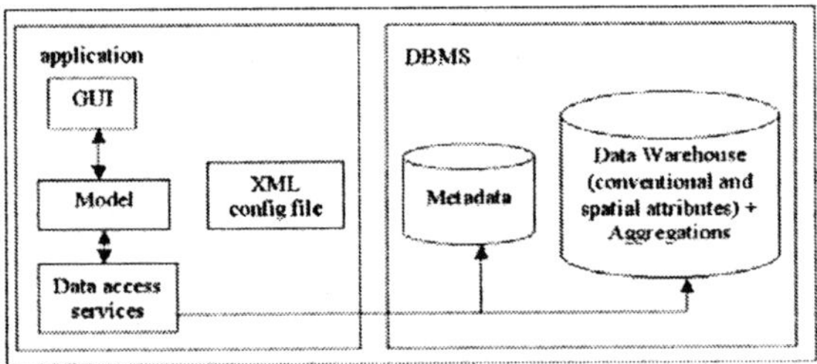

Figure 4. PostGeoOlap Architecture

4.4 PostGeoOlap Functionalities

Use cases are resumed as follows.

- *Create Schema*: creates a connection with a PostGreSQL database.
- *Create Cube*: creates a cube inside the schema selecting the fact table and defining its numeric items and the desired operations over these items.

- *Add Dimension*: creates a perspective for analysis of the data contained in the fact table, selecting one of the database tables. Defines the dimension hierarchy to allocate a level for each attribute. It deals with conventional data in the Fact table and with conventional or geographic data in the dimensions.
- *Process Cube*: verifies the mass of the stored data using the metadata and attempts to infer the query performance (execution time). The queries evaluated as low performance are optimized by aggregations. This involves the cube analysis under any perspective within reasonable time. During the cube processing, the tool always starts with the generation of aggregations of the highest perspective. That is, for each dimension the attributes must receive a hierarchy level, from 9 (less-aggregated information) to 1 (most-aggregated information). Many attributes can share the same hierarchy level.
- *Add Non-Aggregate Dimension*: a non-aggregate dimension is a dimension of geographical nature. It does not participate in the cube processing and it does not generate aggregations (so the name *non-aggregate*). The only purpose of non-aggregate dimensions is to serve as reference for comparisons with other geographical dimensions. The creation of non-aggregate dimensions is not a mandatory step in cube processing. There is no difference on adding non-aggregate dimensions before or after the cube processing.
- *Data Analysis*: provides an interface that allows the attributes selection for a query using conventional and/or geographic restrictions. It visualizes the query result as tables for analysis of non-spatial data and as maps for spatial data.

The `Create Schema`, `Create Cube` and `Add Dimension` functions build the structure of the cubes that will be verified and processed by PostGeoOlap.

4.5 Implementation Details: Cube Processing

Cube processing means the evaluation of the need of generation of aggregations to improve the performance of the queries. The big challenge faced by an OLAP tool is to obtain an acceptable performance of queries when the fact and dimension tables have a great amount of records. The cube-processing algorithm proposed in PostGeoOlap is:

```
Algorithm ProcessCube
   Input: FactAttributesCol: fact table attributes
          DimensionCol: collection of dimensions to be processed
   Begin
    DimCount=DimensionCol.Size // number of dimensions in aggregation
    Dimension1=DimensionCol[1] // Dimension instance
    LevelCount= minimum hierarchical level from Dimension1
    Dim1AttribCol= collection containing all attributes from Dimension1
    // create new stacks, adding to each one a level with the value from hierarchy
    Push 0 to NewStack //each stack is a sequence of elements at a level
    Add NewStack to StackCol          // StackCol: collection of stacks
    For i = LevelCount To 9       // LevelCount: number of levels
     NewStack = {}
```

```
  Push i to NewStack
  Add NewStack to StackCol
 End For
 While StackCol.Size <> 0
  Assigns last element from StackCol to ActiveStack and removes it from
     collection
  If ActiveStack.Size = DimCount //9 refers to the basic level of the DW
   If not (all levels are equal to 9) //executes the aggregation
    ProcessDimension(ActiveStack) //index, if cost-benefit is not worthless
   Else ActiveDimension = DimensionCol[ActiveStack.Size + 1]
  LevelCount = minimum hierarchical level from ActiveDimension
  Reset NewStack
  Copy to NewStack the contents of ActiveStack
  Push 0 to NewStack
  For j = LevelCount To 9
   Copy to NewStack the contents of ActiveStack
   Push j to NewStack
   Add NewStack to StackCol
  End For
 End While
End
```

After the definition of the schema and the cube, the tool processes the cube to check the execution performance. If the performance of a query falls below the predefined threshold, the OLAP tool creates a new aggregation structure represented by a table. The aggregation structure is performed in three steps: (1) creates the table containing the aggregated data, (2) puts the aggregated data into the new table, and (3) creates indexes for the new table (using B-Tree for conventional attributes and Generalized Search Trees - GiST - for the spatial ones).

A complex query can delay very seconds, minutes or even some hours to be executed, depending on the volume of data. To execute a query in an arbitrary acceptable lapse of time, it is necessary to create aggregations useful for the query. Cube processing analyzes the cost/benefit relation of creating new aggregation structures for each combination of levels in each hierarchy.

Considering a cube with four dimensions and supposing each letter is a hierarchical level for each dimension, we have a structure as shown in Figure 5. The first step is the creation of a stack structure whose elements are lists. Initially, for each level of the first dimension, one list containing the level is put on stack, as shown in Figure 6(a). While the stack is not empty, it pops the list from the top and checks if the number of elements in the list is equal to the number of dimensions (in this case, 4). In negative case, it is performed the combination of this list with each level in the next dimensions. It puts on the stack one list for each level in the (next) dimensions.

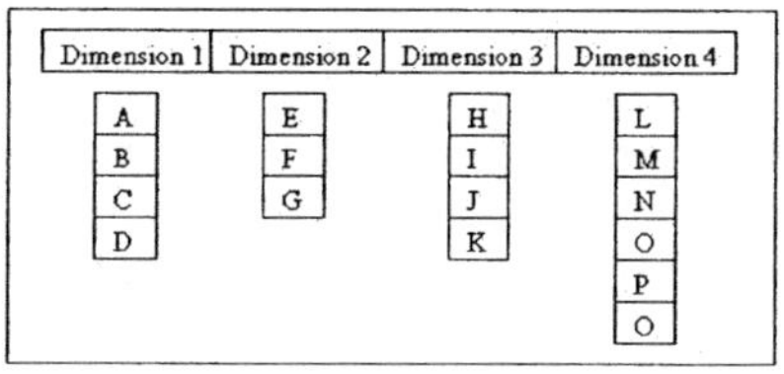

Dimension 1	Dimension 2	Dimension 3	Dimension 4
A	E	H	L
B	F	I	M
C	G	J	N
D		K	O
			P
			O

Figure 5. Dimensions to be Processed and Their hierarchic Levels

Figure 6(b) shows the second and third steps of the algorithm. The loop iterations guarantee all possible combinations for each list with the dimension levels. At the end, the number of elements in the list is equal to the number of dimensions and the element is ready to be submitted to cost/benefit analysis to generate (or not) a new aggregation structure.

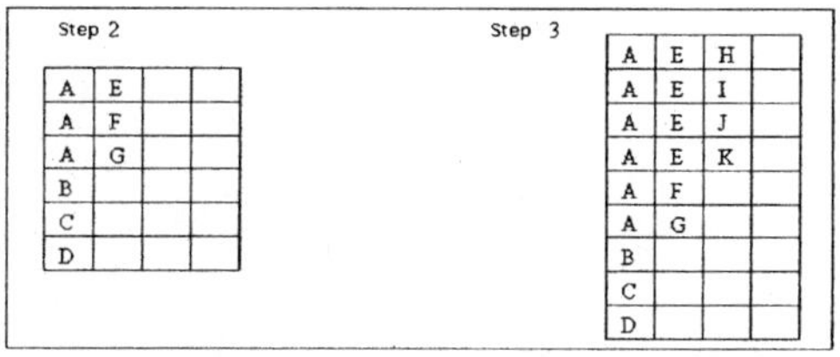

Step 2

A	E		
A	F		
A	G		
B			
C			
D			

Step 3

A	E	H	
A	E	I	
A	E	J	
A	E	K	
A	F		
A	G		
B			
C			
D			

Figure 6. (a) Initial Stack (b) The Second and Third Steps of the Cube-processing Algorithm

4.6 Case Study: Magazine Retailer

As a case study is presented a magazine retailer that distributes its products (newspapers and magazines) for sale to many stores geographically distributed along regions of Rio de Janeiro State. It's very important to answer questions like: *How much products are sold during the year of 2002 in 'Scientific Research' category and near to schools? (for example: 100 meters maximum).* In order to answer it, the model uses a point stereotype associated to store, a polygon stereotype for quarter. The reference point serves as a geographical reference to the store (schools at 100 meters maximum). The results are then presented in a spreadsheet frame, and the geographical ones are passed to a visualization component for displaying the objects in a map (as shown in Figure 7).

Once specified the attributes collection and constraints even conventional or geographical predicates, the tool starts the search for aggregations from the most to the less aggregated level. Consequently, the result aggregation will be the one with the smallest computational cost. Next, it submits the query and returns the results.

5. CONCLUSION

The motivation of this project is the lack of decision support tools that allow to model data integration natively. In GeoOlap, the unified model can be directly mapped into an application where GIS and OLAP functionalities are native. It also described PostGeoOlap, an open source general-purpose tool. The purpose is to ease the work of application implementors in the development of decision support applications. A real study case about a magazine retailer was described in order to validate the tool. PostGeoOlap shows its general purpose character. It demonstrates to be an easy-to-work tool to build DSS. At the current time, tests are being prepared to evaluate the performance potential of PostGeoOlap and future work includes optimization issues at cube processing. The PostGeoOlap project is available at http://pgfoundry.org/projects/postgeoolap.

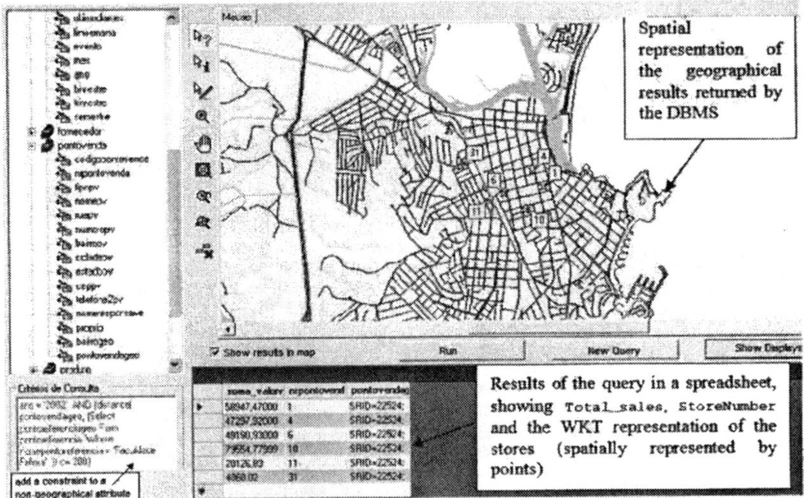

Figure 7. Query Results

REFERENCES

1. Z. Kouba, K. Matouek, and P. Mikovsk, On Data Warehouse and GIS integration, in *Proc. of the IEEE International Conference on DEXA'2000* (Greenwich, London, UK, 2000).
2. A. Ferreira, M. Campos, and A. Tanaka, *An architecture for spatial and dimensional analysis integration*, in *Proc. of World Multiconference on Systemics, Cybernetics and Informatics (SCI), volume XIV Computer Science Engineering. Part II* (2001).

3. R. Fidalgo, V. Times, and F. Souza, Golapa: Uma arquitetura aberta e extensível para integração entre SIG e OLAP, in *Proc. of III Brasilian Workshop of Geoinformática*, Instituto Militar de Engenharia, Rio de Janeiro (2001).
4. N. Stefanovic, J. Han, and K. Koperski, Selective materialization: An efficient method for spatial data cube construction, in *Proc. of the 7th International Symposium on Advances in Spatial and Temporal Databases* (ACM Records, 2001).
5. D. Papadias, P. Kalnis, J. Zhang, and Y. Tao, Efficient OLAP operations in spatial data warehouses, *Lecture Notes in Computer Science*. Volume 21, (2001).
6. G. Colonese,*Uma ferramenta aberta de desenvolvimento integrado de sistemas de informação para processamento analítico e geográfico,* Master's Thesis, Universidade Candido Mendes, Campos dos Goytacazes/RJ, Brazil (2004).
7. J. Trujillo, M. Palomar, J. Gomez, and I.-Y. Song, Designing data warehouses with OO conceptual models, *IEEE Computer*. Volume 34, Number 12, pp.66-75, (2001).
8. E. Cunha and M.S. Sunye, Benchmarking PostgreSQL for data warehousing, in *Proc. of the IADIS International Conference on Applied Computing, IADIS* (Algarve, Portugal, 2005), pp.185-192.

An Information System Integration Method Based on Controllable Genetic Algorithm

Geying Liang and Zongjian Tang

College of Mathematics and Information Science, Guangxi University, Nanning 530004, P.R. China lgy2680@163.com tang2680@tom.com

Abstract. The essential for an enterprise to construct an information system is to integrate the information system with the legacy system. We introduce a biological genetic controllable method into the process of information system integration, and apply self-adaptive genetic algorithm to simulate the process of information system integration. By controlling the original population and the transformation of gene, we can find an optimal integrating effect and an information system integration method.

Keywords: *Information system integration, Genetic algorithm, Genetic controllable, Self-adaptive*

1. INTRODUCTION

When a modern enterprise is to construct an information system, its essential is to integrate the information system with the original system of the enterprise. The objective is to introduce information technology and information system to the enterprise operation process, to raise its efficiency and effectiveness, gain the competition advantage. Because there are many factors influencing the information system integration process, and there are many uncertain factors in the process, the enterprise often can not predict the integration effect. Specially, the enterprise can't know what information system match with it in selection model of information system. Therefore, this paper applies the biological genetic controllable method, from the point of information system integrating with the original system of an enterprise, searches a way to integrate information system.

2. DESCRIPTION OF THE OBJECTIVE OF INFORMATION SYSTEM INTEGRATION

To integrate information system is a complex social-technology system project. In the process of implementing information system integration, people will consider many factors. (1)The objectives of organization, organization structure, business process, human resource, information technology. (2)Information system functions,

Please use the following format when citing this chapter:

Liang, G., Tang, Z., 2007, in IFIP International Federation for Information Processing, Volume 254, Research and Practical Issues of Enterprise Information Systems II Volume 1, eds. L. Xu, Tjoa A., Chaudhry S. (Boston: Springer), pp. 371-376.

performance, structure, and management ideas contain in the information system. (3) How to fully utilize various resources existing in the organization? (4) How to coordinate resources, so that the organization can raise the efficiency and benefit? Except these, the enterprise hopes the cost of information system integration is the lowest. So the objectives of information system integration can be expressed as below.

Suppose in the process of information system integration, the original state of the system is $X = (x_1, x_2, \cdots, x_m)$, m is the number of factors that people will consider in the process of information system integration. $x_i (i = 1, 2, \cdots m)$ is the state of the *i th* factor in the original system, the range of value is the integer in [0,7], its value expresses the degree of the factor realizing the expected system objective, *0* expresses not realizing the expected objective of the system, 7 expresses realizing the expected objective of the system completely. Different factors have different effect degrees to the information system integration, we can adopt expert evaluation method to give the value of weight $a_i (i = 1, 2, \cdots, m)$, a_i expresses the factor x_i effect degree to original system status, $a_i > 0$ and $a_1 + a_2 + \cdots + a_m = 1$.

Suppose the state of realized information system, for example the commercial information system, can be expressed by $Y = (y_1, y_2, \cdots, y_m)$, $y_i (i = 1, 2, \cdots m)$ coincides with x_i factor of original system, the range of value is the integer in [0,7], its value expresses the degree of the factor realizing the expected system objective, 0 expresses not realizing the expected objective of the system, 7 expresses realizing the expected objective of the system completely. Different factors have different effect degrees to the information system integration, we can adopt expert evaluation method to give the value of weight $b_i (i = 1, 2, \cdots, m)$, b_i expresses the factor y_i effect degree to information system state, $b_i > 0$ and $b_1 + b_2 + \cdots + b_m = 1$.

The process of information system integration is to coordinate information system with original system, and produce a new system $Z = (z_1, z_2, \cdots, z_m)$, $z_i = (a_i x_i + b_i y_i)/2$. The effect degree to the new system of z_i is $\theta_i (i = 1, 2, \cdots m)$, and we use expert evaluation method to set the value of θ_i, $\theta_i > 0$ and $\theta_1 + \theta_2 + \cdots + \theta_m = 1$. In the case of not considering interaction of factors, the benefit objective of the information system integration in the organization is

$$MaxZ, Z = \sum_{i=1}^{m} \theta_i (a_i x_i + b_i y_i) \tag{1}$$

In order to realize the objective of informization, it needs to reconstruct the original system, and adjust the status of information system in the process of an organization implementing information system integration. To get z_i , the cost coefficient is $c_i (i = 1, 2, \cdots m)$, $c_i \geq 0$ and $c_1 + c_2 + \cdots + c_m = 1$. Then, the cost objective of the information system integration in the enterprise is:

$$MinC, C = \sum_{i=1}^{m} c_i z_i \tag{2}$$

This is a multi-objective problem [2]. Considering that different organization have different preference to benefit and cost, set benefit preference is $\alpha (\alpha > 0)$, cost preference is $\beta(\beta > 0)$, and $\alpha + \beta = 1$, synthesize (1) and (2) to construct an object function,

$$MaxQ, Q = \alpha Z - \beta C \tag{3}$$

3. THE PROCESS OF USING GENETIC ALGORITHM TO IMPLEMENTING INFORMATION SYSTEM INTEGRATION

In the process of information system integration, original system and information system will adjust continually in the process of informization, matching with each other. According to this characteristic, we adopt self-adaptive genetic algorithm to solve the problems in the process of evolution. We don't use random approach to define the original population, apply expert assess approach to produce the population of original system and the population of information system, and apply XOR algorithm to make a match randomly between the two populations and get the prime population at the beginning of genetic algorithm. This can acquire the prime population corresponding with actuality, and enhance the efficiency of evolution.

3.1 The Code of Problem

This problem will adopt the method of binary code. According to the basic principal of genetic algorithm, every factor effecting on the process of information system can be expresses as a gene. The sequence of gene is decided by the project preference sequence, a_i and b_i. Every gene can be represented by 3 bits, and can get the any integer value between [0, 7]. Therefore, $X = x_1x_2 \ldots x_{m-1}x_m$, $Y = y_1y_2 \cdots y_{m-1}y_m$, the length of gene-string is $l = 3m$.

3.2 The Design of Fitness

The formula (3) is a problem of evaluating maximum, so design a fitness function as below:

$$F = \alpha Z - \beta C + \lambda \tag{4}$$

In the formula (4), λ is a proper small number, when $\alpha Z - \beta C + \lambda \leq 0$, $F = 0$.

3.3 The Design of Genetic Operator

3.3.1 Selection Operators

Suppose the size of population is N, sort on the adaptive values descending, adopt excellent individual proportion-conservation strategy, that is, set a proper ratio, such as $d = 0.1$, let the front dN individuals as the next generation individuals, choose the left individuals to next generation according to roulette wheel method, until the sum of individuals is N.

3.3.2 Crossover Operators and Mutation Operators

In the self-adaptive genetic algorithm [3], the probability of individual crossover and the probability of mutation are not constant, they are adjusted by the fitness of individual, crossover operator and mutation operator are decided by whether the individual fitness is larger than average fitness. If the larger fitness f is less than the average fitness f_{avg} between two individuals which execute crossover operation, the probability of crossover between the two individual are equal and are constant values. If the larger fitness f is larger than the average fitness f_{avg} between two individuals which execute crossover operation, adjust the probability of crossover as below: the probability of crossover is the function of the max fitness $f_{\max}$ and the min fitness $f_{\min}$. And the self-adaptive crossover probability P_c can be represented as below:

$$P_c = \begin{cases} P_{c0}\,, & f \le f_{avg} \\ P_{c1} + \dfrac{f_{\max} - f}{f_{\max} - f_{\min}}(P_{c0} - P_{c1})\,, & f > f_{avg} \end{cases} \tag{5}$$

In formula (5), P_{c0} is a larger probability of crossover, P_{c1} is a less probability of crossover, and $P_{c0} > P_{c1}$. That is, the individual that has a less fitness will adopt a larger probability of crossover, so that it can evolve more rapidly. But the individual that has a larger fitness will adopt a less probability of crossover, so that it can keep on its excellence characteristics.

The self-adaptive probability of mutation P_m can be represented as below:

$$P_m = \begin{cases} P_{m0}\,, & f' \le f_{avg} \\ P_{m1} + \dfrac{f_{\max} - f'}{f_{\max} - f_{\min}}(P_{m0} - P_{m1})\,, & f' > f_{avg} \end{cases} \tag{6}$$

In formula (6), f' is the individual fitness which execute the mutation operation, P_{m0} is a larger probability of mutation, P_{m1} is a less probability of mutation, and $P_{m0} > P_{m1}$. That is, the individual that has less fitness will adopt the larger probability of mutation, and the individual that has larger fitness will adopt the less probability of mutation, that can ensure multiformity of population, and overcome the premature convergence of the algorithm.

4. THE DESIGN OF GENETIC ALGORITHM

Step 1: N experts will evaluate X and Y respectively, and get 2N individuals. Match individual among X with individual among Y according to the random principal, the two matching individual will adopt simple XOR operation at the same position to get the new value. For example, X=101101010011, Y=100110011010, than the value of new individual is 001011001001. Through this approach, get N individual as original population. Let the iterative number of generation $t=1$, and the crossover point $k=1$.

Step 2: If the iterative number of generation t is larger than the max iterative number of generation, go to step 5, otherwise go to step 3. If $k>m$, then $k=1$.

Step 3: Calculate the fitness of each individual and the average fitness of all individual according to formula (4), and sort individuals on the value of fitness, select dN individuals in front of the population as next generation individual. Use roulette wheel approach to select two individuals among the left individuals to match crossover according to P_c, that is execute crossover operation on gene chromosome in the $k\ th$ group. Then execute mutation operation to the new individual according to P_m.

Step 4: $t=t+1$, $k=k+1$, go to step 2.

Step 5: Take the optimal individual as the optimal solution, the algorithm is over.

5. CONCLUSIONS

Because there are many factors influencing the information system integration process, and there are many uncertain factors in the process, the enterprise often can not predict the integration effect. This paper put forward a controllable self-adaptive genetic algorithm. By controlling the original population and cross point in the genetic process, it simulates the process of information system integration, and attain to the optimal effect of information system integration.

REFERENCES

1. M. Zhou and S. Sun, *Genetic Algorithms: Theory and Applications* (National Defense Industry Press: Beijing, Beijing, 2005).
2. C.A. Coello, An Updated Survey of GA-based Multi-objective Optimization Techniques, *ACM Computing Surveys*. Volume 32, Number 2, pp.109-143, (2000).

3. L. Tong, Z. Chen, Z. Yuan, and L. An, A Double Population Self-adaptive Genetic Algorithm for Partner Selection of Virtual Enterprise, *Computer Engineering*. Volume 32, Number 8, pp.192-194, (2006).
4. G. Chen and X. Kuan, The Information System Security Technology Scheme Based on Genetic Algorithm, *Journal of National University of Defense Technology*. Volume 27, Number 6, pp.130-134, (2005).

A Study on Workflow Resource Management Based on Workflow Net and Agent

Xiang Chen and Xinglin Li

School of Management and Economics, Beijing Institute of Technology, Beijing 100081, P.R. China chengxiang@bit.edu.cn lxl_1022@sohu.com

Abstract. At present, the resource modeling of workflow net (WF-net) are too simple to describe complex workflow. Thus, its application is not satisfying in practical use. Based on the analysis of resource management problems, unified resources management which gets the identical resource request and release process is proposed. The method of identical resource-modeling reduces complexity of WF-net model. Based on colored Petri net, this paper proposes colored WF-net, which is easy to control and computerize. Furthermore, the design of unified resources manage is carried on using the Agent technology, and a method that transforms process definition of WF-net into abstract structure of Agent is produced. By using the appliance character of Agent technology, the method also provides feasibility for unified resources management.

Keywords: *Workflow net (WF-net), Workflow model, Colored Petri net, Agent, Workflow resource management, Business process analysis*

1. INTRODUCTION

As a key technology for modern enterprises to realize the process management and process control, workflow provides an integrated framework of modeling, management and operation for enterprise business process [1]. Currently, there are a variety of technologies can be used for workflow modeling, and the workflow net (WF-net) theory based on Petri net[2]is one of them. This theory describes and analyzes complex workflow system model from the perspective of process [3, 4], but the model it built is insufficient in resource management, expression ability and application. SchoSmig and Gong Shi-hao and others established business process model based on Colored Petri net [5, 6]. This model overcame the problem of the expression ability, but can not use the method of performance analysis and structural analysis related with WF-net. Needs to be pointed out is that the current workflow models based on Petri net neglect the modeling of resource——an important dimension in workflow, so it will be very difficult to be applied in practical application. In the application aspect, because of independence, cooperation, communication and consultation, ratiocination and other abilities and characteristics [7], Agent is more and more used in workflow management system [8]. However, Agent-based workflow system has deficiencies in process description and inspection of process structure. Based on the research results above, through analyzing the problems of workflow model based on Petri net, we can see that resource Modeling

Please use the following format when citing this chapter:

Chen, X., Li, X., 2007, in IFIP International Federation for Information Processing, Volume 254, Research and Practical Issues of Enterprise Information Systems II Volume 1, eds. L. Xu, Tjoa A., Chaudhry S. (Boston: Springer), pp. 377-387.

can be adopted to solve the problems of the traditional WF-net. Further, this paper presents the uniform resource management and colored WF-net. Finally, this paper introduces Agent technology into the workflow resource management to enhance existing workflow management system function, and it also discusses the workflow modeling systems based on Petri net and the realization project of Agent-based resource management, ordering to eliminate the gap of the theory and practice and to pave the way for practical application.

2. WORKFLOW NET RESOURCES MODELING

WF-net [6, 2] presented by Aalst and others is the workflow model based on Petri net, which is studied extensively now. It builds workflow model by mapping the workflow reference model to the Petri net, and uses transition represent activity ,place represent the condition which fires activity (if activity need to use some resources), and token represent case to build Petri net model of workflow.

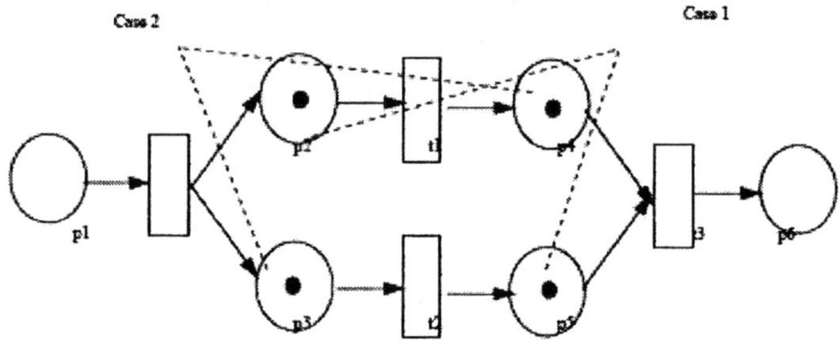

Figure 1. Example of Handling Multi-cases

This traditional WF-net is legible in description of the static workflow model, but in the control of operation process, especially when multi-cases are in the WF-net, there are some problems. Firstly, the workflow model in the course of operation needs to resolve two problems, one is path selection of the uncertainty activity, and another is application for the roles in the resource manager. Both of two problems in the actual operation course of workflow are dynamic, and the traditional WF-net has been unable to resolve them. Secondly, the workflow model in the course of operation needs to run multiple cases, and an instance may appear that two cases start and run two parallel activities simultaneously. As shown in figure 1, Workflow needs to handle a number of cases at one time, and each case has one or more tokens in the model, if considering the delay in the actual system, all tokens will mix together and come into confusion. For example, case 1 and case 2 have access to the model successively. Case 1 did not reach p4 because of the delay t1, but have arrived p5 via t2. Meanwhile, case 2 arrived p3, p4, at this time T4 was in activated state, if consuming token is according to first-in first-out principle, or in accordance with the random principle, then there could be a situation that token of case 1 in p5 is consumed and the token of case 2 in p4 fires t3, all appearance, it is not wish to see this result in the model. Thirdly, in the traditional WF-net model, a state or condition of each object is expressed as a place, and each change or event is express as a transition, but the dynamic character of workflow determines that it has a larger state space. This will make practical application system has more crunodes, which will limit model to be computerized.

In fact, the problem of path selection can be attributed to that: choosing different path is according to different resources. Problem of disordered cases and the large state space can be summed up as that: how to distinguish the states of resources in cases. Thus, the key to solve the problems above is to solve problems of management and resource modeling in the model.

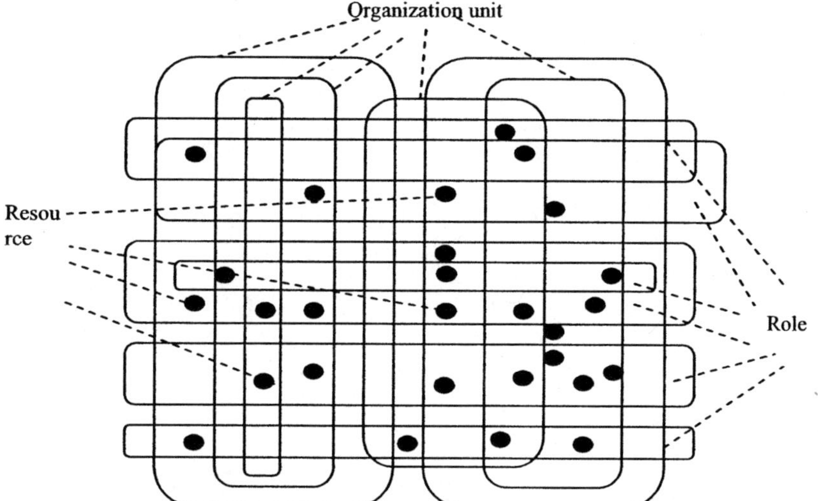

Figure 2. Relation of Organization Unit, Role and Resource

Resource Modeling is the static management of resource information, which is basis of resource allocation in the workflow operation environment. Resource is the implementing entities of task. It is used to analyze composition of Workflow from two logic levels: task logic and organization logic. The former logic reflects the handling process of task——the process definition mentioned above. The latter one reflects the organization structure and relationship inside enterprise. These two logic levels integrate together through the organization strategy. This strategy mechanism is in short that: "which must be executed by whom". It shields the realization of behavior activities, and makes the change of flow divide from individual behavior change, thus enhancing the distribution, flexibility and virtual degree of workflow process.

Resource can be classified in accordance with the function itself, the same type such as printing devices and checkers could be put in one organizational unit, and completes the task by resources which are obtained from the resource class by roles, thus, the resource share will be realized between roles in the model, which increases the flexibility of the model. Moreover, the roles and organization units will organize resources as the orthogonal relationship as shown in Figure 2. Because the activity is fulfilled by the role, therefore, the examination of initiatory state of each activity is to be the fire mechanism of application for roles, and the completion of activity as the fire mechanism of role demobilization. In this way, a whole process of demand of resources is found in the model, from task execution, to role application, to resource distribution, to role demobilization and then to resource release.

Currently, majority of the workflow models integrate organizational factors in the flow. But according to the above analysis, flow should be three-dimensional structure, which contains participant, role and the process. However, process is based on the cases, it is not very suitable to regard resources as a part of the flow. Therefore, we can consider dividing resources from the process as an independent part, which is unified resource manager for resource management. Thus, flow can be seen as the client port in the client / server architecture, which proposes resource request to the server port——resource manager in the course of checking the initiatory conditions of activity, and determines whether to begin activities according to whether resource manager returns resources or not.

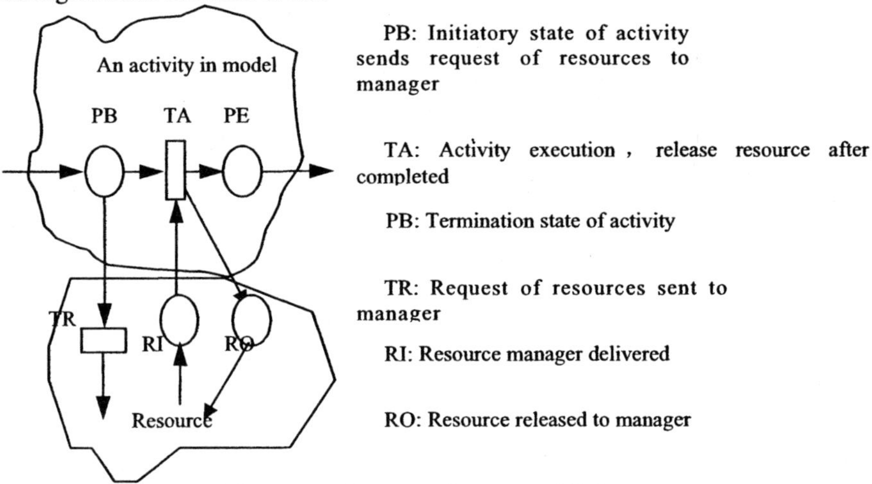

Figure 3. Processes of Resource Request and Release

We build resource manager model for representing the relationship above, as shown in figure 3. Every activity in WF-net will request and release resources through resource manager. When starts an activity, at beginning, PB proposes resource requests to TR——the resource manager application interface, and the request outputs token to the resource request place for firing through TR——the fire transition. Resource manager allocates appropriate resources by the resource allocation arithmetic, and these resources access to the public interface RI in the form of token. Activity TA gains resource tokens from RI, these tokens start and complete activities, which will release resources to RO——resource token collection interface, and recover by unified resource manager at last. For each activity in the model, the process of using, releasing and accessing to resources is consistent, and they only exchange data with three public interfaces, so it is not necessary to describe them in the model.

Dividing the resource modeling from the WF-net reduces its complexity, and compared with the models based on Petri net other scholars established, this model has a better corresponding relationship with the actual workflow ,it is more simple and easier to understand, furthermore, it simplifies the model, which makes the model more easily computerized.

3. COLORED WF-NET

Based on the advantages of expression capacity of Colored Petri net, we can endue WF-net that has a basic flow structure with attribute by coloring the WF-net, making it express more meanings, easier to achieve a feature-rich analysis and application software through computer.

Therefore, the token color set $C(p)$ defined in place p represents the attribute set of cases in the state of p . This set can be divided into two parts. One is called parameter information, which is for recording operating results and operating process control. Parameter is set as case number, activity types can be fired, type and number of resource requirement and other execution attributes of task. Record of case number possesses the operation identifier of the case in work flow. This identifier is the only one to distinguish cases. Activity type can be fired could record that which transition type can be fired by the place at current state, for the path choosing. Resource type is description of the resource. Another part is called description information, it is used to distinguish different objects, such as contract number, contract type and the latest completion dates of a contract and so on, which can be handled in different way according to the different workflow process and cases.

Token color set $C(t)$ defined on transition t represents the color set that $\exists p \in {}^{*}t, C(p)_{MS}$ must include when t could be fired. It is generally composed by three colors: case number, type and number of resource requirement and activity type. The meaning of the first two colors are consistent with the meaning in the place, activity type designates the category of the activity.

Increasing these colors can enhance interpretation capacity of the original model, rich meaning of model, and increase demands of workflow activity and state transfer modeling. Because color parameters can be added appropriately according to different models, therefore the expansible capacity of model strengthens as well. Based on process operation control in the color definition, it can resolve the problem of uncertainty activity modeling and resource application / release by defined a negative / positive correlation function. Defines the color set resolving these two problems as:

$Jobs = \{J_1, J_2, ..., J_J\}$ Activity type

$NO = \{1,2,........n\}$ Case number

$RS = \{R_1, R_2, ..., R_M\}$ Resource requirement type

Defines the color combination as (see the sigh of place and transition as shown in figure 2):

$C(PB) = Jobs \times NO \times RS$ Color combination of activity in initiatory state, RS is resource needed.

$C(PE) = Jobs \times NO$ Color combination of activity after releasing resource at termination condition

$C(TA) = Jobs \times NO \times RS$ Color combination of activity (transition)

$C(RI) = Jobs \times NO \times RS$ Resource applied from resource manager

Define $R = \{R_1, R_2, ... R_R\}$ as set of roles in resource manager, so negative / positive correlation function is defined as:

$$\forall R_r, R_s \in R, \forall J_k, J_l \in Jobs, \forall N_n, N_m \in NO :$$

$$I_+(PB, TR)((J_k, N_m, R_s), R_r) = \begin{cases} 1 & \text{if} \quad R_r = R_s \\ 0 & \text{then} \end{cases} \tag{1}$$

$$I_+(RI, TA)((J_k, N_m, R_s), (J_l, N_n, R_r)) = \begin{cases} 1 \text{ if } J_k = J_l, N_m = N_n, R_r = R_s \\ 0 \quad\quad \text{then} \end{cases} \tag{2}$$

$$I_+(PB, TA) = I_{|C(PB)|} = I_{|C(TA)|} = \begin{pmatrix} 1 & & 0 \\ & \cdots & \\ 0 & & 1 \end{pmatrix} \tag{3}$$

$$I_{-}(RO, TA)(R_r, (J_k, N_m, R_s)) = \begin{cases} 1 & \text{if } R_r = R_s \\ 0 & \text{then} \end{cases} \tag{4}$$

$$I_{-}(PE, TA) = I_{|C(PE)|} = I_{|C(TA)|} = \begin{pmatrix} 1 & & 0 \\ & \cdots & \\ 0 & & 1 \end{pmatrix} \tag{5}$$

Formula 1 represents that model applies resources from resource manager, which are required by the initiatory conditions. Formula 2 represents that the activity could be executed when there are conformable resources in resource manager for the case and activity. Formula 3 represents that the set of resources initiatory condition need to apply is consistent with the set of resources that is needed by transition. Formula 4 represents that activities release resources to resource manager, the released resources must be the ones using when activities were executed. This will solve the role application / release problem. Formula 5 represents that the set of releasing resources in terminated conditions is consistent with the set of resources used by transition. One side, Formula 2 and 3 shows that tokens of the various places in the initiatory state must be in the same case number and the same activity type, only in that way, they can work together to fire the transition, which would resolve the chaotic situation when process multi-cases. The other side, at the initiatory state color Jobs choose the activity could be fired， and all places linked with the activity must choose the type of activities consistent with it, thus, the activity can be fired. This way resolves the problem of the modeling of the uncertainty activities.

Here， define the WF-net add to colors as the colored WF-net:

Definition 1 An Colored WF-net is a seven-tuples

$W = (P, T, F, C, I_{-}, I_{+}, i)$:

1） P, T, F, i accord with the definition of WF-net[3,6];

2） C, I_{-}, I_{+} in the precondition of definition of colored Petri net， its control part is as noted above .

4. AGENT-BASED COLORED WF-NET RESOURCE MANAGEMENT

As a groupware system, Workflow Management System has some similar characteristics with the Agent system. They are all distributed cooperative work system, and all need to have the self-adaptive and self-automatic and other characteristics. Therefore, the Agent system is very fit for workflow management system, in particular the design of distributed workflow control structure.

In application, using Agent can effectively solve resources confliction, mode petrifaction in execution and other issues in workflow. Therefore, we can use Agent technology to establish a unified resource manager. In the Agent-based workflow management, each resource in organization structure (including person, equipment and database, etc.) is in connection with an Agent.

According to different functions Agent achieves, it can be divided into the following three categories:

Task Agent: Its main function is to explain the workflow process definition, operation states of cases in control process.

Resource Agent: It is connected with the resources to be allocated in workflow.

Role disclaimer Agent: It is for organization, and it ensures to make reasonable arrangements for human resources, constitute the best mode of appointment of personnel.

According to the assume based on separation of resource management and process management , the further work is to transform WF-net process definition and execution process into the abstract structure Agent can cognize, and complete coordination and control of resources in workflow through the interaction, response and coordination mechanism of Agent. Firstly defines the Agent in unified resource manager.

Definitions 2 Agent in resource manager is formally to represent as a entity descript by a five- tuples set, namely $Agent =< N, I, E, Ac, K >$, of which:

1) N is the unique name or logo of Agent and can describe the type of Agent.

2) I is interface definition of Agent, which descript human-computer interface and communication interface(including communication protocol and I/O) shown in front of the user, generally following the principle that interface separates with the Agent function.

3) $E = \{e, e',...\}$ is the state set of Agent, which describes internal state of Agent, behaviors of Agent is actually the process transferred from one state to another state.

4) $Ac = \{\alpha, \alpha',...\}$ is Services set of Agent, defining behaviors , embodying the functions, and containing reasoning mechanism of Agent.

5) K is knowledge origin of Agent, describing knowledge, data, inference rules and the reflective resources behaviors of Agent needed, such as data structure, database (and Knowledge Base),etc.

On the state $E = \{e, e',...\}$ of execution of the workflow, it is the limited set of the discrete and instantaneous state. $Ac = \{\alpha, \alpha',...\}$ is the (limited) action set. WF-net uses P short for place and T short for transition. Therefore, the state set E of Agent and P can establish one-to-one correspondence, namely: $E \Leftrightarrow P$. The same as the action set Ac of Agent and T , namely: $Ac \Leftrightarrow T$.

The basic model of Agent action is as follows, starting from a certain state, Agent chooses an action to act on the state. The result of action is a certain state the environment may reach. However, only one state can be truly realized, of course, Agent does not know in advance which state will be realized. Base on the second state, Agent keeps on choosing an action to execute, which may reach a centralized state. Then, Agent will choose another action, so continue. Therefore, an execution r of Agent is a sequence that the state and action are alternate:

$$r : e_0 \xrightarrow{\alpha_0} e_1 \xrightarrow{\alpha_1} e_2 \xrightarrow{\alpha_2} e_3 \xrightarrow{\alpha_3} \ldots \xrightarrow{\alpha_{u-1}} e_u$$

The action model of Agent has similar characteristics with fire sequence used as WF-net model, and mapping relations can be established between them. Presumed that R is finite sequences set of all possibility, and then can think that R has corresponding mapping relationship with coverable tree of WF-net.

For the point that how Ac define the action of Agent, assume that R^E is the subset of R composed by sequence with end state, import a Agent model, which represents a function, mapping an execution to the action:

$$Ag : R^E \rightarrow AC$$

Thus, Agent decides which action will be executed according to the current system situation. For resources management:

Definitions 3: $Agent\ Ag$ is seen as a three-tuples set, $Ag =< see, action, next >$, Of which :

$see : E \rightarrow Per$, which maps a state to an apperceive. Apperceive of workflow comes from that whether there is a corresponding role to execute activity, and obtains adequate resources, which can be acquired through cooperating with the Resource Agent and the Role disclaimer Agent. Reflecting to the WF-net, it is that the corresponding place gets or losts the corresponding token and it takes the function as the mapping of mark $see : P \rightarrow IN$. For example, place n gets token on M', so $M'(p_n) = M'(p_n) + 1$.

$action : I \rightarrow Ac$, I is the set of all states inside Agent, $action$ defines the mapping from internal states to actions. For WF-net, I can be thought as the current mark, and the mapping from state to action can be defined as fire rule, namely $action : M \rightarrow M'$, defined as $M' = M + N\vec{\sigma}, if \exists \sigma, M', M[\sigma > M'$, of which σ is transition sequence.

$next : I \times Per \rightarrow I$, achieve the mapping from the internal states to their perception. It is still the change of mark for WF-net, namely $next : M \times P \rightarrow M$.

Agent behavior can be summarized as follows:

Agent begins with a certain initial internal state i_0, observes the environment e, and has a perception $see(e)$, then updates the internal state of Agent through the $next$ function, finally turns into $next(i_0, see(e))$. Agent chooses actions by $action(next(i_0, see(e)))$. Working out this action makes Agent enter anther circle, keeping on apperceiving world outside via see, updating states by $next$, choosing actions to implement through $action$.

Other Agent reasoning mechanism, the application of knowledge and interface definition is unique characteristics of intelligent and interactive of Agent, which WF-net doesn't have, and that is the main reason why introduced the Agent formally also. Existing research results of Agent can be continued to use. Thus, we establish mapping of the main elements in basic Petri net and the abstract structure of Agent, so that Agent can cognize the process definition and execution process of WF-net.

5. CONCLUSIONS

This paper focus on solving problems of resource management modeling and application in workflow, and divides resource management from the WF-net model as a uniform resource manager, reduces the difficulty of establishing WF-net modeling, increases the readability of the WF-net. Colored Petri net is introduced to enhance the expression of the model, and solves problem that in the actual operation control, the basic model is difficult to decide dynamic path and may arise the confusion when deal with a number of cases at the same time, which makes model has a very strong adaptability. Meanwhile, this model includes an integrated set of concept, a corresponding representation and the necessary rules, which provide a more comprehensive model framework for expressing workflow abstractly. Based on the model, transforms process definition and execution process of WF-net into the abstract structure that Agent can cognize, enables unified resource manager can be combined with Agent, eliminated contradiction of the theory and application. However, the establishment of workflow model also involves the problems such as data sharing and performance analysis, etc. These are pending further study.

ACKNOWLEDGEMENTS

Foundation item: Project supported by the National Natural Science Foundation, China (Grant No. 70502021)

REFERENCES

1. *Workflow Management Coalition* (John Wiley and Sons: New York, 1997).
2. W.M.P. Van Der Aalst, Three Good reasons for Using a Petri-net-based Workflow Management System, *Information and Process Integration in Enterprises: Rethinking documents*, eds. T. Wakayama (Kluwer Academic Publishers: Norwell, 1998), pp.161-182.
3. X. Chen and G. Xia, Workflow modeling based on colored Petri nets and its soundness analysis, *Computer Integrated Manufacturing Systems*. Volume 10, Number 4, pp.381-487, (2004).
4. W.M.P. Van Der Aalst, The application of Petri nets to workflow Management, *The Journal of Circuits, Systems and Computers*. Volume 8, Number 1, pp.21-66, (1998).

5. A. SchoSmig and H. Rau, *A Petri Net Approach for the Performance Analysis of Business Processes*, Research Report Series 116, Institute of Computer Science, University of Wurzburg (1995).
6. S. Gong, J. Yang, Y. Chai, and M. Li, Business Process Modeling Based on Colored Petri nets, *Information and Control*. Volume 29, Number 1, pp.1-5, (2000).
7. K. Sycara and A. Pannu, Distributed Intelligent Agent, *IEEE Expert*. Volume12, pp.36-46, (1996).
8. J.W. Shepherdson, S.G. Thompson, and B.R. Odgers, *Cross Organizational Workflow Co-ordinate by Software Agent* (Oct. 19, 2000). http://www.zurich.ibm.com/hlu/WACCworkshop/papers/Shepherdson/

Analysis of the Interaction Design for Mobile TV Applications Based on Multicriteria

Ana Lisse Carvalho, Marília Mendes, Plácido Pinheiro and Elizabeth Furtado

University of Fortaleza (UNIFOR), Graduate in Applied Computer Science (MIA), Av. Washington Soares, 1321 - Fortaleza, Ceará, Brazil
{ana.lisse, marilia}@edu.unifor.br {placido, elizabet}@unifor.br

Abstract. Since mobile TV represents a new paradigm for interaction design, many different candidate solutions of interaction can be possible. There is not yet any work that explores how to consider the users' experience with technology to analyze the best solution(s) to the interaction design of a mobile TV application. This report brings an experience about what criteria addressing users' experience influence designers to make a decision. A qualitative analysis was performed for different solutions and was based on a multicriteria approach. These criteria were classified in accordance with users' preferences and their intentions of use, which were obtained from a ranking modeled with the ZAPROS III multicriteria method. Results revealed great influence of the users' familiarity with applications in the ease of navigation.

Keywords: *DTV, Mobile Interaction Design, ZAPROS, Multicriteria, HCI*

1. INTRODUCTION

In domains (as digital TV, smart home, and tangible interfaces) that represent a new paradigm of interactivity, the decision of the most appropriate interaction design solution is a challenge. Researchers of Human-Computer Interaction (HCI) field have promoted in their works the validation of design alternative solutions with users before producing the final solution. Taking into account users satisfaction and their preferences is an action that has also gained ground in these works when designers are analyzing the appropriate solution(s). Recent research reveals that the understanding of subjective user satisfaction is an efficient parameter for evaluating interface [1]. In domain of interaction design for digital TV, we claim that it is necessary to consider both international aspects for supporting the accessibility for all and digital contents for supporting a holistic evaluation (content and user interface) of the TV applications that show a content through their user interfaces.

Structured methods for tasks generally consider quantitative variables (such as: quantity of errors, number of times that the user consulted help, time taken to find a new function, etc). The users generally are encouraged to judge the attractiveness of the interface, and from these comments, evaluators produce qualitative texts [2]. The aesthetic quality of a product influences users' preferences but other qualitative aspects influence judgments that transcend the aesthetic appearance [3]. When dealing

---

Please use the following format when citing this chapter:

Carvalho, A. L., Mendes, M., Pinheiro, P., Furtado, E., 2007, in IFIP International Federation for Information Processing, Volume 254, Research and Practical Issues of Enterprise Information Systems II Volume 1, eds. L. Xu, Tjoa A., Chaudhry S. (Boston: Springer), pp. 389-394.

with Digital Television applications, new interface project and evaluation paradigms have been developed, as shown by Angeli [3]. No work however has integrated qualitative criticisms in order to obtain a ranking of interface solutions.

Furthermore understanding subjective questions, another problem deliberated for this research is about traditional means of evaluation. It is quite rigid and not flexible to the emergence of new project alternatives and new ways of considering these alternatives. For example, designers evaluated two interface solutions applying usability tests, and choose one to implement. During a system development, more three design solutions arisen as a result of new usability pattern. How can designers consider these new alternatives? How does evaluate if a new pattern is better than an old solution? At traditional means, usability tests should be applied to all alternatives. With a multicriteria model, these decisions are efficient and only some alternatives would be evaluated. In this project, three interface solutions for Mobile Digital Television Application were evaluated qualitatively by applying verbal decision analysis. This strategy adequately mapped user preferences furnished information which helped to judge solutions for the project. Provide a holistic evaluation of interactions situations and more information to understand and organize subjective questions. A ranking generated by the model is a tool which makes it easy to insert new alternatives and judgments for interfaces.

In order to be able to use the model, hypotheses were elaborated. From these hypotheses, criteria were established as well as usability tests applied in order to obtain information on user preferences. The ZAPROS III method, which belongs to the Verbal Decision Analysis framework, was used [4]. Applying to problems having nature qualitative and difficult to be formalized, called unstructured [5].

2. HYPOTHESES AND EVALUATION SCENARIO

The following hypotheses were the basis for elaborating the multi-criteria model which adheres to the reality of evaluations for applications of mobile Digital Television:

- Hypothesis 1: The user's experience with similar types of applications for navigation influences the choice of standard which is easier to use, more exact and more satisfying to the user;
- Hypothesis 2: If the content is interesting, the user will choose the project of his preference;
- Hypothesis 3: The user interacting with the interface while moving, leads him to choose the easiest interface to use;
- Hypothesis 4: Although the user may have experience with a similar interface, he may choose another interface while in movement;
- Hypothesis 5: If access to unattractive content is easy for the user, he tends to prefer the interface with which he has more familiarity.

Once the hypotheses were defined, usability tests with three mobile TVD prototypes were elaborated. The tests served to elicit user preferences. The results of the tests were entered as data for the model. The usability tests were applied with younger users who had wide experience with palms, DTV and desktop computing devices. The users evaluated were 12 university students and the duration of the test for each user was between 10 and 20 minutes. Two different locations were used: the usability laboratory and a natural environment (field study). Interface Designers and Usability Specialists were present during the tests. For each user, the test began with a sample portal application for digital TV on a television. This was done so that the user would have knowledge of how the application would work on digital TV.

3. COMPUTATIONAL RESULTS

The ZAPROS III can be applied to problems with the following characteristics [4]: the rule of the decision is developed in the form of alternatives; there is a large number of alternatives; evaluations of the alternatives can only be established by humans and not by measuring devices; the graduations of quality inherent to the criteria are verbal definitions that represent the subjective values of the decision maker.

The criteria used in the evaluation of this work were established with the assistance of specialists in the usability of mobile TVD of the Usability and Quality of Software Laboratory. The specialists wished to analyze the aspects that had the greatest influence in the choice of a determined interface project. According to the hypotheses, the following criteria were modeled verbally:

1. Familiarity of the user with a determined technology; if a standard is similar to a determined technology familiar to the user, this standard is preferable to him, since it is easier for him to use.
2. Attractiveness of the task to be carried out; if the standard allows for good visibility of the content, does the user prefer this standard in relation to the standard that has a familiar appearance to the applications that he is used to using?
3. Locomotion of the user during the manipulation of the interface; if the standard allows for good spatial orientation, which doesn't demand much of the user's attention to manipulate, will it be preferred in relation to the standard that has a familiar appearance to the applications that he is used to using, and at the same time allow for excellent viewing of the content?

With conditions thus defined, the ZAPROS III method can be applied according to our following presentation. In table 1, the values are shown for the criteria directed to the aspects on which the definition of the levels of attractiveness among the standards is based.

The order of preference among the criteria values was established during the application of the tests by means of observation. It was found for example that when the users were moving and trying to execute a task in a determined prototype, they complained that: it was difficult to move and manipulate the prototype at the same time. After the tests, the responses to the questionnaires were collected and interpreted. Questions such as "What prototype did you prefer? And Why?" indicated the order of preference among the project alternatives and also which criteria values were decisive for the choice. The Joint Scale of Quality Variation – JSQV which was gradually elaborated and validated with information from the tests. The scale is then elaborated and it is possible to use the transitive operation [6] to diminish the quantity of necessary comparisons. JSQV resulted: $A1 \prec A2 \prec B1 \prec C1 \prec C2 \prec A3 \prec C3 \prec B2 \prec B3$.

Table 1. Criteria and Associated Values

Representation	Criteria	Values
A	Familiarity of the user with a determined technology	A1. No familiarity is required with similar applications of determined technology A2. Requires little user familiarity with applications of determined technology A3. Manipulation of the prototype is fairly easy when the user is familiar with similar applications
B	Attractiveness of the task	B1. Allows high accessibility to the content B2. Allows medium accessibility to the content B3. Accessibility to the content is quite difficult
C	Locomotion of the user during the manipulation of the interface	C1. The user was not hindered in any way when manipulating the prototype while moving C2. The user was occasionally confused when manipulating the prototype while moving C3. The spatial orientation of the application is hindered when the user is moving

The next step of the method was to carry out the comparisons of the alternative standards. Each alternative was studied in order to define which criteria values materialized the prototypes. The usability tests also supplied important information on how the users described the standards (for example, the majority of users said that access to content using prototype 3 (three) was quite easy – a criteria value of B1, but that it required a lot of familiarity with Desktop applications – criteria value A3). Finally, the established relationship was: Alternative 1, prototype 1 - A1 B2 C1; Alternative 2, prototype 2 - A2 B2 C1 and Alternative 3, prototype 3 - A3 B1 C2.

Each Quality Variation - QV of JSQV is numbered in ascending order from 1 (one) to 9 (nine). The sum of the determining QV numbers for each alternative is the Formal Index of Quality - FIQ [4]. The calculation for each alternative is presented in table 2. With the FIQ values, the ranking of the prototypes is organized assuming that the alternative with the lowest FIQ value represents the highest rank and the best alternative. The alternative with the highest FIQ value is the least preferred prototype. Table 2 shows the ranking.

Table 2. FIQ Values for Each Alternative

Alternative	QV determinants	FIQ	RANK
Prototype 1: A1 B2 C1	B1	3	1
Prototype 2: A2 B2 C1	A1, B1	$1+3=4$	2
Prototype 3: A3 B1 C2	A3, C1	$6+4=10$	3

4. DISCUSSION

The resulting rank and the preference scale between two criteria values prove the validity of the hypothesis: The user's experience with similar types of applications of navigation influences the choice of the standard, which is easier to use, more exact and more satisfying for the user. This influence is a determining factor for the choice of the most preferable project solution. A1 was the value at the top of the scale of criteria values, as Hypothesis 1 demonstrated. The interesting content leads the user to choose the project with which he had the greatest affinity. This affinity is determined by the degree of similarity with applications commonly used by the user. The criteria value B1 came just after A1 and A2, showing that affinity is even more important a determinant than the content accessed, no matter how important or attractive this content is. Then, Hypothesis 2 proved. Considering in detail Hypothesis 3. Since C1 was less preferred than the criteria values for A1 and B1, we observed that when the user is moving and interacting with the interface, he chooses the interface that is easiest to use (that with which he has more affinity and ease of access to more interesting content). Hypothesis 4 was refuted because even when users had some experience with similar interfaces, when they were moving, they chose interfaces according to the criteria of ease of use. This is shown by the order of preference that C3 is preferable to B2 and B3. But the user's experience with similar devices is still a determiner in that we can see that A3 is preferable to C3. Hypothesis 5 "If access to unattractive content is easy for the user, he tends to prefer the interface with which he is more familiar," cannot be demonstrated completely with the criteria used up to now. In the current model we can perceive that if the content is attractive or not is less preferred than the influence of experience with similar applications. However, we cannot yet verify that access to unattractive content exercises a different influence than access to more attractive content.

The ranking of the alternatives showed prototype 1, similar to TVD applications, as being the most preferred. Prototype 2, similar to palm applications, with a Formal Index of Quality value very close to that of prototype 1, showed that the difference in attractiveness between the two is quite modest. Prototype 3, similar to desktop applications, proved inadequate for the content of TVD. The very high FIQ value in relation to the two other prototypes shows the low attractiveness for this type of TVD application.

5. CONCLUSIONS

A discussion of user-centered development process taking into account real people's needs is described in [3]. On the contrary of this study, that shows an experience which three solutions of design for different devices were defined and analyzed based on how users experience each solution. In [7] the authors describe a multi-criteria approach in which the execution of its steps allows to identify the order of attractiveness of a list of usability patterns for a certain interactive task of DTV applications. In this experiment and using the ZAPROS III approach, a qualitative analysis about the users' preference and their intentions of use with executable prototypes could be better appreciated. The standards of usability for mobile Digital Television applications should strongly consider which applications are most used by the target clientele. It proved to have characteristics such as flexibility, such that new project alternatives can be added, allowing researchers to better understand the needs and opinions of the target users of mobile TVD. It even assisted the usability specialists themselves to understand the relationship (order of preference) among the commonly used criteria for the interface project using standards. Research is also being developed to discover how to validate the hypotheses with quantitative metrics. What metrics are possible for each hypothesis? Could these metrics be entry points for information used to elaborate a multicriteria model such as ZAPROS III?

It is important to point out our intention was not to compare navigation techniques (as scrollbars, tap-and-drag, and so on) on mobile devices to identify the best one when users are performing navigation and selection tasks. Our goal was to help designers understand how criteria related to users' experience could influence their preference for a solution. In addition, we showed how to integrate two different areas (HCI and OR - Operational Research) describing an approach for evaluating the Interaction design in a subjective perspective of OR. It means researchers interested in making qualitative analysis of the interaction, which leads to more objective results can use this proposal.

REFERENCES

1. K. Chorianopoulos and D. Spinellis, User interface evaluation of interactive TV: a media studies perspective, *Univ Access Inf Soc.* Volume 5, (2006), p.209.
2. N. Tractinsky, A.S. Katz, and D. Ikar, What is beautiful is usable, *Interacting with Computers.* Volume 13, Number 2, pp.127-145, (2000).
3. A. Angeli, A. Sutcliffe, and J. Hartmann, Interaction, Usability and Aesthetics: What Influences Users' Preferences?, in *Symposium on Designing Interactive Systems, Proc. of the 6th ACM conference on Designing Interactive systems* (2006), pp.271-280.
4. O. Larichev, Ranking Multicriteria Alternatives: The Method ZAPROS III, *European Journal of Operational Research.* Volume 131, pp.550-558, (2001).
5. H. Simon and A. Newell, Heuristic Problem Solving: The Next Advance in Operations Research, *Operation Research.* Volume 6, pp.4-10, (1958).
6. O. Larichev and H. Moshkovich, Verbal Decision Analysis for Unstructured Problems (Kluwer Academic Publishers: Boston, 1997).
7. K.S. Sousa, H. Mendonça, and M.E.S. Furtado, Applying a Multi-Criteria Approach for the Selection of Usability Patterns in the Development of DTV Applications, in *IV IHC'2006* (Natal, 2006).

Function Point Metrics Improvement and Application in E-Commerce

Siping He

School of Information, Renmin University of China, Beijing 100872, P.R. China
hesiping@hotmail.com

Abstract. Function point measurement is one of the approaches in measuring functionality of software products, but it has many limitations. In this paper, we improve the function point measurement. The improvement mainly includes adding new factors and adjusting the calculation process. This improvement is applied in one of E-commerce project and gets appropriate result which can guide the process of software development.

Keywords: *Electronic commerce, J2EE, Quality control, Testing, Function point, Measurement*

I. INTRODUCTION

E-Commerce develops quickly in recent years, and promotes the usage of new technology, such as new frame, design pattern and program language. Tradition software development is based on integrate application software, which is composed by various modules, developing for special application, environment or organization. New software development is based on components which provide multi-application and different structure environments and organizations. Software development which based on components emphasizes interface and regulation, i.e. function. Implement is encapsulation of components, so that the requirement of clients can be realized independently. This face-on-function pattern which emphasizes on realization independently inosculates with function point analysis naturally.

Above-mentioned usage of new technology in E-commerce requires new concepts and methods in software metrics. The strength comes from key requirements in E-commerce: popularization of Web operation model and extend application, time shortage of coming into the market, shortage of skillful developers, rapid evolution of technology, generally recognize of component-based regulation, globalization tendency and the last but not the least—expectation of the client. The strength of this transition of the pattern is the mainstream of the software development, which is Java and related enterprise regulation: Enterprise JavaBean (EJB) and Java2 Enterprise Environment (J2EE). Although other standard component is still here, EJB and standard of J2EE have become fact standard in E-Commerce.

In software metrics, the amount of functionality inherent in a product paints a picture of product size. As a distinct attribute, functionality captures an intuitive

---

Please use the following format when citing this chapter:

He, S., 2007, in IFIP International Federation for Information Processing, Volume 254, Research and Practical Issues of Enterprise Information Systems II Volume 1, eds. L. Xu, Tjoa A., Chaudhry S. (Boston: Springer), pp. 395-398.

notion of the amount of function contained in a delivered product or in a description of how the product is supposed to be. Function Point (FP) measurement is an approach brought forward by Albrecht [1] to measure the functionality of software products. In this paper, the approach of function point measurement will be improved under new technology framework and will be used in a new E-commerce mode.

2. INTRODUCTION OF E-COMMERCE AND FRAMEWORK

E-commerce is the abbreviation for electronic commerce. A way of doing real-time business transactions via telecommunications networks, when the customer and the merchant are in different geographical places. Electronic commerce is a broad concept that includes virtual browsing of goods on sale, selection of goods to buy, and payment methods. Electronic commerce operates on a bona fide basis, without prior arrangements between customers and merchants. E-commerce operates via the Internet using all or any combination of technologies designed to exchange data (such as EDI or e-mail), to access data (such as shared databases or electronic bulletin boards), and to capture data (through the use of bar coding and magnetic or optical character readers) [2].

New information technology is widely used in E-commerce, such as new frameworks: Struts, Spring and Hibernate. These are all new frameworks in J2EE development. Framework is composed by a lot of classes, which provide a reusable design for application programs or we called it—a layer in a software. The code in the application call the class library to carry out the task and the framework take charge of calling the application code to manage the flow of the program. This is a so-called Hollywood principle that 'Don't call us, we will call you.' In the runtime, developer's code will be called by the framework.

3. IMPROVEMENT IN FUNCTION POINT METRICS

Function points are intended to measure the amount of functionality in a system as described by a specification. Function points can be computed without forcing the specification to conform to the prescripts of a particular specification model or technique. In tradition approach, to compute the number of function points, FP, we first compute an unadjusted function point count, UFC. To do this, we determine from some representation of the software the number of items of the following types: external inputs, external outputs, external inquiries, external files and internal files. After this, we calculate an adjusted function point count, FP, by multiplying UFC by a technical complexity factor.

Function points are also used in other ways as a size measure. For example, we can express defect density in terms of defects per function point. They are also used in contracts, both to report progress and to define payment. For instance, Onvlee claims that 50-60% of software contracts in the Netherlands have their costs tied to a function-points specification [3]. In other words, many companies write software contracts to include a price per function point, and others track project completion by reporting the number of function points specified, designed, coded and tested.

Although function points are proposed as a technology-independent measure of size, there are several problems with the function-points measure, and users of the technique should be aware of its limitations especially when technology has developed so quickly. Comparing with traditional Client/Server model, new E-commerce software normally based on Web whose development has many new characters. The GUI (Graphical User Interface) in Web application is different which affect the computing of external input, external output and external inquiries. Web GUI generally use different components which need complex dynamic queries, so the proportion between external inquiries and external input/external output is higher than traditional Client/Server model.

In order to overcome above-mentioned limitations, we should adjust the method in computing function points. First we design a function point estimate table and organize a team of experts to fill in the table. Those experts include project manager, senior structure designer, senior function point expert. After finishing the table, project manager will discuss it with customers and affirm that every function point in the table is exact and self-contained. In this table, we add new factors: subjective risk factor and reuse factor. Subjective risk factor is divided into three grades: low, middle, high, and reuse factor has two sides: reuse and no-reuse. In our improvement, we will consider above new factors.

4. APPLICATION IN E-COMMERCE

In a new E-commerce model—BAB [4], the improvement of function point measurement is used and estimate the workload in the project. First of all, let's see the meaning of the new model BAB. As we known, E-commerce can be divided into three traditional models: B to B, B to C and B to G. Here B means Business; C means Client and G means Government. All of these three models do not pay attention to the middle node. But in this new E-commerce model, the middle node is emphasized and called Agent. Agent is a economics term, an entity which has independent status, and should not be considered as person or software narrowly.

For the whole E-commerce model project, we use the improvement method to evaluate the function points and get results as follow. Take one function, show the order form, as example, external inputs are 6, external outputs are 0, external inquiries are 0, external files are 0, and internal files are 25, the sum is 31. Other factors include function points complexity weight is average, reuse factor is R—reuse, and subjective risk factor is M—middle. Therefore based on average productivity, 33.3 function points per month per person, we can estimate that it will take 20 days person to finish this function point. For the whole project, there are 302 function points and will take 276 days person.

5. CONCLUSION AND FUTURE WORK

In this paper we improve the measure of the function points and apply it on an E-commerce project. The improvement mainly adds two new factors and adjusts the calculation process. Comparing with tradition method, the new method considers more factors and the advancement of the technique. The result is more exactly and can be used in many aspects such as project control. In the middle of the project, FPE table can be used to master the plan of the whole project and it will be adjusted after discussion to decide the size and remain time of the project. The adjustment in function points measurement can still be improved in many aspects such as considering the components and adjusting the weights in the calculation.

REFERENCES

1. A.J. Albrecht, Measuring application development, in *Proc. of IBM Applications Development Joint SHARE/GUIDE Symposium* (Monterey, CA, 1979), pp. 83-92.
2. M. Fang, *Electronic Commerce* (Tsinghua University Press: Beijing, Beijing, 2002), pp. 4-5.
3. J. Onvlee, Use of function points for estimation and contracts, in *Software Quality Assurance and Measurement*, eds. N. Fenton, R.W. Whitty, and Y. Iizuka (International Thomson Computer Press: Boston, MA, 1995), pp. 88-93.
4. Y. Chen and M. Fang, *Research and Practice in BAB Based on Resource Management*, Renming University of China (2006). http://www.cnbab.com/bab/bab.jsp (Accessed March 4, 2007).

How to Resolve Conflict in Strategic Alliance: A Cognitive-Map-Based Approach

Tao Zhang and Yanping Liu

School of Economics and Management, Beijing Jiaotong University, Beijing100044, P.R. China enmasse@126.com mf001455@263.net

Abstract. With the business environment become more complex and dynamic, organizations have been faced with more pressures of competition. Organizations are often compelled to form strategic alliances with other organizations to survive and prosper. The inter-organizational arrangement can become favorable seedbed for inter-organization conflict. The participants in the strategic alliance often spend a substantial proportion of time and energy to handle conflict situations and realize collaboration. The effectiveness of the efforts depends on their comprehension on the characteristics of conflict, but it is often difficult for relative participants in conflict to understand cognitively conflict situation and manage it efficiently. Cognitive map can represent conceptual causal relationships between different variables, so it can be used to describe the perceptions of participants about the subjective conflict situation. In this paper, we introduce a method based on NPN logic cognitive map to capture and resolve strategic alliance conflicts.

Keywords: *Strategic alliances, NPN logic, Cognitive map, Conflict resolution*

1. INTRODUCTION

With the business environment become more complex and dynamic, organizations have been faced with more pressures of competition. Organizations are often compelled to form strategic alliances with other organizations to survive and prosper. The inter-organizational arrangement can bring some advantages to participants in alliance such as access of important resources, knowledge creation, and risk sharing etc, but it can also become favorable seedbed for inter-organization conflict. Moderate conflict is considered necessary for the efficiency and effectiveness of strategic alliance, but intense conflict can produce negative residues, even undermine the basis of strategic alliance. Therefore, conflict management and resolution in strategic alliance is of significance on the success of strategic alliance.

Conflict in strategic alliance is a process in which one partnering organization perceives that its interests are opposed or negatively affected by another partnering organization. The participants in strategic alliance often spend a substantial proportion of time and energy to handle conflict situations and realize collaboration. The effectiveness of the efforts depends on their comprehension on the characteristics of conflict, but it is often difficult for relative participants in conflict to understand cognitively conflict situation and manage it efficiently. Cognitive map (CM) can

Please use the following format when citing this chapter:

Zhang, T., Liu, Y., 2007, in IFIP International Federation for Information Processing, Volume 254, Research and Practical Issues of Enterprise Information Systems II Volume 1, eds. L. Xu, Tjoa A., Chaudhry S. (Boston: Springer), pp. 399-403.

represent conceptual causal relationships between different variables, so it can be used to describe the perceptions of participants about the subjective conflict situation. Through cognitive maps construction, partnering organizations in strategic alliance can identify the cause-effect relationships related to conflict situation, and then they can understand each other better and transform their opinions into collective synergy.

In this paper, we introduce a method based on negative-positive-neutral (NPN) logic cognitive map to capture and resolve strategic alliance conflicts. The remaining sections are organized as follows. We first introduce NPN logic which constructs a logical framework for cognitive map modeling, and the concepts of NPN logic cognitive map. Then we describe a generic method to detect and resolve conflict in strategic alliance. And in the end, we propose the managerial implications and an identification of avenues for future research.

2. LITERATURE REVIEW

In this part, we will introduce NPN fuzzy logic which constructs a logical framework for cognitive map modeling, and then present general cognitive map concept and NPN logic cognitive map concept.

In NPN fuzzy logic, a singleton variable can assume any real value in the interval $[-1,1]$, or it can be assumed an ordered NPN value pair (x, y), where x and y assume real values in $[-1,1]$, which indicates a negative strength and a positive strength simultaneously considered. Since each singleton value x can also be represented as a pair (x, x), any NPN logic value can be represented as an ordered pair. Thus the ordered pairs (by $\leq$) in $[-1,1]\times[-1,1]$ form a complete representation space for all NPN logic values.

An NPN relation R in $X \times Y$ was defined as a collection of ordered pairs or a subset of $X \times Y$ characterized by a membership function μ_R that associates each pair (x_i, y_i) in $X \times Y$ with strength of relationship by using an NPN logic value. An NPN relation R in $X \times X$, where $X = \{x_1, x_2 \cdots x_n\}$, is NPN $\max-*$ transitive if, for all $i, j,$ and k, $0 < i, j, k \leq n$ we have

$$\mu_R(x_i, x_k) \geq \max(\mu_R(x_i, x_j) * \mu_R(x_j, x_k)) . \quad (1)$$

In (1), the operator $*$ stands for a general conjunction operator that may be any T-norm extended from the interval $[0,1]$ to $[-1,1]$. The $\max-*$ composition of two NPN relations $R \subseteq X \times Y$ and $Q \subseteq Y \times Z$, denoted by $R \circ Q$, is defined by

$$\mu_{R \circ Q} = \max(\mu_R(x, y) * \mu_Q(y, z)) , \ x \in X , y \in Y , z \in Z . \quad (2)$$

The operator max is equivalent to OR . The n-fold composition of R is denoted as $R^n = R \circ R \circ \cdots \circ R$. A $\max-*$ transitive closure of an NPN relation R in $X \times X$ is defined as the smallest $\max-*$ NPN transitive relation containing R. A theorem proved states: given $X = \{x_1, x_2 \cdots x_n\}$ finite set, the $\max-*$ transitive closure $\overline{R}$ of an NPN relation R in $X \times X$ exists and can be computed as

$$\overline{R} = R^1 + \cdots + R^{2n} = (R^1 + \cdots + R^n) \circ ([I] + (R^1 + \cdots + R^n)) \text{ [1]}. \quad (3)$$

Cognitive Map is a clear representation of the causal relationships that are perceived to exit among the attributes and/or concepts of a given environment [2]. It comprises nodes that represent the crucial factors most relevant to the decision circumstances, and arcs that indicate different causal relationships among factors. CM has been widely used for knowledge acquisition and processing in different disciplines and research domains where both the system concepts and relationships are basically complex. When the relationships are numerically characterized, the CM approach is an inference mechanism that allows the complex causal relations among factors to be identified and their impact to be constructed. The causal relationships are often indicated through weighted directed connections presented in two-valued logic or classical fuzzy logic which has internal deficiencies mentioned above in assessing the impact of positive and negative causalities when stimuli are exerted on one or more elements in a CM. In NPN logic CM, all the strengths of the relationships can be normalized to real value pair (x, y) in $[-1, 1]$, so both negative and positive effects can be retained and integrated in the decision analysis for further reference.

3. COGNITIVE-MAP-BASED METHOD FOR CONFLICT RESOLUTION IN STRATEGIC ALLIANCE

Four processes compose the cognitive-map-based model for conflict resolution in strategic alliance, that is, goal identification, cognitive map composition, cognitive derivation and decision analysis process. In the goal identification process, partnering organizations in strategic alliance confirm the common expected goals of strategic alliance. Based on the uniform goals, each partnering organization constructs the local cognitive map respectively to gather structured information about own present operational situations. Then gathered information is pooled together by integrating assertions and local cognitive maps to form a combined cognitive, which is called a primary cognitive map (PCM). In the cognitive map derivation process, $\max-*$ heuristic transitive closure, which can be used to identify the maximum causalities between any two concepts in PCM, is derived as an advanced CM (ACM) in which implications and inconsistencies of PCM are clarified. Based on ACM, two most effective casual paths, which cause, respectively, a positive and a negative maximum effect, can be confirmed. In decision analysis process, several strategic alliance conflicts are identified based on the computed causal impact paths and values and some approaches for conflict intervention and resolution can be presented.

Strategic agreement on the overall goals of the alliance is a strong foundation for a supportive overall collaborative environment. Goals structured in strategic alliances determine that partnering organizations interact and their interaction pattern determines outcomes. When common goals identified, partnering organizations can develop the cognition of cooperative interdependence which will contribute to long-term relationships. In goal identification process, common goals descriptions are determined in strategic alliance. While common goals have been identified, partnering organization in strategic alliances has individual and diverse goals which are often in conflict with the goals of other partnering organizations. Conflict in strategic alliances can be described as the inter-organizational behavior that occurs when one partnering organization perceives that other partnering organizations counteract its goal achievement and expectation. There are many techniques which can be used to determine and validate the common goals descriptions of strategic alliance such as brainstorm, interview, and document analysis. In this process, 2-3 concepts representing common goals are determined.

Cognitive map construction can be regarded as a knowledge pooling process [1]. In this process, different managers' schema or cognitive structures, which reflect their mental understanding of a particular domain, is integrated to form a combined PCM. The importance of knowledge pooling lies in the fact that no one has perfect and complete knowledge about a large and distributed environment [2]. The construction of PCM includes several phases as follows. First, the appropriate sample size is determined, and then initial structured interview with managers at different levels in partnering organizations is conducted. Second, causal concepts are identified and clustered, and adjacency matrices are completed based on pairwise comparison or structural equation modeling technique. Third, individual cognitive maps are augmented and integrated together to form local cognitive maps of partnering organizations based on the identical causal concepts between individual cognitive maps. At last, global PCM based on the identical causal concepts between local cognitive maps is generated. In cognitive map composition process, both positive and negative assertions are weighted and kept separately to form an NPN compound value. Because both positive and negative effects are important in decision analysis, they should not be summed together if they are not counteractive to each other at the same time or they are not caused by the same path.

In the cognitive map derivation process, $\max-*$ heuristic transitive closure is derived as ACM in which implications and inconsistencies of PCM are clarified. In this process, two algorithms suggested in [1] can be adopted, that is, a heuristic transitive closure (HTC) algorithm and a heuristic path searching (HPS) algorithm. The HTC algorithm implements logic arithmetic mentioned above, which computes the heuristic transitive closures of NPN relations. The HPS algorithm confirms two most effective casual paths, which cause a positive and a negative maximum ripple causalities effect. If the positive path is desirable, the negative path will cause the maximum side effect, and vice versa. HTC and HPS algorithm enhance the coherence in PCM and clear up implications among PCM node connections. In PCM, there are many unrelated object pairs and many pairs which are related only by either a negative or positive edge. The HTC algorithm completes the PCM via transitivity, and the HPS algorithm elicits the new relationship between object pairs. Then the pieces of partial knowledge in the PCM are integrated and the new relationships are derived based on overall coherence and completeness in the $\max-*$ transitive sense.

In decision analysis process, The elements of $\overline{R}$ is regarded as a more or less steady state which identifies network expectations on the effects caused by stimuli, and then can be used to guide a dynamic decision process until one or more goals are reached. Through this way, several conflicts between partnering organizations can be identified based on the computed causal impact paths and values. Furthermore, the maximum causality factors in a closure, which present the conflict situations between partnering organizations, can be used as the criteria for finding the most effective paths corresponding to some potential solutions. The major advantage in using NPN relations lies in the fact that both positive and negative causalities are retained in the model. The integrated representation can be used to support multi-criteria decision analysis and the reason about the potential consequences of an action by a partnering organization. Based on the representation, alternative solutions to conflict situations can be arranged in the order as follow: the most effective ones with least side effects, the least effective ones with least side effects, the least effective ones with the most side effects and the ones with both maximum effects and side effects [2].

4. CONCLUSIONS AND IMPLICATION

This article proposed a cognitive map method to analyze the conflict in strategic alliance based on the NPN logic which can represent both positive and negative causalities simultaneously. The method comprises four processes for conflict resolution in strategic alliance, that is, goal identification, cognitive map composition, cognitive derivation and decision analysis process.

There are some implications in this method for the practitioners and researchers who interest in conflict resolution in strategic alliance. Primarily, the method can help to facilitate the identification of the causal interactions in partnering organizations in strategic alliance. Second, the method can eliminate the ambiguity in partnering organizations on the sources of conflict and the ways of resolutions. However, there are still several limitations in the method. Whereas this article suggests a pairwise-comparison-based technique and/or structural equation modeling technique in causal values confirmation, the appropriateness of these approaches still remains to be further examined. In addition, the method does not consider the cause-effect relationships with time dimension between interrelated causal concepts. Hence, one of the future directions of this research is to represent the time dimension in the interrelated causal concepts.

REFERENCES

1. W. Zhang, S. Chen, W. Wang, and R. S. King, A cognitive-map-based approach to the coordination of distributed cooperative agents, *IEEE Transaction on System, Man, and Cybernetics*. Volume 22, Number 1, pp.103-114, (1992).
2. W. Zhang, S. Chen, and J. C. Bezdek, POOL2: a generic system for cognitive map development and decision analysis, *IEEE Transaction on System, Man, and Cybernetics*. Volume 19, Number 1, pp.31-39, (1989).

Optimizing Supply Chains through Service-Oriented Architecture

Xin Liu, Zhijun Zhang, Tingjie Lu and Wei Fan

School of Economics and Management, Beijing University of Posts and Telecommunications, Beijing 100876, P.R. China liuxin1919@gmail.com zhangzhj@bjtelecom.net lvtingjie@bbn.cn fanwei@buptinfo.com

Abstract. Supply chain is defined as a system of suppliers, producers, distributors, retailers and customers where material, financial and information flows connect participants in the directions. Most supply chains are composed of independent agents with individual preferences. It is expected that no single agent has the power to optimize the supply chain. Supply chain management is now seen as a governing element in strategy and as an effective way of creating value for customers. Service Oriented Architecture (SOA) is a systems architectural tool that support mission-critical transactions and improve systems integration for enterprises. A discussion on how to optimize enterprise's supply chains by the entire development service-oriented architectures, to centralize information, and to increased information flows, reduced uncertainty, and a more profitable supply chains. In the paper, Modeling Dynamic Supply Chain Management (MDSCM) system is put forward, it allows a producer to select, dynamically from the MDSCM Registry, suppliers of components, based on the price, availability, and delivery time of those components. A producer can use one of several strategies to aggregate customers' orders before it processes them and to accumulate suppliers' quotes before it decides on a particular supplier. The use of a Service Oriented Architecture, such as MDSCM, can substantially improve the efficiency of a supply chain.

Keywords: *Supply chain management (SCM), Service-oriented architecture (SOA), Service management, Supply chain, Electronic business (E-business)*

1. INTRODUCTION

Supply chain is defined as a system of suppliers, producers, distributors, retailers and customers where material, financial and information flows connect participants in the direction.

Service Oriented Architecture (SOA) has been viewed as a strategic approach to IT that provides increased flexibility. While the benefit of SOA in terms of organizational agility is well accepted, managers are increasingly becoming concerned about the net performance impact of SOA adoption. Applications communicate with each other in such architectures through services. Services are self describing components, which can be recognized by client applications through look up from a registry. The client application and the service provider communicate via

Please use the following format when citing this chapter:

Liu, X., Zhang, Z., Lu, T., Fan, W., 2007, in IFIP International Federation for Information Processing, Volume 254, Research and Practical Issues of Enterprise Information Systems II Volume 1, eds. L. Xu, Tjoa A., Chaudhry S. (Boston: Springer), pp. 405-414.

standard protocols and exchange information using standard data formats. SOA has come to prominence as previous software architectures base on object-oriented approaches suffer from a lack of standards when compared to SOA [1].

Business partners in a supply chain compose a business community, in which a set of enterprises shares a common market sector, holds existing mutual business relationships, has heterogeneous roles, sizes and technology, and has coordination with coordination support offered by some business authority. In order to satisfy requirements of partners in a supply chain each business community must meet following requirements. First, availability, security, extensibility as quality of services is the main key factors for service distribution in heterogeneous environments [2]. Second, interoperability, dynamic behavior, and many-to-many approach provide flexibility for supply chains [3]. Third, loose coupling, technical independence, and openness provide cost-effective software development. The SOA approach, used in the software development as an integration paradigm, is suggested as a solution to software complexity [4]. Service Oriented Architecture has been paid an increasing attention in both academic and industrial communities since software systems based-on it adapt well to the continuous changes of requirements and application environments.

In this paper, we propose the model of using SOA in the construction of innovative and supply chain management of an enterprise. The paper starts with an introduction of the SOA and then gives a description of supply chain management.

Supply chain management benefits from a variety of concepts that were developed in several different disciplines as marketing, information systems, economics, system dynamics, logistics, operations management, and operations research. There are many concepts and strategies applied in designing and managing supply chains; In giving modeling of sharing information in supply chains, the proposed model is a discrete dynamic model and the cooperation of units is based on contracts and formal agreements achieved in negotiation process; in modeling of sharing information in industry chain, the proposed model is a discrete dynamic model and the cooperation of units is based on protocols and formal agreements achieved in negotiation process; In giving a model of sharing services, the proposed model is a sharing service can be represented by four components.

SOA is a new paradigm in distributed systems aiming at building loosely-coupled systems that are extendible, flexible and fit well with existing legacy systems. SOA will be able to offer solutions that are both cost-efficient and flexible. An increasing number of companies in the world subscribe to the idea that using SOA can significantly improve the efficiency of supply chains and provide a way to ensure competitive advantage. In this paper, we propose to investigate the feasibility of using SOA in the construction of innovative and advanced Supply chains. The paper starts with an introduction of the Supply Chain and then gives a description of the Service - Oriented Architecture: its definition and functions, advantages; In section 4, the paper gives an introduction of Modeling Dynamic Supply Chain Management: Supply chain by physical layer of MDSCM and Information flow model between producers and customers; in section 5, MDSCM Architecture for supply chain is presented thereafter.

2. SUPPLY CHAIN MANAGEMENT

Supply chain management has generated a substantial amount of interest both among managers and researchers. Supply chain management is now seen as a governing element in strategy and as an effective way of creating value for customers. A structure of supply chains is composed from potential suppliers, producers, distributors, retailers and customers etc. The units are interconnected by material, financial, information and decisional flows. Most supply chains are composed of independent units with individual preferences. Each unit will attempt to optimize his own preference. Behavior that is locally efficient can be inefficient from a global point of view. In supply chain behavior is much inefficiency. An increasing number of companies in the world subscribe to the idea that developing long-term coordination and cooperation can significantly improve the efficiency of supply chains and provide a way to ensure competitive advantage.

The overall business environment is becoming increasingly dynamic. Demand and supply for custom products can be very dynamic. Supply chains operate in a network environment. Dynamic information and decision-making models are called to accommodate these changes and uncertainties.

There are some approaches to model and analyze the supply chain dynamics. Dynamic models of supply chains try to reflect changes in real or simulated time and take into account that the network model components are constantly evolving. An information asymmetry is a source of inefficiency in supply. Information exchange is a very important issue for coordinating actions of units. The expected result is a mutually beneficial, win-win partnership that creates a synergistic supply chain in which the entire chain is more effective than the sum of its individual parts. Supply chain partnership leads to increased information flows, reduced uncertainty, and a more profitable supply chain. The ultimate customer will receive a higher quality, cost-effective product in a shorter amount of time.

Supply chains involve identifying a market for offering, creating the offering, supplying products to customers, getting paid for them, managing the customer relationship, and repeating the process. Over the last decade, with the emergence of the Internet, the World Wide Web, related technologies, and globalization has affected how businesses interact with other businesses [5]. In this new environment, companies are seeking ways to become more flexible and adaptive in response to the competitive international economic environment.

A supply chain moves a product or service from the supplier to the customer. It typically consists of suppliers providing raw materials or services, producers putting different components together to produce products, warehouses storing raw materials and manufactured goods, distributors providing finished goods or services to customers, and customers purchasing goods or materials. The main objective of supply chain management is to achieve the most efficient use of resources to meet the customers' demands [6].

Typically, supply chain management deals with three types of flows:

1. Product flow -Movement of goods from a supplier to a customer as well as customer returns
2. Information flow - Transmitting orders and updating the status of delivery

3. Financial flow - Credit terms, payments, payment schedules, consignment, and title ownership

Supply chain management benefits from a variety of concepts that were developed in several different disciplines as marketing, information systems, economics, system dynamics, logistics, operations management, and operations research. There are many concepts and strategies applied in designing and managing supply chains.

3. SERVICE ORIENTED ARCHITECTURE

3.1 SOA's Definition and Functions

There are currently many definitions of the Service Oriented Architecture which are rather divergent and confusing. We choose to adopt the definition inspired by Sayed Hashimi [7]:

In SOA, software applications are built on basic components called services. Processes, etc., defined in terms of what it does, typically carrying out a business-level operation.

A service in SOA is an exposed piece of functionality with three properties:

1. The interface contract to the service is platform in dependent.
2. The service can be dynamically located and invoked.
3. The service is self-contained. That is, the service maintains its own state.

There are basically three functions that must be supported in a service-oriented architecture:

1. Describe and Publish service;
2. Discover a service;
3. Consume/interact with a service.

3.2 SOA's Advantages

There are many shades of meaning when you start digging into the details of what someone means when they use the term. We only describe SOA's advantages, Marks, Eric A. (2004) describe SOA's advantages [8]:

The SOA's key advantage is flexibility. Unlike previous paradigms such as client-server and mainframe environments, it offers IT functionality as cross-platform shared services. This offers a number of benefits, but the most immediate is a clear ROI arising from asset reuse. Once a portfolio of Web services is available in an SOA, these reuse benefits multiply exponentially in an "SOA network effect." The value of SOA increases with the number of available services, and the number of different applications or users that access those services. This value compounds over time and becomes even greater if SOA is leveraged both internally and externally.

SOA's flexibility also benefits an organization through faster application development and lowered costs by allowing hardware and software components to be reused.

Applications developed this way can even be of higher quality than those developed independently because the components are retested and the Web services interfaces have already been proven.

SOA's flexibility is particularly important when trying to integrate several different systems, such as those that result from mergers. After organic growth and multiple acquisitions, for example, office supply retailer Staples found itself with five duplicate systems for credit card authorizations. Rather than transition to just one authorization system or create multiple interfaces to each back-end application, Staples implemented a Web service for use by all five. An SOA provides the run-time, management, and security functionality, allowing Staples to route each of its 100 million annual credit card transactions through whichever one of the five banks and clearinghouses provides the best value for that particular payment.

SOA refers to any system that exposes its functionality as services. The next question, naturally, is "what's a service?" We will turn to a metaphor to explain that one: think of services as a mechanical watch with hands, numbers, and an internal mechanism. The hands and numbers are the "interface," and the mechanism is the "code." To do more than simply tell time—to function as a stopwatch, for example—a watch would need additional components, such as mechanisms to start and stop the time, to display the elapsed time, and to reset the timer. Those operations are essentially simple services.

SOA has led to the creation of many related terms, some that were created because of SOA and others that were given new life. The term loosely coupled, for example, refers to a property of systems in which the complexity of the system is partitioned inside a small number of building blocks that are connected in clearly defined ways. Loose coupling means that the building blocks do not depend on each other in complex ways and can easily be rearranged to meet new challenges. The idea of the service grid has also gained a lot of currency. A service grid is an infrastructure of many different services all designed to work together.

4. THE INTRODUCTION OF MDSCM

4.1 Supply Chain by Physical Layer of MDSCM

MDSCM is appropriate to proposed modeling framework for dynamic multilevel supply network.

The MDSCM language consists of four basic building and one space-saving tool. The four building blocks are:

Stock, represent something that accumulates;

Flow, activity that change magnitude of stock;

Converter modifies an activity;

Connector transmits inputs and information.

Figure1 shows the icons of blocks. This approach enables to model and to solve a broad class of dynamic problems.

Figure 1. Block of the MDSCM Language

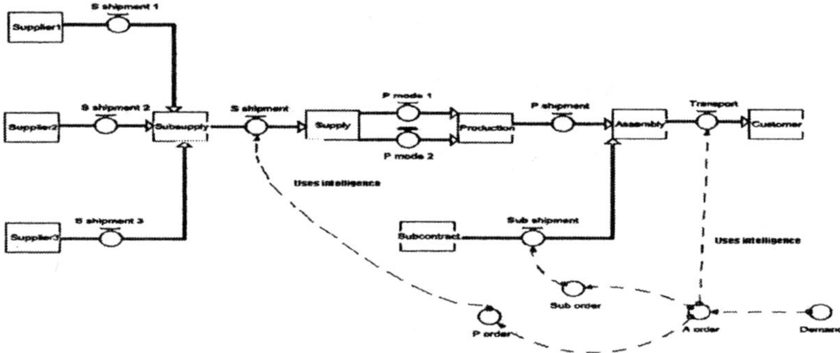

Figure 2. Supply Chain by Physical Layer of MDSCM

In MDSCM system, physical layer contains many functions that can facilitate dynamic modeling of supply chain (Figure2).

In Figure2, the intelligence (information) from producer's clients is producer's business secret, it don't let producer's rivals to acquire, so in the paper, intelligence represents producer's business information from clients.

4.2 Information Flow Model Between Producers and Customers

In the context of the MDSCM defined in Section 3, the usage of our modeling framework is illuminated in Section 4.1. Since the services are elicited from business requirements, their related service components can be specified. Then, for architectural reuse and interoperability, the system architecture should be defined. The architecture specification should be given. Hereinto, it involves service component searching problem. And our before work on SE4SC [9] can support the query of matched service components in the repository.

With respect of the high dynamic nature, dynamic configuration and reconfiguration of SOA according to the changing requirements and environments at runtime and evolving as execution processes are supported here. SOA allows its services consumer to replace services at run-time when there are some new services, which is a better alternative to the former one concerning functionality or quality. And our method can support the dynamic configuration and reconfiguration of SOA by remove or modifying the usage dependency between different service components. Besides, graph transformation rules referred in [10] may be helpful, too.

We can refine the architecture specification defined in figure 3. We suppose that there are an alternative retailer service component and an alternative producer service component in the MDSCM. On account of that the instance of the retailer service component are running on the unsteady thread in the Internet, it may collapse or stop without notification. In these cases, in order to satisfy the needs of customer all the time, it may require the instance to restart or request a substitute. Otherwise, when the published services provided by a service component have higher quality and reliability, consumer will be notified and it may rebind the new service component. According to above discussion, the refined architecture in the MDSCM is defined in Figure3.

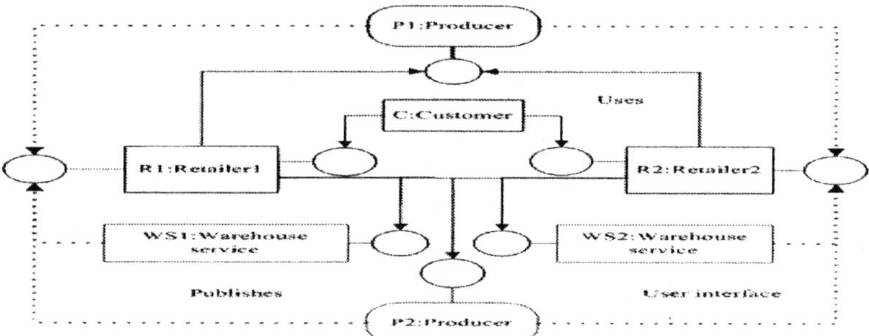

Figure 3. Refined Architecture about Information Flow Model in MDSCM

In Figure3, the information from producer's clients is business secret, it don't let producer's rivals to acquire, because it don't let producer's rivals to acquire, it is called intelligence. The information that producers publish to their clients is not very important to the rivals.

5. MDSCM ARCHITECTURE

MDSCM provides a dynamic environment for customers, producers, and suppliers to cooperate as they have never done before. The MDSCM services in one enterprise dynamically interact with the MDSCM services in other enterprises, which are dynamically accessed over the World Wide Web. MDSCM supports communication between the producer and suppliers, even if the producer did not have any prior business with them.

The advantages of MDSCM for supply chains that it increases business flexibility and lets businesses adapt more quickly to changing business needs. Moreover, it enables applications to be composed in a loosely-coupled fashion, and allows software services to be reused because it has been designed with modularity in mind. A Service Oriented Architecture is fronted by a client user interface, and end users see only the user interface. Although the MDSCM client user interface that we have developed is specific to computer manufactured from components obtained from different suppliers. The underlying MDSCM architecture is general and can be reused by producers and suppliers of other kinds of products.

Although we consider only a three-level supply chain and a single producer here, the MDSCM strategy generalizes to deeper supply chains with N levels, N ≥3, as shown in Figure 4, where a producer is a supplier of the products it produces and a supplier is a producer of the supplies it offers. Note that MDSCM is present at the enterprises in the supply chain that act as both producer and supplier. By considering the entire supply chain, MDSCM provides a better understanding of supply chain needs and faster adaptation to changing demand and supply.

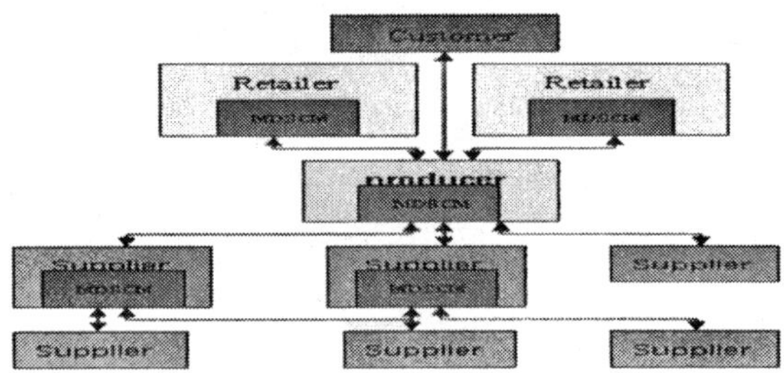

Figure 4. Use of MDSCM in the Supply Chain

The MDSCM system at the producer consists of the following components: the Materials Manager, the Orders Manager, the Database (DB) Monitor, the Registry (Directory Service), and the Quotes Manager. These components are shown in Figure5.

Customers obtain information, from the Materials Manager, about the materials that are available. According to the information in the Orders Database, the Materials Manager relates a material to its components and relates a component to supplies at one or more suppliers. Receiving orders from customers, the Materials Manager passes the information to the Orders Manager. The Orders Manager inserts into the Orders Database information about the customer and products, that the customer is interested in purchasing, and manages the status of the components of each customer's product order. On receiving an order, the Orders Manager informs the DB Monitor to scan the orders. The DB Monitor checks the Orders Database and decides, depending on the particular strategy chosen, whether to inform the Quotes Manager to initiate a search for suppliers and to communicate with them.

All of these components play a role in the different phases of an order from a customer. There are two phases in processing a customer's order:

1. Waiting phase, which involves the collection of orders from the customers before making a Quote request for a component from the suppliers

2. Quotes phase, which involves the collection of Quote replies from the suppliers, and deciding on which supplier will provide the component.

The MDSCM architecture has interfaces on the customer side and the producer side. Each interface involves different components of MDSCM, and some components of MDSCM serve as a bridge between these two interfaces.

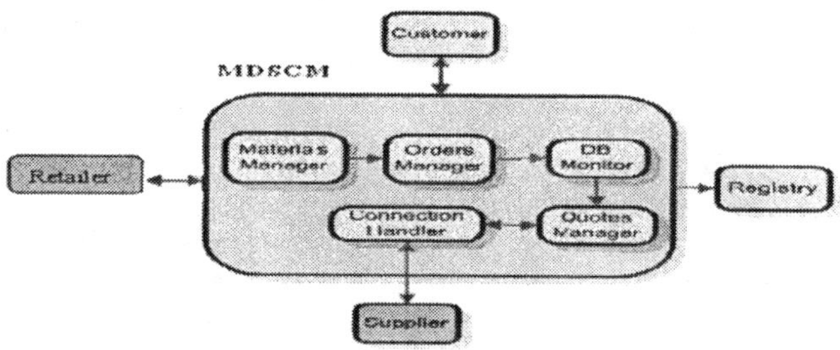

Figure 5. The Components of MDSCM

6. CONCLUSIONS

We have presented the MDSCM system, a Service Oriented Architecture for dynamic supply chain management. We have designed and implemented the services of MDSCM related to information flow. The MDSCM architecture as presented here deals with business processes up to the point where the decision to do business with a specific supplier is completed. However, the status of an order might change after the producer has placed an order with a supplier.

Supply chains need interoperability of business partners and business software and have specified business process and workflow management. Partners also agree their mutual relationships in MDSCM. Business process transformation to information system is done using a workflow notation with transactional properties and compensation. The implementation phase of the composite service uses coordination protocols, negotiation between partners, and WS-specifications.

Moreover, relationships and dependencies between the components that constitute a product might exist. We augment MDSCM with a work flow component that handles the relationships and dependencies between the components of a product.

Supply chains need interoperability of business partners and business software and have specified business process and workflow management. Partners also agree their mutual relationships in MDSCM. Business process transformation to information system is done using a workflow notation with transactional properties and compensation. The implementation phase of the composite service uses coordination protocols, negotiation between partners, and WS-specifications.

In this article we have shown how important it is to analyze business processes and design proper workflows based on the SOA. The proposed MDSCM pattern clarifies the most important concepts needed in the composite service implementation in the supply chain.

The performance of the MDSCM Registry that allows the producer to discover suppliers dynamically needs to be analyzed in terms of the overhead of the Quote messages and the synchronization messages. We expect that this overhead will affect the overall performance of the Query phase. If the Quotes Manager has all of the information it needs to make a decision, it can skip the Query phase and initiate purchases from the suppliers immediately.

REFERENCES

1. B. Lim and J. Wen, Web services: An Analysis of the Technology, Its Benefits, and Implementation Difficulties, *Information System Management*. Volume 20, Number 2, pp.49, (2003).
2. P. Baglietto, M. Maresca, A. Parodi, and N.I. Zingir, Deployment of Service Oriented Architecture for a Business Community, in *Proc. of the Sixth International Enterprise Distributed Object Computing Conference* (EDOC'02) (Lausanne, Switzerland, 2002), pp.293-304.
3. J. Bosch, *Design and Use of Software Architectures, Adopting and Evolving a Product-Line Approach* (Addison-Wesley: New York, NY, USA, 2000).
4. D. Linthicum, *10 Thinks to Think about When Building Perfect SOA*, SOA Web Service Journal (2005). http://webservices.sys-con/ read/121940_p.htm (Accessed December 2, 2006).
5. R. Murch, *Autonomic Computing* (Prentice Hall, Englewood Cliffs, NJ, USA, 2004).
6. Wikipedia, Supply Chain (2006). http://en.wikipedia.org/wiki/ supply chain (Accessed December 4, 2006).
7. A.E. Marks, Build a Better Enterprise Application, *Network Magazine*. Volume 19, Number 8, pp.18-24, (2004).
8. S. Hashimi, *Service-Oriented Architecture Explained*, O'Reilly ONDotnet.com (2003). http://www.ondotnet.com/pub/a/dotnet/2003/08/18/soa_explained.html (Accessed December 3, 2006).
9. H. Chen, S. Ying, J. Liu, and W. Wang, SE4SC: a Specific Search Engine for Software Components, in *Proc. 4th International Conf. on Computer and Information Technology* (Wu Han, China, 2004), pp.863-868.
10. L. Baresi, R. Heckel, S. Thöne, and D. Varró, Modeling and Analysis of Architectural Styles based on Graph Transformation, in *Proc. 25th Int. Conf. Software Engineering Workshop on CBSE6: Automated Reasoning and Prediction* (Portland, 2003), pp.67-72.

A Research on the Authorization Model Based on Organizational Management in E-Gov

Jiangnan Qiu, Jiang Tian and Yanzhang Wang

School of Management, Dalian University of Technology, Dalian 116024, P.R.China
qiu_jn@tom.com tian_jiang@126.com yzwang@dlut.edu.cn

Abstract. Firstly considering the problems in e-government authorization model, we analyze the features of government business process. Then an inner-organization authorization model based on organization is proposed. Then based on the proposed model, an authorization model for inter-organizational business process collaboration is designed. This model can resolve the problem of separating organization and authorization, reduce the difficulty of authorization management to make it more suitable for government management mechanism, and be of great application values.

Keywords: *Authorization model, Organization management, Inter-organizational systems*

1. INTRODUCTION

In the trend of network, informatization, economic globalization, government information system as a basis of national information technology infrastructure, has a direct impact on the country's competitiveness and socio-economic development process. Along with the continuous deepening building of e-government, the government system complexity is growing. As for orienting different service client, government has different application system, such as OA, DSS and Administrative License Procedure System, etc. In the procedure of these systems integration, organization and authorization management has become a crucial problem needed to be resolved.

Modern computer systems become more and more complex, and security management has become increasingly difficult. With the business complexity increasing, organizations need to collaborate with each other to form virtual organizations to share resources. Virtual organization is a combination of heterogeneous and independent organizations. When a new virtual organization establishes its security policy, each participant's identity and roles need to be identified. Therefore, security models like RBAC provided such useful concept in this area.

RBAC (Role-based Access Control) realized the separation of user and access permissions, and has been widely used in the procedure of system construction. But when facing to complex government information system composed of multi-systems, if we still use RBAC model to realize authorization management, there will be some

Please use the following format when citing this chapter:

Qui, J., Tian, J., Wang, Y., 2007, in IFIP International Federation for Information Processing, Volume 254, Research and Practical Issues of Enterprise Information Systems II Volume 1, eds. L. Xu, Tjoa A., Chaudhry S. (Boston: Springer), pp. 415-424.

problems[1]. RBAC model only consider user, role and operation authorization management in a single system, furthermore, from the perspective of management, it did not resolve the problem of authorization problems in complex systems, and emerging a lot of duplicate work. When a user belongs to different roles in multi systems, it requires repetitious assignment. If the responsibility of the user changed, it need to repetitious modify the relationship between user and roles, thus, making heavy permission management work. Additionally, from the perspective of management mechanism, the changing situation of positions is only known by human resource department, in particular, the internal functions of adjustment is generally not informed to outsiders. At this time as a system administrator (generally some staff working in information department) will not be able to make timely adjustment of the corresponding relationships between users and roles, leading to the competence of permission management accuracy, or even the turmoil of the entire system empowering management.

However, the security policy must adapt to the new requirements: according to the environment, not static but dynamic [2]. They must be self-adaptable based on temporary conditions, user location, and prior actions. Organizations participated in virtual organizations must express its own policies. Therefore, appropriate security policies should be able to demonstrate their own rules in a single framework. Classical access control model is not flexible enough to meet this demand for independent context.

To solve these problems above, on the basis of large number of exploration and practice, this paper firstly designed a meta-organization model, and then analyzes the process features of government systems which solved the problems of the separation of organization management and permission assignment in complex government information systems, significantly reduces management complexity overhead. At last, based on this model, we further showed an inner and inter organizational authorization architecture. The proposed authorization model based on organization management is very useful to deal with these new requirements. In this model, access control will not be applied directly to the subject, action and object. Instead, within organization roles execute activities on views. This is used to make static permission assignment, and this model also allows administrators assign more complex and dynamic authorization.

2. GOVERNMENT ORGANIZATION META-MODEL

Organization is an organic system composed of elements according to certain structures and relationships, in order to accomplish certain objectives, and advancing to an orderly state in space, time and functions. Traditional organization models played an important role in the history of organization development, but for their stiff structures, they are not suitable for the requirement of inter-organizational business process integration technology which need to be based on a flexible organization model supporting authority, resources and activity assigning with high efficiency.

Nowadays, the society environment is continuously changing, which requires the organization structures should be more agile and flexible to make information interchanging expedite and active agilely, as well as be adaptable to environment.

This kind of flexible organization is called Flexible Organizations. E-government business integration has a close relationship with organization structures. Organization meta-model is basis for flexible organization modeling and collaboration between distributed organizations. The under using organization models are the instances of meta-model classes which are also the interchanging standards in collaboration models.

According to the analysis above and related works, this paper design an organization meta-model oriented to business processes, as shown in Figure 1. This meta-model constitutes 4 parts: static organization model (SOM), authority and access control model (ACM), process model (PM) and resource model (RM). The SOM is the basis of the entire framework; ACM provides authority and authentication mechanism for task assignment and using resources; PM is responsible for executing tasks and relies on RM to assist it to finish the processes.

Essentially, organization meta-model is the way the organization elements affected and contacted each other. The different property elements are the basis of organization building, and the number and the combination manner affect the complexity and the degree of order. Formally, according to the model in Figure 1, organization meta-model and its related definition in government organization information system are defined as following:

Organization meta-model is defined as a duple having five basic elements: OMM= {Resource, OP, OU, Role, Task}, and there into:

1) Resource includes Human Resource (HR) i.e. personnel and Non-Human Resource (NHR), Resource= {HR, NHR}. Personnel is the subject of organization behaviors, diversified decision making and concrete work are done by them. In other words, organization behaviors are the personnel's actually. Personnel is the crucial element, as well as the most important and active one. Besides, HR has ability property. Non-human resource includes Info Resource and Application Service. Info resource is aggregated with Info Object which serves as digital resources and assists Activity executing; Application service is aggregated with Business Process and serves as encapsulated service package to be registered outside and used by other organizations in collaboration work [3].

2) OP (Organization Position) is a component in static organization model. It is aggregated with personnel according to their ability, and can recur into more complex ones through OP structure. For the state of government organization structure is relatively steady, an authority framework based on positions is built, instead of traditional based on the changeful authority mapping between personnel and roles. Organization meta-model just need to configure the mapping relationship between personnel and position only once, but not need to configure mapping relationship between personnel and all application roles. This method not only resolve the problem in government authority management, but also suitable for government interior management mechanism.

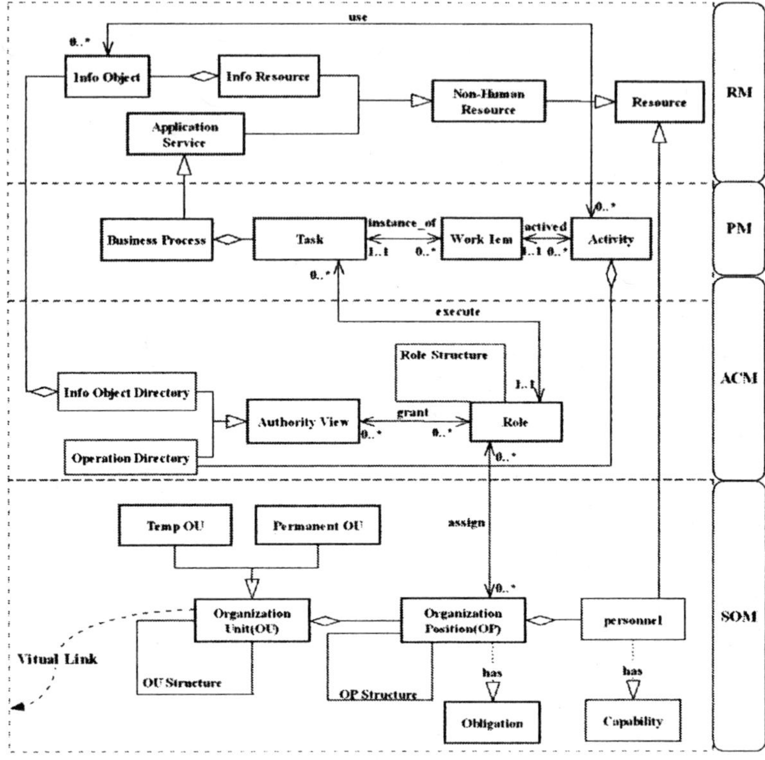

Figure 1. Organization Meta-model [4]

3) OU (Organization Unit) is composed of positions. OU is the parent class of Permanent OU and Temp OU. The former generally indicates the departments with relatively steady functions, and that the latter will be dynamically formed according to the requirement of projects with dynamic, effectiveness and flexibility features. Meanwhile, Temp OU is also an important component when conducting business integration process through Virtual Link.

4) Role is an information system component describing the status and responsibility of personnel in workflow systems, and it is the subject executing business activities. There is an aggregation relationship between roles, and can compose into more complex ones with more authority view which is an abstraction of resources. The authority view includes Info Object Directory composed by Info Object and Operation Directory. Operation Directory stores operation which is lowest activity granularity unit (such as add, delete, update, etc).

5) Task is the basic unit of business process having multi tasks in a certain sequence to achieve defined goals of organizations. Work item is the instance of a task in a defined process. If a work item is executed, it is called activity which is composed of operations.

3. INNER ORGANIZATION AUTHORIZATION MODEL

In government information systems, organization structure is set up based on positions and mapping relationship between positions and roles is relatively steady. Therefore, we set positions as the entire system roles. We construct an integrated role model through mapping between user and position, as well as position and roles in every application systems, instead of original relatively volatile mapping between user and roles.

Before designing the authorization, we would like to explain some related concepts and definition for establishing a good foundation for authorization model in theory. This paper defines the concepts as follows:

1) User: Any person who interacts directly with a computer system.

2) Subject: An active entity, generally in the form of a person, process, or device, that causes information to flow among objects or changes the system states[1]. In our model subject is user.

3) Object: A passive entity that contains or receives information.

4) Access: A specific type of interaction between a subject and an object that results in the flow of information from one to the other.

5) Access control: The process of limiting access to the resources of a system only to authorized programs, processes, or other systems (in a network) [5].

6) Role: A job function within the organization that describes the authority and responsibility conferred on a position assigned to the role. In our model role is actually a set of permissions.

7) System Administrator: The individual who establishes the system security policies, performs the administrative roles, and reviews the system audit trail.

8) Permission: A description of the type of authorized interactions a subject can have with an object .

9) Hierarchy: A partial order relationship established among entities, such as roles, positions, system admin.

According to the analysis above all, an inner organization authorization model (as show in Figure 2) is designed.

This authorization model is designed based on the organization meta-model above, and divided into three parts according to government business system: 1) Business layer; 2) System Management layer; 3) Business Management layer;

As shown in Figure2, business layer is the set of resource, activity and context. System administrator is responsible for abstract entities in concrete layer and assigns permissions to roles. Positions in business management layer do the activities according the permission assigned [6].

Business layer is the basis of entire framework. In our model, the entity Object will mainly cover inactive entities such as data files, emails, printed forms, etc. Seeing that we will also have to structure the objects and to add new objects to the system, we believe that an entity regarding objects is needed: the entity View. That is View is a set of objects having the same properties. And this job is done by system administrator through USE relationship. Entity Activity is the abstraction of actions having the same security policies also done by system administrator through Consider relationship [7]. Context environment impact authorization policies, and is a crucial factors set to be evaluated before permitting a subject access an object in the procedure of authorization using the rules. Context can exam the existing constraints, whether the authorization is validate, and which constraints need to be updated, etc.

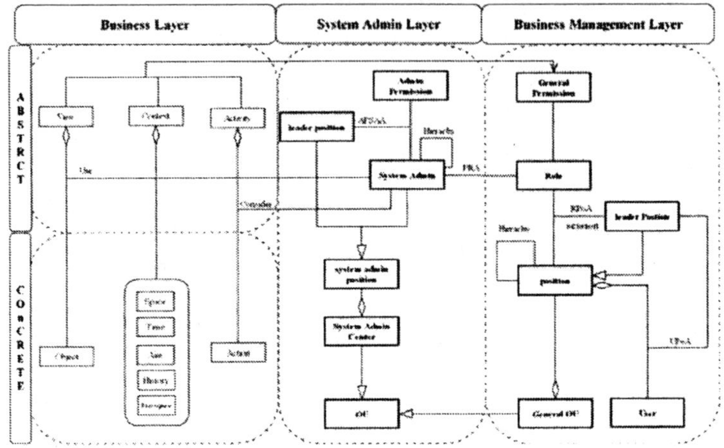

Figure 2. Inner Organization Authorization Model

There are five types of context: The Time context depends on the time at which the subject is requesting for an access to the system, and the Space context depends on the subject location, and the Aim context depends on the subject objective (or purpose), and the Prerequisite context depends on characteristics that join the subject, the action and the object, and the History context depends on previous actions the subject has performed in the system. View, Context and Activity compose the general permission to be assigned to role.

System admin layer include two kinds of positions: system administrators and their leader. Leader position is responsible to set up system administer positions and assign admin permission to them. System administrators assign general permissions to roles which actually are sets of general permission according their given admin permissions.

In general OU, leader position sets up positions according their own business process within OU. Then leader position assigns users to positions and roles to positions. Thus there is a mapping relationship between users and roles which make users get corresponding general permissions.

Through the abstraction of the entities in concrete layer and definition of permission assignment, this model provided a very efficient way to structure organization with authorization, and structured security policies rules which are very suitable for the security requirement in government information systems.

4. INTER-ORGANIZATION AUTHORIZATION MODEL

With the government business complexity growing, the collaboration opportunity between organizations is more and more. Hence, there is need to consider about the security issues across organizations, and construct inter-organizational authorization model.

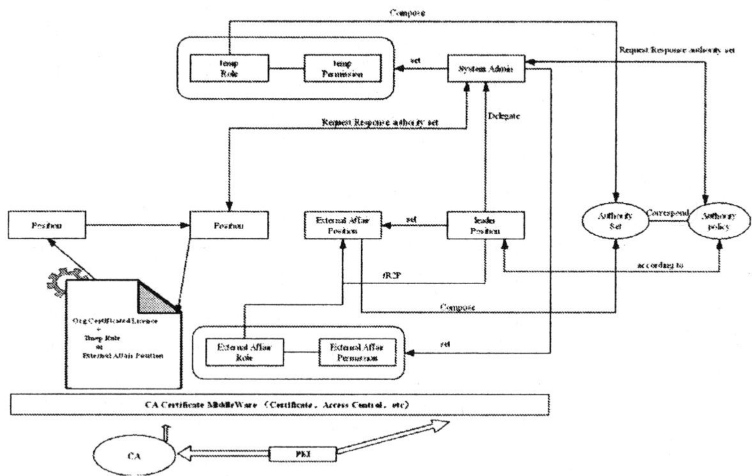

Figure 3. Inter-Organization Authorization Model

From the perspective of management, we designed the inter-organizational authorization model as shown in Figure 3. Leader position in OU B firstly defines the authority policies with its OU and delegate system administrator to set up two entities: external positions or temp roles. External position is a kind of special position which is responsible to deal with external affairs, just like a service window within an organization; Temp roles is a set of temp permissions to be granted to positions from other OU for them to directly participate in OU B's business processes and use resources under the authorized permission . When system administrators receive the delegation request from leader position, they start to assign temp permissions to temp roles and setup external roles according to defined security policies. Then leader position assigns the external affair roles to external positions.

If a position in OU A (called PA) send collaboration request to a position in OU B (called PB), PB firstly identify the PA's identity. If passed, PB transfers this request to system administrator, the latter queries the authority policy database to get corresponding authority set, and then send back to PB with organization certificated license and session time. PB again sends these results to PA. Thus PA can do the collaboration work with temp role or with the staff occupy the external affair positions.

The advantages of this inter-organizational authorization model are as following: 1) It supports the normal collaboration process between government organizations from management perspectives. 2) It realizes the minimal permission principle which means just giving the proper permissions to requesters. 3) Session time guarantee the requester can only hold the permissions in a certain time period, which make prohibit the requesters do illegal actions out of security time.

5. SECURITY PRINCIPLES AND CONSTRAINT

In this paper, the basic idea of authorization model is that the role is a set of permissions; positions can get general permission by mapping them to roles. Through many to many mapping relationship among positions, roles and permissions, we can realize or modify access control polices. This model supports the security principles as following:

1) Minimal permission principle. When assigning permissions to roles, we only give the permissions needed to execute tasks, and only give proper roles to positions. Thus when users are executing the tasks, the permissions they hold will not more than the tasks needed.

2) Responsibility separation principle. To make constraint on conflict roles, there are two ways: One is static separation, in position to role assignment, assign conflict roles to different positions; The other is dynamic separation, that is, decide to activate which roles when positions executing the sessions [8].

3) Entity abstraction principle. When defining permissions, we do not directly define the concrete layer into permissions; instead, from the perspective of application layer, we abstract them [9].

The context we defined in this paper can realize the dynamic constraint mechanism. Dynamic constraint mechanism can make business process be more suitable to actual application rules. Our model can realize the following constraints:

1) Time constraint. Some tasks need to be finished in specified time period, or can only be executed in specified time point.

2) Executing order constraint. The possible executing order can the following sequence: a. Serial order that is the next task must be executed until the former one is finished; b. parallel order that is two tasks can be executed at the same time; c. select order that is only one task can be executed, the other should be cancelled.

3) Delegation constraint. That is a user in a position can define who will do the next step of the tasks by getting the permission from leader positions and system administrator. As shown in Figure 4.

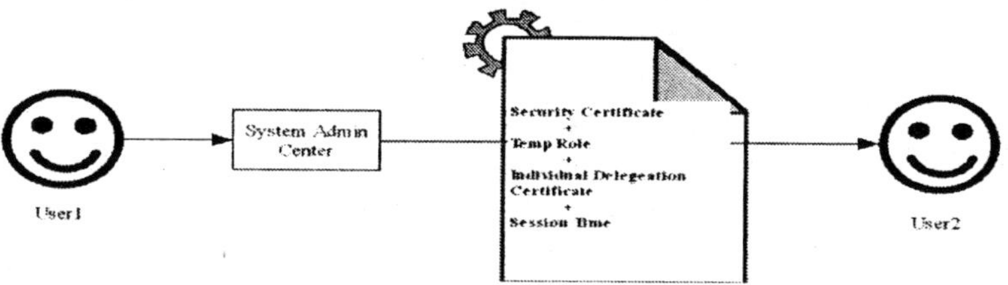

Figure 4. Inter-Organization Authorization Model

6. IMPLEMENTATION STEPS

Suppose that an organization plans to develop an access control system. To this purpose, the security administrator (hereafter denoted by SA) must identify which data have to be protected, how data can be accessed, and who can access those data under which privileges. These activities can be performed in three main steps, described in the following.

1) During the first step, the SA must choose an access control policy. For example, the SA may decide to adopt a discretionary policy because of its flexibility.

2) During the second step, the SA must specify an access control model compliant with the chosen discretionary policy. To this purpose, the SA must specify: a. relevant domain components (for example, groups and/or roles); b. a set of rules specifying how domain components are hierarchically organized (for example, role inheritance hierarchies [10]); c. a set of rules specifying how conditional authorizations are automatically derived by the system, starting from the authorizations explicitly specified; d. a set of rules specifying the integrity constraints the generated authorizations must satisfy. If the chosen model supports both positive and negative authorizations, the SA must also specify a mechanism to deal with conflicts that can possibly arise in the set of entailed authorizations.

3) Once the model has been specified, the SA can start the analysis of the specified model, to identify possible weaknesses and interesting properties. For example, he/she can check whether constraints are well defined, that is, they admit the existence of at least one model instance, or examine the dependencies existing among authorizations. Based on the analysis results, the model can be refined, for example adding or deleting some integrity constraints.

7. CONCLUSIONS

This paper has presented a new security policy model that aims to solve several limits of previous models. This model is centered on the concept Organization. The work we do is as following:

1) We define and clarify the basic government organization meta-model which is the basis of the entire framework.

2) In inner organization authorization model section we define the access control related concepts, abstract entities and give an inner organization authorization model which is very suitable for the actual government need.

3) According to the actual collaboration method, we designed an inter-organizational authorization model for better sharing resources and do collaboration work in virtual organizations.

4) At last, we give the security principles, constraints and implementation steps to give readers a guide to make a new security system.

The work above has made a good foundation of the entire government information system construction. In the future, we will base on them to do research on the business process model of E-Government form a systematic in fracture to give some reference guide for E-Government construction in theory.

REFERENCES

1. E. Bertino, P.A. Bonatti, and E. Ferrari, TBAC: A Temporal Role-Based Access Control for the World Wide Web, in *Proc. of Fifth ACM Workshop on Role-Based Access Control* (Berlin, Germany, July, 2000).
2. R. Viviani, A Type/Domain Security Policy for Internet Transmission Sharing and Archiving of Medical and Biological Data, *International Workshop, Policies for Distributed Systems and Networks (Policy 01)* (Bristol, January, 2001).
3. E. Kohen, R.K. Thomas, W. Winsborough, and D. Shands, Models for Coalition-Based Access Control (CBAC), *Seventh ACM Symposium on Access Control Models and Technologies (SACMAT' 02)* (Monterey, California, June, 2002).
4. Q. Jiang and T. Jiang, A Distributed and Hierarchical Government Organization Model, *Inter-organizational Business Integration. ICICIC2007* (2007).
5. E. Bertino, S. Jajodia, and P. Samarati, Supporting Multiple Access Control Policies in Database Systems, in *Proc. of IEEE Symposium on Security and Privacy* (Oakland, USA, 1996).
6. S. Oh and R. Sandhu, A Model for Role Administration Using Organization Structure, *Seventh ACM Symposium on Access Control Models and Technologies (SACMAT)* (Monterey, California, June 3-4, 2002), pp.155-162.
7. G. Dinolt, L. Benzinger, and M. Yatabe, Combining Components and Policies, *Proc. of the Computer Security Foundations Workshop VII* (Franconia, 1994).
8. G.-J. Ahn and R. Sandhu, Role-Based Authorization Constraints Specification, *ACM Transactions on Information and System Security*. Volume 3, Number 4, (2000).
9. F. Cuppens, L. Cholvy, C. Saurel, and J. Carr`ere, Merging Regulations: analysis of a practical example, *International Journal of Intelligent Systems*. Volume 16, Number 11, (2001).
10. J.B.D. Joshi, E. Bertino, and A. Ghafoor, Temporal Hierarchies and Inheritance Semantics for GTRBAC, *Seventh ACM Symposium on Access Control Models and Technologies* (Monterey, California, June, 2002).

A Case Study of Enterprise Application Integration Based on Workflow Management System

Baosen Yang and Lu Liu

Department of Information Systems, School of Economics and Management, Beihang University, Beijing 100083, P.R. China ybs@buaa.edu.cn liulu@buaa.edu.cn

Abstract. Work flow management system (WFMS) is a flexible tool for enterprise application integration (EAI). The EAI implement with work flow technology is cheap and convenient. This enlarges the view of enterprises and gives them an opportunity to integrate their legacy applications by advanced IT technology. By study on environment and stratagem of enterprises, this paper establishes a solution of the EAI based on work flow management system and presents an EAI framework with an embedded workflow management component to support business-to-business operations. Nowadays, however, such system is not common. A case study of EAI implement in Tianjin Port is presented and a brief overview of the current enterprise applications and information systems in this enterprise are also presented.

Keywords: *EAI, Work flow management system, Enterprise systems, Virtual enterprises*

I. INTRODUCTION

Most of enterprises in China have stepped on the Nolan-Stage IV: integration of information systems. Business organizations today face a complex and competitive environment. E-commerce is becoming more dynamic. It is now termed open E-commerce [1]. Different enterprises put their services and resources together so that they appear to be virtual enterprises (VE) [2]. The relationship between members is thus different from that within a traditional enterprise, because the members are independent, constituent, and dynamic and the business process is scattered over multiple enterprises and subject to frequent change. However, the agility of a company's response to customer demand has been recognized as a critical success factor in meeting competition.

This implies that a cross-enterprise information system is imperative. It should aim at implementing interoperability among independent enterprises, smoothing the information flow between them, and reforming business processes over multiple enterprises. To satisfy and respond quickly to the requirements, many companies are now focusing on enterprise application integration (EAI) in order to strengthen their ability to compete. This has therefore been recognized as an important area for IT innovation and investment [3].

Please use the following format when citing this chapter:

Yang, B., Liu, L., 2007, in IFIP International Federation for Information Processing, Volume 254, Research and Practical Issues of Enterprise Information Systems II Volume 1, eds. L. Xu, Tjoa A., Chaudhry S. (Boston: Springer), pp. 425-431.

Workflow is the automation of a business process. It has now been adopted as a way to implement the cross organization management needed to carry out businesses. The internet's world-wide web has become the prime driver of contemporary electronic commerce (E-commerce). Phan [4] holds the view that the most successful new business models are probably those that can integrate IT to all activities of the enterprise wide value chain.

2. EAI AND WFMS

2.1. EAI: Enterprise Application Integration

Enterprise application integration namely EAI aims to make more than one legacy system in enterprise connected each other by IT so that all systems can cooperate mutually , sufficiently share and use the information resources and eliminate the existing isolated island of information from enterprise.

The traditional EAI adopts the way of peer to peer connection to realize electronic data exchange. But some large enterprise usually owns many application systems. Some of these systems may be old and the other may be new so the integration of them is very complex, difficulty and expensive. This makes enterprise seek new way to solve the problem.

2.2. WFMS: Work Flow Management System

Conventionally, business processes were implemented by hard-coding embedded into the organization's software systems. This led, however, to inflexible systems that were hard to modify and maintain. Work flow is a technology that addresses such problems by separating and abstracting business processes from the software systems [5]. It is the automation of a business process, during which documents, information, or tasks are passed from one participant to another for action, according to a set of procedural rules [6]. A WFMS is used to define, create, and manage the execution of work flows through the use of software running on one or more work flow engines. The engines can interpret the process definition, interact with work flow participants, and, where required, invoke the use of IT tools and applications. Work flow has now become a leading tool in modeling enterprise business rules by taking advantage of continuous advancements of IT. Its inherent characteristics make it suitable to implement cross organizational management. Unfortunately, today's work flow management systems are generally designed to support the work flow within one business unit rather than between business units. Moreover, those from different vendors have problems in cooperation [7]. Thus, a committee, the WFMC, is working on standards for workflow interoperability. The WFMC has focused on developing a variety of interoperable scenarios that can operate at a number of levels from simple task passing to full work flow interoperability.

However, the real issue is not to connect systems but to develop fundamentally new concepts and architectures to support inter-organizational work flow. When developing an information management system for Tianjin Port Petrochemicals Terminal Company (TPPTC), we developed an inter-enterprise work flow architecture that used the internet. The main part of the architecture was a workflow-supported internet information system and an integrated interface.

3. A CASE STUDY

In this section, a case study conducted at Tianjin Port Petrochemicals Terminal Company (TPPTC) investigating the implementation of EAI is discussed. The case study starts with introducing the company and its background, presenting the current status of IT and giving the detail scheme phase of the implementation of EAI in TPPTC. Also, the research methodology is discussed.

3.1. The Background

Tianjin port is the biggest artificial harbor in China. It is a very important international port in north China and is the gateway of capital Beijing to ocean. Also it is the nearest to the inland of north China and north-west China in Bohai bay. Tianjin Port Petrochemicals Terminal Company(TPPTC) backing on the biggest harbor in north China——Tianjin port, by means of the vast inland, convenient and swift transportation, perfect facilities and other advantages has established the good cooperative relationship with numerous petrochemical enterprises. The throughput, oil storage, delivered amount and trade amount have increased quickly in near three years. It is gradually becoming an important trade and distribution center of petrochemicals in north China.

3.2. IT at TPPTC and Analyzing

During the period of "the 10th five-year program of development" TPPTC information system construction had got supports strongly from Tianjin Port Group Company and the infrastructure of IT became advanced. Currently, the state of network and hardware is as follows:

By now TPPTC has invested 6 million ￥ to purchase 5 computers as servers, 125 computers as workstations so that every manager has one computer at least. There is a 1000M fiber cable to connect with Tianjin Port Group Company. Also there is a local area network to connect every office and there is a virtual private network for middle-class managers to connect interior server from outside of his or her office.

Since 1998 especially 2003 based on database management systems TPPTC have successively developed and put to use 20-30 applied information systems, such as human resource management, finance management, facilities management, measurement management, safety management, freight transportation management, customer management, office automation, administration management, file management etc. After investigating and analyzing the status quo of TPPTC information architecture, we think that there is some characteristics and problems as follows:

- Vertical Applications

Most of applications are vertical applications which the functions are set for the superior company Tianjin Port Group Company and few applications consider the business requirement of TPPTC itself, for example:

The scheduling system and freight transportation system is portion of Tianjin port business management system. They can provide the forecast of freight, the month plan and the information of distribution, but they can not provide the key management means of TPPTC: five-day scroll plan and other necessary statistical reports.

The other systems such as human resource management, finance management, facilities management, measurement management, safety management etc. are similar and all belong to vertical applications.

- Poor Integrality

There is no uniform organization model, no uniform user management model and no uniform foundation data in the existing information system. The foundation data include data of human, machine, material, method, environment etc. The fields of existing information systems are divided according to organization not business process, so the data format in a system is much different from another, for example:

Every system has a set of authority policy and if a user wants to use more than one set of information system he or she must remember each account in each system. This is not benefit to access the information safely.

- Isolated Island of Information

All existing information systems own independent database respectively so they can not share data and cooperate with each other. The designer of existing information systems are absent in thinking of integration and cooperation, so the mechanism of integration is also absent and the need of enterprise cooperative business can not be satisfied, for example: the information of freight and charge must be repeat inputting in finance department after production department has done.

- Lacking of Restriction of Standards

Almost 30 information systems are running in TPPTC but there is no uniform design criterion and IT standards. Most of them were designed in Client/Sever architecture. This makes the farther development of information system in TPPTC embarrassed and the IT management has a trend of decentralization.

- No uniform user interface

The legacy applications were developed in deferent periods and there are deferent styles of user interface and operation way. This makes the users feel difficulty to learn and use. Although the legacy applications may provide many functions to users, but the users may give up since they can not easily control the computers, for example, some legacy applications have developed for long time but have not put them into practice yet now.

3.3. The Target of EAI in TPPTC

With above analyzing, we conclude that:

The future Information System Platform of TPPTC is to be established as a business management and network information platform for all employees, customers and outer authorized users of TPPTC. The platform is based Internet/Intranet/Extranet and is real time, integrated, interactive. Through electronic business gateway according with electronic commence standards TPPTC can share and exchange its data with Tianjin Port Group Company, administration, customs and partners. Then the virtue information system will be built and the logistics information, trade information and currency information etc. can pass easily across the whole petrochemical supply chain.

3.4. EAI based on Work Flow Management System (EAI-WFMS)

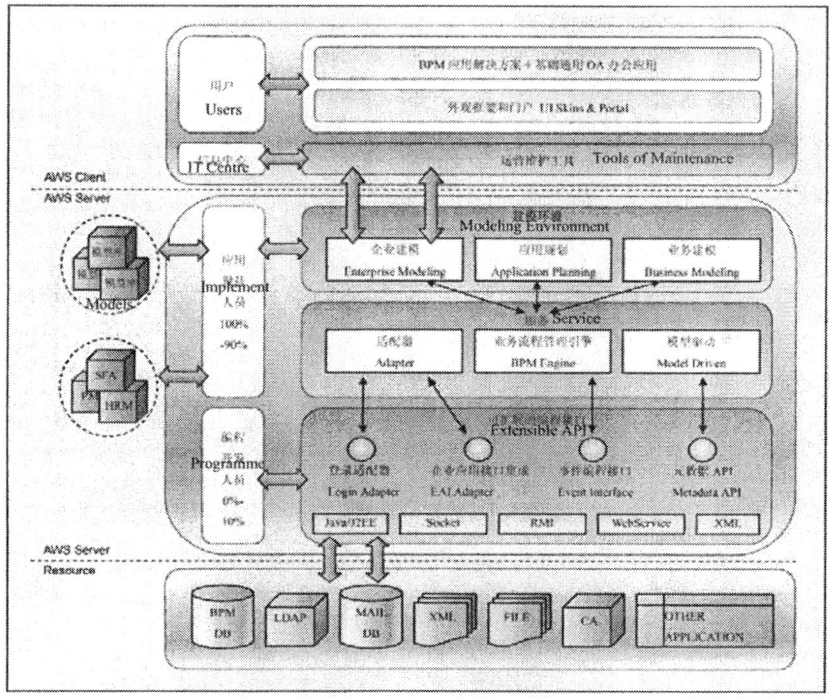

Figure 1. The Architecture of EAI Based on Work Flow Management System

The technology of EAI-WFMS comes from Actionsoft Company (ASC). AWS Enterprise is a product of WFMS based on JAVA/J2EE and is a multi-layer web application oriented to model driven. The modeling tools provided by AWS

Enterprise can realize 90% of zero coding for complex requirements. Through the programmed interface the integration ability can satisfy diversified requirements. Figure 1 shows the architecture of EAI based on AWS workflow management system.

3. 5. Illustration of Integration

U8 is ERP software of User Friend Company. The employee inputs the data of expense account by AWS Enterprise and when selecting the item of expense, the corresponding category of general ledger can be drawn out off U8 finance management system. Then U8 can keep debited and credited accounts.

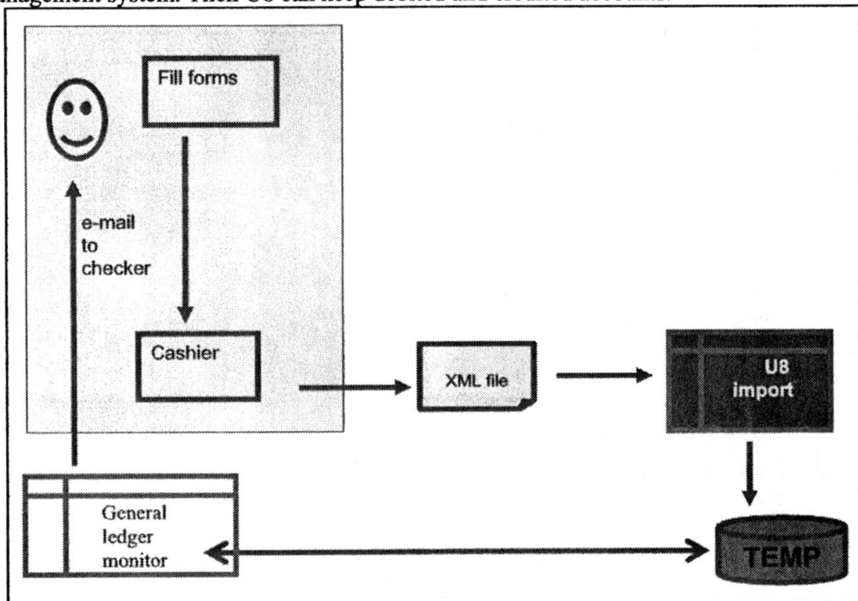

Figure 2. Illustration of Integration of AWS and U8

4. SUMMARY

The EAI project workgroup was made up of a management team of specialists from the external outsourcing company Actionsoft Company (ASC). ASC also have the specialized talents of EAI consultants. The project workgroup consisted of specialist internal managers and staff that had vital knowledge of cross-functional business relationships and experience of the old internal systems. The project construction cycle is about 3 years (from 9/2006 to 12/2008). EAI implementation team has understood the business, cultural and technical difficulties of such a large project. The team has used the specialist skills of consultancy specialists. The partnership has produced a sound architectural framework for the project, thus allowing TPPTC to concentrate its efforts on production and safety management. A project of this size would never run smoothly and difficulties have occurred throughout the implementation and will no doubt occur in the future.

ACKNOWLEDGEMENTS

The research is supported by the National Natural Science Foundation of China under Grant No.70671007 and the PhD Program Foundation of Education Ministry of China under Contract No. 20040006023.

REFERENCES

1. W.M.P. Van Der Aalst, Loosely coupled interorganizational workflows: modeling and analyzing workflows crossing organizational boundaries, *Information and Management.* Volume 37, Number 2, pp.67–75, (2000).
2. G. Dimitrios, S. Hans, C. Andrzej, and B. Donald, Managing process and service fusion in virtual enterprises, *Information System.* Volume 24, Number 6, pp.429-456, (1999).
3. J. Bowersox and J. Calantone, Logistics paradigms: the impact of information technology, *Journal of Business Logistics.* Volume 16, Number 1, pp.65-68, (1995).
4. D. Phan, E-business development for competitive advantages:a case study, *Information and Management.* Volume 40, Number 6, pp.581-590, (2003).
5. M. Kradolfer, *A Workflow Metamodel Supporting Dynamic, Reuse-based Model Evolution*. Ph.D Thesis, University of Zurich (2000).
6. A. Rob, *Workflow: An Introduction*, WfMC (1999). http://www.wfmc.org/standards/docs/Workflow_An_Introduction.pdf (Accessed May 4, 2007)
7. W.M.P. Van Der Aalst, Process-oriented architectures for electronic commerce and interorganizational workflow, *Information Systems*. Volume 24, Number 8, pp.639-671, (1999).

An SVR-Based Data Farming Technique for Web Application

Jian Lin[1] and Minjing Peng[2]

[1]School of Economics and Management, Beihang University 100083 Beijing, P.R. China Jianlin@wyu.cn
[2] Institute of Systems Science and Technology, Wuyi University, Jiangmen 529020, Guangdong, P.R. China reggiepeng@163.com

Abstract. In order to solve the problem that the performance of web application can't meet users' expectation when many users access dynamic data through the application, a data farming optimizing technique for web application is proposed. In the proposed technique, the web application is based on XML and the data are converted into XML format before being presented through XSL. To reduce page response time, SVR is employed to forecast user's requests. And based on the requests, a data farming agent is used to create web pages that may be needed by users. At last, experiments are conducted to compare page response time for three web sites: a dynamic web site without data farming optimization, a data farming optimized web site, and a SVR based data farming optimized web site. It is proved that page response time for the last web site is the least, which proves that the proposed technique is effective.

Keywords: *Data farming, Web application, SVR, XML, Agent*

1. INTRODUCTION

In the e-commerce era, dynamic information customized for each user in web applications provides business the opportunity of success. And performance of web applications is a critical factor to the success of the business. However, the dynamic information is presented from dynamic data in database through dynamic web pages, which require much processing time, and hence the process would lower the performance when there are many users accessing the web application. At this time, opportunities are that the operating systems are over-worked. There are two ways to solve the problem. One solution is upgrading the hardware supporting web applications. However, the upgrade requires more expenditure and more maintenance efforts. The other solution is utilizing the processing capability in the idle time through the technique of data farming. And it is also proposed in this paper. Data farming means that the processing ability of the idle time is used to generate static web pages that are possibly be used in next operational session. In the proposed technique, Support Vector Regression, or SVR, is employed to forecast users' needs so that the appropriate static pages can be prepared.

The rest of this paper is organized as follows. In section 2, concepts of web application are introduced. And as an important measure of performance, response

Please use the following format when citing this chapter:

Lin, J., Peng, M., 2007, in IFIP International Federation for Information Processing, Volume 254, Research and Practical Issues of Enterprise Information Systems II Volume 1, eds. L. Xu, Tjoa A., Chaudhry S. (Boston: Springer), pp. 433-441.

time is described and analyzed. In section 3, concepts, strengths and applications of data farming are presented. In section 4, fundamentals of SVR are shown. And then, in section 5, the framework of the proposed technique is illustrated. And in section 6, experiments of three web sites: a dynamic web site without data farming optimization, a data farming optimized web site, and a SVR based data farming optimized web site are conducted to prove that the proposed technique is effective.

2. WEB APPLICATION

A web application is a multi-tier application system, which communicates with an application server through Hypertext Transfer Protocol (HTTP) and Transmission Control Protocol / Internet Protocol (TCP/IP). It is capable of dynamically processing data and then presenting the information to users through web browsers.

Strengths of web applications are: a) User-friendly interface. All information of web application is presented through web browsers, which makes the application easy to use and the users don't need specialized training; b) Easy maintenance and upgrades. Because that there is no need to install specialized software in the client side, the only job needed to upgrade the system is upgrading the software system in the server side, and it reduces maintenance and upgrade costs; c) Scalability. The use of standard TCP and HTTP enables the module independent and thus makes system easy to expand; and d) High degree of information sharing. Web applications use HTML/XML to transmit information, which means the data format is an open standard. And hence the industry has given web application broad supports.

Due to above strengths, web applications have been widely used to provide customers and partners with customized, convenient, cheap, and efficient information services. And thus, competitiveness of enterprises is promoted. However, large accesses hinder web applications from meeting user performance expectation, which would consequently hinder the success of business.

The performance is measured with response time [1]. Response time of Web applications is the time spent in a HTTP request. It starts when the client sends a HTTP request and ends when the client receives the first byte data from the server. Response time under multi-user requests refers to the response time for a user who randomly accesses the websites with some other users. The response time under multi-user requests is denoted by τ_n^i , where superscript i refers to the user identification, and subscript n refers the total users. Assume that the response times for n users who concurrently access the web application are $\tau_n^1,\cdots,\tau_n^i,\cdots,\tau_n^n$, the average response time $\overline{\tau}_n$ could be computed using equation (1).

$$\overline{\tau}_n = \frac{\tau_n^1 + \cdots + \tau_n^i + \cdots, \tau_n^n}{n} \tag{1}$$

3. DATA FARMING

Data farming maximizes system performance by ensuring that information delivered to users by web application is available when the users require them. The data farming process is executed by a data farming agent, which are called as a data farmer. It is an independent computer process that is constantly looking for opportunities to improve the ability of web application to serve customers. It watches the web application server performance statistics and starts framing at any point in which the demand on the server drops below a defined threshold. And the process consists of four steps: a) Select seeds, b) Grow, c) Harvest and d) Store. The process is illustrated in figure 1.

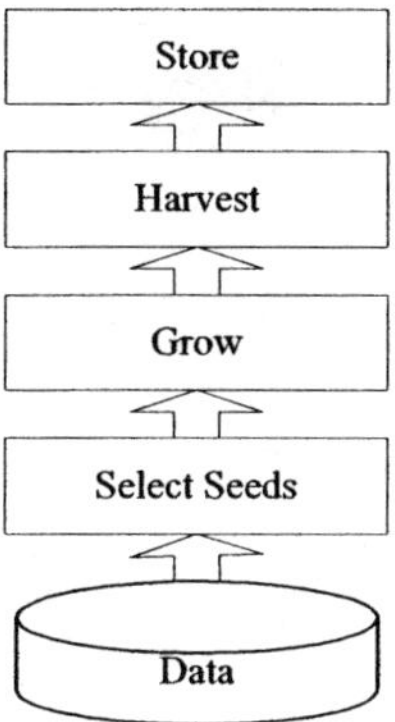

Figure 1. The Process of Data Farming

3.1 Select Seeds

Achieving largest profits by providing right products or services to customers is the purpose of e-commerce web application. And what products or services customers will choose could be predicted through historical transaction records [2, 3]. This research focuses on the data of enterprise customers and profitable products these customers may purchase, and takes them as seeds and grows them into prepared web pages presenting information to customers.

Seed is a combination of features from users and products or services that are to be delivered by a web application. In this step, seeds that are to be nurtured are selected according to the forecasting results based on features of users and products or services using SVR. The criterion for choosing is the probability of users may interest in the services or products.

3.2 Grow

In this step, selected seeds need to grow into static web pages. These seeds and some relevant data will be collected together to form the information that users need. The relevant data are classified into three classes: relevant data of customers, relevant data of products, and system information. For example, product recommendation page needs user's information of login status, information about products and user's profile. And the information from these sources is collected in this step.

3.3 Harvest

The collected data are structured using XML format and transformed into web pages via XSL [4]. XML stands for eXtensible Markup Language. It was designed to describe data and to focus on what data is. And XSL is a family of recommendations for defining XML document transformation and presentation. The process of harvest is illustrated in figure 2.

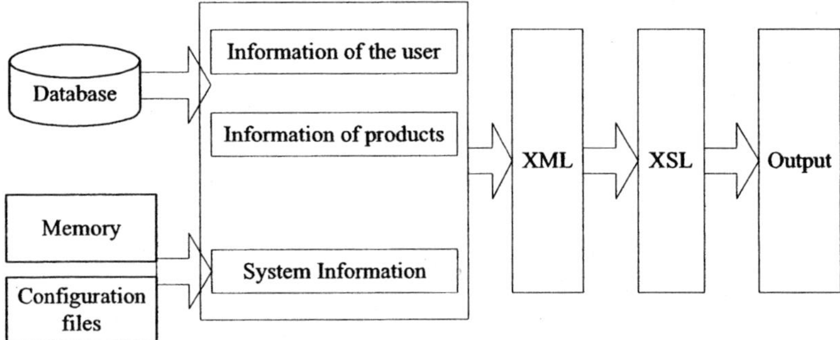

Figure 2. The Process of Harvest

The process fully exploits the benefits of XML through its 'virtual XML tree' approach. Each output pages from the system derives from an XML source.

3.4 Store

These pages are stored in somewhere in file system of web server, so that they can be accessed when users request. And those frequently accessed pages are cached to improve the performance of the application.

4. SVR

In this technique, SVR is employed to forecast the probability of a customer purchasing a product. According to the probability, seeds are selected to grow into static web pages to reduce workload of application in busy time.

Statistical Learning Theory proposed by Vapnik is a theory specialized on the learning problem through a limited number of observations [5]. Support Vector Machine (SVM) proposed based on the theory is a new way for solving nonlinear problems. Through introducingε- insensitive loss function, SVM has been extended to solve problems of nonlinear regression. And the new technique is called as Support Vector Regression.

For a sample dataset $\{(x_1,y_1),\cdots,(x_l,y_l)\}\subset X\times\mathbb{R}$, the purpose of linear regression is to find the weight coefficient w in equation (2).

$$y = Xw+\sigma \tag{2}$$

Where, σ is a coefficient to be minimized. Considering the purpose of regression function and ε -insensitive loss function, linear regression problem can be transformed into following optimizing problem:

$$\min\Phi(w,\xi^*,\xi)=\frac{1}{2}(w\cdot w)+C\sum_{i=1}^{l}\left(\xi_i+\xi_i^*\right) \tag{3}$$

Where, l is the number of observation, C is a fixed value that is used to split the regression error and function feature. Above equation can be transformed into the following optimizing problem:

$$\begin{aligned}\max W(\alpha,\alpha^*)=&\sum_{i=1}^{l}\left(\alpha_i^*(y_i-\varepsilon)-\alpha_i(y_i+\varepsilon)\right)\\&-\frac{1}{2}\sum_{i,j=1}^{l}\left(\alpha_i^*-\alpha_i\right)\left(\alpha_j^*-\alpha_j\right)\left(x_i\cdot x_j\right)\end{aligned} \tag{4}$$

$$s.t.\begin{cases}0\le\alpha_i\le C, i=1,2,\cdots,l\\0\le\alpha_i^*\le C, i=1,2,\cdots,l\\\sum_{i=1}^{l}(\alpha_i^*-\alpha_i)=0\end{cases} \tag{5}$$

For nonlinear regression, the kernel function is introduced to replace the inner product $\left(x_i\cdot x_j\right)$. And the optimizing problem in equation (4) could be transformed into the following equation.

$$\max W(\alpha,\alpha^*) = \sum_{i=1}^{l}\left(\alpha_i^*(y_i-\varepsilon)-\alpha_i(y_i+\varepsilon)\right) \\ -\frac{1}{2}\sum_{i,j=1}^{l}\left(\alpha_i^*-\alpha_i\right)\left(\alpha_j^*-\alpha_j\right)K\left(x_i,x_j\right) \tag{6}$$

Constraints in equation (6) are the same as in equation (5). Values of parameters α_i and α_i^* can be obtained by solving equation (6). On the basis of KKT conditions, there are not many α_i and α_i^* that are unequal to 0. Samples (X_i, y_i) corresponding to α_i and α_i^* are referred as support vectors. The regression function is in the following form:

$$f(x) = \sum_{SVs}(\alpha_i - \alpha_i^*)K(x_i, x) + b \tag{7}$$

Where,

$$b = -\frac{1}{2}\sum_{SVs}(\alpha_i - \alpha_i^*)[K(x_r, x_i) + K(x_s, x_i)] \tag{8}$$

And x_r, x_s are support vectors. Equation (7) is the SVR model. From above discussion, we can find that it has two advantages. First, it is based on kernel mapping which ensures its nonlinear processing ability. Second, it is based on statistical learning theory, so it synthetically takes fitting error and function characteristics of regression model into account, so that its generalization ability is also guaranteed.

5. SVR BASED DATA FARMING TECHNIQUE

5.1 Framework

The whole application can be in two phases: busy time phase and idle time phase.

In the busy time phase, the process of application is busy with the requests from web users. When the process can't find a corresponding static web page for a request, the job of response would be completed by dynamic pages. And the only job data farmer does is watching CPU, when the percentage of idle time is larger than a predefined a threshold, the application gets into idle time phase [6].

In the idle time phase, data farmer needs to do a job besides watching CPU: farming data of customers and products, and generating static web pages. When the percentage of idle time is below the predefined threshold, the process goes into the busy time phase again.

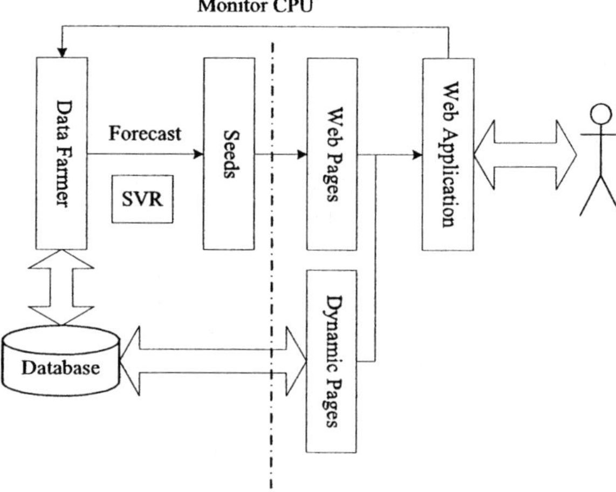

Figure 3. Framework

5.2 Implementation

The database includes historical database and the customer database. All customer transactions records are stored in historical memory database, and all customers' profiles are stored in customer database. Database is based on Microsoft SQL Server 2000 platform.

As SVR is in MatLab code [7], and application server is Microsoft .Net 2005, Combuilder of MatLab is employed to compile SVR MatLab code into COM dll [8], and then SVR can be called by .NET 2005.

Data farmer is implemented as an independent process, which is responsible for monitoring CPU and generating static web pages.

6. EXPERIMENTS

A website without data farming optimization, a data farming optimized web site, and a SVR based data farming optimized web site are built to verify the performance of a web application. The web application is a Blog web site and provides free basic service. However, its extra services such as theme services charge.

The services are provided by a PC server with 2G memory. And the operating system is windows 2003 server standard version. Experiment parameters are shown in table 1.

Table 1. Experiment Parameters

Parameter	Value
Records for training	317
SVR kernel function	$\exp\left(-\|x_i - x_j\|^2 / \sigma^2\right)$
SVR insensitive loss function ε	0.1
SVR punishment factor C	60
σ^2	6

LoadRunner 8.0 is used to conduct the test [9]. And the range of the number of concurrent users is from 50 to 500. Experiment results are plotted in figure 4.

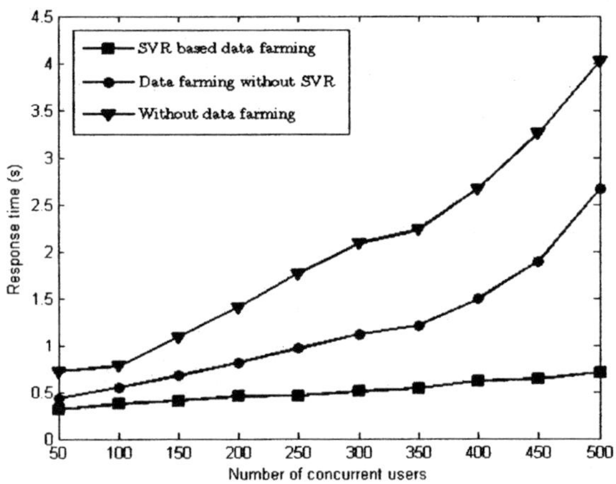

Figure 4. A Comparison of Experimental Results

The results indicate that data farming is an effective technique for improving performance of web application in busy time by transforming dynamic web pages into static web pages in the idle time. And the proposed SVR based data farming technique performs best in that SVR helps select suitable seeds and hence improve the efficiency of data farming.

7. CONCLUSIONS

Data farming is an effective technique for improving performance of web application in busy time by transforming dynamic web pages into static web pages in the idle time. Through the forecast of SVR, the proposed technique performs well in improving efficiency of web application.

REFERENCES

1. Anonymous, *Response Time,* TechTarget (2007). http://searchnetworking.techtarget.com/sDefinition/0,sid7_gci212896,00.html (Accessed July 14, 2007).
2. D.C. Schmittlein, D.G. Morrison, and R. Colombo, Counting your customers: who are they and what will they do next, *Management Science.* Volume 33, Number 1, pp.1-24, (1987).
3. D.C. Schmittlein and R.A. Peterson, Customer base analysis: an industrial purchase process application, *Marketing Science.* Volume 13, Number 1, pp.41-67, (1994).
4. Anonymous, *Extensible Markup Language*, W3C (2007). http://www.w3.org/xml (Accessed July 14, 2007).
5. V.N. Vapnik, *Statistical Learning Theory* (Wiley: New York, 1998).
6. D. Burnell, A. Al-Zobaidie, G. Windall, and A. Butler, Self-Optimising Data Farming for Web Applications, in *Proc. of the 15th International Workshop on Database and Expert Systems Applications (DEXA 2004)*, eds. F. Galindo, M. Takizawa, and R. Traunmüller (Springer: Boston, MA 2004), pp.436-440.
7. G.C. Cawley, *MATLAB Support Vector Machine Toolbox (v0.55\beta)*, School of Information Systems, University of East Anglia, U.K. (2000). http://Theoval.sys.uea.ac.uk/svm/toolbox/ (Accessed July 14, 2007).
8. Anonymous, *Create MATLAB based .NET and COM components*, Mathworks (2006). http://www.mathworks.com/products/netbuilder/ (Accessed July 14, 2007).
9. Anonymous, *Load Testing Software: Automated Performance Testing and Web Testing Software*, Mercury (2007). http://www.mercury.com/us/products/performance-center/loadrunner/

Enterprise Business Intelligence Data Preparation Using RDF Data Sources

Wajee Teswanich and Suphamit Chittayasothorn

Department of Computer Engineering, Faculty of Engineering, King Mongkut's Institute of Technology Ladkrabang, Bangkok, Thailand {s9060012,suphamit}@kmitl.ac.th

Abstract. Business Intelligence (BI) plays important roles in executive decision making in organizations. Up-to-date information from good data sources always gives advantages to the organization. Nowadays, information in Semantic Webs is considered important source of BI data. It provides machine readable information using the Resource Description Framework (RDF). To perform BI activities on RDF documents, many research works propose direct mining on RDF documents. This paper presents a different approach for preparing BI project information from RDF data sources. A conceptual meta schema is used to describe RDF information. The meta schema is transformed into meta tables which are used to keep both RDF schema and document information. A transformation algorithm is proposed to transform the information into 5NF relational database schemas and relations which are finally transformed into BI project data structures.

Keywords: *Resource description framework, Conceptual meta schema, Relational database, Data warehousing,*

1. INTRODUCTION

Most organizations want to gain advantages in decision making and planning of the business. The success of business needs enough up-to-date information. Since Internet comes to be one of the most popular communication channels, information over the Internet is always a good source for the organizations. Semantic Web allows information on the Internet to be shared and understood by machines. Resource Description Framework (RDF) is the data format of Semantic Web presented over the Internet nowadays. RDF Schemas (RDFS) help RDF defined properties (attributes), kinds, and relationships of resources in RDF documents.

Business Intelligence (BI) supports executives' requirements of making the decisions and planning. BI tools from many vendors are available. The tools have drivers to connect many types of data source, except RDF/RDFS documents. So there are needs to make RDF/RDFS documents ready to be used for the tool. Most relational databases (RDBs) are supported by BI tools. Furthermore, RDB has database management system (DBMS) support in order to take care of query processing and other important data management facilities such as concurrency control and recovery control. Storing a RDF/RDFS document in a relational database

Please use the following format when citing this chapter:

Teswanich, W., Chittayasothorn, S., 2007, in IFIP International Federation for Information Processing, Volume 254, Research and Practical Issues of Enterprise Information Systems II Volume 1, eds. L. Xu, Tjoa A., Chaudhry S. (Boston: Springer), pp. 443-453.

allows the document to be the data source for BI tool and also manageable by the DBMS.

There are attempts to store RDF/RDFS documents in relational databases [1]. However, most of them only keep the RDF documents, not the schemas so many properties including the object-oriented properties such as subclass and subproperty are lost. Some of them purpose the design of relational database schema for only a particular application using prior knowledge about the data in order to optimize the relational tables [2]. In the case where RDFS is also kept, such as in Oracle10g [3] many complex non-relational tables are required together with new methods for table manipulations.

2. RDF/RDFS

Resource Description Framework (RDF) document is a computer and human understandable format of data widely used in Semantic Webs. RDF documents use XML syntax and define relationships among XML elements within RDF documents. An RDF Schema (RDFS) [4] defines types, constraints, and relationships of the resources in RDF documents. Ontologies using OWL Web ontology language [5] can be defined for the RDF documents in order to share vocabulary extension of RDF. This paper mainly defines the transformation from RDF/RDFS document to RDB. Ontologies are not referred to in this paper.

3. SYSTEM ARCHITECTURE

The system architecture comprises two parts: data source and BI platform. In data source, each RDF/RDFS document is mapped to meta tables, which are obtained from the conceptual meta schema of RDFS. The meta tables will generate relational database tables, which can directly be data source of multidimensional cube or data to be generated as data mart or data warehouse before loading into the cube. The BI server in the BI platform part will use data from the cube to generate reports, analyzed reports, planning, or forecasting.

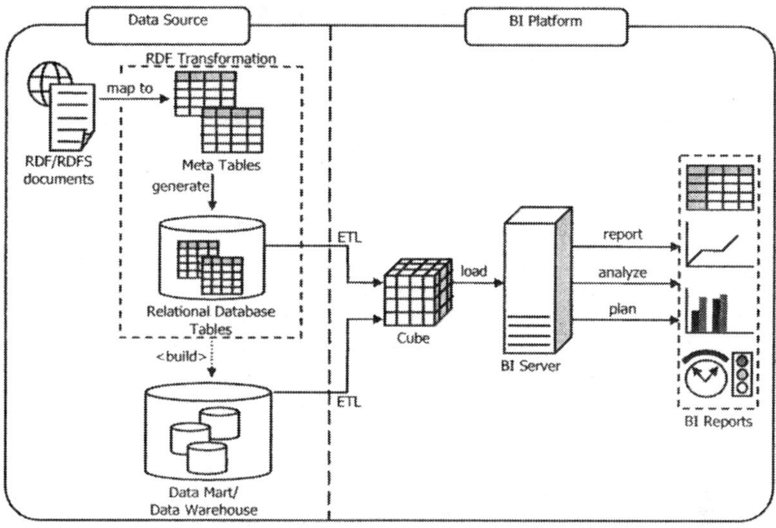

Figure 1. System Architecture

4. CONCEPTUAL META SCHEMA OF RDFS

From the data source in the system architecture in Figure 1, RDF transformation needs complete meta tables describing RDF/RDFS document before generates relational database tables. Since RDFS defines relationships among RDF elements, the corresponding complete conceptual meta schema of RDFS need to be defined.

The conceptual meta schema of RDFS can be described by a diagram of a semantic data model or a conceptual schema model e.g., an Entity-relationship (ER) diagram [6], a class diagram [7], a Nijssen's Information Analysis Method (NIAM) diagram [8,9], etc. The diagram should be able to present subclass relationships among classes and then be transformed to set of meta tables in RDB. In this research paper, the NIAM diagram [8,9] is used to explain RDFS and clarify RDF/RDFS graphs or documents.

4.1 NIAM Conceptual Meta Schema of RDFS

The RDFS specification [4] is described by the NIAM conceptual meta schema in Figure 2. The schema defines relationships among resources in RDF documents. From the schema, meta tables are generated as shown in Figure 3.

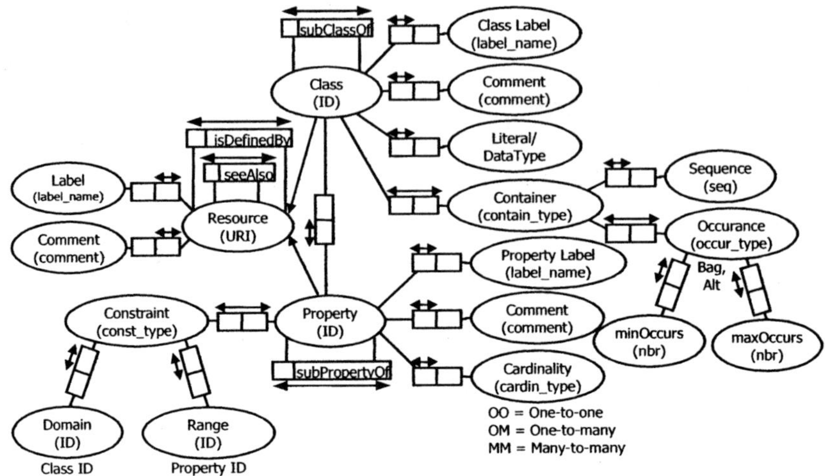

Figure 2. A Conceptual Meta Schema of RDFS

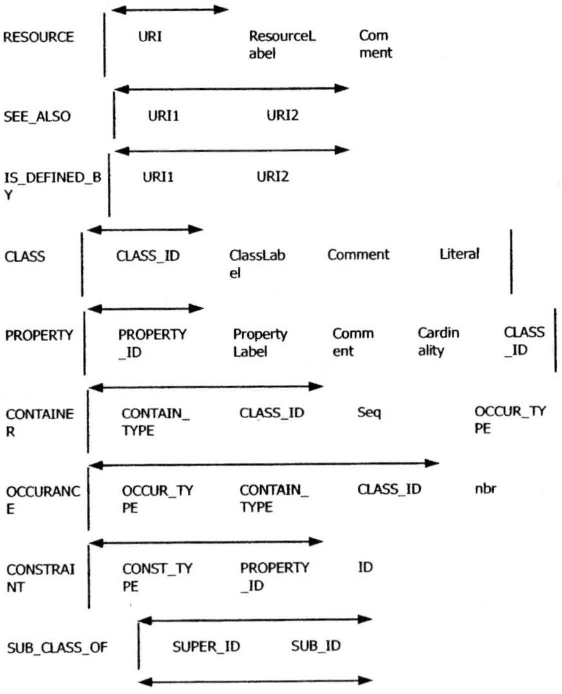

SUB_PROPERTY_OF	SUPER_ID SUB_ID

Figure 3. Meta Tables of RDFS

4.2 Transformation of RDF/RDFS Document to RDB

In the RDF transformation in the system architecture in Figure 1, the RDF document and its schema are first mapped into meta tables in Figure 3. Then, the meta tables will derive relational database tables. However, there is some information that needs to be obtained from the RDF document such as the type of relationships between classes. If the ontology [5] is given along with RDF document, some information is also gathered from the ontology such as minCardinality, maxCardinality, allValueForm, etc.

Figure 4-7 illustrate an example of RDF transformation process.

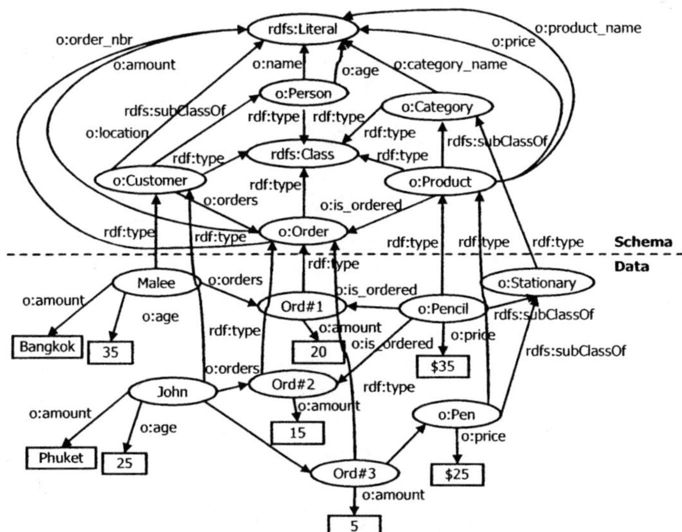

PREFIX o: http://example.org/sample_orders/

Figure 4. A Sample RDF/RDFS Graph

From the sample RDF/RDFS document in Figure 4, meta tables are populated as shown in Figure 5.

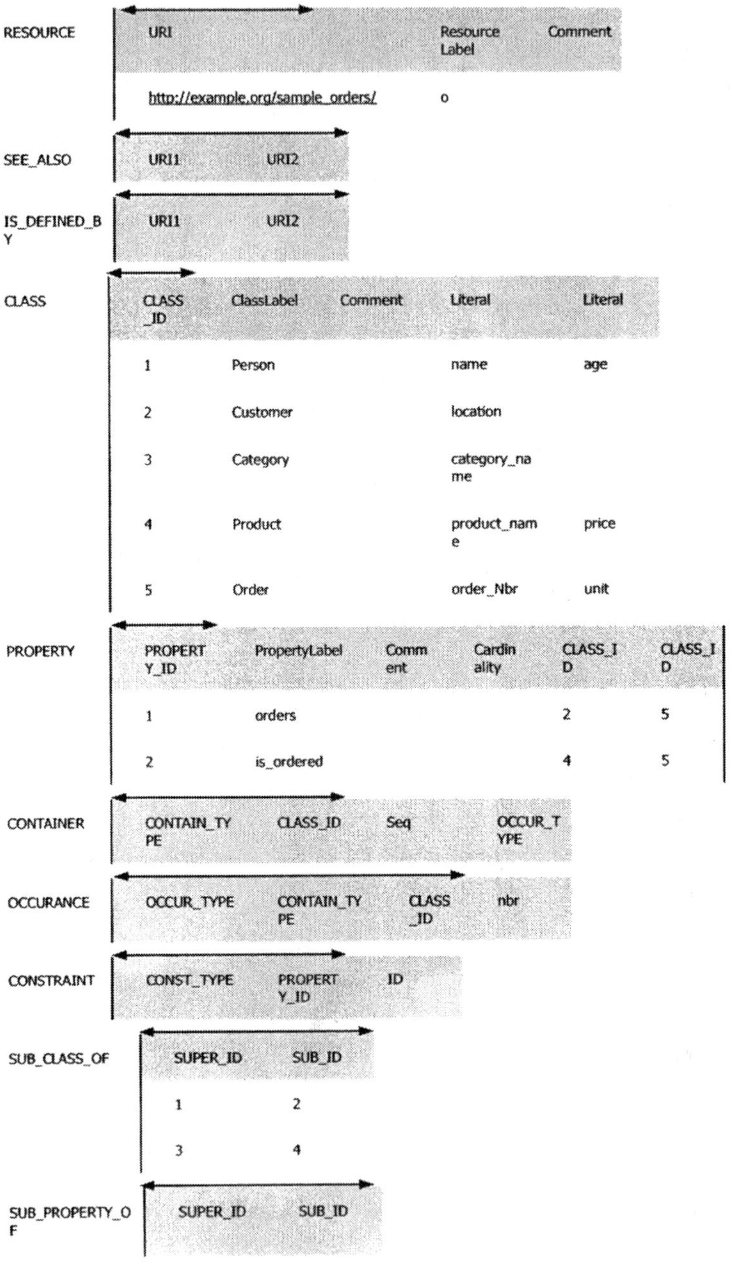

RESOURCE

URI	Resource Label	Comment
http://example.org/sample_orders/	o	

SEE_ALSO

URI1	URI2

IS_DEFINED_BY

URI1	URI2

CLASS

CLASS_ID	ClassLabel	Comment	Literal	Literal
1	Person		name	age
2	Customer		location	
3	Category		category_name	
4	Product		product_name	price
5	Order		order_Nbr	unit

PROPERTY

PROPERTY_ID	PropertyLabel	Comment	Cardinality	CLASS_ID	CLASS_ID
1	orders			2	5
2	is_ordered			4	5

CONTAINER

CONTAIN_TYPE	CLASS_ID	Seq	OCCUR_TYPE

OCCURANCE

OCCUR_TYPE	CONTAIN_TYPE	CLASS_ID	nbr

CONSTRAINT

CONST_TYPE	PROPERTY_ID	ID

SUB_CLASS_OF

SUPER_ID	SUB_ID
1	2
3	4

SUB_PROPERTY_OF

SUPER_ID	SUB_ID

Figure 5. Meta Tables Populated from the RDFS Example

Using the meta tables in Figure 5, the relational database tables in Figure 6 can be obtained. Database tables are populated from each record in class and property tables of meta tables.

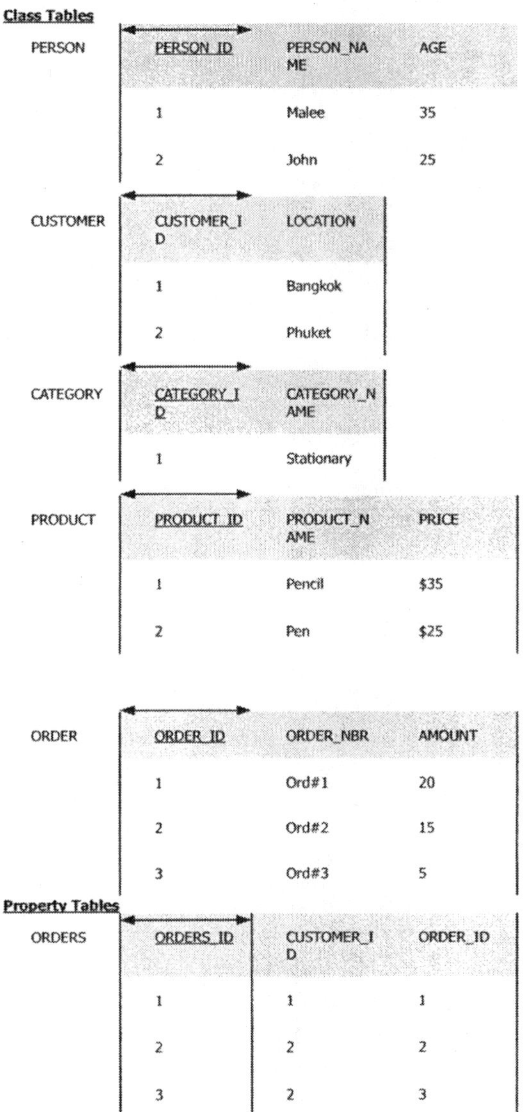

Class Tables

PERSON

PERSON_ID	PERSON_NAME	AGE
1	Malee	35
2	John	25

CUSTOMER

CUSTOMER_ID	LOCATION
1	Bangkok
2	Phuket

CATEGORY

CATEGORY_ID	CATEGORY_NAME
1	Stationary

PRODUCT

PRODUCT_ID	PRODUCT_NAME	PRICE
1	Pencil	$35
2	Pen	$25

ORDER

ORDER_ID	ORDER_NBR	AMOUNT
1	Ord#1	20
2	Ord#2	15
3	Ord#3	5

Property Tables

ORDERS

ORDERS_ID	CUSTOMER_ID	ORDER_ID
1	1	1
2	2	2
3	2	3

IS_ORDERED

IS_ORDERED_ID	PRODUCT_ID	ORDER_ID
1	1	1
2	1	2
3	2	3

Figure 6. Relational Database Tables

In case of two property tables contain a common class id as in Figure 6, the tables can be combined as shown in Figure 7.

ORDERS

ORDERS_ID	CUSTOMER_ID	PRODUCT_ID
1	1	1
2	2	1
3	2	2

Figure 7. Property Tables Redefined by Obtaining Relationships of Data in RDF Documents

4.3 RDF Data Sources

To use RDF as a data source of data warehouses or multidimensional cubes, a transformation to relational databases is required. At present, the processing of RDF/RDFS documents as databases is not efficient due to the lack of database management system (DBMS) support of RDFS as a database model. Query processing and optimization technologies and other important data management facilities such as concurrency control and recovery control which are commonly found in a Relational DBMS are not available in an RDF engine. Querying RDF/RDFS documents is based on tree traversal and simple pattern matching. From the productivity point of view, SQL requests made on relational databases are considered simpler and take less time to formulate than using the RDF-based language such as SPARQL [10]. Also, from the availability point of view, relational DBMS and supported Business Intelligence Software Tools which are widely available are mostly based on relational databases. A transformation from RDF and RDFS to relational databases so that they are in the easy-to-use and widely available form is therefore a logical approach of data management.

SPARQL is currently a working draft under development by W3C's RDF Data Access working group (DAWG). Since SPARQL is not a state-full protocol, using cursors with a special isolation and locking level on relational database could not be applied [11]. SPARQL does not support the data modification operations like INSERT, UPDATE, or DELETE in SQL. The query using SPARQL on RDF document still does not support aggregate functions like COUNT, MAX, MIN, or AVG in SQL in this current version (see Example 1 and 2). Finding the rank of the result cannot be applied using SPARQL (see Example 2). The calculation on returned value cannot be done using SPARQL (see Example 3).

The query processing on RDB makes process of building data warehouse or cube on RDF/RDFS document easier. SQL can be used in order to do the queries.

Example 1: Find customer(s) that send more than one order.

SQL

```
SELECT person.person_name
FROM orders
INNER JOIN [order] ON orders.order_id=[order].order_id
INNER JOIN person ON orders.customer_id=person.person_id
GROUP BY person.person_name
HAVING COUNT(*) > 1
```

Result:

person_name
John

Example 2: Find the product which has highest order amount

SQL

```
SELECT product.product_name, SUM ( [order].amount )
AS sum_amount
FROM orders
INNER JOIN [order] ON orders.order_id=[order].order_id
INNER JOIN product ON
orders.product_id=product.product_id
GROUP BY product.product_name
HAVING SUM([order].amount) =
 ( SELECT TOP 1 SUM(amount) AS amt
   FROM orders AS orders2,[order] AS order1
   WHERE orders2.order_id = order1.order_id
   GROUP BY orders2.product_id
   ORDER BY amt DESC )
```

Result:

person_name	sum_amount
Pencil	35

Example 3: Calculate the total price for each particular order

SQL

```
SELECT [order].order_nbr, ( [order].amount * product.price )
AS total_price
FROM orders
INNER JOIN [order] ON orders.order_id=[order].order_id
INNER JOIN product ON orders.product_id=product.product_id
```

Result:

order_nbr	total_price
Ord#1	$700
Ord#2	$525
Ord#3	$125

5. BUSINESS INTELLIGENCE

Business Intelligence (BI) technologies are employed in decision support systems (DSS) and executive-level support systems (ESS). Data warehouses whose data sources are mostly ETL (Extract, Transform and Load) from operation-level relational databases are used to keep and represent data in an easy-to-use format such as multidimensional cubes. Since RDF/RDFS documents are good source of information, they should be first accumulated for later ETL into the cube format. The accumulation and integration of RDF/RDFS information from various sources is an apparently complex task. We therefore propose that they be transformed into the relational database format before the integration and ETL activities.

The multidimensional cube is designed based on executives' requirements. From an application in section 4, the executives might want to see the orders based on product, location, and age of customer in order to make the suitable marketing on each product for the particular type of customers. The cube then can be designed as in Figure 8 and the example of executives' reports is given in Figure 9.

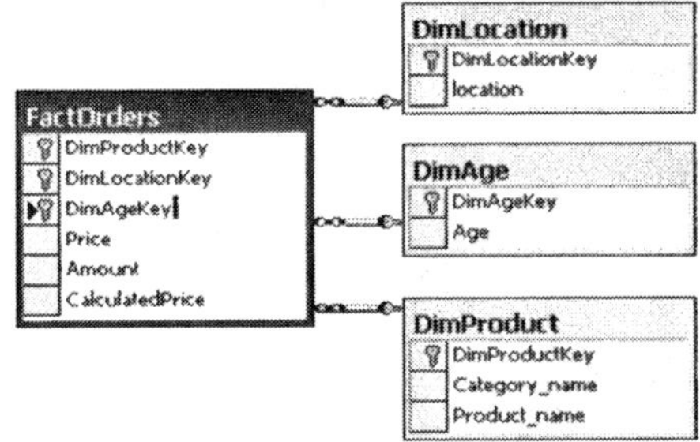

Figure 8. A Cube Design Example

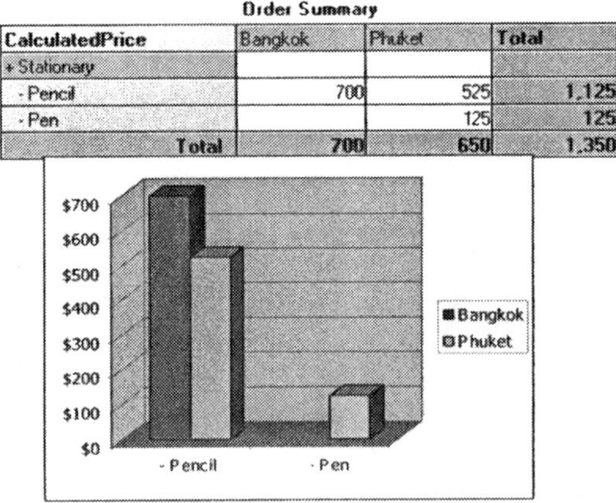
Order Summary

CalculatedPrice	Bangkok	Phuket	Total
+ Stationary			
- Pencil	700	525	1,125
- Pen		125	125
Total	700	650	1,350

Figure 9. A BI Report Example

6. CONCLUSIONS

This paper presents a methodology for transforming RDF documents and schemas to relational database. Complete conceptual meta schema and meta tables of RDFS are introduced and the examples illustrate how RDF documents and their schemas are transformed and stored in relational tables. After the conversion from RDF data source to relational tables is done, multidimensional cubes and executive reports can be defined based on the organization needs.

REFERENCES

1. S.K. Kim, B.G. Kim, J. Lee, and H.C. Lim, The Strategies for storing RDF Documents using RDBMS, in *Proc. of The 6th International Conference on Advanced Communication Technology,* Volume 2 (2004), pp.1027–1029.
2. L. Ding, K. Wilkinson, C. Sayers, and H. Kuno, Application-Specific Schema Design for Storing Large RDF Datasets, in *Workshop on Practical and Scalable Semantic Systems* (Sanibel Island, Florida, October 2003).
3. Oracle, *Oracle® Spatial Resource Description Framework (RDF)*, 10g Release 2, (October 2005). http://download-east.oracle.com/docs/cd/B19306_01/appdev.102/b19307.pdf (Accessed May 10, 2007).
4. D. Brickley and R.V. Guha, *Resource Description Framework (RDF) Schema Specification 1.0,* W3C Candidate Recommendation (March 27, 2000). http://www.w3.org/TR/2000/CR-rdf-schema-20000327 (Accessed May 10, 2007).
5. D.L. McGuinness and F.V. Harmelen, *OWL Web Ontology Language Overview,* W3C Recommendation (February 10, 2004). http://www.w3.org/TR/2004/REC-owl-features-20040210/ (Accessed May 10, 2007).
6. C.J. Dates, *An Introduction to Database Systems*, Sixth Edition (Addison Wesley Publishing Company: 1995), pp.347-365.
7. D. Bell, *An introduction to structure diagrams in UML 2* (September 15, 2004). http://www128.ibm.com/developerworks/rational/library/content/RationalEdge/sep04/bell/ (Accessed May 10, 2007).
8. G.M. Nijssen and T.A. Halpin, *Conceptual Schema and Relational Database Design* (Prentice Hall of Australia Pty Ltd: 1989), pp.291-302.
9. T. Halpin, *Object-Role Modeling* (ORM/NIAM), Handbook on Architectures of Information Systems (1998).
10. E. Prud'hommeaux and A. Seaborne, *SPARQL Query Language for RDF,* W3C Working Draft (October 4, 2006). http://www.w3.org/TR/2006/WD-rdf-sparql-query-20061004 (Accessed May 10, 2007).
11. V. Bonstrom, A. Hinze, and H. Schweppe, Storing RDF as a Graph, in *Proceedings of the First Latin American Web Congress* (November 10-12, 2003), pp.27-36.

Modeling Enterprise Intelligence Component Based on Multi-Agents

Rui Fan and Lingxi Peng

School of Software, Guangdong Ocean University, Zhanjiang 524088, P.R. China
fanrui@gdou.edu.cn scu.peng@gmail.com

Abstract. The large-granularity software component is the basis for structuring complex enterprise software system. However, current components are small, and their coupling is close. Furthermore, a software entity is broken up and distributed in tiers, and different entity pieces in same level are interweaved. All these limitations lead to unclear component boundary, complicated internal structure and inflexible interaction, which increase difficulties for component to be updated, replaced and maintained. This paper proposes a Multi-agent (M-Agent) component formal method, which encapsulates the enterprise subject domain in the enterprise entity component, encapsulates the enterprise subject process in the intelligent connector, and dynamically assembles them in P2P nodes. The theoretical analysis proves that the proposed method will change enterprise intelligence component to a large granularity, loose coupling and independent evolvement grid component model.

Keywords: *Enterprise intelligence component, Enterprise entity component, Intelligence connector, P2P*

1. INTRODUCTION

For adapting dynamic changes of complex enterprise information system, several solutions are already presented. The virtual enterprise whole world supply chain organization net is proposed, which the modeling concept, the method as well as reference architecture is given [1].An M-Agent ERP prototype system is proposed, which completes the widespread enterprise integration. Agents can be assembled fast, which deals with the change demands of enterprise [2]. The dynamic organization network's software component architecture is presented. A engine component runs above the ERP, which provides the essential intelligence and flexible for the dynamic supply chain integration [3].The active services is proposed, which use program mining frame on Internet, dynamically retrieves related components and assembles software system, which satisfies user need [4].

The dynamic changes demand that complex software system can evolve independently. The great granularity component may be the key. Currently, granularity of component is small, their coupling is close, and it is broken up and distributed in tiers, in same level different entity pieces are mixed together. That lead component boundary is unclear, internal structure is complicated, and interaction is inflexibility, increase difficulties for component to renew, replace and maintain. With

Please use the following format when citing this chapter:

Fan, R., Peng, L., 2007, in IFIP International Federation for Information Processing, Volume 254, Research and Practical Issues of Enterprise Information Systems II Volume 1, eds. L. Xu, Tjoa A., Chaudhry S. (Boston: Springer), pp. 455-460.

the M-Agent component formalization method, encapsulates the enterprise subject domain into enterprise entity component, encapsulates the enterprise subject process into the intelligent connector, and dynamically assembles them in P2P nodes. Let the enterprise intelligence component become into a large granularity, loose coupling, and independent evolvement grid component model.

2. ENTERPRISE MODEL TO M-AGENT COMPONENTS

By customizing enterprise subject domain and process with M-agent components, the enterprise model is transformed into the enterprise intelligent component model.

2.1 The Enterprise Entity Component

Define 1 The Enterprise entity component, which is shown in Figure 1

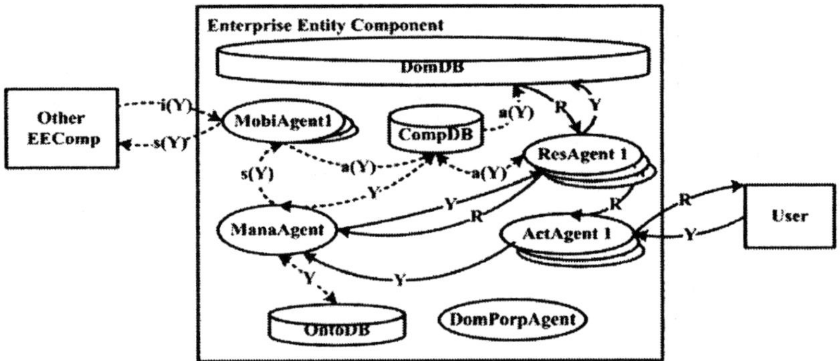

Figure 1. The Enterprise Entity Component Model

$$EEComp ::= (ID,\ DomDB,\ OntoDB,\ CompDB,\ ManaAgent,\ MobiAgentSet,\ ResAgentSet,\ ActAgentSet,\ EC) \qquad (1)$$

Thereinto:
ID is an only identifier;
DomDB is a subject domain database;
OntoDB is an ontology knowledge library;
CompDB is a base components library;
ManaAgent is a management agent, which is control and administrative center;
MobiAgentSet is mobile agent set. MobiAgent plays a role of dynamical interface, which goes to goal nodes for carries out servers and returns results from nodes;

ResAgentSet is resources agent set. ResAgent carries on the inquiry, renewal to the subject domain database as well as other internal resources;

ActAgentSet is participant agent set. ActAgent is interactive windows for user;

DomPropAgent is an attribute value agent, which is a window for viewing and customizing attributes of EEComp.

EC is the π-calculus description about evolution of EEComp. In figure 1, the evolution is described as follows:

$$\overline{User}Y.ActAgent(Y).\overline{ActAgent}Y.ManaAgent(Y).([Y \in RegTable].ResAgent(Y).\overline{ResAgent}Y.$$
$$DomDB(Y).\overline{DomDB}R.ResAgent(R).\overline{ResAgent}R.ActAgent(R).\overline{ActAgent}R.User(R) +$$
$$[Y \notin RegTable].([Y \in OntoDB].([Y \in CompDB].(ResAgent(a(Y)) \mid DomDB(a(Y))).$$
$$\overline{DomDB}R.ResAgent(R).\overline{ResAgent}R.ActAgent(R).\overline{ActAgent}(R).User(R) +$$
$$[Y \notin CompDB].MobiAgent(s(Y)).\overline{MobiAgent}s(Y).Other(s(Y)).\overline{Other}l(Y).MobiAgent(l(Y)).$$
$$\overline{MobiAgent}a(Y).CompDB(a(Y)).(ResAgent(a(Y)) \mid DomDB(a(Y))).\overline{DomDB}R.ResAgent(R).$$
$$\overline{ResAgent}R.ActAgent(R).\overline{ActAgent}R.User(R))$$
$$+[Y \notin OntoDB].MobiAgent(s(Y)).\overline{MobiAgent}(s(Y)).Other(s(Y))))$$

When request Y is sent to ManaAgent via ActAgent, ManaAgent inquires the RegTable for confirming relative services, activates related agents and resources to carry out the corresponding services, and returns the result R. If doesn't have related services, a compare is made with the OntoDB, if Y belongs to this subject, ManaAgent demands related agents to add base components from the CompDB for new functions. If doesn't have need components in CompDB, ManaAgent dispatches MobiAgent to search outside, download and load need components to agents and resources for evolution. If Y doesn't belong to this subject, ManaAgent dispatches MobiAgent to interact with other entity components for request Y.

2.2 The Intelligent Connector

Define 2 The Intelligent connector, is shown in Figure 2

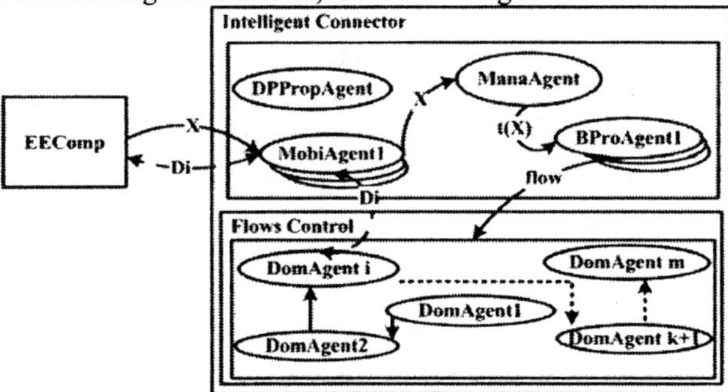

Figure 2. The Intelligent Connector Model

$$IConn ::= (ID, ManaAgent, MobiAgentSet, DomAgentSet, BProAgentSet, EI) \quad \mathbf{(2)}$$

Here:

ID is an only identifier;

ManaAgent is a management agent;

MobiAgentSet is mobile agent set;

DomAgentSet is domain agent set. DomAgent is a proxy of EEComp;

BProAgentSet is subject process agent set. BProAgent dynamically rebuilds and controls business chain;

PPropAgent is an attribute value agent, which is a window for viewing and customizing attributes of IConn.

EI is the π-calculus description about evolution of IConn. In figure 2, the dynamic intelligent evolution mechanism is described as follows:

$$\overline{EEComp}X.MobiAgent(X).\overline{MobiAgent}X.ManaAgent(X).\overline{ManaAgent}t(X$$
$$\overline{BProAgent}flow.(\overline{DomAgent1}D1.MobiAgent1(D1).\overline{MobiAgent1}D1.EEC$$
$$\overline{DomAgent2}D2.MobiAgent2(D2).\overline{MobiAgent2}D2.EEComp2(D2)|...|$$
$$\overline{DomAgentm}Dm.MobiAgentm(Dm).\overline{MobiAgentm}Dm.EECompm(Dm))$$

When X send from EEComp, MobiAgent transmits X to ManaAgent. ManaAgent outputs tasks t(X) to BProAgent. With the contract net, BProAgent classes tasks and sends to each DomAgent, which has registered. According to own ability, DomAgent gives up or returns the bid. BProAgent evaluates, and puts selected DomAgents into the flows control model; the dynamical evolution of structure is achieved by rebuilding business chains. Then, BProAgent controls these DomAgents to interact with related enterprise entity components, cooperatively finish related services.

2.3 The Enterprise Intelligent Component

Define 3 The Enterprise intelligent component is shown in Figure 3.

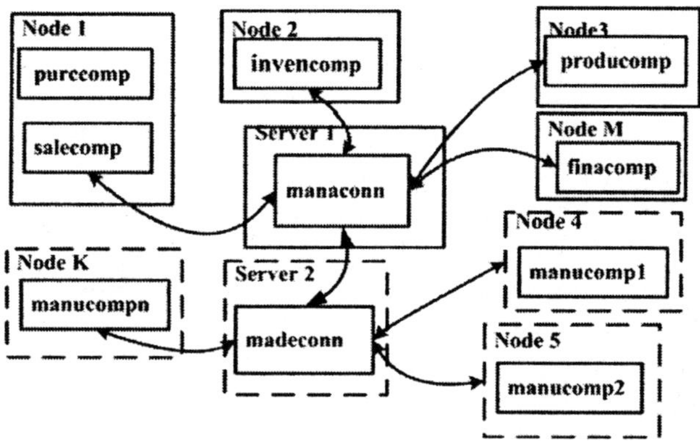

Figure 3. The Enterprise Intelligent Component Model

$$\text{EIComp} ::= (\text{EEComp}, \text{IConn}, \text{EE}) \tag{3}$$

Thereinto:

EEComp is the enterprise entity component;

IConn is the intelligent connector;

EE is the π-calculus description about evolution of EIComp;

Figure 3 shows the deployment of EIComp in P2P nodes, the formal description is as follows:

```
IConn : ManaConn, MadeConn; /* management ,..., manufacture intelligent connector */
EEComp : SaleComp, InvenComp, PurcComp, ..., ManuCompn; /* sale, inventory,
                                        purchase, ..., makesn entity component */
Conf(node1 ,(PurcComp, SaleComp)); /* purcComp & saleComp in node1 */
Conf(node2, InvenComp); /* invenComp in node2 */
...
Conf(nodek, MauCompn); /* mauComp n in nodek */
Conf(Server1, ManaConn); /* manaConn in sever1 node */
Conf(Server2, MadeConn); /* MadeConn in server2 node */
...
manaconn_flow(salecomp, invencomp, producomp, finacomp);
madeconn_flow(manucomp1, manucomp2, ..., manucompn) .
...
```

The Conf ( ) describes the dynamic deployment about node with EEComp or IConn, and the IConn_flow ( ) describes the dynamic rebuilding business chain, which include those EEComps.

3. CONCLUSIONS

In order to construct the great granularity autonomy software component, this paper propose the M-Agent component formal method, it encapsulates the enterprise subject domain into reusable, autonomous enterprise entity component. It also encapsulates the enterprise subject process into the dynamic intelligent connector. Furthermore, it dynamically assembles them in the P2P nodes. Finally, the method makes the enterprise intelligence component become one kind of big granularity, clear boundary, loose coupling, and independent evolution grid component model.

REFERENCES

1. A. Zaidat, X. Boucher, and L. Vincent: A framework for organization network engineering and integration, *Robotics and Computer-Integrated Manufacturing.* Volume 21, pp.259-271, (2005).
2. B.R. Lea, C. Mahesh, W. Gupta, and B. Yu, A prototype multi-agent ERP system: an integrated architecture and a conceptual, *Technovation.* Volume 25, pp.433-441. (2005).
3. M. Verwijmeren: Software component architecture in supply chain management, *Computers in Industry.* Volume 53, pp.165-178, (2004).
4. Y. Zhang and C. Fang, *Active Services: Concepts, Architecture and Implementation* (Science publish house: Beijing, 2005).

Constructing the Knowledge Model in ERP Implementation

Jiangao Deng and Yijie Bian

Business School, Hohai University, Nanjing 210098, Jiangsu, P.R.China
djgwmdkx@163.com byj@hhu.edu.cn

Abstract. Successful knowledge transfer is an effective guarantee for ERP implementation. This paper introduces knowledge types used in ERP implementation, sorts out structure components of such knowledge, analyses the key points of knowledge and its transfer involved in the three ERP implementation entities, and then constructs three-dimensional knowledge models at two main ERP implementation stages, confirming stage and implementing stage, at last it gives a detailed decomposition.

Keywords: *ERP, Knowledge transfer, Knowledge model*

1. INTRODUCTION

As an important means to facilitate and realize innovation in system, technology and management, informationization has become a popular strategy among enterprises. ERP (Enterprise Resource Planning), which reflects today's most advanced enterprise management theory, has realized an optimum management of enterprise's resources, by offering the best scheme for informationization integration [1]. Nevertheless, whether an enterprise can integrate information technology with its organization, overall management and culture, in order to advance its scientific management and its core competition ability, lies on the effective knowledge management during the ERP implementation process. As we all know, most enterprises, who invested in informationization, usually fail to fully realize their original purpose. Therefore, a research on knowledge models in ERP implementation becomes necessary. According to several years of experience in ERP implementation, the author of this paper sorts out knowledge types and puts forth a 3-dimensional knowledge model (3-D KM) in ERP implementation, in hopes of benefiting the ERP implementation practice.

2. ERP IMPLEMENTATION KNOWLEDGE TYPES

ERP Implementation Knowledge (ERP-IK), which is distributed among all ERP implementation participating parties, falls into two categories, namely explicit knowledge and tacit knowledge.

Please use the following format when citing this chapter:

Deng, J., Bian, Y., 2007, in IFIP International Federation for Information Processing, Volume 254, Research and Practical Issues of Enterprise Information Systems II Volume 1, eds. L. Xu, Tjoa A., Chaudhry S. (Boston: Springer), pp. 461-466.

Explicit knowledge refers to the reports and the lectures from experts, manuals on software and hardware, and other documents. Explicit knowledge is quite general, to which enterprises can have easy access at a certain cost.

Tacit knowledge, on the contrary, is quite empirical, which is hard to be materialized or transmitted in words or formulas, as well as in conventional ways. Tacit knowledge is mainly embodied in 3 aspects: Firstly, the methodology, templates and technical knack used in the ERP implementation process; Secondly, management ideas, business process designs and professional experience incarnated in an ERP software; and thirdly, the impact of ERP implementation exerted on an enterprise organization, management system and culture[2].

3. STRUCTURE COMPONENTS OF ERP-IK

In the ERP implementation process, knowledge needing transfer is in various forms and at different levels of difficulty, according to which, structure components of ERP-IK can be divided into two parts: Structure components of knowledge type and Structure components of knowledge state [3-4].

Table 1. Structure Components of ERP-IK

		Name	Symbol
Structure Components	Structure Components of Knowledge Type	Data Knowledge	DK
		Program Knowledge	PK
		Function Knowledge	FK
		Management Knowledge	MK
		Integral Knowledge	IK
		Renewed Knowledge	RK
	Structure Components of Knowledge State	Formalized Knowledge	FOK
		Emerging Knowledge	EMK
		Experiential Knowledge	EXK

DK is the most fundamental data in ERP implementation. PK refers to the rules, regulations, and protocols. FK is the efficient workflow and process. MK is the logical and systematic Management models and knowledge systems. IK is the effective application of administration knowledge. RK means renewed knowledge. FOK is the formalized knowledge, which belongs to explicit knowledge. EMK is the emerging knowledge, which is composed of both explicit and tacit knowledge. EXK is the experiential knowledge, which belongs to tacit knowledge.

4. KNOWLEDGE TRANSFER AMONG ERP IMPLEMENTATION ENTITIES

There are the three organizational entities in ERP implementation, including ERP Applying Enterprise (EAE), ERP Software Provider (ESP) and Professional

Consultant (PC). The most important work of ERP implementation is to transfer technology and knowledge among these three entities [5].

Knowledge transferred from EAE to ESP and PC includes knowledge of the profession, of enterprise demands and individualized demands, etc. Knowledge transferred from ESP to EAE and PC includes knowledge of ERP theories, of project solutions, of project implementation methodology, etc. Knowledge transferred from PC to EAE and ESP includes knowledge of judgment of enterprise demands, of venture evaluation, etc.

The knowledge mentioned above is disseminated in its various structure components, all of which transfer at a different degree of difficulty. As a result, it is necessary to construct an ERP implementation knowledge model (ERP-IKM).

5. CONSTRUCTING THE ERP IMPLEMENTATION KNOWLEDGE MODEL

By summarizing CIM enterprise modeling theories, especially the CIM-OSA modeling theory and Professor Congdong Li's modeling thought [6-9]. The paper puts forward a three-dimensional ERP-IK model (3-D ERP-IKM). This 3-D ERP-IKM, which describes ERP-IK belonging to the three entities, forms the basic theory of ERP-IK transfer. The main panel of the model is composed of knowledge type components and knowledge state components, which describe the ERP-IK contents, forms, transfer difficulty, and transfer strategy at different implementation stages.

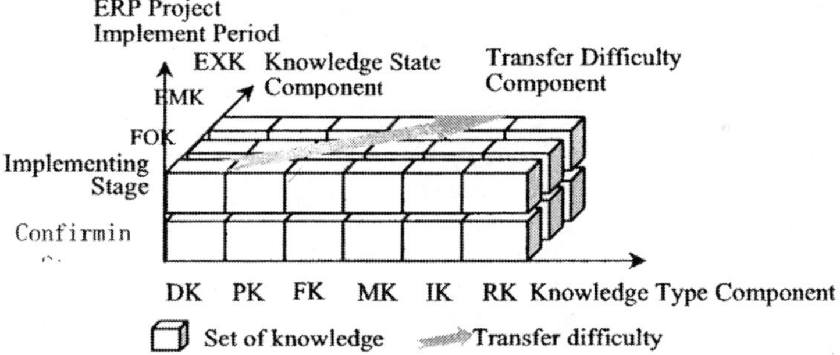

Figure 1. 3-D ERP-IKM

The knowledge transfer difficulty component is also one kind of ERP-IK components. It is intrinsic feature of knowledge and its causal ambiguity that causes great obstacles to knowledge transfer and duplication.

Now, the knowledge transfer difficulty component in this 3-D ERP-IKM rises to such occasions by describing the characteristics of such implicit knowledge explicitly. In the 3-D ERP-IKM, the X-axis shows the six structure components of knowledge type, namely DK, PK, FK, MK, IK and PK, with an increasing transfer difficulty; the

Y-axis shows the three structure components of knowledge state, namely FOK, EMK and EXK, with an increasing transfer difficulty.

5.1 Further Development of ERP-IKM

In order to ensure a successful knowledge transfer in ERP implementation, this paragraph puts forward ERP-IKM at the confirming stage and implementing stage of the project respectively [10-11].

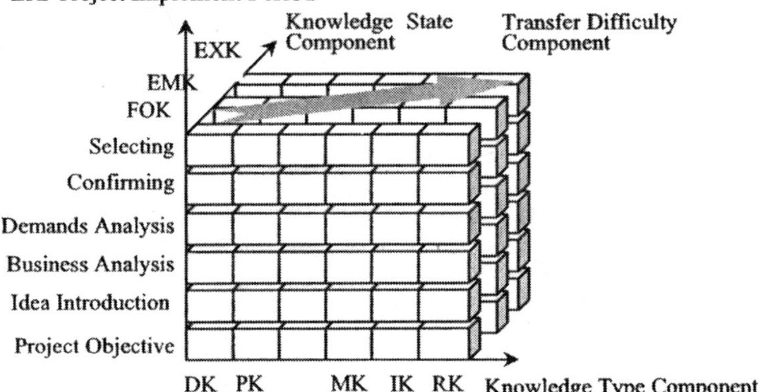

Figure 2. ERP-IKM at the Confirming Stage Knowledge

Figure 2 describes the main contents of ERP-IK at the confirming stage of the project, including knowledge of the project's objectives (enterprise background, project's objective), of ERP ideas (basic conceptions about ERP, preliminary functions of ERP modules), of enterprise transactions (procedures, functions, and existing problems of enterprise transactions), of the project's demands, of ERP software providers, and knowledge of project's management, etc.

Figure3 describes the main contents of ERP-IKM at the implementation stage of the project, including knowledge of implementation preparation, of business blueprint, and of specific implementation, etc.

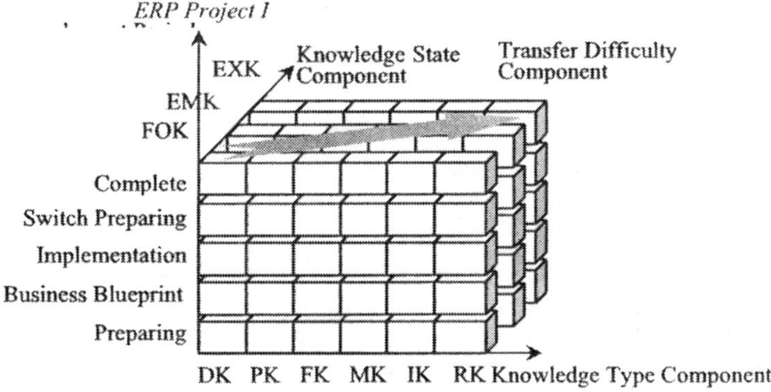

Figure 3. ERP-IKM at the Implementing Stage

6. CONCLUSIONS

To sum up, the course of ERP implementation is the process of knowledge transfer. In such a course, several entities are involved, as well as the two knowledge types, i.e. explicit knowledge and tacit knowledge. Having analyzed the structure components of ERP-IK, and carried out a preliminary research on them, this paper puts forward a three-dimensional knowledge management model, which is used in turn to instruct ERP implementation practice. However, there are still some important aspects which have not been explored, for example, knowledge transfer system involved with software providers, professional consultants and implement enterprises, which can also contribute to a successful ERP implementation.

REFERENCES

1. W. Skokl and M. Legge, Evaluating enterprise resource planning systems using an interpretive approach, *Knowledge and Process Management*. Volume 9, Number 2, pp.72-82, (2003).
2. L. Jeffrey, F. Cummings, and B. Teng, Transferring R&D knowledge: the key factors affecting knowledge transfer success, *Journal of Engineering and Technology*. Volume 20, Number. 2, pp.39-68, (2003).
3. K. Joshi, S. Sarker, and S. Sarker, Knowledge transfer within information systems development teams: Examining the role of knowledge source attributes, *Decision Support Systems*. Volume 41, Number 2, pp.456-460, (2006).

4. M. Alavi and D. Leidner, Review knowledge management and knowledge management systems conceptual foundations and research issues, *MIS Quarterly*. Volume 4, Number 25, pp.11-20, (2001).
5. C. Mary, D. Jones, M. Cline, and H. Ryan, Exploring knowledge sharing in ERP implementation: an organizational culture framework, *Decision Support Systems*. Volume 41, Number 2, pp.411-434, (2006).
6. A. Vincent, D. Mabert, A. Soni, and M. Venkataramanan, Model based interpretation of survey data: a case study of enterprise resource planning implementations, *Mathematical and Computer Modeling*. Volume 44, Number 1, pp.16-29, (2006).
7. H. Du, C. Li, and X. Li, Knowledge transfer architecture for ERP implementation, *Journal of Industrial Engineering*. Volume 19, Number 2, pp.110-113, (2005).
8. S. Newell, J. Huang, R. Galliers, and S. Pan, Implementing enterprise resource planning and knowledge management systems in tandem: fostering efficiency and innovation complementarity, *Information and Organization*. Volume 9, Number 23, pp.32-46, (2003).
9. E. Daniel and O. Leary, Knowledge management across the enterprise resource planning systems life cycle, *International Journal of Accounting Information System*. Volume 8, Number 5, pp.99-100, (2002).
10. F. Eppler, J. Martin, and O. Sukowski, Managing team knowledge: Core process, tools and enabling factors. *European Management Journal*. Volume 10, Number 18, pp.334-341, (2000).
11. D. Malone, Knowledge management: a model for organizational learning, *International Journal of Accounting Information Systems*. Volume 3, Number 2, pp.111-123, (2002).

Research on the Costing and Data Mining Based on ABC in Logistics Firms

Dong Mu, Lingyun Zhou and Shoubo Xu

School of Economics and Management, Beijing Jiaotong University, Beijing 100044, P.R. China mueast@163.com

Abstract. The costing and data mining of logistics costs will become increasingly important to all firms seeking competitive advantages. Activity Based Costing (ABC) is considered as the optimized and most promising method of costing and controlling logistics cost now, and logistics cost data mining based on ABC is playing a very important role in business management. The paper firstly analyses the costing principle of ABC for logistics projects, and according to the basic principles of ABC and business management, the paper puts forward the basically technical route of logistics project costing and data mining based on ABC for business management and decision-making, moreover, the concrete costing process and model of applying ABC are deduced, then the further application forms of data mining based on ABC are summarized and elaborated for business management and decision-making.

Keywords: *Activity based costing, Costing, Data mining, Model, Decision-making*

I. INTRODUCTION

With the development of economy, the importance of logistics has been noticed by all countries. The growth in the importance of the logistics function has significant implications for a firm's cost accounting system and the management of logistics costs has become increasingly important due to their significant impact on product profitability, product pricing, customer profitability, and ultimately, corporate profitability. Logistics can offer a key source of competitive advantage through service differentiation or by reducing costs and increasing corporate profitability. Nowadays it develops fleetly, and it is playing a very important role in economy development, so the accounting and control of logistics costs will become increasingly important to firms seeking a competitive advantage. Logistics business is often operated according to logistics projects by logistics firms, thereby the cost of logistics project is more and more important for logistics project management and enterprise decision, so it must be calculated exactly. At present, most enterprises in China calculate the cost respectively with the traditional cost accounting method. However, the traditional costing method has limitations in the costing of logistics, which prominently displays that costing has not achieved the target of cost content integrity and indirect expense assignment rationality, so the costing results lose the objectivity and the policy-making relativity. Then, the cost accounting and

Please use the following format when citing this chapter:

Mu, D., Zhou, L., Xu, S., 2007, in IFIP International Federation for Information Processing, Volume 254, Research and Practical Issues of Enterprise Information Systems II Volume 1, eds. L. Xu, Tjoa A., Chaudhry S. (Boston: Springer), pp. 467-474.

management not only is the bottle neck of the market development for logistics firms, but also is the sticking point of effective operation management and decision-making. So Chinese logistics firms will require more accurate and detailed logistics cost information from their cost accounting systems, and Chinese logistics managers require detailed information to determine how different products, customers, or supply channels affect the costs of providing logistics services. The detail and complexity of the cost information will correspond to the diversity products handled, customer requirements, or supply channels used. Activity Based Costing, which is considered the optimized and most promising method of costing and controlling logistics cost, so it is necessary and urgent to be introduced into the cost management of logistics firms [1]. And at present, more and more enterprises in China adopt ABC in cost management and get better effects.

2. THE PRINCIPLE OF COSTING AND DATA MINING BASED ON ABC IN LOGISTICS FIRMS

2.1 Costing Principle Based on ABC for Logistics Projects

Logistics business is often operated through logistics projects in Chinese logistics firms. According to the operation characteristics of logistics projects and the basic principle of ABC, namely that product manufacture induces activity and activity consume resources, then it induces cost[2], the consequence conclusion that the operation of logistics service project induces logistics activity and logistics activity consumes resources and induces logistics service cost is deduced. In order to narrate expediently, three concepts of proper cost, direct cost and overhead cost are introduced. Proper cost is the cost which can be carried up to specific logistics project and be paid to other enterprises or organizations directly, it includes the consigned logistics cost, compensation of breach of faith, insurance cost, cost of applying to customs and checkout cost, etc. Direct cost is the cost which can be carried up to cost object directly, so it concludes direct material, direct manpower and proper cost. Overhead cost is the cost which can not be carried up to cost object directly.

2.2 Data Mining Technical Route Based on ABC for Logistics Projects

According to the basic principle and implementation step of ABC[3], the operation process of logistics project and the application route of logistics projects costing and cost management in Chinese enterprises[4], the technical route of applying ABC for logistics projects in china is studied, then is got and illustrated in Figure 1.

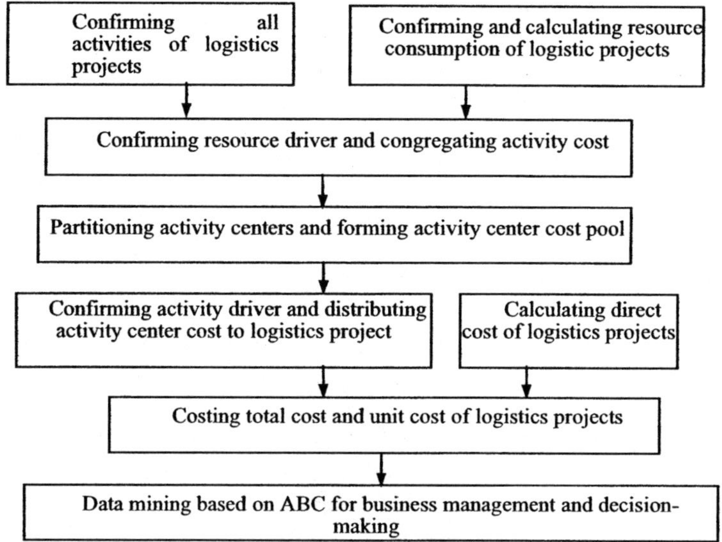

Figure 1. Technical Route of Applying ABC for Logistics Projects

3. COSTING STEP AND MODEL OF APPLYING ABC FOR LOGISTICS PROJECTS

3.1 Confirming Activities of Logistics Project

Confirming activities of logistics projects should follow the process.

(1) Firstly, activity information should be collected by using flow chart or gathering news.

(2) Secondly, activities are identified according to cost-benefit principle, and activity tache and amount are decided according to the cost nicety degree demand of logistics projects and enterprise management.

3.2 Confirming and Calculating Resource Consumption

The application of ABC doesn't change the total amount of resource. It changes the distributing rate of total cost between cost objects, so all resource consumption information can be gained from the accountant sort book.

3.3 Confirming Resource Driver and Congregating Activity Cost

The process should conform to the following approach.

The first step is confirming resource driver. At first, the amount of resource driver should be confirmed. The decision depend on these factors: the correlation degree between cost driver and resource cost, the expectation definition of cost, the complex degree of logistics service and so on. Then the right resource driver should be chosen. The choosing process should follow these principles, such as the cost-benefit principle, correlation principle, important principle and plenitude principle[5].

The second step is calculating resource driver rate by equation (1).

$$r_i = \frac{c_i}{a_i} \qquad (i=1, 2, \cdots\cdots, n) \tag{1}$$

r_i, c_i and a_i are resource driver rate, resource cost and resource driver amount of resource i respectively.

The third step is distributing the resource cost to activity and forming activity cost pool. Activity cost can be calculated by equation (2).

$$c_j = \sum_{i=1}^{n} r_i \times q_{ij} \qquad (j=1, 2, \cdots\cdots, m) \tag{2}$$

c_j is activity cost of activity j and q_{ij} is consumed resource i amount of activity j.

3.4 Partitioning Activity Center

There are some principles of partitioning activity centers, such as homogeneity principle, certain scale principle, cost costing veracity principle. Then activity center cost can be calculated according to these principles and equation (3).

$$B_k = \sum_{j=1}^{m} c_j \times w_{jk} \qquad (k=1,2, \cdots\cdots, q) \tag{3}$$

w_{jk} means whether j belong to activity center cost pool k or not. If j belong to activity center cost pool k, its value is 1, otherwise its value is 0. B_k is the total cost of activity center cost k.

3.5 Confirming Activity Driver and Distributing Activity Center Cost

There are some factors of confirming activity drivers, such as quantitative factor, homogeneity, the connection of between cost and benefit, the correlation degree of activity and consumed resources [6]. Then activity driver can be calculated by equation (4) .

$$R_k = \frac{B_k}{A_k} \tag{4}$$

A_k is activity driver amount of activity center cost pool k . R_k is activity driver rate of activity center cost pool k . Then cost is distributed to cost object from cost pool by equation (5).

$$C_p = \sum_{k=1}^{q} R_k \times Q_{kp} \quad (p = 1,2,\cdots\cdots, s) \tag{5}$$

Q_{kp} is activity driver amount of activity center cost pool k by object p . C_p means the total overhead cost of object p .

3.6 Calculating Direct Cost of Logistics Project

Direct cost should be respectively calculated according to direct material, direct manpower and Proper cost. Direct material can be calculated by equation (6).

$$M_p = (1-w)\sum_{u=1}^{v} Y_u G_{up} \quad (u = 1,2,\cdots\cdots, v) \tag{6}$$

In the equation, M_p is the direct cost of object p , w is the proportion of callback scrap relative to all materials, Y_u is the unit price of direct material u and G_{up} is consumed amount of direct material u by object p . Direct manpower can be calculated by equation (7).

$$L_p = \sum_{\alpha=1}^{x} T_{\alpha p} \mu_\alpha (1+\lambda) \quad (\alpha = 1,2,\cdots\cdots, x) \tag{7}$$

L_p is the direct manpower cost of object p , $T_{\alpha p}$ is work time amount of work type α , μ_α is the average standard pay per an hour of work type α and λ is the proportion of accessional pay relative to standard pay. Because the range of proper cost is big and proper cost of different logistics objects is different, proper cost of object p, namely Z_p, must be calculated according to idiographic conditions.

3.7 Calculating Total Cost and Unit Cost of Logistics Projects

According to above results, the total cost of logistics project p, namely T_p, can be calculated by equation (8).

$$T_p = M_p + L_p + Z_P + C_p \tag{8}$$

According to the above got equations, outspread the equation step by step, equation (9) is gained.

$$T_p = (1-w)\sum_{u=1}^{v} Y_u G_{up} + \sum_{\alpha=1}^{x} T_{\alpha p}\mu_\alpha(1+\lambda) + Z_p + \sum_{k=1}^{q}\sum_{j=1}^{m}\sum_{i=1}^{n} \frac{c_i q_{ij} w_{jk}}{A_k a_i} Q_{kp} \tag{9}$$

Because each logistics project can be cost and get accurate cost results, then unit cost of cost object can be also calculated through equation (10).

$$T_p^{'} = \frac{T_p}{Q_p} = \frac{M_p + L_p + Z_P + C_p}{Q_p} \tag{10}$$

$T_p{'}$ in the equation is the unit cost of logistics project p. Q_p is the unit amount of logistics project p. Every logistics enterprise can get different cost results according to different costing unit, then get wished data for cost management and enterprise innovation.

3.8 Calculating Total Logistics Cost of Enterprises

Because ABC is a complete cost calculating method, all logistics cost can be got through equation (11).

$$T = \sum_{p=1}^{s} T_p = \sum_{p=1}^{s} (M_p + L_p + Z_P + C_p) \tag{31}$$

T of the equation means the total logistics project cost of one enterprise. It can offer a standard for cost control, capital budget, etc.

4. DATA MINING BASED ON ABC FOR BUSINESS MANAGEMENT AND DECISIONS

Activity Based Costing is the optimized and most promising method of costing and controlling logistics cost. The establishment of its application step and costing model is the kernel of applying ABC for any logistics project in Chinese enterprises. It decides the definition of enterprise cost data, then, it affects the enterprise innovation and decision.

However the ABC application of logistics enterprises is not merely one method accurate calculation cost, its real value should be the significantly auxiliary decision-making functions of using obtained correlative ABC cost data in different enterprise management aspects.

The main purpose of using the ABC for enterprises is as follows: the enterprise can obtains the particular and accurate cost data of each logistics activity of operation through the implementation of ABC [7], then enterprises use obtained cost data and make the further data mining and processing, thereby make ABC provide the supporting basis and the guidance function for enterprise's daily digitization operation and information management as well as the related forecast and evaluation analysis and so on According to the correlation analysis, the support business management applications of using obtained ABC cost data are elaborated for logistics enterprises, namely the application patterns based on ABC are concluded for logistics enterprises, such as the pricing decision-making application of logistics service projects, the application in logistics cost budget system, the application in logistics business process reengineering, the application in the performance evaluation based on activity, the analysis application of customer profit ability and decision-making, the cost control application of logistics activity and so on [8].The data mining modes based on ABC for business management and decisions is illustrated in Figure 2.

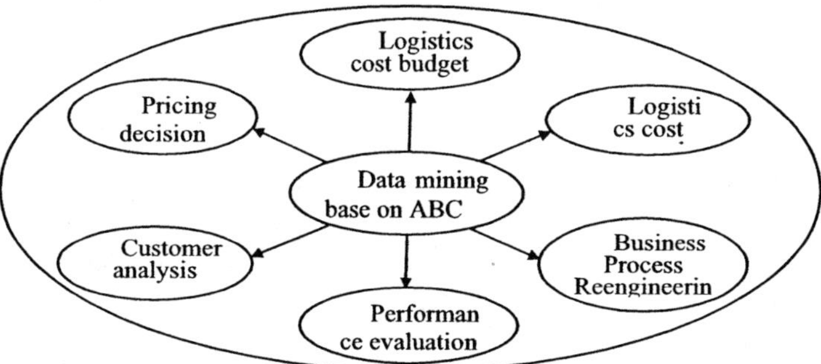

Figure 2. Data Mining Modes of ABC for Logistics Enterprises

In addition, the information obtained from ABC can support such key logistics decisions as determining needs for warehouse space, identifying warehouse locations, choosing between public or private ownership, implementing automation, etc.

5. CONCLUSIONS

According to the research, here we may draw the following conclusions.

(1) ABC achieves greater accuracy of logistics for Chinese logistics firms than traditional costing techniques by using multiple cost drivers. Traditional techniques typically rely on one to three volume based cost drivers to trace overhead costs to products. ABC uses multiple cost drivers to reflect different relationships occurring between activities and the resources they consume.

(2)The analyzed costing principle, step and model of applying ABC for logistics projects are logical and feasible in this paper. It can provide tracking of logistics costs for Chinese logistics firms. This can be of particular value in tracking logistics products or customers for Chinese logistics firms.

(3) ABC can provide financial support data structured for logistics projects in a fashion fundamentally different from accounting data provided in the general ledger. By associating cost to the logistics activity, a clear relationship can be established between sources of logistics activity demand and the related costs. This association can benefit the Chinese logistics firms in determining where logistics costs are being incurred, what is initiating the logistics costs and where to apply efforts to control inflationary logistics costs.

(4) The application of ABC is not merely one method of costing accurately, its real value should is the significantly auxiliary decision-making function in business management of Chinese logistics firms. ABC is a management decision-making tool. Chinese logistics firms can use obtained cost data and develop the further data mining and processing for cost management and relevant decisions. The increased visibility of logistics costs will serve several purposes for the Chinese logistics firms: the identification of more direct costs, a better understanding of price/volume relationships, the opportunity to address significant cost reduction opportunities, better evaluation and justification of logistics investments and customer, the budget of logistics cost budget, the cost controlling of logistics cost and so on.

REFERENCES

1. S. Dan and B. Douglas, ABC/M: Which companies have success?, *The Journal of Corporate Accounting & Finance*. Volume 12, Number 3, pp.35-38, (2001).
2. R. Copper, The rise of activity-based costing-part one: what is an activity-based cost system? *Journal of Cost Management*. Volume 2, Number 2, pp.45-54, (1988).
3. A. Bharara and C.Y. Lee, Implementation of an activity-based costing system in a small manufacturing company, *Journal of International Production Research*. Volume 34, Number 4, pp.1109-1130, (1996).
4. G.L. Fu, *Logistics Cost Management* (China Material Press: Beijing, 2004).
5. X. Zhao and L. Xu, Combination of activity driver of ABC, *Industry Engineering*. Volume 7, Number 6, pp.30-32, (2004).
6. Y.S. Li and H. Yin, *Logistics Cost Management* (China Machine Press, Beijing, 2005).
7. I. John, The use of activity-based information: A managerial perspective, *Management Accounting*. Volume 77, Number 11, pp.80-81, (1999).
8. P. Mike and P. Lew, An integrated framework for activity-based decision making, *Management Decision*. Volume 36, Number 9, pp.580-588, (1998).

Systematization of Requirements Definition for Software Development Processes with a Business Modeling Architecture

Delmir de Azevedo Junior[1] and Renato de Campos[2]

[1]Petrobras University, Republican do Chile, 65, Rio de Janeiro, Brazil, CAP 20.031-912
delmir@petrobras.com.br
[2]UNESP – São Paulo State University, av Luiz E C Coube nº 14-01, Bauru, 17033-360
rcampos@feb.unesp.br

Abstract. There are several modeling methods, techniques and tools available in order to facilitate the understanding and the analysis of the complexity of the modern organizations. Such methods, techniques and tools are used to make the complex organizational practice more understandable. Some of them support information systems development methodologies. Nevertheless, what is observed is lack of integration of the analysis between two domains: the business domain and the system domain. The alignment between the software requirements and the actual need for the business informatization can be improved by means of business modeling techniques. In this work, it was proposed activities for the business modeling to be inserted in the UP (Unified Process) based methodologies or in any other methodology basing on the same principles, with the purpose of systematizing the identification of software requirements aligned with the business objectives. The activities defined in the method comply with the iterative and incremental model, as well as with interfaces well established with the UP pre-established activities, showing some advantages.

Keywords: *Enterprise modeling, Unified process, Information system*

1. INTRODUCTION

The modern business organizations need to be constantly evolving in order to maintain their competitiveness. It is necessary to implement frequent changes and innovations in the business processes and, consequently, in the information systems which support them. The integration among the business objectives, the business processes and the information systems is an important factor for the organizational dynamics and also a challenge to the managers. There are several modeling methods, techniques and tools available in order to facilitate the understanding and the analysis of the complexity of the modern organizations [1]. Such methods, techniques and tools are used to make the complex organizational practice more understandable. There are also several methodologies employed in the information system development. Nevertheless, what is observed is lack of integration of the analysis between the two domains: the business domain and the system domain [2, 3]. Among

Please use the following format when citing this chapter:

de Azevedo Junior, D., de Campos, R., 2007, in IFIP International Federation for Information Processing, Volume 254, Research and Practical Issues of Enterprise Information Systems II Volume 1, eds. L. Xu, Tjoa A., Chaudhry S. (Boston: Springer), pp. 475-485.

all the software system development methodologies, the Unified Process (UP) has been currently highlighted. However, even in the UP, the requirement survey is still an empiric process, not taken systematically into consideration the importance of the focus on the business objectives.

In this context, it is evidenced in the software development processes the need for a closer approximation between the software system requirements and the actual business needs. In the object-oriented paradigm, the requirement analysis has been carried out based on a UML modeling element called Use Case. Although there is some heuristics proposed in order to identify the use cases, such as the ones presented in Schneider and Winters [4], Jacobson et al. [5] and Lilly [6], there are no established methods to make this activity more systematic. The alignment between the software requirements and the actual need for the business informatization can be optimized by means of business modeling techniques.

Thus, this paper presents some definitions regarding the Requirements Engineering, the Unified Process (UP) and some concepts related to the business processes modeling with the UML and issues related to the identification of business use cases. Therefore, the activities proposed to be inserted in UP-based methodologies are described, and the final considerations are presented.

2. REQUIREMENTS ENGINEERING AND UP

The software engineering follows a set of steps. Each of the phases may comprise methods, tools and procedures. Their structuring is mentioned as a software engineering model [7]. Pressman [7] considers that, regardless of the software development model, the software development process has three generic phases: definition, development and maintenance. Four software engineering models have been widely discussed: The classic life cycle (or cascade), the prototyping, the spiral model and the Fourth generation techniques [7]. A new model has been currently used, that is, the iterative and incremental model [5, 8]. The requirement analysis is a phase which is always present in the software definition phase, regardless of the software engineering model adopted. It links the need for process informatization to the software project meeting such needs. A series of analysis methods and requirement specifications was developed. However, there are few propositions aiming at requirement identification systematization in order to make this activity less subjective.

The Unified Process (UP) is a process established to the software development which resulted from three decades of development and practical use. Jacobson *et al.* [5] presents the UP origins from the Objectory process (the first version in 1987), passing through the contributions of the Rational Objectory Process (in 1997), up to the Rational Unified Process – RUP [9]. The UP purpose, as any other development process, is to determine a set of necessary activities to make requirements into software systems. It uses the UML as a language to the modeling of software artifacts produced during the development process. The UML was adopted by the Object Management Group (OMG) in 1997 as a standard language to the modeling of object-oriented systems. It is a language for the specification, visualization, construction and documentation of software system artifacts, as well as for the business modeling and other systems, except for software systems. This language represents a collection of the best engineering practices which proved to be successful in the modeling of large and complex systems [10].

3. BUSINESS PROCESS MODELING BY UML

According to Johansson et al. [11], a business process is a set of connected activities which receives input and transform it into output. In theory, the transformation of the business process must add value and create a useful and effective result to the receiver, above or below the chain. There are several techniques, methodologies and notations to the business modeling [12]. In order to make a company adaptable to the changes, it needs to have a simple and unified description of its entities. Although this is the purpose of many modeling efforts, they provide an extensive, inflexible and fragile description [13]. Recently, UML, which is already consecrated to the software systems modeling, has been proposed to the business modeling by means of its extension mechanisms. According to OMG [10], the UML has extension mechanisms allowing its adjustment to new things and specific domains. The extensions defined by the UML users take place by means of stereotypes, tagged values and constraints that extend and adapt the UML to a specific domain. In the next subsection, a proposal of extensions for the business modeling by using UML will be presented.

The Eriksson and Penker's proposals [14] form a UML-based Architecture for the business modeling in which a business architect can add convenient stereotypes, tagged values and constraints for their business domain. Their work is based primarily on UML extensions in order to represent: processes, resources, rules and objectives. Their proposal is based on the hypothesis that a business can be modeled by means of objects and the relations among them. A modeling architecture provides view for the modeling with a focus on significant aspects. Each view can be modeled by one or more types of diagrams. The proposed Architecture offers the following view [14]:

- Business Vision: It models concepts and objectives to be followed according to the business strategies;
- Business Process: It models the business processes and their relations to the resources, to be followed in order to achieve the objectives;
- Business Structure: It models the (physical, informational, human) resource structure;
- Business Behavior: It models the behavior and interaction among resources and among processes.

Within this Business Process view, it is highlighted the Business Process Diagram and the Assembly Line Diagram. The Business Process Diagram describes the business processes by means of its relations to Objects (Objectives, Inputs, Outputs, Suppliers and Controls). At the top of the Assembly Line Diagram, there is a Business Process Diagram. Below, there are various horizontal packages, which are called assembly line packages, each one representing a group of objects. The objects of a package may be from specific or different classes. An assembly line package is a UML package item stereotyped to << *assembly line* >> and designed as a long horizontal rectangle. It supports the identification of use cases related to the business process. The purpose of this diagram is to demonstrate how the process in the upper part of the diagram uses and generates objects in the assembly line. The reference of an object in an assembly line is indicated by an object flow (represented by a dashed line in the UML) between the process and the object within the packet, in the assembly line. The assembly line diagram can be used as a technique to the use case survey of the system or systems which will support the business processes. The identification of use cases by means of this technique makes the business objectives and the requirements of the system (represented as use cases) be aligned with the global objectives of the business, since they are analyzed based on the business processes, which were defined in terms of the business objectives.

4. ACTIVITY PROPOSAL FOR THE SYSTEMATIZATION

This paper recommends the insertion of a workflow in the UP for the business modeling, based on the modeling technique proposed by Eriksson and Penker [14]. Updates on some UP pre-established activities are also proposed. Such activities are proposed so that they can be applied to any UP-based methodology. The construction technique of business architecture proposed by Eriksson and Penker is, considering all the researched UML business modeling proposals, the only one which has a systematic approach in the transition of the business architecture into a software architecture. However, Eriksson and Penker do not explore the systematization of this transition within a context of system development process or methodology. In the UP, workflow activities to the requirement analysis can be used in all phases of the software development, especially in the Conception and Elaboration phases. In the Conception phase, the requirements identification of the system is emphasized, however, the detailed specification must be performed in the Elaboration phase. A requirement identification method which derive the use cases of a UP software architecture must define activities and their flows, as well as the expected artifact state generated by such activities, in each phase of the process (Conception, Elaboration, Construction and Transition), considering such structure as iterative and incremental. The application of the Eriksson and Penker technique to the UP is performed by means of the definition of a workflow to the business modeling and updates in the activities established for other workflows, so that they can be integrated. Some activities are added and others are only updated, by inserting sub-activities. It is also defined the approach that each activity proposed must have in the Conception and Elaboration phases. As previously shown, these are the phases in which the requirement analysis activities must be more present.

4.1 Business Modeling Workflow

The workflow defined to the business modeling is presented in Figure 1. Following, the descriptions for each activity and the approach for each phase of the development process are presented. Figure 2 shows a part of the development process related to the Concept phase.

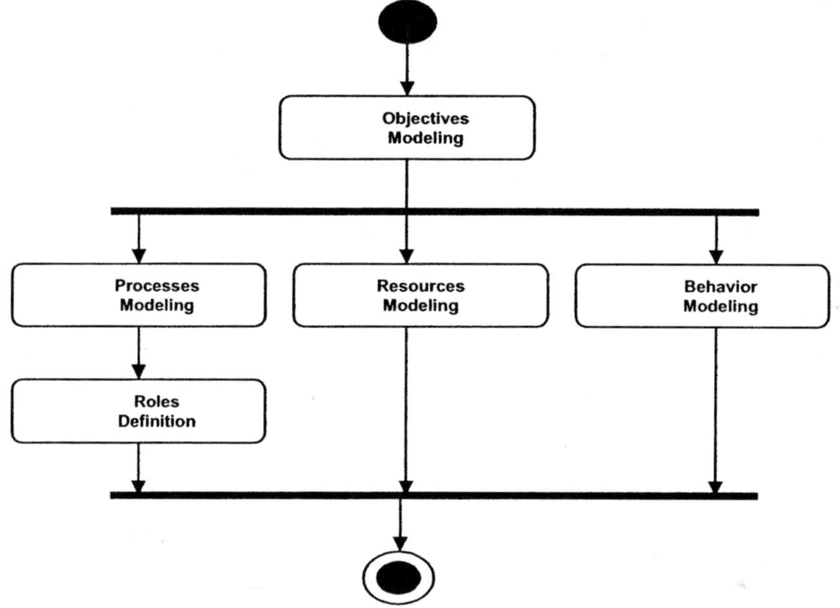

Figure 1. Workflow for Businesses Modeling

4.1.1 Modeling the Business Objectives

The objectives modeling activity must identify the main objectives and sub-objectives of the business in a hierarchical structure that allow the visualization of the dependence aspect among such objectives. This model will be the base for defining the business processes. The business objective modeling must be performed based on interviews with the businesspeople. Resulting product: Objectives Model Diagram. Approaches for each phase:

Conception phase – the Objectives Model must comprehend the objectives relevant to the project, from the strategic ones to those related to the business process objectives themselves.

Elaboration phase – the Objectives Model in terms of possible clarifications must be updated.

4.1.2 Modeling the Business Processes

The business processes must be defined by searching for the achievement of the businesses objectives identified in the Objectives Model. However, there is no need to exist a 1-to-1 relation between the business processes and objectives, because many auxiliary processes will not be necessarily related to an objective of the Objectives Model. It is imperative that interviews with the involved ones also be performed in order to provide subsides to define the business processes. Resulting product: Business Process Diagram.

The approaches for each phase are:

Conception phase – the main business processes must be identified, as well as their relations to the resources (inputs, outputs, suppliers, controls and objectives), and the sequence for their accomplishment. However, it is not necessary to describe in details the event flow taken place internally in the process.

Elaboration phase – To detail the event flow of the processes which will be approached at the iteration.

4.1.3 Modeling the Involved Resources

The resources, information and organizational units must be modeled by means of the Business Structure View diagrams. The modeling of these elements must be performed paralelly with the Business Process Modeling activities, in order to have a better understanding of the terms related to the business, and, consequently, a greater consistence in its modeling. Resulting product: Resource Model Diagram, Information Model Diagram and Organization Model Diagram. Approach for each phase:

Conception phase – all the significant resources identified in the Business Process Model defined in the Conception phase must be modeled, so that the dependence between such resources and the properties can be analyzed.

Elaboration phase – to model all the significant resources identified during the detailing process of the event flow in each business process.

4.1.4 Modeling Resource Behavior

A Resource State (Statechart) Diagram can be created in order to facilitate the determination of the business processes when it is characterized by refining of a same object along the value chain. For example, taking into consideration a sales business, the order can be regarded as an object whose state is being altered (refined) along all the value chain, from the start of the order to the confirmation of the order delivered to the client. In a case like this, the identification of the possible states for the object (such as requested order, order to be verified in the inventory, order in production, order in expedition and order delivered), can facilitate the identification of business processes needed to the accomplishment of the changes in the state of the product. Resulting product: Statechart Diagrams and Interaction Diagrams. Approach for each phase:

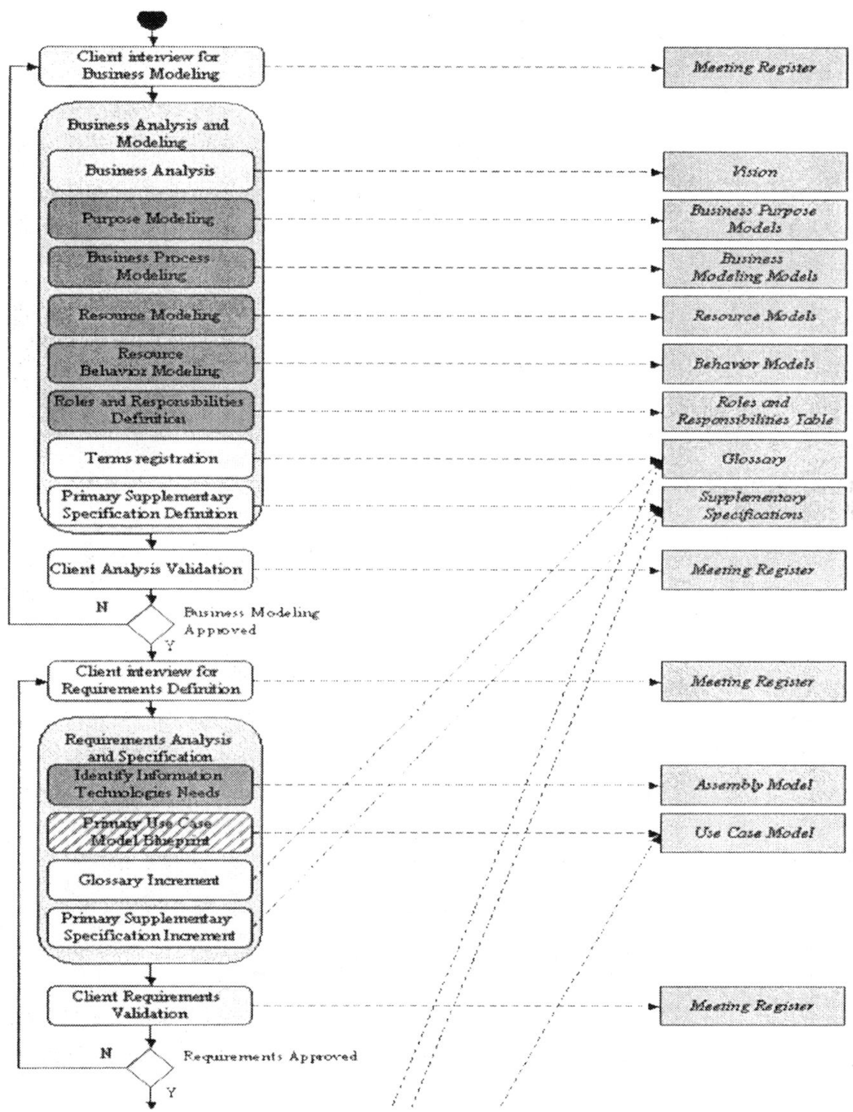

Figure 2. Part of the Development Process Related to the Concept Phase

Conception phase – to model the behavior of the resources when they undergo several changes during the business processes, and this changes dynamic must be better understood.

Elaboration phase – to detail the Statechart Diagrams, in case they have been created in the Conception phase, based on the detailing process of the event flow of the processes.

4.1.5 Defining Roles and Responsibilities

Each business process must have a person in charge, since it will not be connected to only one organizational unit, but passing through many of them. Each process defines an event flow which can involve one or more actors. It is necessary to define which actors act in each one of the processes. It can be done by means of an analysis of the event flow and their association with the actors involved in the process. Resulting product: Table of Roles and Responsibilities. Approach for each phase:

Conception phase - to define solely the people in charge for each business process, whether they are organizational units or functions.

Elaboration phase – to define the roles (actors) associated with the events which take place in the event flow of each business process.

4.2 Requirement Analysis Workflow

Following, activities added to the Requirement Analysis Workflow are described.

4.2.1 Identifying Informatization Needs

In this activity, it is necessary to associate the business processes to the information systems supporting them, thus identifying the possible needs for news information systems through the identification of lacking of automatized support for information and operations to the processes. It is suggested the use of the Assembly Line Diagram as the base for the accomplishment of this activity. Resulting product: Assembly Line Diagram with the identified assembly line packages. Approach for each phase:

Conception phase – to identify software systems which support the business processes as well as to identify the need for new systems and sub-systems. It is used the Assembly Line Diagram as a supporting tool in the development of this activity. One must start with the packages at a high abstraction level, representing the systems which already exist and the nature of the reference information that the systems produce at each analyzed business process. Next, it is necessary to perform an evaluation with regard to the nature of the information and the operations needed in the process, as well as their accomplishment by the existing systems. So, it is possible identify the types of information and operations which are not being held by the software systems available. Such needs for information and operations must be referenced to another representative package of the system (or systems) to be constructed in order to meet such requirements.

Elaboration phase – it is imperative to update and deepen the analysis started at the Conception phase, based on the description of event flow of the processes. It is necessary to evaluate each event flow and to identify events which can be aided by information systems, but that still are not. Such aid must be represented as references (relations) of processes to the systems which support them. Considering the scope of a system identified in the conception, one must represent each assembly line as a system class and distribute the responsibilities among the classes by means of references mentioned to each one of them by the processes. Each event to be informatized must result in a reference to the class that will perform it, and in case this class does not exist, it must be created as a new assembly line. This last step must be performed by following the "encapsulation" concept.

4.2.2 Deriving Use Cases of the Business Processes

The use cases must be identified based on the business processes. This activity must result in a list of Use Case in which one must associate each identified use case with the business process. It is suggested the use of the Assembly Line Diagram as the base for the accomplishment of this activity. The identification of the use cases in the Assembly Line Diagram is performed by means of references cluster (between the processes and the systems) of the same nature. Resulting product: Assembly Line Diagram and Use Cases. Approach for each phase:

Conception phase – the activity must aim at identifying the use cases architecturally significant. These use cases represent functionalities at a high abstraction level. These use cases serve as the base for defining the logic view of the software architecture which will perform them.

Elaboration phase – the activity aims at identifying all the system's use cases based on the reference analysis between the detailed processes and the software systems which will support them.

4.3 Workflow for Analysis

The Use Case Realization activity, which is original from UP, was updated by means of the sub-activity Identifying Classes from the Business Architecture.

4.3.1 Identifying Classes from the Business Architecture

This activity consists of the identification of Classes from Business Structure View models and from the Business Process View. Resulting product: Class Diagram. Approach for each phase:

Conception phase - it is attempted to identify the main system Classes based on the analysis of Resource and Information Models.

Elaboration phase - it is imperative to perform a re-evaluation of the identified Classes based on the references of the Assembly Line Diagram developed in this phase. By means of the reference analysis, it is imperative to identify which classes will be in charge of the use cases realizations identified in the Assembly Line Diagram.

5. FINAL CONSIDERATIONS

In the business modeling domain, the business construction technique proposed by Eriksson and Penker is, considering UML business modeling proposals, the only one that has a systematic approach with the transition of the business architecture into a software architecture which is supportive to the first one. However, Eriksson and Penker do not explore the systematization of this transition within a context of system development process or methodology. In this paper, it was proposed activities for the business modeling, based on the technique proposed by Eriksson and Penker, to be inserted in the UP or in any other methodology basing on the same principles.

The activities have the purpose of systematizing the identification of software requirements aligned with the business objectives. The activities defined in the method comply with the iterative and incremental model, as well as with interfaces well established with the UP pre-established activities, showing two advantages: (i) the systematic identification of informatization needs, from the event flow of the processes established in the activity; (ii) the systematic identification of the use cases under an iterative approach, established in the "Deriving Use Cases of the Business Processes" activity. The identification of use cases from the assembly line diagram turned out to be an efficient procedure, thus facilitating the identification of the actual informatization needs in the business processes.

As a proposal for future studies, it is suggested the comparison of this technique with other requirement identification techniques, and the construction of a CASE tool that allows for a larger automation of the activities defined in this paper.

REFERENCES

1. B. Kalpic and P. Bernus, Business process modelling in industry - the powerful tool in enterprise management, *Computers in Industry*. Volume 47, Number 3, pp.299-318, (2002).
2. H. Shen, B. Wall, M. Zaremba, Y. Chen, and J. Browne, Integration of Business Modelling Methods for Enterprise Information System Analysis and User Requirements Gathering, *Computers in Industry*. Volume 54, Number 3, pp.307-323, (2004).
3. M. Odeh and R. Kamm, Bridging the Gap Between Business Models and System Models, *Information and Software Technology*. Volume 45, pp.1053-1060, (2003).
4. G. Schneider and J.P. Winters, *Applying use cases: a practical guide* (Addison Wesley: Boston, 1998).
5. I. Jacobson, G. Booch, and J. Rumbaugh, The Unified Software Development Process (Addison Wesley: Boston, 1999).
6. S. Lilly, Use Case Pitfalls: Top 10 problems from real projects using use cases, in *Proc. of Technology of Object Oriented Languages and Systems* (1999), pp.174-183.
7. R.S. Pressman, Software Engineering: a practitioner's approach (McGraw-Hill: 2001).
8. W.P.F. Paula, Engenharia de software – fundamentos, métodos e padrões (Rio de Janeiro, LTC, 2001).
9. P. Kruchten, The Rational Unified Process: An Introduction (Pearson, 2003).
10. OMG, UML specifications, Object Management Group (1997). http://www.rational.com/uml (Accessed Nov. 10 2003).

11. H.J. Johansson, P. Mchugh, J. Pedlebury, and W. Wheller III, *Processos de negócio* (Rio de Janeiro, Pioneira, 1995).
12. F.B. Vernadat, *Enterprise Modeling and Integration: Principles and Application* (Chapman & Hall: London, 1996)
13. C. Marshall, *Enterprise modeling with UML* (Addison-Wesley: USA, 1999).
14. H.E. Eriksson and M. Penker, *Business Modeling with UML* (John-Wiley & Sons: USA, 2000).

A Research on the Project of Digital Comprehensive Capability Platform for Shipbuilding

Nan Ren[1], Jianyi Liu[2], Xiang Su[3], Ping Wang[4] and Juan Yin[5]

[1,3,4,5]Economic and Management School, Jiangsu University of Science and Technology, Zhenjiang 212003, Jiangsu, P.R. China rennan_hb@sohu.com susoft@jzerp.com Sdwangp1975@sina.com bamhill@163.com
[2]Business Administration School, Jiangsu University, Zhenjiang 212003, Jiangsu, P.R.China bjliujianyi@163.com

Abstract. This paper is, centering on the requirement of the modern shipbuilding mode, to study on the project of digital comprehensive capability platform for shipbuilding. The purpose was to realize high integration and collaboration among the functions of design, manufacturing and management in shipbuilding enterprises, and form a high collaborated industry chain with its suppliers and client-industries through such solution project, which includes shipbuilding enterprise innovation development platform, advanced shipbuilding management platform, collaborative business comprehensive management platform, resources supply and demand on industry chain collaboration management platform. As the core competencies of shipbuilding enterprises, a manufacturing resources data standard was also suggested.

Keywords: *Shipbuilding, Digital comprehensive capability platform, Enterprise Information Systems (EIS), Enterprise management, Enterprise integration*

1. INTRODUCTION

To implement the modern shipbuilding mode, a total assembly shipbuilding mode featured by middle-products, is the key to the state-of-the art shipbuilding industry. This mode requires a platform to integrate designing, production and business management, and to ensure the concert collaboration among the supply chain of thousands collaborated enterprises.

This article discusses the key elements in building the digital platform.

2. THE COMPONENTS OF DIGITAL SHIPBUILDING COMPREHENSIVE CAPABILITY PLATFORM

The total framework of the digital shipbuilding comprehensive capability platform is shown in figure 1.

Please use the following format when citing this chapter:

Ren, N., Liu, J., Su, X., Wang, P., Yin, J., 2007, in IFIP International Federation for Information Processing, Volume 254, Research and Practical Issues of Enterprise Information Systems II Volume 1, eds. L. Xu, Tjoa A., Chaudhry S. (Boston: Springer), pp. 487-491.

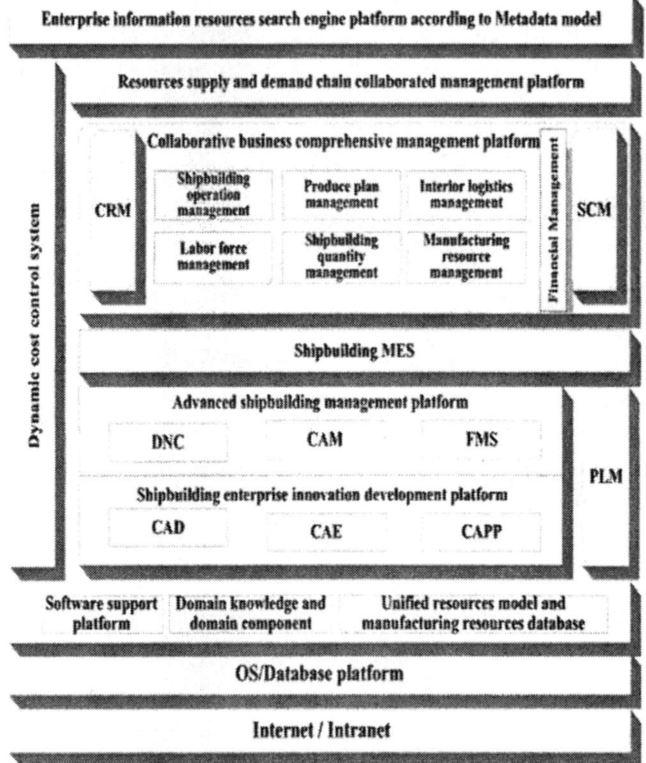

Figure 1. The Structure of Digital Shipbuilding Comprehensive Capability Platform

2.1 Research and Develop Product Data Code of WBS Standards in the Shipbuilding Business

Using the WBS （Work Breakdown Structure ） as a guide, all jobs of the whole life cycle of a project or product are decomposed step by step into the mission packets (WOP). According to the craft processes the mission packets (WOP) are subdivided into work orders (W/O). Each WBS unit is an independent part, can be one or many work packets and then is convenient to distribute or outsource missions. The main components of a mission packet (WOP) include the work specialties, labor hours, material information, elements of WBS, diagram paper, the CBS (cost subdivides structure) elements etc. The work order (W/O) mainly includes the work specialties, labor hours, materials, quantity, the construction diagram etc. Integrated system solution should extend the ideology of WBS into workshops areas to get production ability balanced.

2.2 Set up the Shipbuilding Design Innovation Development Platform

Contract design and detailed design are always designed by experienced shipbuilding design institutes, and production design is always done by mature software. So the emphasis for the integrated design is the establishment of the data standard, unification of the resources code system, and management of the technical documents in the designing process, more over, it should be designed as a collaborated working platform for all the production designers, developers and managers.

2.3 Set up the Integrated Platform of Shipbuilding Production Manufacturing

To utilize the process data in the complicated dynamic production management system, we should introduce the product process data management (PPDM), which serves as a connecting link in the whole shipbuilding design platform, realizing the integrated CAD/CAM upward, and integrating to the complicated dynamic production management downward. Because the EBOM is dynamic and information-increasing, the integration with PPDM up and down should also be dynamic and information-increasing [1]. Based on the statistics and analysis on actual data, developing engineering plans for similar type of ships will get more and effective foundations by accumulating knowledge and genetic optimized production manufacturing resources [2].

2.4 Set up the Business Process Collaboration Management Platform of Shipbuilding Enterprises

Driven by sale management, based on technology and centered by deadline and cost control, the business process collaboration management of shipbuilding includes sale management platform, the reconfigurable and dynamic production plan management system with the ideology of concurrent engineering, quality management platform, and labor force management platform which mainly addresses the problem of who are responsible for the jobs.

2.5 Set up the Collaborated Resources Management Platform of Shipbuilding Manufacturing Industry Supply Chain

It is necessary to implement effective control on shipbuilding combining logistics management and target cost management. Given the characteristics of the multi-collaboration shipbuilding, the collaborated resources management platform includes materials stock management, supply chain architecture, purchase and manufacture integration, logistics optimization. In the process of BPR, business management and operation procedures are standardized. Meanwhile such platform can provide information about materials preparation and cost on entire project dynamically and concurrently, which can help enterprises to realize target cost management.

2.6 Set up Dynamic Cost Control System of Shipbuilding Manufacturing

Within the projects, the all-processes cost management includes quoting price, target cost budget, design cost control, purchase cost control, manufacturing process cost control, accounting and checking cost, which is required by the modern shipbuilding mode [3]. This target cost management system combines the pre-control, ongoing control, and post-control, which integrates the cost planning, cost control and cost analysis. As the cost management involves in the whole processes of enterprise manufacturing and management, therefore, the emphasis is to realize the evolution of BOM in the entire PLM, which attaches monitoring and evaluation information to BOM.

2.7 Set up the Enterprise Information Resources Search Engine Platform according to Metadata Model

With the shipbuilding industry domain ontology as the meta-model for capturing requirements, the EIS can integrate the knowledge of different levels. Meanwhile, such meta-model can optimize its own structure by analyzing the relationship of the available data [4]. By building the meta-model, we can classify resources, and check them according to the rule of code system, provide users with different defined rights, to access and browse different information or knowledge mining in the enterprise information resources search engine platform. This platform supports the decision-making analysis for the active intelligent recommendation.

2.8 The Support System Structure and the Related Technology

It is necessary to make sure that the platform can be expanded and reusable and can realize component-businesses, flexible processes, standard interfaces, and professional security. It is based on unified resources model and manufacturing resources database, which includes the metadata model describing the shipbuilding enterprises resources, and provides much more effective technique support for planning similar ships.

3. CONCLUSIONS

Establishing a digital comprehensive capability platform to realize the dynamic deadline control and cost control, and to build-up a manufacturing resources data standard reflecting the core competency of a shipbuilding enterprise, can improve the management level of the shipbuilding industry of our nation and make it more stronger and competitive.

ACKNOWLEDGEMENTS

This research was supported by National Natural Science Foundation of China: *Study on Data Model for Large-piece One-of-a-kind Production Enterprise* (Grant NO. 70472005).

REFERENCES

1. X. Su, X. Ning, Y. Pan, and X. Ma, Study on Unification of Informationization Catering to Shipbuilding Enterprises, *Shipbuilding of China*. Volume 46, Number 4, pp.78-85, (2005).
2. Q. Ling, The Pivot for Informatization of Manufacturing Industry is MES, *China Computer* (Aug. 9, 2006).
3. Y. Pan and J. Wu, The Cost Control Method in Small-batch Factories, *Mie of China*. Volume 34, Number 12, pp.23-26, (2005).
4. S. Ge and Y. Pan, *Enterprise Information Model for Large-piece one-of-a-kind Production Enterprise* (Science Press: Beijing, 2006).

A Study of Intelligent Information Processing in Human Resource Management in China

Li Zhang and Lunqu Yuan

School of Economics and Management, Beijing Jiaotong University, Beijing 100044, P.R. China lzhang@bjtu.edu.cn lqyuan@bjtu.edu.cn

Abstract. More and more HRM systems today are being changed to e-HRM systems in China. This is mainly due to the advent of Internet technology and the emerging concept of business intelligence. This study shows the evolution of information systems and information processing in the HRM domain and provides an implementation case in a large Chinese state-run enterprise. The experiences and lessons learned from this case reveal several common problems in developing information systems in the HRM domain.

Keywords: *Chinese enterprise, Intelligent information processing, E-HRM,*

1. INTRODUCTION

The advent of information technology (IT) and information systems, together with Internet technology, has inspired many changes in today's business world [1,2]. The impact of IT on today's business is obvious in at least two categories: (1) the improvement of business in efficiency, effectiveness and productivity; (2) the transition of business in the way people create, organize, manage and operate an enterprise. This study shows how information systems and IT are being used in human resource management (HRM) domains through an implementation case in a Chinese enterprise. The experiences and lessons learned from this case reveal several common problems in developing information systems in the HRM domain. HRM practices have a long history. Before the mid-1980s, most practices had focused on the low level, routine tasks such as recruiting, record-keeping, rewards and wages [3]. It is believed that Fombrun et al. pioneered the development of the concept of strategic HRM and started linking HRM functions with the organizational overall strategy [4]. Strategic HRM mainly focuses on activities involving HR planning and HR policies such as internal career opportunities, training systems, performance appraisals, profit-sharing plans, employment security, voice mechanisms, participation in decision-making, and the degree to which jobs are defined [3, 5]. Strategic HRM perceives people as critical organizational investments, strategic resources and competitive advantages which determine the success and failure of an organization [6, 7, 8, 9]. Therefore, HRM has gone through the transition from task-oriented HRM to people-oriented strategic HRM. As one of the driving factors that help today's business transit, IT inevitably should play an important role in the HRM domain [10].

Please use the following format when citing this chapter:

Zhang, L., Yuan, L., 2007, in IFIP International Federation for Information Processing, Volume 254, Research and Practical Issues of Enterprise Information Systems II Volume 1, eds. L. Xu, Tjoa A., Chaudhry S. (Boston: Springer), pp. 493-502.

Information systems have been applied to HRM for decades. However, the way of using information systems and the way of processing information for HRM have evolved, and dramatically improved, over the last decade. This is mainly due to the advent of Internet technology and the emerging concept of business intelligence. In the mid-1990s, the Internet cracked into business operations and the concept of e-business was born. Using Internet technology or IT in general to run business functions, including HRM, is widely accepted as electronic business (e-business). Correspondingly, using IT in HRM is called e-HRM. Dave Ulrich [11] is one of many early e-HRM advocates. Straus et al. researched several impacts of Internet technologies on managing human resources and concluded that the "advances in communication technologies and organizational form suggest the re-evaluation of traditional personnel practices" [10, 11]. Although the literature has explored the opportunities provided by IT to dramatically transform organizations and to help organizations in gaining competitive advantages [12-13], Powell and Dent-Micallef [14] argued that IT alone has not produced competitive advantages, but using IT to leverage intangible, complementary human and business resources has helped organizations gain competitive advantages [12-14]. The proper application of IT in HRM has been proved to be a successful way of running today's business.

2. THE CURRENT STATUS OF E-HRM AND EXISTING PROBLEMS IN CHINA

2.1 The Current Status

Using the customer database of www.chinahr.com, www.ehr4u.com has done research on the current situation of Chinese enterprise's e-HRM over the past days. This research collected 2005 questionnaires from various enterprises in China, 1775 of which were valid. Among all the enterprises surveyed, Chinese domestic enterprises accounted for 78.37% and foreign invested companies took up the remaining 21.63%.

The research showed that even though most enterprises in China take a positive attitude towards e-HRM using computers, networking, business intelligence and Internet technology, they are just taking the first step in revolutionizing HRM with IT. Over 70% of them have not introduced any HRM systems. Most HR managers do not possess sufficient knowledge in IT and information systems to help them in using e-HRM systems. The study showed that over half of the HR managers surveyed have a mediocre ability in applying IT, among whom those from enterprises without use of HRM systems perform worse in applying IT (58% answered levels of poor and very poor, which means that they are just able to use office software and to get information from the Internet). 55% of the managers from enterprises that have used HRM systems, however, have above-average ability in applying IT.

Another result from this study showed the levels of communication and cooperation between the IT department and the HR department. Enterprises preparing to use HRM systems are facing more problems of cooperation between IT and HR departments than those that have adopted HRM systems. Our case study shows that it is quite common that two departments play buck-passing to relieve themselves of responsibilities. In general, most enterprises face a certain level of problems in communications and cooperation between the IT department and the HR department. The results also showed that 71% of enterprises have not used HRM systems. Most of them are enterprises with a size of less than 500 employees and enterprises of this type are in more urgent need of using HRM systems. The research showed that 55% of the enterprises have used HRM systems for less than two years while those who have used it for over two years only account for 29%. Thus Chinese enterprises' efforts in revolutionizing HRM with IT did not start until two years ago.

In today's HRM systems market of mainland China, no prominent HRM systems suppliers or brands have emerged. In terms of market share, no one has more than 10%. Enterprises that develop their own systems take up a share as big as 38.2%, and other unnamed brands account for another 24.3%. HRM systems products manufactured by Chinese enterprise resource planning (ERP) enterprises have not fully grown. HRM systems manufactured by foreign ERP enterprises are restrained in market share due to factors such as price and localization. Professional HRM systems suppliers in China are still in their infancy and most of them are still able to establish complete HRM systems solutions and remain generic software developers.

2.2 Existing Problems

Several major problems exist in today's Chinese enterprises that may hamper the process of adopting e-HRM. We summarize them in the following four categories.

1. There is a misperception of e-HRM from top management. Many VIPs regard HRM as a kind of unavoidable cost instead of realizing the importance of HRM for the development of enterprises; nor do they have sufficient understanding of in-depth questions such as how to carry out e-HRM, what problems they may encounter in this process and what value it may bring to the enterprise. In addition, they have various misunderstandings about e-HRM.

2. There is an unbalanced development in enterprises' digitization which predetermines whether e-HRM can be carried out successfully. Many enterprises either spend too much on e-HRM development or repeat what they already have and waste money. When undertaking e-HRM, enterprises should carefully evaluate what they have already developed, e.g. the computer systems, network systems, and other business applications such as accounting and finance, sales and marketing, manufacturing, and HRM. When choosing e-HRM systems, enterprises should choose those which fit their current organization and satisfy their organizational demands.

3. HRM systems or e-HRM in Chinese enterprises are still in their infancy stage. There are three important parts in e-HRM development: (1) electronic data management; (2) procedural management; (3) strategic management. At present, the strategic functions of e-HRM software such as HR planning, personnel professional development planning and core capability management are still not being emphasized in many Chinese enterprises.

4. There is a lack of competent staff. In the e-HRM development process, HRM knowledge must be organically integrated with IT. However, most enterprises do not have sufficient staffs that possess both HRM and IT knowledge. Those who are experts in HRM have little knowledge about IT techniques and those who know IT do not know HRM well, have little managerial experience and do not have adequate knowledge about the needs of HR businesses. Meanwhile, many managers are not ready to enter the information age. They are short of decent skills in computer operation, Internet applications and information systems usage. Therefore, e-HRM has become a burden for them.

3. A CASE STUDY OF AN ENTERPRISE E-HRM SYSTEM IN CHINA

3.1 Brief Introduction to Plant A

With a history of nearly 70 years, Plant A is a large state-owned enterprise in China. It is one of the top 500 industrial enterprises in China, and is the major researching and manufacturing center of electronic track towing equipment in China. Plant A primarily researches, manufactures and sells high-speed electronic locomotives, metro trains, light-rail trains and electric rail trains, with an annual output of 300 mainline electric locomotives. Plant A owns the biggest workshop for final assembly of electric locomotives and modernized manufacturing centers of locomotive veering shelves, high power electric towing machinery, towing and electric transformers, and resin grit foundry production lines. It owns large quantities of advanced equipment such as high-precision numerically controlled processing centers, robot welders, and numerically controlled cutting, punching, folding and pressing machine tools. Plant A currently has over 10,000 employees, and nearly 3000 of these are engaged in research and development.

3.2 The Overall Demand of Plant A for an E-HRM System

The strategic transformation and rapid development in Plant A caused a managerial revolution in many aspects. Starting from innovation and revolution in HRM, and further infiltrating into marketing, financing, manufacturing and researching, Plant A has found the best way to gain an upper hand in competition via managerial innovation. Facing the situation of Plant A, an HRM consulting team has decided that its consulting objective is regrouping HR to improve performance. In early January of 2002, after a systematic investigation and a lengthy communication with Plant A, the consulting team figured out that an e-HRM system for Plant A has the following specific demands.

1. The system must normalize the HRM system and make HRM more intelligent, networked and knowledge-driven, using e-HRM to make the enterprise's HRM dynamically controllable, which includes overall control, dynamic control and proper personnel–position matching.

2. The e-HRM system must cover all aspects of HRM. It should achieve the automation of HRM operations, the normalization of HRM procedures and the systematization of the management, making the e-HRM system become a platform for an informational and professional enterprise's HRM. The HRM department should become an organic entity to make communication smooth and feedback prompt.

3. The system must update old concepts via the execution of the e-HRM program and build up a proper enterprise culture. The enterprise culture includes giving employees who contribute the most the economic benefits they deserve, and then fulfilling the principle of getting paid according to contribution.

4. It must perfect the management system and form a specific set of rules and regulations, contracts of labor and other related regulations (security and privacy policies, attendance records etc.) via execution of the e-HRM program.

5. The e-HRM system should be as advanced, complete, practical, efficient, flexible, open and automatic as possible. It should also be easy to operate, maintain and expand, be fault-tolerant, be safe and reliable and be able to handle and coordinate different events at the same time. It should have a strict multiple-user authorization management and functions such as database visiting, data copying, operation and visiting log records and system restoration.

6. The e-HRM system should be developed by using mainstream instruments. It should be ensured that it is open, flexible and stable. The system should be based on the browser/server structure, using a uniform platform with a simple and friendly interface. The database should be structured properly, be easy to maintain and be safe (using databases such as MS SQL DB2 or Oracle). At the same time, the system should have a qualified data interface and be compatible with various kinds of databases. The interface should allow the HRM system to seamlessly connect to the ERP system, financial system, office automation system and attendance records system, and to conveniently transmit historical data, such as Excel documents, into the database. It should guarantee the smooth data flow in the system (changes to the data in the attendance records system

3.3 Solutions and the Implementation

After a complete investigation and analysis, the consulting team and Plant A were ready to find some solutions for the plant's HRM. In March 2002, in line with the solution to Plant A's HRM, the consulting team began to implement the e-HRM system.

3.3.1 The General Criteria

1. Put forward the managerial principle to enable the managers to grasp the essence of HRM.

2. Carry out goal management to scout and control the whole process and enable each department/each position to reach its set goal.

3. Optimize managerial procedures to ensure the shortest procedure, the strongest functions, the lowest cost and simplicity of operation. This also makes each job go smoothly according to the procedures.

4. Regulations should be clear, reasonable, scientific and applicable and ensure normalized HRM.

5. Develop software modules out of normalized managerial procedures.

3.3.2 Implementation Model

Step 1 HRM
-HR diagnosis
-Design medium and long-term strategic system for HRM
-Assess and design wage and stimulation system
-Stipulate functions for top officials of the enterprise
-Design talent recruitment and selection process
-Design performance assessment system
-Direct job duty arrangements and job analysis
-Provide an HRM policy system

Step 2 Organizational transformation and structural regrouping
-Diagnose organizational behavior
-Solve disputes between organizational structures and the enterprise's developing strategies
-Set up an authority distribution system
-Optimize organizational structures and managerial procedures
-Organize cultural construction and forge organizational concepts
-Establish academic organizations

Step 3 Enterprise training and course designs
-Analyze on training needs and design training courses
-Share cases interactively
-Design an in-enterprise training system and procedures
-Establish a sophisticated training assessment system

Step 4 Provide user instructions and collect feedback for future maintenance

Plant A completed the construction of the e-HRM system by the end of 2002. The system has been running well.

3.3.3. Value Analysis

Value 1 The e-HRM system makes it easier for Plant A to strengthen its internal cooperation. Along with the principle of new hired loyalty, a noteworthy phenomenon is that the relationship between the staff and managers as well as that between managers and the teams are gradually becoming the crucial factor in determining whether they are willing to stay in the team.

From a daily perspective, the personnel mainly deal with the teams they belong to rather than the enterprise. Strengthening communications between the personnel and their supervisors adds to the sense of their belonging to the enterprise. The e-HRM system provides a platform for prompt communication, and makes a seamless cooperation relationship among the personnel come true through management, electronic magazines and e-mails. The system's personnel self-help terminals and managers' self-help terminals provide horizontal and vertical communication tools.

Value 2 The e-HRM system paves the way for the enrichment of an enterprise culture and a healthy development of Plant A. The enterprise culture of Plant A comes with the enterprise itself. It is based on the dominating fundamental values, consisting of its exterior expressions such as personnel behavior, management style and management policy.

By applying the e-HRM system and introducing the HRM consultation service, Plant A further carries out its enterprise culture and works on a unitary value. The e-HRM system has helped Plant A establish a new working approach of creative thinking, circumventing traditions and seeking innovation and a new system of rewards and stimulation.

Value 3 The e-HRM system brings down Plant A's management costs and raises its productivity. The great functions of an e-HRM system in procedure control and quantified management can be used to ensure that HRM follows a pattern of people first in real terms. Networking computers is an effective means to achieve procedure control. For example, software is used to complete the whole process of a recruitment plan, from drawing the plan, choosing the recruiting channel, and setting it into motion by selecting applicants, giving interviews and undertaking assessments, to making decisions and calculating costs. From an information management perspective, the e-HRM system collects, processes, analyzes and disseminates information for the whole enterprise. Compared to manual work, it makes the procedure more normative, more effective and more accurate. . Plant A's increase in efficiency after the application of the e-HRM system is mainly reflected in the following aspects: (1) It takes less time to make replies; (2) Traveling cost is reduced. Recruitment, training and assessments are all done online which eliminates a huge amount of traveling cost;(3) It takes less time for decisions to be put into action.; (4) Since there are personnel self-help service platforms, most of the trivial personnel affairs can be processed online.

4. THE FUTURE TRENDS OF E-HRM IN CHINA

There are four areas that appear to be popular in China for future e-HRM development.

4.1 Digitization

Over the last decade, people have experienced a lot of e-terms such as e-commerce, e-business, e-government, e-manufacturing, e-procurement, e-learning and e-HRM. It is true that more and more organizations or enterprises have started using IT to run their businesses. China is one of the fastest growing countries in the world, and digitization has been a major topic in most Chinese enterprises [15, 16]. The first step of an e-HRM strategy is office digitalization. It uses computer technology to handle office work which mainly includes the making, transporting and stocking of documents and materials. Office automation is spreading more and more widely, paving the way for e-HRM development. A computer network-connected environment is highly needed by e-HRM.

4.2 More Information Systems to be Developed and Used

Various types of information systems provide a means of collecting, processing, storing, analyzing and applying information to meet various demands from enterprises. By using information systems, we can optimize the current managerial and organizational structures and adjust managerial mechanisms. The coordination between different departments can be strengthened through information systems. Efficiency and effectiveness will be improved for decision-making processes since the required information can be provided to decision-makers in a more timely manner and more accurately. Information systems in e-HRM can help us achieve an integrated management covering various aspects such as personnel affairs, wages, statistics, report forms, documents, securities, contracts and authority approval. They provide a seamless connection between different business departments, avoid duplicate data collection and ensure consistency and accuracy of data. They provide valuable information in a comprehensive, accurate and prompt way, fully and effectively satisfying the needs of HRM activities.

4.3 E-HRM Becomes a Solution for HRM

IT infrastructure is upgraded year after year. Hardware platforms have experienced different forms over the past several decades, from independent computers and networked computers to the client/server architecture and the Internet. Most enterprises today have started using the Internet in their business operations, ranging from the most fundamental Internet service such as getting business information and news and providing enterprise information, to more advanced applications such as online transactions and online services. The concept of e-HRM was born in such a business environment. e-HRM promotes the comprehensive development of HRM and emphasizes an organic binding of information with HR development. Its functions include HR development; talent forecasting; decision-making support by providing precise HR data and analytical reports to decision-makers; performance assessment; and online recruitment and professional training.

4.4 More Qualified E-HRM Users are Need

The HRM personnel are the main body of HRM information and a qualified and professional HRM team is a guarantee of its success. The high quality of HRM personnel means that the HRM personnel must possess the most current and advanced knowledge. They must build and strengthen information awareness, learn the information management concept, and gain the skills in using information systems, Internet technology and applications. They also need to know the new content and the new requirement of HRM in today's information age. Instead of only doing daily routines, e-HRM needs to provide information and analysis of HR data at a strategic level of the enterprise and help top management make decisions for the whole enterprise. Such an intelligent system requires intelligent users. It is the key of successful e-HRM.

5. CONCLUSIONS

The advent of the knowledge economy and widespread application of computer technology and the Internet require today's enterprise management to be digitized. This digitization in turn requires HRM to be changed. E-HRM is born in such an environment. Through the analysis of the current status of HRM in Chinese enterprises and through a case study, we show why e-HRM is needed and how e-HRM is developed. We hope the experiences and the lessons we learned in this case will help people in developing their own e-HRM systems. E-HRM in China is still in its infancy. Many enterprises, particularly small and medium-sized ones, have not accepted the concept of information and have not undertaken any sort of construction of it. On the other hand, some large enterprises set out blindly to develop their e-HRM systems without really knowing what e-HRM is and how to develop it. They just follow the fashion which only backfires on them. This study has shown how to prepare the enterprises themselves to start an e-HRM project and do it successfully.

REFERENCES

1. L. Xu, The contribution of systems science to information systems research, *Systems Research and Behavioral Science*. Volume 17, Number 2, pp.105-116, (2000).
2. L. Xu, C. Wang, X. Luo, and Z. Shi, Integrating knowledge management and ERP in enterprise information systems, *Systems Research and Behavioral Science*. Number 23, pp.147-156, (2006).
3. J. Storey, *Developments in the Management of Human Resources* (Blackwell: London, 1992).
4. C.J. Fombrun, N.M. Tichy, and M.A. Devanna, *Strategic Human Resource Management* (Wiley: New York, 1984).
5. J.A. Sonnenfeld and M.A. Peiperl, Staffing policy as a strategic response: a typology of career system, *Academy of Management Review*. Volume 13, pp.588-600, (1988).
6. J. Barney, Firm resources and sustained competitive advantage, *Journal of Management*. Volume 17, pp.99-120, (1991).
7. D. Ulrich, HR of the future: conclusions and observations, *Human Resource Management*. Volume 36, Number 1, pp.175-179, (1997).
8. J. Pfeffer, *The Human Equation: Building Profits by Putting People First* (Harvard Business School Press: Boston, MA, 1998).
9. B.E. Becker, M.A. Huselid, and D. Ulrich, *The HR Scorecard: Linking People, Strategy and Performance* (Harvard Business School Press: Boston, MA, 2001).
10. S.G. Straus, S.P.Weisband, and J.M. Wilson, *Human resource management practices in the networked organization: impacts of electronic communication systems*, *Trends in Organizational Behavior*. Volume 5, eds. C.L. Cooper and D.M. Rousseau (Wiley: New York, pp.127-154, 1998).

11. D. Ulrich, From e-Business to e-HR, *Human Resource Planning*. Volume 23, Number 2, pp.12-21, (2000).
12. M.J. Culnan and M.L. Markus, Information technologies, in *History of Organizational Communication*, eds. F.M. Jablin, L.L. Putman, K.H. Roberts and L.W. Porter (Newbury Park, CA: Sage, 1987), pp.420-443.
13. G.P. Huber, A theory of the effects of advanced information technologies on organizational design, intelligence, and decision-making, *Academy of Management Review*. Volume 15, pp.47-71, (1990).
14. T.C. Powell and A. Dent-Micallef, Information technology as competitive advantage: the role of human, business, and technology resources, *Strategic Management Journal*. Volume 18, Number 5, pp.375-405, (1997).
15. C. Wang and L. Xu, ERP research, development and implementation in China: an overview, *International Journal of Production Research*. Volume 43, Number 18, pp.3915-3932, (2005).
16. S. Guo, C. Wang, and X. Luo, A study on knowledge management in enterprise information systems, in *Research and Practical Issues of Enterprise Information Systems* (2006).
17. L. Zhang, S. Guo, Y. Liu, and J. Choi, Study of systems methodology in ERP implementation in China, *in Research and Practical Issues of Enterprise Information Systems, International Federation for Information Processing, Volume 205,* eds. A. Tjoa, L. Xu and S. Chaudhry (Springer: Boston, MA, 2006), pp.665-666.

A Framework for Secure Message Transmission Using SMS-Based VPN

MohammadReza Gholami[1], Seyyed Mohsen Hashemi[2] and Mohammad Teshnelab[3]

[1] Islamic Azad University, Science & Research Branch, Tehran, Iran
mr_gholami@yahoo.com
[2] E-Commerce & Computer Engineering Department, Science & Research Branch, Islamic Azad University, Tehran, Iran hashemi@sr.iau.ac.ir
[3] KNTU University, Tehran, Iran

Abstract. As a convenient and low-cost mobile communication technology, short messaging service (SMS) is experiencing rapid growth and our findings provide practical implications for promoting SMS based Virtual Private Network successfully. Secure communication is an important aspect of any networking environment and also is an especially significant challenge in data transmission, fund transfers, important messages sending, etc, especially in e-commerce. Achieving secure communications in networks has been one of the most important problems in the information technology. I designed and developed a VPN framework based on PKI, including Certification Authority, Asymmetric Cryptography Algorithms, using Short Message Service to transmit small data from one computer to another party through Internet or GSM network that can be used in some enterprise organizations like Newspaper corporations, AZAD University (Science & Research). This framework for effecting the secure message transmission to another system uses Smartcards or SAM modules for storing the keys to guarantee the security of the message transmission. In this paper, we study necessary and sufficient conditions for achieving secure communications and present a solution to this problem using Smartcard and GSM network as a transfer platform.

Keywords: *E-business, E-commerce, EDI, EAI, Security, Trust, Privacy*

1. INTRODUCTION

People increasingly rely on computers to do business or send financial data or even confidential messages in their own computers or even in an organization's PC's. But accessing the PC and sending the messages invariably requires typing a username and password to prove one's identity to the remote service and transfer the plain-text message via short message service if the system use SMS for message transferring. This creates significant security vulnerability since the user's confidential message is in plain-text format and can be captured by a hostile party.

In this paper we present a solution to this problem designing a VPN framework to create a Software engine for Enterprise organization and End-Users that accepts messages from clients and encrypt it by keys retrieved from Smart card and

Please use the following format when citing this chapter:

Gholami, M. R., Hashemi, S. M., Teshnelab, M., 2007, in IFIP International Federation for Information Processing, Volume 254, Research and Practical Issues of Enterprise Information Systems II Volume 1, eds. L. Xu, Tjoa A., Chaudhry S. (Boston: Springer), pp. 503-511.

cryptographic methods then store and transmit the encoded message to the remote side via SMS, and also in the remote side the engine retrieve and store the message and decode to deliver to the recipient.

In this Framework a client that wishes to send a message to the remote side first must be authenticated by the engine installed on the server in the enterprise organization then create a message and submit it. The engine automatically Encrypt the message and split it if greater than a standard SMS size, then adds header for client information and the sequence number to the split parts and transmit them by number of SMS(s), in the remote-side the engine do reverse actions of the explained above to retrieve the sender information of the message and number of parts, then remove headers and Concatenate the parts and store it when all of the parts completely received.

The goal is to create a system that is both secure and highly usable. For Encryption and Decryption of the messages this Framework uses digital signatures and for storing the client's keys uses Smart Cards.

2. WHY WE NEED TO SECURE SMS?

SMS (Short Message Service) is a widely used service for brief communication. Occasionally the data sent using SMS services is confidential in nature and is desired not to be disclosed to a third party.

SMS messages are sometimes used for the interchange of confidential data such as social security number, bank account number, password etc. Most mobile operators encrypt all mobile communication data, including SMS messages but sometimes this is not the case, and even when encrypted, the data is readable for the operator. Among others these needs give rise for the need to develop and Engine for additional encryption for SMS messages, so that only accredited parties are able to engage communication.

Short message service (SMS) deliver short text messages to mobile transceivers operating in a communication network, and a service is implemented in the network according to the industry-standard SMS protocol. An SMS message typically consists of a relatively small number of alphanumeric characters, and a mobile transceiver operating in such network may be implemented to receive and/or transmit SMS messages. SMS messages may also be transmitted to the mobile transceiver in other ways, for example by generating the SMS message on a computer terminal coupled to the internet. The message is then forwarded to a Central SMS service center (SMSC), coupled through a network backbone to a switching center of the network, via the internet. The SMSC then transmits the SMS message to the mobile transceivers [1].

3. METHODS FOR SECURING THE MESSAGES

3.1 Defining the VPN

Many different definitions of Virtual Private Network are floating around the marketplace; many of these definitions have been tweaked to meet the product lines and focus of the vendors. I've settled on one rather simple definition for VPN(s) that I'll use throughout my solution – *Virtual Private Network is a network of virtual circuits for carrying private message traffic.*

A Virtual circuit is a connection set up on a network between a sender and a receiver in which both the route for the session and bandwidth is allocated dynamically. VPN(s) can be established between two or more Local Area Networks (LANs), or between remote users and a LAN [2].

Until now there has always been a clear division between public and private networks. A public network, like the public telephone system and the internet, is a large collection of unrelated peers that exchange information more or less freely with each other. The people with access to the public network may or may not have anything in common, and any given person on that network may only communicate with a small fraction of his potential users [3].

A private network is composed of computers owned by a single organization that share information specifically with each other. They're assured that they are going to be the only ones using the network, and that information sent between them will (at worst) only be seen by others in the group. The typical corporate Local Area Network (LAN) or Wide Area Network (WAN) is an example of a private network. The line between a private and public network has always been drawn at the gateway router, where a company will erect a firewall to keep intruders from the public network out of their private network, or to keep their own internal users from perusing the public network [3].

There also was a time, not to long ago, when companies could allow their LANs to operate as separate, isolated islands. Each branch office might have its own LAN, with its own naming scheme, email system, and even its own favorite network protocol – none of which might be compatible with other offices' setups. As more company resources moved to computers, however, there came a need for these offices to interconnect. This was traditionally done using leased phone lines of varying speeds. By using leased lines, a company can be assured that the connection is always available, and private. Leased phone lines, however, can be expensive. They're typically billed based upon a flat monthly fee, plus mileage expenses. If a company has office across the country, this cost can be prohibitive [3].

3.2 Encryption/Decryption Using Digital Signature

In cryptography, a digital signature or digital signature scheme is a type of asymmetric cryptography used to simulate the security properties of a signature in digital, rather than written, form. Digital signature schemes normally give two algorithms, one for signing which involves the user's secret or private key, and one for verifying signatures which involves the user's public key. The output of the signature process is called the "digital signature"[4].

Digital signatures, like written signatures, are used to provide authentication of the associated input, usually called a "message." Messages may be anything, from electronic mail to a contract, or even a message sent in a more complicated cryptographic protocol. Digital signatures are used to create public key infrastructure (PKI) schemes in which a user's public key (whether for public-key encryption, digital signatures, or any other purpose) is tied to a user by a digital identity certificate issued by a certificate authority. PKI schemes attempt to unbreakably bind user information (name, address, phone number, etc.) to a public key, so that public keys can be used as a form of identification [4].

Digital signatures are often used to implement electronic signatures, a broader term that refers to any electronic data that carries the intent of a signature, but not all electronic signatures use digital signatures in some countries, including the United States, and in the European Union, electronic signatures have legal significance. However, laws concerning electronic signatures do not always make clear their applicability towards cryptographic digital signatures, leaving their legal importance somewhat unspecified [4].

Authentication: Although messages may often include information about the entity sending a message, that information may not be accurate. Digital signatures can be used to authenticate the source of messages. When ownership of a digital signature secret key is bound to a specific user, a valid signature shows that the message was sent by that user. The importance of high confidence in sender authenticity is especially obvious in a financial context. For example, suppose a bank's branch office sends instructions to the central office requesting a change in the balance of an account. If the central office is not convinced that such a message is truly sent from an authorized source, acting on such a request could be a grave mistake.

Integrity: In many scenarios, the sender and receiver of a message may have a need for confidence that the message has not been altered during transmission. Although encryption hides the contents of a message, it may be possible to change an encrypted message without understanding it. (Some encryption algorithms, known as nonmalleable ones, prevent this, but others do not.) However, if a message is digitally signed, any change in the message will invalidate the signature. Furthermore, there is no efficient way to modify a message and its signature to produce a new message with a valid signature, because this is still considered to be computationally infeasible by most cryptographic hash functions

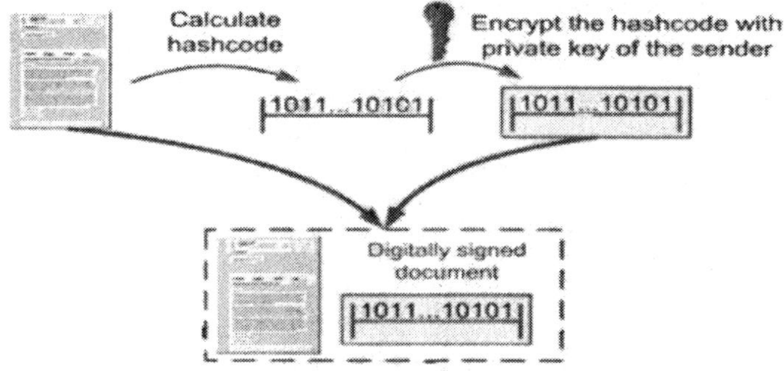

Figure 1. Creation of a Digitally Signed Document (Sender)

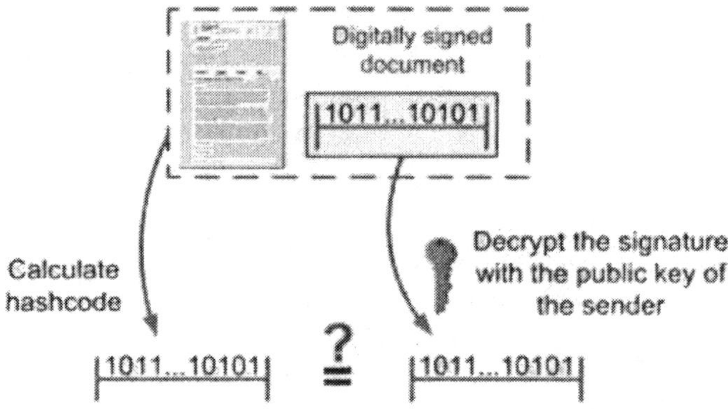

Figure 2. Verifying the Digital Signature (Receiver)

3.3 Using a Smart Card to Store Private-key

All public key / private key cryptosystems depend entirely on keeping the private key secret. A private key can be stored on a user's computer, and protected by, for instance, a local password, but this has two disadvantages:

The user can only sign documents on that particular computer.

The security of the private key completely depends on the security of the computer, which is notoriously unreliable for many PCs and operating systems.

A more secure alternative is to store the private key on a smart card. Many smart cards are deliberately designed to be tamper resistant (however, quite a few designs have been broken, notably by Ross Anderson and his students). In a typical implementation, the hash calculated from the document is sent to the smart card, whose CPU encrypts the hash using the stored private key of the user and returns it. Typically, a user must activate his smart card by entering a personal identification number or PIN code (thus providing a two-factor authentication). Note that it can be sensibly arranged (but is not always done) that the private key never leaves the smart card. If the smart card is stolen, the thief will still need the PIN code to generate a digital signature. This reduces the security of the scheme to that of the PIN system, but is nevertheless more secure than are many PCs [5].

4. AN OVERVIEW OF OTHER SOLUTIONS

Develop an application that can be used in mobile devices to encrypt messages that are about to be sent. Naturally decryption for encrypted messages is also provided. The encryption and decryption are characterized by a secret key that all legal parties have to posses. Several mobile device manufacturers have adopted Java as their platform offered for software developers. To certain extent Java applications are portable between devices of different vendors. Some mobile device manufacturers provide an application programming interface (API) for SMS services, which can be used for our purposes. These facts make Java a natural choice for our application.

In addition to cryptographic strength, things to consider when developing this type of an application for mobile devices are limitations in memory and processing capacity [6].

A system and method is presented for establishing a secure conduit for SMS communication between a center and a wireless terminal. The center encrypts an authorization key in response to a wireless terminal's SMS message containing a public key and a request for the authorization key, sends back to the wireless terminal an SMS message containing the encrypted authorization key, decrypts another SMS message received from the wireless terminal which contains an authentication code and a request for a traffic key, authenticates the SMS message, encrypts the traffic key, and sends to the wireless terminal another SMS message containing the traffic key[7].

5. DESCRIPTION OF THE SOLUTION

Figure 3 illustrates the transmission of a secure message between two clients through secure channel between software installed on both of computers. In this Figure you can see two media for transmission of the encrypted message, (1) is Internet connection for the places that have internet or LAN connection and (2) is GSM modems that send and receive the encrypted message.

The steps are: (1) Client A inserts the Smart Card into Card reader and submits a message. (2) Software on Client A reads the key information of a client and encrypts the message. (3) Software in client A Splits the message if the size exceeds maximum length of a short message, and adds the header for sender information and sequence number. (4) Software sends the parts of the encrypted message by the number of short messages by GSM A. (5) Software on client B Reads the Short messages that received by GSM B. (6) Software on client B removes header and concatenates the encrypted message when all of them received. (7) Software on client B Decrypts the message by key information stored in the Smart card and store the receive message for Client B. (8) Client B reads the received message.

Consider that this method id two-way and Client B can send a secure message too.

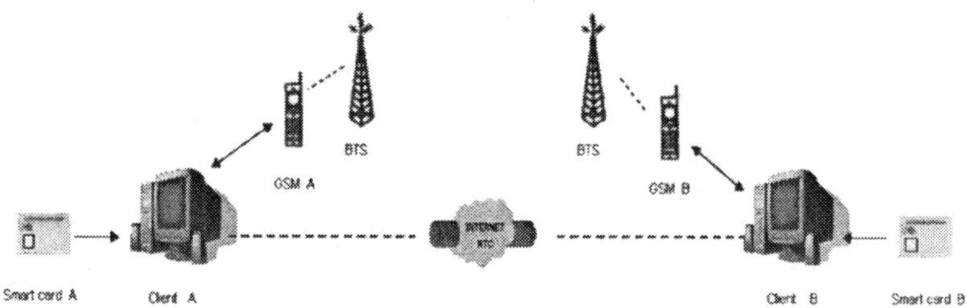

Figure 3. Transmit / Receive Secure Message Between Two Clients

Figure 4 illustrates the transmission of a secure message between two clients in an enterprise environment through secure channel between software installed on both local and remote servers in two different organizations. In this Figure, the media for transmission of the encrypted message is GSM modems that connected to the servers, and send / receive the encrypted message. In this method the main software installed on the server and generates interfaces for the client in the organization to accept the submit requests. On the other hand the Smart card is connected to the server and all the messages Encrypts / Decrypts with single key information and clients can be authenticated by separate database to use the system for using the private messaging service.

The steps are: (1) Client A login to server and submits a message. (2) Engine A reads the key information and encrypts the message. (3) Engine A stores the encrypted message with sender information and time-stamp it for further usage. (4) Engine A splits the message if the size exceeds maximum length of a short message, and adds the header for sender information and sequence number. (5) Engine A sends the parts of the encrypted message by the number of short messages by GSM A. (6) Engine B Reads the Short messages that received by GSM B. (7) Engine B stores the encrypted message with sender information and time-stamp it for further usage. (8) Engine B removes header and concatenates the encrypted message when all of them received. (9) Client B login to server and checks for new message. (10) Engine B Decrypts the message by key information stored in the Smart card and store the receive message for Client B. (11) Client B reads the received message.

Consider that this method id two-way and Client B can send a secure message too, and because of enterprise organization the clients can send and receive messages simultaneously, and the engine can handle the traffic and can use multiple GSM modems.

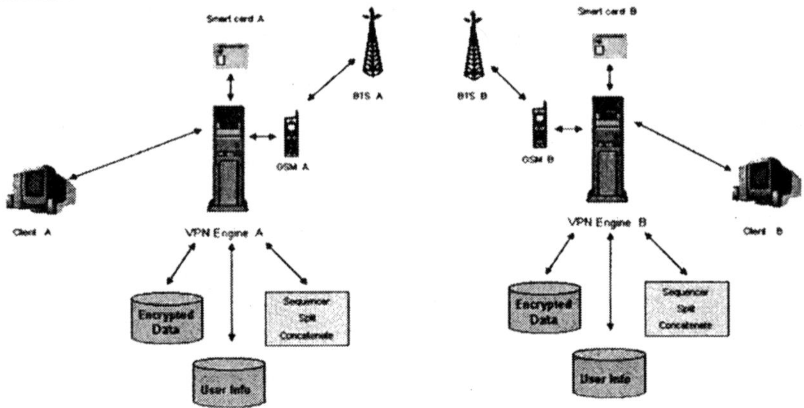

Figure 4. Transmit / Receive Secure Message in Enterprise by SMS

Figure 5 illustrates the transmission of a secure message between two clients in an enterprise environment like Figure 4, but in this Figure, the media for transmission of the encrypted message, is internet or LAN connection.

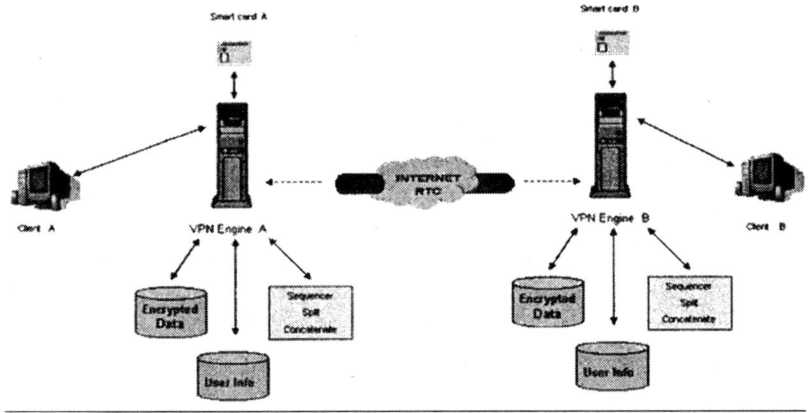

Figure 5. Transmit / Receive Secure Message in Enterprise by Internet

6. CONCLUSIONS

In this paper, I have shown that SMS is not secure. And I presented a framework to ensure the confidentiality and integrity for transmitting/receiving a long message by SMS (Short Message Service). The message will be encoded in the source and decoded in the destination by using private key that stored in the Smart card. The media transmitter of the message can be short message service or even the internet.

Every messages created from any software can be considered to be sent by the system that created by this framework, if confidentiality is very important.

REFERENCES

1. Y. Sabo, U. Benchetrit, and P. Alper, *Secure Short Message Service* (Patent No: US 7082313 B2, 2006).
2. D. Kosiur, *Building and Managing Virtual Private Networks: Virtual Private Networks* (Wiley Computer Publishing: 1998).
3. C. Scott, P. Wolfe, and M. Erwin, *Virtual Private Networks*, Second Edition (O'Reilly, 1999).
4. Wikipedia, *the free encyclopedia: Digital Signature.* http://en.wikipedia.org/wiki/Digital_signature (Accessed May 1, 2007).
5. Wikipedia, *the free encyclopedia: Digital signature, putting the private key on a smart card.* http://en.wikipedia.org/wiki/Digital_signature#smartcard (Accessed May 1, 2007).
6. M. Hassinen, *Smile Markovski: Secure SMS messaging using Quasigroup encryption and Java SMS API,* SPLST (2003), p.187.
7. V. Koukoulids, G. Stamatelos, and R. Jezierny, *Use of Short Message Service for Secure Transactions* (Patent No: US 7076657 B2, 2006).

A Review of Technology and Products Supporting E-Learning System

Yanping Liu and Ying Wang

School of Economics and Management, Beijing Jiao Tong University, Beijing100044, P.R.China mf001455@263.net wywywy0511@sina.com

Abstract. With the development of modern information technology and the increases of demand for building and maintaining ongoing capabilities, e-learning has played more and more important role of all the technologies in the supporting knowledge management. A successful e-learning system is supported by many critical success factors and technology has become the key factor among these factors. Consequently, the review of basic technologies and corresponding products that support e-learning will be in favor of further study on e-learning. This paper generalizes the advanced technologies and products that support the design and operation of e-learning system. At the end of this paper, we analyze the main trends of the development direction of e-learning technology.

Keywords: *E-learning, Knowledge management, Products, Technology*

I. INTRODUCTION

Knowledge Management, is nothing new, but instead is newly practices and has become the most prevalence method to enhance the learning capabilities of organizations and organizational members [1]. Many technologies can be used to support knowledge management system, such as business intelligence, collaboration and e-learning. As the demand for building and maintaining ongoing capabilities increases, e-learning has played more and more important role of all the technologies in the supporting process of knowledge management. Thus, it is urgent for researchers to pay more attention to the theory and technologies development of e-learning.

E-learning system as a just-in-time training delivery system need much help from modern techniques and tools to accomplish the delivery of information. Researchers proposed many advanced technologies and products to support the design and operation of e-learning. So this paper tries to make a literature review of these technologies and corresponding products from the perspective of knowledge management. Based on the review, we put forward the main trends of the development direction of e-learning technology.

Please use the following format when citing this chapter:

Liu, Y., Wang, Y., 2007, in IFIP International Federation for Information Processing, Volume 254, Research and Practical Issues of Enterprise Information Systems II Volume 1, eds. L. Xu, Tjoa A., Chaudhry S. (Boston: Springer), pp. 513-518.

2. LITERATURE REVIEW OF TECHNOLOGY AND PRODUCT SUPPORTING E-LEARNING SYSTEM

2.1 Review of the Development of Technology Supporting E-Learning System

A successful e-learning system is supported by several critical success factors (CSFs) and technology has become the key factor among the CSFs. Different scholars put forward different information technologies to design and support e-learning system. There technologies enhance the learning efficiency and develop the knowledge management of organization. We summarize the basic technologies that playing important role in e-learning system design and operation in Table 1.

Table 1. Development of Information Technologies of E-Learning

Technology	Presenter	Proposed Year
DHTML	Pellegrino, Goldman[2]	1999
VRML	Janet Johns[3]	2000
Portals	Brandon Hall[4]	2000
KnowledgeTree	Peter Brusilovsky, Hemanta Nijhavan [5]	2002
LiveNet	Quang Vinh Nguyen [6]	2004
Ajax	Jesse James Garrett [7]	2005
E-dap	Bonastre [8]	2005
Central LASAR system	Andre Luiz[9]	2007
CAT	Mu-Jung Huang[10]	2007

From Table 1we can see that the technologies developed for e-learning system are mainly information technologies. Information technologies have become the most important technology for the development and operation of e-learning system. How to make full use of these information technologies for the establishment and operation of e-learning system will become one of the most important strategies for all organizations that engaged in the promotion of learning capability.

2.2 Review of Products Supporting E-Learning System

Successful operation of an e-learning system needs products to transfer knowledge to members of organization. There are many products supporting e-learning and Table 2 captures main examples. The products proposed by different scholars to support e-learning system are mainly developed on the basis of information technologies. The function of these products to e-learning system is similar as the function of software to computer. These products make the delivery and share of knowledge in organization come true.

Table 2. Products Supporting E-Learning System [11-12]

Product	Description
Linux Operating system	The product is object-oriented projected to be easily customized for each type of Linux system installation. This product was made using the facilities of IDE Delphi.
Product	Description
E-Learning Suite	The eLearning suite, consisting of e-learning and Siebel Distance Learning, provides automated content management, methods of measuring learning, and course content delivery.
Vuepoint Learning System 3.0	Four modules make up this e-learning and content management system: a Web-based evaluation, teaching, and research tool; a student testing and course tracking program; a template-based content creator; and an off-line viewer for asynchronous learning.
Human Capital Management Suite	The suite includes trademark KP, Performance, KP Learning, and KP Content. Learners can create customized blended online learning curricula. Products test and track learner progress and activities.
TrainNet	It integrates full-screen video with live interaction, using audio conferencing, synchronized Web content, application sharing, embedded email, and whiteboard and Q&A features.

3. THE TECHNOLOGY DEVELOPMENT TRENDS OF E-LEARNING SYSTEM

The review brings us a scene of the actuality of e-learning theory and application. Because of the fast change and complication of market environment, any changes of a slight factor may become the important reason of success or failure of e-learning system. To promote learning efficiency and learning ability of organization, we must consider every factor that supports the operation of e-learning system and integrate synthetically many kinds of technologies and means. By integrating different kinds of technologies, every key element in the e-learning system will coordinate and will give play to its greatest benefit [13]. So integration of different information technologies and integration of information technology with other technologies will be basic direction of e-leaning technology development.

3.1 Development of Technology Integrating Knowledge Management with E-Learning System

Although e-learning system and knowledge management have their unique characteristics, the relationship between them has become more and more closed. Many scholars have found that the emphasis on e-learning has become shifting to "performance support" with the integration of Knowledge Management capabilities [14]. With the highly competitive and dynamic environment, the integration of knowledge and e-learning system has become the critical requirement of improving the learning and innovation capability of organization. E-learning users need a suitable knowledge management system to obtain correct and complete information they need. Knowledge management system needs an advanced e-learning system to help it realize the effective transmission of knowledge. Therefore, the technologies and products that integrate knowledge management and e-learning will be the urgent need for the development of e-learning.

3.2 Development of Collaborative E-Learning Technologies

Collaborative technologies will improve the operability of e-learning system and accelerate the generalization of e-learning system. So a great many owners turn their focus on how to build up a more perfect learning environment for collaborative e-learning. Collaborative e-learning includes man-machine interactions and man-man interactions. Compared with the development of man-machine interaction technology, man-man interactions need more rapid development. Because of the defects of e-learning system, such as lack of interpersonal communication, baldness and aridity, interpersonal communication has become an important direction for e-learning. Collaborative technologies and products that improve interpersonal communication in e-learning system will be one basic trend of the development of e-learning.

3.3 Combination of Technical Domination and Technical Assistant

Technical domination and technical assistant are two basic views about the development direction of e-learning since the birth of e-learning. In the term of the nature of e-learning, an effective e-learning is not decided by whether it is a technical domination or a technical assistant. In terms of characteristics of learning content, the e-learning platform of technical domination more suits for explicit, cognitive and technical knowledge, while the e-learning platform of technical assistant more suits for an academic or soft technology one. A learner no matter where he is-in an enterprise or college-needs both of these two learning modes. Thus a platform that combine the views of technical domination and technical assistant is a promising one that accords with the develop trend of e-learning platform.

4. CONCLUSIONS

This paper makes a review about advanced technologies and products that support the design and operation of e-learning system. With these reviews of e-learning, we find that more theory about technology and corresponding products is needed to guide the design, delivery, and implementation of e-learning. At the end of this paper, we analyze the main trends of the development direction of e-learning technology. With the development of information technology, we believe that more advanced technologies and more effective products that support e-learning will be put forward. E-learning will have a very promising future in the new millennium.

REFERENCES

1. M.T. Hansen, N. Nohria, and T. Tierney, What's your strategy for managing knowledge? *Harvard Business Review.* Volume 77, Number 2, pp.106-116, (1999).
2. J.W. Pellegrino and S.R. Goldman, The new languages, *Training and Development.* Volume 53, Number 8, pp.35-46, (1999).
3. T. Barron, The future of digital learning, *E-learning.* Volume 1, Number 2, pp.46-57, (2000).
4. T.L. Wentling, C. Waight, J. Gallaher, J.L. Fleur, C. Wang, and A. Kanfer, E-learning-A Review of Literature, *Knowledge and Learning Systems Group.* Volume 6, Number 9, pp.37-51, (2000).
5. P. Brusilovsky and H. Nijhavan, A framework for adaptive e-Learning based on distributed re-usable learning activities, in *Proc. of World Conference on E-Learning* (AACE, Canada, 2002), pp.154-161.
6. Q.V. Nguyen, M. Huang, and I. Hawryszkiewycz, A new visualization approach for supporting knowledge management and collaboration in e-Learning, in *Proc. of the Eighth International Conference on Information Visualisation* (Computer Society: London, England, 2004), pp.693-700.
7. J.J. Garrett, *Ajax: A New Approach to Web Applicatio*ns, Adaptive Path (2005). http://www.35dx.com/html/web/1/web386.html (Accessed July 8, 2007).
8. O.M. Bonastre, A.P. Benavent, and M.A. Ortuno, E-dap: An e-learning tool for Managing, Distributing and Capturing Knowledge, in *Proc. of ITHET 6th Annual International Conference,* eds. J. Dolio (IEEE: Dominican Republic, 2005), pp.S3B11-15.
9. A.L.M. Oliveira and C.A. Schneider, Metrology on-the-job e-learning through remote services, *Measurement.* Volume 40, Number 7, pp.183-191, (2007).

10. M. Huang, H. Huang, and M. Chen, Constructing a personalized e-learning system based on genetic algorithm and case-based reasoning approach, *Expert Systems with Applications*. Volume 33, Number 5, pp.551-564, (2007).
11. B. Marshall, E. Zhang, H. Chen, A. Lally, R. Shen, E. Fox, and L.N. Cassel, *Convergence of knowledge management and e-learning: the GetSmart experience*, IEEE (2006). http://ieeexplore.ieee.org/iel5/8569/27127/01204907.pdf?arnumber=1204907 (Accessed July 10, 2007).
12. M.E. Jennex, *Case studies in knowledge management* (Idea Group Inc Publishing: New York, NY, 2005).
13. S. Liu and G. Xiang, Research on the Integration of Knowledge Management and E-Learning, *Modern Educational Technology*. Volume 14, Number 4, pp.10-14, (2004).
14. A. Sadler, *The future of e-learning: an expanding vision,* IBM MindSpan (2001). http://www-3.ibm.com/software/mindspan/distlrng.nsf (Accessed June 10, 2007).

Supply Chain System Integration in Retailing: A Case Study of LianHua

Guoling Lao and Lei Xing

School of Information Management and Engineering, Shanghai University of Finance and Economics, Shanghai 200433, P.R. China gllao@shufe.edu.cn

Abstract. Supply Chain Management (SCM) is one of the most important concepts, which focuses on customer requirement and sets Core Company in the centre, integrating the suppliers, distributors and customers as a whole. Integration is the trend and advantage of SCM. It is necessary for the retail industry to introduce the concepts and methods of SC Integration Management. Through close cooperation and systematical integration with upper enterprises, retailers can effectively improve the operation level of enterprises, reduce cost and improve customer's service level. This thesis introduces SCM theory and development in retailing industry, and then discusses implementation of SC integration according to problems existing in Lian Hua Supermarket. Lian Hua will collaborate with IBM to do a project about supply chain integration. We analyze the information and put forward supply chain integration plan that includes a framework, transaction applications, an IT framework and operation service. We also give some suggestions after analyzing the results of Supply Chain Integration Management.

Keywords: *EIS, SCM, Integration, Retailing*

1. THE CONCEPT OF SUPPLY CHAIN MANAGEMENT

Because supply chain is a complex system, we should plan unitedly and manage harmoniously to have a good performance. The concept of Supply Chain Management is put forward in this environment. Various scholars have various opinions about Supply Chain Management, as well as Supply Chain. Jones and Riley [1] and Langeley and Houlcomb [2] explain the Supply Chain Management from the aspect of function chain, they argued that the key point of Supply Chain Management is Invetory Managemetn, and the supply chain is connected by procurement, production, stock, distribution and selling. Manordt and Harrington [3] studied the information flow in supply chain, which is a course for buyers and sellers to exchange information and data, and they argued that the information should be shared by all sides, not possessed exclusively by only one enterprise, in order that all enterprise in a supply chain can know the logistic situation and make decision more accurately. So the key of Supply Chain Management is transmitting and sharing information. Hewitt, Lambert and Cooper [4] argued that Supply Chain Management should be able to coordinate and unify all business process, including customer relationship management processes, customer service management process, need management

Please use the following format when citing this chapter:

Lao, G., Xing, L., 2007, in IFIP International Federation for Information Processing, Volume 254, Research and Practical Issues of Enterprise Information Systems II Volume 1, eds. L. Xu, Tjoa A., Chaudhry S. (Boston: Springer), pp. 519-528.

process, order satisfaction process, production management process, production process, product research and marketing process, crap and returned purchase process, which is not limited to information flow management and logistic management.

2. INTEGRATING THE SUPPLY CHAIN IN RETAILING INDUSTRY

Supply Chain Integration is coordinating and making an effort for each other in all enterprises of supply chain, to enhance the overall competitive strength [5]. Current studies about supply chain integration in retailing industry are mostly focused in production planning, marketing channels, inventory management and cooperation. The main research achievements include: the analysis of prediction about selling amount of European food grocer through case observation by Johanna Smaros [6]; the application of design method called fuzzy object program in s constructing the Synergetic production and selling planning by Hasan Selim [7]; Jianxin (Roger) Jiao [8] introduces an associative classification-based recommendation system for personalization in B2C e-commerce applications; Bernhard [9] constructed the selling-distribution model of supply chain integration, explained the method that changing the key factories and capability indexes into the environment variables and analyzing how to use decision making system to improve the supply chain; Charles S. Tapiero [10] used NPQ model to analyze the risk and quality controlling of raw material suppliers and manufacturers; Caroline Emberson [11] studied the collaboration between the retailers and suppliers, expatiating on the competitive and cooperative relationship; Piet van der Vlist [12] studied the collaboration between retailers and suppliers in VMI.

In retailing industry, in order to manage more and more products and services effectively, retailers and companies in supply chain should change traditional business model, rebuild supply chain system and realize the integration of supply chain. The supply chain management is not mature in our country, so supply chain management can be solved not only by participators' self-adjusting, but by leaders' support and coordination.

3. CASE STUDY: SC INTEGRATION OF LIANHUA SUPERMARKET

3.1 Brief Introduction of LianHua Supermarket

Lian Hua supermarket organized in May, 1991, is first one supermarket characterized by chain-store operations. After the 14 year's development, Lian Hua created scale developing advantage , including big mall, supermarkets, and convienience stores, which are polynary complementation and progradation. Now, Lian Hua is a leader in Chain's retailing industry, having more than 3500 chain stores.

Lian Hua's current business consists of big mall, standard supermarkets and convenience stores.

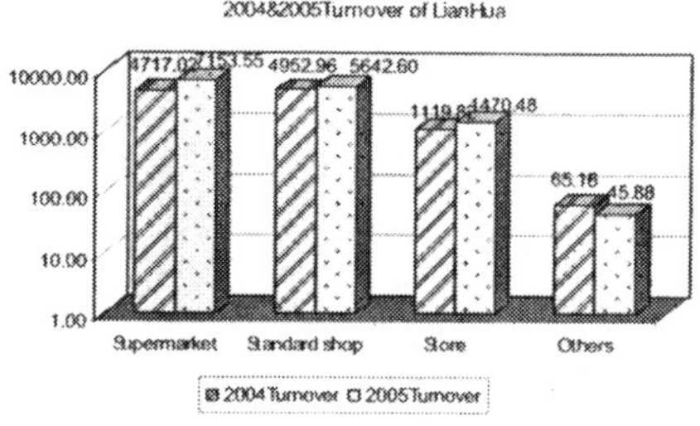

Figure 1. The Sales Turnover of Different Business

3.2 Problem Analysis of Lian Hua Supermarket

Through the analysis of the seven main operation procedures (order operation, receiving operation, returning operation, clearing operation, payment operation, obtaining business and searching operation, marketing operation) in Lian Hua's supply chain at that time, we discover that Lian Hua had established small-scale B2B platform in some business, and had certain application base, but some problems remain in the system and transaction operation, as in showing below:

(1) Ways of interaction

The platform at that time mainly provides a one-way information display through websites, and the suppliers just cooperate passively;

Lian Hua doesn't make its system butted with the suppliers' system, which affects big suppliers' response initiative;

(2) The function of the platform and its integrity

The function of the existing platform is imperfect, with too many interfaces and inadequate stability, security, and processing capability. Different suppliers face different interfaces and have different account numbers of Lian Hua.

(3) Application scope and management depth

Huge number of suppliers (over 8000 all together), but few are online and the charging standards are not unified. Lack support for the monitoring of key performance indicators and lack of information sharing mechanisms. Lack support for strategic plan of Group development.

(4) Difficult to coordinate with the Group Business Resource Integration

The Group needs to enhance its bargaining ability through joint procurement;

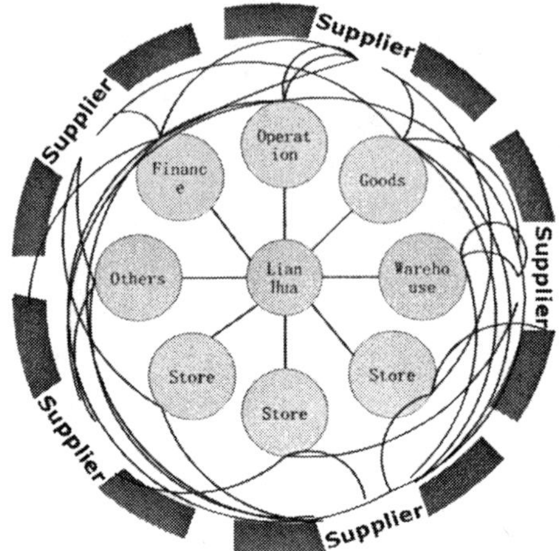

Figure 2. The Current Supplier Management Situation Analysis of Lian Hua

Analysis shows that the current supply chain has been unable to meet Lian Hua Group Co.'s needs of development. Based on the idea of integrated supply chain management, and taking into account the features of Lian Hua's retail chain, the author explored the application of integrated supply chain in the retailing industry. This exploration was made under the background of the implementation of supply chain integration project in Lian Hua and IBM. It considered the problem Lian Hua was facing and its actual demand, used IBM's supply chain management solution for reference, and implements the integrated supply chain management thought. The following illustration will be from the aspects of implementation strategy, solution, progress and evaluation.

3.3 Exploration of the Implementation of Lian Hua Group Supply Chain Integration

3.3.1. Design of an Integrated Supply Chain

Century Lian Hua Supermarket mainly sells daily products, processed foods at normal temperature, and fresh food. According to Fischer's product-based supply chain design strategy, daily products and processed foods at normal temperature are functional foods with stable, predictable demand and long lifecycle, so companies have to choose a supply chain which is more efficient-sensitive; while fresh food is innovative products with instable demand, so companies have to choose a supply chain which is more market-sensitive [13]. Therefore, the supply chain design is shown in the following table 1:

Table 1. Supply Chain Design for a Supermarket

goods / Supply chain	Daily products, pressed foods at normal temperature	Fresh food, daily necessities
main objective	Ensure the supply with lowest cost	Quick response to market demand to reduce the supply shortage and excessive stock loss
suppliers selection criteria	Focus on cost and quality	Focus on supplying speed, flexibility, and quality
Inventory strategy	Accelerate inventory turnover, and reduce inventory quantity	Determine proper purchasing quantity
Predate of delivery	Try to shorten the predate within the scope of cost	Reduce the predate through initiative investment

3.3.2. The Integrated Supply Chain Platform of Lian Hua Supermarket

(1) Platform framework

Guided by the above established strategy, the author provides a B2B overall supply chain management solution for Century Lian Hua. The solution includes four main parts: platform building, suppliers' promotion, customer service of suppliers and retailers, and platform maintenance. This solution provides two users of the supply chain platform-Century Lian Hua and its supplier-a full range of service. The overall function diagram of this solution is as following:

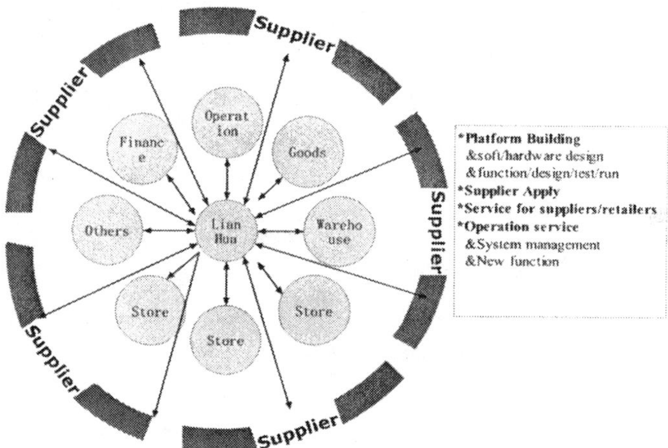

Figure 3. Overall Function of Platform

We can see from this figure, the overall solutions not only includes suggestion work of technology structure, including software and hardware planning, installing and platform function planning, the customers' services provided by retailers, management and maintenance of the platform system and the development and application of new function, ensuring this platform's quick response to changing transaction.

(2) The transaction application

This platform provide with following application support to Lian Hua and its suppliers:

Suppliers' contracts and products research: members' basic information (company information/ factory information), products electronic catalog and contracts checking;

Inquiring quoted price and bargain: new products invoice, quoting files, file management and file limits of authority;

Purchasing and returned purchasing: purchase order receiving/checking, receiving report receiving/checking, returned purchasing inform report receiving/checking, returned purchasing inform replying, sales promotion cooperation inform and sales promotion cooperation replying.

Receiving/selling/inventory management and inventory performance management: sales inventory summary, detail checking, order short delivery report, order overdue, submitted order overdue, summary of returned goods and particulars checking.

Delivering management and payment tasks: an account payable checking, deduction statement checking, deduction projects collection checking, obligated balance checking, bank cable transfer accounts checking, payment on invoice checking and cost of delayed goods checking.

(3) IT structure

From the perspective of IT technology, this framework provides an Internet-based platform for the trusteeship council, sets up an integrated supply chain management system for users from Century Lian Hua and vendors:

Different vendors log on to the platform through dial-up, ADSL, GMB and other access side, System Provide security identification for each vendor to confirm the identity of users and ensure that information security ; Meanwhile, original applications procedures of Century Lian Hua such as the internal network and headquarters of systems, shop operating systems, payment systems, and ERP also integrated with the supply chain management system, and ensured the safety of application through network firewalls. The solution to the functional structure is shown in the figure 5.

Network data center from IBM in Shanghai provided this supply chain management with trusteeship service for hardware and platform software; meanwhile application systems provided by IBM's strategic partnership B&S Link were integrated into the entire System through Gateway.

Without large-scale change to original system, Century Lian Hua and its suppliers acquired a highly reliable, on-demand integrated supply chain management platform. So, in this solution, subsystems between Century Lian Hua, IBM, B&S Link had also created a highly integrated "partnership", together supported the core business of Century Lian Hua.

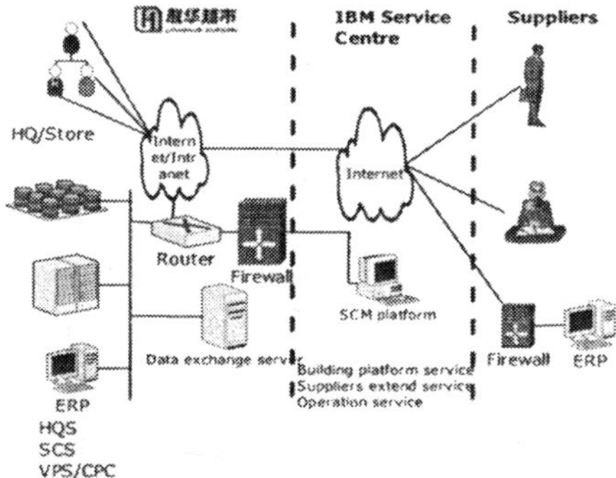

Figure 4. Solutions to the Functional Structure

(4) Operation service

As stated earlier, this solution is an overall plan, which included not only technology platform build, but also the promotion and services after the build platform. The following chart shows the solution to the contents of operation service. IBM, and B&S Link and Century Lian Hua together in close cooperation, after the completion of the first phase of the platform and build functional lines, immediately developed corresponding steps to promote vendor. Along with the continuous build of platform functions, the promotion process is continuous follow-up. At the same time of continued progress of reciprocating in "build—promote—rebuild-re-promote", IBM and B&S Link provided Century Lian Hua and its suppliers with a full range of customer services and maintenance platform management services.

Platform built: Major steps mainly include function planning, function descriptions and demand collection, differences analysis, needs identification, hardware and software investment, development and testing, user acceptance, internal training, and on the line. According to the plan, the two phases of Century Lian Hua will be completed in succession in the 18 months.

Vendors' promotion: Major steps include plan promotion echelon, exploration and selected for manufacturers and sites, delivery of documentation preparation, Vendors contact, platform training, environment preparation, vendors training, and tracking and services for usage situation

Platform operation: adopt three lines service systems to provide Century Lian Hua and suppliers with services, concretely include that the first-line provides operation instructions, function explanations, business advice and platform window; the second line provides a platform issue management; the third line provides platform application with the function maintenance and platform systems management for software / hardware / network.

3. Lian Hua Supermarket Supply Chain Logistics Distribution Centre in Integration

(1) Build a modern logistics distribution centre

As already introduced major Lian Hua Group Distribution Center, Logistics center uses advanced information technology and automated systems, including automatic transmission, automatic pallet lifts system, automatic sorting and handling system, and the systems which load and unload height adjustment plate for cargo platform installed on the platform, all significantly improving Lian Hua Supermarket distribution and overall operating efficiency. Meanwhile, the Group has been adopting wireless handheld terminals, bar code reading technology and wireless signal transmission technology and other hi-tech on such main links as receiving, display, warehouse transfer. Effectively establishing a headquarters and the retailing network and quickly providing real-time operational information facilitate headquarters at any time control the operation. Also, the logistics distribution center installs GPS tracking device and discharge end plates in delivery Vehicles. In addition to real-time handling the passers-delivery vehicles operation, further it improves the discharging efficiency of the shop.

(2) Shorten the logistics flow

① Shorten the time on the way.

Give full play to the network in the role of marketing; organize purchase according to different demand of different customers, improve marketable commodity rate. Only by sticking to formulate marketing can reasonable commodity structure be able to establish. Only having good commodity structure, can effectively reduce the stay time from purchase, storage, display to sale. With the shortest time in-transit (including transportation, distribution, inventory time), send product to the customers.

② Reduce garments ration link, Shorten the logistics distance. Effective methods is reducing distribution links and Shortening logistics corridor.

(3) Use logistics service form third parties

Lian Hua choosing logistics services outsourcing should experience processes as following:

① Inner analysis and estimation of Lian Hua. Make certain the relationship between operation gains and outsourcing; Make certain what logistics services need to outsourcing; collect large material and data to make sure that what outsourcing logistics operation can bring the fast and the best return; adequately communicate with specific operational departments.

② Estimate its own demand, and chose service providers. Store out its own demand in detail and completely, use bidding mode to choose suitable logistics service providers, analyze and chose each enterprise data.

③ The implementation and management of outsourcing. You should keep touch with the business performance of the outsourcing all the way, and exchange your proposal with suppliers immediately, also you should help your employee adapt the new business style.

(4) The alliance strategy of Lian Hua Supermarket with its suppliers

If you want to build an effective and successful supply chain, the key is strategy alliance of retailers and manufactures also distributors. Lian Hua Group wants to set up the collaboration with its suppliers, it should follow below:

① Lian Hua should establish the demand analysis of collaboration with its suppliers

The foundation of establish the strategy alliance include belief each other, improve the information sharing between the chain, the operation is better than operate respectively, and everyone should follow the basic operation rule, also the regular of the alliance. That is to say, Lian Hua should consider its condition and demand first, and then establish a demand report that fit for it.

② Confirm the standard and select the partners

③ Lian Hua establish the formal symbiosis with its manufactures and distributors

④ Implement and enforce the relationship between strategy partners

The figure below illustrates the theory model of strategy alliance between Lian Hua and its suppliers.

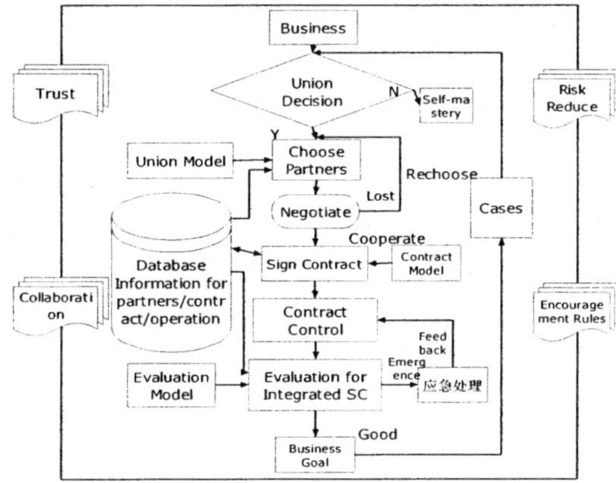

Figure 5. Theory Model for the Union between LianHua and Others

4. CONCLUSIONS

Now, the industry of retail is still in its development phase and the enterprise are all not strong in our country, they may in inferior position in the fierce global competition, there is a big gap between them and the topping global companies. We think the key of improving their competitive capability is combining themselves with all other companies and establish the Supply Chain Web. But actually, the Supply Chain Management in our country just involved the supply chain information management system of a single enterprise, the enterprise and its suppliers are still use the old and out the system's style to communicate with each other, it should enforce the collaboration of the supply chain. Aimed at the feature of Lian Hua, we propose we should pay attention to several problems when we implement the supply chain integrating.

(1) Break the traditional concept and establish the consciousness of win-win
(2) Pay attentions to belief, promises and flexibility protocol
(3) Enforce the core competitive capability
(4) Know and adopt collaboration technology correctly
(5) Recombine the supply chain in the right time

REFERENCES

1. A.B. Christian and J. Jayanth, Supply Chain Management: A Strategic Perspective, *International Journal of Logistics Management.* Volume 8, Number l, pp.15-34, (1997).
2. G.P. Cachon and P.H. Zipkin, *Competitive and cooperative inventory policies in a two-stage supply chain* (Fuqua school of business, Duker university, 1997).
3. F. Chen, Z. Drezner, J.K. Ryan, and D.S. Levi, Quantifying the Bullwhip Effect in a Simple Supply Chain: the Impact of Forecasting, Lead Times, and Information, *Management Science.* Volume 46, Number 3, pp.436-443, (2000).
4. A. Akintoye, G. McIntosh, and E. Fitzgerald, A Survey of Supply Chain Collaboration and Management in the UK Construction Industry, *European Journal of Purchasing & Supply Management.* Volume 6, pp.159-168, (2000).
5. K. Petrson and L. Cecere, Supply Collaboration is a Reality - but Proceed with Caution, *A SCET.* Volume 6, Number 3, (2001).
6. J. Smaros, Forecasting collaboration in the European grocery sector: Observations from a case study, *Journal of Operations Management.* Volume 25, Number 3, pp.702-716, (2007).
7. H. Selim, C. Araz, and I. Ozkarahan, *Collaborative production–distribution planning in supply chain: A fuzzy goal programming approach, Transportation Research Part E: Logistics and Transportation Review.* http://doi:10.1016/j.tre.2006.11.001 (Accessed February 14, 2007).
8. Y. Zhang and J. Jiao, An associative classification-based recommendation system for personalization in B2C e-commerce applications, *Expert Systems with Applications.* Volume 33, Number 2, pp.357-367, (2007).
9. B.J. Angerhofer and M.C. Angelides, A model and a performance measurement system for collaborative supply chains, *Decision Support Systems.* Volume 42, Number 1, pp.283-301, (2006).
10. C.S. Tapiero, Consumers risk and quality control in a collaborative supply chain, *European Journal of Operational Research.* Volume 182, Number 2, pp.683-694, (2007).
11. A. Emberson and J. Storey, Buyer–supplier collaborative relationships: Beyond the normative accounts, *Journal of Purchasing and Supply Management.* Volume 12, Number 5, pp.236-245, (2006).
12. P. Van der Vlist and R. Broekmeulen, Retail consolidation in synchronized supply chains, *Zeitshrift fur Betriebswirtschaft.* Volume 76, pp.165-176, (2006).
13. X. Li and Y. Tian, Analysis on retailing supply chain rebuilding in China, *Business Research.* Number 1, pp.1-3, (2000).

Design and Implementation of 3D Resources Management System for SMMEs Based on Ajax and Web3D

Ming Zu, Tiemeng Li, Xiaowei Liu and Wenjun Hou

Automation School, Beijing University of Posts & Telecommunications, Beijing 100876, P.R. China diysimon@gmail.com tiemeng2000@gmail.com liuxiaowei1983@me.buaa.edu.cn wenjunh2113@263.net

Abstract. Three-dimensional (3D) files are very important resources for Small & Middle-sized Manufacturing Enterprises (SMMEs). In this paper we present a system for management and exhibition of product in 3D form. Virtual Reality Modeling Language (VRML) and extension 3D (X3D) in our system are used to achieve the visualization of model on the internet. Users could view these models only through a web browser. Asynchronous JavaScript and XML (Ajax) also are used in our system to enhance the user experience. Web Services is also introduced in our system. Users only need to access some services that they want to build a virtual exhibition platform without lots of development work. A simple prototype will be introduced in the end.

Keywords: *Ajax, Manufacturing, Virtual reality, Web Services, X3D*

1. INTRODUCTION

In the process of the SMMEs' operation, 3D model files play two important roles. One is 3D model files used in the system such as CAD, CAM and CAPP are very important file resource for improving the automation degree of the enterprise. On the other hand, 3D model files can be used in virtual display, and this is an effective, intuitionistic method for product publicity.

Based on these requirements mentioned above, we present a platform built with Web Services. On this platform users can conveniently build a distributed system as an effective management system for the 3D files or a 3D virtual exhibition environment through the services which they need.

In this system, X3D is used to describe and storage the 3D models. We assume that Browser - Server structure (B/S) will be adopted when they build themselves' system. We use Ajax which is a powerful technology for building rich internet application to exchange the data and enhance the interaction.

In this paper, we present the concept and architecture of the system, and discuss some important work and key points.

Please use the following format when citing this chapter:

Zu, M., Li, T., Liu, X., Hou, W., 2007, in IFIP International Federation for Information Processing, Volume 254, Research and Practical Issues of Enterprise Information Systems II Volume 1, eds. L. Xu, Tjoa A., Chaudhry S. (Boston: Springer), pp. 529-533.

2. USING X3D AND AJAX

There are many methods to realize the 3D sense viewing in the browser. Currently, the most popular technology is VRML/X3D, after installed VRML/X3D plug-in on the client, user can view the 3D scene and do some simple interaction with the model in the browser directly with a VRML/X3D plug-in, e.g. BS Contact VRML, Cortona VRML Client.

Using VRML/X3D to realize the display in the browser of the 3D products refers to the follow key points: the linkages between different products; the interaction between the products and sense; the interaction between the sense and users; the interaction between different users.

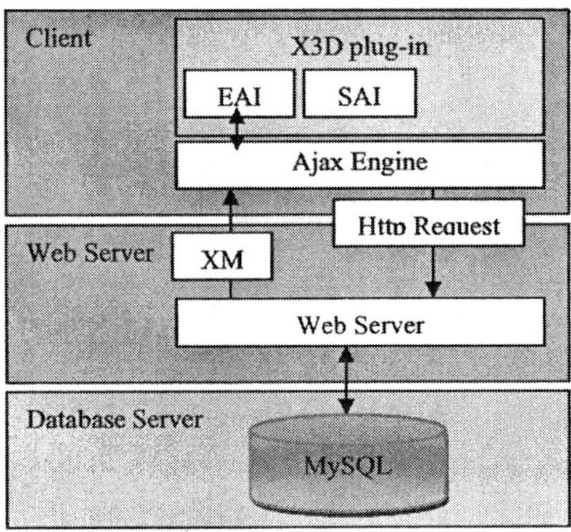

Figure 1. System Architecture

VRML/X3D will not help us to solve all the problems, but X3D provide SAI (Scene Application Interface) and EAI (External Application Interface) that make the VRML/X3D can exchange data with external script language and applications. Usually people use JAVA as an external language to communicate with VRML/X3D directly. But in this way, the efficiency and interaction are generally not excellent.

So we use Ajax to be a middleware. We transmit the XML data through JavaScript running on client. It just refreshes some part of web page which is modified. This method breaks the traditional practice of reload pages. Using Ajax, Web pages can be partially reloaded directly without interruption to the interaction flows. This makes it possible that user can build a Web application close to the local desktop application.

This makes the data' communication and control from sever to 3D sense come true, so we will be able to achieve many functions in 3D environment.

3. USING WEB SERVICES

The feeling of immersion is one of key experience in the virtual reality environment. In a virtual reality environment we not only want to examine a product itself, sometimes the environment which the product is in is necessary that it could help users understand the product. The environment can enhance the authenticity and immersion, this can make users feel they are there, and get a good display result.

But we have to face a fact that if each enterprise has to build different environment for their different products, which make the cost high. Moreover, building 3D model and X3D programming are not very easy for every developer.

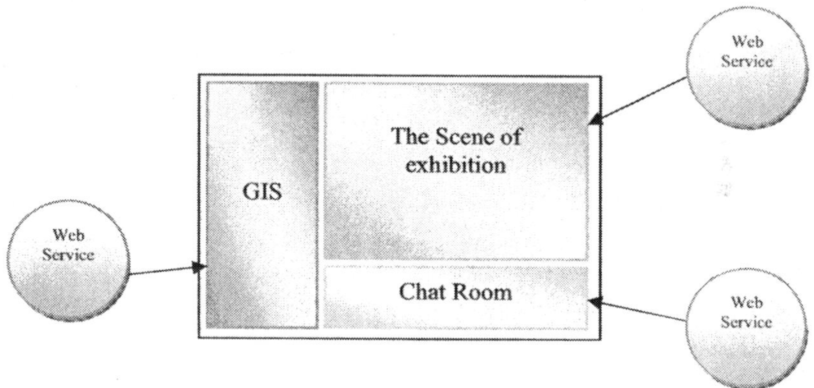

Figure 2. A Prototype Using Web Services

Trough the Web Services, we can pack different environment and scene into several services, and provide them to users who want to build virtual platform. That makes having a products virtual display much easier for developers. Obviously it will encourage users to publish their products in this way. e.g. we build a gallery scene for electrical exhibition, then if an electrical manufacture wish to have an virtual products display the only thing he need to do is using our gallery scene and put his 3D model files of products in.

Besides the scene, we can add a lot of subsidiary functional modules as many web services such as in the part of Chat Room, Product News, etc, the services from different places will be put into one platform, which just likes the Google Personalized Home. This will greatly reduce the development costs and improve efficiency.

4. PROTOTYPE DESIGN

4.1 Interaction of 3D models

The most of X3D plug-in support the zooming, rotation, displacement of models. These actions are all view action. In addition, we also need some acts that are active control behavior, the most important thing is selecting object.

X3D provides a series of event interface, which include mouse click event. When user clicks one model, X3D will trigger the event "eventOut_mouseDown". Then it will map to a corresponding function in JavaScript program. At the same time, the information of node in model will be transmitted to JavaScript. JavaScript procedures for handling such information or transmits to the server. When a result is returned from server, JavaScript will announce the X3D to modify the information of model. This is a flow of interaction in system.

4.2 Navigation

During viewing the virtual scene, every model is a part of the virtual scene. When the space of virtual scene is very big, visitor needs a navigation helping him to find the information he want. Basic on different needs we design two kinds of navigations for visitors.

Two-dimensional map navigation: in a big virtual scene, the visitor's experience of viewing in it is just like walking in a real environment, so it is helpful to be provided a two-dimensional map. We set a background clock, and every clock cycle X3D will tells JavaScript program the location of visitor. And then JavaScript program will judge the distance between the location of this clock cycle and last one, if the distance is long enough to show on the two-dimensional map, JavaScript will conversion the visitor' location information in order to complete the two-dimensional map updates.

Three-dimensional navigation: sometimes user need to view some part of object by select it intuitively. We supply a 3D view of the whole object. System could response to click from users and catch the part which is selected by user. Then show it in the main view.

4.3 Web Services

We divide web services into two categories, one is about 3D, and the other is not.

The services about 3D are scene supply. This type of services needs the VRML model and X3D file of scene. When the system accesses the scene services, the scene will be loaded in the system.

The services unrelated to 3D mostly include message boards, chat rooms, news and a series of traditional web application.

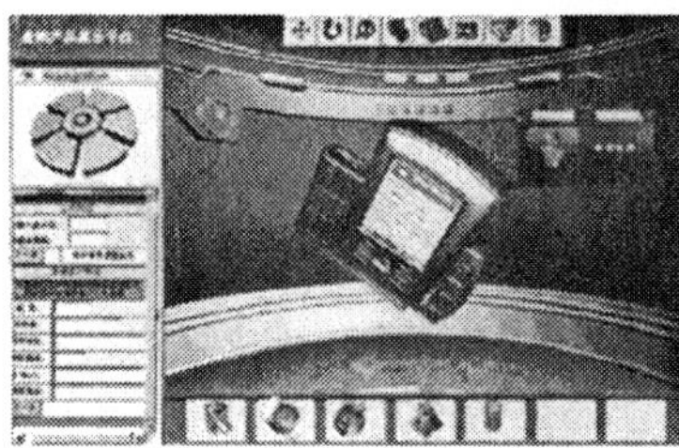

Figure 3. Prototype

5. CONCLUSIONS

In this paper, we have presented the concept of 3D virtual reality environment for management and exhibition the 3D models of SMMEs' products. We mainly introduce the transmission of 3D data between the server and client and building the distributed platform using Web Services. We can implement a 3D rich internet application with X3D and Ajax. These two technologies not only solve the communication problem but also improve the interaction of 3D scene. The development cost of enterprise could be reduced because Web Services enhance the reusability of function model.

In the future, we will study the multi-user collaboration problem. In particular people how to work together in 3D virtual reality environment.

REFERENCES

1. D. Crane and E. Pascarello, *Ajax in Action* (2006). http://www.turingbook.com
2. J.J. Garrett. Ajax: A New Approach to Web Applications, Adaptive Path (Feb. 2005).
3. L.D. Paulson, Building rich web applications with Ajax, *Computer, IEEE*. Volume 38, Number 10, pp.14-17, (2005).
4. X. Tian, C. Huang, and H. Chen, Cache Hint Generation Based on a Profile of an OPT Cache Replacement, *Computer Engineering*. Volume 31, pp.85-87, (2005).
5. W. Hou, Y. Yan, W. Duan, and H. Shun, Research On Three Dimensional Computer Assistance Assembly Process Design System, *Journal of Wuhan University of Technology*. Volume 28, Number 83, pp.1088-1092, (2006).

A Semantic Web Service-Oriented Architecture for Enterprises

Jing Ni[1], Xinli Zhao[2] and Lijun Zhu[3]

[1]Department of Information Management and Information System, Beijing Institute of Petrochemical Technology, Beijing 102617, P.R. China nijing@bipt.edu.cn
[2]China Science and Technology Exchange Center, Beijing 100045, P.R. China zhaoxl@cstec.org
[3]Institute of Scientific & Technical Information of China, Beijing 100038, P.R. China zhulj@istic.ac.cn

Abstract. Developing an interoperable system is one of today's challenging issues in ubiquitous enterprise systems. Initial Web Service-Oriented solutions have enabled the use and combination of distributed functional components within and across company boundaries, but they offer only syntactical description that failed to hold the promise of automatically interacting, dynamically composed web service. Semantic Web Services (SWSs) are an extension of Web Services, with an explicit representation of meanings, to improve their usage and ease scalability. In this paper, we present a Semantic Web Service-Oriented Architecture for enterprise in which data sources and services are made available through SWSs, described by ontologies, allowing interoperability as well as reasoning to create a comprehensive response adapted to user goals, and presenting a use case scenario in the context of an apparatus market, it can also be taken into e-government consideration.

Keywords: *Ontology, Web services semantic web, Service-oriented architecture*

1. INTRODUCTION

The increasing amount of knowledge and information required by a wide variety of users has made it increasingly difficult to share and exchange knowledge between companies. Service-oriented architectures (SOA) build on the decoupled nature and technological independence of services, resulting in more versatile and flexible systems. However, the lack of machine readable semantics is hampering their usage in complex business environment. The Semantic Web, the next generation of World Wide Web, aims to provide a new framework that can enable knowledge sharing and reusing, can be a candidate solution to these problems. SWSs as the combination of the better of the two worlds come along.

SWSs are an extension of Web Services (WSs) with an explicit representation of meanings, facilitating automated discovery, dynamic binding, and invocation of services within an open environment, which can be utilized by applications or other services without human assistance and immune to highly constrained agreements on

Please use the following format when citing this chapter:

Ni, J., Zhao, X., Zhu, L., 2007, in IFIP International Federation for Information Processing, Volume 254, Research and Practical Issues of Enterprise Information Systems II Volume 1, eds. L. Xu, Tjoa A., Chaudhry S. (Boston: Springer), pp. 535-544.

interfaces or protocols. Efforts like the Web Service Modeling Framework (WSMO) [1] propose a formal representation of Web Services that allow access to machine process-able semantics.

The rest of the paper is structured as follows: In section 2, we provide a general overview of SOA. In section 3, we discuss the state-of art in service-oriented enabling technologies. In section 4, we present the proposed semantic web service-oriented approach for enterprise and its implementation architecture. In section 5, we deal with the use case scenario. Finally, we draw our conclusion.

2. RELATED WORK

SOA is critical for making IT more responsive to enterprise requirements. Throughout the years, the following core technology advancements have brought us to where we are today. They are including: Object-oriented analysis and design, Component-based design, Service-oriented design, Interface-based design, Layered application architectures and SOA. Service-oriented architecture presents an approach for building distributed systems that deliver application functionality as services to either end-user applications or other services [2]. Zimmermann et al. [3] discussed the Service-oriented Analysis and Design approach, which aims at helping organizations to discover new business opportunities and threats. Solutions engineered following this approach should be based on reusable services, which in turn must use and provide well defined, standard-compliant interfaces. The high-level activities of identification, specification and realization, and some artifacts of service-oriented modeling were introduced in Ref. [4]. Still, many solutions were published in SOA.

Unlike our approach, such projects takes into account neither the use of SWS technology as the base for developing an enterprise portal nor the use of ontologies for describing services, therefore, they didn't talk about the semantic layer in SOA solution.

The Semantic Web aims to transform the current web into a computer readable web, while WSs provide the tools for the automatic method. Thus, the concept of SWS has been established: Efforts in this area focus on providing rich and machine-understandable representation of services properties, capabilities, and behavior as well as reasoning mechanisms to support automation activities. Examples of such efforts include OWL-S [5], WSMF (Web Services Modeling Framework) [6], and METEOR-S [7]. Work in this area still remains some limitation. Many of the objectives of the SWS paradigm, such as description of service capabilities, dynamic service discovery, and goal-driven composition of WSs, have yet to be reached. Ref. [8] presented that Semantic Web technologies are neither mature nor in state of practice in the industry.

3. SEMANTIC WEB SERVICE ENABLING TECHNOLOGY

3.1 Web Service

Web Services (WSs) provide a set of standards for the provision of functionality over the web, WSs have the advantages of integrating business operations, reducing the time and cost of web application development and maintenance as well as promoting reuse of code over the World Wide Web. A WS is an interoperable unit of application logic that transcends programming languages, operating systems, network communication protocols, and data representation dependencies and issues. It is an infrastructure for developing and deploying distributed applications. WSs are based on the following industry standards: Simple Object Access Protocol (SOAP), Web Service Description Language (WSDL), and Universal Description, Discovery, and Integration (UDDI).

SOAP [9] is fundamentally a stateless, one-way message exchange paradigm, but applications can create more complex interaction patterns (e.g., request/response, request/multiple responses, etc.) by combining such one-way exchanges with features provided by an underlying protocol and/or application-specific information. SOAP is silent on the semantics of any application-specific data it conveys, as it is on issues such as the routing of SOAP messages, reliable data transfer, firewall traversal, etc. However, SOAP provides the framework by which application-specific information may be conveyed in an extensible manner. Also, SOAP provides a full description of the required actions taken by a SOAP node on receiving a SOAP message.

WSDL [10] is the W3C recommended language for describing the service interface. WSDL is used to describe a WS: to specify its location and to describe the operations the service provides. WSDL-based document provides enough information about how to interact with the target WS.

As services become available, they may be registered with a UDDI registry [11], UDDI provides an interoperable, foundational infrastructure for a web services-based software environment for both publicly available services and services only exposed internally within an organization. Advanced through an open process, UDDI is commonly regarded as a cornerstone of WS, defining a standard method for publishing and discovering network-based software components in a SOA.

However, as no explicit semantic information is normally defined, automated comprehension of the WSDL description is limited to cases where the provider and requester assume pre-agreed ontologies, protocols and shared knowledge about operations.

3.2 Semantic Web

In very broad terms, the Semantic Web is a concept wherein all the data and documents on the World Wide Web have some degree of meaning associated with them. From the IT viewpoint, the Semantic Web is a vision of a web which can be interpreted by computer programs. The purpose of Semantic Web is sharing and reusing knowledge. Users will be able to search more accurately of the information and the services they need from the tools provided. Semantic Web focuses on metadata, ontologies, logic and inference, and software agents [12-13]. Among these, the most important concept is ontology.

The most commonly quoted definition (from Tom Gruber of Stanford) of an ontology is "a specification of a conceptualization." Ontology, typically comprises the classes of entities, relations between entities and the axioms which apply to the entities, is useful because in any system, we need to have agreement on the meaning and their interrelationships in order to share understanding. Software and agents are committed to ontologies, and the ontologies are designed to share common knowledge among the agents. Further, its value comes from the ability to share and re-use knowledge between agents in the system. Ontologies are often developed in a collaborative manner by domain experts.

The Semantic Web provides the necessary infrastructure for publishing and resolving ontological descriptions of terms and concepts. In addition, it provides the necessary techniques for reasoning about these concepts, as well as resolving and mapping between ontologies, thus enabling semantic interoperability of WSs through the identification (and mapping) of semantically similar concepts.

3.3 Semantic Web Service

Semantic Web Services (SWSs) aim to combine concepts of the Semantic Web with WS technologies. SWSs expand the capabilities of a WS by associating a semantic description of the WS in order to enable automatic search, discovery, selection, composition, and integration across heterogeneous users and domains, furthermore, enlarging the notion of SOA by applying SWS technology and using ontologies and Semantic Web markup languages to describe data structures and messages passed through WSs interfaces, lead to the development of Semantically-enriched Service-Oriented Business Applications.

There are several approaches to define SWSs, the most prominent proposals are OWL-S and WSMO. Both proposals have been submitted to the World Wide Web Consortium for standardization.

OWL-S [14] is a WS ontology that specifies a conceptual framework for describing SWSs. OWL-S is also a language that enriches WS information from OWL [15] ontologies. The structure of the OWL-S consists of a service profile for service discovering, a process model which supports composition of services, and a service grounding, which associate profile and process concepts with the underlying service interfaces.

The Web Service Modeling Ontology (WSMO) [16] is a formal ontology for describing the various aspects of services in order to enable the automation of WS discovery, composition, mediation and invocation. Its main components are Ontologies, Goals, Web Services and Mediators. Ontologies provide the formally specified terminology of the information used by all other components. Goals represent the objectives that users would like to achieve via the WSs. A goal can import existing concepts and relations defined elsewhere, by either extending or simply re-using them as appropriate. WS descriptions describe the functional behavior of an actual WS. The description also outlines how WSs communicate (choreography) and how they are composed (orchestration). Mediators define mappings between components: (between ontologies (oo), goals (gg), goals and services (wg) and services (wx).

Both OWL-S and WSMO map to UDDI API adding semantic annotation, also OWL-S and WSMO share a default WSDL/SOAP Grounding. However, a WS description within WSMO contains an interface definition. An interface includes a definition of orchestration – how a composite WS invokes subsidiary web services - and choreography. In contrast OWL-S does not provide an explicit definition of choreography but instead focuses on a process based description of how complex web services invoke atomic web services.

4. SEMANTIC WEB SERVICE APPROACH TO ENTERPRISE PROVISION

4.1 Building an Enterprise Ontology

Enterprises are facing a wide range of data processing. Some of this information is structured in databases, some of it is unstructured in documents or semi structured in content management systems. In any large enterprise, employees have to collaborate with a wide variety of people in order to perform different kinds of tasks.

One of the most time-consuming activities that enterprise information professionals suffer is to integrate information from heterogeneous applications. The reason typically is not because the information is on different platforms or in different formats, but because subtle, semantic differences between the applications. So the aim of the enterprise ontology is to provide a "lingua franca" to allow, in order that all the systems within an enterprise to talk to each other, and for the enterprise to talk to its trading partners and the rest of the world.

The task of building enterprise ontology is not very complex. Companies, like IBM, have an ontology editor or manager. The analytical work is similar to building a conceptual enterprise data model for the ontologies are not limited to the restricted set of relationships between nodes that is usually found in a thesaurus. So it involves many of the same skills: the good abstractions ability, the elicited information from interviews with users, and the concepts index through existing documentation and data. [17].

4.2 Enterprise Conceptual Ontology Proposing

Our proposed SW based conceptual portal is based on three ontologies: core ontology, domain ontology and service ontology.

The Core Ontology, describes the common terms used in the given application domain, is a very basic and minimal ontology consisting only of the minimal concepts required to understand the other concepts. It should contain a number of generic concepts and method independent definitions and it is extremely useful for reuse purposes. This ontology represents the general knowledge in different domains (e.g. date, time)

The Domain Ontology, contains specific concepts, encodes concepts of the domain, they are the building blocks for the definition of Core Ontology and Service Ontology concepts. Domain ontologies are specialized for description of parameters of the information. For example, an ontology for Visa and MasterCard related WSs specifies the sub-class and super-class relationships for the relevant entities and properties. In this ontology, Gold Card is defined as a subclass of the MasterCard that is the subclass of Credit Card. The properties of Gold Card include apply name, date, location and capital, etc.

The Service Ontology makes whole the representation of the scenario, modeling the service delivery knowledge level by means of the SWS technology. The Service ontology contains the SWS definitions. They correspond to instances of the Goal, Web Service and Mediator classes used in the IRS-III module, following the WSMO definitions. We start by introducing the Enterprise Ontology [18]. This work was undertaken by the Artificial Intelligence Applications Institute at The University of Edinburgh and its collaborative partners during the Enterprise Project, with the goal of creating a collection of terms and definitions relevant to business enterprises. Since its publication, building the service ontology around it can save time and energy.

The Enterprise Ontology defines concepts within four broad categories: activity, organization, strategy and marketing; it also imports a standard ontology of time. The concepts formally defined within the Enterprise Ontology are listed in Table 1.They are fully defined in [18].

4.3 An Enterprise Architecture Provision

This architecture is not specific for generating a particular type of enterprise service, but is a common architecture which will be useful for establishing and developing any kind of e-business service. The modules (Fig. 1) are organized in three layers.

User Interaction supports the user to identify and collect information for service execution.

The middleware layer is the primary layer. Ontology component, including core ontologies, domain ontologies, ontology describes service, is the core component of the portal, responsible for the interoperability and service integration. It allows the semantic description, publishing of the available services, and also the description, identification, instantiation and invocation of services. The activities such as processing and executing the user goal; discovering web services; selecting the most appropriate one; resolving any mismatches at the ontological level; invoking the relevant set of WSs satisfying any data, and control flow and invocation requirements are mainly supported by IRS-III infrastructure.

Table 1. Overview of the Enterprise Ontology

Activity	Activity, Activity Specification, Execute, Executed Activity Specification, T-Begin, T-End, Pre-Condition, Effect, Doer, Sub-Activity, Authority, Activity Owner, Event, Plan, Sub-Plan, Planning, Process Specification, Resource, Resource Allocation, Resource Substitute, Capability, Skill
Organization	Person, Machine, Corporation, Partnership, Partner, Legal Entity, Organizational Unit, Manage, Delegate, Management Link, Legal Ownership, Non-Legal Ownership, Ownership, Owner, Asset, Stakeholder, Employment Contract, Share, Shareholder
Strategy	Purpose, Hold Purpose, Intended Purpose, Purpose-Holder, Strategic Purpose, Objective, Vision, Mission, Goal, Help Achieve, Strategy, Strategic Planning, Strategic Action, Decision, Assumption, Critical Assumption, Non-Critical Assumption, Influence Factor, Critical Influence Factor, Non-Critical Influence Factor, Critical Success Factor, Risk
Marketing	Actual Customer, Potential Customer, Customer, Sale, Potential Sale, For Sale, Sale Offer, Vendor, Reseller, Product, Asking Price, Sale Price, Market, Need, Market Need, Segmentation Variable, Market Segment, Market Research, Brand, Image, Feature, Promotion, Competitor
Time	Time Line, Time Interval, Time Point

There will be queries which our defined ontologies wouldn't be able to support inference, in such cases we can store them as New Terms Tank. The New Terms will be analyzed by the domain experts and will be accommodated in the existing ontologies.

IRS-III [19], the Internet Reasoning Service, is a framework and platform for developing SWS which utilizes the WSMO ontology, which allows the description, publication and execution of SWS, according to the WSMO conceptual model. Based on a distributed architecture communicating via XML/SOAP messages, it provides an execution environment for SWS. Ontologies are stored by the server, and used in WSMO descriptions to support discovery, composition, invocation and orchestration of WSs. Especially, it can automatically transform programming code into a WS, by automatically creating an appropriate wrapper. Hence, it is very easy to make existing standalone software available on the net, as WSs.

A request presented by the user (i.e. the other companies) through the portal interface is processed by the Business Manager module, which discovers all related events, allowing the user to select the appropriate event. Information is described through the domain ontology, while the Goals are described via the Service Ontology. When the user invokes one of the goals, the Business Manager calls the IRS-III module, which retrieves the semantic description of the goal. Then, it creates an instance with specific data items, and identifies and invokes the WSs addressing the user needs by means of their semantic description. Finally, the WS is executed and the result is presented to the user.

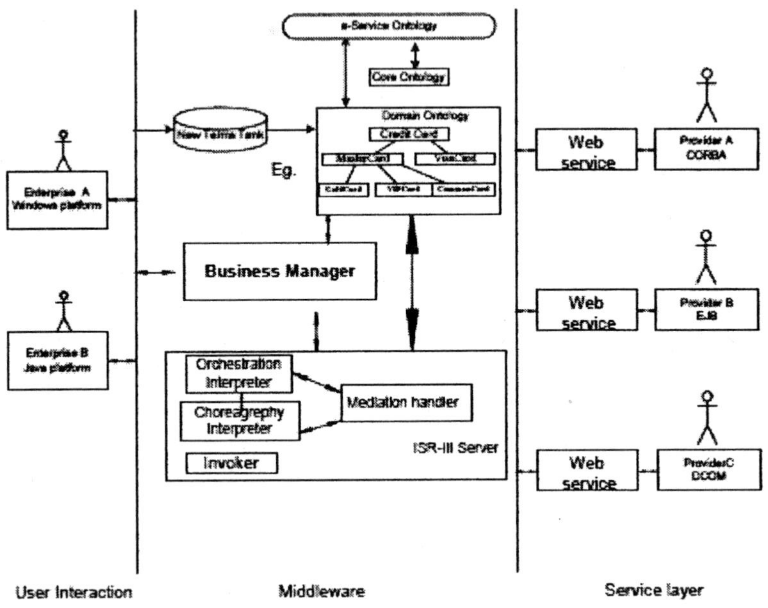

Figure 1. An Architecture Provision

Service Layer is responsible for the execution of services for an event. Each provider supplies services through the WS technology. Each one is connected to the E-marketplace and semantically described via the IRS-III module of the Middleware layer.

5. USE CASE SCENARIO

We think of a real world scenario in the context of a market, where a company wants to sell its produce (e.g. camera) and the possible buyers are an Apparatus Product Market and brokers associated with APM. The company wants to know the market place address. By putting some constraints, the company can place his query through the search interface of the portal.

On the other hand, the service providers create the WSs for supplying a service through the portal. The developers provide the goal description which represents the objectives that users would like to achieve via WSs. The developer semantically describes its WS and associates it to the goal. So when a user query is executed, the process manager discovers the potential buyers, taking into account the buyers' constraints. When doing this, the goal is invoked and the IRS Server detects and calls the WS that match the data. A matching WS could be composed of different integrated WSs that realize the event.

6. CONCLUSIONS

WSs provide a mechanism to connect applications regardless of the underlying software/hardware platform and their location. Business organizations can thus use WS technology to expose elements of their processes. SWSs enable the formal specification of services, allowing their automated, goal-driven, location and usage. WSMO provides a framework for the description of SWSs that enables seamless business integration through formal descriptions, maximal decoupling of components, and strong mediation support.

Developing enterprise application using Semantic Web technology is in early stages. Though there are few success stories (projects) which have successfully completed their projects, but still have a long way to go in implementing the models. In this work, we have presented an integrated, layered semantic service architecture and transformation framework. We propose a Semantic Web Services-Oriented Architecture and make an attempt to integrate the development of SWSs using the WSMO into ISR-III framework.

ACKNOWLEDGEMENTS

This research was supported by the National Natural Science Foundation of China under Grant 70573103.

REFERENCES

1. H. Lausen, A. Polleres, and D. Roman, *Web Service Modeling Ontology (WSMO)* (June 3, 2005). http://www.w3.org/Submission/WSMO/
2. M. Endrei, J. Ang, A. Arsanjani, S. Chua, P. Comte, P. Krogdahl, M. Luo, and T. Newling, *Patterns: Service-Oriented Architecture and Web Services* (April, 2004). http://www.redbooks.ibm.com/abstracts/sg246303.html
3. A. Zimmermann, P. Krogdahl, and C. Gee, *Elements of Service-oriented Analysis and Design: An Interdisciplinary Approach for SOA Projects* (June 2, 2004). http://www-128.ibm.com/developerworks/library/ws-soad1/
4. A. Arsanjani, Service-Oriented Modeling and Architecture (November 9, 2004). http://www-128.ibm.com/developerworks/library/ws-soa-design1/

5. D. Martin, M. Paolucci, S. McIlraith, M. Burstein, D. McDermott, D. McGuinness, B. Parsia, T. Payne, M. Sabou, M. Solanki, N. Srinivasan, and K. Sycara, *Bringing Semantics to Web Services: The OWL-S Approach* (June 6, 2004). http://www.daml.org/services/owl-s/OWL-S-SWSWPC2004-CameraReady.doc
6. D. Fensel, and C. Bussler, The Web Service Modeling Framework WSMF, *Electron Commerce Research and Application.* Volume 1, Number 2, pp.113-137, (2002).
7. K. Verma, K. Gomadam, A.P. Sheth, J.A. Miller, and Z. Wu, *The METEOR-S Approach for Configuring and Executing Dynamic Web Processes* (June 24, 2005). http://lsdis.cs.uga.edu/projects/meteor-s/
8. L. Cabral, J. Dominguez, E. Motta, T. Payne, and F. Hakimpour, *Approaches to Semantic Web Services: An Overview and Comparison* (May 10-12, 2004). http://kmi.open.ac.uk/projects/irs/cabralESWS04.pdf
9. N. Mitra, *SOAP Version 1.2 Part 0: Primer (Second Edition) W3C Recommendation* (April 27, 2007). http://www.w3.org/TR/soap12-part0/
10. E. Christensen, F. Curbera, G. Meredith, and S. Weerawarana, *Web Services Description Language (WSDL) 1.1*, W3C Note (March 15, 2001). http://www.w3.org/TR/2001/NOTE-wsdl-20010315
11. L. Clement, A. Hately, C.V. Riegen, and T. Rogers, *UDDI Version 3.0.2* (Novenber 19, 2004). http://uddi.org/pubs/uddi-v3.0.2-20041019.htm
12. G. Antoniou, and F.V. Harmelen, *A Semantic Web Primer* (The MIT Press: London, 2004).
13. T.B. Passin, *Explorer's Guide to the Semantic Web* (Manning Press: Greenwich, 2004).
14. D. Martin, M. Burstein, J. Hobbs, O. Lassila, D. McDermott, S. McIlraith, S. Arayanan, P. Paolucci, B. Parsia, T. Payne, E. Sirin, E. Srin, N. Sirnivasan, and K. Sycara, *OWL-S Semantic Markup for Web Service* (November 24, 2004). http://www.w3.org/Submission/OWL-S/
15. D. McGuinness, and F. D. Harmelen, Owl Web Ontology Language Overview (Februry 10, 2004). http://www.w3.org/TR/owl-features/
16. D. McComb, *The Enterprise Ontology* (2006). http://www.semanticarts.com/DesktopModules/ViewArticle.asp
17. M. Uschold, M. King, S. Moralee, and Y. Zorgios, *The Enterprise Ontology* (1998). http://www.aiai.ed.ac.uk/project/enterprise/enterprise/ontology.html /
18. J. Domingue, L. Cabral, F. Hakimpour, D. Sell, and E. Motta, *Demo of IRS III: A Platform and Infrastructure for Creating WSMO-based Semantic Web Services* (2004). http://iswc2004.semanticweb.org/demos/45/paper.pdf

On Localization of Enterprise Information Systems

Goutam Kumar Saha

CDAC, Salt Lake, Sector-V, Kolkata 700091, India
sahagk@gmail.com

Abstract. This paper describes how to localize various output information, including alert messages of an enterprise information system by the XML based Computational Linguistics Markup (CLM). To display a web document or program message or to display a user interface in an appropriate, locale and culture specific translated form, is an important and complex task in the I18N & L10N or Globalization process. In L10N we need to address various locale and cultural aspects, for examples, Naming, formats of date and time, number, icons, symbols and colors etc including legal aspects for proper customization of a product. Language localization denotes the process of translating a product into different languages. Software localization addresses the messages that a program of an Enterprise Information System (EIS) presents to a user need to be translated into various languages. This is very important in the Internationalization & Localization process for addressing language and locale specific various must-do issues as an aid to an easier faster and more meaningful translation process for an EIS web content and answers of the web applications in an EIS. The approach presented here relies on a 3-Layered XML Schematic scheme. By using the CLM, while internationalizing a product, we can do localization easily even without having much linguistic resources on a source human language. The work of this paper is a significant step forward toward globalizing the information system of an enterprise at lower cost for higher gain. A next generation EIS would provide such challenging features of dynamically localized presentation layer with this CLM.

Keywords: *Enterprise information systems (EIS), Enterprise language, Web-based logistics, XML and XML schema, Internationalization and localization of Web content, Computational linguistic markup, ontology, Interoperability models, Software architecture*

1. INTRODUCTION

Today, in the era of global competition, localization of the information system [1-3] of an enterprise is must enabling easy reach to its customers at every part of the globe irrespective of its language and culture. The term "Internationalization" refers to the process involved in the design and development of a product, application or document-content that enables easy localization for target-audiences that vary in culture, region, or language. "Localization" is the process on adaptation of a product, application or document content to meet the language, cultural and other requirements of a specific target market or a "locale". Localization is abbreviated as "L10N", after the number of letters between 'L' and 'N'. We can view internationalization (I18N) as

Please use the following format when citing this chapter:

Saha, G. K., 2007, in IFIP International Federation for Information Processing, Volume 254, Research and Practical Issues of Enterprise Information Systems II Volume 1, eds. L. Xu, Tjoa A., Chaudhry S. (Boston: Springer), pp. 545-551.

a process that enables L10N. To display a web document or program message or to display a user interface in an appropriate, locale and culture specific translated form is an important and complex task in the I18N & L10N or Globalization process. In L10N we need to address various locale and cultural aspects, for examples, Naming, formats of date and time, number, icons, symbols and colors etc including legal aspects for proper customization of a product. Language localization denotes the process of translating a product into different languages. Software localization addresses the messages that a program of an Enterprise Information System (EIS) presents to a user need to be translated into various languages. This paper describes how to localize various output information of an enterprise information system by the XML based Computational Linguistics Markup (CLM). This is very important in the Internationalization & Localization process for addressing language and locale specific various must-do issues as an aid to an easier faster and more meaningful translation process for an EIS web content and answers of the web applications in an EIS. The approach talked about here relies on a 3-Layered XML Schematic scheme. On using the CLM, while internationalizing a product, we can do localization easily even without having much linguistic resources on a source human language. The work of this paper is a significant step forward toward globalizing the information system of an enterprise at lower cost for higher gain. The next generation EIS would provide user interactions at users' local languages dynamically apart from an overwhelming functional complexity combined with the requirements of higher interoperability, flexibility, extensibility, adaptive- ness and of course with higher dependability.

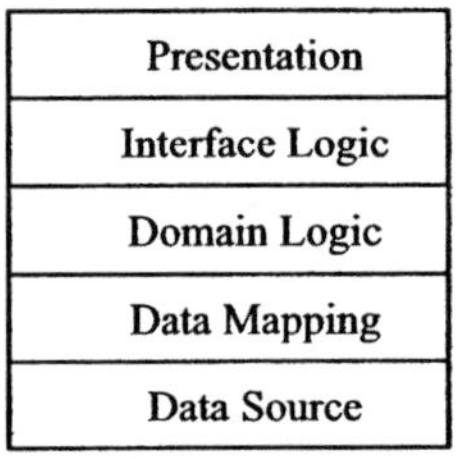

Presentation
Interface Logic
Domain Logic
Data Mapping
Data Source

Figure 1. Logical Architecture of Enterprise Information System

Nowadays, logical architecture of an EIS in [2] has five logical layers (as shown in figure 1) viz., *Presentation, Interface Logic* for User Interface, *Domain Logic, Data Mapping, and Data Source.* Such model is to add a mediating layer that works among the primary layers (e.g., User Interface, Domain Logic, Data Source) to obtain a higher independence among them and, then, to permit their evolution or substitution autonomously, decreasing considerably their impact in the other parts of the system.

2. THE THREE-LAYERED XML – BASED CLM

The proposed 3-Layered XML Schema [4-5] aids to markup for both the syntactic as in [6] and semantic metadata information in the structure of an XML document. This approach is a low-cost solution to I18N and L10N [2,7-10] for producing meaningful translation as the various formative, semantic, grammatical and locale specific embedded information of EIS are found to be very important to both the internationalization and localization processes. An XML schema is any type of model document that defines the structure of an XML document. We can create XML schemas using basic XML. In human languages, we often find that a word has several meanings (i.e., word sense ambiguity) at various content contexts (or content domain of a paragraph of a web page). Similarly, a word may have several linguistic parts of speech (i.e., POS ambiguity). For an example, the word "light" has several POS namely, verb, adjective, noun. Again, a metadata about a sentence helps in parsing during the machine translation of web content. The proposed 3-Tier XML Schema approach uses three schemas for web content. The first schema is meant for content domain, the second schema is for sentence level metadata and the third one is meant for the word level metadata or markups. We need to validate an XML document against the proposed three schemas to examine whether the XML content is well formed to conform to the schemas. This 3-tier schema scheme is also useful for the Translation Memory processes to keep context markups when Internationalization & Localization developers use this scheme for both source and target text. We develop the first XML schema that contains various categories on content domain. The second XML schema contains various categories on sentences. The third XML schema contains various Parts-of-Speech categories on words. The proposed scheme uses three XML elements namely, content domain, sentence category and POS category. The schematic block diagram of the proposed 3-Tier or 3-Layered XML Schema approach is shown in figure 2. Content domain includes various contexts namely, sports, information technology, medicine, travel, personal, mathematics and romance etc. Sentence categories include simple, compound, complex, proverbial, taunt, suspicion, active & passive voice, direct and indirect speech etc. Parts-of-Speech categories include noun, pronoun, verb, adjective, adverb, preposition, postposition, interjection, conjunction and indeclinable etc. A content author for EIS having school level grammatical knowledge will not find any difficulty on using such markups because this scheme does not limit one to add an appropriate markup as an attribute. Content author may not use such three level markups at all parts (not for all words and sentences) of a document. Markups need to be used only at the sensitive or difficult parts or ambiguous parts of a document. For some languages, a content author even may not need to add finer sub-category markups at his /her document. Metadata information about the domain, sentence type or specific words will help translators to do better quality work or to do the work quickly. If translators know that a word belongs to a specific domain then they can go to a terminology database and check the word; thus, even for human translators this 3-Tier or 3-layer schema will be helpful. One cannot do an accurate translation without such information. The proposed 3-tiers model for dealing with various information on Metadata annotation, sentences and linguistic unit annotations, is illustrated in example 1. The result of such segmentation is an annotated document, which is very useful to auto-construct Translation Memory and linguistic resources. The first level schema on content domain helps in finding appropriate terminology for the document words. The translation parser gets benefited from the syntactic or formative markup in the second level schema meant for sentence level and the semantic information helps in getting more meaning translation for a given sentence in the content written in a source human language. The third level schema is to embed word level syntactic and semantic metadata information for a word in a sentence. Importance of the 3-layered schema is to find solution for both word sense disambiguation and POS-level disambiguation. For example, in English: the word "bat" has multiple meanings- (a) "a bird" (in the content-domain of zoology/animal) or (b) in the content domain of sports it means "a playing instrument" to hit a ball (like cricket bat). In both cases, parts-of-speech (POS) of "bat" is noun (finer category- common noun) only. In many languages, there are many common words that have multiple meanings (word sense ambiguity) at various contexts (though POS category may remain same). Only based on the context of content domain and sentence, we understand the appropriate meaning of such words having word sense ambiguities. For example, the English word "bank" may mean a financial institution or a stretch of rising land at the edge of a stream. The 1st level schema (content domain markup) is useful for marking the context information for a paragraph of translatable content. The 2nd level schema (sentence level markups) takes care of translatable proverbs, idioms, dialect and usage etc for any human language in the world. The 3rd level schema (word level markups) is to obtain the most appropriate meaning of "a word" (having POS ambiguity with multiple POS and word sense ambiguity) in a sentence inside text content. Content author will not find any difficulty on using such markups because this scheme does not limit one to add an appropriate markup as an attribute. Content author may not need to use such three level markups at all parts (not for all words and sentences) of a document. Markups may be used only at the sensitive or difficult parts or ambiguous parts of a document. For some languages, a content author even may not need to add finer sub-category markups at his/her document. Finer POS categories are useful for handling pragmatic (deeper semantic) issues of content.

3. THE CLM FOR INTERNATIONALIZATION & LOCALIZATION OF EIS

CLM approach incorporates morphology, syntax, semantics and pragmatics of human languages, which are very essential for better machine translation. In order to translate one language into another, one has to understand the grammar of both languages, including both morphology (the grammar of word forms) and syntax (the grammar of how words are combined to form sentences). In order to understand syntax, one has to also understand the semantics of the vocabulary, and even to understand something of the pragmatics of how the language was being used. The novelty of the CLM- based document modeling approach is that it helps us to translate one language to another without knowing grammar of the source language.

CLM enables machine translation even if we do not have much linguistic resources of source language. Metadata information about the domain, sentence type or specific words will help translators to do better quality work or to do the work quickly. If translators know that a word belongs to a specific context domain then they can go to a terminology database and check the word, thus, even for human translators this 3-layered schema will be helpful. One cannot do an accurate translation without such information. XML Schema authors should prefer to use attributes for metadata information because of their better flexibility and portability. XML element tag is in between “<” and “ >”. XML element tag is used to hold metadata on author’s text that helps a machine translator in translation process. Author’s text (for translation) is in between “<>” and “</>”. Remark or comment is in between “<! –“ and “ -->”. Examples have been added as tutorial so that readers can apply this 3-tier or 3-layered scheme at their work. We may consider an author text or web content that has a sentence, for example, "She played in Shakespeare." CLM Markup as shown in example-1 is meant for word - sense disambiguation.

Example-1 CLM Based EIS Information Annotation

```
<content_domain name="literature" type="drama">
.... <sentence_category name="semantic" type="demonstrative">
She <pos_category name="verb" meaning="acted"> played </pos_category> in
<pos_category name=noun type="proper" meaning="a title of a Drama">Shakespeare
</pos_category>.
<!-- here, "played" implies the verb "acted" -->
</sentence_category>
......... </content_domain>
```

Example-2. An example on Markup for Javascript ToolTips Text

```
<sentence_cat name="scripttitle_value">
<!-- Markup for Javascript ToolTips text on events like ONMOUSEOVER -->
<A HREF="/tips/page2.asp"    ONMOUSEOVER="this._tip='We <FONT COLOR=red>
                  <B>simplify</B></FONT>
                  DHTML'">      DHTML </A> </sentence_cat>
```

Example-3. Markup for ToolTip in EIS

```
<!-- Word-Level Markup for Tool Tip text word embedded inside an Image -->
<para> Click here
<image source="begin.jpg" alt="begin" />
<pos_cat name="alt_value"> begin </pos_cat>
to play now.
</para>
```

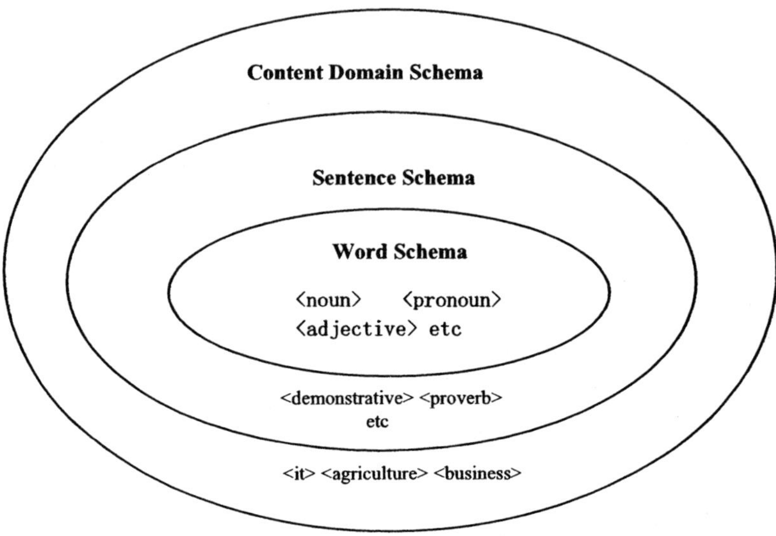

Figure 2. Computational Linguistic Markup Based on 3-layered XML Schema

Example-4. I18n/Localization sensitive Markups used in Postal Address

```
<pos_cat name="noun" meaning="Post Office Box">P.O. Box</pos_cat>4123
<!-- P.O. Box or Postfach (Germany) Or Case Postale (France) in Mailing Address -->
<pos_cat name="noun" meaning="Postal Index Number or ZIP">PIN</pos_cat>700059
<!-- PIN (India) or ZIP (USA) in Mailing Address -->
<pos_cat name="noun" type="common" meaning="Village">Gram</pos_cat> Dignagar
<!-- here, Gram indicates a village or county (not the measurement unit) -->
<!-- Markup example using Road and lane -->
 Netaji Subhas Road,
Shastribagan<pos_cat name="noun" type="common" meaning="lane">Goli</pos_cat>
<!-- here, Goli indicates a narrow road or a lane -->
```

---

4. CONCLUSIONS

The computational linguistic markup based on three- layered XML schema approach is of an immense help in the process of Internationalization and Localization of EIS at the presentation layer. If content author follows CLM based

Internationalization, then Localization to any target language becomes easier. The work aims to ease Localization to any target human language without having knowledge in the source human language at the cost of extra metadata added while internationalizing a web content or software. XML code here is tested as well formed and is tested on web browsers. CLM – based XML document is also validated against the schemas. The paper provides a sound and functional schema, which takes into account the content domain, sentence and word. All the techniques, as described in this paper, relate to how it can be applied from the computation linguistics domain. In addition, with the word, it could be a multi-modal schema, incorporating sound bites of pronunciation. In future, we may describe word meaning in some other standard way, perhaps to hook it up with UNL or WordNet (relations between synonym sets) sense numbers which might further help in automating translation process.

REFERENCES

1. M. Fowler, *Patterns of Enterprise Applications Architecture,* (2007). http://martinfowler.com/isa/index.html (Accessed May 7, 2007).
2. M. Daniel, *The Architecture of Enterprise Information Systems,* (2006). http://moisesdaniel.com/wri/eisa.pdf (Accessed May 3, 2007).
3. Y. Yusuf, A. Gunasekaran, and M.S. Abthorpe, Enterprise information systems: a case study of ERP in rolls-royce, *International Journal of Production Economics.* Volume 87, pp.251-266, (2004).
4. G.K. Saha, *Computational Linguistic Markup (CLM),* W3C Archive, (2005). http://esw.w3.org/topic/its0908LinguisticMarkup (Accessed May 2007).
5. G. K. Saha, A novel 3-tier xml schematic approach for web page translation, *ACM Ubiquity.* Volume 6, Number 43, pp.1-16, (2005).
6. R.P. Sinha, *Current English Grammar and Usage* (Oxford University Press: 2003).
7. *W3C Archive* (2006). http://www.w3.org/TR/its (Accessed May 5, 2007).
8. *W3C Archive* (2006). http://www.w3.org/TR/2006/WD-its-20060222 (Accessed May 5, 2007).
9. R. Ishida and S. K Miller, *Localization vs. Internationalization,* W3C Archive (2006). http://www.w3.org/International/questions/qa-i18n (Accessed May 4, 2007).
10. F. Sasaki, From characters tow web services to internationalization is everywhere, *ACM Ubiquity.* Volume 6, Number 47, pp1-6, (2005).
11. *W3C Archive* (2006). http://www.w3.org/International/quicktips (Accessed May 6, 2007).
12. G.K. Saha, English to bangla translator – the banganubad, *International Journal of Computer Processing of Oriental Languages.* Volume 18, Number 4, pp.281-290, (2005).

Extending Enterprise Services Descriptive Metadata with Semantic Aspect Based on RDF

Lei Zhang, Yani Yan and Jianlin Wu

Beijing Key Laboratory of Intelligent Communications Software and Multimedia, Beijing University of Posts and Telecommunications, Beijing 100876, P.R. China
zlei@bupt.edu.cn kimsky61@gmail.com jlwu@bupt.edu.cn

Abstract. In the area of enterprise information integration, enterprise services are usually pre-defined and constructed before being supplied to users traditionally. However, with the rising of users' individuation needs, constructing and offering every user with the very service that can meet their needs by service provider is impossible and costly. In order to solve this problem, a new method of dynamic constructing and offering services defined by users themselves is put forward in this paper. Firstly, the framework of the service integration system is illustrated. Then, a formalized definition of enterprise services is brought forward. Based on the definition, a meta-model extended with semantic is constructed by RDF (Resource Describe Framework). Metadata defined based on the meta-model can describe the constructive components of a service and their communications. Users can define specific service by subscribing service descriptive metadata. After subscription, services can be called and system will parse the service metadata and dynamic create the service according to the service structure and components operation logic specified in the metadata. At last, a scenario is provided to demonstrate how the meta-model can be used to support the dynamic component-based construction of services.

Keywords: *Component-oriented architecture, Enterprise information integration*

I. INTRODUCTION

Every enterprise faces the challenge of integrating components of diverse IT systems. Components are the basic building blocks of enterprise and distributed applications [1]. How to integrate these components together to dynamic create services that can be offered to enterprise customers to make use of existent enterprise resources furthest and to make enterprise gain from it? The post facto integration of independent components has not been particularly successful. [2]Lack of agreed upon technological standards and the absence of semantic integration models are two major contributing factors [2].

The dominating component standards including Common Object Request Broker Architecture(CORBA), Component Object Model (COM), Enterprise Java Beans (EJB) etc.. CORBA is a communication Middleware that can separate the applications from communication details. CORBA [3] can offer components of distributed systems through consistent interface specification. EJB [3] emphasize on reuse of components.

Please use the following format when citing this chapter:

Zhang, L., Yan, Y., Wu, J., 2007, in IFIP International Federation for Information Processing, Volume 254, Research and Practical Issues of Enterprise Information Systems II Volume 1, eds. L. Xu, Tjoa A., Chaudhry S. (Boston: Springer), pp. 553-562.

EJB offers component operating environment to make business developers can concentrate on developing business applications [4]. However, they are inefficient in dynamic integration of components [4] because they are inefficient in describing components behavior semantic [5].

Web Service Business Process Execution Language (WS-BPEL) [6] is an XML-based standard for modeling business process flows within the Web services architecture [7]. WS-BPEL can effect as a component integration standard. However, WS-BPEL can only be used to integrate Web services components into business process [6]. Other resources, like EJB or COM. Components have to be encapsulated into Web services to be integrated.

Other component integration and dynamic service composition systems lack extensibility and understandability and are inefficient in service specialization. Also some systems cannot support operation dependency and soft-state information. With the rising of users' individuation needs, constructing and offering every user with the very service that can meet their needs by service provider merely is impossible and costly. In order to solve this problem, a new method of dynamic integrating components to construct services based on the component integration model specified in service descriptive metadata subscribed by users is put forward in this paper. Services have not to be constructed before being supplied to users and they can meet users' needs furthest as they are defined by users themselves. The new method can provide several benefits: flexibility, adaptability, and availability.

Section 2 will introduce some background knowledge. The framework of the service integration system is illustrated in section 3. A formalized definition of services is described in section 4 and the service specification meta-model is built by RDF based on the formalization in section 5. At last, in section 6, an example on how to build metadata for specific service based on the meta-model is given.

2. BACKGROUND KNOWLEDGE

2.1 Metadata

Metadata has traditionally been defined as "data about data" or "information about information". Metadata was invented to help computer systems and humans more efficiently and effectively organize, access, and interpret data. [8] Metadata is about knowledge, which is the ability to turn information and data into effective action. Meta-model supplies the template for constructing metadata. Meta-model is simply the elements that are used to describe the data, information and knowledge.

In this paper, we will define the dynamic service descriptive meta-model. Metadata based on the meta-model contains semantic information which describes the dynamic service, including components that constitute the service and their operation sequence.

2.2 RDF

The Resource Description Framework (RDF) is a language for representing information about resources in the World Wide Web [9]. RDF is intended for situations in which this information needs to be processed by applications, rather than being only displayed to people [9]. RDF provides a common framework for expressing this information and application designers can leverage the availability of common RDF parsers and processing tools.

RDF is based on the idea of identifying things using Web identifiers (called Uniform Resource Identifiers, or URIs [9]), and describing resources in terms of simple properties and property values. RDF provides an XML-based syntax (called RDF/XML[9]) for recording and exchanging information.

RDF is particularly intended for representing metadata about Web resources [9]. RDF provides a way to express simple statements about resources. However, RDF user communities also need the ability to define the vocabularies they intend to use, specifically, to indicate that they are describing specific kinds of resources, and will use specific properties in describing those resources. RDF itself provides no means for defining such application-specific classes and properties [9]. Instead, such classes and properties are described as an RDF vocabulary, using extensions to RDF provided by the RDF Vocabulary Description Language 1.0: RDF Schema [9]. RDF Schema does not provide a vocabulary of application-specific classes.

In this paper, we will define our service-specific RDF vocabulary, including RDF classes and properties that can be used to construct the dynamic service descriptive metadata.

3. FRAMEWORK

The service management system needs to be setup. Through the system, user can submit service descriptive metadata and call the service after subscription. And the system will dynamic parse the service metadata and offer service to users by executing related components according to the execution logic specified in the metadata.

Figure1 below will show the framework of the enterprise service management system.

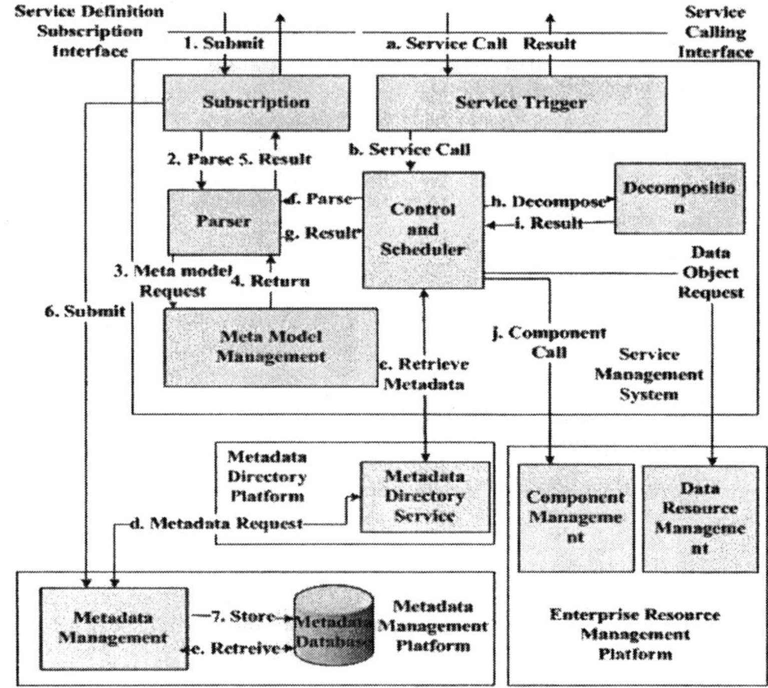

Figure 1. Framework of Enterprise Service Management System

Subscription module is the interface for subscribing service metadata. It first communicates with the Parse module to parse and validate the metadata before subscribing it to the metadata management platform. The Parse module will request meta-model from the Meta-model Management module to parse metadata based on the meta-model. At last, metadata will be stored to the Metadata DB by the Metadata Management module. Messages marked from 1 to 7 describe the procedure.

Service Trigger module is the interface for calling services. It will deliver service requests to the Control and Scheduler module which is the central controller for executing services. The Control and Scheduler module first requests the service metadata through the Metadata Directory service and then call the Parser module to parse it in order to understand the service operation logic. Then, the Decomposition module will be called by the controller to decompose the service into smaller tasks. During executing the tasks, the controller will communicates with the Enterprise Resource Management Platform to utilize related system components and access related data resource. Messages marked from a to j describes the procedure.

The Parser, the Control and Scheduler, the Decomposition and the Meta Model Management modules are under development. The following sections of this paper will concentrate on describing how to construct the service meta-model based on RDF and how to build service metadata based on the meta-model.

4. FORMALIZATION

This section will give a formalized definition of enterprise services. Services can be formalized as: Service (SID, CD, SIFD, CPC, ISC, DOC, PC). SID refers to Service ID, which is the universal service identity within the enterprise. CD refers to Context Description.

CD can be formalized as: CD (FD, UD, ID, RAP). FD refers to Function Description. FD describes the functional characters of services; UD refers to User Description and UD describes users who have privilege of calling the service; ID refers to Environment Description and ID describes the desirable executing environment of the service; RAP refers to Resource Access Privilege.

SIFD refers to Service Interface Description. SIFD describes the service interface through which service can be called by users.

CPC refers to Component Collection. CPC can be formalized as: CPC (CPID).CPID refers to Component ID. Furthermore, component can be formalized as: C(CPID, CPD, AC). CPD represents Component Description and AC represents collection of actions that constitute the component.

ISC represents Inter Sequence of Components, which can be formalized as: ISC((Action1, Action2), (Time1 (Action1), Time2 (Action2), ST)). ISC is comprised of an action collection and an expression which explains the temporal executing sequence of actions included in the collection. Action represents dynamic executing of specific component function. Action can be formalized as: Action (CPID). CPID indicates the component to which the action belongs. Time represents the states of execution of actions. There are two types of states: Begin and End. Begin indicates the start point of an action and End indicates the ending point of the action. ST refers to Sequence of Time. ST indicates the temporal relationship between two action Times and there are three types of ST: Before, After and Simultaneity. For example, the ISC expression ((Action1, Action2), (End (Action1), Begin (Action2), Before)) indicates that Action2 can only be triggered after Action1 has reached its ending point. So, Before means that the former occurs before the latter and After means the reverse against Before as well as Simultaneous means synchronous.

DOC represents Data Objects Collection. Data Objects are logical data resource within the enterprise that can be accessed by services. DOC can be formalized as: DOC (DOID). DOID represents Data Object ID, which is the universal identity within the enterprise. Data Object can be formalized as: DO (DOID, DOD, PDC). DOD represents Data Object Description. DOD describes the owner, access privilege, update time and other characteristics of data objects. PDC represents Physical Data Collection, which indicates the physical data storage to which the logical data object can be mapped. We assume that one logical data object can be mapped to several physical data storages which have the similar data structure. For example, we can define a train ticket sales data object and map it to train ticket sales data of different provinces. Train ticket sales data of different provinces are different physical data storages. Thus, PDS which represents Physical Data Storage can be formalized as:

PDS (PDID, PDD, L, DSD). PDID is the universal identity within the enterprise and PDD represents Physical Data Description, which describes the owner, access privilege, update time and other characteristics of the data storage. L indicates the physical location of the data storage and DSD represents Data Structure Description, which describes the physical structure of the data storage. PC represents Parameter Collection. The following sections will explain how to construct meta-model of dynamic services.

5. SERVICE SPECIFIC RDF VOCABULARY

Meta-model offers the template for defining metadata. Meta-model need to be built to make service descriptive metadata constructed according to conformable criterion that can be comprehended by the service executing system.

In this paper, we will construct the service-specific RDF vocabulary to setup the service meta-model. The service-specific RDF vocabulary includes definition of RDF classes and properties.

5.1 Definition of RDF Classes

Figure 2 shows part of the definition:

```
<?xml version="1.0"?>
<!DOCTYPE rdf:RDF [<!ENTITY xsd "http://www.w3.org/2001/XMLSchema#">]>
<rdf:RDF
   Xmlns:rdf="http://www.w3.org/1999/02/22-rdf-syntax-ns#"
   Xmlns:rdfs="http://www.w3.org/2000/01/rdf-schema#"
   Xmlns:base= "http://service/metadata/rdf-schema#">
<rdfs:Class rdf:ID="Service"/>
<rdfs:Class rdf:ID="Component"/>
<rdfs:Class rdf:ID="DataObject"/>
<rdfs:Class rdf:ID="PhysicalData"/>
<rdfs:Class rdf:ID="Parameter"/>
<rdfs:Class rdf:ID="Action"/>
<rdfs:Class rdf:ID="InterSequence"/>
<rdfs:Class rdf:ID="TimeSequence"/>
</rdfs:RDF>
```

Figure 2. Definition of RDF Classes

Definition of class Action is similar to the formalized definition of Action described in section 4. Action represents dynamic executing of specific function of specific component. Definition of class InterSequence is similar to the formalized definition of ISC ((Action1, Action2), (Time1(Action1), Time2(Action2), ST)) described in section 4. It describes the executing sequence of different actions. Object of class TimeSequence represents the (Time1(Action1), Time2(Action2), ST) part of object of class InterSequence.

5.2 Definition of RDF Properties

Figure 3 shows part of the definition:

```
<rdf:Property rdf:ID="serviceID"> <rdfs:domain rdf:resource="#Service"/> </rdf:Property>
<rdf:Property rdf:ID="componentCollection"> <rdfs:domain rdf:resource="#Service"/> </rdf:Property>
<rdf:Property rdf:ID="dataObjectCollection"> <rdfs:domain rdf:resource="#Service"/> </rdf:Property>
<rdf:Property rdf:ID="interSquenceCollection"> <rdfs:domain rdf:resource="#Service"/> </rdf:Property>

<rdf:Property rdf:ID="componentID"> <rdfs:range rdf:resource="&xsd;integer"/> </rdf:Property>
<rdf:Property rdf:ID="memberAction"> <rdfs:domain rdf:resource="#Component"/> </rdf:Property>

<rdf:Property rdf:ID="actionCollection"></rdf:Property>
<rdf:Property rdf:ID="timeSequenceCollection"></rdf:Property>

<rdf:Property rdf:ID="actionTime">
   <rdfs:domain rdf:resource="#TimeSequence"/>
   <rdfs:range rdf:resource="&xsd;string"/>
</rdf:Property>
<rdf:Property rdf:ID="sequenceType">
   <rdfs:domain rdf:resource="#TimeSequence"/>
   <rdfs:range rdf:resource="&xsd;string"/>
</rdf:Property>
```

Figure 3. Definition of RDF Properties

6. EXAMPLE AND SCENARIO

The service-specific RDF vocabulary can effect as the service meta-model for defining service descriptive metadata. An example on how to build service descriptive metadata based on the service-specific RDF vocabulary is given below:

Suppose that enterprise A offers data mining components which can be utilized by users to define data mining services that can meet their needs. Some of the components can be combined to offer classification and forecast service which can be used for customers churn prediction, credit card fraud identification, heart disease diagnose etc.. In order to build the service, three kinds of components: Data Reader component, Classification Modeling component and Classification Forecast component are essential and the Discretization component is optional.

Data Reader component reads data from files and prepare it for constructing classification and forecast model. Classification Modeling component is responsible for building and validating the model based on classified historical data and Classification Forecast component uses the model built to forecast the attributive class of unclassified data. Discretization component disperses continuous data attributes to discrete values because only discrete data attributes can be used to build classification model. Discretization component offers two kinds of discretization: discretization according to specific standard and discretization by auto-learning.

Users may need different classification and forecast services. E.g. customer B who wants to identify credit card fraud may choose to use standard discretization function of Discretization component and essential components to build the service because some attributes of the consumption data are continuous. Whereas customer C who wants to predict customer chum may like to combine the auto-learning discretization function of the Discretization component and essential components to build the service because auto-learning discretization can produce more accurate result. Besides, customer D who wants to diagnose heart disease doesn't need the Discretization component at all because data of symptom is already discrete. Customer B, C and D can define services that can meet their needs by constructing service specification metadata based on the RDF vocabulary defined in section 5.

```
<rdf:RDF
   Xmlns:base= "http://service/metadata/rdf-schema# ">
   Xmlns:ex="http://service/metadata/ex#">
  <ex:Service rdf:ID= "classificationAndForecast">
    <rdfs:comment>Defined by user to offer classification and forecast service</rdfs:comment>
    <ex:componentCollection rdf:parseType="Collection">
    <rdf:Description rdf:about="http://service/metadata/ex#dataReader"/>
    <rdf:Description rdf:about="http://service/metadata/ex#discretization"/>
    <rdf:Description rdf:about="http://service/metadata/ex#classificationModeling"/>
    <rdf:Description rdf:about="http://service/metadata/ex#classificationForecast"/>
  </ex:componentCollection>
  <ex:interSquenceCollection rdf:parseType="Collection">
    <rdf:Description rdf:about="http://service/metadata/ex#classificationAndForecastInterSequence"/>
  </ex:interSquenceCollection>
</rdf:RDF>
```

Figure 4. RDF Definition of Service of Classification and Forecast

```
<ex:Component rdf:ID= "discretization">
    <rdfs:comment>Disperse continuous data into discrete value for modeling</rdfs:comment>
    <ex:componentID rdf:datatype= "&xsd;integer">2628</ex:componentID>
    <ex:memberAction rdf:resource="http://service/metadata/ex#autoLearningDiscretizationAction"/>
</ex:Component>
<ex:Component rdf:ID= "classificationModeling">
    <rdfs:comment>Build and validate classification model based on historical training data</rdfs:comment>
    <ex:componentID rdf:datatype= "&xsd;integer">2629</ex:componentID>
    <ex:memberAction rdf:resource="http://service/metadata/ex#classificationModelBuildAction"/>
    <ex:memberAction rdf:resource="http://service/metadata/ex#classificationModelValidationAction"/>
</ex:Component>
```

Figure 5. RDF Definition of Service Component

```
<ex:Action rdf:ID= "autoLearningDiscretizationAction">
    <ex:actionID rdf:datatype= "&xsd;integer">262801</ex:actionID>
    <ex:componentID rdf:datatype= "&xsd;integer">2628</ex:componentID>
</ex:Action>
<ex:Action rdf:ID= "classificationModelBuildAction">
    <ex:actionID rdf:datatype= "&xsd;integer">262901</ex:actionID>
    <ex:componentID rdf:datatype= "&xsd;integer">2629</ex:componentID>
</ex:Action>
<ex:Action rdf:ID= "classificationModelValidationAction">
    <ex:actionID rdf:datatype= "&xsd;integer">262902</ex:actionID>
    <ex:componentID rdf:datatype= "&xsd;integer">2629</ex:componentID>
</ex:Action>
<ex:Action rdf:ID= "forecastAction">
    <ex:actionID rdf:datatype= "&xsd;integer">263001</ex:actionID>
</ex:Action>
```

Figure 6. RDF Definition of Service Action

```
<ex:InterSequence rdf:ID= "classificationAndForecastInterSequence">
  <ex:actionCollection rdf:parseType="Collection">
    <rdf:Description rdf:about="http://service/metadata/ex#autoLearningDiscretizationAction"/>
    <rdf:Description rdf:about="http://service/metadata/ex#classificationModelBuildAction"/>
    <rdf:Description rdf:about="http://service/metadata/ex#classificationModelValidationAction"/>
    <rdf:Description rdf:about="http://service/metadata/ex#forecastAction"/>
  </ex:actionCollection>
  <ex:TimeSequenceCollection rdf:parseType="Collection">
    <rdf:Description rdf:about="http://service/metadata/ex#discretizationAndBuildTimeSequence"/>
    <rdf:Description rdf:about="http://service/metadata/ex#validationAndForecastTimeSequence"/>
  </ex:TimeSequenceCollection>
</ex:InterSequence>
```

Figure 7. RDF Definition of Service InterSquence

```
<ex:TimeSequence rdf:ID= "discretizationAndBuildTimeSequence">
   <ex:actionTime rdf:parseType=" Resource"
     <ex:keyword rdf:datatype= "&xsd;string">end</ex:keyword>
     <ex:actionID rdf:datatype= "&xsd;integer">262801</ex:actionID>
   </ex:actionTime>
   <ex:actionTime rdf:parseType="Resource"
     <ex:keyword rdf:datatype= "&xsd;string">begin</ex:keyword>
     <ex:actionID rdf:datatype= "&xsd;integer">262901</ex:actionID>
   </ex:actionTime>
   <ex:sequenceType rdf:datatype= "&xsd;string">before</ex:sequenceType>
</ex:TimeSequence>
<ex:TimeSequence rdf:ID= "validationAndForecastTimeSequence">
   <ex:actionTime rdf:parseType=" Resource"
     <ex:keyword rdf:datatype= "&xsd;string">begin</ex:keyword>
     <ex:actionID rdf:datatype= "&xsd;integer">263001</ex:actionID>
   </ex:actionTime>
   <ex:actionTime rdf:parseType="Resource"
     <ex:keyword rdf:datatype= "&xsd;string">begin</ex:keyword>
     <ex:actionID rdf:datatype= "&xsd;integer">262902</ex:actionID>
   </ex:actionTime>
   <ex:sequenceType rdf:datatype= "&xsd;string">simultaneous</ex:sequenceType>
</ex:TimeSequence>
```

Figure 8. RDF Definition of Service TimeSequence

The above figure 4 to 8 show part of the definition of the service metadata defined by customer C who wants to predict customer churn.

Definition of timeSequence "discretizationAndBuildTimeSequence" indicates that action "classificationModelBuildAction(actionID=262901)" can only be triggered after action "autoLearningDiscretizationAction(actionID=262801)" has finished executing.Definition of timeSequence "ValidationAndForecastTimeSequence" indicates that action "classificationModelValidationAction(actionID=262902)" and action "forecastAction(actionID=263001)" can execute concurrently.

Users can subscribe the service descriptive metadata to the service system. Since subscription, once the service is called, system will load and parse the service metadata and dynamic create the service according to the service structure and components operation logic specified in the metadata.

7. CONCLUSION AND FUTURE WORK

A new method of dynamic offering user-defined services was put forward in this paper. Firstly, the framework of the service management system was illustrated. Then, in order to let user define services that can meet their needs, the service-specific RDF vocabulary was built to define service meta-model based on which service descriptive metadata can be constructed. At last, an example was given.

In the future, we will keep on working at development of the system core modules. At the same time, we will concentrate on analysis of service performance, model validation and design of transaction management mechanism.

REFERENCES

1. L. Roger, H. Ashok, C.-C. Chiang , H.-S. Yang, and H.-K. Kim, A framework for dynamically converting components to web services, in *Proc. of Third ACIS International Conference on Software Engineering Research, Management and Applications, SERA 2005,* eds. R. Lee, K. W. Lee, and B. Malloy (IEEE Computer Society: Piscataway, NJ, 2005), pp.431-437.
2. J. Leon, Towards semantic integration of components using a service-based architecture, *Journal of Integrated Design and Process Science.* Volume 9, Number 3, pp.1-13, (2005).
3. S. Michael, CORBA 3, in *Proc. of the 34th International Conference on Technology of Object-Oriented Languages and Systems, TOOLS 34*, eds. Q. Li, D. Firesmith, R. Riehle, G. Pour, and B. Mayer (IEEE Computer Society: Piscataway, NJ, 2000), pp.397.
4. E. Wolfgang and K. Nima, Component technologies: Java Beans, COM, CORBA, RMI, EJB and the CORBA component model, in *Proc. of the 8th European software engineering conference held jointly with 9th ACM SIGSOFT international symposium on Foundations of software engineering,* eds. Volker Gruhn (ACM Press: New York, NY, 2001), pp.311-312.
5. Y. Wu, K. Zhang, X. Wang, J. Tian, and Y. Chen, Extending Metadata with Semantic Aspect in Component-based Distributed System, *Computer Engineering.* Volume 32, Number 12, pp.68-70, (2006).
6. A. Arkin, S. Askary, B. Bloch, F. Curbera, Y. Goland, N. Kartha, C. Liu, S. Thatte, P. Yendluri, and A. Yiu, *Web Services Business Process Execution Language Version 2.0*, OASIS (2005). http://www.oasis-open.org/committees/tc_home.php?wg_abbrev=wsbpel (Accessed May 18, 2007).
7. Anonymous, *Web Services Architecture*, W3C (2004). http://www.w3.org/TR/ws-arch (Accessed May 18, 2007).
8. S. John and S. Peter, Metadata standards roundup, *IEEE Multimedia.* Volume 13, Number 2, pp.84-88, (2006).
9. Anonymous, *RDF Primer Recommendation*, W3C (2004). http://www.w3.org/TR/rdf-primer(Accessed May 18, 2007).

Research on Information Integration Oriented Supply Chain of Telecom Value-added Service

Guoli Wang and Shoulian Tang

Economics and Management School, Beijing University of Posts and Telecommunications, Beijing 100876, P.R. China
wgl996@tom.com tangshoulian@263.net

Abstract. This paper discusses information integration oriented supply chain of telecom value-added service. Firstly, it uses a series strategic method. Secondly, it argues how to integrate the supply chain within the web service. Thirdly, the paper describes an example that explains how to manage value-added services for banks. The dynamic system has enabled a more complex type of interaction and collaborations among partners.

Keywords: *Web service, Parla, Corba, Integration, Dynamic system*

1. INTRODUCTION

Telecom value-added services (TVAS) have become so important that all enterprises in telecom industry look regard or view their own value-added services as a new source of growth. The ultimate success of a company will depend on how the company constructs, controls and integrates the supply chain formed with its business partners [1].

How to integrate supply chain effectively, how to research services and contents which have no relation to the telecom network and how to make value-added services transferred and manage them more effectively are the theoretical and practical exploring issues. The author attempts to discuss these problems from the perspective of information integration of a value-added services supply chain, and obtain some useful insight.

1.1 Known Results

The Web Services technologies are comprised of XML/SOAP/WSDL/UDDI [2]. Web Services establish interoperability of distributed applications for the new platform [3]. Standardization initiatives like those leaded by Parlay or OMA, have been specifying several standard Web Service interfaces to the most common Telco functionalities [2].

Please use the following format when citing this chapter:

Wang, G., Tang, S., 2007, in IFIP International Federation for Information Processing, Volume 254, Research a Practical Issues of Enterprise Information Systems II Volume 1, eds. L. Xu, Tjoa A., Chaudhry S. (Boston: Springe pp. 563-567.

1.2 Our Results

We study information integration oriented supply chain of telecom value-added service. Our solution is that Web services combine with telecom system and traditional CORBA [4] interface is used between application server and Parlay gateway. This kind of Web-based integrated information system is not only loosely coupled, but also can be controlled. Otherwise it is compatible with the former system.

2. PRELIMINARIES

2.1 Problem Description

Telecom Value-added supply chain has upstream units and downstream units, and especially increasing upstream suppliers. Now, various intelligent application platforms for corresponding services are being used, which brings more and more complex different platforms and interfaces. In the beginning it is possible that telecom value –added supply chain has a number of platforms. But with the technology and business development, there must be a suitable method of integrated supply chain information. Standardization initiatives like those leaded by Parlay or OMA, have been specifying several standard Web Service interfaces to the most common Telco functionalities [2]. But these new solutions could not be perfectly controlled like the former. Traditional Information integration of telecom value-added supply chain is a tight coupling, because the intelligent network integrates it. Different services have different intelligent networks. When intelligent networks have formed a large group in a supply chain, optimization and coordination become very badly, particularly for operators to provide more and more interfaces. Upgrade and management for these platforms are very complex. Furthermore, the heterogeneous information processing needs middleware technology, so researching services has many obstacles. Thus, a tight coupled and controlled system is needed.

2.2 Web Service

Web Services establish interoperability of distributed applications for the new platform [3]. Web Service platform is a set of standards which defines how applications on the Web achieve interoperability. Web Service is a service-oriented architecture [2] that defines a set of standard protocols, which is used to define the interface, to invoke methods, to register components, and to achieve various applications based Internet. Currently, there is no exact definition for the Web Services. Generally it is believed that web service is a new type of Web applications, which are self-contained, self-descriptive, and of the modular characteristics that can be published through the Web. Web services can realize the function of a simple response to customer requests, and accomplish a complex business processes. Once configured, Web Services can be directly found and used by the other applications and web services. The Web Services technologies are comprised of XML/SOAP/WSDL/UDDI [5], which empowers the Web Services differently from the traditional technologies. Web Services Architecture [3] is a service-oriented analysis and design (Application of OOAD). It is a service-oriented architecture that is used for designing, implementing and deploying the components of a logical development. Figure 1 presents the Web Services Architecture -- Service-Oriented Architecture (SOA) Map.

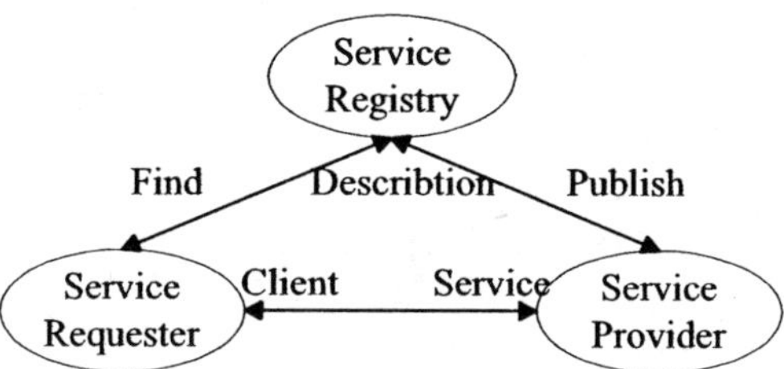

Figure 1. Web Architecture

3. INTEGRATION OF TELECOM VALUE-ADDED SUPPLY CHAIN

3.1 Web-based Information Integration System of Telecom Value-added Supply chain

Telecom system has several open platforms for value-added systems. The Parlay\OSA system is the most important open system. Web Services combine with the promising open telecom system. Web-based integrated information system is not only a loosely coupled system, but also can be controlled as illustrated in figure 2.

Application servers are the clients, which implement service logic and search corresponding services from Web service Registration center. Registration Web service center is responsible for the registration and management of Web services. Parlay Web Gateway provides various basic telecom services.

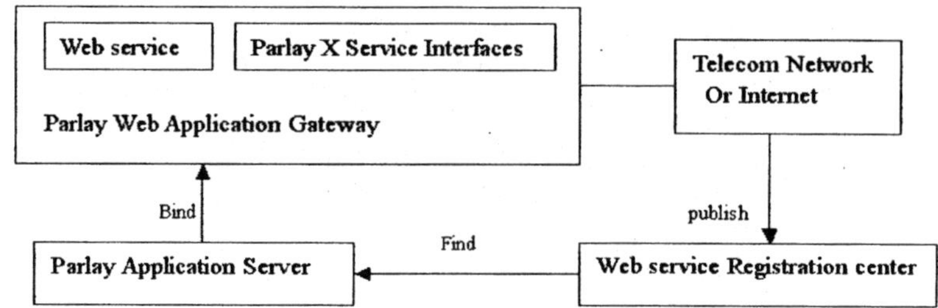

Figure 2. Web-based Open System

3.2 Prominent Aspects

Web service will be integrated with Parlay interface and traditional CORBA interface of telecommunications networks. Operator interface is the key for integrating telecom supply chain by Web service. This technology has four prominent aspects.

(1) Easy integration: Services Based on the Parlay Web Services or Parlay X are more easily integrated with Application systems of other enterprise to configure loosely coupled supply chain, to offer services easily and quickly, to enhance the whole value of the supply chain.

(2) Deployment and operation: UDDI of the Web Services can be introduced to the UDDI deployment environment to offer new ways to discover Gateway for service or to publish various network capabilities. Various Parlay Gateways can be registered in the UDDI registration center, and suitable Parlay Gateway can be searched and chosen to access Network.

3) The influence on third-party application and development: Research and Development of TVAS can be comparatively easy because the researchers need not to understand the telecom technology to make use of Web Services application interfaces, particularly the high-level interface such as Parlay X. Web Services that are open and standard, make far-ranging applications easy to access the Gateway.

4. AN EXAMPLE: BANKCARDS VALUE-ADDED SERVICES

For the customers using bankcards at services terminal, the services can be controlled as illustrated in figure 3. Parlay Gateway requests these services from Parlay Application Server. After Parlay application server receives the request, it looks up the services in the Web services center. And after services confirmed, it implements the bankcard services logic that is located at the Parlay application server. This logic of the bankcard services uses the bank cards Web Services operation by parlay application services. The Bank Card Web Services operation invokes corresponding operation at Parlay Gateway Interface, sends protocol to the bankcard control center. And the control center takes out user information and requests by analyzing the data. Then the control center makes a decision according to the data available in the control center's database. A certain amount of funds may be transferred to the retailer from the customer account and generate corresponding information, which is being sent to the users and stored in a database.

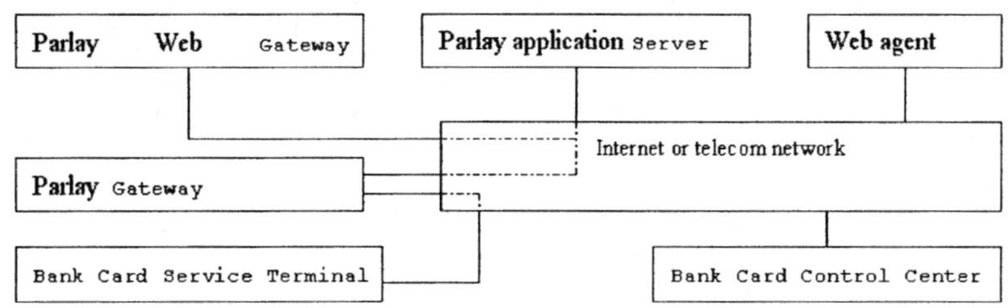

Figure 3. Bankcards Value-added Services Map

5. CONCLUSIONS

This paper discusses the information integration of TVAS in the perspective of supply chain and gives some suggestions. A Web-based Information Integration System of TVAS is advanced. The integration of Web services and telecom system is loosely coupled and can be controlled, which do not only meet the requirement of supply chain, but also meet the requirement of telecom management. Finally this paper gives an example of bankcards value added services.

REFERENCES

1. D.M. Lambert and M.C. Copper, Issues in supply chain management, *Industrial Marketing and Management*. Volume 29, Number 1, pp.65-83, (2000).
2. Anonymous, *Parlay X Web Services Specification*, Parlay (June, 2004). http://www.parlay. org/specs/index. asp(Accessed October 6, 2006).
3. G. Alonso, F. Casati, H. Kuno, and V. Machiraju, *Web Services: Concepts, Architectures and Applications* (Springer: Heidelberg, Berlin, 2004).
4. Anonymous, *Common Object Request Broker Architecture: Core Specification, version 3.0.2,* Object Management Group (OMG) (June, 2002). http://www.omg.org/cgi-bin/apps (Accessed October 20, 2006).
5. Anonymous, *W3C Proposed Recommendation,* World Wide Web Consortium (W3C) (May 7, 2003). http://www.w3c.org/TR/2003/PR-soap12-part1-20030507 (Accessed January 4, 2007).

A Research on the Mechanism and Platform Construction of Public Geological Achievements Sharing

Jianping Ge, Bing Zhong and Yalin Lei

School of Humanities and Economic Management, China University of Geosciences, Beijing 100083, P.R. China
duoduo198229@163.com zhongbing0126@163.com leiyalin@cugb.edu.cn

Abstract. Public geological achievement platform is a part of science and technology infrastructure and related to sustainable development of the economy and society. By literature research, expert's discussion and case study, the paper proposes that centralized sharing with local sharing mechanism and multi-layers network have to be set up to achieve public geological achievements sharing. The operating mechanism regarding integrating mechanism, grading mechanism, sharing manners as the kernel, and sharing guaranteeing mechanism mainly including the outlay investment, policies and legislation, organizational operation, human resources, technical standards and criteria are discussed in detail in this paper. The paper also puts forward two problems which concerns secrecy and rational pricing of public geological achievements, which need further discussion.

Keywords: *Public geological achievements, Platform construction, Sharing mechanism*

1. INTRODUCTION

Public geological achievements are those valuable geological information and material information achieved by geologists, who applied scientific knowledge of geology and exploration technical measure into the research on geologic bodies, including geological map, geological database, and mineral information report, related serial publications, special report and so on. Public geological achievements are supported by public finance, shared by the society. For example, geological maps that collected from geological mapping work which are financed by the government are provided to the society at the price of producing cost, all the social members have the equal usufruct.

The sharing of public geological achievements is necessary. On the one hand, public geological achievements thanks to the work of geologists have powerful practical value and increase social benefits constantly. They could achieve the most utility only by sharing. On the other hand, the taxpayers support the public finance by paying taxes, and the public finance offers the necessary cost of the achievements. According to the principle that people should benefit from his invests, public geological achievements should be shared.

Please use the following format when citing this chapter:

Ge, J., Zhong, B., Lei, Y., 2007, in IFIP International Federation for Information Processing, Volume 254, Research and Practical Issues of Enterprise Information Systems II Volume 1, eds. L. Xu, Tjoa A., Chaudhry S. (Boston: Springer), pp. 569-578.

The services of public geological achievements sharing in foreign developed countries are ahead of that in China. They have set up the modern geological information service systems. Since the WWW server of USGS started to run in 1993, these developed countries have initiated online geological information services successively. In terms of the service provider, in addition to the traditional service providers, such as national, provincial or state Geological Survey and their professional institution, Geological Survey also bring some privately owned geologic research institutions, universities, even individuals into geological information providers through partnership mechanisms in the United States, Britain, Canada, Australia and other developed countries. They have established agent or value-added agent mode simultaneously. In terms of the service content, the United States, Canada, Australia, Britain and other countries have enacted Freedom of Information Act to determine the sharing of resources including simulated information resources, physical geological data and a variety of digital information and databases, while the services have continuing extended. For example, Australia information services have been expanded to various outdoor recreations [1]. In terms of clients, in addition to the traditional government institutions, enterprises, research and education institutions and the public, these developed countries have pointed out definitely the strengthening of information services for special groups (disabled and aboriginal peoples). USGS has set up a special website to satisfy this requirement [2]. In terms of the service approach, public geological achievements are shared through the online services system on the network, such as query and search system of various catalogues, browser and search system of special topic, Web Mapping system and one-stop service system, etc.

Comparing with foreign countries, domestic public geological achievements sharing service system in China has the main gaps as following [3]: In terms of the service provider, there is no unified providers, no multi-levels and multi-units to provide related services in our country; there is no agent and value-added services on the whole; it's lack of coordination among service providers. In terms of the service content, domestic services are mainly about borrowing, reading and duplication of the papery documents; the content of information services are limited greatly; CGS website provides very little online service and practical valuable professional information; most content of the websites just like "about us " in foreign corresponding websites [4-5]. In terms of the clients, the main users are professional geological survey staff in China. Among the readers and users of geological documents in 2003, the geological and mining industry units accounted for 31% of the total users, of which is the highest proportion; the metallurgical, chemical, nonferrous metals, earthquake and other industries units accounted for more than 20% of the total users [6]. In terms of service approach, the domestic services manners are the combination of traditional service and modern service, while the former is the primary one. Data processing and providing of the databases basically adopt the offline manner. Generally speaking, one database has one system only to support the online search, browse and downloading of part of the information [7].

From the above analysis, it's needed to establish harmonized sharing platform which can provide practical valuable information and online services to improve the technical level of information services and develop the systems which support integrated services. From this perspective, the paper discusses the building framework of sharing platform, sharing operating mechanism and sharing guaranteeing mechanism of public geological achievements for the purpose of efficient and real-time sharing. The construction of framework is regarding sharing as the core, achievement data clusters as the foundation, users as the terminal, platform as the physical approach, policies and rules as the guarantee. The sharing platform is made up of multi-layers organizations such as physical layer, data layer and network layer, and integrates related technology. The domestic platform needs to joint the foreign platform when it has been built completely in order to realize the intercommunion and mutual aid. Sharing operating mechanism is the manner and approach to share the achievements. The sharing process is completed by the achievement providers and users. The achievement providers appear in the form of virtual alliance to offer the standardized achievement data and entity. Under the guidance of sharing principle, those providers choose the appropriate sharing manner and provide sharing services to the achievement users followed by the established procedures. Achievement users should feedback the scientific data to platform and those providers after finishing sharing in order to promote the renewal of the achievement data. Sharing guaranteeing mechanism is the various measures to achieve the normal running and sharing of the platform, including the outlay investment mechanism, policies and regulations guaranteeing mechanism, operation guaranteeing mechanism of an organization, human resources guaranteeing mechanism, technical standards and criteria mechanism and so on.

2. METHODS

The main methods are literature surveying and Delphi method. At the same time, we consulted many related experts of the geological museum of China and national geological archives of China. Through the literature survey, we grasped the status and features of socialized services of foreign public geological information and understood the technical methods and models of information sharing. It is helpful to absorb all the useful ideas, grasp the status and features of public geological achievements sharing and improve the sharing scheme and mechanism by Delphi method. At last, we could make the construction of sharing platform and sharing mechanism feasible and scientific by consulting the practitioners and testing run with the examples.

3. THE BUILDING FRAMEWORK OF PUBLIC GEOLOGICAL ACHIEVEMENTS PLATFORM

The platform of public geological achievements is an important component part of national innovation system and the basic support system which provide services for geosciences progress and technological innovation. The platform utilizes fully the information, the network and other modern technique, integrates and optimizes systematically the public geological achievements in order to promote high-efficient allocation and comprehensive utilization of the achievements within the range of the whole society, and maximize the benefits of achievements.

3.1 Idea of Construction

The sharing achievements include the achievements having been public, the achievements to be public in the future and some confidential achievements because of security and intellectual property rights. Therefore, the platform combines centralized sharing with distributed sharing, builds network centre and sub-centre which combines distributed sharing and centralized sharing [8]. Currently, we should continue to perfect distributed and centralized database cluster on the basis of the construction of fundamental geological database of more than 30 different fields and part of geological achievement database; set up achievement data standards and criteria that many units would follow together; establish a set of technology integration of software and hardware on the network to guarantee sharing. Referred to present research result [9], the basic idea of the construction of public geological achievements platform is illuminated as figure 1.

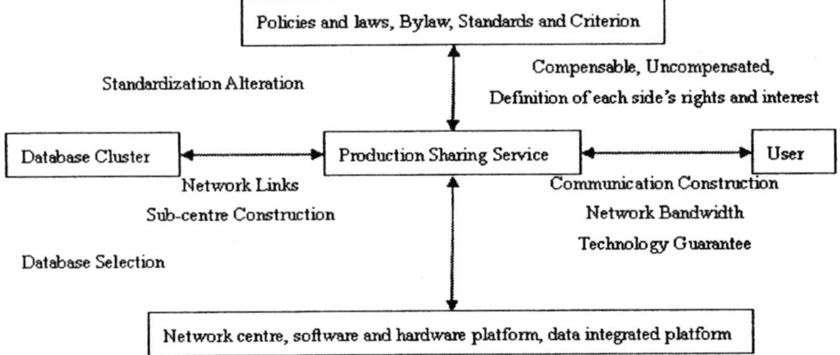

Figure 1. The Basic Idea of the Construction of Public Geological Achievements Platform

3.2 Sharing Network Centre and Sub-centre [9-10]

Both network centers and sub-centers, as the support of achievements sharing network system link with Internet. Network centers have the function of user authentication and own Web server, GIS and application server and database server. Through public geological achievements sharing website and metadata server, the users could browse and query the texts, statistics and spatial data in the public geological achievement sharing database quickly and conveniently. In addition, the network systems also include network system, development platforms, various of hardware and software of server, subsystems of communications, interfaces, security strategy, optimization of hardware and software system integration channel, and the construction of distributed database.

3.3 The Construction of Multi-layers Architecture of Sharing Platform

As a network platform of achievements sharing, we must build a multi-layers architecture to provide users with various services by integrating related technology. The structure of public geological achievements platform include the achievement physical layer, database layer and the network layer, as illustrated in figure 2. Hereby, some research results may be referred to [11].

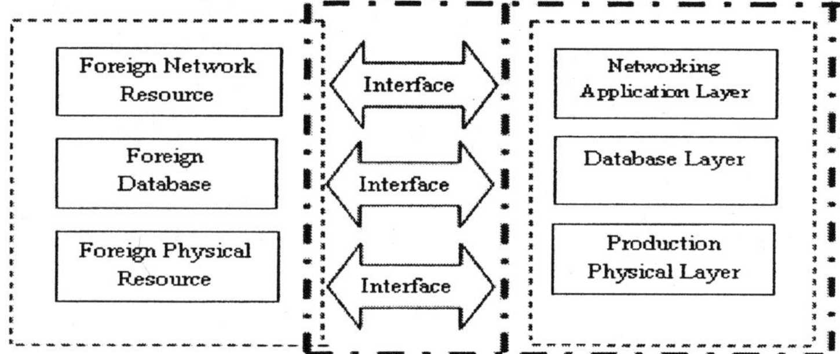

Figure 2. The Structure of Public Geological Achievements Platform

Physical layer is the physical performance of platform resources carrier of public geological achievements. It is mainly about public geological physical achievements, such as geological map, papery form of various reports, hardware equipment and support software system in the network technological environment.

Database layer is a digitized form expression of containing resources of physical layer. It is the integration of the digitized resources of the platform; at the same time, the database layer is the foundation of information resources of network layer of the platform. The organic combination of the database layer, the physical layer and the networking application layer form jointly the overall structure of the platform, including various-scales geological map database, mineral area database, geochemistry database and physical geographic database etc.

Networking application layer is the most basic support system of the construction of public geological achievements sharing platform, the important information service form of the platform and the important approach that the users could obtain the achievement information, including network application environment and management information & service information system of the achievement resources.

The construction of these three layers has to be done in order. Database layer could only be established after finishing the integration of the physical layer. Then the sharing of the network layer may be realized.

Linking with the foreign resources could help to improve further the technology of the platform and the mechanism after completing the construction of the domestic platform. This interface is the construction of talent and resources, the integration of technology and standards, and the unblocked mechanism as well as the cooperative channel [12].

4. THE OPERATING MECHANISM OF PUBLIC GEOLOGICA L ACHIEVEMENTS SHARING

Public geological achievement sharing is the process that achievement owner provides certain public geological achievement to user while sharing platform and sharing manners and achievement user should feedback the information and data produced in the sharing course to sharing platform and achievement owner. It is necessary to set up and realize the achievements' combining, grading mechanism and sharing manners to support the sharing process.

4.1 Achievements' Combining and Grading Mechanism of Sharing

Public geological achievements' combining is the foundation of sharing realizing. At present, public geological achievements' obtaining is mainly supported by governmental investment in our country. But because of lacking top floor designing of investment and macroscopically coordinating management, the exchanging of achievement becomes to be an obstacle. For a long time, these public geological achievements are distributed in different organization units and individuals. Therefore, combining achievements from different sources which can be shared and confirming the sharing range and setting up a unified norm and filing for achievement information are the inalienable contents of achievements' combining mechanism.

The value of utility of public geological achievements will differ if the concrete contents that each achievement displays or the purpose of users are different. So achievement sharing not only needs to be thought about the entire social benefits increasing progressively, but also should be considered to guarantee the national security and the intellectual property rights. Only good sharing order and sharing grading mechanism are establishing and perfecting gradually, the effective achievement sharing can be realized. Sharing grading mechanism mainly based on whether the sharing behavior endangers national security and benefit. This foundation is used to determine that some achievements are brought into secret operation mechanism or make strict and explicit using stipulation.

4.2 Sharing Manners

Sharing manners are the concrete operating modes which both sides achieve achievements exchanging through the corresponding form, method and procedure.

Sharing manners decide adjustment of benefit relations among the country, the society and both sides and act as the core and the key to stimulate the vitality of the sharing platform work.

The establishment basis of sharing manners includes the sharing goal and the security.

1. The Sharing Goal

Sharing manners can be divided into free sharing and paid sharing according to whether sharing behavior takes seeking to make a profit as the goal.

Free sharing refers to the achievement owner no longer to demand achievement cost fee when offers user sharing. Achievement cost fee has included the expenses of gathering, processing as well as preserving. Free sharing can be divided into the following three kinds:

Free entirely sharing refers to achievement owner does not charge any fee when provides achievement sharing.

For certain achievements which do not have the direct sharing condition or should be retreated according to user's request, achievements' owners could charge the retreating expense when provide these achievement.

For certain achievements whose sharing need manpower disbursement and cartage expense, users should pay the corresponding service fee.

Paid sharing is the way that achievement owner gather certain proportion of the achievement cost from user by different methods when provides achievement sharing. The public geological achievements here refers are whose investors cover the country, the collective and the individual. One kind of paid sharing is state investment. In this situation, the main constitution of the achievement funds is financial allocation and the few is the collective accumulation; perhaps the achievement gainer originally is the governmental agency or the enterprise organization and the gainer recently transferred to company which had left behind the state financial allocations ingredient. Paid sharing can be divided into profit-making sharing and non-profit-making sharing according to the using goal.

Non-profit-making paid sharing refers to enterprise units demand achievement to develop themselves or undertake the duty which the country issues.

Profit-making paid sharing refers to the following two kinds of situations: first kind is using achievement to develop achievement or management; second kind is deep processing achievement and gaining profit by forming achievement and information which the market requires.

Regarding non-profit-making paid sharing, achievement owner should gather lower achievement cost. On the contrary, regarding profit-making paid sharing, achievement owner could gather higher achievement cost.

2. The Security

The achievement security refers to the sharing behavior whether possibly threatens the national security, the resources security, the public health security and the biological security.

For the achievement which has the possibility of safety threat, the user must apply for the administration to permit beforehand and only can carry on sharing after obtaining the administrative permission. It is called administrative permission sharing way.

In “Mapping Supervisory work Country Secret Scope Stipulation”, the second item has stipulated country confidential grade and the table of the mapping supervisory work and these achievement sharing scope receive the strict limit. Like “the mutual transformed parameter among the national earth coordinate system, the geocentric coordinate system and the independent coordinate system” is the national top-secret item, the sharing scope is controlled strictly in “the mapping achievement storage unit and the user who has been authorized by the national survey service”, “the military mapping achievement storage unit and the user who has been authorized by the general staff survey service”. Without permission and authorization by department concerned, these achievements all can not be shared.

Based on the above two foundation, the sharing manners of public geological achievements can be divided into paid sharing, free sharing and administrative permission sharing. Certainly, the sharing manners can also be specifically divided into transacting sharing, renting sharing, cooperating research sharing and exchanging sharing and so on according to the different sharing behavior.

5. THE GUARANTEEING MECHANISM OF PUBLIC GEOLOG ICAL ACHIEVEMENTS SHARING

The guaranteeing mechanism of public geological achievements sharing is to secure efficient sharing and sustainable development of the platform, including various measures, policies, laws, regulations, management systems and so on.

In the aspect of outlay investment, it is to change the one-off investment of the construction at present, reinforce the running support of later stage and build up a set of investment system which is diversified and sustainable development.

In the aspect of policies, laws and regulations, it is to consummate the "Mineral Resource Law" and other fundamental laws, "Provide and Utilization of the Public Geological Data Interim Measure" and other administrative laws, "National Geological Data Collection Management Measure " and other administrative rules and regulations, suggest enacting "Technological Resource Sharing Law" and other fundamental laws, "Public Geological Achievement Sharing Regulation" and other administrative laws and related administrative rules and regulations, solve the problems such as the protection of the intellectual property rights, rational pricing and the protection of sharing rights and interests of each side.

In the aspect of the guarantee of the running of the organization, vertically, it is to establish unified leadership organization which takes Chinese Geological Survey as the platform, management organization which takes geological survey centers directly under China Geological Survey in 6 areas as sub-platform, in order to take charge of the construction, maintenance and running of the central and local platform; horizontally, the platform adopts the council system which takes the council as the highest decision-making organization, the platform administrative center as the decision implementing organ, the expert consultative committee as the decision support organ and the supervise council as the platform supervise organ.

To guarantee the supply of required human resource, effective talent employment mechanism, reasonable structure of talents, and scientific post setting and employment system as well as the realization of effective incentives should be established.

For technical standards and criteria, we need to establish the unified description standards, scientific data standards and quality administrative measurements of data.

6. DISCUSSION AND CONCLUSIONS

Public geological achievement sharing has just started in our country. Many achievements have been obtained while lots of insufficiencies still exist. The construction of the public geological achievement platform is to solve the problem of barriers of sharing, promote the establishment of national innovation system and the sustainable development of the resources.

The public geological achievement platform is built up on the basis of more than 30 fundamental geological databases and the achievement resources database at present. Considering confidentiality, intellectual property rights and other factors, the platform needs to achieve the object-oriented services, adopt the combination of centralized sharing and distributed sharing, establish the networking centers and sub-centers, and construct a multi-layers structure of the platform. This is the conception of platform construction which the article proposes.

In addition to the entities guarantee, the realization of achievement sharing also needs to establish the operating, guaranteeing and other mechanisms. The operating mechanism mainly includes the integrating and sharing graduation mechanism, the sharing manners. The guaranteeing mechanism includes the outlay investment, the policies laws and regulations, the running of organization, the human resources and the technical standards and criteria. Only on the basis of the guarantee of the coordination and integrity of the entities and soft mechanism, public geological achievements sharing could realize. Certainly, in the process of the constant communication with other countries, domestic technology development and the experience accumulation, it also needs to update the platform and sharing mechanism constantly to achieve sustainable development.

Limited by condition, the following two problems need to be further studied in the future.

1. The Problem of the Sharing Confidentiality

Parts of the public geological achievements aren't able to be public temporarily. The reason is the technical problem or the related national security requirements. But there has not been an explicit standard to define the scope of secret information yet. From the experience of abroad, the way to solve this problem is possibly to grasp the scale of confidentiality through "the use conditions", which is to limit sharing by the users' verification, such as in Australia, but this manner is affected deeply by the influence of subjective judgment factor.

2. The Problem of Rational Pricing

One part of the public geological achievement is non-profit, the other part is profit. Both of them are related to the problem of pricing. For the former, the achievement providers should provide the achievements to the users free of charge or at a price only with necessary cost, the service fee etc. However, the cost of each kind of the achievements is different, and the sharing groups are indefinite. How to calculate the expense needs to be defined. For the latter, the achievement providers could confer with the users on the price in the principle of the marketing. If both sides are to negotiate a price, the price may be too high or too low. Too high would hinder the transform of the geological achievements, while too low will damage the devaluation of the state assets. Therefore, whether a guide price should be and how to be fixed by the government needs further discussion.

REFERENCES

1. Z. Jiang, The current situations and characteristics of geological information service in developed country, *Strategic Research References on Geological Work* (Inside). Volume 7, pp.1-15, (2006).
2. USGS, *U.S. Geological Survey 2000-2005 Strategic Plan*, USGS (1999). http://www.usgs.gov/stratplan/ (Accessed May 20, 2007).
3. M. Zhang and Q. Lee, *Geoinformation work today at China geological Survey*, Map Asia (2004). http://www.gisdevelopment.net/application/geology/geomorphology/ma04296.htm (Accessed May 22, 2007).
4. Website of China Geological Survey, CGS. http://www.cgs.gov.cn (Accessed May 20, 2007).
5. Website of Development and Research Center of China Geological Survey, DRCCG. http://www.drc.cgs.gov.cn/ (Accessed May 20, 2007).
6. Development and Research Center of China Geologic Survey, Research on the Strategy of Geological Work, in *Proc. of Youth Branch of the Institute of Geological Economics in China Annual Conference*, eds. Youth Branch of the Institute of Geological Economics in China (Earth Publishing House of China: Beijing, December, 2005), p.79.
7. Website of National Geological Archives of China, NGAC. http://www.ngac.cn/ (Accessed May 20, 2007).
8. X. Fu, T. Chi, Y. Shao, and J. Bi, The research and development on China's sustainable development information sharing system, *Geographical Information World*. Volume 12, pp.32-36, (2003).
9. X. Fu, X. Li, and J. He, Research and Construction Progress on China Sustainable Development Information Sharing Based on The Network, *China Basic Science*. Volume 1, p.71, (2003).
10. S. Quaglini, Information models for data sharing, *Neurol Sci*. Volume 27, pp.281-283, (2006).
11. The seminar of the implementing scheme of the National Science and Technology Basic Terms Platform Building, *The Overall Research Paper of the Implementing Scheme of the National Science and Technology Basic Terms Platform Building* (Inside), p.15, (2005).
12. F. Harvey, W. Kuhn, H. Pundt, Y. Bishr, and C. Riedemann, Semantic interoperability: A central issue for sharing geographic information, *The Annals of Regional Science*. Volume 33, pp.213-232, (1999).

The Impacts of Enterprise Resource Planning Systems on Firm Performance: An Empirical Analysis of Chinese Chemical Firms

Lu Liu, Rui Miao and Chengzhi Li

School of Economics and Management, Beihang University, Beijing 100083, P.R. China
liulu@buaa.edu.cn miaorui@sem.buaa.edu.cn lichengzhigg@sohu.com

Abstract. Chinese firms heavily invest in enterprise resource planning systems (ERP) in recent years and expect that ERP can help them gain superior financial performance. Given the high costs and high risk of ERP investments, to quantify the financial benefits of ERP implementation is an important research issue. This paper empirically examines the impacts of ERP implementation on firm performance using the financial data from 50 Chinese chemical firms that implemented ERP. The firms' abnormal performance during the two-year implementation period and three-year post-implementation period was analyzed based on the guideline of Barber et al. on event studies. The results find no significant performance improvement during the implementation period and the three-year post-implementation period and a decline in performance in the first two years after implementation. However, a slight performance improvement in the third year after implementation may indicate that the financial benefits of ERP may show after a long-term ERP use. These results provide insight for Chinese firms that want to invest in ERP.

Keywords: *Enterprise resource planning systems (ERP), Financial performance, Chinese chemical firms, ROS, ROA, COGS*

1. INTRODUCTION

With the development of information technology, Chinese firms begin to realize that a firm's competitive advantages do not only depend on traditional manufacture capabilities but also depend on IT applications in today's highly competitive market. Hence, many firms heavily invest in IT applications and expect that IT can help them enhance the firms' competitive advantages. Taking the Chinese chemical firms as an example, the Chinese chemical firms invested RMB 371 millions on information systems in 2005 and RMB 148 millions out of those investments are invested in enterprise resource planning systems (ERP) [1]. Industry and professional reports often claim that the basic drivers motivating firms to invest in ERP include: more accurate and timely information, high quality decision-making, cost reduction, improved efficiency, reduction of order cycle time and improved customer satisfaction.

However, ERP is an investment with high costs and high complexity. The firms need to commit significant resources to ERP implementation and face with a great

Please use the following format when citing this chapter:

Liu, L., Miao, R., Li, C., 2007, in IFIP International Federation for Information Processing, Volume 254, Research and Practical Issues of Enterprise Information Systems II Volume 1, eds. L. Xu, Tjoa A., Chaudhry S. (Boston: Springer), pp. 579-587.

deal of difficulty in integrating ERP with their operations. Those make quantifying the financial benefits of ERP implementation an important research issue. To examine the impacts of ERP implementation on firm financial performance can shed light on the value of ERP systems and provide beneficial guidance on ERP investments.

The issue of whether ERP is associated with improved financial performance has been studied by a great deal of literature, but there is relatively little literature to investigate the relationship between ERP implementation of Chinese firms and firm performance using objective financial data. Therefore, this paper also contributes to the literature on the impacts of ERP implementation on firm performance in China.

This paper selects the publicly traded Chinese chemical firms that implemented ERP between 1998 and 2005 as the sample and empirically examines the impacts of ERP implementation on firm performance. The paper is organized as follows. Section 2 reviews the literature on the relationship between ERP implementation and firm performance. Section 3 briefly illuminates the benefits of ERP and proposes the research hypothesis. Section 4 describes sample selection and the method used to estimate the change in financial performance of the sample firms after ERP implementation. The results of this study are presented in Section 5. Section 6 discusses the results and suggests the direction of future research.

2. LITERATURE REVIEW

The existing literature using objective financial data to examine the relationship between ERP implementation and firm performance provides ambiguity for the impacts of ERP on firm performance, while some studies indicate that the firms adopting ERP can acquire better performance, other evidence suggests that there are little relationship between ERP implementation and firm performance.

Poston and Grabski use paired t-test to compare the performance ratios in the year before ERP implementation with the performance ratios after implementation and find no significant improvement in the ratio of residual income and selling, general and administrative expenses (SG&A) in each of the three years after adoption [2]. The research of Hunton et al. indicates that there is no significant pre- and post-adoption performance improvement for ERP adopters, but the performance of non-adopters decline significantly comparing to ERP adopters [3]. Hitt et al. analyze the data of firms that implemented SAP systems and the results show that the firms implementing ERP show higher performance in different financial ratios. Although there is a slow down in performance and productivity shortly after implementation, the financial markets consistently reward the ERP firms with higher market value [4]. Nicolaou studies 247 public traded firms and finds that the ERP firms show higher performance only after two years of use. In addition, controlling for vendor selection, implementation goals, modules implemented and implementation time period helps explain the effects of ERP implementation on firm performance [5]. Hendricks et al. investigate the effects of investing in ERP, SCM and CRM on a firm's stock price, return on assets and return on sales and provide insufficient evidence to support a positive relationship between firm performance and the investments of ERP, SCM and CRM [6].

Most of the above literature chooses some financial ratios as performance indicators, while some also considers the firm's gains on stock market. Some of the literature uses non-adopters as control group matched by size and industry, but little eliminates the influence of macro-economy and other factors unrelated to ERP implementation.

3. BENEFITS OF ERP AND RESEARCH HYPOTHESES

A key benefit of ERP is that all the enterprise data are collected immediately during the initial transaction, stored and processed centrally and updated in real time. This ensures that the employees can share information and the managers can acquire more comprehensive, accurate and timely information to support their decision-making. Therefore, this improves the decision-making quality and the firm's capability to take advantage of market opportunity. Information transferring costs and opportunity costs due to poor decision-making are reduced and the profitability is improved.

Second, ERP realizes the standardization and automation of business process and tracks down the employees' responsibility electronically. This facilitates the governance of the firm, reduces human errors and the monitoring costs, increases the efficiency and makes the management process more transparent. Further, ERP can be integrated with the firm's e-business and supply chain management systems. The integration with other systems automates the purchase and order management process, reduces the order cycle time, the transaction costs and the inventory holding costs, quickens the response time to customer demand and improves customer satisfaction.

Taken together, ERP systems can reduce the firm's costs and boost the profitability. Hence, the following hypothesis is advanced:

H1. ERP implementation leads to improvement in financial performance.

4. SAMPLE SELECTION AND METHOD

4.1 Sample Selection

The sample was selected by identifying public traded Chinese chemical firms that publicly disclosed ERP implementation between 1998 and 2005. The reason of selecting chemical firms as the sample is that there is a heat wave of ERP investments in the chemical industry in China in recent years. An initial sample was identified by searching the firms' news and reports with the keyword as "the firm name ERP implementation" for each firm using searching engines such as Google, Baidu and Yahoo. Then, the initial sample was reduced to 50 firms using the following filter conditions:

1. There is specific year when the firm's ERP implementation was started;
2. The financial data before and after the ERP implementation was available;
3. ERP implementation must have begun before December 2005.

The distribution of the sample firms by implementation year and the descriptive statistics of the sample firms are shown in Table 1 and Table 2.

Table 1. The Distribution of the Sample Firms by Implementation Year

Implementation year	Number of implementations	Percent
1998	2	4.0
1999	1	2.0
2000	3	6.0
2001	10	20.0
2002	11	22.0
2003	6	12.0
2004	9	18.0
2005	8	16.0
Total	50	100.0

Table 2. The Descriptive Statistics of the Sample Firms in the Year before ERP Implementation

	Mean	Median	S. D.	Maximum	Minimum
Total assets (￥million)	2183.18	1278.75	4054.03	27580.83	114.22
Sales (￥million)	1777.65	810.48	4364.61	29567.14	123.16
COGS (￥million)	1483.74	668.07	3739.18	25242.21	82.01

4.2 Choosing the Period over Which to Measure Performance Impacts

To better understand the impacts of ERP implementation on firm performance, this paper examines the financial performance during the implementation period as well as the post-implementation period. 16 adopting firms, nearly one third of the firms in the sample, disclosed both the start and ending dates for their ERP implementation. Based on the detailed timeline information from those firms, we estimate that the average time from start of implementation to live is 17.5 months, which is close to the results of Mabert et al. [7]. Given the above evidence, a two-year implementation period is chosen. As the benefits of ERP seem to be shown only after a long time of continue use, a three-year post-implementation period, and overall a five-year period is chosen to measure the financial performance impacts of ERP. This paper uses $T0$, $T1$ to denote the two years in the implementation period and $T2, T3, T4$ to denote the three years in the post-implementation period. Then the year before implementation is coded as $T-1$.

4.3 Research Method

In order to analyze the impacts of ERP implementation on financial performance, this paper selects return on assets (ROA), return on sales (ROS) and the ratio of costs of goods sold (COGS) to sales as performance indicators. ROA is the ratio of pre-tax income to total assets, and ROS is the ratio of operating income to sales, where operating income is defined as sales less COGS and SG&A. These two indicators are the measures of firm's profitability, while the ratio of COGS to sales is a measure of the firm's operating efficiency. The financial data needed to calculate the three indicators is collected from WIND database.

This paper analyzes the abnormal performance of sample firms in the implementation and the post-implementation period to examine the impacts of ERP implementation on firm performance. The abnormal performance of firm i in year t (AP_{it}) is defined as the real performance of firm i in year t (P_{it}) less the expected performance of firm i in year t ($E(P_{it})$), while the expected performance in year t is the expected performance of the firm i in the absence of ERP implementation. The abnormal performance in the implementation period and the post-implementation period can be expressed by the following equation:

$$AP_{it} = P_{it} - E(P_{it}), t = T0, T1, T2, T3, T4 \tag{4}$$

Based on the research of Barber and Lyon on the methods of event studies, an expectation model incorporates a firm's pre-event performance yields well-specified and powerful test statistics [8]. Therefore, this paper chooses the following expectation model to calculate the expected performance of firm i in year t:

$$E(P_{it}) = P_{i,T-1} + (PI_t - PI_{T-1}), t = T0, T1, T2, T3, T4 \tag{2}$$

Where $P_{i,T-1}$ represents the performance of firm i in the year before ERP implementation, and ($PI_t - PI_{T-1}$) represents the change of the median performance of the control group between the year before ERP implementation and the year t. The introduction of the control group eliminates the influence of macro-economy and other factors unrelated to ERP implementation. Hence, the abnormal performance can be finally expressed as follows:

$$AP_{it} = P_{it} - P_{i,T-1} - (PI_t - PI_{T-1}), t = T0, T1, T2, T3, T4 \tag{3}$$

Barber and Lyon found that selecting the control group that have similar size as that of the sample firms yields well-specified test statistics and they also emphasize the importance of using a portfolio of firms as the control group [8]. This paper follows their findings and uses a three-step to select the control group.

1. For each sample firm, identify all firms that have the same industry code as that of the sample firm and whose sales in the year before ERP implementation is within 70%–130% of the sample firm. All firms that meet the criteria are considered part of the control group for the sample firm. The 70%-130% filter on performance is used because this range yields well-specified test statistics [8].
2. If not find any firms in step 1, identify all firms whose sales in the year before ERP implementation is within 70%-130% of the sample firm, without regard to the industry code.
3. If not find any firms in step 2, choose firms whose sales is closest to the sample firm, without regard to the industry code.

5. RESULTS

In order to test the hypothesis in this paper, a t-test for the mean is used to test whether the means of abnormal performance during the ERP implementation and post-implementation period are significantly from zero. Before t-test, the Kolmogorov-Smirnov test is used to test whether the abnormal performance distributions are normally distributed. The hypothesis can not be rejected in every case. Therefore, a t-test could be used to test the hypothesis in this paper.

Table 3. T-test Results for the Mean of the Sample Firms' Abnormal Performance

	Implementation period (T0-T1)		Post-implementation period (T2-T4)		
Year	T0	T1	T2	T3	T4
Number of observations[1]	50	42	33	27	16
Mean of abnormal change in ROA (%)	-0.5493 (-0.857)	-0.4697 (-0.434)	-1.8950 (-1.751)[2]	-0.9723 (-0.753)	0.5789 (0.423)
Mean of abnormal change in ROS (%)	0.1754 (0.26)	0.0362 (0.037)	-0.8430 (-0.834)	0.4105 (-0.359)	-0.0866 (-0.057)
Mean of abnormal change in COGS / sales (%)	0.1122 (0.152)	0.5481 (0.569)	2.9386 (2.356)[3]	2.3475 (1.532)	-0.0228 (-0.01)

As can be seen from Table 3, during the two-year implementation period and the first two years after implementation, the means of abnormal changes in ROA are negative. But only the abnormal change in the first year after implementation is significantly from zero at the 10% level (t=-1.751, p=0.089). In the third year after implementation, the mean of abnormal change in ROA is positive, but not statistically

[1] Sample size varies due to the non-availability of implementation and post-implementation data for sample firms.

[2] Significantly different from zero at the 10% level for two tails

[3] Significantly different from zero at the 2.5% level for two tails

significant. The abnormal changes in ROS during the two-year implementation period are positive, but none are significant. During the three-year post-implementation period, the abnormal changes in ROS are negative but not significantly. During the implementation period and the first two years after implementation, the means of abnormal changes in the ratio of COGS to sales are positive, and the change in the first year after implementation is significantly from zero at the 2.5% level (t=2.356, p=0.025). In the third year after implementation, the mean of abnormal change in the ratio of COGS to sales is -0.028, insignificantly below zero.

As outliers may influence the results of t-test for the mean, a non-parametric test, Wilcoxon sign rank test for the median is also used to test the sample. The results of Wilcoxon sign rank test are basically consistent with those of t-test. All the evidence suggests that the financial performance of firms implementing ERP is not improved significantly, and during the first two years after implementation, the financial performance declines. The hypothesis in this paper is not supported.

6. CONCLUSIONS

Based on an analysis of 50 sample firms that have implemented ERP between 1998 and 2005, this paper examines the impacts of ERP implementation on firm performance. The results find no significant improvement in ROA, ROS and the ratio of COGS to sales during the two-year implementation period and the three-year post-implementation period and a decrease in all the three performance ratios during the first two years after implementation. To fully understand the results, we discuss the findings of this study further.

First, in order to implement ERP, the firm needs to invest on software and hardware and commit a great deal of organization resources. This may raise the firm's costs and expenses. Furthermore, ERP implementation is accompanied with some integration problems, such as the integration with legacy systems, the integration with internal business process and external partners. These problems may hamper the firm's daily operation and lead to an increase in costs and a decline in financial performance. ERP may integrate with the firm's daily operation only after a long-term use and the financial benefits of ERP may show. This indicates that the impacts of ERP implementation on performance improvement have a time-lagged effect. The three-year post-implementation period used by this paper may be insufficient to capture the impacts of ERP on financial performance, but the lack of long-term post-implementation financial data for most of the samples make it infeasible to use a longer time for analysis. Future research should lengthen the time window to ensure an adequate time period for studying the impacts of ERP on firm performance.

Second, a more detailed analysis of the distribution of abnormal performance of the sample firms suggests that some firms gain superior financial performance, but some firms experience adverse financial performance. This may be because the disparities among firms in their capabilities to manage the critical factors influencing the ERP implementation. The firm's leadership, organization structure, culture, human resource and the implementation experience of IT projects and other tangible and intangible resources could influence the successful implementation of ERP and mediate the effects of ERP on firm performance. Based on the resource-based view of the firm (RBV), Bharadwaj testifies that firms with high IT capabilities tend to show high financial performance [9]. The study of Bharadwaj provides a beneficial perspective to study what organization resources influence whether firms can realize the expected benefits from ERP use. Future research should investigate how the firms realize the expected benefits from ERP use and what organization resources influence the successful use of ERP on the basis of RBV.

Finally, this paper only chooses the sample firms in the chemical industry, and the method to identify sample firms using keywords search may exclude firms implementing ERP but not willing to make known. These firms may be included in the control group. Future research should choose sample firms from a variety of industries and identify samples using surveys or interviews to avoid the potential bias. In conclusion, this paper provides insight for the Chinese firms that want to invest in ERP. ERP does not necessarily help them gain superior financial performance especially in the years shortly after implementation. Due to the high costs of ERP implementation, firms' performance may decline in the years shortly after ERP implementation. Hence, firms should set rational implementation goal before ERP implementation and put more emphasis on managing the implementation process.

ACKNOWLEDGEMENTS

Funding for this research was supported by the National Natural Science Foundation of China under Grant No.70671007 and the PhD Program Foundation of Education Ministry of China under Contract No. 20040006023.

REFERENCES

1. Anonymous, *CCW Research data: a heat wave of software investments in the chemical industry*, CCW Research (2006). http://cio.ccw.com.cn/data/ccw/xb/htm2006/20060427_13Q46.asp (Accessed May 19, 2007)
2. R. Poston and S. Grabski, The financial impacts of enterprise resource planning implementations, *International Journal of Accounting Information Systems*. Volume 2, pp.271-294, (2001).
3. J. E. Hunton, B. Lippincott, and J. L. Reck, Enterprise resource planning systems: comparing firm performance of adopters and nonadopters, *International Journal of Accounting Information Systems*. Volume 4, pp.165-184, (2003).
4. L. M. Hitt, D. J. Wu, and X. Zhou, Investment in enterprise resources planning: business impact and productivity measures, *Journal of Management Information Systems*. Volume 19, Number 1, pp.71-98, (2002).
5. A.I. Nicolaou, Firm performance effects in relation to the implementation and use of enterprise resource planning systems, *Journal of Information Systems*. Volume 18, Number 2, pp.79-105, (2004).

6. K.B. Hendricks, V.R. Singhal, and J.K. Stratman, The impact of enterprise systems on corporate performance: A study of ERP, SCM, and CRM system implementations, *Journal of Operations Management.* Volume 25, pp.65-82, (2007).
7. V.A. Mabert, A.K. Soni, and M.A. Venkataramanan, Enterprise resource planning survey of US manufacturing firms, *Production & Inventory Management Journal.* Volume 41, Number 20, pp.52-58, (2000).
8. B.M. Barber and J.D. Lyon, Detecting abnormal operating performance: the empirical power and specification of test statistics, *Journal of Financial Economics.* Volume 41, pp.359-399, (1996).
9. A.S. Bharadwaj, A resource-based perspective on information technology capability and firm performance: an empirical investigation, *MIS Quarterly.* Volume 24, Number 1, pp.169-196, (2000).

On Demand Integration of Dynamic Supply Chain Application Based on Semantic Service Oriented Architecture

Juanqiong Gou[1], Xi Yang[2] and Wei Dai[3]

[1, 2] School of Economics and Management, Beijing Jiaotong University, Beijing 100044, P.R. China jq_gou@263.net 06120693@bjtu.edu.cn
[3] School of Information Systems, Victoria University, Australia Wei.Dai@vu.edu.au

Abstract. Dynamic Supply Chain is flexible to support various needs of enterprises. The integration and collaboration of enterprise systems offer significant challenges, while the problem is the difficulty for the integration of distributed heterogeneous information system as the partnership changes. The emerging technologies of Service-Oriented Architecture (SOA) and Semantic Web offer promising solutions by enhancing the reusability and interoperability of different systems and promoting cooperation among business partners.

This paper analyzes the requirements for On-Demand Integration of supply chain applications and discusses various integration solutions and their challenges. The analysis indicates that an approach combining the Semantic Grid and SOA technologies will be an appropriate solution. Therefore, a generic conceptual architecture for the integration by using Semantic Grid enabled SOA approach is proposed. An example scenario is presented to show a potential application of this architecture with a prototype adopting the WSMX (Web Service Modeling Execution Environment) as the basis of its implementation and deployment.

Keywords: *Dynamic supply chain, On-Demand integration, Semantic grid, Service-oriented architecture, Ontology, WSMX (Web Service Modeling Execution Environment)*

1. INTRODUCTION

The rapid changes of external environments and the uncertain factors within an enterprise (such as malfunction of manufacture equipments, delayed delivery of raw materials, etc.) put significant pressure on the company's performance, and at the same time offering collaboration opportunities among business partners along the supply chain. The core business partners can be formed dynamically according to customers' orders.

Dynamic Supply Chain (DSC) usually contains different cooperation relationships covering from upstream raw material suppliers, manufactures that play a core role in the process, to downstream distributors and retailers. Although the business

Please use the following format when citing this chapter:

Gou, J., Yang, X., Dai, W., 2007, in IFIP International Federation for Information Processing, Volume 254, Research and Practical Issues of Enterprise Information Systems II Volume 1, eds. L. Xu, Tjoa A., Chaudhry S. (Boston: Springer), pp. 589-598.

agreements are reached prior to any business deals among the business partners in a B2B scenario, multiple delivery channels may be available for a buyer business. Therefore, on-demand supply chain channels are generated (dynamically) to meet individual business needs. Figure 1 describes the company relationships along the supply chain which consists of several supply chains distinguished by distinct colors initiated by OrderA , OrderB and OrderC respectively.

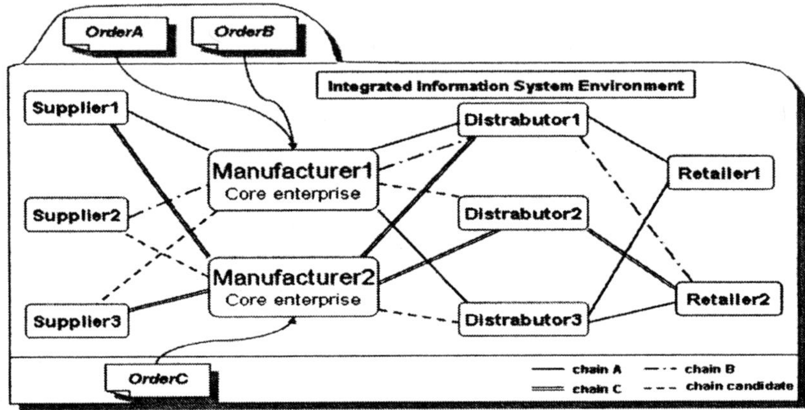

Figure 1. Dynamic Supply Chain Practice

To achieve the automated formation of a dynamic supply chain and enable the enterprises to cooperate effectively, there still exist two cruxes of the matter awaiting settled.

Firstly while manufacturers searching for the potential partners by means of mobile agent technology, the vast amount of heterogeneous information available on the Web actually becomes a obstacle against the right ones, which mainly because of the absence of a effective searching mechanisms and denotation of the online knowledge resources. Secondly, once the cooperation chain is set, how to integrate distributed information systems of other companies for synergy, i.e. on-demand integration, and afterwards detachment of the integrated systems remain the challenging issues [1].

To tackle the first-mentioned problem, we must be able to aggregate the relevant knowledge from the heterogeneous knowledge resources that require semantically enabled technologies to efficiently and precisely discover. At the same time the emerging technologies of Service Oriented Architecture (SOA) to a large extent enhance the interoperability of distributed heterogeneous systems[2], and the Semantic Web (SW) technologies make information and knowledge machine accessible and understandable rather than displaying them for interpretation by human. In addition, the emerging Grid technologies foster the coordination and sharing of computing, application, and data, storage, and network resources in a distributed environment [3]. Therefore, the solution for On-Demand integration of dynamic supply chain application may come from an approach to combine Semantic Grid (SG) and SOA technologies into the development of supply chain management.

2. EMERGING TECHNOLOGIES

The key to achieve the automation relies mainly on solutions to three issues: (1) how to make Web services of supply chain interoperable both syntactically and semantically; (2) how to automatically discover, based on the syntactic and semantic descriptions, the most appropriate information and services; and (3) assemble them to build the composite service. The emerging technologies of SOA and Semantic Grid along with its related technologies are briefly introduced in the following.

2.1 SOA

A SOA is 'a set of components which can be invoked, and whose interface description can be published and discovered over the network' [4]. Services are network addressable entities with a well defined, easy-to-use and standardized interface. Services like components are loosely coupled and often designed independently from the context in which they are used and composed. SOA typically involve multiple organizations that interact with networked systems where there is no single designer having full knowledge, control and ownership. In this sense, services are more coarse-grained than components.

Within a SOA, all applications are in the form of Web services including system functions for monitoring and controlling activities. Each service can invoke other services through shared communication protocols, infrastructures and interface specifications. It offers an ideal environment for applications integration.

Syntactical interoperability of Web services is achieved mainly using two common Web service standards: Web service description language (WSDL) and simple object access protocol (SOAP). WSDL is used to describe a Web service in terms of its interfaces and SOAP formalizes the XML-based message transportation between Web services.

2.2 Semantic Grid

The WS approach of SOA only resolves syntactic heterogeneities. For semantic heterogeneity, Semantic-Web-based technologies are required.

The Semantic Grid addresses the challenges in grid computing and applications by adding meaning through Semantic Web technologies (like ontology, annotation and negotiation process) to the grid [5]. Ontology as the core technology of SW is a formal, explicit specification of a conceptualization that provides a common vocabulary for a knowledge domain and defines the meaning of the terms and the relations between them[6]. Semantic heterogeneity can be handled dynamically by providing ontology mapping, merging, and versioning of ontologies through Semantic Web Services (SWS). SWS is WS semantically annotated based on ontology. The most widespread standard language for the Semantic Web is Web Ontology Language (OWL). Furthermore, the Semantic Web services initiative (SWSI) introduces OWL-

S as the representative technology for describing the semantics of individual Web services. OWL-S can be used to specify the semantics of the exchanged data, the functionality (through the reference to some service classification outside OWL-S), pre/post conditions, and other aspects of a Web service. These explicit specifications make the capabilities of individual Web services machine understandable so that automated Web service discovery is possible.

In this way, the semantic grid not only provides a general semantic-based computational network infrastructure, but a rich, seamless collection of intelligent, knowledge-based services for enabling the management and sharing of complex resources and reasoning mechanisms .

3. REQUIREMENTS FOR ON-DEMAND INTEGRATION

The integration issue in DSC management arises as the collaboration among enterprises becomes more and more frequent. In traditional methods, for companies adopting respective systems programmed by different source codes, in order to offer clients a complete set of services or to integrate the existing business applications (such as EAI and B2Bi) that are based on different architecture, communication protocols and data format, the inchoate E-business technologies such as EDI, Web EDI, are intended as joint solutions for complicated applications.

The SOA is well fit in terms of DSC applications. In this architecture a new mechanism for data interchange is proposed. An enterprise only provides and publishes a standard data searcher component where other partners can acquire it without providing different programs to different partners. Any one that uses company's core datum shall search from the database and package it in the format that its own system can understand. Taking the DSC system as an example for composition of a series of services, SOA aims at solving the dynamic problem of integrations in the means of adding, modifying, deleting services. In a DSC, every company can be a service provider and a service requestor at one time, forming a services sharing system consisting of different kinds of services.

For a sophisticated task, we may have to dynamically configure a collection of appropriate services including raw material stocking, transportation, wholesaling, retailing, etc., and automatically compose and execute them. In many cases, the constituent services are in a distributed heterogeneous environment, which may be geographically dispersed. Moreover, some constituent services may involve utilization of high computational power and large amounts of data. To address these issues, a list of requirements on DSC management solutions for On-Demand Knowledge is as following:

SOA/WS compliant: Adopt the SOA and Web Service standard such as WSDL, UDDI and SOAP to describe, publish/register and invoke knowledge services to increase their reusability and interoperability. Non service-oriented existing knowledge services, e.g. legacy KS, should be wrapped as WS.

Semantic Web based: WS should be semantically annotated base on ontology as SWS to facilitate matchmaking and service discovery.

SG enabled: Non Grid-enabled knowledge services which involve utilization of high computational power and huge amounts of data should be semantically annotated and wrapped as SGS.

Hybrid Reasoning: Ontology reasoning should incorporate with inference services in supply chain domain specific knowledge-based systems to facilitate automated service composition and execution.

Semantic Service Discovery and Negotiation: Use Semantic Web technologies and hybrid reasoning to enable automatic service discovery by matchmaking between SW-based services and the goals which is specified by the cooperating program via client orders.

Semantic Service composition and execution: Hybrid reasoning, BPM and choreography technologies should be incorporated together to enable dynamic configuration and automatic composition and execution of a collection of appropriated DSC services, and to ensure compatible choreographies between them.

4. CONCEPTUAL ARCHITECTURE FOR SG-ENABLED SOA APPROACH TO DSC

To meet the aforementioned requirements for On-Demand Integration, a generic conceptual architecture for Semantic Grid enabled SOA approach to DSC management is proposed and shown in Figure 2. The conceptual architecture

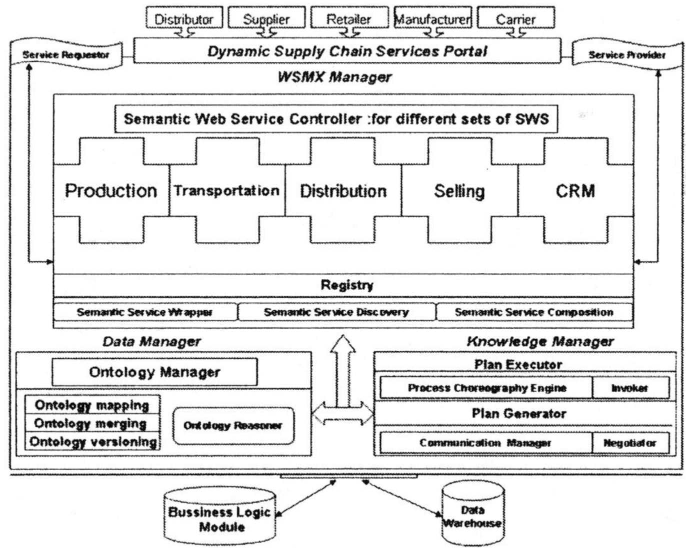

Figure 2. Conceptual Architecture for SG-enabled SOA Approach to DSC

encompasses four parts: *the Dynamic Supply Chain Services Portal, the WSMX*[7] *Manager, the Knowledge Manager* and *the Data Manager.*

The Dynamic Supply Chain Services Portal is provided as an entrance point to facilitate the process of searching for and utilizing the collection of SWS/SGS registered and published in the WSMX Manager.

The WSMX Manager contains basic several categories of supply chain services including production, transportation, distribution, selling, CRM and so on, which are through SWS Controller semantically annotated and wrapped as SWS or SGS. The manager may contain additional un-annotated WS or GS for temporary storage or for future semanticization. The Registry allows the Service Provider to register and publish its SWS/SGS through the portal. This Manager is a key part of the architecture that is responsible for the registry of SWS/SGS and automatic service discovery, composition and publication.

The Knowledge Manager plays the roles of Plan Generator (PG) and Plan Executor (PE) [8]. PG consisting of Communication Manager (CM) and Negotiator, is to communicate with Business Logic Modules and negotiate with Data Manager in order to be able to generate a desired optimized cooperation program of the supply chain into the service configuration. PE consisting of Process Choreography Engine (PCE) and Service Invoker, is to implement the program conveyed from PG by deploying and employing collection of SWS/SGS. PCE is a special container in charge of the sequence to initiate SWS/SGS and consequently defining a specific business process corresponded to SWS/SGS components. Container-provided functions enable long-running process executions that can even span enterprise boundaries, survive planned and unplanned outages, and facilitate Business-to-Business (B2B) collaboration. The Invoker is responsible for the actual invocation of the Web Services based on a standard API.

The Data Manager mainly emphasizes its maintenance on ontologies, among which mapping, merging and versioning are the most basic operations. Mapping could provide a common layer from which several ontologies could be accessed and therefore could exchange information in semantically sound manners[9]. Merging is to solve the problem that more and more ontologies are overlapping with the development of Semantic Web. Versioning is about the ability to manage ontology changes and their effects by creating and maintaining different variants of the ontology [10]. The Ontology Reasoner encompasses DL and Rule Reasoners to check the consistency and taxonomy.

5. RUN-TIME DEMONSTRATION WITH APPLICATION SCENARIO

In the context of Figure 1 supplied earlier, Figure 3 further illustrates driven by client *OrderA*, how a dynamic supply chain can respond to dynamic needs in an integrated information system environment. Manufacturer1 (M1) takes Supplier1 (S1) and Supplier3 (S3) as its main raw material provider, Supplier2 as candidate. M1 sends Material Order (MO) to S1 and S3, S1 intends to corporate with M1 whereas S3 does not. S1 then informs M1 of its stock situation, if stock is in shortage, M1 also can conveniently send MO to S2 to seek for a corporation. After the product is finished, M1 sends to a Product Inventory (PI) to its distributor candidates and distributor. Once the intent of the corporation confirms, a new real-time supply *ChainA* comes into being.

To support this Business Process (BP), we create three types of ontology: Entity Ontology, BP Ontology and Execution Ontology.

Entity Ontology contains different roles of the business world of the supply chain sector covering manufacturer, distributor, retailer, transporter, supplier, etc. Correspondingly the data and information exchanged among them such as product inventory, order, quotation, etc, serve as the foundation of communication and are important parts of entity ontology.

BP Ontology is used to describe the workflow of different BPs, reflecting business logic. It demands an effective abstraction, storage, re-utilization of the real-time BP knowledge.

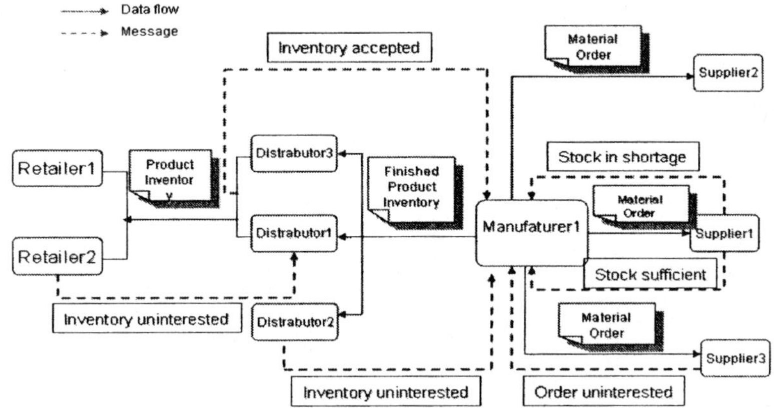

Figure 3. The Chain: A Formation Illustration

Execution Ontology is relevant to some specific activity bounded to the different roles of supply chain. Normally these activities can either change the internal or external management state, such as delivery of the stock control, or choose the decision-making methods such as transportation modes, lines and tools.

In this application scenario, *M1, S1, S2, S3, D1* (Distrabutor1), *D2, D3, R1* (Retailer1), *R2, MO, PI* are classified as Entity Ontology. Table1 shows a section of the owl file of the MO ontology.

Table 1. MO Ontology Example

```
<owl:Class rdf:ID="Material Order">
    <rdfs:subClassOf rdf:resource="&Raw Material;Order"/>
        <owl:ObjectProperty rdf:ID="hasMO_ID"/>
```

```
<owl:ObjectProperty rdf:ID="sent to">
  <rdfs:domain rdf:resource="#Order"/>
  <rdfs:range  rdf:resource="Supplier"/>
 <owl:/ObjectProperty>
   ................
   <owl:Restriction>
  <owl:onProperty rdf:resource="#sended to"/>
<owl:minCardinality
  rdf:datatype="&xsd;nonNegativeInteger">2
  </owl:minCardinality>
   </owl:Restriction>
</owl:Class>
```

The above code shows that MO has to be sent to the type of "Supplier", and at the same time being sent to at least to two suppliers. This constraint makes the non-suppliers' systems automatically skip to process the MO by checking the restriction rdfs:range rdf:resource="Supplier" if receiving the unexpected orders by mistake.

The business logic rule for cooperation of this application in the form of BP Ontology is given in Table 2. The business rules specify the conditions and consequences for business tasks to proceed.

Table 2. Example Business Rule to Deal with MO

RuleID	R001
Event	Received MO from M1(the trigger)
Type	Order Processing
Priority	1
State	Running
Condition	Null
Action	Confirmation of accepting MO or Not
Exception	Handle Exception Message
Pre-Action	Analyzing the MO ontology

In the WSMX architecture, Table 3 shows how the respective WSDL to describe the above service. With the use of Semantic Web markup languages data structures passed through Web Service interfaces are expressed by ontologies.

Table 3. WSDL Service Description

```
<?xml version="1.0" encoding="UTFi8"?>

<!ii Namespace Defintion ii> [...]

<message name="OrderSent">

<part name="hasSupplier" type="xsd:date"/>

<part name="hasManufacturer" type="xsd: string "/>

</message>

<message name=" ">

<part name="hasRule" type="xsd: Integer "/>

</message>

<portType name="MO_Processing">

<operation name="GetMO_Detail">

<input message="tns:OrderSent"/>

<output message="tns:OrderRespone"/>

</operation>

</portType>
```

Once the confirmation of cooperation from supplier sent back to the Manufaturer, the order details can be monitored at any time.

6. SUMMARY AND CONCLUSIONS

The proposed framework for ontology development has research and practical implications. From the research perspective, we cannot claim that the proposed ideas are final and complete since research on DSC problems is continually evolving. On the contrary, new research can be carried out at a more detailed level, such as how problem identification can be accomplished or how ontology can be linked with data repositories. These and other findings can bring the proof of the proposed methodology, its revision and enhancement. From a practical perspective, SWS applications can be built based on the proposed framework to implement ontology-based IS for a DSC or for any other enterprise domain.

ACKNOWLEDGEMENTS

This research was supported by the Peking University Luen Tai center for Supply Chain System R&D.

REFERENCES

1. Z. Hai, Special Section: Semantic Grid and Knowledge Grid, *Future Generation Computer Systems.* Volume 23, Number 2, pp.281-282, (2007).
2. C.J. Yao, An Industry View on Service-oriented Architecture and Web Services, in *Proceedings - SOSE 2005: IEEE International Workshop on Service-Oriented System Engineering* (2005), pp.59.
3. C.D. Goble and D. Roure, The Grid: An application of the Semantic Web, *SIGMOD Record.* Volume 12, Number 2, pp.65-70, (2002).
4. T. Kaihara, Multi-agent Based Supply Chain Modeling with Dynamic Environment, *International Journal of Production Economics.* Volume 2, Number 22, pp.263-269, (2003).
5. M. Zaremba and E. Oren, *WSMX Execution Semantics*, WSMX Working Draft D13.2 v0.2 (2005). http://www.wsmo.org/2005/d13/d13.2/v0.2/20050202/ (Accessed October 2, 2006)
6. D. Booth, H. Haas, and A. Brown, *Web Services Glossary, Technical report,* World Wide Web Consortium (W3C) (2004). http:// www.w3.org/TR/ws-gloss/ (Accessed March 23, 2007)
7. W. Dai, *Collaborative Real-Time Information Services via Portals* (Idea Group Publication, 2007)
8. K. Yannis and S. Marco, *Ontology Mapping:The State of The Art* (2004), http://drops.dagstuhl.de/opus/volltexte/2005/40/ (Accessed June 2, 2006)
9. T. Gruber, *What is an Ontology?* (2002) http://www-ksl.stanford.edu/kst/what-is-an-ontology.html (Accessed June 3, 2006)
10. M. Klein and D. Fensel, *Ontology Versioning on the Semantic Web* (2005) http://www.cs.vu.nl/~mcaklein/presentations/2001-07-31-SWWS-Stanford.pdf

A Research on the Architecture of ERP for Small & Medium-Sized Enterprise Based on Agent and SOA

Ruixue Fu[1], Zhanhong Xin[2] and Jianzhang Wu[3]

[1,2]School of Economics and Management, Beijing University of Posts and Telecommunications, Beijing 100876, P.R. China brucefrx@gmail.com
Key laboratory of Information Management and Economics, MII, P.R. China xinzhanhong@263.net
[3] School of Management Science and Engineering, Shijiazhuang University of Economics, Shijiazhuang 050031, P.R. China

Abstract. With the rapid development of information technology and the gradual extension of information technology to enterprise, ERP systems become more and more complex and some new requirements that focus on both manufacturing activities and the supply chain are brought forward. To address these problems, a MAERP system architecture based on agent and SOA has been developed. To illustrate the architecture, an experiment system has been proposed in detail. This simulation implied that the architecture provides a very efficient method to design ERP systems for small & medium-size Enterprises with the purposes of flexibility to achieve the business agility, reusability of the intelligent component, and cooperation between application systems to assure a global optimization. The objectives of this paper is to illustrate the architecture of ERP systems based on agent for small & medium-size Enterprises, and the approach of how a web services-based SOA supports our MAERP system.

Keywords: *Software architecture, Enterprise resource planning (ERP), Service-oriented architecture, Web services, Agent*

1. INTRODUCTION

ERP (Enterprise Resource Planning) systems reflect the most advanced management theory of enterprise nowadays and supply for the best strategy of CIMS [1]. It is a famous conception put forward by Gartner Group, the famous IT Analysis Company in America, in the 20 century [2]. ERP systems that developed from Material Requirement Planning integrate and automate core corporate activities from inventory control, to sales, production, and supply chain [3, 4].

ERP systems become more and more complex and some new requirements that focus on both manufacturing activities and the supply chain are brought forward. They require ERP for some advantages, such as integration, flexibility and reengineering to respond to changing business requirements and complex transaction processing to extend quickly, more informed decisions making, communication directly with suppliers and customers, etc.

Please use the following format when citing this chapter:

Fu, R., Xin, Z., Wu, J., 2007, in IFIP International Federation for Information Processing, Volume 254, Research and Practical Issues of Enterprise Information Systems II Volume 1, eds. L. Xu, Tjoa A., Chaudhry S. (Boston: Springer), pp. 599-608.

For this reason, the agent has introduced as one of the solutions in future software environments. Since the agent had introduced from AI community, it has extended to various applications, such as e-mail filtering, and Air-traffic Control. Moreover, in distributed and heterogeneous environments such as Electronic Commerce applications, the concepts of agent are widely applied [5]. In the past years, researchers engaged in applying agent technology to the development of ERP systems, and presented various architectures. For examples, Bih-Ru Lea etc. introduce an architecture, called MAERP that includes four types of basic agents [6]; Ye Bin etc. propose an architecture called DIERPS [1].

Previous researches and developments pave a fundamental basis for the application of agent technologies in ERP systems. Although there are many literatures for agent technology, web services-based SOA, and ERP systems respectively, it seems that a lack of literature discusses applying agent technology and web services-based SOA to implement ERP systems for small & medium size enterprises with the purposes of scalability, extensibility, flexibility and reusability of the intelligent component. Based upon multi-agent technology, this paper proposes the architecture aimed at providing a practical solution for ERP systems. Different to the literatures mentioned before, this paper has mainly been concerned with applying agent technology and web services-based SOA to implement ERP systems for small & medium size enterprises with the purposes of scalability, extensibility, flexibility to achieve the business agility, reusability of the intelligent component, and cooperation between application systems to assure a global optimization.

The paper is organized as follows. In section 2, we introduce the concept of Agent, MAS. In section 3, we present our MAERP system architecture consists of five types of agents and web service-based architecture of agents consists of three types of agents. In section 4, we give the communication method between Agents in detail. In section 5, we introduce our simulation of the architecture we proposed in detail. Finally, in section 6 we conclude the present problems and future directions.

2. AGENT AND MAS

The concept of agent was started from John McCarthy in the mid-1950's and established by Oliver G. Selfridge several years later. In the early days, many researchers have been studied about agent in boundary of AI. Since 80's the agent has been widely applied [5]. There is a general agreement that an agent is a reusable component that exhibits a combination of the six characteristics: Autonomous, Adaptable, Mobile, Knowledgeable, Collaborative and Persistence [7, 8]. So in software system, agent means software component that has inference capability, and can interacts autonomously as a surrogate for its user with its environment and other agents to achieve the predefined goal, and reacts to changes in the environment. There are three categories of agents based on the function of agents [7, 8]: Personal agents, Mobile agents, and Collaborative agents.

Inspired by distributed artificial intelligence, a MAS (Multi-Agent System) consists of autonomous, generally heterogeneous and potentially independent agents which work together to solve special problems. As described by Brennan, autonomous, cooperative, and scalable are the typical characteristics of a MAS that has the following capabilities [9]: Independent decision-making, Interacting with other agents and humans, Perceiving changes in their environment and acting as a consequence, and Taking initiative to reach certain objectives.

These distinctive characteristics of a MAS can facilitate ERP systems with effective means to integrate various software systems over a net work in distributed manner. It is appropriate to adopt the MAS technology in a distributed ERP systems to resolve the distributed project scheduling and management problems.

3. THE SOFTWARE ARCHITECTURE

3.1 The SOA

To achieve business agility and IT flexibility, Service-Oriented Architecture (SOA) is becoming the mainstream of system integration [10]. SOA is an architectural framework that supports integrating business tasks as linked services that can be accessed when needed over a network. It allows the user to place multiple service applications into a process or processes. Each application function needs to be transformed into services which are then assembled into processes. Figure 1 presents the relationship between service, processes and applications in SOA. Within SOA architecture, all functions, such as check service inventory, and software distribution are defined as services [11].

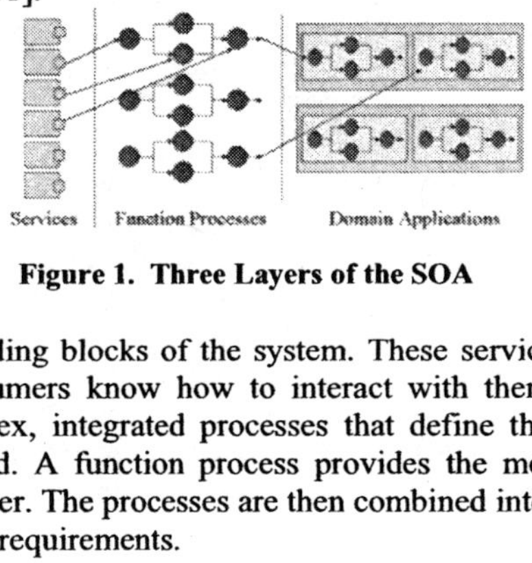

Figure 1. Three Layers of the SOA

Services are the building blocks of the system. These services have well-defined interfaces that let consumers know how to interact with them. They are grouped together to form complex, integrated processes that define the sequence in which services will be invoked. A function process provides the means for coordinating services in a specific order. The processes are then combined into domain applications that fit specific business requirements.

3.2 The MAERP System Architecture

A group of agents can form a MAS to achieve the common global goals by connecting with each other through a LAN, the Intranet or Internet. We assume there is a MAS within each functional area such as department, factory and workroom.

To achieve flexibility of system and business agility, we apply Service Oriented Architecture (SOA) concept to design the system. As indicated in Figure 2, the framework for ERP system consists of five types of agents with different functionalities which are discussed next. Figure 2 illustrates the abstract level of MAERP system architecture with coordination agents communicating with each other over the company's network [6], [12].

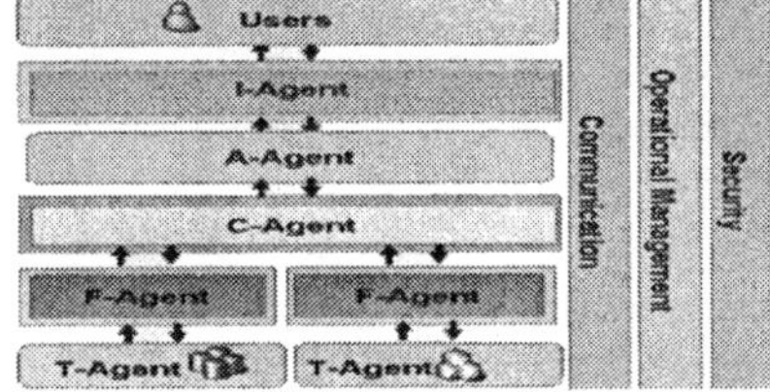

Figure 2. The MAERP System Architecture

A-Agent is used to realize an application of the whole ERP systems which will be divided into three application levels: operation level, management level and decision level. Operation level is the basis of the whole ERP system, its major function is to deal with business and collect the data. Management level is responsible for helping middle-level manager understand work condition in his department in time and make assistant strategy in tactic problem. Decision supporting level is responsible for providing high-level decision staff with information support of all kinds of data and knowledge and some best solving-problem plans. According to the above analysis, we design three types of A-Agents: Operation A-Agent, Management A-Agent and Decision A-Agent to realize the above three applications.

F-Agent is used to realize a function or business process which is the important base for operation of enterprise, to define the sequence in which T-Agents will be invoked, and to be further combined into domain applications that fit specific business requirements.

C-Agent is the heart of this MAERP architecture and is the controller of the other agents within an application. An application can have one or many C-Agent depending on the nature of task complexity. The C-Agent can communicate and collaborate with other agents, react to various requests, assign tasks to F-Agents, receive instructions and report to user through A-Agent, assign data collection to and receive data from F-Agent, assign tasks and receive feedback from F-Agents, as well as communicate with and provide request data for other C-Agents.

T-Agent usually can carry autonomously out some specific functions in terms of their own domain knowledge without the intervention of coordination agents. We look upon T-Agents as services, which are the building blocks of the MAERP and have well-defined interfaces that let other agents know how to interact with them. They are grouped together to form complex, integrated processes that define the sequence in which services will be invoked. Some T-Agents possess the ability to collect data, perform data analysis, query specific databases within the application, retrieve information requested by F-Agent, and perform data warehousing and prepare dataset upon request from F-Agent.

I-Agent can communicate between users and MAERP system, prepare reports for users, and interpret results for users. It can monitor and inform users when tasks have been completed without the inquiry of users, learn and store preferences of users, and record the user's disposition to usage of the MAERP system.

All agents in the system have the ability to communicate through SOAP and KQML (see Agents communication). Each agent has a defined type (denoting a set of messages which are accepted and understood by the agent) and it is identified within the network by its distinct name and a given identification number [9], [4], [13].

3.3 Web Services

By using the service-oriented approach, the MAERP system will have a flexible infrastructure, which can easily adapt to user requirements. We apply web services to implement the MAERP system based on SOA. Web services provide a standard means of interoperating between different software applications, running on a variety of platforms and/or frameworks.

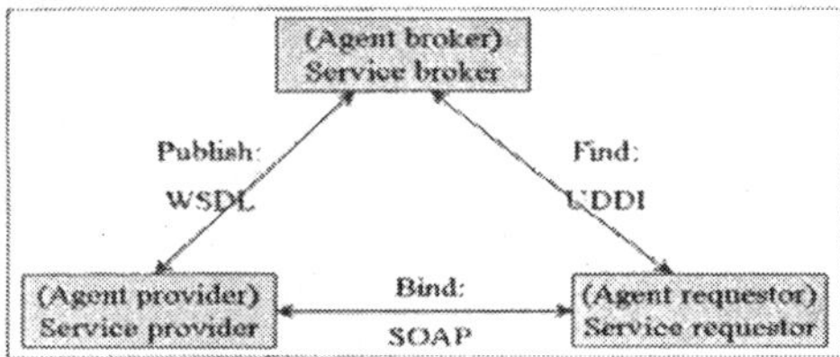

Figure 3. Web Service Based Architecture of Agents

The conceptual architecture of Web services mainly includes three roles and three operations as Figure 3 shows. Each service provider can publish service descriptions to the service broker, which is the description of service interface and of implementation details with WSDL (Web Service Description Language) including data types and operations of Web service, binding and invoking information and its location. To catalog service descriptions, we use a standard registry definition called Universal Discovery, Description and Integration (UDDI). It registries contain white pages for each registered provider. When a service requester needs a service, it will query and find the suitable service in the catalog. After it acquires the suitable service's information, the requester will directly bind and access the service [10].

Web services rely on the functionalities: publish, find, and bind. The equivalent agent-based functionalities depicted in Figure 3 are shown in parentheses, and all interactions are via an agent-communication language that we use KQML. The Web service based architecture of agents consists of three types of agent [14], [15].

Agent provider publishes service descriptions to the Agent broker, asks Agent broker to register their capabilities and physical areas, and provides other agents with the service. Agent requester asks Agent broker to discover the information about Agent provider and bind to the Agent provider to obtain the service. Agent broker registers yellow pages for each registered Agent provider and plays match-maker between Agent providers and Agent requesters by considering their locations, capabilities and requirements.

4. AGENTS COMMUNICATION

To express communication and negotiation required and organize communications between agents, we use the KQML. The basic assumption is that agents can be located on separate machines or at least separate processes within one machine. Hence the communication between them must be constituted by some kind of network protocol-in our case it is TCP/IP. But this protocol represents only the lowest layers of the communication which is extended by five other protocols on the top two levels of the OSI model-they are SOAP, WSDL, UDDI, KQML and the content language itself [10, 3, 14], as shown in Figure 4.

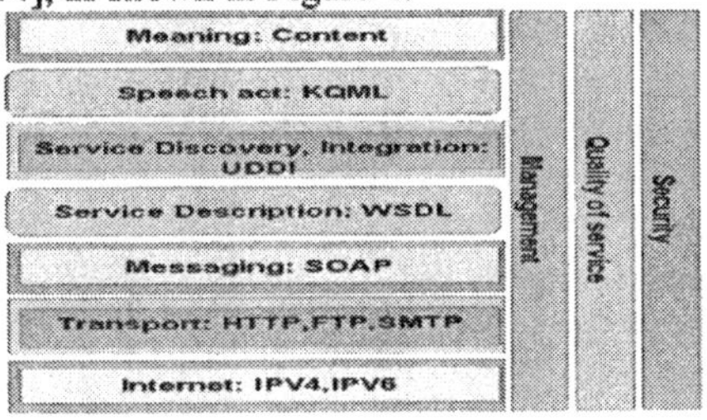

Figure 4. The Communication Layers

The simple object access protocol (SOAP) provides the common protocol systems need to communicate with each other so that they can request services, such as to schedule appointments, order parts, and deliver information. The Web Services Description Language (WSDL) describes the agents in a machine-readable form, where the names of functions, their required parameters, and their results can be specified. Finally, Universal Description, Discovery, and Integration (UDDI) gives Agent requestor a way to find needed agents by specifying a registry or "yellow pages" of agents.

As shown in Figure 4, the inter-agent message-transporting layer is constituted by SOAP [10, 15, 3]. Above UDDI layer which facilitates the connection between agents, there is a KQML layer. The Knowledge Query and Manipulation Language (KQML) language defined by KSE (Knowledge Share Effort) is based on the linguistic theory of the speech act. The KQML is a language and protocol exchanging information and sharing knowledge, which provides basic format of expressing and processing messages and supports sharing information among agents.

So we design architecture of communication based on KQML and SOAP, as shown in Figure 5. We realize knowledge expression and cooperation requests among agents with KQML. Agent sends message to Communication Switch Agent (CSA), CSA wraps the message of KQML to the access format of SOAP message. We realize communication and information exchange between agents (based on KQML and SOAP) by means of Communication Switch Agent [15]. The communication among the agents that used in our architecture is described as follows: The sender agent sends a KQML request message to CSA, the CSA converts the semantics of KQML to the access format of SOAP message, and the CSA sends the message to the receiver agents in terms of the same method over transport network [15, 3].

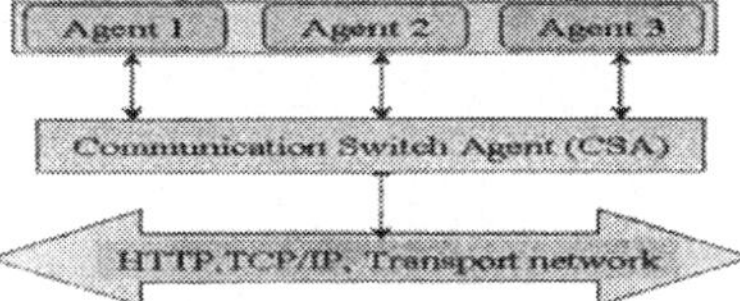

Figure 5. The Architecture of Agent Communication Based on SOAP

5. SIMULATION STUDY

We apply the architecture we proposed to an experiment system as Figure 6 shows to estimate the architecture. We assume that a user in a planning department needs to make the production planning. We assume for simplicity that there are six functions or business processes: sales, transport, planning, materials, purchasing, and distribution centers in the XX Company. Each function has its own information system, database, and data architecture [6, 16].

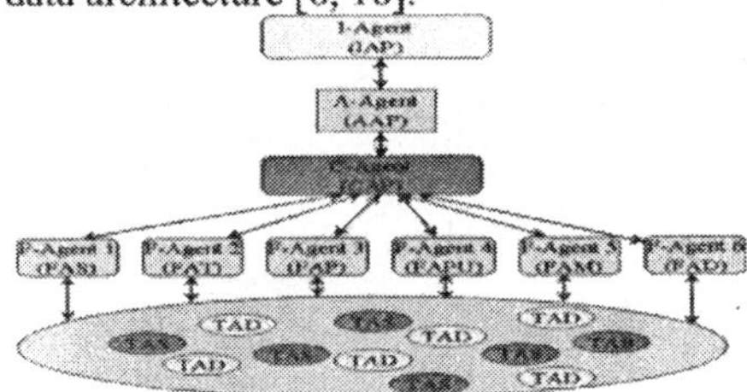

Figure 6. The Architecture of Simulation System

We assume that one Operation A-Agent is assigned to the planning department (i.e., AAP), one C-Agent (i.e., CAP), and one I-Agent (i.e., IAP). We further assume that one function agent is assigned to the sales (i.e., FAS), transport (i.e., FAT), materials (i.e., FAM), purchasing (i.e., FAPU), planning (i.e., FAP), and distribution centers (i.e., FAD). Further, for each function agent, one data collection agent (TAD), and several tasks agents (TAS) [17, 6, 18]. Figure 6 provides an overview of MAS which will be used to answer the above production planning in six steps as follows.

In the planning application, IAP communicates the question about production planning to AAP. And then AAM starts to deal with this question as follows:We realize the production planning through lists of goals for this week and some future weeks. These plans go upstream through the internal supply chain, and come back downstream as plans of delivery. On the way upstream each agent contributes with its own knowledge. To explain the conversation plans and rules, we begin with looking at the issuing of demand-forecasts, which give the expected number of units ordered for this or coming weeks and start production planning.

Step 1:

By exercising domain knowledge, FAS organizes four tasks concurrently by means of C-Agent CAM. Create a demand-forecast-conversation; Compute the demand-forecast by means of T-Agent; Prepare the data for sending, and send the message to the distribution center agent (FAD); and Monitor the status of requested information from various agents.

Step 2:

When FAD receive the demand-forecast message form FAS, the FAD create a demand-plan-conversation which use knowledge of the DC's inventory levels. DC-demand-plans, which define the targeted quantity of each product arriving at the DC at the end of this and coming weeks, are made and send to the Transport agent which creates a corresponding conversation.

Step 3:

Transport agent (FAT) knows how much is expense to the DC and make ship-plans, which define the quantity of each product that should be shipped from a plant to a given DC at the end of this week and coming weeks. The ship-plans are sent to the planning agents of the plants concerned.

Step 4:

The aim of a plant's planning agent (FAP) is to convert the incoming ship-plan (if it has external customers) and materials-demand-plans from the next downstream plants (if it has internal customers) to the plant's own materials-demand-plans that define the number of units of a given product the plant needs this week and coming weeks for all internally supplied parts. To calculate the materials-demand-plans the Planning agent will use data from the other agents in the plant. These plans are sent to the next agent upstream.

Step 5:

FAP will make delivery-plan that defines the number of units the plant will deliver this week and coming weeks for each customer. The delivery-plan includes the total demand and is limited by part availabilities and production capacities. And the planning agent (FAP) decides the actual-production-plan of the plant according to domain knowledge, which is the production goals for this and coming weeks.

Step 6:

From the actual-production-plan, the materials agent can calculate a materials-order-plan for parts. The plans are sent to the purchasing agent, in which they are converted to part orders for the suppliers. When receiving acknowledgment messages from the supplier, FAM update their order data base and inventory data base.

Upon notification of FAM, AAP will inform the user through IAP about the new plan. IAP will also record the user's decision, which will be used to predict the preference in the future.

6. CONCLUSIONS

With the assumption that there is a MAS in each functional area such as department and factory, one ERP architecture is established to meet some new requirements with five types of agent, and present Web service based architecture of agents that is based on three types of agents.

To estimate the architecture, we propose an experiment system. This simulation implies that the architecture provides a very efficient method to design and implement ERP systems for small & medium-size Enterprises to assure a global optimization, flexibility of system, business agility, and the reusable ability of sub-systems or legacy systems in distributed and heterogeneous environments. However, there are many limitations of this paper. One of them is that we have not provided monitoring mechanism to supervise the process when agents communicate with each other. Secondly, the security issues are not resolved.

ACKNOWLEDGEMENTS

This work is supported by Key Laboratory of Information Management and Information Economics, MII, P.R.C, Grant No. F0607-35.

REFERENCES

1. B. Ye, Z. Ma, and X. Tu, Research on the Architecture of ERP System Based on Intelligent Autonomous Decentralized System, in *Proc. of The ISADS 2005 Proceedings* (2005), pp.616-619,
2. Q. Chen, *ERP-Step forward from Internal Integration* (Publishing House of Electronics Industry: Beijing, 2005).
3. C. Wu and Z. Gong, A Study of Web Service and Agent Technology, *Microprocessors*. Volume 4, pp.28-32, (2006).
4. N. Gibson, C.P. Holland, and B. Light, Enterprise Resource Planning: a Business Approach to Systems Development, in *Proc. of the 32nd Annual Hawaii International Conference, Volume 7* (1999), pp.9-13.
5. M. Kim, S. Lee, I. Park, J. Kim, and S. Park, Agent-Oriented Software Modeling, in *The Proc. of Software Engineering Conference (APSEC) Sixth Asia Pacific* (1999), pp.318-325.
6. B. Lea, M.C. Gupta, and W. Yu, A Prototype Multi-Agent ERP System: An Integrated Architecture and a Conceptual Framework, *Technovation*. Volume 25, Number 4, pp.433-441, (2005).

7. G. Pour, Integrating agent-oriented enterprise software engineering into software engineering curriculum, *Frontiers in Education*. Volume 3, pp.8-12, (2002).
8. M.L. Griss and G. Pour, Accelerating Development with Agent Components, *Computer*. Volume 34, Number 5, pp.37-43, (2001).
9. S. Wu and D. Kotak, Agent-Based Collaborative Project Management System for Distributed Manufacturing Systems, in *Proc. of The Man and Cybernetics of IEEE International Conference, Volume 2* (2003), pp.1223-1228.
10. F. Liu, L. Yao, W. Zhang, H. Liu, and H. Zhang, A Conceptual Model of Agent Mediated Web Service, in *Proc. of The Services Computing Proceedings of IEEE International Conference* (2004), pp.638-642.
11. I. Chen and C. Huang, An SOA-Based Software Development Management System, in *Proc. of The Web Intelligence of IEEE/WIC/ACM International Conference* (2006), pp.617-620.
12. Y. Huang, J. Zhang, Q. Zhang, and S. Wang, Intelligent Resource Planning of Testing Lab Based on CORBA and Multi-agent, in *Proc. of Machine Learning and Cybernetics, 2002 International Conference, Volume 1* (2002), pp.492-495.
13. M.L. Griss and G. Pour, Accelerating Development with Agent Components, *Computer*. Volume 34, Number 5, pp.37-43, (2001).
14. M.N. Huhns, Agents as Web services, *The Internet Computing (IEEE)*. Volume 6, Number 4, pp.93-95, (2002).
15. A. Sashima, N. Izumi, and K. Kurumatani, Location-Mediated Coordination of Web Services in Ubiquitous Computing, in *Proc. of The Web Services Proceedings of IEEE International Conference* (2004), pp.22-823.
16. Z. Xu and H. Wang, Research on Service Selection-Oriented Web Service Architecture Based on Agent, *Computer Technology and Development*. Volume 16, Number 9, pp.59-61, (2006).
17. M. Barbuceanu, R. Teigen, and M.S Fox, Agent Based Design and Simulation of Supply Chain Systems, in *Proc. of The Enabling Technologies: Infrastructure for Collaborative Enterprises of Proceedings Sixth IEEE workshops* (1997), pp.36-41.
18. X. Liu, Y. Sun, Y. Hao, and J. Xu, Research on Group-Oriented Enterprises Resource Planning: A Solution to Multiregional, Heterogeneous and Distributed Group Enterprises Application, in *Proc. of the Intelligent Control and Automation of WCICA, Volume 2* (2006), pp.7186-7190.

Constructing the Business Process of an Application System Based on Windows Workflow Foundation

Miao Cui, Jia Chen and Yu Jiang

School of Economics and Management, Dalian Maritime University, Dalian 16026, P.R China Jackychen6662000@yahoo.com.cn chenjia_8008@sina.com miaocui@newmail.dlmu.edu.cn

Abstract. The developing of the Application System always set the Business Process into the entire structure directly, each time the modification of the business process may make the program change largely. This structure adds the complexity to the system and hinders the flexibility of the system. Combining WWF and traditionally information system development theory to construct the Business Process can satisfy the need of the enterprise and make it easy to rebuild and update the Business Process.

Keywords: *Business process modeling, Business transformation, Workflow analysis, Workflow model*

1. INTRODUCTION

Today that is under the information-based tide, mostly business enterprise, especially the business enterprises of certain scale all carry on information-based construction. The developing of the Application System always set the Business Process into the entire structure directly, each time the modification of the business process may make the program change largely. This stiff structure increases the complexity of the system and baffles the flexibility of the system. The business enterprise which wants to exist under this exterior environment that full of competition and variety, have to meet the emergency with need, continuously adjusts itself, optimizes various business process of the business enterprise, and reconstructs the process. The integrated information management system should be an information collection, saving, handling, releasing and supporting the process reconstruction process, but the normal information management system is hard to do this.

The concept of the workflow comes into being under the construction of the modern information system. Workflow is a key technique which supports the business process reorganization and automation and can be supported and circulated by computer.

Please use the following format when citing this chapter:

Cui, M., Chen, J., Jiang, Y., 2007, in IFIP International Federation for Information Processing, Volume 254, Research and Practical Issues of Enterprise Information Systems II Volume 1, eds. L. Xu, Tjoa A., Chaudhry S. (Boston: Springer), pp. 609-615.

2. WINDOWS WORKFLOW FOUNDATION

2.1 Workflow Model and Composition

Microsoft Windows Workflow Foundation is a free, general and extensible framework, used for developing and performing application program that base on workflow. WWF provide a united platform for the products of Microsoft, customers and independent software developing company. It aims to provide a singular engine for workflow execution for all applications built on the Windows platform.

As a part of the upcoming Microsoft's next generation development Framework, WWF provides a workflow engine, a .NET trusteeship API (application program interface), runtime services, visible designer and debugger that integrate with Microsoft Visual Studio 2005, and can create and perform workflow that span client point and server point in the meantime, and can perform in all types .NET program.

2.2 The Control of WWF to Process Reconstruction

The most mature and most attraction side of workflow is the flexibility to set, perform and control process [1]. Figure 1 shows an examination and approve process model. In this process, carry on one class examination and approve to the application first, if pass to carry on the next operation, otherwise clue on do not pass. Figure 1

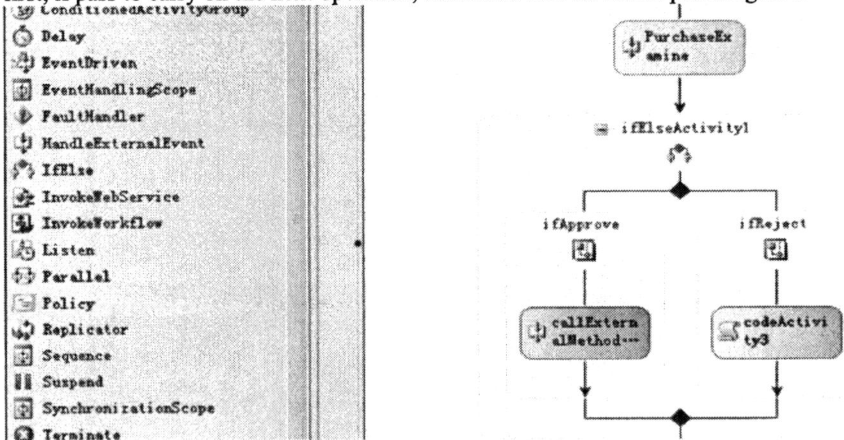

Figure 1. Old Examine Flow

shows the workflow model under WWF designer, as it shown, the left side of interface are some activity control, developer can add or delete them conveniently by dragging.

For the need of management, one class examination and approve has already can't satisfy the requirement of the original examination, based on the one class examination and approve, carry on secondary class examination and approve. In the WWF designer it is very conveniently to make an improvement to the old process. Just adds an ifElse activity to the original process. The new model shown as the figure 2, the activity callExternalMethod in figure 2 performs the same function as callExternalMethod in figure 1, the activity codeActivity1 and codeActivity3 in figure 2 also perform the same code as codeActivity1 in figure 1. CodeActivity1 is the replication of codeActivity3. On the contrary, if the secondary class examine and approve dose not needed, can delete it from the model conveniently, and does not influence the normal work of other workflows.

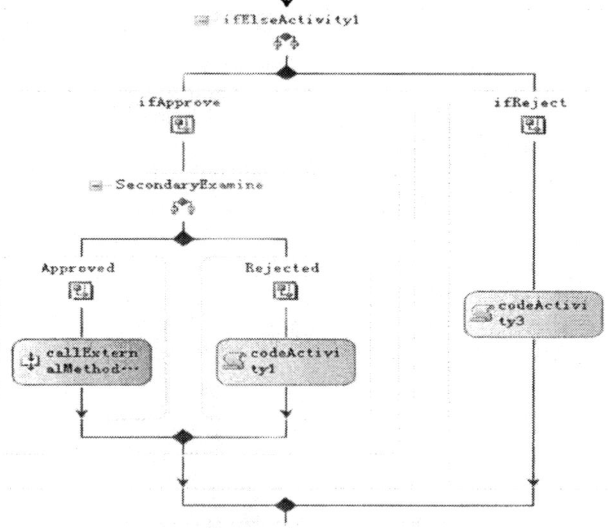

Figure 2. New Examine Flow

Therefore, the management information system which adopts WWF technique can consumedly raise the efficiency of the system develop, lower the development cost, promise the system better extensibility, flexibility.

3. PROCESS MODELLING OF WORKFLOW

3.1 The Definition of UML Activity Diagram

UML activity diagram is one of the graphics tools which is used to modelling for the dynamic behaviour of the system. UML activity diagram is substantively also a kind of flow chart, expresses the control flow from one activity to another, supports the expression of subsequent behaviour and conditional choice behaviour, and still supports the description of data flow. Especially suit the description of workflow.

UML activity diagram is a special kind of state machine, also a special kind of state graph. In a state graph, if most activities denote activity of the operation, and the transfer triggered by the activity, namely all or most events are performed by inner activities, is activity diagram [2]. Therefore, what activity diagram describes is the action of the object class which responds to the inner processing. It emphasizes the control flow from one activity to another. Usually, the activity diagram is on the supposition that there is no break off caused by the exterior events during the computer processing. UML activity diagram catch the result of the action (the work or activity that will be carried out) according to the variety of state. One activity will immediately get into the next activity after ending in an activity diagram.

3.2 UML Modelling of Warehouse Management System

The article will take warehouse management system for example, to explain the application of WWF in business process constructing. The system includes location management and in the location management module includes insert, delete, edit, and auto create location function.

Create location means based on the information of the selected warehouse (such as line, row, and layer) create the location circularly. If want to create location which have been created in the selected warehouse, should judge whether there are cargoes in the grid of the location first. If there are not cargoes, then can create, or can not create, the activity diagram shown as figure 3:

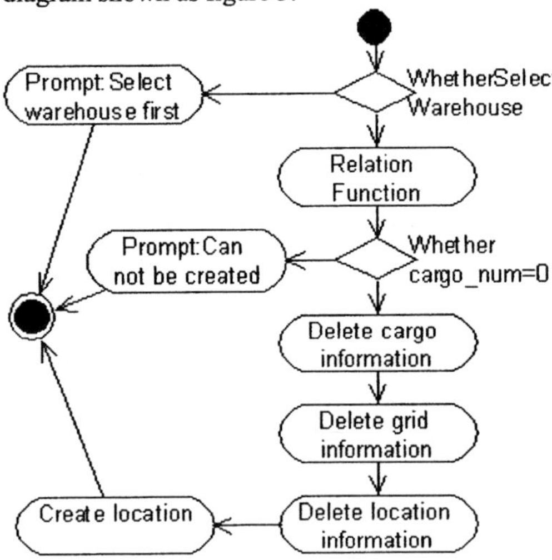

Figure 3. Activity Diagram of Creating Location

4. CARRY OUT WAREHOUSE MANAGEMENT SYSTEM

4.1 The Designing Thought of Process Management

There are two models supported by WWF: Sequential workflow model – comprising activities that execute in a predictable sequential path, and State machine model – a flow driven by events triggering state transitions [3].

There is no fixed model for designing workflow, take state machine model as main flow to control the state and take sequential workflow model as sub flow to carry out operation is not a bad way [4].

In the warehouse management system, include a lot of modules, each module perform different function and transfer many different sub modules, but what time is needed to transfer the sub modules is not sure beforehand. Thus adopt the state machine model is more suitable. In each state, the respond to the events can be carry out by sequential workflow model.

4.2 The Designing and Realization of Process Management

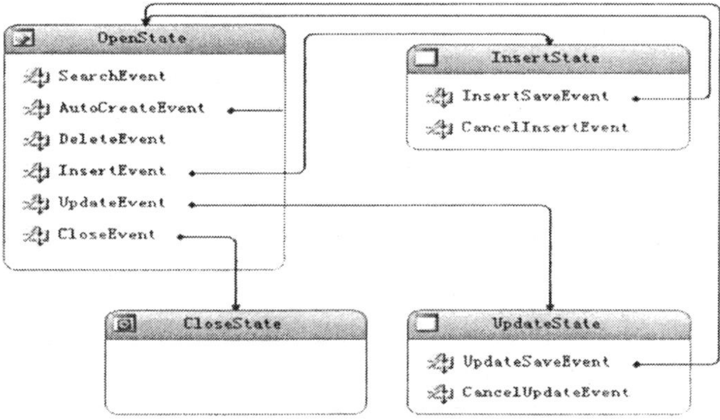

Figure 4. State Machine Model of Location Management

Location management module is a state, defined as initial state (OpenState). According to Figure 1, it includes search, insert, delete, edit and create function, and insert and edit function transfer insert and edit sub module which are defined as InsertState and UpdateState separately. InsertState and UpdateState are triggered by InsertEvent and UpdateEvent in the initial state. The events InsertSaveEvent and UpdateSaveEvent in the sub module perform save operation that is send the data into the database, and return to the initial state after operating successfully. The state machine model described shown as Figure 4.

The event AutoCreateEvent in the initial state is used for performing create location function. In the article 3.2, the activity diagram of create location has been given, still take it for example, the corresponding sequential workflow to Figure 4 shown as Figure 5:

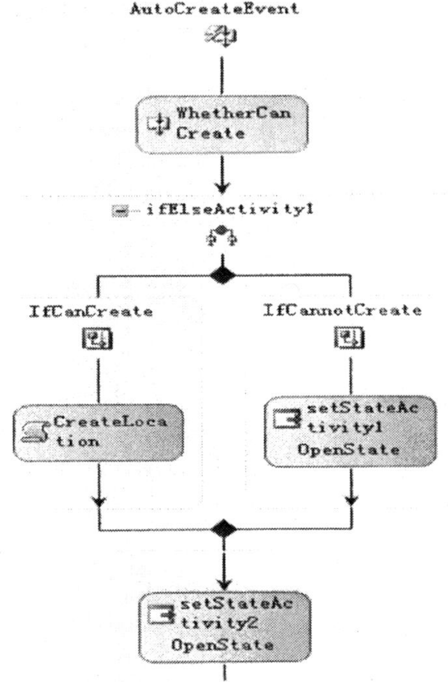

Figure 5. Sequential Workflow of Create Location

Event WhetherCanCreate judge whether can create location by implement the event FunRelationLocation of the interface IAutoCreate, if there are no cargoes in the grid, then implement the left side flow of ifElse, and circularly create location by implement code CreateLocation which include delete the information of the cargo, grid, and location, if there are still cargoes in the grid, then implement the right side flow of ifElse and the flow return to the initial state.

5. CONCLUSIONS

The article makes use of WWF framework which is released by Microsoft lately to construct warehouse management system based on .NET platform, constructs UML model of the location management module, and introduces a visible designing method based on WWF model. Combining traditionally developing technology of system and workflow technology make the manager supervise and optimize the flow exactly and conveniently, and make the business enterprise acquire larger income.

REFERENCES

1. F. Yushun, *Workflow Management Foundation* (Qinghua University Press: Beijing, 2001).
2. J. Arlow and I. Neustadt, *UML2 and the Unified Process* (China Machine Press: Beijing, 2006).
3. V. Yen, A node-centric analysis of metagraphs and its applications to workflow models, *Enterprise Information Systems*. Volume 1, Number 1, pp.139-159, (2007).
4. P. Andrew and J. Conard, *Presenting Windows Workflow Foundation*, Sams Publishing (2006). http://msdn.microsoft.com/workflow (Accessed October 1, 2006).

Linking Organizational Culture and Hospital Information Systems Implementation

Shan Wang[1], Norm Archer[2] and Yanli Pei[3]

[1]Department of Management Science, School of Business, Renmin University, 59 Zhong Guan Cun Avenue, Haidian District, Beijing 100872, P.R. China wangs7@gmail.com
[2]DeGroote School of Business, McMaster University, Hamilton L8S 4M4, ON, Canada archer@mcmaster.ca
[3]School of International Business, Beijing Foreign Studies University, Beijing 100089, P.R. China peiyanli@bfsu.edu.cn

Abstract. The impact of organizational culture on the successful implementation of information systems (IS) has been studied by some researchers. However, a close examination of the literature shows that researchers examined different attributes of organizational culture, and for the same culture attributes, researchers donot agree with the actual impact of these attributes on IS implementation. This paper seeks to identify a comprehensive set of relevant organizational attributes that have the potential to impact IS implementation in the healthcare setting. Seven organizational values are investigated through case studies, and most of the attributes are found to affect IT implementation success.

Keywords: *Enterprise Information Systems (EIS), IS success, Organizational culture*

1. INTRODUCTION

The use of information technology (IT) offers hospitals tremendous opportunities to attain operational and strategic benefits and positive financial performance[1]. The development and use of Hospital Information System (HIS) in the USA can be traced back to the 1960s, but in China it is a recent initiative [2]. The Golden Health project launched by Ministry of Health of P. R. China in 1995 marked the beginning of HIS development and adoption by hospitals.

Despite the push from the Chinese government, HIS diffusion in Chinese hospitals is limited. A survey showed that in China, 31% of hospitals implemented HIS, only 7% of which are the integrated HIS involving most functional departments across the entire hospitals[3]. The slow diffusion of HIS is attributed partly to its complexity. It is an enterprise information system (EIS) and is called hospital ERP. Organizational characteristics of Chinese hospitals also account for the slow diffusion. Chinese hospitals are normally subsidized and controlled by the government. They are less cost cautious and emphasize operational stability in their management. Organization decision making is centralized but communication is informal. These create barriers to the diffusion of HIS. Less cost cautious hospitals have limited incentives to deploy

Please use the following format when citing this chapter:

Wang, S., Archer, N., Pei, Y., 2007, in IFIP International Federation for Information Processing, Volume 254, Research and Practical Issues of Enterprise Information Systems II Volume 1, eds. L. Xu, Tjoa A., Chaudhry S. (Boston: Springer), pp. 617-626.

HIS, whereas centralized structure may lead to a lack of communication about HIS goals and importance between the top management and employees. Since some of the above potential reasons for the slow HIS diffusion are related to organizational culture, in this research we seek answers to the research question: what attributes of organizational culture affect HIS implementation success?

In the next section, we will provide a brief review of the concepts of organizational culture, and how organizational culture is linked to information system implementation and adoption. Hypotheses are then derived to guide data collection and analysis. We adopted a case study approach to illustrate our hypothesis. This paper contributes to the theories about the role of culture in HIS implementation by investigating a more comprehensive but relevant set of cultural attributes, and to practice by providing key directions for organizational change that would help hospitals to achieve greater HIS success.

2. LITERATURE REVIEW

2.1 Organizational Culture

There is no universally accepted definition of organizational culture, and some of the most cited culture definitions can be found in [4, 5]. The characteristics of culture are summarized as the following:

Firstly, culture is normally defined as the shared assumption and value of an organization, which can influence organizational behavior through the formation of norms, rule and practices. It is natural to link culture with organizational performance since by definition, values are assumed to influence or control employee behavior, which is in turn the source of organizational performance[6].

Secondly, culture is hard to observe and articulate. So researchers define them in three levels: value, norm and practice[4]. These three levels of culture are more and more observable and increasingly being able to be articulated.

Thirdly, due to the vague definition of culture and value, it is impossible to exhaust attributes of culture. We could see this from burgeon of organizational culture measurements: to name a few, Competing Value Framework, Organizational Cultural Inventory [7], Hofstede's five cultural dimensions [5], etc.

2.2 The Role of Culture in IS implementation

IS Researchers also tried to link organizational culture to the success of IS implementation[8-11]. Leidner and Kayworth[12] provided an excellent overview of the role of culture in IS adoption and implementation. Based on Competing Value Framework, McDermott and Stock [11]examined how different culture type(market, adhocracy, development and hierarchy) are linked to different IT benefits, including satisfaction, operational, organizational, and competitive benefits).

A detailed examination of previous research results showed that researchers do not agree on how IT effectiveness is affected by culture. For example, Harper and Utley[9]'s and Kanungo[10]'s conclusions contradict with each other. Harper verified that people-oriented culture lead to greater chance of successful IT implementation, whereas Kanungo's work showed that such a culture is not related to the satisfaction of IT implementation. Contradiction in the results can also be found in Ruppel and Harrington[8]'s and McDermott[11]'s work.

These contradictions may be partly due to the use of different measurement of organizational culture and IT effectiveness, but it also implies that more empirical work is needed to verify what organizational culture attributes affect IT implementation effectiveness. Most previous researchers also focus on investigating one culture attribute or instrument, but in our research, we try to include a more comprehensive set of relevant cultural attributes that may affect the HIS implementation, including professional culture and IT culture.

3. HYPOTHESIS

Our work is based on Detert et al [13]'s culture framework, which summarized important organizational attributes that are potentially conducive to the implementation of Total Quality Management (TQM). Their culture framework also has overlap with the cultural instruments that are mentioned in the literature review.

In Detert et al.'s framework, seven culture attributes are considered relevant to IS implementation: (1) the basis of truth and rationality, (2) long- or short-term orientation (3) stability vs. change (4) production and people orientation (5) isolation vs. collaboration (6) centralized vs. decentralized control (7) internal vs. external focus. These dimensions are also used by Jones et al. [14] to develop IS implementation culture, and to explain how implementation culture affects the effectiveness of ERP implementation. In this research, we use these seven attributes as general organizational culture attributes, rather than IS implementation culture.

The basis of truth and rationality refers to the extent to which an organization's decision making is based on systematical collection of data and facts, scientific modeling, and statistical analysis, or are experiential and intuitive in nature[13]. If an organization's decision making tends to be scientific and rational, the organization may value the support of information systems. Information systems are not suitable for experiential decision making style since they are poor media that can only accommodate codified knowledge. In China, why the failure rate of ERP system in state owned enterprises(SOEs) is much higher than that of private ventures is attributed to SOEs' experiential decision making style[15].

Hypothesis one: Rational decision making culture leads to greater HIS success.

Long- vs. short-term orientation refers to the time horizon of an organization that "*helps determine whether leaders and other organizational members adopt long-term planning and goal setting or focus primarily on the here-and-now*"[13]. Long-term horizon culture fits HIS more since HIS is a long term undertaking, with lagged benefits, relatively long implementation time and ongoing improvement of software.

The hospital management must be patient and farseeing, in order to see a successful HIS implementation. So we propose:

Hypothesis two: A hospital with long-term oriented culture will achieve a higher HIS success than a short term oriented culture.

Stability vs. change culture refers to the extent to which an organization is more stable in nature, or tends more to encourage innovation, personal growth, continuous organizational improvement and changes [16]. The failure of many EISs is frequently attributed to organizational inertia and a lack of organizational change. Since HIS is an innovation for hospitals, it also demands significant organizational innovation capacity and changes in the hospital structure and work process. So we propose:

Hypothesis three: change oriented organizational culture tends to favor the HIS implementation

Production vs. people oriented cultures put different emphases on task and people issues[16]. In a production oriented culture, individuals focuses more on getting the task done efficiently (also called efficiency-oriented culture), whereas in people oriented culture, individuals value social relationships and "being comfortable" in the workplace more, and similar to collectivism culture. The effects of production or people oriented culture on information system implementation are among the most frequently tested cultural attributes. However, their results are quite different. People-oriented culture could be conducive for IS implementation since it encourages user involvement by trusting employees to do a good job and by bringing more ideas to the implementation process[9], whereas efficiency oriented culture could also encourage IS adoption since IS is an impersonal tool that help computers to finish job efficiently . Temporarily, we suppose:

Hypothesis four: people-oriented organizational culture tends to favor the HIS implementation.

Isolation vs. collaboration cultures refers to the extent to which individual work or cooperation among employees is valued in an organization. It is similar to team oriented culture, and is also among the most investigated culture attributes. For an EIS, cross functional communication and collaboration are important. Martinson found that ERP implementation with a cross functional team will achieve greater success. Since HIS is an enterprise level information system, we assume:

Hypothesis five: Collaboration-oriented culture tends to favor HIS implementation.

Centralized and decentralized control refers to the extent to which the decisions are centralized to the top management, and the activities in the organization are tightly controlled. It is normally said that decentralized control is favorable for IS implementation since participating in decision making and more flexibility and autonomy in the use of IS will encourage user involvement and enthusiasm. So we propose:

Hypothesis six: decentralized control tends to favor HIS implementation and use.

Internal vs. external orientation refers to the extent to which organizational improvements are driven by a focus on internal process, improvements or by external, stakeholder desires. External oriented organizations also search actively for new ideas and leadership from outside their traditional bounds. The effect of internal vs. external orientation on HIS success is two sided. Firstly, an internal focus of an organization may adopt an HIS for internal motivation that uses HIS to improve internal process.

Secondly, researches showed that the use of external consultants is helpful for the adoption of e-business and ERP systems[17]. So we temporally propose that

Hypothesis seven: Internal-oriented culture and the tendency to proactive use of external information tend to favor HIS implementation and use.

4. METHODOLOGY

A case study approach was adopted to preliminarily test the above hypotheses. This is because the relationship between culture and HIS implementation must be studied in real organizational setting[18] and few studies have done on this topic, especially in Chinese hospitals.

We studies two hospitals in China: a Chinese medicine hospital in a big city in north china (Hospital I), and a county hospital in middle China (Hospital II). Both are public hospitals that are sponsored and supervised by the local government. For each hospital, we visit them on site, observing how users use information system, finding indicators of the hospital culture, and interviewing staffs either onsite or through telephone. The study last 5 months, including two visits to hospital I, which last one – three days for each, and one visits to hospital II, which lasts two days. The interviews are done both during site visits and through telephones, and were guided by a semi-structured questionnaire. In each hospital, we interviewed doctors, nurses and the managers who know the HIS adoption and implementation decisions well.

5. CASE STUDY RESULTS

5.1 Case Introduction

Hospital I is located in the capital city of a province in North China, and is one of the biggest Chinese medicine hospitals in China. This is a comprehensive class-3, grade-A hospital (the highest level of hospital rank in china). It is affiliated with a famous Chinese medicine university, has 744 beds, and 913 staffs including doctors (many of which are also professors), nurses and administrative staff.

This hospital started to implement HIS in 2000, and is claimed to be the earliest hospital that implemented HIS in the city. However in 2005 they changed their system vendor since the old vendor went out of business. The current HIS has the following functions: patient admission and registration, inpatient management, payment processing, order communication between departments, pharmacy management, and material management. During our interview, we found that the users in general were satisfied with the use of this system. However, problems exist. Most users mentioned that the system is too slow, sometimes even slower than manual processing. A few users, especially some young staffs complain the inflexible of system interfaces and functions.

Hospital II is the best local hospital in a county in Middle China. It is a class-2, grade-A hospital, with 325 beds and 674 staffs (including 387 professionals). It is a teaching hospital that provides training to students from several medical schools that are close to this county. Hospital II implemented HIS in 2006. Before HIS, the drug department and accounting department have used single PCs to record drug and do bookkeeping. The currently used HIS includes most functions as those implemented in hospital I, except for doctor workstation, information access by hospital management, and some workflow and parameter variations. Overall, the hospital users are satisfied with the use of HIS, although a few nurses complained the extra work they need to do, such as entering the order according to prescriptions. However, due to other benefits of HIS, such as reduced travel between wards, pharmacy, financial department, they seem to be satisfied.

5.2 Results

The case study results are arranged by case comparison across each attributes since we believe that comparison and cross case difference will better enable us to illustrate and test the hypothesis. Since the system in Hospital I is much more advanced, so we evaluate the success of HIS in hospital I is greater than that of hospital II. The results are summarized in Table 1, and are explained in detail.

Table 1 Cross Case Comparision

Culture attributes	Hospital I	Hospital II	Hypothesis Evaluation
The basis of truth and rationality	Medium rational level due to relatively higher managerial skill	Less rational due to limited managerial skill	Y
Long vs. short term orientation	Long-term orientation	Relatively short term orientation	Y
Stability vs. change culture	Relatively change oriented	More Stability	Y
Production vs. people oriented cultures	Production oriented	People oriented	Y
Isolation vs. collaboration cultures	Collaboration	Collaboration	N
Centralized vs. decentralized control	Centralized	centralized	N
Internal vs. external orientation	Internal orientation and professional advice from external software company	External orientation	Y

Note: Y/N refers to "yes"/ "no", which means that the hypothesis corresponding to each cultural attribute is supported/not supported.

The basis of truth and rationality: Senior managers in both hospital claim that data were important to their decision. One manager in Hospital II commented that since they were public hospitals, the tactic and operational decisions were made in the hospital but the strategic decisions about the hospital were made in the local Bureau of Health and were greatly affected by policies of Ministry of Health. At the lower tactic and operational level of decisions, a reliance on data is necessary. The reports from the accounting and statistical department were submitted to the managers every week. Managers in hospital I made similar comments. They deemed management control and access to more information that was not available before as one of the biggest benefits and a major incentive to adopt such as a system. However, we noticed that some managers in Hospital I accessed computerized information directly, while most managers in hospital II still relied on printed reports. The limited management knowledge of managers in hospital II also constrained their level of rational decisions. So we think the level of rationality is slightly lower in hospital I. This illustrate that a culture with less rationality of decisions will lead to lower HIS success due to limited incentive and desire for more data.

Long vs. short term orientation: Managers in both hospitals suggested that IT should be a long investment. But for the implementation process, their view and practices were different. The usage of HIS in hospital I lasted for 7 years whereas it has existed for only one year in hospital II. The system in hospital I was customized, which took time to develop and test. So during the implementation, software engineers stayed onsite for half a year. The situation is different in hospital II. The system in hospital II was a off the shelf product that has already been tested in another hospital. The software engineers stayed onsite for only two weeks. However, one common characteristic between them is that, once the system launched, all the employs were required to learn how to use it within one week. This was to guarantee that it caused minimum interference to the daily operation to the hospitals.

From the above argument, we can see that the hospital I has a more long term vision to the IT investment, and leave more time for its implementation. So its system is more success in terms of degree of diffusion.

Stability vs. Change: Hospital I is relatively more changed oriented than hospital II. This can be explained mainly by two factors.

First, hospital I is a research oriented hospital that's affiliated to a Chinese medicine university. It has a tradition to encourage innovation. The excellent pool of staffs, including Ph.Ds, numerous master graduates, renders the innovation possible.

Second, hospital II is a local hospital. They are not research oriented but service oriented. Since it is a small city, it's hard to attract talented people, and undergraduates from medical schools are staffs with highest degree in this hospital. The limited technical skill restricts the hospital to be innovative in treatments. Another issue that makes hospital I so conservative is the poor hospital-patient relationship, which is partly attributed to rocketing charges by hospitals in China right now. Patients' distrust puts high pressure on doctors and hospital management, so that they became conservative and more formal in procedures in order to protect themselves. We noticed that poor doctor-patient relationships also affected bigger hospitals such as hospital I, but the effect was much less, since patients still trusted their technical skill. Furthermore, when patients are transferred from local to bigger hospitals in big cities, they are away from local "guanxi" network and is less willing to conflict with doctors.

Due to the above two reasons, we think hospital I is more changed oriented than hospital II. As for the implementation of IT, hospital I made adaptation either to their workflow or to the system, to ensure better performance, whareas in hospital II, only parameters were changed to accommodate hospital specific situation.

Production vs. people oriented cultures: A mixed people and production oriented culture is observed in both hospitals. Hospital service is special since it is about people's life. So doctors and nurses are cautious and try best to do jobs well. Sometimes in order to provide the right treatment, they have to sacrifice personal relationships. So in either hospital, the culture is not entirely production or people oriented. However, the following observation made us to evaluate the culture of hospital I more production oriented and that of hospital II more people oriented.

(1) The sense of competition among doctors and nurses are slightly stronger in hospital I, whereas in hospital II, local people are more satisfied with status quo.

(2) In IT implementation, we found that in hospital II, employee tended to help each in learning how to use HIS, whereas in hospital I, people were at a distance, being less willing to seeking help from friends but more from the IT department.

Since HIS in hospital I is more successful than that in hospital II, it seems that production oriented culture foster greater success of HIS, for the reason that the efficiency oriented culture drives people to learn how to use HIS efficiently, and to seek services from professionals.

Isolation vs. collaboration cultures: In both hospitals, different functional departments collaborate a lot since hospital service is patient centered. In order to cure a patient, collaboration frequently happens between outpatient and inpatient departments, between financial, drug and clinical departments, between nurses and doctors, and between different clinical departments. So we observed that despite the cross enterprise characteristic of HIS, conflict in departmental interfaces seldom occurred, and even if happened, can be resolved quickly. It seems that collaboration oriented culture are favorable for HIS implementation. But due to the similar level of collaboration, we can not explain the difference of HIS success between two hospitals from the collaboration culture perspective. More evidence is needed to make a solid conclusion.

Centralized and decentralized control: Both hospitals are quite centralized. The decision makings in both hospitals are centralized to the top management. Employees are distant from the top management, and are controlled by hospital procedures and policies. Centralization is favorable to the diffusion of HIS, since employees may perceive the use of HIS as an imperative. As one manager in hospital I said: "sometimes keeping a distance with employee is better for management by maintaining a sense of authorization". Again due to the lack of evidence to justify that the level of centralization in two hospitals' are different, we can not explain the difference of HIS success between them from a centralization cultural perspective. More evidence is needed to make a conclusion.

Internal vs. external orientation: As for non IT internal vs. external orientation, both hospitals have connections with external entities, such as governments, other hospitals and universities. However, due to the local nature of hospital II, the doctors also admitted that their opportunities to study in other hospitals were much less than those in big hospitals such as hospital I. When it comes to HIS implementation, hospital I tends to have a clear goal of greater management control, whereas in hospital II, the launch of HIS is more a result of studying other hospitals. A manager in hospital I commented that by implementing HIS, they could save at least 600,000RMB each year, just on the loss of charges due to previous poor management control. Hospital I seemed to have a clear internal motivation to adopt such a system, and seeked professional advices from software engineers. So the conclusion is that internal-oriented culture and the tendency to proactively use of external advice tend to favor HIS implementation and use.

6. CONCLUSIONS

We have investigated the role of nine culture attributes on HIS success, including the basis of truth and rationality, long- or short-term orientation, stability vs. change, production- and people-oriented culture, isolation vs. collaboration, centralized vs. decentralized control, internal or external focus, physician-dominated authoritarian culture, and positive IT value. We found the support for most hypotheses, except for those about isolation vs. collaboration; centralized or decentralized control, and professional culture. The managerial implication of this research is that the hospital leaders can take measures to change the cultural environment that is favorable for HIS implementation.

The future research direction includes investigating each cultural attribute in depth, and measuring them quantitatively. Another research direction is to include more hospitals, especially private hospitals, in the case study. Although we concluded that physician-dominated authoritarian professional culture, which was found affecting HIS adoption in western countries, were less relevant in china, more Chinese professional culture could be explored in the future.

ACKNOWLDGEMENTS

This research was generally supported by Beijing Foreign Studies University Research funds (Grant IDs are 06040 and 032117)

REFERENCES:

1. E. Ammenwerth, S. Gräber, T. Bürkle, and C. Iller, *Evaluation of Health Information Systems: Challenges and Approaches, in E-Health Systems Diffusion and Use: The Innovation, the User and the UseIT Model*, eds. T. Spil and R.W. Schuring (Idea Group Publishing: Hershey, PA, 2005), pp.212-236.
2. X. Zhang, Present status and development of hospital information system, *Chinese Medicine Modern Distance Education of China.* Volume 9, Number 9, pp.10-, (2005).
3. B. Li, Seven Challenges Faced by Hospital Information System in China, *Discovering Value.* Volume 2, Number 5, pp.86-, (2004).
4. E.H. Schein, *Organizational Culture and Leadership* (Jossey Bass Wiley: San Francisco, 1985).
5. G. Hofstede, The Cultural Relativity of Organizational Practices and Theories, *Journal of International Business Studies.* Volume 14, Number 2, pp.75-89, (1983).

6. R.E. Quinn and G.M. Spreitzer, The Psychometrics of the Competing Values Culture Instrument and an Analysis of the Impact of Organizational Culture on Quality of Life, *Research in Organizational Change and Development.* Number 5, pp.115-142, (1991).
7. R. Cooke and J. Szumal, The Reliability and Validity of the Organizational Culture Inventory, *Psychological Reports.* Volume 72, Number 3, pp.1299-330, (1991).
8. C.P. Ruppel and S.J. Harrington, Sharing Knowledge through Intranets: A Study of Organizational Culture and Intranet Implementation, *IEEE Transactions on Professional Communication.* Volume 44, Number 1, pp.37-52, (2001).
9. G.R. Harper and D.R. Utley, Organizational culture and successful information technology implementation, *Engineering Management Journal.* Volume 13, Number 2, pp.11-, (2001).
10. S. Kanungo, An Empirical Study of Organizational Culture and Network-based Computer Use, *Computers in Human Behavior.* Volume 14, Number 1, pp.79-91, (1998).
11. C.M. McDermott and G.N. Stock, Organizational culture and advanced manufacturing technology implementation, *Journal of Operations Management.* Volume 17, Number 5, pp.521-533, (1999).
12. D.E. Leidner and T. Kayworth, Review: A Review of Culture in Information Systems Research: Toward a Theory of Information Technology Culture Conflict, *MIS Quarterly.* Volume 30, Number 2, pp.357-399, (2006).
13. J.R. Detert, R.G. Schroeder, and J.J. Maurie, A Framework for Linking Culture and Improvement Initiatives in Organizations, *The Academy of Management Review.* Volume 25, Number 4, pp.850-863, (2000).
14. M.C. Jones, M. Cline, and S. Ryan, Exploring knowledge sharing in ERP implementation: an organizational culture framework, *Decision Support Systems.* Volume 41, Number 2, pp.411-434, (2006).
15. M.G. Martinsons, ERP in China, One package, Two Profiles, *Communications of the ACM.* Volume 47, Number 7, p.65, (2004).
16. R. Cooke and J. Lafferty, *Organizational Culture Inventory* (OCI) (Human Synergistics: Plymouth, MI, 1987).
17. P. Ifinedo and N. Nahar, ERP systems success: an empirical analysis of how two organizational stakeholder groups prioritize and evaluate relevant measures, *Enterprise Information Systems.* Volume 1, Number 1, pp.25-48, (2007).
18. R.K. Yin, *Case Study Research: Design and Methods* (International Educational and Professional Publisher: Thousand Oaks, 1994).

A Study on the Integration Model of EIS Based on SOA

Xu Yang and Zhanhong Xin

School of Economics and Management, Beijing University of Posts and Telecommunications, Beijing 100876, P.R. China yangx.china@gmail.com

Abstract. Recently, the enterprise application integration has been a crucial requirement for the progress of EIS. However, the integration of those heterogeneous or distributed information systems often encounters problems related to complex management and maintenance, as well as low compatibility. Nevertheless, to totally abandon the former system or to re-develop a new great EIS may result in costly investment, lengthy development cycle and tremendous risk accompanying with the rapid service changes. While, Service-oriented architecture by adopting the loose coupling application program component technology, provides precisely defined and standardized service interface and reusable service that can assist the EIS engineers to dynamically construct the entire system more speedy, more reliable, and more reusable, and to cope with the demand changes more easily. This paper focuses on the integration model of EIS based on SOA. It proposes the implementation suggestions on SOA system and the rational risk analysis. Then, taking a telecommunication operator as an example, it presents a propositional framework for EIS integration based on SOA.

Keywords: *EIS, SOA, EAI*

1. INTRODUCTION

Nowadays, facing with the rapid change of market demand and the intensifying competition situation, the enterprises gradually shift their management pattern from product-oriented to customer-oriented. Therefore, the enterprises must build fluent information flow, break barriers within the enterprise information systems (EIS), eliminate information silos, and develop a holistic enterprise application platform. There is no wonder that enterprise application integration (EAI) tops the priority list of many CIOs [1]. The integration of enterprise IT system undergoes the following stages:

Stage 1: Integration of Isolated Systems. The integration is usually realized by direct access to data source. Due to the fact that the former information systems were developed to meet the specific demand of customers, the foundation of those IT systems were heterogeneous, distributed or isolated. Therefore, the need for specific program interfaces will result in tremendous numbers of interfaces, with expensive management and maintenance expenditure.

Stage 2: EAI. The enterprise starts to pay attention to the layout of EIS; EAI has occupied the main stream of integration. The usual way is to abandon the old application and to build a large complex enterprise application platform, which adopts

Please use the following format when citing this chapter:

Yang, X., Xin, Z., 2007, in IFIP International Federation for Information Processing, Volume 254, Research and Practical Issues of Enterprise Information Systems II Volume 1, eds. L. Xu, Tjoa A., Chaudhry S. (Boston: Springer), pp. 627-633.

ETL and Data Warehouse technique to integrate the old data, applies middleware (or integration adapter) to integrate the applications. This method realizes tight coupled structure, but results in low flexibility, complex structure and costly investment. What's more, this structure often implies huge risk accompanying with the rapid service changes, and long mature period accompanying with continuous update.

Stage 3: Service-Oriented EAI. Service-Oriented is regarded as the benchmark of EAI progress. The application systems could be invoked by other systems through uniform service interfaces. Meanwhile, the gradual maturity of Web Service provides the standard system architecture for integration, and meets the requirements on flexibility and interoperability, which together lead to a new stage of integration.

The paper discusses how SOA can be used to achieve EAI with loose coupling, high flexibility and making use of uniform infrastructures.

2. INTEGRATION MODEL OF EIS BASED ON SOA

Service-Oriented Architecture (SOA) is a component model, which connects the units with distinct application functions, as "Services", under the assistance of well-defined interfaces and contracts [2]. However, SOA is not a specific technique, but firm-level service-oriented system architecture. SOA enjoys the following characteristics and advantages:

1. Loosely coupled service architecture: SOA suffices the application environment with high agility and easy maintenance or correction. Those features establish the flexibility and diminish the complexity and dependency of services. Therefore, SOA can be chosen as the best IT architecture to satisfy the unknown future business demand.
2. Standardized uniform interface: SOA accomplishes the interaction between various services in a uniform and general way with the help of the neutral interface. In this way, both the location transparency of the application program and the independence of platform and protocol are realized, as well as the universal implement of SOA within firm or outside integration.
3. Combination and re-usage of services: SOA achieves dynamic and reusable service, and the by-products of this method are the protection of existing IT assets, the reduction of development and maintenance expenditure, the shortening of developing cycle, as well as the simplification of basic architecture and the lessening of risks.

2.1 SOA Reference Architecture

SOA is designed to be a holistic IT architecture, and the integration model based on SOA usually takes the following form, as shown in figure 1[3].

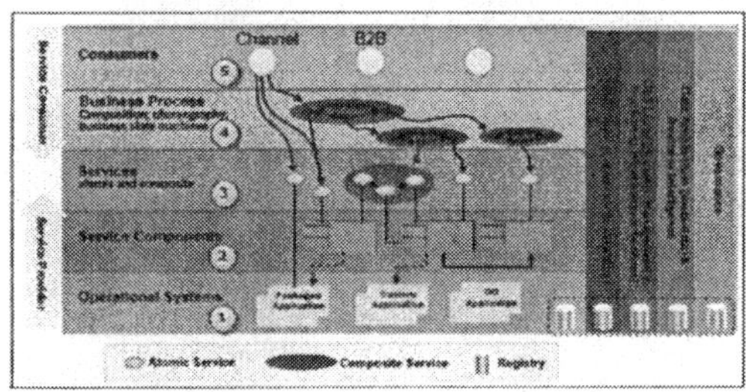

Figure 1. SOA Foundation Reference Architecture

This model consists of several layers. The lowest layer is the existing program or application software owned by the firms. The second one is called the Component Layer, which encapsulates the functions of the systems in the lowest layer into different service components. The third layer is the core one in SOA, which builds the function components of the lower layers into services with different functions. The forth one is called the Business Process Layer. Within this layer, the encapsulated services are used to construct the business process between systems. The fifth layer is viewed as the Expression Layer, which provides customers with interface services, such as portal. The five layers mentioned above require an integrated environment to support their operation, which is furnished by ESB (see the followings). Some complementary functions are also included in SOA systems, such as QoS, safety management, and so on.

Within the architecture of SOA, Enterprise Service Bus (ESB) plays a crucial role. ESB is a logical architecture, providing interconnection service such as Service Transform, Route, Notify and Augment between service consumer and service provider, as shown in figure 2. ESB simplifies the integration and flexible reuse of business components by providing a dependable and scalable infrastructure that connects disparate applications and IT resources, mediates their incompatibilities, orchestrates their interactions, and makes them broadly available as services for additional uses [4].

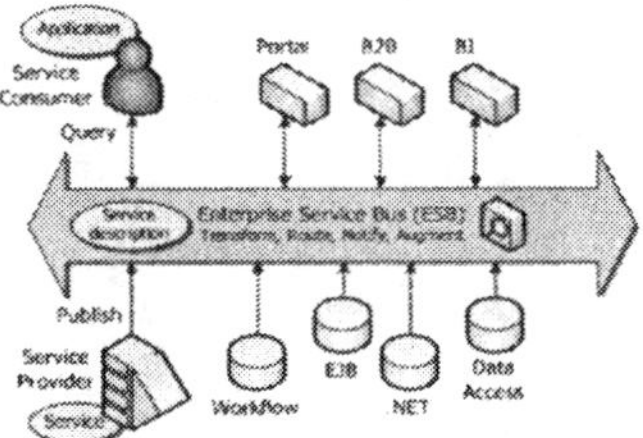

Figure 2. Enterprise Service Bus

2.2 The Application of SOA

SOA is related with the holistic IT architecture, which implies a lengthy time of construction. The way of top-down implementation is often accomplished with large scale of risks, including risks such as whether quick service response can be provided, whether security and QoS can be ensured, and whether lengthy deployment and large investment are needed, etc. Considering the agility of the services, the application of SOA could be based on the service-oriented modeling and architecture (SOMA [5]), start from the basic business demand, and adopt the bottom-up way of implementation, which has four stages:

In stage 1, construction of independent service: encapsulate the object-oriented applications into service functions, which are often the basic and reusable services or processes. In stage 2, integration of services based on business functions: combine the encapsulated services using ESB, to realize the whole business process. In stage 3, firm-level IT transformation: transform the existing EIS, recombine business processes under service-oriented rules, and accomplish the EIS based on SOA. In stage 4, flexible business application according to demand: timely develop the future business process and application systems with the help of SOA. The application frame of SOA is shown in figure 3.

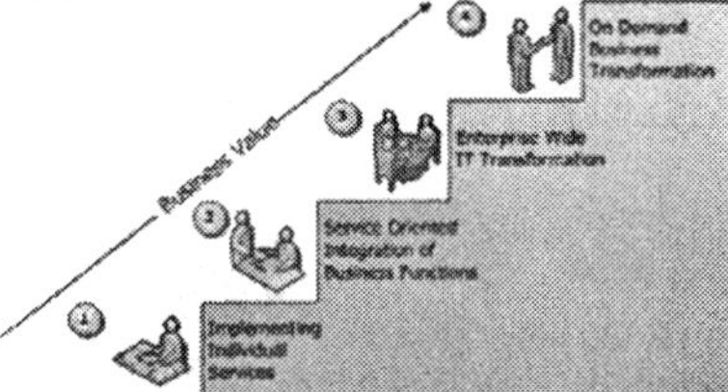

Figure 3. The Application Frame of SOA

3. A CASE STUDY OF TELECOMMUNICATION OPERATOR

3.1 Problem Description

The development of EIS of Chinese telecommunication operators has stepped into the integration stage. All of the Chinese telecom operators built large business support system (BSS, such as Charging and Settling System for telecommunication service), operation support system (OSS, such as Network Management System), management support system (MSS, such as OA, HR, Financial, etc.). For example, through the centralization of multi-local-level systems into a single-province-level system, the business and operation support system (BOSS) of China Mobile has been a core business support platform involving functions such as mobile service commission and allocation, charging and settling, accounting, and so on. China Mobile also attempt to construct Uniform Data Platform and Integrated Application Platform to integrate data and application in firm-scope. However, lack of holistic plan, those systems still can not satisfy the development of telecom services and network.

Customer relationship management (CRM) is a representative system for this situation. Even though the management emphasis is shifting from service-centered to customer-centered, a uniform CRM application has not been formed at this moment. Due to the fact that the data is stored in different IT systems, there is a barrier for quick and accordant response when customers make a consultation, ask for a changing of service, or require other demand by different channels such as business hall, 10086(Call Center of China Mobile), 12580(Mobile Information Interactive Inquiry Center of China Mobile) or China Mobile website. The fail of quick response lowers the quality of service, prohibits the experience of customers, and results in the reduction of customer satisfaction, as shown in figure 4.

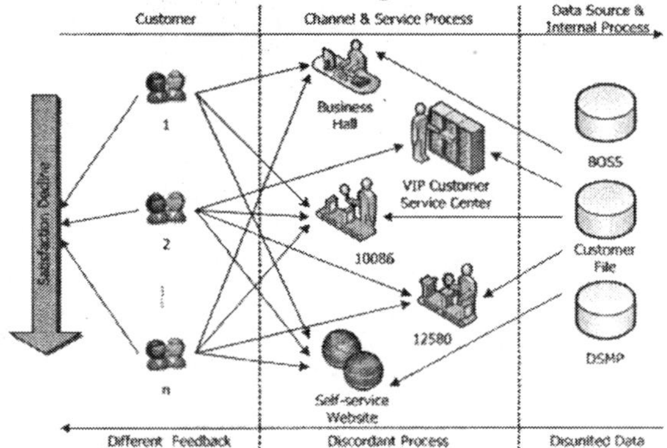

Figure 4. A CRM Lacking a Uniform Customer View

Under this condition, the operators launch on the construction of a holistic CRM system. Their primary consideration is to combine the services such as 10086, 12580 into the BOSS system, to build Uniform Customer View and to realize the customer-oriented service support system. However, the problems related to the large scale and heterogeneous of legacy systems would disadvantageously influence the holistic IT architecture and result in high expenditure.

3.2 Solution of SOA

To solve the above problems, a uniform CRM system could be build by SOA: first, componenting the inner-process functions (service commission and allocation, etc.) of BOSS or DSMP and the outer-process functions (customer inquiry, service alteration requisition, customer feedback, etc.) of 10086 or 12580, and then encapsulate into reusable services, and in turn, combine a series of services into a complete customer serving process (e.g. service alteration process). This process can be adopted by the upper service systems, and finally the uniform CRM is realized. Because the uniqueness of services, the status of all services through all channels are identical from the perspective of customers, and thus, the Uniform Customer View is formulated. The transformation into customer-centered could be successfully completed through the integration of channels. The uniform CRM based on SOA is shown in figure 5.

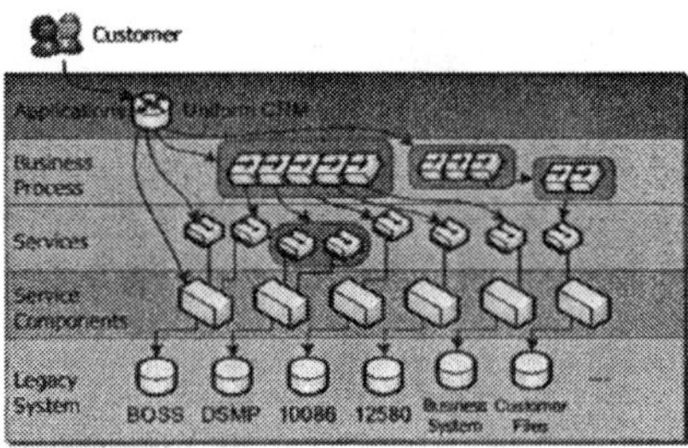

Figure 5. The Uniform CRM Based on SOA

4. CONCLUSIONS

Compared with other EIS architectures, the superiority of SOA is relying on flexibility, interoperability and reusability. By adopting loose coupling application program component model, it is possible to improve the value of business and the value of enterprises through analyzing and implementing of SOA.

For those telecom operators, who are experiencing transformation and facing with enormous subscribers and various telecom services with different tariffs and QoS, the deployment of SOA could integrate the former applications and provide powerful supports for BRP in one way of maintaining the existing flexible service applications and in the other way of constructing firm-level IT architecture to satisfy the future demand by quick response.

ACKNOWLEDGEMENTS

This work is supported by the Open Fund Project F0607-35, Key Laboratory of Information Management and Economics, MII, P.R.C.

REFERENCES

1. K.Channabasavaiah, K.Holley, and Jr.E.Tuggle, *Migrating to a service-oriented architecture*, IBM (2003). http://www.ibm.com/developerworks/library/ws-migratesoa/ (Accessed Apr. 2007).
2. Y. Liu and B. Li, The Operation Support Systems Based on SOA, *Microcomputer Information*. Volume 23, Number 1, pp.248-249, (2007).
3. *Best Practices for SOA Management*, IBM (2007). http://www.redbooks.ibm.com/abstracts/redp4233.pdf (Accessed Jun. 2007).
4. Anonymous, *Enterprise Service Bus (ESB)*, Progress Software. http://www.sonicsoftware.com/solutions/service_oriented_architecture/enterprise_service_bus/index.ssp (Accessed Jun. 2007).

5. N. Bieberstein, S. Bose, M. Fiammante, K. Jones, and R. Shah, *Service-Oriented Architecture Compass: Business Value, Planning, and Enterprise Roadmap* (IBM Press: 2005).
6. *Web Services Architecture*, W3C Working Draft (2002).
7. S. Pan, EAI and Its Application in Telecom Industry, *Telecommunications Science*. Number 7, pp.18-20, (2005).
8. S. Liu, W. Han, J. Liu, and G. Yin, Research on a Framework of Application Integration Based on SOA, *Microelectronics & Computer*. Volume 23, pp.199-201, (2006).

A Research on Data Modeling of Enterprises Based on Control System

Shilun Ge, Nan Ren and Hong Miao

School of Economics and Management, Jiangsu University of Science and Technology, Zhenjiang 212003, Jiangsu, P.R. China jzgsl@jzerp.com rennan_hb@sohu.com miaohong98@hotmail.com

Abstract. The key to establish enterprise information system successfully is to make a comprehensive planning of enterprise data. This paper, taking large-piece one-of-a-kind production as its background, based on the analysis on enterprise objects, enterprise products and management activities according to enterprise control system elements, put forward the classification of enterprise data on enterprise state, enterprise feature, enterprise behavior and enterprise performance, and a new description frame to express them by using the quintuple expression and situation calculus from first-order predicate. The result of it records enterprise management activities, reflects enterprises' state, and offers data support for management decision-making, which is also to provide the initial data criterion for enterprise information systems.

Keywords: *Control system, Data model, Data criterion, Situation calculus, Enterprise information system (EIS)*

1. INTRODUCTION

Enterprise information systems help to describe the enterprise and its products, to record the management activities, to show the enterprise state, to guide and control enterprise behaviors and to provide support for decision-making [1].

This paper took the Large-piece One-of-a-kind Production Enterprise as study background, and got the components of enterprise control system by the ideology of cybernetics. Correspondingly, we classified the enterprise data into 4 types. Then we introduced the description method by using a quintuple expression and situation calculus [2] based on first order predicate to discuss the data on the static and dynamic sides of real business at the level of concept. With the advantage of concept base, the data model can get deduction capability. Lastly we get the result of 8 subject databases, the data in which comprise 39 state data items, 3 feature data items, 26 event data items and 16 control data items.

2. ENTERPRISE CONTROL SYSTEM

The essence of enterprise management system is a control system. From the perspective of information processing, it is also the information movement of being

Please use the following format when citing this chapter:

Ge, S., Ren, N., Miao, H., 2007, in IFIP International Federation for Information Processing, Volume 254, Research and Practical Issues of Enterprise Information Systems II Volume 1, eds. L. Xu, Tjoa A., Chaudhry S. (Boston: Springer), pp. 635-640.

collected, filtered, mined and used to implement organization goals, while the essence of information is just a series of processed valuable data. Therefore it is the point, for EISs development, to build up the enterprise-wide data model with the comprehensive planning [3-6]. Enterprise control system is as the following figure 1.

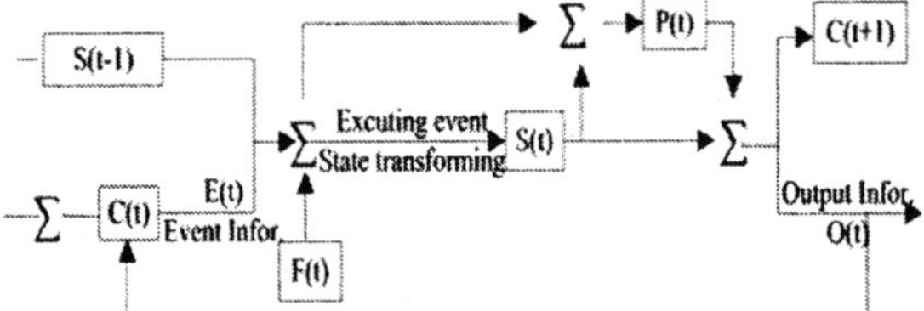

Figure 1. The Model of Enterprise Control System on Discrete Time

So one of the enterprise activities at the time of t can be defined as:

$$A(t) = < C(t),E(t),F(t),S(t-1),S(t),P(t),O(t) > \quad (1)$$

As seen in Fig.1, in enterprise control system enterprise behavior (C(t), E(t)) changes enterprise state (S(t)), such change is also affected by enterprise features (F(t)). The effect by enterprise behavior (C(t), E(t)) is evaluated by enterprise performance (P(t)) according to enterprise features (F(t)).

Therefore we can conclude that the components of enterprise control system include four aspects of state, feature, behavior and performance, by which we will get the four types of enterprise data to set up the enterprise-wide data model.

3. ENTERPRISE-WIDE DATA MODEL

3.1 Description Method For Enterprise-wide Data

$Enterprise\_data = \{C, A^C, R, A^R, H\}$ is a quintuple expression, where C represents a set of concepts; AC represents a collection of attribute sets, one for each concept; R represents a set of relationships; AR represents a collection of attribute sets, one for each relationship; H represents a concept hierarchy [7]. With the deep analysis on each management domain in manufacturing enterprise, such expression can be used as the main frame to capture the detailed concepts on the respect of static side of real business processes. With the captured detailed concepts, the method of situation calculus based on first order predicate is perfect to describe the dynamic side of real business processes, activities and behaviors. For the logic base of these description methods, the enterprise-wide data model can have the capability of deduction and has the potential to be evaluated, justified, improved and get more perfect [8].

3.2 Four Types of Enterprise Data

With the description methods introduced above, to expand the five elements in the quintuple expression and abstract the relevant typical situation calculus models in enterprise domains by conducting the business process analysis according to the four components in the enterprise control system. Note that we just introduced the scope of each type of enterprise data, as for what items are included in each and how they were got and described with the detailed application of those description methods was simplified.

1. Enterprise State Data

For implementing effective control on enterprise, we firstly need to know the enterprise state and identify the state variables to describe the enterprise control system trends and get the effective decision input. Enterprise is composed of objects, the attributes of which just determine the enterprise state, which is just the description on enterprise external features at a time moment, and can be described by the states of tangible entities or objects, which are also the representation of intangible entities. They are just the existing materials including personnel, finance and materials.

2. Enterprise Feature Data

Enterprise features, also the essence of enterprise, determine the mechanism how to implement control on enterprise and what results from enterprise control behaviors. Enterprise feature data is the symbol. For manufacturing, we consider their products and manufacturing methods are the symbol to distinguish them, which are just the enterprise features. The relationship between enterprise feature data and its production type is shown as Figure 2.

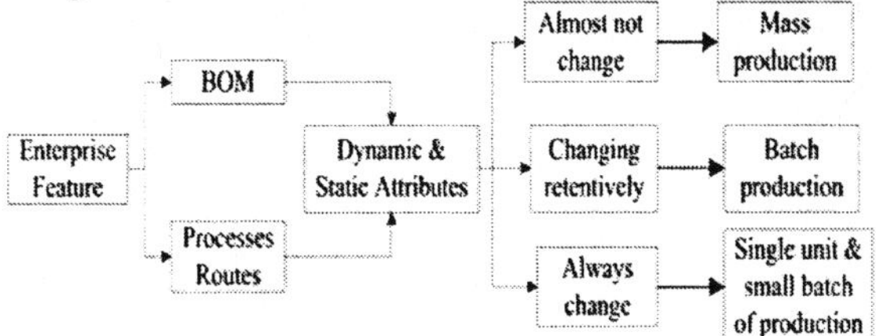

Figure 2. Enterprise Feature Data

So, we can educe the following proposition:

I : For manufacturing enterprises, the difference among them is just their different products, that is to say the product data represents the most essential feature of the enterprise;

II : For the same production type of manufacturing enterprises, their differences are made up of the ones between their BOMs and between their processes routings;

III: The production type, a manufacturing enterprise belongs to, is determined by the dynamic and static attributes of BOM and processes routings;

Meanwhile BOMs and processes routings are also the key for such enterprise to implement ERP successfully. To analyze why many enterprises failed implementing ERP on the aspect of technique, the reason is just the disordered organization and description of enterprise feature data, which is important to develop data criterion for information integration and data exchange between ERP and CAD/CAPP/PDM.

3. Enterprise Behavior Data

Enterprises change their states by executing enterprise behaviors. Enterprise behavior data is to describe management activities and connect the states and behaviors. According to the principle whether the enterprise behavior data change its state directly or indirectly, we classified the behavior data into 16 control data items and 26 event data items. Control data is the gist to execute enterprise behaviors and drive a series of operation indirectly. It is also a certain constraints for enterprise events, for example the developed plan or standards etc. To build up the enterprise behavior data model, it is necessary to identify the enterprise structure and business activities, just the dynamic aspect of business happened on the enterprise entities or objects.

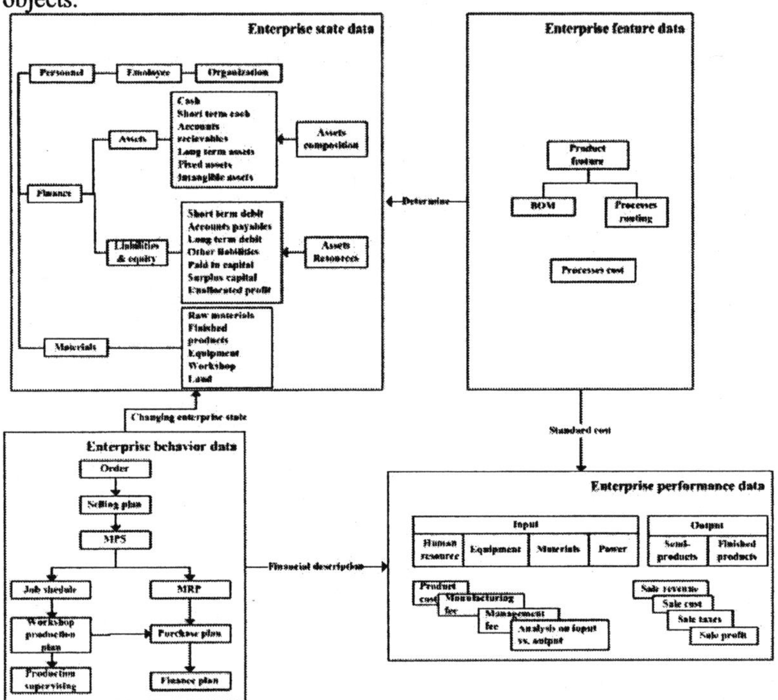

Figure 3. Relationship in Enterprise State, Feature, Behavior and Performance Data

4. Enterprise Performance Data

Enterprise performance data is to describe its business results. By the statistics on enterprise products, including the quantity calculation on semi-products and finished products and on labor hours, materials, power and accessorial staff spent in the production, we can get the cost in the production and its revenues. Enterprise performance data is obtained by analysis and calculation on state data, feature data and behavior data. The management can adjust its control behaviors according to the performance data to realize the business goal.

There is such a relationship among enterprise state data, feature data, behavior data and performance data as shown in Figure 3.

3.3 Enterprise-wide Data Model

After analyzing the management processes and activities of large-piece okp enterprise, we got the data models on different domains, including Sale & Marketing department, R & D department, Material department, Production department, Accounting and finance department, Human resources department. Meanwhile we collected the enterprise entities, represented them unified, classified them into four main data types and finally formed the 8 subject databases, the data in which comprise 39 state data items, 3 feature data items, 26 event data items and 16 control data items [1]. They are represented as:

EDM = [S, F, E, C]
S = [S1, S2, S3,..., S39]
F = [F1, F2, F3]
E = [E1, E2, E3,..., E26]
C = [C1, C2, C3,..., C16]

4. CONCLUSIONS

Such enterprise-wide data model got in the paper has been applied in the ERP product, developed by JinZhou software ltd., which is implemented successfully in China Shipbuilding Industry Corporation and more than 10 subsidiaries. From the perspective of enterprise data description, the other manufacturing mode or production type can be viewed as a special example of large-piece OKP with simple BOM and unchanging processes routings. Therefore the study report also can serve the EIS for other types of enterprises. Research on enterprise data model and data standard can promote the upgrade of EIS and its wide application.

ACKNOWLEDGEMENTS

This research was supported by National Natural Science Foundation of China. *Study on Data Model for Large-piece One-of-a-kind Production Enterprise* (Grant NO. 70472005).

REFERENCES

1. S.L. Ge and Y.H. Pan, *Information Model of Large-scale: single-piece and Small Batches Manufacturings* (Science Press: Beijing, 2006).
2. A.W. Scheer, *Architecture of Integrated Information System-foundations of Enterprise Modeling* (Springer-Verlag Press: Berlin, 1992).
3. M.S. Fox and M. Gruninger, Enterprise modeling, *AI Magazine*. Volume 19, Number 3, pp.109-121, (1998).
4. F.X. Gao, *Information Resource Planning: Fundamental Engineering of Informationization Construction* (Tsinghua University Press: Beijing, 2002).

5. J.Martine, *Strategic Data Planning Methodologies* (Prentice-Hall: Englewood Cliff, New Jersey, 1982).
6. Y.S. Fan and J.W. Cao, *Object-Oriented Modeling, Analysis and Design for Complex System* (Tsinghua University Press: Beijing, 2000).
7. M.M. Naing, E.P. Lim, and D.G. Hoe-Lian, Ontology-Based Web Annotation Framework For HyperLink Structures, in *Proc. of the Third International Conference on Web Information Systems Engineering (DASWIS'02)*, eds. B. Huang, T.W. Ling, M. Mohania, W.K. Ng, J.R. Wen, and S.K. Gupta (2002), pp.184-193.
8. H. Miao and S.L. Ge, Building-up of an enterprise data model supported by ontology, *Journal of Tsinghua University (Sei & Tech)*. Volume 46, Number S1, pp.1131-1137, (2006).

Research and Analysis of Ajax Technology Effect on Information System Operating Efficiency

Xiao Zhang, Yi Zhang and Jun Wu

School of Economics and Management, Beijing University of Posts and Telecommunications, Beijing 100876, P.R. China
newzhangxiao@126.com zhy@bupt.edu.cn junwu@bupt.edu.cn

Abstract. In recent years, information system based on browse/server architecture (namely B/S architecture) received more favor by enterprises. Ajax technology consists of five parts. They are HTML, JavaScript, DHTML, DOM and XML. With the help of cooperation and collaboration of these technologies, they can optimize the conventional enterprise information system by using an asynchronous way. Meanwhile, a quickly-responded and smoother user interface was provided. Enterprise information system with Ajax can be operated in a more efficient way, which means even use the current hardware, it can provide more load capacity, be more stable and serve more clients in parallel. In this paper: we present two kinds of information system models, one use conventional B/S architecture and the other use Ajax enhanced B/S architecture. First, we build both of the systems in accordance with typical business applications (search files, database access, etc.). Second, we use standard web pressure test tool such as Microsoft Web Application Stress tool to test both of the systems to get information like concurrent user number and average response time. Finally, with those experimental data, I compare and found out the difference between the two systems. The results presented in this paper propose a good way for enterprises, to enhance the information system performance, capacity and stability under a definite hardware facilities circumstance.

Keywords: *AJAX, Asynchronous transfer, Enterprise information system, System performance*

1. INTRODUCTION

Ajax (also known as AJAX), shorted for "Asynchronous JavaScript and XML"[1], is a web development technique for creating interactive web applications. The intent is to make web pages feel more responsive by exchanging small amounts of data with the server behind the scenes, so that the entire web page does not have to be reloaded each time the user requests a change. This is meant to increase the web page's interactivity, speed, and usability.

As we know, widely used information systems such as mySAP, IBM WebSphere [2], Microsoft SharePoint [3] are all based on browse/server architecture. Meanwhile, this kind of system is consisted of thousands of web pages. So it is a good practice to combine the Ajax technology with those information system in order to get a more

Please use the following format when citing this chapter:

Zhang, X., Zhang, Y., Wu, J., 2007, in IFIP International Federation for Information Processing, Volume 254, Research and Practical Issues of Enterprise Information Systems II Volume 1, eds. L. Xu, Tjoa A., Chaudhry S. (Boston: Springer), pp. 641-649.

user friendly UI and other benefits? This is the main issue that we will talk about in this paper.

2. AJAX OVERVIEW

Ajax (Asynchronous Javascript And XML technique) consists of five parts. They are HTML, JavaScript, DHTML, DOM and XML. With the help of cooperation and collaboration of these technologies, they can optimize the conventional web interactive mode (User triggers a HTTP request by clicking hyperlinks -->Server gets the request , processes it and visits the database for data -->server generates a HTML page and sends back to the client) by using a asynchronous way(See Figure 1). In this way, there is no interactive process like "Click -> Wait -> Click -> Wait". Meanwhile, a quickly-responded and smoother user interface was provided.

After using Ajax to optimize the information system of browse/server architecture, clients get better experiences. Furthermore, it's also means a lot for the servers. Because Ajax reduce the redundant and duplicated data that were generated and transferred before, now enterprise information system can be operated in a more efficient way, which means even use the current hardware, it can provide more load capacity, be more stable and serve more clients in parallel.

3. EVALUATION CRITERIA

To compare the two kinds of system, I need to set up an evaluation criteria first.

Considering the aspect of TCO (total cost of ownership) of the information system, I define the less bytes transferred the better, on the premise of finishing the same function. This criterion is set base on the following reasons: firstly, process less data will lower the CPU's workload for generating web pages; secondly, transfer less data can save the bandwidth and cost especially for the network that are charged by volume; thirdly, less data means less energy and less usage of the devices, this in turn reduce the cost of device replacement and energy consumption.

Considering the aspect of user experience, I define the average response time as a parameter to measure. The average response time is calculated by TTFB (Time To First Byte) and TTLB (Time To Last Byte), which shows the delay between system opens the web page and finishes it. Using this parameter, it is easy to judge which is better. Because less opening time means less wait and enhanced user experience.

Considering the aspect of system performance, I define the successful requests per second (RPS) as a key criterion. Due to this criterion can effectively reflect system concurrent performance especially when system works under a very heavy workload.

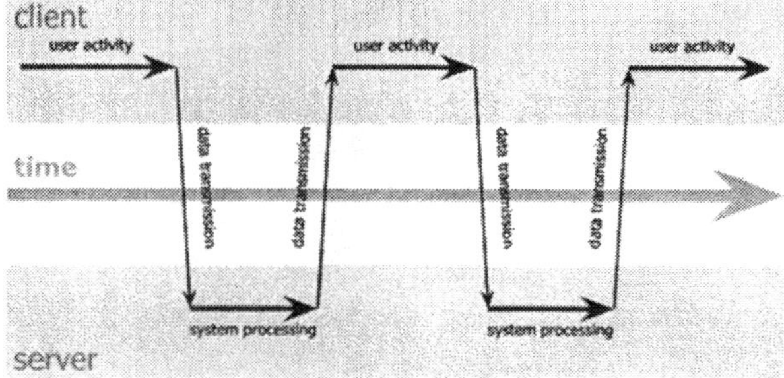

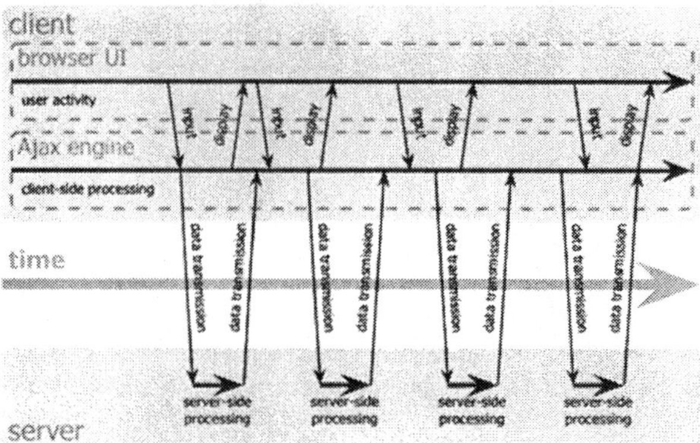

Figure 1. Compare Conventional Web Data Transfer Mode with Ajax Asynchronous Interactive Mode

To display the formula clearly, I set Ax for Ajax optimized information system and Cx for conventional information system based on browse/server architecture. So we have:

$$\text{Data Efficiency Index} = \frac{\sum_{i=1}^{x} \frac{A_{\text{BytesforFunction}}(i)}{C_{\text{BytesforFunction}}(i)}}{i} \tag{1}$$

$$\text{Page Display Efficiency Index} = \frac{\sum_{i=1}^{x} \frac{A_{\text{TTFBforPage}}(i)}{C_{\text{TTFBforPage}}(i)}}{i} \tag{2}$$

$$\text{Page Load Efficiency Index} = \frac{\sum_{i=1}^{x} \frac{A_{TTLBforPage}(i) - A_{TTFBforPage}(i)}{C_{TTLBforPage}(i) - C_{TTFBforPage}(i)}}{i} \quad (3)$$

$$\text{System Performance Efficiency Index} = \frac{A_{RPS}}{C_{RPS}} \quad (4)$$

These four indicators will show the difference between the two kinds of information system.

4. SIMULATION

To compare the two kinds of system, I set up several scenes to simulate the actual working action such as looking for internal news update, search for some file in database, surf specific pages in knowledge base, etc [4-7] .

Scene 1: Looking for Internal News Update

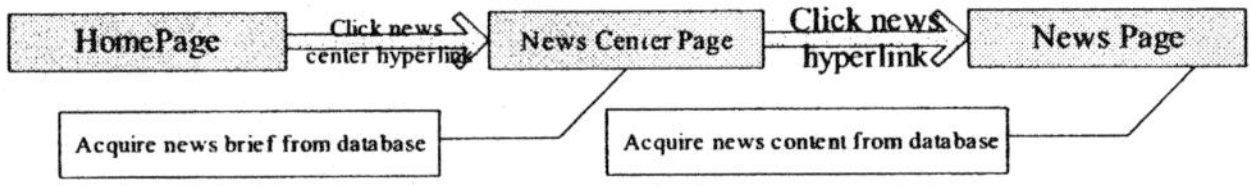

Scene 2: Searching for Some File in Database

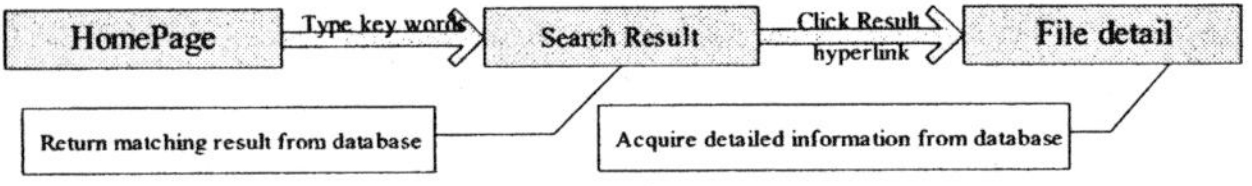

Scene 3: Surf Specific Pages in Knowledge Base

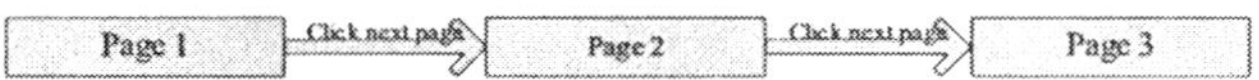

All the pages which are designed to simulate the conventional information system include the same header and footer part in the very top and very bottom of the page. And the main content was put into a form in the middle of the page. This is a very typical layout because in this way, it's easy for system administrator to maintain the navigation bar and other fixed content on the top and bottom of all the pages.

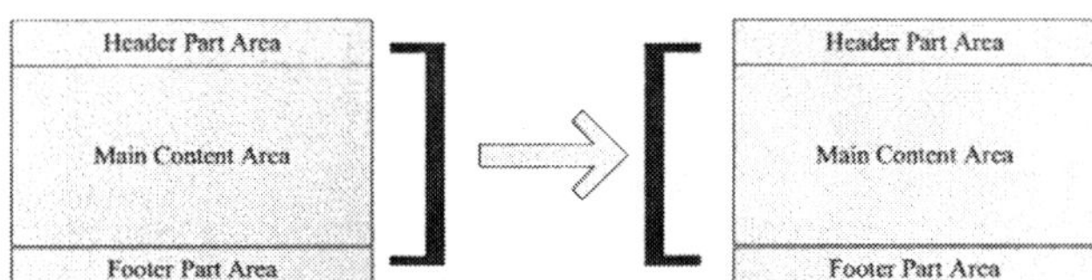

Figure 2. Footer and header layout

All the pages which are designed to simulate the Ajax optimized information system also include the same header and footer part in the very top and very bottom of the page. But the difference between this and the former one is that all the main content was loaded and unloaded dynamically using the Ajax way, that means loading and unloading the main content will not effect the data on the header part and the footer part.

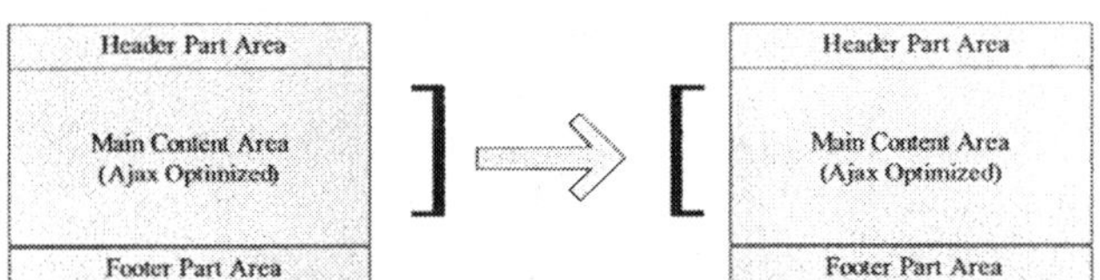

Figure 3. Simulating the Ajax Optimized Information System

Except this, all the content and database are the same, which helps to minimize the effect that different programming method brings to the coming simulations.

5. SIMULATION RESULT

In the simulation, I use Microsoft Web Application Stress Tool (MWAST) [8] as my simulation engine. I choice MWAST because it is designed to realistically simulate multiple browsers requesting pages from a web site. Use this tool I can gather performance and stability information about the web application of the two kinds of information systems. This tool simulates a large number of requests with a relatively small number of client machines. It creates an environment that is as close to production as possible.

Simulation environment is:

Intel Pentium M 1700MHZ with 768MB Memory running Windows XP SP2 and Internet Information Service.

Simulation Results: (All the test were tested for three times, I use the average of the three as the final result)

Table 1. Simulation Result

Scene	Total Hits	Bytes Sent	Bytes Received	Bytes/Hit
	KB			time KB
Scene1(1st)/C	1494	697.34	1778.5	1.657
Scene1(2nd)/C	1475	688.02	1754.34	1.656
Scene1(3rd)/C	1448	675.42	1722.2	1.656
Average			1.656	
Scene1(1st)/A	1523	553.3	1548.15	1.380
Scene1(2nd)/A	1454	528.24	1477.99	1.380
Scene1(3rd)/A	1520	552.21	1545.1	1.380
Average				1.380
Scene2(1st)/C	1460	737.62	1611.27	1.609
Scene2(2nd)/C	1392	703.25	1536.35	1.609
Scene2(3rd)/C	1510	763.38	1667.6	1.610
Average			1.609	
Scene2(1st)/A	1443	527.97	1203.48	1.200
Scene2(2nd)/A	1469	537.52	1225.34	1.200
Scene2(3rd)/A	1399	512.27	1167.77	1.201
Average			1.200	
Scene3(1st)/C	18343	8365.85	15411.24	1.296
Scene3(2nd)/C	18584	8475.78	15613.73	1.296
Scene3(3rd)/C	18988	8659.54	15952.29	1.296
Average			1.296	
Scene3(1st)/A	19701	6772.62	11072.94	0.906
Scene3(2nd)/A	20170	6933.81	11336.3	0.906
Scene3(3rd)/A	20146	6925.56	11322.81	0.906

Average	0.906

Table 2. Simulation Result (Continue)

Scene	TTFB ms	TTLB ms	Page Load Time ms	Request/Second
Scene1(1st)/C	37.573	37.640	0.067	
Scene1(2nd)/C	37.957	38.013	0.057	
Scene1(3rd)/C	38.943	38.993	0.050	
Average	38.158	38.216	0.058	
Scene1(1st)/A	37.013	37.043	0.030	
Scene1(2nd)/A	38.753	38.807	0.053	
Scene1(3rd)/A	36.900	36.940	0.040	
Average	37.556	37.597	0.041	
Scene2(1st)/C	21.463	38.603	17.140	
Scene2(2nd)/C	22.263	40.700	18.437	
Scene2(3rd)/C	20.997	37.360	16.363	
Average	21.574	38.888	17.313	
Scene2(1st)/A	39.030	39.070	0.040	
Scene2(2nd)/A	38.290	38.330	0.040	
Scene2(3rd)/A	40.340	40.377	0.037	
Average	39.220	39.259	0.039	
Scene3(1st)/C	1.480	1.507	0.027	247.4
Scene3(2nd)/C	1.440	1.467	0.027	238.23
Scene3(3rd)/C	1.403	1.420	0.017	244.35
Average	1.441	1.464	0.023	243.33
Scene3(1st)/A	1.330	1.343	0.013	275.32
Scene3(2nd)/A	1.295	1.303	0.008	305.67
Scene3(3rd)/A	1.315	1.330	0.015	289.81
Average	1.313	1.325	0.012	290.27
Data Efficiency Index				0.759
Page Display Efficiency Index				1.238
Page Load Efficiency Index				0.405
System Performance Efficiency Index				1.193

6. RESULT ANALYSIS AND CONCLUSIONS

From the simulation results, I can get the following conclusion:

Compare with the conventional information system (hereinafter referred to as MIS C), the Ajax optimized system (hereinafter referred to as MIS A) enhanced data transfer efficiency remarkably. This enhancement was not caused by the increase of network bandwidth; however, it is because the MIS A saved near 25% of total bytes that system transferred. Meanwhile, MIS A didn't need to transfer the header part and footer part, the same content on all of the pages. But for MIS C, this is a necessity to do on every page. For this simulation, I only put a few texts on the header and footer parts without any picture, but for the real MIS people always use pictures to make the navigation bar and logo, so I believe MIS A will have much better data efficiency than MIS C in real.

Page Display Efficiency Index shows that MIS C has better display effect for users than MIS A, which means the content (partial content, not the whole content of the page) on MIS C comes out quicker than MIS A. The reason for this is Ajax works in an asynchronous way. So in some simulations which Ajax needs to get data from database, the system has to wait until the database finish its work.

Although MIS A has worse result for Page Display Efficiency Index, it also has its advantages. In simulation for Page Loading Efficiency Index, MIS A have excellent result. In average, it only spend 40% of time that MIS C need to load the complete content, which means MIS C will display the partial content very quickly, but visitor has to wait for longer time to get the whole page loaded. Personally, I think the result shown by Page Display efficiency Index is more important because the reason people visit the website is to get the full content, not the partial one. So MIS A will have a better experience for the visitors.

For the stress test part, I simulated numbers of clients to visit the server. Let the server became exhausted in order to get the maximal workload the server can handle. So under this maximal workload, we will know in which architecture (Conventional or Ajax), system can finish more requests from the clients. From the simulation data, we could see, MIS A handles nearly 20% more requests than MIS C. That means, using the same hardware, MIS A can deal with more customers at the same time.

So from these simulation data we could draw this conclusion: the Ajax technology indeed optimized the system. Management information system in Ajax architecture not only reduced the consumption of server resource, enhanced the efficiency and stability of the servers, but also improved the user experience by lessening the page loading time. For the enterprise who will build the new information system, it is reasonable to involve the Ajax in the system. Because this won't increase the cost for building the system, but it will reduce the cost for purchasing hardware and its maintenance. For the enterprise that already has information system, it should compare the cost for maintaining the hardware and the cost for migrating the system from conventional one to Ajax one. Because reduce the total cost of ownership and increase the performance and efficiency is our original goal of deploying Ajax technology.

REFERENCES

1. J.J. Garrett, *AJAX : A New Approach to Web Applications*, Adaptive Path (2005). http://www.adaptivepath.com/publications/essays/archives/000385.php (Accessed May 7, 2007).
2. U. Wahli, *WebSphere Studio Application Developer Version 5 Programming Guide*, IBM Redbooks, International Business Machines Corporation (2003).
3. S. Tu, M. Xiong, X Chen, and W. Du, *Microsoft Office SharePoint Portal Server 2003 Advanced Guide* (Publishing House of Electronics Industry: Beijing, China, 2006).
4. J. Gehtland, B. Galbraith, and D Almaer, *Pragmatic Ajax: A Web 2.0 Primer* (Pragmatic Bookshelf: Lewisville, TX, 2006).
5. D. Crane, E. Pascarello, and D. James, *Ajax in Action* (Manning Publications: Greenwich, CT, 2005).
6. Z. Ke, *Ajax Development Brief ---- Concept, Example and Framework* (Publishing House of Electronics Industry: Beijing, Beijing, 2006).
7. M. Chen and M. Shen, *ASP technology and dynamic web page development* (Tsinghua University Press: Beijing, Beijing, 2007).
8. FECIT Product Research & Development Center, *Practical Software Testing Method and Application* (Publishing House of Electronics Industry: Beijing, China, 2003).

Collective Intelligence in Knowledge Management

Wenyan Yuan[1], Yu Chen[1], Rong Wang[1, 2] and Zhongchao Du[1]

[1]School of Information, Renmin University of China, Beijing 100872, P.R. China
dongtinghu1982@163.com rong@ruc.edu.cn yuchen318@gmail.com duzc@ruc.edu.cn
[2]Key Laboratory of Information Management and Information Economics, Ministry of Education P.R.C, Beijing 100876, P.R. China rong@ruc.edu.cn

Abstract. This paper traces the history of research for Collective Intelligence, and describes new forms of Collective Intelligence on the Internet so far especially from the view of Web2.0, to figure out what Collective Intelligence is, then makes analyses on those forms to make clear the mechanism of Collective Intelligence on the Internet. As one Complex Adaptive System, Collective Intelligence is the emergence of group behaviors, and is stored on the platform of the Internet. So, it is one new kind of the Knowledge Management on the Internet. We finally think about future work for this field to promote the emergence of Collective Intelligence on the Internet.

Keywords: *Collective intelligence, Social software, Web2.0, Complex adaptive system, Knowledge management, Data mining, Semantic Web*

1. INTRODUCTION

The words "Collective Intelligence" may first be widely used in ant-based research, which later developed as "Swarm Intelligence" [1, 2]. And many scholars believe that one antecedent for Collective Intelligence is "Global Brain" [3]. Howard Bloom [4, 5] stresses the biological adaptations that have turned most of this earth's living beings into components of what he calls "a learning machine". One CI pioneer, George Pór, defined the Collective Intelligence phenomenon as "the capacity of a human community to evolve toward higher order complexity thought, problem-solving and integration through collaboration and innovation."[6]

With new communication technologies—especially the Internet—huge numbers of people all over the planet can now work together in ways that were never before possible in the history of humanity. It is thus more important than ever for us to understand Collective Intelligence at a deep level so we can create and take advantage of these new possibilities.

This paper will have a description for some important styles and technologies related to Collective Intelligence on the Internet, and analyze the mechanism for it on the Internet, finally think about future work for this field.

Please use the following format when citing this chapter:

Yuan, W., Chen, Y., Wang, R., Du, Z., 2007, in IFIP International Federation for Information Processing, Volume 254, Research and Practical Issues of Enterprise Information Systems II Volume 1, eds. L. Xu, Tjoa A., Chaudhry S. (Boston: Springer), pp. 651-655.

2. COLLECTIVE INTELLIGENCE ON THE INTERNET

Collective Intelligence is now occurring in dramatically new forms on the Internet. The popularity of Social Software, and the springing up of workshop of Web 2.0, are all characterized by harnessing Collective Intelligence. To have an analysis for these new forms, we here, will have a description for some important styles and technologies of Collective Intelligence. Before all this, we draw one figure below to facilitate coming illumination.

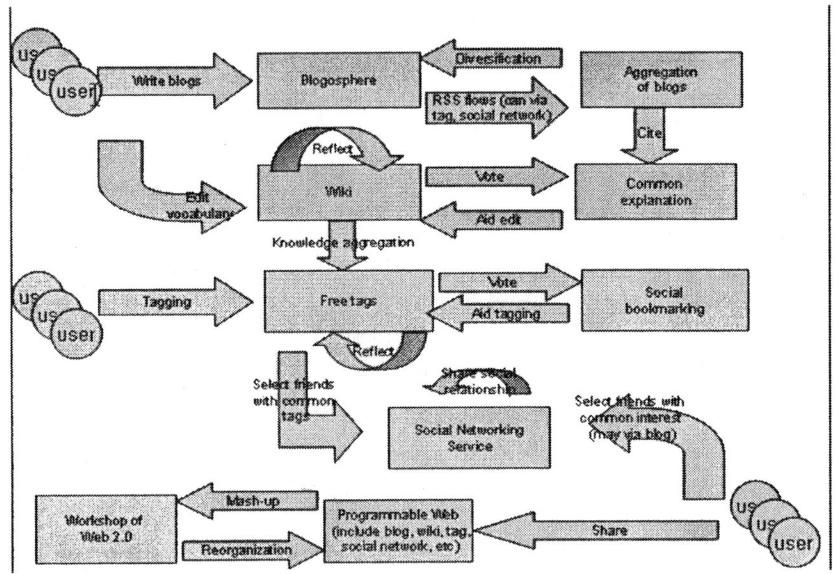

Figure 1. Collective Intelligence Mechanism on the Internet

2.1 Social Software

Blog, Social Bookmarks, Social Networking Service, and Wiki, are the four main kinds of Social Software that are known today by thousands of networks people, and are deemed as Classical Social Software.

1) Blogs

The first main difference between web 1.0 and web 2.0 just lay at whether users can write besides traditional read on the web. Although sharing ideas, facts, and opinions in electronic communities was not new, by opening the "means of production" to non-programmers everywhere, blogs introduced that highly combustible fuel—critical mass, and forming blogosphere.

2) Social Bookmarks

Introduced in 2003, the del.icio.us social bookmark manager was one of the first of its type and has enjoyed an early and large base of committed users[1]. The emergent social bookmarks coming from the collaboration of individual intelligence of free tagging is named by Thomas Vander Wal as Floksonomy (which is the combination of Folks and Taxonomy) [7].

3) Wikis

Wiki pages are editable and changeable by anyone. In the worldwide encyclopedia Wikipedia[2], the forming of stable explanation for vocabulary (common vocabulary in the figure) is the emergence of Collective behaviors, in which people reflect each other by voting or changing other's explanations.

4) Social Networking Service

First, people may find their friend by selecting people with common interest on the blogs or with common tags. Further, because these systems record the social network, enable the share and transferring of social relationship, so they provide one global social relationship view. Through this global view, strangers can become friends via their friends' friendship, and this promotes the aggregation of users with common interest, and the forming the self-organization in the social network.

2.2 Technologies to Motivate Collective Intelligence

The application of RSS (Syndication) and Programmable Web actually do not involve new technologies, but truly make convenience to the environment to activate Collective Intelligence.

1) RSS

To aggregate other RSS files and to be aggregated by other RSS aggregators, the remixing and remixed files which syndicated towards different kinds of taste from users motivate the aggregation of individual intelligence. Information flows are mainly via RSS, which promotes the aggregation of individual intelligence. Via this important process, the Internet becomes really active and diversiform, with each adaptive agent changing every moment according to each other..

2) Share and Mash-ups for Programmable Web

Social Softwares open their APIs to allow other systems to use for further developing. If one system can be used as plug-in for other systems, and even can used entirely as one plug-in for another system, then this system is seen as programmable web. Web 2.0 is feathered as "share, reorganization, mash-ups", and these feathers can produce the systems that are called the workshop of web 2.0, one form of which is the mash-ups of programmable web.

---

1 Del.icio.us; http://del.icio.us/.

2 See www.wikipedia.com

3. COLLECTIVE INTELLIGENCE AND ITS MECHANISM ON THE INTERNET

We have talked too much, but what is Collective Intelligence, and what's its mechanism on the Internet. We are going to explore this.

3.1 Definition for Collective Intelligence

From the Handbook of Collective Intelligence, there is: Collective Intelligence is Groups of individuals doing things collectively that seem intelligent[3].

That is, Collective Intelligence is the combination of individual intelligence, but as one Complex Adaptive System, it is more than the addition of individual intelligence. As the adaptive agents (individual intelligence) acted individually and mutually, Collective Intelligence gradually emerges.

3.2 Mechanism on the Internet for Collective Intelligence

Collective Intelligence has its own characteristics emerging on the Internet. We induced them as seven basic ones: Aggregation, Tagging, and Nonlinearity, and Information flows, Diversity, Selectivity, building blocks

People may find these characteristics are similar with the ones listed for CAS [8], and since we deem Collective Intelligence as CAS, we will be sure to reference it a lot.

The characteristics listed above are implicated in the Fig.1. No mater with blog, wiki, or Social Bookmarking, Social Networking Service, there is aggregations, just with different contents, for example, aggregation of common vocabulary, social relationship, and Floksonomy. Tagging helped aggregation when people select their friends, and selectivity from individuals accomplished this aggregation too. In this picture, the information flows are mainly via RSS, and this makes the Internet active, diversiform, and changing, so that new intelligence emerges.

Each system, with the reflection mechanism embedded, is not linear any more. So they are nonlinear. This nonlinearity makes Collective Intelligence complex and emergent. And with Programmable Web, the Internet is divided into one and one building blocks, which by mixing, facilitate the building more new and complex systems. The Internet is becoming vivid.

Each individual, as one adaptive agent, contributes knowledge, communicates with another, refer to another, votes for others, and modifies other's knowledge, and accomplish the emergence of Mass Intelligence. As one CAS, Collective Intelligence is the emergence of group behaviors, but is stored on the platform of the Internet. So, from this view, we can also say that, Collective Intelligence is also the Knowledge Management on the Internet.

---

[3] This definition is from "the Handbook of Collective Intelligence" from the MIT Centre for Collective Intelligence, see http://www.socialtext.net/mit-cci-hci/index.cgi?handbook_of_collective_intelligence.

4. CONCLUSIONS

We are going to interpret mechanism of Collective Intelligence on the Internet more detailed in the future. The research of this field to promote the emergence of Collective Intelligence needs the help from the field of Date Mining and Semantic Web.

Scholars summarized that there are three main components of Web 2.0: social software, the semantic web and information retrieval. Right now, the idea for semantic web and information retrieval being characteristic by harnessing Collective Intelligence is coming out, and in our opinion, will later become flourishing just like Social Software. We are eager to see that and will continue to keep an eye on the development of Collective Intelligence on the Internet.

ACKNOWLEDGEMENTS

This work is supported by National Social Science Foundation Grant #06BTQ016 and Open Foundation of Key Laboratory of Information Management and Information Economics, Ministry of Education P.R.C, Grant #F0607-16.

REFERENCES

1. E. Bonabeau, M. Dorigo, and G. Theraulaz, *Swarm Intelligence: From Natural to Artificial Systems,* Santa Fe Institute Studies in the Sciences of Complexity (Oxford University Press: New York, 1999).
2. J. Kennedy and R. C. Eberhart, *Swarm Intelligence* (Morgan Kaufmann Publishers: San Francisco, 2001).
3. B. Goertzel, *Creating Internet Intelligence, Wild Computing, Distributed Digital Consciousness, and the Emerging Global Brain* (Plenum Press: New York, 2001).
4. H. Bloom, *Global Brain, The Evolution of Mass Mind from the Big Bang to the 21st Century* (Wiley: New York, 2000).
5. H. Bloom, *The Lucifer Principle: A Scientific Expedition into the Forces of History* (Atlantic Monthly Press: New York, 1995).
6. G. Pór, Blog of Collective Intelligence (May 10, 2006). http://www.community-intelligence.com/blogs/public/(Accessed March 4, 2007).
7. T. Vander Wal, *Folkonomy*. http://www.vanderwal.net/essays/051130/folksonomy.pdf (Accessed March 4, 2007).
8. J.H. Holland, *Hidden order: how adaptation builds complexity* (Addison-Wesley: Massachusetts, 1995).

An Extended Logistics Model with the Theory of Constraints: Applying TOC in Telecom Industry

Shenghan Zhou[1] and Fajie Wei[2]

[1]Economics and Management Center for National Defense, Beihang University, Beijing 100083, P.R. China
[2]Economics and Management School of Beihang University, Beijing 100083, P.R. China
Godbus@sem.buaa.edu.cn Weifajie@buaa.edu.cn

Abstract. The telecommunication industry depends on unit level mobility to respond to unexpected demands occurring over a large geographical range. If the response is not timely and comprehensive, these units may fail to meet the customer' required. Therefore, many telecom enterprises prepared abundant spare part. The arrangement provides "timely and wonderful" service while they raise the debt-to-asset ratio to an uncompromisable level. However, the classical ERP system is far less effective in the service industry, especially in telecom. The first problem comes from the business process, the finance department debate any fixed assets is in their authority. Another problem is the risk to attempt to reduce the stock of the spare part. To make the solution, the study redefined the concept of stock and the fixed assets in telecom industry, firstly. Then the study developed an extended logistics model according to aforesaid definition. In the definition, any assets which may be redeployed belong to the stock, instead of fixed assets. And the business process was reengineered to transfer the authority of stock management to the extended-logistics department. To improve the effect of the model, the study applies the theory of constraints. The application of the model makes a good performance.

Keywords: *TOC, Service industry, Business process, Workflow*

1. INTRODUCTION

The theory of constraints comes from the introduction of optimized production timetables scheduling software [1]. Goldratt [2] furnishes an excellent accounting of the evolution of his thinking. And the TOC encompass three interrelated areas: logistics/production, performance measurement, and problem solving/thinking tools [3]. The critical chain concept remained unstudied until Goldratt's Critical Chain appeared in 1997[4]. Umble and Srikanth [5, 6] believe buffers maintain a small amount of inventory used to protect due date performance.

The CNC Co, Ltd is the main ISP of China. In the operation, different operating units all follow the long-term operating methods. Under this model of operation, the logistics system works slow and ineffective. However, the cut-throat market competition environment leads to the rapid reaction ability of the telecom industry

Please use the following format when citing this chapter:

Zhou, S., Wei, F., 2007, in IFIP International Federation for Information Processing, Volume 254, Research and Practical Issues of Enterprise Information Systems II Volume 1, eds. L. Xu, Tjoa A., Chaudhry S. (Boston: Springer), pp. 657-662.

faced to the changing market. In order to solve this problem, this study begins with the logistics model as well as its management system, and makes a study of the mechanism of logistics and spare part. Meanwhile, through the study of the buffer of bottleneck links in logistics system, the application of the model has improved a lot. The result of the research has indicated that the application of the model can save a great deal of outstanding funds for spare part, simultaneously it can reduce the debt-to-asset ratio in an effective way.

2. EXISTING LOGISTICS MODEL AND MANAGEMENT SYSTEM

The existing logistics model as well as its management system has included two main aspects: the logistics mechanism and the spare part mechanism. There the logistics mechanism mainly includes the internal circulation process and management system of logistics in the operating units. While the spare part mechanism mainly covers the reasonable quantity of spare part stored by the two levels-central nodes and sub nodes everywhere in the service system, which is to satisfy the needs of maintenance and substitution in the inventory system.

2.1 The Problem in the Existing Logistics System

During the practical operation of the telecom operator, reasonable inventory has played a role of buffer. It can also shorten the logistics activity and accelerate reaction speed of operator faced to market. All allocating work must follow the decision of the financial department. Accordingly, there exists contradiction between the utilizing department and the purchasing center .In addition, the lengthy process of logistics results in the low reaction speed of the EPR, therefore the logistics efficiency has been reduced by a large margin. As a result, there exists an enormous gap between the better service to customers and the increasingly climbing cost.

2.2 The Spare Part Management System

The telecom operator has a variety of inventory; generally speaking, the materials are divided into four types. According to the study of Liu Hong Wei et. al, these materials are usually managed in accordance with two levels : central nodes of purchasing and regional units demanding the materials[7]. The distributing proportion is about 40% in sub node and the left in center. In order to guarantee the normal operation of the EPR and service, the study has to maintain a certain number of inventories. However, the traditional inventory with large quantities and multi-varieties increases the cost of inventory and the complexity of management with no doubt. The inventory is usually stored and managed according to two levels-the central node and regional sub-node .However, because of the different service scope, as to different sub-nodes, the emphasis over management also vary in some extent. In this way, the contradiction between the nodes with different levels occurs.

3. EXTENDED LOGISTICS MODEL WITH TOC

In order to solve the first problem, this study develops an expanded logistics model. This model emphasizes a new classification of the existing inventory materials. According to the internal survey of CNC, 95% of spare part in sub-nodes has never been used until scrapped in the year of 2005. The spare part is considered as fixed assets. The transfer of spare part becomes very complicated. The method is that the spare part is subdivided into two types-core spare part and secondary spare part, each with different storage proportion. Simultaneously, in order to redress the bias, we have to establish a reasonable set of calculating system to balance the proportion between central nodes and sub-nodes in spare part. Under this situation, it actually amounts to increase a reasonable buffer to the spare part before the core service ability. The specific calculating method of buffer will be introduced in detail in section 4. The model makes a good performance as shown the Table1.

Table 1. The Improved Ascription of Different Logistics Type

	Stored in sub-nodes	Stored in center
Logistics materials	40%	60%
spare part	60%	40%
Market type logistics	15%~40%	60%~85%
Consumables	40%	60%
Logistics materials	5%~10%	90%~95%

To make sure that the company can restore problems occurred to it promptly, study must regulate the allocating scope of each sub-node beforehand. It has already been realized, the system allocates the spare part according to two mechanisms. In the demonstration, the average time which the sub-point gets the required spare part from center node is about 3.5 hours. And the time from other neighbor sub-point is only about 1.8 hours.

4. EXPLOITING THE SYSTEM CONSTRAINT

The model above has improved the old logistics system as far as the process and definition aspects concerned. However, how to measure the ratio of spare part in the expanding model has become a new difficulty. In order to measure the ratio of spare part effectively, this study has revised the service model.

4.1 Improve the Existing Service System

In the standard service, system is divided into two parts-pretreatment and service centers. There the pretreatment includes two service requirements, and the service center makes separate response to the result of pretreatment. In order to guarantee the normal operation, traditional service system has prepared large numbers of spare part. In fact, the study by Cui Rongchun [8] had pointed out that the ratio of practical failure in most equipment is very low; therefore, this mechanism of spare part is ineffective. Accordingly, we have revised the spare part mechanism of the standard service model. The spare part mechanism which has already been revised happens to be a part of the expanding logistics system illustrated before. In figure 1, spare part is subdivided into the core spare part and the secondary spare part. While the potential service ability of the core spare part is considered as the buffer of the service center.

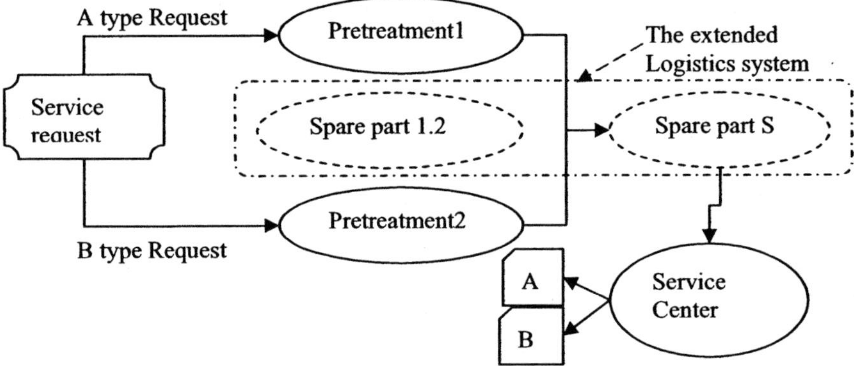

Figure 1. The Extended Service System Model

4.2 The Computation of the Spare-part Buffer

It is shown in Figure 1, there are two equipments to pretreat the services request; they are named pretreatment1 and 2. And there is a service center to provide the service to different result of pretreatment. It is assumed that pretreatment1 may meet the problem with the probability of the negative exponential distribution [9]. The planning service cycle is defined as T. F (t)=1-eft (f-the probability of problem), H (t) =1-e-ht (h- the probability of repaired). Some parameters display as:

I-Inventory buffer, h(t)-pretreatment1's distributing function of repair time. Wb- The average loss of center for repair pretreatment, CI- the cost of every Inventory Unit,P1- Pretreatment1 product of every time unit, P2- Pretreatment2 product of every time unit, Pa-product of every time unit of service A, P_b-product of every time unit of service B. T1- Adjust time of provide service A, T2- Adjust time of provide service B

When the pretreatment equipment1 fails to service, the average repaired time will be t (t<=T). The average space between two continuous problems will be u (u<=T).

$$t = \int_0^L t dH(t) = \int_0^L t d(1 - e^{-ht}) = \frac{1}{h}(1 - e^{ht}) - Le^{-ht} \tag{1}$$

$$u = \int_0^L t dF(t) = \int_0^L t d(1 - e^{-ft}) = \frac{1}{f}(1 - e^{-ft}) - Le^{-ft}$$

We suppose the center will fail to serve the A type service request when the pretreatment equipment 1 meet some problem. Then the probable waste time was set as T_0. There are two cases of the service system while the pretreatment equipment 1 fails to service.

The average loss of service center is:

$$W_{b1} = W \int_{\max\{\frac{I}{P_a}, T_2 + \frac{I}{P_b}\}}^{T} (t - \max\{\frac{I}{P_a}, T_2 + \frac{I}{P_b}\}) h(t) dt \tag{2}$$

$$W_{b2} = W \int_{\max\{\frac{I}{P_b}, T_1 + \frac{I}{P_a}\}}^{T} (t - \max\{\frac{I}{P_b}, T_1 + \frac{I}{P_a}\}) h(t) dt$$

Then the cost of inventory is: C1=CII+W_{b1}/u C2=CI+W_{b2}/u. And the possible cases may include four results:

$$\frac{I}{P_a} \le T_2 + \frac{I}{P_b};\ 2.\ \frac{I}{P_a} \ge T_2 + \frac{I}{P_b};\ 3.\ \frac{I}{P_b} \le T_1 + \frac{I}{P_a};\ 4.\ \frac{I}{P_b} \ge T_1 + \frac{I}{P_a} \tag{3}$$

It is able to get four possible buffer inventories from these cases, B1, B2, B3, B4. And the best buffer inventory is max {min (B1), min (B2), min (B3), min (B4)}. In fact, the really application get the 120% inventory of the result.

5. CONCLUSIONS

The expanding logistics model illustrated in this journal is based on the TOC, it is an improvement of the purchasing and logistics department in traditional telecom industry. The improvement has mainly includes two aspects: 1.an expansion of function of the logistics system; 2.an improvement to the circulation mode of logistics. This study also discusses the calculation of the crucial spare part buffer existing in the improved logistics system. In the future, the predictable study approach is centered on the further discussion about the developing and operating mechanism of buffer that existing in the telecom service system.

REFERENCES

1. E.M. Goldratt and J. Cox, *The Goal* (North River Press: Croton-on- Hudson, NY, 1984).
2. E.M. Goldratt, Computerized shop floor scheduling, *International Journal of Production Research*. Volume 26, Number 3, pp.443-455, (1988).

3. Spencer, M.S., Cox III, J.F., Optimum production technology (OPT) and the theory of constraints (TOC): analysis and genealogy, *International Journal of Production Research.* Volume 33, pp.1495-1504, (1995).
4. E.M. Goldratt, *Critical Chain* (North River Press: Great Barrington, MA, 1997).
5. K.R. Graham, Critical chain: the theory of constraints applied to project management, *International Journal of Project Management.* Volume 18, pp.173-177, (2000).
6. M. Umble and M.L. Srikanth, *Synchronous Manufacturing: Principles for World Class Excellence* (Spectrum Publishing Company: Wallingford, CT, 1995).
7. H. Liu, The study on the optimization of inventory management in telecom industry, *china storage & transport magazine*. Volume 3, pp.104-106, (2006).
8. R. Cui, The study on the optimization of spare part in telecom industry, *Telecommunications Technology*. Volume 3, pp.83-85, (2006).
9. R.C. Newbold, *Project management in the fast lane: applying the theory of constraints. Boca Raton* (The St. Lucie Press: 1998).

The Impact of Transportation Disruptions on Performance of E-Collaboration Supply Chain

Tianjian Yang and Jun Wu

School of Economics and Management, Beijing University of Posts and Telecommunications, Beijing 100876, P.R. China frankytj@sohu.com

Abstract. In this paper, we analyze the impact of a transportation disruption on supply chain performance by using system dynamics simulation. Performances of three different supply chains with Internet e-collaboration tools are compared with the assumption that a transportation disruption occurs within two echelons in a five-echelon supply chain. Numerical results are shown to reveal that from Non-collaborative supply chain to Collaborative Forecasting and Collaborative Planning (or VMI) supply chains more and more robust is revealed under certain transportation disasters.

Keywords: *Supply chain, Supply chain risk management, Disruption management, System dynamics, Transportation disruption*

1. INTRODUCTION

The vulnerability of supply chains has undoubtedly received more attention since the attacks on the World Trade Centers on September 11, 2001, even though supply chains have always been faced with assessing their vulnerabilities and managing risk. Risks faced by supply chains are quite diverse, arising from sources both within and external to the supply chain. Christopher (2005) defined SCRM (supply chain risk management) as "the management of supply chain risks through coordination or collaboration among the supply chain partners so as to ensure profitability and continuity." Based on the definitions of SCRM, it appears that one can address the issue of SCRM along two dimensions: 1.Supply Chain Risk—operational risks or disruption Risks; 2.Mitigation Approach—supply management, demand management, product management, or information management.

We find that existing quantitative models are designed for managing operational risks primarily, not disruption risks. Since there are few supply chain management models for managing disruption risks, we would like to look into this field.

This paper investigates how a transportation disruption affects the supply chain performance of traditional supply chain and e-collaboration supply chains. Applying system dynamics simulation, this study determines how each of these structures responds to a transportation disruption at certain echelon in the supply chain. Supply chain response is measured by the number of service level, inventory fluctuations. Finally, this paper suggests strategies for mitigating the risk from a transportation disruption.

Please use the following format when citing this chapter:

Yang, T., Wu, J., 2007, in IFIP International Federation for Information Processing, Volume 254, Research and Practical Issues of Enterprise Information Systems II Volume 1, eds. L. Xu, Tjoa A., Chaudhry S. (Boston: Springer), pp. 663-667.

2. MODEL DESCRIPTION

We use the system dynamics model which Oscar Rubiano Ovalle [5] developed.

2.1 Non-collaborative Supply Chain

When collaboration does not exist in the SC, an inventory manager only has operative information about the order placed by its direct downstream partner(s). And the causal diagram of the NC (Non-collaborative supply chain) system is shown in Figure 1.

$$\hat{\mu}_t^i = \alpha^i D_{t-1}^{i+1} + \left(1-\alpha^i\right)\hat{\mu}_{t-1}^i \tag{1}$$

$$OP_t^i = Max\left(\hat{\mu}_t^i + \beta_S\left(\hat{\mu}_t^i ss^i - Y_t^i\right) + \beta_{SL}\left(\hat{\mu}_t^i L^i - P_t^i\right) - B_{t-1}^{i-1}, 0\right) \tag{2}$$

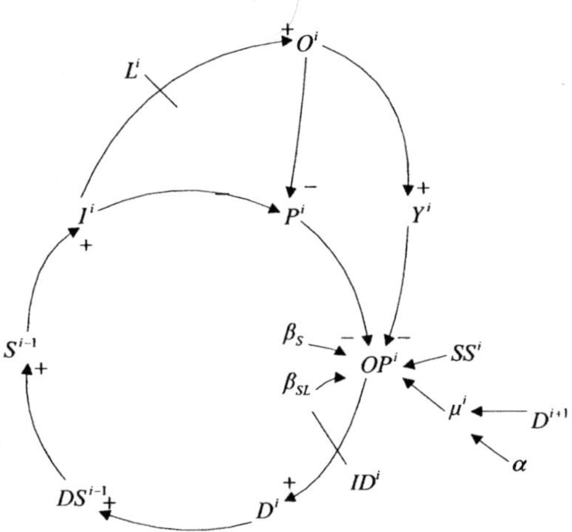

Figure 1. Causal Diagram of the NC System

2.2 Collaborative Forecasting Supply Chain

In this kind of collaboration, Eq. (1) is replaced by the following formulation:

$$\hat{\mu}_t^i = \hat{\mu}_t^n, \forall i = 1,\ldots,n; \tag{3}$$

$$\hat{\mu}_t^i = \alpha^n D_{t-1}^{customer} + \left(1-\alpha^n\right)\hat{\mu}_{t-1}^n, 0 < \alpha^n \leq 1, \forall i \tag{4}$$

and $D_{t-1}^{customer}$ is the last time period demand for the end customer of the chain. Once the new Firm forecast is obtained, the orders are calculated as in (2).

Fig.2 shows the unique modification to the causal loop and the stock and flow diagrams.

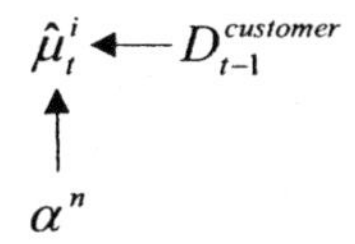

$$\hat{\mu}_t^i \leftarrow D_{t-1}^{customer}$$

$$\uparrow$$

$$\alpha^n$$

Figure 2. Forms Forecast in Collaborative Forecasting Process

2.3 Collaborative Planning and VMI Supply Chain

For the case, (3) and (4) are still applicable, but the following formulation (5) is introduced, replacing (2).

$$OP_t^i = Max\left(\hat{\mu}_t^i + \beta_S\left(\hat{\mu}_t^i ss^i - Y_t^i\right) + \beta_{SL}\left(\hat{\mu}_t^i L^i - P_t^i\right) - B_{t-1}^{i-1} + ib_t^i, 0\right) \quad \textbf{(5)}$$

$$ib_t^i = \hat{\mu}_t^i\left(ss^{i+1} + L^{i+1}\right) - \left(Y_t^{i+1} + P_t^{i+1}\right) + ib_t^{i+1} \quad \textbf{(6)}$$

These new relationships are included in the causal loop diagram (Figure 3). Note that no delay time exists between OP^i and D_i variables.

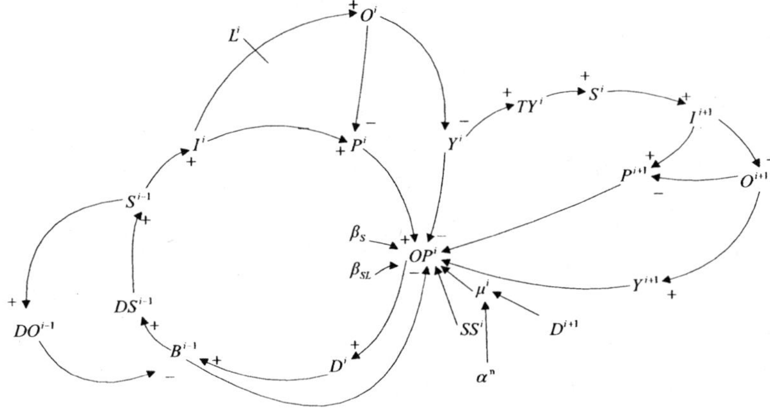

Figure 3. Causal Loop Diagram of the CP and VMI Structure

3. SIMULATION RESULTS

3 types of models (NC, CF and CP) are built, and each of them is a 5-echelon supply chain. And 3 different input functions are tried on the system dynamics models, and it is assumed that transportation should be disrupted between the wholesaler and retailer when 100 to 104 weeks arrive. We focus on inventory and service level fluctuation in each case.

The experiment results are as follows: curve 1 donates the NC structure, curve 2 donates CF structure and No.3 donates the CP and VMI structure.

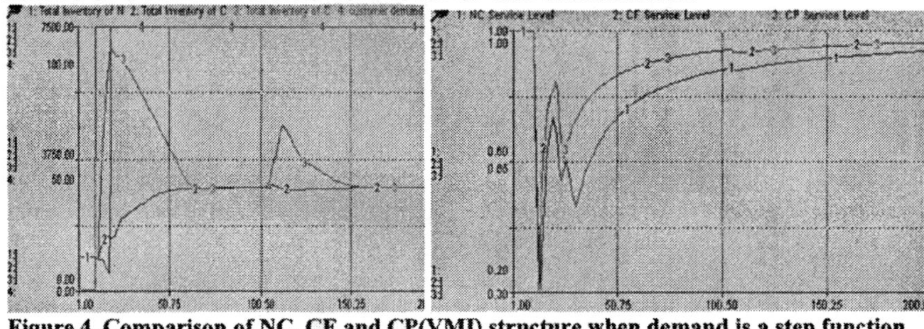

Figure 4. Comparison of NC, CF and CP(VMI) structure when demand is a step function

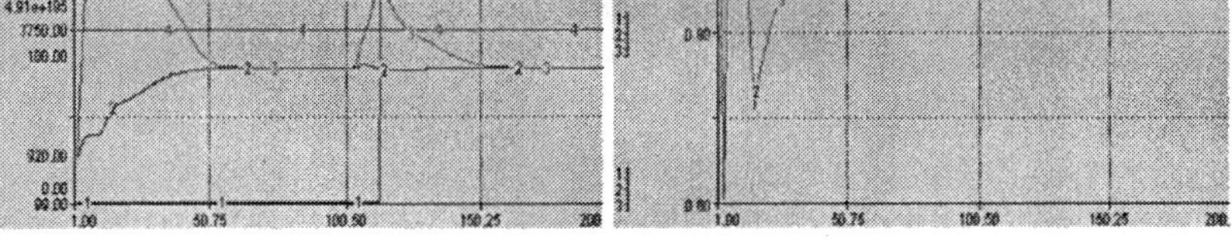

Figure 5. Comparison of NC, CF and CP(VMI) structure when demand is constant

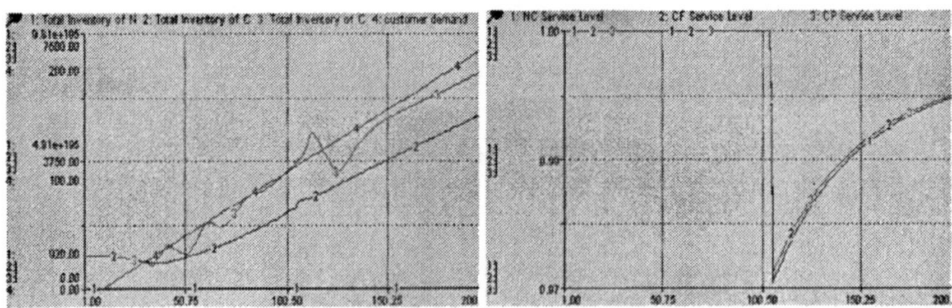

Figure 6. Comparison of NC, CF and CP (VMI) structure when demand is a ramp function

4. DISCUSSION AND CONCLUSIONS

According to the experiment results, a few suggestions have been revealed in a calamitous supply chain:

The diagrams show that the NC structure have much more average inventory than the other two. And the CF structure has the least inventory. But we should note that the CP structure's inventory exceeds that of the CF only when the inventory fluctuation is not in a stable state.

The CP structure has the best service level. Although the NC has the most average inventory, the CP structure has the best service level. But we note that the CF structure is almost as good as the CP in most cases.

The CP structure is the most sensitive. It responds to the disruption by adding to inventory quickly and also responds to the transportation recovery by reducing the inventory quickly. By contrast, the CF structure respond by a much more gentle way, that is to say, the inventory rises and falls little by little. Different from the two, the NC inventory may keep fixed for a long while and suddenly go up a very, very high step.

Although a transportation disruption may lead to service level drops in all the three supply chain structure, we can say CP is the most robust of the three, with good emergency handling mechanics and the best service level.

REFERENCES

1. C.S. Tang, Perspective in supply chain risk management, *Int. J. Production Economics.* Volume 103, Number 2, pp.451-488, (2006).
2. A. Otto and H. Kotzab, Does supply chain management really pay? Six perspectives to measure the performance of managing a supply chain, *European Journal of Operational Research.* Volume 144, Number 2, pp.306-320, (2003).
3. M.C. Wilson, The impact of transportation disruptions on supply chain performance, *Transportation Research Part E: Logistics and Transportation Review.* Volume 43, Number 4, pp.295-320, (2007).
4. D. Vlachos, P. Georgiadis, and E. Iakovou, A system dynamics model for dynamic capacity planning of remanufacturing in closed-loop supply chains, *Computers & Operations Research.* Volume 34, Number 2, pp 367-394, (2007).
5. O.R. Ovalle and A.C. Marquez, The effectiveness of using e-collaboration tools in the supply chain: an assessment study with system dynamics, *Journal of Purchasing & Supply Management.* Volume 9, Number 4, pp.151-163, (2003).
6. S.M. Disney, A.T. Potter, and B.M. Gardner, The impact of vendor managed inventory on transport operations, *Transportation Research (Part E).* Volume 39, Number 5, pp.363-380, (2003).

Analysis of Open Source Software in Enterprise Informatization

Chunli Bi[1], Li Zhao[2], Jinsong Liu[1] and Huaying Shu[1]

[1]School of Economics and Management, Beijing University of Posts and Telecommunications, Beijing 100876, P.R. Chinabicl@163.com liujinsong@bupt.edu.cn shuhy@bupt.edu.cn
[2]School of Law, Renmin University of China, Beijing 100872, P.R. China zhaoli2830@sina.com

Abstract. Enterprise informatization experiences three phases - information islet modeling, intranet modeling and integrated enterprise modeling. The traditional market failure argument suggests that innovation is characterized by high investment and low copy cost, and firms have difficulty in internalizing the fruits of their innovative effort. Thus, technology firms are seeking more patents, expanding their scope and overhauling their business models around intellectual property. Yet paradoxically, with the progress and development of information technology, open source software (OSS) plays an important role in expanding enterprise informatization. For example, Linux is developed quickly by this open way. Some firms have found the ways of making money by opening up their treasure-chest of innovation and sharing it with others. The rise of open-source software is one example.

In this article, the author introduces a model of OSS based on its network effects to understand how the enterprises decide their activities in this open market competition. This article describes the inherent reasons of open source movement from the view of the oligopoly structure. At the same time, this article analyses the effect of leader enterprise and follower enterprise on market structure and the different activities of these enterprises after the source has been opened. Finally, we make suggestions that companies at the leading edge are often in such a strong position that they do need the support of down-streams companies to broaden their technologies successfully and to decrease their risks in order to leverage the value of the technological portfolio. On the other hand, this article suggests that follower enterprises have incentive to take part in the development of open-source software only when the market has grown up.

Keywords: *Open source software, OSS model, Enterprise normalization*

Please use the following format when citing this chapter:

Bi, C., Zhao, L., Liu, J., Shu, H., 2007, in IFIP International Federation for Information Processing, Volume 254, Research and Practical Issues of Enterprise Information Systems II Volume 1, eds. L. Xu, Tjoa A., Chaudhry S. (Boston: Springer), pp. 669-676.

1. INTRODUCTION

While the informationization is unceasingly progressing, how to integrate different enterprise information resources into enterprise's comprehensive competence is getting more and more important. As early as in 1980s, Alvin Toffler, an American renowned sociologist, has proposed in his famous work "Third Tide" that the humanity has experienced the agriculturalization tide, the industrialization tide. Now, the third tide - informationization tide will be forthcoming. He also has forecasted scientifically that the information revolution will bring the humanity a new huge change, and the digital network will be the kernel of the third tide [1].

Enterprise informationization experiences three phases –information islet modeling, intranet modeling and integrated enterprise modeling. Integrated enterprise modeling adopts various information-applied modes, e.g., internet, E-Commerce (EC), Enterprise Resources Planning (ERP), Product Data Management (PDM), Customer Relation Management (CRM), Computer Integration Manufacture System (CIMS) etc. In order to adapt to the highly effective and fast development of the world economics, science and technology, the application technologies in open source code software which emphasize on implementing open computation and open standard foundation are rapidly developing, and also causing the giant echoes in the field and has partially succeed. On January 11, 2005, IBM announced that more than 500 software patents would be put into the opening source code community and would be used for free. Afterwards, Nokia, Ret Hat, Computer Associates and Sun also successionally put their own software patents in open source community. Forrester Research Corporation estimated that there are about 50% of enterprises around the worldwide are using open source software [2].

The goal of enterprise is maximizing the shareholder's value. The way of open sources seems to be paradoxical. Multinational corporations invest massive manpower and financial resources to focus on the improving enterprise core competence through the patent competition. Their basic logic is the one who win the cutting edge technology position will win the market. Tom Bethell said "people who own resources may benefit from opening their resources to other people [3], but it highly depends on the market structure where enterprises are located. According to different competition degree, the western economists classify the market into the four categories: Perfect Competition Market, Monopolistic Competition Market, Oligopoly Competition Market and Complete Monopoly Market.

Figure 1. The Classify of Market Structure

In the real market situation, both complete competition and perfect monopoly are very rare. Moulton Karman and Nanci Schwartz [4] proposed that the market structure that is mostly advantageous to the technology innovation should be positioned between complete competition and perfect monopoly, namely monopolistic competition market and oligopoly market. But under the background of economic globalization, both Chinese and overseas experts hold the opinion that the most beneficial market for the competition among different patents should surely be oligopoly market [5].

Under the assumption of oligopoly market, this article will mainly analyze those inherent factors which is relevant to Open Source Movement and caused by the enterprise informationization, Furthermore, study on how leader enterprise and follower enterprise will react on the market scale selection and decision making strategy will also included in this article.

2. MECHANISM ANALYSIS ON THE OPEN SOURCE MOVEMENT IN THE OLIGOPOLY MARKET

Open Source has different definitions, one of them which comes from the Open Source initiator (OSI) was defined as "it refers to the software with its own source code being widely used by the public; the use, revision and distribution of the software can be realized without any license fee[6]. Here one thing should be noticed that the open-source code software usually has the copyright. The license of OSS usually contains some limits: the original status of the open-source code software should be protected strictly; software author's identification data should be marked clearly; or related development activity can be somehow limited, etc.

This open-source movement can be traced back to a software engineer named Richard Stallman in 1980s, he proposed a so-called "copy left" movement, and founded the free software foundation ("FSF") which aimed at opposing the limitation usage of copyright and the patent of the software. A huge amount of free software had been issued according to those provisions in GPL. According to the GPL provision, "free software" refers to "the free software", not refer to software charge free. In his opinion, the software should be used and revised by the public as freely and equally as like they use the Holy Bible. But this did not mean no cost would be incurred[6].

Researching on the OSS market, we can easily find that almost all kinds of open source code were backed by technical strategies alliance, which is controlled by several enterprises. For example, one open source software like the LAMP framework, are composed of Linux – open-source operating system, Apache – open-source page server, MySQL--- open-source database, except for that, some script languages like PHP, Perl, Python etc. also play an important role in the LAMP framework. Compared with J2EE framework (Java) led by IBM, Sun, and the dot Net framework (C#) led by Microsoft, the triangle competition situation appeared. In 2005, IBM provided 500 patents covering 14 regions freely. The main service targets of these patents are the Linux operating system software users and the Apache homepage service software users. These two kinds of software have already occupied certain market share. One of the reasons why IBM would firmly support the Linux operating system is that IBM wants to weaken the hegemonic position of Microsoft (Microsoft Corp., MSFT) in this field.

The perdurability of the oligopoly in technology market depends on the potential entry barriers to market [7]. Clarkson and Miller (1989) suggested that entry barriers were composed of seven sources, respectively are distinct scale of economy, demand of capital, possession of critically important resources, patents and licenses, advertisement, product differentiation and variety of pattern, and superfluous throughput. Most of these oligopoly enterprises leverage some of these barriers to protect themselves, which is distinctly characteristic by keeping other enterprises away, for example, patent and license. The patents of IBM exceeded two thousand and nine hundred in 2005 and IBM has continued to keep the patent championship for 13 years. In the year 2004, IBM earned over one billion dollars licenses fee through his over 40 thousands ownership of patents [8].

Arrow thought that existing market forces would restrain the motivation of technology innovation, because new products' introduction competed not only with the products of other manufacturers in the niche market, but also cannibalized with their own existing products. The more market shares the manufacturer possessed, the stronger the latter effect showed. Just because Arrow Substitute Effect functioned are popular applied, innovation may harm more on manufacturer with leading position in the market. The leading manufacturer therefore will be inclined to stay on the current championship and not pursue further advancement in technology and product innovation [9]. Kelly, the director of IBM's Intellectual Property Department, told the real reason why they opened the original codes: IBM was afraid if they had too much protection of intellectual properties, they would face the risk of weakening innovation gradually. Patent essentially is used to help to recover one kind of balance, but if the balance is much too far away in certain direction, the industry will be ruined, and then IBM will be ruined.

From Arrow's Substitute Effect, we can easily find that oligopoly market structure is not always advantageous to oligarchs. Under the market environment of high-tech and continual innovation, oligarchs prefer not to supplant all the small companies. On the contrary, these fresh bloods can benefit them in promoting the innovation and also keeping their innovation motivation and consciousness. But, those big companies who want to open part of patents resources is not equal to they will give up all of the patents. If they want to open their patents from very beginning, why do they spend large amount of money in researching/developing and applying for patents? Under the environment of realistic economic market, manufacturers who own patents do not always win the market monopoly. For enterprises, turning patents into business application and production successfully is the final goal. Furthermore, the existing high and new technology enterprise has not yet been able to catch the monopoly position only through only one single patent. It must have core patents or basic patents. Only in this way, enterprises have influences in the related technology field.

In the game theory model, which was adopted by K&Y to explore the uncertainty and Spillover Effect leading to RJV (Research Joint Venture), he suggested that the company which first successfully implemented R&D, cannot assure itself holding the market completely [10]. He suggested that only successfully applied for the core patent, can they truly achieve the" winner" situation. The patents they provided for free are only those fringe patents in that technology field, or the patents with which the current oligarchs can hold the future development trend in control [3].

3. MODEL ANALYSIS

Through the analysis of the actual OSS, we find that only when these open source software reach a considerate scale, or win a number of users, can the follower enterprises participate in the second development or the market expanding. Take the Linux for example; although the Linux source code just occupies 3%-5% of the OSS source code, but its wide range of users make it on leading and fundament position in the entire open source software field. In an open source community, the enterprises that adopt the open source software are numerous, and among these enterprises, which adopt the open source software and take active part in it are also not small amount. According to the above analysis, we know that most of the OSS market structures are oligopoly. For facility, we suppose two enterprises, the OSS leader enterprise A (one of the oligopolies) and the OSS follower enterprise B (other small enterprises). The model for discussion is confined to the sub game perfect Nash equilibrium. The detailed assumption is listed below:

1. The information is perfect, e.g. all information the enterprise acquired is credible, avoiding from the un-trusty threaten;
2. The technology adopted in the OSS has attained a certain portion in the market;
3. All enterprises are equal-efficient in the R&D progress;
4. A certain tech is monopolized by several oligopolies. But in the OSS, only enterprise A opens, while only the enterprise B follows;
5. The market sales volume is indicated as the volume related to the OSS tech.

3.1 The Model Analysis of OSS on Market Scale

Supposing that before the OSS, the market share of A and B is respectively marked as i_A and i_B, and $i_A>0$, $i_B=0$.

The sales volume of A is Q_1, Q is the total market sales volume, thus

$$\mathrm{i}_{\mathrm{A}} = \frac{Q_1}{Q} \tag{1}$$

By the use of opening source code, technology improved, enterprise B gets increased sales volume at: $\Delta Q \geq 0$, $i_B \geq 0$. Meanwhile, the increased sales volume of enterprise B substantially leads to technology market share of enterprise A increased, that is:

(1) It means that the sales volume of other enterprises is decreasing if the total volume is stable. Then:

$$i_A' = \frac{Q_i + \Delta Q}{Q} \geq i \tag{2}$$

(2) If the total volume has been increased due to new users and sales volume of other enterprises remain unchanged, then:

$$i_A^{//} = \frac{Q_i + \Delta Q}{Q + \Delta Q} \geq i \tag{3}$$

It's benefit all technical market, both enterprise A and B through opening source code. Enterprise A expands their developed technology to new application users, which will therefore provide a good opportunity to develop their core patent to control market. At the same time, enterprise B also strengthens its technology capability and broadens technical market. Of course, Enterprise A must be able to control the whole technical trend. It will be very dangerous if it is out of control, wasting their investment will be the result in the situation of losing control. On the other hand, enterprise B is also taking a risk because it may have to give up some their own technology advantages by following the technology of Enterprise A.

3.2 The "Prisoner's Dilemma" Analysis, Enterprise Strategy Selection Analysis in Opening Source Code Situation

From the above analysis, open source code increases the whole market sale volume and profit amount. In order to simplify model, we can set assumptions that the market will keep a basic and stable profit before enterprise A opens source code. We assume the basic profit is zero to simplify thereafter comparison with that enterprise A opened source code. We also assume that the increased profit are 4 after Enterprise A opened its source to the market. If enterprise A opened the OSS, enterprise B followed to use OSS, the total profit will increase to 4, enterprise A and B shared the gross profit, that is (2,2). If Enterprise B refused to follow, the increased profit will be zero according to formula ②, ③ , $\Delta Q = 0$, it means the gross profit of the market increased zero. Similarly, the increased market profit will also be zero on the condition of Enterprise A's no open and B's no follow. If enterprise A refused to open the OSS, enterprise B still wanted to follow this technology, Enterprise would invest research & development cost in this new technology. No doubt that Enterprise B will reduce its profit. Therefore the whole game will be as follows:

Table 1. The Game of Enterprise A and Enterprise B

		Enterprise B	
		Entering	No entering
Enterprise A	Opening	(2, 2)	(0, 0)
	No opening	(0, -2)	(0, 0)

The above diagram shows two Nash Equilibriums, namely, enterprise A opened source and enterprise B follow, or conversely, enterprise A did not open source and enterprise B did not follow. Obviously, enterprise A and B will choose the strategy to maximize their own profits, that is to say, Nash Equilibriums (enterprise A opened and enterprise B followed) is an optimum one. Accordingly, whatsoever purposes that oligarchic enterprises conceived, either for promoting innovations or for snatching market shares, open source offers an invaluable opportunity for small followers to learn advanced technologies and explore more practice in the technology market.

The actual open source movement also substantiated correctness of this model. Taking Linux for example, at the inception stage, some big companies including IBM, Compaq and Sun willingly contributed their own source codes to jointly fight with their common rival – Microsoft, which in the end led to the birth of Linux. Today, there are two mainstream Linux enterprises, i.e. RedHat and TurboLinux and 309 Linux solutions across the world. Some Chinese software enterprises have also been involved in Linux development, such as Linux software platform providers: Red Flag, Co-Create, CS2C, TurboLinux China and SWL. Except for strong momentum from the world's mainstream Linux enterprises, they also need the participation from more and more enterprises to pursue their combat against Microsoft. Therefore, they choose to open source codes through General Public License (GPL), which will allow Chinese Linux enterprises have more opportunity to get themselves involved in the technology market and therefore integrated their specific resources to possess one position in Linux's coming day.

4. CONCLUSIONS

Open source is benefit to increasing social welfare and expanding market in the technology field. Both oligarchic enterprises and small followers will create new values in this movement. Just as some scholars such as Levin H. Campbell said, patent system is simply a kind of second-best efficiency mechanism [11].

Under oligopoly competition market, industry-leading enterprises will also take the responsibility to consider the future development of industry and dig out the potential market requirement [12]., while they snatch the monopoly profits. However, in order to lower risk, they may intentionally disclose to their rivals or publicize a portion of their R&D information, or open their source codes so as to achieve future development and maximize their long-term profits. For the follower, which is relative weak in technology, open source undoubtedly offers them a premium opportunity to get acquainted with the development trend of advanced technologies. They can keep their technical development strategies on the right track and will not diverge from the mainstream. However, huge following risk (surrendering their own technology) is also a problem, which they should carefully consider in advance.

For most Chinese software enterprises, as there is little technical leadership in the industry, they should take sensible strategy when facing the massive open source movement. On the one hand, they should take full use of these advanced technologies; on the other hand, they should take prudent approaches with in-depth analysis so that they will not spent huge amount of resources in research of open source movement, and at the same time they surrender their advantages.

ACKNOWLEDGEMENTS

This paper is funded from "The Fund for PhD Candidate Paper of Beijing Science & Technology Committee" with the fund No. ZZ0640.

REFERENCES

1. X. Pu and Z. Si, Network Economic (Machinery Publish House: 2006).
2. Anonymous, the new opportunity for Chinese software, CNII (2005). http://www.enet.com.cn/article/2005/1229/A20051229488111.shtml (Accessed July 14, 2007).
3. J.D. Gwartney, R.L. Stroup, and R.S. Sobel, Economics Private and Public Choice (CITIC Publish House), p.34.
4. J. Ma, Re-clearance of Relationship between Technology Innovation and Market Structure, Technology Economic. pp.19-20, (1996).
5. R. Dai and S. Gao, The Effect of Market Structure on Patent Race, Forecasting. Number 2, (2003).
6. K. Coar, The Open Source Definition (Annotated) (2006). http://www.opensource.org/docs/definition.php(Accessed July 14, 2007).
7. J. Liu, Reform on Monopoly Industry – analysis based on network perspective (Economic Management Publish House: Beijing, 2005), pp.26.
8. Anonymous, the strike of IBM to Windows (2005).
9. http://live.intozgc.com/049/49624.html(Accessed July 14, 2007)
10. J. Liu, Reform on Monopoly Industry – analysis based on network perspective (Economic Management Publish House: Beijing, 2005).
11. S. Gao and X. Jiang, Patent Competition Theory - pre-empt right model remark, Management Engineering Journal. Volume 3, pp.47-51, (2003).
12. Anonymous, Survey: An open secret, The Economist. Volume 377, Number 8449, p.17, (2005).
13. R.C. Levin, A.K. Klevorick, R.R. Nelson, and S.G.. Winter, Appropriating the returns from industrial research and development, Brookings Papers on Economic Activity. pp.783-820, (1987).
14. G.D. Fraja, Strategic spillovers in Patent Race, International Journal of Industrial Organization. pp.139-146, (1993).

Quality Assurance in the ERP5 Development Process

Rogério Atem de Carvalho[1], Renato de Campos[2] and Rafael Manhaes Monnerat[3]

[1]Federal Center for Technological Education of Campos (CEFET Campos), R. Dr. Siqueira, 273, Campos/RJ, CEP 28030-130, Brazil ratem@cefetcampos.br
[2]Sao Paulo State University (UNESP).Av. Eng. Luiz Edmundo C. Coube n 14-01, Bauru, SP, Brazil rcampos@feb.unesp.br
[3]Nexedi SARL, Bd. Clémenceau 59700, Marcq-en-Baroeul, France monnerat@cefetcampos.br

Abstract. The design and implementation of an ERP involves capturing the information necessary for implementing a system that supports integrated enterprise management, starting at the enterprise modeling level and finishing at the coding level. Unfortunately, in both academic and industrial communities, large quantities of papers focus on ERP deployment management, keeping specific development issues aside most of times. Research on specific techniques for developing ERP software – open source or proprietary, is rather deficient. This paper aims to help filling this gap by presenting a development process for the open source ERP5 system, highlighting the Quality Assurance (QA) techniques used, and the tools that support it. The proposed process covers the different abstraction layers involved, and supplies customized Enterprise, Requirements, Analysis, Design, and Implementation workflows. Each of these workflows is accompanied by one or more QA activities to assure the quality of every modeling and implementation artifact delivered.

Keywords: *Enterprise engineering, Enterprise Resources Planning (ERP), Software development processes, Software quality assurance, Free/open source software*

1. INTRODUCTION

Modeling an ERP software means to deal with the aspects related to the different abstraction layers that must be taken into account in enterprise-integrated management. The ultimate goal of developing an ERP system should be going from the highest abstraction level considered, enterprise modeling, down to code generation, without loosing modeling information, guaranteeing that the software is in complete conformity with business requirements. To accomplish this, it is necessary to define a process that can keep modeling information during its execution and that supplies a high-quality final product. The analysis and documentation of business and software requirements by means of models are essential for the system development, making necessary the use of proper techniques and tools [1]. In this sense, a modeling architecture that properly contemplates business processes aspects can facilitate reuse and promote better functionality, better performance, and a better system understanding [2].

Please use the following format when citing this chapter:

de Carvalho, R. A., de Campos, R., Monnerat, R. M., 2007, in IFIP International Federation for Information Processing, Volume 254, Research and Practical Issues of Enterprise Information Systems II Volume 1, eds. L. Xu, Tjoa A., Chaudhry S. (Boston: Springer), pp. 677-687.

On the other hand, Free/Open Source ERP (FOS-ERP) are increasingly gaining acceptance due to their lower costs and the perception that if customization is inevitable, why not adopt a solution that exposes its code to the adopting organization, which can freely adapt the system to its needs [3]? For FOS-ERP, modeling methods have their importance increased, since they can empower the availability of source code by extending and changing it in a way adherent to enterprise models, which can bring more innovation to integrated management.

However, FOS-ERP projects currently don't follow enterprise systems modeling techniques [3]. Moreover, they lack a more including Software Quality Assurance (SQA) approach, like all other open source projects – an exploratory study had show that SQA methods in FOSS projects are limited to testing, bug tracking, and Software Configuration Management [4], in other words, they only use code-related SQA techniques.

This paper aims to help filling these gaps by presenting a development process for the FOS-ERP ERP5, highlighting the SQA techniques used, and the tools that support it – a work initially proposed in [5]. Moreover, since that large quantities of papers focus on ERP deployment project management and deployment techniques [6], and research on specific techniques for developing ERP software, in special in a quality driven fashion, is rather deficient, this article also aims to contribute by discussing aspects of ERP development. The next section introduces briefly ERP5 main concepts, the following describe process' phases, highlighting SQA techniques used, and finally conclusive remarks are presented at the end.

2. ERP 5

ERP5 aims at offering software for integrated management based on the open source Zope platform, written in the Python scripting language [7]. This platform delivers an object database (ZODB), a workflow engine (DCWorkflow), and rapid GUI scripting based on XML. Additionally, ERP5 incorporates data synchronization among different object databases, through the implementation of the SyncML XML based protocol, and a object-relational mapping scheme that allows much faster object search and retrieval and also analytical processing and reporting. ERP5 is named after the five core business entities that define its Unified Business Model (UBM, Figure 1):

Resource: describes an abstract resource in a given business process (such as individual skills, products, machines etc).

Node: a business entity that receives and sends resources. They can be related to physical entities (such as industrial facilities) or abstract ones (such as a bank account). Metanodes are nodes containing other nodes, such as companies.

Path: describes how a node accesses needful resources.

Movement: describes a movement of resources among nodes, in a given moment and for a given period of time.

***Item*: a physical instance of a resource.**

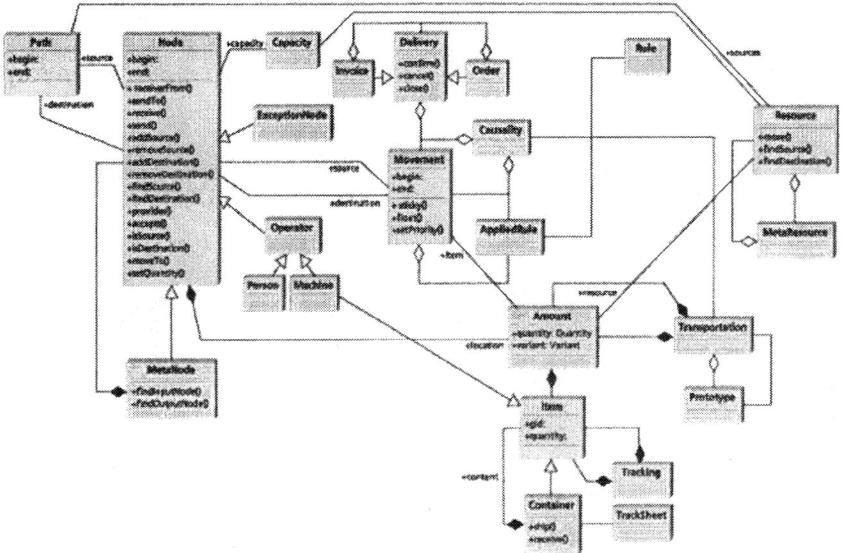

Figure 1. ERP5 Unified Business Model. The Five Main Classes Form the Basis for Creating New ERP5 Instances

The structure of ERP5 instances is defined through mappings of the particular domain concepts to the five core concepts and supportive classes or, in very rare cases, through the extension of the UBM. This mapping is documented by a proper instance's lexicon. Its behavior is implemented through workflows, which implement the business processes, and consider the concept of Causalities (chains of related events). Very flexible and extensible modules, called Business Templates, are also provided for Accounting, Production Planning, Payroll, Finance, MRP, CRM, Trading, Electronic Commerce, Reporting, and others.

ERP5 development process covers the different abstraction layers involved, and supplies customized workflows and SQA techniques. The process is based on the Generalized Enterprise Reference Architecture and Methodology (GERAM), which provides a description of all elements recommended in enterprise engineering and a collection of tools and methods to perform enterprise design with success [8]. Following the classical – but still effective – work of McCall [9], next sections will present SQA techniques and tools used in each workflow.

3. ENTERPRISE MODELING

This workflow stands between Concept and Requirements phases of the Unified Process [10], and concentrates on the modeling of function, information, resources, and organization views, according to the GERAM modeling framework. For the sake of addressing enterprise integration [11], models can be built on top of CIMOSA [12] or Eriksson & Penker approaches [13], depending on the kind of enterprise being modeled and the preferences of modelers. The Enterprise Modeling workflow consists of the activities shown in Figure 2, and can be summarized as follows:

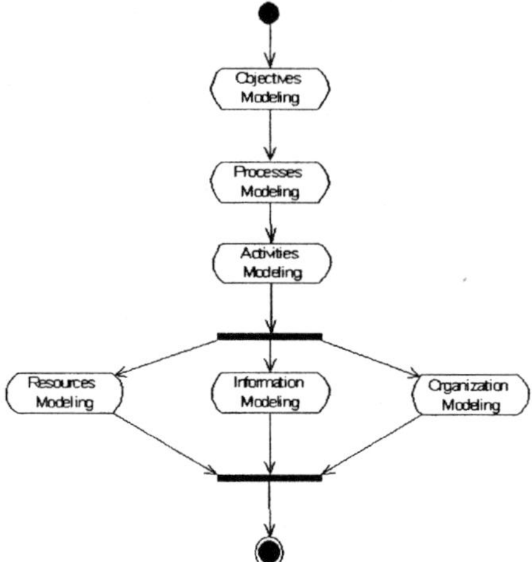

Figure 2. Enterprise Modeling Workflow

1. Objectives Modeling: define the strategic objectives of the entity.
2. Process and Activities Modeling: define the behavioral and functional aspects of the organization (Business Modeling Discipline).
3. Resources Modeling: describes the human, informational and technological resources.
4. Information Modeling: describe, using a high abstraction level, the information handled by the organization.
5. Organization Modeling: describe the structure of the organization.

SQA Techniques: model documenting, using both textual and diagrammatic modeling artifacts. Model quality is guaranteed by Formal Technical Reviews.

SQA Tools: Any UML CASE tool for Information and Process and Activities Modeling. Text editors for Objectives, Resources, and Organization Modeling.

4. REQUIREMENTS

The information captured by the Enterprise Modeling workflow is detailed and consolidated as requirements for the information system, following the Requirements Workflow, shown on Figure 3. Its activities are:

1. System Requirements Definition: provides a basic requirements document. These requirements are a composition of features identified by the Process and Activities Modeling phases of the Enterprise Modeling workflow with some more detailed system's functionalities that can be identified at this point and are necessary to the consolidation of the business process information needs.

2. Use Case Identification: Use Cases are identified from the activities of an Activity Diagram that represents a specific business process. This activity defines the basic system's architecture, and helps driving requirements detailing.
3. Basic Iteration Planning: establish use case development priorities according to their criticality.

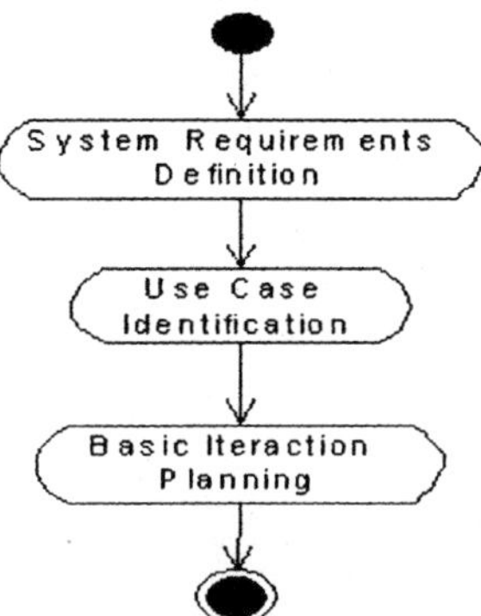

Figure 3. Requirements Workflow

SQA Techniques: Quality is guaranteed by Formal Technical Reviews, which check if all user requirements were captured and documented.

SQA Tools: ERP5 Feature is a tool that aims to help register, control and manage system requirements. This tool is integrated with ERP5 Use Case and ERP5 Project, creating a chain that associates a requirement to one or more use cases (for functional requirements), and then the use cases to project activities. With these tools it is possible to keep track of all requirements implementation and associated resources and costs, in every development phase. Customer inquiries on implementation status are easily answered and change management is facilitated for both the product and the process.

5. ANALYSIS

After the enterprise modeling stage it is necessary to define the activities that will transform structural and behavioral models into source code that reflects integrated business requirements. The workflow for this phase, presented in Figure 4, is executed for every Use Case:

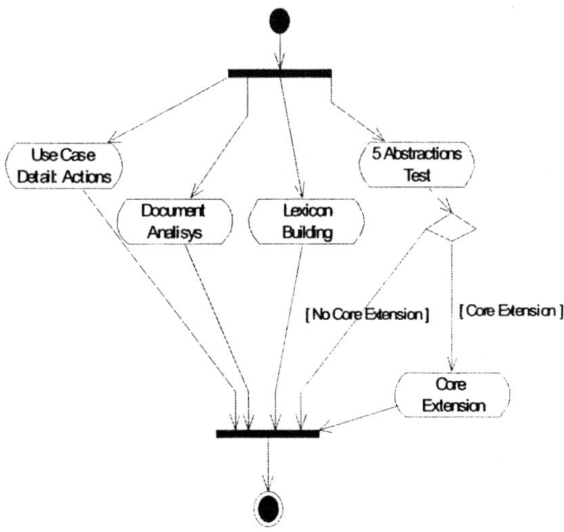

Figure 4. Analysis Workflow

1. Use Case Detail – Actions: it is used two-column Use Cases, one for describing actors' actions and other for describing system's responsibilities or reactions [14]. For this incremental process, in the Analysis activities only the actions and some basic reactions are described, since detailed reactions are identified only during the Design activities. Security issues can also be addressed in this activity.
2. Documents Analysis: ERP5 is a document oriented ERP based on document workflows, since documents are considered a common language understood by all personnel in any organization. This activity consists of identifying the documents that support a given Use Case, starting by ERP5 default document templates that provide a basis for customization.
3. 5 Abstractions Test: the goal of this test is to find out if the UBM can support the Use Case, or in other words, if the resources flows described in a given business process can be represented by ERP5 core model. If not, Core Extensions are implemented.
4. Lexicon Building: maps concepts from the business world of the client to ERP5. This is necessary because, to support reuse, ERP5 names are quite general.

SQA Techniques: Quality is guaranteed by Formal Technical Reviews, which check requirement covering by use cases. Additionally, abstraction tests highly promote reuse, also facilitated by the presence of a lexicon.

SQA Tools: ERP5 Use Case module allows the definition of Use Cases, including their actors and scenarios. ERP5 Document Analysis module helps the identification and naming of documents and their items. ERP5 Lexicon module helps mapping domain terms into ERP5 terms. Any XMI compatible [15] CASE Tool can be used to create UML models.

6. DESIGN

The Design workflow is based on an adapted version of the Workflow, Object Oriented Method (WOOM) [16]. This method focuses on tying structure (classes) to behavior, modeling the second as state machines. The activities of this phase are represented by Figure 5, and described as follows:

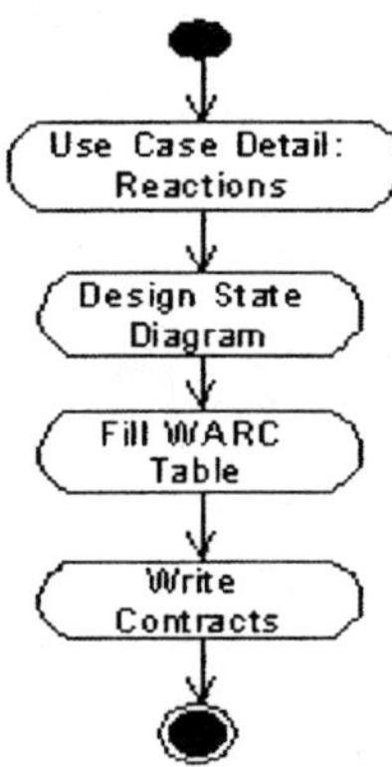

Figure 5. Design Workflow

1. Use Case Detail – Reactions: the reactions correspond to the second column of the UC, they define what the system is suppose to do according to an actor's action.
2. Design Statechart Diagram: states names correspond to the state of the system in a particular moment. From the UC, verbs in the actions column identify state transitions; in the reaction column verbs identify states internal activities. Figure 6 shows an example of a single UC row with a correspondingly transition in a statechart diagram.
3. Fill WARC Table: a new modeling artifact, named WARC Table (Workflow – Action/Reaction – Responsible – Collaborators), is used to associate structure to behavior, guaranteeing encapsulation in object-oriented design. For the process here proposed, a different use of the WARC table is considered: a state transition is associated for each action, and a state internal action to each reaction – forming the Responsible column of the table. The objects that are manipulated by the transition or internal action are listed in the Collaborators column (the objects that participates on the UC were already identified in the Analysis phase). Table 2 shows the rows that represent in the WARC Table the UC step exemplified on Figure 6.
4. Write Contracts: This final step takes care of writing a contract [17] for each action and reaction. Contracts will determine what each transition/internal activity must

do to collaborate to the workflow correct realization. For describing operation's responsibilities, pseudo-code, proto-code, plain text, Object Constraint Language (OCL) and Activity Diagrams can be used.

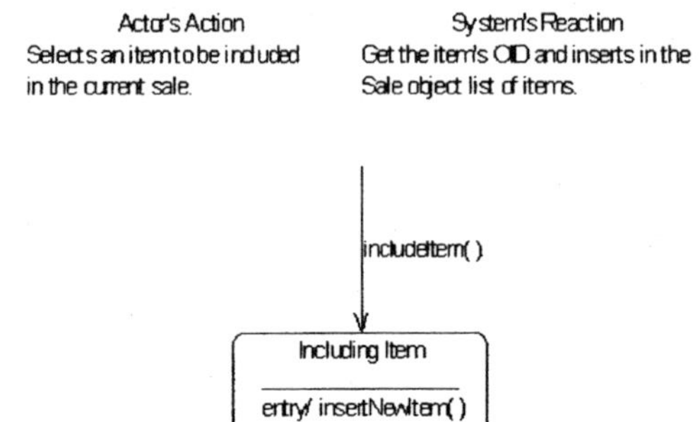

Figure 6. Example Transformation from a Use Case Row to a Statechart Diagram's Transition and State in WOOM

SQA Techniques: use of a well-defined modeling method (WOOM), formal technical reviews for checking the quality of models developed under this method, and Model Checking for checking the consistency of workflows.

SQA Tools: Any XMI compatible CASE Tool can be used to create UML models. For supporting WOOM, currently is in development ERP5 *Deployér*, which will provide integration between use cases and WARC tables. Additionally, formal methods based on Model Checking [18] are under investigation to make *Deployér* check workflow consistency automatically, reducing the necessity for testing code. A plug-in for the Use Case Module will implement WARC tables with some basic features such as selection lists of available classes, transitions, and state activities and automatic updating of class diagrams. These features will avoid ordinary modeling mistakes and accelerate code transformation.

Table 1. Example WARC Table Row for Figure 6

Action/Reaction	Responsible	Collaborators
Select item	includeItem()	Product
Insert item on list	InsertNewItem()	Purchase, Item

7. IMPLEMENTATION

Implementation in ERP5 Process consists of generating code from UML diagrams, writing algorithms for completing this code, and testing. Implementation workflow is executed for every use case as shown in Figure 7, and described as follows:

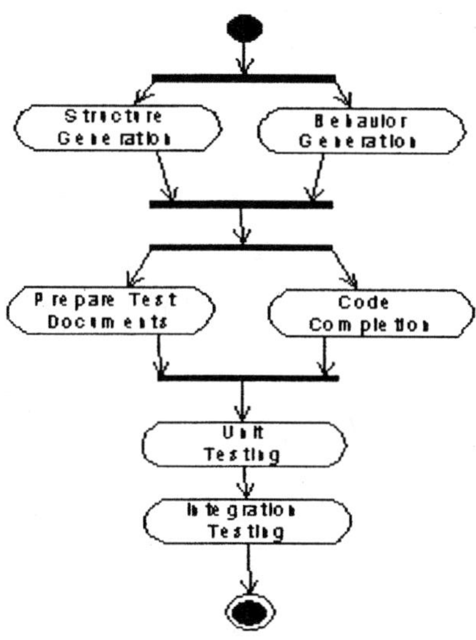

Figure 7. Implementation Workflow

1. Structure and Behavior Generation: using a code generation tool – ERP5 Generator, the new type and related workflow are automatically generated from a XMI file.
2. Prepare Test Documents: these documents are instances of each scenario of each Use Case with specific values.
3. Code Completion: represents the implementation in source code of the algorithms of the workflow's transactions and internal activities.
4. Unit Testing: is run by a testing script, which automates the steps described in the Test Documents. This activity is supported by the ERP5 testing framework.
5. Integration Testing: the Use Case is tested in conjunction with others to check consistency among functionalities that must work integrated.

SQA Techniques: Black and White box testing is used at this stage, since it comprises of both coding and module integration activities. Software Configuration Management is accomplished through the use of a proper tool. Code generation avoids common programming mistakes, reducing testing activities to the code manually written during the code completion activity.

SQA Tools: ERP5 Generator is a tool that generates structural, behavioral, and GUI elements from specific artifacts. From Class Diagrams, Python classes, their relational mapping and basic GUI for object maintenance (create, destroy, getters and setters) are generated. From Statechart Diagrams workflows are generated. ERP5 Generator parses XMI files exported by a compatible CASE tool, check it against a WARC Table, and creates the portal type and associated workflow. Complementing Generator, ERP5 Subversion integrates version control with testing and project management. Finally, ERP5 Test Case provides template testing scripts that automate most of Unit and Integration tests, and Zelenium, a Zope GUI test tool provides user interface testing.

8. CONCLUSIONS

This paper presented ERP5 architecture, its proposed development process and associated SQA techniques quite briefly, given space limitations. It is believed that ERP5 framework addresses all the eleven McCall's quality factors, being highly reusable, easy to maintain, strongly secure, and very usable. Also, ERP5 Process defines a clear flow of model transformations, with consistency checks supported by proper techniques and tools in each transformation. Aiming to enhance even more the use of tools during the development, ERP5 *Déployer*, a tool fully adherent to the proposed development process and integrated with all others cited on this work, is in development. This tool will automate the development workflows, provide template documents for managers – based on the Project Management Body of Knowledge (PMBoK), and improve consistency checks among the successive model transformations that occur during the process, automating it even more.

It is important to note that the goal of the presented process is to supply ERP5 adopters with the option of a model-driven development method based on proper practices and tools, but they are not obliged to follow it entirely.

REFERENCES

1. M. Odeh and R. Kamm, Bridging the Gap Between Business Models and System Models, *Information and Software Technology*. Volume 45, pp.1053-1060, (2003).
2. R.D. Campos, R.A.D. Carvalho, and J.S. Rodrigues, Enterprise Modeling for Development Processes of Open Source ERP, in *Proc. 18th Production and Operation Management Society Conference* (Dallas, USA, 2007).
3. R.A.D. Carvalho, Issues on Evaluating Free/Open Source ERP Systems, in *Proc. of Research and Practical Issues of Enterprise Information Systems (IFIP Series)* (Springer-Verlag: New York, 2006), pp.667-676.
4. L. Zhao and S. Elbaum, Quality assurance under the open source development model, *The Journal of Systems and Software*. Volume 66, pp.65-75, (2003).
5. R.A.D. Carvalho and R.D. Campos, A Development Process Proposal for the ERP5 System, in *Proc. of 2006 IEEE International Conference on Systems, Man, and Cybernetics* (Taipei, Taiwan, 2006).
6. V. Botta-Genoulaz, P.A. Millet, and B. Grabot, A Survey on the recent research literature on ERP systems, *Computers in Industry*. Volume 56, pp.510-522, (2005).

7. J.P.S. Solanes and R.A.D. Carvalho, ERP5: A Next-Generation, Open-Source ERP Architecture, *IEEE IT Professional*. Volume 5, pp.38-44, (2003).
8. *IFIP – IFAC GERAM: Generalized Enterprise Reference Architecture and Methodology*, IFIP – IFAC Task Force on Architectures for Enterprise Integration (1999).
9. J.A. McCall, P.K. Richards, and G.F. Walters, *Factors in Software Quality*. Volumes. 1, 2, 3 - AD/A-049-015/055 (Springfield, 1977).
10. J. Arlow and I. Neustadt, *UML and the Unified Process – Practical Object-Oriented Analysis & Design* (Addison Wesley: London, 2002).
11. V. Botta-Genoulaz, P.-A. Millet and B. Grabot, A Survey on the recent research literature on ERP systems, *Computers in Industry*. Volume 56, pp.510-522, (2005).
12. F.B. Vernadat, Enterprise Modeling and Integration (EMI): Current Status and Research Perspectives, *Annual Reviews in Control*. Volume 26, pp.15-25, (2002).
13. K. Kosanke, F. Vernadat, and M. Zelm, CIMOSA: Enterprise Engineering and Integration, *Computers in Industry*. Volume 40, Number 2, pp.83-97, (1999).
14. H. E. Eriksson and M. Penker, *Business Modeling with UML* (John Wiley & Sons: New York, 2000).
15. R. Wirfs-Brock, *Designing Scenarios: Making the Case for a Use Case Framework*, Smalltalk Report (SIGS Publications: NY, Nov-Dec 1993).
16. Object Management Group, *MOF 2.0/XMI Mapping Specification*, v2.1 (2005).
17. R.A.D. Carvalho, Device and Method for Information Systems Modeling, *Brazilian Patent PI0501998-2* (June 09, 2005).
18. B. Meyer, Applying Design by Contracts, *IEEE Computer*. Volume 25, Number 10, (1992).
19. K.S. Merz, Model Checking and Code Generation for UML State Machines and Collaborations, in *Proc. 5th Workshop on Tools for System Design and Verification* (Augsburg, 2002).

Applications of ICT Services for E-Government

Jiantong Cao and Zhike Che

School of Economics and Management, Beijing University of Posts and Telecommunications, Beijing 100876, P.R. China tony000@263.net

Abstract. ICT (Information and Communication Technology) has been recognized as one main revenue stream for telecom industry, and widely be used for lots of fields, such as government, automobile, health and some others. This article, which aims to explore ICT service for e-government application, focuses on the current products & services provided by telecommunication operators. After studying Verizon business, NTT DATA, Orange, BT and T-system, which are the top ICT service providers in government market. This article describes the general government market, and then, followed by the analysis of the current products & services which can be cataloged by voice, data, IT and BPO. And the discussion will be made on each service. Finally the article shows the important of ICT in the e-government and potential application and service for telecom operators.

Keywords: *E-government, ICT, Telecom operator*

1. INTROUDCTION

In order to provide better service for the citizens and businesses, more and more governments take advantage of information and communication technologies (ICT) to complete the e-government strategies, so that eliminate existing bureaucracy and therefore achieve significant economic and operational efficiencies. It is obvious that governments and governmental institutions are the most complicated organizations in the society providing the legal, political and economic infrastructure to support the daily needs of citizens and businesses [1]. The internet was been seen a convenient and cost-saving channel for governments delivering information and providing online transactions.

In the past, the implementation of e-government was divided into two parts: IT infrastructure and telecommunication services, which were provided separately by IT companies and telecom operators [2]. With the convergence of IT and communications, the distinction between IT and telecom became vague [3]. The IT companies showed great interests in ICT, from 2002, Britain Telecom (BT for short) began ICT strategy as a innovative service [4]. Nortel and Microsoft allied for Communication convergence. All these action can be seen as the sign of convergence. The Figure 1 is the general ICT capability [5].

Please use the following format when citing this chapter:

Cao, J., Che, Z., 2007, in IFIP International Federation for Information Processing, Volume 254, Research and Practical Issues of Enterprise Information Systems II Volume 1, eds. L. Xu, Tjoa A., Chaudhry S. (Boston: Springer), pp. 689-694.

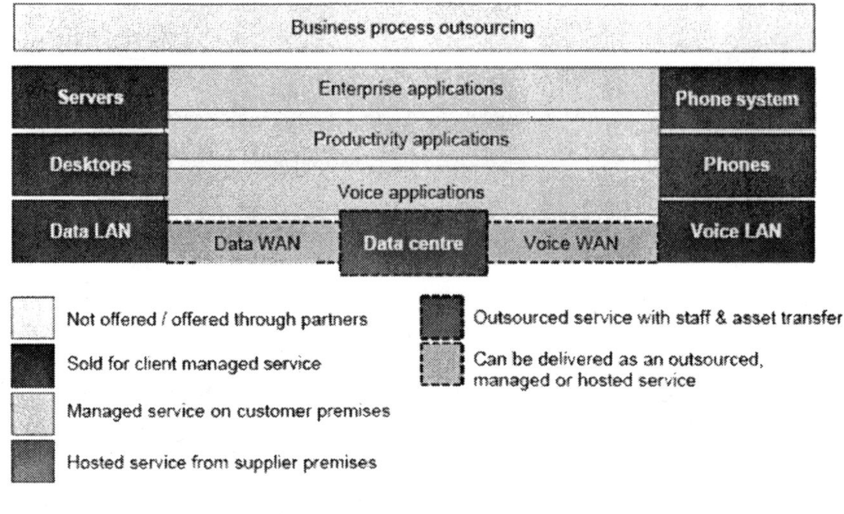

Figure 1. ICT Capability Map

So, it's possible for government to create a single, uniform, high-capacity network that allows data to flow quickly and reliably alongside telephony, helping to enhance productivity and reduce operating costs. In addition, a converged network makes it simple and affordable to integrate new applications and embrace new approaches such as flexible working.

At this moment, the governments face a choice: which would be better provider of ICT service? Telecom operators or IT companies? In this paper, I would like to analyze the ICT service for e-government provided by Telecom operators, and the suggestion would be given.

2. EXISTING ICT SERVICE FOR E-GOVERNMENT

In this chapter, the authors carefully analyze the international telecom operators which include: NTT DATA, Deutsche Telekom (T-Systems), BT, Verizon business, AT&T. These companies are all the top-level ICT providers globally, of course, also perform excellent in e-government application.

Government is the main customer. Here the government involves central government, state and local government and defense department. The Table 1 showed the importance of government for the operators.

Table 1. ICT Department of Operators for e-Government

T-system	AT&T	Verizon	BT	NTT DATA
Real ICT for public sector	AT&T government solution	Verizon Federal Verizon state, local government & defense	Public sector (central, local, defense & devolved government)	Public administration sector

ICT services provided by telecom operators for government can be categorized into:

2.1 System Integration Service

As system integrators, operators can help government departments plan and harness the right technology and networks that are critical in facilitating agile, secure, reliable and compliant information management systems. These system integrations include design of project, purchase, implementation and adjustment of software and hardware, and also the after-sales service under contract.

I Operators provide network telecommunication integration. Many authorities today have a patchwork of different networks, with several carriers and incorporating a wide variety of applications and requirements. The result: high cost of maintenance and which includes WAN/ LAN/ VPN equipment, network security, PBX and so on. These services were quite meet the strength of telecom operators.

II Network application integration embraces call center, video communication (conference and inspect) and network security application. Call center has been one of important channels for government to provide service for citizen and business. BT help the Britain government built call center, so as to improve efficiency and cut cost [6]. Security, a genuine IT service, is another important ICT service for government. Verizon business bought NetSec (a IT security company), so that can serve government customers [7].

III For the e-government, telecom operators provide the industrial services: portals and collaboration.

E-government mainly is seen as a way of dealing with local, national and federal authorities through the Internet, saving time and travel and simplifying and speeding up procedures. T-Systems can build Internet Portals for government, so that government agencies are offering citizens and businesses a better service [8].

The government's IT system is so complex that the collaboration between different departments poses a key challenge for the government. BT offer Shared services that can allow several organizations to operate as a single entity based on standard good practice and sound performance management [6]. So it can be a key enabler of effective, efficient government.

Integrating and re-designing these above essential processes to achieve optimum efficiency has been madc easier.

2.2 Outsourcing Services

A range of Public sector organizations are increasingly looking at outsourced solutions as a way to reduce internal costs and improve service delivery [9].

The benefits of outsourcing are clear - particularly in the case of ICT, which is potentially expensive and labor intensive when dealt with 'in-house'. By enlisting the help of a trusted operator, government departments can benefit both from specialist expertise and technology, and significant economies of scale. BT is currently working on significant outsourcing projects for Department for Work and Pensions (DWP) and HM Revenue & Customs [6].

The outsourcing can also be cataloged by two kinds:

I. Network telecommunication, the government outsources management of core switch equipments, core routers, WAN switches, gateway and other related network equipments. The operators were in charge of the maintenance and operation.

II. Network application. This mean the government outsource maintenance and management of call center, video communication (conference and monitoring)

By managing outsourced functions, telecom operator enables government and allied organizations to concentrate on core activities and achieve significant savings through more effective use of internal resources.

2.3 Professional Services

The telecom operators can provide integrated solution for the government, which include the network communication, network application as requested. These services mainly include:

I Backup and Restore service involves data protection of remote servers and desktops delivers data backup from multiple locations. Government's information is backed up at remote sites thereby lowering the probability of disaster-related data loss. So that keeps the critical business operation up and running. BT Datasure is a simple, easy and cost-effective solution for backing up server data, applications and operating systems [6].

II Management service

Harnessing technology to create more responsive and inclusive government can help to achieve higher levels of citizen satisfaction and deliver efficiency gains [7].

CRM, as a tool of higher citizen satisfaction, plays an integral part in providing effective service delivery in government, thanks to the telecom operators, like BT, T-Systems. This comes to true.

Moreover, T-Systems deliver financial management [8]. With an integrated budgeting and accounting system from T-Systems, authorities can control the costs.

AT&T offers Lifecycle Management, which includes software updates, protocol modifications and/or changes in hardware configurations enable optimum performance of government network [10].

Public Key Infrastructure (PKI), e-legal transaction also belongs to this service.

2.4 Knowledge Support

The operators have many experts of rich experience, so they can provide expertise for governments and improve the development of e-government.

Network Planning and Consulting service, include network planning, network optimizing consulting, business procedure planning, IT system planning, IT system test and risk assessment, business continuity, as well as Disaster Recovery。

Verizon business gives government invaluable advice and analysis from qualified experts. Working with Strohl Systems, the professional services consultants can help government improve their existing business continuity plan or devise and implement a brand new plan designed to readily accommodate rapid advances in technology [7].

2.5 Mobile Government

Everything goes to mobile. Mobile is expected to be the next gold mine for ICT. Wireless technology can help government make more efficient use of its resources. By offering maximum flexibility and mobility, it can help enable staff to be productive and responsive, anywhere, anytime - ideal if they regularly visit other agencies or departments. In addition, wireless technology can free up valuable 'fixed' office space and offer a more versatile working environment.

Based on high-speed Wireless Local Area Networks (WLAN), WiFi technology allows you to connect a range of devices - PCs, Laptops, PDAs, and mobile phones to the Internet without using cables or wires. This enables staff to exchange voice and data, and access vital information and applications, at high-speed, whenever they're in range of a wireless hub.

BT, T-Systems Verizon business and orange all began delivering mobile application for government. This trend would continue, and affect the future of ICT.

3. TELECOM OPERATORS WOULD PLAY A BIG ROLE IN E-GOVERNMENT

From the above products, it's clear that the operators have showed significant advantage in E-government market. Following is the advantage of operators for ICT product, when comparing with the traditional IT companies.

Better understand on network. Public telecommunication network is the infrastructure of ICT. It's convenient for operators expand ICT service for government. Lots of products are network-central.

Network effect meets the characteristic of government. Operators manage a whole network around the country even extending abroad. Accordingly the government scattered all over the country. The traditional IT companies couldn't eliminate this gap between.

It's not a long time for operators to provide ICT for government. And the government's IT request is differ from the telecom demand. So challenge facing the operators is still heavy: first is the talent, there are too many network experts, but lack of real ICT expert. Second is the industrial experience. Today's ICT service is much more complex and customized. Lack of experience pose a key challenge for telecommunication companies.

At present, the telecom operators try their best to exert their strength and avoid the weakness. BT Called their ICT service as networked IT. So do other operators.

4. CONCLUSIONS

From the above analysis, we will propose some suggestion for the government and telecom operators.

For the governments, they should rethink the former impression of telecom operators. Under heavy financial pressure and shortage of experienced ICT staff, outsourcing should be regarded as an invaluable method for government, so that they can concentrate on the core-business, and build an efficient and cost-effective e-government.

For the telecom operators, as newcomers in IT field, are expected to offer integrated IT service to the total ICT solution. Firstly Partnership, merger are both important path to improve operators' IT strength. Secondly the operators have served government for many years; however, they are required to explore government deeply, especially comparing with IBM, SAP, big IT companies.

REFERENCES

1. A. Bouguettaya, A. Rezgui, B. Medjahed, and M. Ouzzani, Internet Computing Support for Digital Government, *Practical Handbook of Internet Computing,* eds. M.P. Singh (CRC Press, 2004).
2. S. He, *The challenges of e-government development in China,* EBchina (2006), pp.45.
3. D.J. Leu, Jr. Charles, and K. Kinzer, The Convergence of Literacy Instruction with Networked Technologies for Information and Communication, *Reading Research Quarterly.* Volume 35, Number 1, pp.108-127, (2000).
4. *Annual report,* BT (2002).
5. X. Liu, *Broadband, Wireless ICT- the Revelation of BT transition telecommunication world 2005 10th* (2005), pp.1009-1564.
6. Chris Lewis, Katy Ring and Jan Dawson, *ICT strategy for Telecos,* by OVUM report (unpunished, 2005), pp.29.
7. www.bt.com (Assessed Apr.20, 2007).
8. www.verizonbusiness .com (Accessed Apr.20, 2007).
9. www.tsystems.com (Accessed Apr.20, 2007).
10. M. Hancox and R. Hackney, Information technology outsourcing: conceptualizing practice in the public and private sector, in *Proc. of the 32nd Annual Hawaii International Conference System Sciences, Volume 7* (Maui, HI, 1999).
11. www.att.com (Accessed Apr.20, 2007).

Research on High-Tech Virtual Enterprise Integrated Information Management Methods and Systems

Changyuan Gao and Zidan Shan

School of Economics and Management, Harbin University of Science and Technology, Harbin 150040, Heilongjiang, P.R. China Gaocy2002@126.com shanzidandana@163.com

Abstract. High-tech Virtual Enterprise (HTVE) is a complicated open tremendous system. It should deal with collaborative manufacture between independent entities with different functions in cooperated enterprises and effective integration of existing information system, business process and commerce rules. This paper combines the characteristics of separated topology organization structure in HTVE to establish its information management model and operational mechanism applying the Distributed Artificial Intelligence approach. Then the Integrated Information Management Systems for Virtual Business in High-tech Enterprise under internet environment is constructed from the aspects of system arrangement, network module and function design. Therefore, the reconfigurable, reusable, scalable and dynamic mutual network-based cooperative commerce chains are realized.

Keywords: *High-tech virtual enterprise, Information management mechanism, Integrated information management system, Distributed artificial intelligence, Work flow, Web services*

1. INTRODUCTION

At present, many countries are exploring and attempting novel growing patterns of high-tech enterprises [1]. Analyzing from the development status and strategic guidance, establishing virtual enterprise should be an effective way to make up deficiency and bring up persistent core competitive ability [2]. High-tech Virtual Enterprise (HTVE) takes the core ability or the superiority ability of high-tech enterprises as support, uses the information technology to obtain the functions that the organization's own resources are not provided with. In addition, it realizes function mutation to meet the dynamic requirements through resource reorganization, function combination, parallel cooperation, and non-property right cooperates with selected correlative enterprises. The new characteristics of HTVE make it difficult to research with traditional management theories and methodologies.

HTVE operation manner requires effective support of integrated information management methods and system platforms. HTVE is a complicated open tremendous system. It should base on entire targets of alliances to deal with distributed and parallel collaborative manufacture among independent entities, as well as effective integration of existing information system, business process and commerce rules. However, existing enterprises have adopted themselves two kinds of integrated

Please use the following format when citing this chapter:

Gao, C., Shan, Z., 2007, in IFIP International Federation for Information Processing, Volume 254, Research and Practical Issues of Enterprise Information Systems II Volume 1, eds. L. Xu, Tjoa A., Chaudhry S. (Boston: Springer), pp. 695-700.

information management styles: information transmission mode and information centre mode. Neither of these two ways is able to solve the questions of information coordination and information security in HTVE. Distributed Artificial Intelligence (DAI) origins from the late 1970s [3], which is capable of overcoming limitations of resource, space-time distribution and functions existing in single intelligence system, with the advantages of parallel, distribution, openness and fault-tolerance, etc. DAI could meet various demands for processing information in HTVE very well.

Hence, how to reform the integrated information management mode which can guarantee the independence of partners and realize resource sharing in HTVE, and how to comprehensively apply existing information systems of the enterprises and HTVE information management platform, have become key problems restraining HTVE from being successful in management.

2. HTVE ORGANIZATION AND BEHAVIOR MODEL

In the distributed system, the organized units have intelligence and autonomy, and are equal in cooperation with each other. The principal and subordinate (sup-sub) between the units of traditional organizations have not been applied. The topological structure solves physically or logically interconnected relationship among units. HTVE is formed by numerous units, divided into core unit organization and non-core unit organization, such as hegemonic enterprises and partnership enterprises. There into, Hegemonic enterprises include original enterprises (VOT) and intimate enterprises (VIT) i.e. $VIT = \{VIT_1, VIT_2, \cdots, VIT_m\}$. VOT and VIT set up the integrative Management Centre in HTVE $(VIMC = \{VOT, VIT_i\}\ \ (i = 1,2,\cdots,m))$ together, which is responsible for the management, coordination, control, lead and get in touch to the outside of the whole HTVE. In addition, VOT and VIT take on the conductors (VCR) of the virtual project team (VTM) respectively. Different VCR chooses unit (VU) in VTM, the project is decomposed to several sub tasks $VAT = \{VAT_1, VAT_2, VAT_3, \cdots, VAT_m, VAT_{m+1}\}$, which distribute to

$VTM = \{VTM_1, VTM_2, \cdots, VTM_m, VTM_{m+1}\}$, over here,

$VTM_i = \{VCR_j, VU_j\}\ \ (j = 1,2,\cdots,m+1)$, even $VCR = VOT \bigcup VIT$,

$$
\begin{aligned}
VU &= VU_1 \bigcup VU_2 \bigcup \cdots \bigcup VU_m \bigcup VU_{m+1} \\
&= \{VU_1{}^1, VU_2{}^1, \cdots, VU_k{}^1\} \bigcup \{VU_{k+1}{}^2, VU_{k+2}{}^2, \cdots, VU_{k+l}{}^2\} \cdots \bigcup \{VU_{r+1}{}^{m+1}, \cdots, VU_{r+s}{}^{m+1}\}
\end{aligned}
$$

After finishing sub tasks, VTM would disaggregate, so VCR turns to regression state.

It is especially important to establish interior and exterior HTVE information behavior model for constructing the integrated information management system (IMS) and exploring the distributional artificial intelligence technology (such as Figure 1). Correspondingly, HTVE information behavior model includes conceptual model, process model and coordinated model. (1)The conceptual models are composed of VCR model and VU model. (2)The process model is the information modeling among VTMs in HTVE. (3)The coordinated models deal with synthesis management of VTMs to form coordinated and harmonious decision-making process.

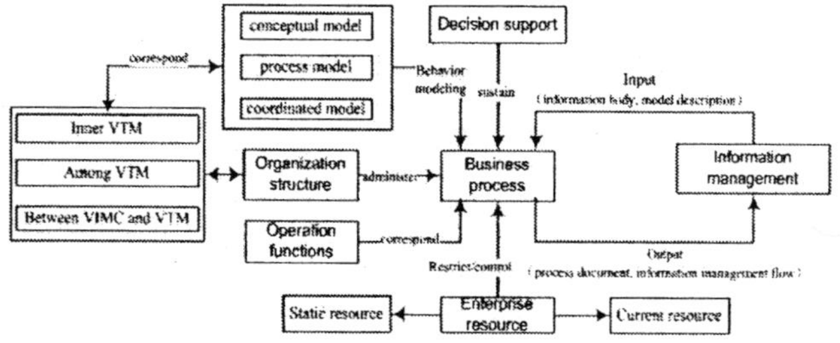

Figure 1. Relations of HTVE Information Behavior Model

3. INTEGRATED IMS OF HTVE

The design standards of the system structure meet the characteristic of DAI and have very high flexibility [3]. Construction of design should proceed from three different angles corresponding to HTVE information behavior mode, first, enterprise's information management system inside VTM, second, enterprise's information management system between VTM, and third, enterprise's information management system between VIMC and VTM.

3.1 Entire Architecture and Network Modules of HTVE Integrated IMS

The paper bases on information technologies and relevant standards of Internet, Web Service, distributed Work Flow etc. It proposes four-layer integration-information-management-system-framework (Figure 2), including operation control layer, decision support layer, user problem dealing layer, and technology support layer. The Four layers structure of the system is suitable for the information management system of VOT and VIT, within VTM (between VCR and many VUs) and between VTM.

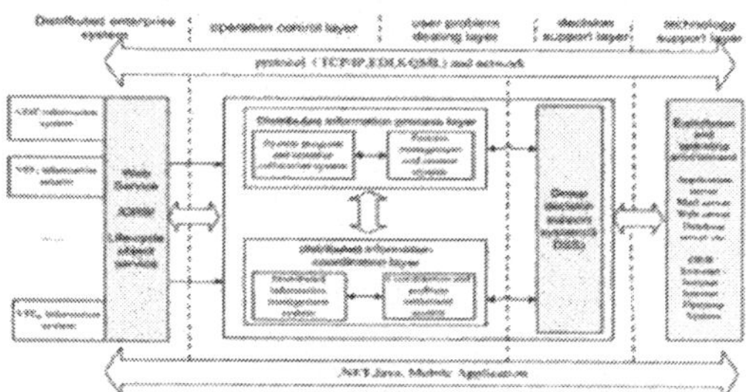

Figure 2. Four Layers Structure of HTVE Integrated Information Management System

In order to support the operation of HTVE distributed information management, each member enterprise acts as one node in network, possessing inside information system and coordination system and DSS between enterprises. Divide each node into five pieces of module (Figure 3). Internal module (IM) represents an independent autonomy member, including the information management system and production control system of VIT, VOT and VU, administering intact information structure, all internal decision-making processes and enterprise activity inside member's enterprises. IM forms the information process layer. Distributed Information Management Module (DIMM) symbolizes the module that manages information among different organizations and with VOT and VIT, and within VTM, and between VTM. CM and DIMM form information coordination layer, and is mainly controlled by VIMC. Decision Module (DM) deals with non-structural problems among the enterprises of the members, DM forms the decision support layer. Communication Infrastructure (CI) supports mutual agreements between HTVE nodes. In correspondence with inside and outside organizations, it divides into Internal Communication Protocol (ICP) and External Communication Protocol (ECP). CI forms the technology support layer.

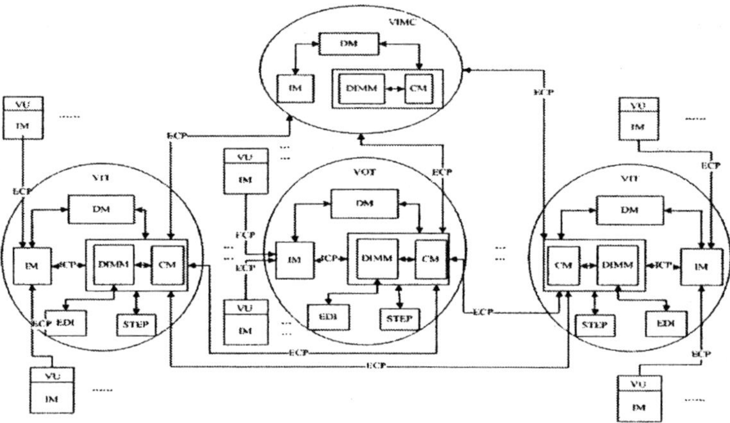

Figure 3. Information Network Module Structure in HTVE

Operation control layer is composed of information process layer and information coordination layer. The information process layer is mainly about the analysis and design of IM. IM is divided two parts. The former is to carry out reasonable plans and distributions to organizations, resources, information database of VOT, VIT, and VU. The later completes the tasks and orders from former, controls the implementations of tasks in real-time, while feedback to program and resource collocation system takes prompt action. Information coordination layer concerns itself mainly of analyses and design of DIMM and CM. DIMM. It exchanges information process through ICP with IM, and its partial outputs for CM, DM and other DIMM to use. With the support of workflow management system, CM transmits workflow data, which deal with work processing engine from distributed process management information of IM to integrated process management system of CM, finally finishes supporting process-running status by enterprise task lists shown. The agreement management system guarantees the normal operation of HTVE integrated information management system, and supervises and controls its course. Decision support system depicts the design of DM. Spacial and systematical distribution determines that the decision support system is GDSS.Technology support layer is formed by supporting milieu, system service, exploitation environment and the tools [4]. Based on the differences between cooperating relationship and the consanguineous grades of member enterprises, it offers mail service and ORB [5] which is systematic encapsulating tool.

3.2 Function Design in HTVE Integrated IMS

According to the characteristics of HTVE whole architecture and network modules constructed by the integrated information management system in hegemony enterprises and partner enterprises, the paper describes functions of three different entities as VU, VCR and VIMC (Figure 4). HTVE public information centre as workspace needs to truss up the large mainstream quantities of application software platforms, and also support various basic platforms and application server for VU, VCR and VIMC.

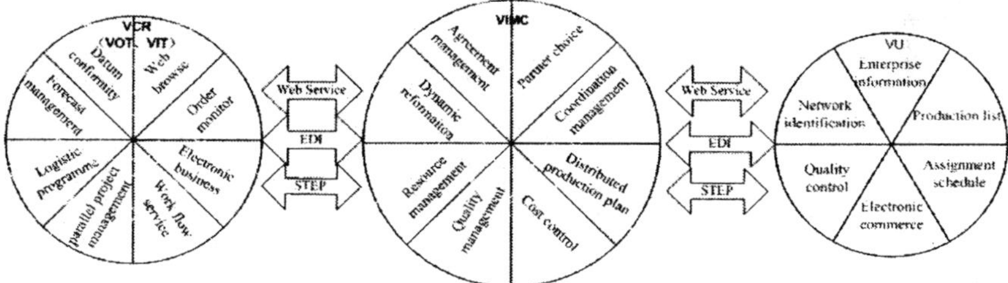

Figure 4. Function Design Frame of VU, VCR and VIMC

4. CONCLUSIONS

HTVE Integrated information management system applies DAI method, expanded by high-tech enterprise existing systems, which guarantees the independence of member enterprises and keeps the relevance of the entrepreneurial alliances. The core technology of member enterprises is mostly left in IM, the users inside the enterprise can only visit its information, and other enterprises can only visit the information in DIMM and CM. Accordingly, the reconfigurable, reusable, scalable and dynamic mutual network-based cooperative commerce chains are realized. However, on account of dynamic and complex organization in HTVE, we need to explore and research more, i.e. negotiation mechanism of and members' credit in HTVE etc.

ACKNOWLEDGEMENTS

This research was supported by two projects: (1) Project 70373058 supported by NSFC (2) Project 06D070 supported by Heilongjiang Social Science Foundation.

REFERENCES

1. C. Henry, W. Lau, and E.T. Wong. Partner Selection and Information Infrastructure of a Virtual Enterprise Network, *Int J. Integr Manuf.*. Volume 14, Number 2, pp.186-193, (2001).
2. R.E. Giachetti, A Framework to Review the Information Integration of the Enterprise, *Int J. Product Res.*. Volume 42, Number 6, pp.1147-1166, (2004).
3. K.H. Choi, D.S. Kim, and Y.H. Doh, Multi-agent-based Task Assignment System for Virtual Enterprises, *Robot Comput Integr Manuf.*. Volume 2, Number 3, pp.1-6, (2007).
4. B.G. Bernsttein and W. Ruh, *Enterprise Integration: the Essential Guide to Integration Solutions* (Addison-Wesley: Boston, MA, 2005)
5. V. Ermolayev and N. Keberle, Towards a Framework for Agent-enabled Semantic Web Service Composition, *Int J. Web Serv Res.*. Volume 1, Number 3, pp.63-87, (2004).

A Strategic Framework for Enterprise Information Integration of ERP and E-Commerce

Zaojie Kong, Dan Wang and Jianjun Zhang

School of Management, Hebei University of Technology, Tianjin 300130, P.R.China
kongzj@sina.com moyuhun_007@163.com zh_jianjunhaohao@163.com

Abstract. At the end of last century, E-commerce and ERP become the main methods to improve competitive power, but the integration of enterprise information of ERP and E-commerce system puzzled many enterprises, so in this article, the integration importance and the main problems that are faced in the integration process are analyzed firstly, and then the enterprise information integration frame of ERP and E-commerce based on Web Services and Multi-Agent is proposed to solve platform heterogeneous, language differences, and achieve the two systems information alternation.

Keywords: *Enterprise information integration, ERP, E-commerce, Agent, Web Services*

1. INTRODUCTION

With the technology of computer and Internet swift and violent development, E-commerce and ERP have become the main means of enterprise management. For the enterprise, E-commerce and ERP system like front and the rear relations, both are closely linked. For example, enterprises getting orders from e-commerce, should sent the order information immediately to the internal ERP system for Procurement, Production, Finance, Sales department arranging raw materials, capital, production and sale. If front-end E-commerce and the backstage ERP system come apart, this can cause lots of key information and data to be enclosed in mutually independent system. Sales order and market information obtaining from E-commerce platform cannot transmit into the backstage ERP system promptly; EC system can't read the product prices, customer information from ERP. The enterprise logistics, fund flow and information flow can't be unified organically, the uniformity, integrity and accuracy of data cannot be guaranteed. Departments cannot make the rapid, prompt, effective response to the customer, so it causes the enterprise working efficiency drop as well as the operation cost rise. Therefore, the E-commerce and ERP integration can not be ignored.

There are many differences in languages, platforms, communication protocols, and so on, between ERP and E-commerce. How to overcome the high cost of system integration arising from the differences is the key to solve this problem. For integration, information is the key. How to select the relevant information and how to achieve the two systems integrating fast and efficiently, which also don't allow to be ignored.

Please use the following format when citing this chapter:

Kong, Z., Wang, D., Zhang, J., 2007, in IFIP International Federation for Information Processing, Volume 254, Research and Practical Issues of Enterprise Information Systems II Volume 1, eds. L. Xu, Tjoa A., Chaudhry S. (Boston: Springer), pp. 701-705.

2. THE ENTERPRISE INFORMATION INTEGRATION FRAME OF ERP AND E-COMMERCE

From above we know that achieving the systems integration is mainly to resolve heterogeneous and information alternation. Web Services technology based on XML is the best mean to resolve the heterogeneous, Agent can achieve information obtain, organization and transmission by its reactivity and intelligence.

Web Services [1] technology is the compilation of technologies (XML [2], Simple Object Access Protocol (SOAP) [3], Web Services Description Language (WSDL) [4], and Universal Discovery, Description, and Inventory (UDDI) [5]) that allow users to develop, catalog, and publish business services for delivery and use on the Web [6]. Web Services provide a distributed computing technology for revealing the business services of applications on the Internet or intranet using standard XML protocols and formats. The use of standard XML protocols makes Web Services platform, language, and vendor independent. Web Services eliminate the interoperability issues of existing solutions, such as CORBA and DCOM. Web Services are simpler, cheaper, based on open standards and more efficient, dynamic, and flexible [7].

The concept of Agent generates form Distributed Artificial Intelligent. It is a particular entity existing in the environment. Agent has following characteristics :(1) Autonomy: Agent has its own resources (data) and behavior control mechanism (process); it can operate without people. (2) Sociability: Agent and others (including people) can communicate with some language for coordination and cooperation. (3) Reactivity: Agent observes the environment, make responses to the change. (4) Pro-activity: Agent not only reacts to the environment, but also accepts certain message, to take the initiative action, which is goal-oriented behavior. (5) Intelligence: Agent has intelligence including reasoning and learning by itself.

It is obvious that the integration problem can be solved by using web services and agent, the enterprise information integration frame is as shown in figure 1.

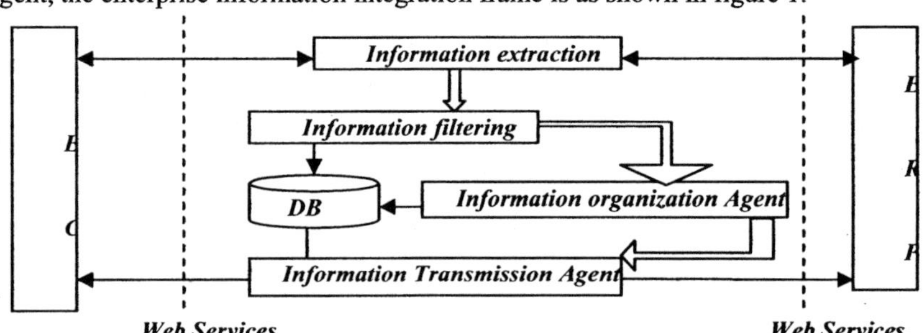

Figure 1. The Enterprise Information Integration Frame of ERP and E-commerce

The frame consists of Information extraction Agent, Information filtering Agent, Information organization Agent and Information Transmission Agent. Web services shields platform heterogonous, data and language differences, the information extraction agent communicate with EC and ERP systems, and extract the integrating information, but there also may be some dirty data ,so the data should be filtered into

DB by Information filtering Agent, then all information is organized by Information organization Agent, at last, the integrating information can be transferred quickly and efficiently by Information transmission Agent, therefore the integration of ERP and E-commerce can be achieved.

3. SYSTEM WORK MECHANISM

3.1 Web Services

All kinds formats information from the two systems can be transformed into XML by Web Services, so all information can be transferred. And all the output information can be transformed the right format by XSLT. Web Services provide the sharing platform for the information systems, all information can be read.

3.2 Agents Function

3.2.1 Information Extraction Agent

Information extraction Agent mainly learns the extraction rules and extracts the integrating information. Agents who want to achieve its functions depend on Knowledge Base and database. The knowledge base of Information extraction Agent includes the domain knowledge base, the extraction request base and the extraction rule base. The domain knowledge base is the knowledge of the basic concept, attribute, entity, rules and so on, which is contained in the field of the extraction information. The extraction request base records use history, memories the extraction requests .When meet the similar request, it will take the optimized request from the base to users. The extraction rule base memory extraction rules. Its main body can be divided into two parts, one is the information format knowledge is relevant to description format; the other is semantic knowledge to describe the information content. When there is new information, Information extraction Agent starts the system by autonomy, accepts the initial extraction request, optimizes the extraction request constantly, learns the rules, then extracts the information. At last results will be taken to deal with by information filtering agent.

3.2.2 Information Filtering Agent

The goal of Information filtering Agent is to help users to eliminate the information that they don't want to get. Information filtering Agent filters the extraction information, and then put the information into database. It can automatically obtain external dynamic information; then information is filtered into Eigen value and special symbols. These values or symbols are stored into database; they can directly lead to action or are processed in deeper level by information organization agent after further polymerization.

For lots of relevant extraction information, Information filtering Agent must filter the data according to the system needs. At present, there are four information filter methods which usually are used [8]: based on keywords vector information filtering methods, based on articles information filtering methods, Multi-Agent filtering methods and evolutionary information filtering method. System can take based on keywords vector information filtering methods. The system needs and the extraction information can be described in VSM, by calculating the two models similarity, when the similarity is over a threshold, put the information into database, otherwise give it up.

3.2.3 Information Organization Agent

Information organization Agent organizes the information in database. It will change information format and manage the information resource by organization, addition, deletion, modify, sorting and inquiry, etc. It not only makes a response quickly, but also manages effectively.

It organizes the information according to the thought of Data warehouse. Data warehouse is the data aggregation which is facing theme, compositing, non-volatile, and supporting the decision-making of enterprises with the time. The data in Data warehouse is from many different data resources. When the data gets into Data warehouse, it will be converted, reformatted, rearranged and exchanged. The result is that the data in Data warehouse has single physical corporate image, so we can organize the data according the characteristic of Data warehouse.

The focus of Data warehouse design is theme, which is always decided by the enterprise needs. When theme selected, it is decided database dimension, dimension attributes and facts table attributes based on granularity. So the filtered information can be organized effectively and transferred into EC and ERP systems efficiently and accurately.

3.2.4 Information Transmission Agent

Information Transmission Agent mainly completes initiative transferring. It searches the integration information, and provides the new inquiry result into EC and ERP systems according to information integration needs. It will notify the systems timely when monitoring the dynamic changes of data, as information expired, update or lost, to achieve the enterprise information alternating.

3.3 Agent Communication Pattern

The system uses SOAP communication mechanism to achieve interoperability between agents. SOAP is a cross-platform protocol standard, it can allocate the object and communicate at heterogeneous platforms by combination with XML.

Figure 2 is a simple agent communication model. Information extraction agent is the sender of SOAP message, Information Transmission agent is the receiver. Information filtering Agent and Information organization Agent is also the sender and the receiver. The sender sends the SOAP message to the receiver; the receiver receives the message, parses the message and obtains the content.

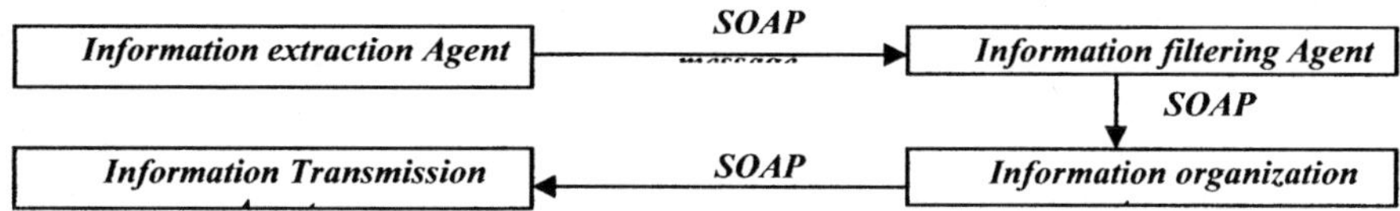

Figure 2. Agent Communication Model Based on SAOP

4. SUMMARY

The enterprise information integration system takes full advantage of Web Services to solve platform heterogeneous and the intelligence of agent. It greatly improves the information transmission speed and accuracy. It only puts forward a conceptual model. The specific construction strategies and methods need summarizing and exploring in practice. However, analysis indicates that the integration strategy is a new idea for resolving the problem of enterprises information isolated islands, it also can be used in other enterprise information systems integrating.

REFERENCES

1. R. Bhatti, E. Bertino, and A. Ghafoor, XML-based specification for web services document security, *IEEE Comps*. Volume 37, Number 4, pp.41-49, (2004).
2. T. Bray, J. Paoli, and C.M. Sperberg-McQueen, *XML extensible markup language (XML) 1.0*. (2004). http://www.w3.org/TR/2004/REC-xml-20040204 (Accessed March 4, 2007).
3. Anonymous, *W3C.SOAP1.2,* W3C(2003). http://www.w3.org/2000/XP/Group (Accessed February 4, 2007).
4. Anonymous, *W3C.WSDL2.0,* W3C(2004). http://www.w3.org/2002/ws/desc (Accessed March 4, 2007).
5. Anonymous, *UDDI ORG.UDDI3.0* W3C (2003). http://uddi.org/pubs/uddi_v3.htm. (Accessed March 4, 2007).
6. K.K.E Venugopal and J.G. Kupper, *Web services and EAI-what'it'is* (2002). http://www.webservices.org/article-php?sid=421 (Accessed March 4, 2007).
7. G. Samtani and D. Sadhwani, *EAI and web services easier enterprise application integration?* (2002). http://www.webservicesarchitect.com/content/articles/samtani01.asp (Accessed February 4, 2007).
8. H. Chen, W. Li, and S. Liu, the Design and Implementation technology of intelligent information filtering Agent, *Guangdong University of Technology Journal.* Number 9, pp.33-35, (2001).

An Integrated Modeling Method Supporting Product Development Process Optimization

Min Li[1], Xiansheng Qin[2] and Yabin Xu[2]

[1]School of Mechatronics, KunMing University of Science & Technology, Kunming 650093, P.R. China leah163@163.com
[2]School of Mechatronics, Northwestern Polytechnical University, Xi'an 710072, P.R. China xsqin@nwpu.edu.cn yabinxu@nwpu.edu.cn

Abstract. Constructing an effective process module is groundwork for product development process optimization. This paper imposes an activity/process based modeling idea which supports the integrated management and optimization of process development process. This idea uses the activity/process as the modeling basic cell. At first, the activity/process based PDP modeling theory is studied; Second, the product Development process Modeling based on the Process/Action (DMP/A) method is forwarded. The basic elements and their properties are defined, then the steps of DMP/A are given in the paper. Through integrating the definition and description of process structure and activity/process attribute, input and output, the process model by DMP/A method helps to programmer, supervise and control the product development activities/processes, as well as communicate messages with each other. This provides a supporting tool for process development process integrated optimization.

Keywords: *Product life cycle systems, Life cycle process, Business process modeling, Modeling and description languages, Activity/Process*

1. INTRODUCTION

Product development process (PDP) should be geared to the needs of manufacturing globalization and normalization. Manufacturing enterprises had employed some advanced manufacturing system theory and methods, such as Concurrent Engineering (CE) and Agile Manufacturing (AM), for the improvement and optimization of the product development process (PDP). These theory and methods are based on the analysis, operation and control of the business and product development process. It founded on PDP modeling. A good modeling method should support the application of advanced manufacturing theories and technologies like CE. Therefore, the study of process modeling is fundamental and significant for the mode optimization of advanced manufacturing system, the application and realization of advanced manufacturing technologies and the performance indexes improvement of product development system [1].

Please use the following format when citing this chapter:

Li, M., Qin, X., Xu, Y., 2007, in IFIP International Federation for Information Processing, Volume 254, Research and Practical Issues of Enterprise Information Systems II Volume 1, eds. L. Xu, Tjoa A., Chaudhry S. (Boston: Springer), pp. 707-716.

Process modeling should support process integration. This means not only the integration and share of process information, but also the cooperation, optimization and management of process. So, new modeling technology is needed to support effectively the process programming and management [2]. The existed research works mostly have no overall consideration of product, process information and process management. For solving this problem, this paper studies the integration of process modeling technology and contemporary PDP management methods to promote the application of PDP model, based on the comprehensive consideration of product, process information and process management.

2. PROBLEMS PDP MODELING FACES

Product development is a complicated process which involves a great deal of activities, information, personnel and resources. The collection of information and management of processes are two key factors among them. In PDP, activities are interrelated. Some activities execute with provision and support of many other related activities. Information of activities is dispersive and dynamic, and executants of activity often do not know which activities information their activity produced will influence. Then how to send the activity information to the product developer and process manager accurately and promptly is a problem PDP faces. In PDP, a tool that manages the activity information is cried for, and it is the goal of process modeling in this paper.

Another problem in PDP is how to support the cooperation among activities and process management under the environment of networks [3]. Because product development system is a very complex and gigantic system with non-linearity, local disorder may trigger chaos in the overall PDP, even the decline of system's whole performance. To manage and control such a system scientifically, an applicable model should be established at first. In other words, an operable and controllable system model or process model is needed to manipulate and analyze the system or process dynamically.

Process model supports mainly the process execution and process management. Process model could describe PDP more accurate than pure language and concept. With a describing and supporting tool of process, developer may simulate PDP, and then acquire information needed of PDP via communication among processes; manager may design and program PDP and supervise the progression and cost situation of processes. Furthermore, based on the process model, simulator and analyzer could be used to improve and optimize PDP.

3. BASIC THEORY OF PDP INTEGRATED MODELING

3.1 Activity/Process Definition

Process and activity are two basic concepts in process modeling. Usually process is regarded as the set of activities and relation among them, and activity is abstraction of product development task; process emphasizes relation and activity emphasizes independence. Their definition is as follow:

3.1.1 Process Definition

$$P=(A,R) \tag{1}$$

P represents a process, and A represents the set of activities within process P. R represents the set of relation among activities within process P, which called process structure. In the following equation, n is the number of activities within process P.

$$A=\{A[i], i=1,2\ldots n, n\in N, n>1\} \tag{2}$$

3.1.2 Activity Definition

An activity could be expressed by its input, output, items and its attribute state space (Figure 1). Activity A could be expressed as:

$$A[i]=\{ I[i], O[i], AC[i], AR[i]\} \tag{3}$$

I [i] represents the set of A[i]'s inputs; O[i] represents the set of A[i]'s outputs; AC [i] represents the set of A[i]'s items; AR [i] represents the set of A[i]'s attributes state space which includes activity attributes and activity item attribute. At a given time, activity attributes and activity item attribute have given value, then these values compose matrix ar [i]. ar [i] is an element in state space AR [i] which called an attribute state.

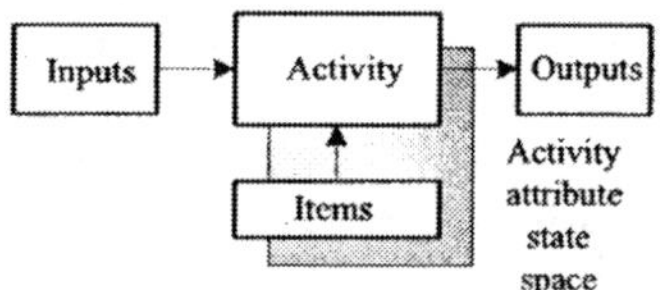

Figure 1. Expression of an Activity

1. Set of inputs: I [i]

Set of inputs, I [i], could be divided into two kinds: IC[i] and ID[i]. IC[i] is the inputs with control attribute and ID[i] is the inputs without control attribute. The difference between them is that inputs in IC[i] may cause the change of activity's state.

2. Set of outputs: O[i]

Like I [i], set of outputs, O[i], could be divided into two kinds: OC[i] and OD[i]. OC[i] is the outputs with control attribute and OD[i] is the outputs without control attribute. The difference between them is that outputs in OC[i] are caused by change of activity's state.

In a system, elements interact by three ways. They are exchange of material, information and energy. PDP has the property of system. Activities in PDP interact by these three ways. The interaction is activity's input and output. Because material exchange and energy exchange could be described by information, set of inputs I[i] and set of outputs O [i] of activity A [i] could be described by information.

3. Set of items: AC [i]

Set of items, AC [i], represents the A[i] related object entity which is non-activity, non-input and non-output. In PDP, activity items include mainly organization and resources.

$$AC [i]=\{ AG[i], U [i]\} \tag{4}$$

AG[i]: Organization, which is the organizational structure of activity;
U[i]: Resources, which is the equipments and tools needed by activity execution.
04. Attribute state space: AR [i]

AR [i] represents the attribute state space of activity A[i] (Table 1).

$$AR [i]=[RAR[i], RAG[i], RU [i], RI [i], RO [i]] \tag{5}$$

Table 1. Attribute State Space of Activity A [i]

attribute state space	name	type	Func-tion	site	start-time	end-time	state	Requi-rement	cost
activity RAR[i]	√	√	√	√	√	√	√		√
organizationRAG[i]	√	√	√				√		
resource RU [i]	√	√	√				√	√	
input RI [i]	√	√			√	√	√	√	
output RO [i]	√	√			√	√	√	√	

3.1.3 Activity Output Function

Activity output function g is a mapping which represents the transform of I[i] to O[i] when the activity is under the attribute state ar [i]. Then activity output

$$O[i]= g(I[i], ar [i]) , ar [i]\in AR [i] \tag{6}$$

3.2 Relation among Activities

To analyze the relation among activities with an eye to time, the following equation expresses relation between activity A_i and A_j:

$$f(ar[i](t),R'_{ij}(t),ar[j](t))=0, ar [i], ar [j]\in AR [j] \tag{7}$$

ar[i](t)and ar[j](t)represent separately an attribute state of AR [i] and AR [j] at the moment t. R'_{ij} represents the activity relation caused by ar[i](t)and ar[j](t).

We know from equation (7) that relation equation is decided by the impersonal rules of process. It is objective thing and determinate to any process. But because of the limitation of the knowledge of product, enterprise and society, we could not work out the relation equation of every process. The management and control of PDP requires participation of human being because of the complexity of process environment.

In equation (7), when any two variables of ar[i](t), $R'_{ij}(t)$and ar[j](t)is given, the other one variable is decided by the corresponding relation equation.

3.3 Process Structure Definition

Process structure R is the abstract of relation among activities. Under given environment, if there exists relation $R_{ij}(t)(1\leq i\leq n,\ 1\leq j\leq n;\ i\neq j,\ n>1)$in the moment t between activity A_i and A_j in process P, then the set of all relation $R_{ij}(t)(1\leq i\leq n,\ 1\leq j\leq n;\ i\neq j,\ n>1)$is called process structure, R(t).

$$R(t)=\{ R_{ij}(t)|1\leq i\leq n,\ 1\leq j\leq n;\ i\neq j,\ n>1\} \quad \textbf{(8)}$$

From definitions in equation (7) and (8), we know that various activity attributes show various relation. The progression attribute of activity shows certain activity relation, and resource attribute shows another activity relation. This leads to the difference among process expression. A uniform process modeling method is needed.

3.4 Breaking Activity/Process Down

PDP expansion simplifies the process research, so method breaking process down layer by layer is employed to describe activity/process (Figure 2). Activity/process is broken down from up to bottom and more detailed step by step. Each son-activity/process is regarded as a local and independent module, and then it has inputs, outputs, control information, task and goal etc., and has certain duties, attributes and behaviors as its father-activity/process.

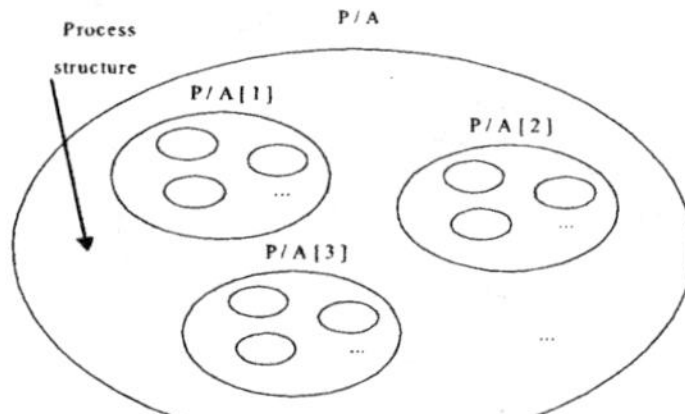

Figure 2. Breaking Down Activity/Process

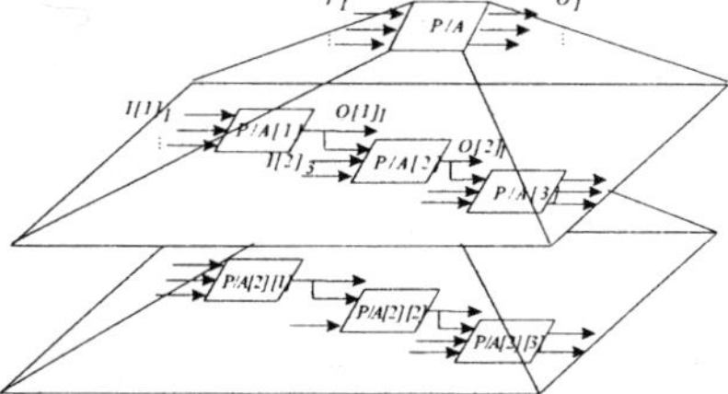

Figure 3. Breaking Down Inputs and Outputs of Activity/Process

3.5 Breaking down Inputs and Outputs of Activity/Process

The key point of activity/process management is to manage the relation among activities. Activity attribute state space is the foundation of activity relation. Inputs and outputs of activity show the task relation and information, material flow relation, on which other activity relation based. In process model, if inputs and outputs of an activity is defined, then they could be broken down and their attributes, including time, quality standard and type, etc., could be endued with. Moreover, all kinds of activity relation could be programmed and managed in the light of activity attributes and relation between inputs and outputs.

In process model, inputs and outputs of activity/process could be described by information. As the deployment of activity/process, a large, fuzzy input (output) is gradually transferred into those detailed input (output) information (Figure 3).

If breaking activity/process, P/A[i], down as follow:

$$P/A[i]=(\{P/A[i][j], j=1,2\ldots n, n\in N, n>1\}, R[i]) \tag{9}$$

n is the number of sub-activity/process, P/A[i][j], in P/A[i]; R[i] represents the process structure of P/A[i].

If there is no coupling between input, I[i], and output, O[I], of activity/process P/A[i], then

$$I[i]=\sum_{j=1}^{n} I[i][j]-\sum_{j=1}^{n}(I[i][j]\cap\sum_{k=1,k\neq j}^{n} O[i][k]) \tag{10}$$

$$O[i]=\sum_{j=1}^{n} O[i][j]-\sum_{j=1}^{n}(O[i][j]\cap\sum_{k=1,k\neq j}^{n} I[i][k]) \tag{11}$$

I[i][j] is the input of sub-activity/process, P/A[i][j]; O[i][j] is the output of sub-activity/process, P/A[i][j]; n is the number of P/A[i]'s son-activity/process, P/A[i][k].

External input and output of P/A[i][j] are as follow:

$$I'[i][j]=I[i][j]-I[i][j]\cap\sum_{k=1,k\neq j}^{n} O[i][k] \tag{12}$$

$$O'[i][j]=O[i][j]-O[i][j]\cap\sum_{k=1,k\neq j}^{n} I[i][k] \tag{13}$$

Then

$$I[i]=\sum_{j=1}^{m} I'[i][j] \tag{14'}$$

$$O[i]=\sum_{j=1}^{m} O'[i][j] \tag{15'}$$

In equation(6), O[i]= g(I[i], ar [i] , ar [i]∈AR [i]). If activity attribute state space, ar [i], could meet the need of transferring input into output, then

$$O[i]=g'(I[i]) \tag{16}$$

From equation (6),(10)',(11)', there is

$$g'(I[i])=\sum_{j=1}^{m} g'(I'[i][j]) \tag{17}$$

Considering the coupling between input and output as well as the interaction among activity attributes, then

$$g(I[i]) = \sum_{j=1}^{m} g(I[i][j] + f[i]) \tag{18}$$

f[i] represents the function of information transferring, managing and harmonizing among A[i]'s son-activities.

4. DMP/A MODELING METHOD

On the basis of PDP integrated modeling theory, we propose Product Development Process Modeling based on the Process/Action (DMP/A) method. The elements of DMP/A methods include activity/process block, link and joint (Figure 4). Process model is described by figure, table and embedded file. Here introduce briefly DMP/A method.

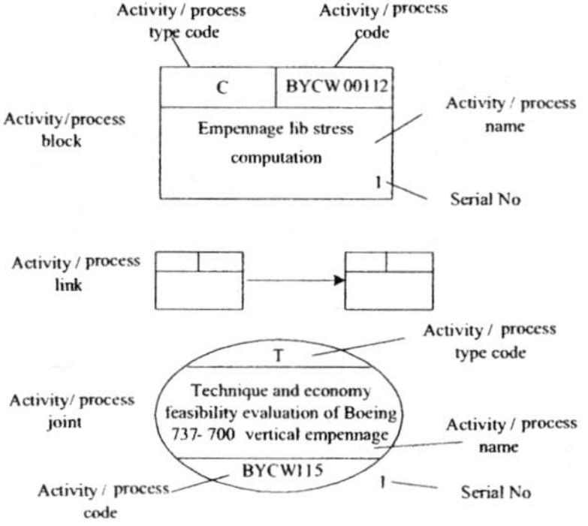

Figure 4. Activity/Process Block, Link and Joint

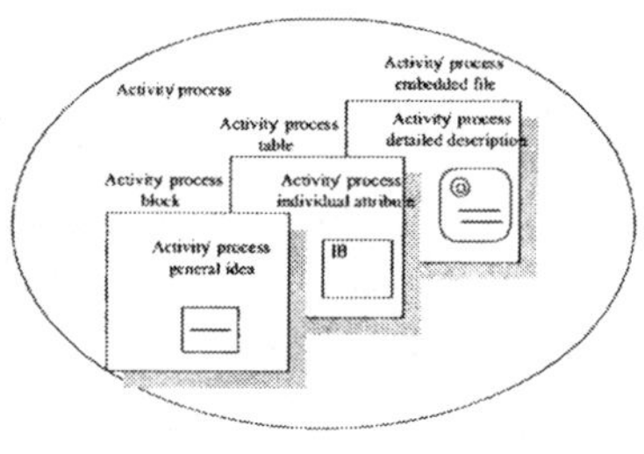

Figure 5. Relationship among Activity/Process Block, Table and Embedded File

4.1 Activity/process Description

DMP/A method uses activity/process block (joint), activity/process table and activity/process embedded file to describe activity/process. Activity/process block (joint) describes activity/process in general with visible figures; activity/process table describes activity/process resources, personnel, time and cost etc. by their individual character or attributes; activity/process embedded file is a more detailed description by explaining activity/process task, goal, rules and restrictions. Figure 5 shows the relationship among them.

4.2 Activity/Process Link Description

Activity/process link describes relation among activity/process in three ways: quality and quantity, direction and time.

- Quality and quantity

Relation among activity/process is character with quality and quantity and could be described by figures, words or graphics document. Figures could be used to analyze quantitatively relation among activity/process, and words or graphics could be used to analyze qualitatively relation among activity/process. So, quantitative analysis and qualitatively analysis are combined.

- Direction

Product development system is ordered, which is displayed by the direction of interaction and relation among activity/process.

- Time

Time is a characteristic of relation among activity/process. Relation among activity/process exists during certain period and might disappear in other period. Relation is changing along with the time's changing.

The describing means of activity/process link include activity/process connecting line, link table and link embedded file. Activity/process connecting line uses arrow to express the direction of interaction and relation among activity/process. Link table and link embedded file describe the quality and quantity of relation among activity/process. Link table shows attributes of activity/process link, including time attribute. Link embedded file shows the content and other explanation of activity/process link. It is different with activity/process embedded file in that it includes not only the description file of task and goal of activity/process link, but also the description file of inputs and outputs of activity/process. These inputs and outputs usually could not be expressed by simple data type like integer or character string, but could only be stored as file, such as product blue print. Two types of activity/process link are displayed in Figure 6. Internal activity/process link represents the information or material flow within a father-activity/process, and external activity/process link is on the contrary.

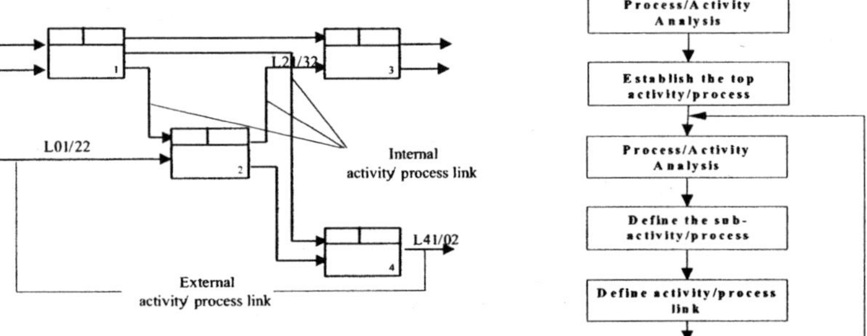

Figure 6. Internal and External Activity/Process Link **Figure 7. Procedure of DMP/A**

4.3 Activity/Process Joint Description

Joint is a special activity/process in DMP/A. It represents the general analysis or decision-making unit in PDP. Joint is displayed by ellipse (Figure 4). This ellipse is divided into three parts by two horizontal lines: the upper is filled with joint type code, the under with joint code and the middle with joint name. The joint serial No. is marked on the right under corner. Process routes may diverge or converge through the joint. Divergence and convergence are shown with activity/process connecting line of different direction.

The activity/process block and the joint use the uniform code, with the same code method. Usually, joint is not broken down. The joint table and embedded file is similar with the activity/process table and embedded file in structure and content. Compared with activity/process table, joint table is added with judging principle of process path. These judging principles may be text or formula, and they are the basis of choosing process path on joint. For example, 'if it passed the design examine' is the judging principle on joint 'design examine'. Further, judging principle could be divided into some rules. According to the information input and judging principle, a joint determines the process path.

4.4 Process/Activity Module

For different product or different parts from one product, object of process/activity dealt with may be differ in thousands ways, but their function and attributes in the attribute state space (ex. time, cost, etc.) are finite. The process/activity which have same or similar functions have the similar personnel constitute, resources type and input, output type. So, these process/activity and its personnel constitute, resources type and input, output type could be distilled for reuse. Then the deployment of product development process could use these standard modules, like the standard parts product, after deploying locally the process/activity, assembling the local process/activity to form the product development system.

Process/activity module is introduced like the toy bricks to construct a product development system. Every process/activity module has special relationship with its personnel constitute, resources type and input, output type, which are encapsulated into the module as well as the function. Through the process/activity module, the relationship among process/activity class and organize class, resource class, input and output could be established. Relating the process/activity with enterprise information system helps reorganize the product information and management information.

4.5 Procedure of DMP/A Modeling (Figure 7)

1. Process/activity analysis

Through process/activity analysis, concept of a certain field product development process is established, and process/activity type, process/activity function, personnel and resources needed in the product development are confirmed.

2. Establish the top process/activity

The top process/activity should be established firstly, and top process/activity table filled, with process/activity name, personnel, resources and inputs, outputs defined.

3. Process/activity breaking down

Process/activity should be broken down into a series of sub-process/activity in the process/activity table. When there existed similar process/activity, it could be transferred and modified to form new process/activity table.

4. Define the sub-process/activity

The table of process/activity broken down should be filled, with process/activity name, personnel, resources and inputs, outputs be defined. Those process/activity that transfer process/activity modules, because the corresponding resources type, personnel type and inputs, outputs have been defined in the process/activity module warehouse, only need to choose from corresponding type of resources, personnel and inputs, outputs.

5. Define process/activity link

Draw the process/activity link, fill in its corresponding link table, define its name, code and product information code, etc.

Repeating step 3 to 5, until every level of process/activity and process/activity link are established.

5. CONCLUSIONS

According to DMP/A method introduced in this paper, combined with the 863/CIMS projects, 'the Study of Double Integrated Framework/Platform and its Object-Oriented Application under Concurrent Engineering Overall Environment in CIMS' and 'Integrated Process Modeling Technology during Product Life Cycle', and the cooperation research project 'New Product Trial-Manufacturing Process Management System', a PDP management integrated application system, Design/PA, was established with the airplane's vertical empennage rib as research object. Through definition and description of process structure, activity/process attributes, activity/process inputs and outputs, Design/PA realized visibly the decomposition and programming of PDP, which could make better use of the process information and reduce the repetition in process programming. Moreover, Design/PA realized information integration based on activity/process and uniform information model. It provides a favorable environment for programming, supervising and managing PDP.

REFERENCES

1. W. Bernhard, Integrated Product and Process Management for Engineering Design Applications, *Integrated Computer Aided Engineering*. Volume 3, Number 1, pp.20-31, (1996).
2. Y. Xu, *Study on Product Development Process Modeling*. Ph.D Thesis, Northwestern Polytechnical University (2000).
3. M. Li, *Study on Integrated Optimization Management of Product Development Process and its Key Technology*. Ph.D Thesis, Northwestern Polytechnical University (2004).

A Model of Lean Supplier Management Based on the Lean Production

Yixun Guo[1] and Zhiduan Xu[2]

[1]Department of Statistics, College of Economics, Xiamen University, Xiamen 361005, Fujian, P.R. China xm-gyx@263.net
[2]MBA Education Center, School of Management, Xiamen University, Xiamen 361005, Fujian, P.R.China zhiduanx@xmu.edu.cn

Abstract. In this paper, we present a model of lean supplier management between an OEM and its suppliers for the objectives of eliminating wastes, reducing cost and improvement continuously based on the lean production. This model includes supplier selection and categorization, supplier improvement, supplier certification and supplier evaluation. First, the supplier selection process and some basic principals about selection criteria are developed, and all suppliers will be categorized so that different management measures can be used effectively. Then, we design the Supplier Quality Assessment process that focus on a comprehensive, continuous improvement of supplier's quality system and processes utilizing benchmarked and time-proven techniques. Finally, the index system of performance evaluation on lean suppliers is given in order to understand what performances a supplier has achieved over the past period, to identify chances that a supplier will be improved, and to provide evidences for re-certification of suppliers during next period.

Keywords: *Lean production, Supplier relationship management, Lean supplier management, Operations management, Quality assurance, Performance evaluation*

I. INTRODUCTION

With uncertainty in competitive business environment, OEMs placed in the middle of supply chain are facing challenges about product variety, lower cost and better quality. Lean thinking which aims eliminating wastes, reducing cost and improvement continuously provides a strategic guiding tool for OEMs so as to gain competitive advantages [1]. Therefore, the lean production approach pioneered by Toyota is being adopted by lots of OEMs, especially in the electronic industry, such as DELL and KODAK. The term 'lean' embodies a system that uses less of all inputs to create outputs similar to the mass production system but offering an increased choice to the end customers [2]. For full effectiveness, the lean production system must be extended down through the supply chain. The need for minimal inventory for cost and quality reasons and early detection of defects requires a kanban supply arrangement [3]. Suppliers need to deliver frequently, in small quantities, as required to the point of use with total quality guaranteed eliminating the need for incoming inspection. Suppliers are also involved in the design of components with assemblers, organizing

Please use the following format when citing this chapter:

Guo, Y., Xu, Z., 2007, in IFIP International Federation for Information Processing, Volume 254, Research and Practical Issues of Enterprise Information Systems II Volume 1, eds. L. Xu, Tjoa A., Chaudhry S. (Boston: Springer), pp. 717-726.

their supply base into a tired hierarchical structure. It means that an OEM adopting lean production approach and its key suppliers (called lean suppliers) should be locked together in long term. Suppliers are not only the most direct outer element which influences manufacturers' production and business, but also the key factor which guarantee the quality, price, delivery and service of the product. This paper focuses on an electronic manufacturer and its suppliers from an OEM's perspective. For the sake of convenience, an electronic manufacturer will be referred to as 'the Company' throughout the paper. In this paper, we will present a framework for lean supplier management based on the lean production. Then, we will focus on how to select lean suppliers, control quality of lean suppliers, and evaluate performances of lean suppliers.

2. A FRAMEWORK FOR LEAN SUPPLIER MANAGEMENT

Lean production system can not be realized without a lean supply. A lean supply arrangement should provide a flow of goods, services and technology from suppliers to the Company (with the associated flows of information and other communications in both directions) without waste [4]. The nucleus of a lean supply is lean supplier management. Figure 1 shows a framework for lean supplier management.

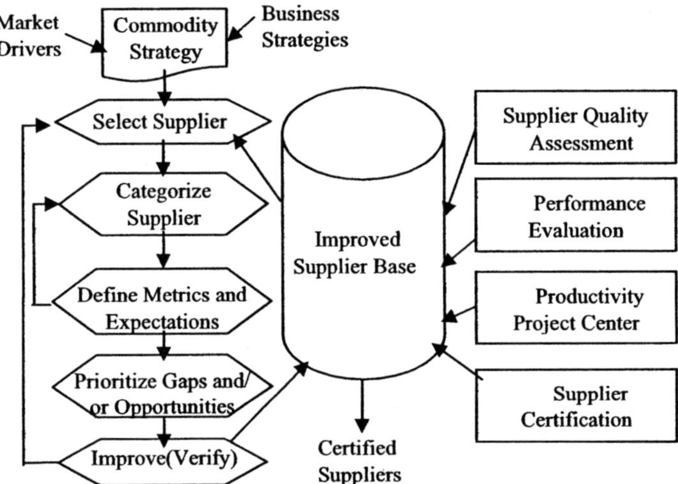

Figure 1. The Framework for Lean Supplier Management

The framework covers all aspects of lean supplier management including business strategy, supplier categorization, supplier improvement, supplier certification and supplier evaluation. The purpose of the framework is to manage the Company's portfolio of suppliers, utilizing Total Quality Management techniques, so that increased productivity results from the optimal deployment of resources. Based on this framework, supplier management activities may be divided into two parts: the first part is aimed at selecting a new supplier; the second part is to manage those suppliers who have been in the Company's supplier base. If a new supplier is selected and verified, it will enter into the Company's supplier base and then can be managed by the second part activities. The first part will be described in Section 3. The second part includes the followings:

(1) Supplier quality assessment: This is a comprehensive, on-site evaluation of supplier's quality system and processes. Utilizing benchmarked and time-proven techniques, a supplier is assessed for its ability to meet the Company's quality and cycle time expectations. This aggressive, evidence-based approach is used to identify the supplier's current capabilities, focus on continuous improvement and ability to meet ever-increasing demands. Section 4 will give the details.

(2) Performance evaluation: Performance evaluation is to examine those suppliers in the Company's supplier base over past period by way of some indexes such as quality, delivery, cost, responsiveness & support and innovation. So the Company may know on which level its each supplier will be placed and then should take some corresponding effective measures to improve. Section 5 will describe the specific evaluating methods.

(3) Productivity project center: Productivity here refers to the ability to "cash" quality and/or reliability improvements. It is expected that suppliers who are in the Company's top 80% spend will provide a number of productivity ideas to the Company each year. In fact, the Company can establish a supplier on-line idea database in which a supplier is encouraged to connect to and put forwards proposals for productivity. Productivity project center is a process to manage these proposals and track information about the adoption of these proposals. The information is very helpful for the specific commodity manager to make sourcing decisions.

(4) Supplier certification: Certification is the designation/status earned by a supplier who consistently demonstrates excellent levels of quality, productivity, and delivery performance. By means of certification, suppliers may benefit from systematic improvements which potentially increase the supplier's profit margin, first consideration for new business and visible recognition from the Company; the Company may benefit from confidence in the supplier's quality systems to consistently produce defect-free and reliable products/services, products/services are received when needed, and continual (year- over- year) productivity improvements. If a degradation of supplier performance occurs at any time, and causes significantly negative impact on the Company operations, the supplier's certification status will be withdrawn. Although certification is not the prime objective of supplier management, it is the Company's vision to have all of key suppliers (top 90% spend and critical) become certified. In this way, the Company may build a competitive and world-class supply base and ensure optimal deployment of valuable resources.

In this framework, the improved supplier base is dynamic. Maybe new selected and verified suppliers are input. Meanwhile, a supplier's data will be upgraded based on its performance over past period. Those suppliers who don't pass the certification will be kicked out.

3. SELECTION AND CATEGORIZATION OF LEAN SUPPLIERS

Lean supplier management starts from the selection of lean suppliers. According to the characteristics of the lean production, key lean suppliers may play significant roles as co-producers. So the selection of lean suppliers is one of critical success factors for the lean production [5]. In this section, the supplier selection process will be described first, then some basic principals about criteria for lean suppliers have to be discussed, and finally all suppliers will be categorized so that different management measures can be used effectively.

3.1 The Supplier Selection Process

Supplier Selection is the process of developing criteria and representative importance weightings by which potential suppliers will be evaluated. The best candidates proceed to the negotiation phase for final determination of who will be chosen to fulfill the strategy. Because of the risk of bias, the supplier selection process is summarized below:

(1) Develop criteria based on market and business needs

(2) Weight the criteria based on importance

(3) Identify all potential suppliers

(4) Reduce the number of suppliers to be considered based on required criteria

(5) Visit Supplier and perform Supplier Quality Assessment to further evaluate

(6) Perform final evaluation and rating of the supplier "finalists"

(7) Negotiate and Select "best" supplier or combination of suppliers

(8) Feedback learning to selected supplier(s) for subsequent quality planning

3.2 The Basic Principals of Developing Criteria for Lean Suppliers

It is important to emphasize on lean supply seamlessly between the Company and suppliers. So the selection criteria for lean suppliers are usually focused on quality, cost, cycle time and delivery. It depends on the Company's specific situation. The selection criteria is not a 'one size fits all'. But there are some basic principals to develop the selection criteria. In order to meet the need for lean production, the potential suppliers may be examined through the followings: quality assurance system; flexibility of production; responsiveness to changeable plans; capability for managing inventories; flexibility of delivery; reputations.

In a word, a strategy should have been developed for sourcing that has taken into consideration particular market drivers and business strategies. Suppliers are selected based on this strategy. Then suppliers need to be categorized based on short-term and long-term needs. The categorization determines the extent and responsibility for the metrics definition/expectations, gaps/opportunities, and improvement phases.

3.3 Supplier Categorization

Categorization or grouping is a way to manage a large base of suppliers, in a way that maximizes results in each category by minimizing both the amount and intensity of resources expended in each category. Categorization will determine the nature and level of resources utilized and what expectations are placed on the supplier. Guidelines for categorizing suppliers include, but are not limited to: Product/Industry growth (declining versus increasing); Market drivers (price versus technology); Length of desired involvement (short-term versus long-term); Criticality (low versus high); Requirements (standard versus custom); Types of projects with suppliers (tactical versus strategic); Switching costs (low versus high).

The above is to be used as a guideline only. The business needs and value of opportunities will determine the ultimate decision of the supplier's category. Usually, there are four types of suppliers as follows: Type Ⅰ, Low value/low risk and convenience sources; Type Ⅱ, High value/low risk and multiple Sources; TypeⅢ, Low value/high risk or sole sources; TypeⅣ, High value/high risk and/or single sources[4].

Based on these four types of suppliers, we divide suppliers into four categories as follows:

(1) Strategic suppliers: Suppliers are designated as "Strategic" when the Company desires a longer-term relationship, possibly due to product or service co-development opportunities. A supplier in this category is a Type I supplier.

(2) Key item suppliers: Key Item suppliers are those who require involvement with the Company due to the criticality of the product or service they provide. This involvement is usually a medium-term effort in order to receive a level of assurance prior to a "ship to use" status. This is most likely Type II suppliers, and possibly some I's and III's.

(3) Manage-By-Exception suppliers: Whether caused by a change in the Company's processes, or a problem or change caused by the Supplier, it may become necessary to engage in a short-term project with the supplier. This supplier could come from any of the four types.

(4) Approved suppliers: Any supplier who has not been identified as belonging to one of the other categories (Strategic, Key Item, and Manage-By-Exception) but in the Company's supply base is in the approved category. It is in the Company's best interests to reduce the key supply base (90% spend) to a manageable number of suppliers. Being competitive within their industry is an expectation common to all approved suppliers. The Company's resources will be minimally utilized for this category. If additional resources are necessary beyond general communication or the setting of expectations, this is an indication that the supplier may not be categorized properly or that the supplier should be removed from the base.

Based on the category chosen for the supplier, subsequent efforts will be different. The Table 1 below provides a summarization.

Table 1. Different Efforts on the Supplier Based on the Category

Suppliers	Define Metrics and Expectations	Identify Gaps / Opportunities	Improve (verify)
Strategic	Consider certification criteria plus client needs.	Jointly identify and prioritize.	Close gaps and show results jointly. Re-categorize supplier if/when needed.
Key Item	Client needs.	Use some specific standards of the Company to develop plan.	Work quality plan to completion then re-categorize supplier.
Manage-by-Exception	Specific to problem.	Establish target expectations.	Report progress until gap closed. Maintain data monitoring system and move back to "approved."
Approved	Communicate Certification criteria, generic expectations.	Supplier responsible.	Supplier responsible; provides data to Commodity Manager, as requested.
Not yet selected	Supplier quality assessment and other needed information.	Select best supplier based on assessment results and information obtained.	Categorize supplier and continue as noted.

4. Quality Systems and Assessments of Lean Suppliers

4.1 Quality Systems

It is generally believed that quality does not happen by chance, especially over the long term. As the Company desires to have higher levels of assurance with regards to supplier quality, reliability, serviceability, and delivery, additional attention is placed on the supplier's quality system. Therefore, the following expectations are placed on a supplier:

(1) Have a documented quality system.

(2) Use process controls and stress defect prevention rather than defect detection.

(3) Maintain records that support lot traceability.

(4) Maintain records that support reliability and serviceability performance metrics.

(5) Characterize all processes.

(6) Achieve designs and processes that result in $Cp > 2$ and $Cpk > 1.5$.

(7) Strive for continual improvement in quality and reliability in all facets of operations.

The following Table 2 may help to distinguish where quality tools may be best utilized. It is meant to be used a guideline only.

Table 2. Quality Tools Matrix

Category	Define Metrics	Identify Gaps	Improve (verify)
Strategic	Concurrent product / process design; Voice of the Customer (VOC); Quality Function Deployment (QFD); Cycle time methodology; Defect measurement / 6 sigma; Failure Modes and Effects and Criticality Analysis (FMECA) / Failure Modes and Effects Analysis (FMEA); Reliability methods; Process capability; Data interpretation / presentation; Design of Experiments (DOE);Decision and risk analysis	Value Analysis and Value Engineering (VA/VE); Pugh Concept Selection; Process Mapping; Process capability; Descriptive statistics; Graphical techniques	Management-By-Fact(MBF); Concurrent product / process design; Design for "x" (DFX); Mistake proofing / fail-safing; Seven basic quality tools; Data interpretation / presentation
Key Item	VOC; QFD; Defect measurement / 6 sigma; Item Quality Process; FMECA /FMEA; Reliability methods; Process capability; Data interpretation / presentation; DOE; Decision & risk analysis	VA/VE; Pugh Concept Selection; Process Mapping; Cycle time methodology; Tolerating; Item Quality Process; Process capability; Descriptive statistics; Graphical techniques	MBF; Design for "x" (DFX); Item Quality Process; Mistake proofing / fail-safing; Seven basic quality tools; Data interpretation / presentation
Manage-By-Exception	Defect measurement / 6 sigma; FMECA /FMEA; Reliability methods; Seven basic tools; Data interpretation / presentation; Decision & risk analysis	Process Mapping; Graphical techniques	MBF; Design for "x" (DFX); Cycle time methodology; Mistake proofing / fail-safing; Seven basic quality tools; Data interpretation / presentation; Statistical software
80% Spend (subset of Approved)	Defect measurement / 6 sigma; Data interpretation / presentation	Process Mapping; Graphical techniques; Benchmarking	7 basic quality tools; Data interpretation / presentation; Strategic Cost Analysis
100% Spend(Approved)	Defect measurement / 6 sigma; Data interpretation / presentation	Graphical techniques	7 basic quality tools; Data interpretation / presentation

4.3 The Supplier Quality Assessment

The Supplier Quality Assessment process is a comprehensive, on-site evaluation of supplier's quality system and processes. Utilizing benchmarked and time-proven techniques, a supplier is assessed for its ability to meet the Company's quality and cycle time expectations. This aggressive, evidence-based approach is used to identify the supplier's current capabilities, focus on continuous improvement and ability to meet ever-increasing demands. Elements of the assessment include:

(1) Management of the quality system and business

Organization, commitment, measurement and reporting, training, cost analysis, continuous improvement activities and teams, and customer feedback

(2) Process capability

Understanding of customer requirements, specification review, order entry, use of process flow maps, capability studies, and identification of key process parameters that affect ability to meet customer requirements, and process control.

(3) Change control

Customer notification of supplier caused changes, audit trails, and revision management.

(4) Process control

Training, data collection and usage, ongoing control criteria, use of statistical and problem-solving tools, and process evaluation and improvement.

(5) Control of purchased and non-conforming materials

How data is defined, tracked, analyzed, and used to improve the purchasing, design, contract, and production processes.

(6) Corrective and preventive action

Analysis of problems, implementation of solutions to prevent recurrence of problems, usage of data to identify trends and prevent potential problems, internal auditing, and verification of effectiveness of solutions.

Although the assessment utilizes several ISO900X concepts, it goes beyond ISO documentation evaluation, into the effectiveness of the processes themselves. ISO registration does not necessarily correlate to a successful Supplier Quality Assessment result.

5. PERFORMANCE EVALUATION ON LEAN SUPPLIERS

The purposes of performance evaluation on lean suppliers are to understand what performances a supplier has achieved over the past period (a year usually), to identify chances that a supplier will be improved, and to provide evidences for re-certification of suppliers during next period. Obviously, the objectives of performance evaluation are those who have been approved in the Company's supplier base and are active over the past period. Based on the lean production, the index system of performance evaluation on lean suppliers may be adopted as shown in Figure.2.

In Figure.2, the second level has eighteen indexes in which each index is evaluated a score between 0 and 5; the first level has five indexes, i.e. quality, delivery, cost, responsiveness & support and innovation, where the score of each index is equal to its weight (shown in Figure.2) multiply the average score of its second level indexes. All scores of the first level indexes are summed to be the final score of a supplier. The full score is 100. In general, the evaluators may be those who contact with suppliers daily inside the Company, usually from the plan department, the purchasing department, the product development department, the quality management department, the production department and etc.

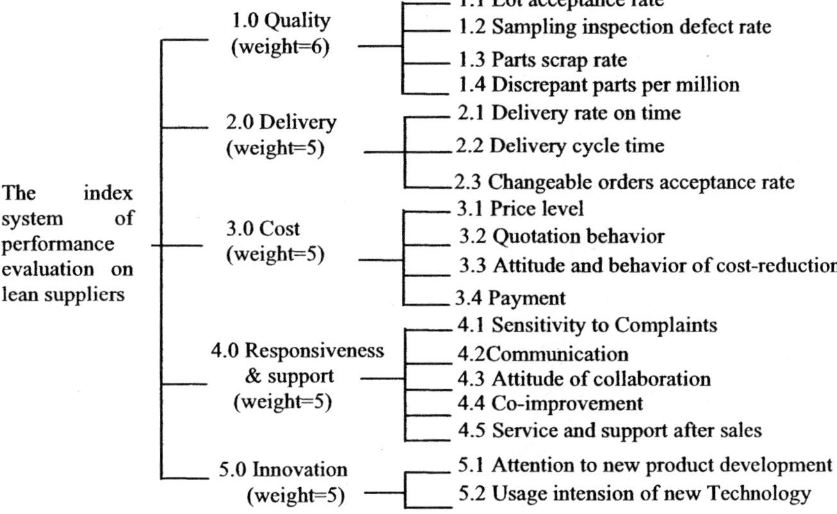

Figure 2. The Index System of Performance Evaluation on Lean Suppliers

6. CONCLUSIONS

Modern enterprises have begun to realize the suppliers' great influence on them and regard the establishment and development of the cooperation relation with suppliers as their business strategy. Lean production needs lean supply that puts forward much stricter requirements on suppliers. No doubt, lean supplier management has become one of the key success factors for an OEM. In this paper, we describe some practices on lean supplier management such as supplier selection and categorization, quality control and assessment, performance evaluation. Of course, lean supplier management covers more than these. The purpose of this paper is just to provide some useful tools and methods for those who want to improve their supplier management based on the lean production.

REFERENCES

1. M.A. Lewis, Lean Production and Sustainable Competitive Advantage, International, *Journal of Production and Operations Management*. Volume 28, Number 8, pp.959-978, (2000).
2. J.P. Womack and D. T. Jones, From Lean Production to the Lean Enterprise, *Harvard Business Review*. Volume 75, pp.93-103, (1994).
3. M. Ronan, Lean Supply: the Design and Cost Reduction Dimensions, *European Journal of Purchasing and Supply Management*. Volume 7, pp.227-242, (2001).
4. R. Lamming, Squaring Lean Supply with Supply Chain Management, *International Journal of Operations and Production Management*. Volume 16, Number 2, pp.183-196, (1996).
5. S. New and J. Ramsay, A Critical Appraisal of Aspects of the Lean Chain Approach, *European Journal of Purchasing and Supply Management*. Volume 2, Number 2, pp.93-102, (1997).

Implementation Evaluation Modeling of Selecting ERP Software Based on Fuzzy Theory

Xukan Xu[1], Yadong Jiang[1] and Zheng Shi[2]

[1]Information Management Department, Changzhou Campus, Hohai University, Changzhou 213022, Jiangsu, P.R. China xxkwh@hhuc.edu.cn
[2]Management Department, Changzhou Campus, Hohai University, Changzhou 213022, Jiangsu, P.R. China

Abstract. Selecting ERP software is a key strategy for enterprises to fully succeed in ERP practice. In this paper, the problem of Chinese medium-sized and small enterprises software selection is a lack of scientific and reliable choosing method, which is mentioned firstly. By combining the features of medium-sized and small enterprises, a special ERP software valuation index system is established based on the serviceability and designing thought of ERP software. Next, a more efficient and precise evaluation model is provided by means of fuzzy evaluation while the subordination degree of property indexes and numeral indexes are defined according to different judges' weight. Furthermore, a fuzzy synthetic evaluation matrix has been modeled. Compared with the traditional evaluation method, this model improves in precision and complexity, which can leads to an impersonal ERP software selection that's more precise and scientific. Finally, a case of an enterprise ERP software selection has been provided.

Keywords: *Enterprise resource plan, Software, Fuzzy theory, Evaluation model, Selection*

1. INTRODUCTION

Recently, Chinese enterprises have been in great development and expand their scales a lot. With the improving of the information technology, more and more enterprises wake up to the importance of it and consider it as a basic tool to upgrade their management level. The significant role of ERP (Enterprise Resource Planning) in enterprises management attracts public attention. Several Chinese enterprises have started to construct ERP projects, but the practical efficiency is not good because of many reasons such as the shortage of scientific and reliable choosing method.

ERP (Enterprise Resource Planning) is a synthetic project and the large integrate management information system for modern enterprises [1]. It combines information technology and advanced management theories together to optimize the resource, reduce the storage rate and cost, and shorten the production cycle, which becomes to the necessary means for enterprises existing and developing in the fierce market competitions of information times. Executing ERP software is a system project. In the initial stages of it, selecting of ERP software becomes to be the main part of the

Please use the following format when citing this chapter:

Xu, X., Jiang, Y., Shi, Z., 2007, in IFIP International Federation for Information Processing, Volume 254, Research and Practical Issues of Enterprise Information Systems II Volume 1, eds. L. Xu, Tjoa A., Chaudhry S. (Boston: Springer), pp. 727-737.

process to execute ERP software under the precondition of completing making analysis on enterprises and market demand. It can influence the final result and the future profits while it is the basis to ensure the enterprises target realization on strategy and special demands. In another word, a synthetic evaluation method with scientific, impersonal and numeral is significantly necessary to make the careful consideration and compare of the selecting of ERP software as well as the basis to make sure the succeeding of ERP establishing and the enterprises targets. According to the practical and fuzzy theory, this paper provides a special ERP fuzzy evaluation method for medium-sized and small enterprises, which can establish a better evaluation system to sort and calculate the index. In a word, this method can support medium-sized and small enterprises on reliable theory and decision-making to select ERP software.

2. THE SITUATION OF ERP SOFTWARE SELECTION

All Based on the latest report, more than 90% enterprises in china are medium-sized and small enterprises and their contribution have taken over 40% on national GDP, which become to the most active part of the national economy. Because of the market competition and the demand of themselves developing, their strong wishes of information construction tend to more urgent. The application of ERP becomes the main strategy for most medium-sized and small enterprises to improve their management level and the production capability. But how to make the selection is a hard problem for them to make the decision, and the success of information construction and enterprises existing will be influenced directly by it as well[2].

Medium-sized and small enterprises haven't paid enough attention to the evaluation of ERP selection. Though there are some evaluations methods tried to study this problem but just from the aspect of numeral measurement, which can't realize the optimization for enterprises resource. Nowadays, more than ten kinds of ERP software available in the market and every of them has their different technical features and applicable environment. Therefore, selecting the proper ERP software is an important decision for enterprises to make. Recently, Chinese enterprises accept numeral analysis as the bases to make ERP software selection, but it can't reflect their efficient level about the evaluation structure. Bidding invitation and bidding selection are two main methods be used and both of them analysis questions from macroscopical point of view. In application, bidding invitation &selection and experts' judgment are included to invite and select the bidding of ERP software. For some extent, they are impersonal and impartial. But, because ERP system is intangible, which can't be defined well by precise specifications and standards. It is hard to get a same evaluation result of ERP software selection. But for the method of experts' judgment, it is lack of the consideration of enterprises target. Every expert can't do judgment of ERP software under the same precondition and the judgment result tends to be influenced by personal opinion, so it is said this evaluation method is limited.

Under the situation about selecting of ERP software for medium-sized and small enterprises, a more reliable and logical Selecting of ERP software is in great need. This new method can solve the problems both in classic mathematics model, measurement and make sure the optimization to their enterprises. There are a lot of factors can influence selecting of ERP software and some of them can't be calculated by a precise value. These factors can reflect the different subjective opinion among different people. In other word, they have ambiguous property. Therefore, establishing a fuzzy based evaluation method of ERP software selection is significant under current information situation [1, 2].

3. THE PRINCIPLE OF ERP SOFTWARE

3.1 Confirming the Significance of Selecting of ERP Software

Selecting of ERP software is defined as a special evaluation strategy only for a certain medium-sized and small enterprise but not for all enterprises. So the selected ERP software should be the most proper one but not the most expensive one.

3.2 Index Setting Principle in ERP Software Selection

In order to successfully evaluate different ERP software, the relative evaluation standards which be called as evaluation index system must be set up, and the selecting of these evaluation index should be up to the following principles.

(1)Adaptability principle: Based on the adaptability to medium-sized and small enterprises, evaluation index system should represent the features of the evaluated subject from aspects of management, technology and efficiency.

(2)Relativity principle: Evaluation index should represent the correlative nature property between evaluated subjects and its purpose.

(3)Arrangement principle: Setting evaluation index should precisely represent the dominative relationship among different levels. Every index should have a definite intention to consist of a logical and reasonable evaluation system on hierarchy rotation.

(4)Conciseness principle: Scope of index system should be appropriate. The index which has great influence to the evaluated subject should be subdivided into the subindex and vice versa to save workload.

(5)Measurability principle: Significance of index should be definite and calculated to ensure the comparability and maneuverability among different indexes.

(6)Independency principle: Evaluation indexes should keep the minimum correlation between every two indexes. In other words, it is mutually exclusive and has no any effect among them.

3.3 Evaluation Index System of ERP Software

During the evaluation of ERP software selection, evaluation indexes should be confirmed on the investigation and analysis of medium sized and small enterprises bases instead of personal opinion [3]. The evaluation index system can be analyzed and calculated into three levels as figure 1.

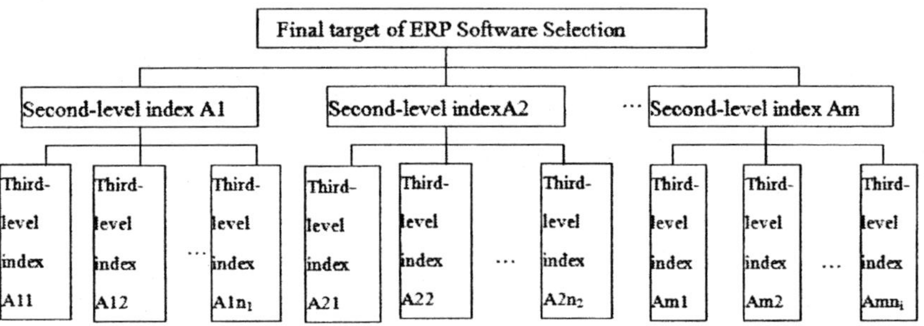

Figure 1. Evaluation Index System

4. INTRODUCTION OF FUZZY EVALUATIONS MODEL

Ambiguous calculation can handle the imprecise ambiguous input information and effectively reduce the demand of sensitivity and precision. Besides, it can save storage and catch the main conflict during the information processing to make sure their multifunction and satisfaction. This model is a special working method based on fuzzy theory[4].

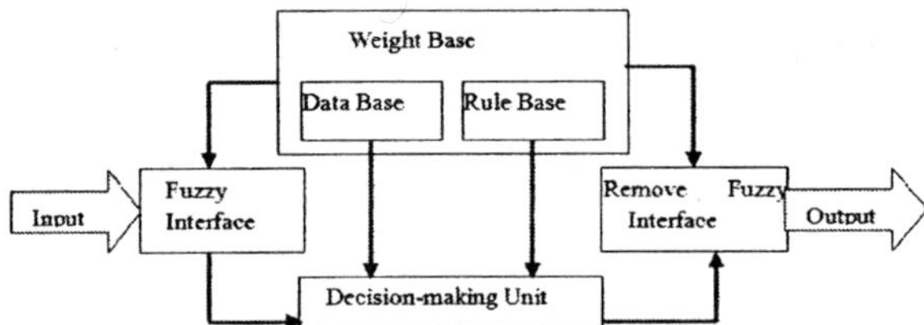

Figure 2. Ambiguous Decision-Making Theory

Ambiguous decision-making system is consisted of technology base, decision-making system, fuzzy input connection and removes fuzzy output. Technology base includes ambiguous "if-then" rule base and data base. Ambiguous rule of rule base defines and provides the relative experts' experience or technology while data base defines the subjection function within ambiguous rule. According to these principles and the decision-making process, decision-making system can lead to reasonable output and result, such as the evaluation value of a certain project. Ambiguous input connection can successfully translate the input into the corresponding ambiguous language of subjection function as well as the removing fuzzy connection can do it reversely.

Fuzzy evaluation model takes ambiguous rule as bases and has the capability of dealing with ambiguous information. The reason of that is this evaluation model can express people's experience and knowledge by means of computer, which can evaluate the software more scientific, precise and impersonal[5,6].

5. BUILDING FUZZY EVALUATION MODEL OF ERP SOFTWARE SELECTION

Fuzzy evaluation model of ERP software selection is consisted of evaluated object, evaluation purpose, evaluation index system & weight, fuzzy evaluation and so on.

5.1 Evaluated Objects

The evaluated object of ERP software should be the adaptable software to medium-sized and small enterprises. This kind of software can prove the enterprises' benefits and achieve the expected strategy target, which can realize the advanced management thought of the enterprises by software application. This pattern can increase the efficiency and reduce costs. There are three sections are included in ERP software. They are management thought, ERP manufacture and consulting services [6].

5.2 Evaluation Purposes

The final purpose of fuzzy evaluation model is to select the most proper ERP software for an enterprise and realize the optimization. Besides, the evaluation can lead a healthy developing of ERP software and help the software developer to do stricter control during the software developing to perfect ERP software and improve the enterprises' benefits [7].

5.3 Evaluation Index System & Weight

During the ERP software selection, a series of evaluation index system should be set up and make the modeling and evaluation by fuzzy theory. Based on the principle of adaptability, system, application, combination between numeral indexes and property indexes, and referred to the evaluation standard of ISO/IEC 9126 and the Walters&McCall three-tier software quality metrics model, evaluation index and their respective weights have been discussed widely and shown as the following table 1.

Table 1. Indexes and Weights of ERP Software Selection

Second-level and Weight	Third-level Index and Weight	Evaluation Result and Weight				
		Best	Better	Good	Qualified	Unqualified
Practical Degree to Enterprises A1 (0.25)	Capital Support Degree A11 (0.4)	0.60	0.20	0.20	0.10	0.00
	Process Redesign Degree A12 (0.3)	0.30	0.25	0.20	0.15	0.10
	Employee Education DegreeA13 (0.2)	0.50	0.30	0.10	0.10	0.00
	Basic Data Adequate Degree A14 (0.1)	0.50	0.20	0.10	0.10	0.10
Function of ERP Software A2 (0.2)	Practical Degree of Software Management A21 (0.3)	0.50	0.20	0.10	0.10	0.10
	Satisfaction Degree of Current FunctionA22 (0.3)	0.65	0.25	0.10	0.05	0.05
	Satisfaction Degree of Developing FunctionA23 (0.2)	0.60	0.20	0.10	0.10	0.00
	Standardization of Financial Software A24 (0.2)	0.60	0.20	0.10	0.10	0.00
Technology of ERP Software A3 (0.15)	Software Modularization Degree A31(0.30)	0.50	0.25	0.15	0.05	0.05
	System Opening A32 (0.20)	0.55	0.20	0.10	0.10	0.05
	Data Base Property A33 (0.30)	0.60	0.20	0.10	0.10	0.00
	Running Effectively A34 (0.10)	0.55	0.20	0.15	0.05	0.05
	Difficulty Degree of Update and Meatiness A35 (0.10)	0.50	0.20	0.15	0.05	0.10
Property of ERP Software A4 (0.1)	Operating Convenience A41 (0.3)	0.60	0.20	0.10	0.10	0.00
	System Security A42 (0.3)	0.45	0.30	0.15	0.10	0.00
	Tracing Property A43 (0.2)	0.40	0.30	0.15	0.10	0.05
	Fault-tolerance Capability A44 (0.1)	0.35	0.25	0.20	0.10	0.10
	Functional expanding Property A45 (0.1)	0.40	0.30	0.10	0.10	0.10
Price of ERP Software A5 (0.2)	Software Purchasing Cost A51 (0.30)	0.50	0.25	0.15	0.05	0.05
	Relative Hardware Cost A52 (0.30)	0.60	0.20	0.10	0.10	0.00
	Consulting CostA53 (0.2)	0.60	0.20	0.10	0.10	0.00
	Software Modifying Cost A54 (0.1)	0.50	0.20	0.10	0.10	0.10
	Training Cost A55 (0.1)	0.60	0.30	0.10	0.00	0.00
Maintenance &Service of ERP Software A6 (0.1)	Standard of Software Development A61(0.3)	0.50	0.20	0.10	0.10	0.10
	Adequate Degree of Technical Material A62 (0.2)	0.60	0.20	0.10	0.10	0.00
	Software Service Level A63 (0.2)	0.50	0.30	0.10	0.10	0.00
	Software Stability and upgrading A64(0.3)	0.50	0.30	0.10	0.10	0.00

5.4. Fuzzy Evaluation Modeling

In fuzzy evaluation model, ambiguous collection is presented by a uniform evaluation collection V{best, better, good, qualified, unqualified}. The second-level index collection is A{A1,A2,...,An} as well as the third-level index collection is Aij={Ai1, Ai2 Ai3,...,Aij}. In this paper, A={enterprises practical degree A1, practice of ERP software A2, technology of ERP A3, property of ERP software A4, price of ERPsoftwareA5, reputation and service level of ERP softwareA6}. In this system, the index I is described by the evaluation vector Ri={Ri1, Ri2 Ri3, Ri4, Ri5} and every index has five evaluation levels.

Let's suppose the collection F(X) is consisted of the whole ambiguous collection and U is index set while V is remark set. If $\forall u_i \in U$, then $J: U \to \xi(U \times V)$, $J(U) = (r_i(1), r_i(2),..., r_i(m))$. This mapping is called fuzzy evaluation mapping[4,8].

5.4.1. Accurate the Fuzzy Input Value

Every third-level evaluation index is found by using subjection function, the formula is:

$$r_{ij}(k) = \frac{n_{ij}(k)}{\sum_{l=1}^{5} n_{ij}(l)}$$

Where:

$n_{ij}(k)$ is the population of remarks

$\sum_{l-1}^{5} n_{ij}(l)$ is the total population per group

$\sum_{i=1}^{5} r_{ij}(l) = 1$ $r_{ij}(l) \in [0,1]$

For example, the weight of second-level index "degree of current function satisfaction" can be defined by calculating the subordination degree about every evaluation collection. After investigating twenty medium-sized and small enterprises in Changzhou of China, the gathered information includes issues of ERP software, such as function and property and price and maintenance of ERP software, practical degree to enterprises, etc. According to statistic of 20 different evaluation collections and the above indexes of ERP software selection, the evaluation result of best, better, good, qualified, unqualified respectively are 14, 3, 2, 1, and 0. Therefore, the evaluation value of every evaluation item can be determined by it. The degree of excellent is 0.70. The degree of better is 0.15. The degree of good is 0.10. The degree of qualified is 0.05. The degree of unqualified is 0. The same way can be used to get every index weight in figure 4-1 and reflect the influence degree to ERP software selection.

5.4.2. Setting up Index Evaluation Matrix

Based on the fuzzy value, every expert can give a evaluation value to every second-level evaluation index, which can be presented by Si= （s_{i1}, s_{i2}, s_{i3},…,s_{ik}） . Let's supposed the index of "software modularization degree" of ERP software is 0.3. Then, founded by the weight base of figure 4-1,

$$w_i^p = (w_{i1}^p, w_{i2}^p, ..., w_{il}^p) \text{ and } \sum_{m-1}^{l} w_{im}^p = 1 .$$

Referred to the principle of maximum subordination degree, this index vector can be expressed by （0,1,0,0,0） . If the index of "degree of software modularization" is 0.6 then the corresponding index vector is （1,0,0,0,0） .

Every second-level evaluation index Ai includes j third-level evaluation index. Combined with the every weight and the calculated vector of second-level evaluation index, the evaluation vector Ai can be found by fuzzy synthetic evaluation [6,9].

$$A_i = \left(\mathrm{w}_{i1} \quad \mathrm{w}_{i2} \quad \cdots \quad \mathrm{w}_{ij}\right) \circ \begin{bmatrix} R_{11} & R_{12} & \cdots & R_{1k} \\ R_{21} & R_{22} & \cdots & R_{2k} \\ \vdots & \vdots & \vdots & \vdots \\ R_{j1} & R_{j2} & \cdots & R_{jk} \end{bmatrix}$$

Where " ∘ " stands for arithmetic operator

Evaluation matrix is described as following;

$$\mathrm{A} = \begin{pmatrix} a_{11} & a_{12} & a_{13} & \cdots & a_{1k} \\ a_{21} & a_{22} & a_{23} & \cdots & a_{2k} \\ a_{31} & a_{32} & a_{33} & \cdots & a_{3k} \\ \vdots & \vdots & \vdots & \vdots & \vdots \\ a_{j1} & a_{j2} & a_{j3} & a_{j4} & a_{jk} \end{pmatrix} .$$

5.4.3. Fuzzy Calculation of Evaluation Matrix

Every According to the weight of second-level evaluation index w=(w_1,w_2,w_3,…,w_k) and the subordination degree of the third-level evaluation index by experts' judge, the original experts' analysis matrix can be calculated, and the second-level evaluation index matrix can be got by fuzzy operating the eight of the third-level index, then which can lead to the calculation of the first-level evaluation index matrix B[10]. The result matrix of fuzzy evaluation is presented as following:

B=W×A,

$$B=\begin{pmatrix} w_1 & w_2 & w_3 & \cdots & w_k \end{pmatrix} \circ \begin{pmatrix} a_{11} & a_{12} & a_{13} & \cdots & a_{1k} \\ a_{21} & a_{22} & a_{23} & \cdots & a_{2k} \\ a_{31} & a_{32} & a_{33} & \cdots & a_{3k} \\ \vdots & \vdots & \vdots & \vdots & \vdots \\ a_{j1} & a_{j2} & a_{j3} & a_{j4} & a_{jk} \end{pmatrix}$$

Where B stands for the result matrix of fuzzy evaluation, The result matrix of fuzzy evaluation can be found as $B=(b_1,b_2,\ldots,b_k)$. For the convenient compare among different selections, the final result matrix of fuzzy evaluation should be translated to specific value by giving the different weight to remark collection. Weights can be described as Q={q1,q2,q3,q4,q5}.

Where:

$$q_i = \frac{(K+1-i)}{K} \times 100$$

K=5

Then: Q={100,80,60,40,20}

The evaluation among different selection cases can be analyzed by the above method and get the corresponding b value ($b=B\times Q^T$). Supposed there are totally p selection cases of ERP software selection and b refers to the final evaluation result [3, 5, 10], every evaluation result is ranked as $b^{(i)} > b^{(j)} > \ldots > b^{(l)}$, then it is concluded that the selection case (i) should be the best.

6. APPLICATION OF EVALUATION MODEL

Take an idiographic case for example. Supposed there are three ERP software selecting decisions to a medium sized and small enterprise where the decision numbers separately are S1, S2 and S3. For the decision S1, the user representatives, managers of this enterprise and experts make the evaluation such as the second-level "enterprises practical degree" and give the scores to its third-level index by subjection principle. After that, the evaluation matrix can be got as R_1, and fuzzy multiply with the weight to get the second-level index vector A_1.

$$A_1 = \begin{pmatrix} 0.4 & 0.3 & 0.2 & 0.1 \end{pmatrix} \circ \begin{pmatrix} 1 & 0 & 0 & 0 & 0 \\ 0 & 1 & 0 & 0 & 0 \\ 0 & 0 & 1 & 0 & 0 \\ 0 & 1 & 0 & 0 & 0 \end{pmatrix} = \begin{pmatrix} 0.4 & 0.4 & 0.2 & 0.1 & 0.0 \end{pmatrix}.$$

Every second-level index vector can be calculated by its second-level index and six second-level index vector can make up of a second-level index evaluation matrix A as following:

$$A=\begin{pmatrix} 0.4 & 0.4 & 0.2 & 0.0 & 0.0 \\ 0.0 & 0.6 & 0.4 & 0.0 & 0.0 \\ 0.3 & 0.2 & 0.4 & 0.1 & 0.0 \\ 0.0 & 0.3 & 0.5 & 0.2 & 0.0 \\ 0.3 & 0.3 & 0.3 & 0.1 & 0.0 \\ 0.0 & 0.7 & 0.3 & 0.0 & 0.0 \end{pmatrix}$$

Then the matrix B is found as:

$$B=V\times A=\begin{pmatrix}0.21 & 0.41 & 0.33 & 0.06 & 0\end{pmatrix}$$

Through the fuzzy evaluation, result matrix is found as B and make the calculation $b^{(s1)}=76$. The same way can be used to analyze the other two selecting decision $b^{(s2)}=53.3$ and $b^{(s3)}=45.2$. A rank of the result can be given as following:

$b^{(s1)}>b^{(s2)}>b^{(s3)}$

Therefore, among the three ERP software, Based on the above fuzzy evaluation model, it is concluded that decision S1 is the best ERP software selecting decision to this enterprise.

7. PROSPECTING

ERP software is a kind of management system with highly complexity and synthesis and it is significant for enterprises to select proper ERP software. Besides the consideration of the management thought of the software, software technology, expending property, maintenance property and implement cost[11], the adaptability of this ERP software is more necessary to be considered. In this paper, this ERP software selection model. pays a lots attention to reduce the man-made mistake and deal with the important element of ERP software by arithmetic to make sure the results can be calculated more conveniently and precisely, which can successfully give the reliable decision support to enterprises' managers.

With the development of information technology, the software development trends to network and intelligence so the evaluation index system and their eights should change correspondingly to ensure the evaluation result more scientific, precise and impersonal, which can advance the development level of ERP software, enhance its practical property and optimize the ERP software application in medium-sized and small enterprises [12].

REFERENCES

1. Y. Zhou and B. Liu, *ERP theory and its application* (China Machine Press: Beijing, PK, 2003).
2. Y. Li, X. Liao, and H.Z. Lei, A knowledge management system for ERP implementation, *Syst. Res. Behav. Sci.*. Volume 23, pp.157-168, (2006).
3. Y. Gao and J. Su, Research of ERP Selecting Based on the FAHP Method, *Statistics and Decision*. Volume 2, pp.42-44, (2005).

4. P. Liu and M. Wu, *Fuzzy theory and its application* (Publishing House of National University of Defense Technology: ChangSha, 2000).
5. L.A. Zadeh, Fuzzy Sets and systems, *International Journal of General Systems*. Volume 17, Number 2 & 3, pp.129-138, (1990).
6. Z. Zhou, Research of ERP index, *Enterprise Economics*. Volume 5, pp.20-22, (2002).
7. S. Wang and M. Xian, Study on synthetic evaluation method of software quality, *Computer Engineer and Design*. Volume 23, Number 4, pp.16-18, (2002).
8. C.E. Bozdag, C. Kahraman, and D. Ruan, Fuzzy group decision making for selection among computer integrated manufacturing systems, *Comput. Ind.*. Volume 51, pp.13–29, (2003).
9. D.F. Li and J.B. Yang, Fuzzy linear programming technique for multi-attribute group decision making in fuzzy environments, *Inform. Sci.*. Volume 158, pp.263-275, (2004).
10. A.L. Jensen, Building a web-based information system for variety selection in field crops-objectives and results, *Computer and Electronics in Agriculture*. Volume 32, pp.195-211, (2001).
11. C.C. Wei, C.F. Chien, and M.J.J. Wang, An AHP-based approach to ERP system selection, *Int. J. Prod. Econom.*. Volume 96, pp.47-62, (2005).
12. J. Xie, N. Cui, and R. Chen. Fuzzy evaluation model and its application of selecting ERP software, *Journal of Huazhong University of Science and Technology*. Volume 30, Number 5, pp.37-40, (2000).
13. M. Morisio, and A. Tsoukiàs, IusWare, a methodology for the evaluation and selection of software products, in *Proc. of IEE Proceedings Software Engineering* (1997), pp.162-174.
14. I. Vlahavas, I. Refanidis, I. Stamelos, and A.Tsoukiàs, ESSE: an expert system for software evaluation, *Journal of Knowledge Based Systems*. Volume 12, pp.183-197, (1999).

Critical Success Factors for ERP System Implementation

Jun Wu

School of Economics and Management, Beijing University of Posts and Telecommunications, Beijing100876, China wujun1127@vip.sina.com

Abstract. As more and more enterprises move from functional to process-based IT infrastructure, ERP system becomes one of today's most widely used IT solutions in many large enterprises. In spite of the widely used IT solutions, many ERP implementations are not successful. It takes longer time and costs more money than expected. Given the large investment that an ERP project requires and the potential benefits it can offer if successfully implemented, it is important to understand what is needed to ensure a successful ERP Implementation. In this paper, we try to explore the critical success factors (CSFs) for the implementation of an ERP system both from the management perspective and technology perspective. Based on the lessons learnt from the previous literature and case studies, we propose a conceptual framework for successful implementation of an ERP system. This framework summarizes the CSFs that need to be addressed during a whole process of ERP implementation, i.e.: pre implementation phase, implementation phase and post-implementation phase. Limitations and future research directions are concluded in the end.

Keywords: *Critical success factors, ERP implementation, Conceptual framework*

I. INTRODUCTION

In today's fiercely competitive business environment, there is a strong need for the enterprises to be closer to the customer and deliver value added product and services in the shortest possible time. In order to achieve improved efficiency and effectiveness, more and more large enterprises move from functional to process-based IT infrastructure. Enterprise Resource Planning (ERP) system is such a strategic tool, which integrates information and information-based processes within and across functional areas in an organization. In general, the benefits ERP systems offer, as Davenport [1] notes, include not only increased decision making-speed, improved control of operations and costs, and cost reductions, but also improved enterprise-wide information dissemination. However, many ERP implementations are not successful. Surveys conducted by Harvard Business School revealed that despite the high investments in ERP systems, ERP implementations are still mired by cost and schedule overruns, resistance to business process change, unavailability of adequate skills, and overall underachievement relative to the expectation of benefits accruing from ERP [2]. Given the large investment that an ERP project requires and the potential benefits it can offer if successfully implemented, it is important to

Please use the following format when citing this chapter:

Wu, J., 2007, in IFIP International Federation for Information Processing, Volume 254, Research and Practical Issues of Enterprise Information Systems II Volume 1, eds. L. Xu, Tjoa A., Chaudhry S. (Boston: Springer), pp. 739-745.

understand what is needed to ensure a successful ERP Implementation. The objective of this paper is to develop a critical success factors (CSFs) research framework that the ERP practitioner should address during the whole process of the system implementation. Compare to previous similar study, the framework groups the CSFs from the technical and management perspectives. Moreover, the success measures and associated critical issues affecting ERP implementation during each phase of the ERP system implementation are discussed.

The rest of this paper is organized as follows: we first synthesize an ERP system implementation process model and develop a set of success measures for ERP system implementation based on previous literatures. After that, the proposed CSFs conceptual framework is developed and further explained. Finally, implications and future research directions are concluded.

2. THE ERP IMPLEMENTATION PROCESS

Previous researchers described the implementation process of the ERP system by models having three to six stages [4]. Markus and Tanis [5] developed a four-phase ERP implementation process model. The phases are chartering, project, shakedown, and onward and upward. Ross [6] presented a model using the following five stages: design, implementation, stabilization, continuous improvement and transformation. Based on these researches, we propose a 3-stage process model shown below in Fig. 1. The pre-implementation stage includes both the broader business focus of the Markus and Tanis chartering phase and the Ross design phase. More specifically, implementation strategy describes plan for change that ensures alignment with overall

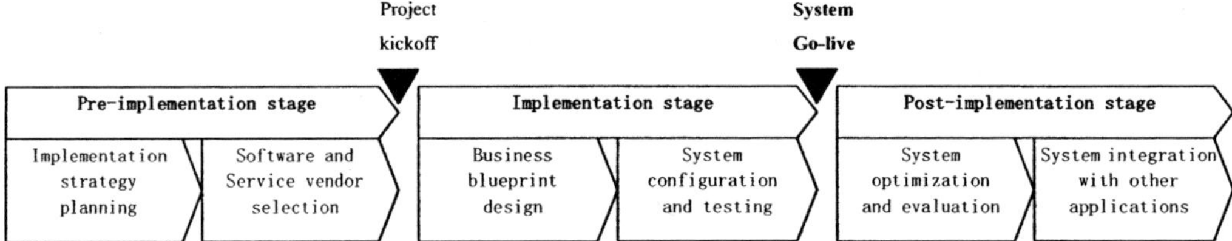

Figure 1. Synthesized Process Model for ERP Implementation

corporate strategy, and determines organizational principles and approach of implementation. While most enterprises nowadays purchasing standard ERP packages from outside ERP vendors rather than developing an ERP system in-house, software and service vendor selection become more important to ensure the perfect match between the ERP system and their specific business requirements. The second implementation stage includes business blueprint design and system configuration and testing. These are taken and extended from the Ross model. The final stage is post-implementation and includes both incremental and radical improvements to business process and technical infrastructure enabled by the implemented ERP system corresponding to the onward and upward phase of Markus and Tanner. Two stage gates, project kickoff and system go-live, represent a distinct milestone in the ERP process. It is crucial that management conduct a review at the end of each stage to make sure everyone agrees on its outcome before moving on to the next stage.

3. SUCCESS ISSUES FOR ERP IMPLEMENTATION

3.1 Success Measures for ERP Implementation

Markus et al. [7] argue that the definition and measurement of ERP success are thorny matters and success depends on the point of view from which you measure it. Thus, there are no agreed measures on how to define ERP system implementation success. Delone and McLean [8] classified six dimensions of ISs success including system quality, information quality, Use, User satisfaction, Individual impact and Organizational impact. Zhang et al. [9] summarized seven measures from previous literature used as surrogates of ERP implementation success. These measures are user satisfaction, intended business performance improvements, Oliver White's ABCD Classification Scheme, on time, within budget, system acceptance and usage and predetermined corporate goals. In reality, IT staffs generally talk about success when the project completes within budgets, timeframe and/ or when the new system "works". However, in the eyes of the business managers, success is achieved when the organization is able to better perform all its business processes and when the integrated ERP system can support the performance development of the company.

From the process viewpoint, we find that the notion of "success" changes as the implementation project unfolds. Thus, we need define different success measures for each stage of the project. For the pre-implementation stage, success measures are ERP organizational readiness and competent ERP package and consultant service vendor. The former one helps the management have a thorough strategic thinking to gain better understanding of the alignments between ERP and corporate goals. The latter shows its significance in shaping the ultimate outcome of the implementation. For the implementation stage, success is mainly concerned with completion of the ERP project, to predefined technical standards, on time and within budget. For the last stage, success is more concerned with the user satisfaction and perceived contribution of the system to organizational performance. Throughout, the success should be assessed both from the information technology (IT) and general management perspectives.

3.2 Critical Success Factors for ERP Implementation

Critical success factors have been defined as "those few critical areas where things must go right for the business to flourish" [10]. They are particularly useful to practitioners as they provide clear guidance on where to focus attention and resources in planning an ERP implementation project. Most of the previous researches on critical success factors in ERP systems implementation have developed prioritized lists of factors. Based on a review of the literature and with extensive personal interviews with ERP practitioners that culminated to the development of the three stages of ERP implementation, we group a set of the fourteen most important critical success factors for the ERP project along with the technical and management dimensions. These are shown in the table 1.

Table 1. Critical Success Factors for the ERP System Implementation

Management perspective	Technical perspective
Top management support [7,11,12]	Data accuracy and integrity [11,12]
Clear goals and objectives [11,12]	Enterprise IT infrastructure and legacy system [9]
Company wide business process reengineering(BPR) and change management [11,12,13]	Suitability of hardware and software [12]
Effective project management [12]	System reliability and flexibility [12]
Stakeholder active involvement [14]	Organizational IT skill [15]
Organizational culture [12,13]	Software and service vendor competency [12,13]
User education and training [11,13]	System perceived usefulness and learnability [15]

4. CONCEPTUAL RESEARCH FRAMEWORK

Drawing from the discussions above, we propose an integrative conceptual research framework, which is comprised of a set of theoretically important constructs. The framework has been developed based on the project life cycle approach, illustrating the critical factors that need to be addressed at all three stages: pre-implementation, implementation, and post-implementation stage. The framework is shown in figure 2.

4.1 Critical Success Factors in Pre-implementation Stage

ERP implementation has been characterized as a "root canal" surgery [16]. The pain is extremely unbearable during the surgery but things get better soon after the surgery. Company should first have a thorough strategic thinking and evaluate whether the organization are ready for the massive changes that would occur. Thus, factors such as clear goals and objectives, organizational culture and organizational IT skills should be more considered. On the other hand, during this stage, successful companies draw their process requirement needs and select the software packages that best fit these needs to the greatest extent possible. To increase the chance of success, two aspects should be cared when selecting software and hardware: (1) Compatibility of software/hardware and company's needs; (2) Ease of customization. By the way, qualified ERP vendor and service consultant are also important as they can provide continuous support throughout the system lifecycle.

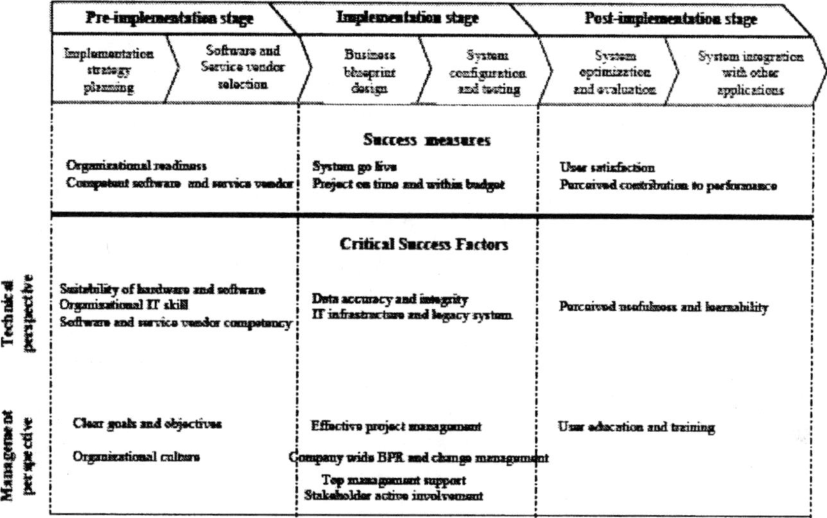

Figure 2. Conceptual Framework of ERP Implementation Success

4.2 Critical Success Factors in Implementation Stage

Since ERP system integrates information and information based processes within and across all functional areas in an organization, ERP implementation is usually accompanied by enterprise-wide business process re-engineering. It requires that the basic business practices embedded in the ERP system be adapted to the organizational processes. Generally, one of the main obstacles facing ERP implementation is resistance to change. In this respect, careful management of changes to business processes and continued support from top management is required to overcome such resistances. On the other hand, effective project management acts as a significant condition for achieving overall success with an ERP system. By having ERP users and other stakeholder work with the implementation team from the beginning of the project, this would facilitate the implementation process and lead to speedy and successful implementation of the ERP system.

From the technical perspective, data accuracy and IT infrastructure are also two key determinants of ERP success. Since ERP system modules are intricately linked to one another, inaccurate data input into one module will adversely affect the functioning of other modules. Data must be cleansed and transferred to the ERP system to ensure no disruption to performance. ERP implementation involves a complex transition from legacy information systems to an integrated IT infrastructure.

Thus, adequate IT infrastructure, hardware and networking are crucial for an ERP system's success.

4.3 Critical Success Factors In Post-implementation Stage

Users training and education is an important factor of the successful ERP implementation as many projects fail in the end due to lack of proper training. It makes the user comfortable with the system and increases the expertise and knowledge level of the people. Features of ERP system and hands on training are all important dimensions of training program for end users. According to Calisir [15], both perceived usefulness and learnability are determinants for end-user technical acceptance with ERP systems, leading to a successful ERP implementation.

5. CONCLUSIONS

In this short paper we have developed a conceptual research framework to identify those factors that are critical to the implementation of ERP systems. Our contributions are twofold: First, relating ERP success measures and critical success factors with implementation methodologies; second, grouping critical success factors into management and technology dimensions. We believe our work would assist both practitioners and academicians. The framework presented in the study could provide practitioners with insights on how to better implement the ERP system and the critical factors that need to be focused on in each stage of implementation. Also, the critical constructs identified in the framework can be used by academicians for further empirical studies. There is a need for empirical studies to test ERP success in relationship to these factors. More over, we feel more empirical research needs to be conducted to better understand the different roles played by various stakeholders viewing success in ERP implementation.

ACKNOWLEDGEMENTS

This paper is based upon work supported by F0607-35, Key Laboratory of Information Management and Economics, MII, P.R.C. The author would like to thank Professor Xu Yang for his kindly help.

REFERENCES

1. T. Davenport, Putting the Enterprise into the Enterprise System, *Harvard Business Review.* Volume 76, Number 4, pp.121-131, (1998).
2. R.D. Austin, M.J. Cotteleer, and C.X. Escalle, Enterprise Resource Planning: Technology Note, *Harvard Business School Publishing.* Number 9-699-020, pp. 1-8, March 2003.

3. T.M. Somers and K.G. Nelson, taxonomy of players and activities across the ERP project life cycle, *Information and Management*. Volume 41, Number 3, pp.257-278, (2004).
4. M.L. Markus and C. Tanis, *The enterprise systems experience – from adoption to success*, Working Paper, Claremont Graduate University (1999).
5. J.W. Ross, *The ERP revolution: surviving versus thriving*, Working Paper, Centre for Information Systems Research, Sloan School of Management, MIT (1998).
6. M.L. Markus, S. Axline, D. Petrie, and C. Tanis, Learning from adopters' experiences with ERP: Problems encountered and success achieved, *Journal of Information Technology*. Volume 15, Number 2, pp.245-265, (2000).
7. W.H. Delone and E.R. McLean, Information systems success: The quest for the dependent variable, *Information Systems Research*. Volume 7, Number 3, pp.60-95, (1992).
8. L. Zhang, M.K.O. Lee, Z. Zhang, and P. Banerjee, Critical success factors of enterprise resource planning systems implementation success in China, in *36th Annual Hawaii International Conference on System Sciences (HICSS'03)*. eds. P. Banerjee (Springer: Big Island, Hawaii, 2003), pp.212-219.
9. J.F. Rockhart, Critical Success Factors, *Harvard Business Review*. Volume 32, Number 1, pp.81-91, (1979).
10. E.J. Umble, R.R. Haft, and M.M. Umble, Enterprise resource planning: Implementation procedures and critical success factors, *European Journal of Operational Research*. Number 146, pp.241-257, (2003).
11. Y. Yusuf, A. Gunasekaran, and M.K. Abthorpe, Enterprise information systems project implementation: A case study of ERP in Rolls-Royce, *International Journal of Production Economics*. Number 87, pp.251-266, (2004).
12. J. Motwani, D. Mirchandani, M. Madan, and A. Gunasekaran, Successful implementation of ERP projects: Evidence from two case studies, *International Journal of Production Economics*. Number 75, pp.83-96, (2002).
13. H.H. Chang, Technical and management perceptions of enterprise information systems importance, implementation, and benefits, *Information Systems Journal*. Volume 16, Number 3, pp.263-292, (2006).
14. S. Aral and P. Weill, IT Assets, Organizational Capabilities and Firm Performance: Do Resource Allocations and Organizational Differences Explain Performance Variation? *MIT Sloan WP*. Number 4632, 2006.
15. F. Calisir, The relation of interface usability characteristics, perceived usefulness, and perceived ease of use to end-user satisfaction with enterprise resource planning (ERP) systems, *Computers in Human Behavior*. Volume 20, Number 4, pp.505-515, (2004).
16. V.A. Mabert, A. Soni, and M.A. Venkatarama, Enterprise Resource Planning: Common Myths Versus Evolving Reality, *Business Horizons*. Volume 12, Number 3, pp.71-78, (2001).

Research and Application of Enterprise Knowledge Management System Based on Ontology

Tiedong Chen[1], Ziyu Liu[2] and Lei Huang[1]

[1]College of Economics and Management, Beijing Jiaotong University, Beijing 100044, P.R. China Chentiedong815@sina.com
[2]College of Information Science & Engineering, Hebei University of Science & Technology, Shijiazhuaug 050018, P.R. China

Abstract. With the coming of knowledge economy, the pattern of enterprise management is going through a great change. Nowadays, in an enterprise, knowledge management has become a key technology to increase intelligence of technique, competition, business and strategy. The key factors for the enterprise to survive the competitive environment lie in how to extract the needed knowledge from numerous of external and internal information, and how to manage the acquiring, producing and spreading of knowledge and the ability to upgrading of the enterprises based on knowledge. This paper proposes an ontology-based knowledge management framework. Then an application case is presented, which is an examples of knowledge management system based on ontology for a logistics enterprise.

Keywords: *Knowledge management, Ontology, Knowledge acquisition and collation, Knowledge storage, Knowledge reuse*

I. INTRODUCTION

Facing economic globalization and fierce market competition, knowledge-intensive enterprises have paid attention to which how to effectively reuse relevant knowledge that are included in the enterprise and outside information system to improve operating efficiency and market competitiveness. More and more enterprises hope that their core competitiveness should be founded on the basis of knowledge innovation, so they want to adopt a knowledge management strategy to achieve this purpose [1]. Under such circumstances, knowledge management technology emerged. Knowledge management was raised earliest by the United Nations International Labor Organization in 1986. In the enterprise context, we adopt the definition of knowledge management as a "concerted effort to capture, organize and share what they know" [2].

Under such circumstances, how to effective retrieve information has become an important research topic [3]. Ontology can solve this problem. Ontology can determine the precise meaning of concept through the strict definition for concept and the relationship between these concepts and these concepts can express the knowledge that can be common recognized and shared. The efficiency of knowledge search, knowledge accumulation and knowledge sharing will be greatly enhanced under the

Please use the following format when citing this chapter:

Chen, T., Liu, Z., Huang, L., 2007, in IFIP International Federation for Information Processing, Volume 254, Research and Practical Issues of Enterprise Information Systems II Volume 1, eds. L. Xu, Tjoa A., Chaudhry S. (Boston: Springer), pp. 747-751.

support of such a series of concepts, so that the true meaning of knowledge reuse and knowledge sharing become possible. In this paper an application case is presented, which is an examples of knowledge management system based on ontology for a logistics enterprise.

2. ONTOLOGY

Ontology that originates from philosophy is widespread paid attention to among the field of information science in recent years [4-5], and its importance has been demonstrated in many ways and has been widely recognized [4][6-7]. Ontology can be regarded as a vocabulary of terms and relationships between those terms in a given domain. Ontology facilitates capture and construction of domain knowledge and enables representation of skeletal knowledge to facilitate integration of knowledge bases irrespective of the heterogeneity of knowledge sources. There are a number of definitions about the ambiguous term "ontology", and Gruber's definition is at large accepted: ontology is an explicit specification of a conceptualization.

3. PROPOSED SOLUTION

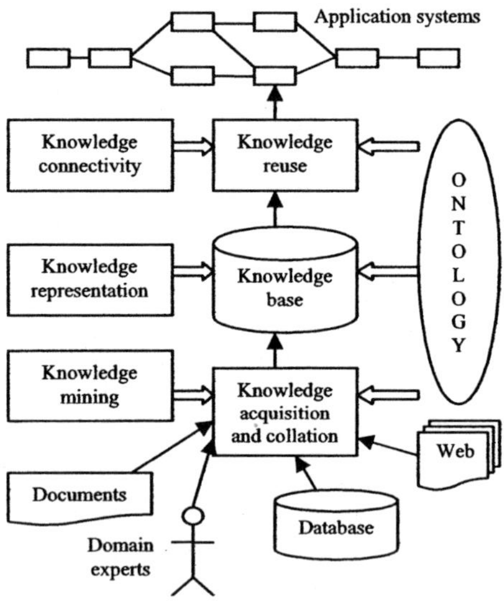

Figure 1. Open Knowledge Management Architecture Based on Ontology

In our ontology-based enterprise knowledge management frame, the knowledge management process is concisely divided into three phases: knowledge acquisition and collation, knowledge storage and knowledge reuse. It uses knowledge connectivity and transformation mechanisms to drive the process of acquisition and reuse. The system architecture is shown in figure 1, and in figure 1 the fine black lines indicate knowledge flow.

3.1 Knowledge Acquisition and Collation

Knowledge acquisition and collation refers to adding meta-information to information. It is a transformation process from structured, semi-structured and unstructured information to the structured information. According to the source of information, there are four categories: (1) Background information of individuals and groups. (2) Various homogeneous or heterogeneous databases. (3) Various documentations. (4) Knowledge over the web including information that is originated from data mining [8].

Knowledge acquisition is the foundation and main technology of knowledge management systems, and it includes knowledge extraction and knowledge acquisition form knowledge base. Knowledge extraction is knowledge's abstract process in which knowledge is extracted from the raw data and information according to concepts that are defined by ontology. In traditional knowledge engineering there are a number of mature knowledge extraction methods and tools, such as Text Miner of IBM, OntoEdit of OntoPrise and Protégé of StanFord [9]. The original data and information may not be electronic, and electronic information may be structured, semi-structured or unstructured information. Non-electronic information can be transformed into structured information by ontology developing tools or OCR tools.

3.2 Knowledge Storage

Knowledge storage can store the knowledge that has been transformed in knowledge base. The knowledge that has been transformed is divided into two parts: one is structured meta-knowledge, the other is semi-structured or unstructured information.

3.3 Knowledge Reuse

Knowledge reuse is the process of using knowledge in application systems, and the reuse of knowledge is achieved by the link between people and knowledge. There are four mainly link: (1) Linking people to knowledge. You can find relevant content at different levels by using visual query and retrieval tools, which is acquiring knowledge through pull. (2) Linking people to people. Knowledge workers can find relevant experts and result to or discuss with them through knowledge management system. (3) Linking knowledge to people. Knowledge management system can push the relevant knowledge to people according to personal preference or immediate needs. (4) Linking knowledge to knowledge. It achieves hyperlink between knowledge and knowledge.

4. CASE STUDY

On the basis of the frame that we proposed, we developed a knowledge management system of three-layer structure for a logistics enterprise. As shown in Figure 2. At the client user agent send the request to intermediate layer through SOAP protocol. The middle layer search the required knowledge from ontology knowledge base according to the user's request and return them to the users. The middle layer also can automatically acquire knowledge from the outside and store them in the knowledge base. The database layer is responsible for the storage and sharing of knowledge. The specialized knowledge engineers are responsible for the work of knowledge maintenance.

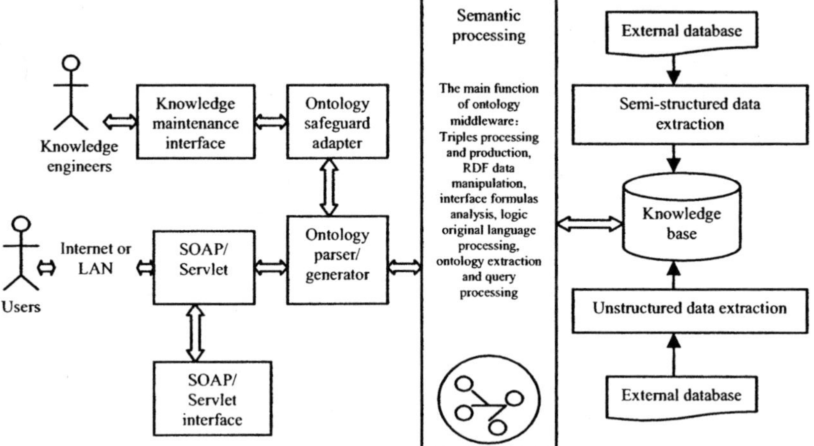

Figure 2. Knowledge Management System Based on Ontology

The function of the main module:

(1) SOAP / Servlet: Finishing the client agency, automatically adapting the changes of the client and finishing interaction with the server's servlet are its main function [2].

(2) SOAP / Servlet interface: These interfaces are application program interfaces that are defined to meet the requirements of knowledge management system, such as query interface, visit interface etc. It can recall the corresponding interface processing according to customer request.

(3) Ontology parser/generator: It is responsible for parsing or generating ontology information.

(4) Ontology middleware: It is the core of knowledge management system. It is responsible for extracting knowledge information from knowledge warehouse and achieving the knowledge's sharing and using. It has the function of querying and reasoning, and it can directly connect with the database system.

(5) Knowledge warehouse: It is responsible for storing knowledge information and achieving the storage and sharing of knowledge.

(6) Unstructured/semi-structured data extraction module: It is responsible for extracting knowledge information from external data sources and storing them in knowledge base.

5. CONCLUSIONS

At present, the internet is moving forward the direction of the semantic web, and knowledge management is increasingly becoming the core of enterprise management. Ontology can solve a series of issues of knowledge management. Because the current knowledge management systems have a common limitation: they are insufficient in dynamic interaction with users, which is denoted by the static usage of knowledge and the closed maintenance of system. According to this, we construct an ontology-based open knowledge management system. On the basis of these, we developed a knowledge management system based on ontology for a logistics enterprise. The practical application shows that system has achieved expected results for supporting compatibility matching, meaning understanding, knowledge networking and establishing and maintaining ontology of knowledge workers etc.

REFERENCES

1. F. Li, J. Gao, L. Zhong, and M. Zhou, OKMF: an ontology-based knowledge management system framework, *Journal of computer-aided design & computer graphics*. Volume 15, Number 12, pp.1538-1543, (2003).
2. A. Stuart, *Knowledge Management Uneasy Pieces*, C10 Magazine site on the World Wide Web, Part 2 (1996). http ://www. cio. com/CIO/060196_uneasy_ 1 .html (Accessed December 7, 1996)
3. B. Shen, Research on knowledge management system of enterprise based ontology, *National Business: Research on Economic Theory*. Number 2, pp.70-72, (2006).
4. N. Guarino, Formal ontology and information systems, in *Proc of the 1st Int'l Conf on Formal Ontology in Information Systems*, Trento (IOS Press: Italy, 1998), pp.3-15.
5. M. Uschold and M. Gruninger, Ontologies: Principles, methods, and applications, *Knowledge Engineering Review*. Volume 11, Number 2, pp.93-155, (1996).
6. T.B. Lee, J. Hendler, and O. Lassila, The semantic Web, *Scientific American*. Volume 284, Number 5, pp.34-43, (2001).
7. T.B. Lee, Semantic Web road map (1998). http://www.w3.org/DesignIssues/Semantic.html
8. B. Liu, Study on key technologies of ontology based knowledge management, *JCSSTI*. Volume 24, Number 1, pp.75-81, (2005).
9. X. Huang, X. Xu, and G. Xu, Research of knowledge management system based ontology, *Science technology and engineering*. Volume 5, Number 6, pp.351-356, (2005).

SOA Oriented Web Services Operational Mechanism

Meiyun Zuo and Bei Wu

School of Information, Renmin University of China, Beijing 100872, P.R. China
zuomeiyun@263.net wubeiwb@gmail.com

Abstract. SOA is a very important guiding theory in constructing information systems recently, the design granularity of information systems will gradually evolve from module to component. At first, this paper shows a SOA oriented information system architecture based on web services. Then it points out that getting web services reasonably and legally is the primary problem in the process of this architecture's realization. According to the different managers of web services, this paper proposes three possible operational mechanisms of web services: (1) Web Service predominant characteristic mechanism guided by large enterprises, (2) Web Services portal mechanism guided by industrial category, (3) Web Service Uniform Alliance (WSUA) mechanism. These three mechanisms may exist and compete with each other at the same time. And the authors think that the ideal operational mechanism is to build a Web Service Uniform Alliance from the perspective of utilizing and saving global intellectual resources.

Keywords: *Service-oriented architecture, Web services, Service management, Service science, Operations management*

1. INTRODUCTION

It is very important for enterprises to respond to the market changes as quickly as they can, which also becomes an important element of their core competitiveness. However, while the business processes change rapidly, the information systems they are using are relatively fixed. Hence, the conflict becomes an annoying problem to enterprises. It is high time to discuss how to change the framework model of enterprise information systems fundamentally, and how to reconstruct a dynamic enterprise information system from the bottom layer, which will assure that the information systems will adapt to the change of business requirements. This paper proposes a SOA oriented enterprise dynamic information system architecture. Whereas we must firstly figure out how to get web services reasonably and legally before we implement this architecture. According to the different managers of web services, this paper proposes three possible operational mechanisms of web services: (1) Web Service predominant characteristic mechanism guided by large enterprises, (2) Web Services portal mechanism guided by industrial category, (3) Web Service Uniform Alliance (WSUA) mechanism.

Please use the following format when citing this chapter:

Zuo, M., Wu, B., 2007, in IFIP International Federation for Information Processing, Volume 254, Research and Practical Issues of Enterprise Information Systems II Volume 1, eds. L. Xu, Tjoa A., Chaudhry S. (Boston: Springer), pp. 753-762.

The rest of this paper is organized as follows: Section 2 designs a SOA oriented information system architecture, Section 3 proposes three web services operational mechanisms, Section 4 is the conclusion, some ideas about future work are presented.

2. DYNAMIC INFORMATION SYSTEM ARCHITECTURE

2.1 Change: a Permanent Problem in the Information Systems Application

Nowadays, more and more enterprises adopt information systems such as ERP (Enterprise Resources Planning) to assist their daily operation works and management process. Information systems play an important role in improving enterprise efficiency, reducing business costs, optimizing business processes and increasing customer satisfaction [1].

But with the pass of time, many enterprises find that most of their running information systems can't meet the new business needs flexibly. For example, in some manufacture enterprises, since the demands of product types and structures from different customers are different, the information systems are supposed to respond to the changing business needs rapidly [2]. On the other hand, a competitive environment driven by technological change and shorter product life-cycle have created a big challenge for enterprises, which should rebuild their business processes with information technology (IT) [3]. Obviously, it asks for more agility and flexibility for the information systems.

Additionally, IT itself develops very fast. Because of the lack of universal design standards in the past, a lot of legacy systems can’ t access with each other. In the meantime, less and less people grasping the language of legacy systems can be found with the development of new programming language and software systems [4]. However, many enterprises having invested heavily in legacy systems want to find ways to integrate them with the newer system instead of scraping them [5].

Furthermore, a common problem when adopting package software is the issue of "misfits" [6], which means there exist the gaps between the functionality offered by the package and the requirements presented by the adopting organization.

Apparently, changing is a permanent problem in the application of information systems. The full potential of IT will be achieved only when software process and business processes are able to be integrated by using a standard process integration model [7]. Then, can we find a solution to make the systems so dynamic that they can adapt to not only the demand changing but also technical changing, and also offer some basis for the matching of these two changing? Combining with the concept of SOA, in the next part, we propose a web services based information system architecture to solve the problems we mentioned above.

2.2 SOA Oriented Information System Architecture

SOA (Service Oriented Architecture) is a method to organize IT infrastructure resources rather than a certain technology essentially. With the advantages of architecture, SOA can bring the enterprise many benefits: full use of the information assets the enterprise now own; persistent business processes improvement; better integration; more agility, usability and maintainability; better support for the enterprise strategy and so forth.

SOA committed to providing application functions as services offered on the Internet (or an intranet) environment which is very distributed, heterogeneous, and dynamic. It tries to bridge the boundaries between systems and organizations. The most common form of SOA is the framework based on the web services. More and more IT companies release applications and their interfaces as web services, playing the role of service provider. And then they can construct application information systems flexibly on the basis of those web services, according to the work flow in the customer businesses [8]. Once the enterprise's core functions are modeled as web services, the question of the application system integration becomes the integration of all kinds of web services [9].Obviously, the theme of SOA is to help enterprises get rid of the constraint from fixed solutions, and face the change of business and technique easily.

On the basis of SOA concept, we propose a SOA oriented enterprise dynamic information system architecture, which is shown in figure 1. This is only a system logic framework, neglecting the operating system, middleware application server and other factors existing in bottom layer.

As is shown in Figure 1, we divide the enterprise information system architecture into three low-coupling layers: data layer, enterprise domain model layer, application platform layer. These three layers are surely related with each other, but they keep relatively independent through certain way: the data layer and the enterprise domain model layer use object or relation mapping in decoupling, while the enterprise domain model layer and the application platform layer realize decoupling through interface invoked and separation between system development and deployment. Thus, one layer can change easily while the other layers are not affected too much.

In the middle of Figure 1, viz. the enterprise domain model layer, we can construct enterprise domain objects by using business process modeling and Object-oriented analysis method comprehensively, then expose some interfaces and deploy them as web services, which will be considered as the meta functional components of enterprise information systems. The business process modeling method can analyze enterprise functions thoroughly, abstract meta-functions from business processes as service components. The Object-oriented analysis will ensure the reusability, while the standardized technology of web services ensures easy integration. After getting the meta-function components, summarizing industry best practices and enterprise special needs, industrial standard process library of the certain industry and enterprise specific process library will be constructed respectively using workflow modeling technology. For some mature industrial processes, enterprises can build their own business processes directly by using industry process templates. Moreover, for some enterprise special processes, they can go through with a secondary assembled development. In this procedure mentioned above, all the processes are assembled flexibly by web services from the meta-function components library, and then deployed on the application platform, making sure that the workflows in information systems will change with business processes.

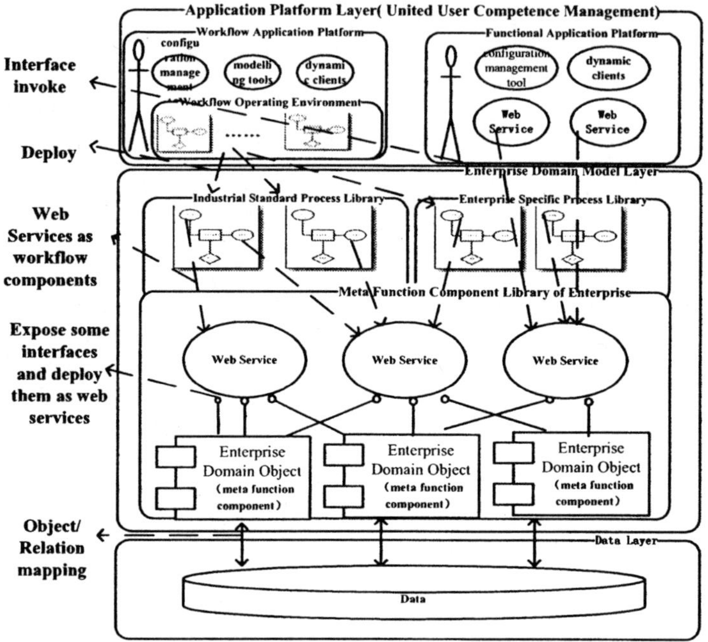

Figure 1. Enterprise Dynamic IS Architecture Model

In the top of Figure 1, there is a uniform platform. It consists of a workflow application platform and a functional application platform to meet the needs from operations related both business process and functional applications. These two platforms are administrated by uniform user authority. Only users who have the matched authority can operate on certain workflow or function. The client software is dynamically created on the application platform according to the user's actual requirements, which will keep its agility and avoid secondary development which is unnecessary.

In the process of implementation, this model can map the actual business processes of the customer enterprise quickly into its information systems by referring to the enterprise optimal business processes. After the mapping work, web services will be configured in the information systems automatically and work in the way that the enterprise wants.

3. THREE WEB SERVICES OPERATIONAL MECHANISMS

However, if we want to realize the architecture showed in Section 2, how can we get web services reasonably and legally from the Internet? Since the emergence of web service concept, many software enterprises and developers in the market began to deploy and release their own application packaged as web services. Web services are all described with WSDL and registered using UDDI, whereas, how to find the right services from all kinds of similar web services for a specific user company? In another word, can there be anyone in charge of works of discriminating, classifying and managing those web services? And who is responsible for the assembly and integration works?

SLA (Service-Level Agreement) is used to not only measure the quality and cost of web services offered by service providers but also as a criterion in choosing and judging web service providers. However, SLA simply protects consumers' benefits technically [10]. Because of the expansion and virtualization of network, almost all the intellectual products on the network are facing a plight, that is, how to protect intellectual property and charge normal fees from the file-sharing network [11]. The authors believe that it is necessary to build up a set of operational mechanisms to protect the benefits of web service consumers, while web services providers' benefits will not be damaged. According to the different managers of web services, we propose three kinds of web services operational mechanisms: (1) Web Service predominant characteristic mechanism guided by large enterprises, (2) Web Services portal mechanism guided by industrial category, (3) Web Service Uniform Alliance (WSUA) mechanism.

3.1 Web Service Predominant Characteristic Mechanism Guided by Large Enterprises

In the IT market, there are many mainstream IT companies in each application field. Hence, we can define the mechanism in which the web services are managed by mainstream software providers as the web service predominant characteristic mechanism guided by large enterprises, shown in Figure 2. The real line arrows show a value-added process, including web services' choosing, assembly, integration and delivery. In contrast, the dotted line arrows have two meanings: firstly, they present the transportation of customers' demands, from the customers, through consultants and mainstream providers, finally to the web services providers; secondly, they show the payment transformation in this whole process (the arrows in Figure 3 and 4 have the same meaning, it will not be pointed out again later).

In this web services mechanism dominated by large enterprises, it is the mainstream software providers who have specialty in certain field that face so many web service components providers directly (including components personally developed, the same in the following parts). For example, Microsoft is one of the generic software mainstream vendors, while SAP is one of the management software mainstream vendors and the like. Certain internal evaluation and selection mechanisms on web services are made by these enterprises. Accordingly they will pick up qualified web services components from diverse web service providers and then assemble them into web services component products with larger granularity. Afterward, encapsulated and value added component products will be supplied to web services consumers by implementation consultants.

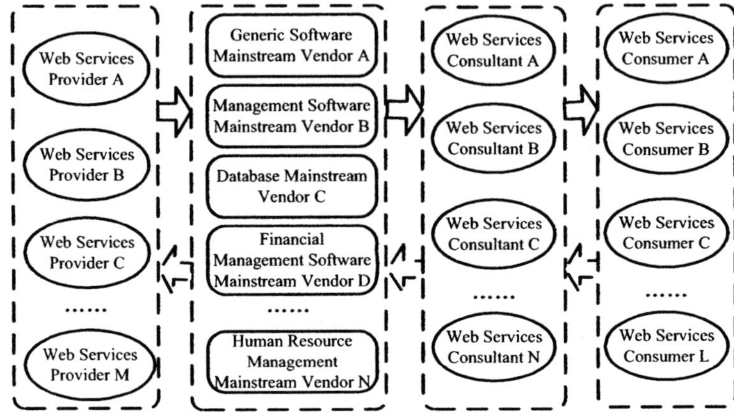

Figure 2. Web Service Predominant Characteristic Mechanism

With the pass of time, more and more web services are developed, but a majority of them are "repeated works" with similar functionality and content. There are so many similar web services that it becomes difficult for consumers to make decision in selecting them unless difference advantage can be established through different added value offered by providers. Besides, due to the diversity of the products, consumers put more emphasizes on reliability in addition to functionality. In this context, web services provided by mainstream enterprises will show their huge brand effects. Their brand advantage is much larger than the other similar products, plus professional skill and management advantage, all of the above make web services products from mainstream enterprises easy win out in the fierce competition. Generally, these mainstream enterprises can not only pick up qualified web services from various providers but also produce their own web services component products. As each of the mainstream enterprises has their own specialty field, the web service predominant characteristic mechanism guided by large enterprises is formed gradually.

In this mechanism, mainstream enterprises are responsible for choosing and evaluating web services, and then they pay for web services they have chosen, classify them and assemble new web services with larger granularity. Implementation consultants shown in the figure collect customers' demands, and buy web services with different granularities from mainstream enterprises. After assembling them and doing some secondary development works, consultants deliver these value-added web services to customers.

Certainly, if some customers have technical strength themselves, in pursuit of lower cost, they can surely cross the mainstream enterprises and consultants, and cooperate with the web service providers directly. The mainstream enterprises can also serve customers directly, without certain consultant.

3.2 Web Services Portal Mechanism Guided by Industrial Category

In reality, there already exist some sorts of industrial association or organizations. Thus we can define the mechanism in which the web services are managed by industrial organization as the web services portal mechanism guided by industrial category reasonably, as is shown in Figure 3.

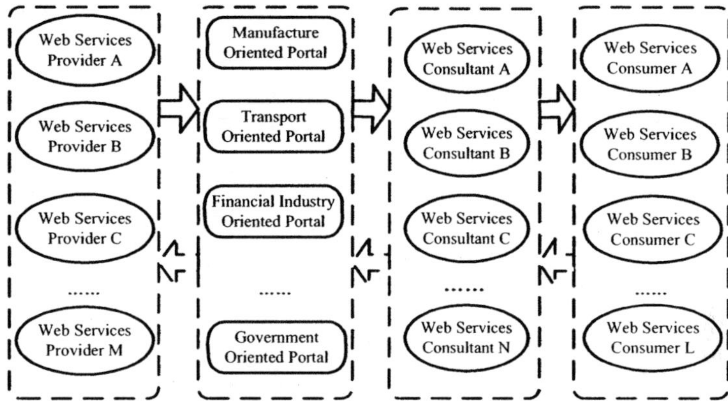

Figure 3. Web Services Portal Mechanism Guided by Industrial Category

In this kind of mechanism, according to the applications fields of the web services, the providers deploy them in different industrial portal platforms, such as manufacture oriented portal, transport oriented portal, government oriented portal and so on.

Once certain customers want to use web services, they will find the implementation consultant first. The consultant will go to the corresponding industrial portal system to find appropriate web service components they need after investigating the customer’ s requirement in detail. Then the consultant assembles and integrates these web services components, and supplies the customer with final product and training.

As to the formation of industrial portal, we have two proposals: (1) There may be some leader enterprises that have been developing a lot of application software in this industry for a long time. Just like what we discussed in the first mechanism, this kind of enterprises have large brand effect and mature management processes, then these industrial leader enterprises can be in charge of the management of industrial portal; or (2) In fact, it is the industrial associations that constitute, monitor and maintain the industrial criteria, so they know business processes, demands and criteria of their own industrial field better. Then, web services management institutions can also be set by industrial associations. These institutions are responsible for developing, evaluating and choosing appropriate web services for their industrial field. Undoubtedly, the industrial leader enterprises can cooperate with the industrial association to management the industrial portal.

3.3 Web Service Uniform Alliance (WSUA) Mechanism

According to Cheng et al [12], their analysis result in 2006 shows that application service strategy of independent service vendors is always dominated by the service alliance, implying that providers will benefit from the increased interoperability of web services, for its low integration cost and the possibility of creating new functionalities through integrating web services. That is to say, it is better for web services providers to be joint venture or form an alliance.

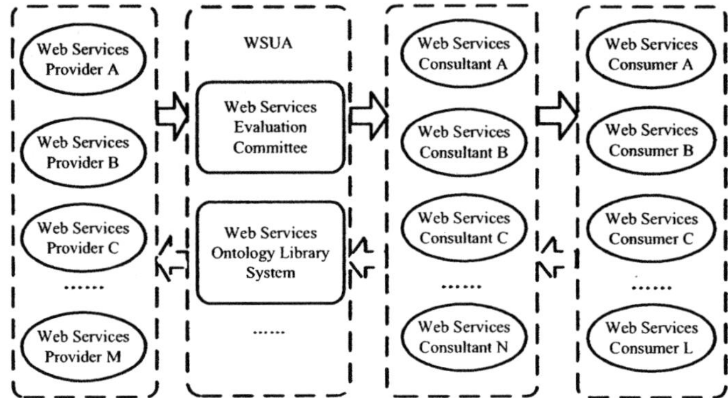

Figure 4. Web Service Uniform Alliance (WSUA) Mechanism

Actually, because there are many web services intercrossing between the industrial mechanism and the mechanism guided by mainstream enterprises, an ideal status is to form a web service uniform alliance (WSUA) which will be in charge of the management of web services in the global area. And we can define the mechanism in which the web services are managed by WSUA as the WSUA mechanism, as shown in Figure 4.

WSUA is obviously an ideal manager of the web services market. In this mechanism, all the web service providers get together via the Internet and form an alliance to choose, classify, evaluate, release and deploy web services. Furthermore, it is essentially a web service practitioners' industrial association, which is made up of web service evaluation committee, web services ontology library system [13], and etc. It is responsible for standardizing and unifying web service supply market, maintaining versions and copyrights of web services products, avoiding vicious competitions among web services providers. Figure 5 shows some responsibilities of WSUA.

Once some web services providers want to be on the WSUA provider list, they have to apply first. Unless they are committed by WSUA evaluation committee, viz., when their web service components pass the evaluation, their web service products can be added into the WSUA products list. WSUA will categorize those web service products and be in charge of their version update.

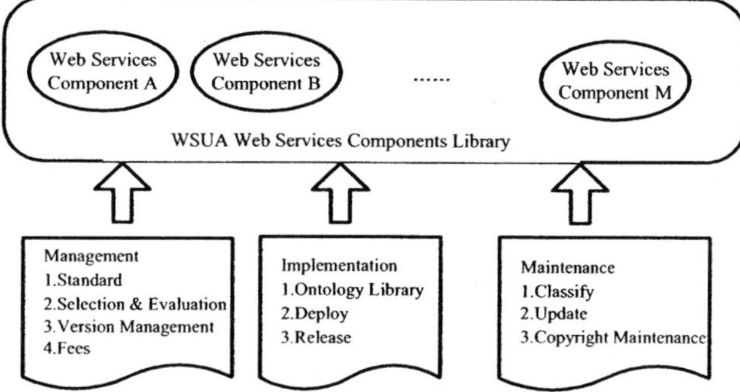

Figure 5. Descriptions of WSUA Functions

In the same way, when some user enterprises want to use web services in their new information systems, they should look for an implementation consultant at first, and then propose their requirements in detail. Once their business models are built up, the consultant will look for the corresponding web services in the WSUA ontology model system, finally assemble them into the final software product for the user enterprise. Of course, the consultant should pay the WSUA for all the web services got from it. And once the web services are updated, WSUA will be responsible for the related informing and updating works.

Some rules or declarations should be constituted to keep the related rights to the web service providers. Meanwhile, it should be noticed that the WSUA plays a very important role in offering all those web service providers a platform for fair competition and mutual cooperation. Then, vicious competitions caused by different scales will be avoided because of the agreement formed among providers.

These three mechanisms above may exist and compete with each other at the same time. Obviously, the ideal operational mechanism is to build a Web Service Uniform Alliance from the perspective of utilizing and saving global intellectual resources.

4. CONCLUSION AND FUTURE WORK

This paper proposes a SOA based information system architecture, and then three available web service operational mechanisms are presented according to the different managers. This will help in normalizing current web service operation. The three mechanisms are: (1) Web Service predominant characteristic mechanism guided by large enterprises, (2) Web Services portal mechanism guided by industrial category, (3) Web Service Uniform Alliance (WSUA) mechanism. The ideal operational mechanism is to build a Web Service Uniform Alliance from the perspective of utilizing and saving global intellectual resources.

However, we only presented three mechanisms and built these corresponding models. In those figures of the models, what we discussed are just the real line arrows, we didn't discuss the dotted line arrows deeply, which contains payment mechanism. In addition, much work about selection mechanism, evaluation mechanism and upgrade mechanism in the models needs to be discussed in the future.

ACKNOWLEDGEMENTS

This research was supported by a research grant from the Foundation of Key Laboratory of Information Management and Information Economics (Project No. F0607-42). And the first author also has a special grant from the Fok Ying Tung Education Foundation.

REFERENCES

1. D.L. Olson and F. Zhao, CIOs' perspectives of critical success factors in ERP upgrade projects, *Enterprise Information Systems.* Volume 1, Number 1, pp.129-138, (2007).
2. M. Holmquvist and K. Pessi, Agility through scenario development and continuous implementation: a global aftermarket logistics case, *European Journal of Information Systems.* Volume 15, Number 2, pp.146-158, (2006).
3. V.L. Mitchell and R.W. Zmud, Endogenous Adaptation: The Effects of Technology Position and Planning Mode on IT-Enabled Change, *Decision Sciences.* Volume 37, Number 3, pp.325-355, (2006).
4. S. Chandra, J.D. Vries, J. Field, and H. Hess, Using Logical Data Models for Understanding and Transforming Legacy Business, *IBM Systems Journal.* Volume 45, Number 3, pp.647-655, (2006).
5. K. Furumo and A. Melcher, The Importance of Social Structure in Implementing ERP Systems: A Case Study using Adaptive Structuration Theory, *Journal of Information Technology Case and Application Research.* Volume 8, Number 2, pp.39-58, (2006).
6. C. Soh, S.S. Kien, and J. Tay-Yap, Enterprise resource planning: cultural fits and misfits: is ERP a universal solution? *Communications of the ACM.* Volume 43, Number 4, pp.47-51, (2000).
7. J.Y. Lee, S. Lee, K. Kim and H. Kim, A process-centric engineering web services framework, *The International Journal of Advanced Manufacturing Technology.* Volume 26, Number 9-10, pp.1173-1183, (2005).
8. S. Zhao and M. Zuo, A SOA Based Research on Enterprise Dynamic Information System Architecture, in *Proc. of the 1st conference of China Association for Information Systems* (2006), pp.295-299.
9. R. Khalaf, A. Keller, and F. Leymann, Business processes for web services: principles and applications, *IBM Systems Journal.* Volume 45, Number 2, pp.425-446, (2006).
10. L.J. Jin, V. Machiraju, and A. Sahai, *Analysis on Service Level Agreement of Web Service*, HP Laboratories Technical Report, HPL (2002).
11. R. Dannenberg, Copyright Protection for Digitally Delivered Music: A Global Affair, *Intellectual Property & Technology Law Journal.* Volume 18, Number 2, pp.12-16, (2006).
12. H. Cheng, Q. Tang, and J. Zhao, Web Services and Service-Oriented Application Provisioning: An Analytical Study of Application Service Strategies, *IEEE Transactions on Engineering Management.* Volume 52, Number 4, pp.520-533, (2006).
13. Y. Ding and D. Fensel, Ontology Library Systems: The key for successful Ontology Reuse, in *Proc.s of the 1st Semantic web working symposium* (Springer-Verlag Heidelberg: Heidelberg, 2001), pp.93-112.

A Study on Tacit Knowledge Sharing in ERP Enterprises

Binli Sun

School of Economic Management, Beijing Institute of Petrochemical Technology, Beijing 102617, P.R. China sunbinli@bipt.edu.cn

Abstract. With the fast developing knowledge economy, one of the major challenges facing enterprise managers is aligning knowledge management (KM) with business strategy and processes, especially after an enterprise has applied Enterprise Resource Planning (ERP). Since knowledge sharing (KnS) is one of the most critical steps in KM activities, it is necessary to study the effective sharing of tacit knowledge in ERP enterprises. In an ERP environment, KnS system should have two functions. One is to support the enterprise business and the other is to support employees' communication. Most researches have thus far focused on the first function trying to find out management mechanism to improve the effect of KnS while ignoring the other function. In the KnS with the communication function, this research finds out that knowledge is exchanged naturally and freely. The KnS system can also make employees feel better about their work by making greater contribution to building an active culture environment to support knowledge exchange. In this paper, these two types of KnS are called business-oriented knowledge-sharing and subject-oriented knowledge-sharing. It also designs their constructions, propose their management mechanism and discuss some relevant practice problems. When these two types of KnS are applied in ERP enterprises they not only can provide channels for employees to exchange knowledge, but can also help enterprises to get tacit knowledge from ERP users and to make tacit knowledge more effectively be converted to explicit knowledge. Though ERP and KnS are performed as two separate systems, this research provides guidance to enterprise managers to develop tacit knowledge-sharing system on their ERP implementation and keep the same goal with it.

Keywords: *Knowledge management, Enterprise resource planning (ERP), Enterprise systems*

1. INTRODUCTION

In an ever-flattening world, organizations must quickly learn and adapt to changes in the marketplace. While we have become better at implementing new business processes and new management information system, such as ERP, we found that we spent too much time on cyber-business line and lost many chances to communicate with our partners. Nowadays, the end users are more involved in ERP implementations than they were in their previous traditional business process [1].

Please use the following format when citing this chapter:

Sun, B., 2007, in IFIP International Federation for Information Processing, Volume 254, Research and Practical Issues of Enterprise Information Systems II Volume 1, eds. L. Xu, Tjoa A., Chaudhry S. (Boston: Springer), pp. 763-770.

To make matter worse, ERP requires the end users to have more divergent knowledge. However, there is often a large gap in knowledge among ERP users, and they do not easily share what they know during their daily work [2]. Some researches have paid attention to the long-term impact of ERP implementation in organizations, and emphasized the importance of organizational learning in ERP implementation [3]. In ERP environment, enterprises will have greater challenges in knowledge management, especially those challenges related to the sharing and integration of knowledge. It is necessary, therefore, to discuss how to build up an effective knowledge sharing models in enterprises. When these models are put into practice, it will improve the organizational learning, knowledge exchange, tacit externalization, and to enhance organizational competitive edge.

In addition of the Introduction Section, the remainder of this paper is organized as follows: Section II provides an analysis to functions and types of knowledge sharing in ERP enterprises. Section III provides the construction of business-oriented KnS and its further analysis. Discussions about the subject-oriented KnS are presented in Section IV. Finally, Section V is the conclusions.

2. FUNCTIONS AND TYPES OF KNOWLEDGE SHARING IN ERP ENTERPRISES

ERP implementation relates closely to knowledge management in manufacturing enterprises. An ERP system stores a company's data, processes its information, and embeds its knowledge in business activities. Such knowledge may reside in company database such as explicit transaction knowledge. Some knowledge such as the process knowledge is embedded in the business activities. Other knowledge may be recorded in process manuals on a regular basis [4]. In addition, there is much more knowledge embedded in the heads of individuals who work directly with the ERP systems. The knowledge stored in database is explicit knowledge -- a kind of formal knowledge, and it can support the employees' work according to certain knowledge management process. Most of the knowledge stored in individuals' heads is tacit knowledge -- an informal knowledge, and it can only be used by communication among concerned people.

2.1 Functions of Knowledge Sharing in ERP Enterprises

The functions of knowledge management are often described as a knowledge support system to personnel in an enterprise. They provide intelligence to knowledge analysis and employees' interests and behavior in support of personalized access to the knowledge base [5]. This type of knowledge sharing is often described as value knowledge exchanging in a certain community, such as seeking and giving advice, sharing individual experience, new solutions to some problems, and supporting each other's work, and so on. To make these functions effective there is a need to research the motivation of KnS, and evaluation mechanism and some external rewards [6].

In ERP enterprises, beside the functions of KnS discussed above, we should notice that KnS in ERP enterprise should have another function, which is to provide a way for ERP users to communicate with each others freely. In this way, employees can exchange their idea, their feeling, their questions and anything which they are interested in. Communicating to other people is a common human behavior. This kind of KnSs dose not need much more external rewards. It has been used in Lenovo company in China and has received a good evaluation from employees.

In general, we can see that there are two major functions of KnS in ERP enterprises, one is a working-support function, and the other is a daily communicating-support function. They are two sides of KnS in ERP enterprises.

2.2 Types of Knowledge Sharing in ERP Enterprises

In traditional enterprises, only small circles of colleagues and work groups commonly share their tacit knowledge, but in an ERP system, if we can get support from IT technology, the circles of colleagues and work groups sharing knowledge have been greatly extended. Such a sharing process is also more complex. According to the functions discussed above, we found the two functions of KnS need different support mechanism. The working-support KnS is commonly related to problems that employees met or discovered in their daily work. These problems have to be solved quickly so that the effect of KnS application will influence the ERP business and enterprise operations. To do this well some kinds of encourage mechanisms is needed to insure the system can work effectively. The communication-support KnS is commonly related to activities that employees' took part during their daily life. This type of activities has a wider scope which may include their work, their feeling and their life. This communication does not need some special encouraging mechanism. The practice methods are different between the two types of KnS. In order to easily discuss KnSs, we divided them into two types: one is business-oriented knowledge-sharing, and the other is subject-oriented knowledge-sharing. We will discuss each of them in following sections.

3. BUSINESS-ORIENTED KNOWLEDGE-SHARING MODEL

The knowledge framework used in the business-oriented knowledge-sharing model is same as the framework in ERP. This means that the content of knowledge is similar to the ERP business. The managers and ERP line workers use the business function modules to finish their daily work. When this kind of KnS system is used on the internal platform, workers will quickly understand the knowledge framework, without much more training, because they have much more knowledge already about the ERP business. Such a KnS system can facilitate the process of knowledge sharing and reduce the time of training. When related materials and Q&As in one business field can be collected together, it will be of great convenience for the employees to discuss the similar questions and promote the efficiency in solving problems.

3.1 Construction of Business-oriented Knowledge-sharing Model

Business-oriented knowledge communication is similar to a kind of formal communication. There is a lot of knowledge exchange under this framework of KnS. Workers in an enterprise can load up some materials, such as words, audio, and video materials, and store them in knowledge database after treatment. Workers can write anything that is related with their work and load-up to knowledge center. The tacit knowledge that cannot be expressed clearly can be recorded or kinescoped as audio or video materials and load-up in an enterprise's knowledge database. Question and answer method is another important channel for workers to exchange their knowledge. By asking and answering, worker can get the solution to the problem occurred in their work. In this way, KnS can get more knowledge from their workers. Meanwhile, Q&A often focuses on the difficult area in employees' work, so the knowledge came from this channel is more important than the knowledge from subject-oriented KnS. Generally, we need certain managers who know the enterprise very well to process the knowledge, such as select the valuable knowledge and give deep treatment before storing. The logic construction of business-oriented knowledge-sharing model is shown in fig.1.

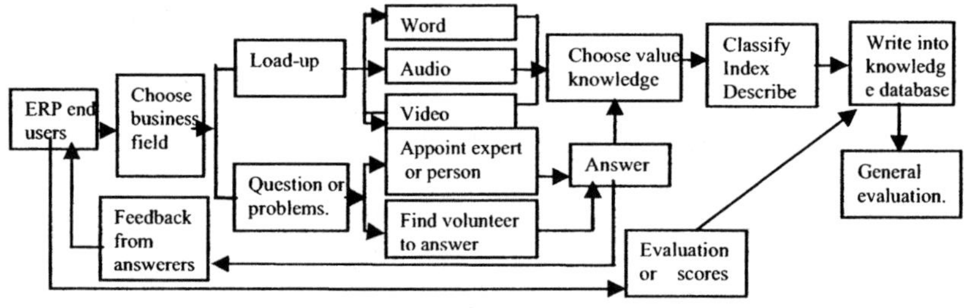

Figure 1. Business-oriented KnS Process Model

3.2 Classification and Restricted Using

In order to keep a close relationship between knowledge and ERP business, business-oriented KnS system should be divided into different fields that are fit to different ERP business modules. ERP end users choose related field to load up their knowledge achievements or hand over their problems, the answers from others will be stored in the same field, so the classification will base on ERP business fields, such as material requirements planning, capital requirements planning, bill of materials, purchase, inventory management, human resource, and so on[7]. This is the center part of business-oriented KnS.

Considering the importance of knowledge to enterprise operation, we need to identify the restricted knowledge and give a sign in order to provide to certain group to use. Not all knowledge is public to all internal employees. Before storing them in databases, the knowledge should be identified by a qualified knowledge manager. It is necessary to do that if we want to make each of the databases useful.

Besides, we know that one of ERP advantages is to help enterprises change from mass production to mass customization production, so the customer's service will become the heart of enterprise operation. Managers and employees will pay much more attention to the knowledge related with customers' interest. This knowledge should be singled out before storing them in knowledge database according to certain attributes to the knowledge entity. In this way, a particular knowledge can be quickly selected out when needed.

3.3 Knowledge Storage

The knowledge provided in business-oriented KnS is almost a kind of formal knowledge, and it doesn't need strict checking. Most of the knowledge will be stored in database after classifying, indexing and describing. Because the existence of a variety of knowledge formats, there are different storage methods. In general, knowledge database should have two basic parts: data-based and document-based. Some knowledge forms, such as audio, video, and some word materials, should be stored into document-based part, but the description of these materials and the other knowledge should be stored into the relative database (data-based part). It is important to remember, however, that there must be a link between the document materials and their description records in relative database. That can insure the needed materials can be found quickly.

3.4 Effective Evaluation Mechanism

Many researchers have indicated that knowledge-sharing processes may fail if they are not backed by a supportive culture. But the culture can't be set up in one night. Without the culture, few employees would like to make their effort to exchange knowledge without any return. If an enterprise has no such culture environment, it is difficult to begin practicing business-oriented KnS. Therefore, the effective evaluation mechanism becomes the key for successful implement of business-oriented KnS. The key steps to effective application of business-oriented KnS at the beginning of tacit knowledge-sharing application are to develop supportive technology functions and build effective management mechanism. The following management mechanisms should be integrated into the tacit KnS system at the beginning of KnS practice.

- Feedback record function: Contentment to knowledge answer is the key criteria to evaluate the knowledge quality. Askers have their feeling to the answers of their question, and the feeling should be recorded by a certain method, such as giving scores, special signs, or evaluation.
- Effective identification mechanism: To identify person who provided much more individual knowledge than others will help top managers to better understand their workers, and the person may gain reputation as a knowledgeable source or receive the enterprise's rewards, such as promotion [8].

• General evaluation mechanism: Enterprises need to incorporate knowledge-sharing proficiencies as part of annual job performance evaluations (as is already the case at Lenovo Company and Shanghai Mechanical Computer Company).

4. SUBJECT-ORIENTED KNOWLEDGE-SHARING MODEL

Subject-oriented knowledge-sharing flat is perceived as a replacement for a face-to-face interaction. During ERP implement, there are fewer opportunities for enterprise worker to make contact with others. Some researches have showed that the enterprise knowledge will only emerge as individual knowledge workers interact with other knowledge workers and the environment. Therefore, it is necessary for enterprises to make their efforts to build a platform for their workers to exchange their ideas. Though they still spend much more time facing their computers, they are keeping contact with their partner in cyberspace. The main function of the Subject-oriented knowledge-sharing flat is to create a friendly, freely and relax environment for their workers.

4.1 Construction of Subject-oriented Knowledge-sharing Model

In order to create a free and relax cyberspace for employees, the Subject-oriented knowledge-sharing needs to simulate the traditional natural communication environment. In natural environment, people have right to choose their partner(s), to choose their like topic and have right to keep their talk secret. Subject-oriented knowledge-sharing should have these functions, so the logic model of Subject-oriented knowledge sharing is shown as fig.2.

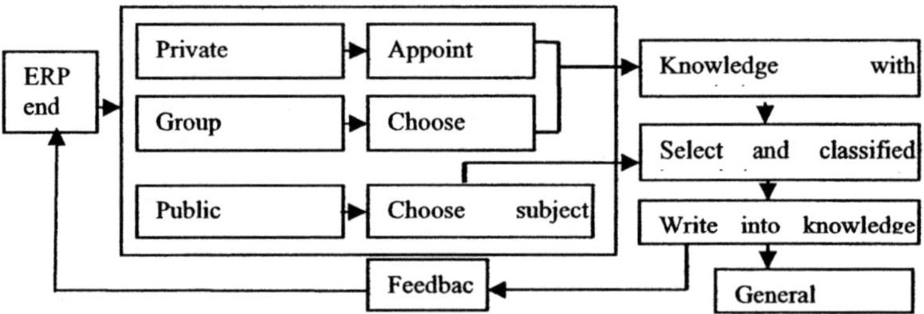

Figure 2. Subject-oriented KnS Process Model

From fig.2, we can see that there are three kinds of communication channels in Subject-oriented KnS process: private communication (which is between two persons), group communication (which is among a group, include teleconferencing), and public communication (which is to the public). The enterprise workers can freely choose one of them to interact with others or environment. Among the three channels, private and group communication should be kept secret, free and safe. Knowledge communication under this framework of KnS is just like the traditional face-to-face communication, and it refers to chat rooms. It allows workers to post their message publicly or privately. They post their public messages and questions on message board (to the public), or directly send to an appointed person (to individual), then wait for someone, either another worker or an expert, to answer the question. Sometimes it may take days to receive an answer, especially if one expects it to be answered by an expert. The public communication is a free field for anybody in an enterprise.

4.2 Knowledge Classification and Storage

Public communication is a place for workers to deliver their ideas to the public. In order to centralize the relative information, public communication fields should be divided into different subjects. The subjects should cover most of employs' interest, and they should be far beyond ERP business boundary, such as sport, travel, hot issues and so on. These subjects should be kept update according to the change. We can see the subjects are much different from that used in business-oriented KnS.

Before storing into database, the knowledge should be selected seriously. For knowledge from public communication, the knowledge manager must first check whether it is of value, only value knowledge to enterprise operation can be further processed and stored into database. For knowledge from private or group communication field, the knowledge can be further processed only after received the permission or recommendation from participants in the group. Generally, two methods can be used for this work: computer programming and knowledge workers determining. The computer programming can judge the useful knowledge by evaluation, and special signs or scores that are provided by private or group communication participants. Compare to the computer programming, knowledge workers' decision has the flexibility and the veracity.

The process storage has two steps: first, communication content is recorded in temporary database and wait for checking; second, the knowledge that fits to enterprise demands is classified, indexed and then stored into formal database. After that, the knowledge can be provided to others. It is important to note that the private and the group process can be recorded only after getting their permission.

Unlike business-oriented KnS, the practice process of subject-oriented KnS does not need much more external rewards. It is a natural process, and the motivation comes from human nature. In subject-oriented KnS model, there is no feedback or scores from the users. If the function is to be added, they are mainly to be used as an element to identify the value knowledge. This will be useful for computer programming to judge the value knowledge.

5. CONCLUSIONS

In this paper, two types of KnS, business-oriented knowledge-sharing and subject-oriented knowledge-sharing, are discussed. There are both sides of KnS in ERP enterprise and support the two important functions: supporting business operation and employees' communication. Neither of these functions should be ignored. They are also important ways to get tacit knowledge from ERP end users and make tacit knowledge convert into explicit knowledge by IT technology support.

In recent years, more and more enterprises use ERP system in their main business process. Successful ERP system can greatly raise enterprise productivity. Meanwhile, many relevant researches and practices have showed that effective knowledge sharing can promote the competitive ability of enterprise. It is very important, therefore, to research the combination of KnS with ERP implementation. This paper has discussed the way to improve the integration of tacit KnS and ERP implementation in enterprises with the hope that it will help enterprise to effectively practice KnS in their ERP environment.

REFERENCES

1. M.C. Jones and R.L. Price, Organizational knowledge sharing in ERP implementation: Lessons from industry, *Journal of organizational & end user computing.* Volume 16, Number 1, pp.21-40, (2004).
2. M.C. Jones, Tacit knowledge sharing during implementation: A multi-site case study, *Information Resources Management Journal.* Volume 18, Number 2, pp.1-23, (2005).
3. L. Wu, Y.W. Hsu, and C.S. Ong, ERP implementation: a quantitative model for organizational learning, *International Journal of Information Technology & Management.* Volume 6, Number 1, p.5, (2007).
4. L.L. Hsu and M. Chen, Impacts of ERP systems on the integrated-interaction performance of manufacturing and marketing, *Industrial management & data systems.* Volume 104, Number 1, pp.42-45, (2004).
5. A.T.Pardo, A.M. Cresswell, J. Zhang, and F. Thompson, Interorganizational knowledge sharing in public sector innovations, in *Proc. of Academy of Management Proceedings, PNP: A1* (2001).
6. D.G. Bobrow and J. Whalen, Community knowledge sharing in practice: the Eureka story, *Reflections.* Volume 4, Number 2, pp.47-61, (2002).
7. Q. Chen, *ERP-step Forward from Internal Integration*, 2nd ed. (Publishing House of Electronics Industry: Beijing, 2006)
8. J. Liebowitz and Y. Chen, Developing knowledge-sharing proficiencies, *Knowledge Management.* Volume 3, Number 3, pp.12-17, (2004).

Research on Customer Profile Integration of Telecom Enterprises Based on Ontology

Jianlin Wu, Yan Xiong, Shuangshuang Lou and Bai Wang

Beijing Key Laboratory of Intelligent Communications Software and Multimedia, Beijing University of Posts and Telecommunications, Beijing 100876, P.R. China
jlwu@bupt.edu.cn xiongyan2001@gmail.com loushuangshuang@gmail.com wangbai@bupt.edu.cn

Abstract. In the product-centered marketing times of telecom industry, BOSS (Business Operations Supporting System) was established step by step, which resulted in the two critical difficulties in customer profile integration: semantic inconsistency and semantic conflict. In this article, ontology theory is introduced to solve these problems. Firstly, the skeleton method is adopted to build telecom customer profile ontology. Besides, a web based ontology building and query environment—Webtege is developed to give the formal definition in OWL. Then a new approach is proposed to achieve customer profile integration in telecom enterprise in both new system and legacy system scenarios from functional and data view. Therefore, this customer profile ontology could give a guideline in constituting and exchanging unified customer profile data through various systems.

Keywords: *Ontology, Customer relationship management, OWL*

1. INTRODUCTION

As the competition in global telecommunication industry becomes more and more fierce, the focus of telecommunication service is transferring from the product to the customer. However, the information systems of telecom operators are built step by step, there are two significant problems: semantic inconsistency and semantic conflict, which decreases the satisfaction of customer services.

The problem of semantic inconsistency has two dimensions: first, because the different systems are built in different times, the systems can not reach an agreement on the information model; second, in the information models, the attributes of table with the same meaning have different codes, resulting that even though various systems have the same logical models, data can not be understood and exchange by different systems. On the other hand, the problem of semantic conflict also has two dimensions: first, the customer information is short of verification; second, the customer information in different systems is updated in different time, so the profiles of one customer in different systems are quite various.

It is critical to handle the above two problems for the integration of customer information of telecommunication enterprises. Ontology can effectively describe the various concepts and the relationships between them on the semantic and knowledge

Please use the following format when citing this chapter:

Wu, J., Xiong, Y., Lou, S., Wang, B., 2007, in IFIP International Federation for Information Processing, Volume 254, Research and Practical Issues of Enterprise Information Systems II Volume 1, eds. L. Xu, Tjoa A., Chaudhry S. (Boston: Springer), pp. 771-780.

level, leading to the share of the concept relationships among various systems. This paper tries to utilize the ontology model methodology to solve the mentioned semantic problems. First, we establish the customer profile ontology of telecommunication operators to achieve the agreement on customer profile models. Then we use the established customer profile ontology to handle the semantic heterogeneous and conflicting problems.

2. RELATED WORK

Information integration could be viewed as there levels: physical, logic and semantic. In physical and logic information integration level, technologies such as COM, CORBA and Agent, have also been developed to solve the technical problem of information integration [1].

In semantic level, many efforts are made. Wang [2] gives the structure, consistency checking and development process of ontology-based metadata model whose research is supported by National Nature Science Foundation of China: Customer Ontology in CRM Study. In his dissertation, Wang tries to establish simple customer ontology to be applied in all industry. In this research group, Lu [3] proposes customer features extraction based on customer ontology; Wang [4] makes efforts on the mechanism of information retrieval based on customer ontology. The above mentioned research is devoted in the common customer information ontology or integration metadata, but there is also customer ontology research in specific domain. Zhu [5] makes research on customer information sharing in the supply chain of automobile. Yan [6] establishes contract ontology in OWL to express semantic relations. Huhns [7] build personal ontology to filtrate information in the web. However, when we refer to telecom industry the ontology concept is rarely used to settle the specific problem of information integration. Here is the meaning of this paper—introducing ontology to telecom industry.

3. BUILDING CUSTOMER ONTOLOGY

3.1 Methodology of Building Customer Ontology

Ontology was original a philosophy concept which is the description of concepts and relationship between concepts. The application of ontology experiences the development from philosophy to artificial intelligent area and is now widely used in information and other areas [8]. Studer [9] defined Ontology as explicit formal specification of shared concept model in 1998. The language describing ontology could be divided as based on framework and logic. The language OWL [10] used in this article is one description language based on logic. Skeleton method is also called Ushold and King Method [11], which is derived from Enterprise Ontology building experiences by Edinburgh University in England. There are four steps to develop the ontology using skeleton methodology: 1. Define ontology objective and scope; 2. Building ontology, including concept extracts and define, codify and integration exists ontology; 3. Evaluation, evaluate the build ontology in technical aspect; 4. Documentation, suggestion about strategy and effection of the building ontology.

3.2 Objective and Scope

In this paper, we circumscribe the scope of ontology building on telecom operator customer. As described in SID (Shared Information Data) [12], the overall information in telecom enterprise could be divided into eight domains. Here we restrict the discussion of data and information in customer domain. According to eTOM (enhanced Telecom Operation Map) [13], telecom customer information could be viewed as three themes: Customer, Subscriber and Account. The definition of Customer and subscriber could be found in eTOM documents. We give definition of Customer Account. See table 1 for the definition and characteristic of those three important concepts which are also our main objectives in ontology building.

Table 1. Customer, Subscriber and Account' Definition and Characteristics

Concept	Definition	Characteristic
Customer	The Customer buys products and services from the Enterprise or receivers free offers or services. A customer may be a person or a business.[13]	Social related data of a person or a company
Subscriber	The Subscriber is responsible for concluding contracts for the services subscribed to and for paying for these services. [13]	Usage related data generated when a customer subscribe or use a product or service
Account	The Account is owing to one or several Customers to dealing with bills for subscribers' product usage.	Finance related data generated when a customer deposits cash in telecom operator in order to pay for usage of products

3.3 Customer Ontology

As discussed before, there are four criteria to follow when we are building the ontology: conceptualization, explicit, formal and share. We adopt these criteria for our telecom customer ontology. Here, we define two kinds of entities in the customer ontology: Substantial Entity and Information Entity.

Definition 1:

Substantial Entity: Substantial Entity is a kind of entity representing a substantial concept which could refer to a corresponding role in the real physical world.

Definition 2:

Information Entity: Information Entity is a kind of entity which represents information concept or a set of data which could not refer to a corresponding role in the real physical world but are generated according to the substantial entity activities.

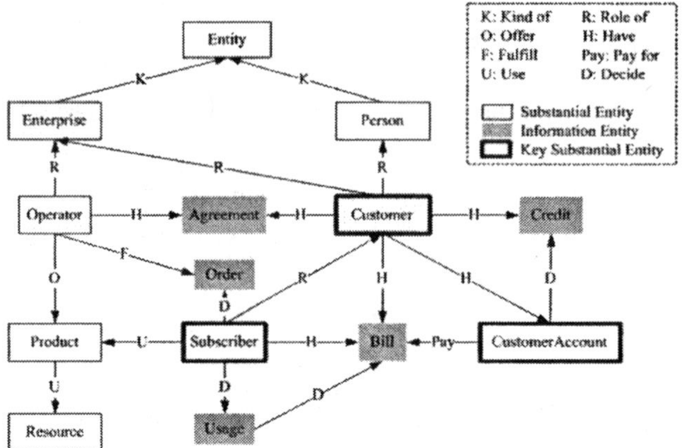

Figure 1. Concept-Relationship Description of Telecom Customer Ontology

For the authors' experiences in telecom industry and the study into information model from many telecom operators, we could abstract the concepts and relationship as Figure 1. We have nine substantial entities, five information entities and eight kinds of relationships in telecom customer ontology. Key substantial entity represents the three theme model which is the centre of the whole model.

Each relationship connects two entities: from domain to range. Relationship *K: Kind of* implies the inherited characteristic from some upper class entity like Subclass of. *R: Role of* also implies Subclass of relationship, but different from *Kind of* that it means an entity performed especially in a particular operation or process. *O: offer* means provide in performance. *H: Have* means hold or maintain as a related information entity. *Pay: Pay for* means make due return to for services rendered. *U: Use* means the act or practice of employing some services. *D: Decide* means the activities of domain substantial entity would determine the data in information entity. *F: Fulfill means* to meet the requirements of a business order.

Besides entity and relationship, the attribute is also an important part of ontology model. Here we list the 2nd level entity and attributes of the entities above. These may not include all the attributes since the limited pages of this article.

3.3 OWL Description of Customer Ontology

As the telecom customer ontology we put forward, we choose OWL as a formal description language in this paper. We use the ontology building and query environment based on web technology—Webtege which is developed by our research team recently. It provides the user graphic webpage to build a new ontology model, convert it into OWL files and query certain relationship or entity in the ontology. Figure 2 are pictures of customer ontology and OWL files built in Webtege.

Table 2. Concept-Attributes Description of Telecom Customer Ontology

Entity	2nd level Entity	Attributes
Customer	Personal customer profile	Name, Gender, Age, Vocation, Contact, Security ID, Affiliation, Customer level
	Enterprise customer profile	Enterprise customer number, Address, Customer manager, Status, Level
Subscriber	Basic services related information	Telephone number, SIM, Package fee used, Terminal unit type, Personal services, Fulfill channel, Status
	Value-added services related information	Service type, Preferential plan
Customer Account		Account ID, Name, Type, Status, Valid period, Balance, Contact person, Telephone, Open time, Calling up of balance
Agreement		Customer Service Level Agreement, Type, ID, Responder, Responsibility person, Customer responsibility person, Start time, Expire time
Order		Order ID, Order association
Credit		Customer credit information, Customer credit history
Bill		Bill format, Bill type, Bill requirement, Bill entry, Bill receipt
Usage		Local call record, Long term call record, Roam call record

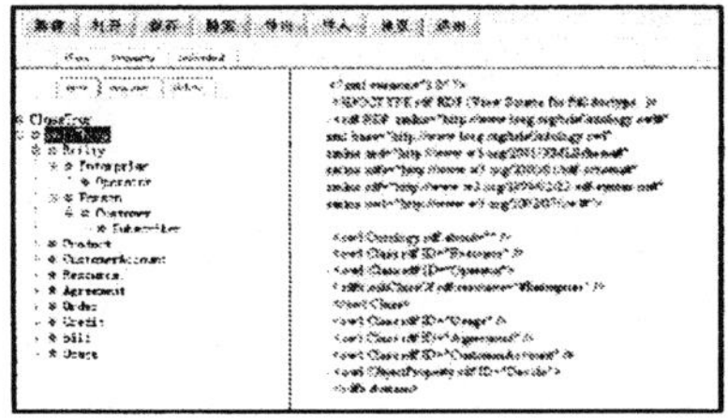

Figure 2. Customer Ontology and OWL Description in Webtege

4. CUSTOMER PROFILE INTEGRATION BASED ON ONTOLOGY

The purpose of customer ontology is to reach the integration of customer profile in telecom enterprise. The customer ontology is a kind of domain ontology and thus reach an agreement on customer profile understand throughout the different enterprise in telecom industry. Here, we propose a new method to achieve customer profile integration based on the customer ontology. We divide this problem into two scenarios: the integration in new systems and the integration in legacy systems.

4.1 Customer Profile Integration in New Systems

Once the customer ontology is approbated among telecom domain, the customer profile in new systems would be built under the direction of customer ontology. We present the integration process in both functional view and data view.

4.1.1 Functional View

In functional view we describe the mainly steps for integration. It may not contain the detail tech but the approach or in another words technique roadmap to achieve the integration purpose. As described in Figure 3, there are three steps to fulfill the customer profile integration in new systems: Generating, Directing and Restricting. In generating step we convert the customer ontology to customer profile standard metadata, i.e. E-R model for customer profile in logic level. The detail principles of generating would be presented in the data view below. Then in directing step we take E-R model into standard table, i.e. data structure in physical level. Finally, restricting step is used to make sure the data in table would follow the restrictions of E-R model and further the ontology constrains. For example, the restriction would be the data type of each row of table; constrains would be the union of, disjoint with and etc. restrictions between entities of customer ontology. Therefore, the problem of semantic conflicts would be settled.

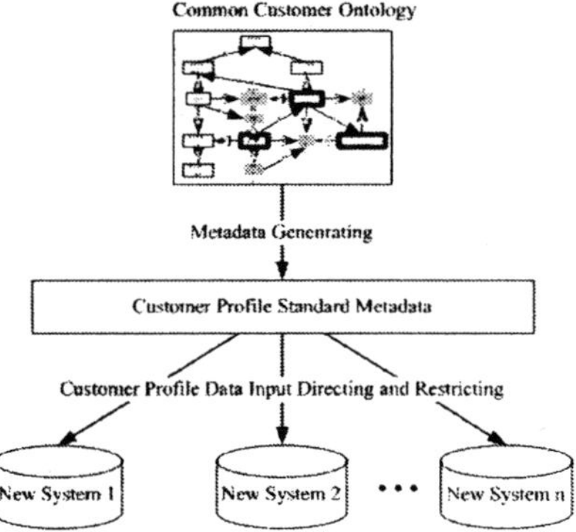

Figure 3. Customer Profile Integration in New systems——Functional View

4.1.2 Data View

The customer ontology built in section 3.3 of this article is a prototype ontology base. While applying it in the real circumstance, we need more detailed information in table or attributes level. Here, in data view we take four entities in ontology for example to show how essential tables are determined according to ontology. We focus on Customer, Customer Account, Credit and Bill ontology. In generating step we makes mapping from ontology to E-R model. Here we define two rules for the mapping:

Generating Rule 1:

Entity generating: One entity in ontology could correspond to at least one entity in E-R model which should express complete information of that entity.

Generating Rule 2:

Relation generating: One relationship in ontology could correspond to one or more relation in E-R model.

As we describe in Figure 4, four entities in ontology correspond six entities in E-R model. The relations are draw as diamonds which is the same as relationship described in ontology. In directing step we detail the E-R model into data table format in physical data level. The rules could be found in database principles of book [14]. In the example here in E-R model three entities--Customer, Personal Customer, Company Customer, could refer to eight tables. The attributes in the table are expanding to the attributes of entities in ontology. In restricting step we take additional vocabulary of ontology such as disjointWith, intersectionOf and etc. for the purpose of expressing more semantic relations and restrictions such as disjoint, intersection, union, complement, enumeration, property restrictions, and cardinality into constrains for table. For example, if we define the maxCardinality of relationship "have" from Customer to Customer Account as 10, and then the relationship table should reflect this cardinatlity. Through these steps, guidance could be given from ontology to table building. Therefore, the customer profile table in new systems could be build according to a unified standard. So we could achieve the integration in this new system scenario.

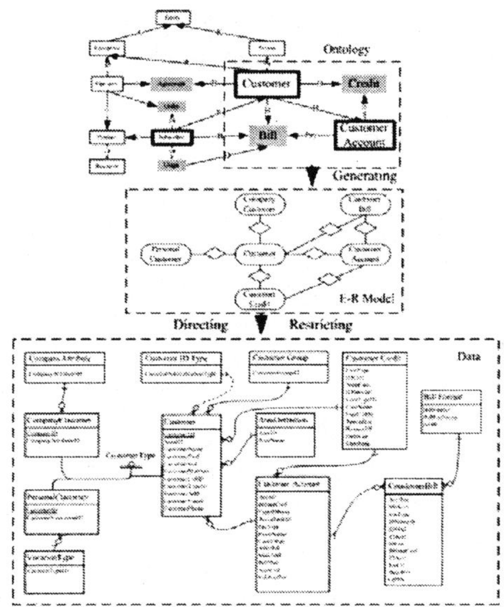

Figure 4. Customer Profile Integration in New systems - Data View

4.2 Customer Profile Integration in Legacy Systems

Besides the new system scenario mentioned above, there exists difficulties in customer profile integration among different legacy systems. Now in telecom business and operating systems, the established customer profile does not conform to certain unified standard. We take advantage of the above customer ontology to solve these problems. We also present the integration process in both functional view and data view.

4.2.1 Functional View

As described in Figure 5, there are four steps to fulfill the customer profile integration in legacy systems: Extracting, Generating, Mapping and Restricting. The Generating and Restricting steps would be the same as described in 4.1.1. Here we describe the Extracting and Mapping steps.

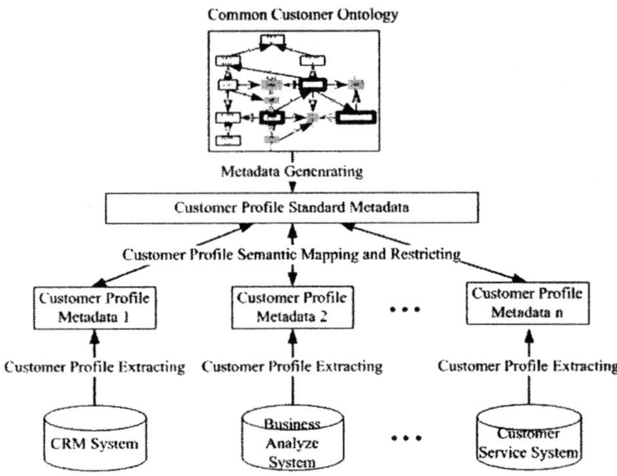

Figure 5. Customer Profile Integration in Legacy Systems—Functional View

In Extracting step we take customer related metadata from legacy systems such as CRM, Business Analyze System, Customer Service System and etc. We can extract metadata according to customer theme or domain from the database's logic model. Or we can use extract tools such as Powermart [15], a data extracting tool from Informatica Inc., to get the metadata. Then in mapping step, we compare the metadata extracted from legacy system to the standard metadata generated from ontology. The detailed mapping explanation refers to 4.1.2. After the comparison of metadata, the legacy metadata might be converted into part of standard metadata, or expand the standard one on the base of which customer data exchange between different systems would be realized and thus solve the problem of semantic inconsistency.

4.2.2 Data View

As in Figure 6 the generating and restricting steps of data view of customer profile integration in legacy systems are the same as described in 4.1.2. The extracting step is the reverse operation of directing step in 4.1.2. Its rules could be found in database principles—abstract physical level data to logic level data. The mapping step might relate to some semantic aspects since the metadata might have the same meaning but use different name. For example, the attributes record Customer universal identification in Customer table of standard metadata might be marked as "CusID", but in legacy system the corresponding attributes might be marked like "C_id".

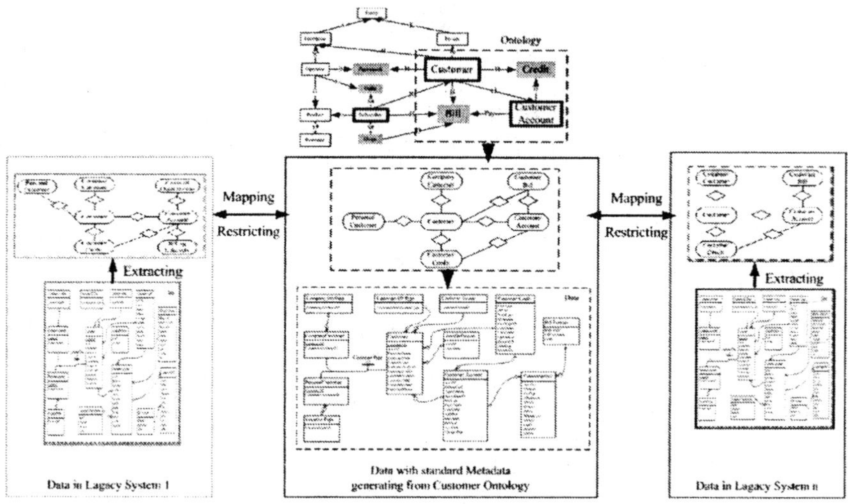

Figure 6 Customer Profile Integration in Legacy Systems—Data View

5. CONCLUSIONS

In conclusion, the building of telecom ontology has significant bearing in solving the semantic inconsistency and semantic conflict problem and thus in realizing the customer profile integration. The customer ontology and integration approach proposed in this paper could give a guideline in constituting customer profile in new systems and achieving the integration over various legacy systems. As a result, according to customer service-centered goal of telecom enterprise, customer profile integration could make the execution of customer relationship management strategy more effectively and thoroughly and the integrated customer information could be (re)used and analyzed for diverse marketing purposes in the coming 3G times of China.

In the future, first we are going to reify, evaluate and improve our telecom customer ontology by using them in the real situation, inviting other telecom industry peers to evaluate our ontology. Second we are going to propose more detailed feasible technique to realize the integration approach and develop a demo to verify.

REFERENCES

1. R.E. Filman, D.J. Korsmeyer, and D.D. Lee, CORBA Extension for Intelligent Software Environments, *Advances in Engineering Software*. Volume 31, Number 8, pp.727-732, (2000).
2. H. Wang, *Research on the Construction of Metadata Models Based on Ontology*. Ph.D Thesis, Shanghai Jiao Tong University (2004).
3. X. Lu, F. Jiang, and L. Hou, Customer Features Extraction Based on Customer Ontology, *Computer Engineering*. Volume 31, Number 5, pp.31-33, (2005).
4. F. Wang, *Research on the Mechanism of Information Retrieval Based on Customer Ontology*. Master Thesis, Shanghai Jiao Tong University (2005).
5. J. Zhu, J. Wu, and F. Jiang, Study on Customer Information Sharing in the Supply Chain of Automobile, *Information Science*. Volume 23, Number 7, pp.1094-1097, (2005).
6. Y. Yan, J. Zhang, and M. Yan, Ontology Modeling for Contract Using OWL to Express Semantic Relations, in *Proceedings of the 10th IEEE International Enterprise Distributed Object Computing Conference (EDOC'06)*, eds. B. Werner (IEEE Computer Society: New York, NY, 2006), pp.409-412.
7. M.N. Huhns and L.M. Stephens, Personal Ontologies, *Internet Computing*. Volume 3, Number 5, pp.85-87, (1999).
8. Z. Deng, S. Tang, and M. Zhang, Overview of Ontology, *Acta Scientiarum Naturalium Universitatis Pekinensis*. Volume 38, Number 5, pp.730-738, (2002).
9. R. Studer, V.R. Benjamins, and D. Fensel, Knowledge Engineering, Principles and Methods, *Data and Knowledge Engineering*. Volume 25, Number 122, pp.161-197, (1998).
10. M.K. Smith, C. Welty, and D.L. McGuinness, *OWL Web Ontology Language Guide*, W3C (2004). http://www.w3.org/TR/2004/REC-owl-guide-20040210/ (Accessed May 20, 2007).
11. M. Uschold, M. King, S. Moralee, and Y. Zorgios, The Enterprise Ontology, *The Knowledge Engineering Review*. Volume 13, Number 1, pp.31-89, (1998).
12. TM Forum, *Shared Information/Data (SID) Model Addendum 2 Customer Business Entity Definitions Release 6.0* (TeleManagement Forum: Morristown, NJ, 2005).
13. TM Forum, *Enhanced Telecom Operations Map (eTOM), The Business Process Framework Release 6.0* (TeleManagement Forum, Morristown, NJ, 2005).
14. A. Silberschatz, H.F. Korth, and S. Sudarshan, *Database System Concepts Fourth Edition* (McGraw-Hill: Columbus, OH, 2001).
15. Anonymous, *Data Integration Software – Informatica Products,* Informatica Inc., (2007). http://www.informatica.com/products/default.htm (Accessed May 20, 2007).

A Research on the Integration Between ERP System and ABCM

Ying He

School of Economics and Management, Beijing University of Post and Telecommunications, Beijing 100876, P.R. China
Heyingcn2001@yahoo.com.cn

Abstract. In recent years, with the widespread application of ERP System, it creates an appropriate environment for implementing ABCM. Many enterprises produce the strong demands on the integration between ERP System and ABCM which is process-focused. As a result, the integration of ERP System and ABCM is regarded as an important strategic choice of fastening the step of information level by many enterprises. This paper mainly makes a detailed discussion on the possibility of the integration between ERP System and ABCM. It describes the benefits of the integration between ERP System and ABCM and the relationship between ERP System and ABCM in the process management. At last, it discusses the existing basic forms for the integration between ERP System and ABCM from the perspective of theory and practice. A successful integration between ERP System and ABCM can minimize the costs of operation and maximize the Enterprise Value, while improving the quality of decision support information available to decision-makers within an organization.

Keywords: *Activity-Based Costing (ABC), Enterprise Resource Planning (ERP)*

1. INTRODUCTION

From the perspective of the historical evolution of ERP, an important progress from MRP、MRP II、to ERP lies in realizing the same step of both finance system and produce system. It means the integration of cash flow and logistics. It is well-known that the traditional procedures and accounting thoughts are run through in ERP system and the traditional cost accounting is designed in ERP system, the information generated from ERP system are distorted. They are hard to provide decision support information for strategic cost analysis such as value chains analysis、cost performance analysis and so on. This discounts the function of ERP system. ABC is the most accurate cost accounting methods as yet. It may accurately measure the profitability on the product and the customer. It also may gain the cost information on the activity process and make aimed controls in order to make the internal supply chains more effective. ABCM can implement process excellent and process management by activity cost and cost drivers. This makes many enterprises produce the strong demands on the integration of ERP System and ABCM which is process-focused. As a result, the integration of ERP System and ABCM is regarded as an

Please use the following format when citing this chapter:

He, Y., 2007, in IFIP International Federation for Information Processing, Volume 254, Research and Practical Issues of Enterprise Information Systems II Volume 1, eds. L. Xu, Tjoa A., Chaudhry S. (Boston: Springer), pp. 781-786.

important strategic choice of fastening the step of information level by many enterprises.

2. THE POSSIBILITY ANALYSIS ON THE INTEGRATION BETWEEN ERP SYSTEM AND ABCM

2.1 Unanimous ERP System and ABCM

Although ABC comes from the veracity motivation of product cost calculation, its meaning has completely exceeded this level, and has gone deeply into the reconstruction on activity chain-value chain of the corporation, even involves the problem about the design of organization structure. Not all activities can create value in the activity chain of the corporation. The aims of ABC are customer chain-oriented, focusing on the activity chain and the value chain, reengineering 'the activity process' fundamentally and thoroughly, emphasizing how to coordinate the relationship between the customers in and out of the corporation, and the relationship among each department. Also, it requires the activities of materials supply, production and distribution coming into 'a activity process' continuously and synchronously, eliminating the activity that can't create value in the activity chain, making the corporation keep a state of continuous improvement, promoting the optimization of the value chain of the corporation , and establishing the competitive edge of the corporation in itself profession.

On the basis of manufacturing resource planning, the ERP System extends the scope of management, advances new construction, and integrates the customers' (include suppliers and distributors) demands out of the corporation with production operations in corporation organically, including the resources of the corporation. Regarding the process of the operation in the corporation as a chain (the activity chain in fact) that joined tightly is the essence of ERP System. ERP system has become popular in recent years because it typically integrates financial system, marketing system, production manufacturing system, quality control system, materials supply management system, human resource management system and so on using a relational database. The use of a relational database permits functional areas to share information without reentering the data or duplicating the data in databases throughout the organization[1]. The goal of ERP System is coordinating the resources in and out of the corporation and establishing the core competitive edge.

The demand of market brings activity and activity consumes resource, so the emergence of activity means the use of resource. In fact, the possible arrangements of activity through ABCM equivalents to the efficient arrangements of resource, thus corporation improves its activity efficiency means to advance the use efficiency of resource.

2.2 Enterprise Transfers from Traditional Cost Management to ABCM

ERP is a kind of system which is composed of many plans, and the operation of the corporation which has implemented ERP system is controlled by all kinds of plans and management. The rationality of plans ensures the routine operation of ERP System. Because the precise data ensures the rationality of plans, the key of bringing ERP System into effect successfully is the accuracy of all kinds of data. However, it is usually anamorphic and tortuous of the production cost information provided by the ERP System basing on traditional cost calculation, and it will have a seriously effect on the manager to make the right estimation on the operation status of the corporation, especially for the corporation which the distribution cost takes a good proportion of production cost (telecommunications corporation etc.). Then, ERP System based on traditional cost management doesn't reveal the cost drivers, this makes the corporation can't recognize the causality of cost and control the cost effectively. At last, ERP System based on traditional cost management prevents the corporation from making the strategic cost analysis on value added, value chain, cost-benefit, etc., for its cost accounting method can't create working procedure and process cost information.

Seeing from the ABCM itself, it emphasizes the consolidation of pre-plan, control and feedback, which embodies fully the cost management method that includes the function of forecasting, decision, planning, controlling and analysis. So this method still stresses the function of the pre-estimation of standard cost, the analysis of cost difference after the real cost, and the responsibility cost management focusing on cost center. Therefore, it's necessary to integrate ERP System with ABCM for many corporations which pay more attention to the cost controlling.

2.3 The Solid Technology Foundation for Successfully Putting ABCM in Practice

The basic idea of ABCM sprouts in the 1930s', but it didn't come into peoples' notices until 1980s'. To the technology of the cost calculation, the difference between traditional costing and ABC is to use many distribution standards of the overhead expenses. Obviously, the complicated calculation of the production expenses would cause the cost exceeding the benefit without the rapid development and application of the ERP System, even in a environment that has possessed the technological base、the society base and the idea base. Thus, the activity costing will be difficult in putting into practice, but just an idea. The development and application of ERP System improves the ability of data collecting and arrangement of the corporation, and it establishes the technique base for the implementation of ABCM.

In a word, the integration between ERP System and ABCM has become the important choice for corporation to accelerate the information. On the basis of implementing ERP system, many corporations practice and apply ABCM, put their cost management procedure on the same data source, use a standard reporting system, realize the identical structure, all these applications enhance the operability of system. And it makes to control the cost and the benefit throughout all functional departments, which really improves the ability to control cost in the overall process of the corporation.

3. THE BENEFITS OF INTEGRATION BETWEEN ERP SYSTEM AND ABCM AND THE RELATIONSHIP BETWEEN ERP SYSTEM AND ABCM IN THE PROCESS MANAGEMENT

Baxendale[1-2] stated that ERP system can provides reliable activity cost-driver information by integrating production planning, materials management, and cost and management accounting in order to increase the accuracy of the product-cost information and to develop activity-based budgets(ABB). Brodeur[3] thought that integrating ERP System and ABCM is to capitalize on the opportunity to improve the ongoing maintenance of the ABC models, increase the likelihood that ABC results will be utilized by decision-makers, and improve the design、implementation and early use of ABC and ERP system. Altogether, the integration between ERP System and ABCM will enable the view of value chain management and process management goes through into the operation level, and it is a major breakthrough in the management ideas. The integration is favorable to obtain the source, improve the efficiency of value chain management, and achieves the ultimate objective, which is maximizing the Enterprise Value. Figure 1 shows the position and relationship between ERP System and ABCM in the process management.

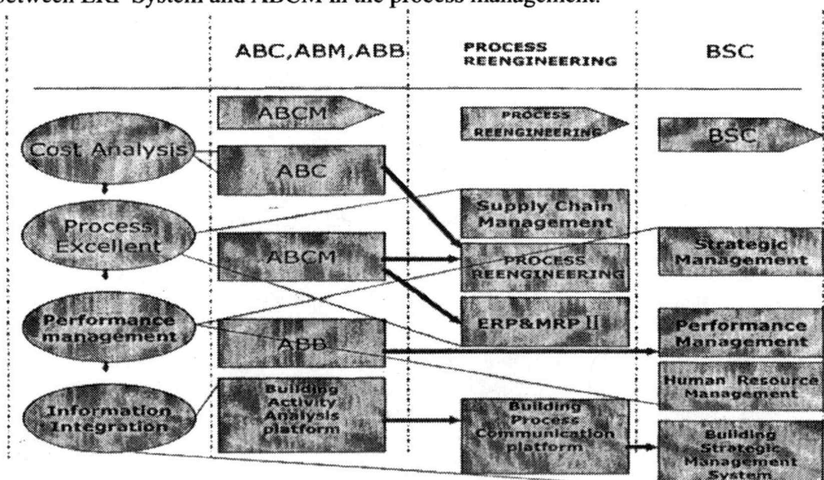

Figure 1. The Position and Relationship between ERP and ABCM in the Process Management

4. THE EXISTING BASIC FORMS FOR THE INTEGRATION BETWEEN ERP SYSTEM AND ABCM

Theorists have different ideas on the existing basic forms for the integration between ERP System and ABCM. Some people states that ERP System and ABCM are two kinds of information systems, which are independent but related to each other. For example, in the discussion about ERP manufacturers and ABCM integration, Russell Shaw [4] considered that ERP System and ABCM are two stand-alone information systems, but maintains a relation of partnership. However, Brodeur [2] thought that ERP system could be used effectively by ABCM and ABCM could rapidly access a lot of non-financial data by ERP system, so the integration of them could promote their implementation(See Figure 2). Other people said that ABCM would be brought into each function-module completely after integrated. In other words, there were no independent sub-module to represent ABCM or was established by ABCM, therefore, the essence of the integration for ABCM is to modify the function-module of ERP by using the concepts and methods of ABCM. Yaping Ning [5] considered that through integration, the technology and management ideas of ABC and ABM (part of ABCM) are integrated to the ERP, which makes a few modules of ABCM separate away from the original ERP. So to say, a few modules are created for ABCM, such as the sub-modules of activity-based accounting and activity efficiency analysis are added to the functional module of management accounting.

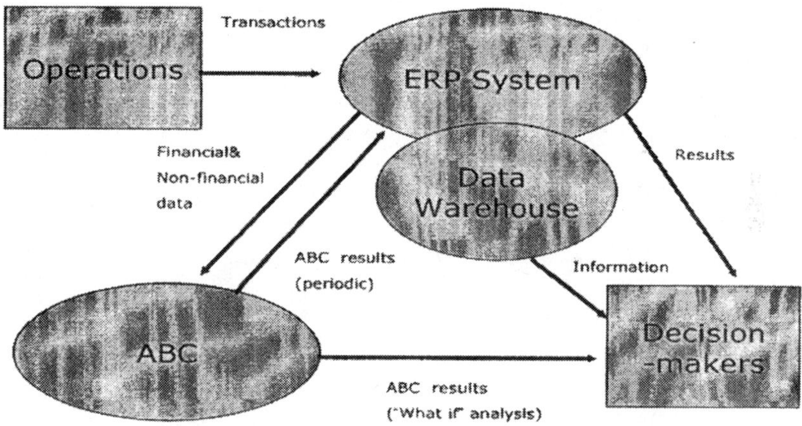

Figure 2. The Relationship between ERP System and ABC

In practice, a kind of special ABCM software which keeps a partnership between ERP system and ABCM, has become a key focus of many software developers. Many business management software suppliers all actively invest in this realm. And certainly there are also some companies, which add the function-modules of ABCM in the management systems of themselves(such as ABCM, SCM etc.) in order to meet the needs of the customers in and out of the corporation. For example, SAS、ALG Software and QPR provide specialized ABCM software. In domestic, there are also some companies which are pushing forward the cost management system based on ABCM, and start the tentative application and implementation in several professions.

In a word, as the ERP and the ABCM are both under developing in the theory and practice, so the existing basic forms for the integration between ERP System and ABCM will also be in the process of groping and optimizing.

5. CONCLUSIONS

Allocating the resource efficiently and manufacturing for making the needs of customers are the core concepts which ERP System and ABCM continuously pursue. The integration between ERP System and ABCM is to cancel the non-value added process and improve the value added process put to the best use in order to create more added values in the process management.

REFERENCES

1. S. Baxendale and F. Jama, What ERP can offer ABC, *Strategic Finance*. Volume 8, Number 1, pp.54-57, (2003).
2. S. Baxendale and P. Jokinen, Interactions between ERP and ABCM systems, *Journal of Cost Management*. Volume 3, Number 1, pp.40-46, (2000).
3. E. Brodeur, Integrating ABC and ERP systems, *Focus Magazine*. Volume 1, Number 1, pp.1-10, (2003).
4. R. Shaw, ABC and ERP: Partners at last?, *Management Accounting*. Volume 5, Number 1, pp.56-58, (1998).
5. Y. Ning, A study and analysis of the integration of ERP with ABCM, *Financial and Accounting Communication*. Volume 1, Number 1, pp.8-10, (2006).
6. Y. Hu, A design on ERP and ABC, *Financial and Accounting Monthly*. Volume 2, Number 1, pp.20-21, (2002).

An Integrated Information Platform for Intelligent Transportation Systems Based on Ontology

Jun Zhai, Zhou Zhou, Zhiman Shi and Lixin Shen

School of Economics and Management, Dalian Maritime University, Dalian 116026, P.R. China zhaijun_dlmu@yahoo.com.cn

Abstract. In semantic web environment, the integration of transportation information systems develops toward semantic integration. Ontology facilitates the integration of heterogeneous data sources by resolving semantic heterogeneity among them. In this paper, we propose the system architecture of integrated information platform for intelligent transportation systems (ITS) based on ontology, including three main layers: distributed heterogeneous data source layer, information integration layer, and application system layer. Its core is the information integration layer including the ontology server and the integrated database. Key technique applied in the ontology server is studies. Firstly, the domain ontology model for transport system is presented. Then we discuss the approach to semantic integration of XML documents based on ontology. At the end we conclude that ontology is a good tool to integrate traffic information among various heterogeneous traffic management systems on semantic level.

Keywords: *Application integration, Data integration, Ontology, Enterprise information architecture, Enterprise information integration (EII), Enterprise information systems (EIS), Semantic integration, Intelligent transportation systems (ITS)*

1. INTRODUCTION

Intelligent Transportation System (ITS), a developing conformation of transportation system in the information times, has been integrating a variety of advanced technologies, especially information technology [1].

Now many kinds of urban traffic management systems are established on their own data storage style (such as database or data files), which operate the data source directly, lacking data share and exchange. It is vital to solve that how to share and exchange the data among various transportation management systems, and how to utilize the data sufficiently and improve the level of urban traffic management. It is vital to solve the problems that how to share and exchange the data among various transportation management systems and how to utilize the data sufficiently to improve the level of urban traffic management. It is necessary to establish an Integrated

Please use the following format when citing this chapter:

Zhai, J., Zhou, Z., Shi, Z., Shen, L., 2007, in IFIP International Federation for Information Processing, Volume 254, Research and Practical Issues of Enterprise Information Systems II Volume 1, eds. L. Xu, Tjoa A., Chaudhry S. (Boston: Springer), pp. 787-796.

Information Platform (IIP) for ITS, which processes various data from different traffic data sources located in various traffic management systems. It can serve as a bridge of data share and exchange among different application systems and data sources, which provides traffic management decision-making support, information service function etc [2-4].

We found some projects similar to the integrated information platform in some countries. In 2001, the MOST (Ministry of Science and technology) of China appointed ten cities as ITS demonstration cities, including Beijing, Shanghai, Guangzhou, Shenzhen etc. The integrated information platform is an important part in the ITS planning of each city. Meanwhile many scholars and some companies have begun the research and development of the integrated information platform and achieved some valuable results. In other countries, such as England, Singapore, America, etc, there are also some similar research and implement project as IIP for ITS [5].

IIP for ITS mainly solves the heterogeneity among diverse information sources. Amit Sheth [6] has classified heterogeneity into four categories: system, syntax, structure and semantic. The system heterogeneity includes hardware and operating systems; the syntax heterogeneity includes different languages and data representations; the structure heterogeneity includes different data models; and semantic heterogeneity includes the semantics of user's information request and those of information sources. Many of the heterogeneity will overcome if XML/DTD is going to be adopted for data publishing, which is used in present research works. However the semantic heterogeneity remains [7].

In the WWW environment, the integration of current information systems turns to semantic level due to the more diversity and heterogeneity of data.

The semantics of diverse information sources are captured by their ontologies, i.e., the terms and relationships among them. Ontologies are emerging as an important tool for constructing sharable and reusable knowledge repositories and supporting their interaction [8-10].

In this paper, we present an IIP system architecture based on ontology to achieve the semantic integration for ITS. The remainder of the paper is structured as follows. In section 2 the IIP system architecture is described. In section 3 the domain ontology model for transportation system is introduced. In sections 4 we discuss the approach to semantic integration of XML documents based on ontology. Finally, in section 5 we present some conclusions and indicate directions for future work.

2. IIP SYSTEM ARCHITECTURE BASED ON ONTOLOGY

IIP forms an abstract homogeneous environment for the application system through integrating the distributed heterogeneous subsystems and providing transparent service based on semantic for users. The system architecture of IIP is shown as Figure 1, including three layers: distributed heterogeneous data source layer, information integration layer, and application system layer.

2.1 Distributed Heterogeneous Data Source Layer

The distributed heterogeneous data source layer is mainly consisted of various traffic management systems, such as traffic signal control system, emergency management system, public transport management system, video monitoring system, and variable message sign system etc, which are the main data sources of IIP. The compatible data sources of IIP include relational database, real-time database, web data, XML documents etc. As the data sources of IIP, various traffic management systems can share and exchange data through integrated transportation information platform on semantic level. The main types of traffic data are shown in Table 1.

Table 1. The Main Kinds of Traffic Data

Type	Content
Space geographical data	The city transportation concerned spatial data and spatial attribute data, which include the elements of city-road-net such as road, crossing and park.
Traffic infrastructure data	Hardware infrastructure data exclude space geographical data, which include communicate, examination and control infrastructure in transportation.
Traffic management operation data	The real-time data of traffic flow, traffic signal control, electric polite, equipment fault etc.
Historical data	The historical data of traffic flow, accident and peccancy.
Other concerned data	The transportation concerned data (such as transfer info, weather report and schedules) and other traffic service concerned yellow page information (such as hotel, train, service station etc).

2.2 Information Integration Layer

The information integration layer is the key of integrated information platform, which mainly includes two parts: ontology server and integrated database. The main functions of ontology server are as follows:

1. To achieve the semantic upgrade of data sources. The server uses the software reverse engineering approach to extract an initial ontology from given data sources and their application programs. Ontology designers will refine this initial ontology. Thus every data source generates own local ontology. Ontology reasoning then is used to check ontology consistency and to merge ontologies to obtain the global ontology, which provides the user access to the data with a uniform query interface to facilitate the formulation of a query on all the data sources. The server includes the mapping database, which records the mapping information between ontologies, and ontology and data sources. These mappings are primitive concept mappings.

2. To achieve the semantic annotation to the integrated database. A set of XML schema or DTDs derived from the global ontology. The global ontology defines the semantics of the terms used to model the data. The set of XML schema or DTDs is used to mark up the data in the integrated database. When an application or agent requires data from the information platform, it will construct a set of queries over the encoded data source. If the application or agent does not understand the tags of the XML schema or DTDs associated with the data, it will query the ontology server. The ontology server is capable of mapping terms, returning relationships between terms and attributes associated with the terms.
3. To manage the ontology. Ontology editor and browser are tools that allow users to visually manipulate ontologies. The editor and browser display ontology in a tree-like structure with nodes denoting concepts. The details of the concepts can be displayed by highlighting nodes. In the editor mode, definitions can be modified, nodes can be added or removed. Ontology relationships can also be displayed.

In section 3 and section 4 we discuss the ontology model and integration approach, which are the key technique applied in the ontology server.

2.3 Application System Layer

Achieving the semantic integration, the IIP can deeply, synthetically utilize various traffic data and information. Based on a large amount of traffic data stored in IIP integrated database, with the Data Fusion, Data Mining technology, some application systems may be developed, such as information service system, decision-making support system etc, to provide information service for traffic managers, travelers and other people. Through these ways, traffic data and information can be used more efficiently, and the intelligent level of urban traffic management can be improved as well.

3. THE DOMAIN ONTOLOGY MODEL FOR ITS

Gruber [11] defines ontology as an explicit specification of a conceptualization, i.e. an abstract and simplified representation of real-world entities. An ontology can be viewed as a model of a domain that defines the concepts existing in that domain, their properties and the relationships between them and is typically represented as a knowledge base.

An ontology (O) organizes domain knowledge in terms of concepts (C), properties (P) and relations (R) and can be formally defined as follows.

Definition (Ontology) – An Ontology O is a triplet of the form $O = (C, P, R)$, where:

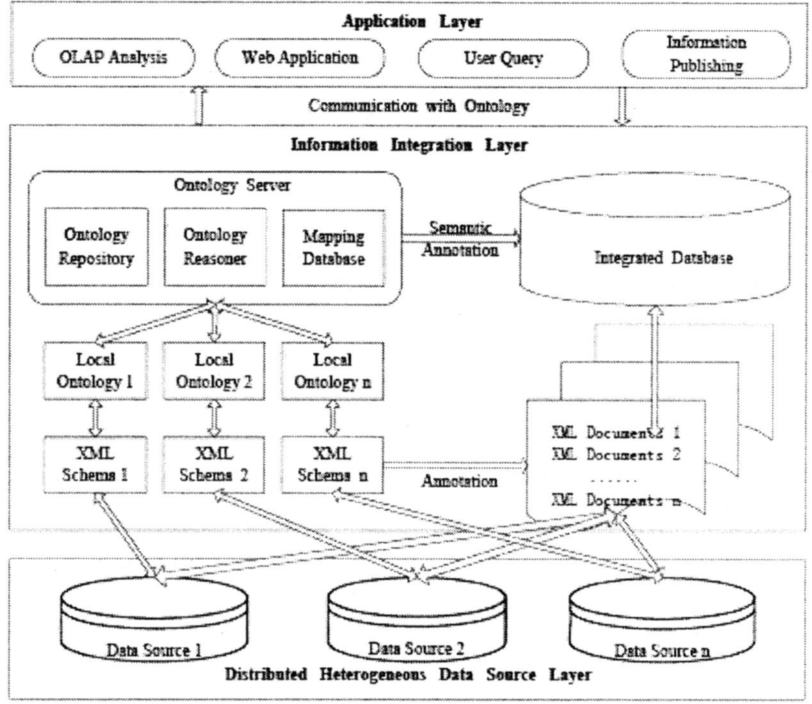

Figure 1. IIP System Architecture Based on Ontology for ITS

1. C is a set of concepts defined for the domain. A concept is often defined as a class in an ontology.
2. P is a set of concept properties. A property $p \in P$ is defined as an instance of a ternary relation of the form $p(c, v, f)$, where $c \in C$ is an ontology concept, v is a property value associated with c and f defines restriction facets on v. Some of the restriction facets are – type (f_t,) cardinality (f_c), and range (f_r). The type facet f_t may be any one from the standard data types supported by ontology editors i.e., $f_t \in$ {Boolean, integer, float, string, symbol, instance, class …}. The cardinality facet f_c defines the upper and lower limits on the number of values for the property. The range facet f_r specifies a range of values that can be assigned to the property.
3. $R = \{r \mid r \subseteq C \times C \times R_t\}$ is a set of binary semantic relations defined between concepts in O. R_t = {one-to-one, one-to-many, many-to-many} is the set of relation type.

A set of basic relations is defined as $R_b = \{\approx, \uparrow, \nabla\}$ which have the following interpretations:

1. For any two ontological concepts $c_i, c_j \in C$, $\approx$ denotes the equivalence relation. $c_i \approx c_j \Rightarrow c_i$ is equivalent to c_j. The synonym relation of natural language is

modeled in an ontology using the equivalence relation. If two concepts c_i and c_j are declared equivalent in an ontology then instances of concept c_i can also be inferred as instances of c_j and vice-versa.

2. $\uparrow$ denotes the generalization relation. $c_i \uparrow c_j \Rightarrow c_i$ is a generalization of c_j. When an ontology specifies that c_i is a generalization of c_j, then c_j inherits all property descriptors associated with c_i, and these need not be repeated for c_j while specifying the ontology.
3. $c_i \nabla c_j \Rightarrow c_i$ has part c_j. In an ontology, a concept which is defined as aggregation of other concepts is expressed using the relation ∇.

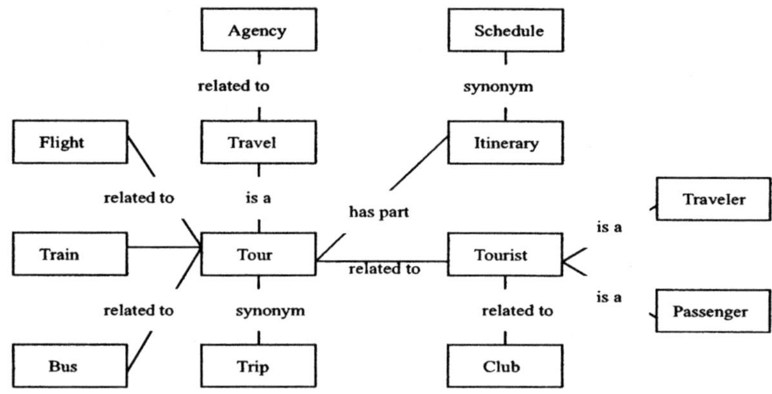

Figure 2. Partial Tourist Information Services Domain Ontology

The individual information services are the vital part of the traveler information services, which assemble correlative information from multi-data-sources (weather bureau, news, agency etc.) for satisfying the personal needs of travelers. The typical application is the travel information afforded for the tourist, in which the partial travel domain ontology is shown in Figure 2. The main concepts include tourist, agency, trip, itinerary etc. The concepts can be related in various ways. The four most commonly used are synonym (equivalent), is-a (generalization), whole-part (has part) and related-to where the semantics of the first three are described above. "Related-to" is used for generic associations between concepts.

In RDFS the concepts of domain ontology are represented as follows:

```
<rdfs:Class rdf:ID="Agency"></rdfs:Class>
<rdfs:Class  rdf:ID="Travel product"></rdfs:Class>
<rdfs:Class  rdf:ID="Tour">
    <rdfs:SubClassOf  rdf:resource="#Travel product"/>
</rdfs:Class>
```

The relations are represented as follows:

```
<rdf:Property  rdf:ID="has part">
 <rdfs:domain  rdf:resource="#Tour">
<rdfs:range  rdf:resource="# Itinerary">
```

```
</rdf:Property>
<rdf:Property rdf:ID=" synonym">
 <rdfs:domain rdf:resource="#Tour">
<rdfs:range rdf:resource="# Trip">
</rdf:Property>
```

The property is represented as follows:

```
<rdf:Property rdf:ID="Agency Name">
 <rdfs:domain rdf:resource="#Agency">
 <rdfs:range rdf:resource="#String">
</rdf:Property>
```

The instance of a concept is represented in RDF as follows:

```
<rdf:Description rdf:ID="Dalian Agency">
    <rdf:type rdf:resource="#Agency"/>
 <Agency Name>Dalian Agency</Agency Name>
</rdf:Description>
```

4. THE APPROACH TO SEMANTIC INTEGRATION OF XML DOCUMENTS BASED ON ONTOLOGY

XML is becoming the standard for data interchange on the web and a web-friendly technology for IIP information exchange [4]. However, XML and its schema languages do not express semantics but rather structure, such as nesting information [7]. RDF (Resource Description Framework) and RDFS (RDF Schema) is a data model and support mechanism for representing meta-data of schemas. XML and RDF are the current standards for establishing semantic interoperability on the Web. RDF better facilitates interoperation because it provides a data model that can be extended to address ontology representation techniques [12].

In this section, we discuss the integration approach of XML sources into the global ontology. The ontology integration process contains two steps: schema transformation and ontology merging. In the first step, we use RDFS to model each XML source as a local RDF ontology to achieve a uniform representation basis for the ontology-merging step. The key operation is the preservation of the nesting structure of the XML documents. In the second step, we merge all the local RDF schemas to generate the global ontology. In this process, additional domain-related knowledge (e.g., inheritance) may be introduced. During the merging process, a mapping table is produced to contain the mapping information between the global RDF ontology and local RDF ontologies.

4.1 Schema Transformations

Taking into account XML elements, attributes and their relationships, the transformation from XML to RDF can further include element-level transformation and structure level transformation.

The element-level transformation defines the basic classes and properties of the local RDF ontology according to the transformation correspondences shown in Table 2. No new RDF metadata needs to be defined here because rdfs: Class and rdfs: Property is enough for the specifications of classes and properties.

The structure-level transformation encodes the hierarchical structures of the XML schema into the local RDF ontology. The encoding involves two relationships: element-attribute relationship and element-subelement relationship. Following the element-level transformation, it is natural to encode the element-attribute relationship as a class-to-literal relationship, and the element-subelement relationship as a class-to-class relationship in RDFS. We define a new RDFS predicate rdfx: contain to represent class-to-class relationships. Specifically, we add a new property with its domain being one class (converted from the parent element), its range being the other class (converted from the subelement), and its name being rdfx: contain.

Table 2. Element-level Transformation

XML Schema concepts	RDF Schema concepts
Attribute	Property
Simple-type element	Property
Complex-type element	Class

4.2 Ontologies Merging

The process of ontology merging takes multiple local ontologies (encoded in RDFS) as the input and returns a merged ontology as the output. Ontology merging and ontology alignment are widely pursued research topics. In this paper we do not intend to introduce a new technique for ontology merging. Instead, we utilize existing techniques to generate the integrated ontology from the local ontologies. In particular, we use the approach that provides the following functionalities [13]:

1. Merging of classes where multiple conceptually equivalent classes are combined into one class.
2. Merging of properties where multiple conceptually equivalent properties of a class are combined into one property.
3. Merging relationships between classes where conceptually equivalent relationships from one class c_1 to another class c_2 are combined into one relationship (i.e., an RDF property taking c_1 as its domain and c_2 as its range).
4. Copying a class and/or its properties if the same or equivalent class/property does not exist in the target ontology.
5. Generalizing related classes into a more general superclass. The superclass can be obtained by searching an existing knowledge domain or reasoning over a thesaurus.

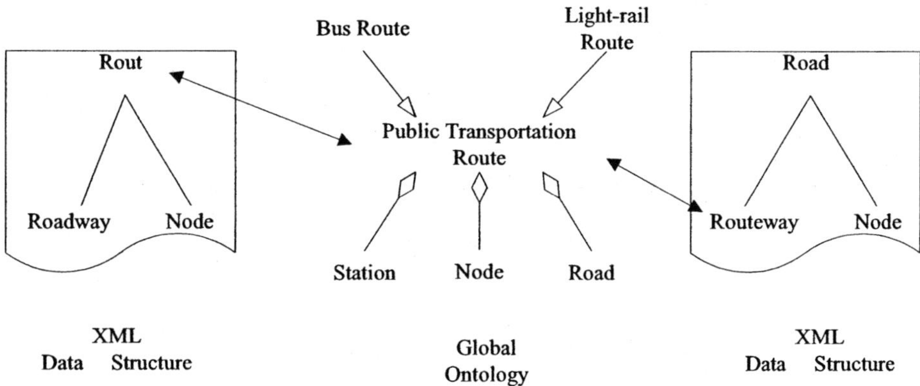

Figure 3. Global Ontology and XML Documents

Figure 3 gives an example, in which the elements "Rout" and "Routway" of two XML data structures are semantically integrated to the "Public Transportation Route" concept of the global ontology.

5. CONCLUSIONS

Ontology-based integrated information platform is motivated by the following properties:

1. Precise description of data and information. IIP uses standardized terms of the ontology and its inherent semantics to provide a formal description of its data. Queries based on the uniform semantics are less prone to misinterpretation of local information semantics.
2. Dynamic support for multiple contexts or interpretation of data. Traditional schema-based database integration of systems requires costly updates to accommodate new semantics. Using the terms of ontology as meta-constructs or meta-attributes allows proper dynamic interpretation of the different contexts.

Our further researches lay on the automatic integration among different domain ontology, especially among the transportation ontology and other domain ontology such as the GIS ontology and urban ontology.

ACKNOWLEDGEMENTS

The authors would like to thank peer reviewers for commenting this article. This work is supported by the National Natural Science Foundation of China (Grant NO.70540005).

REFERENCES

1. L. Figueiredo, I. Jesus, J.A.T. Machado, J.R. Ferreira, and J.L.M.D. Carvalho, Towards the Development of Intelligent Transportation Systems, in *Proc. of 2001 IEEE Intelligent Transportation Systems Conference* (USA, 2001), pp.1206-1211.
2. W. Liu, D. Sun, W. Song, and L. Fu, A Virtual Common Information Platform For Intelligent Transportation Systems, in *Proc. of the 2004 IEEE Intelligent Transportation Systems Conference* (Washington, D.C., USA, October 36), pp.136-141, (2004).
3. Q. Shi and W. Zheng, Architecture Analysis of Common Information Platform for Intelligent Transportation Systems (ITS) and Its Construction Means, *Journal of Transportation Engineering and Information.* Volume 1, Number 1, pp.41-47, (2003).
4. R. Li, H. Lu , Z. Qian, and Q. Shi, Research of the Integrated Transportation Information Platform Based on XML, in *Proc. of the 8th International IEEE Conference on Intelligent Transportation Systems* (Vienna, Austria, 2005), pp.214-219.
5. R. Qiu, ITS development of Singapore, *ITS communication.* Volume 5, Number 1, pp.5-11, (2003).
6. A.P. Sheth, Changing Focus on Interoperability in Information Systems: from System, Syntax, Structure to Semantics, *Interoperation Geography Information Systems* (Academic Publishers, 1998), pp.5-30.
7. I.F. Cruz, H. Xiao, and F. Hsu, An Ontology-based Framework for XML Semantic Integration, in *Proc. of the International Database Engineering and Applications Symposium (IDEAS'04)* (2004), pp.50-58.
8. Z. Cui and P. O'Brien, Domain Ontology Management Environment, in *Proc. of the 33rd Hawaii International Conference on System Sciences* (2000), pp.1-9.
9. Y. Li, J. Zhai, and Y. Chen, Using Ontology to Achieve the Semantic Integration of the Intelligent Transport System, in *Proc. of 2005 International Conference on Management Science & Engineering (12th) (Volume III)* (2005), pp.2528-2532.
10. J.J. Samper, V.R. Tomás, J.J. Martinez, and L.V.D. Berg, An Ontological Infrastructure for Traveller Information Systems, in *Proc. of the 2006 IEEE Intelligent Transportation Systems Conference* (Toronto, Canada, 2006), pp.1197-1202.
11. T.R. Gruber, A Translation Approach to Portable Ontology Specification, *Knowledge acquisition.* Volume 5, Number 2, pp.199-220, (1993).
12. M. Klein, Interpreting XML Documents via an RDF Schema Ontology, in *Proc. of the 13th International Workshop on Database and Expert Systems Applications (DEXA'02)* (2002), pp.1-5.
13. F. Noy and M.A. Musen, PROMPT: Algorithm and Tool for Automated Ontology Merging and Alignment, in *Proc. of the Seventeenth National Conference on Artificial Intelligence and Twelfth Conference on Innovative Applications of Artificial Intelligence, AAAI/IAAI* (2000), pp.450-455.

A Research on Synergic and Spiral-Propulsion Mechanism of Enterprise Information Systems Growth

Xinhua Bi and Cuiling Yu

School of Management, Jilin University, Changchun 130022, P.R. China
fasthome@yeah.net yucuiling0908@sina.com

Abstract. The mechanism of information system (IS) growth is an important part of IS growth theory and has attracted much attention of scholars and entrepreneurs. As validated by many studies, the process of IS growth is influenced by various factors within the enterprise and from external environment. The external factors are mainly governmental propulsion, competitive pressure, linkage demand of cooperative enterprises and IT suppliers' propulsion. The internal factors are top management support, middle management support, IT department propulsion and other organizational personnel's cooperation and participation. The synergic effect of internal and external factors promotes the development of IS construction and the growth of enterprise information systems. This paper pays more attention to the microcosmic mechanism of IS growth and proposes that IT absorption is a direct impetus to IS growth. It analyzes synergic effect of the subjects and elements of IT absorption. Furthermore, a mathematic model is used to describe the spiral-propulsion mode of IS growth. Viewed from a holistic perspective, IS growth presents itself as a dynamic and spiral process.

Keywords: *Enterprise information systems (EIS), Information systems growth (IS growth), Synergic and spiral-propulsion mechanism, Information technology absorption (IT absorption)*

1. INTRODUCTION

With increasing drastic commercial competition, multiplex customer demand and expedite change speed, it has become a hot topic in information system (IS) research field that how organizations utilize information technology (IT) to improve its competence continuously and achieve competitive advantages [1-2]. Therefore, IS growth theory has attracted much attention of scholars and entrepreneurs. IS growth is characterized as a continuously rising process in which IS application evolves from lower stage to higher, from simplicity to complexity, from local implication to systematic integration [3]. Many studies have demonstrated that IS growth is influenced by various factors within the organization and from external environment. The complexity of growth process requires mutual coordination and cooperation of different power to reach maximum synergy and promote enterprise information systems to evolve to higher stages. The whole process presents itself as a spiral mode.

Please use the following format when citing this chapter:

Bi, X., Yu, C., 2007, in IFIP International Federation for Information Processing, Volume 254, Research and Practical Issues of Enterprise Information Systems II Volume 1, eds. L. Xu, Tjoa A., Chaudhry S. (Boston: Springer), pp. 797-806.

Viewed from microcosmic level, enterprise information systems stem from a series of IS construction engineering which enable it to gain continual growth through absorbing new technologies. Within the enterprise, nonlinear interactions of the subjects and various elements related to information systems engender state fluctuation which produces order parameters promoting IS construction. In fact, the introduction of an IS project is a great fluctuation caused by magnification of the nonlinear interactions. Using the method of theory analysis together with mathematic model, this paper tries to make a further analysis on the synergic and spiral-propulsion mechanism of IS growth.

2. THE SYNERGIC AND SPIRAL-PROPULSION MECHANISM OF IS GROWTH

2.1 A Synergic and Spiral-Propulsion Mechanism Model of IS Growth

Many studies have demonstrated that IS growth is influenced by factors both from internal and external environment of an enterprise. Since there are interactions of lots of subsystems during the synergy process, the synergic equation would be very complex because of the impact of too many variables. However, servo principle provides us with a practical and operable methodology which suggests that it needn't to concern all variables and factors but to grasp the most primary and influential variables and neglect minor and trivial variables, thus to approach order state step by step [4]. Based on this idea, we divide these key factors into two classes according to the subjects of this process. The first is external factors, including governmental propulsion, competitive pressure, linkage demand of cooperative enterprises and IT suppliers' support. The second is internal factors, including top management support, middle management support, IT department propulsion and other organizational personnel's participation and cooperation.

The action mechanism of these factors on IS construction is shown as Figure 1. External power refers to the impact of external factors on IS construction. Internal power refers to the impact of internal factors. According to synergic principle, with the increasing strengthening of external parameters, viz. propulsion of governmental policy, informationization act of competitors, linkage demand of supply chain and propulsion of IT supplier, enterprise state of production and operation would be effected, which would changes the main conflicts of the enterprise, causing the organizational system to become unstable. Enterprise must seek a new ordered structure to adapt external environment. While IT solution helps to satisfy this change demand, organizational leader would be motivated to adopt the technology. The synergic effect of top management, middle management, IT department and other organizational personnel produces internal propulsion for information systems. Furthermore, under the guidance of attractors, it evolves into a cohesion which makes various power synergize in the direction of IS construction and promote IS growth.

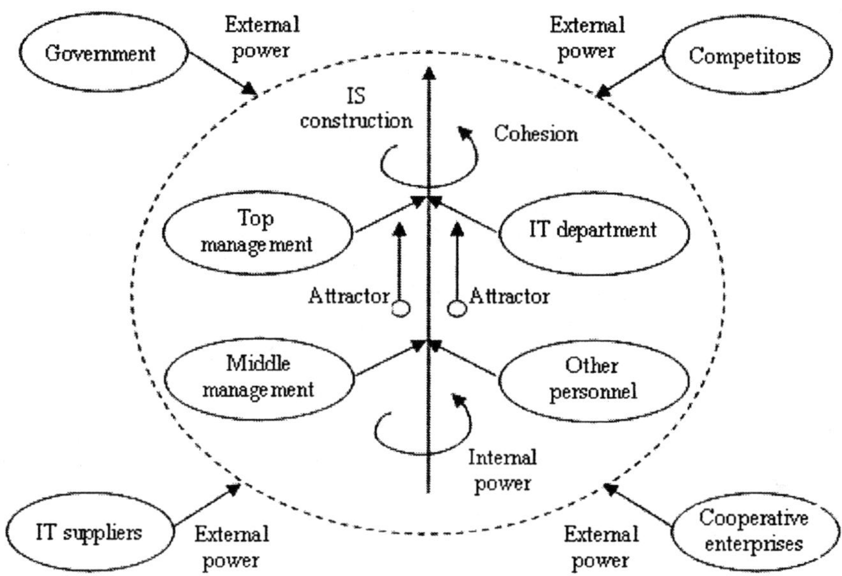

Figure 1. A Synergic and Spiral-Propulsion Mechanism Model of IS Growth

This paper emphasizes on the mechanism of IS growth at microcosmic level. For an enterprise, IS growth stems from a series of IS construction engineering, which conforms to a fundamental law that it is a process beginning from system analysis to system design, then system implementation, till system application. Viewed from a dynamic behavioral perspective, it is a process in which the organization identifies, adopts, adapts, accepts and infuses related IT solution. It is called IT absorption which has been addressed as a special topic by the authors [5]. Based on the stage model of IT implementation proposed by Kwon and Cooper [6-7], a process model of IT absorption is developed which describes IT absorption as a dynamic closed loop composed of five stages, viz. identification, adoption, adaptation, acceptance and infusion, and it integrates a role of "knowledge base" into these five stages.

The process of IT absorption begins from identifying enterprise demand and corresponding IT solutions. Then the enterprise evaluates and compares these solutions to make an adoption decision of whether to make an investment, and puts the one adopted into practice. The most important thing in the next stage is to achieve well mutual adaptation between the organization and information technology. Gradually, organizational personnel accept it through practice and learning. Then IT application spreads and diffuses continuously until the usage of it becomes a conventional activity in the organization. Consequently, information technology infuses into the organization. These five stages proceed and circulate unceasingly, forming a closed loop. The "knowledge base" located in the middle of the model interacts with the five stages and external environment, enabling organizational comprehension of related IT knowledge and experience to accumulate and increase ceaselessly. Viewed from an initiative process perspective, the essential of IS growth is a spiral process propelled by these five stages. Therefore, it can be regarded that the process of IT absorption reflects the microcosmic mechanism of IS growth. Hereby, a microcosmic mechanism model of IS growth is developed as shown in Figure 2.

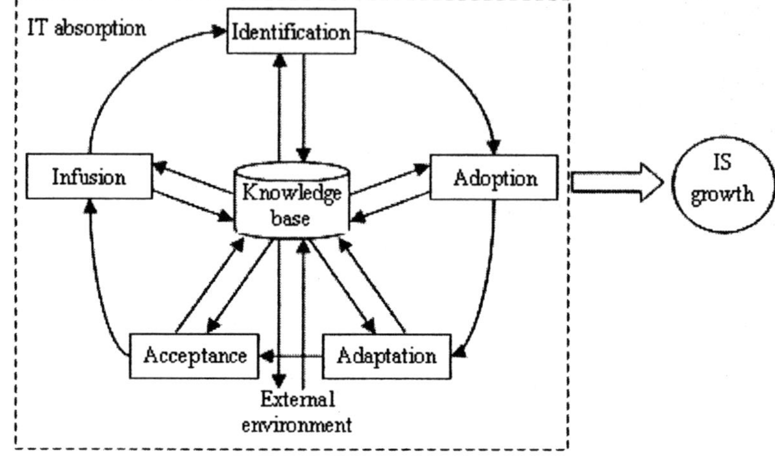

Figure 2. A Microcosmic Mechanism Model of IS Growth

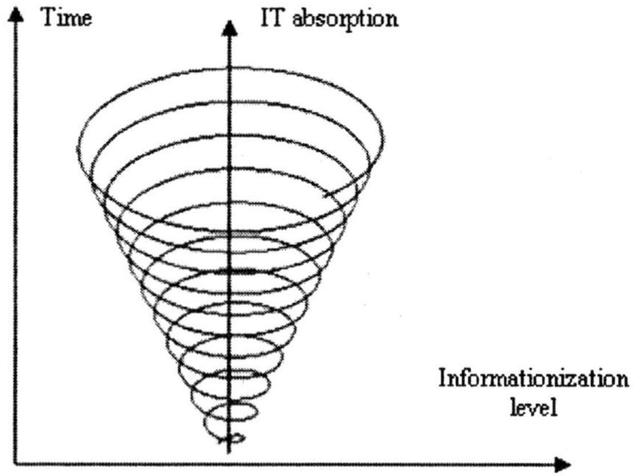

Figure 3. A Spiral Model of IS Growth

The synergic effect of various powers within the enterprise impels it to absorb and utilize information technology effectively. With the development of business strategy, enterprise may introduce new information technology and begin another circle of IT absorption. This process circulates continuously, and every circulation is based on experience accumulation of the prior. Viewed from a holistic perspective, IS growth presents itself as a dynamic and spiral process as shown in Figure 3.

2.2 Subjects Synergy in IS Growth Process

IT absorption is a complicated system engineering related to top management, middle management, IT department and other organizational personnel of the enterprise. We call these key personnel as the subjects of IT absorption. Cooperation and synchronization requirements of IS application demand that all subjects examine their functions from a perspective of maximizing the holistic benefit.

In the stage of identification, management of the enterprise should observantly apperceive enterprise problems, environmental changes and the trends of IT development to set down corresponding IT solutions. Simultaneity, it needs the cooperation of IT department and all organizational personnel.

In the stage of adoption, the decision-maker must consider demands put forward by personnel of all departments; otherwise the adopted solution probably might be difficult to implement and spread. Moreover, management of the enterprise should provide necessary resources IT department

In the stage of adaptation, IT department cooperates with software provider to implement information system and provides training to organizational employee. At the same time, enterprise management needs to coordinate and control the conflicts and contradiction to make the organization synergize with IT solution.

In the stage of acceptance, management of the enterprise should make a good communication with employee to motivate them to convert inherent idea and behavioral inertia to support IT application. IT department should provide technological training for organizational personnel and help them master related knowledge and skills.

In the stage of infusion, IT department needs to make continuous improvement for information systems to realize more comprehensive and integrated application. Management of the enterprise needs to cultivate "IT culture" to infuse information technology into the organization.

Knowledge management needs collaboration and cooperation of all organizational personnel which can promote knowledge accumulation, share, conversion and protection, thus to gain continuous accumulation of IT absorptive capacity.

2.3 Elements Synergy in IS Growth Process

IS growth is a complicated nonlinear process, also a system with various elements which need comprehensive management. G. Zheng proposed a diamond model for comprehensive synergy of innovation elements and pointed out six critical elements of innovation process, viz. technology, strategy, market, organization, culture and institution [8]. Using his viewpoints for reference, this paper proposes six crucial elements at microcosmic level, viz. technology, strategy, organization, culture, personnel and institution.

For various elements, their categories, manners and means to acquire information and energy from external environment are different, and they are distinct in the intensity, intention and methods of their effect in different conditions or stages, fluctuation and conflict inevitably exist in the system. To realize the evolution from disorder (beginning from IT introduction) to order (infusing information technology into organization), various elements interact with each other and finally engender order parameters which propel information system to evolve into advanced state. Therefore, it needs good synergy of all elements.

At technology aspect, the introduced IT solution must meet enterprise demand. Meanwhile, technology must synergize with other elements to impel IT absorption. Many studies have indicated that the primary failure reason of most IS projects is not technology but lies in its ineffective coordination with non-technology elements including strategy, culture, organization, personnel and institution.

At strategy aspect, information system planning (ISP) should match with business planning (BP). Lack of ISP or Lack of match of ISP with BP usually causes short-term benefit oriented, sightless and random decision, which make it difficult to achieve expected goal of IS construction. Only under the guidance of ISP could all elements run effectively and ensure the correctness of synergic direction.

It is needed to adjust and optimize organizational structure and business process during the process of IS implementation. Disordered hierarchy, intersected structure and slack business process impact implementation process and the performance of IT application. Therefore, it is needed to establish a structure which can support elements synergy and enhance coordination of different departments and function units.

To IT application, corporate culture is a two-edge sword which impacts the whole process of IT absorption inherently. On one hand, IT application can gain more support and positive participation in an innovative and adventurous culture; On the other hand, IT application would suffer resistance if it threatens current culture.

IS construction is a complicated process that relates to all organizational personnel. Viewed from a dynamic perspective, the main factors which directly determine the impetus are the subjects and their actions in this process, that is, the personnel concerned with information system. So, organizational personnel have a quite active impact on IS construction.

Institution provides concrete guarantee mechanism and tool to adjust and control the behaviors of organizational personnel, and to solidify related experience and fruit of IS construction.

Comprehensive synergy of all these elements guarantees the success of IS construction. The essence of synergy is multi-coordination which enables them to exert advantage and achieve symbiosis and coexistence, thus to promote IS growth.

3. A MATHEMATICAL MODEL

As mentioned in section 2, there are complex relations of the factors during the process of IS growth, which may be promotion or restraint. When information systems become more and more advanced and complex, its improvement would become more and more difficult. For the diversity of factors, complexity of system and increase of difficult in the process of IS growth, it can be regarded as a Self-Increasing-Difficulty System (SIDIS), and the effective strategy for its development is "Spiral Combining Propulsion Principle" (SPIPRO principle) [9]. Viewed from system science, it is a spiral process driven by synergic effect of critical factors and can be reflected by improvement of informationization level. Using the SPIPRO mode which describes technological catching-up and technological leapfrogging for reference [10], this paper makes a further analysis on the synergic and spiral-propulsion mechanism of IS growth with a mathematic model.

3.1 Conception Definition

Definition 1. When enterprise introduces an information technology/information system, enterprise information system would gain a growth if IS construction is successful, that is, it absorbs the technology successfully. We use P(t) to represent the probability of achieving a success of IS construction, $P(t) \in [0,1]$. We hypothesize that the probability of achieving a success of IS construction is greater while P(t) is larger.

Definition 2. We propose the conception of absorptive capacity for information technology which expresses organizational abilities of identification, adoption, adaptation, acceptance, infusion and knowledge management for IT solution in the process of IT absorption, and use A(t) to represent it.

Definition 3. We use D(t) to represent system difficulty which must be conquered when enterprise constructs information systems at time t.

Definition 4. We hypothesize that technological level of enterprise informationization at time t is a(t) and that of expected after adopting new technology is b(t); a(t) and b(t) are monotonic increasing function. Therefore, the result of subtracting a(t) from b(t) is technological gap marked by h(t), h(t)=b(t)-a(t). In fact, IS construction changes the logic and efficiency of information management and is also a reengineering for enterprise system, which is represented by improvement of economic effectiveness and organizational order of the enterprise [11]. m(t) is used to represent economic effectiveness and n(t) is used to represent organizational order at time t. We take r(t) to record the total gap of informationization level between that of original and expected, r(t) is the sum of h(t), m(t) and n(t).

3.2 Mathematic Model and Its Meanings

The following mathematic model is used to describe the synergic and spiral-propulsion path of IS growth.

$$\rho = \frac{eP(t)}{1 - e\cos(w(t)t)} \tag{1}$$

$$S(t) = \frac{1}{2}\int_0^t \rho^2 \omega(x)dx \tag{5}$$

Equation (1) refers to accumulative plane equation and equation (2) refers to accumulative area equation. The two are used to describe the "spiral" path of IS growth. Their meanings are: the projection of the path of IS growth on x-y plane is a cone curve; x-y is accumulative plane and the enclosed cone curve forms accumulative area.

In equation (1), e refers to the eccentricity. The actual input of IS construction is absolutely consistent with its goal if e=0. But there is a departure from expected direction if e≥1. ω refers to the accumulative speed in the spiral process. It is represented by the functions of critical factors of IS construction, w(t)=f(technology, strategy, organization, culture, personnel, institution). On the other hand, viewed from the subjects of IT absorption, w(t)=f(top management, middle management, IT department, other organizational personnel).

It is hypothesized that system difficulty at time t positively correlates with the gap of informationization level which is embodied by technology level, economic effectiveness and organizational order. It is represented by equation (3).

$$D(t)=\begin{cases} r(t) & r(t)>0 \\ 0 & r(t)\le 0 \end{cases},\ r(t)=h(t)+m(t)+n(t) \tag{3}$$

3.3 Description of the Synergic and Spiral-Propulsion Path

For the "spiral" process, it is important to accumulate absorptive capacity of information technology. The area enclosed by curve projection on accumulative plane is marked by S. $S=S(t)=\frac{1}{2}\int_0^t \rho^2\omega dt$, S(0)=0. We hypothesize that $S(t_0)=S_0$, S_0 is a threshold which is the area necessary to accumulate for the enterprise. In this process, it is necessary to complete absorptive capacity accumulation of all aspects, including identification, adoption, adaptation, acceptance, infusion and knowledge management. The projection curve moves on the plane $Z=Z_0$ during the spiral process. Only when the accumulation of absorptive capacity reaches certain extent could enterprise information systems gain growth. Enterprise completes accumulation process when $S=S_0$. Therefore, only when the accumulation of absorptive capacity exceeds the threshold S_0, that is, when $\frac{1}{2}\int_0^t \rho^2\omega(x)dx > S_0$, could enterprise information system gain "propulsion" following "spiral"; when $\frac{1}{2}\int_0^t \rho^2\omega(x)dx \le S_0$, there is only "spiral" but no "propulsion". It is necessary to accelerate the speed of capacity accumulation in order to shorten the time for accumulation. However, only a good synergy among various elements of this process can enable absorptive capacity to accumulate continuously and promote IS construction.

During the process of information system construction, the probability of success correlates positively with IT absorptive capacity of the enterprise while correlates negatively with system difficulty which depends on not only the progress of time but also the gap of informationization level. Therefore, it is hypothesized that

$$P(t)=\frac{A(t)}{D(r(t),t)} \tag{4}$$

Differential coefficient of P(t) is that

$$\frac{dP(t)}{dt}=\frac{\frac{dA(t)}{dt}D(r(t),t)-\frac{dr(t)}{dt}\frac{\partial D(r(t),t)}{\partial r(t)}A(t)-\frac{\partial D(r(t),t)}{\partial t}A(t)}{D(r(t),t)^2} \qquad (5)$$
$$=\frac{1}{D(r(t),t)}\frac{dA(t)}{dt}(1-\varepsilon_r-\varepsilon_t)$$

In equation (5),

$\varepsilon_r=\frac{\partial D(r(t),t)}{\partial r(t)}\frac{A(t)}{D(r(t),t)}\frac{dr(t)}{dA(t)}$, and ε_r refers to the elasticity of system difficulty to informationization level gap;

$\varepsilon_t=\frac{\frac{\partial D(r(t),t)}{\partial t}}{\frac{dA(t)}{dt}}\frac{A(t)}{D(r(t),t)}$, and ε_t refers to the relative change of system difficulty to IT absorptive capacity through time.

Equation (5) indicates that, when $\frac{dA(t)}{dt}(1-\varepsilon_r-\varepsilon_t)>0$, the differential coefficient of P(t) exceeds 0, which means an increase of the probability for IS growth. It is deduced that P(t) is larger when ε_r and ε_h are smaller. Therefore, for the elasticity of system difficulty to informationization level gap and the relative change of system difficulty through time, the smaller, the better; but for the relative change of IT absorptive capacity through time, the larger, the better. Since informationization level gap is objective and system difficulty engendered by it is uncontrollable, only IT absorptive capacity is controllable. Therefore, enterprise should attach great importance to strengthen its absorptive capacity, thus to increase the probability of success for IS construction and promote IS growth.

Many studies have demonstrated that information system growth presents as an "S" curve, which just validates that it is a spiral process. This paper uses a mathematical model to describe the synergic and spiral-propulsion path of IS growth. Through it we conclude that only when it possesses IT absorptive capacity at some extent could enterprise assimilates advanced technology effectively thus to propel IS growth. The data from our investigation also validate the synergic and spiral-propulsion model of IS growth. Using this model and considering the especial condition of its own, enterprise can find out the critical factors of IS construction and impel their synergy and cooperation, thus to improve the accumulative speed of absorptive capacity and promote the growth of information systems.

4. CONCLUSIONS

This paper summarizes the factors which influence the growing process of enterprise information systems and develops a model for synergic and spiral-propulsion mechanism of IS growth. It proposes that the synergic effect of internal and external factors enables IS construction to advance continuously thus to promote IS growth. Viewed from a holistic perspective, IS growth presents itself as a dynamical and spiral process. This paper emphasizes research on the microcosmic mechanism of IS growth and proposes that IT absorption is the direct impetus to it. A detailed analysis is made on subjects synergy and elements synergy of the enterprise in the process of IS construction. A mathematic model is used to describe the synergic and spiral–propulsion mode of IS growth. It concluded that enterprise should attach great importance to strengthen its absorptive capacity thus to increase the probability of success for IS construction and promote IS growth. This research work is likely to shed light on the mechanism of enterprise information system growth at some extent and provide theoretical foundations and instructions for IS construction.

ACKNOWLEDGEMENTS

This research was supported by the National Natural Science Foundation of China under Grant 70471014.

REFERENCES

1. F.J. Mata, W.L. Fuerst, and J.B. Barney, Information technology and sustained competitive advantage: A resource-based analysis, *MIS Quarterly*. Volume 19, Number 4, pp. 487-505, (1995).
2. E.K. Clemons, R.M. Dewan, and R.J. Kauffman, Special issues: competitive strategy, economics, and information systems, *Journal of Management Information Systems*. Volume 21, Number 2, pp.5, (2004).
3. X. Bi, W. Shang, and Y. Xu, Comprehensive and comparative analysis on the models of IS growth theory, *Information Science*. Volume 23, Number 11, pp.1601-1605, (2005).
4. H. Haken, *Advanced synergetics* (Springer-Verlag: Berlin, 1983).
5. X. Bi and C. Yu, Research on absorptive capacity of information technology and its process model, *Science of Science and Management of S.&T.*. Number 12, pp.42-46, (2006).
6. T.H. Kwon and R.W. Zumd, Unifying the fragmented models of information systems implementation, in *Critical Issues in Information Systems Research*, eds. R. J. Boland and R.A. Hirscheim (John Wiley: New York, NY, 1987), pp.227-252.
7. R.B. Cooper and R.W. Zumd, Information technology implementation research: A technological diffusion approach, *Management Science*. Volume 36, Number 2, pp.123-139, (1990).
8. G. Zheng, *TIM based research on the total synergy mechanism of all the innovation agents during innovation process*. Ph.D Thesis, Zhejiang University (2004).
9. H. Wang, A kind of systems methodology-the SPIPRO principle, *Systems Engineering*. Volume 12. Number 5, pp.9-12, (1994).
10. D. Chen, SPIPRO mode research from catching-up to leapfrogging, *Studies in Science of Science*. Volume 24, Number S, pp.67-73, (2006).
11. X. Bi, Enterprise information systems construction and management change (Jilin University Press: Changchun, Jilin, 2002).

Printed in the United States of America